ELENCHUS OF BIBLICAL BIBLIOGRAPHY

17

ROBERT ALTHANN S.J.

ELENCHUS OF BIBLICA

2001

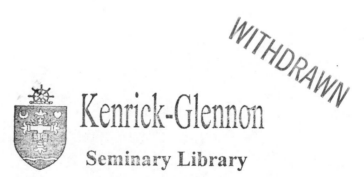
EDITRICE PONTIFICIO ISTITUTO BIBLICO
ROMA 2004

© 2004 E.P.I.B. – Roma

ISBN: 88-7653-626-4

EDITRICE PONTIFICIO ISTITUTO BIBLICO
Piazza della Pilotta, 35 - 00187 Roma, Italia

Urbes editionis—Cities of publication

AA	Ann Arbor	Lv(N)	Leuven (L-Neuve)
Amst	Amsterdam	M/Mi	Madrid/Milano
B	Berlin	Mkn	Maryknoll/
Ba/BA	Basel/Buenos Aires	Mp	Minneapolis
Barc	Barcelona	Mü/Müns('r)	München/Münster
Bo/Bru	Bologna/Brussel	N	Napoli
C	Cambridge, England	ND	NotreDame IN
CasM	Casale Monferrato	Neuk	Neukirchen/Verlag
Ch	Chicago	NHv	New Haven
CinB	Cinisello Balsamo	Nv	Nashville
CM	Cambridge, Mass.	NY	New York
ColMn	Collegeville MN	Oxf	Oxford
Da:Wiss	Darmstadt, WissBuchg	P/Pd	Paris/Paderborn
DG	Downers Grove	Ph	Philadelphia
Dü	Düsseldorf	R/Rg	Roma/Regensburg
E	Edinburgh	S	Salamanca
ENJ	EnglewoodCliffs NJ	Sdr	Santander
F	Firenze	SF	San Francisco
Fra	Frankfurt/M	Shf	Sheffield
FrB/FrS	Freiburg-Br/Schweiz	Sto	Stockholm
Gö	Göttingen	Stu	Stuttgart
GR	Grand Rapids MI	T/TA	Torino/Tel Aviv
Gü	Gütersloh	Tü	Tübingen
Ha	Hamburg	U/W	Uppsala/Wien
Heid	Heidelberg	WL	Winona Lake IN
Hmw	Harmondsworth	Wmr	Warminster
J	Jerusalem	Wsb	Wiesbaden
K	København	Wsh	Washington D.C.
L/Lei	London/Leiden	Wsz	Warszawa
LA	Los Angeles	Wu	Wuppertal
Lp	Leipzig	Wü	Würzburg
LVL	Louisville KY	Z	Zürich

Punctuation: To separate a subtitle from its title, we use a COLON (:). The *semicolon* (;) serves to separate items that in other respects belong together. Hence, at the end of an entry a *semicolon* indicates a link with the following entry. This link may consist in the two entries having the same author or in the case of multiauthor works having the same book title; the author will be mentioned in the first entry of such a group, the common book title in the last entry, that is the one which concludes with a fullstop [period] (.).
Abbreviations: These follow S.M. Schwertner, **IATG**[2] (De Gruyter; Berlin 1992) as far as possible. A list of **other** abbreviations appears below.
Price of books: This is sometimes rounded off ($10 for $9.95).

Index systematicus — Contents

The present volume contains all the 2001 material of the Elenchus. Thanks are due the staff of the Editrice Pontificio Istituto Biblico which assures the publication of the Elenchus. I should also like to express gratitude to colleagues: Fr. Jean-Noël Aletti, S.J. for his patience and readiness to help in matters electronic and to Fr. Robert North, S.J. who continues to send data.. I further thank graduates of the Institute for their invaluable contribution.

The materials for this volume were gathered principally from the libraries of the Pontifical Biblical Institute, the Pontifical Gregorian University and the University of Innsbruck. I thank the staff of these libraries for being so obliging and ready to help. The Department of Biblical Studies at the University of Innsbruck continues to be an important and dependable source of bibliographical information. After an interval and some change of method we are again supplying the Department with lists of book reviews which may be accessed through the University's electronic catalogue, BILDI, at the following address: http://bildi.uibk.ac.at.

Acronyms: Periodica - Series (small).
8 fig.=ISSN; *10 fig.*=ISBN.

A: in Arabic.
ABiG: Arbeiten zur Bibel und ihrer Geschichte; Lp.
AcBib: Acta Pontificii Instituti Biblici; R.
ACCS: Ancient Christian Commentary on Scripture; DG.
ActBib: Actualidad Bibliográfica; Barc.
AcTh(B): Acta Theologica; Bloemfontein.
Ad Gentes; Bo.
AETSC: Annales de l'Ecole Théologique Saint-Cyprien; Yaoundé, Cameroun.
AfR: Archiv für Religionsgeschichte; Stu.
AGWB: Arbeiten zur Geschichte und Wirkung der Bibel; Stu.
AHIg: Anuario de historia de la iglesia; Pamplona.
AJPS: Asian Journal of Pentecostal Studies;
AJSR: Association for Jewish Studies Review; Waltham, MA.
Ä&L: Ägypten und Levante; Wien.
Alei Etzion; Alon Shvut.
Al-Mushir [**Urdu**]; Rawalpindi.
Alpha Omega; R.
Alternativas; Managua.
AltOrF: Altorientalische Forschungen; B.
AnáMnesis; México.
AnBru: Analecta Bruxellensia; Bru.
Ancient Philosophy; Pittsburgh.
Ancient West & East; Lei.
ANESt [<Abr-n]: Ancient Near Eastern Studies; Melbourne.
Anime e corpi; Brezzo di Bedero, Va.
Annali Chieresi; Chieri.
Annals of Theology [**P.**]; Kráków.
AnnTh: Annales Theologici; R.
AnScR: Annali di Scienze Religiose; Mi.
Antologia Vieusseux; F.
APB: Acta Patristica et Byzantina; Pretoria.
Archaeology in the Biblical World; Shafter, CA.

ARET: Archivi reali di Ebla, testi; R.
ARGU: Arbeiten zur Religion und Geschichte des Urchristentums; Fra.
ARJ: The Annual of Rabbinic Judaism; Lei.
ASJ: Acta Sumerologica; Kyoto, Japan.
ATT: Archivo teologico torinese; Leumann (Torino).
AtT: Atualidade teológica; Rio de Janeiro.
Atualizaçâo; Belo Horizonte.
AuOr: Aula Orientalis (**S**: Supplement); Barc.
Auriensia; Ourense, Spain [I, 1998].
BAIAS: Bulletin of the Anglo-Israel Archaeological Society; L.
Bailamme; Mi.
Barnabiti Studi; R.
Bazmavep; Venise.
BBR: Bulletin for Biblical Research; WL.
BCSMS: Bulletin of the Canadian Society for Mesopotamian Studies; Toronto.
BEgS: Bulletin of the Egyptological Seminar; NY.
Bib(L): Bíblica; Lisboa.
BiblInterp (BiblInterp): Biblical Interpretation; Lei.
Biblioteca EstB: Biblioteca de Estudios Bíblicos; S.
BnS: La bibbia nella storia; Bo.
Bobolanum [**P.**]; Wsz.
Bogoslovni Vestnik [**S.**]; Ljubljana.
BolT: Boletín teológico; BA.
BoSm: Bogoslovska Smotra; Zagreb.
BOTSA: Bulletin for Old Testament Studies in Africa; Stavanger.
BRT: The Baptist Review of Theology / La revue baptiste de théologie; Gormely, Ontario.
BSÉG: Bulletin de la Société d'Égyptologie; Genève.
BSGJ: Bulletin der Schweizerischen Gesellschaft für Judaistische Forschung; Z.
BSLP: Bulletin de la Société de Linguistique de Paris; P.

BuBB: Bulletin de bibliographie biblique; Lausanne.

Bulletin of Ecumenical Theology; Enugu, Nigeria.

Bulletin of Judaeo-Greek Studies; C.

Bulletin of Research of Christian Culture; Okayama, Japan.

BurH: Buried History; Melbourne.

BWM: Bibelwissenschaftliche Monographien; Gießen.

C: in Chinese.

CAH: Cambridge Ancient History[2]; Cambridge Univ.

Cahiers de l'Atelier; P.

Cahiers Ratisbonne; J.

CahPhRel: Cahiers de l'Ecole des Sciences philosophiques et religieuses; Bru.

CamArchJ: Cambridge Archaeological Journal; C.

Carmel(T); Toulouse.

Carmel(V); Venasque.

Carthaginensia; Murcia.

Catalyst; Goroka, Papua New Guinea.

Catechisti parrocchiali; R.

Cathedra; Bogotá.

Cathedra [**H.**]; J.

Centro pro unione, Bulletin; R.

Chemins de Dialogue; Marseille.

Choisir; Genève.

Chongshin Review; Seoul.

Cias; Buenos Aires.

CICat: Caietele Institutului Catolic; Bucharest.

CMAO: Contributi e Materiali di Archeologia Orientale; R.

Colloquium; Brisbane.

Comunidades; S.

ConAss: Convivium Assisiense; Assisi.

Confer; M.

ConnPE: Connaissances des Pères de l'Église; Montrouge.

Contacts; Courbevoie.

Contagion; Rocky Mount.

Convergência; São Paulo.

CoSe: Consacrazione e Servizio; R.

CredOg: Credereoggi; Padova.

CritRR: Critical Review of Books in Religion; Atlanta.

Crkva u Svijetu; Split.

Croire aujourd'hui; P.

CTrB: Cahiers de traduction biblique; Pierrefitte, France.

CuesTF: Cuestiones Teológicas y Filosóficas; Medellin.

Cuestion Social, La; Mexico.

Cultura e libri; R.

CurResB: Currents in Research: Biblical Studies; Shf.

[D]: Director dissertationis.

Diadokhē [ΔΙΑΔΟΧΗ]. Revista de Estudios de Filosofía Platónica y Cristiana; B.A.

Didascalia; Rosario, ARG.

Dimensioni e problemi della ricerca storica; R.

Direction; Fresno, CA.

DiscEg: Discussions in Egyptology; Oxf.

DissA: Dissertation Abstracts International; AA/L. -A [= US etc.]: 0419-4209 [C = Europe. 0307-6075].

DosB: Les Dossiers de la Bible; P.

DQ: Documenta Q; Leuven.

DSBP: Dizionario di spiritualità biblico-patristica; R.

DSD: Dead Sea Discoveries; Lei.

[E]: Editor, Herausgeber, a cura di.

Ecclesia orans; R.

Eccl(R): Ecclesia; R.

EfMex: Efemérides Mexicana; Tlalpan.

EgArch: Egyptian Archaeology, Bulletin of the Egypt Exploration Society; L.

Emmanuel; St. Meinrads, IN.

Emmaus; Gozo, Malta.

Encounters; Markfield, U.K.

ERSY: Erasmus of Rotterdam Society Yearbook; Lexington.

EscrVedat: Escritos del Vedat; Valencia.

Esprit; P.

EThF: Ephemerides Theologicae Fluminenses; Rijeka.

Ethics & Medicine; Carlisle.

ETJ: Ephrem's Theological Journal; Satna, India.

EurJT: European Journal of Theology; Carlisle.

Evangel; E.

Evangelizzare; Bo.

EvV: Evangelio y Vida; León.

Exchange; Lei.
F: Festschrift.
Faith & Mission; Wake Forest, NC.
Feminist Theology; Shf.
FgNT: Filologia Neotestamentaria; Córdoba.
Filosofia oggi; Genova.
Firmana; Fermo.
Florensia; S. Giovanni in Fiore (CS).
FolTh: Folia theologica; Budapest.
Forum Religion; Stu.
Forum; Sonoma, CA.
Franciscanum; Bogotá.
Freiburger Universitätsblätter; FrB.
Fundamentum; Basel.
Furrow; Maynooth.
G: in Greek.
Georgica; Konstanz.
G: in Greek.
Gnosis; SF.
Graphè; Lille.
H: in Hebrew.
Hagiographica; F.
Hamdard Islamicus; Karachi.
HBO: Hallesche Beiträge zur Orientwissenschaft; Halle.
Hekima Review; Nairobi.
Henoch; T.
Hermenêutíca; Cachoeira, Brasil.
HIL: Das Heilige Land; Köln.
History of European Ideas; Oxf.
Hokhma; Lausanne.
Holy Land; J.
Horeb; Pozzo di Gotto (ME).
Horizons; Villanova, PA.
HorWi: Horizonty Wiary; Kraków.
Ho Theológos; Palermo.
IAJS: Index of Articles on Jewish Studies; J.
Ichthys ΙΧΘΥΣ; Aarhus.
ICMR: Islam and Christian-Muslim Relations; Birmingham.
ICSTJ: ICST Journal, Vigan, Philippines. [New 1999]
Igreja e Missão; Valadares, Cucujaes.
IHR: International History Review; Burnaby, Canada.
IJCT: International Journal of the Classical Tradition; New Brunswick, NJ.
IJSCC: International Journal for the Study of the Christian Church; E.
Image; Seattle.

INTAMS.R: INTAMS [International Academy for Marital Spirituality] review; Sint-Genesius-Rode, Belgium.
Inter Fratres; Fabriano (AN).
Interpretation(F). Journal of Political Philosophy; Flushing.
Iran; L.
Isidorianum; Sevilla.
IslChr: Islamochristiana; R.
ITBT: Interpretatie; Zoetermeer.
ITE: Informationes Theologiae Europae; Fra.
Iter; Caracas.
Itin(M): Itinerarium; Messina.
J: in Japanese.
JAAT: Journal of Asian and Asian American Theology; Claremont, Calif.
JAB: Journal for the Aramaic Bible; Shf.
Jahrbuch Politische Theologie; Mü.
JANER: Journal of Ancient Near Eastern Religions; Lei.
Japan Mission Journal; Tokyo.
JATS: Journal of the Adventist Theological Society; Collegedale, Tennessee.
JECS: Journal of Early Christian Studies; Baltimore.
Jeevadhara; Alleppey, Kerala.
JEGTFF: Jahrbuch der Europäischen Gesellschaft für theologische Forschung von Frauen; Mainz.
JGRChJ: Journal of Graeco-Roman Christianity and Judaism; Shf.
JHiC: Journal of Higher Criticism; Montclair, NJ.
Jian Dao; Hong Kong.
JMEMS: Journal of Medieval and Early Modern Studies; Durham, NC.
JIntH: Journal of interdisciplinary history; CM.
JISt: Journal of Interdisciplinary Studies; Pasadena, CA.
JJTP: Journal of Jewish Thought & Philosophy; Ba.
JKTh: Jahrbuch für kontextuelle Theologien; Fra.

JNSL: Journal of Northwest Semitic Languages; Stellenbosch.
Journal of Ancient History; Moscow.
Journal of Medieval History; Amst.
Journal of Psychology and Judaism; NY.
Journal of Social History; Fairfax, VA.
JPentec: Journal of Pentecostal Theology; Shf (**S**: Supplement).
JPersp: Jerusalem Perspective; J.
JPJRS: Jnanadeepa, Pune Journal of Religious Studies; Pune.
JProgJud: Journal of Progressive Judaism; Shf.
JRadRef: Journal from the Radical Reformation; Morrow, GA.
JRTI: Journal of Religious and Theological Information; Harrisburg, PA.
JRTR: Jahrbuch für Religionswissenschaft und Theologie der Religionen; FrB.
JSem: Journal for Semitics; Pretoria.
JSQ: Jewish Studies Quarterly; Tü.
JSSEA: Journal of the Society for the Study of Egyptian Antiquities; Toronto.
JTrTL: Journal of Translation and Textlinguistics; Dallas.
Jud.: Judaism; NY.
K: in Korean.
Kairos(G); Guatemala.
KaKe: Katorikku-Kenkyu [**J.**]; Tokyo.
Kerux; Escondido, CA.
KUSATU: Kleine Untersuchungen zur Sprache des Alten Testaments und seiner Umwelt; Waltrop.
Landas. Journal of Loyola School of Theology; Manila.
Laós; Catania.
Leqach; Lp.
Literary and linguistic computing; Oxf.
Living Light; Wsh.
LSDC: La Sapienza della Croce; R.
Luther-Bulletin; Amst.
Luther Digest; Crestwood, Miss.
M.: Memorial.
MastJ: Master's Seminary Journal; Sun Valley, CA.
Mayéutica; Marcilla (Navarra).

MEAH: Miscellánea de Estudios Árabes y Hebraicos (**MEAH.A**: Árabe-Islam. **MEAH.H**: Hebreo); Granada.
MESA.B: Middle East Studies Association Bulletin; Muncie, IN.
Mid-Stream; Indianapolis.
Miles Immaculatae; R.
MillSt: Milltown Studies; Dublin.
Missionalia; Menlo Park, South Africa.
MissTod: Mission Today; Shillong, India.
Mitteilungen für Anthropologie und Religionsgeschichte; Saarbrücken.
Mondo della Bibbia, Il; T.
Moralia; M.
MST Review; Manila.
NABU: Nouvelles Assyriologiques Brèves et Utilitaires; P.
NAC: New American Commentary; Nv.
NEA: Near Eastern Archaeology; Boston.
Nemalah; K.
Neukirchener Theologische Zeitschrift; Neuk.
NewTR: New Theology Review; Ch.
NHMS: Nag Hammadi and Manichaean Studies; Lei.
NIBC: New International Biblical Commentary; Peabody.
Nicolaus; Bari.
NIntB: The New Interpreter's Bible; Nv.
NotesTrans: Notes on Translation; Dallas.
NTGu: New Testament Guides; Shf.
NTTRU: New Testament Textual Research Update; Ashfield NSW, Australia. 1320-3037.
Nuova Areopago, Il; Forlì.
Nuova Europa, La; Seriate (Bg).
Nuova Umanità; R.
Obnovljeni Život; Zagreb.
Oecumenica Civitas: Livorno.
Omnis Terra; R.
OrBibChr: Orbis biblicus et christianus; Glückstadt.
OrExp: Orient-Express, Notes et Nouvelles d'Archéologie Orientale; P.

Orient; Tokyo.
Orientamenti pastorali; Bo.
Orientamenti pedagogici; R.
P: in Polish.
Pacifica; Melbourne.
Paginas; Lima.
PaiC.: Paideia Cristiana; Rosario, ARG.
Paléorient; P.
Palestjinskji Sbornik [**R.**]; Moskva.
Parabola; NY.
Passaggi; Terni.
Path; Città del Vaticano.
Pensiero politico, Il; F.
Phase; Barc.
Philosophiques; Montréal.
Physis; F.
PJBR: The Polish Journal of Biblical Research; Kraków.
PoeT: Poetics Today; Durham, NC.
PoST: Poznańskie studia teologiczne; Poznán.
Presbyteri; Trento.
Presbyterion; St. Louis.
PresPast: Presenza Pastorale, R.
ProcGLM: Proceedings of the Eastern Great Lakes and Midwest Bible Societies; Buffalo.
Pro dialogo; Città del Vaticano.
ProEc: Pro ecclesia; Northfield, MN.
Proyección; Granada.
ProySal: Proyecto Centro Salesiano de Estudios; BA.
Prudentia [.S]; Auckland, NZ.
Przegląd Tomistyezny; Wsz.
PzB: Protokolle zur Bibel; Klosterneuburg.
Qol; México.
Qol(I); Novellara (RE).
Quaderni di azione sociale; R.
Quaderni di scienze religiose; Loreto.
Qumran Chronicle; Kraków.
QVC: Qüestions de Vida Cristiana; Barc.
R: in Russian.
R.: *recensio*, book-review.
RANL.mor.: Rendiconti dell'Accademia Nazionale dei Lincei, Cl. di scienze morali; R.
RBBras: Revista Bíblica Brasileira; Fortaleza.
RBLit: Review of Biblical Literature; Atlanta.

Reason and the Faith, The; Kwangju.
Recollectio; R.
Reformation, The; Oxf (Tyndale Soc.).
Religion; L.
Religious Research; Wsh.
RelT: Religion and Theology; Pretoria.
RenSt: Renaissance Studies; Oxf.
ResB: Reseña Bíblica; Estella.
RevCT: Revista de cultura teológica; São Paulo.
Revista católica; Santiago de Chile.
Revue d'éthique et de théologie morale; P.
RF(CR): Revista de filosofia: San José, Costa Rica.
RGRW: Religions in the Graeco-Roman World; Lei.
Ribla: Revista de interpretação biblica latino-americana; Petrópolis.
RICAO: Revue de l'Institut Catholique de l'Afrique de l'Ouest; Abidjan.
Ricerche teologiche; Bo.
Rivista di archeologia; R.
Rivista di science religiose; R.
Roczniki Teologiczne; Lublin
RRT: Reviews in Religion and Theology; L.
R&T: Religion and theology = Religie en teologie; Pretoria.
RTLit: Review of Theological Literature; Leiderdorp.
RTLu: Rivista Teologica di Lugano; Lugano.
S: Slovenian.
SAA Bulletin: State Archives of Assyria Bulletin; Padova.
SAAS: State Archives of Assyria, Studies; Helsinki.
Saeculum Christianum; Wsz.
San Juan de la Cruz; Sevilla.
SaThZ: Salzburger Theologische Zeitschrift; Salzburg.
SBL.SCSt: Society of Biblical Literature, Septuagint and Cognate Studies; Atlanta.
Science and Christian Belief; Carlisle.

Scriptura; Stellenbosch.
SdT: Studi di Teologia; R.
SEAP: Studi di Egittologia e di Antichità Puniche; Pisa.
Search; Dublin.
Sedes Sapientiae; Chéméré-le-Roi.
Segni e comprensione; Lecce.
SeK: Skrif en Kerk; Pretoria.
Semeia; Atlanta.
Seminarios; M.
Semiotica; Amst.
Servitium; CasM.
SetRel: Sette e Religioni; Bo.
Sève; P.
SIDIC: Service International de Documentation Judéo-Chrétienne; R.
SMEA: Studi micenei ed egeo-anatolici; R.
Sources; FrS.
Spiritual Life; Wsh.
Spiritus(B); Baltimore.
Spiritus; P.
SPJMS: South Pacific Journal of Mission Studies; North Turramurra NSW.
SRATK: Studia nad Rodzina, Akademia Teologii Katolickiej; Wsz, 1429-2416.
STAC: Studien und Texte zu Antike und Christentum; Tü.
Stauros; Pescara.
StBob: Studia Bobolanum; Wsz.
StEeL: Studi epigrafici e linguistici; Verona.
Storia della storiografia; Mi.
St Mark's Review; Canberra.
StSp(K): Studies in Spirituality; Kampen.
Studia Textus Novi Testamenti; Osaka.
Studi Fatti Ricerche; Mi.
Stulos; Bandung, Indonesia.
StWC: Studies in World Christianity; E.
SUBB: Studia Universitatis Babeş-Bolyai; Cluj-Napoca, Romania.
Synaxis; Catania.
T: Translator.
TCNN: Theological College of Northern Nigeria; Bukuru.
Teocomunicaçâo; Porto Alegre, Brasil.
Tertium Millennium; R.

TGr.T: Tesi Gregoriana, Serie Teologia; R.
TEuph: Transeuphratène; P.
Themelios; L.
Theoforum; Ottawa.
Theologia Viatorum; Potenza.
Theologica & Historica; Cagliari.
Theologika; Lima.
Théologiques; Montréal.
Theologischer; Siegburg.
ThEv(VS): Théologie évangélique; Vaux-sur-Seine.
ThLi: Theology & Life; Hong Kong.
Theotokos; R.
ThirdM: Third Millennium: Pune, India.
T&K: Texte und Kontexte; Stu.
TrinJ: Trinity Journal; Deerfield, IL.
Una Voce-Korrespondenz; Köln.
VeE: Verbum et Ecclesia; Pretoria.
Verbum Vitae; Kielce.
Vie Chrétienne; P.
Vie, La: des communautés religieuses; Montréal.
Vivarium; Catanzaro.
VivH: Vivens Homo; F.
VO: Vicino Oriente; R.
Volto dei volti, Il; R.
Vox latina; Saarbrücken.
Vox Patrum; Lublin.
VoxScr: Vox Scripturae; São Paulo.
VTW: Voices from the Third World; Bangalore.
WaW: Word and World; St. Paul, Minn.
Way, The; L.
WBC: Word Biblical Commentary; Waco.
WUB: Welt und Umwelt der Bibel; Stu.
YESW: Yearbook of the European Society of Women in Theological Research; Lv.
ZAC: Zeitschrift für antikes Christentum; B.
ZAR: Zeitschrift für altorientalische und biblische Rechtsgeschichte; Wsb.
ZNT: Zeitschrift für Neues Testament; Tü.

I. Bibliographica

A1 Opera collecta .1 Festschriften, memorials

1 AHITUV, Shmuel: Homage to Shmuel: studies in the world of the bible.
ᴱTalshir, Zipora; Yona, Shamir; Sivan, Daniel: J 2001, Bialik (10)
436 pp. NIS134.55. 965-342-824-1.

2 BARASCH, Moshe: Representation in religion: studies in honor of Moshe
Barasch. ᴱAssmann, Jan; Baumgarten, Albert I.: SHR 89: Lei 2001,
Brill xvii; 363 pp. 90-04-11939-6.

3 BARRUFFO, Antonio: Credo ecclesiam. ᴱCattaneo, Enrico; Terracciano,
Antonio: 2000 ⇒16,7. ᴿMF 101 (2001) 400-402 (*Eldarov, Giorgio*).

4 BECKER, Jürgen: Das Urchristentum in seiner literarischen Geschichte.
ᴱMell, Ulrich; Müller, Ulrich B.: BZNW 100: 1999 ⇒15,9. ᴿCBQ 63
(2001) 581-583 (*Pelser, Gert M.M.*).

5 BETZ, Hans Dieter: Antiquity and humanity: essays on ancient religion
and philosophy: presented to Hans Dieter Betz on his 70th birthday.
ᴱCollins, Adela Yarbro; Mitchell, Margaret M. Tü 2001, Mohr xx;
561 pp. €139. 3-16-147585-2. Bibl. Betz 501-512.

6 BEUKEN, Willem A.M.: Studies in the book of Isaiah. ᴱVan Ruiten, Jacques T.A.G.M.; Vervenne, Marc: BEThL 132: 1997 ⇒13,12... 16,10.
ᴿVT 51 (2001) 570-571 (*Dell, Katharine J.*).

7 BOGAERT, Pierre-Maurice: Lectures et relectures de la bible. ᴱAuwers,
Jean-Marie; Wénin, André: BEThL 144: 1999 ⇒15,14; 16,14. ᴿREJ
160 (2001) 268-270 (*Rothschild, Jean-Pierre*); EstB 59 (2001) 381
(*Ibarzábal, S.*).

8 BONNER, Gerald: AUGUSTINE and his critics. ᴱDodaro, Robert; Lawless,
George: Christian origins: 2000 ⇒16,15. ᴿJECS 9 (2001) 284-286
(*Harmless, William*).

9 BORDONI, Marcello: Gesù Cristo speranza del mondo. ᴱSanna, Ignazio:
2000 ⇒16,16. ᴿRSR 89 (2001) 308-310 (*Fédou, Michel*); Rivista di
teologia dell'evangelizzazione 5/9 (2001) 176-178 (*Lodi, Enzo*).

10 BORGER, Rykle: Festschrift für Rykle Borger. ᴱMaul, Stefan M.:
Cuneiform Monographs 10: 1998 ⇒14,12. ᴿBiOr 58 (2001) 631-634
(*Pearce, Laurie*).

11 BOYLE, Leonard E.: Itineraria culturae medievalis. ᴱHamesse, Jacqueline: Textes et Études du Moyen Age 10: 1998 3 vols ⇒14,13. ᴿDA 57/1
(2001) 197-204 (*Jasper, Detlev*).

12 BRINNER, William M.: Judaism and Islam: boundaries, communication
and interaction. ᴱHary, B.H.; Hayes, J.L.; Asten, F. 2000 ⇒16,18.
ᴿHenoch 23 (2001) 396-398 (*Tottoli, Roberto*).

13 BRUEGGEMANN, Walter: God in the fray. ᴱLinafelt, Tod; Beal, Timothy
K. : 1998 ⇒14,16. ᴿEvQ 73 (2001) 172-173 (*Bodner, Keith*).

14 BÜRKLE, Horst: Die Weite des Mysteriums. ᴱKrämer, Klaus; Paus,
Ansgar: 2000 ⇒16,22. ᴿFKTh 17 (2001) 234-235 (*Haneke, Burkhard*).

15 CAGNI, Luigi: Studi sul Vicino Oriente Antico: dedicati alla memoria di
Luigi Cagni. ᴱGraziani, Simonetta: SMDSA 61: N 2001, Istituto Uni-
versitario Orientale. 4 vol. Collab. Maria C. Casaburi e Giancarlo
Lacerenza; bibl. Luigi Cagni: v.1 xxxv-xlviii.

16 CAMPBELL, Edward F.: Realia Dei. ᴱWilliams, Prescott H.; Hiebert,
Theodore: 1999 ⇒15,15. ᴿBASOR 321 (2001) 93-95 (*Wiggins, Steve
A.*); CBQ 63 (2001) 778-780 (*Roberts, Kathryn L.*); RBLit 3 (2001) 155-
157 (*Power, Bruce A.*).

17 CARMEL, Alex: Das Erwachen Palästinas im 19. Jahrhundert: Alex Carmel zum 70. Geburtstag. ᴱPerry, Yaron; Petry, Erik: Judentum und Christentum 9: Stu 2001, Kohlhammer 142 pp. 3-17-017094-5.
18 CLEMENTS, Ronald Ernest: In search of true wisdom. ᴱBall, Edward JSOT.S 300: 1999 ⇒15,18; 16,29. ᴿJThS 52 (2001) 133-135 (Davidson, Robert).
19 Crenshaw, James L.: Shall not the judge of all the earth do what is right?. ᴱPenchansky, David; Redditt, Paul Lewis: 2000 ⇒16,31. ᴿRBLit 3 (2001) 170-172 (Grundke, Christopher L.K.).
20 CROATTO, José Severino: Los caminos inexhauribles de la Palabra: las relecturas creativas en la biblia y de la biblia: homenaje de colegas y discípulos a J. Severino Croatto en sus 70 años de vida, 40 de magisterio, y 25 en el ISEDET. ᴱHansen, Guillermo: BA 2000, LUMEN 684 pp. 987-00-0057-6.
21 DENZ, Adolf: Sachverhalt und Zeitbezug: semitische und alttestamentliche Studien Adolf Denz zum 65. Geburtstag. ᴱBartelmus, Rüdiger; Nebes, Norbert: Jenaer Beiträge zum Vorderen Orient 4: Wsb 2001, Harrassowitz viii; 166 pp. 3-447-04272-9.
22 DESROCHES NOBLECOURT, Christiane: La femme dans les civilisations orientales et miscellanea aegyptologica: Christiane Desroches Noblecourt in honorem. ᴱCannuyer, Christian; Fredericq-Homes, D. Acta Orientalia Belgica 15: Bru 2001, Société Belge d'Études Orientales: xxxii; 332 pp. €37. Bibl. Noblecourt xxii-xxxii.
23 DEURLOO, Karel Adriaan: Unless some one guide me...: Festschrift for Karel A. Deurloo. ACBET.S 2: Maastricht 2001, Shaker xv; 422 pp. 90-423-0140-6. Bibl. 393-414.
24 DIETRICH, Wendell S.: Ethical monotheism, past and present: essays in honor of...Dietrich. ᴱVial, Theodore M.; Hadley, Mark A.: BJSt 329: Providence, RI 2001, Brown Univ. ix; 347 pp. $60. 1-930675-06-2.
25 DION, Paul Eugène: The world of the Aramaeans I & II: biblical studies in honour of Paul-Eugène Dion. ᴱDaviau, Michèle; Wevers, John William; Weigl, Michael: JSOT.S 324-325: Shf 2001, Sheffield A. 2 vols. $252. 1-84127-158-6/78-0. Bibl. v.1, 289-296.
26 DUCREY, Pierre: Recherches récentes sur le monde hellénistique. ᴱFrei-Stolba, Regula; Gex, Kristine: Echo 1: Berne 2001, Lang 321 pp. €47. 30. 390-6758-478. Actes du coll. international, Lausanne 20-21.11.1998.
27 EASTERLING, Pat E.: Homer, tragedy and beyond: essays in honour of P.E. Easterling. ᴱBudelmann, Felix; Michelakis, Pantelis: L 2001, Society for the Promotion of Hellenic Studies xiii; 262 pp. 0-902984-19-5. Bibl. Easterling, 1960-2003 ix-xiii.
28 ESSE, Douglas L.: Studies in the archaeology of Israel and neighboring lands in memory of Douglas L. Esse. ᴱWolff, Samuel R. SAOC 59; ASOR Books 5: Ch 2001, The Oriental Institute of the University of Chicago xvii; 703 pp. 1-885923-15-5. Bibl. Esse 699-700.
29 FAIVRE, Antoine: Ésotérisme, gnoses & imaginaire symbolique: mélanges offerts à Antoine Faivre. ᴱCaron, Richard; Godwin, Joscelyn, al., Gnostica 3: Lv 2001, Peeters xii; 948 pp. €70. 90-429-0955-2. Bibl. Faivre (1960-2000) 875-917.
30 FESTORAZZI, Franco: Initium sapientiae. ᴱFabris, Rinaldo: SRivBib 36: 2000 ⇒16,38. ᴿRivBib 49 (2001) 113-123 (Crocetti, Giuseppe).
31 FITZGERALD, Aloysius: Imagery and imagination in biblical literature: essays in honor of Aloysius Fitzgerald, F.S.C. ᴱBoadt, Lawrence E.; Smith, Mark S.: CBQ.MS 32: Wsh 2001, The Catholic Biblical Association of America ix; 221 pp. $9. 0-915170-31-0. Bibl. Fitzgerald 191-9.

32 FITZMYER, Joseph A.: Joseph A. Fitzmyer, S.J. celebrating eighty years. CBQ 62/4: Wsh 2000, Catholic Biblical Association of America 607-816 pp. Books, articles, and reviews by...published since 1985, 609-20.

33 FRERICHS, Ernest S.: Hesed ve-Emet. ᴱ**Magness, Jodi; Titin, Seymour**: BJSt 320: 1998 ⇒14,28; 16,39. ᴿBiOr 58 (2001) 660-663 (*Barstad, Hans M.*).

34 GILBERT, Maurice: Treasures of wisdom. ᴱ**Calduch Benages, Nuria; Vermeylen, Jacques**: BEThL 143: 1999 ⇒15,37; 16,44. ᴿJThS 52 (2001) 189-191 (*Dell, Katharine*); RivBib 49 (2001) 358-362 (*Prato, Gian Luigi*);

35 Toute la sagesse du monde. ᴱ**Mies, Françoise**: 1999 ⇒15,36; 16,43. ᴿCivCatt 152/2 (2001) 417-419 (*Prato, G.L.*).

36 GLEMP, Józef: Czynic sprawiedliwosc w milosci: Ksiega pamiatkowa od Universytetu Kardynala Stefana Wyszynskiego dla Jego Eminencji Józefa Kardynala Glempa w dwudziesta rocznice poslugi Prymasowskiej. ᴱ**Chrostowski, Waldemar**: Wsz 2001, Wydawnictwa Uniwersytetu Kardynala Stefana Wyszynkiego. 502 pp. 83-7072-198-2.

37 GRANFIELD, Patrick: The gift of the church. ᴱ**Phan, Peter C.**: 2000 ⇒16, 49. ᴿTS 62 (2001) 391-393 (*Krieg, Robert A.*).

38 GROSS, Walter: Gott, Mensch, Sprache: Schülerfestschrift für Walter Groß zum 60. Geburtstag. ᴱ**Michel, Andreas; Stipp, Hermann-Josef**: ATSAT 68: St. Ottilien 2001, EOS (8) 155 pp. 3-8306-7075-3.

39 HAAS, Volkert: Kulturgeschichten: altorientalistische Studien für Volkert Haas zum 65. Geburtstag. ᴱ**Richter, Thomas; Prechel, Doris; Klinger, Jörg**: Saarbrücken 2001, SDV Saarbrücker xxiv; 500 pp. 3-930843-74-9. Bibl. Haas xiii-xxiv.

40 HAGEN, Kenneth: Ad fontes LUTHERI: toward the recovery of the real Luther: essays in honor of Kenneth Hagen's sixty-fifth birthday. ᴱ**Maschke, Timothy; Posset, Franz; Skocir, Joan**: Milwaukee 2001, Marquette Univ. Pr. 332 pp. $30. 0-8746-2677-3.

41 HAHN, Ferdinand: 'was ihr auf dem Weg verhandelt habt': Beiträge zur Exegese und Theologie des Neuen Testaments, Festschrift für Ferdinand Hahn zum 75. Geburtstag. Neuk 2001, Neuk 223 pp. 3-7887-1857-9. ᴿOrthFor 15 (2001) 230-231 (*Frey, Jörg*).

42 HAINZ, Josef: Pneuma und Gemeinde: Christsein in der Tradition des Paulus und Johannes: Festschrift für Josef Hainz zum 65. Geburtstag. ᴱ**Eckert, Jost; Schmidl, Martin; Steichele, Hanneliese**: Dü 2001, Patmos 403 pp. 3-491-70344-1.

43 HAMILTON, James Russell: De Dunhuang à Istanbul: hommage à James... Hamilton. ᴱ**Bazin, Louis; Zieme, Peter**: Silk Road Studies 5: Turnhout 2001, Brepols 435 pp. 2-50351-1872. 53 pl.; Bibl. Hamilton 17-23.

44 HARMAN, Allan Macdonald: Israel and the church: essays in honour of Allan Macdonald Harman on his 65th birthday and retirement. ᴱ**Milne, D.J.W.**: Melbourne 2001, Theological Education Committee of the Presbyterean Church of Victoria vi; 157 pp. AU$15.

45 HAY, David M.: In the spirit of faith: studies in Philo and early christianity in honor of David Hay. ᴱ**Runia, David T.; Sterling, Gregory E.**: BJSt 332; StPhilo 13: Providence 2001, Brown Univ. xii; 304 pp. 1-930675-10-0. Bibl. Hay 1999-2001, 282-290.

46 HETZRON, Robert: New data and new methods in Afroasiatic linguistics: Robert Hetzron in memoriam. ᴱ**Zaborski, Andrzej**: Wsb 2001, Harrassowitz xix; 230 pp. 3-447-04420-9. Bibl. xi-xix.

47 HEYER, C.J. den: Joden, christenen en hun schrift: een bundel opstellen aangeboden bij het afscheid van... ᴱHoutman, C.; Peerbolte, L.J. Lietaert: Ten Have 2001, Baarn 251 pp. €18.10. 90-259-5270-4 [Streven 69,948s—Beentjes, Panc].

48 HOFFMANN, Paul: Von Jesus zum Christus: christologische Studien. ᴱHoppe, Rudolf; Busse, Ulrich: BZNW 93: 1998 ⇒14,42; 15,45. ᴿSNTU.A 25 (2000) 277-280 (*Fuchs, Albert*).

49 HSIAO, Andrew K.H.: Theology & life: Festschrift for Prof. Dr. Andrew K.H. Hsiao's 75th birthday. ᴱTai, Nicholas Ho Fai; Tang, Andres S.K.: Theology & Life 24 (2001) 1-269. Hong Kong 2001, Lutheran Theological Seminary.

50 HUOT, Jean-Louis: Études mésopotamiennes: recueil de textes offerts à Jean-Louis Huot. ᴱBreniquet, Catherine; Kepinski, Christine: Bibliothèque de la Délégation Archéologique Française en Iraq 10: P 2001, Éditions Recherche sur les Civilisations xxv; 517 pp. 2-86358-280-X.

51 HUß, Werner: Punica—Libyca—Ptolemaica: Festschrift für Werner Huß, zum 65. Geburtstag dargebracht von Schülern, Freunden und Kollegen. ᴱGeus, Klaus; Zimmermann, Klaus: OLA 104: Lv 2001, Peeters vi; 405 pp. €70. 90-429-1066-6.

52 ISRAELIT-GROLL, Sarah: Structuring Egyptian syntax: a tribute to Sarah Israelit-Groll. ᴱGoldwasser, Orly; Sweeney, Deborah: Lingua aegyptia 9: Gö 2001, Seminar für Ägyptologie viii; 332 pp. Bibl. 5-8.

53 JANKOWSKI, Augustyn B.: Duch I oblubienica Mówia: "Przyjdz": Ksiega Pamiatkowa dla Ojca Profesora Augustyna Jankowskiego OSB w 85. rocznice urodzin. ᴱChrostowski, Waldemar: Wsz 2001, "Vocatio" 493 pp. 83-7146-170-4. Bibl. Jankowski 21-30.

54 JANZEN, Waldemar: Reclaiming the Old Testament: essays in honour of Waldemar Janzen. ᴱZerbe, Gordon: Winnipeg 2001, CMBC 260 pp. CAN$22/US$16.

55 JEPPESEN, Knud: Alle der ånder skal lovprise Herren!: det Gamle Testamente i tempel, synagoge og kirke [Let everybody that breathes praise the Lord! The O.T. in the temple, the synagogue, and the church]. ᴱHolt, Else K.: 1998 ⇒14,46... 16,57. ᴿSEÅ 66 (2001) 218-220 (*Norin, Stig*).

56 KAISER, Otto: Gerechtigkeit und Leben im hellenistischen Zeitalter: Symposium anläßlich des 75. Geburtstags von Otto Kaiser. ᴱJeremias, Jörg: BZAW 296: B 2001, De Gruyter ix; 116 pp. €49. 3-11-016823-5.

57 KAROTEMPREL, Sebastian: Be my witnesses: essays in honour of Sebastian Karotemprel SDB. ᴱVarickasseril, Jose; Kariapuram, Mathew: Shillong 2001, Vendrame xi; 300 pp. Rs300/$25. 81-85408-00-29. Bibl. 295-300.

58 KASPER, Walter: Divinarum rerum notitia: la teologia tra filosofia e storia: studi in onore del Cardinale Walter Kasper. ᴱRusso, Antonio; Coffele, Gianfranco: La Cultura 81: R 2001, Studium xxxvii; 827 pp. 88-382-3864-2. Bibl. 783-827. ᴿCivCatt 152/4 (2001) 415-416 (*Vanzan, P.*).

59 KROBATH, Evi: Anspruch und Widerspruch: Evi Krobath zum 70. Geburtstag. ᴱHalmer, Maria; Heyse-Schäfer, Barbara; Rauchwarter, Barbara: 1999 ⇒15,55. ᴿYESW 9 (2001) 282-284 (*Scholz, Susanne*).

60 KURTH, Gottfried: Jericho und Qumran. ᴱMayer, Bernhard: ESt 45: 2000 ⇒16,65. ᴿSNTU.A 26 (2001) 283-284 (*Fuchs, Albert*).

61 LANDES, George M.: On the way to Nineveh. ᴱCook, Stephen L.; Winter, S.C.: 1999 ⇒15,57. ᴿBS 158 (2001) 124-125 (*Chisholm, Robert B.*).

62 LE RIDER, Georges: Travaux de numismatique grecque. ^E**Amandry, Michel; Hurter, Silvia**: 1999 ⇒15,58. ^RREG 114 (2001) 673-675 (*Martinez-Sève, Laurianne*).

63 LEHMANN, Karl: Weg und Weite: Festschrift für Karl Lehmann. ^E**Raffelt, Albert**: FrB ²2001, Herder lvi; 808 pp. 3-451-27572-4. Collab. Barbara Nichtweiß.

64 LEROY, Herbert: Johannes aenigmaticus. ^E**Schreiber, Stefan; Stimpfle, Alois**: BU 29: 2000 ⇒16,67. ^RThRv 97 (2001) 493-495 (*Scholtissek, Klaus*).

65 LINDNER, Manfred: Nach Petra. ^E**Hübner, Ulrich; Knauf, Ernst Axel; Wenning, Robert**: BBB 118: 1998 ⇒14,62. ^RSyr. 78 (2001) 261-264 (*Nehmé, Laïla*).

66 LONG, Burke O.: "A wise and discerning mind". ^E**Olyan, Saul M.; Culley, Robert C.**: BJSt 325: 2000 ⇒16,70. ^RCBQ 63 (2001) 774-775 (*Nicol, George G.*).

67 MALINA, Bruce J.: Social scientific models for interpreting the bible: essays by the Context Group in honor of Bruce J. Malina. ^E**Pilch, John J.**: BiblInterp 53: Lei 2001, Brill vi; 438 pp. 9004120564. Bibl. 398-429.

68 MARIN, Bruno: Un padre per vivere: l'esperienza della figura paterna tra istanze religiose e socio-culturali: scritti in onore di Dom Bruno Marin OSB. ^E**Maccarinelli, Mauro**: Scritti monastici 1: Padova 2001, Il poligrafo 349 pp. 88-7115-228-X Pres. card. Martini; Bibl. 339-340.

69 MARTIN, David: Restoring the image: essays on religion and society in honour of David Martin. ^E**Walker, Andrew; Percy, Martyn**: Lincoln Studies in Religion and Society 3: Shf 2001, Sheffield A. 236 pp. 1-84127-064-4. Bibl. 229-233.

70 MEGAW, A.H.S.: Mosaic: Festschrift for A.H.S. Megaw. ^E**Herrin, Judith; Mullett, Margaret; Otten-Froux, Catherine**: British School at Athens studies 8: L 2001, British School at Athens 200 pp. 0-904887-40-5. Bibl. Megaw 181-183.

71 MERKLEIN, Helmut: Die Macht der Nase. ^E**Kügler, Joachim**: SBS 187: 2000 ⇒16,74. ^RCBQ 63 (2001) 773-774 (*Pilch, John J.*).

72 MIKAT, Paul: Rom und das himmlische Jerusalem. ^E**Haehling, Raban von**: 2000 ⇒16,76. ^RThLZ 126 (2001) 1051-1053 (*Buschmann, Gerd*).

73 MILIK, Józef Tadeusz: Józef Tadeusz Milik. ^E**Długosz, Dariusz; Ratajczak, Henryk**: 2000 ⇒16,77. ^RDSD 8 (2001) 309-11 (*Brooke, George*).

74 MILLER, J. Maxwell: The land that I will show you: essays on the history and archaeology of the ancient Near East in honour of J. Maxwell Miller. ^E**Dearman, John Andrew; Graham, Matt Patrick**: JSOT.S 343: Shf 2001, Sheffield A. 320 pp. $90. 1-84127-257-4. Bibl. Miller 32-35.

75 MORSE, Jane: The whirlwind: essays on Job, hermeneutics and theology in memory of Jane Morse. ^E**Cook, Stephen L.; Patton, Corrine L.; Watts, James Washington**: JSOT.S 336: Shf 2001, Sheffield A. 230 pp. 1-84127-243-4. Bibl. 206-221.

76 MOTTE, André: Kêpoi: de la religion à la philosophie: mélanges offerts à André Motte. ^E**Delruelle, Édouard; Pirenne-Delforge, Vinciane**: Kernos.S 11: Liège 2001, Centre international d'étude de la religion grecque antique xvi; 350 pp. Bibl. 337-346.

77 MÜHLSTEIGER, Johannes: Tradition—Wegweisung in die Zukunft: Festschrift für Johannes Mühlsteiger SJ zum 75. Geburtstag. ^E**Breitsching, Konrad; Rees, Wilhelm**: KStT 46: B 2001, Duncker & Humblot xxxi; 1116 pp. €89. 3-428-10489-7.

78 MÜLLER, Hans Peter: Mythos im Alten Testament und seiner Umwelt.
    ELange, Armin; Lichtenberger, Hermann; Römheld, Diethard:
    BZAW 278: 1999 ⇒15,66; 16,78. RBiOr 58 (2001) 221-224 (Spronk,
    Klaas); OLZ 96 (2001) 61-64 (Schmidt, Werner H.).
79 NORTH, J.L.: The Old Testament in the New. EMoyise, Steve: JSNT.S
    189: 2000 ⇒16,80. RCBQ 63 (2001) 185-187 (Brawley, Robert L.).
80 O'BRIEN, Peter: The gospel to the nations. EBolt, Peter; Thompson,
    Mark: 2000 ⇒16,82. RPacifica 14 (2001) 330-331 (Watson, Nigel).
81 O'COLLINS, Gerald Glynn: The convergence of theology: a Festschrift
    honoring Gerald O'Collins, S.J. EKendall, Daniel; Davis, Stephen T.:
    NY 2001, Paulist vii; 407 pp. $30. 0-8091-4015-2. Foreword by George
    Carey; Bibl. 370-398.
82 ÖGÜN, Baki: Studien zur Religion und Kultur Kleinasiens und des ägäi-
    schen Bereiches: Festschrift für Baki Öğun. EIşik, Cengiz: Asia Minor
    Studien 39: Bonn 2000, Habelt 334 pp. €60. 33 3-7749-3018-X.
83 PARPOLA, Asko: Vidyarnavavandanam: essays in honour of Asko Parpo-
    la. EKarttunen, Klaus; Koskikallio, Petteri: StOr 94: Helsinki 2001,
    The Finnish Oriental Society 511 pp. 951-9380-52-3. Bibl. 15-36.
84 PATHRAPANKAL, Joseph: Indian interpretation of the bible. EThottakara,
    Augustine: 2000 ⇒16,85. RVJTR 65 (2001) 70-71 (Gispert-Sauch, G.);
    Jeevadhara 31 (2001) 384-386 (Chethimattam, John B.).
85 PERROT, Charles: Nourriture et repas. EQuesnel, Michel; Blanchard,
    Yves-Marie; Tassin, Claude: LeDiv 178: 1999 ⇒15,70; 16,87.
    RRHPhR 81 (2001) 231-232 (Grappe, Ch.).
86 PIAMENTA, Moshe: Linguistic and cultural studies on Arabic and He-
    brew: essays presented to Professor Moshe Piamenta for his eightieth
    birthday. ERosenhouse, Judith; Elad-Bouskila, Ami: Wsb 2001, Har-
    rassowitz xxvii; 317 pp. 3-447-04370-9. Bibl. xv-xxvi.
87 PIETERSMA, Albert: The Old Greek psalter: studies in honour of Albert
    Pietersma. EHiebert, Robert J.V.; Cox, Claude E.; Gentry, Peter J.:
    JSOT.S 332: Shf 2001, Sheffield A. 346 pp. 1-84127-209-4. Bibl. 9-12.
88 PULZER, Peter: Liberalism, anti-Semitism, and democracy: essays in
    honour of Peter Pulzer. ETewes, Henning; Wright, Jonathan: NY
    2001, OUP x; (2) 300 pp. 0-19-829723-8.
89 PURY, Albert de: Jacob: commentaire à plusieurs voix de Gen 25-36:
    Mélanges offerts à...de Pury. EMacchi, Jean-Daniel; Römer, Thomas:
    MoBi 44: Genève 2001, Labor et F. 399 pp. €36.59. 2-8309-0987-9.
90 QUISPEL, Gilles: From Poimandres to Jacob Böhme: gnosis, hermetism
    and the christian tradition. EVan den Broek, Roelof; Van Heertum,
    Cis: Bibliotheca Philosophica Hermetica 4: Amst 2001, Bibliotheca
    Philosophica Hermetica 432 pp. 90-71608-10-7.
91 RAINEY, Anson F.: Past links. EShlomo, Izre'el; Singer, Itamar; Zadok,
    Ran: IOS 18: 1998 ⇒14,96. RBSOAS 64 (2001) 101-102 (Oelsner,
    Joachim).
92 RICHARD, Jean: Dei gesta per francos: études sur les croisades dédiés à
    Jean Richard: Crusades studies in honour of Jean Richard. EBalard, M.;
    Kedar, B.Z.; Riley-Smith, J.: Aldershot 2001, Ashgate xxiv; 434 pp.
    $105. 07546-04071. RCRAI (2001/4) 1552-1554 (Contamine, Philippe).
93 RICHARDSON, Peter: Text and artifact. EWilson, Stephen G.; Desjardins,
    Michel: 2000 ⇒16,97. RNT 43 (2001) 402-410 (Damm, Alex); TJT 17
    (2001) 304-6 (Crook, Zeba A.); SR 30 (2001) 457-8 (Murray, Michele).
94 ROBERT, Fernand: Dieux, héros et médecins grecs: hommage à F. Robert.
    Littératures et civilisations antiques: Besançon 2001, Presses Univ.
    Franc-Comtoises viii; 225 pp. 28462-70171 [REA 104,575—Cusset, C.].

95 ROBINSON, Haddon W.: The big idea of biblical preaching. ^EWillhite, Keith; Gibson, Scott M.: 1999 ⇒15,75. ^RTrinJ 22 (2001) 138-143 (*Hurst, Larry*).

96 ROBINSON, James M.: From quest to Q. ^EAsgeirsson, Jon Ma.; De Troyer, Kristin; Meyer, Marvin W.: BEThL 146: 2000 ⇒16,100. ^REThL 77 (2001) 211-214 (*Verheyden, J.*); RivBib 49 (2001) 241-247 (*Poppi, Angelico*); JThS 52 (2001) 803-805 (*Downing, F. Gerald*); TJT 17 (2001) 281-282 (*Kirk, Alan*); CBQ 63 (2001) 579-581 (*Fleddermann, Harry T.*).

97 RUSSELL, Letty M.: Liberating eschatology. ^ERussell Farley, Margaret; Jones, Serene: 1999 ⇒15,78. ^RNBl 82 (2001) 95-96 (*Rowland, Chris*).

98 SAUER, James A.: The archaeology of Jordan. ^EStager, Lawrence E.; Greene, Joseph A.; Coogan, Michael D.: 2000 ⇒16,105. ^RWZKM 91 (2001) 384-387 (*Jaroš, Karl*).

99 SCHÄFER, Jörg: Ithaké: Festschrift für Jörg Schäfer zum 75. Geburtstag am 25. April 2001. ^EBöhm, Stephanie; Eickestedt, Klaus-Valtin von: Wü 2001, Ergon xi; 284 pp. 3-935556-62-4. 30 pl.

100 SCHENKER, Adrian: La double transmission du texte biblique: études d'histoire du texte offertes en hommage à Adrian Schenker. ^EGoldman, Yohanan; Uehlinger, Christoph: OBO 179: Gö 2001, Vandenhoeck & R. (6) 114 pp. 3-525-53993-2. Bibl. 105-114.

101 SCHMUTTERMAYR, Georg: Steht nicht geschrieben?: Studien zur Bibel und ihrer Wirkungsgeschichte: Festschrift für Georg Schmuttermayr. ^EFrühwald-König, Johannes; Prostmeier, Ferdinand R.; Zwick, Reinhold: Rg 2001, Pustet 655 pp. 3-7917-1747-2.

102 SEYBOLD, Klaus D.: Prophetie und Psalmen: Festschrift für Klaus Seybold zum 65. Geburtstag. ^EHuwyler, Beat; Mathys, Hans-Peter; Weber, Beat: AOAT 280: Müns 2001, Ugarit-Verlag xi; 315 pp. 3-934628-01-X.

103 SMITH, Harry S.: Studies on ancient Egypt in honour of H.S. Smith. ^ELeahy, Anthony; Tait, John Gavin: Occasional Publications 13: 1999 ⇒15,86. ^RBiOr 58 (2001) 550-555 (*Altenmüller, Hartwig*).

104 STEK, John H.: Reading and hearing the word. ^ELeder, Arie C.: 1998 ⇒14,113; 15,89. ^RTrinJ 22 (2001) 138-143 (*Hurst, Larry*).

105 STUHLMACHER, Peter: Evangelium, Schriftauslegung, Kirche. 1997 ⇒13,92; 14,114. ^RSNTU.A 22 (1997) 209-212 (*Fuchs, Albert*).

106 THISELTON, Anthony C.: After Pentecost: language and biblical interpretation. ^EBartholomew, Craig G.; Green, Colin; Möller, Karl: Scripture and Hermeneutics 2: GR 2001, Zondervan xxxvi; 425 pp. £25. 0-310-23412-3.

107 THOMAS, John David: Essays and texts in honor of J. David Thomas. ^EGagos, Traianos; Bagnall, Roger S.: ASP 42: NHv 2001, The American Society of Papyrologists xxi; 293 pp. $45. 0-9700591-3-2. Bibl. Thomas xiii-xxi.

108 THOMPSON, William G.: The gospel of Matthew in current study: studies in memory of William G. Thompson, S.J. ^EAune, David Edward: GR 2001, Eerdmans xii; 191 pp. $25. 0-8028-4673-4. Bibl. 185-189. ^RCBQ 63 (2001) 780-781 (*Heil, John Paul*).

109 VAN DER VEN, Johannes A.: The human image of God. ^EZiebertz, Hans-Georg , al.: Lei 2001, Brill xiii; 438 pp. 90-04-12031-9.

110 VATTIONI, Francesco: Biblica et semitica. ^ECagni, Luigi: SMDSA 59: 1999 ⇒15,94. ^RSEÅ 66 (2001) 197-200 (*Görtz-Wrisberg, Irene von*).

111 VEENHOF, Klaas R.: Veenhof anniversary volume: studies presented to Klaas R. Veenhof on the occasion of his sixty-fifth birthday. EVan Soldt, Wilfred Hugo: UNHAII 89: Lei 2001, Nederl. Inst. voor het Nabije Oosten viii; 560 pp. €85. 90625-80912. Bibl. Veenhof 553-560.

112 VOGLER, Werner: leqach 1: Mitteilungen und Beiträge. Lp 2001, Thomas 158 pp. 3-86174-073-7. Forschungsstelle Judentum an der Theologischen Fakultät Leipzig.

113 WEITZMAN, Michael Perry: Biblical Hebrew, biblical texts: essays in memory of Michael P. Weitzman. ERapoport-Albert, Ada; Greenberg, Gillian: JSOT.S 333; The Hebrew Bible and its Versions 2: Shf 2001, Sheffield A. 528 pp. 1-84127-235-3. Bibl. 476-501.

114 WELTEN, Peter: Exegese vor Ort: Festschrift für Peter Welten zum 65. Geburtstag. EMaier, Christl; Liwak, Rüdiger; Jörns, Klaus-Peter: Lp 2001, Evangelische 445 pp. 3-374-01895-5.

115 WENTE, Edward F.: Gold of praise: studies on ancient Egypt in honor of Edward F. Wente. SAOC 58: Ch 2000, Oriental Inst.itute of the Univ. of Chicago xxxi; 494 pp. $75. 140 fig.

A1.2 **Miscellanea** *unius* auctoris

116 **Adamo, David T.** Explorations in African biblical studies. Eugene 2001, Wipf and S. iii; 164 pp. $18. 1-57910-682-X [BOTSA 11, 23].

117 **Andreau, Jean** Patrimoines, échanges et prêts d'argent: l'économie romaine. 1997 ⇒14,129. RGn. 73 (2001) 272-273 (*Herz, Peter*).

118 **Assmann, Jan** Religion und kulturelles Gedächtnis: zehn Studien. 2000 ⇒16,127. RThZ 57 (2001) 388-389 (*Sommer, Andreas Urs*).

119 **Baeck, Leo** Aus drei Jahrtausenden; das Evangelium als Urkunde der jüdischen Glaubensgeschichte. *Friedlander, Albert H.; Klappert, Bertold; Licharz, Werner*: Leo Baeck Werke 4: Gü 2000, Gü 488 pp.

120 **Barthélemy, Dominique** Découvrir l'écriture. LeDiv: 2000 ⇒16,129. RATT 7 (2001) 534-543 (*Marocco, Giuseppe*).

121 **Barton, Stephen C.** Life together: family, sexuality and community in the New Testament and today. E 2001, Clark xiv; 256 pp. £17. 0-567-08772-7 [RB 109,153].

122 **Bauckham, Richard J.** The fate of the dead: studies on the Jewish and christian apocalypses. NT.S 93: 1998 ⇒14,132. RThLZ 126 (2001) 45-47 (*Frey, Jörg*); Apocrypha 12 (2001) 273-275 (*Nuvolone, Flavio G.*).

123 **Baumert, Norbert** Studien zu den Paulusbriefen. SBAB 32: Stu 2001, Kath. Bibelwerk 320 pp. 3-460-06321-1.

124 **Beauchamp, Paul** Testament biblique. P 2001, Bayard 202 pp. €18.90. 2-227-47034-8. Préf. de Paul Ricoeur.

125 **Bergmeier, Roland** Das Gesetz im Römerbrief. WUNT 121: 2000 ⇒ 16,132. RThLZ 126 (2001) 632-634 (*Klaiber, Walter*).

126 **Betz, Hans Dieter** Gesammelte Aufsätze. Antike und Christentum 4: 1998 ⇒14,134; 16,133. RThG 44 (2001) 297-298 (*Giesen, Heinz*); SMSR 67 (2001) 193-203 (*Lancellotti, Maria Grazia*); RBLit 3 (2001) 495-499 (*Hock, Ronald F.*).

127 **Black, C. Clifton** The rhetoric of the gospel: theological artistry in the gospels and Acts. St Louis 2001, Chalice xvii; 224 pp. $23. 0-8272-3218-7 [ThD 49,59—Heiser, W. Charles].

128 **Bosse-Griffiths, Kate** Amarna Studies and other selected papers. EGriffiths, John Gwyn: OBO 182: Gö 2001, Vandenhoeck & R. 244 pp. FS74. 3-525-53997-5. Bibl. Bosse-Griffiths 222-236.

129 **Braulik, Georg** Studien zum Deuteronomium und seiner Nachge-
schichte. SBAB 33: Stu 2001, Kath. Bibelwerk 303 pp. €40.39. 3-460-
06331-9. Bibl. 286-293.
130 **Brenk, Frederick E.** Clothed in purple light: studies in VERGIL and in
Latin literature, including aspects of philosophy, religion, magic,
Judaism, and New Testament background. 1999 ⇒15,108. RREA 103
(2001) 566-567 (*Liou-Gille, Bernadette*).
131 **Broshi, Magen** Bread, wine, walls and scrolls. JSPE.S 36: Shf 2001,
Sheffield A. 312 pp. £65. 1-84127-201-9. Bibl. 1968-2000: 296-300.
132 **Brueggemann, Walter** Deep memory. E*Miller, Patrick D.*: 2000 ⇒16,
139. RCBQ 63 (2001) 769-771 (*Janzen, Waldemar*).
133 **Burchard, Christoph** Studien zur Theologie... des NT. E*Sänger, Dieter*: WUNT 107: 1998 ⇒14,140; 16,142. RJThS 52 (2001) 209-211
(*Barrett, C.K.*); ThG 44 (2001) 298-300 (*Giesen, Heinz*).
134 **Chirilă, Ioan** Fragmentarium exegetic (Exegetisches Bruchstück). Cluj
2001, Limes 186 pp.
135 **Chopineau, Jacques** Quand le texte devient parole: anthologie de ses
études bibliques offerte à Jacques Chopineau à l'occasion de sa retraite
comme professeur d'exégèse de l'Ancien Testament. Analecta Bruxellensia 6: Bru 2001, Faculté Univ. de Théologie Protestante 183 pp.
136 **Curto, Silvio** Attraverso l'egittologia: scritti di Silvio Curto. T 2001,
Soprintendenza al Museo delle antichità egizie di Torino xxxv; 622 pp.
88-86130-11-2. Bibl. xxiii-xxxv.
137 **Dautzenberg, Gerhard** Studien zur paulinischen Theologie und zur
frühchristlichen Rezeption des AT: E*Sänger, Dieter*: GSTR 13: 1999
⇒15,118. RBZ 45 (2001) 145-146 (*Wehr, Lothar*).
138 **Davis, Ellen F.** Getting involved with God: rediscovering the Old
Testament. CM 2001, Cowley x; 208 pp. $14. 1-56101-197-5.
139 **Drane, John** Cultural change and biblical faith. 2000 ⇒16,152.
REvangel 19 (2001) 59-60 (*McKay, W. David J.*).
140 **Ehrlich, Ernst Ludwig** Reden über das Judentum. E*Stegemann, Ekkehard W.*: Judentum und Christentum 6: Stu 2001, Kohlhammer 197 pp.
€17. 3-17-016898-3.
141 **Ellis, Edward Earle** History and interpretation in New Testament perspective. BiblInterp 54: Lei 2001, Brill xvi; 177 pp. €71. 90041-20262.
142 **Elm, Kaspar** Umbilicus mundi: Beiträge zur Geschichte Jerusalems,
der Kreuzzüge, des Kapitels vom Heiligen Grab... und der Ritterorden.
1998 ⇒14,149. RAEM 31/1 (2001) 495-497 (*Jaspert, Nikolas*).
143 **Fee, Gordon D.** To what end exegesis?: essays texual, exegetical, and
theological. GR 2001, Eerdmans x; 378 pp. $26. 0-8028-4925-3.
144 **Ferraro, Giuseppe** Gli autori divini dell'insegnamento: il Padre, Cristo, lo Spirito: studi di esegesi e di teologia biblica. Letture bibliche
16: Città del Vaticano 2001, Vaticana 295 pp. €18.80. 88-209-7154-2.
Bibl. 5-20.
145 **Fiorenza, Elisabeth Schüssler** Cristología feminista crítica: Jesús,
hijo de Miriam, profeta de sabiduría. Estructuras y procesos, religion:
M 2000, Trotta 268 pp. 84-8164-430-7.
146 **Fitzmyer, Joseph A.** The Dead Sea scrolls and christian origins. 2000
⇒16,156. RVJTR 65 (2001) 541-543 (*Meagher, P.M.*); REJ 160
(2001) 513-514 (*Mimouni, Simon C.*); IThQ 66 (2001) 273-274
(*McConvery, Brendan*); Henoch 23 (2001) 383-386 (*Monti, Ludwig*).
147 **Frankemölle, Hubert** Jüdische Wurzeln christlicher Theologie: Studi-
en zum biblischen Kontext neutestamentlicher Texte. BBB 116: 1998
⇒14,151. RThZ 57 (2001) 382-384 (*Weber, Beat*).

148 **Freyne, Seán** Galilee and gospel. WUNT 125: 2000 ⇒16,159. [R]JThS
52 (2001) 775-778 (*Edwards, Ruth B.*); REJ 160 (2001) 514-516 (*Mimouni, Simon C.*); ThLZ 126 (2001) 395-397 (*Zangenberg, Jürgen*);
SNTU.A 26 (2001) 281-283 (*Schreiber, S.*).

149 **Gadamer, Hans-Georg** Hermeneutische Entwürfe: Vorträge und Aufsätze. 2000 ⇒16,162. [R]ThRv 97 (2001) 505-7 (*Hammermeister, Kai*).

150 **Gilbert, Maurice** Il a parlé par les prophètes: thèmes et figures bibliques. 1998 ⇒14,155... 16,163. [R]RThom 101 (2001) 676-678
(*Macaire, David*); EstB 59 (2001) 388-389 (*Asenjo, J.*).

151 **Goldenberg, Gideon** Studies in Semitic linguistics. 1998 ⇒14,156.
[R]JRAS 11 (2001) 58-59 (*Ullendorff, Edward*); BiOr 58 (2001) 219-221 (*Baasten, Martin F.J.*).

152 **Grässer, Erich** Forschungen zur Apostelgeschichte. WUNT 137: Tü
2001, Mohr xi; 359 pp. 3-16-147592-5. Bibl. 352-353.

153 **Greenfield, Jonas C.** 'Al kanfei Yonah: collected studies of Jonas C.
Greenfield on Semitic philology. [E]*Paul, Shalom; Stone, Michael; Pinnick, Avital*: Lei 2001, Brill 2 vols. €171. 90041-21706. Bibl. 945-951.

154 **Grottanelli, Cristiano** Kings & prophets. 1999 ⇒15,132; 16,168.
[R]ZRGG 53 (2001) 77-78 (*Stroumsa, Guy G.*).

155 **Gunkel, Hermann** Water for a thirsty land: Israelite literature and religion. [E]*Hanson, K.C.*: Fortress classics in biblical studies: Mp 2001,
Fortress x; 182 pp. $16. 0-8006-3438-1. Bibl. 168-171

156 **Hahn, Ferdinand** Mission in neutestamentlicher Sicht: Aufsätze, Vorträge und Predigten. MWF 8: Erlangen 1999, Erlanger Verlag für Mission und Ökumene 143 pp. €17.50. 3-16-147242-X.

157 **Hauerwas, Stanley** Wilderness wanderings: probing twentieth century
theology and philosophy. L 2001, SCM xi; 242 pp. £15. 03340-28590.

158 **Heine, Susanne** Frauenbilder—Menschenrechte. 1999 ⇒15,136.
[R]SaThZ 5 (2001) 215-218 (*Arzt, Silvia*).

159 **Heise, Jürgen** Auslegen durch Nachdenken: Exegese johanneischer
Texte und hermeneutische Überlegungen. Theologie 33: Müns 2001,
Lit 122 pp. 3-8258-5267-9.

160 **Hengel, Martin** Kleine Schriften I. WUNT 90: 1996 ⇒12,128... 16,
170. [R]SNTU.A 23 (1998) 239-242 (*Fuchs, Albert*);

161 Kleine Schriften II. WUNT 109: 1999 ⇒15,139; 16,171. [R]ThG 44
(2001) 301-303 (*Giesen, Heinz*).

162 **Hermisson, Hans-Jürgen** Studien zu Prophetie und Weisheit. FAT
23: 1998 ⇒14,161; 16,172. [E]*Barthel, Jörg; Jauss, Hannelore;
Koenen, Klaus*: [R]RBLit 3 (2001) 196-200 (*Brown, William P.*).

163 **Hofius, Otfried Friedrich** Neutestamentliche Studien. WUNT 132:
2000 ⇒16,174. [R]DBM 20 (2001) 138-146 (*Karacolis, Christos*).

164 **Holter, Knut** Yahweh in Africa: essays on Africa and the OT. 2000 ⇒
16,175. [R]BiBh 27 (2001) 76-78 (*Puthenveettil, Jose*); BOTSA 10
(2001) 23-4 (*Boshoff, Willem*); OTEs 14 (2001) 550-52 (*Baloyi, M.E.*);
RBLit 3 (2001) 163-166 (*Adamo, David Tuesday*).

165 **Kaiser, Otto** Gottes und der Menschen Weisheit. BZAW 261: 1998 ⇒
14,166. [R]ThLZ 126 (2001) 749-750 (*Krüger, Thomas*);

166 Studien zur Literaturgeschichte des Alten Testamentes. FzB 90: 2000
⇒16,176. [R]JBL 120 (2001) 532-535 (*Berge, Kaare*); RBLit 3 (2001)
166-170 (*Berge, Kaare*).

167 **Kegler, Jürgen** "dass Gerechtigkeit und Friede sich küssen (Ps 85,
11)": gesammelte Aufsätze, Predigten, Rundfunkreden. BEAT 48: Fra
2001, Lang 452 pp. 3-631-37140-3. Bibl. 415-430.

168 **Kirsch, Jonathan** I raconti proibiti della bibbia. Mi 2001 <1997>, Garzanti 410 pp. €20.14.
169 **Köstenberger, Andreas J.** Studies on John and gender: a decade of scholarship. Studies in Biblical Literature 38: NY 2001, Lang xiii; 378 pp. $68. 0-8204-5275-0. Bibl. 353-376.
170 **Lambrecht, Jan** Collected studies: on Pauline literature and on the book of Revelation. AnBib 147: R 2001, E.P.I.B. xv; 435 pp. 88-7653-147-5.
171 **Landy, Francis** Beauty and the enigma: and other essays on the Hebrew Bible. JSOT.S 312: Shf 2001, Sheffield A. 427 pp. 18412-71470.
172 **Legrand, Lucien** The word is near you: collected papers of Lucien Legrand, MEP, vol. 1. *EXavier, A. Aloysius; Kumar, M. David Stanly*: ITS.S 3: Bangalore 2001, St Peter's Pont. Inst. viii; 423 pp. Rs200/$17 [JDh 27/1,120].
173 **Leibowitz, Yeshayahu** La fede ebraica. *EOfran, Mira*; *THaviv, Daniel*: F 2001, Giuntina 108 pp.
174 **Lévinas, E.** Nell'ora delle nazioni: letture talmudiche e scritti fisosofico-politici. 2000 ⇒16,185. *R*StPat 48 (2001) 534-5 (*Grusovin, Marco*).
175 **Loader, James Alfred** Begegnung mit Gott: gesammelte Studien im Bereich des Alten Testaments. Wiener alttestamentliche Studien 3: Fra 2001, Lang 410 pp. 3-631-37713-4.
176 **Loewen, Jacob A.** The bible in cross-cultural perspective. 2000 ⇒16, 181. *R*RExp 98 (2001) 283-284 (*Berry, Donald L.*).
177 **Lohfink, Norbert** Studien zum Deuteronomium und zur deuteronomistischen Literatur, 4. SBAB 31: 2000 ⇒16,183. *R*ThLZ 126 (2001) 1250-1252 (*Perlitt, Lothar*);
178 Hinos dos pobres: o Magnificat, os Hodayot de Qumran e alguns salmos tardios. *TRoyer, Edwino Aloysius*: São Paulo 2001, Loyola 182 pp. 85-15-02211-7. Bibl. sobre os hodayot 1948-1989 por *Ulrich Dahmen*.
179 **Lohse, Eduard** Das Neue Testament als Urkunde des Evangeliums. Exegetische Studien zur Theologie des NT III. FRLANT 192: 2000 ⇒ 16,184. *R*OrdKor 43 (2001) 132-133 (*Giesen, Heinz*).
180 **Luck, Georg** Ancient pathways... morals and magic in the ancient world. 2000 ⇒16,185. *R*HeyJ 42 (2001) 254-255 (*Waterfield, Robin*).
181 **Mack, Burton L.** The christian myth: origins, logic, and legacy. NY 2001, Continuum 237 pp. $26. 0-8264-1355-2 [ThD 49,276—W. Charles Heiser].
182 **Malamat, Abraham** History of biblical Israel: major problems and minor issues. Culture and history of the Ancient Near East 7: Lei 2001, Brill xv; 476 pp. €89. 90-04-12009-2.
183 **Mathys, Hans-Peter** Vom Anfang und Ende. BEAT 47: 2000 ⇒16, 190. *R*StPat 48 (2001) 503-507 (*Lorenzin,Tiziano*).
184 **Moloney, Francis** 'A hard saying': the gospel and culture. ColMn 2001, Liturgical xiv; 297 pp. $30. 0-8146-5953-5. *R*DoLi 51 (2001) 446-447 (*Carroll, Denis*).
185 **Mosès, Stéphane** L'Eros e la legge: letture bibliche. *TVogelmann, Vanna Lucattini*: Schulim Vogelmann 80: F 2001, La giuntina 153 pp. 88-8057-102-8.
186 **Mussner, Franz** Jesus von Nazareth im Umfeld Israels. *ETheobald, Michael*: WUNT 111: 1999 ⇒15,160; 16,194. *R*FrRu 8 (2001) 301-303 (*Keller, Winfrid*); RBLit 3 (2001) 355-359 (*Labahn, Michael*).
187 **Neirynck, Frans** Evangelica III: 1992-2000: collected essays. BEThL 150: Lv 2001, Univ. Pr. xvii; 666 pp. €60. 90-429-0974-9. *R*EThL 77 (2001) 473-475 (*Verheyden, J.*).

188 **O'Daly, Gerard** Platonism pagan and christian: studies in PLOTINUS and AUGUSTINE. CStS: Aldershot 2001, Ashgate viii; 340 pp.
189 **O'Neill, John C.** The point of it all: essays on Jesus Christ. 2000 ⇒16, 198. ^{R}CBQ 63 (2001) 585-586 (*Martin, Francis*).
190 **Otzen, Benedikt** Judisk litteratur på Jesu tid: utvalgte afhandlingar fra 25 år. K 2001, ANIS 248 pp [SEÅ 68,223s—Bengtsson, Håkan].
191 **Patanè, Massimo** Orientalia. Genève 2001, Tellus Nostra 28 pp.
192 **Pearson, Birger A.** The emergence of the christian religion. 1997 ⇒ 13,154; 15,162. ^{R}Religion 31 (2001) 305-307 (*BeDuhn, Jason*).
193 **Penna, Romano** Vangelo e inculturazione: studi sul rapporto tra rivelazione e cultura nel Nuovo Testamento. Studi sulla Bibbia e il suo ambiente 6: CinB 2001, San Paolo 847 pp. 88-215-4434-6.
194 **Perea Yébenes, Sabino** Entre occidente y oriente: temas de historia romana: aspectos religiosos. Graeco-Romanae Religionis Electa Collectio 4: M 2001, Signifer L. 370 pp.
195 **Picard, Jean-Claude** Le continent apocryphe. IP 36: 1999 ⇒15,163. ^{R}JSJ 32 (2001) 335-337 (*Tromp, Johannes*); Apocrypha 12 (2001) 298-301 (*Zamagni, C.*).
196 **Pilch, John J.** Il sapore della parola: lessico della vita quotidiana nella bibbia. 2000 ⇒16,200. ^{R}RdT 42 (2001) 466-467 (*Ska, Jean Louis*).
197 **Rabello, Alfredo Mordechai** The Jews in the Roman Empire. CStS 645: 2000 ⇒16,202. ^{R}REJ 160 (2001) 512-513 (*Mimouni, Simon C.*).
198 **Radcliffe, Timothy** I call you friends. NY 2001, Continuum vi; 225 pp. £10. ^{R}NBl 82 (2001) 348-350 (*Soskice, Janet Martin*).
199 **Rajak, Tessa** The Jewish dialogue with Greece and Rome: studies in cultural and social interaction. AGJU 48: Lei 2001, Brill xix; 579 pp. €148. 90-04-11283-5.
200 **Räisänen, Heikki** Challenges to biblical interpretation: collected essays 1991-2000. BiblInterp 59: Lei 2001, Brill x; 319 pp. €86. 90-04-12052-1.
201 **Rendtorff, Rolf** Der Text in seiner Endgestalt: Schritte auf dem Weg zu einer Theologie des Alten Testaments. Neuk 2001, Neuk 289 pp. 3-7887-1821-8.
202 **Rössler, Otto** Gesammelte Schriften zur Semitohamitistik. ^{E}*Schneider, Thomas*: AOAT 287: Müns 2001, Ugarit-Verlag 848 pp. €103. 3-934628-13-3. Mitarbeit *Oskar Kaelin*.
203 **Rubinstein, Eliezer** Syntax and semantics: studies in Biblical Hebrew and Modern Hebrew. ^{E}*Borokovsky, Esther; Trummer, Penina*: 1998 ⇒ 14,192. ^{R}JSSt 46 (2001) 313-316 (*Azar, Moshe*).
204 **Saebø, Magne** On the way to canon. JSOT.S 191: 1998 ⇒14,194; 16, 204. ^{R}JBL 120 (2001) 345-347 (*Willis, Timothy M.*).
205 **Sanday, William** Essays in biblical criticism and exegesis. ^{E}*Evans, Craig A.; Porter, Stanley E.*: JSNT.S 225; Classics in Biblical and Theological Studies Supplement Series 2: Shf 2001, Sheffield A. 242 pp. 1-84127-281-7. Collab. *Scott N. Dolff*.
206 **Schaller, Berndt** Fundamenta Judaica: Studien zum antiken Judentum und zum Neuen Testament. ^{E}*Doering, Lutz; Steudel, Annette*: StUNT 25: Gö 2001, Vandenhoeck & R. 243 pp. €60. 33 3-525-53379-9. Bibl. 211-218. ^{R}OrdKor 42 (2001) 421-422 (*Giesen, Heinz*).
207 **Schenker, Adrian** Recht und Kult im Alten Testament. OBO 172: 2000 ⇒16,206. ^{R}CBQ 63 (2001) 578-579 (*Morrow, William S.*).
208 **Schmitt, Armin** Der Gegenwart verpflichtet: Studien zur biblischen Literatur des Frühjudentums. ^{E}*Wagner, Christian*: BZAW 292: 2000 ⇒16,207. ^{R}ThRv 97 (2001) 384-385 (*Marböck, Johannes*).

209 **Schmitt, Hans Christoph** Theologie in Prophetie und Pentateuch: ge-sammelte Schriften. [E]*Schorn, Ulrike; Büttner, Matthias*: BZAW 310: B 2001, De Gruyter x; 376 pp. €98. 3-11-017188-0. Bibl. 367-370.

210 **Schroer, Silvia** Wisdom has built her house: studies on the figure of Sophia in the bible. [T]*Maloney, Linda M.; McDonough, William*: 2000 ⇒16,208. [R]MillSt 48 (2001) 152-153 (*Mangan, Céline*).

211 **Schürmann, Heinz** Im Knechtdienst Christi: zur weltpriesterlichen Existenz. [E]*Scholtissek, Klaus*: 1998 ⇒14,198. [R]SNTU.A 25 (2000) 284-285 (*Scheuer, M.*).

212 **Ska, Jean-Louis** La strada e la casa: itinerari biblici. Collana biblica, i temi della casa 1: Bo 2001, EDB 221 pp. €13.94. 88-10-22102-8.

213 **Soares-Prabhu, George M.** Theology of liberation: an Indian biblical perspective. Jnana-Deepa Vidyapeeth Theology Series 3; Collected Writings of George M. Soares-Prabhu, S.J. Volume 3: Pune 2001, Jnana-Deepa Vidyaeth 296 pp.

214 **Speyer, Wolfgang** Kleine Schriften II. WUNT 116: 1999 ⇒15,176; 16,215. [R]ThG 44 (2001) 300-301 (*Giesen, Heinz*).

215 **Spieckermann, Hermann** Gottes Liebe zu Israel: Studien zur Theologie des Alten Testaments. FAT 33: Tü 2001, Mohr x; 234 pp. €80.78 3-16-147653-0.

216 **Stroumsa, Guy G.** Barbarian philosophy: the religious revolution of early christianity. WUNT 112: 1999 ⇒15,177; 16,217. [R]Sal. 63 (2001) 405-406 (*Vicent, R.*); JECS 9 (2001) 277-278 (*Calvert, Kenneth R.*).

217 **Studer, Basil** Mysterium caritatis. 1999 ⇒15,178; 16,218. [R]FZPhTh 48 (2001) 248-252 (*Emery, Gilles*); VetChr 38 (2001) 361-362 (*Carnevale, Laura*).

218 **Sundermann, Werner**, *al.*, Manichaica iranica: ausgewählte Schriften. [E]*Reck, Christiane*: SOR 89: R 2001, Istituto Italiano per l'Africa e l'Oriente xi; 966 pp; 2 vols [LTP 59,568s—Poirier, Paul-Hubert].

219 **Theobald, Michael** Studien zum Römerbrief. WUNT 136: Tü 2001, Mohr ix; 599 pp. €109. 3-16-147519-4.

220 **Tov, Emanuel** The Greek and Hebrew Bible. VT.S 72: 1999 ⇒15, 180. [R]RBLit 3 (2001) 137-140 (*Rösel, Martin*).

221 **Troiani, Lucio** Il perdono cristiano. StBi 123: 1999 ⇒15,181. [R]RSCI 54 (2001) 530-534 (*Ramelli, Ilaria L.E.*).

222 **Tuckett, Christopher M.** Christology and the New Testament: Jesus and his earliest followers. E 2001, Univ. Pr. ix; 246 pp. 0-7486-0869-9. £16. Bibl. 234-238. [R]RRT 8 (2001) 445 (*Wansbrough, Henry*).

223 **Viviano, Benedict Thomas** Trinity—kingdom—church: essays in biblical theology. NTOA 48: Gö 2001, Vandenhoeck & R. (10) 280 pp. FS85. 3-525-53949-5.

224 **Vorster, Willem S.** Speaking of Jesus. [E]*Botha, J. Eugene*: NT.S 92: 1999 ⇒15,183. [R]JT.hS 52 (2001) 212-218 (*Porter, Stanley E.*); EThL 77 (2001) 206-208 (*Verheyden, J.*).

225 **Warfield, Benjamin B.** Rivelazione e ispirazione. Caltanissetta 2001, Alfa & O. 327 pp;

226 La persona e l'opera di Cristo. Caltanissetta 2001, Alfa & O. 535 pp.

227 **Waschke, Ernst-Joachim** Der Gesalbte: Studien zur alttestamentlichen Theologie. BZAW 306: B 2001, De Gruyter x; 339 pp. €98. 3-11-017017-5. Bibl. 283-317.

228 **Winston, David** The ancestral philosophy: Hellenistic philosophy in second temple Judaism. [E]*Stering, Gregory E.*: Studia Philonica Monographs 4; BJSt 331: Providence, RI 2001, Brown Univ. viii; 249 pp. $35. 1-930675-08-9.

A1.3 *Plurium compilationes* biblicae

229 ^E**Adam, A.K.M.** Postmodern interpretations of the bible: a reader. Saint Louis 2001, Chalice 277 pp. $30. 0-8272-2970-4 [BiTod 39, 312—Bergant, Dianne].

230 ^E**Aichele, George** Culture, entertainment and the bible. JSOT.S 309: 2000 ⇒16,227. ^RBiblInterp 9 (2001) 449-451 (*Kreitzer, Larry J.; Rooke, Deborah W.*)

231 **Alegre Aragüés, José,** *al.,* Personajes del Nuevo Testamento. Estella (Navarra) 2001, Verbo Divino 134 pp. 84-8169-434-7.

232 **Anzulewicz, P.,** *al.,* Gesù servo: di Dio e degli uomini. "Cristologia" 6: 1998 ⇒14,210. ^RAsp. 48 (2001) 249-253 (*Scognamiglio, Edoardo*).

233 ^E**Ådna, Jostein; Kvalbein, Hans** The mission of the early church. to Jews and Gentiles. WUNT 127: 2000 ⇒16,226. ^RNZM 57 (2001) 307-308 (*Schelbert, Georg*).

234 ^E**Baker, David W.; Arnold, Bill T.** The face of Old Testament studies. 1999 ⇒15,192. ^RLouvSt 26 (2001) 282-283 (*Eynikel, Erik*).

235 ^E**Baldermann, Ingo; Dassmann, Ernst** Menschenwürde. Jahrbuch für Biblische Theologie (JBTh) 15: Neuk 2001, Neuk xiv; 385 pp. 3-7887-1800-5. In Verbindung mit *Paul D. Hanson, Ulrich Mauser* et al.

236 ^E**Barthe, Claude** L'Exégèse chrétienne aujourd'hui. 2000 ⇒16,1434. ^RRThom 101 (2001) 673-675 (*Bazelaire, Thomas-M. de*).

237 ^E**Bauckham, Richard J.** The gospels for all christians: rethinking the gospel audiences. 1998 ⇒14,213... 16,235. ^REvangel 19 (2001) 55 (*Baxter, Tony*).

238 **Becking, Bob,** *al.,* Only one God?: monotheism in ancient Israel and the veneration of the goddess Asherah. BiSe 77: Shf 2001, Sheffield A. 231 pp. 1-84127-199-3. Bibl. 202-222.

239 ^E**Beutler, Johannes H.** Der neue Mensch in Christus: hellenistische Anthropologie und Ethik im Neuen Testament. QD 190: FrB 2001, Herder 202 pp. €24.50. 3-451-02190-0. ^ROrdKor 42 (2001) 560-561 (*Giesen, Heinz*).

240 **Bianchi, Enzo,** *al.,* La bellezza. PSV 44: Bo 2001, EDB 277 pp. €17.

241 Bible et sciences humaines. LV.F 56/4 (2001) 361-478.

242 ^E**Black, David Alan; Dockery, David S.** Interpreting the New Testament: essays on methods and issues. Nv 2001, Broadman and H. x; 565 pp. $30. 0-8054-1850-4 [BiTod 39318,—Senior, Donald].

243 ^{ET}**Blowers, Paul M.** The bible in Greek christian antiquity. The Bible through the ages 1: 1997 ⇒13,177... 15,198. ^RRBLit 3 (2001) 130-136 (*De Troyer, Kristin*).

244 ^E**Borghi, Ernesto** Leggere la bibbia oggi: dal testo alla vita. Parola di vita: Mi 2001, Àncora 174 pp. 88-7610-881-5.

245 ^E**Bowley, James E.** Living traditions of the bible: scripture in Jewish, Christian, and Muslim practice. 1999 ⇒15,201. ^RHebStud 42 (2001) 394-395 (*Kaminsky, Joel S.*).

246 ^E**Brenner, Athalya** Prophets and Daniel. Feminist Companion to the Bible 2/8: NY 2001, Continuum 317 pp. $28.50. 1-84127-163-2 [ThD 49,387—Heiser, W. Charles];

247 Ruth and Esther. 1999 ⇒15,203; 16,242. ^RJThS 52 (2001) 151-152 (*Lipton, Diana*); SEÅ 66 (2001) 213-216 (*Sjöberg, Mikael*); RBLit 3 (2001) 244-247 (*Davison, Lisa*).

248 ^E**Broyles, Craig C.** Interpreting the Old Testament: a guide for exegesis. GR 2001, Baker 272 pp. $20. 0-8010-2271-1.

249 **Caron, Gérald**, al., Women also journeyed with him: feminist perspectives on the bible. 2000 ⇒16,245. ᴿCBQ 63 (2001) 372-373 (*Wiley, Tatha*).

250 ᴱ**Carroll, R.M.** Daniel Rethinking contexts, rereading texts: contributions from the social sciences to biblical interpretation. JSOT.S 299: 2000 ⇒16,246. ᴿCBQ 63 (2001) 172-174 (*Seeman, Chris*).

251 ᴱ**Carson, D.A.; O'Brien, Peter Thomas; Seifrid, Mark A.** Justification and variegated nomism 1: the complexities of second temple Judaism. WUNT 2/140: Tü 2001, Mohr 619 pp. €49. 3-16-146994-1. ᴿLuThK 25 (2001) 208-209 (*Stolle, Volker*).

252 ᴱ**Chapman, Stephen B.; Helmer, Christine; Landmesser, Christof** Biblischer Text und theologische Theoriebildung. BThSt 44: Neuk 2001, Neuk viii; 247 pp. 3-7887-1835-8.

253 **Chilton, Bruce David; Evans, Craig A.** Jesus in context. AGJU 39: 1997 ⇒13,183; 15,209. ᴿRHPhR 81 (2001) 238-239 (*Grappe, Ch.*).

254 ᴱ**Chilton, Bruce David; Evans, Craig A.** Authenticating the words of Jesus. NTTS 28,1-2: 1999 ⇒15,207. ᴿThLZ 126 (2001) 276-278 (*Frey, Jörg*);

255 James the Just and christian origins. NT.S 98: 1999 ⇒15,208; 16,249. ᴿJThS 52 (2001) 287-290 (*Painter, John*); EThL 77 (2001) 224-226 (*Verheyden, J.*); CBQ 63 (2001) 373-375 (*Wilson, Walter T.*).

256 ᴱ**Chilton, Bruce David; Neusner, Jacob** The brother of Jesus: James the Just and his mission. LVL 2001, Westminster xiv; 210 pp. $20. 0-664-22299-4.

257 **Cipriani, Settimio**, al., La fede nella bibbia. DSBP 21. 1998 ⇒14, 224. ᴿAsp. 48 (2001) 575-579 (*Iaia, Gaetano*).

258 ᴱ**Coogan, Michael D.** The Oxford history of the biblical world. NY 2001, OUP xi; 487 pp. $20. 0-19-513937-2.

259 ᴱ**Donfried, Karl P.; Richardson, Peter** Judaism and christianity in first-century Rome. 1998 ⇒14,228... 16,9847. ᴿVJTR 65 (2001) 539-541 (*Meagher, P.M.*); JSSt 46 (2001) 336-337 (*Williams, Margaret H.*); TJT 17 (2001) 285-287 (*Donaldson, Terence L.*)

260 ᴱ**Dube, Musa W.** Other ways of reading: African women and the bible. Global perspectives on biblical scholarship 2: Atlanta, GA 2001, SBL viii; 254 pp. $25. 1-58983-009-1.

261 ᴱ**Ebner, Martin; Fischer, Irmtraud** Klage. JBTh 16: Neuk 2001, Neuk viii; 421 pp. 3-7887-1863-3.

262 ᴱ**Engberg-Pedersen, Troels** Paul beyond the Judaism/Hellenism divide. LVL 2001, Westminster x; 355 pp. $40. 0-664-22406-7.

263 ᴱ**Evans, Craig A.; Sanders, James A.** Early christian interpretation of the scriptures of Israel. JSNT.S 148: 1997 ⇒13,191. ᴿThLZ 126 (2001) 900-901 (*Saebø, Magne*).

264 ᴱ**Evans, Craig A.** The interpretation of scripture in early Judaism and christianity. JSPE.S 33: 2000 ⇒16,257. ᴿETR 76 (2001) 434-436 (*Singer, Christophe*); TrinJ 22 (2001) 259-262 (*Pao, David W.*).

265 ᴱ**Fiedler, Peter** Studien zu einer neutestamentlichen Hermeneutik nach Auschwitz. SBAB 27: 1999 ⇒15,229. ᴿZNT 8 (2001) 59-62 (*Faßbeck, Gabriele*).

266 ᴱ**Flesher, Paul** Targum and Peshitta. Targum Studies II. SF-SHJ 165: 1998 ⇒14,238...16,1546. ᴿJSSt 46 (2001) 340-41 (*Hayman, A. Peter*).

267 ᴱ**Flint, Peter W.** The bible at Qumran: text, shape, and interpretation. Studies in the Dead Sea Scrolls and related literature: GR 2001, Eerdmans xv; 266 pp. £16/$22. 080-2846-300. Assist. *Kim, Tae Hun*. ᴿRRT 8 (2001) 514-516 (*Norton, Gerard J.*).

268 ^EFrankemölle, Hubert Lebendige Welt Jesu und des NT. 2000 ⇒16, 261. ^RFgNT 14 (2001) 164-165 (*Stenschke, Christoph*).

269 ^EGeoltrain, Pierre Aux origines du christianisme. 'Le Monde' actuel 98: 2000 ⇒16,264. ^RApocrypha 12 (2001) 278-279 (*Amsler, F.*).

270 ^EGrabbe, Lester L. Did Moses speak Attic?: Jewish historiography and scripture in the Hellenistic period. JSOT.S 317; European Seminar in Historical Methodology 3: Shf 2001, Sheffield A. 352 pp. 1-8412-7155-1.

271 ^EGrabbe, Lester L.; Haak, Robert D. 'Every city shall be forsaken': urbanism and prophecy in Ancient Israel and the Near East. JSOT.S 330: Shf 2001, Sheffield A. 226 pp. $95. 1-84127-202-7.

272 ^EGreen, Joel B.; Turner, Max Between two horizons: spanning New Testament studies and systematic theology. 2000 ⇒16,267. ^RRRT 8 (2001) 149-152 (*Cöster, Henry*); AThR 83 (2001)129-130 (*Zahl, Paul F.M.*); CBQ 63 (2001) 181-183 (*Topel, John*).

273 ^EGriffiths, Richard The bible in the Renaissance: essays on biblical commentary and translation in the fifteenth and sixteenth centuries. Aldershot 2001, Ashgate 204 pp. $85. 0-7546-0394-6.

274 Haag, Herbert, *al.*, Schön bist du und verlockend: große Paare der Bibel. FrB 2001, Herder 191 pp. €35. 3-451-27616-X.

275 ^EHabel, Norman C. The earth story in the psalms and the prophets. The Earth Bible 4: Shf 2001, Sheffield A. 261 pp. £18. 1-84127-087-3. Bibl. 230-249.

276 Hengel, Martin; Schwemer, Anna Maria Der messianische Anspruch Jesu und die Anfänge der Christologie: vier Studien. WUNT 138: Tü 2001, Mohr xv; 267 pp. €49. 3-16-147669-7.

277 ^EHermans, Michel; Sauvage, Pierre Bible et histoire: écriture, interprétation et action dans le temps. 2000 ⇒16,273. ^REeT(O)32 (2001) 113-115 (*Dumais, Marcel*); SapDom 54 (2001) 369-371 (*Miele, Michele*); ActBib 38 (2001) 200-201 (*Boada, J.*).

278 ^EHess, Richard Samuel; Wenham, Gordon J. Zion, city of our God. 1999 ⇒15,238; 16,274. ^RLouvSt 26 (2001) 86-87 (*Doyle, Brian*).

279 ^EHilaire, Yves-Marie De RENAN à MARROU: l'histoire du christianisme et les progrès de la méthode historique (1863-1968). 1999 ⇒15, 239. ^RRHE 96 (2001) 555-556 (*Hannick, Jean-Marie*).

280 ^EHolzhey, Helmut; Kohler, Georg In Erwartung eines Endes: Apokalyptik und Geschichte. Theophil 7: Z 2001, Pano 177 pp. 3907576144.

281 ^EHorn, Friedrich Wilhelm Das Ende des Paulus: historische, theologische und literaturgeschichtliche Aspekte. BZNW 106: B 2001, De Gruyter viii; 359 pp. €98. 3-11-017001-9.

282 ^EHorsley, Richard A. Paul and politics. 2000 ⇒16,275. ^RCBQ 63 (2001) 786-788 (*Love, Stuart L.*).

283 ^EHossfeld, Frank-Lothar Wieviel Systematik erlaubt die Schrift?: auf der Suche nach einer gesamtbiblischen Theologie. QD 185: FrB 2001, Herder 289 pp. €24.50. 3-451-012185-4. Bibl. 289.

284 ^EHuber, Konrad; Repschinski, Boris Wort zum Leben—die Bibel: Beiträge zum Jahr der Bibel: mit einer persönlichen Reflexion von Bischof *Alois Kothgasser*. Innsbruck 2001, Tyrolia 192 pp. 370222419X.

285 ^EJanowski, Bernd; Ego, Beate Das biblische Weltbild und seine altorientalischen Kontexte. FAT 32: Tü 2001, Mohr ix; 587 pp. €99. 3-16-147540-2. Zusammenarbeit mit *Annette Krüger*; Bibl. 544-558.

286 ^EJasper, David; Prickett, Stephen The bible and literature: a reader. 1999 ⇒15,246. ^RAThR 83 (2001) 180-181 (*Wallace, Catherine M.*).

287 ^E**Jobling, David; Pippin, Tina; Schleifer, Ronald** The postmodern bible reader. Oxf 2001, Blackwell xvii; 381 pp. £16. 0-631-21962-5.

288 ^E**Kapera, Zdzisław** The Polish Journal of Biblical Research, vol 1, no. 1, September 2000. 2000 ⇒16,279. ^RCoTh (2001/1) 217-220 (*Chrostowski, Waldemar*).

289 ^E**Kraemer, Ross S.; D'Angelo, Mary R.** Women & christian origins. 1999 ⇒15,365; 16,8225. ^RChH 70 (2001)145-147 (*Torjesen, Karen Jo*); JJS 52 (2001) 171-176 (*Ilan, Tal*); Horizons 27 (2001) 395-396 (*Tilley, Maureen A.*); CBQ 63 (2001) 788-789 (*Osiek, Carolyn*).

290 ^E**Kugel, James** Studies in ancient midrash. CM 2001, Harvard University Press vii; 177 pp. 0-674-00258-X.

291 **Lacocque, A.; Ricoeur, P.** Pensar la biblia: estudios exegéticos y hermenéuticos. Barc 2001, Herder 422 pp. ^REstTrin 35 (2001) 447-449 (*Vázquez Allegue, Jaime*).

292 ^E**Lemaire, André** Prophètes et rois: Bible et Proche-Orient. LeDiv hors série: P 2001, Cerf 304 pp. €29.73. 2-204-06622-2.

293 ^E**Linafelt, Tod** Strange fire: reading the bible after the Holocaust. BiSe 71: 2000 ⇒16,290. ^RRBLit 3 (2001) 116-120 (*Kaminsky, Joel S.*).

294 ^E**Longenecker, Richard N.** Into God's presence: prayer in the New Testament. McMaster N.T. Studies: GR 2001, Eerdmans xiii; 292 pp. $28. 0-8028-4883-4 [RB 109,316].

295 ^E**Luker, Lamontte M.** Passion, vitality, and foment: the dynamics of second temple Judaism. Harrisburg, PA 2001, Trinity viii; 327 pp. $32. 1-56338-353-5.

296 ^E**Mainville, Odette; Marguerat, Daniel L.** Résurrection: l'après-mort dans le monde ancien et le Nouveau Testament. Le monde de la Bible 45: Genève 2001, Labor et F. 338 pp. FS45. 2-8309-1012-5. ^RSR 30 (2001) 436-437 (*Vogels, Walter*).

297 ^E**Marchadour, A.** Que sait-on de Jésus de Nazareth?. P 2001, Bayard 299 pp. €18.29. 2-227-35023-7.

298 ^E**Marguerat, Daniel; Norelli, Enrico; Poffet, Jean-Michel** Jésus de Nazareth. MoBi 38: 1998 ⇒14, 253... 16,4469. ^RRThom 109 (2001) 491-495 (*Grelot, Pierre*); Henoch 23 (2001) 386-387 (*Gianotto, Claudio*); RCatT 26 (2001) 201-208 (*Puig i Tàrrech, Armand*).

299 ^E**Mayes, A.D.H.** Text in context: essays by members of the Society for Old Testament Study. 2000 ⇒16,296. ^RScrB 31/1 (2001) 43-44 (*O'Kane, Martin*); JThS 52 (2001) 709-713 (*Coggins, R.J.*).

300 ^E**Mies, Françoise** Bible et droit: l'esprit des lois. Connaître et Croire 7: Namur 2001, Presses Universitaires de Namur 173 pp. €17.72. 2-87037-335-X.

301 ^E**Mikva, Rachel S.** Broken tablets: restoring the ten commandments and ourselves. Woodstock, VT 1999, Jewish Lights xx; 148 pp. 1-58023-066-0.

302 **Mitteilungen und Beiträge 12/13.** 1997. Forschungsstelle Judentum a. d. Theol. Fakultät Leipzig. ^ROLZ 96 (2001) 76-77 (*Wächter, L.*).

303 ^E**Moxnes, Halvor** Jesus 2000 år etter Kristus. 2000 ⇒16,302. ^RTTK 72 (2001) 314-315 (*Sandnes, Karl Olav*).

304 ^E**Niebuhr, Karl-Wilhelm** Grundinformation Neues Testament: eine bibelkundlich-theologische Einführung. UTB.W 2108: 2000 ⇒16,305. ^RThLZ 126 (2001) 404-406 (*Roloff, Jürgen*); SNTU.A 26 (2001) 221-222 (*Fuchs, Albert*).

305 ^E**Nordhofen, Eckhard** Bilderverbot: die Sichtbarkeit des Unsichtbaren. Pd 2001, Schöningh 190 pp. €24.54. 3-506-73784-8 [SaThZ 5, 219—Alois Halbmayr].

306 ᴱ**Otto, Eckart** Mose: Ägypten und das Alte Testament. SBS 189: 2000
⇒16,307. ᴿOLZ 96 (2001) 401-406 (*Boecker, Hans Jochen*).

307 ᴱ**Panimolle, Salvatore A.** Giustizia-giustificazione nella bibbia. DSBP
28: R 2001, Borla 246 pp. €19.11. 88-263-1367-9;

308 Giustizia-giustificazione nei Padri della Chiesa. DSBP 29: R 2001,
Borla 287 pp. €19.11. 88-263-1382-2.

309 ᴱ**Pope-Levison, Priscilla; Levison, John R.** Return to Babel: global
perspectives on the bible. 1999 ⇒15,269; 16,311. ᴿCBQ 63 (2001)
365-367 (*Smith-Christopher, Daniel L.*).

310 **Puig i Tàrrech, Armand**, *al.*, El text: lectures i història. Scripta Biblica 3: Montserrat 2001, Associació Bíblica de Catalunya 373 pp. 84-
8415-292-8. Bibl. 347-351.

311 **Quesnel, Michel; Gruson, Philippe** La Bible et sa culture, 1: AT, 2:
Jésus et le NT. 2000 ⇒16,316. ᴿREG 114 (2001) 341-343 (*Pouderon,
Bernard*); CoTh (2001/1) 215-217 [Vol. 1] (*Warzecha, Julian*).

312 ᴱ**Rhoads, David M.; Syreeni, Kari A.** Characterization in the gospels:
reconceiving narative criticism. JSNT.S 184: 1999 ⇒15,275; 16,317.
ᴿRBLit 3 (2001) 362-365 (*Gowler, David B.*).

313 ᴱ**Saebo, Magne** Hebrew Bible/Old Testament: the history of its interpretation, 1: from the beginnings to the Middle Ages (until 1300): part
2, the Middle Ages. 2000 ⇒16,323. ᴿJThS 52 (2001) 867-868 (*Lange,
N.R.M. de*).

314 ᴱ**Sauter, Gerhard; Barton, John** Revelation and story. 2000 ⇒16,
376. ᴿRRT 8 (2001) 518-520 (*Elkis, William Wesley*).

315 ᴱ**Schmidinger, Heinrich** Die Bibel in der deutschsprachigen Literatur
des 20. Jahrhunderts. 1999 ⇒15,280; 16,326. 2 vols. ᴿBiblInterp 9
(2001) 236-239 (*Exum, J. Cheryl*).

316 ᴱ**Scholtissek, Klaus** Christologie in der Paulus-Schule. SBS 181: 1999
⇒15,281; 16,327. ᴿCBQ 63 (2001) 586-587 (*McMahon, Christopher*);
BZ 45 (2001) 142-143 (*Schmeller, Thomas*); ThLZ 126 (2001) 168-
170 (*Lindemann, Andreas*).

317 ᴱ**Schottroff, Luise; Wacker, Marie-Theres** Kompendium feministische Bibelauslegung. ²1999 ⇒15,283; 16,328. ᴿRTL 32 (2001) 127-
128 (*Dermience, A.*); YESW 9 (2001) 280-282 (*Stenström, Hanna*).

318 ᴱ**Scoralick, Ruth** Das Drama der Barmherzigkeit Gottes: Studien zur
biblischen Gottesrede und ihrer Wirkungsgeschichte in Judentum und
Christentum. SBS 183: 2000 ⇒16,329. ᴿCBQ 63 (2001) 367-369
(*Bernas, Casimir*); ITS 38 (2001) 259-260 (*Legrand, L.*).

319 ᴱ**Scott, James M.** Restoration: Old Testament, Jewish, and christian
perspectives. JSJ.S 72: Lei 2001, Brill xiii; 600 pp. €155. 90-04-
11580-3. In memory of Odil Hannes STECK.

320 ᴱ**Segovia, Fernando F.** Interpreting beyond borders. 2000 ⇒16,331.
ᴿRRT 8 (2001) 140-142 (*Cöster, Henry*); BiblInterp 9 (2001) 340-341
(*Sawyer, Deborah*); CBQ 63 (2001) 380-382 (*Lozada, Francisco*).

321 ᴱ**Shanks, Hershel** Ancient Israel: from Abraham to the destruction of
the temple. ²1999 <1988> ⇒15,287. ᴿJJS 52 (2001) 155-157
(*Grabbe, Lester L.*).

322 ᴱ**Sieg, Franciszek; Kasilowski, P.** Studies on the bible: to commemor-
ate the 400th anniversary... of Jakub Wujek's translation. 2000 ⇒16,
333. ᴿRivBib 49 (2001) 349-350 (*Boschi, Bernardo Gianluigi*).

323 ᴱ**Souletie, Jean-Louis: Gagey, Henri-Jérôme** La bible parole adressée. P 2001, Cerf 210 pp. FF120. 2-204-0657-4. ᴿFV 100/3 (2001) 88
(*Aubert, Philippe*); Brot. 153 (2001) 639-640 (*Silva, I. Ribeiro da*);

RSR 89 (2001) 550-551 (*Gibert, Pierre*); MD 227 (2001) 163-167 (*Wénin, André*).

324 ^E**Steins, Georg** Schweigen wäre gotteslästerlich: die heilende Kraft der Klage. 2000 ⇒16,334. ^RJBTh 16 (2001) 383-396 (*Ehlers, Kathrin*).

325 ^E**Stone, Ken** Queer commentary and the Hebrew Bible. JSOT.S 334: Shf 2001, Sheffield A. 250 pp. 1-84127-237-X. Bibl. 228-244.

326 ^E**Tambasco, Anthony J.** The bible on suffering: social and political implications. Mahwah 2001, Paulist viii; 215 pp. $20 [BiTod 40,136— Senior, D.].

327 ^E**Terrin, A.N.** Apocalittica e liturgia del compimento. Padova 2000, Messagero 382 pp. 88-250-0924-0.

328 ^E**Thompson, William M.; Morse, David Lee** VOEGELIN's Israel and revelation. 2000 ⇒16,338. ^RTS 62 (2001) 861-863 (*Purcell, Brendan*).

329 ^E**Tuckett, Christopher M.** The scriptures in the gospels. BEThL 131: 1997 ⇒13,234...16,339. ^RSNTU.A 23 (1998) 230-234 (*Fuchs, Albert*).

330 ^E**Ubbiali, Sergio** Il sacrificio: evento e rito. 1998 ⇒14,272... 16,340. ^RHum(B) 56 (2001) 303-304 (*Ghia, Francesco*).

331 ^E**Van Fleteren, Frederick; Schnaubelt, Joseph C.** AUGUSTINE: biblical exegete. Augustinian Historical Inst., Villanova Univ.; Collectanea Augustiniana 5: NY 2001, Lang xvii; 397 pp. $70. 08204-22924.

332 ^E**Van Gelder, Craig** Confident witness—changing world: rediscovering the gospel in North America. 1999 ⇒15,295. ^RNewTR 14 (2001) 91-92 (*Gittins, Anthony J.*).

333 ^E**West, Gerald O. Dube, Musa W.** The bible in Africa: transactions, trajectories and trends. 2000 ⇒16,342. ^RBOTSA 10 (2001) 16-20 (*LeMarquand, Grant*).

334 ^E**Wimbush, Vincent** African Americans and the bible: sacred texts and social textures. 2000 ⇒16,344. ^RBOTSA 10 (2001) 16-20 (*LeMarquand, Grant*).

335 ^E**Wischmeyer, Oda; Becker, Eve-Marie** Was ist ein Text?. Neutestamentliche Entwürfe zur Theologie 1: Tü 2001, Francke x; 225 pp. 3-7720-3151-X. Kolloquium Erlangen.

A1.4 *Plurium compilationes* theologicae

336 ^E**Alonso Avila, Angeles** Amor, muerte y más allá en el judaísmo y cristianismo antiguos. 1999 ⇒15,299. ^RSef. 61 (2001) 201-203 (*González Salinero, R.*).

337 ^E**Avery-Peck, Alan J.; Neusner, Jacob** Judaism in late antiquity, 4: death, life-after-death, resurrection and the world-to-come in the Judaisms of antiquity. HO 1/49,4: 2000 ⇒16,348. ^RRBLit 3 (2001) 269-274 (*Suter, David W.*).

338 ^E**Barclay, John M.G.; Sweet, John** Early christian thought in its Jewish context. 1996 ⇒12,43; 14,285. ^REvQ 73 (2001) 185-187 (*Bond, Helen K.*).

339 ^E**Barnes, Michael Horace** Theology and the social sciences. College Theology Society 46: Mkn 2001, Orbis xviii; 317 pp. $20. 1-57075-355-5 [ThD 49,88—Heiser, W. Charles].

340 ^E**Barton, Stephen C.** Where shall wisdom be found?: wisdom in the bible, the church and the contemporary world. 1999 ⇒15,303; 16,350. ^RThTo 58 (2001) 226-228 (*Morgan, Donn F.*); HeyJ 42 (2001) 499-500 (*Penaskovic, Richard*).

341 ᴱBeckerlegge, Gwilym From sacred text to the internet. Religion to-day: tradition, modernity and change 1: Burlington, VT 2001, Ashgate 347 pp. $75 0-7546-0748-8 [ThD 49,157—Heiser, W. Charles].

342 ᴱBiezeveld, Kune; Mulder, Anne-Claire Towards a different trans-cendence: feminist findings on subjectivity, religion and values. Reli-gions and Discourse 9: Oxf 2001, Lang 358 pp. 3-906765-66-0.

343 ᴱBouteneff, Peter; Heller, Dagmar Interpreting together: essays in hermeneutics. Geneva 2001, World Council of Churches 164 pp. ᴿStudies 90 (2001) 459-461 (May, John D'Arcy).

344 ᴱBradshaw, Paul F.; Hoffman, Lawrence A. Passover and Easter: origin and history to modern times. 1999 ⇒15,8035. ᴿJEH 52 (2001) 338-339 (Spinks, Bryan D.).

345 ᴱBraun, Willi; McCutcheon, Russell Guide to the study of religion. 2000 ⇒16,351. ᴿNumen 48 (2001) 117-120 (Stuckrad, Kocku von).

346 ᴱChristen, Eduard; Kirchschläger, Walter Erlöst durch Jesus Chri-stus. ThBer 23: 2000 ⇒16,354. ᴿThRv 97 (2001) 96-99 (Grümme, Bernhard); StMor 39 (2001) 628-630 (McKeever, Martin).

347 ᴱConnolly, Peter Approaches to the study of religion. 1999 ⇒15,310. ᴿPacifica 14 (2001) 335-337 (Langmead, Ross).

348 ᴱD'Lima, Errol; Gonsalves, Max What does Jesus Christ mean?. Bangalore 2001, Dharmaram 204 pp. Rs125/$8.

349 ᴱDi Nola, Gerardo Lo Spirito Santo nella testimonianza dei Padri e degli scrittori cristiani (I-V sec.). 1999 ⇒15,313. ᴿAsp. 48 (2001) 440-444 (Iaia, Gaetano).

350 ᴱEbach, Jürgen, al., 'Leget Anmut in das Geben': zum Verhältnis von Ökonomie und Theologie. Jabboq 1: Gü 2001, Kaiser 268 pp. 3-579-05330-2.

351 ᴱEmery, Gilles; Gisel, Pierre Le christianisme est-il un monothé-isme?. Lieux théologiques: Genève 2001, Labor & F. 396 pp. €25.92. 2-8309-1011-7.

352 ᴱFrankemölle, Hubert Christen und Juden gemeinsam ins dritte Jahr-tausend: 'das Geheimnis der Erlösung heißt Erinnerung'. Pd 2001 (2000 ⇒16,362), Bonifatius 312 pp. €15.40. 3-89710-152-1. ᴿJud. 57 (2001) 296-297 (Domhardt, Yvonne).

353 ᴱFranz, Albert Was ist heute noch katholisch?: zum Streit um die innere Einheit und Vielfalt der Kirche. QD 192: FrB 2001, Herder 320 pp. 3-451-02192-7.

354 ᴱFreedman, David Noel; McClymond, Michael J. The rivers of par-adise: Moses, Buddha, Confucius, Jesus, and Muhammad as religious founders. GR 2001, Eerdmans ix; 702 pp. £33. 0-8028-45401. ᴿRRT 8 (2001) 500-2 (Linney, Barry J.); RExp 98 (2001) 613-4 (Lee, W. Dan).

355 ᴱFrettlöh, Magdalene L.; Döhling, Jan-Dirk Die Welt als Ort Got-tes—Gott als Ort der Welt: Friedrich-Wilhelm Marquardts theologi-sche Utopie im Gespräch. Gü 2001, Gü 173 pp. €28. 3-579-05323-X.

356 ᴱGajano, Sofia Boesch; Modica, Marilena Miracoli: dai segni alla storia. 1999 ⇒15,316. ᴿRSLR 37 (2001) 141-144 (Gotor, Miguel).

357 ᴱGanssle, Gregory E. God and time: four views. DG 2001, InterVar-sity 247 pp. $18 [BS 160,243s—Tsakiridis, G.].

358 ᴱGerhards, Albert; Odenthal, Andreas Kölnische Liturgie und ihre Geschichte. LWQF 87: 2000 ⇒16,364. ᴿThRv 97 (2001) 501-503 (Probst, Manfred).

359 ᴱGill, Robin Theology and sociology: a reader. L ²1996, Cassell 516 pp. ᴿPacifica 14 (2001) 333-335 (Mason, Michael).

360 ^E**Groß, Walter** Das Judentum—eine bleibende Herausforderung christlicher Identität. Mainz 2001, Grünewald 254 pp. €24.50. 3-7867-2344-3.

361 ^E**Gyselen, Rika** Démons et merveilles d'Orient. Res Orientales 13: Bures-sur-Yvette 2001, Groupe pour l'Étude de la Civilisation du Moyen-Orient 186 pp. 2-9508266-7-9.

362 ^E**Janowski, Bernd; Riede, Peter** Die Zukunft der Tiere: theologische, ethische und naturwissenschaftliche Perspektiven. Stu 1999, Calwer 211 pp. 3-7668-3624-2.

363 **Jung, Patricia Beattie; Coray, Joseph Andrew** Sexual diversity and catholicism: toward the development of moral theology. ColMn 2001, Liturgical xxx; 311 pp. $30.

364 ^E**Kofsky, Arieh; Stroumsa, Guy G.** Sharing the sacred: religious contacts and conflicts in the Holy Land first-fifteenth centuries CE. 1998 ⇒14,306. ^RZion 66 (2001) 242-245 *(Boyarin, Daniel)*.

365 La fine del tempo. Quaderni teologici. Seminario di Brescia 8: 1998 ⇒ 14,296; 15,315. ^RRdT 42 (2001) 150-152 *(Marucci, Corrado)*.

366 ^E**Laplanche, Fr.** Histoire du christianisme des origines à nos jours, 14: anamnèsis: origines—perspectives—index. P 2001, Desclée 750 pp. €79. 2-7189-0637-5.

367 ^E**Larkin, William J.; Williams, Joel F.** Mission in the New Testament: an evangelical approach. ASMS 27: Mkn 2001, Orbis 276 pp. $16. 1-57075-169-2.

368 'Lasst euch vom Geist erfüllen!' (Eph 5,18): Beiträge zur Theologie der Spiritualität. Theologie der Spiritualität, Beiträge 4: Müns 2001, LIT 307 pp. €20.90. 3-8258-5195-8. Institut für Spiritualität [OrdKor 44,104—Hugoth, Matthias].

369 ^E**Linke, Bernd Michael** Schöpfungsmythologie in den Religionen. Fra 2001, Lembeck 203 pp. €15,24. 3-87476-369-2. ^RActBib 38 (2001) 275-276 *(Boada, J.)*.

370 ^E**Mizruchi, Susan L.** Religion and cultural studies. Princeton, NJ 2001, Princeton Univ. Pr. xxv; 269 pp. $55/20. 0-691-00502-8/3-6 [ThD 49,83—Heiser, W. Charles].

371 ^E**Moriconi, Bruno** Antropologia cristiana: bibbia, teologia, cultura. R 2001, Città Nuova 948 pp. €80. 88-311-9262-0.

372 ^E**Natale Terrin, A.** Apocalittica e liturgia del compimento. 2000 ⇒16, 373. ^REstTrin 35 (2001) 676-677 *(Pikaza, Xabier)*.

373 ^E**Pesce, M.** Il sacrificio nel giudaismo e nel cristianesimo. ASEs 18 (2001) 9-333.

374 ^E**Piétri, Luce** Histoire du christianisme, 1: le nouveau peuple (des origines à 250). 2000 ⇒16,374. ^RRHPhR 81 (2001) 336-338 *(Roukema, R.)*; REA 47 (2001) 375-376 *(Fredouille, Jean-Claude)*; EeV 38 (2001) 3-13 *(Cothenet, Edouard; Winling, Raymond)*.

375 ^E**Porter, Barbara Nevling** One God or many?: concepts of divinity in the ancient world. 2000 ⇒16,375. ^RJANER 1 (2001) 188-192 *(Hutter, Manfred)*.

376 Ricerche teologiche. Ricerche Teologiche 12,2: Bo 2001, Dehoniane 200 pp. Società Italiana per la Ricerca Teologica.

377 ^E**Rittner, Carol; Roth, John K.** "Good News" after Auschwitz?: christian faith within a post-holocaust world. Macon, Ga. 2001, Mercer Univ. Pr. 304 pp. $40. 0-86554-701-7.

378 ^E**Schneider, Theodor; Wenz, Gunther** Gerecht und Sünder zugleich?: ökumenische Klärungen. Dialog der Kirchen 11: FrB 2001, Herder 464 pp. 3-451-27626-7.

379 ^E**Selengut, Charles** Jewish-Muslim encounters: history, philosophy and culture. St. Paul, MN 2001, Paragon x; 212 pp. 1-55778-809-X.
380 ^E**Stanuli, Emila** Bòg Ojciec I: Przelom Wiekòw w mysli patrystycznej. SAChr 15: Wsz 2001, Wydawnictwo Uniwersytetu Kardynala Stefana Wyszynskiego. 306 pp. 83-7072-206-7. **P**.
381 ^E**Stravinskas, Peter M.J.** Priestly celibacy: its scriptural, historical, spiritual, and psychological roots. Mount Pocono 2001, Newman 172 pp. $15. 0-970-40222-8 [ThD 49,386—Heiser, W. Charles].
382 ^E**Taylor, Mark C.** Critical terms for religious studies. 1998 ⇒14,314. ^RNumen 48 (2001) 116-117 (*Stuckrad, Kocku von*).
383 Un grande segno nel cielo. Theotokos 8/1: R 2000, Monfortane 372 pp. €23.20.
384 ^E**Ward, Graham** The Blackwell companion to postmodern theology. Malden, MA 2001, Blackwell xxvii; 530 pp. $132. 0-631-21217-5.
385 ^E**Yandell, Keith E.** Faith and narrative. Oxf 2001, OUP 271 pp. 0-19-513145-2.

A1.5 *Plurium compilationes* **philologicae vel archaeologicae**

386 AMI 31 (1999). ^ROLZ 96 (2001) 107-110 (*Schippmann, K.*).
387 ^E**Albertz, Rainer** Kult, Konflikt und Versöhnung: Beiträge zur kultischen Sühne in religiösen, sozialen und politischen Auseinandersetzungen des antiken Mittelmeerraumes. AOAT 285; Veröffentlichungen des AZERKAVO/SFB 493/2: Müns 2001, Ugarit-Verlag viii; 332 pp. 3-934628-05-2.
388 ^E**Alcock, Susan E.; D'Altroy, Terence N.** Empires: perspectives from archaeology and history. C 2001, CUP xxii; 523 pp. $95. 0-521-77020-3. Bibl. 448-507.
389 ^E**Ariel, Donald T.** Excavations at the city of David 1978-1985 VI: inscriptions. Qedem 41: 2000 ⇒16,379. ^RBASOR 323 (2001) 100-101 (*Dion, Paul E.*).
390 ^E**Asirvatham, Sulochana R.; Pache, Corinne O.; Watrous, John** Between magic and religion: interdisciplinary studies in ancient Mediterranean religion and society. Greek studies, interdisciplinary approaches. Lanham 2001, Rowman & L. xxix; 212 pp. 0-8476-9968-4. Bibl. 193-205.
391 ^E**Baßler, Moritz; Greenblatt, Stephen Jay** New historicism: Literaturgeschichte als Poetik der Kultur. UTB.W: Tü ²2001, Francke 279 pp. 3-7720-2978-7.
392 ^E**Bellen, H.; Heinen, H.** Fünzig Jahre Forschungen zur antiken Sklaverei an der Mainzer Akademie 1950-2000: Miscellanea zum Jubiläum. FASk 35: Stu 2001, Steiner xiv; 557 pp. €74. 3-515-07968-8 [REA 104,612—Annequin, Jacques].
393 **Briend, Jacques; Quesnel, Michel** La vie quotidienne aux temps bibliques. P 2001, Bayard 236 pp. €21.50. 2-227-317-35-3.
394 ^E**Brodie, Neil; Doole, Jennifer; Renfrew, Colin** Trade in illicit antiquities: the destruction of the world's archaeological heritage. McDonald Institute Monographs: C 2001, McDonald Institute for Archaeological Research xii; 176 pp. 1-902937-17-1.
395 ^E**Buxton, Richard G.A.** From myth to reason?: studies in the development of Greek thought. Oxf 2001, OUP xv; 368 pp. 0-19-924752-8. Bibl. 329-355.

396 ^E**Carpentier, Jean; Lebrun, François** História de Mediterrâneo. 2000 ⇒16,390. ^RBrot. 153 (2001) 630-631 (*Lopes, F. Pires*).

397 ^E**Cecchelli, Margherita** Materiali e tecniche dell'edilizia paleocristiana a Roma. R 2001, De Luca 455 pp. Ministero per i beni culturali.

398 ^E**Cohn-Sherbok, Dan; Court, John M.** Religious diversity in the Graeco-Roman world: a survey of recent scholarship. BiSe 79: Shf 2001, Sheffield A. 237 pp. £15. 1-84127-216-7. Bibl. 196-228.

399 ^E**Collins, John J.; Sterling, Gregory E.** Hellenism in the land of Israel. CJAn 13: ND 2001, Univ. of ND Pr. 360 pp. $19. 0-2680-3051-0 [BiTod 39,380—Bergant, Dianne].

400 ^E**Cowey, James M.S.; Maresch, Klaus** Urkunden des Politeuma der Juden von Herakleopolis (144/3 - 133/2 v. Chr.) (P. Polit. Iud.): Papyri aus den Sammlungen von Heidelberg, Köln, München und Wien. PapyCol 29: Wsb 2001, Westdeutscher xvii; 189 pp. €39. 3-531-0994-8-5. Bibl. ix-xvi..

401 ^E**Dalley, Stephanie** The legacy of Mesopotamia. 1998 ⇒14,328; 15, 344. ^RBSOAS 64 (2001) 102-104 (*George, A.R.*).

402 **Denis, Albert-Marie**, *al.*, Introduction à la littérature religieuse judéo-hellénistique. 2000 ⇒16,397. ^RREG 114 (2001) 344-346 (*Pouderon, Bernard*); JSPE 12 (2001) 125-127 (*Oegema, G.S.*); RBBras 18 (2001) 496-498; SMSR 67 (2001) 400-404 (*Vian, Giovanni Maria*).

403 ^E**Ehlers, Widu Wolfgang** La biographie antique: huit exposés suivis de discussions. Genève 1998, Hardt viii; 290 pp. ^RREG 114 (2001) 304-306 (*Payen, Pascal*); AnCl 70 (2001) 434-436 (*Dondin-Payre, Monique*)..

404 ^E**Foxhall, Lin; Salmon, John** When men were men: masculinity, power and identity in classical antiquity. 1998 ⇒15,352. ^RAnCl 70 (2001) 389-390 (*Mactoux, Marie-Madeleine*).

405 ^E**Fraschetti, A.** Roman women. ^T*Lappin, L.*: Ch 2001, Univ. of Chicago Pr. vi; 249 pp. £28.50/13. 0-226-26093-3/4-1.

406 **Garbini, Giovanni; Gigante, Marcello; Bingen, Jean** Tre scavi archeologici come misura del mondo mediterraneo. Biblioteca europea, Istit.uto italiano per gli studi filosofici 26: N 2001, Vivarium 75 pp. 88-85239-57-9.

407 ^E**Hallo, William W.; Younger, K. Lawson Jr.** Canonical compositions from the biblical world. The context of scripture 1: 1997 ⇒13, 203; 15,237. ^RThLZ 126 (2001) 155-157 (*Janowski, Bernd*); RBLit 3 (2001) 88-91 (*Knoppers, Gary N.*).

408 ^E**Hoffman, Yair** Studies in Judaica. Te'uda 16-17: TA 2001, University xlv; 722 pp.

409 ^E**Høyrup, Jens; Damerow, Peter** Changing views on ancient Near Eastern mathematics. Berliner Beiträge zum Vorderen Orient 19: B 2001, Reimer xvi; 316 pp. 3-496-02653-7.

410 ^E**Huskinson, J.** Experiencing Rome: culture, identity and power in the Roman Empire. 2000 ⇒16,409. ^RClR 51 (2001) 120-22 (*Rees, Roger*).

411 ^E**Jakobielski, Stefan; Scholz, Piotr O.** Dongola-Studien: 35 Jahre polnischer Forschungen im Zentrum des makuritischen Reiches. Bibliotheca nubica et aethiopica 7: Wsz 2001, ZAS PAN xviii; 409 pp. 83-901809-9-5. Bibl. 395-402.

412 **Keel, Othmar; Staubli, Thomas** 'Im Schatten deiner Flügel': Tiere in der Bibel und im Alten Orient. FrS 2001, Universitätsverlag 96 pp. €23.30. 3-7278-1358-X. Ill. [RB 109,477].

413 ^E**Khan, Geoffrey** Exegesis and grammar in medieval Karaite texts. JSSt.S 13: Oxf 2001, OUP vi; 239 pp. 0-19-851065-9.

414 ^E**Klinkott, Hilmar** Anatolien im Lichte kultureller Wechselwirkungen: Akkulturationsphänomene in Kleinasien und seinen Nachbarregionen während des 2. und 1. Jahrtausends v. Chr. Tü 2001, Attempto 255 pp. FS64.50. 3-89308-333-2.

415 ^E**Lewin, Ariel** Gli ebrei nell'Impero Romano: saggi vari. F 2001, Giuntina 334 pp. €24.79. 88-8057-120-6. ^RRasIsr 67/3 (2001) 123-125 (*Davidzon, Irith*).

416 ^E**Lim, Timothy H.; MacQueen, Hector L.; Carmichael, Calum M.** On scrolls, artefacts and intellectual property. JSPE.S 38: Shf 2001, Sheffield A. 269 pp. £50. 1-84127-212-4. Bibl. 259-266.

417 ^E**Mackay, E. Anne** Signs of orality: the oral tradition and its influence in the Greek and Roman world. Mn.S 188: 1999 ⇒15,369. ^RClR 51 (2001) 58-60 (*Yamagata, Naoko*).

418 ^E**Macleod, R.** The library of Alexandria: centre of learning in the ancient world. 2000 ⇒16,421. ^RClR 51 (2001) 149-151 (*Lightfoot, J.L.*).

419 ^E**Mattingly, David J.; Salmon, John** Economies beyond agriculture in the classical world. L 2001, Routledge xii; 324 pp. £50.

420 ^E**Mikasa, H.I.H. Prince Takahito** Essays on ancient Anatolia. 1999 ⇒15,370. ^RBiOr 58 (2001) 426-430 (*Mouton, A.*).

421 ^E**Mirecki, Paul Allan; BeDuhn, Jason** The light and the darkness: studies in Manichaeism and its world. NHMS 50: Lei 2001, Brill (6) 222 pp. 90-04-11673-7.

422 Mitteilungen und Beiträge 17. 1999 ⇒15,373. Forschungsstelle Judentum, Theol. Fakultät, Leipzig. ^ROLZ 96 (2001) 256-257 (*Wächter, L.*).

423 ^E**Neusner, Jacob; Avery-Peck, Alan Jeffery** The Blackwell reader in Judaism. Blackwell Readings in Religion: Oxf 2001, Blackwell xxv; 452 pp. 0-631-20737-6;

424 Judaism in late antiquity, 3: where we stand: issues and debates in ancient Judaism, 4: the special problem of the synagogue. HO 1/55: Lei 2001, Brill xi; 190 pp. €57. 90-04-12000-9;

425 Judaism in late antiquity, 5: the Judaism of Qumran: a systemic reading of the Dead Sea scrolls, 1: theory of Israel. HO 1/56: Lei 2001, Brill xii; 196 pp. €65. 90-04-12001-7;

426 Judaism in late antiquity, 5: the Judaism of Qumran: a systemic reading of the Dead Sea scrolls, 2: world view, comparing Judaisms. HO 1/57: Lei 2001, Brill xii; 271 pp. €69. 90-04-12003-3.

427 ^E**Olsson, Birger O.; Mitternacht, Dieter; Brandt, Olof** The synagogue of ancient Ostia and the Jews of Rome: interdisciplinary studies. Acta Instituti Atheniensis Regni Sveciae 4,57: Sto 2001, Aströms 202 pp. SEK450. 91-7042-165-X. Bibl. 199-202.

428 ^E**Oren, E.D.** The sea peoples and their world: a reassessment. 2000 ⇒ 16,429. ^RDiscEg 49 (2001) 109-118 (*Nibbi, A.*).

429 ^E**Parkins, H.; Smith, C.** Trade, traders and the ancient city. 1999 ⇒ 15,377. ^RClR 51 (2001) 351-352 (*Percival, John*).

430 ^E**Piñero, A.** En la frontera de lo imposible: magos, médicos y taumaturgos en el Mediterráneo antiguo en tiempos del Nuevo Testamento. Córdoba 2001, El Almendro B Univ. Complutense 348 pp.

431 ^E**Pisano, Giovanna** Phoenicians and Carthaginians in the Western Mediterranean. Studia Punica 12: 1999 ⇒15,378. ^RCBQ 63 (2001) 576-578 (*Brody, Aaron J.*).

432 ^E**Porro, Pasquale** The medieval concept of time: studies on the scholastic debate and its reception in early modern philosophy. STGMA 75: Lei 2001, Brill x; 582 pp. 90-04-12207-9. Bibl. 563-572.

433 ^E**Pouthier, Jean-Luc** Quand l'Afrique du Nord était chrétienne. MoBi 132 (2001) 3-53.
434 ^E**Roberts, Deborah H.; Dunn, Francis M.; Fowler, Don** Classical closure: reading the end in Greek and Latin literature. 1997 ⇒13,301; 15,381. ^RREG 114 (2001) 302-304 (*Payen, Pascal*).
435 ^E**Rowlandson, Jane** Women and society in Greek and Roman Egypt: a sourcebook. 1998 ⇒14,9678; 15,10512. ^RSCI 20 (2001) 247-255 (*Fikhman, I.F.*).
436 ^E**Saporetti, Claudio** La decifrazione delle scritture antiche: ciclo di conferenze tenute presso la Fondazione Europea Dragàn, sede di Roma, Anno accademico 1995-1996. Rivista della Fondazione Europea Dragàn 13. Mi 2001, Nagard 94 pp. 88-85010-61-X;
437 Le sette meraviglie del mondo: ciclo di conferenze tenute presso la Fondazione Europea Dragàn...1996-1997. Rivista della Fondazione Europea Dragàn 14. Mi 2001, Nagard 93 pp. 88-85010-71-7;
438 Nabonedo e Sela': numero speciale di "Geo-Archeologia" Geo-Archeologia 2001/1. R 2001, Associazione Geo-Archeologica Italiana 109 pp.
439 ^E**Scheidel, Walter** Debating Roman demography. Mn.S 211: Lei 2001, Brill x; 242 pp. €72. 90-04-11525-0. ^RLatomus 60 (2001) 1026-1028 (*Salmon, Pierre*).
440 ^E**Settis, Salvatore** I greci: storia cultura arte società, 3: i greci oltre la Grecia. T 2001, Einaudi xl; 1550 pp. 88-06-15204-1.
441 ^E**Signer, Michael A.; Van Engen, John** Jews and christians in twelfth-century Europe. Notre Dame Conferences in Medieval Studies 10: ND 2001, Univ. of Notre Dame Pr. 380 pp. $50. 0-268-03254-8.
442 ^E**Signer, Michael Alan** Memory and history in christianity and Judaism. ND 2001, Univ. of Notre Dame Pr. xv; 231 pp. $40/19. 0-268-03454-0/60-5.
443 ^E**Silberman, Neil Asher; Frerichs, Ernest S.** Archaeology and society in the 21st century: the Dead Sea scrolls and other case studies. J 2001, Israel Exploration Society vi; 210 pp. $28. 965-221-045-5.
444 ^E**Späth, T.; Wagner-Hasel, B.** Frauenwelten in der Antike, Geschlechterordnung und weibliche Lebenspraxis. Stu 2000, Metzler xxvi; 494 pp. £40. 3-476-01677-3.
445 ^E**Speidel, Wilfried** Die Sammlung zyprischer Antiken im Kunsthistorischen Museum. Sammlungskataloge des KHM 2: 1999 ⇒15,11869. ^RBASOR 323 (2001) 97-98 (*Hitchcock, Louise A.*).
446 ^E**Swerdlow, Noel M.** Ancient astronomy and celestial divination. 1999 ⇒15,395. ^RBSOAS 64 (2001) 401-402 (*Brown, David*).
447 ^E**Titchener, Frances B.; Moorton, Richard F.** The eye expanded: life and the arts in Greco-Roman antiquity. 1999 ⇒15,396. ^RPrudentia 33/1 (2001) 94-97 (*Salapata, Gina*).
448 ^E**Too, Yun Lee** Education in Greek and Roman antiquity. Lei 2001, Brill xi; 477 pp. €159. 90-04-10781-9. Bibl. 459-472.
449 ^E**Xella, Paolo** Quando un dio muore: morti e assenze divine nelle antiche tradizioni mediterranee. Verona 2001, Essedue (4) 211 pp. 88-85697-53-4.

A2.1 Acta *congressuum* biblica

450 ^E**Abadie, Philippe; Lémonon, Jean-Pierre** Le judaïsme à l'aube de l'ère chrétienne: XVIIIe congrès de l'ACFEB (Lyon, septembre 1999).

LeDiv 186: P 2001, Cerf 412 pp. €44.97. 2-204-06564-1. ᴿNV 76/3 (2001) 107-108 (*Borel, Jean*); Brot. 153 (2001) 949-950 (*Silva, I. Ribeiro da*); EeV 40 (2001) 16-17 (*Cothenet, Edouard*).

451 ᴱ**Armstrong, Donald** Who do you say that I am?. 1999 ⟹15,401. Symposium, Anglican Institute 1998. ᴿAUSS 39 (2001) 135-137 (*Stefanovic, Ranko*); AThR 83 (2001) 307-308 (*Webb, Stephen H.*).

452 ᴱ**Avemarie, Friedrich; Lichtenberger, Hermann** Auferstehung—Resurrection: the fourth Durham-Tübingen research symposium resurrection, transfiguration and exaltation in Old Testament, ancient Judaism and early christianity (Tübingen, September, 1999). WUNT 135: Tü 2001, Mohr S. xii; 401 pp. €121.24. 3-16-147534-8.

453 ᴱ**Bellia, Giuseppe; Passaro, Angelo** Il libro del Qohelet: tradizione, redazione, teologia. Cammini nello Spirito, Biblica 44: Mi 2001, Paoline 408 pp. €21.69. 88-315-2067-9. ᴿStPat 48 (2001) 680-684 (*Lorenzin, Tiziano*); SEL 18 (2001) 126-127 (*Bonnet, Corinne*); OTEs 14 (2001) 346-347 (*Althann, Robert*).

454 ᴱ**Bouwens, Maurice; Geel, Jacobine; Maas, Frans** Jezus, een eigentijds verhaal. Zoetermeer 2001, Meinema 104 pp. €5.85. 90-211-3855-7. Symposium...*Edward Schillebeeckx*; inleiding van *Hermann Häring*.

455 ᴱ**Brenner, Athalya; Van Henten, Jan Willem** Recycling biblical figures: NOSTER colloquium 1997. 1999 ⟹15,407. ᴿJThS 52 (2001) 187-89 (*Guest, Deryn*); ThLZ 126 (2001) 257-259 (*Bauer, Uwe F.W.*).

456 Charism, leadership and community: proceedings of the second annual convention. Manila 2001, Catholic Biblical Association of the Philippines viii; 128 pp.

457 ᴱ**Charlesworth, James H.; Weaver, Walter P.** Jesus two thousand years later. 2000 ⟹16,458. Biblical Symposium, Florida Southern 1998. ᴿCBQ 63 (2001) 180-181 (*Murphy, Frederick J.*).

458 Chi ha scritto la bibbia (a parte Dio)?: come il libro è diventato testo sacro. F 2001, Biblia 210 pp. Atti del convegno nazionale, Urbino 24-25 aprile 1999.

459 ᴱ**Day, John** King and messiah in Israel and the ancient Near East. JSOT.S 270: 1998 ⟹14,378; 16,461. ᴿJJS 52 (2001) 157-159 (*Fitzpatrick-McKinley, Anne*); JThS 52 (2001) 143-145 (*Clements, R.E.*).

460 ᴱ**Delobel, Joël,** *al.,* Vroegchristelijke gemeenten tussen werkelijkheid en ideaal: opstellen van leden van de Studiosorum Novi Testamenti Conventus. Kampen 2001, Kok 223 pp. 90-435-0380-0.

461 ᴱ**Donnelly, Doris** Jesus: a colloquium in the Holy Land. NY 2001, Continuum vii; 166 pp. $20. 0-8264-1307-2. June 2000 [BiTod 39, 319—Senior, Donald].

462 ᴱ**Dunn, James D.G.** Paul and the Mosaic law. GR 2001, Eerdmans 334 pp. $35. 0-8028-4499-5. 3rd Durham-Tübingen Research Symposium 1994; Bibl. ᴿdialog 40 (2001) 240-242 (*Nanos, Mark D.*).

463 ᴱ**Exum, J. Cheryl; Moore, Stephen D.** Biblical studies / cultural studies: the third Sheffield Colloquium. JSOT.S 266 ; Gender, Culture 7: 1998 ⟹14,380; 16,464. ᴿSEÅ 66 (2001) 216-217 (*Sjöberg, Mikael*).

464 ᴱ**Farmer, William R.** Anti-Judaism and the gospels. 1999 ⟹15,413. ᴿJBL 120 (2001) 378-381 (*Feldman, Louis H.*); RBLit 3 (2001) 339-342 (*Feldman, Louis H.*).

465 Fondamenti biblico-teologici della pastorale di evangelizzazione. R 2001, Calamo 224 pp. €12.91. Convegno Roma 15-19.1.2001 [CivCatt 152/4, 634s—Puca, P.].

466 ᴱGetui, Mary ; Holter, Knut; Zinkuratire, Victor Interpreting the OT in Africa, Nairobi, Kenya, October 1999. 2000 ⇒16,467. ᴿBOTSA 10 (2001) 16-20 (*LeMarquand, Grant*).

467 ᴱGreenspoon, Leonard Jay; LeBeau, Bryan F. Sacred text, secular times: the Hebrew Bible in the modern world. 2000 ⇒16,470. ᴿCBQ 63 (2001) 572-573 (*Seeman, Chris*).

468 ᴱGroß, Walter Bibelübersetzung heute: geschichtliche Entwicklungen und aktuelle Anforderungen: Stuttgarter Symposium 2000. Arbeiten zur Geschichte und Wirkung der Bibel 2: Stu 2001, Deutsche Bibelgesellschaft 360 pp. €34.77. 3-438-06252-6.

469 ᴱHeitz, Françoise; Johnson, Annick Les figures du Christ dans l'art, l'histoire et la littérature. P 2001, L'Harmattan 383 pp. €30. 2-7475-1882-5. Colloque Univ. d'Artois, 3-4.3.2000.

470 ᴱHeller, J.; Talmon, S.; Hlaváčková, H. The Old Testament as inspiration in culture, international academic symposium, Prague, September 1995. Třebenice 2001, 205 + 16 pp. 80-902296-8-9.

471 L'interpretazione della bibbia nella chiesa: atti del simposio promosso dalla Congregazione per la Dottrina della Fede. Atti e Documenti 11: Città del Vaticano 2001, Libreria Editrice Vaticana 342 pp. €25.82. 88-2097-123-2. ᴿAugustinus 46 (2001) 369-371 (*Molina, Mario Alberto*).

472 ᴱJohnston, Philip; Walker, Peter The land of promise: biblical, theological and contemporary perspectives. 2000 ⇒16,474. 1999 conf. organized by The Tyndale Fellowship. ᴿRRT 8 (2001) 516-518 (*Wollaston, Isabel*).

474 ᴱKalms, Jürgen U. Internationales Josephus-Kolloquium Amsterdam 2000. Münsteraner Judaistische Studien 10: Müns 2001, LIT 304 pp. 3-8258-5013-7.

475 ᴱKrasovec, Joze Interpretation of the bible: symposium Sept. 1996 Ljubljana. JSOT.S 289: 1998 ⇒14,388; 16,476. ᴿCBQ 63 (2001) 360-364 (*Mathews, Edward G.*); ThLZ 126 (2001) 902-903 (*Söding, Thomas*).

476 ᴱLeBeau, Bryan F.; Greenspoon, Leonard J.; Hamm, M. Dennis The historical Jesus through catholic and Jewish eyes. 2000 ⇒16,477. Seminars, Creighton 1997-8. ᴿCBQ 63 (2001) 783-4 (*Smiga, George*).

477 ᴱLindemann, Andreas The sayings source Q and the historical Jesus. BEThL 158: Lv 2001, Peeters xxii; 776 pp. €60. 90-429-1003-8.

478 ᴱLipschitz, Ora David King of Israel alive and enduring?. 1997 ⇒13, 319; 15,420. ᴿRBLit 3 (2001) 192-193 (*Garber, Zev*).

479 ᴱLombardi, Paolo Male, bibbia e occidente: atti del convegno, Padova 1998. 2000 ⇒16,479. ᴿCivCatt 152/2 (2001) 313-314 (*Scaiola, D.*).

480 ᴱMalecki, Zdzislaw W Drodze do Jerozolimy: materialy z sympozjum biblijnego zorganizowanego przez katedre Starego Testamentu Wydzialu Teologicznego Uniw. Opolskiego 24 maja 2000. Sympozja 44: Opole 2001, Wydzial Teologiczny Uniw. 85 pp. 83-8893-9092. P.

481 ᴱMamiani, Maurizio Scienza e sacra scrittura nel XVII secolo. Biblioteca Europea 21: N 2001, Vivarium. Convegno Univ. di Udine, 9-11 ott. 1995.

482 ᴱMarconot, Jean-Marie Représentations des maladies et de la guérison dans la bible et ses traditions: actes du colloque de Montpellier, 1er et 2 décembre 2000. Montpellier 2001, Univ. Paul-Valéry 307 pp. 284-269-462-7.

483 ᴱMeyer, Marvin; Hughes, Charles Jesus then and now: images of Jesus in history and christology. Harrisburg 2001, Trinity viii; 294 pp. $35. Conf. Chapman Univ., 1999.

484 ᴱMimouni, Simon C. Le judéo-christianisme dans tous ses états: actes du colloque de Jérusalem 6-10 juillet 1998. LeDiv: P 2001, Cerf 464 pp. €33.50. 2-204-06445-9. Collab. *Jones, F. Stanley.*

485 ᴱMoor, Johannes C. de The elusive prophet: the prophet as a historical person, literary character and anonymous artist: papers read at the eleventh joint meeting of the Society for Old Testament Study and Het Oudtestamentisch Werkgezelschap in Nederland en België, Soesterberg 2000. OTS 45: Lei 2001, Brill x; 263 pp. €75/$87. 90-04121609.

486 ᴱNissinen, Martti Prophecy in its ancient Near Eastern context. SBL. Symposium 13: 2000 ⇒16,483. SBL International Meeting, Lahti, Finland, 1999. ᴿBiblInterp 9 (2001) 431-432 (*Lang, Bernhard*).

487 ᴱOsborne,Thomas P.; Poswick, R. Ferdinand, *al.*, Bible et cultures: P 2001, Lethielleux 195 pp. €19.06. 2-283-61027-3. Actes d'un colloque, oct. 2000, Paris.

488 ᴱPadovese, Luigi Atti dell' VIII Simposio di Efeso su S. Giovanni Apostolo. Turchia: la Chiesa e la sua storia 15; Simposio di Efeso su S. Giovanni Apostolo 8: R 2001, Istit. Francescano di Spiritualità 374 pp.

489 ᴱPanier, Louis Les lettres dans la bible et dans la littérature: Actes du colloque de Lyon (3-5 juillet 1996). LeDiv 181: 1999 ⇒15,427. ᴿJThS 52 (2001) 290-293 (*Porter, Stanley E.*).

490 ᴱPuig i Tàrrech, A. Perdò i reconciliaciò en la tradició jueva. Barc 2000, Assoc. Bíblica de Catalunya 246 pp.

491 Räisänen, Heikki; Fiorenza, Elisabeth Schüssler, *al.*, Reading the bible in the global village: Helsinki. 2000 ⇒16,485. SBL International Meeting (1999). ᴿBiblInterp 9 (2001) 446-449 (*Riches, John K.*).

492 ᴱReventlow, Henning Graf Weisheit, Ethos und Gebot: Weisheits- und Dekalogtraditionen in der Bibel und im frühen Judentum. BThSt 43: Neuk 2001, Neuk vii; 232 pp. 3-7887-1832-3.

493 ᴱRowland, Chris; Vincent, John Bible and practice. Shf 2001, Urban Theology Unit 116 pp. £7.50. 0-907490-09-3. Conf., Institute for British Liberation Theology.

494 SBL 2001 seminar papers: one hundred thirty-seventh annual meeting November 17-20, 2001, Denver, Colorado. SBL.SP 40: Atlanta, GA 2001, SBL vi; 320 pp. 1-58983-017-2.

495 ᴱSchwarzbach, Eugene La bible imprimée dans l'Europe moderne. 1999 ⇒15,435. ᴿREJ 160 (2001) 529-531 (*Rothschild, Jean-Pierre*).

496 ᴱSocci, S. Il cinema e la bibbia: atti del congresso internazionale, Genova, 30 ott.-1 nov. 1999. Brescia 2001, Morcelliana 238 pp. €15.49. 88-372-1855-9. Assoc. Laica di Cultura Biblica.

497 ᴱSorci, Pietro Viva ed efficace la parola di Dio: il lezionario romano a trent'anni dalla promulgazione. 2000 ⇒16,488. Atti del VI conv. lit.-past. Palermo '99. ᴿHo Theologos 19 (2001) 473-8 (*Trapani, Valeria*).

498 ᴱStella, Francesco La scrittura infinita: bibbia e poesia in età medievale e umanistica. Millennio Medievale 28: F 2001, SISMEL xi; 628 pp. €93.13. 88-8702-7714. Atti, convegno di Firenze, 26-28 giugno 1997.

499 ᴱTaylor, Bernard Alwyn X Congress of the International Organization for Septuagint and Cognate Studies Oslo, 1998. SBL.SCSt 51: Atlanta, GA 2001, SBL xviii; 581 pp. $70. 1-58983-020-2.

500 ᴱTábet, Miguel Ángel La sacra scrittura anima della teologia: atti del IV simposio internazionale della facoltà di teologia. 1999 ⇒15,440;

16,493. [R]AnnTh 15 (2001) 354-357 (*De Virgilio, G.*); RivBib 49 (2001) 370-373 (*De Virgilio, Giuseppe*).

501 [E]**Van der Kooij, Arie; Van der Toorn, Karel** Canonization and decanonization. Internat. conf. LISOR, Leiden, January 1997. SHR 82: 1998 ⇒14,407. [R]Apocrypha 12 (2001) 294-297 (*Gounelle, R.*).

502 [E]**Van Henten, Jan Willem; Brenner, Athalya** Families and family relations as represented in early Judaisms and early Christianities. 2000 ⇒16,495. NOSTER colloq., Amsterdam, 1998. [R]BiblInterp 9 (2001) 342-344 (*Reinhartz, Adele*); CBQ 63 (2001) 382-383 (*Osiek, Carolyn*).

503 [E]**Van Kempen, Kimberly; Saenger, Paul** The bible as book: the first printed editions. 1999 ⇒15,296. [R]JRTI 4/2 (2001) 96-100 (*Snavely, Iren L.*).

A2.3 Acta *congressuum* theologica

504 [E]**Allen, P.; Mayer, W.; Cross, L.** Prayer and spirituality in the early church, 2. 1999 ⇒15,448. Conference, Sydney, Jan. 1999. [R]VigChr 55 (2001) 107-109 (*Schipper, H.G.*).

505 [E]**Baker, David Weston** Looking into the future: evangelical studies in eschatology. GR 2001, Baker 383 pp. 0-8010-2279-7. Evangelical Theological Society, Meeting (1999).

506 [E]**Beaude, Pierre-Marie: Fantino, Jacques** Le discours religieux, son sérieux, sa parodie en théologie et en littérature: actes du colloque international de Metz (juin 1999). P 2001, Cerf 430 pp. €26.68. 2-204-06725-3.

507 [E]**Bof, Giampiero; Battaglia, Vincenzo** Gesù di Nazaret... figlio di A-damo, figlio di Dio. 2000 ⇒16,499. Congresso delle Assoc. Teologi-che Italiane (CATI) 1: [R]RevAg 42 (2001) 890-891 (*Sabugal, Santos*).

508 [E]**Bonnet, Corinne; Motte, André** Les syncrétismes religieux dans le monde méditerranéen antique: actes du colloque international en l'honneur de Franz Cumont... 1999 ⇒15,452. [R]ClR 51 (2001) 289-291 (*Elm, Susanna*); AnCl 70 (2001) 383-385 (*Van Liefferinge, Carine*).

509 [E]**Botti, Alfonso; Cerrato, Rocco** Il modernismo tra cristianità e secolarizzazione: atti del convegno internazionale di Urbino (1-4 ott. 1997). Urbino 2000, Quattro Venti. [R]Rivista di teologia dell'evangeliz-zazione 5/9 (2001) 196-200 (*Tagliaferri, Maurizio*).

510 [E]**Brueggemann, Walter** Hope for the world: mission in a global con-text: papers from the Campbell Seminar. LVL 2001, Westminster 177 pp. $19. Sem. Decatur Nov. 2000.

511 [E]**Bsteh, Andreas** Christlicher Glaube in der Begegnung mit dem Bud-dhismus: sechste religionstheologische Akademie St. Gabriel: Refera-te—Anfragen—Diskussionen. Studien zur Religionstheologie 6: Mödling 2001, St. Gabriel 606 pp. 3-85264-596-4.

512 [E]**Calduch Benages, Nuria** La Sagrada Familia en la vida consagrada y familiar: actas del 5. congreso internacional sobre la Sagrada Familia en ocasión del 2000 aniv. de la Encarnación del Verbo, Roma/Barcelo-na 10-13 oct. de 2000. Barc 2001, Nazarenum 416 pp. 84-8297-510-2.

513 [E]**Calvo Moralejo, Gaspar; Cecchin, Stefano** L'Assunzione di Maria Madre di Dio: significato storico-salvifico a 50 anni dalla definizione dogmatica: atti del 1° Forum Internazionale di Mariologia Roma, 30-31 ottobre 2000. Forum 1: Città del Vaticano 2001, Pontificia Acade-mia Mariana Internationalis xiii; 711 pp. 88-900609-0-5.

514 ^E**Cereti, G.** Monoteismo cristiano e monoteismi. CinB 2001, San
     Paolo 156 pp. €9.30. Corso 1997; Associazione Teologica Italiana.
515 Christianity and the human body. **Hoy, Michael,** al., St. Louis 2001,
     ITEST iii; 264 pp. $16. 1-88583-09-5. Proc. of the ITEST workshop,
     October 2000, St. Louis [ThD 48,163—Heiser, W. Charles].
516 La cultura en el horizonte de la transmisión del evangelio: perspectivas
     para una nueva evagelización. Città del Vaticano 2001, Comisión Epis-
     copal de Cultura 259 pp. Pontificio Consejo de la Cultura; Puebla, 4-7
     de Junio de 2001.
517 ^E**Dal Covolo, Enrico; Uglione, Renato** Chiesa e impero: da AUGUSTO
     a GIUSTINIANO. BSRel 170: R 2001, LAS 365 pp. €20.66. 88-213-047-
     95. Atti, Prime e Seconde Giornate Patristiche Torinesi, 1994, 1996.
518 ^E**Davis, Stephen; Kendall, Daniel; O'Collins, Gerald** The Trinity.
     2000 ⇒16,503. Symposium, Dunwoodie, 1998. ^RRBLit 3 (2001) 311-
     314 (*Casiday, Augustine*).
519 ^E**De Fiores, S.; Strangio, G.; Vidau, E.** Il mistero della croce e Maria:
     atti del IV Colloquio internazionale di mariologia. Biblioteca di
     Theototkos 4: R 2001, Monfortane 319 pp. €12.91. Santuario di Pol-
     si—San Luca (Rc), 13-14 Sett. 1999.
520 ^E**Dias, Saturnino** Evangelisation and inculturation. Mumbai 2001,
     Pauline 256 pp. Rs95. ^RMissTod 3 (2001) 478-480 (*Michael, S.M.*).
521 ^E**Dieckmann, Bernhard** Das Opfer—aktuelle Kontroversen: religions-
     politischer Diskurs im Kontext der mimetischen Theorie. Beiträge zur
     mimetischen Theorie 12: Müns 2001, Lit 308 pp. €25.90. 3-8258-
     4755-1. Deutsch-italienische Fachtagung der Guardini Stiftung, Villa
     Vigoni Okt. 1999.
522 ^E**Dreyer, Elizabeth A.** The cross in christian tradition: from Paul to
     BONAVENTURE. 2000 ⇒16,506. ^RSpiritus(B) 1 (2001) 113-15 (*Blastic,
     Michael W.*).
523 ^E**Faber, Richard; Goodman-Thau, Eveline; Macho, Thomas** A-
     bendländische Eschatologie: ad Jacob Taubes. Wü 2001, Königshau-
     sen & N. 570 pp. €49. 3-8260-2123-1. Symposium Villigst 1997; Bibl.
     der Texte von J. Taubes.
524 ^E**Filoramo, Giovanni; Gianotto, Claudio** Verus Israel: nuove pro-
     spettive sul giudeocristianesimo. BCR 65: Brescia 2001, Paideia 388
     pp. €29.95. 88-394-0628-X. Atti del Colloq. di Torino (4-5 nov. 1999).
525 ^E**Finan, Thomas; Twomey, Vincent** Studies in patristic christology.
     1998 ⇒14,412; 16,508. Proceedings of the Third Maynooth Patristic
     Conference, 17-20 October 1996. ^RAugSt 32 (2001) 266-278 (*Prusak,
     Bernard*); NBl 82 (2001) 598-600 (*Yarnold, Edward*).
526 ^E**Fisichella, Rino** Comitato Centrale del Grande Giubileo...2000: il
     Concilio Vaticano II: recezione e attualità. 2000 ⇒16,510. Conv. febb.
     2000, Città del Vaticano. ^RSal. 63 (2001) 783-786 (*Amato, Angelo*).
527 ^E**Frede, D.; Laks, A.** Traditions of theology: studies in Hellenistic the-
     ology, its background and aftermath: papers...8th Symposium Helleni-
     sticum, Villeneuve-d'Ascq 1998. PhAnt 89: Lei 2001, Brill 343 pp.
528 ^E**Haddad, Yvonne Yazbeck; Esposito, John L.** Daughters of Abra-
     ham: feminist thought in Judaism, Christianity, and Islam. Gainesville,
     FL 2001, University Press of Florida xiii; 162 pp. $55. 0-8130-2103-0.
     Conf. Georgetown Univ.; Bibl. 147-151.
529 ^E**Hinze, Bradford E.; Dabney, D. Lyle** Advents of the Spirit: an intro-
     duction to the current study of pneumatology. Milwaukee 2001, Mar-
     quette Univ. Pr. 484 pp. $45. 0-87462-679-X. Symposium, Marquette
     1998 [ThD 49,359—Heiser, W. Charles].

530 ᴱHuber, Konrad; Prüller-Jagenteufel, Gunter M.; Winkler, Ulrich Zukunft der Theologie—Theologie der Zukunft: zu Selbstverständnis und Relevanz der Theologie. Theologische trends 10: Thaur 2001, Thaur 293 pp. 3-85400-118-5. Kongress Salzburg 2001.

531 ᴱHünermann, Peter Papato ed ecumenismo: il ministero petrino al servizio dell'unità. ᵀFabbri, Romeo: Nuovi saggi teologici 48: 1999 ⇒ 15,461. ᴿAnton. 76 (2001) 358-360 (Stamm, Heinz-Meinolf).

532 ᴱKreider, Alan The origins of christendom in the West. E 2001, Clark xvi; 371 pp. 0-567-08776-X. Colloquium Paris Sept. 1996.

533 ᴱLavenant, René Symposium Syriacum VII: Uppsala University 11-14 August 1996. OCA 256: 1998 ⇒14,415; 15,465. ᴿCCist 63 (2001) [48]-[50] (Couilleau, Guerric).

534 ᴱLevine, Lee I. Jerusalem: its sanctity and centrality to Judaism, Christianity, and Islam. 1999 ⇒15,466. Conference Tantur 1996. ᴿJud. 57 (2001) 150-151 (Schreiner, Stefan).

535 ᴱMontesinos, José; Solís, Carlos Largo campo di filosofare: Eurosymposium Galileo 2001. La Orotava 2001, Fundación Canaria Orotava de Historia de la Ciencia 985 pp. Tenerife 19-23 febb. 2001.

536 ᴱNiccacci, Alviero Jerusalem: house of prayer for all peoples in the three monotheistic religions. SBFA 52: J 2001, Franciscan Printing Pr. 193 pp. 96551-60068. Proc. symposium, Jerusalem, Feb. 17-18, 1997.

537 ᴱPedico, M. Marcellina; Carbonaro, Davide La madre de Dio un portico sull'avenire del mondo: fede ecclesiale—iconografia—pietà popolare. Biblioteca di Theotokos 5: R 2001, Monfortane xvi; 264 pp. Atti del 5⁰ colloquio internazionale di mariologia, Roma, 18-20 nov. 1999. ᴿMiles Immaculatae 37 (2001) 601-604 (Olszewski, Jan M.).

538 ᴱPeretto, Elio Maria nel mistero di Cristo: pienezza del tempo e compimento del Regno. 1999 ⇒15,469. Atti XI simposio internaz. mariologico, Roma, ott. 1997. ᴿMar. 63 (2001) 533-536 (Bermon, Pascale).

539 Pietro di Giovanni OLIVI: opera edita et inedita. Archivum Franciscanum Historicum 3: 1999 ⇒15,471. Atti d. giornate internaz., Grottaferrata (Roma) 4-5 dic. 1997. ᴿCFr 71 (2001) 244-46 (Maranesi, Pietro).

540 ᴱPorter, Stanley E.; Hayes, Michael A.; Tombs, David Faith in the millennium. Roehampton Papers 7: Shf 2001, Sheffield A. 493 pp. 1-84127-092-X. Conf. London 15.5.1999.

541 ᴱPouderon, Bernard; Duval, Yves-Marie L'Historiographie de l'Église des premiers siècles. ThH 114: P 2001, Beauchesne xv; 586 pp. Actes du IIe colloque intern. d'études patristiques d'expression française, Tours, sept. 2000. ᴿREG 114 (2001) 708-710 (Wartelle, André).

542 ᴱRomagnani, Gian Paolo La bibbia, la coccarda e il tricolore: i valdesi fra due emancipazioni 1798-1848. Società di studi valdesi 18: T 2001, Claudiana 592 pp. €36.15. Atti del XXXVII e del XXXVIII convegno di studi sulla Riforma e sui movimenti religiosi in Italia, Torre Pellice, 31.8-2.9.1997 e 30.8-1.9.1998.

543 ᴱRuiz Sánchez, José-Leonardo Milenarismos: mesianismo y apocalipsis desde la historia y la religión. Sevilla 2001, Universidad 194 pp. 84-600-9705-6.

544 ᴱSchmidt-Leukel, Perry Buddhist perceptions of Jesus: papers of the third conference of the European network of Buddhist-Christian studies (St. Ottilien 1999). ᴱGütz, Thomas Josef; Köberlin, Gerhard: St. Ottilien 2001, Eos 179 pp. €14.32. 3-8306-7069-9.

545 ᴱTaft, Robert F.; Winkler, Gabriele Acts of the international congress: comparative liturgy fifty years after Anton Baumstark (1872-

1948). OCA 265: R 2001, Pontificio Istituto Orientale 1020 pp. 88-7210-333-9. Bibl. Baumstark 31-60.

546 ᴱTeja, Ramón Actas del XIV seminario sobre historia del monacato: profecia, magia y adivinación en las religiones antiguas. Aguilar de Campoo (Palencia) 2001, Fundación Santa María La Real 175 pp.

547 ᴱToniolo, Ermanno M. Maria e il Dio dei nostri padri, padre del Signore nostro Gesù Cristo. R 2001, Marianum 432 pp. 88-87016-58-5. Atti del XII simposio internazionale mariologico, Roma 5-8 ott. 1999. ᴿMiles Immaculatae 37 (2001) 605-608 (*Olszewski, Jan M.*).

548 ᴱTurner, John Douglas; Majercik, Ruth Dorothy Gnosticism and later platonism: themes, figures, and texts. SBL Symposium 12: 2000 ⇒16,526. ᴿJECS 9 (2001) 600-601 (*Anderson, Neil D.*).

549 ᴱVan Henten, Jan Willem; Houtepen, Anton Religious identity and the invention of tradition: papers read at a NOSTER conference in Soesterberg, January 4-6, 1999. Studies in Theology and Religion 3: Assen 2001, Van Gorcum x; 367 pp. €29. 90232-37145. Bibl. 317-50.

550 ᴱVan Oort, Johannes; Wermelinger, Otto; Wurst, Gregor AUGUSTINE and Manichaeism in the Latin West: proceedings of the Fribourg-Utrecht Symposium of the International Association of Manichaean Studies (IAMS). NHMS 49: Lei 2001, Brill x; 337 pp €95/$111. 90-04-11423-8.

551 ᴱVanhoozer, Kevin J. Nothing greater, nothing better: theological essays on the love of God. GR 2001, Eerdmans vi; 217 pp. $23. 0-8028-4902-4. Papers from the 6th Edinburgh Dogmatics Conference [ThD 49,79—Heiser, W. Charles].

552 ᴱWeth, Rudolf Das Kreuz Jesu: Gewalt—Opfer—Sühne. Neuk 2001, Neuk 232 pp. €19.90. 3-7887-1869-2. Tagung Gesellschaft für evangelische Theologie.

553 ᴱWiles, Maurice F.; Yarnold, Edward Papers presented at the Thirteenth International Conference on Patristic Studies held in Oxford 1999. StPatr 34-38: Lv 2001, Peeters 5 vols. €5x100. 90-429-. Assistance of *P.M. Parvis*; v.34, Historica, biblica, theologica et philosophica; v.35, Ascetica, gnostica, liturgica, orientalia; v.36, Critica et philologica, Nachleben, first two centuries, TERTULLIAN to ARNOBIUS, Egypt before Nicaea, ATHANASIUS and his opponents; v.37, Cappadocian writers, other Greek writers; v.38, St AUGUSTINE and his opponents, other Latin writers.

554 ᴱZuber, Valentine Un objet de connaissance, le catholicisme: réflexions autour de l'oeuvre d'Émile Poulat (en Sorbonne, 22-23 octobre 1999). P 2001, Bayard 365 pp. 2-227-31727-2. Bibl. 291-326.

A2.5 *Acta* philologica et historica

555 ᴱAndorlini, Isabella; Bastianini, Guido Atti del XXII Congresso Internazionale di Papirologia. Firenze, 23-29 agosto 1998. F 2001, "G. Vitelli" 3 vols; xiii; 1349 pp. €155. 88-87829-21-7. 46 pl.

556 ᴱBorchers, D.; Kammerzell, F.; Weninger, S. Lingua aegyptia SM 3: Hieroglyphen Alphabete Schriftreformen. Gö 2001, Seminar f. Ägyptologie/Koptologie. 268 pp. 0946-8641. Symp. Fribourg 28.2-1.3.1996.

557 ᴱBriquel-Chatonnet, Françoise Mosaïque de langues, mosaïque culturelle: le bilinguisme dans le Proche-Orient Ancien. 1996 ⇒12,284... 15,481. ᴿSyr. 78 (2001) 238-241 (*Desreumaux, Alain*).

558 ^E**Brodersen, K.** Prognosis: Studien zur Funktion von Zukunftsvorher-
sagen in Literatur und Geschichte seit der Antike. Antike Kultur und
Geschichte 2: Müns 2001, LIT 141 pp. 3-8258-5341-1.

559 ^E**Brulé, Pierre; Vendries, Christophe** Chanter les dieux: musique et
religion dans l'Antiquité grecque et romaine. Histoire: Rennes 2001,
Presses Univ. 358 pp. €22. 2-86847-598-1. Actes du Colloque des 16-
18 déc. 1999, Rennes et Lorient.

560 ^E**Chazon, Esther G.; Stone, Michael E.** Pseudepigraphic perspectives: the Apocrypha and Pseudepigrapha in light of the Dead Sea
scrolls: proc. Intern. Symp. of the Orion Center, Jan. 1997. StTDJ 31:
1999 ⇒15,485; 16,535. ^RSalm. 48 (2001) 340-44 (*Trevijano, Ramón*).

561 ^E**Consani, Carlo; Mucciante, Luisa** Norma e variazione nel
diasistema greco: atti del quarto incontro internazionale di linguistica
greca (Chieti-Pescara, 30 settembre-2 ottobre 1999). Alessandria 2001,
Orso 380 pp. 88-7694-592-X.

562 ^E**Croiselle, Jean-Michel: Martin, René; Perrin, Yves** Neronia V:
NÉRON: histoire et légende. Latomus 247: 1999 ⇒15,488. Actes du Ve
Colloque international de la SIEN, Clermont-Ferrand et Saint-Etienne,
2-6 nov 1994; 26 pl. ^RAnCl 70 (2001) 472-475 (*Benoist, Stéphane*).

563 ^E**Fabre-Serris, J.** Mythe et/ou philosophie dans les textes grecs et
latins sur les origines de l'humanité: actes des journées d'études des 13
et 14 novembre 1998. 2000 ⇒16,541. ^RREA 103 (2001) 545-546
(*Morel, Pierre-Marie*).

564 ^E**Finazzi, Rosa Bianca; Tornaghi, Paola** Cinquant'anni di ricerche
linguistiche: problemi, risultati e prospettive per il terzo millennio: atti
del IX Convegno Internazionale di Linguisti, Milano, 8-9-10 ottobre
1998. Alessandria 2001, Orso 643 pp. 88-7694-526-1.

565 ^E**Gnirs, Andrea M.** Reading The Eloquent Peasant. Lingua Aegyptia
8: Gö 2001, Seminar für Ägyptologie und Koptologie viii; 229 pp.
€80/42. Proc. Internat. Conf., Univ. of California, LA 27-30.3.1997.

566 ^E**Horbury, William** Hebrew study from Ezra to Ben-Yehuda. 1999 ⇒
15,240; 16,544. ^RJJS 52 (2001) 183-5 (*Saenz Badillos, Angel*); OLZ 96
(2001) 407-409 (*Oelsner, Joachim*); REJ 160 (2001) 507-509 (*Rothschild, Jean-Pierre*); ThLZ 126 (2001) 1262-1264 (*Krispenz, Jutta*).

567 ^E**Laffineur, Robert; Hägg, Robin** Potnia: Deities and religion in the
Aegean Bronze Age: proceedings of the 8th international Aegean conference, 12-15 April 2000. Aegaeum 22 (2001) 496 pp. 108 pl.

568 ^E**MacDonald, Dennis R.** Mimesis and intertextuality in antiquity and
christianity. Harrisburg 2001, Trinity xi; 171 pp. $26. Conf. Claremont
Univ.

569 ^E**Muraoka, Takamitsu; Elwolde, J.F.** The Hebrew of the Dead Sea
Scrolls and Ben Sira. StTDJ 26: 1997 ⇒13,369...15,3479. Proc. symposium Leiden Univ. Dec. 1995. ^RVT 51 (2001) 415-6 (*Emerton, J.A.*).

570 ^E**Paschoud, F.; Grange, B.; Buchwalder, C.** La biographie antique.
1997 ⇒15,499. 1997 meeting of Fondation Hardt. ^RClR 51 (2001)
273-276 (*Pelling, Christopher*).

571 ^E**Peachin, Michael** Aspects of friendship in the Graeco-Roman world:
proceedings of a conference held at the Seminar für Alte Geschichte,
Heidelberg, 10-11 June, 2000. Journal of Roman archaeology, Suppl.
ser. 43: Portsmouth 2001, Journ. of Rom. arch. 160 pp. 1-887829-43-1.

572 ^E**Perez Jiménez, Aurelio; Casadesús Bordoy, Francesc** Estudios sobre PLUTARCO: misticismo y religiones mistéricas en la obra de Plutarco: actas del VII simposio español sobre Plutarco (Palma de Mallorca,
2-4 de noviembre de 2000). M 2001, Clásicas 577 pp. 84-7882-461-8.

573 ᴱPouderon, Bernard; Hunzinger, Christine; Kasprzyk, Dimitri Les personnages du roman grec: actes du colloque de Tours, 18-20 novembre 1999. CMOM 29: Lyon 2001, Maison de l'Orient Méditerranéen 460 pp. 2-903264-22-8.

574 ᴱRibichini, Sergio; Rocchi, Maria; Xella, Paolo La questione delle influenze vicino-orientali sulla religione greca: stato degli studi e prospettive della ricerca: atti del colloquio internazionale Roma, 20-22 maggio 1999. Monografie scientifiche, serie scienze umane e sociali: R 2001, Consiglio Nazionale delle Ricerche 440 pp. 88-8080-023-X.

575 ᴱSpäth, Thomas; Coundry, Marianne L'invention des grands hommes de la Rome antique: actes du colloque du Collegium Beatus Rhenanus August, 16-18 septembre 1999. Collections de l'Université Marc Bloch; Études d'archéologie et d'histoire ancienne: P 2001, De Boccard 492 pp. 2-7018-0145-1.

576 ᴱStone, Michael E.; Chazon, Esther G. Biblical perspectives: early use and interpretation of the bible in light of the Dead Sea scrolls: proc. 1st internat. symposium Orion Center May, 1996. StTDJ 28: 1998 ⇒ 14,441; 15,502. ᴿDSD 8 (2001) 204-207 (Hempel, Charlotte); ETR 76 (2001) 120-121 (Tottoli, Roberto).

A2.7 *Acta* **orientalistica**

577 ᴱAbusch, Tzvi, al., Proceedings of the XLVe Rencontre Assyriologique Internationale, 1: historiography in the cuneiform world. Bethesda, Md. 2001, CDL x; 482 pp. 1-883053-67-6.

578 ᴱBriquel-Chatonnet, Françoise; Lozachmeur, Hélène Proche-Orient ancien: temps vécu, temps pensé: actes de la Table-Ronde du 15 novembre 1997. Antiquités sémitiques 3: 1998 ⇒14,445... 16,567. ᴿJSSt 46 (2001) 121-122 (Watson, Wilfred G.E.).

579 ᴱEmmerick, Roland E.; Sundermann, Werner; Zieme, Peter Studia Manichaica, 4: internationaler Kongress zum Manichäismus. 2000 ⇒ 16,568. Berlin 1997. ᴿOLZ 96 (2001) 101-104 (Klein, Wassilios).

580 ᴱFinazzi, Rosa Bianca; Valvo, Alfredo Pensiero e istituzioni del mondo classico nelle culture del Vicino Oriente: atti del Seminario Nazionale di studio (Brescia, 14-15-16 ottobre 1999). L'eredità classica nel mondo orientale 4: Alessandria 2001, Orso 339 pp. 88-7694-525-3.

581 ᴱFortin, Michel Annual symposium of the Canadian Society for Mesopotamian Studies—2000 Québec: Canadian research on Ancient Syria: BCSMS 36: Toronto, Ontario 2001, The Canadian Society for Mesopotamian Studies iv; 242 pp.

582 ᴱHallo, William W. Proceedings of the XLVe Rencontre Assyriologique Internationale, 2: seals and seal impressions. Bethesda, Md. 2001, CDL vi; 254 pp. 1-883053-67-6.

583 ᴱJanssen, C. Het gebroken hart in oosterse literaturen. Gent 2001, Academia 139 pp. €12.50. Symposium Jan. 2001.

584 ᴱJas, R. Rainfall and agriculture in northern Mesopotamia. Lei 2000, Nederlands Historisch-Archaeologisch Instituut te Istanbul xii; 299 pp. €57. 90-6258-089-0. Symposium, Leiden 21-22.5.1999.

585 ᴱKottek, Samuel; Horstmanshoff, Manfred From Athens to Jerusalem: medicine in Hellenistic Jewish lore and in early christian literature: papers of the symposium in Jerusalem, 9-11 September 1996. Pantaleon 33: Rotterdam 2000, Erasmus 278 pp. €40.84. 90-5235-135-X [JNES 62,288s—Robert D. Biggs].

586 ᴱMilano, L., al., Landscapes: territories, frontiers, and horizons in the ancient Near East: XLIV Rencontre Assyriologique Internationale. 2000 ⇒16,570. ᴿJESHO 44 (2001) 363-371 (Smith, Adam T.).
587 ᴱMoers, Gerald Definitely: Egyptian literature: LA 1995. Lingua aegyptia, St. Mon. 2: 1999 ⇒15,511. ᴿOLZ 96 (2001) 678-685 (Jansen-Winkeln, Karl); ZDMG 151 (2001) 431-436 (Gutschmidt, Holger).
588 ᴱNehmé, Laïla Guerre et conquête dans le Proche-Orient ancien: actes de la table ronde du 14 novembre 1998. Antiquités sémitiques 4: 1999 ⇒15,512. ᴿJNSL 27/2 (2001) 135-139 (Muntingh, L.M.).
589 ᴱWhiting, Robert M. Mythology and mythologies: methodological approaches to intercultural influences: proceedings of the second annual symposium of the Assyrian and Babylonian Intellectual Heritage Project, Paris, October 4-7, 1999. Melammu Symposia 2: Helsinki 2001, The Neo-Assyrian Text Corpus Project xxv; 288 pp. $75. 951-45-9049-X.

A2.9 Acta archaeologica

590 ᴱAdams, Colin; Laurence, Ray Travel and geography in the Roman Empire. L 2001, Routledge x; 202 pp. $75. 0-415-23034-9. Roman archaeology conference, Durham 1999; 48 fig.
591 Alexandrie: une mégapole cosmopolite: actes du 9ᵉ colloque de la Villa Kérylos les 2 et 3 octobre 1998. Cahiers de la Villa 'Kérylos' 9: 1999 ⇒15,517. ᴿCÉg 76 (2001) 316-318 (Nachtergael, Georges).
592 ᴱArchibald, Zofia H., al., Hellenistic economies. L 2001, Routledge xvi; 400 pp. £55. 0-415-23466-2. Colloquium Liverpool 1998.
593 ᴱÅström, P. The chronology of base-ring ware and bichrome wheelmade ware: proceedings of a colloquium held in the Royal Academy of Letters, Stockholm, 18-19 May, 2000. Konferenser 54: Sto 2001, Almqvist & W. 252 pp.
594 ᴱBarbet, Alix La peinture funéraire antique: IVᵉ siècle av. J.-C. - IVᵉ siècle ap. J.-C.: actes du VIIᵉ colloque de l'Association internationale pour la peinture murale antique, 6-10 octobre 1998 Saint-Romain-en-Gal - Vienne. P 2001, Errance 334 pp. €39.64. 2-8777-2208-2. 64 pl..
595 ᴱBatsch, C.; Egelhaaf-Gaiser, U.; Stepper, R. Zwischen Krise und Alltag: antike Religionen im Mittelmeerraum. 1999 ⇒15,521. Colloquium Potsdam, 13-15 June 1997. ᴿClR 51 (2001) 71-72 (Rives, J.B.).
596 ᴱBekker-Nielsen, Tonnes; Hannestad, Lise War as a cultural and social force: essays on warfare in antiquity. Historisk-filosofiske Skrifter 22: K 2001, Det kongelige Danske Videnskabernes Selskab 215 pp. 87-7876-187-5. Conference Jan. 1998 Royal Danish Academy.
597 ᴱBietak, Manfred F.K.W. Archaische griechische Tempel und Altägypten: Internationales Kolloquium am 28. November 1997 am Institut für Ägyptologie der Universität Wien. DÖAW 21; Untersuchungen der Zweigstelle Kairo des Österreichischen Archäologischen Institutes 18: W 2001, ÖAW 115 pp. 3-7001-2937-8.
598 ᴱBonfante, Larissa; Karageorghis, Vassos Italy and Cyprus in antiquity: 1500-450 BC: proceedings of an international symposium, Columbia Univ., Nov. 16-18, 2000. Nicosia 2001, Severis Foundation xv; 393 pp. Cyp£35. 9963-8102-3-3 [RB 109,312].
599 ᴱBranigan, Keith Urbanism in the Aegean Bronze Age. Sheffield Studies in Aegean Archaeology 4: L 2001, Sheffield A. x; 181 pp. 1-84127-341-4. Conference Sheffield Jan. 2000.

600 ^E**Bresson, Alain; Descat, Raymond** Les cités d'Asie mineure occidentale au IIe siècle a.C. Bordeaux 2001, Ausonius 294 pp. Séminaire, Bordeaux 1997 [REG 115,427s—Lefèvre, François].

601 ^E**Briant, Pierre** Irrigation et drainage dans l'Antiquité, qanats et canalisations souterraines en Iran, en Égypte et en Grèce. Persika 2: P 2001, Thotm 190 pp. 2-914531-01-X. Séminaire tenu au Collège de France; Bibl. 190.

602 ^E**Cervelló Autuori, Josep** África antigua: el antiguo Egipto, una civilización africana. Aula Aegyptiaca, Studia 1: Barc 2001, Aula Aegyptiaca 300 pp. €33. 84-607-2429-8. Actas de la IX semana de estudios africanos del Centre d'Estudis Africans de Barcelona, 18-22 de marzo de 1996. ^RDiscEg 51 (2001) 135-141 (*Brito, Mark de*).

603 La circolazione illecita delle opere d'arte: principio della buona fede: atti del 6° Convegno Internazionale Italia-Spagna; Roma, Scuola Ufficiali Carabinieri, 12-16 giugno 2000. Bollettino di numismatica, Suppl. 36: R 2001, Ministero per i Beni Culturali e Ambientali 420 pp. Comando Carabinieri Tutela Patrimonio Artistico.

604 ^E**Clarke, Graeme** Identities in the eastern Mediterranean in antiquity. 1998 ⇒14,469; 15,528. Conference Canberra 10-12 November, 1997. ^RBASOR 321 (2001) 90-91 (*Berlin, Andrea M.*).

605 ^E**Cordano, Federica; Grottanelli, Cristiano** Sorteggio pubblico e cleromanzia dall'antichità all'età moderna: atti della tavola rotonda, Università degli Studi di Milano, Dipartimento di Scienze dell'Antichità 26-27 gennaio 2000. Mi 2001, Et 239 pp. 88-86752-18-0.

606 ^E**Curtis, John** Mesopotamia and Iran in the Parthian and Sasanian periods: rejection and revival c.238 BC-AD 642. 2000 ⇒16,581. Sem. in mem. of V. Lukonin. ^RBiOr 58 (2001) 652-6 (*Henkelman, Wouter*).

607 ^E**Drews, Robert** Greater Anatolia and the Indo-Hittite language family: papers presented at a colloquium, Univ. of Richmond, 18-19.3.2000. Wsh 2001, Institute for the Study of Man xiv; 305 pp. $52. 0-941694-77-1.

608 ^E**Fieger, Michael; Schmid, Konrad; Schwagmeier, Peter** Qumran— die Schriftrollen vom Toten Meer: Vorträge des St. Galler Qumran-Symposiums vom 2./3. Juli 1999. NTOA 47: Gö 2001, Vandenhoeck & R. viii; 226 pp. FS68. 3-525-53947-9.

609 ^E**Fikentscher, Wolfgang** Begegnung und Konflikt: eine kulturanthropologische Bestandsaufnahme. ABAW.PH 120: Mü 2001, Verlag der Bayerischen Akademie der Wissenschaft 303 pp. 3-769601-15-7. Konferenz 21-23.9.1999, München.

610 ^E**Fortin, Michel; Aurenche, Olivier** Espace naturel, espace habité: en Syrie du Nord (10e-2e millénaires av. J.-C.). 1998 ⇒14,476; 15,533. Actes du colloque tenu à l'Université Laval (Québec) du 5 au 7 mai 1997. ^RSyr. 78 (2001) 226-227 (*Contenson, Henri de*).

611 ^E**Fredouille, Jean-Claude** Les Mauristes à Saint-Germain-des-Prés: actes du Colloque de Paris (2 décembre 1999). EAug.Moyen Age et Temps Modernes 36: P 2001, Institut d'Études Augustiniennes 131 pp. 2-85121-183-8.

612 ^E**Goodblatt, David M.; Pinnick, Avital; Schwartz, Daniel R.** Historical perspectives: from the Hasmoneans to Bar Kokhba in light of the Dead Sea Scrolls: proceedings of the Fourth International Symposium of the Orion Center, 27-31 January, 1999. StTDJ 37: Lei 2001, Brill x; 201 pp. 90-04-12007-6.

613 ^E**Hardmeier, Christof** Steine—Bilder—Texte: historische Evidenz au-
ßerbiblischer und biblischer Quellen. Arbeiten zur Bibel und ihrer Geschichte 5: Lp 2001, Evangelische Verlagsanstalt 217 pp. €50. 3-374-
01907-2. Congress, Greifswald 2000.

614 ^E**Hausleiter, A.; Reiche, A.** Iron Age pottery in northern Mesopotami-
a, northern Syria and south-eastern Anatolia. Altertumskunde des Vorderen Orients 10: Müns 1999, Ugarit-Verlag xii; 491 pp. $121. 3-927-
120-782. Papers presented at the meetings of the international 'table
ronde' at Heidelberg (1995) and Nieborów (1997) and other contributions. ^ROLZ 96 (2001) 706-711 (*Schachner, Andreas*).

615 ^E**Hägg, R.** Ancient Greek cult practice from the archaeological evidence: proceedings of the 4th international seminar on ancient Greek
cult. Acta Instituti Atheniensis Regni Sueciae 15: 1998 ⇒14,482;
16,589. ^RAJA 105 (2001) 734-735 (*Brown, Shelby*); AnCl 70 (2001)
378-379 (*Prienne-Delforge, Vinciane*).

616 ^E**Hope, Valerie M.; Marshall, Eireann** Death and disease in the
ancient city. 2000 ⇒16,592. Conf. Univ. of Exeter. ^RAnCl 70 (2001)
406-408 (*Gourevitch, Danielle*).

617 ^E**Höckmann, Ursula; Kriekenbom, D.** Naukratis. Möhnesee 2001,
Bibliopolis xii; 276 pp. 3-933925-15-0. Conf. Univ. Mainz; 42 pl.

618 ^E**Hudson, Michael; Levine, Baruch A.** Urbanization and land owner-
ship in the ancient Near East. 1999 ⇒15,539; 16,593. ^RAJA 105
(2001) 114-115 (*Foster, Benjamin R.*).

619 ^E**Karageorghis, Vassos; Morris, Christine E.** Defensive settlements
of the Aegean and the eastern Mediterranean after c. 1200 B.C.: proceedings of an international workshop held at Trinity College Dublin,
7-9 May 1999. Nicosia 2001, Leventis. Cyp£20.20. 9963-36-433-0.
Num. ill. [RB 109,157].

620 ^E**Karageorghis, Vassos** The white slip ware of late Bronze Age
Cyprus. DÖAW 20; Contributions to the chronology of the eastern
Mediterranean 2: W 2001, Verlag der ÖAW. 244 pp. €47.04. 3-7001-
2935-1. Conf. in honour of Malcolm Wiener, Nicosia 29-30 Oct. 1998.

621 ^E**Kleiner, Diana E.E.; Matheson, Susan B.** I, Claudia II: women in
Roman art and society. 2000 ⇒16,595. ^RAJA 105 (2001) 373-374 (*Sebesta, Judith*).

622 ^E**Kugler, Robert A.; Schuller, Eileen M.** The Dead Sea scrolls at
fifty: SBL Early Judaism and Its Literature 15: 1999 ⇒15,544. ^RCBQ
63 (2001) 175-177 (*Cook, Edward M.*); HebStud 42 (2001) 358-361
(*Duhaimé, Jean*); RBLit 3 (2001) 293-297 (*Nitzan, Bilhah*).

623 ^E**Lavagne, H.; Queyrel, F.** Les moulages de sculptures antiques et
l'histoire de l'archéologie: actes du colloque international Paris,
24.10.1997. 2000 ⇒16,596. ^RREA 103 (2001) 608-610 (*Marcadé, J.*).

624 ^E**Machegay, Sophie; Le Dinahet, Marie-Thérèse; Salles, Jean-
François** Nécropoles et pouvoir, idéologies, pratiques et interprétation:
colloque Théories de la nécropole antique, Lyon 21-25.1.1995. 1998
⇒15,546. ^RRAr (2001) 376-377 (*Lamboley, Jean-Luc*).

625 ^E**Mazar, Amihai** Studies in the archaeology of the Iron Age in Israel
and Jordan. JSOT.S 331: Shf 2001, Sheffield A. 337 pp. $93. 1-84127-
203-5. Collab. *Ginny Mathias*; Colloquium, Univ. College, London,
16-17.4.1996.

626 ^E**Mazoyer, Michel,** *al.*, Ville et pouvoir: origines et développements.
Cahiers Kubaba 1-2: P 2001, L'Harmattan 266+265 pp. €24.40+21.35.
2-7475-2609-7. Actes du Colloque 7-8.12.2000, Univ. de Paris I—Inst.
Catholique.

627 ᴱ**Molin, Michel** Images et représentations du pouvoir et de l'ordre social dans l'antiquité. De l'archéologie à l'histoire: P 2001, De Boccard 346 pp. 2-7018-0147-8. Actes du colloque d'Angers, 28-29 mai 1999; 89 fig. [REG 115,819—Hinard, François].

628 ᴱ**Muller, B.** 'Maquettes architecturales' de l'antiquité: actes du colloque de Strasbourg 3-5 déc. 1998. Travaux du Centre de Recherche sur le Proche-Orient et la Grèce Antique 17: P 2001, Boccard 574 pp. 2-911488-03-02. Num. ill.

629 ᴱ**Müller, Walter** Minoisch-mykenische Glyptik: Stil, Ikonographie, Funktion. B 2000, Mann xv; 368 pp. $128. 3-7861-2406-X. V. Internationales Siegel-Symposium, Marburg, 23-25.9.1999.

630 ᴱ**Neusner, Jacob; Strange, James F.** Religious texts and material contexts. Studies in ancient Judaism: Lanham 2001, University Press of America x; 319 pp. 0-7618-2062-0. Conference Univ. of South Florida, 24-25.2.2001.

631 ᴱ**Nielsen, Inge** The royal palace institution in the first millennium BC: regional development and cultural interchange between east and west. Monographs of the Danish Institute at Athens 4: Århus 2001, Aarhus University Press 317 pp. €34. 87-7934-004-0. Coll. Athens 1999.

632 ᴱ**Olmo Lete, G. del** Archaeology of the Upper Syrian Euphrates, the Tishrin Dam area. AulOr.S 15: 1999 ⇒15,550. Internat. Symposium Barcelona, Jan. 1998. ᴿOLZ 96 (2001) 232-240 (*Mazzoni, S.*).

633 ᴱ**Palagia, Olga; Coulson, William D.E.** Regional schools in Hellenistic sculpture. Oxbow Monograph 90: 1998 ⇒14,487; 15,552. International Conf. American School of Classical Studies at Athens, March 15-17, 1996. ᴿAnCl 70 (2001) 520-522 (*Hermary, Antoine*).

634 ᴱ**Perna, Massimo** Administrative documents in the Aegean and their Near Eastern counterparts: international colloquium Naples 1996. 2000 ⇒16,604. ᴿAJA 105 (2001) 543-544 (*Schoep, Ilse*)..

635 ᴱ**Phelps, William; Lolos, Yannos; Vichos, Yannis** The Point Iria wreck: interconnections in the Mediterranean ca. 1200 B.C. 1999 ⇒ 15,553. ᴿAJA 105 (2001) 341-343 (*Bass, George F.*).

636 ᴱ**Salomies, Olli** The Greek east in the Roman context. Papers and Monographs of the Finnish Institute at Athens 7: Helsinki 2001, Finnish Institute 217 pp. 951-988-060-7. Coll. Athens 21-22.5.1999 [AnCl 72, 586s—Martin, Alain].

637 ᴱ**Scarcia Amoretti, Biancamaria** Islam in East Africa: new sources (archives: manuscripts and written historical sources: oral history: archaeology): international colloquium (Rome, 2-4 December 1999). R 2001, Herder 469 pp.

638 Le sceau et l'administration dans la vallée du Nil: Villeneuve d'Ascq 7-8 juillet 2000. Cahier de recherches de l'Institut de Papyrologie et d'Égyptologie de Lille 22: Lille 2001, Université Charles-de-Gaulle—Lille III 215 pp. 2-9504-764-7-3.

639 ᴱ**Schiffman, Lawrence H.; Tov, Emanuel; VanderKam, James C.** The Dead Sea scrolls fifty years after their discovery: proceedings of the Jerusalem Congress, July 20-25, 1997. 2000 ⇒16,609. ᴿJSJ 32 (2001) 346-351 (*Xeravits, Géza*).

640 ᴱ**Scholz, Piotr O.** Von Hiob Ludolf bis Enrico Cerulli, Halle/S. 3.-5. Oktober 1996: Akten der 2. Tagung der Orbis-Aethiopicus-Gesellschaft zur Erhaltung und Förderung der äthiopischen Kultur. Bibliotheca nubica et aethiopica 8: Wsz 2001, n.p. xix; 242 pp. Mitwirkung von *Lij Asfa-Wassen Asserate* und *Walter Raunig*.

641 ᴱShortland, A.J. The social context of technological change: Egypt and the Near East 1650-1550 BC. Oxf 2001, Oxbow x; 273 pp. £28. 1-84217-050-3. Symposium, Oxford 12-14.9.2000.

642 ᴱShulman, D.; Stroumsa, G.G. Dream cultures: explorations in the comparative history of dreaming. 1999 ⇒15,558. ᴿClR 51 (2001) 139-141 (*Rosenberger, Veit*).

643 ᴱSwiny, Stuart; Hohlfelder, Robert L.; Swiny, Helena W. Res Maritimae: Cyprus and the Eastern Mediterranean from prehistory to late antiquity: Symposium Nicosia 1994. ASOR Arch. Reports 4: 1998 ⇒ 14,491; 15,559. ᴿPEQ 133 (2001) 69-70 (*Cobbing, Felicity J.*).

644 ᴱUehlinger, Christoph Images as media: sources for the cultural history of the Near East and the eastern Mediterranean (1st mill. BCE). OBO 175: 2000 ⇒16,611. ᴿDiscEg 50 (2001) 127-136 (*Warburton, David*).

645 ᴱVermeulen, U.; Van Steenbergen, J. Egypt and Syria in the Fatimid, Ayyubid and Mamluk eras III: proc. of the 6th, 7th and 8th International Colloquium, Katholieke Universiteit Leuven in May 1997, 1998 and 1999. OLA 102: Lv 2001, Peeters xii; 471 pp. 90-429-0970-6.

646 ᴱVillanueva Puig, Marie-Christine, *al.*, Céramique et peinture grecques, mode d'emploi: actes du colloque international, Ecole du Louvre, 26-28.4.1995. 1999 ⇒15,561. ᴿRAr (2001) 387 (*Boardman, John*).

647 Il volto dei volti, 5: Cristo. Gorle 2001, Velar 324 pp. €92.96. Istituto internazionale di ricerca sul volto di Cristo.

648 ᴱWenig, Steffen Studien zum antiken Sudan: Akten der 7... Tagung für meroitische Forschungen Sept. 1992 in Gosen bei Berlin. Meroitica 15: 1999 ⇒15,562; 16,613. ᴿBiOr 58 (2001) 385-389 (*Williams, Bruce*).

649 ᴱWestbrook, Raymond; Jasnow, Richard Security for debt in ancient Near Eastern law. Culture and history of the Ancient Near East 9: Lei 2001: Brill vii; 360 pp. €72. 90-04-12124-2. Colloquium 19-20.3.1999 Baltimore.

650 ᴱWilhelm, Gernot Akten des IV. Internationalen Kongresses für Hethitologie Würzburg, 4.-8. Oktober 1999. StBT 45: Wsb 2001, Harrassowitz xxiv; 761 pp. 3-447-04485-3.

651 ᴱWillems, Harco Social aspects of funerary culture in the Egytian [sic] Old and Middle Kingdoms: proceedings of the international symposium held at Leiden University 6-7 June, 1996. OLA 103: Lv 2001, Peeters ix; 372 pp. €70. 90-429-1015-1.

A3.1 *Opera consultationis*—Reference works *plurium* infra

652 Augustinus-Lexikon, 2/5-6: Donatistas (Contra)–Epistulae. ᴱMayer, Cornelius: Ba 2001, Schwabe 641-1057 col.

653 The Blackwell companion to the Hebrew Bible. ᴱPerdue, Leo G.: Blackwell Companions to Religion: Oxf 2001, Blackwell xxx; 471 pp. £80/$125. 0-6312-1071-7. ᴿSJOT 15 (2001) 326-8 (*Lemche, Niels P.*).

654 CAH²: The Cambridge ancient history, 11: the high empire, A.D. 70-192. ᴱBowman, Alan K.; Garnsey, P.; Rathbone, D.: C 2000, CUP xxi; 1222 pp. 0-521-2633-5.

655 LThK³: Lexikon für Theologie und Kirche 10-11: Thomaschristen bis Žytomyr; Nachträge Register Abkürzungsverzeichnis. ᴱKasper, Walter: FrB 2001, Herder 14 pp + 1536 Sp.; 16 pp + 264 Sp. + 151-746 pp. 3-451-22010-5/011-3.

656 Der neue Pauly 10: Pol-Sal; 11: Sam-Tal. [E]**Cancik, Hubert; Schnei-**
     der, Helmuth: Stu 2001, Metzler xi; 1278 Sp. + xi; 1234 Sp. 3-476-
     01480-0/1-9.
657 Der neue Pauly 13: Rezeption: A-Fo. [E]**Landfester, M.**: Stu 1999,
     Metzler c.600 pp. 3-476-61470-3. [R]At. 89 (2001) 296-297 (*Saletti, Ce-
     sare*).
658 New catholic encyclopedia: jubilee volume, the Wojtyla years. Detroit
     2001, Gale xiii; 681 pp. $95. Catholic Univ. of America.
659 The new encyclopedia of Islam. [E]**Glassé, Cyril**: NY 2001, Altamira
     582 pp. $90 [AUSS 41,145—Lepke, Wolfgang].
660 **RAC**: Reallexikon für Antike und Christentum, 19: Itinerarium-Kanni-
     balismus. [E]**Dassmann, E.**: Stu 2001, Hiersemann 1276 col. 3-7772-
     0134-0;
661 Supplement, Band 1: Aaron-Biographie II. Stu 2001, Hiersemann 1376
     col. 3-7772-0103-0.
662 **RGG**[4]: Religion in Geschichte und Gegenwart, 1: A-B. [E]**Betz, Hans
     Dieter**, *al.*,: 1998 ⇒14,496...16,621. [R]RStR 27 (2001) 319-322
     (*Fitzgerald, John T.*); RStR 27 (2001) 322-325 (*Alles, Gregory D.*);
     RStR 27 (2001) 325-328 (*Duke, James O.*); RStR 27 (2001) 328-329
     (*Krentz, Edgar J.*);
663 2: C-E. 1999 ⇒15,569. [R]ETR 76 (2001) 637-639 (*Askani, Hans-
     Christoph*);
664 4: I-K. Tü 2001, Mohr lxxii; 1924 col. €199. 3-16-146904-6.
665 **TRE**: Theologische Realenzyklopädie, 32: Spurgeon-Taylor. [E]**Krause,
     Gerhard; Müller, Gerhard**: B 2001, De Gruyter 783 pp. 3-11-01671-
     2-3.

A3.3 *Opera consultationis* **biblica** *non excerpta infra*—**not subindexed**

666 [E]**Alexander, Pat; Alexander, David** Das große Handbuch zur Bibel:
     der einzigartige Führer durch die Bücher der Bibel faszinierend—be-
     währt—reich illustriert. Wu 2001, Brockhaus 816 pp. €44.80. 3-417-
     24700-4.
667 [E]**Alexander, Patrick H.**, *al.*, The SBL handbook of style: for ancient
     Near Eastern, biblical, and early christian studies. 1999 ⇒15,574.
     [R]JRTI 4 (2001) 112-113 (*Dubis, Mark*).
668 [E]**Alexander, T.D.; Rosner, Brian S.** The new dictionary of biblical
     theology. 2000 ⇒16,624. [R]Pacifica 14 (2001) 326-328 (*Symons, M.*).
669 [E]**Balz, Horst; Schneider, Gerhard** Dizionario esegetico del Nuovo
     Testamento. Kegchreai-ōphelimos 2: 1998 ⇒14,504. [R]Sal. 63 (2001)
     191-193 (*Bracchi, R.*).
670 [E]**Botterweck, G. Johannes; Ringgren, Helmer; Fabry, Heinz-Josef**
     TDOT: Theological Dictionary of the Old Testament, 9: mārad-nāqâ.
     [T]*Green, David E.*: 1998 ⇒14,499; 15,576. [R]JBL 119 (2000) 381-383
     (*Hiebert, Robert J.V.*);
671 10: nāqam-ʿāzab. [T]*Green, David E.*: 2000 ⇒16,625. [R]VJTR 65 (2001)
     144-146 (*Meagher, P.M.*).
672 Dictionnaire encyclopédique de la bible. Turnhout [2]2001 <1987>, Bre-
     pols 1364 pp. €68.80. 2-503-51311-5.
673 [E]**Douglas, J.D.; Hyllier, N.** The illustrated bible dictionary. 1998 3
     vols ⇒15,581. [R]Annales Theologici 15 (2001) 624-626 (*Estrada, B.*).

674 ᴱEvans, Craig A.; Porter, Stanley E. Dictionary of New Testament background. 2000 ⇒16,631. ᴿAnnales Theologici 15 (2001) 604-606 (*Estrada, B.*); AUSS 39 (2001) 329-330 (*Johnston, Robert M.*).

675 ᴱFernández Ramos, Felipe Diccionario de Jesús de Nazaret. Burgos 2001, Monte Carmelo 1344 pp. 84-7239-634-7.

676 ᴱFreedman, David Noel Eerdmans dictionary of the bible. 2000 ⇒16,633. ᴿAnnTh 15 (2001) 343-345 (*Estrada, B.*); TrinJ 22 (2001) 264-266 (*Thompson, Alan J.*); RBBras 18 (2001) 452-453.

677 ᴱGörg, Manfred; Lang, Bernhard Neues Bibel-Lexikon, 3: O - Z. Z 2001, Benziger xi; 1238 pp. 3-545-23076-7.

678 ᴱHayes, John H. Dictionary of biblical interpretation. 1999 ⇒15,584; 16,637. ᴿHeyJ 42 (2001) 71-72 (*Leemans, Johan*); RB 108 (2001) 311-312 (*Murphy-O'Connor, J.*); JRTI 4 (2001) 105-108 (*Bundy, David*); CBQ 63 (2001) 722-723 (*Matties, Gordon H.*).

679 ᴱLéon-Dufour, Xavier Vocabular de teologie biblică. Bucureşti 2001, Ed. Arhiepiscopiei Romano-Catolice de Bucureşti 804 pp. ᴿCICat 2/2 (2001) 199-200 (*Mecu, Nicolae*).

680 ᴱMcKim, Donald K. Historical handbook of major biblical interpreters. 1998 ⇒14,517. ᴿJBL 120 (2001) 591-593 (*Harvey, Paul B.*); EvQ 73 (2001) 91-92 (*Trueman, Carl R.*).

681 ᴱMetzger, Bruce Manning; Coogan, Michael David The Oxford guide to people & places of the bible. NY 2001, OUP xxii; (2) 374 pp. 0-19-514641-7. Bibl. 351-355.

682 ᴱRogerson, John William The Oxford illustrated history of the bible. Oxf 2001, OUP xvi; 395 pp. $40. 0-19-860118-2. Bibl. 371-381.

683 ᴱRyken, Leland; Wilhoit, James C.; Longman, Tremper III Dictionary of biblical imagery. 1998 ⇒14,521; 15,594. ᴿEvQ 73 (2001) 78-80 (*Dickson, Beth*).

684 Soulen, Richard N.; Soulen, R. Kendall Handbook of biblical criticism. LVL ³2001, Westminster 234 pp. $20. 0-664-22314-1 [BiTod 40,327—Bergant, Dianne].

685 ᴱVan der Toorn, Karel; Becking, Bob; Van der Horst, Pieter W. Dictionary of deities and demons in the bible. ²1999 <1995> ⇒15,596; 16,644. ᴿAUSS 39 (2001) 346-347 (*Abrahamson, Karen K.*); BASOR 321 (2001) 92-93 (*Rendsburg, Gary A.*).

686 ᴱWigoder, G. Nuevo Diccionario de la biblia: lugares, concordancias y personajes. Barc 2001, Muchnik 800 pp.

A3.5 *Opera consultationis* theologica *non excerpta infra*

687 ᴱAlberigo, Giuseppe, *al.*, Dekrete der ökumenischen Konzilien, 2: Konzilien des Mittelalters: vom ersten Laterankonzil (1123) bis zum fünften Laterankonzil (1512-1517). Pd 2000, Schöningh xii; 469 pp. €101.24.

688 ᴱAnthony, Michael Evangelical dictionary of christian education. GR 2001, Baker 747 pp. $50. 08010-21847 [ThD 48,268—Heiser, W.C.].

689 ᴱAuffarth, Christoph; Bernard, Jutta; Mohr, Hubert Metzler-Lexikon Religion: Gegenwart—Alltag—Medien, 1: Abendmahl–Guru, 2: Haar–Osho-Bewegung. Stu 1999, Metzler xvii; 532 + iv; 632 pp. €85.90 + 85.90. 3-476-01551-3/2-1. 156 + 146 ill.;

690 3: Paganismus–Zombie. 2000, Metzler iv; 729 pp. €85.90. 3-476-01553-X. 126 ill.

691 ᴱ**Begley, John J.** The welcoming church: christian initiation: a handbook of liturgical and patristic sources. Scranton 2001, Univ. of Scranton Pr. ix; 207 pp. $28. 09408-66900 [ThD 49,91—Heiser, W.].

692 ᴱ**Benazzi, Natale** Archivum: documenti della storia della chiesa dal I secolo a oggi. 2000 ⇒16,648 ᴿAnnales Theologici 15 (2001) 623-624 (*Martínez Ferrer, L.*).

693 ᴱ**Cancik, Hubert; Gladigow, Burkhard; Kohl, Karl-Heinz** Handbuch religionswissenschaftlicher Grundbegriffe: Band V: Säkularisierung - Zwischenwesen; Register. Stu 2001, Kohlhammer 496 pp. 3-17-011304-6.

694 ᴱ**Elwell, Walter A.** Evangelical dictionary of theology. Baker Reference Library: GR ²2001, Baker 1312 pp. $50. 0-8010-2075-1 [ThD 48,268—Heiser, W. Charles].

695 ᴱ**Fabella, Virginia; Sugirtharajah, R.S.** Dictionary of Third World theologies. 2000 ⇒16,655. ᴿCTJ 36 (2001) 430-431 (*Van Baak, Edward*).

696 ᴱ**Fahlbusch, Erwin; Bromiley, Geoffrey William** The encyclopedia of christianity, 2: E-I. GR 2001, Eerdmans xxx; 787 pp. $100. 0-8028-2414-5. ᴿVJTR 65 (2001) 786-787 (*Gispert-Sauch, G.*)

697 ᴱ**Farrugia, Edward G.** Dizionario enciclopedico dell'Oriente. R 2000, Pont. Ist. Orientale xvi; 854 pp.

698 ᴱ**Gill, Robin** The Cambridge companion to christian ethics. C 2000, CUP xv; 290 pp. £37.50/14. 0-521-77070-X/918-9. ᴿET 112 (2001) 217-218 (*Rodd, C.S.*).

699 ᴱ**Kurian, George Thomas** Nelson's new christian dictionary. Nv 2001, Nelson 977 pp. 0-7852-4300-3.

700 ᴱ**Muñoz Delgado, Luis** Léxico de magia y religión en los papiros mágicos griegos. Diccionario Griego-Español, Anejo V: M 2001, Consejo superior de investigaciones científicas xix; 183 pp. €21.56. 84-0007-949-3. Colab. *Juan Rodríguez Somolinos*. ᴿAnalecta Papyrologica 13 (2001) 251-254 (*Maltomini, Franco*).

701 ᴱ**Sawyer, John F.A.; Simpson, J.M.Y.** Concise encyclopedia of language and religion. Amst 2001, Elsevier xxxi; 580 pp. $211.50. 0-08-043167-4.

702 ᵀ**Skrzypczak, Otto** Documentos dos primeiros oito concílios ecumênicos. ²2000 ⇒16,651. ᴿPerTeol 33 (2001) 131-2 (*Taborda, Francisco*).

703 ᴱ**Sodi, Manlio; Triacca, Achille** Dizionario di omiletica. 1998 ⇒14, 533... 16,662. ᴿTheol(A) 72 (2001) 746-748 (*Koukoura, Demetra A.*).

704 ᴱ**Steimer, Bruno** Lexikon der Päpste und des Papsttums. Lexikon für Theologie und Kirche kompakt: FrB 2001, Herder 16*; 718 col. 3-451-22015-6;

705 Lexikon der Kirchengeschichte, 1: A-Ki, 2: Kl-Z. FrB 2001, Herder 1814 col. €50. 3-451-22018-0.

706 ᴱ**Sunquist, Scott W.**, *al.*, A dictionary of Asian christianity. GR 2001, Eerdmans 937 pp. $75.

707 ᴱ**Walsh, Michael** Dictionary of christian biography. L 2001, Continuum 1250 pp. 0-8264-5263-9.

A3.6 *Opera consultationis* generalia

708 ᴱ**Bosworth, C.E.**, *al.*, Encylopédie de l'Islam, 9: San-Sze. Lei 1998, Brill xvi; 959 pp. 90-04-10423-2.

709 ^E**Brunschwig, Jacques; Lloyd,Geoffrey** Diccionario Akal: el saber griego: diccionario crítico. 2000 ⇒16,664. ^REM 69 (2001) 191-192 (*Elías Pérez, Mónica*).

710 ^E**Calmeyer, Peter** Reallexikon der Assyriologie und vorderasiatischen Archäologie, 9: Nab - Nuzi. B 1998-2001, De Gruyter xxii; 648 pp. 3-11-017296-8.

711 **Goulet, Richard** Dictionnaire des philosophes antiques, 3: d'Eccélos à Juvénal. 2000 ⇒16,667. ^RAnCl 70 (2001) 346-348 (*Beets, François*).

712 ^E**Horbury, William; Davies, W.D.; Sturdy, John** The Cambridge history of Judaism, 3: the early Roman period. 1999 ⇒15,613; 16,670. ^RJThS 52 (2001) 322-325 (*Lange, N.R.M. de*); Religion 31 (2001) 198-200 (*Jaffee, Martin*); JR 81 (2001) 323-325 (*Collins, John J.*); BiOr 58 (2001) 238-239 (*Tromp, Johannes*); ThLZ 126 (2001) 379-382 (*Maier, Johann*).

713 **Klose, Albrecht** Sprachen der Welt/Languages of the World/: ein weltweiter Index der Sprachfamilien, Einzelsprachen und Dialekte, mit Angabe der Synonyma und fremdsprachigen Äquivalente/a multilingual concordance of languages, dialects and language-families. Mü ²2001, Saur 556 pp 3-598-11404-4. Bibl. 19-45.

714 ^E**Knellwolf, Christa; Norris, Christopher** The Cambridge history of literary criticism, 9: twentieth-century historical, philosophical and psychological perspectives. C 2001, CUP xiii; 482 pp. 0-521-30014-2.

715 ^E**McAuliffe, Jane Dammen** Encyclopaedia of the Qur'an, v.1: A-D. Lei 2001, Brill xxxiv; 558 pp. €228/$278. 90-0413-668-1.

716 ^E**Neusner, Jacob; Avery-Peck, Alan J.; Green, William S.** The encyclopaedia of Judaism. 2000, 3 vols ⇒16,674. ^RRRT (2001/1) 3-5 (*Faur, José*); NedThT 55/4 (2001) 328-32 (*Van der Horst, Pieter W.*).

717 ^E**O'Neill, Charles E.; Domínguez, J. M.** Diccionario histórico de la Compañia de Jesús: biografico-tematico, 1: AA-Costa Rica; 2: Costa Rossetti-Industrias; 3: Infante de Santiago-Piątkiewicz; 4: Piatti-Zwaans. R 2001, Institutum Historicum S.J. 4 vols; 1032+1056+1120+1066 pp. $580. 84-8468-036-3.

718 **Pikulik, Jerzy** Polskie Graduaty Sredniowieczne. Wsz 2001, Wyd. Uniwersytetu Kardynala Stefana Wyszynskiego 456 pp. 83707-2194X.

719 **Salisbury, Joyce E.** Encyclopedia of women in the ancient world. Santa Barbara, CA 2001, ABC-Clio xxxvii; 385 pp. 1-57607-092-1. Foreword by *Mary Lefkowitz*.

720 ^E**Selden, Raman** The Cambridge history of literary criticism, 8: from formalism to poststructuralism. C 2001, CUP viii; 487 pp. 0-521-30013-4.

721 ^E**Standaert, Nicolas** Handbook of christianity in China, 1: 635-1800. HO 4, China 15,1: Lei 2001, Brill xxviii, 964 pp. €196/$265. 90-04-11431-9.

722 ^E**Vauchez, André**, *al.*, The encyclopedia of the Middle Ages. C 2000, Clarke 2 vols; 1664 pp. £195/€325. 0-227-67931-8. 640 ill. ^RET 112 (2001) 375-376 (*Edden, Valerie*).

A3.8 *Opera consultationis* archaeologica et geographica

723 ^E**Bienkowski, Piotr; Millard, Alan** Dictionary of the ancient Near East. 2000 ⇒16,679. ^RJRAS 11 (2001) 379-381 (*Robson, Eleanor*); AUSS 39 (2001) 328-329 (*Gane, Constance E.*).

724 **Gran-Aymerich, Éve** Dictionnaire biographique d'archéologie 1798-
     1945. P 2001, CNRS 741 pp. €44.97. 2-271-05702-7. Bibl. 19-24.
725 ^E**Hodder, Ian** Archaeological theory today. C 2001, Polity ix; 317 pp.
     0-7456-2268-2.
726 ^E**Joannès, F.** Dictionnaire de la civilisation mésopotamienne. P 2001,
     Laffont xxxviii; 974 pp. €28.80. Ill. ^RAkkadica 122 (2001) 74-77
     (*Gasche, Hermann*).
727 Lexicon topographicum urbis Romae: suburbium, 1: A-B. ^E**La Regina,**
     Adriano: R 2001, Quasar 343 pp. €134. 88-7097-044-2. 221 fig.
728 **Maier, Johann** Judentum von A bis Z: Glauben, Geschichte, Kultur.
     FrB 2001, Herder 462 pp [FrRu 10,64s—Lauer, Simon].
729 ^E**Meyers, Eric M.** The Oxford encyclopedia of archaeology in the
     Near East. 1997, 5 vols ⇒14,10040... 16,685. ^RThLZ 126 (2001) 507-
     509 (*Rüterswörden, Udo*); JBL 119 (2000) 161-63 (*Halpern, Baruch*).
730 ^E**Negev, Avraham; Gibson, Shimon** Archaeological encyclopedia of
     the Holy Land. NY 2001, Continuum 560 pp. $40. 0-8264-1316-1
     [BiTod 39,321—Senior, Donald].
731 ^E**Redford, Donald B.** The Oxford encyclopedia of Ancient Egypt. NY
     2001, OUP 3 vols. £215. 0-19-510234-7. ^RDiscEg 51 (2001) 147-156
     (*Nibbi, Alessandra*).
732 ^E**Russell, Terence M.** The Napoleonic survey of Egypt: Description de
     l'Égypte, 1-2. Aldershot 2001, Ashgate xvi; 244 + ix; 281-603 pp. £95.
     1-8592-9248-2. Num. ill.
733 ^E**Sonnabend, Holger** Mensch und Landschaft in der Antike: Lexikon
     der historischen Geographie. Stu 1999, Metzler xii; 660 pp. €50.11. 3-
     476-01285-9. 112 fig.

A4.0 Bibliographiae, *computers* biblicae

734 BibleWorks 5: software for biblical exegesis and research. Bigfork,
     MT 1998-2001. BibleWorks LLC.
735 Bibliographie. JAB 3 (2001) 249-261.
736 *Böttrich, Christfried* Neues Testament und hellenistisch-römische
     Welt. JLH 40 (2001) 76-108.
737 **BuBB:** Bulletin de bibliographie biblique. ^E**Kaestli, Jean Daniel** Lau-
     sanne 2001, Institut des sciences bibliques de l'Université de
     Lausanne. 3 issues a year.
738 *Clarysse, Willy* The Leuven data-base of ancient books (LDAB). XXII
     Congresso di papirologia, 1. 2001 ⇒555. 237-249.
739 **DiTommaso, Lorenzo** A bibliography of pseudepigrapha research
     1850-1999. JSPE.S 39: Shf 2001, Sheffield A. 1067 pp. £90. 1-84127-
     202-7. ^RRBBras 18 (2001) 498-499.
740 **Elliott, James Keith** A bibliography of Greek NT manuscripts.
     MSSNTS 109: ²2000 ⇒16,697. ^RNT 43 (2001) 89-91 (*Parker, D.C.*).
741 *Gibert, Pierre* Bulletin d'exégèse de l'Ancien Testament: pentateuque
     et prophètes. RSR 89 (2001) 527-560.
742 *Harrington, Daniel* Books on the bible. America 184/8 (2001) 17-26.
743 *Hoppe, Leslie J.* The internet and biblical studies. BiTod 39 (2001)
     307-311.
744 *Ikeda, Yutaka* It's always challenging—biblical studies in Japan. Orient
     36 (2001) 87-106.

745 **IZBG**: International Review of Biblical Studies 48 (2001-2002): ᴱ**Lang, Bernhard**: Lei 2003, Brill xii; 514 pp. €105/$125. 90-04-12889-1.

746 *Lodge, John G.* New Testament studies: 1961 and 2001. ChiSt 40 (2001) 139-151.

747 *Luciani, Didier* Chronique d'Ecriture Sainte. VieCon 73 (2001) 334-345.

748 *Lust, Johann* Scriptura Sacra Veteris Testamenti. EThL 77 (2001) 169*-272*.

749 **Neirynck, Frans; Verheyden, J.; Corstjens, R.** The gospel of Matthew and the sayings source Q: a cumulative bibliography 1950-1995. BEThL 140: 1998, 2 vols ⇒14,564... 16,707. ᴿTJT 17 (2001) 297-298 (*Derrenbacker, Robert A.*).

750 **NTAb**: New Testament Abstracts 45. ᴱ**Harrington, Daniel J.; Matthews, Christopher R.** CM 2001, Weston Jesuit School of Theology. 3 issues a year.

751 **OTA**: Old Testament Abstracts 24. ᴱ**Begg, Christopher T.**: Wsh 2001, Catholic Biblical Association.. 3 issues a year.

752 *Piñero, Antonio* New Testament philology bulletin. FgNT 14 (2001) 167-212.

753 *Poswick, Ferdinand* La fin des saintes écritures?. Rassegna di Pedagogia 59 (2001) 171-183;

754 L'informatique a-t-elle renouvelé le travail des exégètes de métier?. LV.F 56 (2001) 423-434.

755 The essential IVP reference collection. Leicester 2001, IVP. £100. CD with IVP dictionaries. ᴿIBSt 23 (2001) 135-137 (*McCullough, J.C.*).

756 The Society for Old Testament Study: book list 2001. ᴱ**Brooke, George J.**: Shf 2001, Sheffield Academic vi; 190 pp. 1-84127-206-X [=JSOT 94 (2001) 1-190].

757 *Verheyden, Joseph* Scriptura Sacra Novi Testamenti. EThL 77 (2001) 272*-398*.

758 ᴱ**Waite, David** Bibliographia Carmelitana annualis 2000, 4: sacra scrittura. Carmelus 48 (2001) 22-41.

759 **ZAW** 113: ᴱ**Waschke, Ernst-Joachim; Köckert, Matthias**: B 2001, De Gruyter 82-165; 251-329; 431-479.

760 **ZNW** 92: ᴱ**Wolter, Michael**: B 2001, De Gruyter 136-138; 300-302.

A4.2 *Bibliographiae* theologicae

761 An analytical index to Bibliotheca Sacra from 1991-2000. Dallas 2001, Dallas Theological Seminary.

762 *Berlis, Angela* Bibliographie—Bibliography—Bibliographie. YESW 9 (2001) 251-271.

763 Bibliographia Internationalis Spiritualitatis 36. R 2001 Teresianum.

764 Bibliographia Missionaria 65. R 2001, Urban University.

765 ᴱ**Braun, René**, *al.*, Chronica Tertullianea et Cyprianea 1975-1994: bibliographie critique de la première littérature latine chrétienne. Coll. EAug.Ant 157: 1999 ⇒15,655; 16,718. ᴿRSLR 37 (2001) 144-146 (*Gramaglia, Pier Angelo*).

766 ᴱ**Eisele, Markus** Internet-Guide Religion. GTBS 936: Gü 2001, Gü'er 144 pp. 3-579-00936-2.

767 Elenchus bibliographicus. ᴱ**Lust, J.; Verheyden, J.**: EThL 77: Lv 2001, Peeters 741* pp.

768 *Goergen,Ronald* A bibliography of African christology. African Christian Studies 17 4 (2001) 93-97.
769 **ThD** 47: Book survey. [E]*Heiser, W. Charles*: Duluth, MN 2001, Theology Digest. 4 times a year.
770 Theologie im Kontext 21. Aachen 2001, Missionswissenschaftliches Institut. 2 issues a year.
771 [E]**Tolmie, D.F.** Kaleidoskoop 2000: artikels oor teologie: gedenkuitgawe fakulteit teologie. UOVS 1980 - 2000. AcTh(B).S 1: Bloemfontein 2000, UOVS 251 pp. 0-86886-624-5.
772 **Van Belle, Gilbert** Index generalis ETL/BETL 1982-1997. BEThL 134: 1999 ⇒15,663; 16,727. [R]NT 43 (2001) 308-309 (*Elliott, J.K.*).

A4.3 *Bibliographiae* **philologicae** et **generales**

773 *Alonso-Núñez, J.M.* Bulletin de bibliographie critique: historiographie hellénistique postpolybienne. REG 114 (2001) 604-613.
774 **Bérard, François**, *al.*, Guide de l'épigraphiste: bibliographie choisie des épigraphies antiques et médiévales. Guides et inventaires bibliographiques 6: [3]2000 ⇒16,730. [R]AnCl 70 (2001) 412-413 (*Raepsaet-Charlier, Marie-Thérèse*).
775 Bibliographie annuelle du Moyen-Åge Tardif 11: Turnhout 2001, Brepols 574 pp. 2-503-51114-7.
776 *Gauthier, Philippe, al.*, Bulletin épigraphique. REG 114 (2001) 478-603.
777 *Ikeda, Jun* Linguistic studies—approaching the ANE languages from the oriental mind. Orient 36 (2001) 129-146.
778 **Piacentini, Paola** La biblioteca di Marcello II Cervini: una ricostruzione dalle carte di Jeanne Bignami ODIER: i libri a stampa. StT 404: Città del Vaticano 2001, Biblioteca Apostolica Vaticana xxxix; 261 pp. 88-210-0732-4. Bibl. 199-217; Mss. (Vat. lat. 8185/II).
779 *Renz, Johannes* Dokumentation neuer Texte. ZAH 14 (2001) 86-98.
780 **Stos, Jaroslaw** Starodruki Paradyza: Katalog starodruków seminaryjnej biblioteki w Paradyzu. Wsz 2001, Wydawnictwo Uniwersytetu Kardynala Stefana Wyszynskiego 334 pp. 83-7072-195-8. **P.**

A4.4 *Bibliographiae* **orientalisticae**

781 Index of articles on Jewish studies 50: 2000-2001. J 2001, Jewish National Univ. Library
782 **Leslie, Donald Daniel** Jews and Judaism in traditional China: a comprehensive bibliography. Monumenta Serica, Monograph Series 44: 1998 ⇒16,740. [R]ZDMG 151 (2001) 479-480 (*Franke, Herbert*).
783 *Maeda, Tohru* Assyriology part 1: it all started with fifty Sumerian tablets. Orient 36 (2001) 35-41.
784 *Neumann, Hans* Keilschriftbibliographie 59, 2000 (mit Nachträgen aus früheren Jahren). Or. 70 (2001) 1*-109*.
785 *Roos, Johan de* A repertorium of treated passages from Hittite texts. IV. Internationaler Kongress. 2001 ⇒650. 593-597.
786 *Ullmann, Martina* AIGYPTOS—eine Datenbank zur Literaturrecherche im Fachgebiet Ägyptologie. GöMisz 182 (2001) 5.
787 *Watanabe, Kazuko* Assyriology part 2: contributions of the younger generation. Orient 36 (2001) 41-56.

A4.5 *Bibliographiae* **archaeologicae**

788 *Bartolini, P.; Mazza, F.; Ribichini, S.* Bibliografia 29 (1.1.2000-31.12.2000). RSFen 29 (2001) 245-282.
789 *Ciasca, Antonia* Bibliografia degli scritti sul mondo fenicio e punico. RSFen 29 (2001) 7-11.
790 *Dollfus, Geneviève* Bibliographie générale annuelle. Paléorient 27/2 (2001) 153-192.
791 *Matsumoto, Ken; Oguchi, Kazumi* Archaeology: expeditions and discoveries in West Asia by Japanese archaeologists. Orient 36 (2001) 7-34.
792 *Tamura, Takashi* Hellenistic studies in Japan: domination, subordination and Alexander the Great. Orient 36 (2001) 107-122.
793 *Wada, Hiroshi* Byzantine studies—a general view. Orient 36 (2001) 123-128.

II. Introductio

B1.1 *Introductio tota vel VT*—**Whole Bible or OT**

794 **Arnold, Bill T.; Beyer, Bryan E.** Studienbuch Altes Testament. Wu 2001, Brockhaus 496 pp. €48. 3-417-24697-0.
795 ^E**Birch, Bruce C.**, *al.*, A theological introduction to the Old Testament. 1999 ⇒15,688. ^RHBT 23 (2001) 93-98 (*Bowen, Nancy R.*).
796 **Borragán, V.** La biblia, el libro de los libros. M 2001, San Pablo 264 pp. €11.12.
797 **Boshoff, W.S.; Scheffler, E.H.; Spangenberg, I.J.J.** Ancient Israelite literature in context. 2000 ⇒16,750. ^ROTEs 14 (2001) 545-547 (*Coetzee, Johan*).
798 **Brueggemann, Walter** The bible makes sense. LVL ³2001 <1985; 1997>, Westminster ix; 102 pp. 0-664-22495-4.
799 **Burnet, Régis** Petite initiation biblique. P 2001, Desclée de B. 123 pp. €14.
800 *Campbell, Antony F.* Preparatory issues in approaching biblical texts. The Blackwell companion to the Hebrew Bible. 2001 ⇒653. 3-18.
801 **Cappelletto, Gianni; Milani, Marcello** In ascolto dei profeti e dei sapienti: introduzione all'A.T. Strumenti di Scienze Religiose: Padova ³2001, Messagero 384 pp. €20.14. 88-250-0962-3. ^RRivista di science religiose 15 (2001) 451-453 (*Pinto, Sebastiano*).
802 **Ceresko, Anthony R.** Introduction to the Old Testament: a liberation perspective. Mkn ²2001 <1992>, Orbis 384 pp. $25. 1-57075-348-2. Bibl. 351-373 [BiTod 39,313—Bergant, Dianne].
803 **Chance, J. Bradley; Horne, Milton P.** Rereading the bible: an introduction to the biblical story. 2000 ⇒16,753. ^RCBQ 63 (2001) 513-514 (*Minto, Andrew L.*).
804 **Cimosa, Mario** L'ambiente storico-culturale delle scritture ebraiche. 2000 ⇒16,755. ^REstTrin 35 (2001) 663-664 (*Pikaza, Xabier*).
805 **Coggins, Richard James** Introducing the Old Testament. Oxford Bible Series: Oxf ²2001, OUP xiii; 161 pp. $25. 0-19-870063-6. Bibl. 153-155.

806 **Drane, John** Introducing the Old Testament. Mp 2001, Augsburg 366 pp. $26. Rev. ed. [BiTod 40,257—Bergant, Dianne].
807 ᴱ**Dué, Andrea; Rossi, Renzo** La bibbia e la sua storia, 1: l'Antico Testamento. Mi 2001, Jaka 314 pp. €38.73. Nuova ed.
808 **Eissfeldt, O.** Introducción al Antiguo Testamento, 1. ᵀ*Sicre, J.L.* 2000 ⇒16,758. ᴿEsVe 31 (2001) 356-358 (*Ibáñez, M.D.*).
809 **Fant, Clyde E.; Musser, Donald W.; Raddish, Mitchell G.** An introduction to the bible. Nv 2001, Abingdon 472 pp. $35. Rev. ed. [BiTod 40,323—Bergant, Dianne].
810 **Fonsatti, José Carlos** Introdução à bíblia. Cadernos temáticos para evangelização 4: Petrópolis 2001, Vozes 40 pp [REB 61,748].
811 **George, F.J.** The bible truth: a fresh comprehensible reading experience in the new millennium. 2000 ⇒16,761. ᴿVJTR 65 (2001) 318-319 (*Meagher, P.M.*).
812 *Gilbert, Maurice* Biblia sagrada. Diccionario histórico S.J., 1. 2001 ⇒ 717. 437-443.
813 Guía práctica para el lector de la biblia. Instrumentos para el estudio de la Biblia 6: Estella (Navarra) 2001, Verbo Divino 363 pp. 84-8169-388-X. Bibl. 357-362; Asociación Laica de Cultura Bíblica.
814 **Harrison, Roland Kenneth** Old Testament times. Peabody, MASS 2001, Hendrickson xvi; 357 pp. 1-56563-656-2. Bibl. 341-342.
815 **Hinson, David F.** Theology of the Old Testament. SPCK International Study Guide 15; Old Testament Introduction 3: L 2001, SPCK xviii; 212 pp. 0-281-05384-7 [Bibl. 191-192].
816 **Junco Garza, Carlos** 'Escucha Israel...': introducción a la sagrada escritura. Manuales UPM 1: México ²1995, Claveria 431 pp. ᴿEfMex 19 (2001) 282-283 (*López Rosas, Ricardo*).
817 **Kaiser, Otto** Einleitung in das AT; Grundriß der Einleitung in die kanonischen und deutero-kanonischen Schriften des Alten Testaments 1-3; Die alttestamentlichen Apokryphen. 1984-2000 ⇒65,1010... 16,767. ᴿSaThZ 5 (2001) 49-52 (*Reiterer, Friedrich Vinzenz*).
818 **Kugel, James L.** Traditions of the bible: a guide to the bible as it was at the start of the common era. 1998 ⇒14,611; 16,768. ᴿJBL 119 (2000) 110-112 (*Kugler, Robert A.*).
819 **Levin, Christoph** Das Alte Testament. Mü 2001, Beck 128 pp. €7.50. 3-406-44760-0 [RB 108,476].
820 **Matthews, Victor Harold; Moyer, James C.** The Old Testament: text and context. 1997 ⇒13,549; 16,773. ᴿSBET 19 (2001) 118-119 (*Macgregor, Alan*); CTJ 36 (2001) 384-385 (*Karman, Yonky*).
821 **McConville, Gordon** Oude Testament in hoofdlijnen. Zoetermeer 2001, Boekencentrum 207 pp. €17.90. 90-239-0846-5.
822 **Mendenhall, George** Ancient Israel's faith and history: an introduction to the bible in context. ᴱ*Herion, Gary A.*: LVL 2001, Westminster 284 pp. $30. 06642-23133. Bibl. 265-7 [BiTod 39,315—Bergant, D.].
823 **Millet, Olivier; Robert, Philippe de** Culture biblique. Collection Premier Cycle 1: P 2001, PUF xvi; 553 pp. €22.50. 2-13-052297-1. Bibl. 513-514.
824 **Pardes, Ilana** The biography of ancient Israel: national narratives in the bible. 2000 ⇒16,775. ᴿRRT 8 (2001) 136-38 (*Sherwood, Yvonne*).
825 **Potin, Jean** La bible rendue à l'histoire. 2000 ⇒16,776. ᴿSR 30 (2001) 442-444 (*Steigerwald, Diane*).
826 ᴱ*Pouthier, Jean-Luc* Qui a écrit la bible?. MoBi 137 (2001) 12-49.

827 **Sofer, Morry** Questioning the bible: a guide to the most questioned book in the world. Rockville, Md. 2001, Schreiber xvi; 17-328 pp. 1-887563-64-4. Bibl. 317-320.

828 [E]**Stone, Michael Edward; Bergren, Theodore A.** Biblical figures outside the bible. 1998 ⇒14,8207. [R]CBQ 63 (2001) 776-777 (*Grabbe, Lester L.*).

829 **Tábet, Miguel Angel** Introduzione al pentateuco e ai libri storici dell' Antico Testamento: manuale di Sacra Scrittura. Sussidi di Teologia: R 2001, Apollinare S. 401 pp. €25.82. 88-8333-013-7. Bibl. 377-394.

830 [E]**Tworuschka, Udo** Heilige Schriften: eine Einführung. 1999 ⇒15, 720. [R]ThLZ 126 (2001) 153-155 (*Frenschkowski, Marco*).

831 **Van Buren, Paul M.** According to the scriptures: the origins of the gospel and of the church's Old Testament. 1998 ⇒14,626; 16,780. [R]LouvSt 26 (2001) 89 (*Verheyden, Joseph*).

832 **Vermeylen, Jacques** 10 porte per entrare nella bibbia. Bo 2001, EDB 285 pp. 88-10-82005-3.

833 **Vriezen, Th.C.; van der Woude, A.S.** Oud-Israelitische & vroeg-joodse literatuur. Kampen 2001, Kok 580 pp. €35.85. 90-435-0231-6.

834 **Zenger, Erich** Einleitung in das Alte Testament. Kohlhammer-Studienbücher Theologie 1/1: Stu [4]2001, Kohlhammer 548 pp. 3170172786.

B1.2 'Invitations' to Bible or OT

835 Apprivoiser la bible. Le coeur sur la main: Saint-Laurent 2001, Fides 56 pp. Office de catéchèse du Québec.

836 **Adinolfi, Marco** Alle limpide correnti della bibbia. 2000 ⇒16,786. [R]RivBib 49 (2001) 488-490 (*Rolla, Armando*).

837 **Bergant, Dianne** People of the covenant: an invitation to the Old Testament. Come and see: Franklin 2001, Sheed & W. 182 pp. $13.

838 **Carrera, Juan Antonio** Cien rostros de la biblia para la contemplación. M 2001, San Pablo 216 pp.

839 **Dahler, Etienne** Leggere la bibbia in modo diverso, 1: i luoghi della bibbia, 2: feste e simboli. Città del Vaticano 2001, Libreria Editrice Vaticana 135 + 157 pp.

840 **Fischer, Georg** Wege in die Bibel: Leitfaden zur Auslegung. 2000 ⇒ 16,790. [R]ThRv 97 (2001) 293-294 (*Dormeyer, Detlev*); SaThZ 5 (2001) 54-56 (*Egger-Wenzel, Renate*); CBQ 63 (2001) 515-516 (*Bernas, Casimir*).

841 *Gunkel, Hermann* Why engage the Old Testament?. Water for a thirsty land. Fortress classics in biblical studies: 2001 <1914> ⇒155. 1-30.

842 **Hamel, Christopher de** The book: a history of the bible. L 2001, Phaidon 352 pp. £25/$40. 0-7148-3774-1.

843 **Hamel, Christopher F.R. de** The book: a history of the bible. L 2001, Phaidon xi; 352 pp. £25. 0-7148-3774-1. 237 pl. Bibl. 330-340.

844 **Hiers, Richard H.** The Trinity guide to the bible. Harrisburg 2001, Trinity 292 pp. $24 [BiTod 40,324—Bergant, Dianne].

845 **Kaiser, Walter C.** The Old Testament documents: are they reliable & relevant?. DG 2001, InterVarsity 239 pp. $13. 0-8308-1975-4 [ThD 49,74—Heiser, W. Charles].

846 *Lesch, Karl Josef* Den Tisch des Wortes bereiten: Franz Oberhuber als Förderer des Bibellesens. WDGB 62/63 (2001) 475-502.

847 **Martínez Borrego, P.** Luces del Antiguo Testamento. Córdoba 2001, El Almendro 176 pp.

848 **Salvarani, Brunetto** A scuola con la bibbia: dal libro assente al libro ritrovato. Mondialità: Bo 2001, Missionarie Italiane 256 pp. €12.39. Pref. *G. Ravasi.* ^RQol(I) 94 (2001) 17-18.

849 *Smilde, Brian N.* The "say-ings" of God. RefR(H) 54/3 (2001) 221-29.

850 *Swetnam, James* Some thoughts on reading the bible, I-II. Faith 33/1-2 (2001) 20-22, 14-16.

851 **Tenero, F.** La parola della vita: cammini di lettura popolare della bibbia. Celleno 2001, La Piccola 96 pp. €7.75 [RdT 42,640].

852 **Vallet, Ronald E.** The steward living in covenant: a new perspective in Old Testament stories: includes dramas and choral readings by *Wanda Vassallo.* Faith's Horizons: GR 2001, Eerdmans xvi; 251 pp. $20. 0-8028-4727-7. Bibl. 241-243.

B1.3 *Pedagogia biblica*—**Bible-teaching techniques**

853 *Akao, John O.* Old Testament textbooks: a West African perspective. BOTSA 10 (2001) 7-8.

854 *Audinet, Jacques* À la jonction du discours théologique et du discours populaire: le discours des catéchismes. Le discours religieux. 2001 ⇒ 506. 49-70.

855 *Baldermann, Ingo* Kinder entdecken sich selbst in den Psalmen: Kinderfragen, die aufs Ganze gehen. BiKi 56 (2001) 40-45.

856 *Bauer, Dieter* Ist die "Exegese" jemals angekommen?. BiKi 56 (2001) 187-188.

857 *Bech.mann, Ulrike* Herzstück Bibelarbeit—der Weltgebetstag der Frauen. BiKi 56 (2001) 138-142.

858 *Behrendt, Wilhelm* Alle lieben Zachäus: ein Beispiel für freies Arbeiten, selbständiges Lernen und offenen Unterricht. Zeitschrift für Pädagogik und Theologie 53 (2001) 170-179 [Lk 19,1-10].

859 *Betz, Otto* Übersättigt von der Bibel—hungrig nach der Bibel. LS 52 (2001) 280-281.

860 **Birnstein, Uwe; Werding, Juliane** "Sagen Sie mal, Herr Jesus ..." und andere Interviews mit Menschen der Bibel. Gü 2001, Gü'er 160 pp. 3-579-02312-8.

861 *Bitter, Gottfried* Ein biblisch orientierter Firmkurs. Lebendige Katechese 23 (2001) 36-41.

862 **Blair, Christine Eaton** The art of teaching the bible. LVL 2001, Geneva 138 pp. $13. 0-664-50148-6 [BiTod 39,379—Bergant, Dianne].

863 *Blokker, Dries* Rolling the stone from the mouth of the well: teaching Old Testament exegesis in West-Africa. ^FDEURLOO, K. ACEBT.S 2: 2001 ⇒23. 387-392 [Gen 29,1-14].

864 ^E**Bortone, Giuseppe** La Provvidenza divina: approccio pluridisciplinare: XXI corso biblico. Studio Biblico Teologico Aquilano 21: L'Aquila 2001, ISSRA lxviii; 439 pp. 02-0063-.

865 ^E**Brau, Jean-Claude** S'interroger sur la résurrection de Jésus: parcours en catéchèse d'adultes. Sens et foi 2: Bru 2001, Lumen Vitae 150 pp. €14.63. 2-87324-153-5 [PastSc 21/1,135—Arnaud, Richard].

866 ^E**Büttner, Gerhard; Thierfelder, Jörg** Trug Jesus Sandalen?: Kinder und Jugendliche sehen Jesus Christus. Gö 2001, Vandenhoeck & R. 185 pp. €19.90. 3-525-61392-X [BiKi 57,170s—Fiedler, Peter].

867 *Cioffi, Mario* Il vangelo nella cultura dei media. CiVi 156 (2001) 273-278.

868 ^ECurrò, Salvatore; Dimonte, Roberto Giovani in cammino con la bibbia. Gioventù in ascolto, Saggi 8: Mi 2001, S. Paolo 196 pp. 88-215-4413-3.

869 Davison, James E. This book we call the bible: a study guide for a-dults. LVL 2001, Geneva 113 pp. $11 [BiTod 40,257—Bergant, D.].

870 Díaz, Clara María Bibelauslegung in Lateinamerika. BiKi 56 (2001) 172-173.

871 Dormois, Jean-Pierre Étudiants Montbéliardais au "Stift" évangélique de Tübingen du XVIe au XVIIIe siècle. RHPhR 81 (2001) 277-299.

872 Duvall, J. Scott; Hays, J. Daniel Grasping God's word: a hands-on approach to reading, interpreting, and applying the bible. GR 2001, Zondervan 431 pp. $37 [BiTod 40,396—Bergant, Dianne].

873 Eltrop, Bettina Verstehst du auch, was du liest?: Bibelarbeit in den Gemeinden und Erwachsenenbildung. BiKi 56 (2001) 130-134.

874 Ettel, Margarete Thema: Schule—die Bibel in den Lehrplänen. LS 52 (2001) 324-327.

875 Feininger, Bernd Mit der Bibel das Leben erzählen. BiKi 56 (2001) 148-155.

876 Feld, Gerburgis Was heißt gut lehren?: die Hermeneutik des Unbehagens in Lehr-und Lernprozessen. BiKi 56 (2001) 162-164.

877 García Domene, Juan Carlos Conocer la historia del texto. ResB 31 (2001) 63-69.

878 Gastaldi, Silvia; Musatti, Claire People of the bible: life and customs. Cincinnati 2001, St. Anthony Messenger 112 pp. $16. 0-86716-468-9 [BiTod 40,63—Senior, Donald].

879 Giavini, Giovanni La bibbia nei catechismi dell'iniziazione cristiana: schede biblico-catechistiche. Leumann 2001, Elle Di Ci 186 pp.

880 Grahmann, Robert The challenge of reading Scripture within the university context. RefR(H) 54/3 (2001) 169-180.

881 Hecht, Anneliese; Röwekamp, Georg Die Bibel "vor Ort" auslegen: Erfahrungen. BiKi 56 (2001) 165-166;

882 Exegese und Bibliodrama. BiKi 56 (2001) 156-161;

883 Begeistertes Engagement im Dienst der Bibel: das Bibelwerk und sein Angebot für biblisch Interessierte. LS 52 (2001) 308-311.

884 Hecht, Anneliese Bibel erfahren: Methoden ganzheitlicher Bibelarbeit. Stu 2001, Kath. Bibelwerk 150 pp. €12.68. 3-460-25279-0.

885 Hlungwani, S.B.; Henning, I.J.; Lotter, G.A. The need for the teaching of biblical studies in the RSA with special reference to Giyani high schools. AcTh(B) 21/1 (2001) 41-56.

886 Hofrichter, Claudia; Wildermuth, Bernd Die Bibel in Firmvorbereitung und KonfirmandInnenunterricht. LS 52 (2001) 329-333.

887 Hoppe, Matthias Erfahrungsorientierte Katechese mit Jugendlichen am Beispiel von Lk 13,10-17. LS 52 (2001) 334-337.

888 Höfer, Anne Hoffnung lernen: das Gleichnis vom Senfkorn. KatBl 126 (2001) 112-118 [Mt 13,31-32].

889 Jeska, Joachim Zur Vernetzung von Exegese und Praxis in "Netz". BiKi 56 (2001) 169-170.

890 Karle, Isolde Die Bibel als Medium der Identitätsbildung: Überlegungen zum Umgang mit der Bibel im Religionsunterricht. Zeitschrift für Pädagogik und Theologie 53 (2001) 6-22.

891 Kosch, Daniel Exegese und Bibelarbeit. BiKi 56 (2001) 122-129.

892 ^ELachmann, R.; Adam, G.; Reents, Chr. Elementare Bibeltexte: exegetisch—systematisch—didaktisch. Theologie für Lehrerinnen und Lehrer 2: Gö 2001, Vandenhoeck & R. 479 pp. €28. 3-525-61421-7.

893 *Lagarde, Claude: Lagarde, Jacqueline* La bible, paroles d'amour. 2000 ⇒16,842. ᴿSR 30 (2001) 434-435 (*Vogels, Walter*).

894 *Léna, Marguerite* Le retentissement de l'évangile sur nos pratiques de transmission. Com(F) 26/4 (2001) 9-25.

895 *Long, Burke O.* Lakeside at Chautauqua's holy land. JSOT 92 (2001) 29-53.

896 *Mathonnet-VanderWell, Sophie* Opening the bible to the congregation. RefR(H) 54/3 (2001) 214-219.

897 *Meurer, Thomas* Bibelkunde statt Religionsunterricht?: zu Thomas Rusters Konzept einer "Einführung in das biblische Wirklichhkeitsverständnis". rhs 44 (2001) 248-255.

898 *Micheel, Rosemarie* Die Bibelwoche: eine Station auf dem Weg zur "bibelnden Gemeinde". BiKi 56 (2001) 136-137.

899 **Mogstad, Sverre Dag** Trostradisjon og livssituasjon: en systematisk-teologisk analyse av hvordan etablere en korrelasjon mellom fortelling og erfaring med utgangspunkt i Hans STOCKs og Georg BAUDLERs bibeldidaktiske teorier [Faith and life: a systematica-theological analysis of the correlation between narrative and experience according to Hans Stock's and Georg Baudler's bibledidactic theories]. 2001, Diss. Norwegian Lutheran School of Theology, Oslo.

900 *Morales, Xavier* L'entremise de la foi. Com(F) 26/4 (2001) 26-39.

901 *Mödl, Ludwig* Passionsspiele—biblische Verkündigung im "theatrum sacrum". LS 52 (2001) 319-323.

902 *Mukenge, André Mukenge* L'enseignement de l'Ancien Testament et des cours apparentés aux Facultés Catholiques de Kinshasa. BOTSA 10 (2001) 9-13.

903 *Mynatt, Daniel S.; Crawford, Timothy G.* Integrating the Masorah into the classroom. PRSt 28/4 (2001) 373-383.

904 *Nastainczyk, Wolfgang* Lehren und Lernen (aus) der Bibel—wozu und wie?: Konzepte und Typen christlicher Bibeldidaktik im Wandel. ᶠSCHMUTTERMAYR, G. 2001 ⇒101. 481-496.

905 *Paetz, Michael* Die Bibel als Kraft und Hilfe bei Betagten und Sterbenden. LS 52 (2001) 314-316.

906 *Pfaff, Bernhard* Das Ortenauer Evangeliar 2000. LS 52 (2001) 311-313.

907 *Raurell, Frederic* La Scrittura al servizio della catechesi. Laur. 42 (2001) 273-317.

908 *Regalado, Ferdinand O.* Hebrew thought: its implications for christian education in Asia. AJTh 15/1 (2001) 172-188.

909 *Ruessmann, John* Teaching the bible with respect. BiTod 39 (2001) 294-299.

910 *Sanders, Jill* Opening the bible: one congregation's story. RefR(H) 54/3 (2001) 206-212.

911 *Schäffer, Wilhelm* Methoden der Bibelarbeit. LS 52 (2001) 304-308.

912 *Seth, Sanjay* Which good book?: missionary education and conversion in colonial India. Semeia 88 (2001) 113-128.

913 *Sère, Bénédicte* Eléments d'une transmission théologale de la foi. Com(F) 26/4 (2001) 49-57.

914 ᴱ**Simian-Yofre, H.** Metodología del Antiguo Testamento. ᵀ*Ortiz García, Alfonso*: Biblioteca de Estudios Bíblicos 106: S 2001, Sígueme 249 pp. 84-301-1439-4.

915 **Snyder, H. Gregory** Teachers and texts in the ancient world: philosophers, Jews and christians. 2000 ⇒16,865. ᴿRRT 8 (2001) 488-491 (*Royalty, Robert M.*).

916 *Sonnleitner, Rainer; Kurz, Leonhard* Das Gespräch am Jakobsbrunnen: biografiebezogene Christusbilder. KatBl 126 (2001) 357-361.
917 *Stadlmeier, Elisabeth* Gott geht mit dir—biblische Geschichten erzählen davon. LS 52 (2001) 327-329.
918 **Staglianò, Antonio** Vangelo e comunicazione: radicare la fede nel nuovo millennio. Fede e annuncio 41: Bo 2001, EDB 186 pp. 88-10-20338-0. Pref. card. *Camillo Ruini.*
919 *Tepe, Gerhard* Biblische Impulse in der Betreuung älterer Menschen. LS 52 (2001) 316-319.
920 *Then, Reinhold* Die Bibel auf dem Computer—eine Revolution im Textumgang, BiKi 56 (2001) 167-168.
921 *Vidovic, Marinko* Vrednote krscanske novozavjetne poruke. BoSm 71 (2001) 261-290. **Croatian.**
922 *Welten, Peter* "Das Buch kennenlernen": ostdeutsche Atheisten begegnen der Bibel. BThZ 18 (2001) 300-306.
923 *Zinkuratire, Victor* A survey of the textbook situation in East Africa. BOTSA 10 (2001) 2-7.

B2.1 Hermeneutica

924 *Agourides, Savas* The regula fidei as hermeneutical principle past and present (response to the paper of prof. Prosper Grech). L'interpretazione della bibbia nella chiesa. 2001 ⇒471. 225-231.
925 **Amherdt, François-Xavier** L'herméneutique biblique de Paul Rıcoeur en débat avec la New Yale Theology School. Diss. Fribourg 2001, ᴰ*Schenker, Adrian.*
926 *Antón Pacheco, José Antonio* Algunos aspectos de la hermenéutica en la antigüedad. Isidorianum 20 (2001) 403-429.
927 *Archer, Kenneth J.* Early Pentecostal biblical interpretation. JPentec 18 (2001) 32-70.
928 *Armogathe, Jean R.* Les deux livres. RThPh 133/3 (2001) 211-225.
929 *Barbaglia, Silvio* La rilevanza ermeneutica delle disposizioni canoniche dei testi nelle sacre scritture: metodo ed esemplificazioni. RStB 13/1 (2001) 185-268.
930 *Bartholomew, Craig* Before Babel and after Pentecost: language, literature and biblical interpretation. ᶠTHISELTON, A. 2001 ⇒106. 131-170.
931 ᴱ**Barton, John** La interpretación bíblica, hoy. Presencia teológica 113: Sdr 2001, Sal Terrae 392 pp. 84-293-1406-7. ᴿSalTer 89 (2001) 920-922 (*Ramírez Fueyo, Francisco*); ResB 32 (2001) 70-71 (*Tosaus Abadía, J.P.*).
932 *Bayer, Oswald* Titel und Motto von Johann Georg Hamanns: Metakritik über den Purismus der Vernunft;
933 *Becker, Eve-Marie* Was ein Text sein kann: zur Beschreibung eines Text-Inventars. Was ist ein Text?. 2001 ⇒335. 109-115/159-169.
934 **Berger, Klaus** Hermenêutica do Novo Testamento. ᵀ*Schneider, Nélio*: 1999 ⇒15,820. ᴿREB 61 (2001) 738-739 (*Marques, Valdir*);
935 Ermeneutica del Nuovo Testamento. Brescia 2001, Queriniana 260 pp. €23.24. 88-399-2026-9.
936 *Bergmann, Sigurd* "Ich kenne ihre Leiden, darum bin ich herniedergestiegen ...": das neue Paradigma der kontextuellen Theologie. StTh 55 (2001) 4-22.
937 *Boer, Roland* Introduction: vanishing mediators?;

938 Explorer hermeneutics, or fat damper and sweetened tea. Semeia 88 (2001) 1-12/71-95.

939 *Bori, Pier Cesare* Monachesimo, laicità, profetismò. VM 55/218 (2001) 37-45.

940 *Bosman, Hendrik L.* A 'thick description' of two Bible: studies by the Belhar Anglican group. Scriptura 78 (2001) 367-370 [Mt 13,53-58; Lk 4,16-30].

     [E]**Bouteneff, P.; Heller, D.** Interpreting together. 2001 ⇒343.

941 *Boyer, Frédéric* Le texte biblique et la mise à l'épreuve du lecteur. RSR 89 (2001) 335-352.

942 *Böhmisch, Franz* Vom Bibelleser zum Experten—eine Lebensaufgabe für alle. ThPQ 149 (2001) 156-166.

943 *Briggs, Richard S.* The uses of speech-act theory in biblical interpretation. CurResB 9 (2001) 229-276.

944 **Briggs, Richard S.** Words in action: speech act theory and biblical interpretation: toward a hermeneutic of self-involvement. E 2001, Clark xvi; 352 pp. £25. 0-567-08809-X. Diss.; Bibl. 299-337.

945 *Cadwallader, Alan H.* The building of awareness of hermeneutics through the history of interpretations of the Bible. Colloquium 33/1 (2001) 3-21 [Lk 19,11-27].

946 *Clark, Mathew S.* Pentecostal hermeneutics: the challenge of relating to (post)-modern literary theory. APB 12 (2001) 41-67.

947 **Cochrane, James R.** Circles of dignity: community wisdom and theological reflection. Mp 1999. Fortress 214 pp $21. 0-8006-3182-X. [R]Neotest. 35 (2001) 179-180 (*Le Roux, J.H.*).

948 **Coelho, Ivo** Hermeneutics and method: the 'universal viewpoint' in Bernard LONERGAN. Lonergan studies: Toronto 2001, University of Toronto Press xx; 345 pp. $65. 0-8020-4840-4. Bibl. 293-322.

949 **Conradie, E.M.; Jonker, L.C.** Angling for interpretation: a guide to understand the bible better. Study Guides in Religion and Theology 4: Bellville, South Africa 2001, Univ. of the Western Cape iv; 93 pp. $7. 1-86808-486-8 [BOTSA 10,22—Holter, Knut].

950 *Conradie, Ernst M.; Bosman, Hendrik L.; Jonker, Louis C.* Biblical interpretation in established bible study groups: a chronicle of a regional research project. Scriptura 78 (2001) 340-346.

951 *Conradie, Ernst M.; Jonker, Louis C.* Bible study within established bible study groups: results of an empirical research project. Scriptura 78 (2001) 381-398.

952 *Conradie, Ernst M.* Biblical interpretation within the context of established bible study groups. Scriptura 78 (2001) 442-447;

953 A 'thick description' of two bible studies by the Langa Baptist group. Scriptura 78 (2001) 357-361 [Mt 13,53-58; Lk 4,14-24].

954 **Cook, John Granger** The interpretation of the New Testament in Greco-Roman paganism. Studies and Texts in Antiquity and Christianity 3: 2000 ⇒16,912. [R]Salm. 48 (2001) 357-361 (*Trevijano, Ramón*); ThLZ 126 (2001) 63-64 (*Zangenberg, Jürgen*).

955 *Counet, Patrick Chatelion* Gij zult niet lezen: nul keer tien regels om (de bijbel) postmodern te interpreteren. Streven 68 (2001) 974-984.

956 *Curkpatrick, Stephen* Authority of the text: the hermeneutical question. Colloquium 33/2 (2001) 135-152.

957 *Danaher, James* Postmodern hermeneutics and the reconstruction of the christian mind. Evangel 19 (2001) 69-76. Resp. by *Stephen Motyer* 76-79, by author 79-80.

958 *Docker, John* In praise of polytheism. Semeia 88 (2001) 149-172.
959 **Dohmen, Christoph** Die Bibel und ihre Auslegung. 1998 ⇒14,740.
ᴿZRGG 53 (2001) 75-76 (*Jensen, Peder Hald*).
960 *Dumermuth, Carlo F.* Biblical literature: dreams and fiction?. AJTh
15/1 (2001) 189-198.
961 *Ernst, Michael* Die neutestamentliche Wissenschaft im Komplex der
theologischen Disziplinen. Zukunft der Theologie. Theologische trends
10: 2001 ⇒530. 112-115.
962 *Frankemölle, Hubert* Das Neue Testament als Kommentar?: Möglichkeiten und Grenzen einer hermeneutischen These aus der Sicht eines
Neutestamentlers. Wieviel Systematik?. QD 185: 2001 ⇒283. 200-78.
963 *Gibert, Pierre* Qu'est-ce qu'une bible?. RHR 218 (2001) 33-42.
964 *Goldingay, John* What are the characteristics of evangelical study of
the Old Testament?. EvQ 73 (2001) 99-117.
965 **Graafland, C.** Bijbels en daarom gereformeerd. Zoetermeer 2001,
Boekencentrum 180 pp. €15.90. 90-239-0968-2.
966 *Grech, Prosper* The "regula fidei" as hermeneutical principle yesterday
and today. L'interpretazione della bibbia. 2001 ⇒471. 208-224.
967 **Green, Garrett** Theology, hermeneutics and imagination: the crisis of
interpretation at the end of modernity. 2000 ⇒16,946. ᴿMoTh 17
(2001) 258-260 (*Ayres, Lewis*).
968 *Greene, Colin J.D.* 'Starting a rockslide'—deconstructing history and
language via christological detonators. ᶠTHISELTON, A. 2001 ⇒106.
195-223.
969 **Grenholm, Cristina** The Old Testament, christianity and pluralism.
BGBE 33: Tü 1996, Mohr x; 293 pp. 3-1614-6587-3. Bibl. 281-283.
ᴿThLZ 126 (2001) 616-617 (*Saebø, Magne*).
970 *Habermann, Mechthild* Ein Nürnberger Flugblatt von 1583: ein
Gebrauchstext aus sprachwissenschaftlicher Sicht. Was ist ein Text?.
Neutestamentliche Entwürfe zur Theologie 1: 2001 ⇒335. 145-157.
971 *Heise, Jürgen* Auslegen durch Nachdenken. Auslegen durch Nachdenken.. Theologie 33: 2001 ⇒159. 1-5.
972 *Henrici, Peter* Y a-t-il un fondamentalisme catholique?. Com(F) 26/6
(2001) 17-27 [IKaZ 30,497-506; Com(US) 28,599-609 >ThD 50,237-
242].
973 *Hesse, Mary* How to be a postmodernist and remain a christian: a
response to Nicholas Wolterstorff. ᶠTHISELTON, A. 2001 ⇒106. 91-96.
974 *Hébert, Geneviève* Le procès de la parole entre vérité et méthode. La
bible, parole adressée. 2001 ⇒323. 173-204.
975 ᴱ**Horrell, David G.** Social-scientific approaches to New Testament
interpretation. 1999 ⇒15,241; 16,958. ᴿCV 43 (2001) 87-89 (*Peterlin,
Davorin*); EvQ 73 (2001) 259-260 (*Chang, Steve*).
976 *Hossfeld, Frank-Lothar* Einleitung: fundamentalhermeneutische Ver-
schiebungen. Wieviel Systematik?. QD 185: 2001 ⇒283. 7-12.
977 *Huber, Konrad* Von Pianisten und Musikern: Bemerkungen zur theologischen Dimension der Bibelwissenschaft. Zukunft der Theologie. Theologische trends 10: 2001 ⇒530. 116-130.
978 *Ingraffia, Brian D.; Pickett, Todd E.* Reviving the power of biblical
language: the bible, literature and literary language. ᶠTHISELTON, A.
2001 ⇒106. 241-262.
979 *James, Paul* The word set in blood and stone: the book of God from
tribes to kingdom and nations. Semeia 88 (2001) 173-198.

980 *Janowski, Bernd* "Verstehst du auch, was du liest?": Reflexionen auf die Leserichtung der christlichen Bibel. Wieviel Systematik?. QD 185: 2001 ⇒283. 150-191 [Acts 8,26-40].

981 *Janssen, Jacques; Van der Lans, Jan; Dechesne, Mark* Fundamentalism: the possibilities and limitations of a social-psychological approach. Religious identity. 2001 ⇒549. 302-316.

982 *Jonker, Louis C.* Social transformation and biblical interpretation: a report on some of the results of a research project. BOTSA 11 (2001) 17-20;

983 A 'thick description' of two bible studies by the Dutch Reformed Church Ottery group. Scriptura 78 (2001) 347-351 [Mt 13,53-58; Lk 4,14-24];

984 Mapping the various factors playing a role in biblical interpretation. Scriptura 78 (2001) 418-428;

985 Through the eyes of another: a research project on intercultural bible reading. BOTSA 10 (2001) 14-15.

986 *Kim, Hyun Chul Paul* Interpretative modes of Yin-Yang dynamics as an Asian hermeneutics. BiblInterp 9 (2001) 287-308.

987 *King, Nicholas* Society, academy, and church: who can read the bible. FO'COLLINS, G. 2001 ⇒81. 139-158.

988 EKitzberger, Ingrid Rosa The personal voice in biblical interpretation. 1999 ⇒16,972. REThL 77 (2001) 204-206 (*Van Belle, G.*).

989 *Kloocke, Kurt* J.J. ROUSSEAU: 2. Brief an M. de Malesherbes. Was ist ein Text?. 2001 ⇒335. 117-130.

990 *Kok, Johnson L.* Theological hermeneutics: a reading strategy. AJTh 15/1 (2001) 2-13.

991 *Koster, Severin* Wo spät noch eine Rose weilt ... Horaz, carm. 1,38 als Beispiel eines eindeutig mehrdeutigen Textes. Was ist ein Text?. Neutestamentliche Entwürfe zur Theologie 1: 2001 ⇒335. 95-107.

992 *Köstenberger, Andreas J.* Gender passages in the New Testament: hermeneutical fallacies critiqued. Studies on John and gender. 2001 <1994> ⇒169. 203-231.

993 *Laplanche, François* Rationalisme scientifique et interprétations de la bible au XVII. siècle. RThPh 133 (2001) 227-245.

994 *Laughery, Gregory J.* Language at the frontiers of language. FTHISELTON, A. 2001 ⇒106. 171-194.

995 Laughery, Gregory J. Living hermeneutics as a hermeneutics in motion: an analysis and evaluation of Paul RICOEUR's contribution to biblical hermeneutics. Diss. Fribourg 2001, DSchenker, A. [RTL 33,632].

996 *Lawrie, Douglas G.* A 'thick description' of two bible studies by the Belhar Lighthouse group. Scriptura 78 (2001) 371-380 [Mt 13,53-58; Lk 4,16-30].;

997 Reading, interpretation, reinscription: three perspectives on engaging with texts. Scriptura 78 (2001) 399-417.

998 *LeBrun, Jacques* Présupposés théoriques de la lecture mystique de la bible. RThPh 133 (2001) 287-302.

999 *Lee, Nancy C.; Arapović, Borislav* The bible in political context: new republics from old Yugoslavia and the former Soviet Union. Interp. 55 (2001) 378-388.

1000 *Lehmann, Kardinal Karl* Das Alte Testament als Offenbarung der Kirche. Wieviel Systematik?. QD 185: 2001 ⇒283. 279-289.

1001 *Lepore, Luciano* Sincronia e diacronia: due metodi ermeneutici a confronto. RdT 42 (2001) 177-196.

1002 *Liem, Johnson* Contemporary hermeneutics: bane or boon?. Stulos 9/1 (2001) 1-9.

1003 *Liew, Tat-siong Benny* Reading with Yin Yang eyes: negotiating the ideological dilemma of a Chinese American biblical hermeneutics. BiblInterp 9 (2001) 309-335.

1004 *Lim, Johnson Teng Kok* Hermeneutical rules of reading biblical texts. Mission today 4 (2001) 173-179;

1005 Theological hermeneutics: a reading strategy. AJTh 15/1 (2001) 2-13.

1006 *Loader, James Alfred* Stromab—Gedanken zur Hermeneutik biblischer Texte im Kontext der neueren angelsächsischen Diskussion. Begegnung mit Gott. 2001 ⇒175. 303-324.

1007 *Lombaard, Christo J.S.* A comparison and evaluation of four recent works on the interpretation of the Old Testament in South Africa. Scriptura 78 (2001) 467-478.

1008 **Lundin, Roger; Thiselton, Anthony C.; Walhout, Clarence** The promise of hermeneutics. 1999 ⇒15,887; 16,984. ᴿAnton. 76 (2001) 583-586 (*Oviedo, Lluis*); CV 43 (2001) 84-87 (*Čapek, Filip*); ThLZ 126 (2001) 264-265 (*Körtner, Ulrich H.*).

1009 *MacDonald, Neil B.* Illocutionary stance in Hans Frei's *The eclipse of biblical narrative*: an exercise in conceptual redescription and normative analysis. ᶠTHISELTON, A. 2001 ⇒106. 312-328.

1010 *Macek, Petr* Process thought and biblical hermeneutics: an overview. CV 43/2 (2001) 127-152.

1011 *McKinlay, Judith E.* What do I do with contexts?: a brief reflection on reading biblical texts with Israel and Aotearoa New Zealand in mind. Pacifica 14 (2001) 159-171.

1012 *Moloney, Francis J.* Life, healing, and the bible: a christian challenge. 'A hard saying'. 2001 <1995> ⇒184. 237-258.

1013 *Mwombeki, Fidon R.* Reading the bible in contemporary Africa. WaW 21/2 (2001) 121-128.

1014 *Ndungane, Njongonkulu* Scripture: what is at issue in Anglicanism today?. AThR 83 (2001) 11-23.

1015 *Negrov, Alexander* Biblical interpretation in the Russian Orthodox Church: an historical and hermeneutical perspective. VeE 22 (2001) 352-365.

1016 ᵀ**Neri, Umberto** Flacio ILLIRICO: comprendere le scritture. 1998 ⇒ 14,799; 15,12664. ᴿProtest. 56 (2001) 305-306 (*Gajewski, Pawel*).

1017 *Nielsen, Kirsten* Den fortaerende ild: religionsvidenskabelig disputats med teologiske perspektiver. Ment. *Lundager Jensen, Hans J.* DTT 64 (2001) 176-188.

1018 **Oeming, Manfred** Biblische Hermeneutik: eine Einführung. 1998 ⇒ 14,802; 16,1003. ᴿITBT 9/3 (2001) 9-10 (*Spijkerboer, Anne M.*).

1019 *Olhausen, William* A 'polite' response to Anthony Thiselton. ᶠTHISELTON, A. 2001 ⇒106. 121-130.

1020 **Packer, James I.** Hermeneutics and Genesis 1-11. SWJT 44/1 (2001) 4-21.

1021 **Phillips, D.Z.** Religion and the hermeneutics of contemplation. C 2001, CUP xiv; 330 pp. £45/15.75.

1022 **Picardo, G.** Vicina è la parola: scrittura e interpretazione. 1999 ⇒ 15,908. ᴿAsp. 48 (2001) 455-456 (*Di Bianco, Nicola*).

1023 *Pool, Jeff B.* "Non intratur in veritatem, nisi per charitatem": toward a christian hermeneutic of love. CV 43/2 (2001) 159-188.

1024 **Pozzato, Maria Pia** Semiotica del testo: metodi, autori, esempi. R 2001, Carocci 312 pp. ᴿASEs 18 (2001) 704-6 (*Pozzato, Maria Pia*).

1025 *Prevost, Ronnie* Discovering ourselves through knowing God. RelEd 96/3 (2001) 435-439.

1026 *Punt, Jeremy* The call to rewrite the bible: some perspectives. Scriptura 77 (2001) 303-324.

1027 *Räisänen, Heikki* Biblical critics in the global village <2000>;

1028 The New Testament in theology <1995>;

1029 Tradition, experience, interpretation: a dialectical model for describing the development of religious thought <1999>. Challenges to biblical interpretation. BiblInterp 59: 2001 ⇒200. 283-309/227-249/ 251-262.

1030 *Regalado, Ferdinand O.* Hebrew thought: its implications for christian education in Asia. AJTh 15/1 (2001) 172-188.

1031 *Reiser, Marius* Geist und Buchstabe: zur Situation der östlichen und der westlichen Exegese. TThZ 110 (2001) 67-80.

1032 **Ricoeur, Paul** L'herméneutique biblique. ᵀ*Amherdt, F.-X.* La nuit surveillée. P 2001, Cerf 277 pp. €24.39. 2-204-06331-2. ᴿETR 76 (2001) 452-453 (*Causse, Jean-Daniel*).

1033 *Schenker, Adrian* Der biblische Fundamentalismus und die katholische Kirche. IKaZ 30 (2001) 507-512.

1034 *Schner, George P.* Waiting for Godot: scripture, tradition and church at century's end. Ment. *Beckett, S.* TJT 17 (2001) 33-54.

1035 **Schreiner, Josef** Das Alte Testament verstehen. NEB.E.AT 4: 1999 ⇒15,928; 16,1028. ᴿCart. 17 (2001) 209-210 (*Sanz Valdivieso, R.*).

1036 **Sekine, Seizo** Transcendency and symbols in the Old Testament: a genealogy of the hermeneutical experiences. BZAW 275: 1999 ⇒15, 933; 16,1032. ᴿThLZ 126 (2001) 619-621 (*Saebø, Magne*).

1037 *Şerban, Tarciziu* Philosophical hermeneutics and biblical hermeneutics with Paul RICOEUR. CICat 2/2 (2001) 71-81. Rés. 80.

1038 *Shields, Bruce E.* The hermeneutics of Alexander CAMPBELL. RestQ 43/3 (2001) 167-179.

1039 *Stella, Francesco Ad supplementum sensus*: pluralità ermeneutica e incremento di senso nella poetica biblica dal medioevo a DERRIDA: le ragioni di un convegno. La scrittura infinita. 2001 ⇒498. 31-46.

1040 **Stemberger, Günter** Ermeneutica ebraica della bibbia. Studi Biblici 127: 2000 ⇒16,1038. ᴿStPat 48 (2001) 499-503 (*Lorenzin,Tiziano*).

1041 **Stiver, Dan** Theology after RICOEUR: new directions in hermeneutical theology. LVL 2001, Westminster xii; 257 pp. $28. 0664-222-439.

1042 **Stylianopoulos, Theodore G.** The New Testament: an Orthodox perspective. Scripture, tradition, hermeneutics 1: 1997 ⇒13,776; 15, 940. ᴿSVTQ 45 (2001) 213-215 (*Prokurat, Michael*).

1043 **Sugirtharajah, Rasiah S.** Asian biblical hermeneutics and postcolonialism: contesting the interpretations. BiSe 64: 1999 ⇒14,839; 16, 1041. ᴿHeyJ 42 (2001) 354-355 (*Morris, Colin*); RBLit 3 (2001) 120-124 (*Kim, H.C. Paul*).

1044 ᴱ**Sugirtharajah, Rasiah S.** Vernacular hermeneutics. 1999 ⇒15, 806; 16,1042. ᴿJThS 52 (2001) 863-864 (*Rowland, Christopher*).

1045 *Syreeni, Kari* Bibeln och den svenska 1900—talslitteraturen: några personliga randnotiser. SEÅ 66 (2001) 167-176.

1046 *Thiselton, Anthony C.* 'Behind' and 'in front of' the text: language, reference and indeterminacy. ᶠTHISELTON, A. 2001 ⇒106. 97-120.

1047 **Tilliette, Xavier** Les philosophes lisent la bible. P 2001, Cerf 198 pp. €21.34. 2-204-06705-9. ᴿRPL 99 (2001) 738-741 (*Brito, Emilio*).

1048 *Timm, Hermann* Wovon redet die Schrift?: Gottes Autobiographie: aus der Werkstatt einer libristischen Hermeneutik. Biblischer Text. BThSt 44: 2001 ⇒252. 191-210.

1049 *Ukpong, Justin S.* New Testament hermeneutics in Africa: challenges and possibilities. Neotest. 35 (2001) 147-167.

1050 *Van Keulen, Dirk* Bavinck en het "concessionisme". NedThT 55/4 (2001) 301-312.

1051 *Van Toorn, Penny* Before the second reformation: nineteenth-century aboriginal meditations of the bible in Van Diemen's Land. Semeia 88 (2001) 41-69.

1052 *Van Zyl, Danie C.* A 'thick description' of two bible studies by the Sokhanya Bible School. Scriptura 78 (2001) 352-356 [Mt 13,53-58; Lk 4,16-30]..

1053 **Vanhoozer, Kevin** Is there a meaning in this text?: the bible, the reader, and the morality of literary knowledge. 1998 ⇒14,847... 16,1057. [R]ProEc 10/1 (2001) 105-107 (*Black, C. Clifton*); JBL 120 (2001) 594-595 (*Burnett, Fred W.*).

1054 *Vanhoozer, Kevin J.* From speech acts to scripture acts: the covenant of discourse and the discourse of the covenant. [F]THISELTON, A. 2001 ⇒106. 1-49.

1055 *Vignolo, Roberto* "Scriptura secundum scripturas": valenza narrativa e riflessiva del libro nella tôrâ e nei profeti anteriori: per una fenomenologia del testo biblico tra poetica e teologia. RStB 13/1 (2001) 27-83;

1056 Scriptura secundum scripturas: sulla teologia del libro: introduzione ad un seminario di studio. Teol(Br) 26 (2001) 120-128.

1057 *Vonach, Andreas* Seele und kritisches Gewissen der heiligen Theologie: alttestamentliche Bibelwissenschaft im Spannungsfeld christlicher und jüdischer Theologie sowie literatur- und geschichtswissenschaftlicher Hermeneutik. Zukunft der Theologie. Theologische trends 10: 2001 ⇒530. 103-111.

1058 *Vosloo, W.* Hoe om die bybel beter te verstaan: verklarings van die bybel in Afrikaans. VeE 22 (2001) 178-190.

1059 *Waaijman, Kees* The hermeneutics of Emmanuel LEVINAS. Studies in Spirituality 11 (2001) 71-125.

1060 **Wallace, Ronald S.** On the interpretation and use of the bible: with reflections on experience. 1999 ⇒15,964. [R]BS 158 (2001) 488-489 (*Kreider, Glenn R.*); SBET 19 (2001) 235-236 (*Grogan, Geoffrey*).

1061 *Walsh, Richard G.* Mapping myths of biblical interpretation. Playing the Texts 4: Shf 2001, Sheffield A. 192 pp. 1-84127-204-3. Bibl. 175-189.

1062 Wanamaker, Chuck A. A 'thick description' of two bible studies by the Strand Anglican group. Scriptura 78 (2001) 362-366 [Mt 13,53-58; Lk 4,16-30].

1063 **Watson, Francis** Agape, eros, gender: towards a Pauline sexual ethic. 2000 ⇒16,1064. [R]ThTo 58 (2001) 132-133 (*Brawley, Robert L.*); Thom. 65 (2001) 304-311 (*Atkinson, Joseph C.*); ProEc 10 (2001) 374-376 (*Furnish, Victor Paul*); BiblInterp 9 (2001) 424-428 (*Horrell, David G.*); CBQ 63 (2001) 765-767 (*Scroggs, Robin*).

1064 **Webb, William J.** Slaves, women and homosexuals: exploring the hermeneutics of cultural analysis. DG 2001, InterVarsity 301 pp. $25. 0-8308-1561-9.

1065 *Webster, John* "In the shadow of biblical work": BARTH and BONHOEFFER on reading the bible. TJT 17 (2001) 75-91.

1066 *Wendt, Matthias* Die Vernichtung der Wahrheit und des Wissens. Irreale Glaubensinhalte: eine Fortschreibung der Lüdemann-These vom
sexuellen Mißbrauch der Maria: die Verdrängung der Ursache des
Leidens in den Religionen.. ᴱ**Wendt, Matthias**: Gö ²2001 <1999>,
Saitam. 3-9806160-0-2. 59-60.

1067 *West, Gerald* Response: a real presence, subsumed by others: the
bible in colonial and postcolonial contexts. Semeia 88 (2001) 199-
214.

1068 **West Gerald** The academy of the poor: towards a dialogical reading
of the bible. 1999 ⇒15,969. ᴿJThS 52 (2001) 859-863 (*Rowland,
Christopher*).

1069 *Willi-Plein, Ina* Gesprochenes und geschriebenes Wort. ZDPV 117
(2001) 64-75.

1070 *Witting, Gunther* Friederike Kempners Gedicht "Das scheintote
Kind": zum Problem von Intention und Rezeption. Was ist ein Text?.
Neutestamentliche Entwürfe zur Theologie 1: 2001 ⇒335. 131-143.

1071 *Wolterstorff, Nicholas* The promise of speech-act theory for biblical
interpretation. ᶠTHISELTON, A. 2001 ⇒106. 73-90.

1072 *Zinkuratire,Victor* Method and relevance in African biblical interpretation. African Christian Studies 17/4 (2001) 5-13.

B2.4 *Analysis* **narrationis** *biblicae*

1073 **Crouch, Walter B.** Death and closure in biblical narrative. 2000 ⇒
16,1086. ᴿRSR 89 (2001) 551-552 (*Gibert, Pierre*).

1074 **Dooley, Robert A.; Levinsohn, Stephen H.** Analyzing discourse: a
manual of basic concepts. Dallas 2001, SIL 165 pp. 1-55671-115-8.

1075 **Fokkelman, Jan P.** Reading biblical narrative: an introductory
guide. 1999 ⇒15,983; 16,1088. ᴿThLZ 126 (2001) 260-261 (*Reinmuth, Eckart*).

1076 **Goldfajn, Tal** Word order and time in Biblical Hebrew narrative.
1998 ⇒14,865; 16,1090. ᴿJSSt 46 (2001) 143-146 (*Zewi, Tamar*).

1077 **Kawashima, Robert Saiji** Biblical narration and the death of the
rhapsode. Diss. California, Berkeley 2001, 335 pp.; 3019696.

1078 **Lee, Dae Sung** Theological truth and narrative truth in Paul RI-
COEUR's narrative hermeneutics and C.S. SONG's story theology.
Diss. Graduate Theological Union 2001, 181 pp.; 3007736.

1079 *Linsider, Joel A.* Pursuing and overtaking as a type-scene. Arc 29
(2001) 71-80.

1080 **Marguerat, Daniel L.; Bourquin, Yvan** Per leggere i racconti
biblici: la bibbia si racconta: iniziazione all'analisi narrativa. Per leggere: R 2001, Borla 194 pp. 88-263-1353-9. Bibl. 187-192.

1081 *Mazzinghi, Luca* Storie di re e di profeti. PaVi 46/1 (2001) 4-8.

1082 *Minette de Tillesse, Caetano* 'Tu me verras de dos': théologie narrative de la bible, 1-2; [Annexes au vol. 1]. RBBras 12, 14/1-3, 15/1-3
(1995-1998). ᴿRB 108 (2001) 453-457 (*Loza Vera, J.*).

1083 *Moloney, Francis J.* Narrative criticism of the gospels. 'A hard
saying'. 2001 <1991> ⇒184. 85-105.

1084 **Murphy, Francesca Aran** The comedy of revelation: paradise lost
and regained in biblical narrative. E 2001, Clark xvii; 365 pp. £30. 0-
56708-7182. Bibl. 349-362. ᴿNBl 82 (2001) 350-352 (*Kerr, Fergus*).

1085 *Oeming, Manfred; Pregla, Anne-Ruth* New literary criticism. ThR 66
(2001) 1-23.

1086 *Parmentier, Elisabeth* Le récit comme théologie: statut, sens et portée du récit biblique. RHPhR 81 (2001) 29-44.
1087 *Polak, Frank H.* The style of the dialogue in biblical narrative. Studies in Judaica. Teʻuda 16-17: 2001 ⇒408. 47-102. Sum. xiii-xvi. H. = JANES 28 (2001) 53-95 [Eng.].
1088 **Reinhartz, Adele** "Why ask my name?": anonymity and identity in biblical narrative. 1998 ⇒14,883; 16,1109. ᴿJBL 119 (2000) 541-543 (*Landy, Francis*).
1089 **Ska, Jean-Louis** La Parola di Dio nei racconti degli uomini. 1999 ⇒ 15,1002. ᴿCivCatt 152/2 (2001) 511-512 (*Scaiola, D.*)..
1090 **Tolmie, François D.** Narratology and biblical narratives: a practical guide. 1999 ⇒15,1005. ᴿNeotest. 35 (2001) 182-183 (*Van der Watt, Jan G.*).
1091 **Walsh, Jerome T.** Style and structure in Biblical Hebrew narrative. ColMn 2001, Liturgical xiv; 205 pp. $20. 0-8146-5897-0. Bibl. 195-198.
1092 **Weitzman, Steven** Song and story in biblical narrative: the history of a literary convention in ancient Israel. 1997 ⇒13,831... 16,1114. ᴿEstB 59 (2001) 121-123 (*García Santos, A.*).
1093 *Wesselius, Jan-Wim* Collapsing the narrative bridge. ᶠDEURLOO, K. 2001 ⇒23. 247-255 [Gen 37,21-27; 1,1-2,7; 1 Sam 16-17].

B3.1 *Interpretatio ecclesiastica* Bible and Church

1094 *Aparicio, Carmen* Bishop Paul-Joseph SCHMITT and Vatican II: Jesus Christ, the fullness of revelation. ᶠO'COLLINS, G. 2001 ⇒81. 87-108.
1095 *Arens, Edmund* "Intentio textus" und "intentio auctoris". L'interpretazione della bibbia nella chiesa. 2001 ⇒471. 187-207.
1096 *Baxter, Anthony* The bible, knowledge of God and Dei Verbum. HeyJ 42 (2001) 173-191.
1097 *Beutler, Johannes* El pueblo judío y su sagrada escritura en la biblia cristiana: el nuevo documento de la Pontificia Comisión Bíblica. Qol 27 (2001) 79-81.
1098 *Bordeyne, Philippe* L'usage de l'Écriture sainte en *Gaudium et spes*: un accès au discernement théologique et moral de la constitution pastorale du Concile Vatican II. Revue d'éthique et de théologie morale 219 (2001) 67-107.
1099 *Borras, Alphonse* Bible et droit canonique. Bible et droit. Connaître et croire 8: 2001 ⇒300. 121-155.
1100 **Burigana, Riccardo** La bibbia nel concilio: la redazione della costituzione 'Dei verbum' del Vaticano II. TRSR 21: 1998 ⇒14,895... 16,1118. ᴿHum(B) 56 (2001) 458-460 (*Menestrina, Giovanni*).
1101 **Chrostowski, Waldemar** Biblistyka katolicka w Polsce na Progu XXI Wieku. Biblioteczka Katolicka 3: Wsz 2001, "Adam" 86 pp. Bibl. 3-5. **P.**
1102 *Clifford, Richard J.* The authority of the Nova Vulgata: a note on a recent Roman document. CBQ 63 (2001) 197-202.
1103 Commissio de re biblica: Das jüdische Volk und seine Heilige Schrift in der christlichen Bibel. Verlautbarungen des Apostolischen Stuhls 152: Bonn 2001, Sekretariat der Deutschen Bischofskonferenz 167 pp.

1104 Commission Biblique Pontificale: le peuple juif et ses saintes écritures dans la bible chrétienne. P 2001, Cerf 215 pp. €15.24. 2-20406-913-2. Préf. Cardinal J. Ratzinger [RB 109,476].

1105 *Daniels, Andries* Bybelgebruik in die Belharbelydenis se artikel oor 'Eenheid'. Scriptura 77 (2001) 193-209.

1106 **D'Souza, Francis** Jesus the mediator and the fullness of revelation: the christological perspectives according to Dei Verbum, chapter one. R 2001, Urbaniana 172 pp. Extr. Diss.; Bibl. 143-168.

1107 *Grech, Prosper; Aletti, Jean Noël; Simian-Yofre, Horacio* Introduzione / Introduction. L'interpretazione della bibbia nella chiesa. 2001 ⇒471. 9-40.

1108 *Henn, William* The church as easter witness in the thought of Gerald O'Collins. ^FO'COLLINS, G. 2001 ⇒81. 208-220.

1109 *Hubmann, Franz D.* Bibelauslegung im Wandel. ThPQ 149 (2001) 125-135.

1110 *Jensen, Joseph Liturgiam authenticam* and the New Vulgate. America 185/4 (2001) 11-13.

1111 *Lohfink, Norbert* Gewalt und Friede in der Bibel: Hinführung zum Schreiben der deutschen Bischöfe. "Gerechter Frieden". ^FSCHMUT-TERMAYR, G. 2001 ⇒101. 75-87.

1112 **Lubac, Henri de** Die Göttliche Offenbarung: Kommentar zum Vorwort und zum ersten Kapitel der dogmatischen Konstitution "Dei Verbum" des Zweiten Vatikanischen Konzils. ThRom 26: Einsiedeln 2001, Johannes xxvii; 287 pp. €28. 3-89411-369-3.

1113 **Maggioni, Bruno** 'Impara a conoscere il volto di Dio nelle parole di Dio': commento alla 'Dei Verbum'. 2000 ⇒16,1129. ^REThL 77 (2001) 522-523 (*Schelkens, K.*).

1114 **Maggioni, Bruno** 'Impara a conoscere il volto di Dio nelle parole di Dio'. Dabar: Padova 2001, EMP 208 pp. 'Commento alla 'Dei Verbum'; Pres. di *G. Cappelletto.* ^RMF 101 (2001) 393-396 (*Uricchio, Francesco*).

1115 *Moulins-Beaufort, Eric de* Parole de Dieu, parole de l'église, mystère de l'homme. Com(F) 26/1 (2001) 35-46.

1116 ^E**Murphy, Dennis J.** The church and the bible: official documents of the catholic church. Bangalore 2001, Theological Publications in India lviii; 836 pp. Rs320. ^RITS 38 (2001) 260-262 (*Legrand, L.*).

1117 *Norris, Thomas* On revisiting Dei Verbum. IThQ 66 (2001) 315-337.

1118 **O'Collins, Gerald; Kendall, Daniel** Bibbia e teologia: dieci principi per l'uso teologico della Scrittura. 1999 ⇒16,1131. ^RHum(B) 56 (2001) 140-142 (*Montagnini, Felice*).

1119 *Pesce, Mauro* Può la teologia cristiana rispettare la natura ebraica della bibbia?. Studi Fatti Ricerche 95 (2001) 3-10.

1120 *Räisänen, Heikki* Comparative religion, theology, and New Testament exegesis <1998>;

1121 The 'effective history' of the bible: a challenge to biblical scholarship <1992>. Challenges to biblical interpretation. BiblInterp 59: 2001 ⇒200. 209-225/263-282.

1122 **Salvatori, Davide** L'oggetto del magistero definitivo della chiesa alla luce del m.p. Ad Tuendam Fidem: il can. 750 visto. TGr.Diritto Canonico 51: R 2001, E.P.U.G. 461 pp. 88-7652-901-2.

1123 *Salzmann, Jorg Christian Per quem omnia facta sunt*: Schriftauslegung zu einem theologischen Satz. StPatr 34. 2001 ⇒553. 541-551 [Gen 1,1-2; John 1,3].

1124 *Scheffczyk, Leo* Die Heilige Schrift: Wort Gottes und der Kirche. IKaZ 30 (2001) 44-57; Communio 23,154-166.
1125 The bible documents: a parish resource. Ch 2001, Liturgy Training Pub. xi; 224 pp. $15. 1-56854-249-6.
1126 *Van der Kooij, Arie* Bible exegesis in Dutch ecclesial documents on homosexuality. Scriptura 77 (2001) 251-257.
1127 *Vidović, Marinko* Biblija u životu Crkve [The bible in the life of the church]. Crkva u Svijetu 36 (2001) 27-54 Sum. 54. **Croatian**.
1128 *Wicks, Jared* Pieter Smulders and Dei Verbum: 1: a consultation on the eve of Vatican II. Gr. 82 (2001) 241-297;
1129 *Dei Verbum* developing: Vatican II's revelation doctrine 1963-1964. F*O'COLLINS*, G. 2001 ⇒81. 109-125.
1130 **Williamson, Peter S.** Catholic principles for interpreting scripture: a study of the Pontifical Biblical Commissions's The interpretation of the bible in the church. Diss. Gregoriana, D*Swetnam, James*: SubBi 22: R 2001, E.P.I.B. xxii; 400 pp. $28/€25. 88-7653-617-5. Pref. *Albert Vanhoye*; Bibl. 349-377.
1131 *Zanartu, Sergio* Documento de la Comisión Teológica Internacional sobre la redención: presentación con algunos comentarios. TyV 42 (2001) 20-49.
1132 *Zanca, Lino* L'Enciclica Fides et Ratio: dalla filosofia greca alla filosofia biblica. MF 101 (2001) 567-614.

B3.2 *Homiletica*—The Bible in preaching

1133 *Allen, Ronald J.* Preaching and postmodernism. Interp. 55 (2001) 34-48.
1134 **Bergant, Dianne** Preaching the new lectionary: year A. ColMn 2001, Liturgical x; 474 pp. $30. Collab. *Richard Fragomeni* [BiTod 40,62—Senior, Donald].
1135 *Bexell, Oloph* Bibeln i predikan: om bibeln som referens i svensk kyrkopredikan. SEÅ 66 (2001) 55-72.
1136 *Bitter, Gottfried* Bibel und Verkündigung: eine kritische Umschau in Predigtzeitschriften. LS 52 (2001) 296-300.
1137 *Bos, R.* Wat is de mens, dat Gij hem gedenkt?: een bijdrage tot een homiletische antropologie. VeE 22 (2001) 231-251.
1138 ET*Boud'Hors, Anne* TIMOTEWAS: l'homélie sur l'Église du Rocher: attribuée à Timothée Aelure. PO 49/1-2: Turnhout 2001, Brepols 214 pp. Deux textes arabes et traductions par **Ramez Boutros**.
1139 **Boudreau, Paul** Between Sundays. Mystic 2001, Twenty-Third 358 pp. $25 [BiTod 41,199—Senior, Donald].
1140 **Brueggemann, Walter** Cadences of home: preaching among exiles. 1997 ⇒13,875. R*OTEs* 14 (2001) 175-177 (*Maré, L.P.*).
1141 **Burghardt, Walter J.** To be just is to love: homilies for a church renewing. Mahwah 2001, Paulist 272 pp. $20 [BiTod 40,395—Bergant, Dianne].
1142 **Cameron, Peter John** To praise, to bless, to preach: spiritual reflections on the Sunday gospels, cycle A. Huntington 2001, Our Sunday Visitor 188 pp. $16. 0-8797.3824-3 [BiTod 40,132— Senior, D.].
1143 **Carter, Warren**, *al.*, New proclamation: year A, 2002: Easter through Pentecost. Mp 2001, Fortress x; 292 pp. $25. 0-8006-4246-5 [ThD 49,79—Heiser, W. Charles].

1144 *De Zan* Fondamento biblico dell'omelia. Orientamenti pastorali 1 (2001) 35-40.
1145 *Delzant, Antoine* Écriture, esprit et parole. La bible, parole adressée. 2001 ⇒323. 25-48.
1146 **Dowling, Edward T.** Have you heard the good news?. NY 2001, Alba xi; 180 pp. $13 [BiTod 39,386—Senior, Donald].
1147 *Gagnon, Denis* Parutions récentes sur l'homélie. MD 227 (2001) 147-162.
1148 *Gerstenberger, Erhard* "Höre, mein Volk, lass mich reden!" (Ps 50,7). BiKi 56 (2001) 21-25.
1149 *Gibert, Pierre* Exégèse et homélie. MD 227 (2001) 35-46.
1150 **Goldsworthy, Graeme** Preaching the whole bible as christian scripture: the application of biblical theory to expository preaching. Nottingham 2001, IVP xv; 272 pp. 0-85111-539-X. Bibl. 257-262 [2000 ⇒16,1159]. ᴿTrinJ 22 (2001) 287-289 (*Scharf, Greg R.*).
1151 **Greidanus, Sidney** Preaching Christ from the Old Testament: a contemporary hermeneutical method. 1999 ⇒15,1037; 16,1160. ᴿCTJ 36 (2001) 211-214 (*Schuringa, H. David*); EvQ 73 (2001) 347-348 (*Marshall, I. Howard*).
1152 *Hameline, Jean-Yves* Expliquer l'écriture avec le style de l'écriture: relire FÉNELON. MD 227 (2001) 79-108.
1153 **Hamm, Dennis** Let the scriptures speak: reflections on the Sunday readings (Year A). ColMn 2001, Liturgical xi; 122 pp. $12. 0-8146-2555-X;
1154 Let the scriptures speak (Year C). ColMn 2001, Liturgical xi; 122 pp. $12.
1155 *Kegler, Jürgen* Predigten. Gesammelte Aufsätze. BEAT 48: 2001 ⇒ 167. 294-368.
1156 *Konrad, Werner* Homiletische Reflexion und Predigt zu Koh 11,9-12,8: Predigt: Dreierkonferenz für zwei. ꟳSCHMUTTERMAYR, G. 2001 ⇒101. 441-455.
1157 *Larsen, David L.* Heaven and hell in the preaching of the gospel: a historical survey. TrinJ 22 (2001) 237-258.
1158 *Leeto, Mokoto Ephraim; Letsie, Sejakhosi Cosmas; Zwilling, Anne-Laure* Genèse 22,1-19: sacrifice impossible. Lire et Dire 49 (2001) 16-30 [BuBB 33,51].
1159 *Lienhard, Michael* Was heißt biblisch predigen?. LS 52 (2001) 301-303.
1160 *Martin, François* Les noces de Cana (Jean 2,1-11): homélie préparée par François Martin pour le 14 Jan. 2001. SémBib 101 (2001) 4-7.
1161 **Matera, Frank J.** Strategies for preaching Paul. ColMn 2001, Liturgical vi: 186 pp. $20. 0-8146-1966-5. Bibl. 181-183.
1162 *Neufeld, John H.* Preaching and the Old Testament. ꟳJANZEN, W. 2001 ⇒54. 48-66.
1163 **Nieman, James R.; Rogers, Thomas G.** Preaching to every pew: cross-cultural strategies. Mp 2001, Augsburg 159 pp. $16 [BiTod 40,260—Bergant, Dianne].
1164 *Ortkemper, Franz-Josef* Von der Exegese zur Predigt: ein Plädoyer für die alttestamentliche Predigt. BiKi 56 (2001) 143-147.
1165 **Osborn, Ronald E.** Folly of God: the rise of christian preaching. 1999 ⇒15,1048. ᴿCTJ 36 (2001) 435-437 (*Deppe, Dean*).
1166 **Pilch, John J.** The cultural world of the apostles. ColMn 2001, Liturgical xvi; 128 pp. $12 [Cycle A, 2nd readings] [BiTod 39,389—Senior, Donald].

1167 *Pohl-Patalong, Uta* Bibliolog: eine neue Predigtform in der homiletischen Diskussion. PTh 90 (2001) 272-284.

1168 *Prudky, Martin* Jesaja 44:1-5 als Predigttext zu Pfingstsonntag. ^FDEURLOO, K. ACEBT.S 2: 2001 ⇒23. 137-147.
^FROBINSON, H. The big idea of biblical preaching. 1999 ⇒95.

1169 **Robinson, Haddon W.** Biblical preaching: the development and delivery of expository messages. GR ²2001 <1980>, Baker 256 pp. $20. 0-8010-2262-2 [ThD 49,84—Heiser, W. Charles].

1170 *Schaller, Bettina* Genèse 12,1-9: et Abraham partit... Lire et Dire 49 (2001) 3-15 [BuBB 33,51].

1171 **Schöttler, Heinz-Günther** Christliche Predigt und Altes Testament: Versuch einer homiletischen Kriteriologie. Diss.-Habil. Tübingen, ^D*Groß, W.*: Zeitzeichen 8: Ostfildern 2001, Schwabenverlag 733 pp. 3-7966-1021-8 [ZKTh 125,85—Fischer, Georg].

1172 *Schwank, Benedikt* Gegeben—geworden (Joh 1,17). EuA 77 (2001) 63-65.

1173 **Shelley, A. Carter** Preaching Genesis 12-36. Preaching Classic Texts: St. Louis 2001, Chalice 174 pp. $18. 0-8272-2973-9 [Interp. 57,104—Wilfong, Marsha M.].

1174 **Sibbes, Richard** Works of Richard Sibbes. ^E*Grosart, Alexander B.*: E 2001, Banner of Truth Trust. 7 vols. 0-85151-. Memoir by *Alexander B. Grosart*.

1175 **Steck, Odil Hannes** Der Lebensspur Gottes nachgehen: Predigten. Stu 2001, Kohlhammer 196 pp. 3-17-016877-0.

1176 **Stewart-Sykes, Alistair** From prophecy to preaching: a search for the origins of the christian homily. SVigChr 59: Lei 2001, Brill xi; 306 pp. €69. 90-04-11689-3. Bibl. 281-295.

1177 *Sturm, Wilhelm* Neuwerdung des Menschen—Illusion oder Wirklichkeit?: Predigt über Joh 3,1-8 in Auseinandersetzung mit Bert Brechts 'Der gute Mensch von Sezuan'. ^FSCHMUTTERMAYR, G. 2001 ⇒101. 601-608.

1178 ^E**Van Harn, Roger E.** The lectionary commentary: theological exegesis for Sunday's texts, 1: the first readings: the Old Testament and Acts, 2: the second readings: Acts and the epistles, 3: the third readings: the gospels. GR 2001, Eerdmans xx; 622 + xx; 647 + xx; 635 pp. $40 per vol. 0-8028-4751-X/2-8/3-6. ^RRExp 98 (2001) 618-619 (*Graves, Mike*).

1179 *Van Rensburg, J. Janse* Pastoral care and preaching-partners in healing. AcTh(B) 21/2 (2001) 50-64.

1180 *Van Zyl, H.C.* Om te "lotto" of nie te "lotto" nie: gedagtes oor aktuele prediking. AcTh(B) 21/2 (2001) 145-152.

1181 *Weyermann, Andrew M.* Christ-centered preaching. CThMi 28 (2001) 594-599.

1182 ^E**Whitby, Mary** The propaganda of power: the role of panegyric in late antiquity. Mn.S 183: 1998 ⇒14,958. ^RClR 51 (2001) 62-64 (*Nixon, C.E.V.*).

1183 **Wilson, Paul Scott** God sense: reading the bible for preaching. Nv 2001, Abingdon 192 pp. $18. 0-687-00632-5.

1184 **Wright, Stephen** Preaching with the grain of scripture. C 2001, Grove 24 pp. £2.50. 1-85174-468-1.

B3.3 **Inerrantia, inspiratio**

1185 **Achtemeier, Paul J.** Inspiration and authority: nature and function of christian scripture. 1999 ⇒15,1063; 16,1189. ^RSEÅ 66 (2001) 227-229 (*Stenström, Hanna*).

1186 *Beltz, Walter* Zum Problem 'religiöse Texte als Autorität sozialen Handelns'. HBO 31 (2001) 71-81.

1187 *Borgonovo, Gianantonio* Una proposta di rilettura dell'ispirazione biblica dopo gli apporti della Form- e Redaktionsgeschichte. L'interpretazione della bibbia nella chiesa. 2001 ⇒471. 41-63.

1188 *Braaten, Carl E.* A shared dilemma: Catholics and Lutherans on the authority and interpretation of scripture. ProEc 10/1 (2001) 63-75.

1189 *Craig, William Lane* Inspiration and the freewill defense revisited. EvQ 73 (2001) 327-339.

1190 *DiNoia, J.A.; Mulcahy, Bernard* The authority of scripture in sacramental theology: some methodological observations. ProEc 10 (2001) 329-345.

1191 *Fabris, Rinaldo* 'Una dottrina nuova insegnata con autorità' (Mc 1,27). Credere 21/2 (2001) 25-36.

1192 *Forte, Bruno* La parola di Dio nella sacra scrittura e nei libri sacri delle altre religioni;

1193 *Gabel, Helmut* Inspiration und Wahrheit der Schrift (DV 11): neue Ansätze und Probleme im Kontext der gegenwärtigen wissenschaftlichen Diskussion. L'interpretazione della bibbia nella chiesa. 2001 ⇒471. 106-120/64-84.

1194 *Hahn, Eberhard* Wieviel Bibel braucht die evangelische Kirche?. JETh 15 (2001) 37-48.

1195 *Izquierdo, Antonio* Encuentro internacional sobre la inspiración. Alpha Omega 4 (2001) 315-339. Roma, 18-20.9.2001.

1196 **Law, David R.** Inspiration: new century theology. NY 2001, Continuum 234 pp. $23. 0-8264-5183-7. Bibl. 213-223 [ThD 48,381— Heiser, W. Charles].

1197 *Martin, R. Francis Sacra doctrina* and the authority of its *Sacra scriptura* according to St. Thomas AQUINAS. ProEc 10/1 (2001) 84-102.

1198 **Mathison, Keith A.** The shape of sola scriptura. Moscow 2001, Canon 364 pp.

1199 *Ndungane, Njongonkulu* Scripture: what is at issue in Anglicanism today?. AThR 83 (2001) 11-23.

1200 *Paolini, Pier G.* Spirito e parola: alcune riflessioni sull'ispirazione. VivH 12/2 (2001) 329-358.

1201 *Patton, Corrine L.; Cook, Stephen L.* Introduction: Jane Morse and the fuller sense (theoretical framework for a sensus plenior). JSOT.S 336: ^MMORSE, J. 2001 ⇒75. 13-39.

1202 *Peifer, Claude J.* The inspiration and truth of sacred scripture. BiTod 39 (2001) 360-365.

1203 **Reynier, Chantal** Le Christ au cœur de l'histoire: l'autorité du Nouveau Testament. 1999 ⇒15,1077. ^REeV 42 (2001) 27 (*Cothenet, Edouard*).

1204 *Rogerson, John W.* Die Bibel lesen wie jedes andere Buch?: Auseinandersetzungen um die Autorität der Bibel vom 18. Jahrhundert an bis heute. Biblischer Text. BThSt 44: 2001 ⇒252. 211-234.

1205 *Spieckermann, Hermann* Die Verbindlichkeit des Alten Testaments: unzeitgemäße Betrachtungen zu einem ungeliebten Thema. Gottes Liebe zu Israel. FAT 33: 2001 <1997> ⇒215. 173-196.

1206 **Straight, Julie** British women writers in controversies regarding the bible's authority, 1810-1823 [Lamb M; Shelley M; More H; West J]. Diss. North Carolina 2001, 249 pp. 3007892.

1207 *Trembath, Kern* Response to Professor Helmut Gabel's "Inspiration and truth of the writing ...". L'interpretazione della bibbia nella chiesa. 2001 ⇒471. 85-89.

B3.4 Traditio

1208 *Antonelli, Mario* La comunicazione ecclesiale e le condizioni della sua attendibilità in rapporto alla canonicità del testo biblico. ScC 129 (2001) 7-51.

1209 *Barbeau, Jeffrey W.* Scripture and tradition at the council of Trent: reapplying the "conciliar hermeneutic". AHC 33/1 (2001) 127-146.

1210 **Brown, David** Discipleship and imagination: christian tradition and truth. 2000 ⇒16,1211. RTS 62 (2001) 386-388 (*Oakes, Edward T.*); JThS 52 (2001) 980-982 (*Macquarrie, John*); ET 112 (2001) 145-147 (Resp. 148-149) (*Rodd, C.S.*).

1211 *Dulles, Avery* Tradition: l'authentique et l'inauthentique. Com(F) 26/6 (2001) 69-77.

1212 *Fisichella, Rino* Dei verbum audiens et proclamans: sobre la escritura y la tradición como fuente de la palabra de Dios. Communio 23 (2001) 184-195.

1213 *García Trapiello, Jesús* Equilibrio bíblico entre tradición e innovación. Communio 34/1 (2001) 29-54.

1214 **Lyman, Rebecca** Early christian traditions. 1999 ⇒15,1085. RChH 70 (2001) 772-774 (*McGuckin, John*).

1215 **O'Grady, John F.** Catholic beliefs and traditions: ancient and ever new. NY 2001, Paulist x; 356 pp. 0-8091-4047-0. Bibl. 335-347.

1216 *Post, Paul* The creation of tradition: rereading and reading beyond HOBSBAWM. Religious identity. 2001 ⇒549. 41-59.

1217 *Sarot, Marcel* Counterfactuals and the intention of religious traditions. Religious identity. 2001 ⇒549. 21-40.

1218 **Stylianopoulos, Theodore G.** The New Testament: an Orthodox perspective. Scripture, tradition, hermeneutics 1: 1997 ⇒13,776; 15,940. RSVTQ 45 (2001) 213-215 (*Prokurat, Michael*).

1219 **Thiel, John E.** Senses of tradition: continuity and development in catholic faith. 2000 ⇒16,1215. RTS 62 (2001) 843-845 (*O'Keefe, John J.*).

1220 *Van Henten, Jan Willem; Houtepen, Anton* Introduction. Religious identity. Studies in theology and religion 3: 2001 ⇒549. 3-18.

1221 **Williams, D.H.** Retrieving the tradition and renewing evangelicalism: a primer for suspicious Protestants. 1999 ⇒15,1088. RSBET 19 (2001) 236-237 (*Bathgate, Andy*).

B3.5 Canon

1222 **Abraham, William J.** Canon and criterion in christian theology: from the Fathers to feminism. 1998 ⇒14,988... 16,1216. RNT 43 (2001) 190-193 (*Toit, Andrie du*).

1223 **Aichele, George** The control of biblical meaning: canon as semiotic mechanism. Harrisburg, Pennsylvania 2001, Trinity xi; 259 pp. $26. 1-56338-333-0. Bibl. 237-245.

1224 *Auwers, Jean-Marie; Jonge, Henk Jan de* The biblical canons: Colloquium Biblicum Lovaniense L (2001). EThL 77 (2001) 524-537.

1225 [E]**Bisschops, Ralph; Francis, James** Metaphor, canon and community: Jewish, Christian and Islamic approaches. 1999 ⇒15,1096. [R]Jud. 57 (2001) 233-235 (*Dober, Hans Martin*).

1226 **Bohlmann, Ralph Arthur** The criteria of biblical canonicity in sixteenth century Lutheran, Roman Catholic and Reformed theology. AA 2001, UMI Diss. Services [BuBB 33,11].

1227 *Bordreuil, Pierrre; Briquel-Chatonnet, Françoise* La rédaction de la bible à l'époque perse. MoBi 137 (2001) 24-27 [BuBB 35,31].

1228 **Brandt, Peter** Endgestalten des Kanons: das Arrangement der Schriften Israels in der jüdischen und christlichen Bibel. BBB 131: Bodenheim 2001, Philo 493 pp. €48.50. 38257-02588. Bibl. 443-73.

1229 *Broyles, Craig C.* Traditions, intertextuality, and canon. Interpreting the OT. 2001 ⇒248. 157-175.

1230 **Chapman, Stephen B.** The law and the prophets: a study in Old Testament canon formation. FAT 27: 2000 ⇒16,1226. [R]EstTrin 35 (2001) 446-447 (*Vázquez Allegue, Jaime*); JThS 52 (2001) 715-717 (*Clements, R.E.*); Jud. 57 (2001) 293-295 (*Ego, Beate*).

1231 **Cross, Frank Moore** From epic to canon: history and literature in Ancient Israel. 1998 ⇒14,1000; 16,1227. [R]JSSt 46 (2001) 325-327 (*Tomes, Roger*); JBL 119 (2000) 750-753 (*Klingbeil, Gerald A.*).

1232 *Denzey, Nicola* What did the Montanists read?. HThR 94 (2001) 427-448.

1233 *Dettmar, Werner* Mythos—Geschichte—Gottes Wort. DtPfrBl 101 (2001) 127-129.

1234 *Diebner, Bernd Jørg* Die Konzeption der hebräisch-aramäischen 'Bibel' (TNK) und die Definition der judäischen kulturellen Identität 'Israel' gegenüber der samaritanischen Kultgemeinde Israel seit dem 2. Jh. v. Chr. HBO 31 (2001) 147-165.

1235 *Dohmen, Christoph* Reaktion zum Beitrag von James A. SANDERS "Scripture as canon in the church". L'interpretazione della bibbia nella chiesa. 2001 ⇒471. 144-149.

1236 *Ellis, Edward Earle* Pseudonymity and canonicity of New Testament documents. History and interpretation. 2001 ⇒141. 17-29.

11237 **Ellis, Edward Earle** L'Antico Testamento nel primo cristianesimo: canone e interpretazione alla luce della ricerca moderna. 1999 ⇒15, 1104; 16,1230. [R]PaVi 46/5 (2001) 59-61 (*Cappelletto, Gianni*).

1238 *Evans, Craig A.* The Dead Sea scrolls and the canon of scripture in the time of Jesus. The bible at Qumran. 2001 ⇒267. 67-79.

1239 *Groote, Marc de* Bemerkungen zum Entstehen des Kanons in der alten Kirche. ZKG 112 (2001) 372-376.

1240 **Jasper, David** The sacred and the secular canon in romanticism: preserving the sacred truths. 1999 ⇒15,1113. [R]HeyJ 42 (2001) 212-214 (*Knottenbelt, E.M.*).

1241 *Markschies, Christoph* Neue Forschungen zur Kanonisierung des Neuen Testaments. Apocrypha 12 (2001) 237-262.

1242 **Metzger, Bruce Manning** Il canone del Nuovo Testamento: origine, sviluppo e significato. 1997 ⇒13,962; 16,1240. [R]Asp. 48 (2001) 244-246 (*Di Palma, Gaetano*).

1243 *Neri, Marcello* Fides ex auditu: le scritture canoniche, *forma fidei*. ScC 129/1 (2001) 145-210.

1244 **Noble, P.R.** The canonical approach 1996 ⇒12,814... 15,1122. ᴿVT 51 (2001) 131-133 (*Gordon, Robert P.*).

1245 **Paul, André** Et l'homme créa la bible: d'HÉRODOTE à FLAVIUS JOSÈPHE. 2000 ⇒16,1245. RSR 89 (2001) 147-152 (*Abadie, Philippe*); VieCon 73 (2001) 335-336 (*Luciani, Didier*); NRTh 123 (2001) 641-643 (*Radermakers, J.*).

1246 *Peels, H.G.L.* The blood 'from Abel to Zechariah' (Matthew 23,35; Luke 11,50f.) and the canon of the Old Testament. ZAW 113 (2001) 583-601.

1247 *Pistone, Rosario* Ancora su "Primo" o "Antico" Testamento. Ho Theológos 19 (2001) 401-413.

1248 *Rahner, Johanna* Kanonische und/oder kirchliche Schriftauslegung?: der Kanon und die Suche nach der Einheit. ZKTh 123 (2001) 402-422.

1249 *Rendtorff, Rolf* Die Hermeneutik einer kanonischen Theologie des Alten Testaments. Der Text in seiner Endgestalt. 2001 ⇒201. 61-70;

1250 The paradigm is changing: hopes and fears. Der Text in seiner Endgestalt. 2001 ⇒201. 83-102.

1251 *Römer, Thomas C.* Naissance de la bible. MoBi 137 (2001) 18-19.

1252 *Sanders, James A.* Scripture as canon in the church. L'interpretazione della bibbia nella chiesa. 2001 ⇒471. 121-143;

1253 Canon as dialogue. The bible at Qumran. 2001 ⇒ 267. 7-26.

1254 *Schenker, Adrian* L'écriture sainte subsiste en plusieurs formes canoniques simultanées (réaction à l'exposé du prof. Max Seckler). L'interpretazione della bibbia nella chiesa. 2001 ⇒471. 178-186.

1255 *Seckler, Max* Problematik des biblischen Kanons und die Wiederentdeckung seiner Notwendigkeit. L'interpretazione della bibbia nella chiesa. 2001 ⇒471. 150-177.

1256 *Sequeri, Pierangelo* Bibbia e teologia: il luogo del testo. RStB 13/1 (2001) 279-295.

1257 **Steinmann, Andrew E.** The oracles of God: the Old Testament canon. 1999 ⇒15,1130. ᴿCBQ 63 (2001) 532-533 (*Salyer, Gary D.*).

1258 *Stemberger, Günter* Tanach. TRE 32 (2001) 636-639.

1259 *Stone, Michael E.* Armenian canon lists VI—Hebrew names and other attestations. HThR 94 (2001) 477-491.

1260 *Stordalen, Terje* Law or prophecy?: on the order of the canonical books. TTK 72 (2001) 131-150.

1261 *Van de Water, Rick* "Removing the boundary" (Hosea 5:10) in first-century Palestine. CBQ 63 (2001) 619-629.

1262 *Verhoef, Eduard* Pseudepigraphy and canon. BN 106 (2001) 90-98.

1263 **Vian, Giovanni Maria** Bibliotheca divina: filologia e storia dei testi cristiani. R 2001, Carocci 340 pp. €21.69.

1264 *Vogels, Walter* The parallel—chiastic structure of the christian bible. Theoforum 32 (2001) 203-221.

1265 *Waltke, Bruce K.* How we got the Hebrew Bible: the text and canon of the Old Testament. The bible at Qumran. 2001 ⇒267. 27-50.

1266 *Webster, John* The dogmatic location of the canon. NZSTh 43 (2001) 17-43. Zsfg. 43.

B4.1 *Interpretatio humanistica* **The Bible—man; health, toil, age**

1267 **Alonso Schökel, Luis** I nomi dell'amore: simboli matrimoniali nella bibbia. 1997 ⇒13,987; 14,1047. [R]RdT 42 (2001) 619-621 (*Franco, Ettore*).

1268 *Baude, Jeanne-Marie* La maladie comme expérience spirituelle dans la littérature actuelle. Représentations des maladies. 2001 ⇒482. 211-230.

1269 *Boëtsch, Gilles* La peste, Saint Sébastien et Saint Roch en Savoie et en Dauphiné. Représentations des maladies. 2001 ⇒482. 189-204.

1270 *Briend, Jacques; Quesnel, Michel* Die Erziehung der Kinder. WUB 22 (2001) 80-83.

1271 *Capps, Donald* Curing anxious adolescents through fatherlike performance. Interp. 55 (2001) 135-147.

1272 *Carroll, John T.* Children in the bible. Interp. 55 (2001) 121-134.

1273 *Chevé, Dominique* Motifs bibliques et représentations épidémiques dans l'iconographie du 'corps' de la peste au corps pestiféré. Représentations des maladies. 2001 ⇒482. 243-260.

1274 *Devries, Dawn* Toward a theology of childhood. Interp. 55 (2001) 161-173.

1275 **Hull, John M.** In the beginning there was darkness: a blind person's conversations with the bible. L 2001, SCM 176 pp. £10. 0-334-02821-3. [R]Theol. 104 (2001) 439 (*France, R.T.*); ET 112 (2001) 361-362 (*Rodd, C.S.*).

1276 **Longeaux, Jacques de** Amour, mariage et sexualité d'après la Bible. Cahiers de l'École Cathédrale 22: 1996 ⇒12,840. [R]SRATK 9 (2001) 169-170 (*Ozorowski, Mieczysław*).

1277 **Newman, Jay** Biblical religion and family values: a problem in the philosophy of culture. Westport, CT 2001, Greenwood ix; 357 pp. $80. 0-275-97137-6. Bibl. 331-342.

1278 *Parker, Evelyn L.* Hungry for honor: children in violent youth gangs. Interp. 55 (2001) 148-160.

1279 *Pawlak, Leonard* Małżeństwoi rodzina w biblii [Matrimonio e famiglia nella bibbia]. SRATK 5/1 (2001) 65-74. Som. 74. **P.**

1280 *Pelletier, Anne-Marie* L'epreuve de la maladie chez les Pères du Désert. Représentations des maladies. 2001 ⇒482. 121-134.

1281 *Poirson-Dechonne, Marion* Maladie de l'esprit et guérison dans OR-DET de Dreyer et BLEU de Kieslowski. Représentations des maladies. 2001 ⇒482. 291-304.

1282 **Rashkow, Ilona N.** Taboo or not taboo: sexuality and family in the Hebrew Bible. 2000 ⇒16,1275. [R]CBQ 63 (2001) 730-731 (*Mandolfo, Carleen*).

1283 **Ruether, Rosemary Radford** Christianity and the making of the modern family. 2000 ⇒16,1276. [R]Interp. 55 (2001) 194, 196 (*Couture, Pamela D.*).

1284 *Sicre, José Luis* La utopía de la familia humana en la tradición bíblica. Conc(E) 37 (2001) 783-790; Conc(I) 37,905-914; Conc(GB) 2001/5,89-96; Conc(D) 37/5,612-619.

1285 *Stiebert, Johanna* Does the Hebrew Bible have anything to tell us about HIV/AIDS?. Missionalia 29 (2001) 174-185. Sum. 174.

1286 [E]**Stol, Marten; Vleeming, Sven P.** The care of the elderly in the ancient Near East 1998 ⇒14,1066; 15,1158. [R]JNES 60 (2001) 157-158 (*Harris, Rivkah*).

1287 **Wells, Louise** The Greek language of healing from HOMER to New Testament times. BZNW 83: 1998 ⇒14,1070... 16,1281. [R]JBL 119 (2000) 561-564 (*Aune, David E.*).

1288 **Wohlers, Michael** Heilige Krankheit—Epilepsie in antiker Medizin, Astrologie und Religion. MThSt 57: 1999 ⇒15,1162; 16,1282. [R]ThLZ 126 (2001) 763-764 (*Strecker, Christian E.*).

B4.2 *Femina, familia*; Woman in the Bible [⇒B4.1; H8.8s]

1289 [E]**Bach, Alice** Women in the Hebrew Bible. 1999 ⇒15,1164; 16, 1284. [R]HebStud 42 (2001) 331-334 (*Green, Barbara*).

1290 *Bartolini, Elena* La bellezza delle matriarche. La bellezza. PSV 44: 2001 ⇒240. 175-191.

1291 **Bebe, Pauline** Dictionnaire des femmes et du judaïsme. P 2001, Cal-mann-Lévy 440 pp [RThPh 134,96s—Graesslé, Isabelle].

1292 **Blaquière, Georgette** Femmes selon le coeur de Dieu. 1999 ⇒15, 1169. [R]AETSC 8 (2001) 215-219 (*Guillen, Ferdinand*).

1293 *Bowen, Nancy R.* The quest for the historical גְּבִירָה. CBQ 63 (2001) 597-618.

1294 **Brenner, Athalya** A mulher Israelita. [T]*Belinsky, Sylvia Márcia K.* Bíblia e história: São Paulo 2001, Paulinas 216 pp [REB 61,754].

1295 **Camp, Claudia V.** Wise, strange and holy: the strange woman and the making of the bible. JSOT.S 320; Gender, Culture, Theory 9: 2000 ⇒16,144. [R]CBQ 63 (2001) 711-712 (*Farmer, Kathleen A.*); RBLit 3 (2001) 157-160 (*Fuchs, Esther*).

1296 *Dolamo, Ramathate T.* A critical review of Cheryl Exum's feminist interpretation of Hebrew canon patriarchy. VFTW 24/1 (2001) 152-164.

1297 [E]**Eltrop, Bettina; Hecht, Anneliese** Frauenbilder. 2000 ⇒16,1291. [R]OrdKor 43 (2001) 131-132 (*Heinemann, Franz Karl*).

1298 *Gaines, Janet Howe* Lilith: seductress, heroine or murderer?. BiRe 17/5 (2001) 12-20, 43-44.

1299 *Gunkel, Hermann* The Hagar traditions. Water for a thirsty land. Fortress classics in biblical studies: 2001 <1900> ⇒155. 68-84.

1300 *Hain, Regine* Warum Jungs Miriam "uncool" finden: Frauen der Bi-bel—Erfahrungen aus der Praxis. WuA(M) 42 (2001) 120-124.

1301 **Hammer, Jill** Sisters at Sinai: new tales of biblical women. Ph 2001, Jewish Publication Society of America xxvi; 294 pp. 0-8276-0726-1. Bibl. 287-289.

1302 *Harvey, Susan Ashbrook* 2000 NAPS presidential address: spoken words, voiced silence: biblical women in Syriac tradition. JECS 9 (2001) 105-131.

1303 **Ilan, Tal** Integrating women into Second Temple history. TSAJ 76: 1999 ⇒15,1179; 16,1298. [R]CBQ 63 (2001) 151-152 (*McGinn, Sheila E.*); Zion 66 (2001) 382-388 (*Schwartz, Joshua*); ThLZ 126 (2001) 385-387 (*Reichman, Ronen*);

1304 Integrating women into second temple history. Peabody 2001, Hen-drickson 296 pp. $25 [BiTod 40,258—Bergant, Dianne].

1305 *Levine, Amy-Jill* Settling at Beer-lahai-roi. Daughters of Abraham. 2001 ⇒528. 12-34.

1306 *Malamat, Abraham* Naamah, the Ammonite princess, King Solo-mon's wife. History of biblical Israel. Culture and history of the ANE 7: 2001 <1999> ⇒182. 234-239.

1307 **McKenna, Megan** 'Déjala' (Juan 12,7): mujeres en la escritura. Std 2001, Sal Terrae 280 pp.

1308 [E]**Meyers, Carol; Craven, Toni; Kraemer, Ross S.** Women in scripture. 2000 ⇒16,1305. [R]CBQ 63 (2001) 575-576 (*Sivan, Hagith*).

1309 *Mullins, Pat* The religious roles of women in ancient Israel. MillSt 47 (2001) 106-139.

1310 **Pestalozza, Uberto** I miti della Donna-giardino: da Iside alla Sulamita. Hermes 1: Mi 2001, Medusa 221 pp. 88-88130-11-X. Introd. Pier Angelo Carozzi.

1311 **Rapp, Úrsula** Mirjam: eine feministisch-rhetorische Analyse der Mirjamtraditionen in der hebräischen Bibel. Diss. Graz, [D]*Fischer, I.* 2001, 383 pp [RTL 33,633].

1312 *Schmitz-Gieldorf, Uwe* Schön—rein—schön: zur Interpretation der biblischen Susanna-Figur in HÄNDELs "Susanna"-Oratorium (HWV 66). WuA(M) 42 (2001) 125-130.

1313 **Thompson, John Lee** Writing the wrongs: women of the Old Testament among biblical commentators from PHILO through the Reformation. Oxford studies in historical theology: Oxf 2001, OUP xiv; (2) 288 pp. $50. 0-19-513736-1. Bibl. 255-271.

1314 *Weill, Marie D.* La femme épouse et mère dans la bible. Aletheia 20 (2001) 19-42.

1315 *Wu, Rose* Women on the boundary: prostitution, contemporary and in the bible. Feminist Theology 28 (2001) 69-81.

1316 *Zlotnick, Helena* From Jezebel to Esther: fashioning images of queenship in the Hebrew Bible. Bib. 82 (2001) 477-495.

B4.4 *Exegesis litteraria*—**The Bible itself as literature**

1317 **Aaron, David H.** Biblical ambiguities: metaphor, semantics and divine imagery. Brill Reference Library of Ancient Judaism 4: Lei 2001, Brill ix; 221 pp. 90-04-12032-7. Bibl. 201-214.

1318 *Alter, Robert* Northrop FRYE, entre archétype et typologie. RSR 89 (2001) 403-418.

1319 *Amit, Yaira* Gradation as a rhetorical device in biblical literature. [F]AHITUV, S. 2001 ⇒1. 21-48. **H.**

1320 **Amit, Yairah** Reading biblical narratives: literary criticism and the Hebrew Bible. Ph 2001, Fortress xii; 188 pp. $20. 0-8006-3280-X. Bibl. 169-179.

1321 *Anderegg, Johannes* Zum Ort der Klage: literaturwissenschaftliche Erkundungen. JBTh 16 (2001) 185-208.

1322 **Andersen, Øivind** Im Garten der Rhetorik: die Kunst der Rede in der Antike. Da 2001, Primus 335 pp. €39.90. 3-89678-195-2.

1323 *Avis, Paul* The gospel as a work of art. Theol. 104 (2001) 94-101.

1324 *Barré, Michael L.* 'Wondering about' as a *topos* of depression in ancient Near Eastern literature and in the bible. JNES 60 (2001) 177-188.

1325 **Callahan, James Patrick** The clarity of scripture: history, theology & contemporary literary studies. DG 2001, InterVarsity 272 pp. 083-0815-848.

1326 *D'Alessio, Davide* Il racconto e la vita: *lectio biblica* come avventura della mente e del cuore. ScC 129 (2001) 103-144.

1327 **Dancy, John** The divine drama: the Old Testament as literature. C 2001, Lutterworth 800 pp. 0-7188-2987-5. Bibl. 795.

1328 *Dartigues, André* Théologie et esthétique. BLE 102 (2001) 95-110.

1329 *Delorme, Jean* La sémiotique littéraire interrogée par la bible. Sém-Bib 102, 103 (2001) 3-28, 3-21.

1330 **Dormeyer, Detlev** The New Testament among the writings of antiquity. ^T*Kossow, Rosemarie*: BiSe 55: 1998 ⇒14,1139; 16,1322. ^RRBLit 3 (2001) 314-316 (*Öhler, Markus*).

1331 **Dorsey, David A.** The literary structure of the Old Testament: a commentary on Genesis-Malachi. 1999 ⇒15,1664; 16,1323. ^RRBLit 3 (2001) 160-162 (*Lee, Won W.*).

1332 *Dumermuth, Carlo F.* Biblical literature: dreams and fiction. AJTh 15/1 (2001) 189-198.

1333 *Erlemann, Kurt* Anfänge, die das Ganze verbürgen: Überlegungen zu einer frühchristlichen Metapherngruppe. ThZ 57 £60-87.

1334 **Gabel, J.B.; Wheeler, C.B.; York, A.D.** The bible as literature: an introduction. ⁴2000 ⇒16,1324. ^RBiOr 58 (2001) 432-435 (*Van Peursen, Wido*).

1335 **Grelot, Pierre** Le langage symbolique dans la bible: enquête de sémantique et d'exégèse. Initiations bibliques: P 2001, Cerf 237 pp. €22.56. 2-204-06605-2. ^RCEv 117 (2001) 65-66 (*Gruson, P.*); RTL 32 (2001) 537-539 (*Wénin, André*); EeV 46 (2001) 19 (*Cothenet, Edouard*).

1336 *Gunkel, Hermann* Israelite literary history. Water for a thirsty land. Fortress classics in biblical studies: 2001 <1919> ⇒155. 31-41.

1337 **Haines-Eitzen, Kim** Guardians of letters: literacy, power, and the transmitters of early christian literature. 2000 ⇒16,1325. ^RRRT 8 (2001) 491-494 (*Royalty, Robert M.*).

1338 **Heyer, C.J. den; Schellihg, P.** Symbolen in de bijbel: woorden en hun betekenis. 2000 ⇒16,1327. ^RStr. 68 (2001) 375-376 (*Beentjes, Panc*).

1339 **Holland, Glenn S.** Divine irony. 2000 ⇒16,1328. ^RJThS 52 (2001) 704-706 (*McDonald, J.I.H.*).

1340 **Holzberg, Niklas** Die antike Fabel: eine Einführung. Da:Wiss ²2001 <1993>, v; 150 pp. €15.29. 3-534-15040-6.

1341 *Hovdelien, Olav* Moderne litteraturteori og teologisk eksegese. Ung teologi 34/1 (2001) 7-16.

1342 *Jobling, David* Methods of modern literary criticism. The Blackwell companion to the Hebrew Bible. 2001 ⇒653. 19-35.

1343 *Landy, Francis* On metaphor, play, and nonsense. Beauty and the enigma. JSOT.S 312: 2001 <1993>, ⇒171. 252-272.

1344 **Leezenberg, Michiel** Contexts of metaphor. Current Research in the Semantics/Pragmatics Interface 7: Amst 2001, Elsevier x; 321 pp. 0-08-043881-4. Bibl. 305-316.

1345 *Long, V. Philips* Reading the Old Testament as literature. Interpreting the OT. 2001 ⇒248. 85-123.

1346 *Mazzinghi, Luca* L'estetica della parola: l'arte narrativa e poetica nell'Antico Testamento. La bellezza. PSV 44: 2001 ⇒240. 79-92.

1347 *Mésoniat, Claudio* Il problema estetico del conflitto fra bibbia e poesia. La scrittura infinita. 2001 ⇒498. 5-14.

1348 **Moreschini, Claudio; Norelli, Enrico** Histoire de la littérature chrétienne antique grecque...latine, 1: de Paul...Constantin. ^T*Rousset, Madeleine*: 2000 ⇒16,1333. ^RRHPhR 81 (2001) 339-40 (*Prieur, J.-M.*).

1349 **Musche, Brigitte** Die Liebe in der altorientalischen Dichtung. 1999 ⇒15,1224; 16,1334. ^RBiOr 58 (2001) 151-152 (*Böck, Barbara*).

1350 **Niditch, Susan** Oral world and written word: ancient Israelite literature. 1996 ⇒12,896; 14,1149. ᴿOTEs 14 (2001) 354-356 (*Nel, Philip J.*).

1351 *Panier, Louis* Les sémitiques d'A.J. GREIMAS. SémBib 104 (2001)
55-67.

1352 *Panier, Louis* Du style pascal d'un récit de rencontre. SémBib 102
(2001) 57-66.

1353 *Paul, Ian* Metaphor and exegesis. ᶠTHISELTON, A. 2001 ⇒106. 387-
402.

1354 *Pénicaud, Anne* Vers une lecture figurative de la bible: les mutations
de la sémiotique biblique. RSR 89 (2001) 377-401.

1355 *Rölleke, Heinz* De numero XL: zu Charakter und Bedeutung der Zahl
40 in Bibel, Brauchtum und Literatur. CistC 108 (2001) 343-350.

1356 *Scarry, Elaine* The interior structure of made objects. The postmodern bible reader. 2001 <1985> ⇒287. 274-295.

1357 *Smolak, Kurt* Die Bibeldichtung als 'verfehlte Gattung'. La scrittura
infinita. 2001 ⇒498. 15-29.

1358 **Steinhart, Eric Charles** The logic of metaphor: analogous parts of
possible worlds. Synthese 299: Dordrecht 2001, Kluwer vii; 254 pp.
0-7923-7004-X. Bibl. 231-248.

1359 **Stenger, Hermann M.** Im Zeichen des Hirten und des Lammes: Mit-
gift und Gift biblischer Bilder. 2000 ⇒16,1343. ᴿDiak. 32 (2001)
148-150 (*Scharer, Matthias*).

1360 **Sternberg, Meir** Hebrews between cultures: group portraits and
national literature. 1998 ⇒15,1234. ᴿJBL 120 (2001) 739-741
(*Cohn, Robert L.*); RBLit 3 (2001) 172-174 (*Hamilton, Mark W.*).

1361 **Templeton, Douglas A.** The New Testament as true fiction: literature, literary criticism, aesthetics. 1999 ⇒15,1236; 16,1345. ᴿHeyJ
42 (2001) 500-501 (*Brigg, Richard*).

1362 *Thompson, Richard P.* Reading beyond the text: part 2: literary crea-
tivity and characterization in narrative religious texts of the Greco-
Roman world. Arc 29 (2001) 81-122.

1363 *Torres, Milton L.* The stripping of a cloak: a topos in classical and
biblical literature. Hermenêutíca 1 (2001) 45-54.

1364 *Vogels, Walter* The parallel-chiastic structure of the christian bible.
Theoforum 32 (2001) 203-221.

1365 *Vos, C.J.A.* Beeld- en simbooltaal. AcTh(B) 21/2 (2001) 136-144.

1366 *Weinberg, Joel* The phenomenon of 'authorship' in the literature of
the ancient Near East and the bible. ᶠAHITUV, S. 2001 ⇒1. 167-177.
H.

1367 **Weisman, Ze'ev** Political satire in the Bible. SBL.Semeia Studies 32:
1998 ⇒14,1154; 16,1351. ᴿJSSt 46 (2001) 146-147 (*Hens-Piazza,
Gina*).

1368 *Yonah, Shamir* Who's afraid of repetitions?: concerning one of the
patterns of repetition in biblical rhetoric. ᶠAHITUV, S. 2001 ⇒1. 234-
244. **H.**

1369 *Zaborowski, Holger* "Aber sprich nur ein Wort, so wird meine Seele
gesund": zur Theologie der Sprache und zur Sprache der Dichtung.
IKaZ 30 (2001) 58-76.

B4.5 **Influxus biblicus in litteraturam profanam**, *generalia*

1370 *Agosti, Gianfranco* L'epica biblica nella tarda antichità greca: autori
e lettori nel IV e V secolo. La scrittura infinita. 2001 ⇒498. 67-104.

1371 *Alberti, Luciano* 'Moses und Aron'. Il cinema e la bibbia. 2001 ⇒
496. 185-191.

1372 *Bañeza Román, Celso* El *exemplum* de los personajes bíblicos en las
listas de pecados capitales en la patrística y poetas medievales españoles. EE 76 (2001) 259-292.

1373 *Baude, Jeanne-Marie* Paroles de dieu, voix de la sagesse dans la poésie moderne. Le discours religieux. 2001 ⇒506. 373-390.

1374 *Bernabei, Ettore* La bibbia sul piccolo schermo;

1375 *Bernardi, Sandro* Le grandi metafore bibliche nel cinema: alcuni e-
sempi. Il cinema e la bibbia. 2001 ⇒496. 193-197/61-71.

1376 **Billanovich, Giuseppe** Dal medioevo all'umanesimo: la riscoperta
dei classici. ᴱ*Pellegrini, Paolo*: Humanae litterae 1: Mi 2001, CUSL
vii; 164 pp. 88-8132-117-3.

1377 *Bonati, Sabrina; Bernardelli, Milena* Sirene e altri esseri fantastici
dalla bibbia ai testi armeni. Pensiero e istituzioni. 2001 ⇒580. 79-
100.

1378 *Brant, Jo-Ann A.* The sword, the stone and the Holy Grail. ᶠJANZEN,
W. 2001 ⇒54. 165-174.

1379 *Casaretto, Francesco Mosetti* Il genere pastorale e la bibbia: ambiguità dell'immaginario e ridefinizione cristiana del modulo narrativo in
epoca carolingia. La scrittura infinita. 2001 ⇒498. 339-357.

1380 *Chiamenti, Massimiliano* Il modulo della negazione: sul filo di *bibbi-
a-fiore-commedia*. La scrittura infinita. 2001 ⇒498. 187-192.

1381 *Corsani, Alberto* L'asino di Bresson. Il cinema e la bibbia. 2001 ⇒
496. 147-149.

1382 *Cruz Palma, Oscar de la* El tratamiento de las citas de los salmos en
el *Barlaam et Iosaphat*. La scrittura infinita. 2001 ⇒498. 591-599.

1383 *D'Alatri, Alessandro* 'I giardini dell'Eden'. Il cinema e la bibbia.
2001 ⇒496. 199-204.

1384 *D'Ottavi, Stefania D'Agata* Immagine e parola: il poema onirico tar-
do-medievale inglese. La scrittura infinita. 2001 ⇒498. 193-211.

1385 *D'Angelo, Edoardo* La coscienza degli assassini: citazione scritturale
riflessione metalinguistica nei prologhi agiografici suditaliani dei secoli IX e X. La scrittura infinita. 2001 ⇒498. 47-65.

1386 *De Benedetti, Paolo* Un libro da vedere e da raccontare;

1387 *Farassino, Alberto* Godard, il profeta;

1388 *Fava, Claudio G.* La storia del cinema e il 'libro dei libri'. Il cinema
e la bibbia. 2001 ⇒496. 31-35/173-182/23-29.

1389 *Finch, Ann* A star over Bethlehem: from Advent to the Epiphany.
Hyde Park, NY 2001, New City 143 pp. $12. 1-56548-141-0 [ThD
49,87—Heiser, W. Charles].

1390 *Fink, Guido* Le acque della contraddizione: dall'immagine biblica
all'immagine cinematografica. Il cinema...bibbia. 2001 ⇒496. 37-43.

1391 *Frantzen, Allen J.* Tears for Abraham: the Chester play of Abraham
and Isaac and antisacrifice in works by Wilfred Owen, Benjamin
Britten, and Derek Jarman. JMEMS 31 (2001) 445-476.

1392 *Gellner, Christoph* "Geheiligt werde dein zugefrorener Name ...":
moderne Psalmgedichte—spirituell gelesen. BiKi 56 (2001) 46-51.

1393 *Giannarelli, Elena* La poesia sui santi nella tarda antichità: il ruolo
della scrittura. La scrittura infinita. 2001 ⇒498. 303-316.

1394 *Gonnelli, Fabrizio* Le sacre scritture e i generi poetici a Bisancio. La
scrittura infinita. 2001 ⇒498. 393-429.

1395 *Hallam, Paul* From *The book of Sodom*. The postmodern bible
reader. 2001 <1993> ⇒287. 233-246.

1396 Hill, Thomas D. 'The ballad of St Stephen and Herod': biblical his-
      tory and medieval popular religious culture. MAe 70 (2001) 240-249.
1397 **Kasack, Wolfgang** Christus in der russischen Literatur: ein Gang
      durch ihre Geschichte von den Anfängen bis zum Ende des 20. Jahr-
      hunderts. Stu 2000, Urachhaus 409 pp. €30.
1398 ᴱ**Knight, Alan E.** Les mystères de la procession de Lille: le penta-
      teuque. Textes littéraires français 535: Genève 2001, Droz 630 pp.
      FS80. 2-600-00492-0.
1399 Langenhorst, Georg Theologie und Literatur 2001—eine Standortbe-
      stimmung. StZ 219 (2001) 121-132.
1400 **Layzer, Varese** Signs of weakness: juxtaposing Irish tales and the bi-
      ble. JSOT.S 321: Shf 2001, Sheffield A. 241 pp. 1-84127-172-1.
      Bibl. 224-236.
1401 Levi della Torre, Stefano Il linguaggio del volto nella bibbia: proble-
      mi di traduzione figurativa e cinematografica. Il cinema e la bibbia.
      2001 ⇒496. 73-81.
1402 **Lobrichon, Guy** La poésie biblique, instrument théologique: les para-
      phrases bibliques (XIIᵉ-XIIIᵉ siècles). La scrittura infinita. 2001 ⇒
      498. 155-176.
1403 **Maier, Paul** Pilatus: historischer Roman. Zoetermeer 2001, Mozaiek
      422 pp. €19.29. 90-239-9033-1.
1404 ᴱ**Millward, Celia** La estorie del evangelie: a parallel-text edition.
      1998 ⇒15,1266. ᴿSpec. 76 (2001) 764 (Izydorczyk, Zbigniew).
1405 Moses, Gavriel La bibbia nel cinema americano contemporaneo. Il
      cinema e la bibbia. 2001 ⇒496. 97-116.
1406 Nazzaro, Antonio V. Poesia biblica come espressione teologica: fra
      tardoantico e altomedioevo;
1407 Necchi, Elena Richiami biblici in due epitafi per Alessandro Magno;
1408 Orazi, Veronica Riflessi di simbologia biblica nella literatura de de-
      bate spagnola medievale (sec. XIII). La scrittura infinita. 2001 ⇒
      498. 119-153/581-590/359-391.
1409 Pellizzari, Lorenzo Perfidi fratelli: il kolossal biblico tra Cecil B.
      DeMille e John Huston. Il cinema e la bibbia. 2001 ⇒496. 117-128.
1410 Petringa, Maria Rosaria La fortuna del poema dell'"Heptateuchos"
      tra VII e IX secolo. La scrittura infinita. 2001 ⇒498. 511-536.
1411 Pinsent, Pat Some reflections of millenarianism in seventeenth-
      century literature. Faith in the millennium. 2001 ⇒540. 409-422.
1412 Pistoia, Marco Storia di un film mai nato: il 'San Paolo' di Pier
      Paolo Pasolini. Il cinema e la bibbia. 2001 ⇒496. 159-172.
1413 Pittaluga, Stefano Immagini bibliche nella poesia profana mediola-
      tina. La scrittura infinita. 2001 ⇒498. 291-302.
1414 Privat, Jean-Marie La "parodia sacra" dans Boule-de-suif;
1415 Richard, Jean Discours religieux, discours théologique et discours
      littéraire. Le discours religieux. 2001 ⇒506. 189-197/111-122.
1416 Ropa, Giampaolo L'immaginario biblico nella lirica liturgica. La
      scrittura infinita. 2001 ⇒498. 261-290.
1417 Sargent, Joe 'Abramo'. Il cinema e la bibbia. 2001 ⇒496. 205-207.
1418 Sarrazin, Bernard Parodies du discours religieux: de l'ambivalence
      carnavalesque à l'ambiguïté moderne. Le discours religieux. 2001 ⇒
      506. 171-188.
1419 Scardigli, Piergiuseppe Cantori biblici fra Inghilterra e Germania;
1420 Schmidt, Paul Gerhard La bibbia versificata: i testi mediolatini. La
      scrittura infinita. 2001 ⇒498. 433-447/449-457.

1421 *Shapira, Dan* On biblical quotations in Pahlavi. Henoch 23 (2001) 175-183.
1422 *Singh, Amardeep* A Pisgah sight of Ireland: religious embodiment and colonalism in Ulysses. Semeia 88 (2001) 129-147.
1423 *Socci, Stefano* Icone bibliche nel cinema. Il cinema e la bibbia. 2001 ⇒496. 83-93.
1424 *Sonnet, Jean-Pierre* La bible et la littérature de l'occident: langue mère, loi du père et descendance littéraire. LV.F 56 (2001) 375-389.
1425 *Spagnoletti, Giovanni* Un laico politico cinematografico: 'il decalogo' di Krzystof Kieslowski;
1426 *Stefani, Piero* La via delle grandi metafore: Eden, Babele, Esodo, Apocalisse. Il cinema e la bibbia 2001 ⇒496. 151-157/45-60.
1427 *Sturbaut, Françoise* La chute ou la parole d'un "prophète vide pour temps médiocres". Le discours religieux. 2001 ⇒506. 199-215.
1428 *Taddei, Nazareno* La metafora della passione: Dreyer, Bergman, Tarkovskij. Il cinema e la bibbia. 2001 ⇒496. 129-145.
1429 *Vannier, Marie-Anne* Les résonances contemporaines du langage Eckhartien. Le discours religieux. 2001 ⇒506. 71-80.
1430 *Vray, Jean-Bernard* Anna, soror... ou La bible et le tiroir. Le discours religieux. 2001 ⇒506. 289-312.
1431 *Zielińska, Beata* Literatura jako praeparatio evangelica [La littérature comme praeparatio evangelica]. PrzPow 118 (2001) 335-345.
1432 **Ziolkowski, Eric Jozef** Evil children in religion, literature, and art. Cross-currents in religion and culture: Houndmills 2001, Palgrave xvii; 253 pp. 0-333-91895-9.

B4.6 *Singuli auctores*—Bible influence on individual authors

1433 BAYLE; VOLTAIRE: *Robert, Philippe de* Bayle et Voltaire devant la bible. Le discours religieux. 2001 ⇒506. 139-153.
1434 BOCCACCIO: *Pisani Salerni, Maria* Echi di Geremia nel *Filocolo* del Boccaccio (seconda parte). Vivarium 9 (2001) 521-529.
1435 BRONTE C: **Meeks, Mary Frances** Visions of a new heaven and a new earth: inheritance, marriage, and revelation in the novels of Charlotte Bronte. Diss. Drew 2001, 207 pp. 3005861.
1436 BULHAKOWA M: *Krawiecka, Ewa* Apokalipsa według Michaiła Bułhakowa: przestrzeń biblijno-apokaliptyczna *Mistrza i Małgorzaty*. [F]JANKOWSKI, A. 2001 ⇒53. 204-212.
1437 CELAN P; PAGIS D; RÜBNER T: *Lorenz-Lindemann, Karin* Die Tore von Frage-und-Antwort sind verschlossen: Klage im Werk von Paul Celan, Dan Pagis und Tuvia Rübner. JBTh 16 (2001) 233-266.
1438 CHAUCER G: **Wheeler, Lyle Kip** 'Of pilgrims and parables': the influence of the Vulgate parables on Chaucer's 'Canterbury Tales'. Diss. Oregon 2001, 261 pp. 3024538.
1439 CIXOUS H: *Cixous, Hélène* Dreaming in 1990. The postmodern bible reader. 2001 <1993> ⇒287. 117-127.
1440 CLAUDEL G: *Chaudier, Stéphane* Claudel, Grosjean: La passion selon (saint) Pilate. Le discours religieux. 2001 ⇒506. 251-267.
1441 DANTE: **Hawkins, Peter S.** Dante's testaments: essays in scriptural imagination. 1999 ⇒15,1294. [R]ChH 70 (2001)158-160 (*Ferrante, Joan M.*); MAe 70 (2001) 156-157 (*Armour, Peter*);
1442 *Leonardi, Anna Maria Chiavacci* Il tema biblico dell'esilio nella *Divina Commedia*. La scrittura infinita. 2001 ⇒498. 177-185.

1443 DAUMAL R: *Heyer, René* "Je suis mort [...], on vit": sur on poème de René Daumal. Le discours religieux. 2001 ⇒506. 239-250.

1444 D'AUREVILLY B: *Koopman-Thurlings, Mariska* Rêve d'angélisme et héros prométhéen: le catholicisme dans l'oeuvre de Barbey d'Aurevilly: apologie ou parodie?. Le discours religieux. 2001 ⇒506. 155-69.

1445 DESMARETS de Saint-Sorlin J: **Desmarets de Saint-Sorlin, J.** Marie-Madeleine ou le triomphe de la grâce. [E]*Banderier, G.* Grenoble 2001, Millon 219 pp. €9.50.

1446 DICKINSON E: *Edwards, Cliff* The Bible through a poet's prism: reading Emily Dickinson's poems as revelation continued. BiRe 17/2 (2001) 38-42.

1447 ELIOT G: *Hodgson, Peter C.* George Eliot's religious pilgrimage. [F]DIETRICH, W. BJSt 329: 2001 ⇒24. 92-119;

1448 **Hodgson, Peter C.** Theology in the fiction of George Eliot. L 2001, SCM x; 244 pp. £18. [R]NBl 82 (2001) 291-293 (*Edney, Mark*).

1449 ELIOT T: *Rosaye, Jean P.* De l'idée d'absolu au Verbe: l'herméneutique de T.S. Eliot. Graphè 10 (2001) 159-180 [Jn 1,1-18].

1450 FLAMINIO M: *Bottai, Monica* Bibbia e modelli classici nella parafrasi salmica del Flaminio. La scrittura infinita. 2001 ⇒498. 105-115.

1451 GERMAIN S: *Michel, Raymond* Sylvie Germain: Tobie des Marais ou le secret du texte. Le discours religieux. 2001 ⇒506. 331-372.

1452 GERSON J: *Placanica, Antonio* Tradizione, esegesi e teologia nella *Iosephina* di Giovanni Gerson (il *trinubium* di Sant'Anna, la genealogia di Cristo, le nozze di Maria e Giuseppe). La scrittura infinita. 2001 ⇒498. 213-257.

1453 GIONO J: *Henky, Danièle* Reprise de l'apocalypse comme motif littéraire dans l'oeuvre de Jean Giono. Le discours religieux. 2001 ⇒506. 217-238.

1454 GOETHE: *Ullendorff, Edward* Goethe on Hebrew. [M]WEITZMAN, M. JSOT.S 333: 2001 ⇒113. 470-475.

1455 GREEN J: *Thinès, Georges* La quête du sens dans "Léviathan". MSR 58/3 (2001) 7-12.

1456 HAWTHORNE N: *Poole, Gordon* Il contesto biblico de *La casa dei sette comignoli*. [M]CAGNI, L., 4. SMDSA 61: 2001 ⇒15. 1983-1990.

1457 LA TOUR DU PIN P DE: *Renaud-Chamska, Isabelle* Les fondements johanniques d'"'Une somme de poésie" de Patrice de La Tour du Pin. Graphè 10 (2001) 199-217 [Jn 1,1-18].

1458 LAWRENCE D: *Julien, Jacques* L'écrivain D.H. Lawrence, lecteur de l'Apocalypse. SR 30 (2001) 35-50. Rés., sum. 35.

1459 LEOPARDI G: *Cerbo, Anna* Il libro della *Genesi* nell'*Inno ai patriarchi* di Giacomo Leopardi. [M]CAGNI L., 3. SMDSA 61: 2001 ⇒15. 1401-1422.

1460 MARCABRU: *Lazzerini, Lucia* Presenze bibliche nella poesia trobadorica: un'ipotesi sul dittico marcabruniano dell'*Estornel*. La scrittura infinita. 2001 ⇒498. 459-492.

1461 MILLER A: *Theobald, Maria* Zwischen Paradies und Gericht: biblisch inspirierte Themen und Motive in Arthur Millers Drama "After the Fall". [F]SCHMUTTERMAYR G: 2001 ⇒101. 609-624.

1462 MILON: *Bottiglieri, Corinna* L'utilizzazione della bibbia nella *Vita sancti Amandi metrica* di Milone di Saint-Amand. La scrittura infinita. 2001 ⇒498. 317-337.

1463 MILTON J: **Shoulson, Jeffrey** Milton and the rabbis: Hebraism, Hellenism, and christianity. NY 2001, Columbia Univ. Pr. 340 pp. $19.50. 0-2311-2329-9;

1464 **Wood, Derek N.C.** Exiled from divine light: law, morality, and violence in Milton's *Samson Agonistes*. Toronto 2001, Univ. of Toronto Pr. 247 pp. $55. 0-8020-4848X.

1465 PERSE S: *Kopenhagen-Urian, Judith* Anatomie du "Verbe-qui-s'est-fait-chair" dans l'oeuvre de Saint-John Perse face à la tropologie d'ELIOT et de CLAUDEL. Graphè 10 (2001) 181-198 [Jn 1,1-18].

1466 POMILIO M: *Ferroni, Giulio* Il vangelo senza fine: *Il quinto evangelio* di Mario Pomilio. Com(I) 179 (2001) 68-76.

1467 PROUST: ^E**Anguissola, Alberto Beretta** Proust e la bibbia. Pinnacoli 19: 1999 ⇒15,1309. ^RRdT 42 (2001) 463-466 (*Marucci, Franco*).

1468 ROTH J; KASCHNITZ M: *Kuschel, Karl-Josef* "Ein Gleichgültiger hadert nicht": zur Funktion der Anklage Gottes bei Joseph Roth und Marie Luise Kaschnitz. JBTh 16 (2001) 209-231.

1469 ROUBAUD J: *Jérusalem, Christine* Quête spirituelle et enquête policière dans la trilogie *La belle Hortense* de Jacques Roubaud. Le discours religieux. 2001 ⇒506. 269-287.

1470 ROUSSEAU J; REMBRANDT: *Bal, Mieke* Body politic. The postmodern bible reader. 2001 <1994> ⇒287. 142-158 [Judg 19].

1471 SACHS N: *Dust, Silke* "Zu Gott verrenkt"—die Jakobsgeschichte in der Lyrik der Nelly Sachs—ein spannungsvolles theologisches Gespräch. LS 52 (2001) 117-121 [Gen 32,23-32].

1472 SADE D DE: **Schmid, Muriel** Le soufre au bord de la chair: Sade et l'évangile. Genève 2001, Labor et F. 179 pp. €22.87. 2-8309-0986-0. ^REeV 46 (2001) 23-24 (*Wattiaux, Henri*).

1473 SALFI F: *Borrelli, Clara* Saul dal *Primo libro dei Re* al melodramma di Francesco Saverio Salfi. ^MCAGNI L., 3. SMDSA 61: 2001 ⇒15. 1303-1317.

1474 SERRES M: *Serres, Michel* Meals among brothers: theory of the joker. Postmodern bible reader. 2001 <1982> ⇒287. 265-273 [Gn 38-50].

1475 SHAKESPEARE W: **Kaston, David Scott** Shakespeare and the Book. C 2001, CUP 167 pp. $55. 0-521-781-396;

1476 **Marx, Steven** Shakespeare and the bible. 2000 ⇒16,1409. ^RSCJ 32 (2001) 217-218 (*Spencer, Janet M.*);

1477 *Beauregard, David N.* Shakespeare and the bible. Religion and the arts 5/3 (2001) 317-330.

1478 SILONE I: *Guerriero, Elio* Il linguaggio biblico-simbolico di Silone e la sua permanenza in Svizzera. RTLu 6 (2001) 543-552.

1479 STEINBECK J: *Gilmore, Alec* John Steinbeck. ET 112 (2001) 192-196.

1480 TAREEV M: **Röhrig, Hermann-Josef** Kenosis: die Versuchungen Jesu Christi im Denken von Michail M. Tareev. EThSt 77: 2000 ⇒16, 1412. ^REThL 77 (2001) 499-500 (*Brito, E.*).

1481 THIONG'O N: *Anonby, John A.* Grim present, glorious future: millennial implications in the novels of Ngugi wa Thiong'o. Faith in the millennium. 2001 ⇒540. 372-386.

1482 VIGÉE C: *Frank, Évelyne* Claude Vigée: une poétique biblique. Le discours religieux. 2001 ⇒506. 391-406.

1483 VOLTAIRE: **Bessire, François** La bible dans la correspondance de Voltaire. 1999 ⇒15,1319. ^RCrSt 22 (2001) 261-262 (*Pitassi, Maria-Cristina*).

1484 WALZER M: *Stout, Jeffrey* Walzer on Exodus and prophecy. ^FDIETRICH W. BJSt 329: 2001 ⇒24. 307-338.

1485 WIESEL E: *Nadeau, Jean-Guy* Le masque de la citation quand les théologiens citent Élie Wiesel. Discours religieux. 2001 ⇒506. 123-37;

1486 **Van den Berg, Gundula** Gebrochene Variationen: Beobachtungen und Überlegungen zu Figuren der Hebräischen Bibel in der Rezeption von Elie Wiesel. Altes Testament und Moderne 7: Müns 2001, Lit 311 pp. 3-8258-5377-2.

B4.7 *Interpretatio* psychiatrica

1487 *Craddock, Ida* Sexuell-magnetische Kräfte;
1488 Seelische Heirat (Auszug): Gemeinschaft mit dem Göttlichen als drittem Partner in der ehelichen Vereinigung. Irreale Glaubensinhalte. 2001 ⇒1066. 53/57-58.
1489 **Donoghue, Paul J.** The Jesus advantage: a new approach to a fuller life. ND 2001, Ave Maria 190 pp. $13. 0-87793-703-6 [ThD 48, 265—Heiser, W. Charles].
1490 **Drewermann, Eugen** Psychanalyse et exégèse, 1: la vérité des formes: rêves, mythes, contes, sagas et légendes. ᵀ*Trierweiler, Denis*: 2000 ⇒16,1420. ᴿSR 30 (2001) 101-103 (*Pelletier, Pierre*);
1491 Hat der Glaube Hoffnung?: von der Zukunft der Religion am Beginn des 21. Jahrhunderts. 2000 ⇒16,1421. ᴿActBib 38 (2001) 210-202 (*Boada, J.*);
1492 Psychanalyse et exégèse, 2: miracles, visions, prophéties, apocalypses, paraboles. ᵀ*Bagot, Jean-Pierre*: P 2001, Seuil 648 pp. €28.20. 2-02-026059-X.
1493 *Forest, Jean* De quelle oreille lire l'Écriture avec FREUD?. LV.F 56 (2001) 391-400.
1494 ᴱ**Kessler, Rainer; Vandermeersch, Patrick** God, biblical stories and psychoanalytic understanding. Fra 2001, Lang 198 pp. 3-631-37641-3.
1495 *Lacan, Jacques* Introduction to the names-of-the-father seminar. The postmodern bible reader. 2001 <1990> ⇒287. 102-116.
1496 **Merkur, Dan** The mystery of manna: the psychedelic sacrament of the bible. 2000 ⇒16,1425. ᴿReligion 31 (2001) 105-108 (*Ruck, Carl A.*) [Ex 16].
1497 *Philippo, Michel* Le biblique n'est pas accessible en solitaire: comment Balmary relit la bible?. LV.F 56 (2001) 401-412.
1498 **Polka, Brayton** Depth psychology interpretation and the bible: an ontological essay on FREUD. Montreal 2001, McGill xviii; 397 pp.
1499 **Rollins, Wayne Gilbert** Soul and psyche: the bible in psychological perspective. 1999 ⇒15,1326. ᴿNewTR 14 (2001) 90-91 (*Harrington, Daniel J.*); ThTo 58 (2001) 260-261 (*Cosgrove, Mark P.*).
1500 **Schnelzer, Thomas** Archetyp und Offenbarung: die Archetypenlehre ...JUNGs im Rahmen von E. DREWERMANNs Offenbarungskonzeption. APPSR 49: 1999 ⇒15,1327. ᴿActBib 38 (2001) 59-60 (*Boada, J.*).

B5 Methodus exegeticus

1501 **Amador, J. David Hester** Academic constraints in rhetorical criticism of the New Testament: an introduction to a rhetoric of power. JSNT.S 174: 1999 ⇒15,4505; 16,1431. ᴿJBL 120 (2001) 373-376 (*Carey, Greg*); CBQ 63 (2001) 134-136 (*Watson, Duane F.*).
1502 *Artus, Olivier* Quel statut pour l'exégèse historico-critique?. La bible, parole adressée. 2001 ⇒323. 155-172.

1503 *Avalos, Hector* Rubel Shelly's "Prepare to answer" as a case study in current christian apologetics. JHiC 8/1 (2001) 18-40.
1504 *Barthe, Claude* Le rationalisme de l'exégèse biblique: apurer les comptes. Catholica 71 (2001) 96-100.
1505 ^E**Barthe, Claude** L'Éxégèse chrétienne aujourd'hui. 2000 ⇒16, 1434. ^RRThom 101 (2001) 673-675 (*Bazelaire, Thomas-M. de*).
1506 *Bergen, Wesley J.* Can new methods free us to listen to the Old Testament?. ^FJANZEN, W. 2001 ⇒54. 67-82.
1507 *Blanchard, Yves-Marie* La théorie des sens de l'écriture. La bible, parole adressée. 2001 ⇒323. 119-138.
1508 **Brandscheidt, Renate** Theologie betreiben—Glaube ins Gespräch bringen: Exegese des Alten Testamentes. ^E*Kunzler, Michael; Gerosa, Libero*: Pd 2001, Bonifatius 88 pp. €8.90. 3-89710-180-7.
1509 *Byrskog, Samuel* Talet, minnet och skriften: evangelietraditionen och den antika informationsteknologin. SEÅ 66 (2001) 139-150.
1510 **Classen, Carl Joachim** Rhetorical criticism of the NT. WUNT 128: 2000 ⇒16,145. ^RRHPhR 81 (2001) 233-234 (*Grappe, Ch.*).
1511 *Conradie, Ernst M.* What are interpretative strategies?. Scriptura 78 (2001) 429-441.
1512 *Conradie, Ernst M.; Jonker, Louis C.* Determining relative adequacy in biblical interpretation. Scriptura 78 (2001) 448-455.
1513 **Corsani, Bruno** Come interpretare un testo biblico. Piccola collana moderna, serie biblica 90: T 2001, Claudiana 150 pp. 88-7016-392X.
1514 *Ellis, Edward Earle* Historical-literary criticism—after two hundred years. History and interpretation. BiblInterp 54: 2001 ⇒141. 1-16;
1515 Dating the New Testament. History and interpretation. BiblInterp 54: 2001 ⇒141. 31-51.
1516 **Fee, Gordon D.** Exegese van het Nieuwe Testament: een praktische handleiding. Zoetermeer 2001, Boekencentrum 192 pp. €18.50. 90-2390-7175.
1517 **Fenske, Wolfgang** Arbeitsbuch zur Exegese des Neuen Testaments: ein Proseminar. 1999 ⇒15,1349. ^RSNTU.A 25 (2000) 269-271 (*Fuchs, Albert*).
1518 **Gorman, Michael J.** Elements of biblical exegesis: a basic guide for students and ministers. Peabody 2001, Hendrickson 239 pp. $17. 1-56563-485-3. ^RRExp 98 (2001) 441-442 (*Jones, Barry A.*).
1519 *Groß, Walter* Ist biblisch-theologische Auslegung ein integrierender Methodenschritt?. Wieviel Systematik?. 2001 ⇒283. 110-149.
1520 *Günther, Andreas* Wie viele Schwalben machen einen Sommer?: Multiples Testen oder Signifikanzen-Fischen. BN 106 (2001) 28-32.
1521 *Hardmeier, Christof* Zur Quellenevidenz biblischer Texte und archäologischer Befunde: falsche Fronten und ein neues Gespräch zwischen alttestamentlicher Literaturwissenschaft und Archäologie. Steine–Bilder–Texte. 2001 ⇒613. 11-24.
1522 **Hochschild, Ralph** Sozialgeschichtliche Exegese. NTOA 42: 1999 ⇒15,1361. ^RBZ 45 (2001) 124-126 (*Schmeller, Thomas*); ThRv 97 (2001) 309-310 (*Dormeyer, Detlev*); JThS 52 (2001) 849-854 (*Horrell, David G.*); EstB 59 (2001) 415-416 (*González García, F.*); CBQ 63 (2001) 749-751 (*Malina, Bruce J.*); ThLZ 126 (2001) 1154-1155 (*Rebell, Walter*).
1523 *Hughes, Paul Edward* Compositional history. Interpreting the OT. 2001 ⇒248. 221-244.
1524 *Hurley, Robert* La critique biblique et la construction du vrai. Le discours religieux. 2001 ⇒506. 29-48.

1525 **Jack, Alison** Texts reading texts, sacred and secular: two postmodern perspectives. JSNT.S 179: 1999 ⇒15,4507. ᴿRBLit 3 (2001) 330-334 (*Royalty, Robert M.*).

1526 *Jonker, Louis* Social transformation and biblical interpretation: a comparative study. Scriptura 77 (2001) 259-286.

1527 *Kremer, Jacob* Das leere Grab—ein Zeichen: zur Relevanz der historisch-kritischen Exegese für die kirchliche Verkündigung. ThPQ 149 (2001) 136-145.

1528 ᴱ**Kreuzer, Siegfried**, *al.*, Proseminar—Altes Testament: ein Arbeitsbuch. 1999 ⇒15,1365. ᴿBZ 45 (2001) 309-311 (*Baumgart, Norbert*); ThLZ 126 (2001) 513-515 (*Schart, Aaron*).

1529 **Krispenz, Jutta** Literarkritik und Stilstatistik im Alten Testament: eine Studie zur literarkritischen Methode, durchgeführt an Texten aus den Büchern Jeremia, Ezechiel und 1 Könige. BZAW 307: B 2001, De Gruyter ix; 251 pp. €85.90. 3-11-017057-4. Bibl. 216-240.

1530 *Langner, Cordula* De las posibilidades de comunicar la palabra de Dios y de malentenderla. Qol 27 (2001) 47-58.

1531 **Linnemann, Eta** Biblical criticism on trial: how scientific is 'scientific theology'?. ᵀ*Yarbrough, Robert*: GR 2001, Kregel 217 pp. $15. 032-8254-3088-7 [ThD 49,274—W. Charles Heiser].

1532 *Loubser, J.A.* Reconciling rhetorical criticism with its oral roots. Neotest. 35 (2001) 95-110.

1533 **Masini, Mario** La lectio divina: teología, espiritualidad, método. ᵀ*Rodríguez, A.* Estudios y ensayos, espiritualidad 18: M 2001, Biblioteca de Autores Cristianos 436 pp. 84-7914-577-3.

1534 **Meynet, Roland** Wprowadzenie do hebrajskiej retoryki biblijnej. Mysl Teologiczna 30: Kraków 2001, Wydawnictwo WAM 223 pp. 83-7097-813-4. Bibl. 216-220. **P.**

1535 **Nahkola, Aulikki** Double narratives in the Old Testament: the foundations of method in biblical criticism. BZAW 290: B 2001, De Gruyter xii; 226 pp. 3-11-016731-X. Bibl. 197-214.

1536 *Nel, M.* Semiotiese ontleding as nuttige en noodsaaklike eksegetiese hulpmiddel. OTEs 14 (2001) 89-101.

1537 *Oberlinner, Lorenz; Häfner, Gerd* Neuere Entwicklungen in der Exegese des Neuen Testaments. LS 52 (2001) 282-289.

1538 **Ochs, Peter** PEIRCE, pragmatism and the logic of scripture. 1998 ⇒ 14,1208; 15,1381. ᴿHeyJ 42 (2001) 411-414 (*Adams, Nicholas*); ProEc 10 (2001) 496-498 (*Fodor, Jim*).

1539 *Pippin, Tina* Issues in: biblical exegesis and interpretation. QR 21 (2001) 425-431.

1540 **Powell, Mark Allan** Chasing the eastern star: adventures in biblical reader-response criticism. LVL 2001, Westminster (8); 249 pp. 0-664-22278-1.

1541 *Raurell, Frederic* Més enllà de la lletra, però no sense la lletra: lectura del text bíblic. QVC 201 (2001) 46-61.

1542 *Reichert, Angelika* Offene Fragen zur Auslegung neutestamentlicher Texte im Spiegel neuerer Methodenbücher. ThLZ 126 (2001) 993-1006.

1543 **Reiser, Marius** Sprache und literarische Formen des Neuen Testaments: eine Einführung. UTB für Wissenschaft 2197: Pd 2001, Schöningh xiv; 257 pp. €14.90. 3-506-99451-4. Bibl. 224-241.

1544 *Rico, Christophe* Synchronie et diachronie: enjeu d'une dichotomie: de la linguistique à l'interprétation de la bible. RB 108 (2001) 228-265.

1545 *Sale, Giovanni* HARNACK, LOISY e il dibattito sul metodo storico-critico. CivCatt 152/1 (2001) 36-49.

1546 *Sanday, William* Methods of theology: the historical method. Essays in biblical criticism. JSNT.S 225: 2001 <1897> ⇒205. 22-27.

1547 **Schertz, Mary H.; Yoder, Perry B.** Seeing the text: exegesis for students of Greek and Hebrew. Nv 2001, Abingdon 220 pp. $19 [BiTod 40,130—Bergant, D.].

1548 **Schiappa, E.** The beginnings of rhetorical theory in classical Greece. 1999 ⇒15,1388. ᴿCIR 51 (2001) 60-61 (*Hesk, Jon*).

1549 **Seeley, D.** Deconstructing the New Testament. BiblInterp 5: 1994 ⇒ 11/2,1372. ᴿSNTU.A 22 (1997) 229-231 (*Öhler, M.*).

1550 *Soggin, Jan Alberto* Fondamentalismo: un'indagine terminologica. ᴹCAGNI, L., 4. SMDSA 61: 2001 ⇒15. 2143-2152.

1551 **Söding, Thomas** Wege der Schriftauslegung: Methodenbuch zum Neuen Testament. 1998 ⇒16,1492. ᴿRBLit 3 (2001) 334-336 (*Schnabel, Eckhard J.*).

1552 **Steck, Odil Hannes** Old Testament exegesis: a guide to the methodology. ᵀ*Nogalski, James D.*: SBL Resources for Biblical Study 39: 1998 ⇒14,1221. ᴿLouvSt 26 (2001) 367-368 (*Eynikel, Erik*).

1553 **Stuart, Douglas** Old Testament exegesis: a handbook for students and pastors. LVL ³2001, Westminster xx; 179 pp. $15. 066422315X.

1554 *Talstra, Eep; Bosma, Carl J.* Psalm 67: blessing, harvest and history: a proposal for exegetical methodology. CTJ 36 (2001) 290-313.

1555 *Turiot, Cécile; Gagey, Henri-Jérôme* Bible et figure. La bible, parole adressée. 2001 ⇒323. 139-154.

1556 **Untergaßmair, Franz G.** Exegese des Neuen Testaments. ᴱ*Kunzler, Michael; Gerosa, Libero*: Theologie betreiben—Glaube ins Gespräch bringen 6: Pd 2001, Bonifatius 96 pp. €8.90. 3-89710-185-8.

1557 *Wells, George A.* Pentecostal mutterings and evangelical blandishments. JHiC 8/1 (2001) 41-48.

1558 **Weren, Wim J.C.** Finestre su Gesù: metodologia dell'esegesi dei vangeli. ᵀ*Soggin, Thomas*: Strumenti 8: T 2001, Claudiana 284 pp. 88-7016-387-3. Bibl. 263-266.

1559 **Witherup, Ronald D.** Biblical fundamentalism: what every catholic should know. ColMn 2001, Liturgical xiv; 90 pp. $9. 0-8146-2722-6. Bibl. 87-90 [BiTod 40,66—Senior, Donald].

III. Critica Textus, Versiones

D1 Textual Criticism

1560 Bibliothecae Apostolicae Vaticanae Codex Vaticanus graecus 1209... Cod. Vaticanus B. 1999 ⇒15,1410. Fascimile a colori, vol. annesso di 'Prolegomena'. ᴿStPat 48 (2001) 688-693 (*Leonardi, Giovanni*).

1561 **Letis, Theodore P.** The ecclesiastical text: text criticism, biblical authority and the popular mind. ²2000 <1997> ⇒16,1506. ᴿNT 43 (2001) 397-398 (*Elliott, J.K.*).

D2.1 *Biblia Hebraica* **Hebrew text**

1562 *Baker, David W.* Language and text of the Old Testament. Interpreting the OT. 2001 ⇒248. 63-83.
1563 *Blok, Hanna* Chronicle: a bible translation to be read aloud. [F]DEURLOO, K. ACEBT.S 2: 2001 ⇒23. 375-386.
1564 *Dempster, Stephen* From many texts to one: the formation of the Hebrew Bible. [F]DION, P.-E., 1. JSOT.S 324: 2001 ⇒25. 19-56.
1565 [E]**Dotan, Aron** Biblia Hebraica Leningradensia: prepared according to the vocalization, accents, and masora of Aaron ben Moses BEN A-SHER in the Leningrad Codex. Peabody, MASS 2001, Hendrickson xxv; 1264 pp. $50. 1-56563-089-0. [R]CBQ 63 (2001) 716-718 (*O'Connor, M.*).
1566 *Fernández Tejero, Emilia* El texto hebreo del Antiguo Testamento. ResB 31 (2001) 5-14.
1567 *Gelston, Anthony* The ancient versions of the Hebrew Bible: their nature and significance. [M]WEITZMAN, M. JSOT.S 333: 2001 ⇒113. 148-164.
1568 *Haug, Hellmut* Zur abweichenden Kapitel und Verszählung im Alten Testament: ein Fund aus der Hinterlassenschaft von Eberhard NESTLE. ZAW 113 (2001) 618-623..
1569 *Himbaza, Innocent* Quelle massore pour quel texte?. BN 106 (2001) 33-39.
1570 JPS Hebrew-English Tanakh: the traditional Hebrew text and the new JPS translation. [2]1999 <1985> ⇒15,1593. [R]JRTI 4 (2001) 113-115 (*Dubis, Mark*).
1571 **Kelley, Page H.; Mynatt, Daniel Stephen; Crawford, Timothy G.** The Masorah of Biblia Hebraica Stuttgartensia: introduction and annotated glossary. 1998 ⇒14,1245; 15,1421. [R]OTEs 14 (2001) 352-354 (*Naude, J.A.*).
1572 **Levy, B. Barry** Fixing God's torah: the accuracy of the Hebrew Bible text in Jewish law. NY 2001, OUP xvii; 237 pp. £40. 019-51411-3-X.
1573 **Lyons, David** The cumulative masora: text, form and transmission with a facsimile critical edition of the cumulative masora in the Cairo Prophets codex. Beer Sheva 1999, Ben Gurion Univ. Pr. 210; xii pp.
1574 *Miller, Peter N.* The 'antiquarianization' of biblical scholarship and the London Polyglot Bible (1653-57). JHI 62 (2001) 463-482.
1575 *Ognibeni, Bruno* Il problema ecdotico dell'Antico Testamento ebraico. RStB 13/1 (2001) 167-184.
1576 *Pisano, Stephen* Bilancio attuale sulle edizioni del testo biblico. RStB 13/1 (2001) 271-278.
1577 *Rapti, Ioanna* Manuscrits bibliques. MoBi 136 (2001) 34-41.
1578 [E]**Richler, Benjamin** Hebrew manuscripts in the Biblioteca Palatina in Parma: catalogue. J 2001, Jewish National and University Library xxx; 574; lamed-waw pp. Descriptions paléographiqes et codicologiques [by] *Beit-Arié, Malachi*; Préf. *S. Japhet*; 49 pl.
1579 *Schenker, Adrian* Comment l'histoire littéraire, canonique et textuelle concourent toutes les trois dans la première phase de l'histoire du texte de la bible: les versions anciennes de la bible comme reflets d'activités éditoriales officielles dans le texte hébreu avant le début de notre ère. RStB 13/1 (2001) 87-94.

1580 **Tov, Emanuel** Der Text der Hebräischen Bibel: Handbuch der Text-kritik. [T]*Fabry, Heinz-Josef*: 1997 <1992> ⇒13,1241. [R]ThGl 91 (2001) 509-510 (*Herr, Bertram*);

1581 Textual criticism of the Hebrew Bible. Mp [2]2001, Fortress xl; 456 pp. 0-8006-3429-2. Bibl. xxix-xxxiv.

1582 [E]**Weil, Gérard E.** Massorah Gedolah: iuxta codicem Leningraden-sem B19a, 1: catalogi. R 2001 <1971>, E.P.I.B. xxvii; 463 + 69 pp. €90. 88-7653-549-7. Biblia Hebraica Stuttgartensia, pars altera: masora magna.

1583 **Wonneberger, Reinhard** Understanding BHS: a manual for the users of Biblia Hebraica Stuttgartensia. [T]*Daniels, Dwight R.*: SubBi 8: R [3]2001, E.P.I.B. xiv; 104 pp. €9.30/$11. 88-7653-578-0. Bibl. 77-85.

1584 **Zimmermann, Frank** Before the masora. Lanham, MD 2001, Univ. Pr. of America x; 559 pp. $72. 07618-1876-6. [R]HebStud 42 (2001) 381-382 (*Revell, E.J.*).

D2.2 Targum

1585 *Bardski, Krzysztof* Eschatologia mesjańska w targumie do Pieśny nad Pieśniami 7,12-8,14. [F]JANKOWSKI, A. 2001 ⇒53. 47-58.

1586 **Bengstsson, Per Å.** Passover in Targum Pseudo-Jonathan Genesis: the connection of early biblical events with Passover in Targum Pseudo-Jonathan in a synagogue setting. Scripta Minora 2000-2001: 1: Sto 2001, Almqvist & W. 88 pp. 91-22-01927-8.

1587 *Bernstein, Moshe J.* The 'righteous'and the 'wicked' in the Aramaic version of Psalms. JAB 3 (2001) 5-26.

1588 *Brady, C.M.M.* Vindicating God: the intent of Targum Lamentations. JAB 3 (2001) 27-40.

1589 *Chilton, Bruce* Temple restored, temple in heaven: Isaiah and the prophets in the Targumim. Restoration. JSJ.S 72: 2001 ⇒319. 335-362.

1590 *Díez Merino, L.* Interpretación de la toponimia como método herme-néutico en el Targum de Jonás, Miqueas, Nahum, Habaquc, Ageo y Sofonías. EstB 59 (2001) 79-100;

1591 A Spanish Targum Onqelos manuscript from the thirteenth century (Villa-Amil N. 6). JAB 3 (2001) 41-56.

1592 *Ego, Beate* All kingdoms and kings trembled before him: the image of King Solomon in Targum Sheni on Megillat Esther. JAB 3 (2001) 57-74.

1593 *Flesher, Paul V.M.* The translations of Proto-Onqelos and the Palestinian Targums. JAB 3 (2001) 75-100.

1594 [E]**Flesher, Paul V.M.** Targum Studies, II Targum and Peshitta. SF-SHJ 165: 1998 ⇒14,238... 16,1546. [R]JSSt 46 (2001) 340-341 (*Hay-man, A. Peter*).

1595 *Greenfield, Jonas C.; Shaked, Shaul* Three Iranian words in the Tar-gum of Job from Qumran <1972>;

1596 A Mandaic 'targum' of Psalm 114 <1980>. 'Al kanfei yonah, 1. 2001 ⇒153. 344-352/388-396.

1597 **Grossfeld, Bernard** Targum Neofiti, 1: an exegetical commentary to Genesis including full rabbinic parallels. [E]*Schiffman, Lawrence H.*: 2000 ⇒16,1547. [R]PIBA 24 (2001) 114-118 (*McNamara, Martin*).

1598 *Hayward, C.T.R.* Targumic perspectives on Jacob's change of name to Israel. JAB 3 (2001) 121-138 [Gen 32,25-33; 35,9-15].

1599 *Katsumata, Etsuko* Priests and priesthood in the Aramaic Bible. JAB 3 (2001) 139-160.

1600 *McNamara, Martin* Some Targum themes. Justification, 1: second temple Judaism. WUNT 2/140: 2001 ⇒251. 303-356.

1601 *Moor, Johannes de* Multiple renderings in the Targum of Isaiah;

1602 *Müller-Kessler, Christa* The earliest evidence for Targum Onqelos from Babylonia and the question of its dialect and origin. JAB 3 (2001) 161-180/181-198.

1603 *Tal, Abraham* Is there a raison d'être for an Aramaic targum in a Hebrew-speaking society?. REJ 160 (2001) 357-378.

1604 *Van Staalduine-Sulman, E.* Translating with subtlety: some unexpected translations in the Targum of Samuel;

1605 *Wesselius, Jan-Wim* Completeness and closure in targumic literature: the emulation of Biblical Hebrew poetry in Targum Jonathan to the former prophets [Judg 5; 1 Sam 2; 2 Sam 22; 23,1-7]. JAB 3 (2001) 225-236/237-247.

D3.1 *Textus graecus*—Greek NT

1606 [E]**Barrett, David P.; Comfort, Philip W.** The text of the earliest New Testament Greek manuscripts. Wheaton, Ill. 2001, Tyndale H. 704 pp. $45. 0-8423-5265-1.

1607 *Kraus, Thomas J.* Ad fontes: Gewinn durch die Konsultation von O-riginalhandschriften am Beispiel von P. Vindob. G 31974. Bib. 82 (2001) 1-16.

1608 *Litsas, Efthymios K.* The Mount Athos manuscripts in the *Kurzgefasste Liste der griechischen Handschriften des Neuen Testaments*. Kl. 32/A'-B' (2000) 245-250.

1609 **Nestle, E.; Aland, Kurt** Novum Testamentum Graece. Stu [27]2001, Deutsche Bibelgesellschaft 89* + 812 pp. 3-438-05100-1. 8th repr.

1610 [E]**Nolli, Gianfranco** Novum Testamentum graece et latine. Città del Vaticano [2]2001, Libreria Editrice Vaticana 1348 pp. 88-209-7078-3.

1611 *Passoni Dell'Acqua, Anna* Testimoni del testo neotestamentario: il cod. B e i nuovi papiri: in margine ad Angelico Poppi, sinossi quadri-forme dei quattro vangeli greco-italiano vol. I—testo, Edizioni Mes-saggero, Padova 1999. RivBib 49 (2001) 203-210.

1612 *Spottorno, M[a] Victoria* El texto del Nuevo Testamento. ResB 31 (2001) 25-34.

1613 **Swanson, Reuben J.** New Testament Greek manuscripts: variant readings arranged in horizontal lines against Codex Vaticanus. 1995-1996 ⇒12,152. [R]JBL 119 (2000) 383-384 (*Kannaday, Wayne*).

1614 *Tuckett, Christopher M.* P 52 and nomina sacra. NTS 47 (2001) 544-548.

1615 *Vincent, John J.* Outworkings: a gospel practice criticism. ET 113 (2001) 16-18.

D3.2 *Versiones graecae*—VT, Septuaginta etc.

1616 [E]**Dogniez, Cécile; Harl, Marguerite** Le Pentateuque d'Alexandrie: texte grec et traduction. La Bible d'Alexandrie: La Bible des Septante. P 2001, Cerf 922 pp. 2-204-06699-0. €38. Introd. *Monique Alexandre* et al.; Bibl. 21-25. [R]EThL 77 (2001) 467-468 (*Lust, J.*); REG 114 (2001) 711-712 (*Wartelle, André*).

1617 [E]**Sollamo, Rajia; Sipilä, Seppo** Helsinki perspectives on the translation technique of the Septuagint: proceedings of the IOSCS congress in Helsinki 1999. SESJ 82: Helsinki 2001, Finnish Exegetical Society 307 pp. $30. 951-9217-37-1.

1618 [E]**Zenger, Erich** Der Septuaginta-Psalter: sprachliche und theologische Aspekte. Herders Biblische Studien 32: FrB 2001, Herder vii; 347 pp. €51.50. 3-451-27623-2.

1619 *Aejmelaeus, Annel* Übersetzungstechnik und theologische Interpretation: zur Methodik der Septuaginta-Forschung. Der Septuaginta-Psalter. Herders biblische Studien 32: 2001 ⇒1618. 3-18;

1620 What we talk about when we talk about translation technique. X Congress IOSCS. SBL.SCSt 51: 2001 ⇒499. 531-552.

1621 **Beck, John A.** Translators as storytellers: a study in Septuagint translation technique. Studies in biblical literature 25: 2000 ⇒16,1586. [R]JThS 52 (2001) 755-756 (*Salvesen, A.G.*); BiTr 52 (2001) 354-355 (*Scanlin, Harold P.*).

1622 *Boyd-Taylor, Cameron* The evidentiary value of Septuagintal usage for Greek lexicography: Alice's reply to Humpty Dumpty. BIOSCS 34 (2001) 47-80.

1623 *Brodersen, Kai* Die Bedeutung der Septuaginta für die Altertumswissenschaft. BiKi 56 (2001) 101-103.

1624 *Catastini, Alessandro* L'originale ebraico dei LXX: un problema ancora aperto. AnScR 6 (2001) 125-146.

1625 *Cook, Johann* Ideology and translation technique: two sides of the same coin?. Helsinki perspectives. SESJ 82: 2001 ⇒1596. 195-210.

1626 *Cordes, Ariane* Theologische Interpretation in der Septuaginta: Beobachtungen am Beispiel von Psalm 76 LXX. Der Septuaginta-Psalter. Herders biblische Studien 32: 2001 ⇒1618. 105-121.

1627 *Danove, Paul* The grammatical constructions of ἀκούω and their implications for translation. Helsinki perspectives. SESJ 82: 2001 ⇒ 1596. 229-245.

1628 *Dorival, Gilles* Le sacrifice dans la traduction grecque de la Septante. ASEs 18 (2001) 61-79.

1629 [E]**Fabry, Heinz-Josef; Offerhaus, Ulrich** Im Brennpunkt: die Septuaginta: Studien zur Entstehung und Bedeutung der Griechischen Bibel. BZAW 153: Stu 2001, Kohlhammer 261 pp. €38.70. 3-1701-68-21-5.

1630 *Fabry, Heinz-Josef* Die griechischen Handschriften vom Toten Meer. Im Brennpunkt. BWANT 8,13: 2001 ⇒1605. 131-153.

1631 *Falcetta, Alessandro* A testimony collection in Manchester: Papyrus Rylands Greek 460. BJRL 83/1 (2001) 3-19.

1632 *Fernández Marcos, Natalio* La prima traducción de la biblia. ResB 31 (2001) 15-24;

1633 On the borderline of translation: Greek lexicography: the proper names. JNSL 27/2 (2001) 1-22.

1634 **Fernández Marcos, Natalio** Introducción a las versiones griegas de la Biblia. TECC 64: [2]1998 ⇒14,1301... 16,1593. [R]EE 76 (2001) 293-294 (*Spottorno, Maria Victoria*);

1635 La Bibbia dei Settanta: introduzione alle versioni greche della Bib-
      bia. ᴱZoroddu, Donatella: 2000 ⇒16,1594 ᴿETR 76 (2001) 121-123
      (Ubigli, Liliana Rosso).
1636 Fernández Marcos, Natalio Reactions to the panel on modern trans-
      lations. X Congress IOSCS. SBL.SCSt 51: 2001 ⇒499. 233-240;
1637 A Greek-Hebrew index of the Antiochene text. X Congress IOSCS.
      SBL.SCSt 51: 2001 ⇒499. 301-317.
1638 Görg, Manfred Die Septuaginta im Kontext spätägyptischer Kultur:
      Beispiele lokaler Inspiration bei der Übersetzungsarbeit am Penta-
      teuch. Im Brennpunkt. BWANT 8,13: 2001 ⇒1605. 115-130.
1639 Haacker, Klaus Methodische Probleme einer Septuaginta-Überset-
      zung. Im Brennpunkt. BWANT 8,13: 2001 ⇒1605. 51-59.
1640 Hadas-Lebel, Mireille Qui utilisait la LXX dans le monde juif?. Le
      pentateuque d'Alexandrie. 2001 ⇒1616. 42-49.
1641 Hamonville, David-Marc d' La liberté du traducteur grec. MoBi 137
      (2001) 32-33 [BuBB 35,127].
1642 Hanhart, Robert Studien zur Septuaginta und zum hellenistischen
      Judentum. ᴱKratz, Reinhard Gregor: FAT 24: 1999 ⇒15,1493; 16,
      1618. ᴿETR 76 (2001) 609-610 (Rüsen-Weinhold, Ulrich); ThLZ
      126 (2001) 261-262 (Böttrich, Christfried).
1643 Harl, Marguerite La Bible d'Alexandrie dans les débats actuels sur la
      Septante. ᶠSCHENKER, A.: OBO 179: 2001 ⇒100. 7-24.
1644 Harl, Marguerite, al., La Bible d'Alexandrie, 1: the translation prin-
      ciples. X Congress IOSCS. SBL.SCSt 51: 2001 ⇒499. 182-197.
1645 Harl, Marguerite Avant-propos: le rôle du grec dans la diffusion de
      la bible. Le pentateuque d'Alexandrie. 2001 ⇒1616. 5-12.
1646 Heckel, Theo K. Ohne Septuaginta kein Neues Testament. BiKi 56
      (2001) 96-100.
1647 ᴱHengel, Martin; Schwemer, Anna Maria Die Septuaginta zwi-
      schen Judentum und Christentum. WUNT 72: 1994 ⇒10,323a; 14,
      1304. ᴿSNTU.A 23 (1998) 238-239 (Fuchs, Albert).
1648 Jobes, Karen H.; Silva, Moisés Invitation to the Septuagint. 2000
      ⇒16,1601. ᴿEThL 77 (2001) 193-196 (Cook, J.); ThGl 91 (2001)
      508-509 (Herr, Bertram); RExp 98 (2001) 443-44 (Biddle, Mark E.)
1649 Joosten, J. On the LXX translators' knowledge of Hebrew. X
      Congress IOSCS. SBL.SCSt 51: 2001 ⇒499. 165-179.
1650 Kraus, Wolfgang; Karrer, Martin Septuaginta-deutsch. BiKi 56
      (2001) 104-105.
1651 Kreuzer, Siegfried A German translation of the Septuagint. BIOSCS
      34 (2001) 40-45.
1652 Krieger, Klaus-Stefan Von der Tora-Übersetzung zum Alten Testa-
      ment der Kirche: die Entstehung der Septuaginta;
1653 Karriere im Christentum: aus Übersetzern werden Propheten. BiKi
      56 (2001) 66-70/71-75.
1654 Lemmelijn, Bénédicte Two methodological trails in recent studies on
      the translation technique of the Septuagint. Helsinki perspectives.
      SESJ 82: 2001 ⇒1596. 43-63.
1655 Leonas, Alex Patristic evidence of difficulties in understanding the
      LXX: Hadrian's philological remarks in Isagoge. X Congress
      IOSCS. SBL.SCSt 51: 2001 ⇒499. 393-414.
1656 Lust, Johan Syntax and translation Greek. EThL 77 (2001) 395-401.
1657 McLay, Tim Lexical inconsistency: towards a methodology for the
      analysis of the vocabulary in the Septuagint. X Congress IOSCS.
      SBL.SCSt 51: 2001 ⇒499. 81-98.

1658 *Moatti-Fine, Jacqueline* La tâche du traducteur. (*a*) VS 741 (2001) 713-724;

1659 (*b*) Le pentateuque d'Alexandrie. 2001 ⇒1616. 67-76.

1660 **Muraoka, Takamitsu** Hebrew/Aramaic index to the Septuagint: keyed to the Hatch-Redpath concordance. 1998 ⇒14,1308; 16,1604. ᴿANESt 38 (2001) 224-227 (*Falla, Terry C.*).

1661 *Muraoka, Takamitsu* Translation techniques and beyond. Helsinki perspectives. SESJ 82: 2001 ⇒1617. 13-22.

1662 *Murray, Oswyn* Aristeasbrief. RAC, Sup. Bd. 1. 2001 ⇒661. 573-87.

1663 *Orth, Wolfgang* Ptolemaios II. und die Septuaginta-Übersetzung. Im Brennpunkt. BWANT 8,13: 2001 ⇒1605. 97-114.

1664 *Passoni Dell'Acqua, Anna* Il divenire del testo greco. RStB 13/1 (2001) 105-132.

1665 **Peterca, Vladimir** Wege zum Bibelstudium: Midrasch—Targum—Septuaginta—Talmud. Studii biblici 2: Iasi 2001, Sapientia 238 pp. 973-85370-2-9. Bibl. 235-238. ᴿCICat 2/2 (2001) 202-204 (*Bǎltǎceanu, Francisca*).

1666 *Pietersma, Albert* A new English translation of the Septuagint. X Congress IOSCS. SBL.SCSt 51: 2001 ⇒499. 217-228;

1667 A proposed commentary on the Septuagint. Helsinki perspectives. SESJ 82: 2001 ⇒1617. 167-184.

1668 *Schenker, Adrian* La place de la Septante dans la bible. CTrB 35 (2001) 7-12.

1669 *Schröder, Christian* Alphabetische Zusammenstellung auffälliger Neologismen der Septuaginta. Im Brennpunkt. 2001 ⇒1605. 61-69.

1670 **Siegert, Folker** Zwischen Hebräischer Bibel und Altem Testament: eine Einführung in die Septuaginta. Münsteraner judaistische Studien 9: Müns 2001, LIT viii; 342 pp. €25.90. 3-8258-5012-9.

1671 *Sipilä, Seppo* The renderings of the circumstantial כי clauses in the LXX of Joshua and Judges;

1672 *Sollamo, Raija* The Letter of Aristeas and the origin of the Septuagint. X Congress IOSCS. SBL.SCSt 51: 2001 ⇒499. 49-61/329-342;

1673 Prolegomena to the syntax of the Septuagint. Helsinki perspectives. SESJ 82: 2001 ⇒1617. 23-41.

1674 *Spottorno, Mᵃ Victoria* Lexical variants in the Greek text of Reigns and Chronicles. X Congress IOSCS. SBL.SCSt 51: 2001 ⇒499. 63-80.

1675 *Tov, Emanuel* The nature of the Greek texts from the Judean desert. NT 43 (2001) 1-11;

1676 Scribal features of early witnesses of Greek scripture. ᶠPIETERSMA, A. 2001 ⇒87. 125-148.

1677 *Utzschneider, Helmut* Auf Augenhöhe mit dem Text: Überlegungen zum wissenschaftlichen Standort einer Übersetzung der Septuaginta ins Deutsche. Im Brennpunkt. BWANT 8,13: 2001 ⇒1605. 11-50.

1678 *Van der Kooij, Arie* Comments on NETS and La Bible d'Alexandrie. X Congress IOSCS. SBL.SCSt 51: 2001 ⇒499. 229-221.

1679 *Veltri, Giuseppe* Übersetzungsverständnis und Autorität: rabbinische Einstellung zu Septuaginta und Aquila. Der Septuaginta-Psalter. Herders biblische Studien 32: 2001 ⇒1618. 89-104.

1680 *Walser, Georg* A peculiar word order rule for the Septuagint and for cognate texts. X Congress IOSCS. SBL.SCSt 51: 2001 ⇒499. 499-511.

1681 *Walter, Nikolaus* Die griechischen Bücher—kanonisch oder nicht?:
      der unterschiedliche Umgang der Konfessionen mit der Septuaginta.
      BiKi 56 (2001) 81-84;
1682 Die griechische Übersetzung der "Schriften" Israels und die christli-
      che "Septuaginta" als Forschungs- und als Übersetzungsgegenstand.
      Im Brennpunkt. BWANT 8,13: 2001 ⇒1605. 71-96.
1683 *Wevers, John William* The rendering of the Tetragram in the psalter
      and pentateuch: a comparative study. ᶠPIETERSMA, A. JSOT.S 332:
      2001 ⇒87. 21-35;
1684 Aram and Aramaean in the Septuagint. ᶠDION, P.-E., 1. JSOT.S 324:
      2001 ⇒25. 237-251.
1685 *Zipor, M.A.* The use of the Septuagint as a textual witness: further
      considerations. X Congress IOSCS. SBL.SCSt 51: 2001 ⇒499. 553-
      581.

D4 Versiones orientales

1686 *Azzam, Jean* Le Peshitta (A.T.) et le texte massorétique: étude com-
      parative. ParOr 26 (2001) 89-125.
1687 *Borbone, Pier G.* L'origine e lo sviluppo testuale della versione siria-
      ca dell'Antico Testamento "Peshitta". RStB 13/1 (2001) 153-164.
1688 *Dupuy, Bernard* L'édition de Leyde de la Peshitta de l'Ancien Testa-
      ment. Ist. 46 (2001) 127-138.
1689 *Gelston, Anthony* The biblical citations in the Syriac anaphoras of
      James and the Twelve Apostles. StPatr 35 (2001) 271-274.
1690 *Joosten, Jan* Tatian's Diatessaron and the Old Testament Peshitta.
      JBL 120 (2001) 501-523.
1691 **Kiraz, George Anton** Comparative edition of the Syriac gospels.
      NTTS 21/1-4: 1996 4 vols ⇒12,1090... 16,1615. ᴿJThS 52 (2001)
      328-321 (*Taylor, David G.K.*).
1692 **Knibb, Michael A.** Translating the bible: the Ethiopic version of the
      Old Testament. Oxf 1999, OUP xii; 145 pp. 0-19726-1949. Schweich
      lectures in biblical archaeology, 1995; Bibl. 113-129. ᴿJBL 120
      (2001) 758-759 (*Casiday, Augustine*).
1693 **Luisier, Philippe** Les citations vétéro-testamentaires dans les ver-
      sions coptes des évangiles. COr 22: 1998 ⇒14,1335... 16,1616. ᴿNT
      43 (2001) 91-93 (*Boud'hors, Anne*); Bib. 82 (2001) 126-129 (*Plisch,
      Uwe-Karsten*); Or. 70 (2001) 117-127 (*Richter, T.S.*).
1694 *Mahé, Jean-Pierre* La traduction arménienne de la bible. MoBi 136
      (2001) 18-21 [BuBB 35,133].
1695 ᴱMüller-Kessler, Christa; Sokoloff, Michael A corpus of christian
      Palestinian Aramaic, IIA: the christian Palestinian Aramaic New
      Testament version from the early period: gospels; IIB: Acts of the
      Apostles and epistles. 1998-1999 ⇒16,1621. ᴿThLZ 126 (2001) 907-
      908 (*Beyer, Klaus*).
1696 **Nersessian, Vrej** The bible in the Armenian tradition. L 2001, Brit-
      ish Library 96 pp. 0-7123-4698-8. Bibl. 88-93.
1697 ᴱSchüssler, Karlheinz Das sahidische Alte und Neue Tesament:
      vollständiges Verzeichnis mit Standorten, Lfg. 4: sa 93-120. Biblia
      Coptica 1/4: 2000 ⇒16,1623.. ᴿThLZ 126 (2001) 909 (*Luisier,
      Philippe*);
1698 Lfg.1: sa 500-520. Biblia Coptica 3/1: Wsb 2001, Harrassowitz 124
      pp. €54. 3-447-04458-6.

1699 **Shedinger, Robert F.** TATIAN and the Jewish scriptures: a textual and philological analysis of the Old Testament citations in Tatian's Diatessaron. CSCO 591; CSCO.Sub 109: Lv 2001, Peeters viii; 190 pp. €70. 90-429-1042-9. Bibl. 168-177.

1700 *Spottorno, Mª Victoria* Las versiones antiguas de la biblia. ResB 31 (2001) 43-51.

1701 The Syriac New Testament, translated into English from the Syriac Peshitto version. ᵀ*Murdock, James*: Piscataway, NJ 2001 <1893>, Gorgias xlviii; 507 pp. Introd. *H.L. Hastings*; bibliographical appendix by *I.H. Hall*: new foreword by *G.A. Kiraz*.

1702 *Ter Haar Romeny, R.B.* Biblical studies in the church of the east: the case of Catholicos TIMOTHY I. StPatr 34 (2001) 503-510.

1703 *Walter, Donald* Multidimensional scaling (mapping) of Peshitta manuscripts of Numbers and Deuteronomy. ᴹWEITZMAN, M. JSOT.S 333: 2001 ⇒113. 178-199.

1704 **Weitzman, Michael Perry** The Syriac version of the Old Testament: an introduction. UCOP 56: 1999 ⇒15,1552; 16,1627. ᴿNT 43 (2001) 304-305 (*Lane, D.J.*); JSSt 46 (2001) 341-343 (*Gelston, A.*); RBLit 3 (2001) 140-143 (*Shedinger, Robert F.*).

1705 *Williams, P.J.* Some problems in determining the Vorlage of early Syriac versions of the NT. NTS 47 (2001) 537-543.

1706 *Yacoub, Joseph* Les versions araméennes de la Bible. Ist. 46 (2001) 116-126.

D5.0 **Versiones latinae;** *Citationes apud Patres*—**The Patristic Bible**

1707 ᴱ**Brecht, Martin; Zwink, Eberhard** Eine glossierte Vulgata aus dem Umkreis Martin LUTHERs. VB 21: 1999 ⇒15,1555; 16,1631. ᴿThLZ 126 (2001) 542-544 (*Zschoch, Hellmut*).

1708 *Cañas Reíllo, José Manuel* De oriente a occidente: las versiones latinas de la biblia. ResB 31 (2001) 35-42.

1709 ᴱ**Contreni, John J.; Ó Néill, Pádraig P.** The biblical glosses of John Scottus ERIUGENA. 1997 ⇒13,11600. ᴿSpec. 76 (2001) 449-451 (*Herren, Michael W.*); Journal of Medieval Latin 11 (2001) 216-219 (*Franklin, Carmela Vircillo*).

1710 **Dutton, Paul Edward; Kessler, Herbert L.** The poetry and paintings of the First Bible of Charles the Bald. 1997 ⇒13,1326. ᴿSpec. 76 (2001) 155-156 (*Noble, Thomas F.X.*).

1711 ᴱ**Gryson, Roger** Altlateinische Handschriften, 1: Mss 1-275. VL. AGLB 1,2A: 1999 ⇒15,1562; 16,1637. ᴿJThS 52 (2001) 301-306 (*Birdsall, J. Neville*); NT 43 (2001) 398-400 (*Elliott, J.K.*).

1712 *Light, Laura* Roger BACON and the origin of the Paris Bible. RBen 111 (2001) 483-507.

1713 **Lobrichon, Guy** La bible au Moyen Age: bible des clercs, bible des laïcs. Diss.-Habil. Paris I, 2001. ᴰ*Parisse, Michel* [RMab 13,346-50].

1714 *Misonne, Daniel* Les plus anciens manuscrits bibliques de Saint-Hubert. RBen 111 (2001) 181-197.

1715 *Stammberger, R.M.W.* Die Halberstädter Glosse zum Matthäus-Evangelium und zum Buch Josua: zur Wiederentdeckung der Handschrift Halberstadt, Dom-Gymnasium 47 aus der ersten Hälfte des 12. Jahrhunderts. RTPM 68 (2001) 18-33.

1716 *Stramare, Tarcisio* Il cammino della sacra scrittura nella tradizione testuale latina. RStB 13/1 (2001) 133-151;

1717   I vangeli della Vulgata. RivBib 49 (2001) 155-172.
1718   **Thomson, Rodney M.** The Bury Bible. Woodbridge 2001, Boydell xiv; 60 pp. €725. 0-85115-855-2. Ill.
1719   Vetus Latina... Beuron: 44. Arbeitsbericht der Stiftung; 33. Bericht der Instituts. 2000 ⇒16,1649. ᴿThLZ 126 (2001) 1056-1057 (*Haendler, Gert*);
1720   45. Arbeitsbericht der Stiftung, 34. Bericht des Instituts. FrB 2001, Herder 44 pp.

D6 **Versiones modernae** .1 *romanicae*, **romance**

1721   **Alonso Schökel, Luis** Biblia del peregrino: edición de estudio. ²1998 ⇒14,1356. ᴿBiTr 52 (2001) 351-354 (*Sanchez Cetina, Edesio*).
1722   **Anania, Bartolomeu Valeriu** Eine neue Auflage der Heiligen Schrift in rumänischer Sprache. Bucharest 2001, Biblisches Institut der rumänisch-orthodoxen Kirche 1831 pp. 973-9332-86-2 [OrthFor 17/1,107ss—Basarab, Mircea].
1723   *Auwers, Jean-Marie* La bible revisitée: à propos d'une nouvelle traduction de la bible. RTL 32 (2001) 529-536.
1724   La bible: nouvelle traduction. ᵀ**Boyer, Frédéric; Prévost, Jean-Pierre; Sevin, Marc:** P 2001, Bayard 3186 pp. 2-227-35800-9. ᴿChoisir (nov. 2001) 39-40 (*Livio, Jean-Bernard*); RTL 32 (2001) 529-536 (*Auwers, Jean.Marie*); EeV 47 (2001) 3-14 (*Grelot, Pierre; Roullière, Yves; Maldamé, Jean-Michel; Martin de Vivies, Pierre de; Forster, Christian; Monloubou, Louis; Légasse, Simon; Cothenet, Edouard; Carrez, Maurice; Chauvin, Charles*).
1725   La Bible de Jérusalem: édition de référence avec notes et augmentée de clefs de lectures. P 2001, Cerf-Fleurus 2559 pp. €15.09. 2-2150-4399-7.
1726   Bible d'étude: version du Semeur 2000: traduite en français d'après les textes originaux hébreu et grec. Cléon d'Andran 2001, Excelsis 2137 pp.
1727   La bible, parole de vie: nouvelle traduction. 2000 ⇒16,1653. ᴿDosB 90 (2001) 33-35 (*Auwers, Jean-Marie*).
1728   Bíblia Sagrada. São Paulo 2001, Ave-Maria xviii; 1653 pp. 85-1502-346-6. Trad. da CNBB com introd. e notas; ediçao comemorativa dos quinhentos anos de evangelizaçao do Brasil e dos cinqüenta anos da Conferência Episcopal; Confêrencia Nacional dos Bispos do Brasil. ᴿEstudos Bíblicos 69 (2001) 85-87 (*Konings, Johan*).
1729   *Courcelles, Dominique de* Les bibles en Catalogne à la fin du Moyen Âge ou l'occultation de la lettre sacrée. RHR 218 (2001) 65-82.
1730   *De Azcárraga, Mᵃ Josefa* Versiones españolas de la biblia. ResB 31 (2001) 53-62.
1731   **Fellous, Sonia** Histoire de la bible de Moïse ARRAGEL: quand un rabbin interprète la bible pour les chrétiens,Tolède, 1422-1433. P 2001, Somogy 384 pp. €95. 2-85056-516-4.
1732   **Mateos, J.; Alonso Schökel, L.** Nuevo Testamento. Córdoba 2001, Almendro 463 pp.
1733   *Minissale, Antonino* Versioni italiane della bibbia: storia e tipologia. Synaxis 19 (2001) 7-23.
1734   ᵀ**Oltramare, Hugues** Le Nouveau Testament. ᴱ**Armogathe, J.-R.; Clément, Olivier; Schmid, Vincent:** Folio classique 3596: P 2001, Gallimard 980 pp. €4.50. 2-07-04702-6. Collab. *Régis Burnet.*

1735 *Puig i Tàrrech, Armand* Les traduccions catalanes medievals de la
       bíblia. El text. Scripta Biblica 3: 2001 ⇒310. 107-231.
1736 *Sacquin, Michèle* 'Evangélisez la France': les bibles protestantes
       dans la France rurale (1814-1870). RHR 218 (2001) 113-141.
1737 Sagrada Biblia: Antiguo Testamento, 3: libros poéticos y sapien-
       ciales: traducción, notas. Pamplona 2001, EUNSA 1118 pp. 84-313-
       1860-0.
1738 *Varvaro, Alberto* Le traduzioni in versi della bibbia nella letteratura
       francese del sec. XII: committenti, autori, pubblico. La scrittura infi-
       nita. 2001 ⇒498. 493-509.

D6.2 *Versiones anglicae*—English Bible Translations

1739 **Barker, Kenneth L.** The balance of the NIV: what makes a good
       translation. 1999 ⇒16,1662. [R]RExp 98 (2001) 605-606 (*Cosgrove,
       Charles H.*).
1740 [E]**Beacham, Roy E.; Bauder, Kevin T.** One bible only?: examining
       exclusive claims for the King James Bible. GR 2001, Kregel 238 pp.
       $14. 0-8254-2048-2 [ThD 48,383—Heiser, W. Charles].
1741 **Bobrick, Benson** Wide as the waters: the story of the English Bible
       and the revolution it inspired. NY 2001, Simon & S. 379 pp. 0-684-
       84747-7. Bibl. 345-357.
1742 **Boer, Roland** Last stop before Antarctica: the bible and postcoloni-
       alism in Australia. The Bible and postcolonialism 6: Shf 2001, Shef-
       field A. 219 pp. 1-84127-170-5. Bibl. 194-214.
1743 [E]**Coogan, Michael David** The New Oxford Annotated Bible: with
       the Apocryphal/Deuterocanonical books [NRSV]. Oxf ³2001, OUP
       pag. varia. 0-19-528478-X. *Marc Z. Brettler, Carol A. Newsom,
       Pheme Perkins*, associate editors.
1744 **Gutjahr, Paul C.** An American Bible: a history of the Good Book in
       the United States, 1777-1880. 1999 ⇒15,1591; 16,1670. [R]JR 81
       (2001) 130-131 (*Freeman, Maria*).
1745 *Hyman, Ronald T.* Bible translators as arbiters of ambiguity, 1-2.
       JBQ 29 (2001) 96-102, 156-170.
1746 **Lindberg, Conrad** The earlier version of the Wycliffite Bible. 1997
       ⇒13,1363. [R]Spec. 76 (2001) 190-191 (*Besserman, Lawrence*).
1747 [E]**Lindberg, Conrad** King Henry's Bible, MS Bodley 277: the revised
       version of the Wyclif Bible: vol. II: 1 Kings-Psalms. Stockholm
       Studies in English 94: Sto 2001, Almqvist & W. 570 pp. SKr414. 91-
       22-01921-9.
1748 *MacKenzie, Cameron A.* The coming of the kingdom and sixteenth-
       century English bibles. Looking into the future. 2001 ⇒505. 144-56.
1749 *Masenya, Madipoane* What differences do African contexts make for
       English translations?. OTEs 14 (2001) 281-296.
1750 **McGrath, Alister E.** In the beginning: the story of the King James
       Bible and how it changed a nation, a language, and a culture. NY
       2001, Doubleday 320 pp. $25. 0-385-49890-X.
1751 **Morey, James H.** Book and verse...guide to Middle English biblical
       literature. 2000 ⇒16,1678. [R]HeyJ 42 (2001) 207-8 (*Swanson, R.N.*).
1752 *Neff, David* A translation fit for a king [KJV]. ChrTo 45/13 (2001)
       36-39, 75.
1753 *Nowell, Irene* The English bible: troubled beginnings;

1754 English translations of the bible: the last century. BiTod 39 (2001) 105-107/161-163.

1755 *Sloyan, Gerard S.* Some thoughts on bible translations. Worship 75 (2001) 228-249.

1756 **Thuesen, Peter J.** In discordance with the scriptures: American Protestant battles over translating the bible. 1999 ⇒15,1606; 16,1692. ᴿCBQ 63 (2001) 327-329 (*Bundy, David*); ChH 70 (2001) 820-822 (*Lewis, James W.*); RRT (2001/1) 32-34 (*Marlett, Jeffrey*).

1757 *Trautmann, Donald W.* Il futuro dell'ICEL. Il Regno 46 (2001) 410-413 [Cf. America, 4.3.2000]. Risposta di Card. *Medina* 414-416.

1758 *Wallace, Daniel B.* Innovations in text and translation of the NET Bible, New Testament. BiTr 52 (2001) 335-346.

1759 *Waters, Ken* Competing moral visions: ethics and the Stealth Bible. Journal of mass media ethics 16 (2001) 48-61.

1760 **Westbrook, Vivienne** Long travail and great paynes: a politics of Reformation revision. Dordrecht 2001, Kluwer xxxix; 190 pp. $74. 0-7923-6955-6 [ThD 49,91—Heiser, W. Charles].

1761 Holman christian standard bible, New Testament. Nv 2001, Holman $25. 1-58640-008-8.

1762 Holy Bible: English Standard Version. Wheaton, IL 2001, Crossway B. xiii; 1328 pp. $25. 1-58134-316-7. Incl. CD-ROM [ThD 49,159—Heiser, W. Charles].

D6.3 *Versiones germanicae*—**Deutsche Bibelübersetzungen**

1763 ᴱ**Fricke, K.D.; Meurer, S.** Die Geschichte der Lutherbibelrevision: von den Anfängen 1850 bis 1984. Arbeiten zur Geschichte und Wirkung der Bibel 1: Stu 2001, Deutsche Bibelgesellschaft 389 pp. €35. 3-438-06251-8.

1764 *Anderegg, Johannes* Zur neuen Zürcher Bibel—Überlegungen und Erfahrungen aus germanistischer Sicht. Bibelübersetzung heute. 2001 ⇒468. 283-299.

1765 ᵀ**Berger, Klaus; Nord, Christiane** Das Neue Testament und frühchristliche Schriften. Fra ⁵2001, Insel 1413 pp. 3-458-16970-9.

1766 *Besch, Werner* Bibelübersetzungen im 16. Jahrhundert ohne kodifizierte Schriftsprache?: Sprachregionalität in Deutschland als zusätzliches Übersetzungsproblem LUTHERs. Bibelübersetzung heute. 2001 ⇒468. 73-93.

1767 Die beste Nachricht aller Zeiten: das Neue Testament: eine Sonderausgabe der zeitgemässen Bibelübersetzung 'Hoffnung für alle'. Dorsten 1996, International Bible Society 379 pp. ᴿTheol(A) 72/1 (2001) 413-416 (*Simotas, Pan.*).

1768 *Beutel, Albrecht* Auf dem Weg zum 'Septembertestament' (1522): die Anfänge von LUTHERs Dolmetschung des Neuen Testaments;

1769 *Bieberstedt, Andreas* Zur Syntax spätmittelalterlicher Bibelverdeutschungen vor LUTHER—Verfahren zur Umsetzung lateinischer Partizipalkonstruktionen in die deutsche Volkssprache. Bibelübersetzung heute. 2001 ⇒468. 95-116/11-48.

1770 *Breest, Ernst* Erläuterungen zur Entstehung und zur Durchführung der sprachlichen Revision der Lutherbibel 1912/13;

1771 *Burghart, Georg* Die Revisionsgrundsätze von 1928;

1772 *Frick, Otto* Vorwort zur durchgesehenen Ausgabe 1892;

1773 Bericht der von Cansteinschen Bibelanstalt zur revidierten Ausgabe 1883 (sog. Probebibel);

1774 *Fricke, Klaus Dietrich* Bibliographie zur Geschichte der Lutherbibelrevision;

1775 Probleme und Stand der Revision der Apokryphen der Lutherbibel;

1776 Die Fortsetzung der Revisionsarbeit von 1870 bis 1956. Die Geschichte der Lutherbibelrevision von 1850 bis 1984. 2001 ⇒1763. 315-342/351-352/307-314/253-272/365-391/197-217/149-187.

1777 *Groß, Walter* Pragmatische und syntaktische Gesichtspunkte des Hebräischen und deutscher Übersetzungen: Beispiele aus der alttestamentlichen Poesie. Bibelübersetzung heute. 2001 ⇒468. 167-207.

1778 *Gundert, Wilhelm* Die Revision des Alten Testaments 1964;

1779 Die Revision des Neuen Testaments 1975. Die Geschichte der Lutherbibelrevision. 2001 ⇒1763. 188-196/218-228.

1780 *Haug, Hellmut* Ein Vergleich zwischen den großen 'Gebrauchsbibeln': Lutherbibel—Einheitsübersetzung—Gute Nachricht. Bibelübersetzung heute. 2001 ⇒468. 329-364.

1781 *Herrmann, Johannes* Nachwort zum Probetestament 1955 (AT). Die Geschichte der Lutherbibelrevision. 2001 ⇒1763. 353-361.

1782 *Jenni, Ernst* Semantische Gesichtspunkte des Hebräischen und deutscher Übersetzungen am Beispiel von Num 10,29-31. Bibelübersetzung heute. 2001 ⇒468. 209-233.

1783 **Kettler, Wilfried** Die Zürcher Bibel von 1531: philologische Studien zu ihrer Übersetzungstechnik und den Beziehungen zu ihren Vorlagen. Bern 2001, Lang 521 pp. FS105. 39067-55746. Bibl. 497-505.

1784 *Krüger, Thomas* Zur Revision der Zürcher Bibel (Altes Testament)— ein 'Werkstattbericht' aus exegetischer Sicht. Bibelübersetzung heute. 2001 ⇒468. 301-327.

1785 *Lippold, Ernst* Die Revision des Neuen Testaments der Lutherbibel 1981-1984;

1786 *Meurer, Siegfried* Vorwort. Die Geschichte der Lutherbibelrevision von 1850 bis 1984. 2001 ⇒1763. 229-249/13-32.

1787 **Mühlen, Reinhard** Die Bibel und das Titelblatt: die bildliche Entwicklung der Titelblattgestaltung lutherischer Bibeldrucke vom 16. bis zum 19. Jahrhundert. Diss. Wien 1999, ᴰ*Raddatz, Alfred*: Studien zur Theologie 19: Wü 2001, Stephans 240 pp. €45. 3-929-734-19-2. 50 pl.

1788 *Müller, Augustin R.* BUBERs Verdeutschung der Schrift—die wirkliche Übersetzung?. Bibelübersetzung heute. 2001 ⇒468. 267-282.

1789 *Nebe, August; Herrmann, Johannes; Kittel, Gerhard* Einführung in die revidierten Teile der Lutherbibel von 1926;

1790 *Rupprecht, Walter* Die Bedeutung Karl FROMMANNs für die Erhaltung der Lutherbibel;

1791 *Schmidt, Lothar* Die Anfänge der ersten kirchenamtlichen Lutherbibelrevision;

1792 *Schröder, Karl Friedrich* Bericht über die Arbeit der Revisionskommission zur Probebibel 1883. Die Geschichte der Lutherbibelrevision von 1850 bis 1984. 2001 ⇒1763. 343-350/130-148/37-129/273-306.

1793 *Seyferth, Sebastian* Bibelsprachliche Lexemkonstanten in Martin LUTHERs Septembertestament, verglichen mit früheren spätmittelalterlichen Übersetzungen. Bibelübersetzung heute. 2001 ⇒468. 49-71.

1794 ^E**Steurer, Rita Maria** Das Alte Testament: Interlinearübersetzung Hebräisch-Deutsch, 4: Die 12 Kleinen Propheten, Hiob, Psalmen. ²1999 ⇒15,1617. ^RTheol(A) 72 (2001) 710-711 (*Simotas, Pan. N.*).

1795 *Stolt, Birgit* "... und fühl's im Herzen ...": LUTHERs Bibelübersetzung aus der Sicht neuerer Sprach- und Übersetzungswissenschaft. ZThK 98 (2001) 186-208.

D6.4 Versiones slavoniae *et variae*

1796 *Abela, Anthony* Suggestions for changes in the second edition of the Maltese Bible. Sijon 2 (2001) 47-84.

1797 *Albrektson, Bertil* Gamla Testamentet på svenska under det gångna seklet. SEÅ 66 (2001) 13-24.

1798 *Álvarez-Pedrosa, Juan Antonio* Particularidades de la traducción al antiguo eslavo de los nombres de oficios en los evangelios. Pensiero e istituzioni. 2001 ⇒580. 11-25.

1799 *Combrink, Bernard* The Afrikaans translation of the bible for the deaf. Scriptura 77 (2001) 297-302.

1800 *Ejrnæs, Bodil* Den nye danske bibeloversættelse—dens modtagelse og anvendelse. SEÅ 66 (2001) 25-37.

1801 *Fatica, Michele; Sanna, Gianluca* Francesco Saverio WANG e l'adattamento in cinese del Vecchio e Nuovo Testamento in strofe tetrastiche (1894). ^MCAGNI, L., 3. SMDSA 61: 2001 ⇒15. 1493-1528.

1802 **Garzaniti, Marcello** Die altslavische Version der Evangelien: Forschungsgeschichte und zeitgenössische Forschung. Bausteine zur slavischen Philologie und Kulturgeschichte Reihe A 33: Köln 2001, Böhlau vi; 795 pp. 3-412-17500-5.

1803 *Golub, Ivan* Tko je zaustavio tiskanje hrvatske biblije Bartola Kašica. BoSm 71 (2001) 153-170.

1804 **Himbaza, Innocent** Transmettre la bible: critique exégétique de la traduction de l'Ancien Testament: le cas du Rwanda. Diss. 1998. Vatican City 2001, Urbaniana Univ. Pr. [BuBB 33,54].

1805 **Hopkins-James, Lemuel J.** The Celtic gospels: their story and their text. Oxf 2001, OUP lxx (2) 278 pp. 0-19-924494-4.

1806 **Krašovec, Jože** Med izvirnikom in prevodi [Between original and translations]. Studijska zbirka, Svetopisemska druzba slovenije 3: Ljubljana 2001, Svetopisemska Druzba Slovenije 784 pp. 961-6138-53-7. Sum. 549-603; Bibl. 753-757; 56 pl. S.

1807 *Larsson, Göran* Arabiska bibelöversättningar i al-Andalus-ett steg mot konvertering. SvTK 77 (2001) 31-37.

1808 *Mbuwayesango, Dora R.* How local divine powers were suppressed: a case of Mwari of the Shona. Other ways. 2001 ⇒260. 63-77.

1809 *Naudé, J.A.* The Afrikaans bible translations and apartheid. AcTh(B) 21/1 (2001) 106-123.

1810 *Ntloedibe-Kuswani, Gomang Seratwa* Translating the divine: the case of Modimo in the Setswana Bible. Other ways. 2001 ⇒260. 78-97.

1811 *Soesilo, Daud* Translating 'the kingdom of God' in the Malay bible;
1812 Translating the names of God: recent experience from Indonesia and Malaysia. BiTr 52 (2001) 239-244/414-423.

1813 *Stander, H.F.* Afrikaanse bybelvertalings: 'n toekomsvisie. VeE 22 (2001) 379-391.

1814 Sveto pismo Stare in Nove zaveze: Slovenski standardni prevod iz izvirnih jezikov: studijska izdaja. Ljubljana 2001, Svetopisemska Druzba Slovenije 1952 pp. 961-6138-17-0. S.

1815 *Szesnat, Holger* Representing 'the text' in Pacific bible translations. Pacific Journal of Theology 26 (2001) 21-54.

1816 *Vander Stichele, Caroline* The Lord can no longer be taken for granted: the rendering of JHWH in the New Dutch Bible translation. YESW 9 (2001) 179-187.

1817 *Warzecha, Julian* Kilka uwag o V wydaniu Biblii Tysiaclecia. CoTh 71/1 (2001) 113-123. **P.**

1818 *Wendland, Ernst R.* The rhetoric of Christ in a Bantu language: hermeneutics in action during bible translation: with special reference to Christ's hillside discourse (Matt 5-7) in Chichewa. Neotest. 35 (2001) 1-33.

1819 Werk in uitvoring, 2: deeluitgavn van de [Nieuwe Bijbelvertaling], Genesis, 31 psalmen, Zacharia, Tobit, Marcus, 1 Kointhiërs, Openbaring., 2000 ⇒16,1719. [R]KeTh 52 (2001) 194-95 (*Kooyman, Arie C.*).

1820 **Zetzsche, Jost Oliver** The bible in China: the history of the Union Version. 1999 ⇒15,1637. [R]ASSR 114 (2001) 121-122 (*Aubin, Françoise*); NZM 57 (2001) 220-21 (*Meili, Josef*); ThLZ 126 (2001) 850-851 (*Gänßbauer, Monika*).

D7 *Problema vertentis*—Bible translation techniques

1821 *Barrick, William D.* The integration of OT theology with bible translation. Master's Seminary Journal 12/1 (2001) 15-31 [Gen 12,3; 15,5; 19,24].

1822 *Blois, Kees F. de; Mewe, Tamara* Functional equivalence and the new Dutch translation project. BiTr 52 (2001) 430-440.

1823 **Buzzetti, Carlo** Traduzione e tradizione: la via dell'uso-confronto (oltre il biblico "Traduttore traditore"). Studi religiosi: Padova 2001, Messaggero 254 pp. €16.5. 88-250-1041-9.

1824 *Buzzetti, Carlo; Lis, Marek* 'Translating' from medium to medium— what terms are appropriate?. BiTr 52 (2001) 441-445.

1825 *Crisp, Simon* Icône de l'ineffable?: un point de vue orthodoxe sur le langage, et ses implications pour la traduction biblique. CTrB 35 (2001) 26-33.

1826 *De Vries, Lourens* Bible translations: forms and functions;

1827 *Del Corro, Anicia* Bible translation and endangered languages: a Philippines perspective. BiTr 52 (2001) 306-319/201-210.

1828 *Fuchs, Ottmar* Die pragmatische Relevanz semantischer Beweglichkeit von Bibelausgaben. Bibelübersetzung heute. 2001 ⇒468. 235-264.

1829 **Hatim, Basil** Communication across cultures: translation theory and contrastive text linguistics. Exeter Linguistic Studies: Exeter 1997, Univ. of Exeter Pr. xvi; 235 pp. [R]JSSt 46 (2001) 128-131 (*Edwards, Malcolm*).

1830 *Hong, Joseph* Bible translation and endangered languages: some general reflections. BiTr 52 (2001) 210-215.

1831 *Joubert, S.J.* No culture shock?: addressing the Achilles heel of modern bible translations. VeE 22 (2001) 314-325.

1832 **Lapide, Pinchas** Bibbia tradotta bibbia tradita. CSB 36: 1999 ⇒15, 1643. [R]RivBib 49 (2001) 91-92 (*Ghidelli, Carlo*).

1833   **Long, Lynne** Translating the Bible: from the 7th to the 17th century. Ashgate new critical thinking in theology & biblical studies: Aldershot 2001, Ashgate vii; 230 pp. £40. 0-7546-1411-5. Bibl. 213-226.

1834   *Maire, John* Le pupitre du traducteur: un CD-ROM pour les traducteurs de la bible. CTrB 35 (2001) 4-6.

1835   *Meinhold, Arndt* Kriterien wissenschaftlichen Bibelübersetzens an Beispielen alttestamentlicher Kommentare. Bibelübersetzung heute. 2001 ⇒468. 151-165.

1836   **Metzger, Bruce Manning** The bible in translation: ancient and English versions. GR 2001, Baker 200 pp. $15. 0-8010-2282-7 [ThD 49,181—Heiser, W. Charles].

1837   *Noss, Philip A.* Choix lexicaux et lecture théologique—implications pour la formation des traducteurs. CTrB 35 (2001) 34-44;

1838   Wanto and Laaiso and the Gbaya bible: the trickster and his wife in scripture translation. BiTr 52 (2001) 114-132.

1839   *Nowell, Irene* The making of translations: a dilemma. Worship 75 (2001) 58-68.

1840   *Ogden, G.S.* Is it 'and' or 'but'?: ideology and translation. BiTr 52 (2001) 327-335.

1841   **Osimo, Bruno** Propedeutica della traduzione: corso introduttivo con tavole sinottiche. Mi 2001, Hoepli (6) 122 pp. 88-203-2935-2. Bibl. 115-120.

1842   *Porter, Stanley E.* Some issues in modern translation theory and study of the Greek New Testament. CurResB 9 (2001) 350-382.

1843   *Roubaud, Jacques* "Traduire pour les 'idiots'": Sébastien Châteillon et la bible. RSR 89 (2001) 353-376.

1844   **Rountree, Sara Catherine** Testing scripture translation for comprehension. Diss. Fuller Sem. 2001, 348 pp. 3006183.

1845   *Salevsky, Heidemarie* Übersetzungstyp, Übersetzungstheorie und Bewertung von Bibelübersetzungen (ein Beitrag aus übersetzungtheoretischer Sicht). Bibelübersetzung heute. 2001 ⇒468. 119-150.

1846   *Sloyan, Gerard S.* Some thoughts on bible translations. Worship 75 (2001) 228-249.

1847   **Sofer, Morry** The translator's handbook. ³1999 ⇒16,1743. ᴿBiTr 52 (2001) 151-153 (*Ellington, John*).

1848   *Spreafico, Ambrogio* Problemi di traduzione della bibbia. ᴹCAGNI, L., 4. SMDSA 61: 2001 ⇒15. 2153-2163.

1849   *Thomas, Kenneth J.* Allah in translations of the bible. BiTr 52 (2001) 301-306.

1850   *Van Leeuwen, Raymond C.* On bible translation and hermeneutics. ᶠTHISELTON, A. 2001 ⇒106. 284-311.

1851   *Wendland, Ernst* Contextualized translations and readings of the New Testament in Africa. BiTr 52 (2001) 132-144.

1852   *Wynn, Kerry* Disability in bible translation. BiTr 52 (2001) 402-414.

1853   *Zogbo, Lynell* Idéologie et traduction: le cas de *roûah 'elôhîm* et de *roûah YHWH* dans l'Ancien Testament. CTrB 35 (2001) 13-25.

D8   *Concordantiae, lexica specialia*—**Specialized dictionaries, synopses**

1854   **Cervantes Gabarrón, José** Sinopsis bilingüe de los tres primeros Evangelios con los paralelos del evangelio de Juan. 1999 ⇒15,1656; 16,1755. ᴿSalm. 48 (2001) 163-166 (*Guijarro, Santiago*); EstB 59 (2001) 556-558 (*Contreras Molina, F.*).

1855 ᴱElwell, Walter A. Die große Themenkonkordanz zur Bibel. Hänss-
ler-Lexikon. Holzgerlinge 2001, Hänssler xi; 1076 pp. 37751-30942.
1856 Hoffmann, Paul; Hieke, Thomas; Bauer, Ulrich Synoptic concordance... Greek... Acts, 1: introduction; A-D. 1999 ⇒15,1658; 16,
1758. ᴿRBLit 3 (2001) 371-373 (*Whitt, R. Keith*).
1857 Logos Bible Software Series X: original languages library (Libronix
digital library system 1.1a). Bellingham, Wash. 2001, Logos
Research Systems. $400.
1858 MacArthur, John The MacArthur topical bible. 1999 ⇒15,1659.
ᴿBS 158 (2001) 490-491 (*Zuck, Roy B.*).
1859 Sievers, Joseph Synopsis of the Greek sources for the Hasmonean
period: 1-2 Maccabees and Josephus, War 1 and Antiquities 12-14.
SubBi 20: R 2001, E.P.I.B. xii; 336 pp. 88-7653-615-9.

IV. Exegesis generalis VT vel cum NT

D9 Commentaries on the whole Bible or OT

1860 ᴱBarton, John; Muddiman, John The Oxford bible commentary.
Oxf 2001, OUP 1488 pp. £40. 0-19-875500-7. Bibl. 1331-1345.
ᴿNBl 82 (2001) 362-363 (*Kerr, Fergus*).
1861 ᴱBlack, Matthew Peake's commentary on the bible. NY 2001, Routledge 1126 pp. $40 [BiTod 40,192—Bergant, Dianne].
1862 ᴱEynikel, Erik, *al.*, Internationaal commentaar op de bijbel. Kampen
2001, Kok 2244 pp. €158.82. 90-435-0002-X.
1863 ᴱFarmer, William R. The international bible commentary: a catholic
and ecumenical commentary for the twenty-first century. 1998 ⇒14,
1535... 16,1762. ᴿPacifica 14 (2001) 87-88 (*Lawson, Veronica*); JBL
119 (2000) 335-337 (*Hauer, Christian E.*).
1864 Halbfas, Hubertus Die Bibel: erschlossen und kommentiert. Dü
²2001, Patmos 600 pp. €68. 3-491-70334-4.
1865 ᴱKeck, Leander E., *al.*, NIntB 6: Introduction to prophetic literature,
the book of Isaiah, the book of Jeremiah, the book of Baruch, the letter of Jeremiah, the book of Lamentations, the book of Ezekiel. Nv
2001, Abingdon xviii; 1612 pp. $70. 0-687-27819-8;
1866 NIntB 2: Numbers, Deuteronomy, introduction to narrative literature,
Joshua, Judges Ruth, 1&2 Samuel. 1998 ⇒14,1538... 16,1763.
ᴿHeyJ 42 (2001) 489-491 (*McNamara, Martin*);
1867 NIntB 3: Kings, Chronicles, Ezra, Nehemiah, Esther, Tobit, Judith.
1999 ⇒ 15,1669. ᴿCTJ 36 (2001) 385-387 (*Koopmans, William T.*).
1868 ᴱNewsom, Carol A.; Ringe, Sharon H. Women's bible commentary. ²1998 <1992> ⇒15,1673. With Apocrypha. ᴿVJTR 65
(2001) 781-782 (*Meagher, P.M.*).
1869 *Tomes, Roger* A century of The Century Bible. ET 112 (2001) 408-
412.
1870 *Vosloo, W.* Hoe om die Bybel beter te verstaan: verklarings van die
Bybel in Afrikaans. VeE 22 (2001) 178-190.
1871 Walton, John H.; Matthews, Victor Harold; Chavalas, Mark
William The IVP bible background commentary: Old Testament.
2000 ⇒16,1769. ᴿAUSS 39 (2001) 347-349 (*Shea, William H.*).

V. Libri historici VT

E1.1 Pentateuchus, Torah *Textus, commentarii*

1872 *Alexandre, Monique* Ecrits judéo-hellénistiques et pentateuque grec. Le pentateuque d'Alexandrie. 2001 ⇒1616. 86-98.

1873 *Auwers, Jean-Marie* Le pentateuque d'Alexandrie et le Texte Massorétique: enjeux d'une confrontation. Le pentateuque d'Alexandrie. 2001 ⇒1616. 60-66.

1874 ᴱ**Böckler, Annette** Die Tora nach der Übersetzung von Moses MEN-DELSSOHN: mit den Prophetenlesungen im Anhang. B 2001, Jüdische Verlagsanstalt 528 pp. €29.90. Vorwort v. *Tovia Ben-Chorin.*

1875 *Capelli, Piero* Septuaginta: libri sacri della diaspora giudaica e dei cristiani: IV giornata di studio: Gerusalemme ed Alessandria: uno stesso pentateuco?. Henoch 23 (2001) 113-114.

1876 *Casevitz, Michel* D'Homère aux historiens romains: le grec du pentateuque alexandrin. Le pentateuque d'Alexandrie. 2001 ⇒1616. 77-85.

1877 *Dogniez, Cécile* La présente édition du pentateuque d'Alexandrie. Le pentateuque d'Alexandrie. 2001 ⇒1616. 13-19.
ᴱ**Dogniez, C.; Harl, M.** Le pentateuque d'Alexandrie ⇒1616.

1878 *Dorival, Gilles* La traduction de la torah en grec. Le pentateuque d'Alexandrie. 2001 ⇒1616. 31-41.

1879 **Evans, Trevor V.** Verbal syntax in the Greek pentateuch: natural Greek usage and Hebrew interference. Oxf 2001, OUP xxiii; 335 pp. $85. 0-19-827010-0. Bibl. 298-318.

1880 **Friedman, Richard Elliott** Commentary on the Torah: with a new English translation. SF 2001, HarperSanFrancisco xvii; 681 pp. $50. 0-06-062561-9.

1881 *Himbaza, Innocent; Schenker, Adrian* Le Pentateuque samaritain de la Bibliothèque cantonale et universitaire Fribourg (Suisse) L 2057. ThZ 57 (2001) 221-226.

1882 *Joosten, Jan* Greek words shared by the Peshitta and targums to the pentateuch. ᴹWEITZMAN, M. JSOT.S 333: 2001 ⇒113. 165-177.

1883 *Le Boulluec, Alain* Le pentateuque dans la littérature chrétienne de langue grecque. Le pentateuque d'Alexandrie. 2001 ⇒1616. 106-12.

1884 **Leiner, Mordecai Joseph** Living waters: the Mei Hashiloach: a commentary on the Torah. ᴱᵀ*Edwards, Betsalel Philip*: Northvale, NJ 2001, Aronson xxii; 485 pp. 0-7657-6147-5.

1885 ᴱ**Lieber, David L.** Etz Hayim: Torah commentary. Ph 2001, Jewish Publication Society of America xxiv; 1560 pp. 0-8276-0712-1.

1886 ᴱ**Lienhard, Joseph T.** Exodus, Leviticus, Numbers, Deuteronomy. ACCS.OT 3: DG 2001, InterVarsity xxxi; 382 pp. $40. 0-8308-1473-6. Collab. *Ronnie J. Rombs*; Bibl. 361-372.

1887 ᴱᵀ**Mathews, Edward G.** The Armenian commentaries on Exodus-Deuteronomy attributed to EPHREM the Syrian. CSCO 587-588; CSCO.Ar 25-26: Lv 2001, Peeters 2 vols. 90-429-.

1888 ᴱ**Mortari, Luciana** Il pentateuco. La Bibbia dei LXX, 1. 1999 ⇒15, 1682; 16,1776. ᴿBZ 45 (2001) 116-118 (*Schenker, Adrian*).

1889 **Munk, Elie** The call of the torah: an anthology of interpretation and commentary on the five books of Moses. [T]*Mazer, E.S.*; [E]*Kirzner, Yitzchok*: Artscroll Mesorah: Brooklyn, NY 2001, Mesorah 5 vols. 0-899006-.

1890 *Munnich, Olivier* Le texte du pentateuque grec et son histoire. Le pentateuque d'Alexandrie. 2001 ⇒1616. 50-59.

1891 **Polliak, Meira** The Karaite tradition of Arabic bible translation... the pentateuch from the tenth and eleventh centuries C.E. EJM 17: 1997 ⇒13,1466... 16,1622. [R]RBLit 3 (2001) 505-506 (*Wheeler, Brannon*).

1892 **Van Seters, John** The pentateuch: a social-science commentary. 1999 ⇒15,1689; 16,1782. [R]JBL 120 (2001) 529-532 (*Wagenaar, Jan A.*); ThLZ 126 (2001) 519-521 (*Wischnowsky, Marc*).

1893 **Voitila, Anssi** Présent et imparfait de l'indicatif dans le pentateuque grec: une étude sur la syntaxe de traduction. Diss. Helsinki 2001, [D]*Sollamo, R.* SESJ 79: Gö 2001, Vandenhoeck & R. (6) xxxviii; 260 pp. 3-525-53518-X. Bibl. 241-253.

E1.2 *Pentateuchus* **Introductio: Fontes JEDP**

1894 *Bergey, Ronald; Berthoud, Pierre* L'A.T.: évolutions majeures au XXe siècle et perspectives d'avenir pour le XXIe siècle. Ḥokhma 77 (2001) 2-34 [BuBB 37,5].

1895 **Blenkinsopp, Joseph** El pentateuco: introducción a los cinco prime-ros libros de la biblia. 1999 ⇒15,1694. [R]ActBib 38 (2001) 197-198 (*Boada, J.*).

1896 *Boorer, Suzanne* The earth/land (ארץ) in the priestly material: the preservation of the "good" earth and the promised land Canaan throughout the generations. ABR 49 (2001) 19-33.

1897 *Brzegowy, Tadeusz* Kompozycja pięcioksięgu według Johna VAN SE-TERSA [La composition du pentateuqe selon John Van Seters]. ACra 33 (2001) 325-355. Rés. 355. P.

1898 *Dogniez, Cécile* Présentation des cinq livres. Le pentateuque d'Ale-xandrie. 2001 ⇒1616. 113-130.

1899 **Feiler, Bruce S.** Walking the bible: a journey by land through the five books of Moses. NY 2001, Morrow (12) 451 pp. 0-380-97775-3.

1900 **Frevel, Christian** Mit Blick auf das Land die Schöpfung erinnern: zum Ende der Priestergrundschrift. 2000 ⇒16,1789. [R]ThRv 97 (2001) 212-214 (*Otto, Eckart*).

1901 *Friedman, Richard Elliott* Studying Torah: commentary, interpreta-tion, translation. Jdm 50 (2001) 295-306.

1902 **Grauner, Axel** Der Elohist. [D]*Schmidt, W.H.*: Diss.-Habil. Bonn 2001 [RTL 33,632],

1903 *King, Greg* The documentary hypothesis. JATS 12/1 (2001) 22-30.

1904 **Kratz, Reinhard G.** Die Komposition der erzählenden Bücher des Alten Testaments: Grundwissen der Bibelkritik. UTB 2157: 2000 ⇒ 16,1800. [R]ZAR 7 (2001) 415-417 (*Otto, Eckart*).

1905 *Loader, James Alfred* Die redaktionelle Manifestation der Theologie des Pentateuch. Begegnung mit Gott. 2001 ⇒175. 19-30.

1906 *Marx, Alfred* L'impureté selon P: une lecture théologique. Bib. 82 (2001) 363-384.

1907 **Nicholson, Ernest Wilson** The pentateuch in the twentieth century: the legacy of Julius WELLHAUSEN. 1998 ⇒14,1584... 16,1804. [R]JBL 120 (2001) 348-350 (*Watts, James W.*).

1908 *North, Robert* Perspective of the Exodus author(s). ZAW 113 (2001) 481-504.
1909 *Rendtorff, Rolf* Directions in pentateuchal studies. Der Text in seiner Endgestalt. 2001 ⇒201. 103-125.
1910 **Rofé, Alexander** Introduction to the composition of the pentateuch. BiSe 58: 1999 ⇒15,1712. [R]BS 158 (2001) 495-496 (*Chisholm, Robert B.*); ZAR 7 (2001) 417-420 (*Otto, Eckart*); HebStud 42 (2001) 334-336 (*Person, Raymond F.*);
1911 La composizione del pentateuco: un'introduzione. CSB 35: 1999 ⇒ 15,1711; 16,1806. [R]RivBib 49 (2001) 218-225 (*Fanuli, Antonio*).
1912 *Ska, Jean Louis* La structure du pentateuque dans sa forme canonique. ZAW 113 (2001) 331-352.
1913 **Ska, Jean-Louis** Introduction à la lecture du pentateuque. 2000 ⇒ 16,1808. [R]NRTh 123 (2001) 99-100 (*Luciani, D.*); CEv 115 (2001) 65 (*Artus, Olivier*); RTL 32 (2001) 117-119 (*Wénin, A.*);
1914 Introduzione alla lettura del pentateuco. 2000 ⇒16,1807. [R]RivBib 49 (2001) 211-218 (*Fanuli, Antonio*);
1915 Introducción a la lectura del Pentateuco: claves para la interpretación de los cinco primeros libros de la biblia. [T]*Gordón, Francisco*: Estella (Navarra) 2001, Verbo Divino 383 pp. 84-8169-4355. Bibl. 321-358;
1916 Introduction à la lecture du pentateuque: clés pour l'interprétation des cinq premiers livres de la bible. [T]*Pahk, Johan Yeong-Sik*: Seoul 2001, St Pauls 486 pp. 89-8015-446-1. Bibl. 424-463. **K**.
1917 **Thompson, Thomas L.** The origin tradition of ancient Israel, 1: the literary formation of Genesis and Exodus 1-23. 1987 ⇒3,1917... 7, 1748. [R]VJTR 65 (2001) 146-148 (*Raj, M.I.*).
1918 *Vargon, Shmuel* The controversy between I.S. REGGIO and S.D. LUZZATTO on the date of the writing of the pentateuch. HUCA 72 (2001) 139-153.
1919 [E]**Watts, James Washington** Persia and torah: the theory of imperial authorization of the pentateuch. SBL.Symposium 17: Atlanta 2001, SBL xi; 228 pp. $40. 1-58983-015-6. Bibl. 183-213.

E1.3 *Pentateuchus*, **themata**

1920 *Blenkinsopp, Joseph* Was the pentateuch the civic and religous constitution of the Jewish ethnos in the Persian period?. Persia and torah. SBL Symposium 17: 2001 ⇒1919. 41-62.
1921 *Carmichael, Calum M.* Law and the narrative in the pentateuch. The Blackwell companion to the Hebrew Bible. 2001 ⇒653. 321-334.
1922 *Cerutti, Maria Vittoria* La terminologia religiosa e cultuale nel pentateuco greco. AnScR 6 (2001) 191-214.
1923 *Crüsemann, Frank* The torah and the unity of God. WaW 21/3 (2001) 243-252.
1924 *Rendtorff, Rolf* Creation and redemption in the torah. The Blackwell companion to the Hebrew Bible. 2001 ⇒653. 311-320.
1925 **Sassoon, Isaac S.D.** Destination torah: notes and reflections on selected verses from the weekly torah readings. Hoboken, NJ 2001, KTAV xvii; 364 pp. 0-88125-639-0.
1926 *Schmitt, Hans-Christoph* Die Suche nach der Identität des Jahweglaubens im nachexilischen Israel: Bemerkungen zur theologischen Intention der Endredaktion des Pentateuch. Theologie in Prophetie. 2001 <1995> ⇒209. 255-276.

1927 *Seebass, Horst* Jakob im Pentateuch ohne Genesis. [F]PURY, A. DE: MoBi 44: 2001 ⇒89. 329-338.

1928 **Sperling, S. David** The original torah: the political intent of the bible's writers. 1998 ⇒14,1603... 16,1819. [R]JBL 119 (2000) 547-549 (*Levenson, Jon D.*)

1929 **Sysling, Harry** Teḥiyyat ha-metim: the resurrection of the dead in the Palestinian targums of the pentateuch and parallel traditions in classical rabbinic literature. TSAJ 57 1996 ⇒12,1306... 15,1457. [R]RB 108 (2001) 312-313 (*Nodet, Étienne*).

1930 *Vignolo, Roberto* Il libro e la terra: la torah mosaica nella storia deuteronomistica. Teol(Br) 26 (2001) 185-212.

1931 *Warning, Wilfried* Terminological patterns and the verb mwl "circumcise" in the pentateuch. BN 106 (2001) 52-56;

1932 Terminological patterns and the term עצום 'strong, powerful' in the pentateuch. AUSS 39 (2001) 233-240.

1933 *Watts, James W.* Introduction. Persia and torah. SBL Symposium 17: 2001 ⇒1919. 1-4.

1934 **Watts, James Washington** Reading law: the rhetorical shaping of the pentateuch. BiSe 59: 1999 ⇒15,1743; 16,1820. [R]JBL 120 (2001) 350-352 (*Grundke, Christopher L.K.*).

1935 [E]**Wolowelsky, Joel B.** Women and the study of torah: essays from the pages of tradition. Essays from the Pages of Tradition: Hoboken, NJ 2001, KTAV xxi; 148 pp. 0-88125-690-0.

E1.4 Genesis; *textus, commentarii*

1936 [E]**Wénin, André** Studies in the book of Genesis: literature, redaction and history. BEThL 155: Lv 2001, University Press 643 pp. €60. 90-429-0934-X. [R]RSR 89 (2001) 530-531 (*Gibert, Pierre*); LouvSt 26 (2001) 369-370 (*Doyle, Brian*).

1937 [E]**Brenner, Athalya** Genesis. Feminist Comp. to the Bible II/1. 1998 ⇒14,1610; 16,1825. [R]YESW 9 (2001) 273-274 (*Rakel, Claudia*).

1938 **Brodie, Thomas L.** Genesis as dialogue: a literary, historical, & theological commentary. Oxf 2001, OUP xxxii; 579 pp. $65. 0-19-513836-8. Bibl. 533-561.

1939 **Cappelletto, Gianni** Genesi (Capitoli 12-50). Dabar—Logos—Parola, AT: Padova 2001, Messaggero 240 pp. €10.50. Bibl.

1940 *Cook, Johann* The Septuagint of Genesis: text and/or interpretation?. Studies in the book of Genesis. 2001 ⇒1936. 315-329 [Gen 1].

1941 Das erste Buch Mose, genannt Genesis. Fischer Taschenbuch 14501: Fra 2000, Fischer 148 pp. 3-596-14501-5. Mit einer Einleitung von *Joseph von Westphalen*.

1942 **Hendel, Ronald S.** The text of Genesis 1-11: textual studies and critical edition. 1998 ⇒14,1618... 16,1829. [R]JBL 119 (2000) 339-341 (*Greenspoon, Leonard J.*).

1943 *Hiebert, Robert J.V.* Translating a translation: the Septuagint of Genesis and the NETS Project. X Congress IOSCS. 2001 ⇒499. 263-84.

1944 **Johnson, Richard; Johnson, Tricia** Discovering Genesis. Crossway Bible Guide: Leicester 2001, Crossway 187 pp. 1-85684-202-9. Bibl. 186-187.

1945 **Joslin, Mary Coker; Watson, Carolyn C.J.** The Egerton Genesis. British Library Studies in Medieval Culture: L 2001, British Library xxvii; 312 pp. $75. 0-7123-4648-1. Bibl. 289-300; Egerton MS 1894.

1946 **Koudouguéret, David** Poétique et traduction biblique: les récits de la Genèse dans le système littéraire Sango. CNWS Publications 92: 2000 ⇒16,1832. ᴿBiTr 52 (2001) 148-149 (*Ellingworth, Paul*).

1947 **Krochmalnik, Daniel** Schriftauslegung, 1; das Buch Genesis im Judentum. Neuer Stuttgarter Kommentar: Altes Testament 33,1: Stu 2001, Kath. Bibelwerk 158 pp. €16.90. 3-460-07331-4.

1948 ᴱ**Louth, Andrew** Genesis I-II [!]. ACCS.OT 1: Ch 2001, Dearborn lii; 204 pp. $40. 1-57958-220-6. Collab. *Marco Conti* [Gen 1-11].

1949 ᴱᵀ**Mathews, Edward G.** The Armenian commentary on Genesis attributed to Eᴘʜʀᴇᴍ the Syrian. CSCO.Ar 23-24: Lv 1998, Peeters 2 vols. 90-429-0594-8/3-X.

1950 **Millard, Matthias** Die Genesis als Eröffnung der Tora: kompositions- und auslegungsgeschichtliche Annäherungen an das erste Buch Mose. WMANT 90: Neuk 2001, Neuk xii; 439 pp. €69. 3-7887-1830-7. Bibl. 377-410.

1951 **O'Loughlin, Thomas** Teachers and code-breakers: the Latin Genesis tradition, 430-800. Studia Patristica 35: 1999 ⇒15,1766; 16,1834. ᴿMillSt 47 (2001) 160-162 (*Lennon, Paul*).

1952 **Rogerson, John William; Moberly, R.W.L.; Johnstone, William** Genesis and Exodus. OTGu N.S. 1-2: Shf 2001, Sheffield A. 289 pp. $25. 1-84127-191-8. Introd. *John Goldingay*.

1953 *Strauss, Leo* On the interpretation of Genesis. Logos & Pneuma 15 (2001) 61-82.

1954 *Ter Haar Romeny, R.B.; Gentry, P.J.* Towards a new collection of Hexaplaric material for the book of Genesis. X Congress IOSCS. SBL.SCSt 51: 2001 ⇒499. 285-299.

1955 **Towner, Wayne Sibley** Genesis. Westminster Bible Companion: LVL 2001, Westminster x; 296 pp. $25. 0664-25256-7. Bibl. 293-96.

1956 **Trimpe, Birgit** Von der Schöpfung bis zur Zerstreuung: intertextuelle Interpretationen der biblischen Urgeschichte (Gen 1-11). 2000 ⇒ 16,1838. ᴿTThZ 110 (2001) 247-248 (*Haag, Ernst*).

1957 **Waltke, Bruce K.** Genesis: a commentary. GR 2001, Zondervan 656 pp. $40. 0-310-22458-6. With *Cathi J. Fredricks*; Bibl. 629-641.

E1.5 *Genesis*, topics

1958 *Abela, Anthony* Is Genesis the introduction of the primary history?. Studies in the book of Genesis. BEThL 155: 2001 ⇒1936. 397-406.

1959 **Brett, Mark G.** Genesis: procreation and the politics of identity. 2000 ⇒16,1842. ᴿBiblInterp 9 (2001) 336-337 (*Lang, Bernhard*); Pacifica 14 (2001) 328-330 (*Bulkeley, Tim*).

1960 *Brodie, Thomas L.* Genesis as dialogue: Genesis' twenty-six diptychs as a key to narrative unity and meaning;

1961 *Carr, David McLain* Genesis in relation to the Moses story: diachronic and synchronic perspectives. Studies in the book of Genesis. BEThL 155: 2001 ⇒1936. 297-314/273-295.

1962 *Cioli, Gianni* La pace nella *Genesi*. RAMi 26 (2001) 27-32.

1963 ᴱ**Dal Covolo, Enrico; Perrone, Lorenzo** Mosè ci viene letto nella chiesa: lettura delle Omelie di Oʀɪɢᴇɴᴇ sulla Genesi. BSRel 153:

1999 ⇒15,1749. ^RAsp. 48 (2001) 274-275 (*Iaia, Gaetano*); Sal. 63 (2001) 786-787 (*Malina, Anna*); CivCatt 152/4 (2001) 526-528 (*Cremascoli, G.*).

1964 *Frühwald, Wolfgang* Der "große Code der Kunst": das Buch Genesis in der Literatur. ^FSCHMUTTERMAYR, G. 2001 ⇒101. 403-417.

1965 **Gardner, Bruce K.** The Genesis calendar: the synchronistic tradition in Genesis 1-11. Lanham 2001, University Press of America xx; 374 pp. $48.50. 0-7618-1969-X. Bibl. 317-355 [Gen 5,1-32; 11,10-26].

1966 **Gilboa, R.** Intercourses in the book of Genesis: mythic motifs in creator-created relationships. 1998 ⇒14,1632. ^RJSSt 46 (2001) 152-153 (*Jenkins, Allan K.*).

1967 *Hall, Kevin* The theology of Genesis 1-11. SWJT 44/1 (2001) 56-75.

1968 **Humphreys, W. Lee** The character of God in the book of Genesis: a narrative appraisal. Old Testament Studies: LVL 2001, Westminster x; 284 pp. $30. 0-664-22360-5. Bibl. 273-281.

1969 *Kruger, Hennie A.J.* Subscripts to creation: a few exegetical comments on the literary device of repetition in Gen 1-11 [Gen 2,8-15];

1970 *Levin, Christoph* Gerechtigkeit Gottes in der Genesis [Gen 6,5-9,17; 18; 20]. Studies in the book of Genesis. BEThL 155: 2001 ⇒1936. 429-445/347-357.

1971 **Marabella, Lynne** Women and God: dialogues: hermeneutical interpretations of conversations in the book of Genesis. Diss. Pacifica Graduate Institute 2001, 230 pp. 3025061.

1972 *Minissale, Antonino* Elementi mitici in Gen 1-11: implicazioni ermeneutiche. ^MCAGNI, L., 4. SMDSA 61: 2001 ⇒15. 1811-1834.

1973 *Rendsburg, Gary A.* Reading David in Genesis: how we know the torah was written in the tenth century B.C.E. BiRe 17/1 (2001) 20-33, 46.

1974 **Vogels, Walter** Nos origines: Genèse 1-11. 2000 ⇒16,1860. ^RSR 30 (2001) 123-124 (*David, Robert*).

1975 *Wénin, André* La question de l'humain et l'unité du livre de la Genèse. Studies in the book of Genesis. BEThL 155: 2001 ⇒1936. 3-34.

1976 **Williams, Michael James** Deception in Genesis: an Investigation into the morality of a unique biblical phenomenon. Studies in Biblical Literature 32: NY 2001, Lang xviii; 252 pp. £36. 0-8204-5154-1. Bibl. 227-244.

1977 **Witte, Markus** Die biblische Urgeschichte: redaktions- und theologiegeschichtliche Beobachtungen zu Genesis 1,1-11,26. BZAW 265: 1998 ⇒14,1640... 16,1862. ^RThLZ 126 (2001) 34-36 (*Blum, Erhard*); Bib. 82 (2001) 270-273 (*Otto, Eckart*).

1978 **Yoo, Yeon Hee Yani** A rhetorical reading of the Rebekah narratives in the book of Genesis. Diss. New York, Union 2001, ^D*Trible, P.*: 277 pp. 3010000 [RTL 33,635].

E1.6 Creatio, *Genesis 1s*

1979 *Albani, Matthias* "Kannst du die Sternbilder hervortreten lassen zur rechten Zeit...? (Hi 38,32): Gott und Gestirne im Alten Testament und im Alten Orient. Das biblische Weltbild. 2001 ⇒285. 181-226.

1980 *Arnould, Jacques* Au commencement, Dieu créa le ciel et la terre. MoBi 133 (2001) 14-19 [BuBB 35,68].

1981 *Barbiero, Gianni* Il lavoro e il riposo di Dio: riflessioni in margine al racconto sacerdotale della creazione. Horeb 10/2 (2001) 30-35.

1982 *Bauks, Michaela* "Chaos" als Metapher für die Gefährdung der Welt-
      ordnung. Das biblische Weltbild. FAT 32: 2001 ⇒285. 431-464;
1983 Genesis 1 als Programmschrift der Priesterschrift (Pg). Studies in the
      book of Genesis. BEThL 155: 2001 ⇒1936. 333-345.
1984 *Belardi, Walter* Impositio nominum e problemi connessi nella 'Gene-
      si', nei Presocratici e in PLATONE. RANL.mor 12 (2001) 345-394.
1985 *Breukelman, Frans; Dzubba, Horst* Befreiung als kosmisches Drama.
      TeKo 24/2 (2001) 32-41 [Ps 18,1-20; Jer 14,1-17; Jonah 2,2-10].
1986 *Brottier, Laurence* La lecture Chrysostomienne des deux premiers
      chapitres de la *Genèse*: une création ordonnée et offerte en spectacle
      à l'homme. ConnPE 84 (2001) 23-31.
1987 *Burnet, Régis: Morales, Xavier* Créés à l'image de l'homme à venir.
      Com(F) 26 (2001) 11-22 [Gen 1,26].
1988 *Christian, Ed* Genesis 1 as vision: what are the implications?. JATS
      12/1 (2001) 139-159.
1989 *Díez Merino, Luis* El hombre imagen y semejanza de Dios en la lite-
      ratura judía antigua. CTom 128 (2001) 277-315 [Gen 1,26].
1990 *Ego, Beate; Janowski, Bernd* Bibliographie zum biblischen Weltbild
      und seinen altorientalischen Kontexten. Das biblische Weltbild. FAT
      32: 2001 ⇒285. 543-558.
1991 *Fantino, Jacques* La création d'après S. IRÉNÉE. ConnPE 84 (2001)
      10-22;
1992 Nature et création: imaginaire et réalité. Le discours religieux. 2001
      ⇒506. 81-97.
1993 *Greenfield, Jonas C.* A touch of Eden. 'Al kanfei yonah, 2. 2001
      <1984> ⇒153. 750-755 [Gen 2,8].
1994 *Gruber, Meir* 'In the image of God': what is it?. [F]AHITUV, S. 2001 ⇒
      1. 81-87 [Gen 1,26-27].
1995 *Harris, John L.* An exposition of Genesis 2:4-11:32. SWJT 44/1
      (2001) 39-55.
1996 *Hartenstein, Friedhelm* Wolkendunkel und Himmelsfeste: zur Gene-
      se und Kosmologie der Vorstellung des himmlischen Heiligtums
      JHWHs. Das biblische Weltbild. FAT 32: 2001 ⇒285. 125-179.
1997 **Hayes, Zachary** The gift of being: a theology of creation. ColMn
      2001, Liturgical vi; 129 pp. $15. 0-8146-5941-1. [R]MillSt 48 (2001)
      155-158 (*Ryan, Fainche*).
1998 *Janowski, Bernd* Das biblische Weltbild: eine methodologische Skiz-
      ze. Das biblische Weltbild. FAT 32: 2001 ⇒285. 3-26.
1999 *Kegler, Jürgen* Die Ur-geschichte von Welt und Mensch: biblische
      Schöpfungsaussagen—neu gesehen. Gesammelte Aufsätze. BEAT
      48: 2001 <1987> ⇒167. 127-137.
2000 *Kvalvaag, Robert W.* Det gamle testamente og den guddommelige
      livspust. Ung teologi 34/3 (2001) 81-92 [Gen 2,7].
2001 *Lieberg, Godo* Homo imago deorum deive: a *Genesi* et OVIDIO ad S.
      THOMAM. Latinitas 49 (2001) 76-82 [Gen 1,26-27].
2002 *Loretz, Oswald* Gen 1,2 als Fragment aus einem amurritisch-kanaanä-
      ischen Schöpfungsmythos in neuer ägyptischer Deutung. UF 33
      (2001) 387-401;
2003 Genesis 1,2 als Fragment eines amurritisch-kanaanäischen Schöp-
      fungsmythos. [F]VEENHOF, K. 2001 ⇒111. 287-300.
2004 *Lucci, Laila* Il lavoro nei racconti biblici della creazione e nei miti
      mesopotamici. RivBib 49 (2001) 3-41.
2005 **Morales, José** Creation theology. Dublin 2001, Four Courts 261 pp.
      1-85182-264-X.

2006 *Mutius, Hans-Georg von* Der hebräische Text von Genesis 2,1 im Licht der Septuaginta und der rabbinischen Schriftauslegung. ^FDENZ, A. 2001 ⇒21. 107-112.

2007 *Pasquet, Colette* La création chez les Pères syriaques. ConnPE 84 (2001) 44-55.

2008 *Ravasi, Gianfranco* 'Dio vide che era *tôv*' (Gen 1). La bellezza. PSV 44: 2001 ⇒240. 11-20.

2009 *Ravazzolo, Roberto* L'Esamerone nel IV secolo: una pagina di letteratura cristiana antica. StPat 48 (2001) 385-412.

2010 *Smelik, Klaas A.D.* The creation of the sabbath (Gen 1:1-2:3). ^FDEURLOO, K. ACEBT.S 2: 2001 ⇒23. 9-11.

2011 *Stipp, Hermann-Josef* Dominium terrae: die Herrschaft der Menschen über die Tiere in Gen 1,26.28. ^FGROß, W. ATSAT 68: 2001 ⇒ 38. 113-148.

2012 *Van Bemmelen, Peter M.* Divine accommodation and biblical creation: CALVIN vs. McGrath. AUSS 39 (2001) 109-116.

2013 *Vannier, Marie-Anne* La création chez les Pères;
2014 La création et son accomplissement chez S. AUGUSTIN. ConnPE 84 (2001) 2-9/32-43.

2015 *Vervenne, Marc* Genesis 1,1-2,4: the compositional texture of the Priestly overture to the pentateuch. Studies in the book of Genesis. BEThL 155: 2001 ⇒1936. 35-79.

2016 *Vidal, Marie* Homme et femme: il les créa. Christus 48 (2001) 159-166 [Gen 1,27].

E1.7 *Genesis 1s*: Bible and myth [⇒M3.8]

2017 *Brzegowy, Tadeusz* Kosmologia (kosmogonia) biblijna. ^FJANKOWSKi, A. 2001 ⇒53. 68-86. **P.**

2018 *Kaiser, Otto* Die Schöpfungsmacht des Wortes Gottes. IKaZ 30 (2001) 6-17.

2019 *Keel, Othmar* Altägyptische und biblische Weltbilder, die Anfänge der vorsokratischen Philosophie und das ARCHÄ-Problem in späten biblischen Schriften. Das biblische Weltbild. 2001 ⇒285. 27-63.

2020 *Klein, George L.* Reading Genesis 1. SWJT 44/1 (2001) 22-38.
^E**Linke, B.** Schöpfungsmythologie in den Religionen ⇒369.

2021 *Müller, Hans-Peter* History-oriented foundation myths in Israel and its environment. Religious identity. 2001 ⇒549. 156-168.

2022 ^E**Sánchez Leon, María Luisa** Religions del món antic: la creació: II cicle de conferències. Palma 2001, Universitat de les Illes Balears 205 pp. 84-7632-710-2. Bibl. 204-205.

2023 *Schmidt, Josef* Zum Begriff der Schöpfung—theologisch, philosophisch. ZKTh 123 (2001) 129-142.

2024 *Simian-Yofre, Horacio* L'assimilazione di culture straniere nella S. Scrittura: riflessione critica. L'interpretazione della bibbia nella chiesa. 2001 ⇒471. 90-105.

2025 *Talon, Philippe* Enūma Eliš and the transmission of Babylonian cosmology to the west. Mythology and mythologies. 2001 ⇒589. 265-277.

2026 *Waschke, Ernst Joachim* Mythos als Strukturelement und Denkkategorie biblischer Urgeschichte. Der Gesalbte. 2001 <1986> ⇒227. 189-205.

2027 **Wright, J. Edward** The early history of heaven. 2000 ⇒16,1930.
      ᴿJR 81 (2001) 276-278 (*Collins, John J.*); JECS 9 (2001) 291-292
      (*Kelly, Joseph F.*); CBQ 63 (2001) 537-538 (*Hawkins, Ralph K.*);
      HebStud 42 (2001) 315-321 (*Smith, Mark Stratton*).
2028 *Wyatt, N.* The mythic mind. SJOT 15 (2001) 3-56.

E1.8 *Gen 1s, Jos 10,13...*: The Bible, the Church and science

2029 **Aviezer, Nathan** Fossils and faith: understanding torah and science.
      Hoboken, NJ 2001, KTAV xv; 270 pp. $25. 0-88125-607-2.
2030 *Chiyu, Wu* Legend in the *Old Testament* and in the *Huainan zi* on the
      stopping of the solar movement. ᶠHAMILTON, J. 2001 ⇒43. 379-400
      [Josh 10,12-13; 1 Kgs 3,16-27].
2031 **Fripp, Robert** Let there be life: a scientific and poetic retelling of
      the Genesis creation story. Mahwah 2001, HiddenSpring 196 pp.
      $18.
2032 *Giorello, G.* Intrecci e conflitti tra il dato di fede e il dato scientifico.
      CredOg 123 (2001) 19-26.
2033 **Greene-MacCreight, Kathryn E.** Ad litteram: how AUGUSTINE,
      CALVIN and BARTH read the "plain sense" of Genesis 1-3. 1999 ⇒15,
      1859; 16,1936. ᴿProEc 10/1 (2001) 104-105 (*Black, C. Clifton*).
2034 **Griffin, David Ray** Religion and scientific naturalism: overcoming
      the conflicts. 2000 ⇒16,1937. ᴿTS 62 (2001) 413-415 (*Korsmeyer,
      Jerry D.*).
2035 **Harrison, Peter** The bible, Protestantism, and the rise of natural
      science. 1998 ⇒14,1703... 16,1938. ᴿJR 81 (2001) 128-129
      (*Gerrish, B.A.*); JThS 52 (2001) 429-433 (*Mandelbrote, Scott*).
2036 *Jiménez Ortiz, Antonio* Es creíble todavía la fe en Dios creador?. EE
      76 (2001) 639-652.
2037 *Koltermann, Rainer* Evolution, creation, and church documents. ThD
      48 (2001) 124-132.
2038 ᴱ**Lerner, Michel-Pierre** Tommaso CAMPANELLA: apologia pro GALI-
      LEO: apologie de Galilée. Science et humanisme: P 2001, Belles
      Lettres clxxviii; 336 pp. €39.64. Texte, traduction et notes. ᴿSapDom
      54 (2001) 371-373 (*Miele, Michele*); FZPhTh 48 (2001) 496-498
      (*Accietto-Gualtieri, Marie-Jeanne*).
2039 **Levi, Yehuda** Ha-maddaᶜ she-ba-Torah [The science in the torah]. J
      2001, Jerusalem College of Technology 118; x pp. Eng. sum. **H.**
2040 **Lucas, Ernest** Can we believe Genesis today?: the bible and the
      questions of science. Leicester 2001, Inter-Varsity Press 192 pp. £7.
      0-85111-658-2.
2041 *Moda, A.* Invito alla lettura: bibliografia... [scienza e fede]. CredOg
      123 (2001) 123-134.
2042 *Morandini, S.* Il dibattito scienza-fede: coordinate per una mappa.
      CredOg 123 (2001) 7-18.
2043 ᴱ**Motta, Franco** GALILEO Galilei: lettera a Cristina di Lorena sull'uso
      della bibbia nelle argomentazioni scientifiche. 2000 ⇒16,1943.
      ᴿRRFC 95 (2001) 454-458 (*Tugnoli, Claudio*).
2044 *Ong, Walter J.* Where are we now?: some elemental cosmological
      considerations. ThD 48 (2001) 119-123.
2045 *Pesce, M.* Ermeneutica biblica e scienza: un problema storico.
      CredOg 123 (2001) 27-44.

2046   **Rowland, Wade** GALILEO's mistake: the archeology of a myth.
       Toronto 2001, Allen 350 pp. $35.
2047   **Whedbee, J. William** The bible and the cosmic vision. 1998 ⇒14,
       1711; 15,1869. [R]JBL 120 (2001) 393-395 (*Noegel, Scott B.*).

E1.9 *Peccatum originale,* the sin of Eden, *Genesis 2-3*

2048   *Alegre, Xavier* El pecado del mundo: el maligno es mentiroso, encu-
       bridor y asesino. Conc(E) 37 (2001) 733-740 [Conc(I) 37,855-864;
       Conc(GB) 2001/5,51-58; Conc(D) 37/5,574-581].
2049   *Anderson, Gary A.* Biblical origins and the problem of the Fall.
       ProEc 10/1 (2001) 17-30.
2050   *Ansell, Nicholas J.* The call of wisdom—the voice of the serpent: a
       canonical approach to the tree of knowledge. CScR 31/1 (2001) 31-
       57.
2051   *Báez, Silvio José* L'uomo nel progetto di Dio: Genesi 1-3. Antropolo-
       gia cristiana. 2001 ⇒371. 167-205.
2052   *Beuttler, Ulrich* Gestörte Gemeinschaft: das biblische Verständnis
       der Sünde. Glaube und Denken 14 (2001) 43-54.
2053   [E]*Billon, Gérard* Le diable. DosB 89 (2001) 3-29.
2054   **Braaten, Carl E.; Jenson, Robert W.** Sin, death and the devil. GR
       2000, Eerdmans 137 pp. $15. 0-8028-4695-5. [R]VeE 22 (2001) 478-
       479 (*Joubert, S.J.*).
2055   *Bramorski, Jacek* Personalistyczny wymiar grzechu w świetle biblij-
       nej relacji o upadku pierwszych rodziców [Dimension personnaliste
       du péché dans le récit biblique de la chute des premiers parents]. AtK
       554 (2001) 4-16. P.
2056   **Callender, Dexter E.** Adam in myth and history: ancient Israelite
       perspectives on the primal human. HSSt 48: 2000 ⇒16,1957. [R]CBQ
       63 (2001) 309-310 (*Gorman, Frank H.*).
2057   **Delumeau, Jean** History of paradise: the Garden of Eden in myth
       and tradition. [T]*O'Connell, Matthew*: 2000 ⇒16,1969. [R]CTJ 36
       (2001) 391-393 (*Williams, Michael J.*);
2058   Que reste-t-il du paradis?. 2000 ⇒16,1968. [R]Annales 56/1 (2001)
       271-275 (*Boutry, Philippe*); EeV 48 (2001) 11-12 (*Jay, Pierre*).
2059   *Dietrich, Manfried* Das biblische Paradies und der babylonische
       Tempelgarten: Überlegungen zur Lage des Gartens Eden. Das bibli-
       sche Weltbild. FAT 32: 2001 ⇒285. 281-323.
2060   *Eco, Umberto* On the possibility of generating aesthetic messages in
       an Edenic language. The postmodern bible reader. 2001 <1984> ⇒
       287. 78-91.
2061   *Emmrich, Martin* The temptation narrative of Genesis 3:1-6: a pre-
       lude to the pentateuch and the history of Israel. EvQ 73 (2001) 3-20.
2062   **Falmagne, Thomas** Un texte en contexte: les flores paradisi et le
       milieu culturel de Villers-en-Brabant dans la première moitié du 13e
       siècle. IP 39: Turnhout 2001, Brepols 580 pp. 2-503-51067-1.
2063   *Grundke, Christopher L.K.* A tempest in a teapot?: Genesis III 8
       again. VT 51 (2001) 548-551.
2064   *Kruger, H.A.J.* Genesis 3 Part II: myth as vehicle for a polemic
       against religion, ideology and wisdom. OTEs 14 (2001) 214-234.
2065   *Lauer, Stewart E.* Was the tree of life always off-limits?: a critique of
       Vos's answer. Kerux 16/3 (2001) 42-50.

2066 ^E**Luttikhuizen, Gerard P.** Paradise interpreted: representations of biblical paradise in Judaism and Christianity. 1999 ⇒15,422; 16. 1980. ^RJThS 52 (2001) 207-208 (*Barker, Margaret*); JSJ 32 (2001) 317-325 (*Pesthy, Monika*); ThLZ 126 (2001) 266-267 (*Pezzoli-Olgiati, Daria*); Apocrypha 12 (2001) 276-277 (*Zamagni, C.*).

2067 **Messadié, Gerald** História geral do diabo—da antiguidade à época contemporânea. Mem Martins 2001, Europa-América 444 pp. ^RBrot. 153 (2001) 747-748 (*Lopes, P. Pires*).

2068 *Mosès, Stéphane* Adamo ed Eva. L'Eros e la legge. Schulim Vogelmann 80: 2001 ⇒185. 11-31.

2069 **Norris, Pamela** Eve: a biography. NY 1999, New York Univ. Pr. 496 pp. 0-8147-5812-6.

2070 *Pfeiffer, Henrik* Der Baum in der Mitte des Gartens: zum überlieferungsgeschichtlichen Ursprung der Paradieserzählung (Gen 2,4b-3,24): Teil II: prägende Traditionen und theologische Akzente. ZAW 113 (2001) 2-16.

2071 *Rudman, D.* Falling for the wrong woman?: a theological reassessment of Genesis 2-3. ET 113 (2001) 44-47;

2072 A little konwledge is a dangerous thing: crossing forbidden boundaries in Gen 3-4. Studies in the book of Genesis. BEThL 155: 2001 ⇒1936. 461-466.

2073 *Schüngel-Straumann, Helen* Adam & Eva: Buch Genesis, Kapitel 2 und 3. Schön bist du. 2001 ⇒274. 28-37.

2074 *Spieckermann, Hermann* Ambivalenzen: ermöglichte und verwirklichte Schöpfung in Gen 2f. Gottes Liebe zu Israel. FAT 33: 2001 <2000> ⇒215. 49-61.

2075 **Stordalen, Terje** Echoes of Eden: Genesis 2-3 and symbolism of the Eden garden in biblical Hebrew literature. 2000 ⇒16,1987. ^RJBL 120 (2001) 741-744 (*Levison, John R.*).

2076 *Strus, Andrzej* Gn 2,4b-3,24: structure et décodage du message. Studies in the book of Genesis. BEThL 155: 2001 ⇒1936. 447-460.

2077 *Tillesse, Caetano Minette de* Ecclesiologia 5: Gênesis 2-11: matrimônio e aliança; Gênesis 3: o pecado. RBBras 18 (2001) 355-378.

2078 *Wehrle, Josef* Wesen und Wandel der Satansvorstellung im Alten Testament. MThZ 52 (2001) 194-207.

2079 **Williams, Patricia A.** Doing without Adam and Eve: sociobiology and original sin. Theology and the sciences: Mp 2001, Fortress xvii; 227 pp. 0-8006-3285-0. Bibl. 209-219.

E2.1 Cain and Abel; *gigantes, longaevi; Genesis 4s*

2080 **Balmary, Marie** Abel ou la traversée de l'Eden. 1999 ⇒15,1900; 16,1994. ^RETR 76 (2001) 144-145 (*Causse, Jean-Daniel*).

2081 *Butting, Klara* Kain en Abel—en Set. ITBT 9/1 (2001) 5-6.

2082 *Chennattu, Rekha* The story of Cain (Genesis 4,1-16): a cry for divine-human-cosmic harmony. BiBh 27 (2001) 255-270.

2083 *Gillet-Didier, Véronique* Généalogies anciennes, généalogies nouvelles: formes et fonctions. FV 100/4 (2001) 3-12.

2084 **Hughes, Richard A.** Cain's lament: a christian moral psychology. Studies in Biblical Literature 35: NY 2001, Lang xix; 221 pp. 0-8204-5222-X [Gen 4,13-16].

2085 *Kim, Angela Y.* Cain and Abel in the light of envy: a study in the history of the interpretation of envy in Genesis 4,1-16. JSPE 12 (2001) 65-84.

2086 *Kio, Stephen Hre* Revisiting 'the sons of God' in Genesis 6.1-4. BiTr 52 (2001) 234-239.

2087 *Malamat, Abraham* Tribal societies: biblical genealogies and African lineage systems. History of biblical Israel. Culture and history of the ANE 7: 2001 <1973> ⇒182. 41-53.

2088 *Prato, Gian Luigi* Integrità testuale e coerenza ermeneutica per i tempi primordiali di Gen 6,1-4. ^MCAGNI, L., 4. SMDSA 61: 2001 ⇒15. 1991-2016.

2089 *Rizzi, Armido* Parola di Dio e diritti umani. Horeb 28/1 (2001) 58-61 [Gen 4,1-16].

2090 *Schrenk, Sabine* Kain und Abel. RAC 19 (2001) 943-972.

2091 *Stadelmann, Luis* The giants in the bible. Month 34 (2001) 120-122 [Gen 6,1-4].

E2.2 *Diluvium,* the Flood; *Gilgameš (Atraḫasis)*; Genesis 6...

2092 *Abusch, Tzvi* The epic of Gilgamesh and the Homeric epics. Mythology and mythologies. 2001 ⇒589. 1-6.

2093 *Böttrich, Christfried* Die Baumasse der Arche in jüdischer und christlicher Auslegung. Leqach 1 (2001) 90-106 [BuBB 36,137].

2094 *Braarvig, Jens* Gilgamesh-eposets ellevte tavle: en oversettelse til norsk, tilegnet Arvid Tångberg. TTK 72 (2001) 85-96.

2095 **Cavigneaux, Antoine; Al-Rawi, Farouk N.H.** Gilgames et la mort: textes de Tell Haddad VI: avec un appendice sur les textes funéraires sumériens. 2000 ⇒16,2010. ^RBiOr 58 (2001) 411-416 (*Römer, W.H.Ph.*); WZKM 91 (2001) 418-422 (*Selz, Gebhard J.*).

2096 *Chopineau, Jacques* L'histoire de Noé, étude litteraire. Quand le texte devient parole. AnBru 6: 2001 ⇒135. 48-56.

2097 *Dalley, Stephanie* Old Babylonian tablets from Nineveh; and possible pieces of early Gilgamesh Epic. Iraq 63 (2001) 155-167.

2098 *Disse, Andreas* Turmbau oder Sprachverwirrung?: von der Exegese zur Religionspädagogik. ^FGROß, W. ATSAT 68: 2001 ⇒36. 23-44 [Gen 11,1-9].

2099 *Dohmen, Christoph* Untergang oder Rettung der Quellenscheidung?: die Sintfluterzählung als Prüfstein der Pentateuchexegese. Studies in the book of Genesis. BEThL 155: 2001 ⇒1936. 81-104.

2100 **Ebach, Jürgen** Noah: die Geschichte eines Überlebenden. Biblische Gestalten 3: Lp 2001, Evangelische Verlagsanstalt 249 pp. €14.50. 3-374-01912-9.

2101 *Fewell, Danna Nolan* Building Babel. Postmodern interpretations. 2001 ⇒229. 1-16 [Ge 11,1-9].

2102 ^{TE}**Foster, Benjamin Read** The epic of Gilgamesh: a new translation, analogue, criticism. ^T*Frayne, Douglas Ralph; Beckman, Gary M.*: A Norton Critical Edition: NY 2001, Norton xxiii; 229 pp. 0-393-9751-6-9. Bibl. 229. ^RWZKM 91 (2001) 422-433 (*Selz, Gebhard J.*).

2103 *Grottanelli, Cristiano* The story of Combabos and the Gilgamesh tradition. Mythology and mythologies. 2001 ⇒589. 19-27. Contrib. by *Simo Parpola.*

2104 *Heltzer, Michael* Noah's drunkenness: (Gen 9,20-23) and the Greek variant about the first wine-drinking. ᶠHuß, W. OLA 104: 2001 ⇒51. 7-12.

2105 *Jonker, Louis* The biblical legitimization of ethnic diversity in apartheid theology. Scriptura 77 (2001) 165-183 [Gen 10-11].

2106 *Kwong, Andrew P.* Does God repent (Gen 6:6?). Jian Dao 15 (2001) 19-51. Sum. 51. **C**.

2107 *Landy, Francis* Flood and Fludd. Beauty and the enigma. JSOT.S 312: 2001 <1998> ⇒171. 328-370.

2108 *Marchesi, Gianni* ì-a Lullum, ù-luḫ-ḫa sù-sù: on the incipit of the Sumerian poem Gilgameš and Ḫuwawa B. ᴹCAGNI, L., 2. SMDSA 61: 2001 ⇒15. 673-684.

2109 *Millard, Alan R.* Where was Abraham's Ur?: the case for the Babylonian city. BArR 27/3 (2001) 52-53, 57 [Gen 11,31].

2110 *Mulzac, Kenneth* Genesis 9:1-7: its theological connections with the creation motif. JATS 12/1 (2001) 65-77.

2111 *Noel, Ted; Noel, Ken* A scientific paradigm for the Genesis Flood. JATS 12/1 (2001) 106-138.

2112 **Rizzi, Giovanni, Caglioni, Adriano; Redaelli, Raffaella** Il patto con Noè: tradizioni bibliche, giudaiche, cristiane e coraniche a confronto. Sintesi e proposte 21: San Cataldo—Caltanisetta 2001, Centro Studi Cammarata 368 pp. 88-8243-057-X.

2113 **Saporetti, Claudio** Il Ghilgames: l'epopea del più noto personaggio della letteratura sumero-babilonese nell'ultima traduzione effettuata dall'originale cuneiforme delle dodici tavole rinvenute nella biblioteca del re Assurbanipal (VII secolo) a Ninive. Il piacere di raccontare: Mi 2001, Simonelli 187 pp. 88-86792-26-3.

2114 **Schrott, Raoul** Gilgamesh: Epos. Mü 2001, Hanser 342 pp. €25.51. 3-446-20060-6. Wissenschaftlicher Anhang von *Robert Rollinger* u. *Manfred Schretter*; Bibl. 330-334.

2115 *Seely, Paul H.* The date of the tower of Babel and some theological implications. WThJ 63 (2001) 15-38 [Gen 11,1-9].

2116 **Seguin, Maria Susanna** Science et religion dans la pensée française du XVIIIᵉ siècle: le mythe du déluge universel. Les dix-huitièmes siècles 52: P 2001, Champion 536 pp.

2117 **Shehata, Dahlia** Annotierte Bibliographie zum altbabylonischen Atramhasis-Mythos Inuma ilu awilum. Göttinger Arbeitshefte zur altorientalischen Literatur 3: Gö 2001, Seminar für Keilschriftforschung (12) 201 pp. 3-936297-00-2. Bibl. 166-186.

2118 *Van den Eynde, Sabine* The missing link: ברית in the flood narrative: meaning and peculiarities of a Hebrew key word. Studies in the book of Genesis. BEThL 155: 2001 ⇒1936. 467-478.

2119 **Vicari, Jacques** La tour de Babel. QSJ 3555: 2000 ⇒16,2024. ᴿAkkadica 122 (2001) 77-78 (*Veenhof, Klaas R.*);

2120 La Torre di Babele. ᵀ*Teodorani, Alda*: La via dei simboli: R 2001, Arkeios 154 pp. 88-86495-58-7 [Gen 11,1-9].

2121 **Wilson, Ian** Before the flood: understanding the biblical flood story as recalling a real-life event. L 2001, Orion xv; 336 pp. 0-75284-6353. Bibl. 303-309.

E2.3 **Patriarchae, Abraham**; *Genesis 12s*

2122 *Boase, Elizabeth* Life in the shadows: the role and function of Isaac in Genesis—synchronic and diachronic readings. VT 51 (2001) 312-335 [Gen 26].

2123 *Chopineau, Jacques* Texte et parole: l'art du récit dans l'histoire d' Abraham. Quand le texte devient parole. AnBru 6: 2001 ⇒135. 57-73.

2124 *Çığ, Muazzez Ilmiye* Father Abraham-Sara and the god and goddess Dumuzi-Inanna. ᴹCAGNI, L., 3. SMDSA 61: 2001 ⇒15. 1451-1457 [Gen 12,10-20; Prov 19,13; 27,15].

2125 *Dyk, Janet W.* Lack of space and loneliness: Abraham and Lot separate. ᶠDEURLOO, K. ACEBT.S 2: 2001 ⇒23. 13-19 [Gen 13,1-18].

2126 *Evans, Craig A.* Abraham in the Dead Sea scrolls: a man of faith and failure. The bible at Qumran. 2001 ⇒267. 149-158.

2127 *Fackenheim, Emil L.* Assault on Abraham: thoughts after fifty years. TJT 17 (2001) 11-16.

2128 *Fernández Marcos, Natalio* Tradiciones tribales: los hijos de Jacob. AnScR 6 (2001) 147-165 [Gen 29,31-30,24; 49].

2129 *Fischer, Irmtraud* Das Geschlecht als exegetisches Kriterium: zu einer gender-fairen Interpretation der Erzeltern-Erzählungen. Studies in the book of Genesis. BEThL 155: 2001 ⇒1936. 135-152.

2130 *Gosse, Bernard* Les traditions sur Abraham et sur le jardin d'Éden en rapport avec Is 51,2-3 et avec le livre d'Ézéchiel. Studies in the book of Genesis. 2001 ⇒1936. 421-427 [Gen 2,8-15; Ezek 33,24].

2131 *Grohmann, Marianne* Die Erzeltern;

2132 Abraham & Sara: Buch Genesis, Kapitel 11 bis 23. Schön bist du. 2001 ⇒274. 38-39/40-45.

2133 *Guillén Torralba, Juan* Un viaje iniciático: Gn 11,27-13,18. Communio 34/1 (2001) 55-91.

2134 **Heard, R. Christopher** Dynamics of diselection: ambiguity in Genesis 12-36 and ethnic boundaries in post-exilic Judah. Diss. Dallas 2000, ᴰ*Fewell, D.N.* SBL Semeia Studies 39: Atlanta 2001, SBL xii; 212 pp. $30. 1-58983-001-6. Bibl. 185-212.

2135 *Hoop, Raymond de* The use of the past to address the present: the wife—sister—incidents (Gen 12,10-20; 20,1-18; 26,1-16). Studies in the book of Genesis. BEThL 155: 2001 ⇒1936. 359-369.

2136 *Kuschel, Karl-Josef* One in Abraham?: the significance of Abraham for Jews, christians, and Muslims today. Memory and history. 2001 ⇒442. 183-203.

2137 **Kuschel, Karl-Josef** Strijd om Abraham: wat joden, christenen en moslims scheidt en bindt. Zoetermeer 2001, Meinema 304 pp. €20.90. 90-211-3836-0 [Streven 69,949s—Beentjes, Panc].

2138 *Le Roux, Jurie H.* Waar is Abraham dan?. VeE 22 (2001) 326-340;

2139 No theory, no science (or: Abraham is only known through a theory). OTEs 14 (2001) 444-457.

2140 **Lipton, Diana** Revisions of the night: politics and promises in the patriarchal dreams of Genesis. JSOT.S 288: 1999 ⇒15,1967; 16, 2040. ᴿBZ 45 (2001) 105-107 (*Fischer, Irmtraud*); JBL 119 (2000) 753-754 (*Hiebert, Robert J.V.*).

2141 *Oswald, Wolfgang* Die Erzeltern als Schutzbürger: Überlegungen zum Thema von Gen 12,10-20 mit Ausblick auf Gen 20.21,22-34 und Gen 26. BN 106 (2001) 79-89.

2142 *Otero Lázaro, Tomás* Abrahán y la justificación por la fe. Burg. 42/1 (2001) 9-32.

2143 **Pagolu, Augustine** The religion of the patriarchs. JSOT.S 277: 1998
⇒14,1841. ᴿCBQ 63 (2001) 325-326 (*Patton, Corrine L.*): ThLZ
126 (2001) 30-33 (*Wahl, Harald*).
2144 *Pury, Albert de* Le choix de l'ancêtre. ThZ 57 (2001) 105-114 [Hos
12].
2145 *Römer, Thomas C.* Recherches actuelles sur le cycle d'Abraham.
Studies in the book of Genesis. BEThL 155: 2001 ⇒1936. 179-211.
2146 *Rudolph, Anette* 'Abraham' in JUSTINS Dialog mit dem Juden Tryphon. OS 50 (2001) 10-33.
2147 *Signer, Michael A.* Abraham: the one and the many. Memory and history. 2001 ⇒442. 204-212.
2148 *Ska, Jean Louis* Abramo nel Nuovo Testamento;
2149 Abramo nella tradizione musulmana. CivCatt 152/1 (2001) 50-60/
479-484;
2150 Essai sur la nature et la signification du cycle d'Abraham (Gn 11,27-
25,11). Studies in the book of Genesis. 2001 ⇒1936. 153-177.
2151 **Wheaton, Byron L.** Abraham, land, and stewardship: reading the
Abraham narratives for their contribution to Israel's land ethic. Diss.
Westminster Sem. 2001, 256 pp. 3010610.

E2.4 Melchisedech: *Genesis 14*

2152 *Böttrich, Christfried* The Melchizedek story of 2 (Slavonic) Enoch: a
reaction to A. Orlov. JSJ 32 (2001) 445-470.
2153 *Elgavish, David* The encounter of Abram and Melchizedek king of
Salem: a covenant establishing ceremony. Studies in the book of
Genesis. BEThL 155: 2001 ⇒1936. 495-508 [Gen 14,18-20].
2154 *Manzi, Franco* Il fascino di Melchisedek su MARCO il Monaco. EL
115 (2001) 488-503.

E2.5 The Covenant (alliance, Bund): *Foedus, Genesis 15...*

2155 **Aldeeb Abu-Sahlieh, Sami A.** Male & female circumcision among
Jews, christians and Muslims: religious, medical, social and legal
debate. Marco Polo Monographs (MPM): Warren Center, PA 2001,
Shangri-La (12) 400 pp. 0-9677201-6-8. Foreword *Marilyn Fayre
Milos*; Bibl. 378-391.
2156 *Anbar, M.* 'On that day YHWH made a covenant with Abram' (Gen
15:18). Beit Mikra 165 (2001) 115-120. **H.**
2157 **Bruckner, James K.** Implied law in the Abraham narrative: a literary
and theological analysis. JSOT.S 335: Shf 2001, Sheffield A. 260 pp.
1-84127-241-8. Bibl. 236-249 [Gen 18,16-20,18].
2158 *Carden, Michael* Remembering Pelotit: a queer midrash on calling
down fire. Queer commentary. JSOT.S 334: 2001 ⇒325. 152-168
[Gen 18-19].
2159 *Cheon, Samuel* Filling the gap in the story of Lot's wife (Genesis
19:1-29). AJTh 15/1 (2001) 14-23.
2160 *Cordier, Pierre* Les romains et la circoncision. REJ 160 (2001) 337-
355.
2161 *Corsano, Marinella* Lot e il destino di Zoar. Orpheus 22 (2001) 26-
38.

2162 *De Martino, Stefano; Imparati, Fiorella* Observations on Hittite international treaties IV. Internationaler Kongress. 2001 ⇒650. 347-363.

2163 *Feldman, Louis H.* The destruction of Sodom and Gomorrah, according to PHILO, PSEUDO-PHILO, and JOSEPHUS. Henoch 23 (2001) 185-198 [Gen 18,16-19,29].

2164 *Fleishman, Joseph* Name change and circumcision in Genesis 17. BetM 167 (2001) 310-321 Sum. 383. **H.**;

2165 On the significance of a name change and circumcision in Genesis 17. JANES 28 (2001) 19-32.

2166 *Flüchter, Sascha; Schnor, Lars* Die Anrechnung des Glaubens zur Gerechtigkeit: ein rezeptionsgeschichtlicher Versuch zum Verständnis von Gen 15,6 MT. BN 109 (2001) 27-44.

2167 *Greenfield, Jonas C.* An ancient treaty ritual and its targumic echo. 'Al kanfei yonah, 1. 2001 <1986> ⇒153. 405-411;

2168 Some aspects of treaty terminology in the bible. 'Al kanfei yonah, 2. 2001 <1967> ⇒153. 901-906.

2169 *Mattox, Mickey L.* Sainte Sara, mère de l'église: l'exégèse catholique de Genèse 18,1-15 par Martin LUTHER. PosLuth 49/4 (2001) 319-39;

2170 Sancta Sara, mater ecclesiae: Martin LUTHER's Catholic exegesis of Genesis 18:1-15. ProEc 10 (2001) 295-320.

2171 *Morrow, William* The Sefire treaty stipulations and the Mesopotamian treaty tradition. FDION, P.-E. 3. JSOT.S 326: 2001 ⇒25. 83-99.

2172 *Neupert-Eyrich, Elvira* Dreh dich nicht um Frau Lot ... oder: welchen Preis hat der Ausstieg aus einem Mobbing-System?. DtPfrBl 101 (2001) 130-132 [Gen 19,23-26].

2173 *Nikaido, S.* Hagar and Ishmael as literary figures: an intertextual study. VT 51 (2001) 219-242 [Gen 16; 21,8-21].

2174 *Papoutsakis, Manolis* 'A small thing': early Syriac views of Zoar (Gen 19:20-23). StPatr 35 (2001) 484-487.

2175 *Rendtorff, Rolf* Noah, Abraham and Moses God's covenant partners. Der Text in seiner Endgestalt. 2001 ⇒201. 155-163.

2176 **Rendtorff, Rolf** The covenant formula. 1998 ⇒14,1873; 16,2074. REvQ 73 (2001) 170-172 (*Bodner, Keith*);

2177 La "formula dell'alleanza": ricerca esegetica e teologica. EGarrone, Daniele: StBi 128: Brescia 2001, Paideia 158 pp. €13.43. 88-394-0617-4. Bibl. 150-155.

2178 *Schüngel-Straumann, Helen* Abraham & Hagar: Buch Genesis, Kapitel 16 und 21. Schön bist du. 2001 ⇒274. 147-151.

2179 *Singer, Itamar* The treaties between Karkamiš and Hatti IV. Internationaler Kongress. 2001 ⇒650. 635-641.

2180 *Spero, Shubert* '...And Abraham stood yet before the Lord'. JBQ 29 (2001) 102-105 [Gen 18,22].

2181 *Tonson, Paul* Mercy without covenant: a literary analysis of Genesis 19. JSOT 95 (2001) 95-116.

2182 *Warning, Wilfried* Terminologische Verknüpfungen und Genesis 15. Henoch 23 (2001) 3-9.

2183 *Weinfeld, Moshe* The meaning of the political 'covenant of friendship' in Israel and the ancient Near East. FAHITUV, S. 2001 ⇒1. 178-183. **H.**

2184 *Wénin, André* Saraï, Hagar et Abram: une approche narrative et contextuelle de Gn 16,1-6. RTL 32 (2001) 24-54.

E2.6 **The 'Aqedâ, Isaac, Genesis 22...**

2185 *Bardski, Krzysztof* Gen 22,1-14: les intuitions parallèles des traditions juive et chrétienne dans le dialogue créatif entre le texte biblique et la communauté de foi. CoTh 71A (2001) 5-13.
2186 *Bauks, Michaela* L'enjeu théologique du sacrifice d'enfants dans le milieu biblique et son dépassement en Genèse 22. ETR 76 (2001) 529-542.
2187 *Brandscheidt, Renate* Das Opfer des Abraham (Genesis 22,1-19). TThZ 110 (2001) 1-19.
2188 *Causse, Jean-Daniel* Le jour où Abraham céda sur sa foi: lecture psycho-anthropologique de Genèse 22. ETR 76 (2001) 563-573.
2189 *Gillmayr-Bucher, Susanne* Genesis 24—ein Mosaik aus Texten. Studies in the book of Genesis. BEThL 155: 2001 ⇒1936. 521-532.
2190 *Grohmann, Marianne* Isaak & Rebekka: Buch Genesis, Kapitel 24 bis 28. Schön bist du. 2001 ⇒274. 46-50.
2191 **Kundert, Lukas** Die Opferung, Bindung Isaaks: 1. Gen 22,1-19 im Alten Testament, im Frühjudentum und im Neuen Testament. WMANT 78: 1998 ⇒14,1894... 16,2087. [R]JBL 119 (2000) 588-589 (*Basser, Herbert W.*).
2192 *Kurianal, James* "Multiplying I shall multiply you" (Gen 22,17): christians as the multiplicity of progeny promised to Abraham. ETJ 5 (2001) 23-33.
2193 *Landy, Francis* Narrative techniques and symbolic transactions in the Akedah. Beauty and the enigma. JSOT.S 312: 2001 <1989> ⇒171, 123-158.
2194 *Launay, Marc de* La ligature d'Isaac: Genèse XXII,1-19. RMM 106 (2001) 517-533.
2195 *Marx, A.* Sens et fonction de Gen. xxii 14. VT 51 (2001) 197-205.
2196 *Michel, Andreas* Ijob und Abraham: zur Rezeption von Gen 22 in Ijob 1-2 und 42,7-17. [F]Groß, W. ATSAT 68: 2001 ⇒38. 73-98.
2197 **Milgrom, Josephine Berman** The binding of Isaac (the Akedah): a primary symbol in Jewish thought and art. Diss. AA 2001, UMI xv; 322 pp.; Bibl. 312-322.
2198 *Moltz, Howard* God and Abraham in the binding of Isaac. JSOT 96 (2001) 59-69.
2199 **Olumpiou, Nikolaou P.** Ἀπὸ τὴ θυσία τοῦ Ἀβραάμ στὴν 'Akedah Yitzhak: τὸ Γεν. 22,1-19 στὴν Παλαιὰ διαθήκη καὶ τὸν πρώψο Ἰουδαϊσμό. 2000 ⇒16,2090. [R]Theol(A) 72/1 (2001) 416-420 (*Simotas, Pan.*).
2200 *Schäfer-Lichtenberger, Christa* Abraham zwischen Gott und Isaak (Gen 22,1-19). WuD 26 (2001) 43-60.
2201 *Schmitt, Hans-Christoph* Die Erzählung von der Versuchung Abrahams Gen 22,1-19* und das Problem einer Theologie der elohistischen Pentateuchtexte. Theologie in Prophetie. 2001 <1986> ⇒209. 108-130.
2202 *Steins, Georg* Die Versuchung Abrahams (Gen 22,1-19): ein neuer Versuch. Studies in the book of Genesis. BEThL 155: 2001 ⇒1936. 509-519.
2203 *Stolle, Jeffrey* Levinas and the *Akedah*: an alternative to Kierkegaard. Philosophy Today 45 (2001) 132-143.
2204 *Volgger, David* Es geht um das Ganze—Gott prüft Abraham (Gen 22,1-19). BZ 45 (2001) 1-19.

2205 *Warning, Wilfried* Terminogical patterns and Genesis 23. OTEs 14 (2001) 533-543.

2206 **Wénin, André** Isaac ou l'épreuve d'Abraham: approche narrative de Genèse 22. 1999 ⇒15,2013; 16,2099. [R]Istina 46 (2001) 90-92 (*Couteau, Elisabeth*); RivBib 49 (2001) 234-236 (*Heller, Karin*); ScEs 53 (2001) 410-411 (*Hurley, Robert*).

2207 *Wénin, André* Les 'sacrifices' d'Abraham et d'Anne: regards croisés sur l'offrande du fils. ETR 76 (2001) 513-527 [1 Sam 1,1-2,21].

E2.7 Jacob and Esau: ladder dream; *Jacob, somnium, Gen 25...*

2208 *Breitbart, Sidney* The problem of deception in Genesis 27. JBQ 29/1 (2001) 45-47.

2209 *Bühlmann, Alain; Jurissevich, Elena* Genèse 30,25-43—un jeu de probabilité. [F]PURY, A. DE, MoBi 44: 2001 ⇒89. 128-136.

2210 *Dulaey, Martine* La figure de Jacob dans l'exégèse paléochrétienne (Gn 27-33). RechAug 32 (2001) 75-168.

2211 *García López, Félix* Genèse 29,1-14: la rencontre de Jacob avec Rachel et Laban. [F]PURY, A. DE, MoBi 44: 2001 ⇒89. 87-94.

2212 **Golka, Friedemann W.** Jakob—biblische Gestalt und literarische Figur: Thomas MANNs Beitrag zur Bibelexegese. AzTh 91: 1999 ⇒ 15,2049. [R]RBLit 3 (2001) 181-184 (*Rösel, Martin*).

2213 *Grohmann, Marianne* Jakob & Lea & Rahel: Buch Genesis, Kapitel 29 bis 35. Schön bist du. 2001 ⇒274. 51-57.

2214 *Guillaume, Philippe* "Beware of foreskins": the priestly writer as matchmaker in Genesis 27,46-28,8. [F]PURY, A. DE, MoBi 44: 2001 ⇒ 89. 69-76.

2215 *Gunkel, Hermann* The Jacob traditions. Water for a thirsty land. Fortress classics in biblical studies: 2001 <1919> ⇒155. 42-67.

2216 **Hrebík, Josef** Lest cestou k pozehnáni?: pokus o nalezeni hermeneutického klice ke Gn 27, 1-45 pomoci komplexni exegetické analyzy. Praha 2001, Univerzita Karlova 142 pp. 80-246-0280-6. Bibl. 131-140. **Czech**.

2217 **Husser, Jean-Marie** Dreams and dream narratives in the biblical world. BiSe 63: 1999 ⇒15,2019; 16,2104. [R]JThS 52 (2001) 139-142 (*Lipton, Diana*).

2218 *Khan, Pinchas* Jacob's choice in Genesis 25:19-28:9. JBQ 29 (2001) 80-86.

2219 **Klein, Renate-Andra** Leseprozess als Bedeutungswandel: eine rezeptionsästhetisch orientierte Erzähltextanalyse der Jakobserzählungen der Genesis. Diss. Hamburg 2001, [D]Willi-Plein, I. [RTL 33,632].

2220 *Kuntzmann, Raymond* Jacob et le thème de la lutte initiatique dans le livre de la Genèse: pertinence et intérêt d'une lecture symboliste. Studies in the book of Genesis. BEThL 155: 2001 ⇒1936. 533-539 [Gen 28,10-22; 32,23-33; 32,2-3].

2221 *LaCocque, André* Une descendance manipulée et ambiguë (Genèse 29,31-30,24). [F]PURY, A. DE, MoBi 44: 2001 ⇒89. 109-127.

2222 *Marx, Alfred* Genèse 26,1-14a;

2223 *Mathys, Hans-Peter* Genesis 29,15-30. [F]PURY, A. DE, MoBi 44: 2001 ⇒89. 22-33/95-108.

2224 *Meurer, Thomas* Der Gebärwettstreit zwischen Lea und Rahel: der Erzählaufbau von Gen 29,31-30,24 als Testfall der erzählerischen

Geschlossenheit einer zusammenhanglos wirkenden Einheit. BN 107/108 (2001) 93-108.

2225 *Mosès, Stéphane* La voce di Giacobbe. L'Eros e la legge. Schulim Vogelmann 80: 2001 <1965> ⇒185. 33-43.

2226 *Naef, Thomas* Genèse 26,26-35—Isaac at Abimélek. ᶠPURY, A. DE, MoBi 44: 2001 ⇒89. 51-59.

2227 *Normandeau, Denise* Le cheminement de Jacob et les *Exercices spirituels* de saint IGNACE. Cahiers de spiritualité ignatienne 97 (2001) 35-51.

2228 *Oblath, Michael* 'To sleep, perchance to dream...': what Jacob saw at Bethel (Genesis 28.10-22). JSOT 95 (2001) 117-126.

2229 *Peleg, Yitzhak (Itzik)* 'and if I come back in peace to my father's house' (Gen 28:11): the vow and its contribution to understanding and interpreting Jacob's dream. BetM 167 (2001) 335-352. Sum. 382. **H**.

2230 *Pollak, Aharon* Laban and Jacob. JBQ 29/1 (2001) 60-62 [Gen 30-31].

2231 *Pury, Albert de* Situer le cycle de Jacob: quelques réflexions, vingt-cinq ans plus tard. Studies in the book of Genesis. BEThL 155: 2001 ⇒1936. 213-241.

2232 *Rose, Martin* Genèse 28,10-22: l'exégèse doit muer en herméneutique théologique. ᶠPURY, A. DE, MoBi 44: 2001 ⇒89. 77-86.

2233 *Ska, Jean Louis* Genèse 25,19-34—ouverture du cycle de Jacob. ᶠPURY, A. DE, MoBi 44: 2001 ⇒89. 11-21.

2234 *Smith, Craig A.* Reinstating Isaac: the centrality of Abraham's son in the 'Jacob-Esau' narrative of Genesis 27. BTB 31 (2001) 130-134.

2235 *Smyth, Françoise* Genèse 27,01-40: lecture;

2236 *Starobinski-Safran, Esther* Quelques interprétations juives antiques et médiévales du songe de Jacob (Gn 28,12-13). ᶠPURY, A. DE, MoBi 44: 2001 ⇒89. 60-68/373-393.

2237 **Taschner, Johannes** Verheißung und Erfüllung in der Jakoberzählung (Gen 25,19-33,17). 1999 ⇒15,2022. ᴿEstAg 36 (2001) 385 (*Mielgo, C.*).

2238 *Vermeylen, Jacques* De Guérar à Béer-Shéva: Genèse 26,14b-25. ᶠPURY, A. DE, MoBi 44: 2001 ⇒89. 34-50.

E2.8 Jacob's wrestling, the Angels: *Gen 31-36 & 38*

2239 *Bauks, Michaela* Genesis 35,22b-29. ᶠPURY, A. DE, MoBi 44: 2001 ⇒89. 276-290.

2240 *Berger, Klaus* Juda (Patriarch). RAC 19 (2001) 38-63 [Gen 38].

2241 *Blum, Erhard* Genesis 33,12-20: die Wege trennen sich;

2242 *Briend, Jacques* Genèse 35,16-22a. ᶠPURY, A. DE, MoBi 44: 2001 ⇒ 89. 227-238/267-275.

2243 *Cohen, Jeffrey M.* Jacob's paradoxical encounters. JBQ 29/1 (2001) 40-42 [Gen 32].

2244 *Cook, Joan E.* Four marginalized foils—Tamar, Judah, Joseph and Potiphar's wife: a literary study of Genesis 38-39. ProcGLM 21 (2001) 115-128.

2245 *Diebner, Bernd Jørg* Eine "enge Definition" von "Israel": Genesis 35,6-15;

2246 *Dietrich, Walter* Jakobs Kampf am Jabbok (Gen 32,23-33). ᶠPURY, A. DE, MoBi 44: 2001 ⇒89. 257-266/197-210.

2247 *Dünzl, Franz* Gott, Engel oder Dämon?: zur Auslegungsgeschichte von Gen 32,23-33. [F]SCHMUTTERMAYR, G. 2001 ⇒101. 337-348.

2248 *Ebach, Jürgen* Der Kampf am Jabboq: Genesis 32,23-32: eine Geschichte voller Verdrehungen. 'Leget Anmut'. Jabboq 1: 2001 ⇒350. 13-43.

2249 *Gibert, Pierre* Sichem et Béthel, sanctuaires d'Israël (Genèse 35,1-5). [F]PURY, A. DE, MoBi 44: 2001 ⇒89. 248-256.

2250 **Hannah, Darrel D.** Michael and Christ: Michael traditions and angel christology in early christianity. WUNT 2/109: 1999 ⇒15,2032. [R]JSJ 32 (2001) 97-100 (*Tromp, Johannes*); RHPhR 81 (2001) 230-231 (*Grappe, Ch.*); JThS 52 (2001) 781-783 (*Rowland, Christopher*); ThR 66 (2001) 498-501 (*Wehnert, Jürgen*).

2251 *Heintz, Jean-Georges* Genèse 31,43-32,1: un récit de pacte bipartite: son arrière-plan rituel et sa cohérence narrative. [F]PURY, A. DE, MoBi 44: 2001 ⇒89. 163-180.

2252 *Huddlestun, John R.* Unveiling the versions: the tactics of Tamar in Genesis 38:15. Journal of Hebrew Scriptures 3 (2001)[electr. journ.].

2253 *Hurowitz, Victor* Whose earrings did Jacob bury?. BiRe 17/4 (2001) 31-33, 54 [Gen 35].

2254 *Knauf, Ernst Axel* Genesis 36,1-43. [F]PURY, A. DE, MoBi 44: 2001 ⇒ 89. 291-300.

2255 **Krauss, Heinrich** Die Engel: Überlieferung, Gestalt, Deutung. 2000 ⇒16,2126. [R]GuL 74 (2001) 394-395 (*Steinmetz, Franz-Josef*);

2256 Kleines Lexikon der Engel: von Ariel bis Zebaoth. Mü 2001, Beck 220 pp. €11.71.

2257 *Loza Vera, José* La berît entre Laban et Jacob (Gn 31.43-54). [F]DION, P.-E. 1. JSOT.S 324: 2001 ⇒25. 57-69.

2258 *Macchi, Jean-Daniel* Genèse 31,24-42: la dernière rencontre de Jacob et de Laban. [F]PURY, A. DE, MoBi 44: 2001 ⇒89. 144-162.

2259 **Pezzini, Domenico** Giacobbe e l'angelo: il mistero della relazione. Mi 2001, Ancora 93 pp [Eccl(R) 17,278s—Estrella, Juan Manuel] [Gen 32,23-33].

2260 *Poujol, Catherine* Ces boiteux qui font l'histoire. Représentations des maladies. 2001 ⇒482. 173-187.

2261 **Rapp, Hans A.** Jakob in Bet-el: Gen 35,1-15 und die jüdische Literatur des 3. und 2. Jahrhunderts. Diss. Luzern 1998/99, [D]*Thoma, Clemens*: Herders Biblische Studien 29: FrB 2001, Herder xi; 348 pp. €50. 3-451-27558-9. Bibl. 299-327.

2262 *Römer, Thomas* Genèse 32,2-22: préparations d'une rencontre;

2263 *Schenker, Adrian* Le tribunal des femmes et un vol légitime: Gn 31,1-25 et Ex 21,7-11;

2264 *Schmid, Konrad* Die Versöhnung zwischen Jakob und Esau (Genesis 33,1-11). [F]PURY, A. DE, 2001 ⇒89. 181-196/137-143/ 211-226.

2265 **Scholz, Susanne** Rape plots: a feminist cultural study of Genesis 34. 2000 ⇒16,2135. [R]YESW 9 (2001) 278-279 (*Leijnse, Barbara*).

2266 *Schüngel-Straumann, Helen* Juda & Tamar: Buch Genesis, Kapitel 38. Schön bist du. 2001 ⇒274. 58-61;

2267 Sichem und Dina: Buch Genesis, Kapitel 34. Schön bist du. 2001 ⇒ 274. 120-123.

2268 *Van Seters, John* The silence of Dinah (Genesis 34). [F]PURY, A. DE, MoBi 44: 2001 ⇒89. 239-247.

E2.9 **Joseph**; Jacob's blessings; *Genesis 37; 39-50*

2269 *Ausloos, Hans* The Deuteronomist and the account of Joseph's death (Gen 50,22-26);

2270 *Fischer, Georg* Die Josefsgeschichte als Modell für Versöhnung;

2271 *Fleishman, Joseph* Towards understanding the legal significance of Jacob's statement: "I will divide them in Jacob, I will scatter them in Israel" (Gen 49,7b). Studies in the book of Genesis. BEThL 155: 2001 ⇒1936. 381-395/243-271/541-559.

2272 *Fox, Michael V.* Wisdom in the Joseph story. VT 51 (2001) 26-41.

2273 *Görg, Manfred* Wohin ist Josef?: weitere Anfragen anläßlich einer Spurensuche. BN 107/108 (2001) 15-21.

2274 *Gregg, Robert C.* Joseph with Potiphar's wife: early christian commentary seen against the backdrop of Jewish and Muslim interpretations. StPatr 34 (2001) 326-346 [Gen 39].

2275 **Hoop, Raymond de** Genesis 49 in its literary and historical context. OTS 39: 1999 ⇒15,2050; 16,2156. ᴿJBL 120 (2001) 150-151 (*McLay, Tim*); Bib. 82 (2001) 273-277 (*Berry, Donald K.*).

2276 *Kalimi, Isaac* Joseph between Potiphar and his wife: the biblical text in the light of a comparative study on early Jewish exegesis. BN 107/108 (2001) 55-64.

2277 *Lange, Armin* Becherorakel und Traumdeutung: zu zwei Formen der Divination in der Josephsgeschichte. Studies in the book of Genesis. BEThL 155: 2001 ⇒1936. 371-379 [Gen 37,5-11; 40; 41,1-36].

2278 **Lisewski, Krzysztof Dariusz** Studien zu Motiven und Themen zur Josefsgeschichte der Genesis. Diss. Graz 2001, ᴰ*Marböck, J.* [RTL 33,633].

2279 *Loader, James Alfred* Gott "haben" oder "hat"?: Unklarheiten und Einsichten. Begegnung mit Gott. 2001 ⇒175. 31-42 [Gen 45,3-13].

2280 **Lux, Rüdiger** Josef: der Auserwählte unter seinen Brüdern. Biblische Gestalten 1: Lp 2001, EVA 291 pp. €14.50. 3-374-01848-3.

2281 *Pirson, Ron* The sun, the moon and eleven stars: an interpretation of Joseph's second dream. Studies in the book of Genesis. BEThL 155: 2001 ⇒1936. 561-568 [Gen 37,05-11].

2282 **Pirson, Ron** De dromer van Hebron: een herlezing van het verhaal van Jozef en zijn broers. Baarn 2001, Ten Have 156 pp. €13.59. 90-259-5223-2 [Streven 68,1038—Beentjes, Panc].

2283 *Quincoces Loren, Aaron* Nota testuale a Gen. 39,20 nella versione della LXX. Henoch 23 (2001) 39-41.

2284 *Revell, E.J.* Midian and Ishmael in Genesis 37: synonyms in the Joseph story. ᶠDɪᴏɴ, P.-E. 1. JSOT.S 324: 2001 ⇒25. 70-91.

2285 *Schmitt, Hans-Christoph* Die Hintergründe der 'neuesten Pentateuchkritik' und der literarische Befund der Josefsgeschichte <1985>;

2286 Eschatologische Stammesgeschichte im Pentateuch: zum Judaspruch von Gen 49,8-12 <1999>;

2287 Die Josephsgeschichte und das Deuteronomistische Geschichtswerk Genesis 38 und 48-50 <1997>. Theologie in Prophetie. 2001 ⇒209. 89-107/189-199/295-308.

2288 *Schüngel-Straumann, Helen* Josef & die Frau des Potifar: Buch Genesis, Kapitel 39. Schön bist du. 2001 ⇒274. 141-146;

2289 Josef & Asenat: Buch Genesis, Kapitel 41. Schön bist du. 2001 ⇒274. 157-161.

2290 *Schweizer, Harald* Josefsgeschichte: Grammatik-Interpretation-Datierung-Wirkungsgeschichte. BN 107/108 (2001) 120-145.

2291 **Swenson-Mendez, Kristin Marie** The relationship of Judah and Joseph in Genesis 49. Diss. Boston Univ. 2001, 362 pp. 9995603.

2292 *Uehlinger, Christoph* Fratrie, filiations et paternités dans l'histoire de Joseph (Genèse 37-50). [F]PURY, A. DE, MoBi 44: 2001 ⇒89. 303-28.

2293 *Van Hecke, Pierre* Shepherds and linguists: a cognitive-linguistic approach to the metaphor "God is shepherd" in Gen 48,15 and context. Studies in the book of Genesis. BEThL 155: 2001 ⇒1936. 479-493.

2294 **Wallace, Ronald S.** The story of Joseph and the family of Jacob. GR 2001, Eerdmans xii; 135 pp. $16. 0-8028-4808-7.

E3.1 **Exodus event and theme**; *textus, commentarii*

2295 *Albertz, Rainer* Exodus: liberation history against charter myths. Religious identity. 2001 ⇒549. 128-143.

2296 [E]**Beretta, Piergiorgio** Esodo, ebraico, greco, latino, italiano. [T]*Doveri, Cristiana*: CinB 2001, San Paolo 14-284 pp. Traduzione letterale interlineare.

2297 [E]**Casadeum, Thomas** Esodo. 1999 ⇒15,2065. [R]FilTeo 15 (2001) 199-201 (*Rosa, Guglielmo Forni*).

2298 **Coats, George W.** Exodus 1-18. FOTL 2A: 1999 ⇒15,2066; 16,2176. [R]VJTR 65 (2001) 148-149 (*Raj, M.I.*); JBL 120 (2001) 535-537 (*Hauser, Alan J.*); JSSt 46 (2001) 331-33 (*Davies, Eryl W.*); ThLZ 126 (2001) 369 (*Schmidt, Werner H.*).

2299 *Collins, John J.* The development of the Exodus tradition. Religious identity. Studies in theology and religion 3: 2001 ⇒549. 144-155.

2300 **Cox, Dorian Coover** 'How will it be known?': the art of characterization in the book of Exodus. Diss. Dallas Theol. Sem. 2001, 349 pp. 3002961.

2301 *Crüsemann, Frank* Freiheit durch Erzählen von Freiheit: zur Geschichte des Exodus-Motivs. EvTh 61/2 (2001) 102-118.

2302 **Currid, John D.** A study commentary on Exodus, 2: Exodus 19-40. Darlington 2001, Evangelical 398 pp. 0-85234-472-4.

2303 **Gertz, Jan Christian** Tradition und Redaktion in der Exoduserzählung: Untersuchungen zur Endredaktion des Pentateuch. FRLANT 186: 2000 ⇒16,2191. [R]ThLZ 126 (2001) 369-373 (*Schmidt, Werner H.*); RBLit 3 (2001) 184-186 (*Hagedorn, Anselm C.*).

2304 *Gilbert, Pierre* Libre arbitre et déterminisme: une réflexion sur la figure de Pharaon. Theoforum 32/1 (2001) 5-21 [Exod 4-14].

2305 *Hale, F.* Stuart Cloete's construction of Voortrekker religion in Turning wheels. AcTh(B) 21/1 (2001) 24-40.

2306 *Hendel, Ronald* The exodus in biblical memory. JBL 120 (2001) 601-622.

2307 **Houtman, Cornelis** Exodus, 3: chapters 20-40. [T]*Woudstra, Sierd*: Hist. comm. on the OT: 2000 ⇒16,2179. [R]CBQ 63 (2001) 315-316 (*Kugler, Robert A.*); RTLu 6 (2001) 563-566 (*Praximadi, Giorgio*).

2308 **Johnstone, William** Chronicles and Exodus: an analogy and its application. JSOT.S 275: 1998 ⇒14,1973; 16,2946. [R]JBL 120 (2001) 362-364 (*Boda, Mark J.*); RBLit 3 (2001) 262-265 (*Boda, Mark J.*).

2309 *Malamat, Abraham* The Exodus: Egyptian analogies. History of biblical Israel. Culture and history of the ANE 7: 2001 <1997> ⇒182. 57-67.

2310 **Mazzi, Enzo** La forza dell'esodo. La talpa di biblioteca 26: R 2001, Manifestolibri 166 pp. 88-7285-201-3.

2311 *Nickelsburg, George W.E.* Aaron. RAC, Suppl. Bd. 1. 2001 ⇒661. 1-11.

2312 **Oblath, Michael David** The exodus itinerary sites: their locations from the perspective of the biblical sources. Diss. Graduate Theol. Union & Univ. of Calif., Berkeley 2001, 272 pp. 3021412.

2313 *Perani, Mauro* Traduzione ed ermeneutica: a proposito di due recenti traduzioni interlineari del testo ebraico di Esodo. RivBib 49 (2001) 473-483.

2314 [ET]**Petit, Françoise** La chaîne sur l'Exode: édition intégrale, 2: Collectio Coisliniana, 3: Fonds caténique ancien (Exode 1,1-15,21). Traditio exegetica graeca 10: Lv 2000, Peeters xxxi; 357 pp. €95. 90-429-0893-9;

2315 La chaîne sur l'Exode: texte grec établi et traduit par Françoise Petit ... 4: fonds caténique ancien (Exode 15,22 - 40,32). Traditio exegetica graeca 11: Lv 2001, Peeters xiv; 358 pp. 90-429-0993-5;

2316 La chaîne sur l'Exode. Fragments de SÉVÈRE d'Antioche. 1999 ⇒15, 2075; 16,2186. [R]RB 108 (2001) 266-269 (*Malzoni, Cláudio Vianney*); VetChr 38 (2001) 364-365 (*Infante, Renzo*).

2317 **Ponizy, Bogdan** Motyw wyjscia w Biblii: od historii do teologii. Uniw. Mickiewicza...teologiczny, Bibl. Pomocy Naukowych 21: Poznan 2001, Uniw. Mickiewicza 158 pp. 8386-360-712. Bibl. 145-146.

2318 **Propp, William H.C.** Exodus 1-18.: a new translation with introduction and commentary. AncB 2: NY 1999, Doubleday xl; 680 pp. $50. 0-385-1480-46. Bibl. 57-115. [R]ETR 76 (2001) 113-114 (*Vincent, Jean Marcel*); Interp. 55 (2001) 74, 76 (*Fretheim, Terence E.*); JR 81 (2001) 271-272 (*Sommer, Benjamin D.*); AUSS 39 (2001) 148-149 (*Li, Tarsee*); CBQ 63 (2001) 125-127 (*Dozeman, Thomas B.*); JBL 120 (2001) 744-746 & RBLit 3 (2001) 186-189 (*Palmer, David B.*).

2319 **Ravasi, Gianfranco** Esodo. LoB. 1/4: Brescia [6]2001, Queriniana 188 pp. 88-399-1554-0.

2320 [E]**Reggi, Roberto** Esodo: traduzione interlineare in italiano. Bo 2001, EDB 104 pp. 88-10-80636-0.

2321 *Rendsburg, Gary A.* An additional note to two recent articles on the number of people in the exodus from Egypt and the large numbers in Numbers I and XXVI. VT 51 (2001) 392-396.

      Rogerson, J., *al.*, Genesis and Exodus. OTGu 1-2: 2001 ⇒1952.

2322 [T]**Rottzoll, Dirk U.** IBN ESRAS langer Kommentar zum Buch Exodus. 2000 ⇒16,2188. [R]ThLZ 126 (2001) 387-389 (*Arndt, Timotheus*).

2323 **Scharbert, Josef** Esodo. Brescia 2001, Morcelliana 190 pp. 88-372-1839-7. Bibl. 15-18.

2324 *Schrijver, Georges De* The Exodus motif in the theologies of liberation: changes of perspective;

2325 *Van der Toorn, Karel* The Exodus as charter myth. Religious identity. 2001 ⇒549. 169-190/113-127.

2326 *Van Seters, John* The geography of the Exodus. [F]MILLER, J. JSOT.S 343: 2001 ⇒74. 255-276.

2327 **Vogels, Walter** Exodus. Belichting van het bijbelboek: Den Bosch 2001, Katholieke Bijbelstichting 326 pp. 90-6173-716-8.

2328 *Weimar, Peter* Zwischen Hoffnung und Resignation: Visionen und Bilder der Befreiung Israels. rhs 44 (2001) 10-19.

2329 *Witvliet, Theo* Exodus in the African-American experience. Religious identity. 2001 ⇒549. 191-205.

2330 **Zornberg, Avivah Gottlieb** The particulars of rapture: reflections on Exodus. NY 2001, Doubleday (10) 582 pp. $35. 0-385-49152-2. Bibl. 543-547.

2331 Das zweite Buch Mose, genannt Exodus. Fischer Taschenbuch 14502: Fra 2000, Fischer 120 pp. 3-596-14502-3. Mit einer Einleitung von *David Grossman.*

E3.2 **Moyses**—Pharaoh, Goshen—*Exodus 1...*

2332 **Assmann, Jan** Moses der Ägypter: Entzifferung einer Gedächtnisspur. 1998 ⇒14,1991; 15,2099. [R]HerKorr 55 (2001) 186-191 (*Zenger, Erich*); ZRGG 53 (2001) 377-379 (*Mehring, Reinhard*); rhs 44 (2001) 1-9 (*Görg, Manfred*) [⇒2339].

2333 Moïse l'égyptien: un essai d'histoire de la mémoire. [T]*Bernardi, Laure*: P 2001, Aubier 412 pp. €22.80.

2334 *Blanco Wißmann, Felipe* Sargon, Mose und die Gegner Salomos: zur Frage vor-neuassyrischer Ursprünge der Mose-Erzählung. BN 110 (2001) 42-54. [1 Kgs 11].

2335 **Blot, Jean** Moïse: notre contemporain. Spiritualités vivantes 185: P 2001, Michel 261 pp. 2-226-13015-2.

2336 *Den Hertog, Cornelis* Concerning the sign of Sinai (Ex 3:12): including a survey of prophetic and call signs. [F]DEURLOO, K. ACEBT.S 2: 2001 ⇒23. 33-41.

2337 *Ehrlich, Carl S.* Moses, torah, and Judaism. Rivers of paradise. 2001 ⇒354. 11-119.

2338 *Johnstone, William* The portrayal of Moses as Deuteronomic archetypal prophet in Exodus and its revisal. The elusive prophet. OTS 45: 2001 ⇒485. 159-174 [Exod 34,1-4; 34,28-29; Dt 10,1-5].

2339 *Kaiser, Gerhard* War der Exodus der Sündenfall?: Fragen an Jan ASSMANN anläßlich seiner Monographie "Moses der Ägypter". ZThK 98 (2001) 1-24.

2340 *Miller, Robert D.* Moses and MENDENHALL in traditio-historical perspective. IBSt 23 (2001) 146-166 [Exod 19-34; Josh 24,1-28].

2341 **Otto, Eckart** Die Tora des Mose: die Geschichte der literarischen Vermittlung von Recht, Religion und Politik durch die Mosegestalt. Berichte... J. Jungius-Gesellschaft der Wissenschaften Hamburg 19, 2: Gö 2001, Vandenhoeck & R. 74 pp. 3-525-86311-X. Bibl. 64-74.

2342 *Rowley, James E.* Moses in the Dead Sea scrolls: living in the shadow of God's anointed. The bible at Qumran. 2001 ⇒267. 159-181.

2343 **Rozier, Gilles** Moïse fiction. P 2001, Denoël 292 pp. €13.57.

2344 *Römer, Thomas* L'Ancien Testament est-il monothéiste?. Le christianisme. 2001 ⇒351. 72-92.

2345 **Sabbah, Messod; Sabbah, Roger** Les secrets de l'Exode: l'origine égyptienne des hébreux. 2000 ⇒16,2227. [R]CEv 116 (2001) 65-66 (*Abadie, Philippe*).

2346 *Schüngel-Straumann, Helen* Mose & Zippora: Buch Exodus, Kapitel 2, 4, und 18. Schön bist du. 2001 ⇒274. 152-156.

2347 *Stolz, Fritz* Essences et fonction des monothéismes abrahamites. Le christianisme. 2001 ⇒351. 40-59.

2348 *Stolz, Fritz* Wesen und Funktion von Monotheismus. EvTh 61/3 (2001) 172-189.

2349 *Vignal, Marie-Noëlle* Le personnage de Moïse au livre VIII du *Contre Julien* de CYRILLE d'Alexandrie. ConnPE 83 (2001) 56-59.

2350 *Weaver, Dorothy Jean* Beware of burning bushes: a biblical theological foundation for the ministry of political advocacy. [F]JANZEN, W. 2001 ⇒54. 186-197.

2351 *Zenger, Erich* Echnaton und Mose: Gemeinsamkeiten und Unterschiede. WUB 22 (2001) 27-30.

E3.3 Nomen divinum, Tetragrammaton; *Exodus 3,14...*Plagues

2352 *Boer, Roland* Yahweh as top: a lost targum. Queer commentary. JSOT.S 334: 2001 ⇒325. 75-105.

2353 **Brichto, Herbert C.** The names of God: poetic readings in biblical beginnings. 1998 ⇒14,2017; 15,2128. [R]JThS 52 (2001) 147-149 (*Davidson, Robert*).

2354 *Brueggemann, Walter* Symmetry and extremity in the images of YHWH. The Blackwell companion to the Hebrew Bible. Blackwell companions to religion 3: 2001 ⇒653. 241-257.

2355 **Burnett, Joel S.** A reassessment of Biblical Elohim. SBL.DS 183: Atlanta 2001, SBL xv; 172 pp. $50. 1-58983-016-4. Bibl. 153-172.

2356 *Dijkstra, Meindert* El, the God of Israel—Israel, the people of YHWH: on the origins of ancient Israelite Yahwism. Only one God?. BiSe 77: 2001 ⇒238. 81-126.

2357 *Dombrowski, Bruno W.* Another attempt at identification of Yahweh and the Ba`al of Ugarit. PJBR 1/2 (2001) 213-215.

2358 *Ebach, Jürgen* Der eine Gott und die Vielfalt der Menschen: Konkurrenzfragen in der Bibel und an die Bibel. WzM 53 (2001) 462-481.

2359 **Gnuse, Robert Karl** No other gods: emergent monotheism in Israel. JSOT.S 241: 1997 ⇒13,1990... 16,2237. [R]JBL 119 (2000) 113-114 (*Ackerman, Susan*).

2360 *Jennings, Theodore W. Jr.* YHWH as Erastes. Queer commentary. JSOT.S 334: 2001 ⇒325. 36-74.

2361 *Kegler, Jürgen* Zu Komposition und Theologie der Plagenerzählungen. Gesammelte Aufsätze. BEAT 48: 2001 <1990> ⇒167. 228-246.

2362 *Kessler, Rainer* Psychoanalytische Lektüre biblischer Texte—das Beispiel von Ex 4,24-26. EvTh 61/3 (2001) 204-221.

2363 *Langner, Allan M.* The ninth plague JBQ 29 1 2001 48-55 {Exodus} 10,21-23

2364 *Lemmelijn, Bénédicte* Genesis' creation narrative: the literary model for the so-called plague-tradition?. Studies in the book of Genesis. BEThL 155: 2001 ⇒1936. 407-419 [Gen 1,1-2,4; Exod 7,14-11,10; Ps 78,44-51; 105,28-38; Wisd 11,5-15; 16-19];

2365 The so-called 'major expansions' in SamP, 4QpaleoExod[m] and 4QExod[j] of Exod 7:14-11:10: on the edge between textual criticism and literary criticism. X Congress IOSCS. 2001 ⇒499. 429-439.

2366 *Mosès, Stéphane* 'Io sarò colui che sarò'. L'Eros e la legge. Schulim Vogelmann 80: 2001 <1994> ⇒185. 45-66.

2367 *Noblesse-Rocher, Annie* Le nom et l'être de Dieu (Exode 3, 14) selon Thomas d'AQUIN et Martin BUCER. RHPhR 81 (2001) 425-447.

2368 *Odendaal, Marietjie* Who is 'I shall be'?: God in Exodus. OTEs 14 (2001) 297-310 [Exod 3,14-15].

2369 *Pleizier, T.T.* Omdat er slechts één is: enkele overwegingen bij de vertaling van de godsnaam: gereformeerd vertalen of geeft de praktijk de doorslag?. ThRef 44 (2001) 302-316.

2370 *Reggiani, Clara Kraus* Il monoteismo ebraico e il concetto di mediazione. SMSR 67 (2001) 5-35.

2371 *Rendtorff, Rolf* 'El als israelitische Gottesbezeichnung: mit einem Appendix: Beobachtungen zum Gebrauch von *h'lhjm*. Der Text in seiner Endgestalt. 2001 ⇒201. 183-200.

2372 *Römer, Thomas Christian* Der biblische Monotheismus. WUB 22 (2001) 33-36.

2373 **Rösel, Martin** Adonaj—warum Gott 'Herr' genannt wird. FAT 29: 2000 ⇒16,2244. ᴿOLZ 96 (2001) 552-554 (*Rose, Martin*); Sal. 63 (2001) 779-780 (*Vicent, R.*).

2374 *Schmitt, Hans-Christoph* Tradition der Prophetenbücher in den Schichten der Plagenerzählung Ex 7,1-11,10. Theologie in Prophetie. 2001 <1989> ⇒209. 38-58.

2375 *Schneider, Laurel C.* Yahwist desires: imagining divinity queerly. Queer commentary. JSOT.S 334: 2001 ⇒325. 210-227.

2376 *Tropper, Josef* Der Gottesname *Yahwa. VT 51 (2001) 81-106.

2377 *Zenger, Erich* "Wo ist denn ihr Gott?": die Einzigartigkeit JHWHs nach Psalm 115. BiLi 74 (2001) 230-239;

2378 Was ist der Preis des Monotheismus?: die heilsame Provokation von Jan Assmann. HerKorr 55 (2001) 186-191.

E3.4 *Pascha, sanguis, sacrificium*: **Passover, blood, sacrifice, Ex 11...**

2379 **Cardellini, Innocenzo** I sacrifici dell'antica alleanza: tipologie, rituali, celebrazioni. Studi sulla Bibbia e il suo ambiente 5: CinB 2001, San Paolo 574 pp. €30. 88-215-4381-1. Bibl. 491-535. ᴿRdT 42 (2001) 933-935 (*Fanuli, Antonio*).

2380 **Chan, Frank** Baptismal typology in MELITO of Sardis' 'Peri Pascha': a study in the interpretation of Exodus 12 in the second century. Diss. Westminster Theol. Sem. 2001, 449 pp. [Acts 15,36-41].

2381 *Grottanelli, Cristiano* Aspetti de sacrificio nella bibbia ebraica. ASEs 18 (2001) 47-60.

2382 **Hauge, Martin Ravndal** The descent from the mountain: narrative patterns in Exodus 19-40. JSOT.S 323: Shf 2001, Sheffield A. 362 pp. £56/$88. 1-84127-177-2. Bibl. 339-344.

2383 **Heger, Paul** The three biblical altar laws. BZAW 279: 1999 ⇒15, 2170. ᴿCBQ 63 (2001) 112-114 (*Schwartz, Baruch J.*); Bib. 82 (2001) 560-561 (*Niehr, Herbert*).

2384 *Hoftijzer, J.* Description or categorical rule?: some remarks on Ex. 18:16. ᶠVEENHOF, K. 2001 ⇒111. 193-196.

2385 *Horwitz, Liora Kolska* Animal offerings in the Middle Bronze Age: food for the gods, food for thought. PEQ 133 (2001) 78-90.

2386 *Human, Dirk J.* Exodus 15:1-21—Lob an den unvergleichlichen Gott!. OTEs 14 (2001) 419-443.

2387 *Ilan, Nahem* שִׁמָּרם לֵיל [A night of watching]. Beit Mikra 165 (2001) 97-114 [Exod 12,42]. H.

2388 *Jagersma, H.* Structure and function of Exodus 19:3bB-6. ᶠDEURLOO, K. ACEBT.S 2: 2001 ⇒23. 43-48.

2389 *Janowski, Bernd* Tieropfer. rhs 44 (2001) 339-344.

2390 **Jung, Seokgyu** The judicial system in ancient Israel: a synchronic and diachronic reading of Exodus 18:1-27, Deuteronomy 16:18-17:20, and 2 Chronicles 19:1-11. Diss. Claremont Graduate 2001, 339 pp. 9998943.
2391 *Klawans, Jonathan* Pure violence: sacrifice and defilement in ancient Israel. HThR 94 (2001) 133-155.
2392 **Lempert, Bernard** Critique de la pensée sacrificielle. 2000 ⇒16, 2258. ᴿRThPh 133 (2001) 199-200 (*Bubloz, Yvan*).
2393 *Lenhardt, Pierre* Senza il 'servizio dell'altare': il valore dei sacrifici nell'ebraismo di ieri e di oggi. Qol(I) 94 (2001) 4-7.
2394 *Massonnet, Jean* Le sacrifice dans le judaïsme. CEv 118 (2001) 5-12.
2395 ᵀ**Mello, Alberto** Rabbi Jishma'el: il cantico presso il mare: commento a Es 15, 1-21: Mekhilta di Rabbi Jishma'el. 2000 ⇒16,2262. ᴿAsp. 48 (2001) 241-244 (*Castello, Gaetano*).
2396 *Musielak, Jan M.* Obraz Paschy w różnych okresach historycznych. ᶠJANKOWSKI, A. 2001 ⇒53. 281-296. **P.**
2397 *Rendtorff, Rolf* Der Text in seiner Endgestalt: Überlegungen zu Exodus 19. Der Text in seiner Endgestalt. 2001 ⇒201. 71-82.
2398 *Schmitt, Hans-Christoph* Die Geschichte vom Sieg über die Amalekiter Ex 17,8-16 als theologische Lehrerzählung <1990>;
2399 Priesterliches' und 'prophetisches' Geschichtsverständnis in der Meerwundererzählung Ex 13,17-14,31: Beobachtungen zur Endredaktion des Pentateuch <1979>. Theologie in Prophetie. 2001 ⇒209. 155-164/203-219.
2400 *Smith, Mark S.* The poetics of Exodus 15 and its position in the book. ᶠFITZGERALD, A. CBQ.MS 32: 2001 ⇒31. 23-34.
2401 *Snyman, S.D.* Waar is die Moses-figure wat na God wys?. AcTh(B) 21/2 (2001) 113-125 [Exod 14,1-14].
2402 *Steins, Georg* Priesterherrschaft, Volk von Priestern oder was sonst?: zur Interpretation von Ex 19,6. BZ 45 (2001) 20-36.
      ᴱ**Ubbiali, S.** Il sacrificio: evento e rito. 1998 ⇒330.
2403 *Viterbi, Benedetto Carucci* La pasqua ebraica: "passare oltre". RivLi 88 (2001) 57-66.

E3.5 Decalogus, *Ex 20=Dt 5; Ex 21ss*; Ancient Near Eastern Law

2404 *Bast, Robert J.* From two kingdoms to two tables: the ten commandments and the christian magistrate. Luther Digest 9 (2001) 2-5 <Archive for Reformation History 89,79-95.
2405 *Colomo, Daniela* Osservazioni intorno ad un nuovo papiro dell'Esodo (P. Oxy. 4442). XXII Congresso di papirologia, 1. 2001 ⇒555. 269-277 [Exod 20,10-17].
2406 *Cunneen, Joseph* 'Being alive is a gift': Krzyztof Kieslowski's *The Decalogue*. Spiritus(B) 1 (2001) 79-85.
2407 'Entdecken: Lese- und Arbeitsbuch zur Bibel': 'Zehn Gebote'. Stu 2001, Kath. Bibelwerk 144 pp. €9.80. 3-460-20023-5.
2408 **Ferrario, F.** I dieci commandamenti. Cinquanta pagine: T 2001, Claudiana 48 pp. €3 [RdT 43,158].
2409 *Ferry, Joëlle* Le décalogue, une loi pour l'homme?. RICP 80 (2001) 155-170.

2410 **Freedman, David Noel** The nine commandments: uncovering a hidden pattern of crime and punishment in the Hebrew Bible. 2000 ⇒ 16,2286. [R]CBQ 63 (2001) 517-519 (*Brettler, Marc Zvi*).

2411 *Graupner, Axel* Die zehn Gebote im Rahmen alttestamentlicher Ethik: Anmerkungen zum gegenwärtigen Stand der Forschung. Weisheit, Ethos und Gebot. BThSt 43: 2001 ⇒492. 61-95.

2412 *Green, Lowell C.* What does this mean?: LUTHER's exposition of the decalogue in relation to law and gospel with special reference to Johann Michael REU. Luther Digest 9 (2001) 152-154 <Kogia 7/2,3-10.

2413 *Kellermann, Ulrich* Der Dekalog in den Schriften des Frühjudentums: ein Überblick. Weisheit, Ethos und Gebot. BThSt 43: 2001 ⇒ 492. 147-226.

2414 *Krüger, Thomas* Woran orientiert sich die Ethik des Dekalogs?. MJTh 13 (2001) 113-124.

2415 **Ouaknin, Marc-Alain** De tien geboden. [T]*Kunstenaar, Marion Th.*: Amst 2001, Boom 239 pp. €18.10. 90-5352-613-7;

2416 Le dieci parole: il decalogo riletto e commentato dai maestri ebrei antichi e moderni. Mi 2001, Paoline 296 pp. Pres. *Ottavio Di Grazia* e *Alessandra Pontecorvo* [Studi Fatti Ricerche 99,15].

2417 *Pratscher, Wilhelm* Die Bedeutung des Dekalogs im Neuen Testament. SNTU.A 26 (2001) 189-204.

2418 *Sänger, Dieter* Tora für die Völker—Weisungen der Liebe: zur Rezeption des Dekalogs im frühen Judentum und Neuen Testament. Weisheit, Ethos und Gebot. BThSt 43: 2001 ⇒492. 97-146.

2419 *Waschke, Ernst Joachim* 'Es ist dir gesagt, Mensch, was gut ist...' (Mi 6,8): zur Frage nach dem Begründungszusammenhang einer biblischen Ethik am Beispiel des Dekalogs (Ex 20/Dtn 5). Der Gesalbte. 2001 <1993> ⇒227. 221-233.

2420 *Zabłocka, Maria* Reguły prawa rzymskiego do dziesięciu przykazań bożych [Regole del diritto romano attinenti al decalogo]. Zeszyty Prawnicze 1 (2001) 71-78 Som. 78. **P.**

2421 *Rendtorff, Rolf* Die Herausführungsformel in ihrem literarischen und theologischen Kontext. Der Text in seiner Endgestalt. 2001 ⇒201. 226-252 [Exod 20,2; Dt 26,8-9; Hos 12,10].

2422 *Adler, Gerhard* `Du sollst dir kein Gottesbildnis machen'—zur Geschichte des Bilderverbots. COst 56/2 (2001) 84-99.

2423 *Luzzatto, Amos* L'aniconismo ebraico fra immagine e simbolo. Il cinema e la bibbia. 2001 <1992> ⇒496. 211-228.

2424 *Podella, Thomas* Bild und Text: mediale und historische Perspektiven auf das alttestamentliche Bilderverbot. SJOT 15 (2001) 205-256.

2425 *Rendtorff, Rolf* Was verbietet das alttestamentliche Bilderverbot?. Der Text in seiner Endgestalt. 2001 ⇒201. 201-212.

2426 *Schenker, Adrian* La profanation d'images cultuelles dans la guerre: raisons explicites et raisons implicites de l'aniconisme israélite dans les textes de la bible. RB 108 (2001) 321-330 [Dt 4,15-20].

2427 [E]**Van der Toorn, Karel** The image and the book: iconic cults, aniconism, and the rise of book religion in Israel and the ancient Near East. 1997 ⇒13,2073... 16,2315. [R]OLZ 96 (2001) 247-256 (*Podella, Thomas*).

2428 *Wallenhorst, Ansgar* Klangbilder Gottes: Spurensuche an den Grenzen von Gottes-Offenbarung und Klangerfahrung in der Tradition der biblischen Bilderverbotspraxis. WuA(M) 42/1 (2001) 15-21.

2429 *Davis, Ellen Frances* Slaves or sabbath-keepers?: a biblical perspective on human work. AThR 83 (2001) 25-40.

2430 *Dennison, James T.* Vos on the sabbath: a close reading. Kerux 16/1 (2001) 61-70.

2431 *Pahk, Johan Yeong-Sik* 'Thou shalt not steal any man?': the meaning and its implication of *ganabh* in Ex 20:15 (Dt 5:19.) Catholic Theology and Thought 37 (2001) 7-26.

2432 *Lorenzetti, Luigi* 'Non pronunciare falsa testimonianza contro il tuo prossimo'. RTM 33 (2001) 345-351 Sum 345.

2433 *Composta, Dario* I fondamenti biblici del diritto canonico. Div. 44 (2001) 272-298.

2434 **Falk, Ze'ev** Hebrew law in biblical times: an introduction. Provo ²2001 <1964>, Young Univ. Pr. 305 pp. $30. 0-934893-55-1 [RB 109,155].

2435 **Fasano, Vincenzo** L'incriminazione in materia di reati sessuali nell' Antico Testamento. Theses ad Doctoratum in Iure Canonico: R 2001, Pontificia Università Lateranense 108 pp. Bibl. 99-106.

2436 **Fitzpatrick-McKinley, Anne** The transformation of Torah from scribal advice to law. JSOT.S 287: 1999 ⇒15,1728; 16,1813. ᴿThLZ 126 (2001) 746-748 (*Otto, Eckart*).

2437 *Frymer-Kensky, Tikva* Israel. Security for debt in ANE law. 2001 ⇒ 649. 250-263.

2438 *Hays, J. Daniel* Applying the Old Testament law today. BS 158 (2001) 21-35.

2439 **Hoffmann, Heinrich** Das Gesetz in der frühjüdischen Apokalyptik. StUNT 23: 1999 ⇒15,3956. ᴿThLZ 126 (2001) 625-629 (*Deines, Roland*); SNTU.A 25 (2000) 263-264 (*Pratscher, W.*).

2440 **Jackson, Bernard S.** Studies in the semiotics of biblical law. JSOT. S 314: 2000 ⇒16,2293. ᴿET 112 (2001) 292 (*Rodd, C.S.*).

2441 **Limbeck, Meinrad** Das Gesetz im Alten und Neuen Testament. 1997 ⇒13,2092... 16,2340. ᴿThLZ 126 (2001) 903-905 (*Hübner, Hans*); SNTU.A 22 (1997) 228-229 (*Böhmisch, F.*).

2442 *Maier, Johann* Das jüdische Gesetz zwischen Qumran und Septuaginta. Im Brennpunkt. BWANT 8,13: 2001 ⇒1605. 155-165.

2443 *Mosès, Stéphane* Rivelazione e linguaggio secondo le fonti ebraiche. L'Eros e la legge. Schulim Vogelmann 80: 2001 ⇒185. 79-91.

2444 *Otto, Eckart* Die Tora in Max WEBERs Studien zum Antiken Judentum: Grundlagen für einen religions- und rechtshistorischen Neuansatz in der Interpretation des biblischen Rechts. ZAR 7 (2001) 1-188.

2445 **Rothenbusch, Ralf** Die kasuistische Rechtssammlung im 'Bundesbuch' (Ex 21,2-11.18-22,16) und ihr literarischer Kontext im Licht altorientalischer Parallelen. AOAT 259: 2000 ⇒16,2343. ᴿOLZ 96 (2001) 541-545 (*Schmitt, Hans-Christoph*) [Exod 21-23].

2446 *Rothenbusch, Ralf* Die kasuistische Rechtssammlung im 'Bundesbuch' (Ex 21,2-11.18-22,16). ZAR 7 (2001) 243-272.

2447 **Schenker, Adrian** La legge dell'Antico Testamento volto dell'umano: una chiave di lettura per le leggi bibliche. Sussidi biblici 73: Reggio Emilia 2001, San Lorenzo 63 pp. 88-8071-120-2.

2448 *Schmidt, Ludwig* Israel und das Gesetz: Ex 19,3b-8 und 24,3-8 als literarischer und theologischer Rahmen für das Bundesbuch. ZAW 113 (2001) 167-185.

2449 *Ska, Jean-Louis* Le droit d'Israël dans l'Ancien Testament. Bible et droit. Connaître et croire 8: 2001 ⇒300. 9-43.

2450 *Spieckermann, Hermann* Recht und Gerechtigkeit im Alten Testament: politische Wirklichkeit und metaphorischer Anspruch. Gottes Liebe zu Israel. FAT 33: 2001 <1998> ⇒215. 119-140.

2451 **Williamson, James** The book of the covenant: a comparison of diachronic and synchronic approaches. Diss. Belfast 2001, ^D*Hibbert, A.*, 370 pp. [RTL 33,635].

2452 *Allam, Schafik* Ein Erbstreit um Sklaven (Papyrus BM 10568). ZÄS 128 (2001) 89-96.

2453 *Altman, Amnon* Concerning the judgment of the refugee who seeks sustenance in the international law of the ancient Near East. ^FAHITUV, S. 2001 ⇒1. 3-20. **H.**

2454 *Bord, Lucien-Jean* La loi, le droit et la justice: réflexions sur les droits cunéiformes et biblique: à propos de deux livres récents. Bib. 82 (2001) 99-107.

2455 *Bouzon, Emanuel* Einige Bemerkungen zum KH §117 und zur Schuldknechtschaft im alten Israel. ^MCAGNI, L., 1. SMDSA 61: 2001 ⇒15. 47-69.

2456 **Bouzon, Emanuel** Uma coleção de direito babilônico pré-hamurabiano: leis do reino de Eshnunna. Petrópolis 2001, Vozes 207 pp [REB 61,510].

2457 *Cohen, Yoram* The 'unwritten laws' of the Hittites: the case of the *natta āra* expression. IV. Internat.. Kongress. 2001 ⇒650. 73-82.

2458 **Donbaz, Veysel; Parpola, Simo** Neo-Assyrian legal texts in Istanbul. Studien zu den Assur-Texten (StAT) 2: Saarbrücken 2001, SDV Saarbrücker Verlag xxi; 267 pp. €65. 3-930843-64-1.

2459 *Fleishman, Joseph* Child maintenance in the laws of Eshnunna;
2460 Who is parent?: legal consequences of child maintenance. ZAR 7 (2001) 374-383/398-402.

2461 *Freitag, Klaus* Die Schiedsgerichtsbarkeit der panhellenistischen Heiligtümer. Kult, Konflikt. AOAT 285 (2001) 211-228.

2462 *Gandulla, Bernardo* Marriage and adoption: two institutions of Hurrian's [!] family law in the patriarchal traditions. ^MCAGNI, L., 1. SMDSA 61: 2001 ⇒15. 319-331.

2463 *Greenfield, Jonas C.* Some Neo-Babylonian women <1987>;
2464 'Because he/she did not know letters': remarks on a first millennium C.E. legal expression <1993>. 'Al kanfei yonah, 2. 2001 ⇒153. 920-925/939-944.

2465 *Haase, Richard* Zu den Rechtsfolgen falscher Angaben vor altorientalischen Gerichten. ^MCAGNI, L., 1. SMDSA 61: 2001 ⇒15. 433-438;
2466 De fetu abito sive ne se immisceat mulier praegnans rixae inter viros: vom ungewollten Abgang der Leibesfrucht im altorientalischen und biblischen Bereich. ZAR 7 (2001) 384-391 [Exod 21,22];
2467 Der § 36 der hethitischen Rechtssatzung: Versuch einer Deutung [Familie]. ZAR 7 (2001) 392-397.

2468 *Hagedorn, Anselm C.* Gortyn—utilising an archaic Greek law code for biblical research. ZAR 7 (2001) 217-242.

2469 *Kestemont, Guy* Remarques sur la situation de la femme dans le code hittite. ^FDESROCHES NOBLECOURT, C. 2001 ⇒22. 35-42.

2470 **Lafont, Sophie** Femmes, droit et justice dans l'antiquité orientale. OBO 165: 1999 ⇒15,2266; 16,2369. ^RZSRG.R 118 (2001) 388-405 (*Yaron, Reuven*); RBLit 3 (2001) 94-96 (*Melcher, Sarah J.*).

2471 ^E**Lévy, Edmond** La codification des lois dans l'antiquité. 2000 ⇒16, 597. Colloque 1997. ^RMes. 36 (2001) 130-132 (*Saporetti, C.*).

2472 **Richardson, M.E.J.** Hammurabi's laws: text, translation and glossary. BiSe 73: 2000 ⇒16,2373. [R]RA 95 (2001) 181-182 (*Charpin, D.*).
2473 *Roth, Martha T.* Reading Mesopotamian law cases: PBS 5 100: a question of filiation. JESHO 44 (2001) 243-292 Sum., rés. 243;
2474 The because clause: punishment rationalization in Mesopotamian laws. [F]VEENHOF, K. 2001 ⇒111. 407-412.
2475 *Steiner, Gerd* 'Diebstahl' in den 'Reformtexten' des Uru.inim.ginak von Lagaš. [M]CAGNI, L., 2. SMDSA 61: 2001 ⇒15. 1033-1047.
2476 *Weisberg, David B.* Pirqūti or Širkūti?: was Ištar-ab.uṣur's freedom affirmed or was he re-enslaved?. [M]CAGNI, L., 2. 2001 ⇒15. 1163-77.
2477 *Westbrook, Raymond* Social justice and creative jurisprudence in late Bronze Age Syria. JESHO 44 (2001) 22-43.

E3.6 Cultus, *Exodus 24-40*

2478 [E]**Köckert, Matthias; Blum, Erhard** Gottes Volk am Sinai: Untersuchungen zu Ex 32-34 und Dtn 9-10. Veröffentlichungen der Wissenschaftlichen Gesell. f. Theol. 18: Gü 2001, Gü 191 pp. 35790-53469.

2479 **Balentine, Samuel Eugene** The Torah's vision of worship. 1999 ⇒ 15,2274; 16,2380. [R]TS 62 (2001) 154-155 (*Endres, John C.*); JThS 52 (2001) 135-139 (*Bray, Jason*); Interp. 55 (2001) 305-306, 308 (*Olson, Dennis T.*) ; RBLit 3 (2001) 177-181 (*Wagenaar, Jan A.*).
2480 *Borgonovo, Gianantonio* Scrittura e berit in Es 19-40. Teol(Br) 26 (2001) 129-154.
2481 *Carr, David* Method in determination of direction of dependence: an empirical test of criteria applied to Exodus 34,11-26 and its parallels. Gottes Volk am Sinai. 2001 ⇒2478. 107-140.
2482 *Garbini, Giovanni* Il vitello di Bethel. [M]CAGNI, L., 3. SMDSA 61: 2001 ⇒15. 1543-1552 [Exod 32].
2483 *Gertz, Jan Christian* Beobachtungen zu Komposition und Redaktion in Exodus 32-34. Gottes Volk am Sinai. 2001 ⇒2478. 88-106.
2484 **Gleis, Matthias** Die Bamah. BZAW 251: 1997 ⇒13,2137... 16, 2390. [R]RBLit 3 (2001) 146-151 (*Simkins, Ronald A.*) .
2485 *Hartenstein, Friedhelm* Das "Angesicht Gottes" in Exodus 32-34. Gottes Volk am Sinai. 2001 ⇒2478. 157-183.
2486 *Isbell, Charles David* The liturgical function of Exodus 33:16-34:26. JBQ 29/1 (2001) 27-31.
2487 *Jelonek, Tomasz* Żydowskie tradycje święta Szawuot. [F]JANKOWSKI, A. 2001 ⇒53. 150-162.
2488 *Kongolo, Chijika* Les lustrations d'eau dans les écrits bibliques. LTP 57 (2001) 305-318.
2489 **Kung, Matias H.** The ritual dimensions in the tabernacle worship and their missiological implications. Diss. Trinity Evang. Divinity 2001, 302 pp. 3003798.
2490 *Laney, J. Carl* God's self-relevation in Exodus 34:6-8. BS 158 (2001) 36-51.
2491 **LaRocca-Pitts, Elizabeth C.** "Of wood and stone": the significance of Israelite cultic items in the bible and its early interpreters. HSM 61: WL 2001, Eisenbrauns xiii; 385 pp. $40. 1-57506-913-X. Bibl. 355-376.
2492 *Lind, Millard* The prophetic emphasis of the Sinai tabernacle pericope—Exodus 25:11-22. [F]JANZEN, W. 2001 ⇒54. 138-145.

2493 *Loewe, Raphael* Ark, archaism and misappropriation. ^MWEITZMAN, M. JSOT.S 333: 2001 ⇒113. 113-145.

2494 *Lohfink, Norbert* Deuteronomium 9,1-10,11 und Exodus 32-34: zu Endtextstruktur, Intertextualität, Schichtung und Abhängigkeiten. Gottes Volk am Sinai. 2001 ⇒2478. 41-87.

2495 **Millar, William R.** Priesthood in ancient Israel. Understanding biblical themes: Saint Louis 2001, Chalice 126 pp. $18.

2496 *Mosès, Stéphane* La punta di Enoch. L'Eros e la legge. Schulim Vogelmann 80: 2001 <1985> ⇒185. 93-112 [Exod 32].

2497 *Otto, Eckart* Gab es "historische" und "fiktive" Aaroniden im Alten Testament?. ZAR 7 (2001) 403-414.

2498 **Paximadi, Giorgio** "Ed io dimorerò in mezzo a loro": linee interpretative di Es 25-31 a partire dalla struttura retorica del testo: analisi di Es 25,10-40. Diss. Extr. Pont. Istituto Biblico, ^D*Bovati, Pietro*, Lugano 2001, Bassi 79 pp. Bibl. 58-74.

2499 **Rooke, Deborah W.** Zadok's heirs: the role and development of the high priesthood in ancient Israel. OTM: 2000 ⇒16,2403. ^RJThS 52 (2001) 145-147 (*Coggins, R.J.*); BiblInterp 9 (2001) 227-230 (*Hayward, Robert*); HebStud 42 (2001) 378-381 (*Klingbeil, Gerald A.*).

2500 *Rubin, Uri* Traditions in transformation: the ark of the covenant and the golden calf in biblical and Islamic historiography. Oriens 36 (2001) 196-214 [Exod 32; 35-40].

2501 *Schmid, Konrad* Israel am Sinai: Etappen der Forschungsgeschichte zu Ex 32-34 in seinen Kontexten. Gottes Volk am Sinai. 2001 ⇒ 2478. 7-40.

2502 *Schmitt, Hans-Christoph* Die Erzählung vom Goldenen Kalb Ex. 32* und das Deuteronomistische Geschichtswerk. Theologie in Prophetie. 2001 <2000> ⇒209. 311-325.

2503 *Scoralick, Ruth* "JHWH, JHWH, ein gnädiger und barmherziger Gott ..." (Ex 34,6): die Gottesprädikationen aus Ex 34,6f. in ihrem Kontext in Kapitel 32-34. Gottes Volk am Sinai. 2001 ⇒2478. 141-156.

2504 *Simian-Yofre, Horacio* Il volto di Dio clemente e misericordioso. Gr. 82 (2001) 477-486 [Exod 32-34].

2505 *Sindawi, Khalid* 'Ashura' Day and Yom Kippur. ANESt 38 (2001) 200-214.

2506 **Soggin, J. Alberto** Israel in the biblical period: institutions, festivals, ceremonies, rituals. ^T*Bowden, John*: E 2001, Clark xi; (2) 209 pp. £15. 0-567-08811-1. Bibl. 187-192;

2507 *Israele in epoca biblica: istituzioni, feste, cermonie e rituali.* Strumenti 4: 2000 ⇒16,2409. ^RCredOg 123 (2001) 137-138 (*Cappelletto, Gianni*); RivBib 49 (2001) 485-488 (*Prato, Gian Luigi*).

2508 *Sommer, Benjamin D.* Conflicting constructions of divine presence in the priestly tabernacle. BiblInterp 9 (2001) 41-63.

2509 **Ulfgard, Hσkan** The story of Sukkot: the setting, shaping, and sequel of the biblical feast of Tabernacles. BGBE 34: 1998 ⇒14, 2168; 16,2412. ^RRB 108 (2001) 460-462 (*Devillers, Luc*); ThLZ 126 (2001) 40-42 (*Veltri, Giuseppe*).

E3.7 **Leviticus,** *Jubilee*

2510 **Bellinger, W.H.** Leviticus, Numbers. Peabody 2001, Hendrickson 338 pp. $12. 1-56563-213-3 [BiTod 40,256—Bergant, Dianne].

2511 *Berquist, Jon L.* Leviticus and nausea. Postmodern interpretations. 2001 ⇒229. 17-28.
2512 *Buis, Pierre* Le Lévitique: la loi de sainteté. CEv 116 (2001) 5-47.
2513 *Büchner, Dirk; Jackson, Leonora* Interim report: NETS Leviticus. X Congress IOSCS. SBL.SCSt 51: 2001 ⇒499. 319-328.
2514 **Douglas, Mary** Leviticus as literature. 1999 ⇒15,2306; 16,2419. RPrPe 15 (2001) 80-81 (*Robinson, Bernard*); NRTh 123 (2001) 277-278 (*Luciani, D.*); JThS 52 (2001) 725-726 (*Jenson, Philip*).
2515 EFabry, Heinz-Josef; Jüngling, Hans-Winfried Levitikus als Buch. BBB 119: 1999 ⇒15,222. RThLZ 126 (2001) 509-512 (*Reventlow, Henning Graf*).
2516 **Gorman, Frank H.** Divine presence and community: a commentary on the book of Leviticus. 1997 ⇒13,2169... 15,2302. RVJTR 65 (2001) 312-314 (*Beck, Milianus*).
2517 **Grünwaldt, Klaus** Das Heiligkeitsgesetz Leviticus 17-26: ursprüngliche Gestalt, Tradition und Theologie. BZAW 271: 1999 ⇒15,2353. RThLZ 126 (2001) 1023-26 & Bib. 82 (2001) 418-22 (*Otto, Eckart*).
2518 *Jürgens, Benedikt* Wiederherstellung der Schöpfungsordnung: Levitikus (Teil 2): rituelle Kommunikation. BoSm 71 (2001) 133-137;
2519 "Angenommen jemand sündigt ..." (Lev 5,1): eine Entdeckungsreise in die fremde Welt des Buches Levitikus. ThG 44 (2001) 182-190.
2520 **Maccoby, Hyam** Ritual and morality: the ritual purity system and its place in Judaism. 1999 ⇒15,2310; 16,2421. RJThS 52 (2001) 721-722 (*Grabbe, Lester L.*).
2521 **Milgrom, Jacob** Leviticus 23-27: a new translation with introduction and commentary. AncB 3B: NY 2001, Doubleday 1896-2714 pp. $50. 0-3855-0035-1.
2522 *Milgrom, Jacob* הצד השווה בין חוקי המוסר בויקרא יט 11-12 וחוקי המשפט בויקרא ה 20-26 [The common denominator between the moral commandments, *Leviticus* 19:11-12, and the cultic laws, *Leviticus* 5:20-26]. BetM 166 (2001) 244-247 Sum. 286 [Lev 19,11-12; 5,20-26].
2523 North, Robert The Biblical Jubilee: ...after fifty years. AnBib 145: 2000 ⇒16,2455. RAng. 78 (2001) 736-738 (*Jurič, Stipe*); CBQ 63 (2001) 729-730 (*Balentine, Samuel E.*).
2524 *Ost, François* 'Vous sanctifierez la cinquantième année': reflexions sur le temps racheté. Bible et droit. Connaître et croire 8: 2001 ⇒ 300. 47-65.
2525 EPlaut, W. Gunther Die Tora: in jüdischer Auslegung, 3: Wajikra: Levitikus. TBöckler, Annette: Gü 2001, Kaiser 348 pp. €23. 3579-02-648-8. Bearbeitung, Gestaltung *A. Böckler*; collab. *B.J. Bamberger*.
2526 *Regev, Eyal* Priestly dynamic holiness and Deuteronomic static holiness. VT 51 (2001) 243-261.
2527 **Schwartz, Baruch J.** The Holiness legislation: studies in the Priestly Code. 1999 ⇒15,2357. RCBQ 63 (2001) 128-9 (*Anderson, Gary A.*).
2528 *Staubli, Thomas* Warum man Hühner ass, aber keine Schweine: biblische Speisetabus und ihre Folgen. Im Schatten deiner Flügel. 2001 ⇒ 412. 46-48.
2529 *Van Cangh, Jean-Marie* Le jubilé biblique: un temps marqué ouvrant un temps neuf. ScEs 53 (2001) 63-92.
2530 *Van Engen, John* RALPH of Flaix: the book of Leviticus interpreted as christian community. Jews and christians. 2001 ⇒441. 150-170.
2531 *Walton, John H.* Equilibrium and the sacred compass: the structure of Leviticus. BBR 11 (2001) 293-304.

2532 *Rendtorff, Rolf* Priesterliche Opfertora in jüdischer Auslegung. Der Text in seiner Endgestalt. 2001 ⇒201. 213-225 [Lev 1-7].
2533 *Bibb, Bryan D.* Nadab and Abihu attempt to fill a gap: law and narrative in Leviticus 10.1-7. JSOT 96 (2001) 83-99.
2534 *Moskala, Jirí* Categorization and evaluation of different kinds of interpretation of the laws of clean and unclean animals in Leviticus 11. BR 46 (2001) 5-41 [Lev 11].
2535 *Pfeiffer, Henrik* Bemerkungen zur Ritualgeschichte von Lev 16. ^FHAAS, V. 2001 ⇒39. 313-326.
2536 *Stökl, Daniel* The biblical Yom Kippur, the Jewish fast of the Day of Atonement and the Church Fathers. StPatr 34 (2001) 493-502 [Lev 16].
2537 *Kiuchi, Nobuyoshi* A paradox of the skin disease. ZAW 113 (2001) 505-514 [Lev 17].
2538 *Luciani, Didier* La fille 'perdue' et 'retrouvée' de Lévitique 18. ETR 76 (2001) 103-112 [Lev 18].
2539 **Sadler, Madeline McClenney** Recovering the daughter's nakedess: a formal analysis of Israelite kinship terminology and the internal logic of Leviticus 18. Diss. Duke 2001 [RTL 33,634].
2540 *Malamat, Abraham* 'You shall love your neighbour as yourself': a case of misinterpretation?. History of biblical Israel. Culture and history of the ANE 7: 2001 <1990> ⇒182. 401-405 [Lev 19,18].
2541 *Schüle, Andreas* Kamoka—der Nächste, der ist wie Du: zur Philologie des Liebesgebots von Lev 19,18.34. KUSATU 2 (2001) 97-129.
2542 *Schüle, Andreas von* 'Denn er ist wie du': zu Übersetzung und Verständnis des alttestamentlichen Liebesgebots Lev 19,18. ZAW 113 (2001) 515-534.
2543 *Takeuchi, Yu* Redonner sens au précepte de "l'amour du prochain" (Lev19,18ab)-"comme toi-même bien-aimé". AJBI 27 (2001) 3-21.
2544 *Wagenaar, Jan A.* You shall not sow two kinds of seed in your field: Leviticus 19,19 and the formation of the Holiness Code. ZAR 7 (2001) 318-331 [Dt 22,9-11].
2545 **Lefèbvre, Jean-François** Un mémorial de la création et de la rédemption: le jubilé biblique en Lv 25. ConBib 23: Bru 2001, Lumen Vitae 64 pp. €6.25. 2-87324-158-6 [Lev 25].
2546 *Marocco, Giuseppe* Dallo "Yôbel" del testo ebraico al "Giubileo" della Volgata. ATT 7 (2001) 51-61 [Lev 25].
2547 *O'Brien, D.P.* A comparison between early Jewish and early christian interpretations of the Jubilee Year. StPatr 34 (2001) 436-442 [Lev 25; Isa 61].
2548 *Ollenburger, Ben C.* Jubilee: this land is mine; you are aliens and tenants with me. ^FJANZEN, W. 2001 ⇒54. 208-234 [Lev 25].

E3.8 *Numeri*; Numbers, Balaam

2549 **Azcárraga Servert, María Josefa de** Las masoras del libro de Números: Códice M1 de la Universidad Complutense de Madrid. TECC 66: M 2001, Instituto de Filología, C.S.I.C. 265 pp. 84-00-07942-6.
2550 ^E**Basser, Herbert W.** Avraham BEN-DAWID: commentary to Sifre Numbers/Pseudo-Rabad. SFSHJ 189: 1998 ⇒14,2237. ^RREJ 160 (2001) 522-523 (*Rothschild, Jean-Pierre*).
        Bellinger, W.H. Leviticus, Numbers 2001 ⇒2510.

2551 **Domanski, Adam** The figure of Caleb in the O.T. tradition: its role and importance. Diss. Angelicum, Rome 2001, ^D*Agius, J.* [RTL 33, 631].

2552 **Douglas, Mary** Nel deserto: la dottrina della contaminazione nel libro dei Numeri. ^E*Destro, Adriana*: Collana di studi religiosi: Bo 2001, Dehoniane 352 pp. €33.57. 88-10-40799-7. Bibl. 327-334.

2553 **Levine, Baruch A.** Numbers 21-36. AncB 4A: 2000 ⇒16,2501. ^RDiv. 44 (2001) 213-214 (*Stramare, Tarcisio*); BiblInterp 9 (2001) 430-431 (*Pixley, Jorge*); JThS 52 (2001) 727-728 (*Davies, Eryl W.*); Interp. 55 (2001) 426, 428 (*Olson, Dennis T.*); CBQ 63 (2001) 525-526 (*Patrick, Dale*); ThLZ 126 (2001) 750-752 (*Seebass, Horst*).

2554 *Nowell, Irene* Are we there yet?. BiTod 39 (2001) 5-10.

2555 *Patrick, Dale* Depictions of God in the wilderness. BiTod 39 (2001) 11-16.

2556 *Rösel, Martin* Die Septuaginta und der Kult: Interpretationen und Aktualisierungen im Buch Numeri. ^FSCHENKER, A.: OBO 179: 2001 ⇒ 100. 25-40.

2557 **Seebass, Horst** Numeri [15,37-19,22]. BK.AT 4/2/3: Neuk 2001, Neuk'er 161-240 pp. 3-7887-1475-1.

2558 *Warning, Wilhelm* Terminologische Verknüpfungen und der aaronitische Segen. JETh 15 (2001) 5-9 [Num 6,24-26].

2559 *Cotton, Roger D.* The Pentecostal significance of Numbers 11. JPentec 10/1 (2001) 3-10.

2560 *Bledstein, Adrien* Family matters: a multidimensional reading of Miriam's humiliation and healing. BR 46 (2001) 55-61 [Num 12].

2561 *Condie, Keith* Narrative features of Numbers 13-14 and their significance for the meaning of the book of Numbers. RTR 60/3 (2001) 123-137.

2562 *Ausloos, Hans* LXX Num 14:23: once more a 'Deuteronomist' at work?. X Congress IOSCS. SBL.SCSt 51: 2001 ⇒499. 415-427.

2563 *Boer, Dick* Teure Gnade: Numeri 16:1-35. ^FDEURLOO, K. ACEBT.S 2: 2001 ⇒23. 49-56.

2564 **Mbinda Sambu, Théodore** Pouvoir divin et autodetermination de l'homme: étude de Nombres 16,1-17,5. Extr. Diss. Urbaniana, ^D*Spreafico, Ambrogio*: R 2001, xii; 96 pp.

2565 *Lim, Johnson Teng Kok* A puzzle in the pentateuch?. JBQ 29 (2001) 127-130 [Num 20,1-13].

2566 *Lemański, Janusz* Mojzesz i Nehusztan (Lb 21,4-9; 2 Krl 18,4): Próba analizy historii jednej tradycji. CoTh 71/4 (2001) 5-24. **P.**

2567 *Williams, James G.* Serpent and the Son of Man. BiTod 39 (2001) 22-26 [Num 21,8; John 3,14-15].].

2568 *Lenchak, Timothy A.* Puzzling passages: Numbers 21:9. BiTod 39 (2001) 306.

2569 *De Benedetti, Paolo* I pozzi e le sorgenti nella tradizione ebraica. RSEc 19 (2001) 341-343 [Num 21,16-18; John 4,6-15].

2570 *Schmitt, Hans-Christoph* Das Hesbonlied Num. 21,27aβb-30 und die Geschichte der Stadt Hesbon. Theologie in Prophetie. 2001 <1988> ⇒209. 131-154.

2571 **Betto, Frei** A mula de Balaão: versão atualizada do episódio da Bíblia contado em Números, capítulos 22 a 24. São Paulo 2001, Salesiana 56 pp. 85-87997-55-6.

2572 **Gass, Erasmus** "Ein Stern geht auf aus Jakob": sprach- und literatur-wissenschaftliche Analyse der Bileampoesie. ATSAT 69: St. Ottilien 2001, EOS x; 407 pp. €29.65. 3-8306-7076-1. Bibl. 346-400.

2573 *Moore, Michael S.* Prophet or magician?. BiTod 39 (2001) 17-21 [Num 22-24].

2574 *Schmitt, Hans-Christoph* Der heidnische Mantiker als eschatologi-scher Jahweprophet: zum Verständnis Bileams in der Endgestalt von Num 22-24. Theologie in Prophetie. 2001 <1994>. ⇒209. 238-254.

2575 **Schüle, Andreas** Israels Sohn—Jahwes Prophet: ein Versuch zum Verhältnis von kanonischer Theologie und Religionsgeschichte an-hand der Bileam-Perikope (Num 22-24). Diss. Heidelberg, ᴰ*Schmid, K.*, Altes Testament und Moderne 17: Müns 2001, Lit 338 pp. €30. 90. 3-8258-5590-2.

2576 *Zlotnick Sivan, Helena* The rape of Cozbi (Numbers XXV). VT 51 (2001) 69-80 [Gen 34].

2577 *Nwaoru, Emmanuel O.* The case of the daughters of Zelophehad (Num. 27:1-11) and African inheritance rights. VFTW 24/2 (2001) 63-78.

2578 *Mattingly, Keith* The significance of Joshua's reception of the laying on of hands in Numbers 27:12-23. AUSS 39 (2001) 191-208.

E3.9 Liber Deuteronomii

2579 **Araújo, Reginaldo Gomes de** Theologie der Wüste im Deuterono-mium. ÖBS 17: Fra 1999, Lang 376 pp. €53.30. 3-631-3453-1. ᴿThLZ 126 (2001) 1248-1250 (*Finsterbusch, Karin*).

2580 *Braulik, Georg* Das Buch Deuteronomium <³1998>;

2581 Das Deuteronomium und die Bücher Ijob, Sprichwörter, Rut: zur Frage früher Kanonizität des Deuteronomiums <1996>;

2582 'Konservative Reform': das Deuteronomium in wissenssozio-logischer Sicht <1998>;

2583 Durften auch Frauen in Israel opfern?: Beobachtungen zur Sinn- und Festgestalt des Opfers im Deuteronomium <1998>;

2584 Ezechiel und Deuteronomium <2000>;

2585 Von der Lust Israels vor seinem Gott <1999>;

2586 Die Völkervernichtung und die Rückkehr Israels ins Verheißungs-land: hermeneutische Bemerkungen zum Buch Deuteronomium <1997>. Studien zum Deuteronomium. SBAB 33: 2001 ⇒129. 11-37/213-293/39-57/59-89/171-201/91-112/113-150.

2587 **Brueggemann, Walter** Deuteronomy. Abingdon O.T. commentaries: Nv 2001, Abingdon 306 pp. $34. 0-687-08471-7. Bibl. 293-301.

2588 **Carrière, Jean-Marie** Théorie du politique dans le Deutéronome: a-
nalyse des unités, des structures et des concepts de Dt 16,16-18,22.
ÖBS 18: Fra 2001, Lang 515 pp. €63.83. 3-6313-7083-0. Diss. ⇒
13,2272. [R]RSR 89 (2001) 534-535 (*Gibert, Pierre*).

2589 **Christensen, Duane L.** Deuteronomy 1:1-21:9. WBC 6A: Waco
2001, Word cxii; 458 pp. 0-7852-4220-1. Rev. ed.

2590 **Clements, Ronald Ernest** The book of Deuteronomy: a preacher's
commentary. Epworth Commentaries: Peterborough 2001, Epworth
xxiv; 150 pp. 0-7162-0543-2. Bibl. xi.

2591 **Harman, Allan M.** Deuteronomy: the commands of a covenant God.
Fearn 2001, Christian Focus 288 pp. $AU17.

2592 *Hoppe, Leslie J.* Deuteronomy and the law. BiTod 39 (2001) 265-
270.

2593 **Jasnos, Renata** Teologia prawa w Deuteronomium. Kraków 2001,
Wyzsza Szkola Filozoficzno-Pedagogiczna Ignatianum 300 pp. 83-
88209-24-8. Bibl. 11-27. **P.**

2594 *Knoppers, Gary N.* Rethinking the relationship between Deuteronomy and the Deuteronomistic History: the case of Kings. CBQ 63
(2001) 393-415.

2595 *Levinson, Bernard M.* The reconceptualization of kingship in Deuteronomy and the deuteronomistic history's transformation of torah. VT
51 (2001) 511-534.

2596 *McConville, J. Gordon* Metaphor, symbol and the interpretation of
Deuteronomy. [F]THISELTON, A. 2001 ⇒106. 329-351;

2597 Restoration in Deuteronomy and the Deuteronomic literature. Restoration. JSJ.S 72: 2001 ⇒319. 11-40.

2598 **Millar, J. Gary** Now choose life: theology and ethics in Deuteronomy. 1998 ⇒14,2287; 16,2544. [R]HebStud 42 (2001) 336-338 (*Haak,
Robert D.*); EvQ 73 (2001) 169-170 (*Bodner, Keith*).

2599 **Norrback, Anna** The fatherless and the widow in the Deuteronomic
covenant. Diss. Åbo. Åbo Akademis 2001, 285 pp. 951-765-068-X.

2600 **Otto, Eckart** Das Deuteronomium: politische Theologie und Rechts-
reform in Juda und Assyrien. BZAW 284 1999 ⇒15,2417; 16,2549.
[R]BZ 45 (2001) 294-98 (*Dahmen, Ulrich*); ThLZ 126 (2001) 1030-34
(*Hardmeier, Christof*); Bib. 82 (2001) 422-426 (*Morrow, William*).

2601 *Rofé, Alexander* The organization of the judiciary in Deuteronomy
(Deut. 16.18-20; 17.8-13; 19.15; 21.22-23; 24.16; 25.1-3). [F]DION, P.-
E. 1. JSOT.S 324: 2001 ⇒25. 92-112.

2602 *Scalabrini, Patrizio Rota* La scrittura secondo il Deuteronomio, ovvero il libro per i tempi moderni. Teol(Br) 26 (2001) 155-184.

2603 *Sonnet, Jean-Pierre* Le rendez-vous du Dieu vivant: la mort de
Moïse dans l'intrigue du Deutéronome (Dt 1-4 et Dt 31-34). NRTh
123 (2001) 353-372.

2604 *Spieckermann, Hermann* Mit der Liebe im Wort: ein Beitrag zur Theologie des Deuteronomiums. Gottes Liebe zu Israel. FAT 33: 2001 <2000> ⇒215. 157-172.

2605 *Talstra, Eep* Texts for recitation: Deuteronomy 6:7; 11:19. ᶠDEUR-LOO, K. ACEBT.S 2: 2001 ⇒23. 67-76.

2606 **Willis, Timothy M.** The elders of the city: a study of the elders-laws in Deuteronomy. SBL.MS 55: Atlanta, GA 2001 SBL xiii; 353 pp. $45. 1-58983-013-X. Bibl. 313-339 [Dt 21,18-21; 25,4-10; 21,1-9; 22,13-21; 19,1-13].

2607 *Taschner, Johannes* Die Bedeutung des Generationswechsels für den Geschichtsrückblick in Dtn 1-3. WuD 26 (2001) 61-72.

2608 *Houtman, Cees* Autoritative Interpretation im Deuteronomium: beleuchtet anhand von Deuteronomium 1:9-18. ᶠDEURLOO, K. ACEBT. S 2: 2001 ⇒23. 57-65.

2609 **Heckl, Raik** Die 'Ich-Erzählung des Mose': eine Studie zu Kohärenz, literarischer Intention und Funktion von Dtn 1,1-3,29. Diss. Leipzig 2001, ᴰ*Lux, R.* [RTL 33,632].

2610 *Lenchak, Timothy A.* Puzzling passages: Deut 7:2. BiTod 39 (2001) 114-115.

2611 *Tanner, Beth Laneel* Deuteronomy 10:12-22. Interp. 55 (2001) 60-3.

2612 *Derby, Josiah* The evolution of a law. JBQ 29 (2001) 113-117 [Dt 25,5-10].

2613 *Loader, James Alfred* Gerste, Bullen, Land und Levirat. Begegnung mit Gott. 2001 ⇒175. 167-183 [Dt 25,5-10].

2614 *Matlock, Michael D.* Disobeying or obeying the first part of the tenth commandment: alternative meanings from Deuteronomy 25:5-10. ProcGLM 21 (2001) 91-103.

2615 *Rendtorff, Rolf* Sihon, Og und das israelitische "Credo". Der Text in seiner Endgestalt. 2001 ⇒201. 174-180 [Dt 26,5-9].

2616 *Israel, Felice* L'arameo errante e le origini di Israele. ᶠDION, P.-E. 1. JSOT.S 324: 2001 ⇒25. 275-287 [Dt 26,5-11].

2617 *Haraguchi, Takaaki* A rhetorical analysis of Deuteronomy 29-30. AJTh 15/1 (2001) 24-37.

2618 *Breyne, Jean-François* Deutéronome 30,11-20: entre vie et mort, un autre chemin. Lire et Dire 50 (2001) 5-14.

2619 **Welikadaarachchi Daya, Andrew Shelton** Transition of leadership from Moses to Joshua: an exegetico-theological study of Deuteronomy 31:1-8. Diss. Urbaniana 2001, ᴰ*Deiana, G.* [RTL 33,634].

2620 *Dion, Paul E.* Moisés luchando contra los desafios del tiempo: Deuteronomio 31. AnáMnesis 11/2 (2001) 5-16.

2621 *Heiser, Michael S.* Deuteronomy 32:8 and the sons of God. BS 158 (2001) 52-74.

2622 *Greenfield, Jonas C.* Smitten by famine, battered by plague (Deuteronomy 32:24). 'Al kanfei yonah, 2. 2001 <1987> ⇒153. 785-788.

2623 *Frevel, Christian* Ein vielsagender Abschied: exegetische Blicke auf den Tod des Mose in Dtn 34,1-12. BZ 45 (2001) 209-234.

2624 *Polaski, Donald C.* Moses' final examination. Postmodern interpretations. 2001 ⇒229. 29-42 [Dt 34].

E4.1 *Origo Israelis in Canaan: Deuteronomista*; Liber Josue

2625 **Finkelstein, Israel; Silberman, Neil Asher** The bible unearthed: archaeology's new vision of Ancient Israel and the origin of its sacred texts. NY 2001, Free x (2) 385 pp. $26. 0-684-86912-8. Bibl. 356-372. [R]BASOR 322 (2001) 67-77 (*Dever, William G.*).

2626 **Macchi, Jean-Daniel** Israël et ses tribus selon Genèse 49. OBO 171: 1999 ⇒15,2460. [R]EstAg 36 (2001) 140-141 (*Mielgo, C.*); ThLZ 126 (2001) 28-30 (*Seebass, Horst*).

2627 **Schmid, Konrad** Erzväter und Exodus: Untersuchungen zur doppelten Begründung der Ursprünge Israels innerhalb der Geschichtsbücher des Alten Testaments. WMANT 81: 1999 ⇒15,2463; 16,2604. [R]JBL 119 (2000) 341-343 (*Van Seters, John*).

2628 **Thompson, Thomas L.** The mythic past: biblical archaeology and the myth of Israel. 1999 ⇒15,2464; 16,2605. [R]REJ 160 (2001) 263-265 (*Mimouni, Simon C.*); BetM 168 (2001) 25-32 [H., Sum. 95] (*Oded, Bustenay*); RBLit 3 (2001) 151-154 (*Hamilton, Mark W.*).

2629 *Barstad, Hans M.* Deuteronomists, Persians, Greeks, and the dating of the Israelite tradition. Did Moses speak Attic?. JSOT.S 317: 2001 ⇒270. 47-77.

2630 *Braulik, Georg* Die Theorien über das Deuteronomistische Geschichtswerk. Studien zum Deuteronomium. 2001 <[3]1998> ⇒129. 153-169.

2631 **Campbell, Antony F.; O'Brien, Mark A.** Unfolding the Deuteronomistic History: origins, upgrades, present text. 2000 ⇒16,2612. [R]CBQ 63 (2001) 712-713 (*Mullen, E. Theodore*); RBBras 18 (2001) 462.

2632 **Cortese, Enzo** Deuteronomistic work. ASBF 47: 1999 ⇒15,2473; 16,2613. [R]CDios 214 (2001) 511-512 (*Gutiérrez, J.*).

2633 *Gisana, Rosario* I libri di Samuele e Re. PaVi 46/1 (2001) 9-15.

2634 *Halpern, Baruch* The taking of nothing: 2 Kings 14.25, Amos 6.14 and the geography of the Deuteronomistic History. [F]DION, P.-E. 1. JSOT.S 324: 2001 ⇒25. 186-204.

2635 **Hamilton, Victor P.** Handbook on the historical books: Joshua, Judges, Ruth, Samuel, Kings, Chronicles, Ezra-Nehemiah, Esther. GR 2001, Baker 557 pp. $33. 0-8010-2257-6.

2636 *Hunt, Joel H.* The deuteronomists as loyal opposition. AsbTJ 56/1 (2001) 7-16.

2637 **Klaus, Nathan** Pivot patterns in the Former Prophets. JSOT.S 247: 1999 ⇒15,2480. RCBQ 63 (2001) 316-317 (*Walsh, Jerome T.*).

Kratz, R. Komposition der erzählenden Bücher 2000 ⇒1904.

2638 **Nentel, Jochen** Trägerschaft und Intentionen des deuteronomistischen Geschichtswerks...Jos 1; 23; 24; 1 Sam 12...1 Kön 8. BZAW 297: 2000 ⇒16,2661. ROLZ 96 (2001) 560-563 (*Levin, Christoph*).

2639 **Nielsen, Flemming A.J.** The tragedy in history: HERODOTUS and the Deuteronomistic History. JSOT.S 251: 1997 ⇒13,2322; 15,2487. RJBL 120 (2001) 353-354 (*Barrick, W. Boyd*).

2640 **Pakkala, Juha** Intolerant monolatry in the deuteronomistic history. SESJ 76: 1999 ⇒15,2488. REThL 77 (2001) 198-199 (*Lust, J.*).

2641 **Peters, Kathleen Wood** A phenomenological study of divine images in the Deuteronomistic History. Diss. Emory 2001, 284 pp. 3009464.

2642 **Richter, Sandra Lynn** The Deuteronomistic History and the place of the name. Diss. Harvard 2001, 282 pp. 3011544 [HThR 97,112].

2643 *Römer, Thomas* La fin de l'historiographie deutéronomiste et le retour de l'hexateuque?. ThZ 57 (2001) 269-280.

2644 ERömer, Thomas The future of the Deuteronomistic History. BEThL 147: 2000 ⇒16,322. RCart. 17 (2001) 436 (*Sanz Valdivieso, R.*); ETR 76 (2001) 641-642 (*Römer, Thomas*).

2645 **Sacchi, Alessandro** I libri storici: Israele racconta la sua storia. 2000 ⇒16,2638. RRivBib 49 (2001) 350-352 (*Boschi, Bernardo Gianluigi*); RdT 42 (2001) 144-145 (*Ska, Jean Louis*); CivCatt 152/1 (2001) 328-329 (*Scaiola, D.*).

2646 *Saebø, Magne* "Ne bis in idem"?—theologische und kanonische Aspekte der Parallelität von Deuteronomistischem und Chronistischem Geschichtswerk. Biblischer Text. BThSt 44: 2001 ⇒252. 27-51.

2647 *Schmitt, Hans-Christoph* Das spätdeuteronomistische Geschichtswerk Genesis I - 2 Regum XXV und seine theologische Intention. Theologie in Prophetie. 2001 <1997> ⇒209. 277-294.

2648 *Spieckermann, Hermann* Former prophets: the deuteronomistic history. The Blackwell companion to the Hebrew Bible. Blackwell companions to religion 3: 2001 ⇒653. 337-352.

2649 **Erbes, Johann E.** The Peshitta and the versions: a study of the Peshitta variants in Joshua 1-5. AUU.SSU 16: 1999 ⇒15,2513; 16, 2659. RJSSt 46 (2001) 173-175 (*Lane, D.J.*); AUSS 39 (2001) 143-

144 *(Taylor, Richard A.)*; CBQ 63 (2001) 107-108 *(Bundy, David)*; BiOr 58 (2001) 435-438 *(Owens, Robert J.)*.

2650 *Gilead, David* The double ending of the book of Joshua: editorial considerations. [F]AHITUV, S. 2001 ⇒1. 75-80. **H**.

2651 **Hawk, L. Daniel** Joshua. Berit Olam: 2000 ⇒16,2647. [R]ScrB 31 (2001) 112-114 *(Mills, Mary)*.

2652 **Hertzberg, Hans Wilhelm** Giosuè, Giudici, Rut. [T]*Ronchi, Franco*: Antico Testamento 9: Brescia 2001, Paideia 446 pp. €38.73. 88-394-0602-6. Bibl. 441-442.

2653 **Howard, David M.** Joshua. NAC 5: 1998 ⇒15,2494. [R]HebStud 42 (2001) 338-340 *(Moore, Michael S.)*.

2654 **Niessen, Friedrich** Eine samaritanische Version des Buches Yehosua und die Sobak-Erzählung. TSO 12: 2000 ⇒16,2650. [R]FJB 28 (2001) 173-175 *(Dexinger, Ferdinand)*.

2655 *Rösel, Martin* Die Septuaginta-Version des Josuabuches. Im Brennpunkt. BWANT 8,13: 2001 ⇒1629. 197-211.

2656 *Stammberger, Ralf M.* Die Halberstädter Glosse zum Matthäus-Evangelium und zum Buch Josua: zur Wiederentdeckung der Handschrift Halberstadt, Dom- Gymnasium 47 aus der ersten Hälfte des 12. Jahrhunderts. Recherches de théologie et philosophie médiévales 68 (2001) 18-33.

2657 **Van der Meer, M.N.** Formation and reformulation: the redaction of the book of Joshua in the light of the oldest textual witnesses. Diss. R.U. Leiden 2001, [D]*Van der Kooij, A.*: xiv; 464 pp .

2658 **Auld, A. Graeme** Joshua retold: synoptic perspectives. 1998 ⇒14, 2341; 16,2654. [R]OLZ 96 (2001) 554-556 *(Schäfer-Lichtenberger, Christa)*; JBL 120 (2001) 747-748 *(Klein, Ralph W.)*.

2659 *Batto, Bernard F.* Images of God in Joshua and Judges. BiTod 39 (2001) 217-223.

2660 *Cotter, David W.* The Israelite conquest of Canaan. BiTod 39 (2001) 205-209.

2661 *Hens-Piazza, Gina* Violence in Joshua and Judges. BiTod 39 (2001) 197-203.

2662 *Hubbard, Robert L., Jr.* 'What do these stones mean?': biblical theology and a motif in Joshua. BBR 11 (2001) 1-16.

2663 *Jericke, Detlef* Baal-Gad. ZDPV 117 (2001) 129-139 [Josh 11,17; 12,7; 13,5].

2664 *Malamat, Abraham* Conquest of Canaan: Israelite conduct of war according to biblical tradition. History of biblical Israel. Culture and history of the ANE 7: 2001 <1979> ⇒182. 68-96.

2665 *Merling, David* The book of Joshua, part I: its evaluation by non-evidence. AUSS 39 (2001) 61-72;

2666 The book of Joshua, part II: expectations of archaeology. AUSS 39 (2001) 209-221;

2667 Rahab: la mujer que cumplio las palabras de YHWH. Theologika 16 (2001) 128-153.

2668 **Merling, David, Sr.** The book of Joshua: its theme and role in archaeological discussions. Andrews Univ. Sem. Doctoral Diss. 23, ^D*Shea, William H.*: Berrien Springs 1996, Andrews 353 pp. ^RJBL 119 (2000) 344-345 (*Nelson, Richard D.*).

2669 *Spina, Frank Anthony* Rahab the Israelite & Achan the Canaanite. BiRe 17/4 (2001) 25-30, 53-54.

2670 *Van der Meer, Michaël N.* Textual criticism and literary criticism in Joshua 1:7 (MT and LXX). X Congress IOSCS. SBL.SCSt 51: 2001 ⇒499. 355-371.

2671 *Boneva, Krassimira* La puissance du croire dans l'établissement d'un contrat selon le livre de Josué (chapitre 2). SémBib 101 (2001) 42-9.

2672 *Roetman, Jan-Albert* Josué 3: passer à un temps nouveau. Lire et Dire 48 (2001) 3-11.

2673 *Jódar-Estrella, Carlos* Jos 5,13-15: ensayo sobre la coherencia textual. EstB 59 (2001) 243-279.

2674 *Knauf, Ernst Axel* Zeret-Schahar (Jos 13,19). BN 110 (2001) 37.

2675 *Noort, Ed* Der Streit um den Altar: Josua 22 und seine Rezeptionsgeschichte. Kult, Konflikt. AOAT 285: 2001 ⇒387. 151-174.

E4.2 *Liber Judicum*: **Richter, Judges**

2676 **Amit, Yairah** Judges. Mikra Leyisra'el: 1999 ⇒15,2520; 16,2678. ^RCBQ 63 (2001) 709-710 (*Reeves, John C.*); RBLit 3 (2001) 189-192 (*Brettler, Marc Z.*). **H.**

2677 ^E**Dyk, Janet W.** Richteren. ACEBT 19: Maastricht 2001, Shaker 149 pp. €14. 90-423-0177-5. Sum. 177-182.

    Hertzberg, H. Giosuè, Giudici, Rut. 2001 ⇒2652.

2678 **Schneider, Tammi J.** Judges. Berit Olam: 2000 ⇒16,2680. ^RHebStud 42 (2001) 341-343 (*Hess, Richard S.*).

2679 **Andersson, Greger** The book and its narratives: a critical examination of some synchronic studies of the book of Judges. Örebro studies in literary history and criticism 1: Örebro 2001, Örebro universitet 236 pp. 91-7668-276-5.

2680 *Block, Hanna* 'En het land had veertig jaar rust': de bewoners van Israël in het tijdperk van de Richteren. Richteren. 2001 ⇒2677. 37-53.

2681 ᴱ**Brenner, Athalya** Juízes: a partir de uma leitura de gênero. ᵀ*Marques, Fátima Regina Durães*: A Biblia, uma leitura de gênero: São Paulo 2001, Filhas de São Paulo 303 pp [REB 244,1006].

2682 *Kreuzer, Siegfried* Eine Schrift, zwei Fassungen: das Beispiel des Richterbuches. BiKi 56 (2001) 88-91.

2683 *Malamat, Abraham* The period of the Judges <1971>;

2684 Charismatic leadership in the book of Judges <1976>. History of biblical Israel. 2001 ⇒182. 97-147/151-170.

2685 **Mondini, Umberto** La penetrazione militare degli israeliti in Palestina nel libro dei Giudici. R 2001, Pro Deo Univ Pr 49 pp. Bibl. 39-47.

2686 **Sasaki, Tetsuo** The concept of war in the book of Judges: a strategical evaluation of the wars of Gideon, Deborah, Samson, and Abimelech. Tokyo 2001, Gakujutsu T.S. 140 pp.

2687 *Spronk, Klaas* Het boek Richteren: een overzicht van het recente onderzoek. Richteren. 2001 ⇒2677. 1-36. Sum. 177.

2688 **Stanley, Rhona** Charismatic leadership in Ancient Israel: a socialscientific approach. Diss. Fort Worth 2001, ᴰ*Hunt, H.*: 190 pp. 3010755 [RTL 33,634].

2689 *Van Midden, Piet* Lees maar: er staat niet wat er staat: verborgen theologie in Richteren. Richteren. 2001 ⇒2677. 55-63. Sum. 178;

2690 A hidden message?: Judges as foreword to the books of Kings. ᶠDEURLOO, K. ACEBT.S 2: 2001 ⇒23. 77-85.

2691 *Van Wieringen, C.G.* Een dochter in de aanbieding (Ri. 15:2): de wederwaardigheden van de dochters in het boek Richteren als teken van verval. Richteren. 2001 ⇒2677. 125-138. Sum. 181.

2692 **Álvarez Barredo, Miguel** La iniciativa de Dios: estudio literario y teológico de Jueces 1-8. 2000 ⇒16,2686. ᴿRevista teología 41 (2001) 248-250 (*Ranieri, Aldo Adrián*).

2693 *Sima, Alexander* Nochmals zur Deutung des hebräischen Namens עָתְנִאֵל. BN 106 (2001) 47-51 [Judg 1,13].

2694 *Guillaume, Philippe* Dating the Negatives Besitzverzeichnis (Judges 1,27-34): the case of Sidon. Henoch 23 (2001) 131-137.

2695 *Spronk, Klaas* A story to weep about: some remarks on Judges 2:1-5 and its context. ᶠDEURLOO, K. ACEBT.S 2: 2001 ⇒23. 87-94.

2696 *Jagersma, Henk* Geen andere goden: Richteren 3:1-6. Richteren. 2001 ⇒2677. 65-69.

2697 *Gómez-Acebo, Isabel* Débora, una mujer al frente de su pueblo. MisEx(M) 184 (2001) 277-286 [Judg 4-5].

2698 *Spronk, Klaas* Deborah, a prophetess: the meaning and background of Judges 4:4-5. The elusive prophet. OTS 45 (2001) 232-242.

2699 *Wit, Hans de* Lezen met Jaël: op weg naar interculturele hermeneutiek. Richteren. 2001 ⇒2677. 71-96. Sum. 179 [Judg 4,17-22].

2700 *Kegler, Jürgen* Debora—Erwägungen zur politischen Funktion einer Frau in einer patriarchalischen Gesellschaft. Gesammelte Aufsätze. BEAT 48: 2001 <1980> ⇒167. 72-89 [Judg 5].

2701 *Claassens, L. Juliana M.* The character of God in Judges 6-8: the Gideon narrative as theological and moral resource. HBT 23 (2001) 51-71.

2702 **Bluedorn, Wolfgang** Yahweh Versus Baalism: a theological reading of the Gideon-Abimelech narrative. JSOT.S 329: Shf 2001, Sheffield A. 320 pp. £55. 1-84127-200-0. Bibl. 292-305 [Judg 6-9].

2703 *Smelik, Klaas A.D.* Gideon, held of antiheld?: karakterisering van een personage in het boek Richteren. Richteren. 2001 ⇒2677. 97-109 Sum. 180 [Judg 6,11-8,35].

2704 *Himbaza, Innocent* Retour sur Juges 7,5-6. RB 108 (2001) 26-36.

2705 *Malamat, Abraham* Appendix: The punishment by Gideon of Succoth and Penuel in the light of ancient Near Eastern treaties. History of biblical Israel. 2001 ⇒182. 148-150 [Judg 8].

2706 *Rhodes, James N.* 'Safe and sound' (Judges 8.9). BiTr 52 (2001) 246-248.

2707 *Álvarez Barredo, M.* Abimelec: paradigma de una actitud autónoma ante Dios: estudio literario de Jue 9. Cart. 17 (2001) 1-66 Res., sum.

2708 *Castelbajac, Isabelle de* Histoire de la rédaction de Juges IX: une solution. VT 51 (2001) 166-185.

2709 **Jans, Edgar** Abimelech und sein Königtum: diachrone und synchrone Untersuchungen zu Ri 9. Diss. Tübingen 2000, ᴰ*Gross, W.*: ATSAT 66: St. Ottilien 2001, EOS 504 pp. €24.54. 3-8306-7064-8. Bibl. 483-498.

2710 *Álvarez Barredo, Miguel* Jefté, símbolo de una utilización interesada de Dios: rasgos teológicos de Jueces 10,1-12,15. VyV 59 (2001) 465-484. Sum. 465.

2711 *Olson, Dennis T.* Dialogues of life and monologues of death: Jephthah and Jephthah's daughter in Judges 10:6-12:7. Postmodern interpretations. 2001 ⇒229. 43-54.

2712 *Ostriker, Alicia* Jephthah's daughter. CrossCur 51/2 (2001) 201-218 [Judg 11,29-40].

2713 *Sharp, Carolyn* Le prix de l'engagement: vers une lecture politisée du récit de la fille de Jephté (Juges 11,29-40). Theoforum 32 (2001) 367-390.

2714 *Van Wieringen, Willien* 'Wer ... äh, dein Name, bitte?': ein erster Versuch, mit der Frau ohne Name aus Richter 13 Bekanntschaft zu machen. ᶠDEURLOO, K. ACEBT.S 2: 2001 ⇒23. 95-105.

2715 *Hoogewoud, F.J.* Simson revisited: in memoriam Dr. Aleida G. van Daalen, leesmoeder in Amsterdam Richteren. 2001 ⇒2677. 111-124. Sum. 180s [Judg 13-16].

2716 *Kegler, Jürgen* Simson—Widerstandskämpfer und Volksheld. Gesammelte Aufsätze. 2001 <1985> ⇒167. 107-126 [Judg 13-16].

2717 **Meurer, Thomas** Die Simson-Erzählungen: Studien zu Komposition und Entstehung, Erzähltechnik und Theologie von Ri 13-16. BBB 130: B 2001, Philo 405 pp. 3-8257-0238-3. Bibl. 397-405.

2718 *Rowlett, Lori* Violent femmes and s/m: queering Samson and Delilah. Queer commentary. JSOT.S 334: 2001 ⇒325. 106-115 [Judg 13-16].

2719 *Spronk, Klaas* Vrouwen en Simson: enkele opmerkingen over de feministische uitleg van Richteren 13-16. GThT 101 (2001) 11-21.

2720 *Schüngel-Straumann, Helen* Simson & Delila: Buch der Richter, Kapitel 16. Schön bist du. 2001 ⇒274. 135-140.

2721 *Bauer, Uwe F.* Richteren 17-18 als 'anti-verbaal' van teksten uit Genesis - 2 Koningen. Richteren. 2001 ⇒2677. 139-157 Sum. 181.

2722 **Bauer, Uwe F.** 'Warum nur übertretet ihr sein Geheiß?': eine synchrone Exegese der Anti-Erzählung von Richter 17-18. BEAT 45: 1998 ⇒14,2403. [R]JBL 119 (2000) 550-552 (*Block, Daniel I.*).

2723 *Malamat, Abraham* The Danite migration and the Pan-Israelite Exodus-Conquest: a biblical narrative pattern. History of biblical Israel. 2001 <1970> ⇒182. 171-185 [Judg 17-18].

2724 **Mueller, E. Aydeet** The Micah story: a morality tale in the book of Judges. Studies in Biblical Literature 34: NY 2001, Lang xiii; 149 pp. $48. 0-8204-5190-8. Bibl. 129-141 [Judg 17-18].

2725 *Mayes, Andrew D.H.* Deuteronomistic royal ideology in Judges 17-21. BiblInterp 9 (2001) 241-258.

2726 *Bauer, Uwe* Eine metaphorische Ätiologie in Richter 18:12. [F]DEURLOO, K.: ACEBT.S 2: 2001 ⇒23. 107-113;

2727 A metaphorical etiology in Judges 18:12. Journal of Hebrew Scriptures 3 (2001) [electronic journal].

2728 *Van Buuren, Lidwien M.A.* Het raadsel van de 'bijvrouw' te Gibea in Richteren 19. Richteren. 2001 ⇒2677. 159-175. Sum. 182.

2729 *Leshem, Y.* Date of composition of the narrative material in Judges: the 'concubine at Gibeah' story (Judges 19-21). Beit Mikra 165 (2001) 128-145. **H.**

2730 *Stiebert, Johanna; Walsh, Jerome T.* Chaos cries for a king. BiTod 39 (2001) 211-215 [Judg 19-21].

2731 *Organ, Barbara E.* Pursuing Phinehas: a sychronic reading. CBQ 63 (2001) 203-218 [Num 25; 31; Judg 20-21; Josh 22].

E4.3 **Liber Ruth**, '*V Rotuli*', the Five Scrolls

2732 Die Bücher Ruth und Ester. Fischer Taschenbuch 14509: Fra 2000, Fischer 46 pp. 3-596-14509-0. Mit einer Einleitung von *Zoë Jenny*.

2733 **Fischer, Irmtraud** Rut. HThK.AT: FrB 2001, Herder 277 pp. €55. 22. 3-451-26811-6. Bibl. 15-21.

2734 *Gesche, Bonifatia* Ruth. BVLI 45 (2001) 9-11.
Hertzberg, H. Giosuè, Giudici, Rut 2001 ⇒2652.

2735 **Linafelt, Tod; Beal, Timothy Kandler** Ruth and Esther. 1999 ⇒15, 2556. [R]Gr. 82 (2001) 169-171 (*Conroy, Charles*); CBQ 63 (2001) 117-118 (*Day, Linda*).

2736 **Ljungberg, Bo-Krister** Verbal meaning: a linguistic, literary, and theological framework for interpretive categories of the Biblical Hebrew verbal system as elaborated in the book of Ruth. Diss. Lund 2001, Teologiska institutionen, Lunds Univ. 396 pp.

2737 **Lowden, John** The making of the bibles moralisées, 1: the manuscripts; 2: the book of Ruth. 2000 ⇒16,2705. [R]TS 62 (2001) 607-608 (*Greenspoon, Leonard*).

2738 **Niccacci, Alviero; Pazzini, Massimo** Il rotolo di Rut: analisi del testo ebraico. SBFA 51: J 2001, Franciscan 106 pp. $10. 0081-8933. [R]MF 101 (2001) 396-397 (*Holc, Milan*).

2739 *Turner, Kenneth J.* A study of articulation in the Greek Ruth. BIOSCS 34 (2001) 95-114.

2740 **Zakovitch, Yair** Das Buch Rut: ein jüdischer Kommentar. SBS 177: 1999 ⇒15,2560; 16,2709. [R]BZ 45 (2001) 301-304 (*Bohlen, Reinhold*); ThLZ 126 (2001) 377-379 (*Naumann, Thomas*); RBLit 3 (2001) 247-250 (*Nielsen, Kirsten*).

2741 *Dube, Musa W.* Divining Ruth for international relations. Other ways. 2001 ⇒260. 179-195;

2742 Postmodern interpretations. 2001 ⇒229. 67-80.

2743 **Eichrodt-Kessel, Hélène** Ruth: une patri-matriarche: lectures intertextuelles et études des représentations de l'homme et de la femme dans le livre de Ruth. Diss. Strasbourg 2001, [D]*Vincent, G.* 437 pp [RTL 33,631].

2744 *Estévez, Elisa* Función socio-histórica y teológica del libro de Rut. MCom 59 (2001) 685-706.

2745 **Ghini, Emanuela** Nei campi di Betlemme: il libro di Rut. CasM ²2001 <1982>, Portalupi 158 pp. €8.30 [PaVi 48/3,62–Doglio, C.].

2746 *Grohmann, Marianne* Rut & Boas: Buch Rut, Kapitel 1-4. Schön bist du. 2001 ⇒274. 62-67.

2747 **Korpel, Marjo Christina Annette** The structure of the book of Ruth. Pericope 2: Assen 2001, Van Gorcum ix; 288 pp. $65. 90-232-3657-2. Bibl. 235-246.

2748 *Landy, Francis* Ruth and the romance of realism, or deconstructing history. Beauty and the enigma. 2001 <1994> ⇒171. 218-251.

2749   *Loader, James Alfred* David und seine Ahnmutter im Buch Ruth. Be-
       gegnung mit Gott. 2001 ⇒175. 43-54.

2750   *Moore, Michael S.* To king or not to king: a canonical-historical
       approach to Ruth. BBR 11 (2001) 27-41.

2751   *Nadar, Sarojini* A South African Indian womanist reading of the
       character of Ruth. Other ways. 2001 ⇒260. 159-175.

2752   *Polak, Frank H.* דו־שיח ותבניותיו במגילת רות לחקר הדיאלוג ומעמד הדוברים
       בסיפורי המקרא [On dialogue and speaker status in the scroll of Ruth].
       BetM 166 (2001) 193-218. Sum. 288. **H**.

2753   *Yaron, Shlomith* Sperm stealing: a moral crime by three of David's
       ancestresses. BiRe 17/1 (2001) 35-38, 44 [Gen 19; 38].

2754   *Engel, Ulrich* "Wo Du hingehst, da will auch ich hingehen ...": An-
       merkungen zu Rut 1,16. WuA(M) 42 (2001) 115-117.

2755   *Shepherd, David* Violence in the fields?: translating, reading, and re-
       vising in Ruth 2. CBQ 63 (2001) 444-463.

2756   *Loader, James Alfred* Ruth 2,7—eine crux interpretum. Begegnung
       mit Gott. Wiener alttestamentliche Studien 3: 2001 ⇒175. 9-17.

2757   *Moen Saxegaard, Kristin* "More than seven sons": Ruth as example
       of the good son. SJOT 15 (2001) 257-275 [Ruth 4,15].

E4.4 1-2 Samuel

2758   **Cartledge, Tony W.** 1 and 2 Samuel. Bible Commentary: Macon,
       Georgia 2001, Smyth & H. 748 pp. $65. 1-57312-064-2 + CD-ROM
       [BiTod 40,193—Bergant, Dianne].

2759   **Evans, Mary J.** 1 and 2 Samuel: based on the New International
       Version. NIBC.OT 6: 2000 ⇒16,2719. [R]CBQ 63 (2001) 107-108
       (*White, Marsha*); RTR 60 (2001) 151-152 (*Snead, Andrew*).

2760   **Jobling, David** 1 Samuel. Berit Olam: 1998 ⇒14,2427... 16,2720.
       [R]Month 34 (2001) 127-128 (*King, Nicholas*); JBL 120 (2001) 356-
       358 (*Linville, James R.*).

2761   **Morrison, Craig, E.** The character of the Syriac version of the first
       book of Samuel. MPIL 11: Lei 2001, Brill xvi; 173 pp. 90-04-11984-
       1. Bibl. 160-165.

2762   [E]**Salvesen, Alison** The books of Samuel in the Syriac version of
       Jacob of Edessa. MPIL 10: 1999 ⇒15,2601. [R]JThS 52 (2001) 325-
       327 (*Lane, D.J.*); OrChr 85 (2001) 246-249 (*Wehrle, Josef*).

2763   *Bakon, Shimon* The book of Samuel: a literary masterpiece. JBQ
       29/1 (2001) 32-39.

2764 *Corti, Gianluigi* Samuele, capo civile, religioso e profeta. PaVi 46/1 (2001) 17-22.

2765 *Meiser, Martin* Wahrung jüdischer Identität: das 1. Samuelbuch in der Septuaginta. BiKi 56 (2001) 85-87.

2766 *Rendtorff, Rolf* Samuel the prophet: a link between Moses and the kings. Der Text in seiner Endgestalt. 2001 ⇒201. 164-173.

2767 *Menaul, Marjorie* 1 Samuel 1 & 2. Interp. 55 (2001) 174-176.

2768 *Auld, Graeme* From king to prophet in Samuel and Kings. The elusive prophet. OTS 45: 2001 ⇒485. 31-44 [1 Sam 1-3].

2769 *Passaro, Angelo* Samuele e la parola del Signore (1 Sam 1-3). PaVi 46/1 (2001) 23-29.

2770 *Harvey, John E.* Tendenz and textual criticism in 1 Samuel 2-10. JSOT 96 (2001) 71-81 [Ex 6-12; Num 11; 25; Lev 10; 1 Sam 2-10].

2771 *Lorenzin, Tiziano* L'arca dell'alleanza (1 Sam 4-6; 2 Sam 6). PaVi 46/1 (2001) 39-44.

2772 *Tsumura, David Toshio* List and narrative in I Samuel 6,17-18a in the light of Ugaritic economic texts. ZAW 113 (2001) 353-369.

E4.5 *1 Sam 7...Initia potestatis regiae*, Origins of kingship

2773 *Demsky, Aaron* The conflict between Samuel and Saul and the question of the judicial authority of the king. ᶠAHITUV, S. 2001 ⇒1. 98-111. **H.**

2774 *Hentschel, Georg* Król Saul—tragiczna klęska czy słuszne odrzucenie. ᶠJANKOWSKI, A. 2001 ⇒53. 138-149. **P.**

2775 *Knauf, Ernst Axel* Saul, David, and the Philistines: from geography to history. BN 109 (2001) 15-18.

2776 *Kreuzer, Siegfried* "War Saul auch unter den Philistern?": die Anfänge des Königtums in Israel. ZAW 113 (2001) 56-73.

2777 *Master, Daniel* State formation theory and the kingdom of Israel. JNES 60 (2001) 117-132.

2778 *Niemann, Hermann Michael* Königtum in Israel. RGG², 4: I-K. 2001 ⇒664. 1593-1597 col.

2779 *Van Daalen, Liet* Samuel and Saul. ᶠDEURLOO, K. ACEBT.S 2: 2001 ⇒23. 115-128.

2780 *White, Marsha* Searching for Saul: what we really know about Israel's first king?. BiRe 17/2 (2001) 22-29, 52-53.

2781 *Launderville, Dale* Anti-monarchical ideology in Israel in light of Mesopotamian parallels. ᶠFITZGERALD, A. CBQ.MS 32: 2001 ⇒31. 119-128 [1 Sam 8-12].

2782   *Tavolaro, Gianpiero* La caduta di Saul: interpretazione tragica del rifiuto di un eletto. Asp. 48 (2001) 483-502 [1 Sam 8-22].

2783   *Virgili Dal Prà, Rosanna* Saul e la giovane monarchia di Israele (1 Sam 13-15). PaVi 46/1 (2001) 30-38.

E4.6   *1 Sam 16...2 Sam: Accessio Davidis.* **David's Rise**

2784   *Barrick, W. Boyd* Genealogical notes on the 'house of David' and the 'house of Zadok'. JSOT 96 (2001) 29-58.

2785   **Bietenhard, Sophia** Des Königs General: die Heerführertraditionen in der vorstaatlichen und frühen staatlicher Zeit und die Joabgestalt in 2 Sam 2-20; 1 Kön 1-2. OBO 163: 1998 ⇒14,9503... 16,2749. ᴿBiOr 58 (2001) 224-227 (*Hentschel, G.*).

2786   **Cohen, Laurent** Il re David: una biografia mistica. ᵀ*Vogelmann, Vanna Lucattini*: Schulim Vogelmann 93: F 2001, La giuntina 161 pp. 88-8057-132-X. Con una conversazione con *Elie Wiesel*.

2787   *Cortese, Enzo* David tra storia e letteratura. PaVi 46/2 (2001) 4-15.

2788   ᴱ**Desrousseaux, Louis; Vermeylen, Jacques** Figures de David à travers la bible. LeDiv 177: 1999 ⇒15,410; 16,2754. XVIIᵉ congrès de l'ACFEB (Lille, 1ᵉʳ-5 septembre 1997). ᴿREJ 160 (2001) 225-228 (*Pellistrandi, Christine*).

2789   *Edelman, Diana* Did Saulide-Davidic rivalry resurface in early Persian Yehud?. ᶠMILLER, J. JSOT.S 343: 2001 ⇒74. 69-91.

2790   *Firth, David G.* Shining the lamp: the rhetoric of 2 Samuel 5-24. TynB 52 (2001) 203-224.

2791   **Halpern, Baruch** David's secret demons: messiah, murderer, traitor, king. GR 2001, Eerdmans xx; 492 pp. $30. 0-8028-4478-2. ᴿOTEs 14 (2001) 350-352 (*Stiebert, J.*).

2792   *Hendel, Ronald S.* The empire of David—or not?. BiRe 17/5 (2001) 8;

2793   King David loves Bathsheba. BiRe 17/1 (2001) 6.

2794   *Knoppers, Gary N.* The Davidic genealogy: some contextual considerations from the ancient Mediterranean world. TEuph 22 (2001) 35-50.

2795   **Kunz, Andreas** Die Frauen und der König David: Studien zur Figuration von Frauen in den Daviderzählungen. Diss.-Habil. Leipzig 2001, ᴰ*Lux, R.* [RTL 33,632].

2796   *Lefebvre, Philippe* David et Jonathan: un homme rencontre un homme. VS 81 (2001) 199-214.

2797   *Loader, James Alfred* Das Haus Elis und das Haus Davids: wie Gott sein Wort zurücknehmen kann;

2798   Jedidja oder Amadeus: Gedanken über die Thronfolgeerzählung und Weisheit. Begegnung mit Gott. 2001 ⇒175. 55-66/67-97.

2799 *Malamat, Abraham* A political look at the kingdom of David and Solomon and its relations with Egypt <1982>;

2800 Aspects of the foreign policies of David and Solomon <1963>. History of biblical Israel. 2001 ⇒182. 189-207/208-233.

2801 **McKenzie, Steven L.** King David: a biography. 2000 ⇒16,2771 [!]. ᴿJThS 52 (2001) 728-730 (*Auld, Graeme*); CBQ 63 (2001) 728-729 (*Green, Barbara*).

2802 *Pisano, Stephen* Narrativa della successione di David: un'introduzione generale a 2Sam 9-20 e 2Re 1-2. PaVi 46/3 (2001) 4-10.

2803 *Polak, Frank H.* Joab and David in double vision. Bib. 82 (2001) 264-269.

2804 **Seiler, Stefan** Die Geschichte von der Thronfolge Davids (2 Sam 9-20; 1 Kön 1-2): Untersuchungen zur Literarkritik und Tendenz. BZAW 267: 1998 ⇒14,2469... 16,2779. ᴿJBL 119 (2000) 755-756 (*Moore, Michael S.*).

2805 *Sembrano, Lucio* La figura di David nei salmi. PaVi 46/2 (2001) 40-45.

2806 *Snell, Daniel C.* The structure of politics in the age of David. ᴹCAGNI, L., 4. SMDSA 61: 2001 ⇒15. 2131-2142.

2807 *Tarocchi, Stefano* David figura messianica nella bibbia. PaVi 46/3 (2001) 38-43.

2808 *Torti, Rita* David tra politica e fede. PaVi 46/3 (2001) 11-18.

2809 **Vermeylen, Jacques** Histoire de la rédaction des récits davidiques, de 1 Samuel 8 à 1 Rois 2. BEThL 154: 2000 ⇒16,2784. ᴿColl. 31 (2001) 329-331 (*Hoet, Hendrik*).

2810 *Wetzel, Christoph* Frauen um König David;

2811 David & Michal: Erstes Buch Samuel, Kapitel 18 und 19; Zweites Buch Samuel, Kapitel 3 und 6. Schön bist du. 2001 ⇒274. 68-70/71-75.

2812 *Corti, Gianluigi* L'unzione di David (1 Sam 16,1-13). PaVi 46/2 (2001) 16-20.

2813 *Kalimi, Isaac* A transmission of tradition: the number of Jesse's sons: biblical writings, Judeo-Hellenistic arts, rabbinic literature and medieval christian art. ThZ 57 (2001) 1-9 [1 Sam 16-17].

2814 *Duarte Castillo, Raúl* Micol en la ruta real de David. Qol 26 (2001) 3-9 [1 Sam 18-19].

2815 *Termini, Cristina* L'innocente perseguitato (1 Sam 19). PaVi 46/2 (2001) 21-26.

2816 *Boggio, Giovanni* David rifugiato nel deserto (1 Sam 22-26). PaVi 46/2 (2001) 27-33.

2817 *O'Rourke Boyle, Marjorie* The law of the heart: the death of a fool (1 Samuel 25). JBL 120 (2001) 401-427.

2818 *Wetzel, Christoph* David & Abigajil: Erstes Buch Samuel, Kapitel
      25. Schön bist du. 2001 ⇒274. 76-81.
2819 *Catastini, Alessandro* David, Guy de MAUPASSANT è una variante
      qumranica. ᴹCAGNI, L., 3. SMDSA 61: 2001 ⇒15. 1377-1384 [1
      Sam 25,31].
2820 *Leithart, Peter J.* Nabal and his wine. JBL 120 (2001) 525-527 [1
      Sam 25,37].
2821 *Balzaretti, Claudio* La fine di Saul (1 Sam 27-31). PaVi 46/2 (2001)
      34-39 [1 Sam 27-31].
2822 *Angert-Quilter, Theresa; Wall, Lynne* The 'spirit wife' at Endor.
      JSOT 92 (2001) 55-72 [1 Sam 28].
2823 *Fischer, S.* 1 Samuel 28: the woman of Endor—who is she and what
      does Saul see?. OTEs 14 (2001) 26-46.

2824 *Lemański, Janusz* Refleksja historyczno-egzegetyczna nad tekstem 2
      Sm 5,6-8. CoTh 71/3 (2001) 69-85. **P**.
2825 *Ceresko, Anthony R.* The identity of 'the blind and the lame' in 2
      Samuel 5:8b. Charism, leadership. 2001 ⇒456. 99-108;
2826 The identity of "the blind and the lame" (עִוֵּר וּפִסֵּחַ) in 2 Samuel 5:8b.
      CBQ 63 (2001) 23-30.
2827 *Couffignal, Robert* Le transfert de l'arche d'alliance: un récit carnava-
      lesque?. SémBib 103 (2001) 56-62 [2 Sam 6].
2828 *Bodner, Keith* Nathan: prophet, politician and novelist?. JSOT 95
      (2001) 43-54 [2 Sam 7; 12; 1 Kgs 1].
2829 *Calduch-Benages, Nuria* Promessa di Dio e preghiera di David
      (2Sam 7). PaVi 46/3 (2001) 19-23.
2830 *McKenzie, Steven L.* The typology of the Davidic covenant. ᶠMILLER,
      J. JSOT.S 343: 2001 ⇒74. 152-178 [2 Sam 7].
2831 *Waschke, Ernst Joachim* Das Verhältnis alttestamentlicher Überliefe-
      rungen im Schnittpunkt der Dynastiezusage und die Dynastiezusage
      im Spiegel alttestamentlicher Überlieferungen. Der Gesalbte. 2001
      <1987> ⇒227. 105-125 [2 Sam 7].
2832 *Petercă, Vladimir* Messianismul regal: originile sale in 2 Sam 7,1-17
      [Royal messianism: its origins in 2 Sam 7,1-17]. CICat 2/1 (2001) 5-
      14. **Romanian**.
2833 **Pietsch, Michael** 'Dieser ist der Spross Davids...': Studien zur Re-
      zeptionsgeschichte der Nathanverheissung. Diss. Hamburg 2001,
      ᴰ*Timm, S.* [2 Sam 7,1-17] [RTL 33,633].
2834 **Schniedewind, William M.** Society and the promise to David: the
      reception history of 2 Samuel 7:1-17. 1999 ⇒15,2662; 16,2806.
      ᴿJBL 120 (2001) 537-539 (*McKenzie, Steven L.*); HebStud 42 (2001)
      343-346 (*Wright, Benjamin G.*).

2835 *Good, Robert M.* 2 Samuel 8. TynB 52 (2001) 129-138.

2836 *Virgili Dal Pra, Rosanna* Vizi privati e pubbliche virtù (2Sam 9-12). PaVi 46/3 (2001) 24-30.

2837 *Wetzel, Christoph* David & Batseba: Zweites Buch Samuel, Kapitel 11 und 12. Schön bist du. 2001 ⇒ 274. 82-87.

2838 *Schüngel-Straumann, Helen* Amnon & Tamar: Zweites Buch Samuel, Kapitel 13. Schön bist du. 2001 ⇒274. 124-128.

2839 *West, Gerald* Tamar en de assertiviteit van verkrachte vrouwen in Zuid-Afrika. ITBT 9/4 (2001) 13-15 [2 Sam 13,1-22].

2840 *Sasson, Jack M.* Absalom's daughter: an essay in vestige historiography. [F]MILLER, J. 2001 ⇒74. 179-196 [2 Sam 13,1-18,18].

2841 *Scaiola, Donatella* 'Pagherà quattro volte!' (2 Sam 13-21). PaVi 46/3 (2001) 31-37.

2842 *Petercă, Vladimir* Process of consciences: conflicts and tensions at David's court. CICat 2/2 (2001) 7-17 Zsfg. 17 [2 Sam 13,37-14,23]. **Romanian**.

2843 *Lefebvre, Philippe* Le fils enchevêtré: Absalom, Isaac, Jésus. [F]SCHENKER, A. OBO 179: 2001 ⇒100. 75-97 [2 Sam 18].

2844 *Cohen, Matty* II Sam 24 ou l'histoire d'un décret royal avorté. ZAW 113 (2001) 17-40.

E4.7 *Libri Regum*: **Solomon, Temple: 1 Kings...**

2845 *Balzaretti, Claudio* Lo scisma dei due regni. PaVi 46/6 (2001) 11-16.

2846 *Cavedo, Romeo* La storia dei re da Salomone all'esilio: storia o teologia della storia?. PaVi 46/6 (2001) 4-10.

2847 **Cogan, Mordechai** 1 Kings: a new translation with introduction and commentary. AncB 10: NY 2001, Doubleday xvii; 556 pp. $50. 0-385-02992-6. Bibl. 109-149.

2848 *Galil, Gershon* The message of the book of Kings in relation to Deuteronomy and Jeremiah. BS 158 (2001) 406-414.

2849 *Galpaz-Feller, Penina* שלטון ירבעם—דגם מצרי [The Egyptian model for Jeroboam's administration]. BetM 166 (2001) 219-226 Sum. 287.

2850 **Linville, James Richard** Israel in the book of Kings: the past as a project of social identity. JSOT.S 272: 1998 ⇒14,2496. [R]CoTh (2001/1) 220-223 (*Chrostowski, Waldemar*); JBL 119 (2000) 116-118 (*Glatt-Gilad, David*).

2851 *Malamat, Abraham* Organs of statecraft in the Israelite monarchy. History of biblical Israel. 2001 <1964> ⇒182. 240-273.

2852 **Mulder, Martin Jan** 1 Kings 1-11. [T]*Vriend, J.* 1998 ⇒15,2683; 16, 2832. [R]LouvSt 26 (2001) 283-285 (*Eynikel, Erik*); ThLZ 126 (2001) 1027-1030 (*Dietrich, Walter*).

2853 *Na'aman, Nadav* Historical analysis of the book of Kings in the light of royal inscriptions of the ninth century BCE. Cathedra 100 (2001) 89-108 Sum. 403. **H**.

2854 *Trabacchin, Gianni* Il regno di Israele, un regno senza un futuro (931-722) (1Re 14-2Re 17). PaVi 46/6 (2001) 17-23.

2855 ᴱᵀ**Vogüé, Adalbert de** GRÉGOIRE le Grand: commentaire sur le premier livre des Rois tome III (III,38-IV,78). SC 432: 1998 ⇒14, 2499... 16,2836. ᴿREAug 47 (2001) 198-199 (*Weiss, Jean-Pierre*);

2856 GRÉGOIRE le Grand (Pierre de Cava): commentaire sur le premier livre des Rois, 4: IV,79-217. SC 449: 2000 ⇒16,2905. ᴿJThS 52 (2001) 930-931 (*Winterbottom, Michael*).

2857 **Williams, Peter J.** Studies in the syntax of the Peshitta of 1 Kings. MPIL 12: Lei 2001, Brill xv; 202 pp. €64. 90-04-11978-7. Bibl. 188-192.

2858 *Balzaretti, Claudio* Il regno di Salomone tra storia e letteratura. PaVi 46/4 (2001) 4-10.

2859 *Barrick, W. Boyd* Loving too well: the negative portrayal of Solomon and the composition of the Kings history. EstB 59 (2001) 419-450.

2860 *Kitchen, Kenneth A.* How we know when Solomon ruled: synchronisms with Egyptian and Assyrian rulers hold the key to dates of Israelite kings. BArR 27/5 (2001) 32-37, 58.

2861 *Knauf, Ernst Axel* Solomon at Megiddo?. ᶠMILLER, J. JSOT.S 343: 2001 ⇒74. 119-134 [1 Kgs 9,15-19].

2862 *Leach, Edmund* The legitimacy of Solomon: some structural aspects of Old Testament history. AES 42 (2001) 131-74 [1 Sam 4-2 Kgs 2].

2863 *Luke, K.* Solomon's wisdom. BiBh 27 (2001) 134-146.

2864 *Perani, Mauro* La fortuna di Salomone nel giudaismo. PaVi 46/4 (2001) 37-44.

2865 *Polak, Frank H.* The Septuagint account of Solomon's reign: revision and ancient recension. X Congress IOSCS. SBL.SCSt 51: 2001 ⇒ 499. 139-164.

2866 **Särkiö, Pekka** Exodus und Salomo: Erwägungen zur verdeckten Salomokritik anhand von Ex 1-2; 5; 14 und 32. SESJ 71: 1998 ⇒14, 2504; 16,2841. ᴿJBL 119 (2000) 549-550 (*Moore, Michael S.*).

2867 *Spina, Frank Anthony* In but not of the world: the confluence of wisdom and torah in the Solomon story (1 Kings 1-11). AsbTJ 56/1 (2001) 17-30.

2868 **Wälchli, Stefan** Der weise König Salomo. BWANT 141: 1999 ⇒14, 2506. ᴿThRv 97 (2001) 116-118 (*Willmes, Bernd*); ThZ 57 (2001) 469-470 (*Kellenberger, Edgar*).

2869 **Ådna, Jostein** Jerusalemer Tempel und Tempelmarkt im 1. Jahrhundert n. Chr. ADPV 25: 1999 ⇒15,2698; 16,2843. ^RThLZ 126 (2001) 36-37 (*Küchler, Max*).

2870 *Balzaretti, Claudio* La bellezza del tempio. La bellezza. PSV 44: 2001 ⇒240. 21-33.

2871 *Barker, Margaret* Time and eternity: the world of the temple. Month 34 (2001) 15-22.

2872 *Baslez, M.-F.* Le temple de Jérusalem comme lieu de mémoire: à propos de la bibliothèque de Néhémie. TEuph 21 (2001) 31-42 [Ezra 6, 3-12; 7,12-26].

2873 **Bedford, Peter Ross** Temple restoration in early Achaemenid Judah. JSJ.S 65: Lei 2001, Brill xiii; 369 pp. $123. 90-04-11509-9. Bibl. 311-345.

2874 *Blenkinsopp, Joseph* Did the second Jerusalemite temple possess land?. TEuph 21 (2001) 61-68 [Lev 27,14-29; Ezra 9-10].

2875 *Broshi, Magen* The role of the temple in the Herodian economy. Bread, wine. JSPE.S 36: 2001 <1987> ⇒131. 188-196.

2876 *Castello, Gaetano* Il tempio di Salomone. PaVi 46/4 (2001) 27-32.

2877 *Chopineau, Jacques* Les prophètes et le temple. Quand le texte devient parole. AnBru 6: 2001: ⇒135. 91-96.

2878 *Dever, William G.* Archaeology, the Israelite monarchy, and the Solomonic temple. The Blackwell companion to the Hebrew Bible. Blackwell companions to religion 3: 2001 ⇒653. 186-206.

2879 ^E**Ego, Beate; Lange, Armin; Pilhofer, Peter** Gemeinde ohne Tempel. WUNT 118: 1999 ⇒15,218; 16,2846. ^RJSJ 32 (2001) 93-97 (*Hogeterp, Albert*); FrRu 8 (2001) 212-214 (*Thoma, Clemens*); ThRv 97 (2001) 208-211 (*Backhaus, Knut*); RHPhR 81 (2001) 236-238 (*Grappe, Ch.*); CBQ 63 (2001) 781-783 (*Viviano, Benedict T.*).

2880 *Elior, Rachel* The Jerusalem temple: the representation of the imperceptible. Studies in Spirituality 11 (2001) 126-143.

2881 **Faßbeck, Gabriele** Der Tempel der Christen. TANZ 33: 2000 ⇒16, 2847. ^RThLZ 126 (2001) 1040-1042 (*Niebuhr, Karl-Wilhelm*); SNTU.A 26 (2001) 259-261 (*Kügler, J.*).

2882 *Greenberg, Moshe* A house of prayer for all peoples. Jerusalem: house of prayer. SBFA 52: 2001 ⇒536. 31-37 [Isa 19,16-25; 56,2-8; Zech 2,14-15].

2883 *Janowski, Bernd* Der Himmel auf Erden: zur kosmologischen Bedeutung des Tempels in der Umwelt Israels. Das biblische Weltbild. FAT 32: 2001 ⇒285. 229-260.

2884 **Knowles, Melody D.** The centrality of the Jerusalem temple in the religious practice of Yehud in the Persian period. Diss. Princeton Sem.2001, 152 pp. 3006834 [RTL 33,632].

2885 *Ligato, Giuseppe* The temple esplanade in crusader Jerusalem. Jerusalem: house of prayer. SBFA 52: 2001 ⇒536. 141-162.

2886 *Loza Vera, J.* A response to Professor Greenberg's paper. Jerusalem: house of prayer. SBFA 52: 2001 ⇒536. 39-44 [Isa 19,16-25; 56,2-8; Zech 2,14-15].

2887 **Martin, E.L.** The temples that Jerusalem forgot. 2000 ⇒16,2851. ᴿATG 64 (2001) 396-398 (*Verd, G.M.*).

2888 **Paesler, Kurt** Das Tempelwort Jesu. FRLANT 184: 1999 ⇒15, 2719. ᴿThLZ 126 (2001) 286-288 (*Böcher, Otto*); SNTU.A 25 (2000) 253-254 (*Fuchs, Albert*).

2889 **Papa, Sebastiana** Il kotel: un muro metafisico. R 2001, Fahrenheit 72 pp.

2890 *Schiffman, Lawrence H.* Descriptions of the Jerusalem temple in JOSEPHUS and the Temple Scroll. Historical perspectives. StTDJ 37: 2001 ⇒612. 69-82.

2891 *Sudilovsky, Judith* Virtual Temple Mount: computerized exhibit opens at foot of ancient site. BArR 27/4 (2001) 16.

2892 *Trotter, James M.* Was the second Jerusalem temple a primarily Persian project?. SJOT 15 (2001) 276-294 [Ezra 1-6].

2893 **Volgger, David** Verbindliche Tora am einzigen Tempel: zu Motiv und Ort der Komposition von 1.2 Kön. ATSAT 61: 1998 ⇒14,2523; 16,2837. ᴿJSSt 46 (2001) 156-157 (*Coggins, Richard*).

2894 *Wodecki, Bernard* Rola i znaczenie Świątyni według Pierwszego Testamentu. ᶠJANKOWSKI, A. 2001 ⇒53. 413-442. P.

2895 **Zwickel, Wolfgang** Der salomonische Tempel. Kulturgeschichte der antiken Welt 83: 1999 ⇒15,2723. ᴿThLZ 126 (2001) 160-161 (*Knauf, Ernst Axel*).

2896 *Bartelmus, Rüdger* Sachverhalt und Zeitbezug: pragmatisch-exegetische Anwendung eines noetischen Theorems auf 1 Kön 1. ᶠDENZ, A. 2001 ⇒21. 1-20.

2897 **Schenker, Adrian** Septante et texte massorétique dans l'histoire la plus ancienne du texte de 1 Rois 2-14. CRB 48: 2000 ⇒16,2859. ᴿOLZ 96 (2001) 267-270 (*Fernández Marcos, Natalio*).

2898 *Schenker, Adrian* Die zwei Erzählungen von Joabs Tod (1 Kön 2:28-34) im Massoretischen Text und in der LXX. X Congress IOSCS. SBL.SCSt 51: 2001 ⇒499. 27-35.

2899 *Termini, Cristina* Il sogno di Salomone e la sapienza (1Re 3,4-15). PaVi 46/4 (2001) 11-15.

2900 *Scaiola, Donatella* Il giudizio di Salomone (1Re 3,16-28). PaVi 46/4 (2001) 16-20.

2901 *Kamlah, Jens* Die Liste der Regionalfürsten in 1 Kön 4,7-19 als historische Quelle für die Zeit Salomos. BN 106 (2001) 57-78.

2902 *Na'aman, Nadav* Solomon's district list (1 Kings 4:7-19) and the Assyrian province system in Palestine. UF 33 (2001) 419-436.

2903 *Hoppe, Leslie J.* Solomon's prayer (1 Kings 8). BiTod 39 (2001) 133-137.

2904 *Ostinell, Caterina* La preghiera di Salomone nel tempio (1Re 8,1-9, 9). PaVi 46/4 (2001) 21-26.

2905 *Green, Elliott A.* The Queen of Sheba: a queen of Egypt and Ethiopia?. JBQ 29 (2001) 151-155 [1 Kgs 10,1-13].

2906 *Elliger, Katharina* Salomo & die Königin von Saba: Erstes Buch der Könige, Kapitel 10. Schön bist du. 2001 ⇒274. 105-113.

2907 *Le Failler, Françoise* La Reine de Saba ou le rêve incertain. Études juillet-août (2001) 91-100 [1 Kgs 10].

2908 *Van Keulen, P.S.F.* A touch of Chronicles: the provenance of 3 Reigns 10:26-26a. X Congress IOSCS. SBL.SCSt 51: 2001 ⇒499. 441-461.

2909 *Talshir, Zipora* Literary design—a criterion for originality?: a case study: 3 Kgdms 12:24a-z; 1 K 11-14. ᶠSCHENKER, A. OBO 179: 2001 ⇒100. 41-57.

2910 *Hayes, John H.* The beginning of the regnal year in Israel and Judah. ᶠMILLER, J.: JSOT.S 343: 2001 ⇒74. 92-95 [1 Kgs 12,32-33].

2911 *Werlitz, Jürgen* Was hat der Gottesmann aus Juda mit dem Propheten Amos zu tun?: Überlegungnen zu 1 Kön 13 und den Beziehungen des Textes zu Am 7,10-17. ᶠSCHMUTTERMAYR, G. 2001 ⇒101. 109-123.

2912 *Luciani, Ferdinando* 1Re 13,11-32 secondo la traduzione araba della bibbia poliglotta di Londra. ᴹCAGNI, L., 3. SMDSA 61: 2001 ⇒15. 1731-1744.

2913 *Cogan, Mordechai* 'Because there was found in him something pleasing to the Lord God of Israel' 1 Kgs 14:13: the evolution of interpretations. ᶠAHITUV, S. 2001 ⇒1. 269-272. **H.**

E4.8 *1 Regum 17-22: Elias,* **Elijah**

2914 **Arnold, Daniel** Elie: entre le jugement et la grâce: commentaire de 1 Rois 17 à 2 Rois 2. Saint-Légier 2001, Emmaüs 202 pp. 2-8287-0082-8.

2915 **Álvarez Barredo, Miguel** Las narraciones sobre Elías y Eliseo en los libros de los Reyes. 1996 ⇒12,2521; 13,2591. ᴿRBLit 3 (2001) 193-196 (*Ben Zvi, Ehud*).

2916 *Balzaretti, Claudio* Il ciclo di Elia (1Re 17-20; 2Re 1). PaVi 46/5 (2001) 4-9.

2917 **Beck, Martin** Elia und die Monolatrie. BZAW 281: 1999 ⇒15, 2737. ᴿCBQ 63 (2001) 103-104 (*Moore, Michael S.*).

2918 *Benzi, Guido* Elia sul Monte Horeb (1Re 19). PaVi 46/5 (2001) 10-13.

2919 *Cornehl, Peter* Wo ist Gott?: Gedanken zu 1 Kön 19,9-13. Diak. 32 (2001) 417-419.

2920 **D'Ambrosio, Rocco** La vigna di Nabot: saggio di etica politica. Bari 2001, Cacucci 127 pp. 88-8422-074-2. Bibl. 121-127 [1 Kgs 21].

2921 *Grohmann, Marianne* Ahab & Isebel: Erstes Buch der Könige, Kapitel 21; Zweites Buch der Könige, Kapitel 9. Schön bist du. 2001 ⇒274. 88-91.

2922 **Keinänen, Jyrki** Traditions in collision: a literary and redaction-critical study on the Elijah narratives 1 Kings 17-19. Diss. Helsinki 2001, ᴰ*Veijola, T.*: SESJ 80: Gö 2001, Vandenhoeck & R. (8) 207 pp. 3-525-53981-9. Bibl. 194-202.

2923 *Lemaire, André* Achab, l'exil d'Élie et les Arabes. Prophètes et rois. LeDiv: 2001 ⇒292. 133-144.

2924 *Mariaselvam, Abraham* Elijah: a paradigm for priestly ministry. WoWo 34 (2001) 137-148.

2925 *Masson, Michel* Rois et prophètes dans le cycle d'Élie. Prophètes et rois. LeDiv: 2001 ⇒292. 119-131.

2926 *Mazzinghi, Luca* Elia e la voce del silenzio (1Re 19). PaVi 46/5 (2001) 14-19.

2927 *Nocquet, D.* Une manifestation 'politique' ancienne de Yhwh: 1 R 18,17-46 réinterprété. TEuph 22 (2001) 169-184 [1 Kgs 1,2-17; 2 Kgs 10,18-28].

2928 **Otto, Susanne** Jehu, Elia und Elisa: die Erzählung von der Jehu-Revolution und die Komposition der Elia-Elisa-Erzählungen. Diss. Münster 2000, ᴰ*Albertz, R.*: BWANT 152: Stu 2001, Kohlhammer 290 pp. €36.30. 3-17-016764-2. Bibl. 267-282.

2929 *Shemesh, Abraham Ofir* Reviving the children by Eliyau and Elisha: medical treatments or miracles? (1 Kings 17,8-17; II Kings 4,1-8). BetM 166 (2001) 248-260 Sum. 286. **H**.

2930 *Valentini, Alberto* Elia nel giudaismo e nel Nuovo Testamento. PaVi 46/5 (2001) 20-26.

E4.9 2 Reg 1... *Elisaeus, Elisha*... Ezechias, Josias

2931 *Barrick, W. Boyd* Another shaking of Jehoshaphat's familiy tree: Jehoram and Ahaziah once again. VT 51 (2001) 9-25.

2932 **Bergen, Wesley J.** Elisha and the end of prophetism. JSOT.S 286: 1999 ⇒15,2758; 16,2899. ᴿETR 76 (2001) 417-418 (*Sternberger, Jean-Pierre*); ThLZ 125 (2000) 881-882 (*Schmitt, Hans-Christoph*).

2933 *Gutmann, Israel* Manasseh—the worst of all the kings of Judah. [F]A-HITUV, S. 2001 ⇒1. 49-66. **H**.

2934 *Malamat, Abraham* The twilight of Judah: in the Egyptian-Babylonian maelstrom <1975>;

2935 The kingdom of Judah between Egypt and Babylon: a small state within a great power confrontation <1990>. History of biblical Israel. Culture and history of the ANE 7: 2001 ⇒182. 299-321/322-337.

2936 *Priotto, Michelangelo* Il ciclo di Eliseo: linee di teologia profetica (2Re 2,19-8,15; 13,14-21). PaVi 46/5 (2001) 27-32.

2937 **Ruthofer, Andreas** Zefanja und die Reform König Joschijas. Diss. Wien 2001, [D]*Braulik, G*. 373 pp. [RTL 33,634].

2938 **Sweeney, Marvin Alan** King Josiah of Judah: the lost Messiah of Israel. Oxf 2001, OUP xvi; 350 pp. $60. 0-19-513324-2. Bibl. 325-341. [R]ZAR 7 (2001) 420-422 (*Otto, Eckart*).

2939 **Aucker, William Brian** Putting Elisha in his place: genre, coherence and narrative function in 2 Kings 2-8. Diss. Edinburgh 2001, [D]*Auld, A*. 253 pp. [RTL 33,631].

2940 *Abadie, Philippe* L'enlèvement d'Élie, une symbolique prophétique. MoBi 133 (2001) 40-45 [BuBB 35,76] [2 Kgs 2,9-12].

2941 *Nadav, Na'aman* בין כתובת מלכותית לסיפור נבוא: מרד מישע מלך מואב בהאארה היסטורית [Royal inscription versus prophetic story: Mesha's rebellion in historical writing] Zion 66 (2001) 5-40 Sum. iv [2 Kgs 3]. **H**.

2942 *Nepi, Antonio* La stanza del figlio: la sunammita converte Eliseo (2Re 4,8-37). PaVi 46/5 (2001) 33-38.

2943 *Scaiola, Donatella* La guarigione di Naaman il siro (2Re 5). PaVi 46/5 (2001) 40-43.

2944 *Brueggemann, Walter* A brief moment for a one-person remnant (2 Kings 5:2-3). BTB 31 (2001) 53-59.

2945 *Liverani, Mario* 2 Kings 5:5-6 in the light of the Amarna Letters. [M]CAGNI, L., 3: SMDSA 61: 2001 ⇒15. 1709-1717.

2946 *Greenfield, Jonas C.* Doves' dung and the price of food: the topoi of II Kings 6:24-7:2. 'Al kanfei yonah, 2. 2001 <1991> ⇒153. 815-820.

2947 *Irvine, Stuart A.* The rise of the house of Jehu [2 Kgs 9-10]. [F]MILLER, J. JSOT.S 343: 2001 ⇒74. 96-103/104-118.

2948 *Van den Berg, Evert* Fact and imagination in the history of Hezekiah in 2 Kings 18-20. [F]DEURLOO, K.: ACEBT.S 2: 2001 ⇒23. 129-136.

2949 *Nepi, Antonio* L'ombra della meridiana e del piombino: Ezechia e Manasse (2Re 18-21). PaVi 46/6 (2001) 24-33.

2950 *Cogan, Mordechai* Sennacherib's siege of Jerusalem: once or twice?. BArR 27/1 (2001) 40-45, 69 [2 Kgs 18,13-19,37].

2951 *Barker, Margaret* Hezekiah's boil. JSOT 95 (2001) 31-42 [2 Kgs 19-20; 2 Chr 32].

2952 *Kasher, Rimon* The Sitz im Buch of the story of Hezekiah's illness and cure (II Reg 20,1-11; Isa 38,1-22). ZAW 113 (2001) 41-55.

2953 **Stenstrup, Kenneth G.** King Manasseh in early Judaism and christianity: a consideration of text, context and hermeneutics in portrayals of King Manasseh in Jewish and christian scripture and related literature prior to the mid-fifth century C.E. Diss. Claremont Graduate Univ. 2001, 357 pp. 3012312 [2 Kgs 21,1-18].

2954 *Malamat, Abraham* The historical background of the assassination of Amon, King of Judah [2 Kgs 21,23]. History of biblical Israel. Culture and history of the ANE 7: 2001 <1953> ⇒182. 277-281.

2955 *Cappelletto, Gianni* Giosia il riformatore e la sua tragica morte. PaVi 46/6 (2001) 34-41 [2 Kgs 22,1-23,30].

2956 *Handy, Lowell K.* The rise and fall of the *sogennant* Josianic Empire. ProcGLM 21 (2001) 69-79 [2 Kgs 22-23].

2957 *Arneth, Martin* Die antiassyrische Reform Josias von Juda: Überlegungen zur Komposition und Intention von 2 Reg 23,4-15. ZAR 7 (2001) 189-216.

2958 *Malamat, Abraham* Josiah's bid for Armageddon: the background of the Judaean-Egyptian encounter in 609 B.C. [2 Kgs 23,29]. History of biblical Israel. 2001 <1973-74> ⇒182. 282-297.

2959 *Hooker, Paul K.; Hayes, John H.* The year of Josiah's death: 609 or 610 BCE? [2 Kgs 23,29-35];

2960 *Lorenzin, Tiziano* L'esilio: la fine di tutto? (2Re 23,31-25,30). PaVi 46/6 (2001) 42-47.

E5.2 *Chronicorum libri*—**The books of Chronicles**

2961 *Abadie, Philippe* La symbolique du temple dans l'oeuvre du chroniste. TEuph 21 (2001) 13-29.

2962 **Balzaretti, Claudio** I libri delle Cronache. Guide spirituali all'Antico Testamento: R 2001, Città N. 225 pp. 88-311-3746-8. Bibl. 19.

2963 *Beentjes, Pancratius* Prophets in the book of Chronicles. The elusive prophet. OTS 45: 2001 ⇒485. 45-53 [2 Chr 25,107; 15,2-6].

2964 *Ben Zvi, Ehud* Shifting the gaze: historiographic constraints in Chronicles and their implications. [F]MILLER, J. JSOT.S 343: 2001 ⇒ 74. 38-60.

2965 **Dyck, Jonathan E.** The theocratic ideology of the Chronicler. Biblical interpretation series 33: 1998 ⇒14,2570; 16,2941. [R]JThS 52 (2001) 152-156 (*Williamson, H.G.M.*); Bib. 82 (2001) 277-280 (*Labahn, Antje*); JBL 119 (2000) 118-119 (*McKenzie, Steven L.*).

2966 *Glatt-Gilad, David A.* Regnal formulae as a historiographic device in the book of Chronicles. RB 108 (2001) 184-209.

2967 [E]**Graham, Matt Patrick; McKenzie, Steven L.** The Chronicler as author. JSOT.S 263: 1999 ⇒15,235. [R]BiblInterp 9 (2001) 219-221 (*Williamson, H.G.M.*); CBQ 63 (2001) 771-772 (*Endres, John C.*).

2968 **Hooker, Paul K.** First and Second Chronicles. Westminster Bible companion: LVL 2001, Westminster x; 295 pp. $20. 0-664-25591-4. Bibl. 295.

Johnstone, William Chronicles and Exodus ⇒2308;

2969 1 and 2 Chronicles. JSOT.S 253-254: 1997 ⇒13,2647... 16,2945. [R]JBL 119 (2000) 120-121 (*Wright, John W.*).

2970 **Kalimi, Isaac** The book of Chronicles—historical writing and literary devices. Biblical Encyclopaedia Library 18: J 2000, Bialik xxi; 477 pp. $65. 9653427172. [R]RB 108 (2001) 503-10 (*Aberbach, Moses*) **H.**

2971 *Kegler, Jürgen* Das Zurücktreten der Exodustradition in den Chronikbüchern. Gesammelte Aufsätze. 2001 <1989> ⇒167. 214-227.

2972 *Klein, Ralph W.* Narrative texts: Chronicles, Ezra, and Nehemiah. The Blackwell companion to the Hebrew Bible. Blackwell companions to religion 3: 2001 ⇒653. 385-401.

2973 *Levin, Yigal* Understanding biblical genealogies. CurResB 9 (2001) 11-46.

2974 *Mathys, Hans-Peter* Prophetie, Psalmengesang und Kultmusik in der Chronik. [F]SEYBOLD, K. AOAT 280: 2001 ⇒102. 281-296.

2975 *Murray, Donald F.* Under YHWH's veto: David as shedder of blood in Chronicles. Bib. 82 (2001) 457-476.

2976 *Peltonen, Kai* A jigsaw without a model?: the date of Chronicles. Did Moses speak Attic?. JSOT.S 317: 2001 ⇒270. 225-271.

2977 **Steins, Georg** Die Chronik als kanonisches Abschlussphänomen: Studien zur Entstehung und Theologie von 1 / 2 Chronik. 1995 ⇒11/ 1,1314; 13,2660. [R]JBL 119 (2000) 552-553 (*Graham, M. Patrick*).

2978 *Talshir, Zipora* Several canon-related concepts originating in Chronicles. ZAW 113 (2001) 386-403.

2979 **Tuell, Steven S.** First and Second Chronicles. Interpretation: LVL 2001, Westminster xii; 252 pp. $25. 0-8042-3110-9. Bibl. 247-252.

2980 *Van den Eynde, Sabine* Chronicler's usage of the collocation ארון ברית יהוה. ZAW 113 (2001) 422-430.

2981 *Yamaga, Tetsuo* König Joschafat und seine Außenpolitik in den Chronikbüchern. AJBI 27 (2001) 59-154.

2982 *Galil, Gershon* The Jerahmeelites and the Negeb of Judah. JANES 28 (2001) 33-42 [1 Chr 2,25-41].

2983 *Toloni, Giancarlo* Problemi di lessicografia in 1Cr 26,16. [M]CAGNI, L., 4. SMDSA 61: 2001 ⇒15. 2177-2191.

2984   **Vaughn, Andrew G.** Theology, history, and archaeology in the Chronicler's account of Hezekiah. 1999 ⇒15,2814; 16,2961. [R]CBQ 63 (2001) 130-131 (*Throntveit, Mark A.*); RBLit 3 (2001) 259-262 (*Haak, Robert D.*) [2 Chr 29-32].

E5.4 *Esdrae libri*—Ezra, Nehemiah

2985   [E]**Kümmel, Werner Georg; Lichtenberger, Hermann** Unterweisung in lehrhafter Form, Lfg. 1(1974) - 7(2001). Jüdische Schriften aus hellenistisch-römischer Zeit 3: Gü 1974-2001, Mohn 880 pp. 3-579-03928-8.

2986   **Balzaretti, Claudio** Esdra-Neemia. 1999 ⇒15,2828; 16,2964. 88-315-1799-6. [R]RivBib 49 (2001) 94-98 (*Bianchi, Francesco*).

2987   *Barc, Bernard* De Siméon le Juste à Esdras: l'image du grand prêtre réformateur dans la littérature du second temple. Le judaïsme à l'aube de l'ère chrétienne. LeDiv 186: 2001 ⇒450. 97-122.

2988   **Becker, Joachim** Der Ich-Bericht des Nehemiabuches als chronistische Gestaltung. FzB 87: 1998 ⇒14,2597. [R]ThLZ 126 (2001) 363-365 (*Schunck, Klaus-Dietrich*).

2989   **Böhler, Dieter** Die heilige Stadt in Esdras a alpha und Esra-Nehemia. OBO 158: 1997 ⇒13,2674... 16,2966. [R]JThS 52 (2001) 156-159 (*Van der Kooij, Arie*).

2990   *Conklin, Blane* The decrees of God and of kings in the Aramaic correspondence of Ezra. ProcGLM 21 (2001) 81-89.

2991   *Fried, Lisbeth S.* "You shall appoint judges": Ezra's mission and the rescription of Artaxerxes. Persia and torah. 2001 ⇒1919. 63-89.

2992   *Gosse, B.* Le gouverneur et le grand prêtre, et quelques problèmes de fonctionnement de la communauté postexilique: au sujet des rapports entre les charismatiques et l'autorité religieuse et civile dans le cadre de l'empire perse TEuph 21 (2001) 149-173 [Num 27,15-21; Ezra 1; Zech 6,8-15].

2993   *Grabbe, Lester L.* "Mind the gaps": Ezra, Nehemiah and the Judean restoration. Restoration. JSJ.S 72: 2001 ⇒319. 83-104.

2994   **Karrer, Christiane** Ringen um die Verfassung Judas: eine Studie zu den theologisch-politischen Vorstellungen im Esra-Nehemia-Buch. BZAW 308: B 2001, De Gruyter x; 488 pp. €108. 3-11-017055-8. Bibl. 457-473.

2995   **Loken, Israel Peter** A literary analysis of Nehemiah. Diss. Dallas Sem. 2001, 210 pp. 3002966.

2996   **Osterfield, George Thomas** Ezra and Nehemiah in the first person. Diss. Vanderbilt 2001, 283 pp. 3019465.

2997 *Porton, Gary G.* Ezra in rabbinic literature. Restoration. JSJ.S 72: 2001 ⇒319. 305-333.

2998 *Sacchi, Paolo* Re vassalli o governatori?: una discussione. Henoch 23 (2001) 147-152.

2999 **Schaper, Joachim** Priester und Leviten im achämenidischen Juda: Studien zur Kult- und Sozialgeschichte Israels in persischer Zeit. FAT 31: 2000 ⇒16,2971. ^REstAg 36 (2001) 387-388 (*Mielgo, C.*).

3000 **Schunck, Klaus-Dietrich** Nehemia [3,1-5,19]. BK.AT 23/2/2: Neuk 2001, Neuk'er 81-160 pp. €18.50. 3-7887-1611-9.

3001 *Steiner, Richard C.* The *mbqr* at Qumran, the *episkopos* in the Athenian empire, and the meaning of *lbqr'* in Ezra 7:14: on the relation of Ezra's mission to the Persian legal project. JBL 120 (2001) 623-646.

3002 **White, John** Excellence in leadership: the pattern of Nehemiah. Leicester 2001, Inter-Varsity 125 pp. 0-85111-497-0.

3003 *Becking, Bob* The idea of Torah in Ezra 7-10: a functional analysis. ZAR 7 (2001) 273-286.

3004 *Lawson, Steven J.* The pattern of biblical preaching: an expository study of Ezra 7:10 and Nehemiah 8:1-18. BS 158 (2001) 451-466.

3005 **Duggan, Michael W.** The covenant renewal in Ezra-Nehemiah (Neh 7:72B-10:40): an exegetical literary, and theological study. SBL.DS 164: Atlanta 2001, SBL xii; 372 pp. $50. 1589830148. Bibl. 301-29.

3006 **Boda, Mark J.** Praying the tradition: the origin and use of tradition in Nehemiah 9. BZAW 277: 1999 ⇒15,2835. ^RBS 158 (2001) 242-243 (*Anderson, Carl R.*); CBQ 63 (2001) 511-512 (*Duggan, Michael W.*); ThLZ 126 (2001) 613-614 (*Schunck, Klaus-Dietrich*); RBLit 3 (2001) 257-259 (*Becking, Bob*).

3007 *Rendtorff, Rolf* Nehemia 9: an important witness of theological reflection. Der Text in seiner Endgestalt. 2001 ⇒201. 265-271.

3008 *Eskenazi, Tamara Cohn* Nehemiah 9-10: structure and significance. Journal of Hebrew Scriptures 3 (2001) [electronic journal].

3009 *Reinmuth, Titus* Reform und Tora bei Nehemia: Neh 10,31-40 und die Autorisierung der Tora in der Perserzeit. ZAR 7 (2001) 287-317.

3010 *Berger, Klaus* Beobachtungen zur äthiopischen Esra-Apokalypse. ^FHuß, W.: OLA 104: 2001 ⇒51. 385-392.

3011 *Burkes, Shannon* "Life" redefined: wisdom and law in fourth Ezra and second Baruch. CBQ 63 (2001) 55-71.

3012 **Hamilton, Alastair** The apocryphal Apocalypse: the reception of the second book of Esdras (4 Ezra) from the Renaissance to the Enlightenment. OWS: 1999 ⇒15,2864; 16,2991. ^RJR 81 (2001) 109-

110 (*Hogan, Marina Martin*); JEH 52 (2001) 736-737 (*Pettegree, Andrew*); SCJ 32 (2001) 1156-1158 (*Barnes, Robin B.*); CBQ 63 (2001) 720-721 (*Bryan, David J.*).

3013 *Israeli, Edna* 'Ego Salathiel qui et Ezras'. Studies in Judaica. Teʿuda 16-17: 2001 ⇒408. 391-420. Sum. xxvii-xxix. **H**.

3014 **Talshir, Zipora** I Esdras: from origin to translation. SBL.SCSt 47: 1999 ⇒15,2859; 16,2993. ᴿJBL 120 (2001) 587-589 (*McKenzie, Steven L.*); HebStud 42 (2001) 371-375 (*Van Henten, Willem*); RBLit 3 (2001) 265-267 (*Becking, Bob*).

3015 ᴱ**Talshir, Zipora** I Esdras: a text critical commentary. SBL.SCSt 50: Atlanta 2001, SBL xiv; 556 pp. $68. 1-58983-023-7. Bibl. 503-521.

3016 *Wolter, Michael* 5. Esra-Buch, 6. Esra-Buch. Unterweisung in lehrhafter Form. Jüdische Schriften aus hellenistisch-römischer Zeit 3: 2001 ⇒2985. 767-880 pp.

E5.5 Libri Tobiae, Judith, Esther

3017 **Babini, Giuliana** I Libri di Tobia, Giuditta, Ester. Guide spirituali all'Antico Testamento: R 2001, Città N. 129 pp. 88-311-3747-6. Bibl. 31-33.

3018 *Auwers, Jean-Marie* Tobit. BVLI 45 (2001) 11-15.

3019 *Baslez, Marie-Françoise* Le roman de Tobit: un judaïsme entre deux mondes. Le judaïsme à l'aube. LeDiv 186: 2001 ⇒450. 29-50.

3020 **Ego, Beate** Unterweisung in erzählender Form: Buch Tobit. JSHRZ 2/6: Gü 1999, Gü 873-1007 pp. 3-579-03926-1. Bibl. 902-914.

3021 *Greenfield, Jonas C.* Aḥiqar in the book of Tobit. ʿAl kanfei yonah, 1. 2001 <1981> ⇒153. 195-202.

3022 *MacDonald, Dennis Ronald* Tobit and the <u>Odyssey</u>. Mimesis. 2001 ⇒568. 11-40 [BuBB 36,92].

3023 *Portier-Young, Anathea* Alleviation of suffering in the book of Tobit: comedy, community, and happy endings. CBQ 63 (2001) 35-54.

3024 *Schüngel-Straumann, Helen* Tobias & Sara: Buch Tobit, Kapitel 7 und 8. Schön bist du. 2001 ⇒274. 114-119.

3025 *Solhaune, Liliana* El libro de Tobías: itinerario del 'yo' al 'nosotros'. CuMon 36 (2001) 465-479.

3026 *Soll, Will* The book of Tobit as a window on the hellenistic Jewish family. Passion. 2001 ⇒295. 242-274.

3027 *Talshir, Ziporah; Talshir, David* The apocryphal literature: retroversion or translation? (with examples from the book of Tobit and the Testament of Naphtali). ᶠAHITUV, S. 2001 ⇒1. 216-233. **H**.

3028 **Bogaert, Pierre-Maurice** Judith, 1: introduction. BVLI 7/2: FrB 2001, Herder 80 pp. 3-4510-0281-7. Collab. *I. Baise* [RB 109,160].

3029 *Bogaert, Pierre-Maurice* Judith. BVLI 45 (2001) 15-18;

3030 Judith. RAC 19. 2001 ⇒660. 245-258.

3031 *Day, Linda* Faith, character and perspective in Judith. JSOT 95 (2001) 71-93.

3032 *Dicou, Bert* 'Use the guile of my words to strike them down': introducing Judith in a liberal Protestant congregation (Jdt 9:10). ^FDEURLOO, K. ACEBT.S 2: 2001 ⇒23. 265-272.

3033 *Esler, Philip F.* "By the hand of a woman": culture, story and theology in the book of Judith. ^FMALINA, B. BiblInterp 53: 2001 ⇒67. 64-101.

3034 **Gallazzi, Sandro; Rizzante, Ana Maria** Judite: a mão da mulher na história do povo. Comentário Bíblico/AT: Petrópolis 2001, Vozes 143 pp. 85-326-2491-X [REB 61,508].

3035 **Marijnissen, Ernst** Judit, de jodin van Betulia: een gelijkenis. Baarn 2001, Ten Have 176 pp. €17.02. 90-259-5238-0.

3036 *Mulzer, Martin* Das griechische Juditbuch—eine Spätschrift des Alten Testaments. BiKi 56 (2001) 92-95.

3037 *Sawyer, Deborah F.* Gender strategies in antiquity: Judith's performance. Feminist Theology 28 (2001) 9-26;

3038 Dressing up-dressing down: power, performance and identity in the book of Judith. Theology and sexuality 15 (2001) 23-31.

3039 *Schüngel-Straumann, Helen* Judit & Holofernes: Buch Judit, Kapitel 8 bis 16. Schön bist du. 2001 ⇒274. 129-134.

Die Bücher Ruth und Ester. 2000 ⇒2732.

3040 **Beal, Timothy K.** The book of hiding: gender, ethnicity, annihilation and Esther. 1997 ⇒13,2703; 16,3011. ^RBiblInterp 9 (2001) 84-85 (*O'Brien, Julia Myers*).

3041 **Berlin, Adele** Esther: introduction and commentary. Mikra Leyisra'el: J 2001, Magnes (10) 164 pp. 965-13-1422-3. **H**.

3042 **Berlin, Adele** Esther: the traditional Hebrew text with new JPS translation. The JPS Bible Commentary: Ph 2001, Jewish Publication Society of America. lix; 110 pp. $35. 0-8276-0699-0. Bibl. 99-110. ^RCV 43 (2001) 267-269 (*Ber, Viktor*).

3043 *Berman, Joshua A.* Hadassah Bat Abihail: the evolution from object to subject in the character of Esther. JBL 120 (2001) 647-669.

3044 *De Troyer, Kristin* Translation or interpretation?: a sample from the books of Esther. X Congress IOSCS. 2001 ⇒499. 343-353.

3045 **De Troyer, Kristin M.L.L.** The end of the alpha text of Esther: ... MT 8:1-17, LXX 8:1-17, and AT 7:14-41. SBL.SCSt 48: 2000 ⇒16, 3029. ^RBib. 82 (2001) 561-564 (*Vilchez, José*).

3046 *Eisen, Robert* Joseph Ibn KASPI on the secret meaning of the scroll of Esther. REJ 160 (2001) 379-408.

3047 **Fox, Michael V.** Character and ideology in the book of Esther. GR ²2001 <1991>, Eerdmans x; 333 pp. $26. 0802848818. Bibl. 304-18.

3048 *Grohmann, Marianne* Ester & Artaxerxes: Buch Ester, Kapitel 1 bis 10. Schön bist du. 2001 ⇒274. 92-97.

3049 *Haelewyck, Jean-Claude* Esther. BVLI 45 (2001) 18-20.

3050 *Lerner, Berel Dov* No happy ending for Esther. JBQ 29 (2001) 4-12.

Linafelt, T.; Beal, T. Ruth and Esther 1999 ⇒2735.

3051 *Masenya, Mmadipoane* Esther and Northern Sotho stories: an African-South African woman's commentary. Other ways. 2001 ⇒ 260. 27-49.

3052 *Morard, Thomas* À propos du remplage de la verrière d'Esther. ACr 89 (2001) 23-30.

3053 **Oren, Drora** Embodiment in the book of Esther. Diss. Utah 2001, 179 pp. 3002135.

3054 *Pierguidi, Stefano* La storia di Ester nei fregi ad affresco del XVI secolo. ACr 89 (2001) 31-38.

3055 **Prime, Derek** Esther simply explained: unspoken lessons about the unseen God. Darlington 2001, Evangelical 144 pp. £7. 08523-44716.

3056 **Steck, Odil H.; Kratz, Reinhard G.; Kottsieper, Ingo** Das Buch Baruch; der Brief des Jeremia; Zusätze zu Ester und Daniel. ATD.Apokryphen 5: 1998 ⇒14,2653... 16,3024. ᴿJBL 120 (2001) 547-549 & RBLit 3 (2001) 267-26 (*Kugler, Robert A.*).

3057 *Treloar, Richard* The hermeneutics of textual exile: comparing rabbinic and poststructuralist readings of Esther. Pacifica 14 (2001) 31-54.

3058 *Van den Eynde, Sabine M.L.* If Esther had not been that beautiful: dealing with a hidden God in the (Hebrew) book of Esther. BTB 31 (2001) 145-150.

3059 *Wahl, Harald* Esther-Forschung. ThR 66 (2001) 103-130;

3060 Das Buch Esther als methodisches Problem und hermeneutische Herausforderung: eine Skizze. BiblInterp 9 (2001) 25-40;

3061 "Glaube ohne Gott?": zur Rede vom Gott Israels im hebräischen Buch Esther. BZ 45 (2001) 37-54.

3062 *Wechsler, Michael G.* An early Karaite commentary on the book of Esther. HUCA 72 (2001) 101-137;

3063 The appellation βουγαιος and ethnic contextualization in the Greek text of Esther. VT 51 (2001) 109-114 [3,1; 8,5; 9,10.24].

3064 **Weiland, Forrest Sherman** The contribution of literary analysis to the understanding of genre, unity, and message in the book of Esther. Diss. Dallas Sem 2001, 266 pp. 3002972 [HThR 94,500].

E5.8 *Machabaeorum libri*, 1-2[3-4] Maccabees

3065 **Bartlett, John R.** 1 Maccabees. 1998 ⇒14,2656. [R]JBL 120 (2001) 761-763 (*Williams, David S.*).

3066 *Cañas Reíllo, José Manuel* Un testimonio inédito de *Vetus Latina* (1 *Macabeos* 1,1-6,40): el Codex Hubertianus (Londres, British Museum, Add 24142), edición crítica. Sef. 61 (2001) 57-82.

3067 *Eriksson, Lars Olov* "Fruktansvärd var vreden som drabbade Israel"—om berättarteknik och gudsbild i Mackabeerböckerna. SEÅ 66 (2001) 95-117.

3068 *Krentz, Edgar* The honorary decree for Simon the Maccabee. Hellenism in the land of Israel. CJAn 13: 2001 ⇒399. 146-153.

3069 *Orofino, Francisco* A elite e o mercado: uma leitura da crise na elite governante de Judá, a partir do primeiro livro dos Macabeus. Estudos Bíblicos 69 (2001) 32-41.

3070 *Rajak, Tessa* Dying for the law: the martyr's portrait in Jewish-Greek literature. The Jewish dialogue. 2001 <1997> ⇒199. 99-133.

3071 *Van der Kooij, Arie* The Septuagint of Psalms and the first book of Maccabees. [F]PIETERSMA, A.: JSOT.S 332: 2001 ⇒87. 229-247.

3072 *Van Henten, Jan Willem* The honorary decree for Simon the Maccabee (1 Mac 14:25-49) in its hellenistic context. Hellenism in the land of Israel. CJAn 13: 2001 ⇒399. 116-145.

3073 *Williams, David S.* Recent research in 1 Maccabees. CurResB 9 (2001) 169-184.

3074 **Williams, David Salter** The structure of 1 Maccabees. CBQ.MS 31: 1999 ⇒15,2935; 16,3037. [R]JThS 52 (2001) 191-194 (*Bartlett, J.R.*); ATG 64 (2001) 403-405 (*Sicre, J.L.*); ThLZ 126 (2001) 629-630 (*Schunck, Klaus-Dietrich*).

3075 *Nicklas, Tobias* Aus erzählter Geschichte "lernen": eine narrative Analyse von 2Makk 8. JSJ 32 (2001) 25-41.

3076 *Regev, Eyal* ב מקבים בספר המילואים וימי סוכעת ,חנוכה [Hannukkah, Succot and the days of *Milluim* in II Maccabees]. BetM 166 (2001) 227-243 Sum. 287. **H**.

3077 *Zwick, Reinhold* Unterhaltung und Nutzen: zum literarischen Profil des 2. Buches der Makkabäer. [F]SCHMUTTERMAYR, G. 2001 ⇒101. 125-149.

3078 *Alexander, Philip S.* 3 Maccabees, Hanukkah and Purim. [M]WEITZMAN, M. JSOT.S 333: 2001 ⇒113. 321-339.

3079 *Cousland, J.R.C.* Dionysus theomachos?: echoes of the Bacchae in 3 Maccabees. Bib. 82 (2001) 539-548.

3080 *Karlsen Seim, Turid* Abraham, ancestor or archetype?: a comparison of Abraham-language in 4 Maccabees and Luke-Acts. [F]BETZ, H. 2001 ⇒5. 27-42.

VI. Libri didactici VT

E6.1 *Poesis metrica*, Biblical and Semitic versification

3081 *Alexandre, Jean* Que dites-vous des juifs?: la traduction de la poétique biblique par Henri MESHONNIC. FV 100/5 (2001) 87-106.

3082 **Arduini, Stefano** Prolégomenos a una teoría general de las figuras. 2000 ⇒16,3046. [R]Rhetorica 19 (2001) 429-433 (*Martín Jiménez, Alfonso*).

3083 **Ashland, Brian A.** An examination of the rules for Babylonian poetic accentuation. Diss. Wisonsin—Madison 2001, 197 pp. 3020740.

3084 *Cook, Eleanor* The figure of enigma: rhetoric, history, poetry. Rhetorica 19 (2001) 349-378.

3085 **Fokkelman, Jan** Dichtkunst in de bijbel: een hanleiding bij literair lezen. 2000 ⇒16,3049. [R]ITBT 9/2 (2001) 33-4 (*Spijkerboer, Anne*);

3086 Major poems of the Hebrew Bible. 1998 ⇒14,2670... 16,3050. [R]JSSt 46 (2001) 153-155 (*Gillingham, Sue*) [Exod 15; Dt 32; Job 3];

3087 Major poems of the Hebrew Bible, 2: 85 psalms and Job 4-14. SSN 41: 2000 ⇒16,3051. [R]CBQ 63 (2001) 516-517 (*Vogels, Walter A.*);

3088 Reading biblical poetry: an introductory guide. [T]*Smit, Ineke*: LVL 2001, Westminster viii; 243 pp. $25. 0-664-22439-3 [ThD 49,170— Heiser, W. Charles].

3089 *Greenfield, Jonas C.* The cluster in biblical poetry. 'Al kanfei yonah, 2. 2001 <1990> ⇒153. 789-798.

3090 *Landy, Francis* Poetics and parallelism: some comments on James Kugel's *The idea of biblical poetry*. Beauty and the enigma. JSOT.S 312: 2001 <1984> ⇒171. 96-122.

3091 *Rand, Michael* Metathesis as a poetic technique in Hodayot poetry and its relevance to the development of Hebrew rhyme. DSD 8 (2001) 51-66.

3092 *Seybold, Klaus* Akrostichie im Psalter. ThZ 57 (2001) 172-183.

3093 *Smend, Rudolf* Der Entdecker des Parallelismus: Robert Lowth (1710-1787). [F]SEYBOLD, K. AOAT 280: 2001 ⇒102. 185-199.

3094 **Vance, Donald R.** The question of meter in Biblical Hebrew poetry. SBEC 46: Lewiston, NY 2001, Mellen (6) xii; 516 pp. 0-7734-7574-5. Bibl. 499-512.

3095 **Walker, Jeffrey** Rhetoric and poetics in antiquity. 2000 ⇒16,3062.
^RRhetorica 19 (2001) 125-128 (*Graff, Richard*); AJP 122 (2001)
579-582 (*Kirby, John T.*).

3096 ^E**Zenger, Erich** Der Psalter in Judentum und Christentum. 1998
⇒15,2957 ^RThRv 97 (2001) 305-307 (*Jüngling, Hans-Winfried*);
RTL 32 (2001) 402-403 (*Auwers, Jean-Marie*).

E6.2 Psalmi, textus

3097 *Aejmelaeus, Anneli* Characterizing criteria for the characterization of
the Septuagint translators: experimenting on the Greek Psalter. ^FPIE-
TERSMA, A. JSOT.S 332: 2001 ⇒87. 54-73.

3098 ^E**Aejmelaeus, Anneli P.M.; Quast, Udo** Der Septuaginta-Psalter
und seine Tochterübersetzungen: Symposium 1997. MSU 24: 2000
⇒16,3069. ^RETR 76 (2001) 423-425 (*Dorival, Gilles*).

3099 **Barber, Charles Theodore** Psalter CD-ROM: electronic fascimile.
L 2001, Univ. of Illinois Pr. £45. London, BL, ms Add. 19352 [Scr.
55,302*—Büttner, F.O.].

3100 ^T**Bianchi, Enzo** I salmi. Mi 2001, Mondadori 242 pp.

3101 *Boyd-Taylor, Cameron; Austin, Peter C.; Feuerverger, Andrey* The
assessment of manuscript affiliation within a probabilistic framework: a study of Alfred Rahlfs's core manuscript groupings for the
Greek Psalter. ^FPIETERSMA, A.: JSOT.S 332: 2001 ⇒87. 98-124.

3102 ^E**Browne, Gerald Michael** Collectio psalterii BEDAE Venerabili
adscripta. BSGRT: Monachii 2001, Saur xiv; 48 pp. 3-598-71229-4.

3103 *Cook, Johann* Intertextual relationships between the Septuagint of
Psalms and Proverbs. ^FPIETERSMA, A.: 2001 ⇒87. 218-228.

3104 *Cordes, Ariane* Der Septuaginta-Psalter?: zur Geschichte des griechischen Psalmentextes und seiner Edition. Der Septuaginta-Psalter.
Herders biblische Studien 32: 2001 ⇒1618. 49-60.

3105 **Devens, Monica S.** A concordance to Psalms in the Ethiopic version.
ÄthF 59: Wsb 2001, Harrassowitz xv; 546 pp. €53.17. 3447-044527.

3106 **Flint, Peter W.** The Dead Sea Psalms scrolls and the book of
Psalms. StTDJ 17: 1997 ⇒13,2757... 16,3080. ^RVT 51 (2001) 403-
405 (*Emerton, J.A.*); JNSL 27/1 (2001) 149-151 (*Cook, Johann*).

3107 *Gentry, Peter J.* The Greek Psalter and the καιγε tradition: methodological questions. ^FPIETERSMA, A. JSOT.S 332: 2001 ⇒87. 74-97.

3108 *Gzella, Holger* Die Wiege des griechischen David: die Diskussion
um die Entstehung des Septuaginta-Psalters in der neueren
Forschung. Der Septuaginta-Psalter. Herders biblische Studien 32:
2001 ⇒1618. 19-47.

3109 *Hiebert, Robert J.V.* Syriac biblical textual history and the Greek Psalter. [F]PIETERSMA, A. JSOT.S 332: 2001 ⇒87. 178-204.

3110 [E]**Jean-Nesmy, Claude; Solms, Élisabeth de** Bible chrétienne, 5: le psautier et textes en parallèle. Sillery/Québec 2001, Sigier 566 pp [RThPh 134,90s—Borel, Jean].

3111 **Knesebeck, Harald Wolter von dem** Der Elisabethpsalter in Cividale del Friuli: Buchmalerei für den Thüringer Landgrafenhof zu Beginn des 13. Jahrhunderts. Diss. Gö 1998: B 2001, Deutscher Verlag für Kunstwissenschaft 378 pp. €149. 3-87157-184-9. 287 pl.

3112 *Kraft, Robert A.; Wright, Benjamin G.* Coptic/Sahidic fragments of the biblical Psalms in the University of Pennsylvania Museum. [F]PIETERSMA, A. JSOT.S 332: 2001 ⇒87. 163-177.

3113 *Leoni, Aron di Leone* A hitherto unknown edition of the Spanish psalter by Abraham USQUE (Ferrara 1554). Sef. 61 (2001) 127-136.

3114 *Lust, Johan* The *pisqah be'emṣaʿ pasuq*, the Psalms, and Ezekiel 3.16. [F]PIETERSMA, A. JSOT.S 332: 2001 ⇒87. 149-162.

3115 *Marti, Andreas* Der Genfer Psalter in den deutschsprachigen Ländern im 16. und 17. Jahrhundert. Zwing. 28 (2001) 45-72.

3116 *Muraoka, Takamitsu* Pairs of synonyms in the Septuagint Psalms. [F]PIETERSMA, A. JSOT.S 332: 2001 ⇒87. 36-43.

3117 **O'Neill, Patrick P.** King Alfred's Old English prose translation of the first fifty psalms. CM 2001, Medieval Academy of America vii; 362 pp. $50. 0-915651-13-0.

3118 *Pietersma, Albert* The place of origin of the Old Greek Psalter. [F]DION, P.-E. 1. JSOT.S 324: 2001 ⇒25. 252-274.

3119 [E]**Pulsiano, Phillip** Old English glossed psalters, Psalms 1-50. Toronto Old English series 11: Toronto 2001, University of Toronto Press lv (2); 742 pp. $100. 0-8020-4470-0. Bibl. xi-xviii.

3120 *Rösel, Martin* Die Psalmüberschriften des Septuaginta-Psalters;

3121 *Rüsen-Weinhold, Ulrich* Der Septuaginta-Psalter in seinen verschiedenen Textformen zur Zeit des Neuen Testaments. Der Septuaginta-Psalter. Herders biblische Studien 32: 2001 ⇒1618. 125-148/61-87.

3122 *Sollamo, Raija* Repetition of possessive pronouns in the Greek Psalter: the use and non-use of possessive pronouns in renderings of Hebrew coordinate items with possessive suffixes. [F]PIETERSMA, A. JSOT.S 332: 2001 ⇒87. 44-53.

3123 *Stichel, Rainer* Zur Herkunft der Psalmenüberschriften in der Septuaginta. Der Septuaginta-Psalter. Herders biblische Studien 32: 2001 ⇒ 1618. 149-161.

3124 **Tanner, Beth LaNeel** The book of Psalms through the lens of intertextuality. Studies in Biblical Literature 26: NY 2001, Lang xv; 207 pp. 0-8204-4969-5. Bibl. 185-199.

3125 *Ter Haar Romeny, R. Bas* The Hebrew and the Greek as alternatives to the Syriac version in Išoʻdad's commentary on the Psalms. ^MWEITZMAN, M. JSOT.S 333: 2001 ⇒113. 431-456.

3126 **Thompson, J. David** A critical concordance to the Septuagint: Psalms. The Computer Bible 90,1-2: Lewiston, NY 2001, Mellen 0-7734-4045-3.

3127 ^T**Trebolle Barrera, Julio Cesar** Libro de los Salmos: himnos y lamentaciones. Colección Estructuras y Procesos, Religión: M 2001, Trotta 302 pp. 84-8164-460-9. Versión poética de *Susana Pottecher*.
Van der Kooij, A. The Septuagint of Psalms. 2001 ⇒3071.

3128 *Van Rooy, Harry F.* The psalm headings in book one of the Syro-Hexapla Psalms. X Congress IOSCS. SBL.SCSt 51: 2001 ⇒499. 373-392.

3129 **Van Rooy, H.F.** Studies on the Syriac apocryphal psalms. JSSt.S 7: 1999 ⇒15,2972. ^RJBL 120 (2001) 760-761 (*Mathews, Edward G.*).

3130 *Williams, Tyler F.* Towards a date for the Old Greek Psalter. ^FPIETERSMA, A. JSOT.S 332: 2001 ⇒87. 248-276.

E6.3 Psalmi, introductio

3131 ^E**Reid, Stephen Breck** Psalms and practice: worship, virtue, and authority. ColMn 2001, Liturgical xvii; 290 pp. $20. 0-8146-5080-5. ^RNBl 82 (2001) 591-593 (*Hill, Edmund*).

3132 **Barbiero, Gianni** Das erste Psalmenbuch als Einheit: eine synchrone Analyse von Psalm 1-41. ÖBS 16: 1999 ⇒15,2973; 16,3101. ^RRTL 32 (2001) 387-388 (*Auwers, Jean-Marie*).

3133 *Bellinger, W.H.* The Psalms as a place to begin for Old Testament theology. Psalms and practice. 2001 ⇒3131. 28-39.

3134 ^E**Brenner, Athalya; Fontaine, Carole R.** Wisdom and Psalms. The Feminist Companion to the Bible (Second series) 2: 1998 ⇒14,221. ^RYESW 9 (2001) 273-275 (*Rakel, Claudia*).

3135 **Bullock, C. Hassell** Encountering the book of Psalms: a literary and theological introduction. Encountering biblical studies: GR 2001, Baker 266 pp. $25. 0-8010-2245-2. Bibl. 245-248.

3136 **Crenshaw, James L.** The Psalms: an introduction. GR 2001, Eerdmans x; 187 pp. $15. 0-8028-0854-9. Bibl. 170-171. ^RHebStud 42 (2001) 349-352 (*Tate, Marvin E.*).

3137 *Gerstenberger, Erhard S.* The Psalter. The Blackwell companion to the Hebrew Bible. Blackwell companions to religion 3: 2001 ⇒653. 402-417.

3138 **Gunkel, Hermann** An introduction to the psalms: the genres of the religious lyric of Israel. [T]*Nogalski, James D.* 1998 ⇒14,2696; 16, 3107. [R]HeyJ 42 (2001) 205-207 (*Prior, Michael*).

3139 Liter: christelijk literair tijdschrift 2001/1: themanummer Psalmen. Zoetermeer 2001, Boekencentrum 114 pp. €11.50. Musiekbijlage.

3140 **Nasuti, Harry P.** Defining the sacred songs: genre, tradition and the post-critical interpretation of the Psalms. JSOT.S 231: 1999 ⇒15, 2980. [R]ArOr 69 (2001) 38-39 (*Craghan, John F.*); JThS 52 (2001) 747-752 (*Gillingham, Sue*); CBQ 63 (2001) 322-323 (*Craghan, John F.*); ThLZ 126 (2001) 618-619 (*Körting, Corinna*).

3141 *Smith, Mark S.* Taking inspiration: authorship, revelation, and the book of Psalms. Psalms and practice. 2001 ⇒3131. 244-273.

3142 **Trebolle Barrera, Julio Cesar** Libro de los Salmos: religión, poder y saber. Estructuras y Procesos, Serie Religión: M 2001, Trotta 286 pp. €18.50. 84-81164-461-7. Bibl. 267-268.

3143 *Uehlinger, Christoph* Antiker Tell, lebendiges Stadtviertel: das Psalmenbuch als Sammlung von Einzeldichtungen und als Großkomposition. BiKi 56 (2001) 174-177.

3144 **Wénin, André** Le livre des louanges: entrer dans les psaumes. Ecritures 6: Bru 2001, Lumen Vitae 164 pp. €16. 2-87324-157-8 [ETR 78,111—Vincent, Jean M.].

3145 *Zenger, Erich* Von der Psalmenexegese zur Psalterexegese. BiKi 56 (2001) 8-15.

E6.4 Psalmi, commentarii

3146 [T]**Boulding, Maria** AUGUSTINE: exposition of the Psalms: 51-72. [E]*Rotelle, John E.*: Works of Saint Augustine 3/17: Hyde Park, NY 2001, New City 518 pp. $44/28. 1-56548-156-9/5-0 [ThD 49,58—Heiser, W. Charles].

3147 **Brinkman, J.M.** Psalmen IV: een praktische bijbelverklaring. Tekst en toelichting: Kampen 2001, Kok 211 pp. €19.02. 90-435-0363-0.

3148 **Broyles, Craig C.** Psalms. 1999 ⇒15,2985. [R]JThS 52 (2001) 179-180 (*Eaton, J.H.*); HebStud 42 (2001) 352-353 (*Brueggemann, Walter*); CBQ 63 (2001) 710-711 (*Nasuti, Harry P.*).

3149 **Eissler, Friedmann** Der Psalmenkommentar der Karäers Jefet BEN ELI am Beispiel der Königspsalmen: Übersetzung, Kommentierung und Vergleich mit dem Tafsir des Gaon SAADJA Ben Josef. Diss. Tübingen 2001, [D]*Schreiner, S.* 472 + 200 pp. [RTL 33,635].

3150 **Gerstenberger, Erhard S.** Psalms, part 2 and Lamentations. FOTL 15: GR 2001, Eerdmans xxii; 543 pp. $45. 0-8028-0488-8.

3151 ᴱGori, Franco AUGUSTINUS: Enarrationes in Psalmos 101-150, pars 3: enarrationes in Psalmos 119-133. CSEL 95/3: W 2001, Verlag der Österreichischen Akademie der Wissenschaften 340 pp. 3-7001-2981-4. ᴿREA 47 (2001) 418-419 (*Dulaey, Martine*).

3152 Goulder, Michael D. Studies in the psalter, IV: the psalms of the return (Book V, Psalms 107-150). JSOT.S 258: 1998 ⇒14,2714... 16, 3125. ᴿRTL 32 (2001) 389-392 (*Auwers, Jean-Marie*); EvQ 73 (2001) 80-83 (*Brunson, Andrew*).

3153 ᵀHill, Robert Charles THEODORET of Cyrus: commentary on the Psalms, 1: Psalms 1-72. FaCh 101: 2000 ⇒16,3127. ᴿIThQ 66 (2001) 181-182 (*Urbainczyk, Theresa*);

3154 Commentary on the Psalms, 2: Psalms 73-150. FaCh 102: Wsh 2001, The Catholic Univ. of America Pr. xii; 383 pp. $40. 0-8132-0102-0. Bibl. ᴿIThQ 66 (2001) 181-182 (*Urbainczyk, Theresa*);

3155 St. John CHRYSOSTOM: commentary on the Psalms. 1998 ⇒15,2990. ᴿRBLit 3 (2001) 490-492 (*Pulikottil, Paulson*).

3156 Hossfeld, Frank-Lothar; Zenger, Erich Psalmen 2: 51-100. 2000 ⇒16,3128. ᴿStPat 48 (2001) 529-531 (*Lorenzin,Tiziano*); RTL 32 (2001) 380-381 (*Auwers, Jean-Marie*); ThQ 181 (2001) 249-250 (*Groß, Walter*).

3157 ᴱJean-Nesmy, Claude; Solms, Élisabeth de Bible chrétienne, 5*: commentaires: le psautier. Sillery/Québec 2001, Sigier 694 pp [RThPh 134, 90s—Borel, Jean].

3158 Limburg, James Psalms. 2000 ⇒16,3131. ᴿTS 62 (2001) 825-826 (*Brueggemann, Walter*); CBQ 63 (2001) 726-28 (*Culley, Robert C.*).

3159 Lorenzin, Tiziano I salmi: versione, introduzione e commento. 2000 ⇒16,3132. ᴿPaVi 46/1 (2001) 62-63 (*Cappelletto, Gianni*); CivCatt 152/4 (2001) 631-632 (*Scaiola, D.*).

3160 Maggioni, Bruno Davanti a Dio: i salmi 1-75. Sestante 16: Mi 2001, Vita e Pensiero 232 pp. 88-343-0721-6. Bibl. 231-232.

3161 *Norton, Gerard J.* Commentaries, with particular application to the psalms. PIBA 24 (2001) 83-104.

3162 Oeming, Manfred Das Buch der Psalmen, v.1, Psalm 1-41. 2000 ⇒ 16,3135. ᴿBiKi 56 (2001) 53-54 (*Feininger, Bernd*); StPat 48 (2001) 527-529 (*Lorenzin,Tiziano*); BZ 45 (2001) 298-300 (*Zenger, Erich*); ThLZ 126 (2001) 1136-1138 (*Albertz, Rainer*).

3163 Ravasi, Gianfranco I Salmi. Parola di vita: Mi ⁸2001, Àncora 246 pp. 88-7610-921-8.

3164 ᴱᵀSánchez Manzano, Maria Asunción Benito Arias MONTANO: comentarios a los treinta y un primeros Salmos de David. 1999 ⇒15, 2993. ᴿSef. 61 (2001) 203-207 (*Fernández Marcos, N.*).

3165 Schaefer, Konrad Psalms. Berit Olam: ColMn 2001, Liturgical xlv; 399 pp. $50. 0-8146-5061-9. Bibl. 359-361.

3166   **Tromp, Nico** Psalmen 51-100. Belichting van het bijbelboek: Den
       Bosch 2001, Katholieke Bijbelstichting 269 pp. €16.50. 90-6173-
       893-8.
3167   **Weber, Beat** Werkbuch Psalmen, 1: die Psalmen 1 bis 72. Stu 2001,
       Kohlhammer 357 pp. FS43.60. 3-17-016312-4. Bibl. 331-357.
3168   **Wilcock, Michael** The message of the Psalms: songs for the people
       of God: v.1: Psalms 1-72; v.2: Psalms 73-150. The Bible Speaks To-
       day: Nottingham 2001, Inter-Varsity Press 2 vols. 0-8511-1-506-3.

E6.5 **Psalmi, themata**

3169   **Achenbach, Reinhard** Unheilsdrohung und Erlösungshoffnung: zum
       Sitz im Leben mesopotamischer und altisraelitischer Klagegebete.
       Diss.-Habil. München 2001, ᴰ*Otto, E.* [RTL 33,631].
3170   *Austermann, Frank* ʼAvoμία im Septuaginta-Psalter: ein Beitrag zum
       Verhältnis von Übersetzungsweise und Theologie. Helsinki perspec-
       tives. SESJ 82: 2001 ⇒1617. 99-137.
3171   *Auwers, Jean-Marie* Où va l'exégèse du Psautier?: bilan de six
       années d'études psalmiques (1995-2000). RTL 32 (2001) 374-410.
3172   **Auwers, Jean-Marie** La composition littéraire du Psautier: un état
       de la question. CRB 46: 2000 ⇒16,3144. ᴿBiblInterp 9 (2001) 82-84
       (*Goulder, Michael*); JThS 52 (2001) 181-183 (*Cunningham, Sue*);
       VieCon 73 (2001) 258-266 (*Fabre, Véronique*).
3173   *Baldermann, Ingo* Les enfants se découvrent eux-mêmes dans les
       psaumes: des interrogations d'enfants qui posent toutes les questions.
       LV.F 56 (2001) 245-254.
3174   **Bautch, Richard John** Developments in genre between post-exilic
       penitential prayers and the psalms of communal lament. Diss. Notre
       Dame 2001, ᴰ*Blenkinsopp, J.* 266 pp. 3000399.
3175   *Bayer, Oswald* Zur Theologie der Klage. JBTh 16 (2001) 289-301.
3176   **Bouzard, Walter C., Jr.** We have heard with our ears, O God:
       sources of the communal laments in the Psalms. SBL.DS 159: 1997
       ⇒13,2817; 15,3002. ᴿJSSt 46 (2001) 161-164 (*Gillingham, Sue*).
3177   *Chinitz, Jacob* Particularism and universalism in Psalms. JBQ 29/1
       (2001) 13-17.
3178   *Cimosa, Mario* Tendenze escatologiche nella traduzione greca
       (LXX) dei salmi. 'In Lui ci ha scelti' (Ef 1,4): studi in onore del prof.
       Giorgio GOZZELINO. ᴱ**Frigato, Sabino:** R 2001, LAS. 197-210 [Ps
       16; 49; 73].
3179   **Conti, Martino** Presente e futuro dell'uomo nei salmi sapienziali.
       1998 ⇒14,2727. ᴿRTL 32 (2001) 377 (*Auwers, Jean-Marie*).

3180 *Cook, Stephen L.* Relecture, hermeneutics, and Christ's passion in the Psalms. ᴹMORSE, J. JSOT.S 336: 2001 ⇒75. 181-205 [Ps 132; 22].

3181 *Cortese, Enzo* Dio rifugio nella preghiera del re e la storia della formazione delle raccolte davidiche. RB 108 (2001) 481-502 [Ps 17-19; 31; 91; 144].

3182 *Cox, Claude E.* SCHAPER's 'Eschatology' meets KRAUS's 'Theology of the Psalms'. ᶠPIETERSMA, A. JSOT.S 332: 2001 ⇒87. 289-311.

3183 *Davison, Lisa W.* 'My soul is like the weaned child that is with me': the Psalms and the feminine voice. HBT 23 (2001) 155-167.

3184 **Day, John Nathan** The imprecatory psalms and christian ethics. Diss. Dallas Theol. Sem. 2001, 239 pp. 3022979.

3185 *Ehlers, Kathrin* "JHWH ist mein Becheranteil": zum Bechermotiv in den Psalmen 16; 23 und 116. ᶠGROß, W.: 2001 ⇒38. 45-63.

3186 *Ejrnaes, Bodil* "Den lille Bibel": traek af de gammeltestamentlige salmers receptionshistorie. DTT 64 (2001) 161-175.

3187 **Emmendörffer, Michael** Der ferne Gott: eine Untersuchung der alttestamentlichen Volksklagelieder vor dem Hintergrund der mesopotamischen Literatur. FAT 21: 1998 ⇒14,2732... 16,3156. ᴿJSSt 46 (2001) 323-325 (*Dalley, Stephanie*).

3188 **Forster, Christine** Begrenztes Leben als Herausforderung: das Vergänglichkeitsmotiv in weisheitlichen Psalmen. 2000 ⇒16,3157. ᴿThRv 97 (2001) 298-301 (*Schnocks, Johannes*); CBQ 63 (2001) 313-314 (*Culley, Robert C.*); ThLZ 126 (2001) 913-915 (*Köhlmoos, Melanie*).

3189 *Froehlich, Karlfried* Discerning the voices: praise and lament in the tradition of the christian psalter. CTJ 36 (2001) 75-90.

3190 *Gerstenberger, Erhard S.* 'World dominion' in Yahweh kingship psalms: down to the roots of globalizing concepts and strategies. HBT 23 (2001) 192-210.

3191 *Gosse, Bernard* La libération des ennemis, le salut, et la faute. CICat 2/1 (2001) 15-24 [Exod 15; 2 Sam 22].

3192 *Greenstein, Eliezer (Ed)* The lament over city and sanctuary in early Israelite literature. ᶠAHITUV, S.: 2001 ⇒1. 88-97. **H.**

3193 **Grelot, Pierre** Le mystère du Christ dans les Psaumes. CJJC 74: 1998 ⇒14,2737; 15,3017. ᴿRivista di teologia dell'evangelizzazione 5/9 (2001) 178-179 (*Lodi, Enzo*);

3194 Il mistero del Cristo nei salmi. ᵀ*Cestari, Giuseppe*: CSB 38: 2000 ⇒ 16,3163. ᴿEfMex 19 (2001) 280-281 (*Merlos Arroyo, Francisco*).

3195 *Gunkel, Hermann* The religion of the Psalms. Water for a thirsty land. 2001 <1922> ⇒155. 134-167.

3196 **Hartenstein, Friedhelm** Das 'Angesicht JHWHs': Studien zu seinem höfischen und kultischen Bedeutungshintergrund in den Psalmen und in Exodus 32-34. Diss.-Habil. Marburg 2001, ᴰ*Jeremias, J.* [RTL 33,632].

3197 **Hauge, Martin Ravndal** Between Sheol and temple: motif structure and function in the I-Psalms. JSOT.S 178: 1995 ⇒11,1/1507... 13, 2827. ᴿThZ 57 (2001) 471-472 (*Weber, Beat*).

3198 *Jakobzen, Lea* The individual's suffering in Psalms and in Mesopotamian narratives. BetM 168 (2001) 33-56 Sum. 95. H.

3199 *Joffe, Laura* The Elohistic Psalter: what, how and why?. SJOT 15 (2001) 142-166 [Ps 42-83].

3200 **Kleer, Martin** "Der liebliche Sänger der Psalmen Israels": Untersuchungen zu David als Dichter und Beter der Psalmen. BBB 108: 1996 ⇒12,2414. ᴿRTL 32 (2001) 375-376 (*Auwers, Jean-Marie*).

3201 *Krüger, Annette* Himmel—Erde—Unterwelt: kosmologische Entwürfe in der poetischen Literatur Israels. Das biblische Weltbild. FAT 32: 2001 ⇒285. 65-83 [Job 38,4-38; Ps 148; 104].

3202 **Kwakkel, G.** According to my righteousness: upright behaviour as grounds for deliverance in Psalms 7, 17, 18, 26 and 44. Diss. Rijksuniv. Groningen 2001, ᴰ*Noort, E.* [Phoe. 47,4].

3203 *Lane, David J.* 'Come here...and let us sit and read...': the use of Psalms in five Syriac authors. ᴹWEITZMAN, M.: 2001 ⇒113. 412-30.

3204 *Llamas, Román* La experiencia de Dios en los salmos. REsp 60 (2001) 7-48.

3205 *McCann, J. Clinton* Righteousness, justice, and peace: a contemporary theology of the Psalms. HBT 23 (2001) 111-131,

3206 *Menchén Carrasco, Joaquín* El clamor de los pobres en los salmos. ResB 30 (2001) 53-62.

3207 **Mitchell, David Campbell** The message of the psalter: an eschatological programme in the book of Psalms. JSOT.S 252: 1997 ⇒13, 2836... 16,3173. ᴿRTL 32 (2001) 383-386 (*Auwers, Jean-Marie*).

3208 *Mortari, Luciana* La paternità di Dio nel salterio greco. ᶠMARIN, B. 2001 ⇒68. 51-59.

3209 *Nasuti, Harry P.* Historical narrative and identity in the Psalms. HBT 23 (2001) 132-153.

3210 *Olofsson, Staffan* Law and lawbreaking in the LXX Psalms—a case of theological exegesis. Der Septuaginta-Psalter. Herders biblische Studien 32: 2001 ⇒1618. 291-330.

3211 *Pietersma, Albert* Exegesis and liturgy in the superscriptions of the Greek Psalter. X Congress IOSCS. 2001 ⇒499. 99-138.

3212 *Rigby, Cynthia L.* All God, and us: double agency and reconciliation in Psalms 22 and 51. Psalms and practice. 2001 ⇒3131. 202-219.

3213 *Roberts, J.J.M.* God's imperial reign according to the psalter. HBT 23 (2001) 211-221.

3214   *Roberts, Kathryn L.* My tongue will sing aloud of your deliverance: praise and sacrifice in the Psalms. Psalms and practice. 2001 ⇒3131. 99-110.

3215   **Rösel, Christoph** Die messianische Redaktion des Psalters: Studien zu Entstehung und Sammlung Ps 2-89*. CThM.BW 19: 1999 ⇒15, 3036; 16,3179. [R]JThS 52 (2001) 745-746 (*Clements, R.E.*).

3216   *Schaper, Joachim* Die Renaissance der Mythologie im hellenistischen Judentum und der Septuaginta-Psalter. .

3217   *Schenker, Adrian* Götter und Engel im Septuaginta-Psalter: text- und religionsgeschichtliche Ergebnisse aus drei textkritischen Untersuchungen;

3218   *Seiler, Stefan* Theologische Konzepte in der Septuaginta: das theologische Profil von 1 Chr 16,8ff. LXX im Vergleich mit Ps 104; 95; 105 LXX. Der Septuaginta-Psalter. Herders biblische Studien 32: 2001 ⇒1618. 171-183/185-195/197-225.

3219   *Silva, Larry* The cursing psalms as a source of blessing. Psalms and practice. 2001 ⇒3131. 220-230.

3220   **Starbuck, Scott R.A.** Court oracles in the Psalms: the so-called royal psalms in their ancient Near Eastern context. SBL.DS 172: 1999 ⇒ 15,3039; 16,3182. [R]Bib. 82 (2001) 426-429 (*Auwers, Jean-Marie*); JBL 119 (2000) 757-758 (*Creach, Jerome F.D.*).

3221   *Trudinger, Peter L.* Friend or foe?: earth, sea and *Chaoskampf* in the Psalms. The earth story. 2001 ⇒275. 29-41.

3222   *Van der Plancke, Chantal* Apprivoisier le psautier avec des jeunes. LV.F 56 (2001) 255-265.

3223   *Weber, Beat* Der Asaph-Psalter—eine Skizze [Ps 50; 73-83];

3224   *Willi, Thomas* Das *šjr hmʿlwt*: Zion und der Sitz im Leben der "Aufstiegslieder" Psalm 120-134. [F]SEYBOLD, K. AOAT 280: 2001 ⇒102. 117-14/153-162.

3225   *Zegarra Russo, Felipe* El Dios de la alianza en algunos salmos. Páginas 172 (2001) 56-63.

3226   **Zenger, Erich** Ein Gott der Rache?: Feindpsalmen verstehen. 1998 <1994> ⇒10,2952; 11/1,1537. [R]FrRu 8 (2001) 227-228 (*Schwendemann, Wilhelm*).

E6.6 *Psalmi: oratio, liturgia*—Psalms as prayer

3227   **Barber, Michael** Singing in the reign: the Psalms and the liturgy of God's Kingdom. Steubenville, Ohio 2001, Emmaus R. 186 pp. $12. 1-931018-08-1. Introd. *Scott Hahn*: Bibl. 179-186.

3228 *Baumgartner, Konrad* Psalter und Harfe wacht auf!: die Psalmen heute: in Liturgie, Verkündigung und Meditation. ^FSCHMUTTERMAYR, G. 2001 ⇒101. 305-316.

3229 *Beauchamp, Paul* La prière à l'école des psaumes. Etudes (2001) 794-805.

3230 *Berges, Ulrich* Zwijgen is zilver—klagen is goud: pleidooi voor een herontdekking van het bijbelse klagen. TTh 41 (2001) 231-252.

3231 **Bonhoeffer, Dietrich** I Salmi: il libro di preghiere della bibbia. ^T*Lupi, Giuliana*: La parola e le parole: Mi 2001, Paoline. €8.26. 88-315-22-05. ^RRSEc 19 (2001) 580-582 (*Abbà, Maurizio*).

3232 *Butting, Klara* "Die Töchter Judas frohlocken" (Ps 48,12): Frauen beten die Psalmen. BiKi 56 (2001) 35-39.

3233 *Carstens, Pernille* Mellem tavshed og sang: hvad er der blevet af den kultiske tolkning af de gammeltestamentlige salmer?. DTT 64 (2001) 97-110.

3234 *De Miguel González, José María* Salmos del Domingo I: una lectura litúrgica. EstTrin 35 (2001) 373-422.

3235 *Deseille, Placide* Les psaumes: prières de l'église, prières trinitaires. Unité chrétienne 144 (2001) 15-18.

3236 *Dorff, Francis* Interiorizzare i salmi. VitaCon 37 (2001) 544-552.

3237 *Endres, John C.* Praying with Psalms: a school of prayer. Psalms and practice. 2001 ⇒3131. 62-77.

3238 **Endres, John C.; Liebert, Elizabeth** A retreat with the Psalms: resources for personal and communal prayer. NY 2001, Paulist 254 pp. $19. 0-8091-4026-8. Bibl. 247-254.

3239 **Erbele-Küster, Dorothea** Lesen als Akt des Betens: eine Rezeptionsästhetik der Psalmen. WMANT 87: Neuk 2001, Neuk viii; 207 pp. 3-7887-1812-9. Bibl. 189-200.

3240 *Falk, Daniel* Psalms and prayers. Justification, 1: second temple Judaism. WUNT 2/140: 2001 ⇒251. 7-56.

3241 *Farias, Jacir de Freitas* A história como motivo de oração nos salmos. Estudos Bíblicos 71 (2001) 42-52.

3242 *Fuchs, Ottmar* Wer darf die jüdischen Klagepsalmen beten?: praktisch-theologische Überlegungen zu einem ebenso universalen wie unbeliebigen Bibelbezug. Biblischer Text. 2001 ⇒252. 135-161.

3243 **Genion, Michael** Praying the Sunday psalms. Staten Island, NY 2001, St Paul's 204 pp. $13 [BiTod 40,194—Bergant, Dianne].

3244 *Hossfeld, Frank-Lothar* Von der Klage zum Lob—die Dynamik des Gebets in den Psalmen. BiKi 56 (2001) 16-20.

3245 *Howell, James C.* The Psalms in worship and preaching: a report;

3246 *Jacobson, Rolf* Burning our lamps with borrowed oil: the liturgical use of the Psalms and the life of faith. Psalms and practice. 2001 ⇒ 3131. 123-142/90-98.

3247 **Jaki, Stanley L.** Praying the psalms: a commentary. GR 2001, Eerdmans v; 237 pp. $16. 0-8028-4771-4.

3248 *Janowski, Bernd* Die Antwort Israels. BiKi 56 (2001) 2-7.

3249 *Kellenberger, Corina; Kellenberger, Edgar* Psalmen am Krankenbett. [F]SEYBOLD, K. AOAT 280: 2001 ⇒102. 175-181.

3250 **Martin, Jean-Marie** Psaumes d'Israël et harmonies chrétiennes: prier en église dans le Christ. P 2001, Lethielleux 365 pp. €19.67.

3251 *Mattheeuws, Alain* Seigneur, Tu me connais... et je me laisse connaître de Toi. VieCon 73 (2001) 267-277 [Ps 139].

3252 *McCann, J. Clinton* Thus says the Lord: 'Thou shalt preach on the Psalms!'. Psalms and practice. 2001 ⇒3131. 111-122.

3253 **McCann, J. Clinton; Howell, James C.** Preaching the Psalms. Nv 2001, Abingdon 144 pp. $15. 0-687-04499-5.

3254 **Menichelli, Ernesto** I salmi: rileggere la storia nel clima della preghiera. 1998 ⇒15,3060. [R]RivBib 49 (2001) 352-354 (*Gamberoni, Johann*).

3255 *Miguel González, José María de* Los salmos de laudes de la I semana: para celebrar la oración de la iglesia. Salm. 48 (2001) 399-468.

3256 **Monari, Luciano** Come profumo d'incenso: salga a te la mia preghiera (Sl. 141,2): lectio divina sui salmi. Piacenza 2001, Berti 204 pp. 88-7364-004-4.

3257 *Muck, Terry* Psalm, *Bhajan*, and *Kirtan*: songs of the soul in comparative perspective. Psalms and practice. 2001 ⇒3131. 7-27.

3258 *Nasuti, Harry P.* The sacramental function of the Psalms in contemporary scholarship and liturgical practice. Psalms and practice. 2001 ⇒3131. 78-89.

3259 **Nicoli, U.** Un salmo al giorno. CasM 2001, Piemme 414 pp. €23.24 [RdT 43,159].

3260 *Nogalski, James D.* Reading David in the psalter: a study in liturgical hermeneutics. HBT 23 (2001) 168-191.

3261 *Oberforcher, Robert* Poesie der Psalmen: eine Sprachschule für existenzielles Beten. Wort zum Leben. 2001 ⇒284. 57-78.

3262 **Ognibeni, Bruno** Se non fossi tuo: meditazioni e note su quindici salmi e una poesia di GREGORIO di Nazianzo. 1998 ⇒14,2786; 15, 3062. [R]EstB 59 (2001) 413-414 (*Carbajosa, I.*) [Ps 8; 22; 23; 42; 43; 51; 90; 91; 119; 122; 126; 127; 130; 137; 139].

3263 *Rist, Josef* Ein spätantikes Plädoyer für den Psalmengesang: NICETA von Remesiana und seine Schrift De psalmodiae bono (CPL 649). OS 50 (2001) 34-57.

3264 **Rogerson, John** The psalms in daily life. Mahwah 2001, Paulist 112 pp. $11 [BiTod 40,196—Bergant, Dianne].

3265 *Rogerson, John W.* Their place in worship, 3: the psalms. ET 112 (2001) 293-297.

3266 *Sánchez Caro, José Manuel* La biblia, libro sagrado: teología de la inspiración en los últimos diez años. Salm. 48 (2001) 81-121.

3267 *Selander, Inger* Psalmförfattaren och biblen: några iakttagelser. SEÅ 66 (2001) 73-94.

3268 *Tanner, Beth LaNeel* How long, O Lord!: will your people suffer in silence forever?. Psalms and practice. 2001 ⇒3131. 143-152.

3269 *Vos, C.J.A.* Met 'n lied in die hart. VeE 22 (2001) 455-464.

3270 *Wilson, Gerald H.* Songs for the city: interpreting biblical psalms in an urban context. Psalms and practice. 2001 ⇒3131. 231-243.

3271 *Zenger, Erich* 'Ich aber sage: Du bist mein Gott' (Ps 31,14): kirchliches Psalmengebet nach der Schoa. ᶠLEHMANN, K. 2001 ⇒63. 15-31.

E6.7 *Psalmi: versiculi*—Psalms by number and verse

3272 *Auffret, Pierre* Comme un arbre ... étude structurelle du Psaume 1. BZ 45 (2001) 256-264.

3273 *Austermann, Frank* Deshalb werden nicht aufstehen Frevler im Gericht: zur Übersetzungsweise und Interpretation im ersten Septuaginta-Psalm. X Congress IOSCS. SBL.SCSt 51: 2001 ⇒499. 481-497.

3274 *Holgenhaven, Jesper* The opening of the Psalter: a study in Jewish theology. SJOT 15 (2001) 169-180 [Ps 1-2].

3275 *Auffret, Pierre* Étude structurelle du Psaume 2. EstB 59 (2001) 307-323.

3276 *Rosengren, Allan* Parallelismer i det Gamle Testamente: Salme 2 som eksempel. DTT 64 (2001) 1-15.

3277 *Kotzé, Annemaré* Reading Psalm 4 to the Manicheans. VigChr 55 (2001) 119-136.

3278 *Conti, Martino* Gioia per il soccorso divino secondo il salmo 5. Anton. 76 (2001) 407-428.

3279 *Lescow, Theodor* Die Komposition der Psalmen 6 und 55. BN 107/108 (2001) 32-40.

3280 *Talstra, E.* Psalm 8: de lofzang op Christus: bijbel en liturgie. ITBT 9/4 (2001) 20-22.

3281 *Tate, Marvin E.* An exposition of Psalm 8. PRSt 28/4 (2001) 343-59.

3282 *Pitkin, Barbara* Psalm 8:1-2. Interp. 55 (2001) 177-180.

3283 *Van Leeuwen, Raymond C.* Psalm 8.5 and Job 7.17-18: a mistaken scholarly commonplace?. ᶠDION, P.-E. 1. 2001 ⇒25. 205-215.

3284 *Janowski, Bernd* Das verborgene Angesicht Gottes: Psalm 13 als Muster eines Klagelieds des Einzelnen. JBTh 16 (2001) 25-53.

3285 *Tournay, Raymond Jacques* À propos du Psaume 16, 1-4. RB 108 (2001) 21-25.

3286 **Adam, Klaus-Peter** Der königliche Held: die Entsprechung von kämpfendem Gott und kämpfendem König in Psalm 18. WMANT 91: Neuk 2001, Neuk ix; 273 pp. 3-7887-1855-2. Bibl. 245-270.

3287 *Köckert, Matthias* Die Theophanie des Wettergottes Jahwe in Psalm 18. ᶠHAAS, V. 2001 ⇒39. 209-226.

3288 *Smelik, Marian; Smelik, Willem* Twin targums: Psalm 18 and 2 Samuel 22. ᴹWEITZMAN, M.: JSOT.S 333: 2001 ⇒113. 244-281.

3289 *Grund, Alexandra* Auf die ganze Erde geht ihre 'Messschnur' aus—die Ordnung des Himmels in Ps 19,5a und der babylonische Sternenkatalog BM 78161. BN 110 (2001) 66-75.

3290 **Bazylinski, Stanislaw** I Salmi 20-21 nel contesto delle preghiere regali. 1999 ⇒15,3092; 16,3242. ᴿCBQ 63 (2001) 102-103 (*Duggan, Michael*); RTL 32 (2001) 395-397 (*Auwers, Jean-Marie*).

3291 *Bauks, Michaela* Le délivrance de la maladie mortelle selon le Psaume 22. Représentations des maladies. 2001 ⇒482. 27-43.

3292 *Green, Douglas J.* The good, the bad and the better: Psalm 23 and Job. ᴹMORSE, J. JSOT.S 336: 2001 ⇒75. 69-83.

3293 *Kealy, Seán P.* The Lord is my shepherd. DoLi 51 (2001) 291-302.

3294 **Lively, Bob** God help me through today: Psalm 23 revisited. Harrisburg 2001, Morehouse 146 pp. $18 [BiTod 39,383—Bergant, D.].

3295 *Pyper, Hugh S.* The triumph of the lamb: Psalm 23 and textual fitness. BiblInterp 9 (2001) 384-392.

3296 *Schuman, Niek* Quelques relectures anciennes du psaume 23. ᶠDEURLOO, K. ACEBT.S 2: 2001 ⇒23. 181-191 [Mt 18,12-14; Jn 10].

3297 *Knauf, Ernst Axel* Psalm XXIII 6. VT 51 (2001) 556.

3298 **Baby, Mathew** A holy God among his holy people in a holy place: an exegetico-theological study of Psalm 24. Extr. Diss. Angelicum, ᴰ*Stipe, Jurič*: R 2001, ix; 162 pp. Bibl. 128-156.

3299 *Doyle, Brian* Just you, and I, waiting—the poetry of Psalm 25. OTEs 14 (2001) 199-213.

3300 *Gzella, Holger* Das Kalb und das Einhorn: Endzeittheophanie und Messianismus in der Septuaginta-Fassung von Ps 29(28). Der Septuaginta-Psalter. Herders biblische Studien 32: 2001 ⇒1618. 257-290.

3301 *Habel, Norman C.; Avent, Geraldine* Rescuing earth from a storm god: Psalms 29 and 96-97. The earth story. 2001 ⇒275. 42-50.

3302 *Klaus, Nathan* The pivot pattern—Psalm 34:9-13. BetM 168 (2001) 65-79 Sum. 93. **H.**

3303 *Lorenzin, Tiziano* "Presso di te è la fonte della vita" (Sal. 36,10): una lettura intertestuale. RSEc 19 (2001) 327-340 [Ps 35-41].

3304 *Corsato, Celestino* "È in te la sorgente della vita" (Sal 36[35],10): interpretazioni patristiche. RSEc 19 (2001) 345-360.

3305 *Forti, Tova* The image of the moth: a window on a wisdom psalm Psalm 39. ᶠAHITUV, S. 2001 ⇒1. 319-331. **H.**

3306 *Grelot, Pierre* Le texte du Psaume 39,7 dans la Septante. RB 108 (2001) 210-213.

3307 *Auffret, Pierre* J'ai proclamé la justice: étude structurelle du Ps 40 (et du Ps 70). RivBib 49 (2001) 385-416.

3308 *Kaschewsky, Rudolf Introibo ad altare Dei*—Psalm 42 in der Deutung AUGUSTINS und THOMAS' von Aquin. Una Voce-Korrespondenz 31 (2001) 96-105.

3309 **Dockner, Thomas** "Sicut cerva...": Text, Struktur und Bedeutung von Psalm 42 und 43. ATSAT 67: Erzabtei St. Ottilien 2001, EOS viii; 290 pp. 3-8306-7058-3. Bibl. 263-277.

3310 *Strola, Germana* I Sal 42-43 nella storia dell'esegesi. Gr. 82 (2001) 637-688.

3311 *Kessler, Martin* Psalm 44. [F]DEURLOO, K. 2001 ⇒23. 193-204.

3312 *Couffignal, Robert* Les structures figuratives du Psaume 45. ZAW 113 (2001) 198-208.

3313 *Sandherr, Susanne* "Nach der Weise der Lilien": geistliches Wort zu Psalm 45. GuL 74 (2001) 291-295.

3314 *Bateman, Herbert W.* Psalm 45:6-7 and its christological contributions to Hebrews. TrinJ 22 (2001) 3-21.

3315 *Weber, Beat* Formgeschichtliche und sprachliche Beobachtungen zu Psalm 57. SJOT 15 (2001) 295-305.

3316 **Krawczack, Peter** "Es gibt einen Gott, der Richter ist auf Erden"! (Ps 58,12b): ein exegetischer Beitrag zum Verständnis von Psalm 58. Diss. Bonn 2000/01, [D]*Hossfeld, F.-L.* BBB 132: Bodenheim 2001, Philo xiv; 495 pp. €63.50. 3-8257-0259-6. Bibl. 463-491.

3317 *Wallace, Howard N. Jubilate Deo omnis terra*: God and earth in Psalm 65. The earth story. 2001 ⇒275. 51-64.

3318 **Obinwa, Ignatius** Yaweh my refuge: a critical analyis of Ps 71.Diss. Frankfurt, St. Georgen, [D]*Jüngling, H.-W.* 2001 [RTL 33,633].

3319 **Arneth, Martin** 'Sonne der Gerechtigkeit': Studien zur Solarisierung der Jahwe-Religion im Lichte von Psalm 72. ZAR.B 1: 2000 ⇒ 16,3276. [R]JBL 120 (2001) 541-543 (*Moore, Michael S.*); RBLit 3 (2001) 234-236 (*Moore, Michael S.*).

3320 **Cole, Robert L.** The shape and message of book III: (Psalms 73-89). JSOT.S 307: 2000 ⇒16,3282. [R]StPat 48 (2001) 531-533 (*Lorenzin, Tiziano*); CBQ 63 (2001) 311-312 (*McCann, J. Clinton*).

3321 *Greenfield, Jonas C. 'attā pōrartā bĕʿozkā yam* (Psalm 74:13a). ʿAl kanfei yonah, 2. 2001 <1994> ⇒153. 833-839.

3322 *Jensen, Joseph E.* Psalm 75: its poetic context and structure. CBQ 63 (2001) 416-429.

3323 *MacMillion, Phillip E.* Psalm 78: teaching the next generation. RestQ 43/4 (2001) 219-228.

3324 *Hoppe, Leslie J.* Vengeance and forgiveness: the two faces of Psalm 79. ᶠFITZGERALD, A. CBQ.MS 32: 2001 ⇒31. 1-22.

3325 *Weyde, Karl W.* "Hør, mitt folk, jeg formaner deg": formaningstalen i Sal 81,6b-17. TTK 72 (2001) 161-176.

3326 *Auffret, Pierre* Ta justice dans la terre de l'oubli?: étude structurelle du psaume 88. FolOr 37 (2001) 5-18.

3327 *Janowski, Bernd* Die Toten loben JHWH nicht: Psalm 88 und das alt-testamentliche Todesverständnis. Auferstehung—Resurrection. WUNT 135: 2001 ⇒452. 3-45.

3328 *Nowell, Irene* Psalm 88: a lesson in lament. ᶠFITZGERALD, A.: CBQ. MS 32: 2001 ⇒31. 105-118.

3329 *Hossfeld, Frank-Lothar* Akzentsetzungen der Septuaginta im vierten Psalmenbuch: Ps 90-106 (Ps 89-105 bzw. 106 LXX). Der Septuaginta-Psalter. Herders biblische Studien 32: 2001 ⇒1618. 163-169.

3330 *Vignolo, Roberto* Impararea contare, imparare a pregare: un commento al salmo 90. RCI 82 (2001) 577-591.

3331 *Urbrock, William J.* The earth song in Psalms 90-92. The earth story. 2001 ⇒275. 65-83.

3332 *Knight, Leonard C.* I will show him my salvation: the experience of anxiety in the meaning of Psalm 91. RestQ 43/4 (2001) 280-292.

3333 *Witvliet, Theo* Glauben gibt es nur als Hoffen: Andacht über Psalm 91. ᶠDEURLOO, K. ACEBT.S 2: 2001 ⇒23. 205-209.

3334 *Katz, Reuben M.* A suggested translation of Psalm 91:1-2. JBQ 29/1 (2001) 43-44.

3335 *Görg, Manfred* "Schreiten über Löwen und Otter": Beobachtungen zur Bildsprache in Ps 91,13a. ᶠSCHMUTTERMAYR, G. 2001 ⇒101. 37-48.

3336 *Braulik, Georg* Gottes Ruhe—das Land oder der Tempel?: zu Psalm 95,11. Studien zum Deuteronomium. SBAB 33: 2001 <²1987> ⇒ 129. 203-211.

3337 *Doyle, Brian* Heaven, earth, sea, field and forest: unnatural nature in Ps 96. JNSL 27/2 (2001) 23-44.

3338 *Leene, Henk* The coming of YHWH as king: the complementary character of Psalm 96 and 98. ᶠDEURLOO, K. 2001 ⇒23. 211-228.

3339 *Lescow, Theodor* Die literarische Struktur des Psalms 100. BN 110 (2001) 39-41.

3340 *Macholz, Christian* Psalm 100—Israels Todah-Feier mit den Völkern. ᶠSEYBOLD, K. AOAT 280: 2001 ⇒102. 143-152.

3341 **Heijer, C.J. den** De lievelingspsalm van Jezus: consequenties voor de bijbelse theologie. Baarn 2001, ten Have 48 pp. €6.76. 90-259-5280-1.

3342 *Ntreh, Abotchie* The survival of earth: an African reading of Psalm 104. The earth story. 2001 ⇒275. 98-108.

3343 *Walker-Jones, Arthur* Psalm 104: a celebration of the *Vanua*. The earth story. 2001 ⇒275. 84-97.

3344 *Carbajosa, I.* Salmo 107: unidad, organización y teología. EstB 59 (2001) 451-485.

3345 *Van Grol, Harm* The torah as a work of YHWH: a reading of Psalm 111. ᶠDEURLOO, K. ACEBT.S 2: 2001 ⇒23. 229-236.

3346 *Boendermaker, J.P.* Psalm 113 in LUTHERs Magnificat: opgedragen ter nagedachtenis aan Dirk Monshouwer. ITBT 9/4 (2001) 23-24.

3347 *Müller, Hans-Peter* Psalm 113 und Archilochos 58 D. ᴹCagni, L., 4. SMDSA 61: 2001 ⇒15. 1847-1857.

3348 *Zenger, Erich* Götter- und Götterbildpolemik in Ps 112-113 LXX = Ps 113-115 MT. Der Septuaginta-Psalter. 2001 ⇒1618. 229-255.

3349 *Miller, Robert D.* From the songs of Zion: a literary analysis of psalms 113 and 137. DBM 20/1 (2001) 38-51.

3350 *Bauer, Uwe* Eine literarische Analyse von Psalm CXIV. VT 51 (2001) 289-311.

3351 **Mark, Martin** Meine Stärke und mein Schutz ist der Herr: poetologisch-theologische Studie zu Psalm 118. FzB 92: 1999 ⇒15,3160. ᴿCBQ 63 (2001) 121-122 (*Creach, Jerome F.D.*).

3352 **Berder, Michel** "La pierre rejetée par les bâtisseurs": psaume 118, 22-23 et son emploi dans les traditions juives et dans le NT. EtB 31: 1996 ⇒12,2891... 16,3310. ᴿRTL 32 (2001) 405-407 (*Auwers, Jean-Marie*); RThom 101 (2001) 675-676 (*Ramlot, Francis-Léon*).

3353 *Austermann, Frank* Von der Tora im hebräischen Psalm 119 zum Nomos im griechischen Psalm 118: was die Wiedergabe über die Gesetzestheologie des Übersetzers verrät und was nicht. Der Septuaginta-Psalter. Herders biblische Studien 32: 2001 ⇒1618. 330-347.

3354 **Freedman, David Noel** Psalm 119: the exaltation of Torah. 1999 ⇒ 15,3162. ᴿJJS 52 (2001) 359-360 (*Eaton, John*); JBL 120 (2001) 543-545 (*Borger, J. Todd*).

3355 **Leonhard, Clemens** ISHODAD of Merw's exegesis of the Psalms 119 and 139-147: a study of his interpretation in the light of the Syriac translation of THEODORE of Mopsuestia's commentary. Diss. Wien 1999, ᴰ*Braulik, G.* CSCO.Sub 107; CSCO 585: Lv 2001, Peeters vi; 307 pp. 90-429-0960-9. Bibl. 249-272.

3356 **Auffret, Pierre** Là montent les tribus: étude structurelle de la collection des Psaumes des Montées, d'Ex 15,1-18 et des rapports entre eux. BZAW 289: 1999 ⇒15,3165. ᴿETR 76 (2001) 420-421 (*Hüllstrung, Wolfgang*); Theoforum 32 (2001) 239-240 (*Laberge, Léo*); OTEs 14 (2001) 345-346 (*Ashby, G.W.*).

3357 *Booij, Th.* Psalm CXXII 4: text and meaning. VT 51 (2001) 262-266.

3358 *Botha, P.J.* Social values and the interpretation of Psalm 123. OTEs 14 (2001) 189-198.

3359 **Costacurta, Bruna** Il laccio spezzato: studio del salmo 124. CSB 39: Bo 2001, EDB 229 pp. €18. 88-10-40741-5. Bibl. 199-219.

3360 *Masenya, Madipoane* An eco*bosadi* reading of Psalm 127.3-5. The earth story. 2001 ⇒275. 109-122.

3361 *Weippert, Helga* "Deine Kinder seien wie die Schößlinge von Ölbäumen rund um deinen Tisch!": zur Bildsprache in Psalm 128,3. ᶠSEYBOLD, K.: AOAT 280: 2001 ⇒102. 163-174.

3362 *Mosconi, Franco* Invocando, diventiamo speranza: sul Salmo 130 (129). Qol(I) 94 (2001) 11-15.

3363 *Weber, Beat* "Wenn du Vergehen aufbewahrtest...": linguistische, poetologische und theologische Notizen zu Psalm 130. BN 107/108 (2001) 146-160.

3364 *Booij, Th.* Psalm 130:3-4: the words and their context. ᶠDEURLOO, K.: ACEBT.S 2: 2001 ⇒23. 237-245.

3365 *Flor Serrano, Gonzalo* 'Como un niño a hombros de su madre': observaciones sobre el salmo 131. Communio 34/1 (2001) 93-101.

3366 *Reid, Stephen Breck* Power and practice: performative speech and piety in Psalm 132. Psalms and practice. 2001 ⇒3131. 40-51.

3367 *Doyle, Brian* Metaphora interrupta: Psalm 133. EThL 77 (2001) 5-22.

3368 *Zuckerman, Constantine* Psalms 135:25 in Symmachus' translation on a Jewish inscription from Nicaea (Iznik). SCI 20 (2001) 105-111.

3369 *Jinkins, Michael* The virtues of the righteous in Psalm 137: an exercise in translation. Psalms and practice. 2001 ⇒3131. 164-201.

3370 *Krüger, Thomas* 'An den Strömen von Babylon...': Erwägungen zu Zeitbezug und Sachverhalt in Psalm 137. ᶠDENZ, A. 2001 ⇒21. 79-84.

3371 *Maré, L.P.* Psalm 137: 'n (on)christelike psalm?. VeE 22 (2001) 341-351.

3372 *Zakovitch, Yair* 'By the rivers of Babylon': Psalm 137—memory in the shadow of trauma. ᶠAHITUV, S. 2001 ⇒1. 184-204. **H.**

3373 *Harder, Lydia* Reading Psalm 139: opting for a realistic reading. ᶠJANZEN, W. 2001 ⇒54. 128-137.

3374 *Paas, Stefan* A textual note on Psalm 143,6 (אֶרֶץ־עֲיֵפָה—"a weary land"?). ZAW 113 (2001) 415-418.

3375 *Bielefeld, Placida; Brüning, Christian* Psalm 148 im Gebet der Kirche. EuA 77 (2001) 273-284.

3376 *Fernández Marcos, Natalio* David the adolescent: on Psalm 151. ᶠPIETERSMA, A. JSOT.S 332: 2001 ⇒87. 205-217.

E7.1 **Job**, *textus, commentarii*

3377 *Backhaus, Knut* Im Hörsaal des Tyrannus (Apg 19,9): von der Lang-
lebigkeit des Evangeliums in kurzatmiger Zeit. ThGl 91 (2001) 4-23.

3378 Das Buch Hiob. Fischer Taschenbuch 14504: Fra 2000, Fischer 90
pp. 3-596-14504-X. Mit einer Einleitung von *Louis de Bernières*.

3379 **Chauvin, Jacques** Job l'insoumis: Dieu n'est jamais celui qu'on
croit. Poliez-le-Grand 1997, Moulin 89 pp. ^REstB 59 (2001) 106-107
(Asenjo, J.).

3380 **Japhet, Sara** The commentary of Rabbi Samuel Ben Meir (RASH-
BAM) on the book of Job. 2000 ⇒16,3341. ^RJSQ 8 (2001) 80-104
(Lockshin, Martin). **H**.

3381 **Murphy, Roland Edmund** The book of Job: a short reading. 1999
⇒15,3185; 16,3342. ^RScrB 31/1 (2001) 41-42 *(Dale, John)*;
HebStud 42 (2001) 353-355 *(Szlos, M. Beth)*.

3382 **Sitaramayya, K.B.** The marvel and the mystery of pain: a new interpretation of the book of Job. Bangalore 2001, M.C.C. 164 pp.
Rs150/$12.

3383 **Stadelmann, Luís** O itinerário espiritual de Jó. São Paulo 1997, Loyola 124 pp. 85-15-01519-6. Bibl. 121-122.

3384 **Ternay, Henri de** O livro de Jó: da provação à conversão, um longo
processo. Comentário Bíblico/AT: Petrópolis 2001, Vozes 333 pp.
85-326-2593-2.

3385 **Vogels, Walter** Giobbe: l'uomo che ha parlato bene di Dio. CinB
2001, San Paolo 252 pp. €17.56.

3386 **Wharton, James A.** Job. 1999 ⇒15,3188; 16,3346. ^RRBLit 3
(2001) 237-240 *(Cheney, Michael S.)*; HBT 23 (2001) 101-102
(Gowan, Donald E.).

E7.2 *Job: themata*, **Topics**... *Versiculi*, **Verse numbers**

3387 **Asurmendi Ruiz, Jesús Maria** Job: experiencia del mal, experiencia
de Dios. Estella (Navarra) 2001, Verbo Divino 165 pp. 8481694339.

3388 **Barsotti, Divo** Meditazione sul libro di Giobbe. Bibbia e liturgia 40:
Brescia 2001, Queriniana 134 pp. €9.30. 88-399-1640-7.

3389 **Berrigan, Daniel** Job: and death no dominion. 2000 ⇒16,3348.
^RPIBA 24 (2001) 105-107 *(McConvery, Brendan)*.

3390 *Bochet, M.* Job après Job: destinée littéraire d'une figure biblique. Le
livre et le rouleau 9: 2000 ⇒16,3349. ^RVieCon 73 (2001) 340-341
(Luciani, Didier).

3391 **Chirpaz, Fr.** Job: la force d'espérance. P 2001, Cerf 193 pp. €18.29.
       2-204-06647-8.

3392 *Gilbert, Maurice* Les livres sapientiaux de l'Ancien Testament: le
       livre de Job. EeV 43; 44; 45; 46 (2001) 13-17; 14-20; 12-16; 12-17.

3393 *Gutridge, Coralie A.* The sacrifice of fools and the wisdom of
       silence: Qoheleth, Job and the presence of God. ᴹWEITZMAN, M.
       JSOT.S 333: 2001 ⇒113. 83-99 [Qoh 5,1-7].

3394 *Hoffer, Victoria* Illusion, allusion, and literary artifice in the frame
       narrative of Job. ᴹMORSE, J. JSOT.S 336: 2001 ⇒75. 84-99.

3395 *Langer, Michael* Alte Weisheiten für junge Menschen: Gedanken
       zum Buch Hiob im Religionsunterricht der gymnasialen Oberstufe.
       ᶠSCHMUTTERMAYR, G. 2001 ⇒101. 457-480.

3396 *Lawrie, Douglas* How critical is it to be historically critical?: the case
       of the composition of the book of Job. JNSL 27/1 (2001) 121-146.

3397 *Limet, H.* La pensée religieuse des Sumériens et le livre de Job.
       TEuph 22 (2001) 115-127.

3398 *Loader, James Alfred* Hiob—Antwort oder Rätsel?;
3399 Gott mit eigenen Augen sehen: Hiob und die Natur. Begegnung mit
       Gott. 2001 ⇒175. 113-137/99-112.

3400 **Maldamé, J.-M.** Le scandale du mal: une question posée à Dieu. Ini-
       tiations: P 2001, Cerf 132 pp. €16.77. 2-204-06680-X.

3401 *Masenya, Madipoane* Between unjust suffering and the 'silent' God:
       Job and HIV/AIDS sufferers in South Africa. Missionalia 29 (2001)
       186-199 Sum. 186.

3402 *Mathews, Susan F.* All for nought: my servant Job. The bible on suf-
       fering. 2001 ⇒326. 51-71.

3403 **Oeming, Manfred; Schmid, Konrad** Hiobs Weg: Stationen von
       Menschen im Leid. BThSt 45: Neuk 2001, Neuk 144 pp. 3-7887-
       1860-9.

3404 *Pathak, Zakia* A pedagogy for postcolonial feminists. The postmod-
       ern bible reader. 2001 <1992> ⇒287. 219-232.

3405 *Perraymond, Myla* Giobbe: annotazioni iconografiche e tradizione
       esegetica. SMSR 67 (2001) 229-252.

3406 **Popma, K.J.** A battle for righteousness: the message of the book of
       Job. ᵀ*Van Meggelen, Jack*: Belleville, Ontario 1998, Essence 278 pp.
       CDN$19. ᴿCTJ 36 (2001) 147-148 (*Cooper, John W.*).

3407 **Pyeon, Yohan** 'You have not spoken what is right about me': inter-
       textuality in the book of Job. Diss. Claremont Graduate Univ. 2001
       290 pp. 9987690.

3408 *Quezada del Río, Javier* El eslabón perdido de Job. Qol 25 (2001)
       89-108.

3409 *Raguse, Hartmut* Psychoanalytische Erwägungen zum Hiob-Buch.
       WzM 53/1 (2001) 19-35.

3410 *Sitaramayya, K.B.* Suffering in the book of Job: its nature and function: a Hindu approach. VSVD 42 (2001) 497-503.

3411 *Susaimanickam, Jebamalai* Protest: the language of prophecy. JDh 26 (2001) 311-335.

3412 *Sutherland, Martin* "Bringing their gods in their hands": Job and absolute orthodoxy. Pacifica 14 (2001) 144-158.

3413 *Watts, James W.* The unreliable narrator of Job. ᴹMORSE, J. JSOT.S: 336: 2001 ⇒75. 168-180.

3414 *Wilken, Robert L.* Interpreting Job allegorically: the "Moralia" of GREGORY the Great. ProEc 10 (2001) 213-226.

3415 *Zaradija Kis, Antonija* Levijatan i Behemot u hrvatskim glagoljskim brevijarima. BoSm 71 (2001) 485-496. **Croatian**.

3416 *Elliger, Katharina* Ijob & seine Frau: Buch Ijob, Kapitel 1 und 2. Schön bist du. 2001 ⇒274. 162-166.

3417 *Strauß, Hans* Theologische, form- und traditionsgeschichtliche Bemerkungen zur Literargeschichte des (vorderen) Hiobrahmens: Hiob 1-2. ZAW 113 (2001) 553-565.

3418 *McGinnis, Claire M.* Playing the devil's advocate in Job: on Job's wife. ᴹMORSE, J. 2001 ⇒75. 121-141 [Job 1,6-22; 2,1-10].

3419 *Oesch, Josef M.* Ijob 3,3a: "gezeugt" oder "geboren"?: ein Beitrag zur Struktur von Ijob 3. PzB 10 (2001) 121-130.

3420 **Snoek, J.** Antwoorden op het lijden: een bijdrage aan de discussie over contextueel bijbellezen: Job 4-5 in het licht van opvattingen van Nicaraguaanse pinkstergelovigen. 2000 ⇒16,3385. ᴿExchange 30 (2001) 195-196 (*Gooren, Henri*).

3421 **Egger-Wenzel, Renate** 'Von der Freiheit Gottes, anders zu sein': die zentrale Rolle der Kapitel 9 und 10 für das Ijobbuch. 1998 ⇒14, 2984; 15,3238. ᴿTJT 17 (2001) 287-288 (*McLaughlin, John L.*).

3422 *Loader, James Alfred* Job 9:5-10 as a quasi-hymn. OTEs 14 (2001) 76-88.

3423 *Chrostowski, Waldemar* Ludzka cielesność jako obraz Boga. CoTh 70/4 (2000) 5-19 [Job 10,8-13]. P.

3424 *Lacerenza, Giancarlo* 'Con penna di ferro e piombo' (Gb 19,24). ᴹCAGNI, L., 3: SMDSA 61: 2001 ⇒15. 1667-1680.

3425 **Tremblay, Hervé** Job 19,25-27 dans la Septante et chez les Pères grecs: unanimité d'une tradition. Diss. Ottawa, Dom. 2001, ᴰLaberge, L. [RTL 33,634].

3426 *Snapp, Kevin* Job's displaced kidneys: Job 19:27. JBQ 29 (2001) 125-126.

3427 **Tchimboto, Bonifácio** 'A fé dos oprimidos': Jb. 24 e o confronto com as tradições biblicas sobre o pobre. Diss. Urbaniana 2001, ᴰRizzi, G. [RTL 33,641].

3428 *Riede, Peter* Spinnennetz oder Mottengespinst?: zur Auslegung von Hiob 27,18. BN 110 (2001) 76-85.

3429 *Kunz, Andreas* Der Mensch auf der Waage: die Vorstellung vom Gerichtshandeln Gottes im ägyptischen Totenbuch (Tb 125) und bei Hiob (Ijob 31). BZ 45 (2001) 235-250.

3430 *Gold, Sally L.* Making sense of Job 37.13: translation strategies in 11Q10, Peshitta and the rabbinic targum. ᴹWEITZMAN, M.: JSOT.S 333: 2001 ⇒113. 282-302.

3431 *Kegler, Jürgen* 'Gürte wie ein Mann deine Lenden...'—die Gottesreden im Ijob-Buch als Aufforderung zur aktiven Auseinandersetzung mit dem Leid. Gesammelte Aufsätze. BEAT 48: 2001 <1994> ⇒ 167. 278-293 [Job 38-41].

3432 *Viviers, H.* Body and nature in Job. OTEs 14 (2001) 510-524 [Job 38,1-42,6].

3433 *Burns, John Barclay* Is the Ibis yet wise?: a reconsideration of Job 38:36. ProcGLM 21 (2001) 131-136.

3434 *Patton, Corrine L.* The beauty of the beast: Leviathan and Behemoth in light of Catholic theology. ᴹMORSE, J. JSOT.S 336: 2001 ⇒75. 142-167 [Job 40-41].

E7.3 *Canticum Canticorum*, Song of Songs, Hohelied, *textus, comm.*

3435 **Bergant, Dianne** The Song of Songs. Berit Olam: ColMn 2001, Liturgical xvi; 123 pp. $30. 0-8146-5069-4. Bibl. 107-109.

3436 **Bosetti, Elena** Cantico dei Cantici: "Tu che il mio cuore ama": estasi e ricerca. Fame e sete della parola: CinB 2001, San Paolo 111 pp. 88-215-4342-0. Bibl. 107-108.

3437 ᴱ**Brenner, Athalya; Fontaine, Carole R.** The Song of Songs. Feminist companion to the bible (2nd ser.) 6: 2000 ⇒16,3398. ᴿHeyJ 42 (2001) 356-357 (*Van den Eynde, S.*); ThLZ 126 (2001) 744-746 (*Reinmuth, Eckart*); MillSt 47 (2001) 140-141 (*Mangan, Celine*).

3438 **Duarte Castillo, Raúl** El Cantar de los Cantares: estudio introductorio. Más allá de la letra 1: México 2001, Palenque-UPM. ᴿQol 27 (2001) 87-89 (*Figueroa Jácome, Leonor*); 89-91 (*Gómez Noguez, Miriam Aurora*); 91-96 (*López R., Ricardo*); 96-97 (*Maciel del Río, Carlos*).

3439 ᵀ**Hill, Robert C.** THEODORET of Cyrus: commentary on the Song of Songs. Early Christian Studies 2: Brisbane 2001, Centre for Early Christian Studies xi; 131 pp. AUS$43. 0-9577-4832-9 [RHE 98, 118s—Auwers, Jean-Marie].

3440 Das Hohelied Salomos. Fischer Taschenbuch 14506: Fra 2000, Fischer 44 pp. 3-596-14506-6. Einleitung von *Antonia S. Byatt.*

3441 **Longman, Tremper** Song of Songs. NIC: GR 2001, Eerdmans xvi; 238 pp. $35. 08028-2543-5. Bibl. 70-83. [R]RBBras 18 (2001) 492-93.

3442 **Lorenzin, Tiziano** Cantico dei Cantici: introduzione e commento. Padova 2001, EMP 164 pp. €9.50. 88-250-1021-4.

3443 **Murphy, Roland E.; Huwiler, Elizabeth** Proverbs, Ecclesiastes, Song of Songs. NIBC.OT 12: 1999 ⇒15,3284. [R]TJT 17 (2001) 295-297 (*Heskett, Randall*); EvQ 73 (2001) 343-344 (*Rudman, Dominic*).

3444 **Provan, Iain W.** Ecclesiastes, Song of Songs. NIV application commentary: GR 2001, Zondervan 400 pp. $25. 0-310-21372-X [ThD 49,187—Heiser, W. Charles].

3445 [ET]**Schlageter, Johannes** Petri Johannis OLIVI: expositio in Canticum Canticorum. 1999 ⇒15,3260; 16,3414. [R]RHEF 87 (2001) 205-206 (*Paul, Jacques*).

3446 *Schulz-Flügel, Eva* Canticum canticorum. BVLI 45 (2001) 20-24.

3447 [ET]**Schützeichel, Rudolf; Meineke, Birgit** Die älteste Überlieferung von WILLIRAMs Kommentar des Hohen Liedes: Edition—Übersetzung—Glossar. Studien zum Althochdeutschen 39: Gö 2001, Vandenhoeck & R. 357 pp. €62. 3-525-20354-3 [EuA 79,345].

E7.4 **Canticum**, *themata, versiculi*

3448 *Asiedu, F.B.A.* The Song of Songs and the ascent of the soul: AMBROSE, AUGUSTINE, and the language of mysticism. VigChr 55 (2001) 299-317.

3449 *Black, Fiona C.* Nocturnal egression: exploring some margins of the Song of Songs. Postmodern interpretations. 2001 ⇒229. 93-104.

3450 Jean-Baptiste CHASSIGNET: le Cantique des cantiques. Trévoux 2000, Compagnie de Trévoux [LV(L) 258,76].

3451 **De Ena Tardi, Jean Emmanuel** Le conflit des interprétations sur le sens du Cantique des Cantiques: essai théorique et pratique d'une herméneutique articulée du sens au texte: sens textuel, sens directionnel et cadre du texte. Diss. Fribourg 2001, [D]*Schenker, A.* [RTL 33,631].

3452 *Elliger, Katharina* Das Hohelied. Schön bist du. 2001 ⇒274. 98-104.

3453 *Genovese, Armando* Note sull'uso del Cantico dei Cantici in Sant'Agostino. Aug. 41 (2001) 201-212.

3454 **Horine, Steven C.** Interpretive images in the Song of Songs: from wedding chariots to bridal chambers. Studies in the Humanities: Literature-Politics-Society 55: NY 2001, Lang xviii; 235 pp. $57. 0-8204-5156-8. Bibl. 199-220.

3455 **Ka-lun, Leung** Chinese spiritual interpretations of the Song of Songs. Hong Kong 2001, Alliance Bible Seminary xiii; 261 pp. C.

3456 *Keel, Othmar* Zwei Arten von Liebe: biblische Liebeslyrik zwischen Mesopotamien und Ägypten. WUB 21 (2001) 27-33.

3457 *Landy, Francis* Beauty and the enigma: an inquiry into some interrelated episodes of the Song of Songs. Beauty and the enigma. JSOT.S 312: 2001 <1980> ⇒171. 35-95.

3458 *Mazzinghi, Luca* 'Quanto sei bella, amica mia!': il Cantico dei Cantici e la bellezza del corpo. La bellezza. PSV 44: 2001 ⇒240. 35-50.

3459 *Mosès, Stéphane* L'Eros e la legge. L'Eros e la legge. Schulim Vogelmann 80: 2001 ⇒185. 67-78.

3460 *Müller, Hans-Peter* Der Libanon in altorientalischen Quellen und im Hohenlied: Paradigma einer poetischen Topographie. ZDPV 117 (2001) 116-128.

3461 *Reinhardt, Klaus* Die Auslegung des Hohenliedes in der spanischen Mystik und im deutschen Pietismus: TERESA von Avila und GOTTFRIED Arnold. TThZ 110 (2001) 195-213.

3462 **Roberts, D. Phillip** 'Let me see your form': seeking poetic structure in the 'Song of Songs'. Diss. Westminster Theol. Sem. 2001, 812 pp. 3010609.

3463 **Rossi, Rita** Un eterno dialogo d'amore: spunti di meditazione sul Cantico dei Cantici. 2000 ⇒16,3446. [R]Immacolata Mediatrix 1/1 (2001) 140-141 (*Zangheratti, Massimiliano M.*).

3464 *Ryan, Thomas F.* Sex, spirituality, and pre-modern readings of the Song of Songs. Horizons 28/1 (2001) 81-104.

3465 *Uehlinger, Christoph* Anthologie oder Dramaturgie?: ein außergewöhnliches biblisches Buch: das Hohelied der Liebe. WUB 21 (2001) 35-39.

3466 [T]**Verdeyen, Paul; Fassetta, Raffaele** BERNARD de Clairvaux: sermons sur le Cantique, 2: 16-32. SC 431: 1998 ⇒14,3052. [R]CCMéd 44 (2001) 203-204 (*Callerot, Françoise*).

3467 **Walsh, Carey Ellen** Exquisite desire: religion, the erotic, and the Song of Songs. 2000 ⇒16,3449. [R]CBQ 63 (2001) 535-536 (*Carr, David M.*).

3468 **Winsor, Ann Roberts** A king is bound in the tresses: allusions to the Song of Songs in the fourth gospel. 1999 ⇒15,3294. [R]AThR 83 (2001) 890-891 (*Conway, Colleen M.*).

3469 *Young, Frances M.* Sexuality and devotion: mystical readings of the Song of Songs. Theology and sexuality 14 (2001) 80-96.

3470 *Des Rochettes, Jacqueline, al.*, Les mots du Cantique: une polysémie symphonique. BLE 102 (2001) 167-180 [Cant 1,2-4; 3,1-5].

3471 *Regalzi, Giuseppe* "Bella come una grazia, terribile come...": a proposito di Ct 6,4. Henoch 23 (2001) 139-145.

3472 *Eichner, Jens; Scherer, Andreas* "Die >Teiche< von Hesbon": eine exegetisch-archäologische Glosse zu Cant 7,5ba. BN 109 (2001) 10-14.

E7.5 *Libri sapientiales*—Wisdom literature

3473 *Bechmann, Ulrike* Von der Weisheit der Frauen zur Frau Weisheit: zur Entwicklung der Weisheitstheologie im Alten Testament. WuA(M) 42 (2001) 105-110.

3474 *Bennema, Cornelis* The strands of wisdom tradition in intertestamental Judaism: origins, developments and characteristics. TynB 52 (2001) 61-82.

3475 *Böhmisch, Franz* Weisheitliche Krisenbewältigung bei Hermann HESSE und in der alttestamentlichen Weisheitsliteratur. PzB 10 (2001) 85-103.

       ^E**Brenner, A.** Wisdom and Psalms. 1998 ⇒3134.

3476 *Cannuyer, Christian* A propos de la Maât égyptienne et de la ḥokmâh biblique, figures féminines de la sagesse. ^FDESROCHES NOBLECOURT, C. 2001 ⇒22. 17-34.

3477 *Chrostowski, Waldemar* Wychowanie i kształcenie młodego pokolenia w przedwygnaniowym Izraelu. ^FGLEMP, J. 2001 ⇒36. 23-38. **P.**

3478 **Collins, John Joseph** Jewish wisdom in the Hellenistic age. 1997 ⇒ 13,3129... 16,3463. ^ROTEs 14 (2001) 548-550 (*Nel, Philip J.*).

3479 **Conti, Martino** La sapienza personificata negli elogi veterotestamentari (Pr 8; Gb 28; Sir 24; Bar 3; Sap 7). SPAA 36: R 2001, Antonianum 233 pp. €18.07. 88-7257-046-8.

3480 *D'Agostino, Franco* Le sezioni 4 E 4A del 'Dialogo umoristico babilonese sul pessimismo' (un tentativo di interpretazione). ^MCAGNI, L., 1. SMDSA 61: 2001 ⇒15. 135-145.

3481 *Dell, Katharine J.* Wisdom literature. The Blackwell companion to the Hebrew Bible. Blackwell companions to religion 3: 2001 ⇒653. 418-431.

3482 *Eichler, Eckhard* Zur Datierung und Interpretation der Lehre des Ptahhotep. ZÄS 128 (2001) 97-107.

3483 *Fischer, S.* Egyptian personal piety and Israel's wisdom literature. AcTh(B) 21/1 (2001) 1-23.

3484 **Gesche, Petra D.** Schulunterricht in Babylonien im ersten Jahrtausend v. Chr. AOAT 275: Müns 2001, Ugarit-Verlag xxxv; 820 pp. 3-927120-93-6. Bibl. xvii-xxxv; 14 pl.

3485 *Gilbert, Maurice* Il concetto di tempo ('t) in Qohelet e Ben Sira. Il libro del Qohelet. 2001 ⇒453. 69-89;

3486 Les livres sapientiaux de l'Ancien Testament: présentation générale. EeV 38 (2001) 14-19;

3487 La 'sapienza' biblica. Storia della scienza, 1: la scienza antica: EPetruccioni, G.: R 2001, Istituto della Enciclopedia Italiana. 373-377 [AcBib 10,802].

3488 **Gimeno Granero, José Carlos** La sabiduria en Proverbos y Eclesiastico. Diss. Madrid 2001, DBusto Saiz, J.R. [RTL 33,632].

3489 *Gowan, Donald E.* Wisdom. Justification, 1: second temple Judaism. WUNT 2/140: 2001 ⇒251. 215-239.

3490 *Greenfield, Jonas C.* The wisdom of Aḥiqar. 'Al kanfei yonah, 1. 2001 <1995> ⇒153. 334-343.

3491 EHabel, Norman C.; Wurst, Shirley The earth story in wisdom traditions. The Earth Bible 3: Shf 2001, Sheffield A. 213 pp. £18. 1-84-127-086-5. Bibl. 190-203.

3492 *Hanspach, Alexander* Die Rede von der Gottebenbildlichkeit in der alttestamentlichen Weisheitsliteratur. FGROß, W. 2001 ⇒38. 65-72.

3493 *Lemaire, André* Schools and literacy in ancient Israel and early Judaism. The Blackwell companion to the Hebrew Bible. Blackwell companions to religion 3: 2001 ⇒653. 207-217.

3494 *Lips, Hermann von* Jüdische Weisheit und griechische Tugendlehre: Beobachtungen zur Aufnahme der Kardinaltugenden in hellenistisch-jüdischen Texten (Aristeasbrief, Sapientia Salomonis, 4. Makkabäerbuch). Weisheit, Ethos und Gebot. BThSt 43: 2001 ⇒492. 29-60 [Wisd 8,7].

3495 *Loader, James Alfred* The significant deficiency of revelation in Wisdom. OTEs 14 (2001) 235-259;

3496 Weisheit aus dem Volk für das Volk;

3497 Narren erklären, Weise nicht. Begegnung mit Gott. Wiener alttestamentliche Studien 3: 2001 ⇒175. 211-235/341-355..

3498 EMills, Watson Early; Wilson, Richard Francis Wisdom writings. Mercer Commentary on the Bible 3: Macon, GA 2001, Mercer University Press lviii; 250 pp. $20. 0-86554-508-1.

3499 *Perdue, Leo G.* The vitality of wisdom in second temple Judaism during the Persian period. Passion. 2001 ⇒295. 119-154.

3500 **Poirier, J.M.** Sur les pistes du bonheur: la sagesse biblique. Toulouse 2000, Source de Vie 151 pp. €13.57.

3501 *Sanders, Jack T.* When sacred canopies collide: the reception of the Torah of Moses in the wisdom literature of the second-temple period. JSJ 32 (2001) 121-136.

3502 *Spieckermann, Hermann* Ludlul bēl nēmeqi und die Frage nach der Gerechtigkeit Gottes. Gottes Liebe. 2001 <1998> ⇒215. 103-118.

3503 **Terstriep, Dominik** Weisheit und Denken: Stilformen sapientialer
      Theologie. AnGr 283: Roma 2001, E.P.U.G. 525 pp. €36. 88-7652-
      902-0.

3504 ^T**Vernus, Pascal** Sagesses de l'Égypte pharaonique. La Salamandre:
      P 2001, Imprimerie nationale 414 pp. 2-7433-0332-8. Prés., notes;
      Bibl. 393-397.

3505 *Vonach, Andreas* Between transience and fear of God: drafts and
      aspects of human fulfilment in Old Testament wisdom literature. Di-
      sputatio philosophica 3 (2001) 169-179 [Prov 2,1-5; 2,20-3,2; Wisd
      3,1-4; 4,7-14];

3506 "Das Auge wird nicht satt zu sehen und das Ohr nicht voll vom Hö-
      ren" (Koh 1,8b): vom theologischen Umgang mit sich verändernden
      gesellschaftlichen, kulturellen und politischen Gegebenheiten inner-
      halb der alttestamentlichen Weisheitstradition. Die Götter kommen
      wieder: Religion—Religiosität—neue Götter. ^E**Vonach, Andreas**:
      Theologische trends 9: Thaur 2001, Thaur 3-85400-112-6. 116-136;

3507 Glaube im Umbruch: die alttestamentliche Weisheitsliteratur als Ant-
      wort auf eine sich wandelnde Gesellschaft. Wort zum Leben. 2001 ⇒
      284. 79-94.

3508 *Winston, David* Hellenistic Jewish philosophy <1997>;

3509 Freedom and determinism in Greek philosophy and Jewish Hellenis-
      tic wisdom <1974>. Ancestral philosophy. 2001 ⇒228. 11-32/44-56.

E7.6 **Proverbiorum liber**, *themata, versiculi*

3510 **Bartholomew, Craig** Reading Proverbs with integrity. C 2001,
      Grove 23 pp. £2.50. 1-85174-485-1 [SBET 21,125—Meredith, D.].

3511 *Bellia, Giuseppe; Passaro, Angelo* Proverbi e Qohelet: eredità e pro-
      spettive di ricerca. Ho Theológos 19 (2001) 115-132.

3512 **Bridges, Charles** Proverbs. Crossway Classic Commentaries:
      Wheaton, IL 2001, Crossway xiv; 15-286 pp. 1-58134-300-0.

3513 *Calduch-Benages, Núria* Il kairós dei Proverbi. Ho Theológos 19
      (2001) 287-298.

3514 **Clifford, Richard J.** Proverbs: a commentary. OTL: 1999 ⇒15,
      3344; 16,3513. ^RThLZ 126 (2001) 615-616 (*Krispenz, Jutta*).

3515 **Cook, Johann** The Septuagint of Proverbs. VT.S 69: 1997 ⇒13,
      3166; 15,3345. ^RVT 51 (2001) 274-276 (*Aitken, J.K.*).

3516 *Cook, Johann* Intertextual relationships between the Septuagint of
      Psalms and Proverbs. ^FPIETERSMA, A.: 2001 ⇒87. 218-228;

3517 The ideology of Septuagint Proverbs. X Congress IOSCS. SBL.SCSt
      51: 2001 ⇒499. 463-479.

3518 **Frydrych, Tomás** Living under the sun: examination of Proverbs and Qoheleth. VT.S 90: Lei 2001, Brill xv; 255 pp. 90-04-12315-6.

3519 **Fuhs, Hans Ferdinand** Das Buch der Sprichwörter: ein Kommentar. FzB 95: Wü 2001, Echter 396 pp. €19.80. 3-429-02335-1;

3520 Sprichwörter NEB: Kommentar zum Alten Testament mit der Einheitsübersetzung, Lfg. 35. Wü 2001, Echter 189 pp. €19.80. 3-429-02133-2.

3521 *Gilbert, Maurice* Les livres sapientiaux de l'Ancien Testament: le livre des Proverbes. EeV 39; 40; 41; 42 (2001) 13-18; 11-15; 14-20; 16-19.

3522 *Gitay, Yehoshua* The rhetoric and logic of wisdom in the book of Proverbs. JNSL 27/2 (2001) 45-56.

3523 *Grelot, Pierre* Les Proverbes d'Aḥîqar. RB 108 (2001) 511-528.

3524 ᵀ**Hamonville, David-Marc d'** La Bible d'Alexandrie, 17: Les Proverbes. 2000 ⇒16,3520. ᴿContacts 53 (2001) 180-182 (*Larchet, Jean-Claude*); REAug 47 (2001) 165-167 (*Bady, Guillaume*).

3525 **Hyun, Changhak** A study of the translation technique of Peshitta Proverbs. Diss. Wisconsin 2001, 236 pp. 3012397.

3526 **Lisimba, Mukumbuta** Kongo proverbs and the origins of Bantu wisdom. 1999 ⇒15,3356. ᴿAnthr. 96 (2001) 278-280 (*Kabuta, N.S.*).

3527 *Loader, James Alfred* Lernen im Indikativ;

3528 Weise rufen zur Ordnung. Begegnung mit Gott. Wiener alttestamentliche Studien 3: 2001 ⇒175. 201-209/185-199.

3529 *Murphy, Roland E.* Can the book of Proverbs be a player in 'biblical theology'?. BTB 31 (2001) 4-9.

    Murphy, R. Proverbs... Song of Songs 1999 ⇒3443.

3530 **Murphy, Roland Edmund** Proverbs. WBC 22: 1998 ⇒14,3101; 16, 3528. ᴿJBL 120 (2001) 545-547 (*Dell, Katharine J.*).

3531 **Owan, K.J.N.** Moments for meditation. African Proverbial Wisdom 2: Enugu 2001, Ambassador 52 pp. 978-049-077-X [BOTSA 13, 20—Holter, Knut].

3532 *Rofé, Alexander* The 'virtuous wife' (אשת חיל), γυνὴ συνετή, and the editing of the book of Proverbs. ᶠAHITUV, S. 2001 ⇒1. 382-390. **H.**

3533 *Saebø, Magne* Ny aktualitet for gammel visdom: nyere arbeider til Proverbia. TTK 72 (2001) 151-160.

3534 *Spieckermann, Hermann* What is wisdom?: the evidence in the book of Proverbs. SvTK 77 (2001) 13-21.

3535 *Stek, John H.* Proverbs: an introduction. CTJ 36 (2001) 365-371.

3536 *Waard, Jan de* Some unusual translation techniques employed by the Greek translator(s) of Proverbs. Helsinki perspectives. SESJ 82: 2001 ⇒1617. 185-193.

3537 *Weigl, Michael* Compositional strategies in the Aramaic sayings of Ahikar: columns 6-8. ᶠDION, P.-E. 3. JSOT.S 326: 2001 ⇒25. 22-82.

3538 **Fox, Michael V.** Proverbs 1-9. AncB 18A: 2000 ⇒16,3518. [R]JThS
52 (2001) 752-755 (*Wood, D.R.*); RExp 98 (2001) 449-450 (*Biddle,
Mark E.*); CBQ 63 (2001) 718-720 (*Burns, Camilla*).

3539 **Miles, Johnny Edward** When is a wise man a fool?: a semiotic analysis of Proverbs 1-9 as satire. Diss. Baylor 2001, 222 pp. 3003090.

3540 **Müller, Achim** Proverbien 1-9: der Weisheit neue Kleider. BZAW
291: 2000 ⇒16,3543. [R]OLZ 96 (2001) 563-566 (*Delkurt, Holger*).

3541 *Paul, Martin* Die "fremde Frau" in Sprichwörter 1-9 und die "Gelieb-
te" des Hohenliedes: ein Beitrag zur Intertextualität. BN 106 (2001)
40-46 [Cant 3,1-5].

3542 **Schäfer, Rolf** Die Poesie der Weisen: Dichotomie...in Proverbien 1-
9. WMANT 77: 1999 ⇒15,3369; 16,3540. [R]RBLit 3 (2001) 240-244
(*Brown, William P.*).

3543 **Yoder, Christine Roy** Wisdom as a woman of substance: a socioeconomic reading of Proverbs 1-9 and 31:10-31. Diss. Princeton, Sem.
1999-2000. BZAW 304: B 2001, De Gruyter xiii; 165 pp. €58. 3-11-
017007-8. ; Bibl. 115-141. [R]ET 112 (2001) 397-398 (*Rodd, C.S.*).

3544 *Tepox, Alfredo* The importance of becoming wise: Proverbs 1.1-7.
BiTr 52 (2001) 216-222.

3545 *Vignolo, Roberto* Pregnanza e limiti della pedagogia sapienziale di
Proverbi 2. [F]MARIN, B. 2001 ⇒68. 27-49.

3546 *Skarsaune, Oskar* Ordspråkene 8,22-31 som kristologisk tekst. TTK
72 (2001) 113-130.

3547 *Mies, Françoise* "Dame Sagesse" en Proverbes 9 une personnifica-
tion féminine?. RB 108 (2001) 161-183.

3548 *Greenfield, Jonas C.* The seven pillars of wisdom (Prov. 9:1)—a mis-
translation. 'Al kanfei yonah, 2. 2001 <1985> ⇒153. 766-773.

3549 **Gjorgjevski, Gjoko** Enigma degli enigmi: un contributo allo studio
della composizione della raccolta salomonica (Pr 10,1-22,16). TGr.T
72: R 2001, E.P.U.G. 298 pp. 88-7652-884-9. Bibl. 271-290.

3550 **Heim, Knut Martin** Like grapes of gold set in silver: an interpretation of proverbial clusters in Proverbs 10:1-22:16. BZAW 273: B
2001, De Gruyter xiv; 378 pp. €100.21. 311-016376-4. Bibl. 331-
349.

3551 **Scherer, Andreas** Das weise Wort und seine Wirkung: eine Untersu-
chung zur Komposition und Redaktion von Proverbia 10,1-22,16.
WMANT 83: 1999 ⇒15,3377; 16,3554. [R]ThLZ 126 (2001) 374-377
(*Krispenz, Jutta*).

3552 *Bronznick, Nachum M.* The antithesis between עצל and ישרים in Prov.
15,19. Beit Mikra 165 (2001) 171-176. **H**.

3553 *Chiesa, Bruno* Ebr. *delef ṭōrēd*—una strana coppia per un bel prover-
bio. [M]CAGNI, L., 3. 2001 ⇒15. 1423-1449 [Prov 19,13; 27,15].

3554 *Niccacci, Alviero* Proverbi 22,17-23,11 tra Egitto, Mesopotamia e Canaan. ᴹCAGNI, L., 4. SMDSA 61: 2001 ⇒15. 1859-1891.

3555 *Emerton, J.A.* The teaching of Amenemope and Proverbs XXII 17-XXIV 22: further reflections on a long-standing problem. VT 51 (2001) 431-465.

3556 *Hurowitz, Avigdor Victor* Thirty (?) of admonition and knowledge': structural and exegetical notes to 'the words of the wise' (Proverbs 22:17-24). ᶠAHITUV, S. 2001 ⇒1. 146-160 [Zech 7]. **H**.

3557 *Heskett, Randall J.* Proverbs 23:13-14. Interp. 55 (2001) 181-184.

3558 *Shlomo, Sigal* 'rūaḥ ṣāfōn tᵉḥōlēl gašem, ufānîm nizᵉāmîm lᵉšōn sāter' (Proverbs 25:23)—review. BetM 166 (2001) 268-282 Sum. 285. **H**.

3559 *Hurowitz, Victor Avigdor* Proverbs 29.22-27: another unnoticed alphabetic acrostic. JSOT 92 (2001) 121-125.

3560 *Richter, Hans-Friedemann* Hielt Agur sich für den Dümmsten aller Menschen? (Zu Prov 30,1-4). ZAW 113 (2001) 419-421.

3561 *Steinmann, Andrew E.* Three things..four things...seven things: the coherence of Proverbs 30:11-33 and the unity of Proverbs 30. HebStud 42 (2001) 59-66.

3562 *Hurowitz, Victor Avigdor* The seventh pillar—reconsidering the literary structure and unity of Proverbs 31. ZAW 113 (2001) 209-218.

3563 *Brockmöller, Katrin* "Chiasmus und Symmetrie": zur Diskussion um eine sinnvolle Struktur in Spr 31,10-31. BN 110 (2001) 12-18.

3564 *Cholin, Marc* Structure de Proverbes 31,10-31. RB 108 (2001) 331-348.

3565 **Szlos, Mary Beth Bruskewicz** Metaphor in Proverbs 31:10-31: a cognitive approach. Diss. New York, Union 2001, ᴰO'Connor, M. 336 pp. 3009998 [RTL 33,634].

3566 **Wolters, Al** The song of the valiant woman: studies in the interpretation of Proverbs 31:10-31. Carlisle 2001, Paternoster ix (2); 154 pp. 1-84227-008-7.

E7.7 *Ecclesiastes*—**Qohelet**; *textus, themata, versiculi*

Bellia, G; *Passaro, A.* Proverbi e Qohelet 2001 ⇒3511.

3567 **Brandscheidt, Renate** Weltbegeisterung und Offenbarungsglaube: literar-, form- und traditionsgeschichtliche Untersuchung zum Buch Kohelet. TThSt 64: 1999 ⇒15,3399; 16,3579. ᴿThRv 97 (2001) 110-114 (*Willmes, Bernd*); BZ 45 (2001) 304-306 (*Zenger, Erich*).

3568 **Brown, William P.** Ecclesiastes. Interpretation: 2000 ⇒16,3563. ᴿOTEs 14 (2001) 173-174 (*Venter, Pieter M.*)

3569 ᵀ**Fry, G.** JÉRÔME: commentaire de l'Ecclésiaste. CPF 79-80: P 2001, Migne 355 pp. €28.87. 2-908-58744-0.

3570 *Gilbert, Maurice* Les livres sapientiaux de l'Ancien Testament: Qohélèt. EeV 47 (2001) 18-22.

3571 **Longman III, Tremper** The book of Ecclesiastes. NICOT: 1998 ⇒ 14,3125... 16,3567. [R]RBLit 3 (2001) 250-252 (*Laniak, Timothy S.*).

3572 **Motos López, María del Carmen** Las vanidades del mundo: comentario rabínico al Eclesiastés. Biblioteca Midrásica 22: Estella (Navarra) 2001, Verbo Divino 571 pp. 84-8169-453-3. Bibl. 565-571.

   Murphy, R. Proverbs, Ecclesiastes... 1999 ⇒3443.

3573 Der Prediger Salomo. Fischer Taschenbuch 14505: Fra 2000, Fischer 43 pp. 3-596-14505-8. Mit einer Einleitung von *Doris Lessing*.

   Provan, I. Ecclesiastes, Song of Songs 2001 ⇒3444.

3574 *Puech, Émile* Qohelet a Qumran. Il libro del Qohelet. 2001 ⇒453. 144-170.

3575 **Ravasi, Gianfranco** Qohelet: il libro più originale e "scandaloso" dell'Antico Testamento. La parola di Dio: CinB [3]2001, San Paolo 474 pp. 88-215-1624-5.

3576 [E]**Schoors, Antoon** Qohelet in the context of wisdom. BEThL 136: 1998 ⇒14,266... 16,3570. [R]ThRv 97 (2001) 218-220 (*Backhaus, Franz Josef*); RivBib 49 (2001) 355-358 (*Prato, Gian Luigi*).

3577 *Schwab, George M.* Woman as the object of Qohelet's search. AUSS 39 (2001) 73-84.

3578 *Seow, Choon-Leong* Theology when everything is out of control. Interp. 55 (2001) 237-249.

3579 *Támez, Elsa* Ecclesiastes: a reading from the periphery. Interp. 55 (2001) 250-259.

3580 **Támez, Elsa** Da hasste ich das Leben: eine Lektüre des Buches Kohelet. Luzern 2001, Exodus 176 pp. 3-905577-50-X.

3581 *Van der Toorn, Karel* Echoes of Gilgamesh in the book of Qohelet?: a reassessment of the intellectual sources of Qohelet. [F]VEENHOF, K. 2001 ⇒111. 503-514.

3582 *Yoreh, Tzemah* 'Mirth what does it'? (Eccl. II,2). BetM 167 (2001) 353-370 Sum. 381. **H**.

3583 **Zimmer, Tilmann** Zwischen Tod und Lebensglück: eine Untersuchung zur Anthropologie Kohelets. 1999 ⇒15,3430. [R]ThRv 97 (2001) 108-110 (*Backhaus, Franz Josef*); CBQ 63 (2001) 735-736 (*Sneed, Mark*).

3584 *Anderson, William H.U.* A critique of the standard interpretations of the joy statements in Qoheleth. JNSL 27/2 (2001) 57-75.

3585 **Bartholomew, Craig G.** Reading Ecclesiastes. AnBib 139: 1998 ⇒ 14,3139...16,3577. [R]Bib. 82 (2001) 280-2 (*Van Leeuwen, Raymond*).

3586 *Bellia, Giuseppe; Passaro, Angelo* Qohelet, ovvero la fatica di conoscere. Il libro del Qohelet. 2001 ⇒453. 357-390.

3587 *Bellia, Giuseppe* Il libro del Qohelet e il suo contesto storico-antropologico. Il libro del Qohelet. 2001 ⇒453. 171-216.

3588 *Berger, Benjamin Lyle* Qohelet and the exigencies of the absurd. BiblInterp 9 (2001) 141-179.

3589 *Brown, William P.* "Whatever your hand finds to do": Qoheleth's work ethic. Interp. 55 (2001) 271-284.

3590 **Burkes, Shannon** Death in Qoheleth and Egyptian biographies of the late period. SBL.DS 170: 1999 ⇒15,3400. [R]HebStud 42 (2001) 356-358 (*Henze, Matthias*).

3591 *Buss, Martin J.* A projection for Israelite historiography: with a comparison between Qohelet and Nagarjuna. [F]MILLER, J. JSOT.S 343: 2001 ⇒74. 61-68.

3592 *Carasik, Michael* Exegetical implications of the Masoretic cantillation marks in Ecclesiastes. HebStud 42 (2001) 145-165.

3593 *Chopineau, Jacques* Le livre de Qohelet et son image dans l'exégèse contemporaine. Quand le texte devient parole. 2001 ⇒135. 105-113.

3594 **Christensen, Leise** Modsigelsens nødvendighed: kontinuitet via ambiguitet i Ecclesiastes [The necessity of contradiction: continuity via ambiguity in Ecclesiastes]. Diss. Aarhus 2001, [D]*Rosendal, B.*, 192 pp.

3595 **Christianson, Eric S.** A time to tell: narrative strategies in Ecclesiastes. JSOT.S 280: 1998 ⇒14,3142; 16,3581. [R]JThS 52 (2001) 184-186 (*Dell, Katharine*); JBL 120 (2001) 360-362 (*Lee, Eunny*).

3596 **Claustre Solé i Auguets, Maria** Déu, una paraula sempre oberta: el concepte de Déu en el Qohèlet. Sant Pacià 65: 1999 ⇒15,3402. [R]RivBib 49 (2001) 236-238 (*D'Alario, Vittoria*).

3597 *Curkpatrick, Stephen* A disciple for our time: a conversation. Interp. 55 (2001) 285-291.

3598 **Fischer, Stefan** Die Aufforderung zur Lebensfreude im Buch Kohelet und seine Rezeption der ägyptischen Harfnerlieder. [T]*Herz, Dina; Rahveh-Klemke, Smadar*: Wiener Alttestamentliche Studien 2: 1999 ⇒15,3404. [R]BiOr 58 (2001) 663-667 (*Schoors, A.*).

3599 **Fox, Michael Vass** A time to tear down and a time to build up: a rereading of Ecclesiastes. 1999 ⇒15,3405; 16,3584. [R]TS 62 (2001) 155-157 (*Wimmer, Joseph F.*); Bib. 82 (2001) 108-111 (*Schoors, Antoon*); EvQ 73 (2001) 345-346 (*Rudman, Dominic*).

3600 *Frades, Eduardo* ¿No valdrá el hombre más que esta su vida? (una lectura del libro de Qohélet). Iter 26 (2001) 125-157.

Frydrych, T. Living under the sun 2001 ⇒3518.

3601 *Gigliotti, Marcus A.* Qoheleth: portrait of an artist in pain. The bible on suffering. 2001 ⇒326. 72-92.

3602 *Iovino, Paolo* "Omnia vanitas": da Qohelet a Paolo. Il libro del Qohelet. 2001 ⇒453. 337-356.

3603 *Krüger, Thomas* Alles Nichts?: zur Theologie des Buches Qohelet. ThZ 57 (2001) 184-195.

3604 *Manfredi, Silvana* Qohelet in dialogo: una sfida intertestuale. Il libro del Qohelet. 2001 ⇒453. 293-313.

3605 **Mazzinghi, Luca** "Ho cercato e ho esplorato": studi sul Qohelet. Collana biblica: Bo 2001, EDB 461 pp. €33.05. 88-10-22116-8.

3606 *Pahk, Johan Y.-S.* Qohelet e le tradizioni sapienziali del Vicino Oriente Antico. Il libro del Qohelet. 2001 ⇒453. 117-143.

3607 *Pampaloni, Massimo* O gesto interrompido e o grão de trigo: reflexões sobre a morte e sobre o morrer a partir do Qohelet e do mistério pascal. PerTeol 33 (2001) 87-104.

3608 *Passaro, Angelo* Le possibili letture di un libro difficile. Il libro del Qohelet. 2001 ⇒453. 21-39.

3609 **Rose, Martin** Rien de nouveau: nouvelles approches du livre de Qohéleth. OBO 168: 1999 ⇒15,3386; 16,3600. ᴿEstAg 36 (2001) 143-144 (*Mielgo, C.*); BiOr 58 (2001) 232-236 (*Schoors, A.*); RBLit 3 (2001) 253-255 (*Lavoie, Jean-Jacques*).

3610 ᴱ**Rose, Martin** Situer Qohéleth: regards croisés sur un livre biblique. 1999 ⇒15,3385. ᴿLTP 57 (2001) 319-325 (*Lavoie, Jean J.*).

3611 **Rudman, Dominic** Determinism in the book of Ecclesiastes. JSOT.S 316: Shf 2001, Sheffield A. 226 pp. £40/$64. 1-84127-153-5. Bibl. 207-213.

3612 **Salyer, Gary D.** Vain rhetoric: private insight and public debate in Ecclesiastes. JSOT.S 327: Shf 2001, Sheffield A. 443 pp. $95. 1-84-127-181-0. Bibl. 403-431.

3613 *Schoors, Antoon* L'ambiguità della gioia in Qohelet. Il libro del Qohelet. 2001 ⇒453. 276-292.

3614 *Perrin, Nicholas* Messianism in the narrative frame of Ecclesiastes?. RB 108 (2001) 37-60 [Qoh 1,1; 12,9-14].

3615 *Rizzi, Giovanni* Tradizione e intertestualità nell'ermeneutica giudaica di lingua greca e aramaica di Qo 1,1-3: una prospettiva di ricerca. Il libro del Qohelet. 2001 ⇒453. 227-255.

3616 **Spaller, Christina** 'Die Geschichte des Buches ist die Geschichte seiner Auslöschung...': die Lektüre von Koh 1,3-11 in vier ausgewählten Kommentaren. Diss. Salzburg 1998. Exegese in userer Zeit 7: Müns 2001, Lit ix; 291 pp. €25.90. 3-8258-5395-0.

3617 *Vignolo, Roberto* Maschera e sindrome regale: interpretazione ironico-psicanalitica di Qoh 1,12-2,26. Teol(Br) 26 (2001) 12-64.

3618 *Lenchak, Timothy* Puzzling passages: Qoh 2:22-23. BiTod 39 (2001) 48.

3619 *Brisson, E. Carson* Ecclesiastes 3:1-8. Interp. 55 (2001) 292-295.

3620 *Loader, James Alfred* Kohelet 3,2-8—ein "Sonett" im Alten Testament. Begegnung mit Gott. 2001 ⇒175. 5-8.

3621 *Loretz, Oswald* Eiliges Gebet, Eid und Gelübde in Ugarit und Israel nach RS 15.10 und Qohelet 4,17-5,6; 8,2-3. Kult, Konflikt. AOAT 285: 2001 ⇒387. 99-121.

3622 *Fletcher, Douglas K.* Ecclesiastes 5:1-7. Interp. 55 (2001) 296-298.

3623 *Rofé, Alexander* La formula sapienziale "non dire..." e l'angelo di Qo 5,5. Il libro del Qohelet. 2001 ⇒453. 217-226.

3624 *D'Alario, Vittoria* Struttura e teologia del libro del Qohelet. Il libro del Qohelet. 2001 ⇒453. 256-275 [Qoh 6,10-12].

3625 *Bianchi, Francesco* "Un fantasma al banchetto della sapienza?": Qohelet e il libro dei Proverbi a confronto. Il libro del Qohelet. 2001 ⇒ 453. 40-68 [Qoh 7,1-14].

3626 *Andrews, Susan R.* Ecclesiastes 7:1-19. Interp. 55 (2001) 299-301.

3627 *Mazzinghi, Luca* Qohelet tra giudaismo ed ellenismo: un'indagine a partire da Qo 7,15-18;

3628 *Simian-Yofre, Horacio* Conoscere la sapienza: Qohelet e Genesi 2-3. Il libro del Qohelet. 2001 ⇒453. 90-116/314-336 [Qoh 7,23-29].

3629 *Pahk, Johan Yeong Sik* A syntactical and contextual consideration of ᵓš in Qoh. IX 9. VT 51 (2001) 370-380.

3630 *Chrostowski, Waldemar* Alegoryczne przedstawienie starości i śmierci w Koh 12,1-7. ᶠJANKOWSKI, A. 2001 ⇒53. 91-108. **P**.

3631 *Slemmons, Timothy Matthew* Ecclesiastes 12:1-13. Interp. 55 (2001) 302-304.

3632 *Dulin, Rachel Z.* "How sweet is the light": Qoheleth's age-centered teachings. Interp. 55 (2001) 260-270 [Qoh 12,2-5].

E7.8 *Liber Sapientiae*—**Wisdom of Solomon**

3633 **Berrigan, Daniel** Wisdom: the feminine face of God. Franklin, WI 2001, Sheed & Ward 224 pp. $25. 1-58051-100-7. Contrib. by *Robert McGovern* [ThD 49,260—W. Charles Heiser].

3634 **Hübner, Hans** Die Weisheit Salomons: Liber Sapientiae Salomonis. ATD, Apokryphen 4: 1999 ⇒15,3442; 16,3625. ᴿBib. 82 (2001) 434-437 (*Mazzinghi, Luca*).

3635 **Kepper, Martina** Hellenistische Bildung im Buch der Weisheit: Studien zur Sprachgestalt und Theologie der Sapientia Salomonis. BZAW 280: 1999 ⇒15,3455. ᴿJSJ 32 (2001) 308-310 (*Beentjes, P.C.*); ThLZ 126 (2001) 270-272 (*Wagner, Christian*).

3636 **McGlynn, Moyna** Divine judgement and divine benevolence in the book of Wisdom. WUNT 2/139: Tü 2001, Mohr S. xi; 294 pp. €49. 3-16-147598-4. Bibl. 246-264.

3637 **Pereira, Ney Brasil** Livro da Sabedoria: aos governantes, sobre a ju-
      stiça. Comentário Bíblico AT: 1999 ⇒15,3443. ᴿEstudos Bíblicos 69
      (2001) 88-90 (*Andiñach, Pablo*).
3638 *Rosenstock, Heidi* Was ist Weisheit?. WzM 53 (2001) 242-244.
3639 ᴱᵀ**Scarpat, Giuseppe** Libro della Sapienza, 3. 1999 ⇒15,3445; 16,
      3626. ᴿBib. 82 (2001) 430-434 (*Mazzinghi, Luca*); CivCatt 152/2
      (2001) 91-94 (*Prato, G.L.*).
3640 *Volgger, David* Die Adressaten des Weisheitsbuches. Bib. 82 (2001)
      153-177.
3641 *Winston, David* The book of Wisdom's theory of cosmogony.
      Ancestral philosophy. 2001 <1971> ⇒228. 59-77;
3642 Wisdom in the Wisdom of Solomon <1993>;
3643 The sage as mystic in the Wisdom of Solomon <1990>. Ancestral
      philosophy 2001 ⇒228. 83-98/99-113.

3644 *Cheon, Samuel* Three characters in the Wisdom of Solomon 3-4.
      JSPE 12 (2001) 105-113.
3645 *Ponizy, Bodgan* Recognition of God according to the book of Wis-
      dom 13:1-9. PJBR 1/2 (2001) 201-206.
3646 *Schmitt, Armin* Heilung und Leben nach Weish 16,5-14 vor dem Hin-
      tergrund der hellenistischen Zeit. Gerechtigkeit und Leben. BZAW
      296: 2001 ⇒56. 53-86.

ᴱ7.9 *Ecclesiasticus, Siracides*; **Wisdom of Jesus Sirach**

ᴱ**Muraoka, T.** The...Dead Sea Scrolls...Ben Sira 1997 ⇒569.
3647 **Sauer, Georg** Jesus Sirach / Ben Sira. ATD.Apokryphen 1: 2000 ⇒
      16,3650. ᴿJSJ 32 (2001) 344-346 (*Beentjes.P.C.*); ThLZ 126 (2001)
      752-754 (*Marböck, Johannes*).
3648 ᴱ**Talmon, Shemaryahu** Masada VI... the Ben Sira Scroll from
      Masada. 1999 ⇒15,3482; 16,3651. ᴿOr. 69 (2000) 186-188
      (*Beentjes, Pancratius*).
3649 *Thiele, Walter* Sirach / Ecclesiasticus. BVLI 45 (2001) 24-26.
3650 **Thiele, Walter** Sirach (Ecclesiasticus): 8. Lief.: Sir 20,1-23,6. BVLI
      11/2: FrB 2001, Herder 561-640 pp. 3-451-00438-5.
3651 *Van Peursen, Wido* The alleged retroversions from Syriac in the He-
      brew text of Ben Sira revisited: linguistic perspectives. KUSATU 2
      (2001) 47-95.
3652 **Wagner, Christian** Die Septuaginta-Hapaxlegomena im Buch Jesus
      Sirach: Untersuchungen zur Wortwahl und Wortbildung unter beson-
      derer Berücksichtigung des textkritischen und übersetzungstechni-

schen Aspekts. BZAW 282: 1999 ⇒15,3485; 16,3652. ᴿThRv 97 (2001) 491-493 (*Schmitt, Armin*).

3653 *Calduch-Benages, Núria* La situació actual dels estudis sobre el llibre del Siràcida (1996-2000). RCatT 26 (2001) 391-398;

3654 Gli ornamenti sacerdotali nel Siracide: studio del vocabolario. ᴹCAGNI, L., 3: SMDSA 61: 2001 ⇒15. 1319-1330.

3655 *Ebner, Martin* "Weisheitslehrer"—eine Kategorie für Jesus?: eine Spurensuche bei Jesus Sirach. Der neue Mensch in Christus. QD 190: 2001 ⇒239. 99-119.

3656 ᴱ**Egger-Wenzel, Renate; Krammer, Ingrid** Der Einzelne und seine Gemeinschaft bei Ben Sira. BZAW 270: 1998 ⇒14,3230; 16,3657. ᴿThLZ 126 (2001) 735-736 (*Sauer, Georg*).

3657 *Kaiser, Otto* Das Verständnis des Todes bei Ben Sira. NZSTh 43 (2001) 175-192.

3658 *Marböck, Johannes* Gerechtigkeit Gottes und Leben nach dem Sirachbuch: ein Antwortversuch in seinem Kontext. Gerechtigkeit und Leben. BZAW 296: 2001 ⇒56. 21-52.

3659 **Wicke-Reuter, Ursel** Göttliche Providenz und menschliche Verantwortung bei Ben Sira und in der frühen Stoa. BZAW 298: 2000 ⇒ 16,3670. ᴿBiblInterp 9 (2001) 342-343 (*Beentjes, P.C.*).

3660 *Winston, David* Theodicy in Ben Sira and Stoic philosophy. Ancestral philosophy. 2001 <1989> ⇒228. 35-43.

3661 *Winter, Michael M.* Jewish and christian collaboration in ancient Syria. ᴹWEITZMAN, M. JSOT.S 333: 2001 ⇒113. 355-364.

3662 *Wright, Benjamin G.; Camp, Claudia V.* "Who has been tested by gold and found perfect?": Ben Sira's discourse of riches and poverty. Henoch 23 (2001) 153-174.

3663 *Calduch-Benages, Núria* La recompensa del just: estudi de la versió siríaca de Sir 1. El text. Scripta Biblica 3: 2001 ⇒310. 39-60.

3664 **Calduch-Benages, Nuria** Un gioiello di sapienza: leggendo Siracide 2. Cammini nello Spirito, Biblica 45: Mi 2001, Paoline 173 pp. 88-315-2203-5. Bibl. 167-173.

3665 *Rogers, Jessie* Wisdom—woman or angel in Sirach 24?. JNSL 27/1 (2001) 71-80.

3666 *Spatafora, Andrea* La fonction du narrateur en Siracide 24. Theoforum 32 (2001) 303-320.

3667 *Vetrali, Tecle* "Quanti bevono di me avranno ancora sete" (Sir 24,20): sorgente inesauribile e acqua sempre nuova. RSEc 19 (2001) 361-374 [Jn 4,14].

3668 **Linder, Agnes** Lingua tripla, giogo ferreo e l'oro della parola: studio
esegetico di Sir 28,13-26 in parallelo con testi sapienziali egiziani.
Diss. Roma, Angelicum 2001; [D]*Jurič, S.* [RTL 33,633].

3669 *Kügler, Joachim* Der Sohn als Abbild des Vaters: kulturgeschichtliche Notizen zu Sir 30,4-6. BN 107/108 (2001) 78-92.

3670 *Beentjes, P.C.* Scripture and scribe: Ben Sira 38:34c-39:11. [F]DEUR-
LOO, K. ACEBT.S 2: 2001 ⇒23. 273-280.

3671 **Liesen, Jan** Full of praise: an exegetical study of Sir 39,12-35. JSJ.S
64: 2000 ⇒16,3677. [R]JSJ 32 (2001) 106-8 (*Beentjes, Pancratius C.*).

3672 *Reymond, Eric D.* Sirach 40,18-27 as 'Tôb-Spruch'. Bib. 82 (2001)
84-92.

3673 *Greenfield, Jonas C.* Ben Sira 42.9-10 and its talmudic paraphrase.
'Al kanfei yonah, 2. 2001 <1990> ⇒153. 633-639.

3674 *Calduch-Benages, Nuria* L'inno al creato in Ben Sira (Sir 42,15-43,
33). La bellezza. PSV 44: 2001 ⇒240. 51-66.

3675 *Reymond, Eric D.* Prelude to the praise of the ancestors, Sirach 44:1-
15. HUCA 72 (2001) 1-14.

3676 *Witte, Markus* "Mose, sein Andenken sei zum Segen" (Sir 45,1)—das
Mosebild des Sirachbuchs. BN 107/108 (2001) 161-186.

3677 **Mulder, Otto** Simon de Hogepriester in Sirach 50: een exegetisch
onderzoek naar de betekenis van Simon de Hogepriester, als climax
van de lof der vaderen in Ben Sira's concept van de geschiedenis van
Israel. Diss. Utrecht. 2000; [D]*Beentjes, P.C.*: Almelo 2001, O. Mulder
464 pp. $30. 90-9014-167-7 [RB 109,158].

3678 *Xeravits, Géza* The figure of David in the book of Ben Sira. Henoch
23 (2001) 27-38 [Sir 51,12].

VII. Libri prophetici VT

E8.1 Prophetismus

3679 **Arthur, David** A smooth stone: biblical prophecy in historical perspective. Lanham 2001, University Press of America x; 416 pp. $74.
0-7618-2074-4. Bibl. 405-408.

3680 *Barstad, Hans M.* Den gammeltestamentlige profetismen belyst ved
paralleller fra Mari. TTK 72 (2001) 51-68.

3681 **Baumann, Gerlinde** Liebe und Gewalt: die Ehe als Metapher für das
Verhältnis JHWH—Israel in den Prophetenbüchern. SBS 185: 2000
⇒16,3692. [R]YESW 9 (2001) 272-273 (*Siebert-Hommes, Jopie*);

CBQ 63 (2001) 304-305 (*Petersen, David L.*); ThLZ 126 (2001) 268-270 (*Zimmermann, Ruben*).

3682 *Berges, Ulrich* Personifications and prophetic voices of Zion in Isaiah and beyond. The elusive prophet. OTS 45: 2001 ⇒485. 54-82.

3683 *Blenkinsopp, Joseph* The social roles of prophets in early Achaemenid Judah. JSOT 93 (2001) 39-58.

3684 **Blenkinsopp, Joseph** Une histoire de la prophétie en Israël. [T]*Desjardins, M.* 1993 ⇒9,3462; 11/1,2087. [R]Istina 46 (2001) 429-432 (*Couteau, Elisabeth*).

3685 **Brueggemann, Walter** The prophetic imagination. Mp [2]2001 <1978>, Augsburg xxiv; 151 pp. $16. 0-8006-3287-7. Bibl. 147-148 [BiTod 39,379—Bergant, Dianne].

3686 [E]**Brzegowy, Tadeusz**, *al.*, Wielki swiat starotestamentalnych proroków: v.1: Od poczatków profetyzmu do Niewoli Babilonskiej; v.2: Od konca Niewoli Babilonskiej i proroctw Deutero-Izajasza do apokaliptyki Daniela. Wprowadzenie w mysl i wezwanie ksiag Biblijnych 4-5: Wsz 2001, Wyd. Uniw. Wyszynskiego 2 vols. 83-7072-. **P.**

3687 **Butting, Klara** Prophetinnen gefragt: die Bedeutung der Prophetinnen im Kanon aus Tora und Prophetie. Diss.-Habil. Bochum 2000/01, [D]*Ebach, J.* Biblisch-feministische Texte 3: Wittingen 2001, Erev-Rav 232 pp. €12.78. 3-932810-15-5 .

3688 *Carroll, Robert P.* City of chaos, city of stone, city of flesh: urbanscapes in prophetic discourses. Urbanism and prophecy. JSOT.S 330: 2001 ⇒271. 45-61 [Isa 24-27].

3689 *Charpin, Dominique* Prophètes et rois dans le Proche-Orient amorrite. Prophètes et rois. LeDiv: 2001 ⇒292. 21-53.

3690 *Chopineau, Jacques* Les prophètes et le temple. Quand le texte devient parole. AnBru 6: 2001 ⇒135. 91-96.

3691 *Coninck, Frédéric de* Débat démocratique et prophétisme biblique: convergences et divergences. FV 100/3 (2001) 3-13.

3692 *Coote, Robert B.* Proximity to the central Davidic citadel and the greater and lesser prophets. Urbanism and prophecy. JSOT.S 330: 2001 ⇒271. 62-70.

3693 *Deissler, Alfons* Prophet und Volk Gottes. [F]LEHMANN, K. 2001 ⇒63. 33-42.

3694 **Dempsey, Carol J.** The prophets: a liberation-critical reading. 2000 ⇒16,3708. [R]JThS 52 (2001) 176-179 (*Guest, Deryn*); CBQ 63 (2001) 104-106 (*Brueggemann, Walter*).

3695 *Epp-Tiessen, Daniel* The LORD has truly sent the prophet. [F]JANZEN, W. 2001 ⇒54. 175-185.

3696 *Fenton, Terry* Israelite prophecy: characteristics of the first protest movement. The elusive prophet. OTS 45: 2001 ⇒485. 129-141.

3697 *Fischer, Georg* Betroffen von Gottes Wort: Prophetie damals und heute. Wort zum Leben. 2001 ⇒284. 41-55.

3698 *Giorgio, Giovanni* La profezia come comprensione della rivelazione. Ricerche teologiche 12/2 (2001) 5-13.

3699 **Girard, Marc** De Moïse à Jésus: l'option politique chez les prophètes et dans le monde actuel. Parole d'actualité 10: Montréal 2001, Médiaspaul 207 pp. €20. 2-89420-483-3.

3700 *Gitay, Yehoshua* Marginal remarks. BetM 167 (2001) 376-380 Sum. 381. **H.**

3701 **Glazov, Gregory Yuri** The bridling of the tongue and the opening of the mouth in biblical prophecy. JSOT.S 311: Shf 2001, Sheffield A. 449 pp. £58/$90. 1-85075-600-7. Bibl. 384-423.

3702 *Gonçalves, Francolino J.* Les 'Prophètes écrivains' étaient-ils des nabi³im?. ᶠDION, P.-E. 1. JSOT.S 324: 2001 ⇒25. 144-185.

3703 *Grabbe, Lester L.* Introduction and overview to "Every city shall be forsaken": urbanism and prophecy in ancient Israel and the Near East. Urbanism and prophecy. JSOT.S 330: 2001 ⇒271. 15-34.

3704 **Grilli, M.** Il pathos della parola: i profeti di Israele. 2000 ⇒16,3718. ᴿCivCatt 152/1 (2001) 223-225 (*Scaiola, D.*).

3705 *Gunkel, Hermann* The prophets: oral and written. Water for a thirsty land. Fortress classics in bibl. studies: 2001 <1923> ⇒155. 85-133.

3706 **Hardmeier, Christof** Prophetie im Streit vor dem Untergang Judas... II Reg 18-20 und Jer 37-40. BZAW 187: 1990 ⇒6,3916... 9,3711. ᴿRBBras 18 (2001) 475-478.

3707 **Junco Garza, Carlos** Palabra sin fronteras: los profetas de Israel. México 2001, Paulinas 750 pp. ᴿActBib 38 (2001) 40-41 (*Sivatte, R. de*).

3708 *Kegler, Jürgen* Prophetisches Reden von Zukünftigem. Gesammelte Aufsätze. BEAT 48: 2001 <1978, 1981> ⇒167. 10-45;

3709 Prophetischer Widerstand. Gesammelte Aufsätze. BEAT 48: 2001 <1989> ⇒167. 171-213.

3710 *Kizhakkeyil, Sebastian* Mission of the church: inspiration and model from the prophets. ETJ 5/1 (2001) 3-22.

3711 *Knauf, Ernst A.* Prophetie und Dissidenz. Ref. 50 (2001) 200-204 [BuBB 35,57];

3712 Mythos Kanaan: oder: Sex, Lügen und Propheten-Schriften. WUB 21 (2001) 41-44.

3713 *Koch, Klaus* Latter prophets: the major prophets. The Blackwell companion to the Hebrew Bible. 2001 ⇒653. 353-368.

3714 *Lang, Bernhard* Prophet, Priester, Virtuose. Max WEBERs 'Religionssystematik'. ᴱ**Kippenberg, Hans G.; Riesebrodt, Martin**: Tü 2001, Mohr S. 167-191.

3715 **Lange, Armin** Vom prophetischen Wort zur Schriftauslegung: Studien zur Traditions- und Redaktionsgeschichte innerprophetischer Konflikte im Alten Testament. Diss.-Habil. Tübingen 2001, ᴰ*Blum, E.* [RTL 33,632].

3716 *Lemaire, André* Introduction *Prophètes et rois*;

3717 Prophètes et rois dans les inscriptions ouest-sémitiques (IXe-VIe siècle av.J.-C.);

3718 Épilogue: la fin des prophètes?. Prophètes et rois. LeDiv: 2001 ⇒ 292. 11-18/85-115/299-301.

3719 *Malamat, Abraham* Addendum to Luigi Cagni's collection of Mari prophecies. ᴹCᴀɢɴɪ, L., 2. SMDSA 61: 2001 ⇒15. 631-634;

3720 The historical background of two prophecies of the nations. History of biblical Israel. 2001 <1951> ⇒ 182. 370-380 [Jer 47; Zech 9,1-6].

3721 *Manzi, Franco* Il discernimento profetico dei segni di Dio: spunti teologico-biblici alla luce di Isaia 7,1-17 e del vangelo secondo Luca. ScC 129 (2001) 213-271.

3722 **Matthews, Victor Harold** Social world of the Hebrew prophets. Peabody, MASS 2001, Hendrickson xi; 205 pp. $25. 1-56563-417-9. Bibl. 183-190.

3723 **McKenna, Megan** Prophets: words of fire. Mkn 2001, Orbis vii; 271 pp. $15. 1-57075-364-4. Bibl. 269-271.

3724 *McKenzie, Steven L.* Jacob in the Prophets. ꟳPᴜʀʏ, A. de. MoBi 44: 2001 ⇒89. 339-357.

3725 **McLaughlin, John** The marzeah in the prophetic literature: references and allusions in light of extra-biblical evidence. VT.S 39: Lei 2001, Brill xviii; 264 pp. €73. 90-04-12006-8. Bibl. 218-240.

3726 *Minette de Tillesse, Caetano* [Os profetas do AT.] RBBras 18/1-2 (2001) 3-180.

3727 *Möller, Karl* Words of (in-)evitable certitude?: reflections on the interpretation of prophetic oracles of judgment. ꟳTʜɪsᴇʟᴛᴏɴ, A. 2001 ⇒106. 352-386.

3728 *Otto, Randall E.* The prophets and their perspective. CBQ 63 (2001) 219-240.

3729 **Parpola, Simo** Assyrian prophecies. 1997 ⇒13,3409... 16,3746. ᴿWO 31 (2001) 31-45 (*Frahm, Eckart*).

3730 *Petersen, David L.* Introduction to prophetic literature. NIntB 6: 2001 ⇒1865. 1-23.

3731 *Panafit, Lionel* Du peuple d'Israël à la communauté des juifs: la construction religieuse de l'ethnie juive: à propos du *Judaïsme antique* de Max Wᴇʙᴇʀ. REJ 160 (2001) 189-211.

3732 *Rathinam, Selva* Prophetism in the Hebrew Bible. VJTR 65 (2001) 802-815.

3733 *Regt, Lénart de* Person shift in prophetic texts: its function and its rendering in ancient and modern translations. The elusive prophet. OTS 45: 2001 ⇒485. 214-231 [Jer 3,16; 25,4; 7,25; Hos 2,4-25; 11; Amos 8-9; Zeph 2,12; 3].

3734 *Rouillard-Bonraisin, Hedwige* Ésaï, Jérémie et la politique des rois de Juda. Prophètes et rois. LeDiv: 2001 ⇒292. 177-224.

3735 *Schmid, Konrad; Steck, Odil Hannes* Restoration expectations in the prophetic tradition of the Old Testament. Restoration. JSJ.S 72: 2001 ⇒319. 41-81.

3736 *Schmitt, Hans-Christoph* Prophetie und Tradition: Beobachtungen zur Frühgeschichte des israelitischen Nabitums <1977>;

3737 Das sogenannte vorprophetische Berufungsschema: zur 'geistigen Heimat' des Berufungsformulars von Ex 3,9-12; Jdc 6,11-24 und I Sam 9,1-10,16 <1992>. Theologie in Prophetie. 2001 ⇒209. 3-18/59-73.

3738 **Schultz, Richard L.** The search for quotation: verbal parallels in the prophets. JSOT.S 180: 1999 ⇒15,3588; 16,3752. ᴿThLZ 126 (2001) 516-8 (*Nogalski, James*); RBLit 3 (2001) 200-3 (*Pietsch, Michael*).

3739 **Seidl, Theodor** "Der Becher in der Hand des Herrn": Studie zu den prophetischen "Taumelbecher"-Texten. ATSAT 70: St. Ottilien 2001, EOS vii; 170 pp. 3-8306-7084-2. Bibl. 151-159.

3740 **Smith, W. Robertson** †1894. The prophets of Israel and their place in history. New Brunswick, NJ 2001, Transaction cxxii; 146 pp. $35. 0-76580-7483. Introd. *Robert A. Jones* [ThD 49,190—Heiser, W.C.].

3741 *Spieckermann, Hermann* Dies irae: der alttestamentliche Befund und seine Vorgeschichte. Gottes Liebe. 2001 <1989> ⇒215. 34-46.

3742 **Stamos, Colleen** The killing of the prophets: reconfiguring a tradition. Diss. Chicago 2001, ᴰ*Smith, J.* 291 pp. 3019971 [RTL 33,641].

3743 **Steck, Odil Hannes** Gott in der Zeit entdecken: die Prophetenbücher des Alten Testaments als Vorbild für Theologie und Kirche. BThSt 42: Neuk 2001, Neuk xiv; 249 pp. 3-7887-1834-X.

3744 *Taseva, Lora; Yovcheva, Maria* The first comprehensive edition of a Slavonic prophetologion manuscript. OCP 67 (2001) 447-454.

3746 **Vanderhooft, David Stephen** The Neo-Babylonian empire and Babylon in the latter prophets. HSM 59: 1999 ⇒15,3600; 16,3765. ᴿCBQ 63 (2001) 534-535 (*Bellavance, Eric*).

3746 **Wagner, Andreas** Prophetie als Theologie: die alttestamentlichen 'so spricht'-Formeln und ihr Beitrag für das Grundverständnis der Prophetie. Diss.-Habil. Mainz 2001, ᴰ*Zwickel, W.* [RTL 33,634].

3747 *Waschke, Ernst Joachim* Eschatologie als hermeneutischer Schlüssel prophetischen Geschichtsverständnisses. Der Gesalbte. 2001 <1983> ⇒227. 173-187.

3748 **Wischnowsky, Marc** Tochter Zion: Aufnahme und Überwindung der Stadtklage in den Prophetenschriften des Alten Testaments. Diss. Göttingen 2000, ^D*Aejmelaeus, A.* WMANT 89: Neuk 2001, Neuk xi; 323 pp. 3-7887-1831-5. Bibl. 282-314.

3749 *Yocum, Bruce* Prophecy, discernment, community. Charism, leadership. 2001 ⇒109-117

E8.2 Proto-Isaias, *textus, commentarii*

3750 **Berges, Ulrich** Das Buch Jesaja: Komposition und Endgestalt. 1998 ⇒14,3328; 15,3608. ^RZAW 113 (2001) 124-125 (*Pfeiffer, H.*).

3751 **Beuken, Willem A.M.** Isaiah, part 2, vol. 2: Isaiah chapters 28-39. ^T*Doyle, Brian*: Historical Commentary of the OT. 2000 ⇒16,3772. ^RBiOr 58 (2001) 229-232 (*Höffken, Peter*); CBQ 63 (2001) 305-306 (*Heskett, Randall*); RBBras 18 (2001) 472-473.

3752 **Blenkinsopp, Joseph** Isaiah 1-39. AncB 19: 2000 ⇒16,3773. ^RRExp 98 (2001) 444-445 (*Biddle, Mark E.*); CBQ 63 (2001) 509-510 (*Miscall, Peter D.*).

3753 *Brock, Sebastian* Text divisions in the Syriac translations of Isaiah;

3754 *Brooke, George J.* The Qumran Pesharim and the text of Isaiah in the Cave 4 manuscripts. ^MWEITZMAN, M. 2001 ⇒113. 200-221/304-320.

3755 **Childs, Brevard S.** Isaiah. 2000 ⇒16,3776. ^RSvTK 77 (2001) 184-185 (*Bäckersten, Olof*); ^RET 113 (2001) 51-54 (*Reimer, David J.*); RBBras 17/4 (2000) 647-48; RBLit 3 (2001) 1-9 (*Sweeney, Marvin*).

3756 **De Zan, Renato** Isaia [1-39]. Dabar... AT: Padova 2001, Messaggero 235 pp. €11.50. 88-250-1040-0. Bibl. 229-230.

3757 **Goldingay, John** Isaiah. NIBC: Peabody 2001, Hendrickson 397 pp. $12. 1-56563-223-0 [BiTod 40,323—Bergant, Dianne].

3758 *Gosse, Bernard* L'influence de la rédaction bipartite du livre d'Isaïe, jugement du monde (Is 1-34), rachat d'Israël (Is 35-62), sur la rédaction type massorétique du livre de Jérémie. StEeL 18 (2001) 63-69.

3759 **Hollerich, Michael J.** EUSEBIUS of Caesarea's commentary on Isaiah: christian exegesis in the age of CONSTANTINE. 1999 ⇒15,3611; 16,3779. ^RJThS 52 (2001) 892-896 (*Kamesar, Adam*).

3760 **Light, G.W.** Isaiah. LVL 2001, Geneva 118 pp. £6. 0-664-50080-3 [Evangel 21/1,29—Dray, Stephen].

3761 ^E**Melugin, Roy F.; Sweeney, Marvin Alan** New visions of Isaiah. JSOT.S 214: 1996 ⇒12,3331; 14,3333. ^RVT 51 (2001) 413-414 (*Dell, Katharine J.*).

3762 **Quinn-Miscall, Peter D.** Reading Isaiah: poetry and vision. LVL 2001, Westminster 224 pp. $21. 0-664-22369-9 [BS 160,118—Chisholm, Robert B.].

3763 *Schmid, Konrad* Jesaja/Jesajabuch. RGG², 4. 2001 ⇒664. 451-456.

3764 **Sweeney, Marvin Alan** Isaiah 1-39: with an introduction to prophetic literature. FOTL 16: 1996 ⇒12,3346... 16,3784. ᴿBiblInterp 9 (2001) 88-89 (*Hagedorn, Anselm*).

3765 **Tucker, Gene M.** The book of Isaiah 1-39: introduction, commentary, and reflections. NIntB 6: 2001 ⇒1865. 25-305.

3766 *Ulrich, Eugene* The developmental composition of the book of Isaiah: light from 1QIsaᵃ on additions in the MT. DSD 8 (2001) 288-305.

E8.3 Isaias 1-39, *themata, versiculi*

BEUKEN, W. Studies in...Isaiah 1997 ⇒6.

3767 *Blenkinsopp, Joseph* Cityscape to landscape: the "back to nature" theme in Isaiah 1-35. Urbanism and prophecy. JSOT.S 330: 2001 ⇒ 271. 35-44.

3768 *Boadt, Lawrence* Re-examining a preexilic redaction of Isaiah 1-39. ᶠFITZGERALD, A. CBQ.MS 32: 2001 ⇒31. 169-190.

3769 **Davies, Andrew** Double standards in Isaiah: re-evaluating prophetic ethics and divine justice. Bibl.Interp. 46: 2000 ⇒16,3793. ᴿThLZ 126 (2001) 1021-1022 (*Höffken, Peter*); ET 112 (2001) 73-75 (*Rodd, C.S.*).

3770 **Déclais, Jean-Louis** Un récit musulman sur Isaïe. Patrimoines: P 2001, Cerf 181 pp. 2-204-06602-8. ᴿOCP 67 (2001) 499-500 (*Poggi, V.*); IslChr 27 (2001) 275-276 (*Borrmans, Maurice*).

3771 **Fanwar, Wann Marbud** Creation in Isaiah. Diss. Andrews 2001, 240 pp. 3007051.

3772 *Gitay, Yehoshua* Prophetic criticism—'what are they doing?': the case of Isaiah—a methodological assessment. JSOT 96 (2001) 101-127.

3773 *Gordon, Robert P.* The legacy of LOWTH: Robert Lowth and the book of Isaiah in particular. ᴹWEITZMAN, M. 2001 ⇒113. 57-76.

3774 *Goréa-Autexier, Maria* Signes et oracles messianiques dans le Proto-Ésaïe. Prophètes et rois. LeDiv: 2001 ⇒292. 225-248.

3775 **Hagelia, Hallvard** Coram Deo: spirituality in the book of Isaiah, with particular attention to faith in Yahweh. CB.OT 49: Sto 2001, Almqvist & W. 528 pp. SEK342. 91-22-01901-4. Bibl. 499-528.

3776 **Heskett, Randall** Messianism within the book of Isaiah as a whole. Diss. Toronto, St. Michael 2001, ᴰSheppard, G. 453 pp. [RTL 33, 632].

3777 *Johnson, Luke T.* Isaiah the evangelist. MillSt 48 (2001) 88-105.

3778 **Kim, Hae-Kwon** The plan of Yahweh in First Isaiah. Diss. Princeton Sem. 2001, 337 pp. 3006832.

3779 *Landy, Francis (a)* Ghostwriting;
(*b*) Vision and voice in Isaiah <2000>. Beauty and the enigma.
JSOT.S 312: 2001 ⇒171. 392-413/371-391.

3780 **Leclerc, Thomas L.** Yahweh is exalted in justice: solidarity and conflict in Isaiah. Mp 2001m Fortress x; 229 pp. $20. 0-8006-3255-9.
Bibl. 200-217.

3781 **Ma, Wonsuk** Until the Spirit comes: the Spirit of God in the book of
Isaiah. JSOT.S 271: 1999 ⇒15,3638. ᴿCBQ 63 (2001) 526-527
(*Irwin, William H.*).

3782 *Olley, John W.* The wolf, the lamb, and a little child': transforming
the diverse earth community in Isaiah. The earth story. 2001 ⇒275.
219-229 [Hos 2].

3783 *Pfisterer Darr, Katheryn* "Alas, she has become a harlot," but who's
to blame?: unfaithful-female imagery in Isaiah's vision. Passion. 2001
⇒295. 55-76.

3784 *Rendtorff, Rolf* The book of Isaiah: a complex unity: synchronic and
diachronic reading. Der Text in...Endgestalt. 2001 ⇒201. 126-138.

3785 *Sawyer, John F.A.* The gospel according to Isaiah. ET 113 (2001)
39-43.

3786 **Schmidtgen, Beate** Die Stadt als Frau im Buch Jesaja. Diss. Basel
2001, ᴰ*Mathys, H.P.* 342 pp [RTL 33,634].

3787 *Van der Kooij, Arie* Interpretation of the book of Isaiah in the Septuagint and other ancient versions. SBL.SP 2001. SBL.SPS 40: 2001
⇒494. 220-239.

3788 *Waschke, Ernst Joachim* Die Stellung der Königstexte im Jesajabuch
im Vergleich zu den Königspsalmen 2, 72 und 89. Der Gesalbte.
2001 <1998> ⇒227. 141-155.

3789 *Williamson, Hugh G.M.* Isaiah and the Holy One of Israel. ᴹWEITZ-
MAN, M.: JSOT.S 333: 2001 ⇒113. 22-38.

3790 *Willis, John T.* Symbolic names and theological themes in the book
of Isaiah. HBT 23 (2001) 72-92.

3791 *Baer, David A.* It's all about us!: nationalistic exegesis in the Greek
Isaiah (chapters 1-12). SBL.SP 2001. 2001 ⇒494. 197-219.

3792 *Yilpet, Yoilah K.* Righteousness as order in Isaiah 1:21-31. TCNN
Research Bulletin 36 (2001) 28-38.

3793 *Van Duin, Kees* Orgueil ou souveraineté, psychologie ou politique?:
quelques remarques sur l'interprétation de la racine גאה dans le livre
d'Esaïe, notamment dans la Traduction Oecuménique de la Bible.
ᶠDEURLOO, K. ACEBT.S 2: 2001 ⇒23. 149-156 [Is 2,6-22].

3794 *Watts, John D.W.* Jerusalem: an example of war in a walled city
(Isaiah 3-4). Urbanism and prophecy. 2001 ⇒271. 210-215.

3795   *Miscall, Peter D.* Isaiah 5-6: called and sent. Postmodern interpretations. 2001 ⇒229. 105-116.

3796   *Hadson, José* A micro estrutura quiástica do Canto da Vinha de
Isaías 5:1-6. Hermenêutíca 1 (2001) 79-83.

3797   *Lescow, Theodor* Jesaja 5,1-7 und Ezechiel 37,1-14: Anmerkungen
zu Komposition und Interpretation. ZAW 113 (2001) 74-76.

3798   *Malul, Meir* The relationship between tearing the fence down in the
song of the vineyard (Isaiah 5:1-7) and stripping the woman naked in
the Old Testament. BetM 168 (2001) 11-24 Sum. 96. **H.**

3799   *Moberly, R.W.L.* Whose justice?: which righteousness?: the interpretation of Isaiah V 16. VT 51 (2001) 55-68.

3800   *Biton, S.* A new outlook on Isaiah 5,17: 'Then shall the lambs feed as
in their pasture, and fat ones and strangers shall feed in the ruins'.
BetM 168 (2001) 84-91 Sum. 92. **H.**

3801   *Landy, Francis* Strategies of concentration and diffusion in Isaiah 6.
Beauty and the enigma. JSOT.S 312: 2001 <1999> ⇒171. 298-327.

3802   *Persic, Alessio* L'esegesi patristica di *Isaia* 6 in alcuni autori di area
palestinese, cappadoce e antiochena fra IV e V secolo (2ª parte);

3803   *Sacchi, Alessandro* Israele e i gentili: riletture neotestamentarie di
Isaia 6 (seconda parte). AnScR 6 (2001) 277-291/217-237.

3804   *Tampellini, Stefano* Osservazioni sull'esegesi di *Isaia* 6 in TEODORE-
TO: dalla 'prevaricazione' del re Ozia a quella del popolo ebraico.
AnScR 6 (2001) 293-298.

3805   *Greenfield, Jonas C.* Ba'al's throne and Isa. 6:1. 'Al kanfei yonah, 2.
2001 <1985> ⇒153. 892-897.

3806   *Rizzi, Giovanni* Il Tg *Isaia* 6,1-13 come traduzione e come esegesi
interpretativa del testo ebraico. AnScR 6 (2001) 239-276.

3807   *Hurley, Robert* Le Seigneur endurcit le coeur d'Israël?: l'ironie d'Isaïe
6,9-10. Theoforum 32/1 (2001) 23-43.

3808   *Joosten, Jan* La prosopopée, les pseudo-citations et la vocation
d'Isaïe (Is 6,9-10). Bib. 82 (2001) 232-243.

3809   **Lehnert, Volker A.** Die Provokation Israels: die paradoxe Funktion
von Jes 6,9-10 bei Markus und Lukas. 1999 ⇒15,3673; 16,3820.
[R]RBLit 3 (2001) 376-79 (*Holm, Tawny L.*) [Mk 4,10-13; Lk 8,9-10].

3810   *Uemura, Shizuka* Isaiah 6:9-10: a hardening prophecy?. AJBI 27
(2001) 23-57 [Mt 13,14-15; Mk 4,11-12; Jn 12,40; Acts 28,26-27].

3811   *Manzi, Franco* Il discernimento profetico dei segni di Dio: spunti teologico-biblici alla luce di Isaia 7,1-17 e del vangelo secondo Luca.
ScC 129 (2001) 213-271.

3812   *Wong, Gordon C.I.* Faith in the present form of Isaiah VII 1-17. VT
51 (2001) 535-547.

3813 *Vargon, Shmuel* Prophecy of rebuke or consolation? (Isaiah 7:18-25). BetM 167 (2001) 289-303 Sum. 384. **H**.

3814 *Schmidtgen, Beate* Denn meine Kraft und mein Gesang ist Gott: Jesaja 12,1-6. JK 62/2 (2001) 71-74.

3815 *Herrmann, Wolfram* Die Kombination יה יהוה. ZAH 14 (2001) 79-83 [Is 12,2; 26,4].

3816 *Vercruysse, Jean-Marc* Les pères de l'église et la chute de l'ange (Lucifer d'après Is 14 et Ez 28). RevSR 75 (2001) 147-174.

3817 *Zehnder, Markus* Jesaja 14,1f.: widersprüchliche Erwartungen zur Stellung der Nicht-Israeliten in der Zukunft?. [F]SEYBOLD, K.: AOAT 280: 2001 ⇒102. 3-29.

3818 *Heiser, Michael S.* The mythological provenance of Isa. XIV 12-15: a reconsideration of the Ugaritic material. VT 51 (2001) 354-369.

3819 *Croughs, Mirjam* Intertextuality in the Septuagint: the case of Isaiah 19. BIOSCS 34 (2001) 81-94.

3820 *Sedlmeier, Franz* Israel—"ein Segen inmitten der Erde": das JHWH-Volk in der Spannung zwischen radikalem Dialog und Identitätsverlust nach Jes 19,16-25. [F]SCHMUTTERMAYR, G.: 2001 ⇒101. 89-108.

3821 *Haran, Menahem* The prophet Isaiah's going 'naked and barefoot for three years' Isaiah 20. [F]AHITUV, S. 2001 ⇒1. 163-166. **H**.

3822 **Van der Kooij, Arie** The oracle of Tyre: the Septuagint of Isaiah XXIII as version and vision. VT.S 71: 1998 ⇒14,3375; 16,3832. [R]RB 108 (2001) 285-287 (*Gonçalves, Francolino J.*); JBL 119 (2000) 345-347 (*McLay, Tim*).

3823 **Polaski, Donald C.** Authorizing an end: the Isaiah Apocalypse and intertextuality. BiblInterp 50: Lei 2001, Brill xv; 415 pp. $139. 90-04-11607-9. Bibl.

3824 **Scholl, Reinhard** Die Elenden in Gottes Thronrat: stilistisch-kompositorische Untersuchungen zu Jesaja 24-27. BZAW 274: 2000 ⇒16, 3838. [R]ThRv 97 (2001) 303-305 (*Becker, Uwe*); ThLZ 126 (2001) 1140-1142 (*Fechter, Friedrich*).

3825 *Charles, Norman J.* A prophetic (fore)word: 'a curse is devouring earth' (Isaiah 24.6). The earth story. 2001 ⇒275. 123-128.

3826 *Gryson, Roger* "Enfanter un esprit de salut": l'interprétation de Isaïe 26,17.18 chez les Pères grecs. RTL 32 (2001) 189-217.

3827 *Landy, Francis* Tracing the voice of the other: Isaiah 28 and the covenant with death. Beauty...enigma. 2001 <1993> ⇒171. 185-205.

3828 *Emerton, John A.* Some difficult words in Isaiah 28.10 and 13. [M]WEITZMAN, M.: JSOT.S 333: 2001 ⇒113. 39-56.

3829 *Gosse, Bernard* Isa 63,1-6 en relation à la synthèse du livre d'Isaïe en *mšpṭ ṣdqh / yšwʿh ṣdqh*, et la place d'Isa 34-35 dans la rédaction du livre. ZAW 113 (2001) 535-552.

3830   *Howell, Maribeth* A closer look: Isaiah 35:1-10. [F]FITZGERALD, A.
       CBQ.MS 32: 2001 ⇒31. 72-80.

E8.4 Deutero-Isaias 40-52: *commentarii, themata, versiculi*

3831   **Baltzer, Klaus** Deutero-Jesaja. KAT 10,2: 1999 ⇒15,3704; 16,
       3856. [R]ThRv 97 (2001) 40-42 (*Berges, Ulrich*);
3832   Deutero-Isaiah: a commentary on Isaiah 40-55. [T]*Kohl, Margaret.*
       Hermeneia: Mp 2001, Fortress xxv; 597 pp. $78. 0-8006-6039-0.
       Bibl. 491-548.
3833   **Gryson, Roger** Commentaires de Jérôme sur le prophète Isaie: livres
       XVI-XVIII. AGLB 36: 1999 ⇒15,3772. [R]AnBoll 119 (2001) 206-
       207 (*Leroy, François*); RHE 96 (2001) 455-456 (*Jay, Pierre*).
3834   **Koole, Jan L.** Isaiah 3/2: Isaiah 49-55. HCOT: 1998 ⇒14,3403...
       16,3861. [R]BZ 45 (2001) 111-112 (*Berges, Ulrich*); JBL 120 (2001)
       153-155 (*Williamson, H.G.M.*).
3835   **Korpel, Marjo C.; Moor, Johannes C. de** The structure of classical
       Hebrew poetry: Isaiah 40-55. OTS 41: 1998 ⇒14,3405; 16,3053.
       [R]ThRv 97 (2001) 42-44 (*Berges, Ulrich*).
3836   *Seitz, Christopher R.* The book of Isaiah 40-66: introduction, com-
       mentary, and reflections. NIntB 6: 2001 ⇒1865. 307-552.
3837   **Thompson, Michael E.W.** Isaiah Chapters 40-66. Epworth Com-
       mentaries: Peterborough 2001, Epworth xxxiv; 188 pp. 0-7162-0550-
       5. Bibl. xiii-xv.
3838   **Zapff, Burkard M.** Jesaja 40-55. NEB: Wü 2001, Echter 219-442
       pp. €18.20. 3-429-02314-9.

3839   **Albani, Matthias** Der eine Gott und die himmlischen Heerscharen:
       zur Begründung des Monotheismus bei Deuterojesaja. 2000 ⇒16,
       3865. [R]ThLZ 126 (2001) 1131-1134 (*Koch, Klaus*).
3840   *Clements, Ronald E.* Psalm 72 and Isaiah 40-66: a study in tradition.
       PRSt 28/4 (2001) 333-341.
3841   *Clifford, Richard J.* Prophetic leader. BiTod 39 (2001) 69-74.
3842   *Franke, Chris* Is there a God and does God care?. BiTod 39 (2001)
       83-87.
3843   [E]**Grabbe, Lester L.** Leading captivity captive: 'the exile' as history
       and ideology. JSOT.S 278: 1998 ⇒14,3394. [R]JThS 52 (2001) 731-
       733 (*Mein, Andrew*).
3844   *Kaminsky, Joel S.* The concept of election and Second Isaiah: recent
       literature. BTB 31 (2001) 135-144.
3845   **Labahn, Antje** Wort Gottes und Schuld Israels: Untersuchungen zu
       Motiven deuteronomistischer Theologie im Deuterojesajabuch.

BWANT H. 143: 1999 ⇒15,3724; 16,3875. ᴿRBLit 3 (2001) 203-206 (*Sweeney, Marvin A.*).

3846 *McGinnis, Claire Mathews* Engaging Israel's traditions for a new day. BiTod 39 (2001) 75-81.

3847 *Schmitt, Hans-Christoph* Prophetie und Schultheologie im Deuterojesajabuch: Beobachtungen zur Redaktionsgeschichte von Jes 40-55. Theologie in Prophetie. 2001 <1979> ⇒209. 19-37.

3848 **Sommer, Benjamin D.** A prophet reads scripture: allusions in Isaiah 40-66. 1998 ⇒14,3413... 16,3883. ᴿJR 81 (2001) 108-109 (*Schniedewind, William M.*); JSSt 46 (2001) 164-166 (*Williamson, H.G.M.*); JBL 119 (2000) 122-123 (*Linafelt, Tod*).

3849 *Weippert, Manfred* "Ich bin Jahwe"—"Ich bin Ištar von Arbela": Deuterojesaja im Lichte der neuassyrischen Prophetie. ᶠSEYBOLD, K. AOAT 280: 2001 ⇒102. 31-59.

3850 *Ferrie, John J.* Singing in the rain: a meteorological image in Isaiah. 42:10-12. ᶠFITZGERALD, A.: CBQ.MS 32: 2001 ⇒31. 95-104 [Ps 96; 98].

3851 *Schmitt, Hans-Christoph* Erlösung und Gericht: Jes 43,1-7 und sein literarischer und theologischer Kontext. Theologie in Prophetie. 2001 <1992> ⇒209. 74-86.

3852 *Faisandier, Anne* Esaïe 43,16-21: l'exil entre fidélité et rupture. Lire et Dire 50 (2001) 15-24.

3853 *Dempsey, Deirdre A.* The verb syntax of the idol passage of Isaiah 44:9-20. ᶠFITZGERALD, A.: CBQ.MS 32: 2001 ⇒31. 145-156.

3854 *Bieberstein, Klaus* Leiden erzählen: Sinnfiguren der Theodizee im Alten Testament: nur eine Skizze. ᶠGROß, W.: ATSAT 68: 2001 ⇒ 38. 1-22 [Isa 45,5-7].

3855 *Marquardt, Friedrich W.* Lob der Kolporteure: Jesaja 52,7-10. JK 62/6 (2001) 48-49.

E8.5 *Isaiae 53ss. Carmina Servi YHWH*: Servant Songs

3856 ᴱᵀ**Alobaidi, Joseph** The messiah in Isaiah 53: the commentaries of SAADIA Gaon, SALMON ben Yeruham and YEFET ben Eli on Is 52,13-53,12. La Bible dans l'histoire, textes et études 2: 1998 ⇒14,3427. ᴿRBLit 3 (2001) 503-505 (*Mandell, Sara*).

3857 ᴱ**Bellinger, William H.; Farmer, William R.** Jesus and the suffering servant: Isaiah 53 and christian origins. 1998 ⇒14,3430; 15,3747. ᴿJBL 119 (2000) 564-567 (*Kim, H.C. Paul*).

3858 *Landy, Francis* The construction of the subject and the symbolic order: a reading of the last three Suffering Servant songs. Beauty and the enigma. JSOT.S 312: 2001 <1993> ⇒171. 206-217.

3859 **Masini, Mario** Il Servo del Signore: lectio divina dei carmi del profeta Isaia. 1998 ⇒14,3444; 15,3760. REstB 59 (2001) 389-390 (*Ramis Darder, F.*).

3860 *Polan, Gregory J.* Portraits of Second Isaiah's servant. BiTod 39 (2001) 89-93.

3861 *Vanoni, Gottfried* Erwählung, Leiden, Stellvertretung: im 'Gottesknecht' verdichtete Erfahrung Israels. Christlicher Glaube. 2001 ⇒ 511. 125-138.

3862 *Dempsey, Carol J.; Tambasco, Anthony J.* Isaiah 52:13-53:12: unmasking the mystery of the Suffering Servant. The bible on suffering. 2001 ⇒326. 34-50.

3863 *Likins-Fowler, Deborah G.* Sociological functions of the Servant in Isaiah 52:13-53:12. ProcGLM 21 (2001) 47-59.

3864 *Lopasso, Vincenzo* Il Servo sofferente di Yhwh (Is 52,13-53,12). Vivarium 9 £421-438.

3865 **Schenker, Adrian** Knecht und Lamm Gottes (Jesaja 53): Übernahme von Schuld im Horizont der Gottesknechtslieder. SBS 190: Stu 2001, Kathol. Bibelwerk 131 pp. €20.35. 3-460-04901-4. Bibl. 127-131.

3866 *Spieckermann, Hermann* Konzeption und Vorgeschichte des Stellvertretungsgedankens im Alten Testament. Gottes Liebe zu Israel. FAT 33: 2001 <1997> ⇒215. 141-153.

3867 *Wagner, Volker* Die poetische Form des vierten Gottesknechtsliedes. Jes 52,13-53,12. ZAH 14 (2001) 173-199.

3868 *Tångberg, Karl A.* The justification of the Servant of the Lord: light from Qumran on the interpretation of Isaiah 53:11ab. TTK 72 (2001) 31-36.

3869 *Becker, Joachim* Zur Deutung von Jes 54,15. BN 106 (2001) 5-12.

E8.6 [Trito]Isaias 56-66

3870 **Baer, David A.** When we all go home: translation and theology in LXX Isaiah 56-66. JSOT.S 318; The Hebrew Bible and its Versions 1: Shf 2001, Sheffield A. 304 pp. 1-84127-180-2. Bibl. 283-291.

3871 **Croatto, José Severino** Imaginar el futuro: estructura retórica y querigma del Tercer Isaías (Isaías 56-66). Comentario bíblico: BA 2001, Lumen 552 pp. 987-00-0121-1. Bibl. 523-530.

3872 **Koole, Jan L.** Isaiah, 3/3: Isaiah 56-66. [T]*Runia, A.P.*: Historical commentary on the Old Testament: Lv 2001, Peeters xxi; 531 pp. €50. 90-429-1065-8.

3873 **Park, Kyun-Chul** Die Gerechtigkeit Israels und das Heil der Völker: Israel und die Völker in Bezug auf die Themen 'Kultus, Tempel, Eschatologie und soziale Gerechtigkeit' in der Endgestalt des Jesajabuches (56,1-8; 58,1-14; 65,17-66.24). Diss. Bethel 2001; [D]*Crüsemann, F.*, 434 pp [RTL 33,633].

3874 *Ruszkowski, Leszek* Der Sabbat bei Tritojesaja. [F]SEYBOLD, K. AOAT 280: 2001 ⇒102. 61-74.

3875 **Ruszkowski, Leszek** Volk und Gemeinde im Wandel: eine Untersuchung zu Jesaja 56-66. FRLANT 191: 2000 ⇒16,3918. [R]ThLZ 126 (2001) 915-917 (*Koenen, Klaus*).

3876 *Chiesa, Bruno* Isaiah 56:6-7 according to some Jewish exegetes of the 10th century;

3877 *Manns, Frédéric* A response to Professor A.Shinan. Jerusalem: house of prayer. SBFA 52: 2001 ⇒536. 73-80 [Isa 56,7].

3878 *Shinan, Avigdor* Isaiah 56:7 in rabbinic literature—a textual study. Jerusalem: house of prayer. SBFA 52: 2001 ⇒536. 135-140/67-71.

3879 *Nihan, C.* Trois cultes en Ésaïe 57,3-13 et leur signification dans le contexte religieux de la Judée à l'époque perse. TEuph 22 (2001) 143-167.

3880 *Greenfield, Jonas C.* The prepositions b... taḥat... im [!] Jes 57 5. 'Al kanfei yonah, 2. 2001 <1961> ⇒153. 698-700.

3881 *Polan, Gregory J.* Zion, the glory of the holy one of Israel: a literary analysis of Isaiah 60. [F]FITZGERALD, A.: CBQ.MS 32: 2001 ⇒31. 50-71.

3882 *Tsoi, Jonathan T.* 'I am the Lord: in its time I will hasten it!': the dynamic parallelism of Isaiah 60. Jian Dao 16 (2001) 21-55.

3883 **Tsoi Ting Pong, Jonathan** Let Zion live!: a synchronic and diachronic study of Isaiah 60. Diss. Lv 2001, [D]*Beuken, W.* xlviii; 336 pp [EThL 78,278].

3884 **Atawolo, Andreas Leba** The servant in the service of the Lord and his people: a theological-exegetical study of Isaiah 61. Exc. Diss. Gregoriana 2001, [D]*Conroy, Charles*: R 2001, 146 pp.

3885 **Goldenstein, Johannes** Das Gebet der Gottesknechte: Jesaja 63,7-64,11 im Jesajabuch. Diss. Göttingen 2000, [D]*Perlitt, L.*: WMANT 92: Neuk 2001, Neuk xii; 291 pp. €49.90. 3-7887-1858-7. Bibl. 253-274.

3886 *Gardner, Anne* Ecojustice or anthropological justice?: a study of the new heavens and the new earth in Isaiah 65.17. The earth story. 2001 ⇒275. 204-218 [Hos 2].

E8.7 Jeremias

3887 **Brueggemann, Walter** A commentary on Jeremiah. 1998 ⇒14, 3461; 15,3783. ^RVJTR 65 (2001) 543-544 (*Meagher, P.M.*).

3888 *Feder, Frank* La version Copte-Sahidique du Corpus Jeremiae. XXII Congresso di papirologia, 1. 2001 ⇒555. 457-460.

3889 *Fischer, Georg* Jeremia/Jeremiabuch. RGG², 4: 2001 ⇒664. 414-23.

3890 *Greenberg, Gillian* Some secondary expansions in the Masoretic text of Jeremiah: retroversion is perilous but the risk may be worthwhile. ^MWEITZMAN, M.: JSOT.S 333: 2001 ⇒113. 222-243.

3891 **Hoffman, Yair** Jeremiah: introduction and commentary. Mikra Leyisra'el: J 2001, Magnes 2 vols; vi; 512 + iv, vi; 911 + vii pp. 965-13-1493-1. V.1, chapters 1-25, v.2, chapters 26-52. **H.**

3892 **Lundbom, Jack R.** Jeremiah 1-20. AncB 21A: 1999 ⇒15,3786. ^RCBQ 63 (2001) 320-321 (*Friebel, Kelvin G.*).

3893 **McKeating, Henry** The book of Jeremiah. Epworth Commentaries: 1999 ⇒15,3788 ^RRBLi.t 3 (2001) 208-211 (*Fried, Lisbeth S.*).

3894 *Miller, Patrick D.* The book of Jeremiah: introduction, commentary, and reflections. NIntB 6: 2001 ⇒1865. 553-926.

3895 **Stipp, Hermann-Josef** Das masoretische und alexandrinische Sondergut des Jeremiabuches. OBO 136: 1994 ⇒10,3516... 15,3821. ^RRB 108 (2001) 145-147 (*Gonçalves, Francolino J.*).

3896 *Avioz, Michael* The identity of the 'enemy from the north' in the book of Jeremiah. BetM 167 (2001) 322-334 Sum. 383. **H.**

3897 *Baldacci, Massimo* 'Pivotal pattern' nell'ebraico di Geremia. ^MCAGNI, L., 3. SMDSA 61: 2001 ⇒15. 1261-1274.

3898 **Bauer, Angela** Gender in the book of Jeremiah: a feminist literary reading. 1999 ⇒15,3794. ^RHBT 23 (2001) 99-100 (*Fuchs, Esther*); JBL 119 (2000) 554-555 (*Sharp, Carolyn J.*).

3899 *Brueggemann, Walter* An ending that does not end: the book of Jeremiah. Postmodern interpretations. 2001 ⇒229. 117-128.

3900 *Bultmann, Christoph* A prophet in desperation?: the confessions of Jeremiah. The elusive prophet. OTS 45: 2001 ⇒485. 83-93.

3901 ^T**Dal Covolo, E.; Maritano, M.** Omelie su Geremia: lettura origeniana. B.S.R. 165: R 2001, Las 122 pp. €10.33. ^RMar. 63 (2001) 561-565 (*Peretto, Elio*).

3902 ^E**Diamond, A.R. Pete; O'Connor, Kathleen M.; Stulman, Louis** Troubling Jeremiah. JSOT.S 260: 1999 ⇒15,212; 16,3940. ^RJThS 52 (2001) 159-162 (*Bultmann, C.*); ThLZ 126 (2001) 365-368 (*Liwak, Rüdiger*).

3903 **Ferry, Joëlle** Illusions et salut dans la prédication prophétique de Jérémie. BZAW 269: 1999 ⇒15,3802. [R]ETR 76 (2001) 114-115 (*Vincent, Jean Marcel*); CBQ 63 (2001) 108-110 (*Sweeney, Marvin A.*); RBLit 3 (2001) 211-215 (*Gosse, Bernard C.*)

3904 **Friebel, Kelvin G.** Jeremiah's and Ezekiel's sign-acts. JSOT.S 283: 1999 ⇒15,3803; 16,3942. [R]CBQ 63 (2001) 110-111 (*Strong, John T.*); RBLit 3 (2001) 206-208 (*Galambush, Julie*).

3905 **Goldman, Yohanan** Prophétie et royauté au retour de l'exil: les origines littéraires de la forme massorétique du livre de Jérémie. OBO 118: 1992 ⇒10,3493. [R]RB 108 (2001) 141-145 (*Gonçalves, Francolino J.*).

3906 *Hieke, Thomas* "Das Wort des Herrn bringt mir nur Spott und Hohn" (Jer 20,8): der Prophet "Jeremia" als Typus des frustrierten Verkündigers. LebZeug 56 (2001) 5-24.

3907 **Hill, John Edward** Friend or foe?: the figure of Babylon in the book of Jeremiah MT. Bibl. Interp. 40: 1999 ⇒15,3806. [R]ABR 49 (2001) 57-58 (*Boyle, Brian*); RBLit 3 (2001) 218-220 (*Bellis, Alice Ogden*).

3908 **Hung, Emmanuel Yun-wing** Relationship and rebirth: a literary study of the Exodus motif in Jeremiah. Diss. Westminster Sem. 2001, 262 pp. 3010605.

3909 *Kegler, Jürgen* Das Leid des Nachbarvolkes—Beobachtungen zu den Fremdvölkersprüchen Jeremias. Gesammelte Aufsätze. BEAT 48: 2001 <1980> ⇒167. 56-71.

3910 **Lalleman-de Winkel, Hetty** Jeremiah in prophetic tradition. 2000 ⇒16,3945. [R]OLZ 96 (2001) 264-266 (*Fischer, Georg*); Ho Theologos 19 (2001) 469 (*Manfredi, Silvana*); ThLZ 126 (2001) 273-276 (*Schmidt, Werner H.*).

3911 *Langenhorst, Georg* Der "Narr mit dem Holzjoch"—Deutungen Jeremias in der Gegenwartsliteratur. EuA 77 (2001) 20-41.

3912 *Malamat, Abraham* Jeremiah and the last two kings of Judah. History of biblical Israel. 2001 <1951> ⇒182. 381-386.

3913 *Ossom-Batsa, George* The theological significance of the root *šwb* in Jeremiah. AUSS 39 (2001) 223-232.

3914 **Parke-Taylor, Geoffrey H.** The formation of the book of Jeremiah: doublets and recurring phrases. SBL.MS 51: 2000 ⇒16,3949. [R]JBL 120 (2001) 748-751 (*Wells, Roy D.*); RBLit 3 (2001) 215-218 (*Wells, Roy D.*).

3915 **Pschibille, Judith** Hat der Löwe erneut gebrüllt?: sprachliche, formale und inhaltliche Gemeinsamkeiten in der Verkündigung Jeremias und Amos'. BThSt 41: Neuk 2001, Neuk xiii; 226 pp. 3-7887-1833-1. Bibl. 202-226.

3916 *Scalise, Pamela J.* The logic of covenant and the logic of lament in the book of Jeremiah. PRSt 28/4 (2001) 395-401.

3917 *Schmidt, Werner H.* Jeremias Konfessionen. JBTh 16 (2001) 3-23.

3918 *Van den Eynde, Sabine* Taking broken cisterns for the fountain of living water: on the background of the metaphor of the whore in Jeremiah. BN 110 (2001) 86-96 [Jer 2-3].

3919 *Lopasso, Vincenzo* Ger 3: forma, contenuto e scopo. BeO 43 (2001) 197-213.

3920 *Wurst, Shirley* Retrieving earth's voice in Jeremiah: an annotated voicing of Jeremiah 4. The earth story. 2001 ⇒275. 172-184.

3921 *Leene, Hendrik* Blowing the same shofar: an intertextual comparison of representations of the prophetic role in Jeremiah and Ezekiel. The elusive prophet. OTS 45: 2001 ⇒485. 175-198 [Jer 6,9-21; 18,18-23; Ezek 13,1-16; 33,1-9; 7,23-27].

3922 *Mutius, Hans-Georg von* Neues zur hebräischen Textvorlage des Targums zu Jeremia 6,19. BN 107/108 (2001) 46-49.

3923 *Keller, Martin* Jeremia 7: eine Rede und eine Besinnung: von der Gotteslehre zur Gottesleere. ^FSEYBOLD, K. AOAT 280: 2001 ⇒102. 75-78.

3924 *Wypych, Stanisław* 'Będę wam Bogiem, wy będziecie moim ludem' (Jr 7,23): studium egzegetyczno-teologiczne formuły w ekonomii Starego Przymierza. ^FJANKOWSKI, A. 2001 ⇒53. 451-469. **P.**

3925 **Rayappan, Arasakumar** The divine struggle: divine-cosmic-human-relationship in Jer. IX. Diss. Innsbruck 2001, ^D*Fischer, G.* 2001, 204 pp [RTL 33,633].

3926 *Kharanauli, Anna* Das Chanmeti-Fragment aus Jeremia—Fragen seiner Entstehung und seiner Übersetzungstechnik. OrChr 85 (2001) 204-236 [Jer 12; 17-18; 20].

3927 *Stoebe, Hans-Joachim* Gehörtes Gebet: Retraktation einer Predigt über die Konfessionen Jeremias (Jer 12,1-5). ThZ 57 (2001) 227-229.

3928 *Boda, Mark J.* From complaint to contrition: peering through the liturgical window of Jer 14,1-15,4. ZAW 113 (2001) 186-197 [Lev 26; Ezra 9; Neh 1].

3929 *Bogaert, Pierre-Maurice* Jérémie 17,1-4 TM, oracle contre ou sur Juda propre au texte long, annoncé en 11,7-8.13 TM et en 15,12-14 TM. ^FSCHENKER, A.: OBO 179: 2001 ⇒100. 59-74.

3930 *Nagel-Strotmann, Konrad* Von der Zerrissenheit der Anwältinnen und Anwälte für Gerechtigkeit: Jeremia 20,7-13. JK 62/1 (2001) 61-64.

3931 *Dubbink, Joep* Cedars devay, a sprout will blossom: Jeremiah 23,5-6: conclusion of the prophecies on kingship. ^FDEURLOO, K.: ACEBT.S 2: 2001 ⇒23. 157-165.

3932 *Kegler, Jürgen* Prophetisches Reden und politische Praxis Jeremi-as—Beobachtungen zu Jer 26 und 36. Gesammelte Aufsätze. BEAT 48: 2001 <1979, 1981> ⇒167. 46-55.

3933 *Kiernikowski, Zbigniew* Rola przebaczenia grzechów w Nowym Przymierzu według Jr 31,31-34. ᶠJANKOWSKI, A. 2001 ⇒53. 190-203.

3934 **Marafioti, Domenico** Sant'AGOSTINO e la nuova alleanza: l'interpre-tazione agostiniana di Geremia 31,31-34 nell'ambito dell'esegesi pa-tristica. Aloisiana 26: 1995 ⇒11/1,2371... 16,3983. ᴿRecollectio 23-24 (2000-2001) 686-687 (*Rouanet Bastos, Luciano*).

3935 *Robinson, Bernard P.* Jeremiah's new covenant: Jer 31,31-34. SJOT 15 (2001) 181-204.

3936 **Pardo Izal, José Javier** Pasión por un futuro imposible: estudio lite-rario-teológico de Jeremías 32. TGr.T 76: R 2001, E.P.U.G. 406,pp. €23.24. 88-7652-894-6. Bibl. 377-398.

3937 *Wittenberg, Gunther H.* The vision of land in Jeremiah 32. The earth story. 2001 ⇒275. 129-142.

3938 *Hoffman, Yair* The law as a literary shaping device: the law of manu-mission and the story in Jeremiah 34:8-22. BetM 168 (2001) 2-10 Sum. 96. **H.**

3939 *Migsch, Herbert* Zur Interpretation von *wᵉ'et kål-bêt hårekåbîm* in Je-remia XXXV 3. VT 51 (2001) 385-389;

3940 "Eingehalten worden sind die Worte Jehonadabs": zur Interpretation von Jer 35,14. Bib. 82 (2001) 385-401;

3941 Zur Interpretation von Jeremia 35Pesch,14a. BN 107-8 (2001) 41-45.

3942 *Di Pede, Elena* Jérémie 36: essai de structure. RivBib 49 (2001) 129-153.

3943 *Hoffman, Yair* History and ideology: the case of Jeremiah 44. JANES 28 (2001) 43-51.

3944 *Peels, Hendrik G.* "Drinken zùlt gij!": plaats en betekenis van de vol-kenprofetieën in Jeremia 46-51. ThRef 44 (2001) 205-220.

3945 *Schneider, Thomas* Jeremia in Memphis: eine Neusituierung von Je-remia 46,13-24. ᶠSEYBOLD, K.: AOAT 280: 2001 ⇒102. 79-97.

3946 *Scibona, Rocco* Ger. (TM) 46:15=Ger. (LXX) 26:15 e il dio Apis (הַף) ᴹCAGNI, L., 4. SMDSA 61: 2001 ⇒15. 2109-2130.

3947 *Bellis, Alice Ogden* The new exodus in Jeremiah 50:33-38. ᶠFITZGE-RALD, A. CBQ.MS 32: 2001 ⇒31. 157-168.

3948 *Fischer, Georg* Jeremiah 52: a test case for Jer LXX. X Congress IOSCS. SBL.SCSt 51: 2001 ⇒499. 37-48.

E8.8 **Lamentations**, *Threni*; **Baruch**

3949 *Cooper, Alan* The message of Lamentations. JANES 28 (2001) 1-18.
3950 *Dobbs-Allsopp, Fred W.* The enjambing line in Lamentations: a taxonomy (Part 1). ZAW 113 (2001) 219-239;
3951 The effects of enjambment in Lamentations (Part 2). ZAW 113 (2001) 370-385.
       Gerstenberger, E. Psalms, 2...Lamentations 2001 ⇒3150.
3952 **Linafelt, Tod** Surviving Lamentations: catastrophe, lament, and protest in the afterlife of a biblical book. 2000 ⇒16,3997. ᴿThTo 57 (2001) 576, 578 (*Provan, Iain*); MoTh 17 (2001) 401-402 (*Lipton, Diana*); CBQ 63 (2001) 118-120 (*Washington, Harold C.*); JBL 120 (2001) 755-756 (*O'Connor, Kathleen M.*).
3953 *Michaeli, H.* Reconstruction of '*Lamentations*' from Qumran: 4Q179. Beit Mikra 165 (2001) 146-170. **H.**
3954 *O'Connor, Kathleen M.* The book of Lamentations: introduction, commentary, and reflections. NIntB 6: 2001 ⇒1865. 1011-1072;
3955 Prayer in the book of Lamentations. BiTod 39 (2001) 139-144 [1 Kgs 8].
3956 *Pyper, Hugh S.* Reading Lamentations. Ment. *Freud, S.* JSOT 95 (2001) 55-69.
3957 **Renkema, Johan** Lamentations. 1998 ⇒14,3523; 16,4001. ᴿJBL 120 (2001) 155-157 (*Miller, Charles William*); ThZ 57 (2001) 381-382 (*Weber, Beat*); RBBras 18 (2001) 493-494.
3958 *Salters, Robert B.* The unity of Lamentations. IBSt 23 (2001) 102-10.
3959 **Slavitt, David R.** The book of Lamentations: a meditation and translation. Baltimore 2001, Johns Hopkins University xiv; 88 pp. 0-8018-6617-0. Bibl. 87-88.
3960 *West, Mona* The gift of voice, the gift of tears: a queer reading of Lamentations in the context of AIDS. Queer commentary. JSOT.S 334: 2001 ⇒325. 140-151.

3961 *Miller, Charles William* Reading voices: personification, dialogism, and the reader of Lamentations 1. BiblInterp 9 (2001) 393-408.
3962 *Dobbs-Allsopp, Fred W.; Linafelt, Tod* The rape of Zion in Thr 1,10. ZAW 113 (2001) 77-81.

3963 *Harlow, Daniel C.* The christianization of early Jewish pseudepigrapha: the case of 3 Baruch. JSJ 32 (2001) 416-444.
3964 *Nir, Rivka* Christian sacraments in the Syriac Apocalypse of Baruch. Studies in Judaica. Teʻuda 16-17: 2001 ⇒408. 421-473 Sum. xxix-xxxi. **H.**

3965 *Saldarini, Anthony J.* The book of Baruch: introduction, commentary, and reflections. NIntB 6: 2001 ⇒1865. 927-982;

3966 The letter of Jeremiah: introduction, commentary, and reflections. NIntB 6: 2001 ⇒1865. 983-1010.

3967 *Schmid, Herbert; Speyer, Wolfgang* Baruch. RAC, Suppl. Bd. 1. 2001 ⇒661. 962-993.

    Steck, O., *al.*, Baruch; Brief des Jeremia... 1998 ⇒3056.

3968 *Sulavik, Athanasius Baruch secundum decanum Salesburiensem*: text and introduction to the earliest Latin commentary on Baruch. AHDL 68 (2001) 249-296.

3969 *Whitters, M.F.* Testament and canon in the letter of second Baruch (2 Baruch 78-87). JSPE 12 (2001) 149-163.

3970 *Jenni, Hanna* Zum Jeremia-Apokryphon. [F]SEYBOLD, K. AOAT 280: 2001 ⇒102. 99-114.

3971 *Schaller, Berndt* Die griechische Fassung der Paralipomena Jeremiou: Originaltext oder Übersetzungstext?. Fundamenta Judaica. StUNT 25: 2001 ⇒206. 67-103.

E8.9 **Ezekiel**: *textus, commentarii; themata, versiculi*

3972 *Darr, Katheryn Pfisterer* The book of Ezekiel: introduction, commentary, and reflections. NIntB 6: 2001 ⇒1865. 1073-1607.

3973 **Eichrodt, Walther** Ezechiele. Antico Testamento 22/1-2: Brescia 2001, Paideia 2 vols; 729 pp. €27.37. 88-394-0608-5/9-3. [R]Anton. 76 (2001) 571-572 (*Nobile, Marco*).

3974 **Greenberg, Moshe** Ezechiel 1-20. HThK.AT: FrB 2001, Herder 445 pp. €70. 3-451-26842-6. Vorwort *Erich Zenger*; Bibl. 9-18.

3975 **Pohlmann, Karl-Friedrich** Das Buch des Propheten Hesekiel (Ezechiel) Kapitel 20-48. ATD 22/2: Gö 2001, Vandenhoeck & R. xv; 300-631 pp. €34. 3-525-51203-1. Beitrag von *T.A. Rudnig*.

3976 **Rossi, Luiz A. Solano** O livro de Ezequiel: o profeta da esperança. Como ler a bíblia: São Paulo 2001, Paulus 71 pp [REB 61,756].

3977 **Angelini, Giuseppe** Il profeta ammutolito: meditazioni su Ezechiele. 2000 ⇒16,4024. [R]ED 54/1 (2001) 234-235 (*Rizzi, Giovanni*).

3978 *Bodi, Daniel* Le prophète critique la monarchie: le terme *naśi'* chez Ézéchiel. Prophètes et rois. LeDiv: 2001 ⇒292. 249-257.

3979 *Carley, Keith* Ezekiel's formula of desolation: harsh justice for the land/earth. The earth story. 2001 ⇒275. 143-157.

3980 **Drewermann, Eugen** '...auf dass ihr wieder leben sollt': die Botschaft des Propheten Ezequiel. ^E*Marz, Bernd*: Z 2001, Pendo 331 pp. 3-85842-424-2.

    Friebel, K. Jeremiah's and Ezekiel's sign-acts 1999 ⇒3904.

3981 *Galambush, Julie* This land is my land: on nature as property in the book of Ezekiel. Urbanism and prophecy. 2001 ⇒271. 71-94.

3982 *Habel, Norman* The silence of the lands: the ecojustice implications of Ezekiel's judgement oracles. SBL.SP 2001. 2001 ⇒494. 305-320.

3983 *Hauspie, Katrin* Neologismus in the Septuagint of Ezekiel. JNSL 27/1 (2001) 17-37;

3984 πίπτω ἐπὶ πρόσωπόν μου: a set phrase in Ezekiel?. X Congress IOSCS. SBL.SCSt 51: 2001 ⇒499. 513-530.

3985 *Holladay, William L.* Had Ezekiel known Jeremiah personally?. CBQ 63 (2001) 31-34.

3986 *Kasher, Rimon* The 'private' prophecies in the book of Ezekiel: their scope, function and relation to the 'public' prophecies. ^FAHITUV, S. 2001 ⇒1. 273-282. **H.**

3987 **Kutsko, John F.** Between heaven and earth: divine presence and absence in the book of Ezekiel. 2000 ⇒16,4032. ^RHebStud 42 (2001) 346-348 (*Boadt, Lawrence*).

3988 **Lapsley, Jacqueline E.** Can these bones live?: the problem of the moral self in the book of Ezekiel. BZAW 301: 2000 ⇒16,4034. ^RZKTh 123 (2001) 98-99 (*Premstaller, Volkmar*); ThLZ 126 (2001) 1026-1027 (*Krüger, Thomas*).

3989 *Mein, Andrew* Ezekiel as a priest in exile. The elusive prophet. OTS 45: 2001 ⇒485. 199-213.

3990 **Mein, Andrew** Ezekiel and the ethics of exile. Oxford Theological Monographs: Oxf 2001, OUP xii; 298 pp. £45. 0-19-829992-3. Bibl. 264-282.

3991 *Olley, John W.* Animals in heaven and earth: attitudes in Ezekiel. Colloquium 33/1 (2001) 47-57.

3992 **Renz, Thomas** The rhetorical function of the book of Ezekiel. VT.S 76: 1999 ⇒15,3926. ^RJThS 52 (2001) 733-735 (*Mein, Andrew*); RBLit 3 (2001) 220-223 (*Odell, Margaret S.*).

3993 *Stevenson, Kalinda Rose* The land is yours: Ezekiel's outrageous land claim. SBL.SP 2001. SBL.SPS 40: 2001 ⇒494. 175-196.

3994 *Turner, P.D.M.* The translator(s) of Ezekiel revisited: idiosyncratic LXX renderings as a clue to inner history. Helsinki perspectives. SESJ 82: 2001 ⇒1617. 279-307.

3995 **Wong, Ka Leung** The idea of retribution in the book of Ezekiel. VT. S 87: Lei 2001, Brill xiv; 308 pp. €80. 90-04-12256-7. Bibl. 255-282. ^REThL 77 (2001) 471-473 (*Lust, J.*).

3996 **Wright, Christopher J.H.** The message of Ezekiel: a new heart and a new spirit. The Bible Speaks Today: Leicester 2001, InterVarsity 368 pp. 0-85111-548-9. Bibl. 15-16.

3997 *Uehlinger, Christoph; Müller Trufaut, Susanne* Ezekiel 1, Babylonian cosmological scholarship and iconography: attempts at further refinement. ThZ 57 (2001) 140-171.

3998 *Dulaey, Martine* Des roues dans les roues: Ez 1,15-16 chez les Pères. StPatr 34 (2001) 318-325.

3999 *Alford, Anthony M.* Prophecy: rebellion or redemption: Ezekiel 2:1-6. LexTQ 36/1 (2001) 13-21 [BuBB 37,91].

4000 *Lust, J.; Hauspie, K.; Ternier, A.* Ezekiel 4 and 5 in Hebrew and in Greek: numbers and ciphers. EThL 77 (2001) 132-152.

4001 *Stevenson, Kalinda Rose* If earth could speak: the case of the mountains against YHWH in Ezekiel 6; 35-36. The earth story. 2001 ⇒ 275. 158-171.

4002 *Lust, Johan; Hauspie, K.; Ternier, A.* Notes to the Septuagint: Ezekiel 7. EThL 77 (2001) 384-394.

4003 *Wong, Ka Leung* A note on Ezekiel VIII 6. VT 51 (2001) 396-400.

4004 *Scatolini, Silvio S.* Delimiting the contours of Israel in Ezek 12:21-15 and 12:26-28. Journal of Hebrew Scriptures 3 (2001) [electr. journ.].

4005 **Nay, Reto** Jahve im Dialog: ... Untersuchung der Ältestenperikope Ez 14,1-11. AnBib 141: 1999 ⇒15,3938; 16,4051. [R]RBLit 3 (2001) 223-226 (*Renz, Thomas*) [Ezek 8; 20].

4006 *Odendaal, Marietjie* A South African annotation to shame in Ezekiel 16. Scriptura 78 (2001) 479-489.

4007 *Kamionkowski, S. Tamar* The savage made civilized: an examination of Ezekiel 16.8. Urbanism and prophecy. 2001 ⇒271. 124-136.

4008 *Shields, Mary* An abusive God?: identity and power/gender and violence in Ezekiel 23. Postmodern interpretations. 2001 ⇒229. 129-52.

4009 *Lust, Johan* The delight of Ezekiel's eyes: Ez 24:15-24 in Hebrew and in Greek. X Congress IOSCS. SBL.SCSt 51: 2001 ⇒499. 1-26.

4010 *Kumar, David Stanly* Land motif in Ezek 28:20-26 (a social reading). ITS 38 (2001) 279-300.

4011 *Wendland, Ernst R.* 'Can these bones live again?': a rhetoric of the gospel in Ezekiel 33-37. AUSS 39 (2001) 85-100, 241-272.

4012 *Van den Eynde, Sabine* Interpreting 'Can these bones come back to life?' in Ezekiel 37:3: the technique of hiding knowledge. OTEs 14 (2001) 153-165 [Ezek 37,1-14].

4013 **Fitzpatrick, Paul E.** Ezekiel 38-39: cosmogony's finale in Ezekiel's final form. Extr. Diss. Gregoriana, [D]*Conroy, Charles*: R 2001, ix; 105 pp .

4014 **Konkel, Michael** Architektonik des Heiligen: Studien zur zweiten
Tempelvision Ezechiels (Ez 40-48). Diss. Bonn 2000/01, ^D*Hossfeld,
F.-L.* BBB 129: B 2001, Philo xvi; 398 pp. €96.12. 3-8257-0237-5.
Bibl. 375-389. ^REThL 77 (2001) 470-471 (*Lust, J.*).

4015 **Rudnig, Thilo Alexander** Heilig und profan: redaktionskritische
Studien zu Ez 40-48. BZAW 287: 2000 ⇒16,4069. ^REThL 77
(2001) 201-203 (*Lust, J.*); JThS 52 (2001) 735-738 (*Renz, Thomas*);
ThLZ 126 (2001) 1256-1259 (*Liwak, Rüdiger*).

E9.1 Apocalyptica VT

4016 *Abadie, Philippe* Les racines de l'apocalyptique. Le judaïsme à l'aube
de l'ère chrétienne. LeDiv 186: 2001 ⇒450. 209-245.

4017 *Aune, David E.; Stewart, Eric* From the idealized past to the
imaginary future: eschatological restoration in Jewish apocalyptic literature. Restoration. JSJ.S 72: 2001 ⇒319. 147-177.

4018 **Cohn, Norman** Cosmos, chaos & the world to come: the ancient
roots of apocalyptic faith. NHv ²2001, Yale Univ. Pr. 282 pp. $17
[BiTod 40,127—Bergant, D.].

4019 *Collins, John J.* Apocalyptic literature. Blackwell companion to the
Hebrew Bible. 2001 ⇒653. 432-447.

4020 **Collins, John Joseph** The apocalyptic imagination: an introduction
to Jewish apocalyptic literature. ²1998 ⇒14,3581... 16,4079. ^RSal. 63
(2001) 382-384 (*Vicent, R.*).

4021 ^E**Ebertz, Michael N.; Zwick, Reinhold** Jüngste Tage: die Gegenwart der Apokalyptik. 1999 ⇒15,3953. ^RActBib 38 (2001) 48-50
(*Boada, J.*).

4022 *Efron, Joshua* The beginnings of christianity and apocalypticism.
Studies in Judaica. Te'uda 16-17: 2001 ⇒408. 277-313. Sum. xxiii-
xxv. **H**.

4023 **Koenen, Klaus; Kühschelm, Roman** Zeitenwende: Perspektiven
des Alten und Neuen Testaments. 1999 ⇒15,3957; 16,4080. ^RETR
76 (2001) 117-118 (*Vincent, Jean Marcel*).

4024 *Quinto, Riccardo* Giubileo e attesa escatologica negli autori monastici e nei maestri della sacra pagina. Medioevo 26 (2001) 25-109.

4025 *Redditt, Paul L.* The rhetoric of Jewish apocalyptic eschatology.
PRSt 28/4 (2001) 361-371;

4026 The vitality of the apocalyptic vision. Passion. 2001 ⇒295. 77-118.

E9.2 **Daniel**: *textus, commentarii: themata, versiculi*

4027 **Buchanan, George Wesley** The book of Daniel. 1999 ⇒15,3962. ^RCBQ 63 (2001) 308-309 (*Aaron, Charles L.*).

4028 ^E**Collins, John Joseph; Flint, Peter W.** The book of Daniel: composition and reception. VT.S 83/1-2; Formation and interpretation of Old Testament Literature 2/1-2: Lei 2001, Brill xxii; 290 + xxiv; 291-769 pp. €118+118. 9004-11675-3/12200-1. Collab. *C. VanEpps.*

4029 Cumulative bibliography. Book of Daniel. 2001 ⇒4028. 689-713.

4030 *Di Lella, Alexander A.* The textual history of Septuagint-Daniel and Theodotion-Daniel. Book of Daniel. 2001 ⇒4028. 586-607.

4031 **Di Lella, Alexander A.** El libro de Daniel (1-6). 2000 ⇒16,4114. ^RRevAg 42 (2001) 413-414 (*Sánchez Navarro, Luis*); San Juan de la Cruz 27 (2001) 133-134 (*Parejo, Juan Hidalgo*);

4032 Guía espiritual del Antiguo Testamento: el libro de Daniel (7-14). M 2001, Ciudad Nueva 149 pp. 84-89651-92-2.

4033 **Gowan, Donald E.** Daniel. Abingdon Old Testament Commentaries: Nv 2001, Abingdon 172 pp. $22. 0-687-08421-0. Bibl. 163-169.

4034 *Jenner, Konrad D.* Syriac Daniel. Book of Daniel. 2001 ⇒4028. 608-637.

4035 **Koch, Klaus** Daniel [2,1-3,91]. BK.AT 22/4: Neuk 2001, Neuk'er 241-320 pp. €18.50. 3-7887-0788-7.

4036 **Koch, Klaus; Rösel, Martin** Polyglottensynopse zum Buch Daniel. 2000 ⇒16,4093. ^RJBL 120 (2001) 753-4 (*Henze, Matthias*); VeE 22 (2001) 203-04 (*Nel, M.*); RBLit 3 (2001) 255-257 (*Henze, Matthias*).

4037 **Longman, Tremper** Daniel. 1999 ⇒15,3966. ^RAUSS 39 (2001) 331-333 (*Mulzac, Kenneth*).

4038 **Redditt, Paul L.** Daniel. NCBC: 1999 ⇒15,3970. ^RJThS 52 (2001) 172-175 (*Mastin, B.A.*); RB 108 (2001) 427-431 (*Grelot, Pierre*). **Steck, O.** Baruch...Zusätze zu...Daniel 1998 ⇒3056.

4039 *Ulrich, Eugene* The text of Daniel in the Qumran scrolls. Book of Daniel. 2001 ⇒4028. 573-585.

4040 ^E**Ziegler, J.** Susanna; Daniel; Bel et Draco. ^E*Munnich, Olivier; Fraenkel, Detlef*: Septuaginta 16/2: ²1999 ⇒15,3973. ^RRTL 32 (2001) 106-109 (*Bogaert, Pierre-Maurice*); Theol(A) 72 (2001) 711-713 (*Simotas, Pan. N.*).

4041 *Albertz, Rainer* The social setting of the Aramaic and Hebrew book of Daniel. Book of Daniel. 2001 ⇒4028. 171-204.

4042 *Aranda Pérez, Gonzalo* Daniel, el 'Apocalipsis' del Antiguo Testamento. ResB 30 (2001) 5-12.

4043 *Ausín, Santiago* Un reino nuevo y definitivo. ResB 30 (2001) 21-28.

4044 *Barton, John* Theological ethics in Daniel;

4045 *Beyerle, Stefan* The book of Daniel and its social setting. Book of Daniel. 2001 ⇒4028. 661-670/205-228.

4046 *Blumenthal, Fred* The book of Daniel: a guide for Judaism in exile. JBQ 29 (2001) 73-79.

4047 *Boccaccini, Gabriele* The solar calendars of Daniel and Enoch;

4048 *Collins, John J.* Current issues in the study of Daniel. Book of Daniel. 2001 ⇒4028. 311-328/1-15.

4049 *Custer, John S.* Man of desires: eros in the book of Daniel. DR 119 (2001) 217-230.

4050 *Davies, Philip R.* The scribal school of Daniel;

4051 *Dunn, James D.G.* The Danielic Son of Man in the New Testament;

4052 *Eshel, Esther* Possible sources of the book of Daniel;

4053 *Evans, Craig A.* Daniel in the New Testament: visions of God's kingdom. Book of Daniel. 2001 ⇒4028. 247-65/528-49/387-94/490-527.

4054 *Flint, Peter W.* The Daniel tradition at Qumran. Book of Daniel. 2001 ⇒4028. 329-367.

4055 *Gianto, Agustinus* Sejarah, Apokaliptik, dan Kebijaksanaan Daniel [History, apocalyptics, and wisdom thinking in Daniel]. Forum Biblika 12 (2001) 3-9 [AcBib 10,801]. **Indonesian**.

4056 *Glessmer, Uwe* Die "vier Reiche" aus Daniel in der targumischen Literatur. Book of Daniel. 2001 ⇒4028. 468-489.

4057 *Goldingay, John* Daniel in the context of Old Testament theology;

4058 *Grabbe, Lester L.* A Dan(iel) for all seasons: for whom was Daniel important?;

4059 *Hobbins, John F.* Resurrection in the Daniel tradition and other writings at Qumran;

4060 *Knibb, Michael A.* The book of Daniel in its context. Book of Daniel. 2001 ⇒4028. 639-660/229-246/395-420/16-35.

4061 *Koch, Klaus* Die jüdische und christliche Kanonisierung des Danielbuchs als Rezeption unter verändertem geschichtlichen Horizont. Biblischer Text. BThSt 44: 2001 ⇒252. 1-25;

4062 Stages in the canonization of the book of Daniel;

4063 *Lust, Johan* Cult and sacrifice in Daniel: the Tamid and the abomination of desolation. Book of Daniel. 2001 ⇒4028. 421-446/671-688.

4064 **Makujina, John** Old Persian calques in the Aramaic of Daniel. Diss. Westminster Sem. 2001, ᴰ*Corley, B.* 272 pp. 3010606 [RTL 33,639].

4065 *Mathews, Susan F.* When we remembered Zion: the significance of the exile for understanding Daniel. The bible on suffering. 2001 ⇒ 326. 93-119.

4066 *Mosès, Stéphane* I quattro imperi. L'Eros e la legge. Schulim Vogelmann 80: 2001 <1997> ⇒185. 113-136.

4067 *Nel, M.* Danielboek as apokaliptiek. VeE 22 (2001) 366-378.

4068 **Niskanen, Paul Vincent** The human and the divine in history: HERO-DOTUS and the book of Daniel. Diss. Graduate Theol. Union 2001, 225 pp. 3007737.

4069 **Parchem, Marek** Pojęcie królęstwa bożego w księdze Daniela oraz jego recepcja w pismach qumrańskich i w apokaliptyce zydowskiej [La notion de royaume de Dieu dans le livre de Daniel et sa réception dans les écrits de Qumran et dans l'apocalyptique juive]. Diss. Warsaw 2001, ᴰ*Mędala, S.*: 443 pp. [RTL 33,633]. **P**.

4070 *Rowland, Christopher* The book of Daniel and the radical critique of empire: an essay in apocalyptic hermeneutics;

4071 *Smith-Christopher, Daniel* Prayers and dreams: power and diaspora identities in the social setting of the Daniel tales;

4072 *Stuckenbruck, Loren T.* Daniel and early Enoch traditions in the Dead Sea scrolls. Book of Daniel. 2001 ⇒4028. 447-67/266-290/368-386.

4073 *Sweeney, Marvin A.* The end of eschatology in Daniel?: theological and socio-political ramifications of the changing contexts of interpretation. BiblInterp 9 (2001) 123-140.

4074 *Van der Toorn, Karel* Scholars at the oriental court: the figure of Daniel against its Mesopotamian background. Book of Daniel. 2001 ⇒4028. 37-54.

4075 *Vázquez Allegue, Jaime* Trasfondo socio-histórico del libro de Daniel (de la crisis seléucida a la secesión de Qumrán). ResB 30 (2001) 13-20.

4076 *Venter, P.M.* Violence and non-violence in Daniel. OTEs 14 (2001) 311-329.

4077 *Wesselius, Jan-Wim* The writing of Daniel. Book of Daniel. 2001 ⇒ 4028. 291-310.

4078 *Henze, Matthias* The narrative frame of Daniel: a literary assessment. JSJ 32 (2001) 5-24 [Dan 1-6].

4079 *Paul, Shalom M.* The Mesopotamian Babylonian background of Daniel 1-6. Book of Daniel. 2001 ⇒4028. 55-68.

4080 *Husser, J.-M.* Théologie du pouvoir politique dans les récits araméens de Daniel. TEuph 22 (2001) 21-34 [Dan 2-6].

4081 **Melnyk, Janet L.R.** The four kingdoms in Daniel 2 and 7: chapters in the history of interpretation. Diss. Emory 2001, 200 pp. 3009454.

4082 *Kulczak-Rudiger, Friederike Maria, al.,* Jünglinge im Feuerofen. RAC 19. 2001 ⇒660. 346-388 [Dan 3].

4083 *Van Henten, Jan Willem* Daniel 3 and 6 in early christian literature. Book of Daniel. 2001 ⇒4028. 149-169.

4084 **Henze, Matthias** The madness of King Nebuchadnezzar: the ancient Near Eastern origins and early history of interpretation of Daniel 4. JSJ.S 61: 1999 ⇒15,3992. ᴿBib. 82 (2001) 564-68 (*Albertz, Rainer*).

4085 *Henze, Matthias* Nebuchadnezzar's madness (Daniel 4) in Syriac literature. Book of Daniel. 2001 ⇒4028. 550-571.

4086 *Lacocque, André* Allusions to creation in Daniel 7. Book of Daniel. 2001 ⇒4028. 114-131.

4087 *Muñoz León, Domingo* Profecía con futuro: la venida de un hijo de hombre (Dn 7). ResB 30 (2001) 29-36.

4088 *Tuckett, Christopher M.* The Son of man and Daniel 7: Q and Jesus. The sayings source Q. BEThL 158: 2001 ⇒477. 371-394.

4089 *Walton, John H.* The Anzu myth as relevant background for Daniel 7?. Book of Daniel. 2001 ⇒4028. 69-89.

4090 *Kratz, Reinhard G.* The visions of Daniel. Book of Daniel. 2001 ⇒4028. 91-113 [Dan 7-12].

4091 *Gardner, Anne E.* Daniel 7,2-14: another look at its mythic pattern. Bib. 82 (2001) 244-252.

4092 *Royer, Wilfred Sophrony* The Ancient of Days: patristic and modern views of Daniel 7:9-14. SVTQ 45 (2001) 137-162.

4093 *Shea, William H.* Supplementary evidence in support of 457 B.C. as the starting date for the 2300 day-years of Daniel 8:14. JATS 12/1 (2001) 89-96.

4094 *Asurmendi, Jesús María* Las setenta semanas (Dn 9). ResB 30 (2001) 37-43.

4095 *Meadowcroft, Tim* Exploring the dismal swamp: the identity of the anointed one in Daniel 9:24-27. JBL 120 (2001) 429-449.

4096 *Haag, Ernst* Daniel 12 und die Auferstehung der Toten. Book of Daniel. 2001 ⇒4028. 132-148.

4097 *Fournier Mathews, Susan* The numbers in Daniel 12:11-12: rounded Pythagorean plane numbers?. CBQ 63 (2001) 630-646.

4098 **Fabre, Marie-Louise** Suzanne ou les avatars d'un motif biblique. 2000 ⇒16,4125. ᴿASSR 46 (2001) 117-119 (*Vogels, Christian*); FV 100/4 (2001) 102 (*Fabre, Marie-Louise*).

4099 *Tronina, Antoni* Historia Zuzanny (Dn 13) w tradycji rzymskiej. ᶠJANKOWSKI, A. 2001 ⇒53. 405-412. **P.**

4100 *Calduch Benages, Nuria* Un sabio que enseña con historias. ResB 30 (2001) 45-51 [Dan 13-14].

4101 *Haag, Ernst* Bel und Drache: Tradition und Interpretation in Daniel 14. TThZ 110 (2001) 20-46.

E9.3 *Prophetae Minores*, **Dōdekaprophetōn...Hosea, Joel**

4102 **Barton, John** Joel and Obadiah: a commentary. OTL: LVL 2001, Westminster xxi; 168 pp. $40. 0-664-21966-7. Bibl. xiii-xxi.

4103 *Calabria, Nicola* Osea ed Amos. PalCl n..s. 1 (2001) 799-806.

4104 **Carbone, Sandro Paolo; Rizzi, Giovanni** Aggeo, Gioele, Giona, Malachia: secondo il testo ebraico masoretico, secondo la versione greca della LXX, secondo la parafrasi aramaica targumica. Lettura e-braica, greca e aramaica 5: Bo 2001, EDB 544 pp. €54.23. 88-10-20591-X. Bibl. 19-29;

4105 Abaquq, Abdia, Nahum, Sofonia: lettura ebraica greca aramaica. 1998 ⇒14,3619. ᴿRivBib 49 (2001) 93-94 (*Savoca, Gaetano*).

4106 **Coggins, Richard James** Joel and Amos. NCeB: 2000 ⇒16,4127. ᴿRExp 98 (2001) 445-447 (*Biddle, Mark E.*); CBQ 63 (2001) 714 (*O'Brien, Julia Myers*).

4107 *Crenshaw, James L.* Latter prophets: the minor prophets. The Blackwell companion to the Hebrew Bible. 2001 ⇒653. 369-381;

4108 Theodicy in the book of the Twelve;

4109 *De Vries, Simon J.* Futurism in the preexilic minor prophets compared with that of the postexilic minor prophets. SBL.SP 2001. SBL. SPS 40: 2001 ⇒494. 1-18/19-38.

4110 *Dogniez, Cécile* Fautes de traduction, ou bonnes traductions?: quelques exemples pris dans la LXX des Douze Petits Prophètes. X Congress IOSCS. SBL.SCSt 51: 2001 ⇒499. 241-261.

4111 ᵀ**Domínguez García, Avelino** San JERÓNIMO: Obras completas, IIIa: comentarios a los Profetas Menores. 2000 ⇒16,12749. ᴿEstFil 143 (2001) 208-209 (*Aniz Iriarte, Cándido*).

4112 **Floyd, Michael H.** Minor prophets, part 2. FOTL 22: 2000 ⇒16, 4130. ᴿJThS 52 (2001) 163-166 (*Tollington, Janet*); ThLZ 126 (2001) 1245-1247 (*Koenen, Klaus*).

4113 Gioele, Amos, Abdia: versione ufficiale italiana confrontata con e-braico masoretico, greco dei Settanta... ᴱ**Sgargi, Giorgio** 1998 ⇒14, 3632; 16,4147. ᴿRdT 42 (2001) 935-936 (*Fanuli, Antonio*).

4114 ᵀ**Harl, Marguerite** La Bible d'Alexandrie, 23: les douze prophètes, 4-9: Joël, Abdiou, Jonas, Naoum, Ambakoum, Sophonie. 1999 ⇒15, 4003. ᴿCBQ 63 (2001) 111-112 (*Cox, Claude*); JBL 120 (2001) 756-757 & RBLit 3 (2001) 136-137 (*Peters, Melvin K.H.*).

4115 *Jaruzelska, Izabela* Amos et Osée face aux rois d'Israël. Prophètes et rois. LeDiv: 2001 ⇒292. 145-176.

4116 **Prior, David** The message of Joel, Micah, and Habakkuk: listening to the voice of God. The Bible speaks today: 1998 ⇒14,3628. ᴿCTJ 36 (2001) 148-149 (*Vander Vliet, Marvin*).

4117 *Redditt, Paul L.* Recent research on the book of the Twelve as one book. CurResB 9 (2001) 47-80;

4118 The formation of the book of the Twelve: a review of research. SBL.SP 2001. SBL.SPS 40: 2001 ⇒494. 58-80.

4119 *Rendtorff, Rolf* How to read the book of the Twelve as a theological unity. Der Text in seiner Endgestalt. 2001 ⇒201. 139-151;

4120 Alas for the day!: the "Day of the LORD" in the book of the Twelve. Der Text in seiner Endgestalt. 2001 ⇒201. 253-264.

4121 **Roth, Martin** Israel und die Völker: eine Untersuchung zu den Büchern Joel, Jona, Micha und Nahum als Beitrag zur Theologie und Religionsgeschichte des zweiten Tempels. Diss. Basel 2001, ᴰ*Mathys, H.P.*: 319 pp [RTL 33,634].

4122 *Schultz, Richard L.* The ties that bind: intertextuality, the identification of verbal parallels, and reading strategies in the book of the Twelve. SBL.SP 2001. SBL.SPS 40: 2001 ⇒494. 39-57.

4123 **Sweeney, Marvin A.** The Twelve Prophets. 2000 ⇒16,4150. ᴿScrB 31/1 (2001) 46-47 (*O'Kane, Martin*); PIBA 24 (2001) 124-126 (*O' Leary, Anthony*); CBQ 63 (2001) 732-734 (*Craghan, John F.*).

4124 **Beeley, Ray** Wayward but loved: a commentary and meditations on Hosea. E 2001, Banner of Truth Trust viii; 224 pp. 0-85151-797-8.

4125 *Berge, Kåre* Victim and victimizer: plotting God in the book of Hosea. TTK 72 (2001) 69-84.

4126 *Bowman, Craig D.* Prophetic grief, divine grace: the marriage of Hosea. RestQ 43/4 (2001) 229-242.

4127 *Dearman, J. Andrew* Interpreting the religious polemics against Baal and the Baalim in the book of Hosea. OTEs 14 (2001) 9-25.

4128 *Dempsey, Carol J.* Hosea's use of nature. BiTod 39 (2001) 347-353.

4129 **Fuß, Barbara** "Dies ist die Zeit... die expliziten Zitate aus dem Buch Hosea in den Handschriften von Qumran und im Neuen Testament. NTA 37: 2000 ⇒16,4158. ᴿJThS 52 (2001) 769-771 (*Brooke, George J.*); CBQ 63 (2001) 519-520 (*Nogalski, James D.*).

4130 **Jeremias, Jörg** Osea. ᵀ*Ronchi, Franco* 2000 ⇒16,4161. ᴿRivBib 49 (2001) 239-241 (*Virgili dal Pra, Rosanna*).

4131 **Keefe, Alice A.** Woman's body and the social body in Hosea. JSOT.S 338; Gender, Culture, Theory 10: Shf 2001, Sheffield A. 252 pp. 1-84127-247-7. Bibl. 222-243.

4132 *Kessler, Stephan Ch.* Die patristischen Hoseakommentare: zur Rezeption der Kleinen Propheten in der Alten Kirche. StPatr 34 (2001) 413-419.

4133 *Landy, Francis* In the wilderness of speech: problems of metaphor in Hosea. Beauty and the enigma. JSOT.S 312: 2001 <1995> ⇒171. 273-297.

4134 **Macintosh, Andrew Alexander** A critical and exegetical commentary on Hosea. ICC: 1997 ⇒13,3887... 16,4163. ᴿEvQ 73 (2001) 173-176 (*Johnstone, William*).

4135 *O'Kennedy, D.F.* Healing as/or forgiveness?: the use of the term רפא in the book of Hosea. OTEs 14 (2001) 458-474.

4136 **Pfeiffer, Henrik** Das Heiligtum von Bethel im Spiegel des Hoseabuches. FRLANT 183: 1999 ⇒15,4023. ᴿJThS 52 (2001) 167-170 (*Macintosh, A.A.*); ThLZ 126 (2001) 1252-1256 (*Schart, Aaron*).

4137 *Polan, Gregory J.* Hosea's interpretation of Israel's traditions. BiTod 39 (2001) 329-334.

4138 **Solà, Teresa; Raurell, Frederic** Oseas, teologia renovadora des d'una hermenèutica d'amor. 2000 ⇒16,4165. ᴿLaur. 42 (2001) 576-578 (*Tous Mur, Llorenç*); CBQ 63 (2001) 731-732 (*Gossai, Hemchand*); RCatT 26 (2001) 195-201 (*Bosch Veciana, Antoni*).

4139 *Stone, Ken* Lovers and raisin cakes: food, sex and divine insecurity in Hosea. Queer commentary. JSOT.S 334: 2001 ⇒325. 116-139.

4140 **Trotter, James M.** Reading Hosea in Achaemenid Yehud. JSOT.S 328: Shf 2001, Sheffield A. 242 pp. 1-84127-197-7. Bibl. 226-234.

4141 *Vall, Gregory* Hosea and 'knowledge of God'. BiTod 39 (2001) 335-341.

4142 *Yee, Gale A.* "She is not my wife and I am not her husband": a materialist analysis of Hosea 1-2. BiblInterp 9 (2001) 345-383.

4143 *Braaten, Laurie J.* Earth community in Hosea 2. The earth story. 2001 ⇒275. 185-203.

4144 *Gangloff, Frédéric* A l'ombre des déesses-arbres? (Os 4:12-14). BN 106 (2001) 13-20.

4145 *Macintosh, Andrew A.* Hosea: the rabbinic commentators and the ancient versions. ᴹWEITZMAN, M.: JSOT.S 333: 2001 ⇒113. 77-82 [9, 2; 10,7; 13,15; 14,6].

4146 *Klopfenstein, Martin A.* Hosea 9,7-9: ein Lese- und Übersetzungsversuch. ThZ 57 (2001) 135-139.

4147 *Owens, J. Edward* Reflections on Hosea 11. BiTod 39 (2001) 343-6.

4148 *Siebert-Hommes, Jopie* 'With bands of love': Hosea 11 as 'recapitulation' of the basic themes in the book of Hosea;

4149 *Abma, Richtsje* Jacob, a questionable ancestor?: some questions on Hosea 12. ᶠDEURLOO, K.: ACEBT.S 2: 2001 ⇒23. 165-173/175-179.

4150 *Heintz, Jean-Georges* Osée XII 2b à la lumière d'un vase d'albâtre de l'époque de Salmanasar II (Djézirêh) et le rituel d'alliance assyrien: une hypothèse de lecture. VT 51 (2001) 466-480.

4151 *Schmitt, Hans-Christoph* Der Kampf Jakobs mit Gott in Hos 12,3ff. und in Gen 32,23ff.: zum Verständnis der Verborgenheit Gottes im

Hoseabuch und im elohistischen Geschichtswerk. Theologie in Prophetie. 2001 <1998> ⇒209. 165-188.

4152 *Bons, Eberhard* La signification de ἀρκος α[πορουμενη en LXX Osée XIII 8. VT 51 (2001) 1-8.

4153 **Oestreich, Bernhard** Metaphors and similes for Yahweh in Hosea 14:2-9 (1-8): a study of Hoseanic pictorial language. 1998 ⇒14, 3664; 16,4177. [R]RBLit 3 (2001) 226-229 (*Sweeney, Marvin A.*).

4154 *Mathews, Susan F.* The power to endure and be transformed: sun and moon imagery in Joel and Revelation 6. [F]FITZGERALD, A., CBQ.MS 32: 2001 ⇒31. 35-49.

E9.4 Amos

4155 *Carroll R., M. Daniel* Seeking the virtues among the prophets: the book of Amos as a test case. ExAu 17 (2001) 77-96.

4156 **Chung, Hyun Jin** Die theologische Botschaft des Visionszyklus in der Amosschrift. Diss. Mainz 2001, [D]*Zwickel, W.* [RTL 33,631].

4157 **Dahmen, Ulrich; Fleischer, Gunther** Das Buch Amos. Neuer Stuttgarter Kommentar zum AT 23/2: Stu 2001, Kath. Bibelwerk 292 pp. €26.90. 3-460-07232-6 [BiKi 59,47—Schmitz, Barbara].

4158 *Dassmann, Ernst* Amos. RAC, Suppl. Bd. 1. 2001 ⇒661. 333-350.

4159 **Jaruzelska, Izabela** Amos and the officialdom in the Kingdom of Israel. 1998 ⇒14,3680; 16,4187. [R]PEQ 133 (2001) 203-204 (*Williamson, H.G.M.*); JBL 119 (2000) 758-760 (*Moore, Michael S.*).

4160 *Landy, Francis* Vision and poetic speech in Amos. Beauty and the enigma. JSOT.S 312: 2001 <1987> ⇒171. 159-184.

4161 **Park, Aaron W.** The book of Amos as composed and read in antiquity. Studies in Biblical Literature 37: NY 2001, Lang xix; 256 pp. 0-8204-5244-0. Bibl. 223-241.

   Pschibille, J. Hat der Löwe erneut gebrüllt? 2001 ⇒3915.

4162 *Steins, Georg* Amos und Mose rücken zusammen: oder: was heißt intertextuelles Lesen der Bibel?. rhs 44 (2001) 20-28.

4163 *Vitório, Jaldemir* 'Os olhos do Senhor estão sobre o reino pecador' (Am 9,8): profetismo e história na pregação de Amós. Estudos Bíblicos 71 (2001) 32-41.

4164 *Malamat, Abraham* Amos 1:5 in the light of the Til Barsip inscriptions. History of biblical Israel. 2001 <1953> ⇒182. 366-369.

4165 *Pinker, Aron* Observations on some cruxes in Amos, 1, 2, 3. JBQ 29 (2001) 18-26; 87-95; 171-179.

4166 *Collins, Terry* Threading as a stylistic feature of Amos. The elusive prophet. OTS 45: 2001 ⇒485. 94-104 [Amos 3,4].

4167 *Köhlmoos, Melanie* Der Tod als Zeichen: die Inszenierung des Todes in Am 5. BN 107/108 (2001) 65-77.

4168 *Schoblocher, Birgit* "Er ist Finsternis und nicht Licht!": ein Beitrag zur Rede vom Tag YHWHs in Am 5,18-20. ᶠGRoß, W.: ATSAT 68: 2001 ⇒38. 99-111.

4169 *Preez, Jannie du* "Let justice roll on like ..." : some explanatory notes on Amos 5:24. JTSA 109 (2001) 95-98.

4170 *Becker, Uwe* Der Prophet als Fürbitter: zum literarhistorischen Ort der Amos-Visionen. VT 51 (2001) 141-165 [Gen 18,22-32; 7,1-8; 8, 1-2].

4171 *Dijkstra, Meindert* 'I am neither a prophet nor a prophet's pupil': Amos 7:9-17 as the presentation of a prophet like Moses. The elusive prophet. OTS 45: 2001 ⇒485. 105-128.

4172 *Sherwood, Yvonne* Of fruit and corpses and wordplay visions: picturing Amos 8.1-3. JSOT 92 (2001) 5-27.

4173 *Lang, Martin; Meßner, Reinhard* Gott erbaut sein himmlisches Heiligtum: zur Bedeutung von אֲגֻדָּתוֹ in Am 9,6. Bib. 82 (2001) 93-98.

E9.5 Jonas

4174 *Abela, Anthony* When the agenda of an artistic composition is hidden: Jonah and intertextual dialogue with Isaiah 6, the 'Confessions of Jeremiah', and other texts. The elusive prophet. 2001 ⇒485.1-30.

4175 ᴱ**Bedini, Chiara; Bigarelli, Alberto** Il viaggio di Giona: targum, midrash, commento di RASHI. Tradizione d'Israele. 1999 ⇒15,4071. ᴿCivCatt 152/4 (2001) 302-304 (*Prato, G.L.*).

4176 *Blanpain, Jean-Luc* Prier en ville: la surprise de Jonas. LV.F 56 (2001) 305-310.

4177 *Chopineau, Jacques* Avant de relire Jonas: introduction;

4178 Après la relecture de Jonas. AnBru 6 (2001) 122-148/149-172.

4179 *Eagleton, Terry J.L.* AUSTIN and the book of Jonah. The postmodern bible reader. 2001 <1990> ⇒287. 177-182.

4180 *Golka, Friedemann W.* Jona/Jonabuch. RGG², 4. 2001 ⇒664. 567-9.

4181 *Hill, Charles* Jonah in Antioch. Ment. *Theodoret*. Pacifica 14 (2001) 245-261.

4182 **Jiménez Hernández, Emiliano** Jonás, las setenta caras del profeta. Tripode: Bilbao 2001, Grafite 303 pp. 84-95042-51-7.

4183 *Rube-Glatt, Christina* Das Zeichen des Jona. PzB 10 (2001) 41-56 [Isaiah 2,2-4; Joel 4,1-9].

4184 **Simon, Uriel** Jonah. ^T*Schramm, Lenn J.* 1999 ⇒15,4087. ^RRBLit 3 (2001) 229-231 (*Marcus, David*).
4185 *Terrinoni, Ubaldo* Giona o la parabola della disobbedienza. RCI 82/1 (2001) 45-56.
4186 *Willi-Plein, Ina* Jona als Beispiel narrativer Diskussionskultur. ^FSEY-BOLD, K. AOAT 280: 2001 ⇒102. 217-229.

4187 *Hunter, Alastair G.* Jonah from the whale: Exodus motifs in Jonah 2. The elusive prophet. 2001 ⇒485. 142-158 [Neh 9,9-11; Ps 55].
4188 *Chopineau, Jacques* 'La ville de la colombe': Jonas 3 comme relecture actualisante. AnBru 6 (2001) 114-121.
4189 *Lawson, Steven J.* The power of biblical preaching: an expository study of Jonah 3:1-10. BS 158 (2001) 331-346.
4190 *Loader, James Alfred* Gottes Umkehr und prophetische Absurdität: zum umgekehrten Bekenntnis in Jona 4,2-3. Begegnung mit Gott. Wiener alttestamentliche Studien 3: 2001 ⇒175. 139-149.

E9.6 *Micheas*, **Micah**

4191 **Andersen, Francis I.; Freedman, David Noel** Micah. AncB 24E: 2000 ⇒16,4237. ^RJThS 52 (2001) 739-741 (*Tollington, Janet*); RExp 98 (2001) 447-448 (*Jones, Barry A.*); CBQ 63 (2001) 507-508 (*Biddle, Mark E.*).
4192 **Ben Zvi, Ehud** Micah. FOTL 21B: 2000 ⇒16,4238. ^RJThS 52 (2001) 170-172 (*Mason, Rex*); CBQ 63 (2001) 132-134 (*Biddle, Mark E.*); JBL 120 (2001) 751-753 (*Wagenaar, Jan A.*); ThLZ 126 (2001) 743-744 (*Utzschneider, Helmut*); RBLit 3 (2001) 231-234 (*Wagenaar, Jan A.*).
4193 **Jacobs, Mignon R.** The conceptual coherence of the book of Micah. JSOT.S 322: Shf 2001, Sheffield A. 283 pp. $80. 1-84127-176-4. Bibl. 260-268.
4194 **Kessler, Rainer** Micha. HThK.AT: 1999 ⇒15,4097; 16,4242. ^RETR 76 (2001) 115-117 (*Vincent, Jean Marcel*); BZ 45 (2001) 112-115 (*Utzschneider, Helmut*); ThLZ 126 (2001) 1135-1136 (*Thiel, Winfried*).
4195 **McKane, William** The book of Micah: introduction and commentary. 1998 ⇒14,3713... 16,4243. ^RJSSt 46 (2001) 169-170 (*Tomes, Roger*).
4196 **Runions, Erin** Changing subjects: gender, nation and future in Micah. Playing the texts 7: L 2001, Sheffield A. 295 pp. 1-84127-269-8.
4197 *Utzschneider, Helmut* Das griechische Michabuch—zur Probe übersetzt und erläutert im Rahmen des Projekts "Septuaginta-Deutsch—

das Griechische Alte Testament in Übersetzung". Im Brennpunkt BWANT 8,13: 2001 ⇒1629. 213-250.

4198 *Wagenaar, Jan A.* Judgement and salvation: the composition and redaction of Micah 2-5. VT.S 85: Lei 2001, Brill vii; 361 pp. $123. 90-04-11936-1. Bibl. 329-338.

4199 *Mariottini, Claudemiro F.* Yahweh, the breaker of Israel (Micah 2:12-13). PRSt 28/4 (2001) 385-393.

4200 *Wagenaar, Jan A.* You eat the flesh of my people and break their bones: the reversal of fortunes in the judgement of fortunes in the judgement oracle Micah 3:1-4. OTEs 14 (2001) 525-532.

4201 *Sweeney, Marvin A.* Micah's debate with Isaiah. JSOT 93 (2001) 111-124 [Isaiah 2,2-4,5; Micah 4,1-5,14].

4202 *Runions, Eric* Called to do justice?: a Bhabhian reading of Micah 5 and 6:1-8. Postmodern interpretations. 2001 ⇒229. 153-164.

4203 *Schmidt, Ludwig* Micha 5,1-5: ein Beispiel für die historische Auslegung alttestamentlicher Texte. Was ist ein Text?. Neutestamentliche Entwürfe zur Theologie 1: 2001 ⇒335. 15-27.

E9.7 *Abdias, Sophonias...*Obadiah, Zephaniah, Nahum

4204 **Raabe, Paul R.** Obadiah. AncB 24D: 1996 ⇒12,3784; 16,4254. ᴿJBL 119 (2000) 555-558 (*Ben Zvi, Ehud*).

4205 *Johnston, Gordon H.* Nahum's rhetorical allusions to Neo-Assyrian treaty curses. BS 158 (2001) 415-436;

4206 Nahum's rhetorical allusions to the Neo-Assyrian lion motif. BS 158 (2001) 287-307 [Nah 2,11-13].

4207 **Spronk, Klaas** Nahum. 1997 ⇒13,3929; 15,4129. ᴿJBL 120 (2001) 158-159 (*McLaughlin, John L.*); OLZ 96 (2001) 71-76 (*Baumann, Gerlinde*).

4208 *Weigl, Michael* Current research on the book of Nahum: exegetical methodologies in turmoil?. CurResB 9 (2001) 81-130.

4209 *Dogniez, Cécile* La Bible d'Alexandrie, 2: select passage: Sophonie (Zephaniah) 3,8-11. X Congress IOSCS. 2001 ⇒499. 199-216.

4210 *Greenfield, Jonas C.* A hapax legomenon: חרול ממשק. ʿAl kanfei yonah, 2. 2001 <1982> ⇒153. 734-737 [Zeph 2,9].

4211 *Holladay, William L.* Reading Zephaniah with a concordance: suggestions for a redaction history. JBL 120 (2001) 671-684.

4212 *Irsigler, Hubert* Der Freudenaufruf an Zion in Israels Prophetie: Żef 3,14-15 und seine Parallelen. ᶠSCHMUTTERMAYR, G. 2001 ⇒101. 49-74.

4213 **Vlaardingerbroek, Johannes** Zephaniah. 1999 ⇒15,4125. ᴿThLZ 126 (2001) 33-34 (*Neef, Heinz-Dieter*).

E9.8 *Habacuc*, **Habakkuk**

4214 **Andersen, Francis I.** Habakkuk: a new translation with introduction and commentary. AncB 25: NY 2001, Doubleday xxii; 387 pp. $45. 0-385-08396-3.

4215 *Dangl, Oskar* Habakkuk in recent research. CurResB 9 (2001) 131-168.

4216 *Gorgulho, Maria Laura* Habacuc: uma visão bíblica sobre a violência. Estudos Bíblicos 69 (2001) 19-31.

4217 *Herrmann, W.* Das unerledigte Problem des Buches Habakkuk. VT 51 (2001) 481-496.

4218 *Huwyler, Beat* Habakuk und seine Psalmen. ᶠSEYBOLD, K. AOAT 280: 2001 ⇒102. 231-259.

4219 *Dangl, Oskar* "Canonical approach" am Buch Habakuk?: Hab 2,4b als Lebenszusage. PzB 10 (2001) 131-148.

4220 *Penna, Romano* Il giusto e la fede: Ab 2,4b e le sue antiche riletture giudaiche e cristiane. Vangelo e inculturazione. 2001 <1998> ⇒193. 484-511.

4221 *Prinsloo, G.T.M.* Yahweh the warrior: an intertextual reading of Habakkuk 3. OTEs 14 (2001) 475-493.

4222 *Wendland, Ernst R.* "May the whole world hush in his presence!" (Habakkuk 2:20b): communicating aspects of the rhetoric of an ancient biblical text today. JNSL 27/2 (2001) 113-133 [Hab 3].

4223 *Shupak, Nili* The God who comes from Teman and the Egyptian sun god: a new study of Habakkuk 3:3-7. ᶠAHITUV, S. 2001 ⇒1. 409-432. **H.**

E9.9 *Aggaeus*, **Haggai**—*Zacharias*, **Zechariah**—*Malachias*, **Malachi**

4224 *Kessler, John* Reconstructing Haggai's Jerusalem: demographic and sociological considerations and the search for an adequate methodological point of departure. Urbanism and prophecy. JSOT.S 330: 2001 ⇒271. 137-158.

4225 *Sérandour, Arnaud* Zacharie et les autorités de son temps. Prophètes et rois. LeDiv: 2001 ⇒292. 259-298.

4226 *Boda, Mark J.* Oil, crowns and thrones: prophet, priest and king in Zechariah 1:7-6:15. Journal of Hebrew Scriptures 3 (2001) [electr. journ.].

4227 *Bruehler, Bart B.* Seeing through the עינים of Zechariah: understanding Zechariah 4. CBQ 63 (2001) 430-443.

4228 *Hofmann, Yair* The pericope of the fasts in the book of Zechariah: 7: 1-6, 18-19 and the shaping of the national memory. ᶠAHITUV, S. 2001 ⇒1. 112-145. **H.**

4229 *Caldwell, Elizabeth F.* Zechariah 8:1-8. Interp. 55 (2001) 185-187.

4230 *Rudman, Dominic* Zechariah 8:20-22 & Isaiah 2:2-4//Micah 4:2-3: a study in intertextuality. BN 107/108 (2001) 50-54.

4231 **Kunz, Andreas** Zions Weg zum Frieden: jüdische Vorstellungen vom endzeitlichen Krieg und Frieden in hellenistischer Zeit am Beispiel von Sacharja 9-14. Beiträge zur Friedensethik 33: Stu 2001, Kohlhammer 43 pp. €12.50. 3-17-016822-3.

4232 *Hurowitz, Victor Avigdor* Splitting the sacred mountain: Zechariah 14,4 and Gilgamesh V, ii 4-5. BetM 167 (2001) 304-9. Sum. 384. **H.**

4233 *Botha, P.J.* Honour and shame as keys to the interpretation of Malachi. OTEs 14 (2001) 392-403.

4234 **Weyde, Karl William** Prophecy and teaching: prophetic authority, form problems, and the use of traditions in...Malachi. BZAW 288: 2000 ⇒16,4295. ᴿBiblInterp 9 (2001) 338-40 (*McKenzie, Steven L.*).

VIII. NT Exegesis generalis

F1.1 New Testament introduction

4235 **Achtemeier, Paul J.; Green, Joel B.; Thompson, Marianne Meye** Introducing the New Testament: its literature and theology. GR 2001, Eerdmans xii; 624 pp. $35. 0-8028-3717-4.

4236 ᴱ**Bockmuehl, Markus** The Cambridge companion to Jesus. Cambridge companions to religion: C 2001, CUP xviii; 311 pp. £16. 0-521-79261-4/678-4. Bibl. 281-298.

4237 **Broer, Ingo** Einleitung in das Neue Testament, 2: die Briefliteratur, die Offenbarung des Johannes und die Bildung des Kanons. NEB

Erg. Bd. z. N.T. 2/2: Wü 2001, Echter 442 pp. €34.80. 3-429-02316-5. [R]OrdKor 42 (2001) 557-558 (*Giesen, Heinz*).

4238 **Brown, Raymond Edward** Introduzione al Nuovo Testamento. [E]*Boscolo, Gastone*: Brescia 2001, Queriniana 1130 pp. 88399-01051.

4239 **Casalini, Nello** Iniziazione al Nuovo Testamento. ASBF 53: J 2001, Franciscan Printing Pr. 396 pp. 965-516-002-5.

4240 **Cullmann, O.** Introduzione al Nuovo Testamento. Bo 2001, Mulino 163 pp.

4241 **Donelson, Lewis R.** From Hebrews to Revelation: a theological introduction. LVL 2001, Westminster v; 161 pp. $20. 0-664-22236-6 [ThD 48,265—Heiser, W. Charles].

4242 **Drane, John** Introducing the New Testament. Mp 2001, Fortress 480 pp. $29. 0-8006-3272-9. Rev. ed.

4243 **Ellis, Edward Earle** The making of the New Testament documents. BiblInterp. 39: 1999 ⇒15,4171; 16,4310. [R]JThS 52 (2001) 218-222 (*Moule, C.F.D.*); Salm. 48 (2001) 344-351 (*Trevijano, Ramón*); JBL 120 (2001) 767-769 (*Chancey, Mark A.*); RExp 98 (2001) 608-609 (*Givens, J.M.*); ThLZ 126 (2001) 281-283 (*Lindemann, Andreas*); RBLit 3 (2001) 319-321 (*Chancey, Mark A.*).

4244 **Elwell, Walter A.; Yarbrough, Robert W.** Studienbuch Neues Testament. Wu 2001, Brockhaus 448 pp. 3-417-24694-6.

4245 **Houdry, Lucien** La naissance du Nouveau Testament. 1999 ⇒15, 4178. [R]NRTh 123 (2001) 101-102 (*Radermakers, J.*).

4246 **Köster, Helmut** Introduction to the New Testament 1, history and literature of early christianity. NY [2]2000, De Gruyter xxxvii; 374 pp. 3-11-014693-2/2-4.

4247 **Maggioni, Romeo** Vieni al Padre!: un "vangelo" per il terzo millennio. CinB 2001, San Paolo 187 pp. 88-215-4485-0.

4248 [E]**Marguerat, Daniel L.** Introduction au Nouveau Testament. 2000 ⇒16,4322. [R]ETR 76 (2001) 269-273 (*Campbell, Gordon*); Cart. 17 (2001) 441-442 (*Sanz Valdivieso, R.*).

4249 **McDonald, Lee Martin: Porter, Stanley E.** Early christianity and its sacred literature. 2000 ⇒16,4323. [R]Theol. 104 (2001) 447-449 (*Houlden, Leslie*); OCP 67 (2001) 470-473 (*Farrugia, E.G.*).

4250 **Meiser, Martin** Neues Testament—Kirchengeschichte: ein Arbeitsbuch. 2000 ⇒16,4324. [R]ZKG 112 (2001) 379-380 (*Lexutt, Athina*).

4251 **Motyer, Alec** The story of the New Testament. L 2001, Candle 157 pp. £8. 1-85985-400-1.

4252 **Omodeo, Adolfo** Storia delle origini cristiane, 1: Gesù, 2: Prolegomeni alla storia dell'età apostolica, 3: Paolo di Tarso. 2000 <1949-1950> ⇒16,4326. [R]RSLR 37 (2001) 347-351 (*Bolgiani, Franco*).

4253 **Riley, Gregory John** One Jesus, many Christs: how Jesus inspired not one true christianity, but many. 1997 ⇒13,4010. [R]JBL 119 (2000) 131-133 (*Maclean, Jennifer K. Berenson*).

4254 **Rinaldi, Giancarlo** La bibbia dei pagani, 1-2. 1997-98 ⇒14,3808; 15,4533. [R]RivBib 49 (2001) 111-113 (*Penna, Romano*).

4255 **Simoens, Yves** Entrer dans l'alliance: une introduction au Nouveau Testament. P 2001, Médiasèvres 276 pp. 2-900-388-60-9 [ATG 65,323—Peña, E.].

4256 **Strecker, Georg** History of NT literature. [T]*Katter, Calvin*: 1997 ⇒ 13,4019. [R]JBL 119 (2000) 349-351 (*Weidmann, Frederick*).

4257 **Tarazi, Paul Nadim** The New Testament: introduction, 2: Luke and Acts. Crestwood, NY 2001, St Vladimir Seminary Pr. 303 pp.

4258 **Theissen, Gerd** A theory of primitive christian religion. 1999 ⇒15, 4201; 16,4331. [R]StPat 48 (2001) 670-674 (*Segalla, Giuseppe*).

4259 **Thellung, Antonio** Un po' meno della verità: l'antivangelo nel vangelo. R 2001, Borla 150 pp. 88-263-1405-5. Pres., post. *Carlo Molari*.

4260 **Untergaßmair, Franz Georg** Handbuch der Einleitung, 1-2: Evangelien... Offenbarung. Vechtaer Beiträge zur Theologie 4/1-2: 1999 ⇒15,4202; 16,4332. [R]ThRv 97 (2001) 310-313 (*Hübner, Hans*).

4261 **Vouga, François** Il cristianesimo delle origini: scritti, protagonisti, dibattiti. Strumenti, Biblica 7: T 2001, Claudiana 300 pp. €23.21. [R]StPat 48 (2001) 747-748 (*Sartori, Luigi*);

4262 Los primeros pasos del cristianismo: escritos, protagonistas, debates. Agora 7: Estella (Navarra) 2001, Verbo Divino 297 pp. 84-8169-430-4. Bibl. 285-292.

4263 **Wenham, David; Walton, Steve** Exploring the New Testament, 1: a guide to the Gospels and Acts. L 2001, SPCK xii; 302 pp. $25. 0-281-05433-9.

4264 *Winter, Bruce W.* Harvesting evidence for New Testament studies. TynB 52 (2001) 319-320.

F1.2 *Origo Evangeliorum*, the origin of the Gospels

4265 **Black, David Alan** Why four gospels?: the historical origins of the gospels. GR 2001, Kregel 118 pp. $10 0-8254-2070-9 Bibl. 95-112

4266 **Gerhardsson, Birger** The reliability of the gospel tradition. Peabody 2001 <1977>, Hendrickson xxiv; 143 pp. $15. 1-56563-667-8. Foreword *Donald Hagner* [BiTod 40,197—Senior, Donald].

4267 **Hengel, Martin** The four gospels and the one gospel of Jesus Christ. 2000 ⇒16,4337. [R]BiblInterp 9 (2001) 418-421 (*Witherington, Ben*); CBQ 63 (2001) 748-749 (*Collins, Adela Yarbro*); ThLZ 126 (2001) 925-929 (*Heckel, Theo K.*).

4268 *Penna, Romano Kerygma* e storia alle origini del cristianesimo: le narrazioni evangeliche e le più antiche biografie di ALESSANDRO Magno. Vangelo e inculturazione. 2001 <1997> ⇒193. 231-251.

4269 *Sanday, William* The interpretation of the gospels as affected by the newer historical methods. Essays in biblical criticism. JSNT.S 225: 2001 <1903> ⇒205. 33-39.

4270 **Schmithals, Walter** Die Evangelisten als Schriftsteller: zur Geschichte des frühen Christentums. Z 2001, TVZ 127 pp. 3-290-17228-7.

4271 **Schulz, Hans-Joachim** Die apostolische Herkunft der Evangelien. QD 145: 1994 ⇒10,3906... 13,4028. ᴿSNTU.A 22 (1997) 238-241 (*Schreiber, S.*).

4272 *Sim, David C.* The gospels for all christians?: a response to Richard Bauckham. JSNT 84 (2001) 3-27.

4273 **Tragan, Pius-Ramon** La preistoria dei vangeli: tradizione cristiana primitiva: valore storico, forma e contenuto. Quaderni di ricerca 72: Sotto il Monte (BG) 2001, Servitium 205 pp. 88-8166-116-0.

4274 **Wills, Lawrence Mitchell** The quest of the historical gospel: Mark, John and the origins of the gospel genre. 1997 ⇒13,4032... 15,4218. ᴿNT 43 (2001) 180-182 (*Spensley, B.E.*); JBL 119 (2000) 133-135 (*Goodacre, Mark*).

F1.3 Historicitas, *chronologia* Evangeliorum

4275 **Bazec, Dario** La cronologia dei vangeli secondo il calendario ebraico. Trieste 2001, Italo Svevo xiv; 214 pp. 42 tables.

4276 *Bogaert, Pierre-Maurice* Les quatre vivants, l'évangile et les évangiles. RTL 32 (2001) 457-478.

4277 **Byrskog, Samuel** Story as history—history as story: the gospel tradition in the context of ancient oral history. WUNT 123: 2000 ⇒16, 4343. ᴿBS 158 (2001) 245 (*Bock, Darrell L.*); SvTK 77 (2001) 86-87 (*Rydbeck, Lars*); BiblInterp 9 (2001) 422-424 (*Evans, Craig A.*); Sal. 63 (2001) 770-771 (*Vicent, R.*); CBQ 63 (2001) 544-546 (*Carter, Warren*); TynB 52 (2001) 275-294 (*Head, Peter M.*).

4278 **Carrón Pérez, J.; García Pérez, J.M.** Cuándo fueron escritos los evangelios: el testimonio de Pablo. Studia semitica Novi Testamenti 7: M 2001, Encuentro 180 pp. ᴿCDios 214 (2001) 514-515 (*Gutiérrez, J.*); VyV 59 (2001) 582-584 (*Álvarez Barredo, Miguel*).

4279 **Graffy, Adrian** Trustworthy and true: the gospels beyond 2000. Dublin 2001, Columba 258 pp. €12.70. 1-85607-332-7. Bibl. 254. ᴿMillSt 48 (2001) 153-155 (*Rogers, Patrick*).

4280 **Heckel, Theo K.** Vom Evangelium des Markus zum viergestaltigen Evangelium. WUNT 120: 1999 ⇒15,4220. ᴿRBLit 3 (2001) 385-386 (*Syreeni, Kari*); JThS 52 (2001) 297-301 (*Parker, D.C.*); ZRGG 53 (2001) 379-381 (*Horn, Friedrich W.*).

4281 *Sanday, William* The New Testament background. Essays in biblical criticism. JSNT.S 225: 2001 <1918> ⇒205. 59-78.

4282 *Stiver, Dan R.* RICOEUR, speech-act theory, and the gospels as history. ᶠTHISELTON, A. 2001 ⇒106. 50-72.

F1.4 *Jesus historicus*—The human Jesus

4283 ᴱ**Labahn, Michael; Schmidt, Andreas** Jesus, Mark and Q: the teaching of Jesus and its earliest records. JSNT.S 214: Shf 2001, Sheffield A. 296 pp. £40/$64. 1-84127-218-3.

4284 **Abrahamson, Magnus** Jesu uppståndelse som historiskt problem: en studie av Rudolf BULTMANNs och Wolfhart PANNENBERGs tolkningar. Diss. Uppsala: Skellefteå 2001, Norma 265 pp.

4285 **Adinolfi, Marco** A tavola con Gesù di Nazaret. CasM 2001, Portalupi 139 pp. €7.23. 88-8441-010-X.

4286 **Allen, Charlotte V.** The human Christ: the search for the historical Jesus. 1998 ⇒14,3836. ᴿThTo 57 (2001) 533-35 (*Black, C. Clifton*).

4287 **Allison, Dale C.** Jesus of Nazareth: millenarian prophet. 1998 ⇒14, 3837; 16,4350. ᴿJBL 119 (2000) 357-360 (*Patterson, Stephen J.*).

4288 *Awwad, Johnny* The kingdom of God and the state: Jesus' attitude to the power and governing structures of his day. ThRev 22 (2001) 35-60.

4289 *Backhaus, Knut* Undeutlichkeit: von einem deutlichen Vorzug der Jesus-Überlieferung. ThGl 91 (2001) 369-389.

4290 *Bartolomé, Juan J.* Jesús de Nazaret, profeta galileo: Galilea, su patria: Jerusalén, su tumba. CuesTP 28 (2001) 23-35;

4291 La búsqueda del Jesús histórico: una crónica. EstB 59 (2001) 179-242;

4292 "Quién dice la gente que soy yo?" (Mc 8,27): la búsqueda contemporánea del Jesús histórico: una reseña. Sal. 63 (2001) 431-464.

4293 *Barton, Stephen C.* Many gospels, one Jesus?. The Cambridge companion to Jesus. 2001 ⇒4236. 170-183.

4294 *Batey, Richard A.* Sepphoris and the Jesus movement. NTS 47 (2001) 402-409.

4295 **Bennett, Clinton** In search of Jesus: insider and outsider images. L 2001, Continuum xi; 404 pp. £50/15. 0-8264-4916-6. Bibl. 365-388.

4296 **Bolyki, János** Jesu Tischgemeinschaften. WUNT 2/96: 1998 ⇒14, 3855... 16,4366. [R]JBL 119 (2000) 568-570 (*Taussig, Hal*).

4297 *Bruners, Wilhelm* Jesus—Schüler und Lehrer des Gebetes. Lebendige Katechese 23 (2001) 73-78.

4298 **Bultmann, R.** Historia de la tradición sinóptica. [T]*Ruis-Garrido, Con-stantino* 2000 ⇒16,4375. [R]RevAg 42 (2001) 892-893 (*Sabugal, Santos*); ActBib 38 (2001) 38-39 (*Boada, J.*); EstTrin 35 (2001) 445-446 (*Vázquez Allegue, Jaime*).

4299 *Cadavid Duque, Alvaro* Historia y estado actual de la investigación acerca del Jesús histórico. CuesTP 28 (2001) 37-58.

4300 *Carleton Paget, James* Quests for the historical Jesus. The Cambridge companion to Jesus. 2001 ⇒4236. 138-155.

4301 *Cerbelaud, Dominique* La christologie interdite. Théophilyon 6 (2001) 163-187 [BuBB 32,12].

4302 **Childs, Hal** The myth of the historical Jesus and the evolution of consciousness. SBL.DS 179: 2000 ⇒16,4379. [R]BiblInterp 9 (2001) 440-444 (*Crossan, John Dominic*).

4303 **Chilson, Richard W.** Yeshua of Nazareth, spiritual master: the spirituality he lived and taught. ND 2001, Sorin 219 pp. $13. 1-8937-32-27-4.

4304 *Chilton, Bruce* Friends and enemies. The Cambridge companion to Jesus. Cambridge companions to religion: 2001 ⇒4236. 72-86.

4305 *Chittinappilly, Paul* The Q and the Galilean Jesus movement: a social historical perspective, I-II. BiBh 27 (2001) 174-194, 286-308.

4306 *Cnockaert, André* Jésus-Christ et la violence. Telema 106/107 (2001) 38-50.

4307 *Craffert, P.F.* Vernuwing in historiese Jesus-navorsing. VeE 22 (2001) 1-29.

4308 *Crossan, John Dominic* Eschatology, apocalypticism, and the historical Jesus. Jesus then and now. 2001 ⇒483. 91-112.

4309 **Crossan, John Dominic; Reed, Jonathan L.** Excavating Jesus: beneath the stones, behind the texts. SF 2001, HarperSanFrancisco xxi; 298 pp. $30. 0-06-061633-4.

4310 **Cunningham, Phillip J.** A believer's search for the Jesus of history. 1999 ⇒15,4253. [R]EstB 59 (2001) 393-394 (*Ródenas, A.*).

4311 [E]**Dawes, Gregory W.** The historical Jesus quest. 1999 ⇒15,4254. [R]ThLZ 126 (2001) 754-756 (*Schmeller, Thomas*).

4312 **Dawes, Gregory W.** The historical Jesus question: the challenge of history to religious authority. LVL 2001, Westminster xiii; 392 pp. $30. 0-664-22458-X. Bibl. 370-384.

4313 **De Mier, Francisco** Los encuentros de Jesús. M 2001, BAC 300 pp. [R]VyV 59 (2001) 591-592 (*Sanz Montes, Jesús*).

4314 *Doran, Robert* The agraphon at Liber graduum 3.3. CBQ 63 (2001)
      298-303.

4315 *Du Toit, David S.* Redefining Jesus: current trends in Jesus research.
      Jesus, Mark and Q. JSNT.S 214: 2001 ⇒4283. 82-124.

4316 *Dunn, James D.G.* Jesus in oral memory: the initial stages of the
      Jesus tradition. Jesus: a colloquium. 2001 ⇒461. 84-145.

4317 *Eddy, Paul R.* John HICK and the historical Jesus. ᶠO'COLLINS, G.
      2001 ⇒81. 304-319.

4318 **Ehrman, Bart D.** Jesus: apocalyptic prophet of the new millennium.
      1999 ⇒15,4262. ᴿCBQ 63 (2001) 144-145 (*Powell, Mark Allan*);
      BS 158 (2001) 181-197 (*Ingolfsland, Dennis*).

4319 *Ellis, Edward Earle* How Jesus interpreted the bible. History and in-
      terpretation. BiblInterp 54: ⇒141. 121-132.

4320 *Evans, Craig A.* The new quest for Jesus and the new research on the
      Dead Sea scrolls. Jesus, Mark and Q. JSNT.S 214: 2001 ⇒4283.
      163-183;

4321 Context, family and formation. The Cambridge companion to Jesus.
      Cambridge companions to religion: 2001 ⇒4236. 11-24.

4322 *Fabris, Rinaldo* I conflitti di Gesù. Servitium 35 (2001) 624-629.

4323 *Fedalto, Giorgio* Quando è morto Gesù?. StPat 48 (2001) 621-629.

4324 **Fillion, Louis Claude** Nuestro Señor Jesucristo según los evangeli-
      os. 2000 ⇒16,4398. ᴿEstJos 55 (2001) 175-176 (*Llamas, Román*).

4325 **Fiorenza, Elisabeth Schüssler** Jesus and the politics of interpreta-
      tion. L 2001, Continuum xi; 180 pp. 0-8264-1366-8.

4326 *Forthomme, Bernard* La violence évangélique. Christus 48 (2001)
      459-468.

4327 *Francis, James* Childhood and Jesus. PrPe 15 (2001) 439-443.

4328 **Fredriksen, Paula** Jesus of Nazareth King of the Jews. 2000 <1999>
      ⇒15,4281; 16,4403. ᴿTS 62 (2001) 608-610 (*Hamm, Dennis*);
      ᴿCBQ 63 (2001) 550-551 (*Donahue, John R.*): RBLit 3 (2001) 346-
      348 (*Keener, Craig S.*).

4329 *Freyne, Seán* A Galilean Messiah?. StTh 55 (2001) 198-218.

4330 *Funk, Robert* The Jesus Seminar and the quest. Jesus then and now.
      2001 ⇒483. 130-139.

4331 *Gardocki, Dariusz* Wiara Jezusa w ujęciu współczesnej chrystologii
      [The faith of Jesus according to contemporary christology]. Studia
      Bobolanum 1/2 (2001) 53-82 Sum. 81. P.

4332 **González Echegaray, Joaquín** Jesús en Galilea: aproximación des-
      de la arqueología. Agora 5: 2000 ⇒16,4414. ᴿEccl(R) 15 (2001)
      483-485 (*Izquierdo, A.*).

4333 *González Faus, José Ignacio* Memoria subversiva, memoria subyu-
      gante: presentación de Jesús de Nazaret. RLAT 18 (2001) 107-124.

4334 **Good, Deirdre J.** Jesus the meek king. 1999 ⇒15,4683. [R]Horizons 27 (2001) 393-394 (*Sloyan, Gerard S.*).

4335 *Grappe, Christian* Jésus parmi d'autres prophètes de son temps. RHPhR 81 (2001) 387-411.

4336 *Gräßer, Erich* Die Hermeneutik der Jesusgeschichte bei Helmut MERKLEIN. BZ 45 (2001) 161-169.

4337 *Guijarro Oporto, Santiago* Kingdom and family in conflict: a contribution to the study of the historical Jesus. [F]MALINA, B. BiblInterp 53: 2001 ⇒67. 210-238.

4338 *Habermann, Jürgen* Kriterienfragen der Jesusforschung. [F]HAHN, F. 2001 ⇒41. 15-26.

4339 *Hagner, Donald A.* An analysis of recent 'Historical Jesus' studies. Religious diversity. BiSe 79: 2001 ⇒398. 81-106.

4340 *Harvey, John D.* Mission in Jesus' teaching. Mission in the NT. ASMS 27: 2001 ⇒367. 30-49.

4341 **Hegel, G.W.F.** Vita di Gesù. [E]*Tassi, Adriano:* GdT 278: Brescia 2001, Queriniana 147 pp. €11.36. 88-399-0778-5. [R]StPat 48 (2001) 225-226 (*Segalla, Giuseppe*).

4342 **Heiligenthal, Roman; Dobbeler, Axel von** Menschen um Jesus: Lebensbilder aus neutestamentlicher Zeit. DaWiss 2001, 248 pp. €17. 84. 3-89678-411-0.

4343 *Hengel, Martin* Ein Blick zurück im Zorn: Rudolf Augsteins "Jesus Menschensohn". ThBeitr 32 (2001) 158-163;

4344 Jesus als messianischer Lehrer der Weisheit und die Anfänge der Christologie. Der messianische Anspruch Jesu. WUNT 138: 2001 ⇒ 276. 81-131 [Mt 11,28-30].

4345 **Herzog, William R.** Jesus, justice, and the reign of God: a ministry of liberation. 2000 ⇒16,4427. [R]CBQ 63 (2001) 146-148 (*Miller, Robert J.*); BiblInterp 9 (2001) 413-418 (*Bryan, David J.*); JThS 52 (2001) 787-789 (*Dawson, Andrew*).

4346 **Heyer, C.J. den** La storicità di Gesù. 2000 ⇒16,4428. [R]StPat 48 (2001) 26-227 (*Segalla, Giuseppe*); ATT 7 (2001) 548-550 (*Ghiberti, Giuseppe*).

4347 *Holmén, Tom* A theologically disinterested quest?: on the origins of the "Third Quest" for the historical Jesus. StTh 55 (2001) 175-197.

4348 **Holmén, Tom** Jesus and Jewish covenant thinking. BiblInterp 55: Lei 2001, Brill ix; 415 pp. 90-04-11935-3. Bibl. 348-387.

4349 *Hooker-Stacey, Morna D.* Disputed questions in biblical studies, 2: Jesus and christology. ET 112 (2001) 298-302.

4350 **Horsley, Richard A.** Arqueologia, história e sociedade na Galiléia: o contexto social de Jesus e dos rabis. 2000 ⇒16,4433. [R]REB 244 (2001) 984-987 (*Coutinho, Sérgio Ricardo*).

4351 *Irudaya, Raj* Jesus, protagonist of children's dignity and rights. VJTR 65 (2001) 509-519.

4352 **Jaros, Karl** Jesus von Nazareth: Geschichte und Deutung. 2000 ⇒ 16,4435. [R]ActBib 38 (2001) 52-54 (*Boada, J.*).

4353 **Jenkins, Philip** Hidden gospels: how the search for Jesus lost its way. Oxf 2001, OUP vii; 260 pp. £17. 0-19-513509-1.

4354 *Johnson, Elizabeth A.* The word was made flesh and dwelt among us: Jesus research and christian faith. Jesus: a colloquium. 2001 ⇒461. 146-166.

4355 **Johnson, Luke Timothy** Jésus sans parti pris: la quête chimérique du Jésus historique et la vérité des évangiles. [T]*Witt, Fabienne*: 2000 ⇒16,4439. [R]RThom 109 (2001) 495-497 (*Grelot, Pierre*).

4356 **Jonge, Marinus de** God's final envoy: early christology and Jesus' own view of his mission. 1998 ⇒14,3922... 16,4441. [R]RBLit 3 (2001) 337-339 (*Dunn, James D.G.*); EvQ 73 (2001) 263-264 (*Marshall, I. Howard*); SNTU.A 25 (2000) 256-258 (*Niemand, Ch.*).

4357 *Keating, James F.* The invincible allure of the historical Jesus for systematic theology. IThQ 66 (2001) 211-226.

4358 **Keck, Leander E.** Who is Jesus?: history in perfect tense. 2000 ⇒ 16,4447. [R]ThTo 58 (2001) 117-118, 120 (*Meyer, Paul W.*); CBQ 63 (2001) 551-553 (*McKnight, Scot*); WThJ 63 (2001) 456-459 (*Waters, Guy*); RBLit 3 (2001) 348-350 (*Vinson, Richard B.*).

4359 **Kesich, Veselin** The gospel image of Christ. Crestwood, NY [2]1992, St. Vladimir's Seminary Pr. 214 pp. ⇒9,4175. [R]OS 50 (2001) 267-268 (*Hološnjaj, Boris*).

4360 **Kieffer, René** Evangeliernas Jesus—myt och verklighet. Örebro 2001, Libris 175 pp.

4361 *Kister, Menahem* Law, morality, and rhetoric in some sayings of Jesus. Studies in ancient midrash. 2001 ⇒290. 145-154.

4362 **Klausnitzer, Wolfgang** Jesus von Nazareth: Lehrer—Messias—Gottessohn. Rg 2001, Kevelaer 143 pp. €8.90. 3-7867-8381-0 [BiKi 58, 184].

4363 *Krasevac, Edward L.* Two unresolved issues for the third millennium. NBl 82 (2001) 177-181;

4364 Questing for the historical Jesus: need we continue?. DoLi 51 (2001) 598-604.

4365 *Labahn, Michael* Introduction. Jesus, Mark and Q. JSNT.S 214: 2001 ⇒4283. 70-79.

4366 **Lagrange, Joseph M.** Vida de Jesucristo según el evangelio. 1999 ⇒15,4318; 16,4455. [R]EstJos 55 (2001) 169-171 (*Llamas, Román*).
        [E]**LeBeau, B.** The historical Jesus. 2000 ⇒476.

4367 *Leers, Frei Bernardino* O triste cristianismo e Jesus de Nazaré. REB 61 (2001) 586-601.

4368 **Leroy, Herbert** Gesù: tradizione e interpretazione. ᵀ*Palermo, Silvia:* Piccoli saggi 12: R 2001, Salerno 234 pp. 88-8402-354-8. Bibl. di *Anne Dawson* e *Michael Lattke* 187-225.

4369 *Liebich, Franz* Jesus von Nazaret als Kosmopolit: war er bilingual?: oder gar trilingual?. CPB 114 (2001) 20-21.

4370 **Loader, William R.G.** Jesus and the fundamentalism of his day. GR 2001, Eerdmans vi; 156 pp. $14. 0-8028-4796-X. Bibl. 147-151.

4371 **Lüdemann, Gerhard** Jesus nach 2000 Jahren. 1999 ⇒15,4324; 16, 4464. ᴿActBib 38 (2001) 55-57 (*Boada, J.*);

4372 Jesus after 2000 years: what he really said and did. 2000 ⇒16,4348. ᴿICMR 12 (2001) 106-108 (*Forward, Martin*); RRT (2001/1) 87-88 (*Wansbrough, Henry*); CBQ 63 (2001) 755-756 (*Powell, Mark Allan*); PrPe 15 (2001) 39-40 (*Wansbrough, Henry*).

4373 *Mack, Burton L.* Prolog;

4374 The historical Jesus hoopla;

4375 The case for a Cynic-like Jesus;

4376 Epilog. The christian myth. 2001 ⇒181. 11-21/25-40/41-58/195-99.

ᴱ**Marchadour, A.** Que sait-on de Jésus. 2001 ⇒297.

4377 *Marguerat, Daniel* Jésus historique: une quête de l'inaccessible étoile?: bilan de la 'troisième quête'. Théophilyon 6 (2001) 11-55 [BuBB 32,12].

4378 *Marshall, I. Howard* Jesus—example and teacher of prayer in the synoptic gospels. Into God's presence. 2001 ⇒294. 113-131.

4379 **Martin, Raymond** The elusive Messiah: a philosophical overview of the quest for the historical Jesus. 1999 ⇒15,4333; 16,4470. ᴿMillSt 47 (2001) 154-156 (*Rogers, Patrick*).

4380 ᴱ**Martínez Puche, José A.** Fray Luis de Granada: Vida de Cristo. 2000 ⇒16,4473. ᴿEstJos 55 (2001) 172-173 (*Llamas, Román*).

4381 *McClymond, Michael J.* Jesus. Rivers of paradise. 2001 ⇒354. 309-456.

4382 *McEvoy, James* Narrative or history?—a false dilemma: the theological significance of the historical Jesus. Pacifica 14 (2001) 262-280.

4383 **McKnight, Edgar V.** Jesus Christ in history and scripture: a poetic and sectarian perspective. 1999 ⇒15,4334. ᴿRBLit 3 (2001) 353-355 (*Graham, Susan Lochrie*).

4384 *McKnight, Scot* Jesus and his death: some recent scholarship. CurResB 9 (2001) 185-228;

4385 Jesus and prophetic actions. BBR 11 (2001) 197-232.

4386 *Meier, John P.* From Elijah-like prophet to royal Davidic messiah. Jesus: a colloquium. 2001 ⇒461. 45-83.

4387 **Meier, John P.** A marginal Jew: rethinking the historical Jesus, 3: companions and competitors. AncB reference library: NY 2001, Doubleday xiv; 703 pp. $42.50. 0-385-46993-4;

4388 Un ebreo marginale: ripensare il Gesù storico, 1: le radici del problema e della persona. Btc 117: Brescia 2001, Queriniana 466 pp. €38.73. ᴿStPat 48 (2001) 507-510 (*Segalla, Giuseppe*); ATT 7 (2001) 543-548 (*Ghiberti, Giuseppe*).

4389 *Michaud, Jean-Paul* Jésus de l'histoire et Jésus des évangiles: à l'occasion du Jésus de Nazareth de Jacques Schlosser. Theoforum 32/2 (2001) 223-233.

4390 *Millán Romeral, Fernando* La conciencia de Jesús. MCom 59 (2001) 829-876.

4391 *Moloney, Francis J.* Jesus Christ: the question to cultures. 'A hard saying'. 2001 <1988> ⇒184. 183-209.

4392 **Mordillat, G.; Prieur, J.** Jesús contra Jesús: una polémica visión de la figura de Cristo a partir de las contradicciones de los evangelios. Barc 2001, Muchnik 380 pp [EstAg 37,395—Natal, D.].

4393 *Moxnes, Halvor* The construction of Galilee as a place for the historical Jesus, I-II. BTB 31 (2001) 26-37, 64-77.

4394 *Mußner, Franz* Welcher Jesus spricht in den Evangelien?. ᶠSCHMUT-TERMAYR, G. 2001 ⇒101. 201-208.

4395 *Naumowicz, Józef* La date de naissance du Christ d'après DENYS le Petit et les auteurs chrétiens antérieurs. StPatr 35 (2001) 292-296 [Lk 3,1].

4396 **Navone, John J.** Lead, radiant Spirit: our gospel quest. ColMn 2001, Liturgical vii; 128 pp. 0-8146-2594-0.

4397 *Neirynck, Frans* The historical Jesus: reflections on an inventory. E-vangelica III. BEThL 150: 2001 <1994> ⇒187. 631-648.

4398 *Niebuhr, Karl-Wilhelm* Jesus als Lehrer der Gottesherrschaft und die Weisheit: eine Problemskizze. Zeitschrift für Pädagogik und Theologie 53 (2001) 116-132.

4399 **Nouwen, Henri J.M.** Jesus: a gospel. ᴱ*O'Laughlin, Michael*: Mkn 2001, Orbis xvi; 150 pp. $20. 1570753849 [ThD 48,382 Heiser, W.].

4400 *Oakman, Douglas E.* Models and archaeology in the social interpretation of Jesus. ᶠMALINA, B. BiblInterp 53: 2001 ⇒67. 102-131.

4401 **Onimus, Jean** Jesús en directo. ᵀ*Ares Fondevila, Suso* 2000 ⇒16, 4496. ᴿPerTeol 33 (2001) 283 (*Marques,Valdir*).

4402 **Paul, André** Jésus-Christ, la rupture: essai sur la naissance du christianisme. P 2001, Bayard 279 pp. €18.90. 2-227-35022-9. Bibl. [BCLF 642,19].

4403 *Penna, Romano* La figura reale di Gesù e quella virtuale dell'"uomo divino" (*theîos anēr*): un confronto sbilanciato. Vangelo e inculturazione. 2001 <2000> ⇒193. 211-230.

4404 **Perkins, Pheme** Jesús como maestro: la enseñanza de Jesús en el contexto de su época. Grandes temas de Nuevo Testamento: Córdoba 2001, El Almendro 155 pp. 84-8005-031-4.

4405 **Perrot, Charles** Jésus Que sais-je?. 1998 ⇒14,3967; 16,4499. [R]RB
      108 (2001) 627-628 (*Boimard [!], M.-É.*).

4406 **Perrot, Charles** Gesù. 1999 ⇒15,4370. [R]RSEc 19 (2001) 146-148
      (*Abbà, Maurizio*).

4407 *Perrot, Charles* Jésus, le lecteur des écritures. Théophilyon 6 (2001)
      57-87 [BuBB 36,30].

4408 *Pesce, Mauro* Gesù e il sacrificio ebraico. ASEs 18 (2001) 129-168.

4409 **Porter, Stanley E.** The criteria for authenticity in historical-Jesus
      research. 2000 ⇒16,4507. [R]RRT (2001/1) 84-86 (*Wansbrough,
      Henry*); HeyJ 42 (2001) 496-497 (*Turner, Geoffrey*); BiblInterp 9
      (2001) 410-413 (*Fitzmyer, Joseph A.*); JBL 120 (2001) 769-771
      (*Vinson, Richard*); CBQ 63 (2001) 761-763 (*Attridge, Harold W.*).

4410 [E]**Pouthier, Jean-Luc** Jésus le Galiléen. MoBi 134 (2001) 3-53.

4411 **Powell, Mark Allan** Jesus as a figure in history. 1998 ⇒14,3974;
      16,4509. [R]RBLit 3 (2001) 359-362 (*Percer, Leo*).

4412 **Price, Robert M.** Deconstructing Jesus. 2000 ⇒16,4512. [R]CBQ 63
      (2001) 160-161 (*Montague, George T.*).

4413 **Punton, Anne** The world Jesus knew. GR 2001, Monarch 267 pp.
      $13. 0-8254-6004-2. Num. ill.]ThD 49,82—Heiser, W. Charles].

4414 *Pyper, Hugh S.* The secret of succession: Elijah, Elisha, Jesus, and
      Derrida. Postmodern interpretations. 2001 ⇒229. 55-66.

4415 **Rau, Eckhard** Jesus Freund von Zöllnern und Sündern: eine metho-
      denkritische Untersuchung. 2000 ⇒16,4518. [R]ETR 76 (2001) 425-
      426 (*Gloor, Daniel*).

4416 *Räisänen, Heikki* Jesus in context: on *The historical figure of Jesus*
      (1993) by E.P. Sanders. Challenges to biblical interpretation.
      BiblInterp 59: 2001 <1994> ⇒200. 3-13.

4417 *Reed, Jonathan L.* Galilean archaeology and the historical Jesus.
      Jesus then and now. 2001 ⇒483. 113-129.

4418 *Repschinski, Boris* Some trends in life of Jesus research. ThD 48
      (2001) 11-19 <StZ 218 (2000) 455-466.

4419 **Ricciotti, Giuseppe** Vida de Jesucristo. 2000 ⇒16,4520. [R]EstJos 55
      (2001) 359-360 (*Llamas, Román*).

4420 *Sahuc, Louis* Les rigueurs de l'évangile: entretien avec un croyant or-
      dinaire. Sedes Sapientiae 77 (2001) 13-24.

4421 **Salguero, José** Vida de Jesús según los evangelios sinópticos. 2000
      ⇒16,4526. [R]EstJos 55 (2001) 173-175 (*Llamas, Román*).

4422 *Sanday, William* Did Christ speak Greek?—a rejoinder. Essays in
      biblical criticism. JSNT.S 225: 2001 <1878>⇒205. 94-107.

4423 **Sanders, Ed Parish** La figura histórica de Jesús. Agora 6: Estella
      (Navarra) [2]2001, Verbo Divino 332 pp. 84-8169-400-2.

4424 *Sanders, E.P.* Jesus in Galilee. Jesus...colloquium. 2001 ⇒461. 5-26.

4425 **Sarkar, Nirmal Chandra** Who is Jesus?. Delhi 2001, ISCPK xvi; 222 pp. Rs 95. 81-7214-628-0 [VJTR 66,946—D'Mello, Augustine].

4426 **Schlosser, Jacques** Jésus de Nazareth. 1999 ⇒15,4395; 16,4529. [R]RB 108 (2001) 269-273 (*Boismard, M.-É.*); Theoforum 32 (2001) 223-233 (*Michaud, Jean-Paul*); ThLZ 126 (2001) 535-538 (*Roloff, Jürgen*).

4427 *Schmidt, Andreas* Introduction. Jesus, Mark and Q. 2001 ⇒4283. 14-16.

4428 *Schmithals, Walter* 75 Jahre: BULTMANNs Jesus-Buch. ZThK 98 (2001) 25-58.

4429 **Schnackenburg, R.** Amistad con Jesús. 1998 ⇒14,3996. [R]Eccl(R) 15 (2001) 482-483 (*Izquierdo, A.*);

4430 La persona di Gesù Cristo nei quattro vangeli. CTNT.S 4: 1995 ⇒ 11/2,2197... 14,3994. [R]RB 108 (2001) 289-293 (*Devillers, Luc*).

4431 *Schröter, Jens* Jesus als Lehrer nach dem Zeugnis des Neuen Testaments. Zeitschrift für Pädagogik und Theologie 53 (2001) 107-115;

4432 Die Frage nach dem historischen Jesus und der Charakter historischer Erkenntnis. The sayings source Q. BEThL 158: 2001 ⇒477. 207-54.

4433 *Schüssler Fiorenza, Elisabeth* The rhetorics and politics of Jesus research: a critical feminist perspective. Jesus, Mark and Q. JSNT.S 214: 2001 ⇒4283. 259-282.

4434 **Schweitzer, Albert** The quest of the historical Jesus. [E]*Bowden, John* 2000 ⇒16,4531. [R]RRT (2001/1) 1-2 (*Wollaston, Isabel*);

4435 La vita di Gesù: il segreto della messianità e della passione. [T]*Coppellotti, F.* Mi 2001, Mariotti 234 pp. €18.08. [R]ATT 7 (2001) 554-556 (*Casale, Umberto*).

4436 **Schweizer, E.** Jesús, parábola de Dios: ¿Qué sabemos realmente de la vida de Jesús?. [T]*Olasagasti, Manuel* Biblioteca de estudios bíblicos Minor 2: S 2001, Sígueme 142 pp. 84-301-1339-8. [R]EstTrin 35 (2001) 459-460 (*Miguel, José Maria de*).

4437 *Scullion, James* Quest for the historical Jesus. NewTR 14/3 (2001) 73-75.

4438 *Segalla, Giuseppe* Rispensare il Gesù storico. Teol(Br) 26 (2001) 238-245.

4439 *Sharma, Arvind* Did Jesus baptize?. BiBh 27 (2001) 85-89.

4440 *Ska, Jean Louis* Mosè—Giosuè—Gesù. Firmana 27 (2001) 53-72.

4441 *Söding, Thomas* Ein Jesus—vier Evangelien: zur Vielseitigkeit und Eindeutigkeit der neutestamentlichen Jesustradition. ThGl 91 (2001) 409-443.

4442 *Stefani, Piero* Le visioni ebraiche di Gesù. StMiss 50 (2001) 235-250.

4443 **Taussig, Hal** Jesus before God: the prayer life of the historical Jesus. 1999 ⇒15,4414. [R]TJT 17 (2001) 303-304 (*Kirk, Alan*).

4444　**Taylor, Justin** Where did christianity come from?. ColMn 2001, Liturgical xv; 189 pp. $20. 0-8146-5102-X;

4445　Woher kommt das Christentum. Mainz 2001, Matthias-Grünewald 207 pp. 3-7867-2312-5.

4446　**Theissen, Gerd; Merz, Annette** The historical Jesus. 1998 ⇒14, 4019... 16,4545. [R]ThTo 57 (2001) 535-537 (*Black, C. Clifton*); RExp 98 (2001) 455-457 (*Vinson, Richard B.*).

4447　**Theissen, Gerd; Winter, Dagmar** Die Kriterienfrage in der Jesus-forschung. NTOA 34: 1997 ⇒13,4238... 15,4418. [R]RB 108 (2001) 287-289 (*Nodet, Étienne*).

4448　*Theißen, Gerd* Jesus und seine historisch-kritischen Erforscher: über die Menschlichkeit der Jesusforschung. ThGl 91 (2001) 355-368.

4449　*Tilliette, Xavier* Come Cristo visse la sua umanità: un saggio di ese-gesi fenomenologica. Gr. 82 (2001) 527-541.

4450　*Tiwald, Markus* Der Wanderradikalismus als Brücke zum histori-schen Jesus. The sayings source Q. 2001 ⇒477. 523-534.

4451　*Tuckett, Christopher* Sources and methods. The Cambridge com-panion to Jesus. 2001 ⇒4236. 121-137.

4452　*Valentini, Alberto* Il volto di Cristo nel Nuovo Testamento: i molti ri-tratti di un unico volto. Gr. 82 (2001) 487-514.

4453　*Van Aarde, A.G.* Jesus—kind van God, vaderloos in Galilea. VeE 22 (2001) 401-417.

4454　**Van Aarde, Andries** Fatherless in Galilee: Jesus as child of God. Harrisburg 2001, Trinity vi; 246 pp. $28 [BiTod 40,136–Senior, D.].

4455　**Van der Linde, Henk** Het koninkrijk van God is de stad op de berg: wat heeft Jezus zelf gewild?. Zoetermeer 2001, Meinema 158 pp. €15.50. 90-211-3788-7.

4456　*Van Oyen, Geert* How do we know (what there is to know)?: criteria for historical Jesus research. LouvSt 26 (2001) 245-267.

4457　**Van Voorst, R.** Jesus outside the New Testament: an introduction to the ancient evidence. 2000 ⇒16,4555. [R]CBQ 63 (2001) 163-164 (*O'Loughlin, Thomas*); RBLit 3 (2001) 501-03 (*Kerkeslager, Allen*).

4458　*Vanhoye, Albert* Lek Jezusa. Pastores 11 (2001) 20-26 [AcBib 10, 808]. **P.**

4459　*Vassallo Pastor, Manuel* La salud como exigencia del evangelio. Páginas 172 (2001) 6-9.

4460　*Viviano, Benedict T.* The historical Jesus in the doubly attested say-ings: an experiment. Trinity—kingdom—church. NTOA 48: 2001 <1996> ⇒223. 21-63.

4461　*Wagner, Volker* Mit der Herkunft Jesu aus Nazaret gegen die Geltung des Gesetzes?. ZNW 92 (2001) 273-282.

4462　*Watson, Francis* The quest for the real Jesus. The Cambridge com-panion to Jesus. 2001 ⇒4236. 156-169 [Mk 8].

4463 **Weaver, Walter P.** The historical Jesus in the twentieth century, 1900-1950. 1999 ⇒15,4429; 16,4561. ᴿRBLit 3 (2001) 365-367 (*Vinson, Richard B.*).

4464 *Weren, Wim* Is Jezus verdwenen achter het geloof van zijn volgelingen?: nieuwe gegevens uit historisch onderzoek. TTh 41 (2001) 128-144.

4465 *Williams, Rowan* A history of faith in Jesus. The Cambridge companion to Jesus. 2001 ⇒4236. 220-236.

4466 **Witherington, Ben, III** Jesus the seer: the progress of prophecy. 1999 ⇒15,4433; 16,4564. ᴿJThS 52 (2001) 211-212 (*Ziesler, J.A.*); JBL 120 (2001) 163-165 (*Vinson, Richard*).

F1.5 *Jesus et Israel*—**Jesus the Jew**

4467 ᴱ**Bruteau, Beatrice** Jesus through Jewish eyes: rabbis and scholars engage an ancient brother in a new conversation. Mkn 2001, Orbis xvi; 191 pp. $20. 157-075-3881. Bibl. 183 [BiTod 40,62 Senior, D.].

4468 *Addison, Howard Avruhm* What manner of man?. Jesus through Jewish eyes. 2001 ⇒4467. 103-106.

4469 **Ben-Chorin, Schalom** Brother Jesus: the Nazarene through Jewish eyes. ᵀᴱ*Klein, Jared S.; Reinhart, Max*: Athens, GA 2001, Univ. of Georgia Pr. xiv; 252 pp. $40. 0-8203-2256-3. Bibl. 207-215 [ThD 48,353—Heiser, W. Charles].

4470 **Bernard, Jacques** Le Nouveau Testament et les courants du judaïsme de l'époque. Diss. Lille 2001 [RTL 33,636].

4471 **Bronstein, Herbert** Talking Torah with Jesus. Jesus through Jewish eyes. 2001 ⇒4467. 45-60.

4472 *Chouraquil, Jean-Marc* Réflexions d'un juif sur Jésus. Théophilyon 6 (2001) 125-162 [BuBB 32,12].

4473 *Chrostowski, Waldemar* Żydzi i religia żydowska a Jezus Chrystus [Juifs, judaïsme et Jésus Christ]. AtK 136/1 (2001) 7-21. **P.**;

4474 Jesus Christ in the eyes of Jews and Judaism. CoTh 71A (2001) 101-113.

4475 *Cook, Michael J.* Evolving Jewish views of Jesus. Jesus through Jewish eyes. 2001 ⇒4467. 3-24.

4476 ᴱ**Copan, Paul; Evans, Craig A.** Who was Jesus?: a Jewish-Christian dialogue. LVL 2001, Westminster viii; 205 pp. £16.

4477 *Edwards, Laurence* "How do you read?": Jesus in conversation with his colleagues. Jesus through Jewish eyes. 2001 ⇒4467. 137-145.

4478 **Ehrman, B.D.** Jesús, el profeta judío apocalíptico. Paidos Orígenes 20: Barc 2001, Paidós Ibérica 327 pp. 84-493-1027-X.

4479 *Flitter, Lance* Jesus and me. Jesus through Jewish eyes. 2001 ⇒ 4467. 122-133.

4480 **Flusser, David** Jezus: een joodse visie. Hilversum 2001, Folkertsma 246 pp. €29.50. 90-239-0401-X;

4481 Jesus. J ³2001, Magnes 324 pp. 965-223-978-X. Collab. *R. Steven Notley*; Ill.

4482 ᴱ*Fozzati, Renza* L'immagine di Gesù nell'ebraismo. CoSe 12 (2001) 114-120.

4483 *Gelberman, Joseph* My friend, Jesus. Jesus through Jewish eyes. 2001 ⇒4467. 117-118.

4484 **Heschel, Susannah** Der jüdische Jesus und das Christentum: Abraham GEIGERs Herausforderung an die christliche Theologie. ᵀ*Wiese, Ch.* B 2001, Jüdische Verlagsanstalt 406 pp. €49.90. 3-934658-04-0.

4485 *Holmén, Tom* The Jewishness of Jesus in the 'Third Quest'. Jesus, Mark and Q. JSNT.S 214: 2001 ⇒4283. 143-162.

4486 **Isaac, Jules Marx** Gesù e Israele. Radici 16: Genova 2001, Marietti 445 pp. 88-211-8372-6. Prefazione di *Marco Morselli*.

4487 *Kampling, Rainer* "Und da acht Tage um waren, daß das Kind beschnitten würde, da ward sein Name genannt Jesus ...": Jesus von Nazaret in jüdischer Sicht. ThGl 91 (2001) 390-408.

4488 *Kushner, Lawrence* My lunch with Jesus. Jesus through Jewish eyes. 2001 ⇒4467. 119-121.

4489 **Lapide, Pinchas** Predicava nelle loro sinagoghe: esegesi ebraica dei vangeli. StBi 131: Brescia 2001, Paideia 116 pp. 88-394-0613-1.

4490 *Leder, Drew* Yehoshua and the intact covenant;

4491 *Lerner, Michael* Fresh eyes: current Jewish renewal could see Jesus as one like themselves. Jesus through Jewish eyes. 2001 ⇒4467. 148-150/146-147.

4492 **Malka, Salomon** Gesù riconsegnato agli ebrei. 2000 ⇒16,4578. ᴿEstTrin 35 (2001) 450-452 (*Vázquez Allegue, Jaime*).

4493 *Matt, Daniel* Yeshua the Hasid. Jesus through Jewish eyes. 2001 ⇒ 4467. 74-80.

4494 **McKnight, Scot** A new vision for Israel: the teachings of Jesus in national context. 1999 ⇒15,4448; 16,4579. ᴿJBL 120 (2001) 376-378 (*Siker, Jeffrey S.*).

4495 **Moberly, R.W.L.** The bible, theology, and faith: a study of Abraham and Jesus. 2000 ⇒16,4581. ᴿThTo 58 (2001) 257-258 (*Brueggemann, Walter*); CBQ 63 (2001) 348-349 (*Brawley, Douglas J.*); ET 112 (2001) 1-2 (*Rodd, C.S.*).

4496 *Mussner, Franz* Jesus von Nazareth: vero homo judaeus. Cath(M) 55 (2001) 200-207.

4497 *Orth, Stefan* Aufhebung der Grenzen?: die Neutestamentler und der Gott des Juden Jesus. HerKorr 55 (2001) 298-301.

4498 *Penna, Romano* Gesù di Nazaret e la sua esperienza di Dio: novità nel giudaismo. Vangelo e inculturazione. 2001 <1999> ⇒193. 183-210.

4499 *Polish, Daniel F.* A Jewish reflection on images of Jesus;

4500 *Rosenbaum, Stanley Ned* A letter from Rabbi Gamaliel ben Gamaliel. Jesus through Jewish eyes. 2001 ⇒4467. 94-98/81-93.

4501 *Schaller, Berndt* Jesus, ein Jude aus Galiläa: zur Trilogie von Geza VERMES. Fundamenta Judaica. 2001 <1997> ⇒206. 148-155;

4502 Jesus der Jude. Fundamenta Judaica. 2001 <1994> ⇒206. 191-200.

4503 *Secher, Allen* The "J" word;

4504 *Shapiro, Rami M.* Listening to Jesus with an ear for God;

4505 *Sherwin, Byron L.* "Who do you say that I am?" (Mark 8:29): a new Jewish view of Jesus;

4506 *Solomon, Lewis D.* Jesus: a prophet of universalistic Judaism. Jesus through Jewish eyes. 2001 ⇒4467. 109-116/168-180/31-44/151-167.

4507 *Sperling, S. David* Jewish perspectives on Jesus. Jesus then and now. 2001 ⇒483. 251-259.

4508 *Tomson, Peter J.* Jesus and his Judaism. The Cambridge companion to Jesus. Cambridge companions to religion: 2001 ⇒4236. 25-40.

4509 **Tomson, Peter J.** 'If this be from heaven...': Jesus and the New Testament authors in their relationship to Judaism. BiSe 76: Shf 2001, Academic 455 pp. £26. 1-84127-196-9. Bibl. 428-436;

4510 De zaak-Jezus en de Joden. Zoetermeer 2001, Meinema 163 pp. €12.35. 90-211-3840-9.

4511 *Veghazi, Esteban* Jesús, el judío. Revista católica 101 (2001) 33-37.

4512 **Vermes, Geza** The changing faces of Jesus. 2000 ⇒16,4585. ᴿJJS 52 (2001) 375-376 (*Lieu, Judith*); JThS 52 (2001) 792-794 (*Hooker, Morna D.*); Theol. 104 (2001) 444-445 (*Harvey, Anthony*).

4513 **Vidal, Marie** Um judeu chamado Jesus. ᵀ*Teixeira, Guilherme João de Freitas*: 2000 ⇒16,4587. ᴿEstudos Bíblicos 71 (2001) 75-78 (*Farias, Jacir de Freitas*).

4514 *Vogel Ettin, Andrew* That troublesome cousin;

4515 *Waskow, Arthur* Jesus, the rabbis, and the image on a coin [Mk 12, 13-17];

4516 *Wolf, Arnold Jacob* Jesus as a historical Jew. Jesus through Jewish eyes. 2001 ⇒4467. 63-73/99-102/25-30.

F1.6 *Jesus in Ecclesia*—The Church Jesus

4517 **Arias, Juan** Jesús: ese gran desconocido. M 2001, Maeva 247 pp.

4518 *Balter, Lucjan* Jezus Chrystus w spojrzeniu rzymskich katolików [Jé-
sus Christ dans la pensée des catholiques romains]. AtK 136 (2001)
204-215 Rés. 215. **P**.

4519 **Cahill, Thomas** Desire of the everlasting hills: the world before and
after Jesus. 1999 ⇒15,4469. [R]CrossCur 51 (2001) 125-127 (*Hei-
negg, Peter*).

4520 *Fabris, Adriano* Sapere e credere a proposito di Gesù. Hum(B) 56
(2001) 65-78.

4521 **Holmgren, Frederick C.** The Old Testament and the significance of
Jesus: embracing change—maintaining christian identity. 1999 ⇒15,
4474; 16,4595. [R]ThTo 57 (2001) 586, 588 (*Setz, C.R.*); ProEc 10/1
(2001) 107-108 (*McGinnis, Claire Mathews*); RBLit 3 (2001) 114-
116 (*Fischer, Paul*).

4522 **Mahan, Wayne W.** The taming of Jesus by christianity. Lanham
2001, University Press of America ix; 93 pp. 0-7618-2099-X.

4523 **Nolan, Albert** Jesus before christianity. Mkn 2001 <1976>, Orbis
xii; 196 pp. $15. 1-57057-404-7 [ThD 49,183—Heiser, W. Charles].

4524 **O'Collins, G.** Segui la via!: Gesù nostro maestro spirituale. CinB
2001, San Paolo 192 pp. €12.39.

4525 **Placher, William C.** Jesus the savior: the meaning of Jesus Christ for
christian faith. LVL 2001, Westminster x; 230 pp. $20. 0-664-22391-
5 [ThD 49,186—Heiser, W. Charles].

4526 *Roloff, Jürgen, al.*, Jesus Christus. RGG², 4. 2001 ⇒664. 463-485.

4527 **Ruck-Schöder, Adelheid** Der Name Gottes und der Name Jesu: eine
neutestamentliche Studie. WMANT 80: 1999 ⇒15,4478; 16,4598.
[R]JBL 120 (2001) 165-167 (*Hurtado, Larry W.*).

4528 *Sobrino, Jon* Teología de los misterios de la vida de Jesús. Iter 24
(2001) 45-93.

4529 *Torrance, Alan* Jesus in christian doctrine. The Cambridge companion to Jesus. 2001 ⇒4236. 200-219.

4530 **Tupper, Frank E.** A scandalous providence: the Jesus story of the
compassion of God. 1995 ⇒12,4129. [R]RExp 98 (2001) 460-462
(*Stiver, Dan R.*).

4531 **West, Thomas H.** Jesus and the quest for meaning: entering theology. Mp 2001, Fortress xiv; 296 pp. $20. 0-8006-3297-4 [ThD 49,
91—Heiser, W. Charles].

F1.7 *Jesus 'annormalis'*: **to atheists, psychoanalysts, romance...**

4532 *Baugh, Lloyd* La rappresentazione di Gesù nel cinema: problemi teologici, problemi estetici. Gr. 82 (2001) 199-240.

4533 **Bauschke, Martin** Jesus im Koran. Köln 2001, Böhlau xii; 210 pp. €21.47. 3-412-09501-X. [R]OrChr 85 (2001) 291-292 (*Suermann, Harald*).

4534 *Castelli, Ferdinando* Volti di Gesù nella letteratura italiana del novecento. CoSe 12 (2001) 132-146.

4535 **Chilton, Bruce** Rabbi Jesus: an intimate biography. 2000 ⇒16,4604. [R]ASEs 18 (2001) 381-383 (*Neusner, Jacob*).

4536 *Fitzgerald, Michael L.; Machado, Felix A.* L'immagine di Gesù Cristo nelle religioni. CoSe 12 (2001) 104-113.

4537 **Gange, F.** Jésus et les femmes. Tournai 2001, La Renaissance du Livre 443 pp. €24.67. 2-8046-0460-8. [R]NRTh 123 (2001) 445-446 (*Radermakers, J.*).

4538 *Haraway, Donna J.* Ecce Homo, ain't (ar'n't) I a woman, and inappropriate/d others: the human in a post-humanist landscape. The postmodern bible reader. 2001 <1992> ⇒287. 205-218.

4539 **Khalidi, Tarif** The Muslim Jesus: sayings and stories in Islamic literature. CM 2001, Harvard Univ. Pr. 224 pp. $23. 0-67400-477-9. [R]SR 30 (2001) 432-434 (*Nicole, Jean-Thomas*).

4540 **Kuschel, Karl-Josef** The poet as mirror: human nature, God and Jesus in twentieth-century literature. [T]*Bowden, John*: 1999 ⇒15,4494. [R]ER 53 (2001) 279-281 (*Henry, Patrick*).

4541 *Langenhorst, Georg* Niemand wie Er: Jesus in der Literatur des 20. Jahrhunderts. AnzSS 110/7-8 (2001) 19-22.

4542 **Miles, Jack** Jesus: der Selbstmord des Gottessohnes. [T]*Griese, Friedrich*: Mü 2001, Hanser 390 pp. €24.90. 3-446-19997-7. [R]Zeitzeichen 12 (2001) 65-66 (*Hurth, Elisabeth*);

4543 Christ: a crisis in the life of God. NY 2001, Knopf ix; 352 pp. $27. 0-375-40014-1.

4544 **Pelikan, Jaroslav Jan** The illustrated Jesus through the centuries. 1997 ⇒13,4352; 14,4094. [R]HR 40 (2001) 402-405 (*Dungan, David*).

4545 **Sandvoss, Ernst R.** Die Wahrheit wird euch frei machen: SOKRATES und Jesus. Mü 2001, Deutscher Taschenbuch Verlag 166 pp. €9.50. 3-423-30806-0.

4546 **Schmitt, Eric-Emmanuel** L'évangile selon Pilate. 2000 ⇒16,4618. [R]Notes et Documents 60-61 (2001) 72-73 (*Nothomb, Jean-François*).

4547 **Scholl, Norbert** Mein Bruder Jeshua: Erinnerungen des Jakobus an die Zeit in Galiläa und Jerusalem. 2000 ⇒16,4619. [R]GuL 74 (2001) 478-479 (*Kurz, Paul Konrad*).

4548 **Schweitzer, Albert** Les jugements psychiatriques sur Jésus: examen et critique. [T]*Sorg, Jean-Paul*: P 2001, Foyer de l'Ame 125 pp. €16. 2-950-7099-8-2. Notes, introd.

4549 *Viganò, Dario E.* Il cinema: tra inesorabile perdita di sé e rimando all'eterno: la figura di Gesù nel cinema contemporaneo. CoSe 12 (2001) 147-151.

F2.2 *Unitas VT-NT*: **The Unity of OT-NT**

4550 **Albl, Martin C.** "And scripture cannot be broken": the form and function of the early christian testimonia collections. NT.S 96: 1999 ⇒15,4162; 16,4621. [R]RB 108 (2001) 117-120 (*Taylor, Justin*); ThRv 97 (2001) 50-51 (*Frenschkowski, Marco*); JThS 52 (2001) 293-296 (*Stanley, Christopher*); Apocrypha 12 (2001) 279-282 (*Norelli, E.*).

4551 *Beauchamp, Paul* Critères néotestamentaires pour une théologie de l' Ancien Testament (réaction à l'exposé du prof. Thomas Söding). L' interpretazione della bibbia nella chiesa. 2001 ⇒471. 266-272.

4552 **Beauchamp, Paul** L'uno e l'altro Testamento, 2: compiere le scritture. Biblica 1: Mi 2001, Glossa xliv; 482 pp. 88-7105-122-X. Introd. *Angelo Bertuletti*; Selezione bibliografica (1962-2000) 471-482.

4553 *Borse, Udo* Die geschichtliche Absicherung (Lk 23,5-16) des christologischen Psalmwortes (Ps 2,1s/LXX) und seiner Auslegung (Apg 4, 25-28). SNTU.A 26 (2001) 129-138.

4554 *Brueggemann, Walter* Prerequisites for genuine obedience: theses and conclusions. CTJ 36 (2001) 34-41;

4555 The Friday voice of faith. CTJ 36 (2001) 12-21.

4556 *D'Souza, Jerome* The relation between the Old and New Testaments. JPJRS 4/2 (2001) 137-146.

4557 **Dohmen, Christoph** No trace of Christmas?: discovering Advent in the Old Testament. [T]*Maloney, Linda M.* 2000 ⇒16,4624. [R]PIBA 24 (2001) 109-113 (*Kelly, David*).

4558 *Ellis, Edward Earle* The interpretation of the bible within the bible itself. History and interpretation. BiblInterp 54: 2001 ⇒141.99-120.

4559 **Fantato, Sergio** Mosè: stragi e saccheggi per un regno... poi venne Gesù. Luoghi saggistici: Mi 2000, Todariana 151 pp. 88-7015-322-3.

4560 *Geffre, Claude* Révision de la théologie chrétienne du judaïsme?. Le judéo-christianisme. 2001 ⇒473. 383-398 [BuBB 33,28].

4561 *Hahn, Ferdinand* Die Heilige Schrift in jüdischer und christlicher Sicht. [F]LEHMANN, K. 2001 ⇒63. 43-54.

4562 Das jüdische Volk und seine Heilige Schrift in der christlichen Bibel. VApS 152: Bonn 2001, Sekretariat der Deutschen Bischofskonferenz 167 pp. Dokument der Päpstliche Bibelkommission.

4563 *Krieger, Klaus Stefan* Keinen neuen Namen für das Alte Testament. BiKi 56 (2001) 113.

4564 *Meyer, Insa* Die Bibel zwischen Inspirationslehre und funktionalem Kanonverständnis: zum Bibelverständnis bei Wolfgang Trillhaas. KuD 47/2 (2001) 90-110.

4565 *Moberly, R.W.L.* The Christ of the Old and New Testaments. The Cambridge companion to Jesus. 2001 ⇒4236. 184-199.

4566 *Moyise, Steve* The use of analogy in biblical studies. Anvil 18/1 (2001) 33-42.

4567 **Moyise, Steve** The Old Testament in the New: an introduction. Continuum Biblical studies: L 2001, Continuum (6) 153 pp. $22. 0-8264-5414-3. Bibl. 139-144.

4568 *Müller, Mogens* The reception of the Old Testament in Matthew and Luke-Acts: from interpretation to proof from scripture. NT 43 (2001) 315-330.

4569 **Oeming, Manfred** Das Alte Testament als Teil des christlichen Kanons?: Studien zu gesamtbiblischen Theologien der Gegenwart. Z 2001, Pano v; 304 pp. €19.50. 3-907576-45-4. Bibl. 275-304.

4570 *Oeming, Manfred* Unitas scripturae?: eine ProblemskizzeDas Alte Testament als Teil des christlichen Kanons? 1986>;

4571 Biblische Theologie—was folgt daraus für die Auslegung des Alten Testaments? <1985>;

4572 Gesamtbiblische Theologien der Gegenwart: das Verhältnis von Altem und Neuem Testament in der hermeneutischen Diskussion seit Gerhard VON RAD <1985, 1987> Diss.;

4573 Biblische Theologie als Dauerreflexion im Raum des Kanons <1995>;

4574 Vorwort. Das Alte Testament als Teil des christlichen Kanons?. 2001 ⇒4569. 15-40/245-259/41-243/261-274/5-14.

4575 *Rico, Christophe* Contexte, autorité et mode de signification: de la linguistique à l'interprétation de la bible. RB 108 (2001) 598-613.

4576 *Schmitt, Hans-Christoph* Die Einheit der Schrift und die Mitte des Alten Testaments. Theologie in Prophetie. 2001 <1994> ⇒209. 326-345.

4577 **Seitz, Christopher R.** Figured out: typology and providence in christian scripture. LVL 2001, Westminster xii; 228 pp. $25. 0-664-2226-8-4 [BiTod 40,260—Bergant, Dianne].

4578 *Singer, Christophe* Abolir, accomplir, dépasser: quel modèle pour quelle compréhension de la foi chrétienne?. FV 100/4 (2001) 75-91.

4579 *Söding, Thomas* Kriterien im Neuen Testament für eine Theologie des Alten Testaments. L'interpretazione della bibbia nella chiesa. 2001 ⇒471. 232-265.

4580 *Vaage, Leif E.* Jewish scripture, Q and the historical Jesus: a Cynic way with the word?. The sayings source Q. BEThL 158: 2001 ⇒477. 479-495.

4581 *Vahrenhorst, Martin* Gift oder Arznei?: Perspektiven für das neutestamentliche Verständnis von Jes 6,9f. im Rahmen der jüdischen Rezeptionsgeschichte. ZNW 92 (2001) 145-167.

4582 *Vanhoye, Albert* Nuovo documento della Commissione Biblica: 'il popolo ebraico e le sue sacre scritture nella bibbia cristiana'. OR 5 dic. (2001) 6 [AcBib 10,915].

4583 *Viviano, Benedict T.* Origins of christian study. Trinity—kingdom—church. NTOA 48: 2001 <1977> ⇒223. 213-222.

4584 *Williams, Rowan* The unity of the church and the unity of the bible: an analogy. IKZ 91/1 (2001) 5-21.

4585 *Zenger, Erich* Unser Gottesbuch: auf der Suche nach einem neuen Umgang mit dem Alten Testament. Wort zum Leben. 2001 ⇒284. 13-39.

4586 **deSilva, David A.** New Testament themes. Saint Louis 2001, Chalice 151 pp. $16 [BiTod 39,385—Senior, Donald].

F2.5 *Commentarii*—Commentaries on the whole NT

4587 **Carson, D.A.** New Testament commentary survey. GR ⁵2001, Baker 144 pp. 0-8010-2287-8.

4588 [E]**Edwards, Mark J.** Gálatas, Efesios, Filipenses. [TE]*Merino Rodríguez, Marcelo*: La Biblia comentada por los Padres de la Iglesia, NT 8: M 2001, Ciudad N. 382 pp. €30.05. 84-89651-93-0. Bibl. 17-22.

4589 [E]**Gruson, Philippe** Les évangiles: textes et comentaires. P 2001, Bayard 1109 pp. €27.44. 2-227-01109-2.

4590 **Hurault, B. & L.** Les quatre évangiles. La Bible des peuples: P 2001, Le Sarment 446 pp. €10.52. 2-86679-307-2.

4591 **Hübner, Hans** An Philemon: an die Kolosser: an die Epheser. HNT 12: 1997 ⇒13,4404... 16,4655. [R]RBLit 3 (2001) 458-460 (*Sumney, Jerry L.*).

4592 The Navarre Bible: New Testament in the Revised Standard Version with a commentary. Princeton, NJ 2001, Scepter xv; 735 pp. $40. 1-889334-59-6. Compact edition; by members of the Faculty of Theology of the University of Navarre; Bibl. 709-712.

4593 [E]**Stuhlmacher, Peter; Weder, Hans** Das Neue Testament Deutsch–NTD- Wu 2001, Brockhaus 3-417-36057-9. CD-ROM—Laufwerk 18MB [ThG 46,236—Giesen, Heinz].

IX. Evangelia

F2.6 Evangelia Synoptica: *textus, synopses, commentarii*

4594 [E]**Hoffmann, Paul; Hieke, Thomas; Bauer, Ulrich** Synoptic concordance: a Greek concordance...occurences in Acts, 2: E—I; 3: K—O; 4. P—Omega. 2000 ⇒16,4666. [R]NT 43 (2001) 395-397 [vol. 2] (*Elliott, J.K.*); TJT 17 (2001) 289-291 (*Derrenbacker, Robert A.*);

4595 Synoptic concordance, 1-4. 1999-2000 ⇒16,1758. [R]ThLZ 126 (2001) 393-395 (*Schnelle, Udo*).

4596 **Marconcini, Benito** Os evangelhos sinóticos. [T]*Mahl, Clemente R.* Bíblia e história: São Paulo 2001, Paulinas 319 pp [REB 61, 754].

4597 **Meynet, Roland** Una nuova introduzione ai vangeli sinottici. Retorica biblica: Bo 2001, EDB 366 pp. €31. 88102-51024. Bibl. 347-353.

4598 **Neri, Umberto** Introduzione a Matteo, Marco, Luca. Conversazioni bibliche; Catechesi di Monteveglio 10: Bo 2000, EDB 130 pp. 88-10-70976-4.

4599 **Nickle, Keith Fullerton** The synoptic gospels: an introduction. LVL 2001, Westminster viii; 215 pp. $20. 0-664-22349-4. Bibl. 211-215.

4600 **Riches, John Kenneth; Telford, William R.; Tuckett, Christopher M.** The synoptic gospels. Shf 2001, Sheffield A. 359 pp. $25. 1-8-4127-210-8. Introduction by *Scot McKnight*.

4601 **Stein, Robert H.** Studying the synoptic gospels: origin and interpretation. GR [2]2001, Baker 302 pp. $25. 0-8010-2258-4.

4602 [E]**Weder, Hans** Neue Zürcher Evangeliensynopse. Z 2001, Theologischer xii; 363; 30 pp. €27.40. 3-290-17204-X. Erarb. von *K. Ruckstuhl* [ThLZ 127,770—Niebuhr, Karl-Wilhelm].

F2.7 *Problema synopticum*: The Synoptic Problem

4603 *Allison, Dale C.* Q's new exodus and the historical Jesus. The sayings source Q. BEThL 158: 2001 ⇒477. 395-428.

4604 *Amsler, Frédéric* L'Évangile avant les évangiles: la source des paroles de Jésus. BCPE 53/8 (2001) 5-31.

4605 [T]*Amsler, Frédéric* L'évangile inconnu: la source des paroles de Jésus (Q). Essais bibliques 30: Genève 2001, Labor et Fides 126 pp. €11.89. 2-8309-1029-X. Introd., annotation; Bibl. 65.

4606   **Arnal, William Edward** Jesus and the village scribes: Galilean conflicts and the setting of Q. Mp 2001, Fortress xiv; 290 pp. $26. 0-8006-3260-5.

4607   *Aurelius, Erik* Gottesvolk und Außenseiter: eine geheime Beziehung Lukas-Matthäus. NTS 47 (2001) 428-441.

4608   ᴱ**Black, David Alan; Beck, David R.** Rethinking the synoptic problem. GR 2001, Baker 160 pp. $17. 0-8010-2281-9.

4609   *Broadhead, Edwin K.* The extent of the sayings tradition (Q);

4610   *Brodie, Thomas L.* An alternative Q/logia hypothesis: Deuteronomy-based, Qumranlike, verifiable. The sayings source Q. BEThL 158: 2001 ⇒477. 719-728/729-743.

4611   *Carlson, Stephen C.* CLEMENT of Alexandria on the 'order' of the gospels. NTS 47 (2001) 118-125.

4612   **Derrenbacker, Robert A.** Ancient compositional practices and the synoptic problem. Diss. Toronto, St. Michael, ᴰ*Kloppenborg, J.* 2001 345 pp [RTL 33,637].

4613   *Downing, F. Gerald* Dissolving the synoptic problem through film?. JSNT 84 (2001) 117-119.

4614   *Dreyer, Yolanda* The tradition history of the sayings gospel Q and the 'christology' of Q3. Neotest. 34 (2000) 273-285.

4615   **Dungan, David Laird** A history of the synoptic problem: the canon, the text, the composition, and the interpretation of the gospels. 1999 ⇒15,4559; 16,4679. ᴿJBL 120 (2001) 565-567 (*Lukaszewski, A.L.*); RBLit 3 (2001) 368-371 (*Lukaszewski, A.L.*).

4616   *Edwards, Ruth* Challenging Q scholarship. ET 112 (2001) 342.

4617   *Frenschkowski, Marco* Galiläa oder Jerusalem?: die topographischen und politischen Hintergründe der Logienquelle. The sayings source Q. BEThL 158: 2001 ⇒477. 535-559.

4618   **Frenschkowsky, Marco** Q-Studien: historische, religionsgeschichtliche und theologische Untersuchungen zur Logienquelle. Diss.-Habil. Mainz 2001, ᴰ*Böcher, O.* [RTL 33,638].

4619   *Fuchs, Albert* Die Frage nach der Vollmacht Jesu: Mk 11,27-33 par Mt 21,23-27 par Lk 20,1-8;

4620   Die Pharisäerfrage nach der Kaisersteuer: Mk 12,13-17 par Mt 22,15-22 par Lk 20,20-26;

4621   Die Sadduzäerfrage: Mk 12,18-27 par Mt 22,23-33 par Lk 20,27-40;

4622   Mehr als Davids Sohn: Mk 12,35-37a par Mt 22,41-46 par Lk 20,41-44. SNTU.A 26 (2001) 27-58/59-81/83-110/111-128.

4623   **Goodacre, Mark S.** The synoptic problem: a way through the maze. BiSe 80: Shf 2001, Sheffield A. 178 pp. £15. 1-84127-238-8. Bibl. 174-175.

4624   *Heil, Christoph* Die Q-Rekonstruktion des internationalen Q-Projekts: Einführung in Methodik und Resultate. NT 43 (2001) 128-143;

4625 Beobachtungen zur theologischen Dimension der Gleichnisrede Jesu in Q. The sayings source Q. BEThL 158: 2001 ⇒477. 649-659.

4626 [E]**Heil, Christoph** The database of the International Q project, Q 22:28, 30: You will judge the twelve tribes of Israel. Documenta Q: 1999 ⇒15,4571. [R]SNTU.A 25 (2000) 280-282 (*Fuchs, Albert*) [Mt 19,28; Lk 22,28; 22,30].

4627 *Hermant, Dominique* Les redites chez Marc et les deux autres synoptiques (IIIe partie).RB 108 (2001) 571-597.

4628 [E]**Hieke, Thomas** Documenta Q: reconstructions of Q through two centuries of gospel research: excerpted, sorted, and evaluated: Q 6:20-21: the beatitudes for the poor, hungry, and mourning. Lv 2001, Peeters xxxi; 343 pp. 90-429-1043-7.

4629 *Hoffmann, Paul* Mutmaßungen über Q: zum Problem der literarischen Genese von Q;

4630 *Holmén, Tom* Knowing about Q and knowing about Jesus: mutually exclusive undertakings?. The sayings source Q. BEThL 158: 2001 ⇒ 477. 255-288/497-514.

4631 **Horsley, Richard A.; Draper, Jonathan A.** Whoever hears you hears me: prophets, performance, and tradition in Q. 1999 ⇒15, 4301. [R]JBL 120 (2001) 772-774 (*Kirk, Alan*); RBLit 3 (2001) 373-376 (*Kirk, Alan*).

4632 *Horsley, Richard A.* Moral economy, little tradition, and hidden transcript: applying the work of James C. Scott to Q. SBL.SP 2001. SBL. SPS 40: 2001 ⇒494. 240-259.

4633 *Hüneburg, Martin* Jesus als Wundertäter: zu einem vernachlässigten Aspekt des Jesusbildes von Q. The sayings source Q. BEThL 158: 2001 ⇒477. 635-648;

4634 Matthäus und Lukas als Erben der Wunderüberlieferung von Q. Leqach 1 (2001) 137-150 [BuBB 33,116].

4635 **Hüneburg, Martin** Jesus als Wundertäter in der Logienquelle: ein Beitrag zur Christologie von Q. Arbeiten zur Bibel und ihrer Geschichte 4: Lp 2001, Evangelische 287 pp. €35. 3-374-01852-1. Bibl. 229-272.

4636 *Järvinen, Arto* Jesus as a community symbol in Q. The sayings source Q. BEThL 158: 2001 ⇒477. 515-521.

4637 **Kirk, Alan** The composition of the sayings source: genre, synchrony, and wisdom redaction in Q. NT.S 91: 1998 ⇒14,4142... 16,4688. [R]JBL 119 (2000) 353-357 (*Jacobson, Arland*).

4638 *Kloppenborg Verbin, John S.* Discursive practices in the sayings gospel Q and the quest of the historical Jesus. The sayings source Q. BEThL 158: 2001 ⇒477. 149-190.

4639 **Kloppenborg Verbin, John S.** Excavating Q: the history and setting
      of the sayings gospel. 2000 ⇒16,4690. ᴿJThS 52 (2001) 800-803
      (*Downing, F. Gerald*); JBL 120 (2001) 568-570 (*Jacobson, Arland
      D.*); SR 30 (2001) 107-109 (*Arnal, William E.*); CBQ 63 (2001) 752-
      753 (*Goodman, Daniel E.*); RBBras 18 (2001) 527-528; ET 112
      (2001) 342 (*Edwards, Ruth*).

4640 *Lindemann, Andreas* Introduction;

4641 Die Logienquelle Q: Fragen an eine gut begründete Hypothese;

4642 *Lührmann, Dieter* Die Logienquelle und die Leben-Jesu-Forschung;

4643 *Marucci, Corrado* Sprachliche Merkmale der Q-Quelle als Hilfe für
      deren geschichtliche Einordnung. The sayings source Q. BEThL 158:
      2001 ⇒477. xiii-xxii/3-26/191-206/607-615;

4644 La fonte Q e il problema del Gesù storico: annotazione in merito al
      XLIX Colloquium Biblicum Lovaniense. RivBib 49 (2001) 319-336.

4645 ᴱ**McNicol, Allan James** Beyond the Q impasse: Luke's use of Mat-
      thew. 1996 ⇒12,4227... 15,4591. ᴿSNTU.A 23 (1998) 247-250
      (*Fuchs, Albert*).

4646 *Michaud, Jean-Paul* Quelle(s) communauté(s) derrière la source Q?;

4647 *Moreland, Milton C.* Q and the economics of early Roman Galilee;

4648 *Neirynck, Frans* The reconstruction of Q and IQP / CritEd parallels.
      The sayings source Q. 2001 ⇒477. 577-606/561-575/53-147;

4649 Literary criticism, old and new <1993>;

4650 The minor agreements and Q <1995>;

4651 Goulder and the minor agreements <1997>;

4652 Gospel issues in the passion narratives <1994>;

4653 A symposium on the minor agreements <1993>;

4654 The two-source hypothesis: the Jerusalem Symposium 1984 <1990>;

4655 The argument(s) from order <1997>;

4656 Q: from source to gospel <1995>;

4657 Documenta Q: Q 11,2b-4 <1996>;

4658 Note on Q 4,1-2 <1997>;

4659 Ναζαρά in Q: pro and con <2000> [Mt 4,13; Lk 4,16]. Evangelica
      III. BEThL 150: 2001 ⇒187. 65-92/245-266/307-318/319-332/333-
      339/343-362/363-370/419-431/432-439/440-450/451-461.

4660 **Neirynck, Frans** Q-Parallels: Q-Synopsis and IQP/CritEd parallels.
      SNTA 20: Lv 2001, Peeters 119 pp. 90-429-1058-5.

4661 *Piper, Ronald A.* Jesus and the conflict of powers in Q: two Q
      miracle stories. The sayings source Q. BEThL 158: 2001 ⇒477. 317-
      349 [Lk 7,1-10; 11,14-26; 4,1-13].

4662 *Porter, Stanley E.* P.OXY. 655 and James ROBINSON's proposals for
      Q: brief points of clarification. JThS 52 (2001) 84-92 [Mt 6,28].

4663 **Robbins, Charles Michael** The testing of Jesus in Q. Diss. Clare-
      mont Graduate Univ. 2001, 177 pp. 9998949.

4664 *Robinson, James M.* The critical edition of Q and the study of Jesus. The sayings source Q. BEThL 158: 2001 ⇒477. 27-52;

4665 The image of Jesus in Q. Jesus then and now. 2001 ⇒483. 7-25.

4666 ᴱ**Robinson, James McConkey; Hoffmann, Paul; Kloppenborg, John S.** The critical edition of Q: synopsis. 2000 ⇒16,4698. ᴿETR 76 (2001) 427-429 (*Cuvillier, Élian*); NT 43 (2001) 416 (*Elliott, J.K.*); RBBras 18 (2001) 526-527;

4667 The sayings gospel Q in Greek and English with parallels from the gospels of Mark and Thomas. Contrib. to Biblical Exegesis and Theology 30: Lv 2001, Peeters 176 pp. $20. 90429-10569. Bibl. 175-76.

4668 *Rodd, C.S.* The end of the theology of Q?. ET 113 (2001) 5-12.

4669 *Sanday, William* The conditions under which the gospels were written, in their bearing upon some difficulties of the synoptic problem. Essays in biblical criticism. JSNT.S 225: 2001 <1911> ⇒205. 40-58.

4670 *Schlosser, Jaques* Q et la christologie implicite;

4671 *Sevrin, J.-M.* Thomas, Q et le Jésus de l'histoire. The sayings source Q. BEThL 158: 2001 ⇒477. 289-316/461-476.

4672 *Sewell, Peter* The synoptic problem: a stylometric contribution regarding Q. Colloquium 33/2 (2001) 153-168.

4673 **Smith, Daniel Alan** Post-mortem vindication of Jesus in the sayings gospel Q. Diss. Toronto, St. Michael, ᴰ*Kloppenborg, J.S.* 2001, 346 pp [RTL 33,641].

4674 *Verheyden, J.* The conclusion of Q: eschatology in Q 22,28-30;

4675 *Zeller, Dieter* Jesus, Q und die Zukunft Israels. The sayings source Q. BEThL 158: 2001 ⇒477. 695-718/351-369.

F2.8 *Synoptica*: **themata**

4676 *Cothenet, Édouard* Le sacrifice dans les évangiles synoptiques. CEv 118 (2001) 22-30.

4677 **Ebersohn, M.** Das Nächstenliebegebot in der synoptischen Tradition. MThSt 37: 1993 ⇒9,4431. ᴿSNTU.A 22 (1997) 232-233 (*Fuchs, Albert*).

4678 **Ebner, Martin** Jesus—ein Weisheitslehrer?: synoptische Weisheitslogien im Traditionsprozeß. Herders biblische Studien 15: 1998 ⇒ 14,4159; 15,4616. ᴿThLZ 126 (2001) 756-758 (*Lips, Hermann von*).

4679 *Ferraro, Giuseppe* Il termine 'ora' nei vangeli sinottici. Gli autori divini. 2001 <1973> ⇒144. 35-49.

4680 **Guijarro Oporto, Santiago** Fidelidades en conflicto: la ruptura con la familia por causa del discipulado y de la misión en la tradición sinóptica. 1998 ⇒14,4160...16,4707. ᴿBiblInterp 9 (2001) 97-9 (*Aguilar, Mario I.*); RCatT 26 (2001) 408-411 (*Puig i Tàrrech, Armand*).

4681 **Liebenberg, Jacobus** The language of the Kingdom and Jesus: parable, aphorism, and metaphor in the sayings material common to the synoptic tradition and the gospel of Thomas. BZNW 102: B 2001, De Gruyter xiv; 547 pp. €138. 3-11-016733-6. Bibl. 531-547.

4682 **Manhoff, Harry Alan** All of the kingdoms: Semitic idiom in the synoptic gospels and related Jewish literature. Diss. California, Santa Barbara 2001, 239 pp. 3016398.

4683 *Marconot, Jean-Marie* Pauvreté et maladie dans l'évangile. Représentations des maladies. 2001 ⇒482. 57-75.

4684 **Mazzeo, Michele** I vangeli sinottici: introduzione e percorsi tematici. Cammini nello Spirito, Biblica 43: Mi 2001, Paoline 521 pp 88-3-15-2121-7. Bibl. 505-516.

4685 **Meiser, Martin** Die Reaktion des Volkes auf Jesus: eine redaktionskritische Untersuchung zu den synoptischen Evangelien. BZNW 96: 1998 ⇒14,4164; 15,4622. RJBL 120 (2001) 167-69 (*Matson, Mark*).

4686 **Merklein, Helmut** Die Jesusgeschichte—synoptisch gelesen. SBS 156: 1994 ⇒10,4260... 14,4165. RSNTU.A 22 (1997) 242-246 (*Fuchs, Albert*).

4687 **Meynet, Roland** Jésus passe: testament, jugement, exécution et résurrection du Seigneur Jésus dans les évangiles synoptiques. 1999 ⇒ 15,4623. REstB 59 (2001) 394-395 (*Ibarzábal, S.*);

4688 La Pasqua del Signore: testamento, processo, esecuzione e risurrezione di Gesù nei vangeli sinottici. Retorica biblica 5: Bo 2001, EDB 495 pp. €51. 88-10-25103-2. Bibl. 475-479.

4689 **Roh, Taeseong** Die "familia dei" in den synoptischen Evangelien: eine redaktions- und sozialgeschichtliche Untersuchung zu einem urchristlichen Bildfeld. NTOA 37: Gö 2001, Vandenhoeck & R. xi (2) 309 pp. 3-525-53937-1. Bibl. 293-303.

4690 **Tiwald, Markus** Wanderradikalismus: Jesu erste Jünger—ein Anfang und was davon bleibt. Diss. Wien 2001, DKüschelm, R. 295 pp [RTL 33,642].

4691 *Wegenast, Klaus* Lehren und Lernen in den Synoptischen Evangelien—Anleitung für religiöse Bildung im 3. Jahrtausend oder historische Spurensuche?. Zeitschrift für Pädagogik und Theologie 53 (2001) 133-144.

F3.1 **Matthaei evangelium**: *textus, commentarii*

4692 **Barclay, William** The gospel of Matthew: the New Daily Study Bible. E 2001, Saint Andrew Pr. 2 vols. 0-7152-.

4693 *Baum, Armin Daniel* Ein aramäischer Urmatthäus im kleinasiatischen Gottesdienst: das Papiaszeugnis zur Entstehung des Matthäusevangeliums. ZNW 92 (2001) 257-272.

4694 **Boice, James Montgomery** The gospel of Matthew, 1: the King and his kingdom: Matthew 1-17; 2: The triumph of the King: Matthew 18-28. GR 2001, Baker 676 pp. $25 + $25. 0-8010-1201-5/2-3 [ThD 48,258—Heiser, W. Charles].

4695 **Borghi, E.** Il cuore della giustizia: vivere il vangelo secondo Matteo. Cammini nello Spirito—Meditazione 70: Mi 2001, Paoline 278 pp. Pref. di *Giuseppe Segalla*.

4696 *Boscolo, Gastone* Sarà chiamato Emmanuele, che significa 'Dio con noi' (Mt 1,23). CredOg 125-126 (2001) 5-37;

4697 Invito alla lettura [Bibl.]. CredOg 125-126 (2001) 163-167.

4698 **Boscolo, Gastone** Vangelo secondo Matteo. Dabar, NT: Padova 2001, Messaggero 187 pp. 88-250-1003-6. Bibl. 181-182.

4699 *Cuvillier, Élian* Chronique matthéenne VI: 'l'un de ces plus petits de mes frères...' (Mt 25/40). ETR 76 (2001) 575-598 [Gen 22].

4700 [E]**Daniele, Maria Ignazia** ORIGENE: commento al vangelo di Matteo, 2 (libri XIII-XV). [T]*Scognamiglio, Rosario*: CTePa 151: 1999 ⇒ 15,4640. [R]CivCatt 152/4 (2001) 307-309 (*Cremascoli, G.*).

4701 Das Evangelium des Matthäus. Fischer Taschenbuch 14507: Fra 2000, Fischer 94 pp. 3-596-14507-4. Einleitung *Marlene Streeruwitz*.

4702 **Foulkes, Francis** A guide to St. Matthew's gospel. SPCK International Study Guide 37: L 2001, SPCK xvi; 285 pp. $18. 0-281-05173-9. Bibl. xiii.

4703 **Francis, Leslie J.; Atkins, Peter** Exploring Matthew's gospel. Personality type and scripture: NY 2001, Mowbray x; 224 pp. $22. Commentary on the lectionary selection [BiTod 40,265—Senior, D.].

4704 **Frankemölle, Hubert** Matthäus Kommentar, 2. 1997 ⇒13,4467... 16,4728. [R]ETR 76 (2001) 577-578 (*Cuvillier, E.*).

4705 **Heras Oliver, Gloria** Jesús según San Mateo: análisis narrativo del primer evangelio. Teológica 105: Pamplona 2001, EUNSA 287 pp. 84-313-1931-3. Bibl. 279-287.

4706 *Kealy, Seán P.* Matthew's gospel today. ChiSt 40 (2001) 229-238.

4707 **Keener, Craig S.** A commentary on the gospel of Matthew. 1999 ⇒ 15,4652; 16,4732. [R]EThL 77 (2001) 219-220 (*Verheyden, J.*); VJTR 65 (2001) 544-546 (*Meagher, P.M.*); ABR 49 (2001) 61-62 (*Doyle, B. Rod*); Bib. 82 (2001) 112-115 (*Byrskog, Samuel*); RBLit 3 (2001) 379-382 (*Whitt, R. Keith*); ETR 76 (2001) 580-582 (*Cuvillier, E.*).

4708 **Keener, Craig S.** Matthew. The IVP New Testament Commentary 1: 1997 ⇒13,4472. [R]ETR 76 (2001) 580-582 (*Cuvillier, E.*).

4709 ^E**Levine, Amy-Jill** A feminist companion to Matthew. The Feminist Companion to the New Testament and Early Christian Writings 1: Shf 2001, Academic 247 pp. $25. 1-84127-211-6. With *Marianne Blickenstaff*; Bibl. 221-234.

4710 *Löfstedt, Bengt* Zum Matthäuskommentar in CLM 14311. Aevum 75 (2001) 263-266.

4711 **Luz, Ulrich** Das Evangelium nach Matthäus: 3. Teilband: Mt 18-25. Evangelisch-katholischer Komm. zum NT 1/3: 1997 ⇒13,4476. ^RRBBras 18 (2001) 533-534; ETR 76 (2001) 576-577 (*Cuvillier, E.*);

4712 Matthew 8-20: a commentary. ^T*Crouch, James E.*; ^E*Köster, Helmut*: Hermeneia: Mp 2001, Fortress xxxvii; 608 pp. $69. 0-8006-6034-X. Bibl. xx-xxxvi;

4713 El evangelio según San Mateo, 2: Mt 8-17. ^T*Olasagasti Gazteluzmendi, Manuel*: BEB 103: S 2001, Sígueme 699 pp. €39. ^REstTrin 35 (2001) 671-672 (*Pikaza, Xabier*).

4714 **Mani, M.** Il vangelo per la chiesa e per il mondo: itinerario con l'evangelista Matteo nel ciclo liturgico dell'anno A. Leumann 2001, Elledici 240 pp. €8.

4715 **Mello, Alberto** Évangile selon Matthieu: commentaire midrashique et narratif. LeDiv 179: 1999 ⇒15,4658. ^RBrot. 152 (2001) 415-416 (*Ribeiro da Silva, I.*); ETR 76 (2001) 582-583 (*Cuvillier, E.*).

4716 *Neirynck, Frans* The sources of Matthew: annotations to U. Luz's commentary. Evangelica III. 2001 <1998> ⇒187. 371-398.

4717 **Pronzato, Alessandro** Sólo tú tienes palabras: comentario al evangelio de Mateo. S 2001, Sígueme 320 pp. €17.43.

4718 ^{TE}**Schenke, Hans-Martin** Das Matthäus-Evangelium im mittelägyptischen Dialekt des Koptischen (Codex Schøyen). Manuscripts in the Schøyen Collection 2: Coptic Papyri 1: Oslo 2001, Hermes 392 pp. $95. 82-8034-002-5.

4719 **Scholl, Norbert** Ein Bestseller entsteht: das Matthäus-Evangelium. 1998 ⇒14,4197. ^RSNTU.A 25 (2000) 287-288 (*Raml, R.*).

4720 *Schweizer, Eduard* Il vangelo secondo Matteo. NT 2: Brescia 2001, Paideia 520 pp. Bibl. 505-506.

4721 ^E**Simonetti, Manlio** Ancient christian commentary on scripture: New Testament, 1a: Matthew 1-13. Ch 2001, Dearborn lii; 326 pp. 0-8308-1489-8.

      Stammberger, Ralf M. Die Halberstädter Glosse 2001 ⇒2656.

4722 **Stock, Klemens** La liturgia della parola: spiegazione dei vangeli domenicali e festivi: Anno A (Matteo). Bibbia e Preghiera 39: R 2001, ADP 359 pp. 88-7357-252-9.

      ^MTHOMPSON, W. The gospel of Matthew 2001 ⇒108.

4723 ᵀTommaseo, Niccolò Armando TORNO: Il vangelo secondo Matteo. Mi 2001, Vita Felice 127 pp. 88-7799-127-5. Introd. *Armando Torno*; riproduzione di 30 xilografie di *Bartolomeo di Giovanni*.

4724 **Trilling, Wolfgang** Vangelo secondo Matteo. Commenti spirituali del Nuovo Testamento: R 2001, Città Nuova 491 pp. 88-311-3825-1.

4725 **Vangheluwe, Roger** Matteüs aan het woord. Antwerpen 2001, Halewijn 313 pp.

4726 *Zuurmond, Rochus* The textual background of the gospel of Matthew in Ge'ez. Aethiopica 4 (2001) 32-41.

4727 **Zuurmond, Rochus** Novum Testamentum Aethiopice: part III: the gospel of Matthew. ÄthF 55: Wsb 2001, Harrassowitz viii; 488 pp. FS112. 3-447-04306-7.

F3.2 **Themata** *de Matthaeo*

4728 *Anderson, Janice Capel* Matthew: gender and reading. A feminist companion to Matthew. 2001 ⇒4709. 25-51.

4729 *Ascough, Richard S.* Matthew and community formation. ᴹTHOMPSON, W. 2001 ⇒108. 96-126.

4730 **Barnet, John** Not the righteous but sinners: M.M. BAKHTIN's theory of aesthetics and the problem of reader-character interaction in Matthew's gospel. Diss. Duke 2001[RTL 33,636].

4731 *Buckley, Thomas W.* The christology of Matthew. ChiSt 40 (2001) 251-260.

4732 **Carter, Warren** Matthew and empire: initial explorations. Harrisburg, Pa. 2001, Trinity v; 249 pp. $25. 1-56338-342-X.

4733 **Castaño, Adolfo M.** Fonseca Δικαιοσύνη en Mateo: una interpretaciþ teológica a partir de 3,15 y 21,32. TGr.T 27: 1997 ⇒13, 4497; 15,4674. ᴿEstB 59 (2001) 105-106 (*Rodríguez Carmona, A.*).

4734 **Charette, Blaine B.** Restoring presence: the Spirit in Matthew's gospel. JPentec.S 18: 2000 ⇒16,4749. ᴿETR 76 (2001) 590-591 (*Cuvillier, E.*).

4735 *De Marchi, Sergio* 'Chi è mai constui al quale i venti e il mare obbediscono?' (Mt 8,27): la comprensione di Cristo;

4736 *De Zan, Renato* 'Ecco, io sono con voi tutti i giorni' (Mt 28,20): l'uso liturgico del vangelo di Matteo nella chiesa. CredOg 125-126 (2001) 71-81/101-109.

4737 *Deutsch, Celia* Jesus as wisdom: a feminist reading of Matthew's wisdom christology. A feminist companion to Matthew. 2001 ⇒4709. 88-113.

4738 *Eckstein, Hans-Joachim* Die 'bessere Gerechtigkeit': zur Ethik Jesu nach dem Mattäusevangelium. ThBeitr 32 (2001) 299-316.

4739 *Frankemölle, Hubert* Für eine neue Lektüre der Bibel: Antijudaismus im Matthäus-Evangelium (und in der Matthäus-Passion von J.S. BACH)?. Christen und Juden gemeinsam. 2001 ⇒352. 151-182.

4740 *Giesen, Heinz* Galiläa—mehr als eine Landschaft: bibeltheologischer Stellenwert Galiläas im Matthäusevangelium. EThL 77 (2001) 23-45.

4741 *Grasso, Santi* 'Seguitemi, vi farò pescatori di uomini' (Mt 4,19): la sequela. CredOg 125-126 (2001) 91-99.

4742 *Harrington, Daniel J.* Matthew's gospel: pastoral problems and possibilities. ᴹTHOMPSON, W. 2001 ⇒108. 62-73.

4743 *Harvey, John D.* Mission in Matthew. Mission in the NT. ASMS 27 (2001) 119-136.

4744 **Hertig, Paul** Matthew's narrative use of Galilee in the multicultural and missiological journeys of Jesus. Mellen 46: 1998 ⇒14,4226. ᴿETR 76 (2001) 593-594 (*Cuvillier, E.*).

4745 *Huijzer, Richart* Een joodse dissident aan het woord: achtergronden bij het evangelie van Matteus. ITBT 9/2 (2001) 21-23.

4746 *Humphries-Brooks, Stephenson* The Canaanite women in Matthew. A feminist companion to Matthew. 2001 ⇒4709. 138-156.

4747 **Klein, Hans** Bewährung im Glauben: Studien zum Sondergut des Evangelisten Matthäus. BThSt 26: 1996 ⇒12,4318. ᴿETR 76 (2001) 589-590 (*Cuvillier, E.*).

4748 **LaGrand, James** The earliest Christian mission to "all nations" in the light of Matthew's gospel. 1999 ⇒15,4690. ᴿThLZ 126 (2001) 530-32 (*Wrege, Hans-Theo*); ETR 76 (2001) 591-593 (*Cuvillier, E.*).

4749 *Levine, Amy-Jill* Matthew's advice to a divided readership. ᴹTHOMPSON, W.: 2001 ⇒108. 22-41;

4750 Introduction. A feminist companion to Matthew. 2001 ⇒4709. 13-23.

4751 **Luomanen, Petri** Entering the kingdom of heaven: a study on the structure of Matthew's view of salvation. WUNT 2/101: 1998 ⇒14, 4237; 16,4771. ᴿJBL 119 (2000) 135-137 (*Verseput, Donald J.*).

4752 *Luz, Ulrich* Das Matthäusevangelium—eine neue oder eine neu redigierte Jesusgeschichte?. Biblischer Text. BThSt 44: 2001 ⇒252. 53-76.

4753 **Mareček, Petr** La preghiera di Gesù nel vangelo di Matteo: uno studio esegetico-teologico. TGr.T 67: 2000 ⇒16,4774. ᴿCBQ 63 (2001) 345-346 (*Bernas, Casimir*); CivCatt 152/4 (2001) 96-98 (*Scaiola, D.*).

4754 **Mari, Pietro** Gesù, profeta del regno: leggere e pregare il vangelo secondo Matteo. 1999 ⇒15,4696; 16,4775. ᴿEccl(R) 15 (2001) 485-486 (*Izquierdo, Antonio*).

4755 *Matera, Frank J.* Jesus and the law: Matthew's view. BiTod 39 (2001) 271-276.

4756 **Mesters, Carlos; Lopes, Mercedes; Orofino, Francisco** Misericordia quiero y no sacrificios: encuentros bíblicos sobre el evangelio de Mateo. Estella (Navarra) 2001, Verbo Divino 143 pp. 84-8169-4258.

4757 *Miler, Jean* Le travail de l'accomplissement: Matthieu et les écritures. FV 100/4 (2001) 13-29.

4758 **Miler, Jean** Les citations d'accomplissement dans l'évangile de Matthieu. AnBib 140: 1999 ⇒15,4697; 16,4777. [R]RivBib 49 (2001) 490-494 (*Grasso, Santi*); ETR 76 (2001) 596-597 (*Cuvillier, E.*).

4759 *Mora, Vincent* La symbolique de Matthieu, 2: les groupes. LeDiv 187: P 2001, Cerf 394 pp. €37. 2-204-06596-X. Bibl. 391-392.

4760 **Nakano, Minoru** Jesus the Savior of God's people from sin: a study of Matthew's soteriology. Diss. Claremont Graduate Univ. 2001, 344 pp. 9998948.

4761 **Nakanose, Shigeyuki; Paula Pedro, Enilda de** Él está en medio de nosotros!: el sembrador del reino: el evangelio de Mateo. Estella (Navarra) 2001, Verbo Divino 164 pp. 84-8169-432-0.

4762 **Neyrey, Jerome H.** Honor and shame in the gospel of Matthew. 1998 ⇒14,4244; 16,4779. $30. [R]CThMi 28 (2001) 58-60 (*Roth, S. John*).

4763 *O'Grady, John F.* The community of Matthew. ChiSt 40 (2001) 239-250.

4764 *Padovese, Luciano* 'Simile a un padrone di casa che estrae dal suo tesoro cose nuove e cose antiche' (Mt 13,52): la dimensione etica. CredOg 125-126 (2001) 63-69.

4765 **Park, Jeongsoo** Sündenvergebung: ihre religiöse und soziale Dimension im Matthäusevangelium. Diss. Heidelberg 2001, [D]*Theissen, G.* [RTL 33,640].

4766 **Podeszwa, Pawel** 'Misericordia voglio e non sacrificio': la rilettura di Os 6,6 nel vangelo di Matteo. Exc. Diss. Gregoriana 2001, [D]*Grilli, Massimo*: 128 pp. [Mt 9,13; 12,7].

4767 **Repschinski, Boris** The controversy stories in the gospel of Matthew. FRLANT 189: 2000 ⇒16,4784. [R]BZ 45 (2001) 130-132 (*Dobbeler, Stephanie von*); CBQ 63 (2001) 352-353 (*Witherup, Ronald D.*); ThLZ 126 (2001) 1273-1275 (*Becker, Hans-Jürgen*); ETR 76 (2001) 586-588 (*Cuvillier, E.*).

4768 *Rowan, Peter A.* Discipleship and mission: toward an integral mission theology in the gospel of Matthew, 3. Evangel 19/1 (2001) i-xii. EMA Occasional Paper 7.

4769 *Saldarini, Anthony J.* Reading Matthew without anti-semitism. [M]THOMPSON, W. 2001 ⇒108. 166-184;

4770 Absent women in Matthew's households. A feminist companion to Matthew. 2001 ⇒4709. 157-170.

4771 *Sato, Migaku* Ist Matthäus wirklich Judenchrist?. AJBI 27 (2001) 155-173.

4772 *Senior, Donald* Directions in Matthean studies. ᴹTHOMPSON, W. 2001 ⇒108. 5-21.

4773 *Sheffield, Julian* The father in the gospel of Matthew. A feminist companion to Matthew. 2001 ⇒4709. 52-69.

4774 **Söding, Thomas** Exegese und Predigt: das Matthäus-Evangelium: Anregungen zum Lesejahr A. Wü 2001, Echter 86 pp. 3429-023-807.

4775 *Stanton, Graham N.* The early reception of Matthew's gospel: new evidence from papyri?. ᴹTHOMPSON, W. 2001 ⇒108. 42-61.

4776 *Stefani, Piero* 'Non sono stato inviato che alle pecore perdute della casa di Israele...' (Mt 15,24-26): il rapporto chiesa—Israele. CredOg 125-126 (2001) 83-89.

4777 **Steffen, Daniel S.** The messianic banquet as a paradigm for Israel-Gentile salvation in Matthew. Diss. Dallas Sem. 2001, 348 pp. 3002970.

4778 **Stock, Augustine** The method and message of Matthew. 1994 ⇒10, 4340... 13,4535. ᴿSNTU.A 23 (1998) 257-259 (*Fuchs, Albert*).

4779 *Sweetland, Dennis M.* Suffering in the gospel of Matthew. The bible on suffering. 2001 ⇒326. 120-143.

4780 *Talbert, Charles H.* Indicative and imperative in Matthean soteriology. Bib. 82 (2001) 515-538.

4781 **Talbot, Michel** La béatitude des doux chez Matthieu. Diss. Ottawa, Coll. Dominicain 2001, ᴰ*Gourgues, M.* [RTL 33,641].

4782 *Toffanello, Giuseppe* 'Quando il Figlio dell'uomo verrà...' (Mt 25,31): il discorso escatologico. CredOg 125-126 (2001) 39-47.

4783 Il vangelo di Matteo nelle celebrazioni eucharistiche. CredOg 125-126 (2001) 111-155.

4784 *Viviano, Benedict T.* Matthew, master of ecumenical infighting. Trinity— kingdom—church. NTOA 48: 2001 <1983> ⇒223. 187-195.

4785 *Wainwright, Elaine* The Matthean Jesus and the healing of women. ᴹTHOMPSON, W. 2001 ⇒108. 74-95.

4786 *Weiß, Hans-Friedrich* Noch einmal: zur Frage eines Antijudaismus bzw. Antipharisäismus im Matthäusevangelium. ZNT 8 (2001) 37-41.

4787 *Weren, Wim* De geschiedenis en sociale situatie van de gemeente rond Matteüs. Vroegchristelijke gemeenten. 2001 ⇒460. 100-114.

4788 *Williams, P.J.* Bread and the Peshitta in Matthew 16:11-12 and 12:4. NT 43 (2001) 331-333.

4789 *Wills, Lawrence M.* Scribal methods in Matthew and Mishnah Abot. CBQ 63 (2001) 241-257.

F3.3 *Mt 1s (Lc 1s⇒F7.5) Infantia Jesu*—Infancy Gospels

4790 *Bartina, Sebastián* La sagrada familia en el Antiguo Testamento: visión de conjunto. Sagrada Familia en la biblia. 2001 ⇒4792. 19-38.

4791 *Becker-Huberti, Manfred* Ex oriente lux: Weihnachten in judenchristlicher Tradition als "Lichtfest". AnzSS 110/12 (2001) 5-9.

4792 ^E**Calduch-Benages, Nuria** La Sagrada Familia en la biblia. Biblioteca Manual, Desclée 28: Bilbao 2001, Desclée de B. 221 pp. 84-330-1598-2. Bibl. 219-221.

4793 *Calduch-Benages, Nuria* La peregrinación de la familia de Nazaret: reflexiones bíblicas. 5° Congreso sobre la sagrada família. 2001 ⇒ 512. 63-77;

4794 La peregrinación de la sagrada familia;

4795 La sagrada familia en la perspectiva de los salmos mesiánicos;

4796 La sagrada familia en los textos proféticos del Antiguo Testamento;

4797 La sagrada familia a la luz de la tradición sapiencial del Antiguo Testamento;

4798 *Da Campo, Lino* La sagrada familia en el Nuevo Testamento: visión de conjunto. Sagrada Familia en la biblia. 2001 ⇒4792. 197-213/77-93/39-54/55-75/97-121.

Finch, Ann A star over Bethlehem 2001 ⇒1389.

4799 **Freed, Edwin D.** The stories of Jesus' birth: a critical introduction. BiSe 72: Shf 2001, Sheffield A. 184 pp. 1-84127-132-2. Bibl. 171-2.

4800 *Kingsbury, Jack Dean* The birth narrative of Matthew. ^MTHOMPSON, W. 2001 ⇒108. 154-165.

4801 *Kügler, Joachim* Der König als Realpräsenz Gottes und das Geheimnis von Weihnachten. WUB 22 (2001) 39-43.

4802 *Lange, Ulrich-Paul* Was sagt das Neue Testament über die Geburt des Erlösers aus der Jungfrau Maria?. Theologisches 31 (2001) 2-10.

4803 **Lienhard, Joseph T.** St. Joseph in early christianity: devotion and theology: a study and an anthology of patristic texts. 1999 ⇒15, 4732. ^RAugSt 32 (2001) 157-158 (*Fitzgerald, Allan D.*).

4804 **Maier, Paul I.** The first christmas; the true and unfamiliar story. GR 2001, Kregel 96 pp. $15. 0-8254-3330-4 [ThD 48,378—Heiser, W.].

4805 *Marín i Torner, Joan Ramon* El rerefons isaïà de Mt 1-2: aspectes cúltics. El text. Scripta Biblica 3: 2001 ⇒310. 11-38.

4806 **Mayordomo-Marín, Moisés** Den Anfang hören: leserorientierte Evangelienexegese am Beispiel von Matthäus 1-2. FRLANT 180: 1998 ⇒14,4276... 16,4802. ^RETR 76 (2001) 584-586 (*Cuvillier, E.*); JBL 119 (2000) 769-770 (*Nolland, John*).

4807 **Mittmann-Richert, Ulrike** Magnifikat und Benediktus: die ältesten
Zeugnisse der judenchristlichen Tradition von der Geburt des Messias. WUNT 2/90: 1996 ⇒14,4277; 15,5495. ᴿThLZ 126 (2001) 532-
534 (*Walter, Nikolaus*).

4808 *Niclós, Josep Vicent* El text hebreu i preguntes d'un jueu medieval a
l'evangeli de la infància (Mt 1-2). El text. 2001 ⇒310. 75-105.

4809 *Orchard, Bernard* The betrothal and marriage of Mary to Joseph, 1,
2. HPR 102/1-2 (2001) 7-14, 50-56.

4810 **Orchard, Bernard** The betrothal and marriage of Mary to Joseph: a
scriptural meditation. L 2001, Ealing Abbey [ScrB 31,109].

4811 **Salama, Sayed** La huida de la sagrada familia a Egipto: escritura,
tradición y arqueología. Bilbao 2001, Grafite 221 pp. Vers. esp.. re-
visada por *Dra Mᵃ Luz Mangado*; Ill.

4812 *Sánchez Bosch, Jordi* El mundo en que vivió la sagrada familia. La
Sagrada Familia en la biblia. 2001 ⇒4792. 187-195.

4813 *Sánchez Mielgo, Gerardo* Los evangelios de la infancia: ¿historia, relato, teología?. Communio 34/1 (2001) 103-180.

4814 *Trimaille, Michel* Qui est cet enfant?: les évangiles de Noël répon-
dent (Mt 1-2). EeV 48 (2001) 3-5.

4815 *Vanni, Ugo* La sagrada familia desde la óptica del evangelio de Mateo. La Sagrada Familia en la biblia. 2001 ⇒4792. 123-137.

4816 *Vernet, Josep Maria* La presencia de la sagrada familia en Tierra
Santa. La Sagrada Familia en la biblia. 2001 ⇒4792. 169-185.

4817 *Zeller, Dieter; Radl, Walter; Beinert, Wolfgang* Jungfrauengeburt.
RGG², 4: I-K. 2001 ⇒664. 705-708.

4818 *Zenger, Erich* "Dies alles ist geschehen, damit sich erfüllte...": Weihnachten im Licht des Ersten Testaments. AnzSS 110/12 (2001) 15-19
[Isa 7,14; Hos 11,1-11].

4819 *Hutchison, John C.* Women, gentiles, and the messianic mission in
Matthew's genealogy. BS 158 (2001) 152-164 [Mt 1,1-17].

4820 *Teuwsen, Bernward* Die Frauen in der toledot/genealogie des Evangeliums nach Matthäus (Mt 1,1-25). WuA(M) 42 (2001) 111-114.

4821 *Van Deun, Peter* La parenté de la Vierge et du Christ dans une exégèse byzantine de Matthieu 1,15-16. AnBoll 119/1 (2001) 33-39.

4822 *Chilton, Bruce* Jésus, le mamzer (Mt 1.18). NTS 47 (2001) 222-227.

4823 *Giesler, Michael E.* Bʀᴏᴡɴ's "Birth of the Messiah ..." revisited.
HPR 101/5 (2001) 16-24 [Mt 1,18-2,23; Lk 1,5-2,52].

4824 *Menken, Maarten J.J.* The textual form of the quotation from Isaiah
7:14 in Matthew 1:23. NT 43 (2001) 144-160.

4825 *Baudy, Gerhard* Der messianische Stern (Mt 2) und das sidus Iulium:
zum interkulturellen Zeichengehalt antiker Herrschaftslegitimation.
HBO 31 (2001) 23-69.

4826 *Jensen, Robin M.* Witnessing the divine: the magi in art and literature. BiRe 17/6 (2001) 24-32, 59 [Mt 2,1-12].

4827 *Marty, Joseph* Au cinéma, le détail "obscur" peut révéler la "lumière"
de l'évangile: la séquence des mages de "L'Évangile selon Saint Matthieu" de Pier Paolo PASOLINI. VivH 12/1 (2001) 13-16.

4828 *Parpola, Simo* The magi and the star: Baylonian astronomy dates
Jesus' birth. BiRe 17/6 (2001) 16-23, 52-54 [Mt 2,1-12].

4829 **Trexler, Richard C.** The journey of the magi: meanings in history of
a christian story. 1997 ⇒13,4585... 15,4749. [R]HR 40 (2001) 304-306
(*Noble, Thomas F.X.*) [Mt 2,1-12].

4830 *Nocquet, Dany* Matthieu 2,13-23: l'enfant épargné de Bethléem. Lire
et Dire 48 (2001) 31-42.

4831 *McCartney, Dan; Enns, Peter* Matthew and Hosea: a response to
John Sailhamer. WThJ 63 (2001) 97-105 [Hos 11,1; Mt 2,15].

4832 *Sailhamer, John H.* Hosea 11:1 and Matthew 2:15. WThJ 63 (2001)
87-96.

4833 *Menken, Maarten J.J.* The sources of the Old Testament quotation in
Matthew 2:23. JBL 120 (2001) 451-468.

4834 *Zuckschwerdt, Ernst* Abermals: Nazoraîos in Mt 2,23. ThZ 57 (2001)
402-405.

F3.4 *Mt 3...Baptismus Jesu,* Beginnings of the Public Life

4835 *Baudoz, Jean-François* Les tentations de Jésus. Christus 48 (2001)
37-44.

4836 [E]*Billon, Gérard* Le baptême de Jésus. DosB 86 (2001) 3-29.

4837 **Guyenot, Laurent** Jésus et Jean Baptiste: enquête historique sur une
rencontre légendaire. Chambéry 1999, Exergue 369 pp [ETR 78,
438—Couteau, Elisabeth].

4838 *Katz, Friedrich* Hat Johannes der Täufer Jesus getauft?: Überlegungen zu einem erledigten Thema. [F]HAHN, F. 2001 ⇒41. 27-36.

4839 *Keel, Othmar* Warum bei der Taufe im Jordan eine weisse Taube zu
Jesus fliegt: Entstehung und Wandel von Tiersymbolen. Im Schatten
deiner Flügel. 2001 ⇒412. 58-63.

4840 *Lupieri, Edmondo; Afnulf, Arwed* Johannes der Täufer. RGG[2], 4: I-
K. 2001 ⇒664. 514-518.

4841 *Lupieri, Edmondo* 'The law and the prophets were until John': John
the Baptist between Jewish and christian history of salvation.
Neotest. 35 (2001) 49-56.

4842 *Plisch, Uwe-Karsten* Die Perikopen über Johannes den Täufer in der
neuentdeckten mittelägyptischen Version des Matthäus-Evangeliums
(Codex Schoyen). NT 43 (2001) 368-392.

4843 **Pulatt, Sebastian** The baptism of Jesus in Italian christology and pneumatology (1981-1995). Exc. Diss. Gregoriana 2001, ᴰ*O'Collins, Gerald*: viii; 79 pp.

4844 *Román Flecha, José* Juan del desierto. Personajes del NT. 2001 ⇒ 231. 25-35.

4845 **Taylor, Joan** The Immerser: John the Baptist within Second Temple Judaism. 1997 ⇒13,4601... 16,4831. ᴿSNTU.A 23 (1998) 251-257 (*Fuchs, Albert*).

4846 **Yamasaki, Gary** John the Baptist in life and death: audience-oriented criticism of Matthew's narrative. JSNT.S 167: 1998 ⇒14, 4302. ᴿRExp 98 (2001) 606-7 (*Vinson, Richard B.*); ETR 76 (2001) 588-589 (*Cuvillier, E.*); JBL 119 (2000) 572-574 (*Brown, Stephen*).

4847 *Gramaglia, Pier Angelo* La predicazione battesimale del Battista (Mt 3,7-10; Lc 3,7-9). ATT 7 (2001) 18-50 Som., sum. 49.

4848 *Taylor, N.H.* The temptation of Jesus on the mountain: a Palestinian christian polemic against AGRIPPA I. JSNT 83 (2001) 27-49 [Mt 4,1-11; Mk 1,12-13; Lk 4,1-13].

F3.5 **Mt 5...Sermon on the Mount** [...plain, Lk 6,17]

4849 *Diebold-Scheuermann, Carola* Gewaltverzicht und Feindesliebe: die ethische Relevanz der Bergpredigt. CPB 114 (2001) 227-233.

4850 ᴱ**Dulk, M. den** De Bergrede: steunpunt van de vrijheid. Zoetermeer 2001, Meinema 164 pp. €14.75. 90-211-3844-1.

4851 **Hughes, R. Kent** The Sermon on the Mount. Wheaton, IL 2001, Crossway 287 pp. $22. 158-134-063X [BS 160,123—Zuck, Roy B.].

4852 *Kilgallen, John J.* Matthew's Sermon on the Mount. ChiSt 40 (2001) 261-274.

4853 **Lamberigts, S.** Onverdeeld goed: over de bergrede van Jezus. Averbode 2001, Altiora 112 pp [Coll. 31,331s—Hoet, Hendrik].

4854 **Meistad, Tore** Martin LUTHER and John WESLEY on the Sermon on the Mount. Pietist and Wesleyan Studies 10: 1999 ⇒15,4778. ᴿEvQ 73 (2001) 270-271 (*Wellings, Martin*).

4855 **Pelikan, Jaroslav** Divine rhetoric: the Sermon on the Mount as message and as model in AUGUSTINE, CHRYSOSTOM, and LUTHER. Crestwood, NY 2001, St. Vladimir's Seminary Press xiii; 167 pp. $13. 0-8-8141-214-7. Bibl. 157-167.

4856 **Petersen, Walter** Zur Eigenart des Matthäus: Untersuchung zur Rhetorik in der Bergpredigt. Osnabrücker Studien zur Jüdischen und Christlichen Bibel 2: Osnabrück 2001, Rasch 379 pp. €36.80. 3-934-005-91-8. Diss.

4857 **Schegget, G.H. ter** Een hart onder de riem: over de bergrede. Baarn 2001, Ten Have 240 pp. €15.84. 90-259-5232-1.

4858 *Schmidt, Frederick W.* Loyal opposition and the law in the teaching of Jesus: the ethics of a restorative and Utopian eschatology. AsbTJ 56/1 (2001) 31-44 [Mk 10,9; 2,27].

4859 **Stiewe, Martin; Vouga, François** Die Bergpredigt und ihre Rezeption als kurze Darstellung des Christentums. Neutestamentliche Entwürfe zur Theologie 2: Tü 2001, Francke x; 294 pp. €29. 3-7720-31-52-8.

4860 **Vaught, Carl G.** The Sermon on the Mount: a theological investigation. Waco 2001, Baylor Univ. Pr. xiv; 219 pp. $15. 0-918954-76-2 [TD 48,292—Heiser, W. Charles].

4861 *Zager, Werner* Weisheitliche Aspekte in der Bergpredigt. Weisheit, Ethos und Gebot. BThSt 43: 2001 ⇒492. 1-28.

4862 *Parsons, Mikeal C.; Hanks, D. Thomas* When the salt lost its savour: a brief history of Matthew 5.13/Mark 9.50/Luke 14.34 in English translation. BiTr 52 (2001) 320-326.

4863 *Shillington, V. George* Salt of the earth? (Mt 5:13/Lk 14:34f). ET 11/2 (2001) 120-121.

4864 *Fowler, Miles* City on a hill: an interpretation of Matt 5:14B/GThom. 32. JHiC 8/1 (2001) 68-72.

4865 *Vouga, François* Matthäus 5,17-20: der Gott des Tausches und der Geist der Gabe: das theologische und existentielle Programm der Bergpredigt. Was ist ein Text?. 2001 ⇒335. 43-64.

4866 *Hengel, Martin* "Du sollst nicht töten"—"Ich aber sage Euch ..." (Matthäus 5,21-26). ThBeitr 32 (2001) 65-69.

4867 *Duff, Paul B.* Vision and violence: theories of vision and Matthew 5: 27-30. FBETZ, H. 2001 ⇒5. 63-75.

4868 *Kollmann, Bernd* Erwägungen zur Reichweite des Schwurverbots Jesu (Mt 5,34). ZNW 92 (2001) 20-32.

4869 **Davis, James Frederick** Lex talionis in early Judaism and the exhortation of Jesus in Matthew 5:38-42. Diss. Dallas Theol. Sem. 2001, 302 pp. 3002962.

4870 *Vez, Christian* Matthieu 5,38-48: violence/non violence. Lire et Dire 48 (2001) 3-11.

4871 *Salvarani, Brunetto* Interpretazione di 'non resistere al malvagio/al male' (Matteo 5,39). Servitium 35 (2001) 671-675.

4872 *Zöckler, Thomas* Light within the human person: a comparison of Matthew 6:22-23 and gospel of Thomas 24. JBL 120 (2001) 487-99.

4873 *Stenström, Thure* Søren KIERKEGAARD och liljorna på marken. SvTK 77 (2001) 98-106 [Mt 6,24-34].

F3.6 **Mt 5,3-11** (Lc 6,20-22) **Beatitudines**

4874 *Amaladoss, M.* Listen to Spirit: blessed are the peacemakers (Mt 5:9). VJTR 65 (2001) 917-920.

4875 *Cardellino, Lodovico* Le beatitudini (Mt 5,1-16). BeO 43 (2001) 69-129.

4876 ᴱ**Drobner, Hubertus R.; Viciano, Alberto** GREGORY of Nyssa: homilies on the Beatitudes. SVigChr 52: 2000 ⇒16,12641. ᴿJThS 52 (2001) 915-916 (*Gould, Graham*).

4877 **Green, H. Benedict** Matthew, poet of the beatitudes. JSNT.S 203: Shf 2001, Sheffield A. 350 pp. £50/$80. 1-84127-165-9. Bibl. 309-328. ᴿET 112 (2001) 362-364 (*Rodd, C.S.*).

4878 **Maggi, Alberto** Las bienaventuranzas: traducción y comentario de Mateo 5,1-12. Grande temas de Nuevo Testamento 4: Córdoba 2001, El Almendro 188 pp. 84-8005-033-0.

4879 *Martin, Francis* The paradox of the beatitudes: between eschatology and history. Anthropotes 17 (2001) 225-238.

4880 *Nadeau-Lacour, Thérèse* Les béatitudes, entre spiritualité et morale, dans la vie familiale. Anthropotes 17 (2001) 239-254.

4881 **Philippe, Marie-Dominique** Un feu sur la terre: entretiens autour des béatitudes. Hommes de parole: P 2001, Mame 247 pp. €19.

4882 **Jankowski, Stanisław** Geneza i znaczenie klausul mateuszowych: studium historyczno-egsegetyczne [Genèse et signification des clauses de Matthieu: étude historique et exégétique]. Diss. Warsaw 2001, ᴰŁach, J., 299 pp. [RTL 33,638] [Mt 5,32; 19,9]. **P.**

4883 *Schaller, Berndt* Die Sprüche über Ehescheidung und Wiederheirat in der synoptischen Überlieferung. Fundamenta Judaica. StUNT 25: 2001 <1970> ⇒206. 104-124.

4884 *Weibling, James M.* Reconciling Matthew and Mark on divorce. TrinJ 22 (2001) 219-235 [Mt 5,32; 19,9; Mk 10].

4885 *Yiftach, Uri* Was there a 'divorce procedure' among Greeks in early Roman Egypt?. XXII Congresso di papirologia, 2. 2001 ⇒555. 1331-1339.

F3.7 *Mt 6,9-13 (Lc 11,2-4)* **Oratio Jesu,** *Pater Noster,* **Lord's Prayer**

4886 *Apecechea Perurena, Juan* Comentario del Padrenuestro de Joaquín LIZARRAGA, el vicario de Elcano (1745-1835): cuarta petición VII. ScrVict 48 (2001) 109-151.

4887 **Blasi, Rocchina Maria Abbondanza** Tra evangelismo e riforma cattolica: le prediche sul Paternoster di Girolamo SERIPANDO. 1999 ⇒ 15,4811; 16,4878. ᴿSapDom 54 (2001) 376-377 (*Spera, Salvatore*).

4888 *Ceccherelli, Ignazio Marino* Et ne nos inducas in tentationem?. BeO 43 (2001) 55-68.

4889 *Gascou, Jean* Sur la date du *Pater noster* de Vienne: P.Rain. Unterricht 184: ᶠTHOMAS, J. 2001 ⇒107. 19-23.

4890 *Gibson, Jeffrey B.* Matthew 6:9-13//Luke 11:2-4: an eschatological prayer?. BTB 31 (2001) 96-105.

4891 ᴱ**Grossi, Vittorino** Sant'AGOSTINO: commento al Padre Nostro. L'Anima del mondo 44: CasM 2001, Piemme 231 pp. 88-384-69296.

4892 **Guardini, Romano** Das Gebet des Herrn. ⁸2000 <1932> ⇒16,4883. ᴿThGl 91 (2001) 339-341 (*Kreiml, Josef*).

4893 *Hogan, Martin* EPHREM's commentary on the Lord's prayer. PIBA 24 (2001) 48-63.

4894 *Kiley, Mark* Enemies at prayer. BiTod 39 (2001) 151-154.

4895 *Kościelniak, Krzysztof* Modlitwa Pańska w tradycji muzułmańskiej: egzegetyczno-teologiczne studium porównawcze: Mt 6,9-13 a hadis Abu Dawuda, Ṭibb, 19 bab: Kayfa ar-ruqua. CoTh 71/2 (2001) 119-128. P.

4896 **Martini, Carlo Maria** Praying as Jesus taught us. Franklin 2001, Sheed & W. xv; 100 pp. $12 [BiTod 39,389—Senior, Donald].

4897 **Montes Peral, Luis Angel** El Padrenuestro: la oración trinitaria de Jesús y los cristianos. Estella (Navarra) 2001, Verbo Divino 205 pp. 84-8169-436-3. Bibl. 199-200.

4898 *Moreno García, Abdón* Ein trinitarisches Vaterunser: Bemerkungen zu einem Manuskript aus dem 16. Jahrhundert. BZ 45 (2001) 94-100.

4899 *Panaino, Antonio* Il testo del 'Padre Nostro' nell'apologetica mazdaica. ᴹCAGNI, L., 4. SMDSA 61: 2001 ⇒15. 1937-1962.

4900 **Philonenko, Marc** Le Notre Père: de la prière de Jésus à la prière des disciples. P 2001, Gallimard 208 pp. €16.01. 2-07-076122-3. ᴿRevue des Sciences morales & politiques (2001/3) 195-197 (*Chaunu, Pierre*).

4901 **Romaniello, Giuseppe** Interpretazione autentica del "Pater Noster": "I limiti del potere di Satana". Latina 2001, "PHOS" 319 pp. Bibl. 316-317.

4902 **Scarpat, Giuseppe** Il Padrenostro di San FRANCESCO. AClCr 33: 2000 ⇒16,4894. ᴿCFr 71 (2001) 533-534 (*Lehmann, Leonardo*).

4903 **Simonis, Cardinal J.** Our Father: reflections on the Lord's prayer. 1999 ⇒15,4836. ᴿHeyJ 42 (2001) 220-221 (*Cooper, Adam G.*).

4904 *Wright, N.T.* The Lord's Prayer as a paradigm of christian prayer. Into God's presence. 2001 ⇒294. 132-154.

4905 **Zumstein, Jean** Notre Père: la prière de Jésus au coeur de notre vie. Poliez-le-Grand 2001, Moulin 92 pp. €9.91. 2-88469-006-9.

F4.1 *Mt 9-12: Miracula Jesu*—The Gospel miracles

4906 *Alkier, Stefan* Wen wundert was?: Einblicke in die Wunderauslegung von der Aufklärung bis zur Gegenwart. ZNT 7 (2001) 3-15.

4907 *Alvarez Valdes, Ariel* ¿Cuál fue el primer milagro que hizo Jesús?. CuesTP 28 (2001) 129-134.

4908 *Aubin, Melissa* Beobachtungen zur Magie im Neuen Testament. ZNT 7 (2001) 16-24.

4909 *Bartolomé, Juan J.* Jesús de Nazaret, 'ese varón acreditado por Dios con hechos prodigiosos' (Hch 2,22): una reseña de la investigación crítica sobre los milagros de Jesús. Sal. 63 (2001) 225-265.

4910 *Bate, Stuart C.* The mission to heal in a global context. IRM 90 (2001) 70-80.

4911 **Bee-Schroedter, Heike** Neutestamentliche Wundergeschichten im Spiegel vergangener und gegenwärtiger Rezeptionen. SBB 39: 1998 ⇒14,4398; 15,4852. ᴿZNT 4 (2001) 69-71 (*Erlemann, Kurt*).

4912 *Brucker, Ralph* Die Wunder der Apostel. ZNT 7 (2001) 32-45.

4913 *Busch, Peter* War Jesus ein Magier?. ZNT 7 (2001) 25-31.

4914 *Cardona Ramírez, Hernán* Los signos en la biblia: una aproximación bíblico-teológica. CuesTP 28 (2001) 71-115.

4915 ᴱ**Cavadini, John C.** Miracles in Jewish and Christian antiquity. 1999 ⇒15,206. ᴿHeyJ 42 (2001) 501-503 (*Rousseau, Philip*).

4916 **Collins, C. John** The God of miracles: an exegetical examination of God's action in the world. Leicester 2001, Apollos 219 pp. 0-85111-477-6. Bibl. 199-207.

4917 **Cotter, Wendy** Miracles in Greco-Roman antiquity: a sourcebook. The context of early christianity: 1999 ⇒15,4853; 16,4902. ᴿCTJ 36 (2001) 220 (*Deppe, Dean*); JECS 9 (2001) 409 (*Bowe, Barbara E.*).

4918 *Cuvillier, Élian* Récits de miracles dans le Nouveau Testament: éléments de bibliographie. Représentations des maladies. 2001 ⇒482. 77-83.

4919 *Guijarro Oporto, Santiago* Los exorcismos de Jesús. ResB 32 (2001) 53-61.

4920 *Guinan, Patrick* Christ the physician. Linacre Quarterly 68 (2001) 314-318.

4921 *Heiligenthal, Roman* Wunder im frühen Christentum:Wirklichkeit oder Propaganda: Einleitung zur Kontroverse. ZNT 7 (2001) 46-47.

4922 **John, Jeffrey** The meaning in the miracles. Norwich 2001, Canterbury viii; 248 pp. 1-85311-434-0. Bibl. 247-248.

4923 **Johnson, David** HUME, holism, and miracles. 1999 ⇒15,4860. ^RPhilosophy 76 (2001) 312-316 (*Kieran, Matthew*).

4924 *Le Guern, Michel* Expérience et théorie du miracle chez PASCAL. Représentations des maladies. 2001 ⇒482. 163-172.

4925 **Perrot, Ch.; Souletie, J.L.; Thévenot, S.** I miracoli: fatti storici o genere letterario?. 2000 ⇒16,4910. ^RRevAg 42 (2001) 419-421 (*Tejerina Arias, Gonzalo*).

4926 *Petri, Heinrich* Offenbarungskriterien oder Zeichen des Reiches Gottes?: die Wunder Jesu in der neueren Fundamentaltheologie. ^FSCHMUTTERMAYR, G. 2001 ⇒101. 497-518.

4927 **Pilch, John J.** Healing in the New Testament: insights from medical and Mediterranean anthropology. 2000 ⇒16,4911. ^RBTB 31 (2001) 78-79 (*Cotter, Wendy*); PastSc 20 (2001) 191-193 (*Meakes, Elizabeth*); JThS 52 (2001) 778-779 (*Nielsen, H.K.*); ThLZ 126 (2001) 761-763 (*Strecker, Christian E.*).

4928 *Riesner, Rainer* Jesus—Jüdischer Wundertäter und epiphaner Gottessohn. ZNT 7 (2001) 54-58.

4929 **Rusecki, Marian** Gottes Wirken in der Welt: Dimensionen und Funktionen des biblischen Wunderbegriffs. Fra 2001, Lang 247 pp. 3-631-37928-5.

4930 *Stanton, Graham* Message and miracles. The Cambridge companion to Jesus. Cambridge companions to religion: 2001 ⇒4236. 56-71.

4931 *Tabuce, Bernard* Les miracles dans deux manuels catholiques, 1925 et 1999. Représentations des maladies. 2001 ⇒482. 271-289.

4932 **Trunk, Dieter** Der messianische Heiler: eine redaktions- und religionsgeschichtliche Studie zu den Exorzismen im Matthäusevangelium. Herders Biblische Studien 3: 1994 ⇒10,4487... 14,4413. ^RSNTU.A 22 (1997) 246-254 (*Fuchs, Albert*).

4933 **Twelftree, Graham H.** Jesus the miracle worker. 1999 ⇒15,4869; 16,4914. ^RAUSS 39 (2001) 155-156 (*Stefanovic, Ranko*).

4934 *Valdés, Ariel Álvarez* Qual foi o primeiro milagre de Jesus?. REB 61 (2001) 639-645.

4935 **Vendrame, Calisto** A cura dos doentes na Bíblia. São Paulo 2001, Loyola 225 pp. 85-15-02344-X;

4936 La cura dei malati nel Nuovo Testamento. Salute e salvezza 17: T 2001, Camilliane 189 pp. 88-8257-097-5. Bibl. 185-189.

4937 *Wohlers, Michael* Jesus, der Heiler. ZNT 7 (2001) 48-53.

4938 **Woodward, Kenneth L.** The book of miracles: the meaning of the miracle stories in Christianity, Judaism, Buddhism, Hinduism, Islam. 2000 ⇒16,4917. ^RAmerica 184/11 (2001) 27-28 (*Burns, J. Patout*).

4939   **Vledder, Evert-Jan** Conflict in the miracle stories: a socio-exegeti-
       cal study of Matthew 8 and 9. JSNT.S 152: 1997 ⇒13,4717; 15,
       4873. [R]JBL 119 (2000) 137-139 (*Duling, Dennis C.*).

4940   **Landmesser, Christof** Jüngerberufung und Zuwendung zu Gott: ein
       exegetischer Beitrag zum Konzept der matthäischen Soteriologie im
       Anschluß an Mt 9,9-13. WUNT 133: Tü 2001, Mohr S. viii; 204 pp.
       €70.56. 3-16-147417-1. Bibl. 161-179.

4941   *Levine, Amy-Jill* Discharging responsibility: Matthean Jesus, biblical
       law, and hemorrhaging woman. A feminist companion to Matthew.
       2001 ⇒4709. 70-87 [Mt 9,18-26].

4942   *Puthenpurackal, Chacko* The crowds at the centre of mission. LivWo
       107 (2001) 281-299 [Mt 9,35-38].

4943   *Calambrogio, Leone* Missione, violenza e teologia in Mt 10. Laós 8/
       1 (2001) 3-10.

4944   *Sampatkumar, P.A.* The prohibition of foreign mission: a study of Mt
       10:5-6. VJTR 65 (2001) 245-258.

4945   **Laansma, Jon** I will give you rest: the rest motif in the New Testa-
       ment with special reference to Mt 11 and Heb 3-4. WUNT 2/98:
       1997 ⇒13,4733; 15,4884. [R]EvQ 73 (2001) 83-85 (*Baum, Armin
       Daniel*).

4946   *Sánchez Navarro, Luis* La complacencia del padre (Mt 11,26). EstB
       59 (2001) 7-27.

4947   **Ring, Th.G.** Die 'unvergebbare' Sünde wider den Heiligen Geist in
       Mt 12,31f nach der Deutung des hl. AUGUSTINUS. Cassiciacum 48:
       2000 ⇒16,4926. [R]REA 47 (2001) 458-459 (*Stammkötter, Franz-
       Bernhard*).

F4.3 **Mt 13...***Parabolae Jesu*—**The Parables**

4948   *Beavis, Mary Ann* The power of Jesus' parables: were they polemical
       or irenic?. JSNT 82 (2001) 3-30.

4949   **Buttrick, David** Speaking parables: a homiletic guide. 2000 ⇒16,
       4931. [R]CTJ 36 (2001) 140-141 (*Timmer, John*); Interp. 55 (2001)
       430, 432 (*Long, Thomas G.*).

4950   **Carter, Warren; Heil, John Paul** Matthew's parables: audience-
       oriented perspectives. CBQ.MS 30: 1997 ⇒13,4738... 16,4932.
       [R]JBL 119 (2000) 570-572 (*Bauer, David R.*).

4951   **Ellisen, Stanley A.** Parables in the eye of the storm: Christ's
       response in the face of conflict. GR 2001, Kregel 272 pp. $13. 0-
       8254-2527-1 [ThD 48,363—Heiser, W. Charles].

4952   **Ford, Richard Q.** The parables of Jesus. 1997 ⇒13,4743. [R]WThJ
       63 (2001) 453-454 (*Poythress, Vern Sheridan*).

4953 **Gowler, David B.** What are they saying about the parables?. 2000 ⇒16,4939. [R]EstB 59 (2001) 552-554 (*Bartolomé, Juan J.*); CBQ 63 (2001) 745-746 (*Reid, Barbara E.*).

4954 **Harnisch, Wolfgang** Die Gleichniserzählungen Jesu: eine hermeneutische Einführung. UTB 1343: Gö [4]2001, Vandenhoeck & R. 339 pp. 3-525-03602-7.

4955 **Hosein, Fazadudin** The banquet type-scene in the parables of Jesus. Diss. Andrews, [D]*Johnston, Robert M.*: Berrien Springs 2001 [AUSS 40,130s].

4956 **Hultgren, Arland J.** The parables of Jesus: a commentary. 2000 ⇒ 16,4943. [R]EThL 77 (2001) 214-217 (*Friedrichsen, T.A.*); CBQ 63 (2001) 342-343 (*Branick, Vincent P.*); TS 62 (2001) 829-831 (*McGaughy, Lane C.*); WThJ 63 (2001) 450-452 (Poythress, Vern Sheridan); SNTU.A 26 (2001) 257-259 (*Fuchs, Albert*).

4957 [E]**Longenecker, Richard N.** The challenge of Jesus' parables. 2000 ⇒16,4929. [R]EThL 77 (2001) 217-218 (*Friedrichsen, T.A.*); VJTR 65 (2001) 782-783 (*Meagher, P.M.*).

4958 **Maggi, Alberto** Parabole come pietre. Cittadella Incontri: Assisi 2001, Cittadella 127 pp. 88-308-0714-1. Bibl. 123-124.

4959 **Maillot, Alphonse** Le parabole di Gesù. 1997 ⇒13,4753. [R]RdT 42 (2001) 937 (*Marucci, Corrado*).

4960 **Massa, Dieter** Verstehensbedingungen von Gleichnissen: Prozesse und Voraussetzungen der Rezeption aus kognitiver Sicht. TANZ 31: 2000 ⇒16,4945. [R]ThLZ 126 (2001) 402-403 (*Rau, Eckhard*).

4961 **McBride, Denis** Les paraboles de Jésus. La bible tout simplement: P 2001, Atelier 208 pp.

4962 [E]**Mell, Ulrich** Die Gleichnisreden Jesu 1899-1999: Beiträge zum Dialog mit Adolf JÜLICHER. BZAW 103: 1999 ⇒15,4893; 16,4946. [R]CBQ 63 (2001) 789-791 (*Stenschke, Christoph W.*); ThLZ 126 (2001) 53-54 (*Harnisch, Wolfgang*).

4963 **Meynet, Roland** Tu vois cette femme?: parler en paraboles. Lire la Bible 121: P 2001, Cerf 199 pp. €15. 2-204-06658-3. Bibl. 189-193.

4964 *Miller, J. Hillis* Parable and performative in the gospels and in modern literature. Postmodern bible reader. 2001 <1991> ⇒287. 128-41.

4965 *Protus, Kemdirim O.* The portrait of women in the parables. VFTW 24/1 (2001) 139-151.

4966 **Raja, John Joshua** Facing the reality of communication: culture, church and communication. Diss. Edinburgh, Delhi 2001, ISPCK xiv; 339 pp. Rs175/$17/£14. 81-7214-605-1 [Lk 10,25-37].

4967 *Sanday, William* A new work on the parables [A. Jülicher, Die Gleichnis Reden Jesu (1899)]. Essays in biblical criticism: JSNT.S 225: 2001 <1900> ⇒205. 137-154 .

4968 *Schröer, Henning* Jesu Gleichnisse als biblisches Sprachereignis (theo)poetischer Didaktik. Zeitschrift für Pädagogik und Theologie 53 (2001) 144-152.

4969 **Scott, Bernard Brandon** Re-imagine the world: an introduction to the parables of Jesus. Santa Rosa, CA 2001, Polebridge Pr. (12) 167 pp. $18. 0-944344-86-0. Bibl. 163-164.

4970 *Tarasenko, Alexander* Jesus and his parables in the context of rabbinic Judaism. APB 12 (2001) 179-197.

4971 *Toni, Roberto* L'operosità nelle parabole di Gesù. Horeb 10/2 (2001) 44-53.

4972 *Vouga, François* Die Parabeln Jesu und die Fabeln Äsops: ein Beitrag zur Gleichnisforschung und zur Problematik der Literarisierung der Erzählungen der Jesus-Tradition. WuD 26 (2001) 149-164.

4973 **Young, Bradford H.** The parables. 1998 ⇒14,4451; 16,4960. RJThS 52 (2001) 224-227 (*Casey, Maurice*).

4974 **Wierzbicka, Anna** What did Jesus mean?: explaining the Sermon on the Mount and the parables in simple and universal human concepts. Oxf 2001, OUP xiv; 509 pp. $65/30. 01951-37329/3-7. Bibl. 481-95.

4975 *Varickasseril, Jose* Ecclesial perspectives in Matthew 13:1-52. FKAROTEMPREL, S. 2001 ⇒57. 262-271.

4976 **Graber, Philip L.** Context in text: a systemic functional analysis of the parable of the sower. Diss. Emory 2001, 345 pp. 3009434 [Mt 13, 3-23].

4977 **Hartmann, Michael** Der Tod Johannes' des Täufers: eine exegetische und rezeptionsgeschichtliche Studie auf dem Hintergrund narrativer, intertextueller und kulturanthropologischer Zugänge. Diss. Tübingen 2001,DTheobald, M.: SBB 45: Stu 2001, Kathol. Bibelwerk 399 pp. €45.50. 3-460-00451-7. Bibl. 369-399 [Mt 14,3-12].

4978 *Atmatzides, Charalampos I.* Ο χορτασμος των πεντε χιλιαδων (Μτ 14,13-21· Μκ 6,34-44· Λκ 9,10-17· Ιω 6,1-14) -- μια φουνταμενταλιστικη ερμηνευτική προσέγγιση [The feeding of the five thousand (Mt 14,13-21; Mk 6,34-44; Lk 9,10-17; Jn 6,1-14): a fundamentalistic hermeneutical approach]. DBM 20/1 (2001) 52-81. **G.**

4979 *Dobbeler, Stephanie von* Auf der Grenze: Ethos und Identität der matthäischen Gemeinde nach Mt 15,1-20. BZ 45 (2001) 55-78.

4980 *O'Day, Gail R.* Surprised by faith: Jesus and the Canaanite woman. Feminist companion to Matthew. 2001 ⇒4709. 114-25 [Mt 15,21-8].

4981 *Van Andel, Jan* `Eigen volk eerst'!?. ITBT 9/2 (2001) 4-6 [15,21-8].

4982 *Wainwright, Elaine M.* Not without my daughter: gender and demon possession in Matthew 15.21-28. A feminist companion to Matthew. 2001 ⇒4709. 126-137.

F4.5 Mt 16...*Primatus promissus*—The promise to Peter

4983 **Bessière, Gérard** Jésus, Pierre et le pape. P 2001, L'Atelier 192 pp. €14.48.

4984 **Bisconti, Fabrizio,** *al.*, Pietro: la storia, l'immagine, la memoria. 1999 ⇒15,4948. [R]RSCI 54 (2001) 527-530 (*Ramosino, Laura Cotta*).

4985 **Bizot, Catherine** Pierre, l'apôtre fragile. P 2001, Desclée de B 160 pp. €14.94.

4986 **Böttrich, Christfried** Petrus: Fischer, Fels und Funktionär. Biblische Gestalten 2: Lp 2001, Evangelische 288 pp. €13.80. 3-374-01849-1.

4987 [E]**Donati, Angela** Pietro e Paolo. 2000 ⇒16,4973. [R]CivCatt 152/2 (2001) 90-91 (*Lenzi, A.*).

4988 **Gibert, Pierre** Simon Pierre, apôtre et compagnon. Croire aujourd'hui: P 2001, Bayard 144 pp. €12.20. 2-227-35029-6.

4989 *Hagedorn, Dieter* Kein Petrus im Tal der Könige. ZPE 137 (2001) 197-198.

4990 **Perkins, Pheme** Peter: apostle for the whole church. [2]2000 <1994> ⇒16,4976. [R]Dialog 40 (2001) 77-79 (*Hultgren, Arland J.*); JThS 52 (2001) 842-844 (*Horrell, David G.*).

4991 **Pesch, Rudolf** Die biblischen Grundlagen des Primats. QD 187: FrB 2001, Herder 112 pp. 3-451-02187-0. Bibl. 11-12. [R]CoTh (2001/4) 202-205 (*Załęski, Jan*).

4992 **Quinn, R. John** Die Reform des Papsttums. [T]*Schellenberger, Bernardin*: QD 188: FrB 2001, Herder 168 pp. 3-451-02188-9.

4993 **Schima, S.** Caput occidentis?: die römische Kirche und der Westen von den Anfängen bis Konstantin. 2000 ⇒16,4978. [R]Annales Theologici 15 (2001) 616-622 (*Sproll, H.*).

4994 **Wiarda, Timothy** Peter in the gospels: pattern, personality and relationship. WUNT 2/127: 2000 ⇒16,4979. [R]TrinJ 22 (2001) 266-269 (*Davids, Peter H.*).

4995 **Heil, John Paul** The transfiguration of Jesus. AnBib 144: 2000 ⇒ 16,4984. [R]CBQ 63 (2001) 746-748 (*Spencer, F. Scott*).

4996 *Barton, Stephen C.* The transfiguration of Christ according to Mark and Matthew: christology and anthropology [Mt 17,1-9; Mk 9,2-10];

4997 *Fletcher-Louis, Crispin H.T.* The revelation of the sacral Son of Man: the genre, history of religious context and the meaning of the transfiguration. Auferstehung—Resurrection. WUNT 135: ⇒452. 231-246/247-298 [Mt 17,1-9].

4998 *Maggioni, Bruno* Gesù e il denaro. VitaCon 37/5 (2001) 473-479 [Mt 17,27].

4999   *Marzaroli, Davide* 'Dove due o tre sono riuniti nel mio nome, io sono in mezzo a loro' (Mt 18,19-20): dalla comunità all'ekklesia.
CredOg 125-126 (2001) 49-62.

5000   *Pastore, Stefania* A proposito di Matteo 18,15: *correctio fraterna* e
Inquisizione nella Spagna del Cinquecento. RSIt 113 (2001) 323-68.

5001   *Martini, Carlo M.* Perdonare, chiedere perdono, sentirsi perdonati.
VitaCon 37/2 (2001) 115-125 [Mt 18,21-25].

5002   **Lamerson, Samuel Philip** The parable of the unforgiving servant in
its first-century Jewish milieu: the relationship between exile and forgiveness in the gospel of Matthew. Diss. Trinity Evang. Divinity
2001, 303 pp. 3003783 [Mt 18,23-35].

5003   *Moloney, Francis J.* Matthew 19:3-12 and celibacy: a redactional and
form-critical study. 'A hard saying'. 2001 <1979> ⇒184. 35-52.

5004   *Hedrick, Charles W.* An unpublished Coptic fragment of the gospel
of Matthew. Journal of Coptic Studies 3 (2001) 149-51 [Mt 19,6-13].

F4.8   **Mt 20**...*Regnum eschatologicum*—**Kingdom eschatology**

5005   *Marguerat, Daniel* Loi et jugement dernier dans le Nouveau Testament. Bible et droit. 2001 ⇒300. 67-86.

5006   **Riniker, Christian** Die Gerichtsverkündigung Jesu. EHS.T 653:
1999 ⇒15,4969; 16,4993. ^RJThS 52 (2001) 789-790 (*Casey, Maurice*).

5007   **Wilson, Alistair** Matthew's portrait of Jesus the judge: with special
reference to Matthew 21-25. Diss. Aberdeen 2001, ^D*Marshall, I.H.*:
Sum. TynB 54,157-160.

5008   *Göbel, Christian* Übermensch im Weinberg des Herrn: Betrachtung
zu Mt 20,1-16. Ment. *Nietzsche, F.*: PzB 10 (2001) 33-40.

5009   *Sanday, William* The parable of the labourers in the vineyard: Matthew 20.1-16. Essays in biblical criticism. JSNT.S 225: 2001 <1876>
⇒205. 124-136.

5010   **Nieuviarts, Jacques** L'entrée de Jésus à Jérusalem (Mt 21,1-17):
messianisme et accomplissement des écritures en Matthieu. LeDiv
176: 1999 ⇒15,4976; 16,4999. ^RCoTh (2001/3) 221-225 (*Załęski,
Jan*); ETR 76 (2001) 594-596 (*Cuvillier, E.*).

5011   **Ådna, Jostein** Jesu Stellung zum Tempel: die Tempelaktion und das
Tempelwort als Ausdruck seiner messianischen Sendung. WUNT
2/119: 2000 ⇒16,4990. ^RThPQ 149 (2001) 201-203 (*Niemand,
Christoph*); RHPhR 81 (2001) 234-235 (*Grappe, Ch.*); CBQ 63
(2001) 331-332 (*Stenschke, Christoph*); ThLZ 126 (2001) 1035-1037
Heckel, Theo K.) [Mt 21,12-13; 24].

5012 *López Rosas, Ricardo* Mt 21,12-17: la sanitad salvífica o la misericordia del hijo de David. EfMex 19 (2001) 5-26.

5013 *Foster, Paul* A tale of two sons: but which one did the far, far better thing?: a study of Matt 21.28-32. NTS 47 (2001) 26-37.

5014 *Oldenhage, Tania* How to read a tainted text: the wicked husbandmen in a Post-Holocaust context. Postmodern interpretations. 2001 ⇒229. 165-176 [Mt 21,33-41].

5015 *Weren, Wim J.C.* From Q to Matthew 22,1-14: new light on the transmission and meaning of the parable of the guest. The sayings source Q. BEThL 158: 2001 ⇒477. 661-679.

5016 *Viviano, Benedict T.* Social world and community leadership: the case of Matthew 23.1-12,34. Trinity—kingdom—church. NTOA 48: 2001 <1990> ⇒223. 196-212.

5017 *Hurley, Robert* Le lecteur et les chevreaux dans le jugement dernier de Matthieu. SémBib 101 (2001) 21-41 [Mt 25].

5018 *Rosenblatt, Marie-Eloise* Got into the party after all: women's issues and the five foolish virgins. A feminist companion to Matthew. 2001 ⇒4709. 171-195 [Mt 25,1-13].

5019 *Pilch, John J.* The parable of the talents. BiTod 39 (2001) 366-370 [Mt 25,14-30].

5020 **Fumagalli, Anna** Gesù crocifisso, straniero fino alla fine dei tempi: una lettura di Mt 25,31-46 in chiave comunicativa. EHS.T 707: 2000 ⇒16,5013. [R]PaVi 46/3 (2001) 61-62 (*Cappelletto, Gianni*); StPat 48 (2001) 535-536 (*Segalla, Giuseppe*).

5021 *Hjelde, Sigurd; Sauter, Gerhard; Klein, Peter K.* Jüngstes Gericht. RGG[2], 4: I-K. 2001 ⇒664. 710-714 col. [Mt 25,31-46].

5022 *Pokorný, Petr* Matth 25,31-46 und die Globalisierung christlicher Ethik. CV 43/2 (2001) 153-158.

5023 **Pond, Eugene Warren** Interpretive issues pertaining to the judgment of sheep and goats. Diss. Dallas Sem. 2001, 262 pp. 3002969 [Mt 25, 32-33].

F5.1 *Redemptio*, **Mt 26**, *Ultima coena*; **The Eucharist** [⇒H7.4]

5024 *Banaszek, Andrzej* Teologizacja obrazu Judasza. [F]JANKOWSKI, A. 2001 ⇒53. 31-46. **P**.

5025 *Caspers, Charles M.A.* The Lord's Supper and Holy Communion in the Middle Ages: sources, significance, remains and confusion. Religious identity. 2001 ⇒549. 253-264.

5026 *Cavagnoli, Gianni* L'ultima cena di Gesù e il racconto ecclesiale in rendimento di grazie. RivLi 88 (2001) 345-360.

5027 **Clark, Stephen, B.** Catholics and the eucharist: a scriptural introduc-
       tion. 2000 ⇒16,5022. ᴿSVTQ 45 (2001) 99-101 (*Whitters, Mark F.*);
       ProEc 10 (2001) 503-504 (*Keating, Daniel*).

5028 **Crocetti, Giuseppe** Questo è il mio corpo e lo offro per voi: la dona-
       zione esistenziale e sacramentale di Gesù alla sua Chiesa. 1999 ⇒15,
       4993; 16,5024. ᴿED 54/1 (2001) 231-233 (*Biguzzi, Giancarlo*).

5029 *Desiderio, Frank R.* Visual ecclesiology: a priest-producer reflects on
       making the movie *Judas*. Image 33 (2001) 111-118.

5030 Die Eucharistie im Leben der Kirche. ᴱ**Voss, Gerhard**: Una Sancta
       56 (2001) 273-359.

5031 *Forte, Bruno* La ultima cena y la iglesia del amor. Labor Theologicus
       26 (2001) 5-13.

5032 *Immink, F.G.* Meal and sacrament: how do we encounter the Lord at
       the table?. Religious identity. 2001 ⇒549. 265-275.

5033 *Instone-Brewer, David* Jesus's last passover: the synoptics and John.
       ET 112 (2001) 122-123.

5034 *Jonge, Henk Jan de* The early history of the Lord's Supper. Religious
       identity. Studies in theology and religion 3: 2001 ⇒549. 209-237.

5035 *Klawans, Jonathan* Was Jesus' last supper a Seder?. BiRe 17/5
       (2001) 24-33, 47.

5036 *Koch, Dietrich-Alex* The early history of the Lord's Supper: response
       to Henk Jan de Jonge. Religious identity. 2001 ⇒549. 238-252.

5037 **Koenig, John** The feast of the world's redemption: eucharistic ori-
       gins and christian mission. 2000 ⇒16,5033. ᴿThTo 58 (2001) 120,
       122 (*Chilton, Bruce*); Worship 75 (2001) 564-65 (*Johnson, Luke T.*).

5038 *May, George* The Lord's Supper: ritual or relationship?: making a
       meal of it in Corinth, Part 1: meals in the gospels and Acts. RTR 60/3
       (2001) 138-150.

5039 **Mazza, Enrico** L'action eucharistique, développement, interpréta-
       tion. 1999 ⇒15,5002. ᴿMD 228 (2001) 169-71 (*Lanne, Emmanuel*);

5040 The celebration of the eucharist: the origin of the rite and the devel-
       opment of its interpretation. ᵀ*O'Connell, Matthew J.*: 1999 ⇒15,
       5003; 16,5039. ᴿMillSt 48 (2001) 161-164 (*Moloney, Raymond*).

5041 *Moloney, Francis J.* The Eucharist as Jesus' presence to the broken.
       'A hard saying'. 2001 <1989> ⇒184. 211-235.

5042 *Moraldi, Luigi* Ultima Cena dagli Esseni. ᴹCᴀɢɴɪ, L., 4. SMDSA 61:
       2001 ⇒15. 1835-1845.

5043 *Nagy, Agnes Anna* La forme originale de l'accusation d'anthropopha-
       gie contre les chrétiens, son dévelopement et les changements de sa
       représentation au IIe siècle. REAug 47 (2001) 223-249.

5044 **Stewart-Sykes, Alistair** The Lamb's high feast: Mᴇʟɪᴛᴏ, Peri Pascha
       and the Quartodeciman Paschal Liturgy at Sardis. SVigChr 42: 1998

⇒14,4532. [R]RTL 32 (2001) 555-556 (*Auwers, J.-M.*); JECS 9 (2001) 598-599 (*Bowe, Barbara E.*).

5045 *Tillesse, Caetano Minette de* Ecclesiologia 3: ponto de partida duma eclesiologia crítica. RBBras 18 (2001) 296-340;

5046 Ecclesiologia 4: a eucaristia como sacrifício. RBBras 18 (2001) 341-354.

5047 **Tomasi, Giovanni** Il Memoriale del Signore. Seraphicum, Diss. ad Lauream 96: R 2001, n.p. 364 pp. Bibl. 11-50.

5048 **Trummer, Peter** "...dass alle eins sind!": neue Zugänge zu Eucharistie und Abendmahl. Dü 2001, Patmos 183 pp. €17.79. 34917-03387.

5049 *Winter, Karsten* Fragen an das Abendmahl: heilig oder blutig?. TeKo 24/1 (2001) 13-15.

5050 *Köstenberger, Andreas J.* A comparison of the pericopae of Jesus' anointing. Studies on John and gender. 2001 <1992> ⇒169. 49-63 [Mt 26,6-13].

5051 *Kügerl, Johannes* Das letzte Abendmahl des Juden Jesus. CPB 114 (2001) 22-25 [Mt 26,26-9; Mk 14,22-5; Lk 22,15-20; 1 Cor 11,23-6].

F5.3 Mt 26,30...//*Passio Christi*; Passion narrative

5052 **Blinzler, Josef** Il processo di Gesù. [T]*Pellizzari, M.A. Colao*: BCR 6: Brescia 2001, Paideia 472 pp. Bibl. 423-431.

5053 **Bond, Helen Katharine** Pontius Pilate in history and interpretation. MSSNTS 100: 1998 ⇒14,4544; 16,5051. [R]Latomus 60 (2001) 498-500 (*Levick, Barbara*); JBL 119 (2000) 762-764 (*Karris, Robert J.*).

5054 **Brown, Raymond E.** La morte del Messia. BTC 108 1999 ⇒15, 5018; 16,5052. [R]ActBib 38 (2001) 198-199 (*Boada, J.*).

5055 *Cane, Anthony* Contested meanings of the name 'Judas Iscariot'. ET 112 (2001) 44-45.

5056 *Cernuda, Antonio Vicent* ¡Pro Barrabás, contra Jesús!. EstB 59 (2001) 29-46.

5057 *Couvée, Paulien* Judas, één van de twaalf. ITBT 9/3 (2001) 18-19.

5058 **Crossan, John Dominic** Wer tötete Jesus?. 1999 ⇒15,5019; 16, 5056. [R]ZKTh 122 (2001) 226-227 (*Repschinski, Boris*); ThLZ 126 (2001) 521-523 (*Sänger, Dieter*).

5059 **Diebold-Scheuermann, Carola** Jesus vor Pilatus: eine exegetische Untersuchung zum Verhör durch Pilatus (Joh 18,28 - 19,16a). 1996 ⇒12,5616; 13,5887. [R]SNTU.A 23 (1998) 266-267 (*Fuchs, Albert*).

5060 *Fedalto, Giorgio* Quando è morto Gesù?. StPat 48 (2001) 621-629.

5061 **Fenske, Wolfgang** Brauchte Gott den Verräter?: die Gestalt des Judas in Theologie, Unterricht und Gottesdienst. DAW 85: 1999 ⇒15, 5026. ᴿThRv 97 (2001) 257-258 (*Dieckmann, Bernhard*).

5062 *Gangemi, Attilio* 'Dovrà patire molte cose': un possibile sviluppo dalla professione di fede alla narrazione della passione, 2. Synaxis 19 (2001) 25-77.

5063 *Green, Joel B.* Crucifixion. The Cambridge companion to Jesus. Cambridge companions to religion: 2001 ⇒4236. 87-101.

5064 **Hesemann, Michael** Titulus crucis: la scoperta dell'iscrizione posta sulla croce di Gesù. 2000 ⇒16,5064. ᴿEccl(R) 15 (2001) 487-488 (*De Martino, M.*).

5065 **Holtz, Gudrun** Der Herrscher und der Weise im Gespräch: Studien zu Form, Funktion und Situation der neutestamentlichen Verhörgespräche. ANTZ 6: 1996 ⇒12,4671; 14,4560. ᴿRBLit 3 (2001) 325-327 (*Hezser, Catherine*).

5066 *McLaren, James S.* Exploring the execution of a provincial: adopting a Roman perspective on the death of Jesus. ABR 49 (2001) 5-18.

5067 **Meynell, Mark J.H.** Cross-examined: the life-changing power of the death of Jesus. Nottingham 2001, Inter-Varsity Pr. 191 pp. 0-85111-552-7. Bibl. 189.

5068 *Milbank, John* Christ the exception. NBl 82 (2001) 541-556.

5069 *Millar, Fergus* Riflessioni sul processo di Gesù. Gli ebrei nell'impero romano. 2001 <1990> ⇒415. 77-97.

5070 *Noordegraaf, Albert* Wie draagt schuld aan de dood van Jezus?: over de vraag naar het anti-judaïsme in de evangeliën. ThRef 44 (2001) 135-157.

5071 **Paffenroth, Kim** Judas: images of the lost disciple. LVL 2001, Westminster xv; 207 pp. $25. 0-664-22424-5. Bibl. 179-196.

5072 *Quintero, José Luis* Una narración,origen de vida: breve ensayo de teología narrativa a partir de los relatos de la pasión. Staurós 36 (2001) 49-55.

5073 *Rechberger, Walter H.* Der Prozess Jesu. Österreichisches Archiv für Recht und Religion 48 (2001) 177-199.

5074 *Senior, Donald* Matthew's story of the passion: theological and pastoral perspectives. ChiSt 40 (2001) 275-285.

5075 *Speyer, Wolfgang* Kaiphas. RAC 19: 2001 ⇒660. 982-992.

5076 *Stolle, Volker* Braucht man denn Schuldige für den Tod Jesu?: der Kreuzestod Jesu in historischer und unter theologischer Perspektive. LuThK 25/1 (2001) 1-13.

5077 *Synnott, Margarita* Why did Jesus die?. DoLi 51 (2001) 162-169.

5078 *Terbuyken, Peri; Kremer, Christian Josef* Judas Iskariot. RAC 19: 2001 ⇒660. 142-160.

5079   Tomaso MORO: Gesù al Getsemani. Mi 2001, Paoline 233 pp.

5080   **Toro Bedoya, Carlos Maria** La muerte de Jesús: estudio sistemático en algunos teólogos católicos (1974-1988): comparación crítica y perspectivas. Exc. Diss. Gregoriana, ^DO'Collins, Gerald: R 2001, 272 pp .

5081   *Vicent Cernuda, Antonio* La inhibición teatral de Pilato en el caso de Jesús. EstB 59 (2001) 147-177.

5082   **Wroe, Ann** Pilate: the biography of an invented man. 1999 ⇒15, 5055. ^RHPR 101/8 (2001) 78-79 (*Grondelski, John M.*).

5083   *Strola, Germana* Le riprese dell'Antico Testamento nella pericope del Getsemani. Lat. 67 (2001) 7-29 [Ps 41-42; Mt 26,38; Mk 14,34].

5084   *Wick, Peter* Judas als Prophet wider Willen: Mt 27,3-10 als Midrasch. ThZ 57 (2001) 26-35.

5085   *García Macho, Pablo* Palabra y palabras desde la cruz: 'Dios mío, ¿por qué me has abandonado?'. Staurós 36 (2001) 69-85 [Mt 27,45-46].

5086   *Diebner, Bernd Jørg* Warum Joseph von Arimathia Jesus von Nazareth sein Familiengrab zur Verfügung stellte ...: ein Beitrag zur Logik biblischer Erzählungen. ^FDEURLOO, K., ACEBT.S 2: 2001 ⇒23. 325-339 [Mt 27,57; Lk 23,50; Jn 19,38].

F5.6 Mt 28//: Resurrectio

5087   *Bockmuehl, Markus* Resurrection. The Cambridge companion to Jesus. Cambridge companions to religion: 2001 ⇒4236. 102-118.

5088   **Boismard, Marie-Émile** La nostra vittoria sulla morte: 'risurrezione'?. Assisi 2001, Cittadella 180 pp.

5089   *Bostock, D. Gerald* Osiris and the resurrection of Christ. ET 112 (2001) 265-271.

5090   **Brambilla, Franco Giulio** Il Crocifisso risorto: risurrezione di Gesù e fede dei discepoli. BTCon 99: 1998 ⇒14,4598... 16,5091. ^RRSR 89 (2001) 305-306 (*Fédou, Michel*); REB 61 (2001) 732-736 (*Melo, Antônio Alves de*).

5091   *Chester, Andrew* Resurrection and transformation. Auferstehung— Resurrection. WUNT 135: 2001 ⇒452. 47-77.

5092   ^E**Copan, Paul; Tacelli, Ronald K.** Jesus' resurrection: fact or figment?: a debate between William Lane Craig and Gerd Lüdemann. 2000 ⇒16,5094. ^RZKTh 123 (2001) 314-316 (*Lehner, Ulrich L.*).

5093   *Dabney, Delmar L.* "Justified by the Spirit": soteriological reflections on the resurrection. International journal of systematic theology 3/1 (2001) 46-68.

5094 **Durrwell, Fr.-X.** Christ notre Pâque. Racines: Montrouge 2001, Nouvelle Cité 253 pp. €18.29. 2-85313-387-7. [R]AETSC 6 (2001) 391-414 (*Igirukwayo, Antoine M.Z.*).

5095 *Eckstein, Hans-Joachim* Von der Bedeutung der Auferstehung Jesu. ThBeitr 32 (2001) 26-41.

5096 *Eriksson, Stefan* The resurrection and the incarnation—myths, facts or what?. StTh 55 (2001) 129-144.

5097 **Frosini, Giordano** La risurrezione inizio del mondo nuovo. Teologia viva 42: Bo 2001, EDB 324 pp. 88-10-40955-8. Bibl. 307-315.

5098 *Gwynne, Paul* Why some still doubt that Jesus' body was raised. [F]O'-COLLINS, G. 2001 ⇒111. 355-367.

5099 *Habermas, Gary R.* The late twentieth-century resurgence of naturalistic responses to Jesus' resurrection. TrinJ 22 (2001) 179-196.

5100 *Kattackal, Jacob* Christ is risen or Christ is raised?. BiBh 27 (2001) 147-154.

5101 **Kehl, Medard** E cosa viene dopo la fine?: sulla fine del mondo e sul compimento finale, sulla reincarnazione e sulla risurrezione. Giornale di teologia 279: Brescia 2001, Queriniana 237 pp. 88-399-0779-3.

5102 **Kellermann, Ulrich** Das Gotteslob der Auferweckten: motivgeschichtliche Beobachtungen in Texten des Alten Testaments, des frühen Judentums und Urchristentums. BThSt 46: Neuk 2001, Neuk (8) 146 pp. €19.90. 3-7887-1861-7.

5103 **Kessler, Hans** Sucht den Lebenden nicht bei den Toten: die Auferstehung Jesu Christi in biblischer, fundamentaltheologischer und systematischer Sicht. Wü [2]1995 <1985>, 526 pp. Neuausgabe mit ausführlicher Erörterung der aktuellen Fragen [R]RSR 89 (2001) 303-305 (*Fédou, Michel*)

5104 **Lorenzen, T.** Resurrección y discipulado: modelos interpretativos, reflexiones bíblicas y consecuencias teológicas. 1999 ⇒15,5080; 16, 5104. [R]Seminarios 47/1 (2001) 115-117 (*Morata Moya, Alonso*).

5105 *Lowder, Jeffery J.* Historical evidence and the empty tomb story: a reply to William Lane Craig. JHiC 8 (2001) 251-293.

5106 **Lüdemann, Gerd; Özen, Alf** La resurrección de Jesús: historia, experiencia, teología. [T]*Tosaus, José-Pedro*: Estructuras y procesos, Ser. Religión: M 2001, Trotta 158 pp. 84-8164-457-9.

5107 *Lüpke, Johannes von* "... nimm wahr, was heut geschicht": zur Erkenntnis des auferstandenen Christus. WuD 26 (2001) 271-288.

     [E]**Mainville, O.; Marguerat, D.** Résurrection 2001 ⇒296.

5108 **Marguerat, Daniel** Résurrection?: une histoire de vie?. Poliez-le-Grand 2001, Moulin 98 pp. 2-88469-007-7.

5109 *McDonald, Lee Martin* Beyond resurrection?: a review essay. BBR 11 (2001) 123-138.

5110 **Messori, Vittorio** Dicen que ha resucitado: una investigación sobre el sepulcro vacío. M 2001, Rialp 297 pp.;

5111 Dicono che è risorto: un'indagine sul sepolcro vuoto. 2000 ⇒16, 5107. [R]CivCatt 152/2 (2001) 407-408 (*Castelli, F.*).

5112 *Michaud, Jean-Paul* La résurrection dans le langage des premiers chrétiens. Résurrection: l'après-mort. MoBi 45: 2001 ⇒296. 111-28.

5113 **Müller, Ulrich B.** L'origine della fede nella risurrezione di Gesù: a-spetti e condizioni storiche. Orizzonti biblici: Assisi 2001, Cittadella 192 pp. 88-308-0712-5. Bibl. 167-190.

5114 *Myre, André* L'avenir de la résurrection: déblayage. Résurrection: l'après-mort. MoBi 45: 2001 ⇒296. 321-336.

5115 *Park, Eung Chun* The problem of the APOUSIA of Jesus in the synoptic resurrection traditions. [F]BETZ, H.: 2001 ⇒5. 121-135.

5116 [E]**Porter, Stanley E.; Hayes, Michael A.; Tombs, David** Resurrection. JSNT.S 186: 1999 ⇒15,1242. [R]Neotest. 35 (2001) 181-182 (*Van der Watt, Jan G.*).

5117 *Reinsdorf, Walter* The gospel resurrection accounts. BiBh 27 (2001) 241-254.

5118 **Russell, Jeffrey B.** A history of heaven: the singing silence. 1997 ⇒ 13,4996; 14,4641. [R]HR 39 (2000) 379-381 (*Madigan, Kevin*).

5119 *Saint-Arnaud, Guy-Robert* La grâce du "troisième jour". RevSR 75 (2001) 338-364.

5120 *Schlosser, Jacques* Vision, extase et apparition du ressuscité. Résurrection: l'après-mort. MoBi 45: 2001 ⇒296. 129-159.

5121 **Schmid, Johannes Heinrich** Die Auferweckung Jesu aus dem Grab. Ba 2000, Reinhardt 139 pp.

5122 **Vögtle, Anton** Biblischer Osterglaube. [E]*Hoppe, Rudolf:* 1999 ⇒15, 5063; 16,5112. [R]Neotest. 35 (2001) 183-185 (*Van der Watt, Jan G.*).

5123 **Walker, Peter** The weekend that changed the world: the mystery of Jerusalem's empty tomb. GR 1999, Zondervan 208 pp. £10. 0-5510-3135-2. [R]RB 108 (2001) 469-470 (*Murphy-O'Connor, J.*).

5124 **Wedderburn, Alexander J.M.** Beyond resurrection. 1999 ⇒15, 5098; 16,5114. [R]JThS 52 (2001) 308-310 (*Houlden, Leslie*); TS 62 (2001) 390-391 (*Loewe, William P.*); EvQ 73 (2001) 265-267 (*Bennison, Tim*)

5125 **Winling, Raymond** La résurrection et l'exaltation du Christ dans la littérature de l'ère patristique. 2000 ⇒16,5116. [R]Brot. 153 (2001) 855-856 (*Silva, I. Ribeiro da*); TS 62 (2001) 613-615 (*Mueller, Joseph G.*); RSR 89 (2001) 296-297 (*Fédou, Michel*); Gr. 82 (2001) 794-795 (*Dupuis, Jacques*).

5126 *Wright, N.T.* Jesus and the resurrection. Jesus then and now. 2001 ⇒ 483. 54-71.

5127 *Carrier, Richard* The guarded tomb of Jesus and Daniel in the lion's den: an argument for the plausibility of theft. JHiC 8 (2001) 304-318 [Dan 6; Mt 27,63-64].

5128 *Cotter, Wendy J.* Greco-Roman apotheosis traditions and the resurrection appearances in Matthew. ᴹTHOMPSON, W. 2001 ⇒108. 127-153 [Mt 28].

5129 *Boyarin, Daniel* 'After the Sabbath' (Matt. 28:1)—once more into the crux. JThS 52 (2001) 678-688 [Mk 16,1].

5130 *Longstaff, Thomas R.W.* What are those women doing at the tomb of Jesus?: perspectives on Matthew 28.1;

5131 *Osiek, Carolyn* The women at the tomb: what are they doing there? [Mt 28,1]. A feminist companion to Matthew. 2001 ⇒4709. 196-204/205-220.

5132 *Neirynck, Frans* Note on Mt 28,9-10. Evangelica III. BEThL 150: 2001 <1995> ⇒187. 579-584.

5133 *Christudhas, M.* The vision of Jesus and the mission of the disciples in Matthew 28:16-20. ᶠKAROTEMPREL, S. 2001 ⇒57. 163-174.

5134 *Hennig, Gerhard* Matthäus 28,16-20 aus der Sicht der Praktischen Theologie: Beobachtungen und Überlegungen. ThBeitr 32 (2001) 317-326.

5135 *Hertig, Paul* The great commission revisited: the role of God's reign in disciple making. Miss. 29 (2001) 343-353 [Mt 28,16-20].

F6.1 Evangelium Marci—*Textus, commentarii*

5136 **Barclay, William** The New Daily Study Bible: the gospel of Mark. E 2001, Saint Andrew Pr. xxvi; 432 pp. 0-7152-0782-2.

5137 **Black, C. Clifton** Mark: images of an apostolic interpreter. Studies on personalities of the N.T.: Mp ²2001 <1994>, Augsburg xxii; 327 pp. $20. 0-8006-3168-4. [RB 109,154].

5138 *Bonneau, Guy* Saint Marc: nouvelles lectures. CEv 117 (2001) 5-53.

5139 **Broadhead, Edwin K.** Mark. Readings: Shf 2001, Sheffield A. 163 pp. 1-84127-188-8. Bibl. 152-156.

5140 **Eckey, Wilfried** Das Markusevangelium: Orientierung am Weg Jesu: ein Kommentar. 1998 ⇒14,4664; 16,5130. ᴿZKTh 122 (2001) 227-228 (*Repschinski, Boris*).

5141 Das Evangelium des Markus. Fischer Taschenbuch 14508: Fra 2000, Fischer 73 pp. 3-596-14508-2. Mit einer Einleitung von *Nick Cave*.

5142 **Evans, Craig A.** Mark 8:27-16:20. Nv 2001, Nelson xcii; 594 pp.

5143 **Geddert, Timothy J.** Mark. Believers Church Bible Commentary: Scottdale, PA 2001, Herald 454 pp. $25. 0-8361-9140-4 [ThD 48,366—Heiser, W. Charles].

5144 **Lafont, Gh.** Qui est Jésus?: une lecture de l'évangile de saint Marc. Saint-Maur 2001, Parole et Silence 95 pp. €12.04. 2-84573-060-8.

5145 **LaVerdiere, Eugene** The beginning of the gospel: introducing the gospel according to Mark. 1999 ⇒15,5122; 16,5134. [R]VJTR 65 (2001) 546-547 (*Meagher, P.M.*).

5146 **Leonardi, Giovanni** Vangelo secondo Marco: traduzione strutturata, analisi letteraria e narrativa, messaggio e problemi introduttori. 1999 ⇒15,5124. [R]Lat. 67 (2001) 370-371 (*Pulcinelli, Giuseppe*).

5147 [E]**Levine, Amy-Jill** A feminist companion to Mark. The Feminist Companion to the New Testament and Early Christian Writings 2: Shf 2001, Academic 261 pp. $25. 1-84127-194-2. With *Marianne Blickenstaff*; Bibl. 235-251.

5148 **Légasse, Simon** Marco. Commenti biblici: 2000 ⇒16,5136. [R]Civ-Catt 152/4 (2001) 208-209 (*Scaiola, D.*).

5149 **Marcus, Joel** Mark 1-8. AncB 27: 2000 ⇒16,5137. [R]BZ 45 (2001) 268-270 (*Pellegrini, Silvia*); RBLit 3 (2001) 386-391 (*Gundry, Robert H.*).

5150 **Mateos, Juan; Camacho, Fernando** El evangelio de Marcos, 2. Los orígenes del cristianismo 11: 2000 ⇒16,5140. [R]Theoforum 32 (2001) 240-242 [with vol. 1] (*Laberge, Léo*).

5151 **Mitchell, Joan L.** Beyond fear and silence: a feminist-literary approach to the gospel of Mark. NY 2001, Continuum viii; 152 pp. $18. 0-8264-1354-4. Bibl. 133-146.

5152 *Neirynck, Frans* Urmarcus révisé: la théorie synoptique de M.-E. Boismard nouvelle manière <1995>;

5153 Mark and Q: assessment <1995>. Ment. *Fleddermann, H.*: Evangelica III. BEThL 150: 2001 ⇒187. 399-416/505-545.

5154 **Oden, Thomas C.; Hall, Christopher Alan** Evangelio según San Marcos. 2000 ⇒16,5142. [R]RevAg 42 (2001) 414-416 (*Sánchez Navarro, Luis*); San Juan de la Cruz 17 (2001) 247-249 (*García, Juan Carlos*); Alpha Omega 4 (2001) 617-619 (*Izquierdo, Antonio*).

5155 **Runacher, Caroline** Saint Marc. La bible tout simplement: P 2001, L'Atelier 157 pp. €14. 2-7082-3569-9.

5156 **Thurston, Bonnie Bowman** Preaching Mark. Fortress Resources for Preaching: Mp 2001, Fortress xii; 218 pp [BiTod 40,136 Senior, D.].

5157 **Trainor, Michael F.** The quest for home: the household in Mark's community. ColMn 2001, Liturgical vi; 201 pp. $20. 0-8146-5087-2. Bibl. 189-195 [BiTod 39,322—Senior, Donald].

5158 **Trocmé, Étienne** L'Evangile selon saint Marc. 2000 ⇒16,5150. [R]Orpheus 22 (2001) 412-414 (*Osculati, Roberto*); ThLZ 126 (2001) 764-767 (*Schweizer, Eduard*).

5159   **Van Iersel, Bas M.F.** Mark: a reader-response commentary. JSNT.S
       164: 1998 ⇒14,4676; 16,5152. ^RJThS 52 (2001) 234-239 (*Telford,
       W.R.*); JBL 119 (2000) 771-773 (*Liew, Tat-siong Benny*).

5160   **Witherington, Ben** The gospel of Mark: a socio-rhetorical com-
       mentary. GR 2001, Eerdmans xxiv; 463 pp. $35. 0-8028-4503-7.
       Bibl. xiii-xxiv. ^RTS 62 (2001) 826-827 (*Dowd, Sharyn*).

5161   **Wright, Tom** Mark for everyone. L 2001, SPCK xii; 243 pp. 0-281-
       05300-6.

F6.2 *Evangelium Marci*, **Themata**

5162   *Ahearne-Kroll, Stephen P.* `Who are my mother and my brothers?':
       family relations and family language in the gospel of Mark. JR 81
       (2001) 1-25.

5163   *Alomía, K.M.* Como es usado Daniel en Marcos. Theologika 16
       (2001) 2-30.

5164   *Balla, Peter* What did Jesus think about his approaching death?.
       Jesus, Mark and Q. JSNT.S 214: 2001 ⇒4283. 239-258.

5165   *Bayer, Hans F.* The eschatological prospect in the context of Mark.
       Looking into the future. 2001 ⇒505. 74-84.

5166   *Black, Carl Clifton* Does suffering possess educational value in
       Mark's gospel?. PRSt 28/1 (2001) 85-98.

5167   *Blanco Berga, José Ignacio* Marcos: un evangelio para interrogarnos.
       Personajes del NT: 2001 ⇒231. 59-73.

5168   *Bolt, Peter G.* Feeling the cross: Mark's message of atonement. RTR
       60/1 (2001) 1-17.

5169   **Bonilla, Max** Minor characters in the gospel of Mark: a narrative
       analysis towards a theology of discipleship. Ext. Diss. Gregoriana,
       ^D*Swetnam, James*: R 2001, 64 pp.

5170   **Bonneau, Guy** Stratégies rédactionelles et fonctions communautaires
       de l'évangile de Marc. Diss. Montréal 1995. ÉtB 44: P 2001, Gabalda
       405 pp. €46. 2-85021-134-5. Bibl. 359-395.

5171   *Bonneau, Normand* Jesus and human contingency in Mark: a
       narrative-critical reading of three healing stories. Theoforum 32
       (2001) 321-340 [Mk 1,1-12; 5,21-43].

5172   *Brown, Colin* The Jesus of Mark's gospel. Jesus then and now. 2001
       ⇒483. 26-53.

5173   **Casey, Maurice** Aramaic sources of Mark's gospel. MSSNTS 102:
       1998 ⇒14,4688; 16,5162. ^RJBL 120 (2001) 169-171 (*Chilton,
       Bruce*); EvQ 73 (2001) 261-263 (*France, R.T.*).

5174 *Corley, Kathleen E.* Slaves, servants and prostitutes: gender and social class in Mark. A feminist companion to Mark. 2001 ⇒5147. 191-221.

5175 *Danove, Paul L.* The narrative function of Mark's characterization of God. NT 43 (2001) 12-30.

5176 **Danove, Paul L.** Linguistics and exegesis in the gospel of Mark: applications of a case frame analysis. JSNT.S 218; Studies in New Testament Greek 10: Shf 2001, Sheffield Academic 247 pp. $85. 1-84127-260-4. Bibl. 240-245.

5177 **Dawson, Anne** Freedom as liberating power: a socio political reading of the ἐχουσία texts in the gospel of Mark. NTOA 44: 2000 ⇒16, 5166. [R]ThLZ 126 (2001) 1039-1040 (*Lührmann, Dieter*).

5178 **Dechow, Jens** Gottessohn und Herrschaft Gottes: der Theozentrismus des Markusevangeliums. WMANT 86: 2000 ⇒16,5167. [R]ThLZ 126 (2001) 1142-1144 (*Guttenberger, Gudrun*).

5179 **Decker, Rodney J.** Temporal deixis of the Greek verb in the gospel of Mark with reference to verbal aspect. Studies in Biblical Greek 10: NY 2001, Lang xvii; 293 pp. 0-8204-5033-2. Bibl. 253-277.

5180 **Dormeyer, Detlev** Das Markusevangelium als Idealbiographie von Jesus Christus, dem Nazarener. SBB 43: 1999 ⇒15,5160. [R]ThRv 97 (2001) 46-47 (*Backhaus, Knut*); ThLZ 126 (2001) 164-166 (*Lührmann, Dieter*); SNTU.A 25 (2000) 245-246 (*Huber, K.*).

5181 *Downing, F. Gerald* The Jewish Cynic Jesus. Jesus, Mark and Q. JSNT.S 214: 2001 ⇒4283. 184-214.

5182 *Dschulnigg, Peter* Grenzüberschreitungen im Markusevangelium: auf dem Weg zu einer neuen Identität. MThZ 52 (2001) 113-120.

5183 *DuToit, David S.* Prolepsis als Prophetie: zur christologischen Funktion narrativer Anachronie im Markusevangelium. WuD 26 (2001) 165-189;

5184 "Gesalbter Gottessohn"—Jesus als letzter Bote Gottes: zur Christologie des Markusevangeliums. [F]HAHN, F. 2001 ⇒41. 37-50;

5185 Prolepsis als Prophetie: zur christologischen Funktion narrativer Anachronie im Markusevangelium. WD 26 (2001) 165-189.

5186 **Feneberg, Rupert** Der Jude Jesus und die Heiden: Biographie und Theologie Jesu im Markusevangelium. 2000 ⇒16,5173. [R]BZ 45 (2001) 127-128 (*Neubrand, Maria*); FrRu 8 (2001) 214-216 (*Renker, Alwin*); ThQ 181 (2001) 158-159 (*Theobald, Michael*); ThPh 76 (2001) 568-570 (*Baumert, N.*); ThLZ 126 (2001) 1267-1269 (*Pokorný, Petr*).

5187 *Fenton, John* Mark's gospel—the oldest and the best?. Theol. 104 (2001) 83-93.

5188 **Fenton, John** More about Mark. L 2001, SPCK vii; 119 pp. £10.

5189 *Fleddermann, Harry T.* Mark's use of Q: the Beelzebul controversy and the cross saying. Jesus, Mark and Q. JSNT.S 214: 2001 ⇒4283. 17-33 [Mk 3,22-30; Lk 11,14-26].

5190 **Geyer, Douglas W.** Fear, anomaly, and uncertainty in the gospel of Mark. Lanham 2001, Scarecrow 352 pp. $58. 0-8108-4202-5.

5191 **Herranz Marco, Mariano; García Pérez, José Miguel** Milagros y resurrección de Jesús según San Marcos. Studia Semitica Novi Testamenti 8: M 2001, Encuentro 198 pp. 84-7490-629-6. Bibl. 17-20.

5192 **Horsley, Richard A.** Hearing the whole story: the politics of plot in Mark's gospel. LVL 2001, Westminster xv; 296 pp. $30. 0-664-22275-7.

5193 **Jaśko, Andrzej** Gesù e la sua famiglia: contributo allo studio del discepolato nel contesto della parentela con Gesù nel vangelo di Marco. Diss. Rome, Angelicum 2001, ᴰ*De Santis, L.* [RTL 33,638].

5194 *Jonge, Henk Jan de* De markaanse gemeente. Vroegchristelijke gemeenten. 2001 ⇒460. 84-99.

5195 **Jossa, Giorgio** I gruppi giudaici ai tempi di Gesù. BCR 66: Brescia 2001, Paideia 222 pp. €18.59. 88-394-0629-8.

5196 *Jossa, Giorgio* I farisei di Marco e Luca. I gruppi giudaici. 2001 <1990> ⇒5195. 79-104.

5197 *Kasiłowski, Piotr* Problem tożsamości Jezusa w ewangelii św. Marka. ᶠJANKOWSKI, A. 2001 ⇒53. 170-189. **P.**

5198 *Katz, Paul* Von Markus zu Johannes—oder umgekehrt?: mögliche Wege einer Markus und Johannes gemeinsamen Sonderüberlieferung des biblischen Satzeinleiters 'und siehe'. ThZ 57 (2001) 36-59.

5199 *Kealy, Sean P.* My journey with Mark's gospel. PIBA 24 (2001) 64-82.

5200 **Klumbies, Paul-Gerhard** Der Mythos bei Markus. BZNW 108: B 2001, De Gruyter ix; 375 pp. €100.21. 3-11-017120-1. Bibl. 315-54.

5201 *Krause, Deborah* School's in session: the making and unmaking of docile disciple bodies in Mark. Postmodern interpretations. 2001 ⇒ 229. 177-186.

5202 *Levine, Amy-Jill* Introduction. A feminist companion to Mark. 2001 ⇒5147. 13-21.

5203 *López Rosas, Ricardo* Jesús y el templo en el evangelio según San Marcos: trazos para una cristología templaria. Qol 25 (2001) 3-38.

5204 **MacDonald, Dennis Ronald** The Homeric epics and the gospel of Mark. 2000 ⇒16,5180. ᴿCBQ 63 (2001) 155-156 (*Dowd, Sharyn*).

5205 **Maggi, Alberto** Jesús y Belcebú: Satán y demonios en el evangelio de Marcos. 2000 ⇒16,5181. ᴿEfMex 19 (2001) 432-433 (*Landgrave Gándara, Daniel*).

5206 **Malbon, Elizabeth Struthers** In the company of Jesus: characters in Mark's gospel. 2000 ⇒16,5182. ᴿABR 49 (2001) 62-63 (*Webb, Geoff*).

5207 **Malina, Artur** "Non come gli scribi" (Mc 1,22): studio del loro ruolo nel vangelo di Marco. Estr. Diss. Pont. Ist. Biblico, ᴰ*Stock, Klemens*: R 2001, E.P.I.B. 107 pp. Bibl. 71-100.

5208 **Martínez Aldana, Hugo Orlando** "Y todos huyeron" (Mc 14,50): la incomprensión de los discípulos en el evangelio de Marcos. Diss. Roma, Angelicum, ᴰ*De Santis, L.*, R 2001, vi; 196 pp. Bibl. 189-196.

5209 *Matjaž, Maksimilijan* Strah kot slutnja presežnega: kristološki pomen motiva strahu v Markovem evangeliju [Fear as presentiment of transcendence: christological meaning of the motive of fear in Mark's gospel]. Bogoslovni vestnik 61 (2001) 153-165 Sum. 165. S.

5210 **Matjaz, Maksimilijan** Furcht und Gotteserfahrung: die Bedeutung des Furchtmotivs für die Christologie des Markus. FzB 91: 1999 ⇒ 15,5182. ᴿBZ 45 (2001) 128-130 (*Pellegrini, Silvia*); ThRv 97 (2001) 47-49 (*Scholtissek, Klaus*); ThLZ 126 (2001) 758-759 (*Fenske, Wolfgang*).

5211 *Moloney, Francis J.* The vocation of the disciples in the gospel of Mark. 'A hard saying'. 2001 <1981> ⇒184. 53-84.

5212 **Myers, Ched** Binding the strong man: a political reading of Mark's story of Jesus. Mkn ¹²2000, Orbis xxxiii; 500 pp. 0-88344-620-0/1-9.

5213 *Naluparayil, Jacob Chacko Conversion* in the gospel of Mark: a reader-response perspective. Living Word 107/1 (2001) 27-39.

5214 **Naluparayil, Jacob Chacko** The identity of Jesus in Mark: an essay on narative christology. SBFA 49: 2000 ⇒16,5191. ᴿBib. 82 (2001) 569-573 (*Malbon, Elizabeth Struthers*).

5215 *Navone, John* Spiritual pedagogy in the gospel of Mark. BiTod 39 (2001) 231-238.

5216 *Nesse, Knut M.* Har dere ennä ikke tro? (Mark 4,40): en undersøkelse av hvilken rolle disiplene spiller i Markusevangeliet ved hjelp av den narrative metode. Ung teologi 34/1 (2001) 23-35.

5217 *Öhler, Markus* Jesus as prophet: remarks on terminology. Jesus, Mark and Q. JSNT.S 214: 2001 ⇒4283. 125-142.

5218 **Palmer, David G.** The Markan matrix: a literary-structural analysis. 1999 ⇒15,5190. ᴿJThS 52 (2001) 240-245 (*Telford, W.R.*).

5219 *Parker, David C.* Et incarnatus est. SJTh 54 (2001) 330-343.

5220 *Perkins, Larry* Mark's language of religious conflict as rhetorical device. BBR 11 (2001) 43-63.

5221 *Phillips, Victoria* The failure of the women who followed Jesus in the gospel of Mark. A feminist companion to Mark. 2001 ⇒5147. 222-234.

5222 **Poetker, Katrina M.** 'You are my mother, my brothers, and my sisters'; a literary-anthropological investigation of family in the gospel of Mark. Diss. Emory 2001, 256 pp. 3009465.

5223 *Reiser, Marius* Eschatology in the proclamation of Jesus. Jesus, Mark and Q. JSNT.S 214: 2001 ⇒4283. 216-238.

5224 **Reiser, William** Jesus in solidarity with his people: a theologian looks at Mark. 2000 ⇒16,5204. ᴿCBQ 63 (2001) 351-352 (*Beck, Robert R.*); PIBA 24 (2001) 120-122 (*Byrne, Patrick*).

5225 *Riches, John K.* Conflicting mythologies: mythical narrative in the gospel of Mark. JSNT 84 (2001) 29-50.

5226 **Rolin, Patrice** Les controverses dans l'évangile de Marc. ÉtB 43: P 2001, Gabalda (4) 383 pp. €45.74. 2-85021-132-1. Diss. Inst. Prot. de théologie, Paris 1997; Bibl. 369-376.

5227 *Sanday, William* The injunctions of silence in the gospels. Essays in biblical criticism. JSNT.S 225: 2001 <1904> ⇒205. 167-174.

5228 *Sawicki, Marianne* Making Jesus. A feminist companion to Mark. 2001 ⇒5147. 136-170.

5229 *Schröter, Jens* The Son of Man as the representative of God's kingdom: on the interpretation of Jesus in Mark and Q. Jesus, Mark and Q. JSNT.S 214: 2001 ⇒4283. 34-68.

5230 ᴱ**Söding, Thomas** Der Evangelist als Theologe: Studien zum Markusevangelium. SBS 163: 1995 ⇒11/1,3402; 14,4726. ᴿSNTU.A 22 (1997) 254-258 (*Fuchs, Albert*).

5231 *Tassin, Claude* "Pour vous, qui suis-je?" (Mc 8,29): stratégies marciennes de la révélation de Jésus. StMiss 50 (2001) 1-22.

5232 *Taylor, N.H.* Herodians and phrarisees: the historical and political context of Mark 3:6; 8:15; 12:13-17. Neotest. 34 (2000) 299-310.

5233 *Telford, William R.* Maze and amazement in Mark's gospel. Way 41 (2001) 339-348.

5234 **Telford, William R.** The theology of the gospel of Mark. 1999 ⇒15, 5206; 16,5213. ᴿEvQ 73 (2001) 260-261 (*Smith, Stephen H.*).

5235 **Trimaille, M.** La christologie de saint Marc. CJJC 82: P 2001, Désclée 241 pp. €23. 2-7189-0959-5. ᴿITS 38 (2001) 252-254 (*Legrand, L.*); EeV 40 (2001) 18-19 (*Cothenet, Edouard*).

5236 **Van Oyen, Geert** The interpretation of the feeding miracles in the gospel of Mark. CBRA 4: 1999 ⇒15,5208. ᴿTJT 17 (2001) 298-300 (*Damm, Alex*); SNTU.A 25 (2000) 252-253 (*Fuchs, Albert*) [Mark 6,30-44; 8,1-9].

5237 *Varickasseril, Jose* Mark's portrayal of Jesus. MissionToday 3 (2001) 285-291.

5238 *Vermeylen, Jacques* 'Il vous précède en Galilée: c'est là que vous le verrez'. Spiritus 42 (2001) 439-450.

5239 **Vines, Michael E.** The problem of Markan genre: the gospel of Mark and the Jewish novel. Diss. Union Theol. Sem. 2001, 272 pp. 3019385.

5240 **Watts, Rikki E.** Isaiah's new exodus and Mark. WUNT 2/88: 1997 ⇒13,5106... 16,5215. ᴿJBL 119 (2000) 140-141 (*Dowd, Sharyn*).

5241 *Wilkens, Hermann* Der markinische Christusmythos und die Predigt der Kirche. WD 26 (2001) 191-206.

5242 *Williams, Joel F.* Mission in Mark. Mission in the NT. ASMS 27: 2001 ⇒367. 137-151.

5243 **Zager, Werner** Gottesherrschaft und Endgericht in der Verkündigung Jesu: eine Untersuchung zur markinischen Jesusüberlieferung einschliesslich der Q-Parallelen. BZNW 82: 1996 ⇒12,4859... 14, 4733. ᴿSNTU.A 25 (2000) 255-256 (*Fuchs, Albert*).

5244 *Zawadzki, Ryszard* "Ich sende meine Boten vor dir her" (Mk 1,2): die Gestalt des Elija im Markusevangelium. CoTh 71A (2001) 23-52.

F6.3 Evangelii Marci versiculi

5245 *Croy, N. Clayton* Where the gospel text begins: a non-theological interpretation of Mark 1:1. NT 43 (2001) 105-127.

5246 *Maisano, Riccardo* Il prologo di Marco nel codice di Beza. ᴹCAGNI, L., 4: SMDSA 61: 2001 ⇒15. 1745-1773 [Mk 1,1-15].

5247 **Garrett, Susan R.** The temptations of Jesus in Mark's gospel. 1998 ⇒14,4737; 15,5220. ᴿRBLit 3 (2001) 382-385 (*Smith, Abraham*) [Mk 1,12-13].

5248 **Heindl, Bernhard** Jesus, der Arzt, der Sünder heilt: eine leser-orientierte Auslegung von Mk 1,16-2,17. Diss. Innsbruck 2001, ᴰHasitschka, M. [RTL 33,638].

5249 **Peron, Gian Paolo** Seguitemi!: vi farò diventare pescatori di uomini (Mc 1,17): gli imperativi ed esortativi di Gesù ai discepoli come elementi di un loro cammino formativo. 2000 ⇒16,5226. ᴿCart. 17 (2001) 444-445 (*Martínez Fresneda, F.*); Ang. 78 (2001) 738-740 (*Jurič, Stipe*); Anthropos Venezuela 42 (2001) 113-116 (*Pastore, Corrado*); Ben. 48 (2001) 483-485 (*Donghi, Antonio*).

5250 *Wright, Stephen I.* Words of power: biblical language and literary criticism with reference to Stephen Prickett's *Words and the Word* and Mark 1:21-28. ᶠTHISELTON, A. 2001 ⇒106. 224-240.

5251 *Reid, Barbara E.* Puzzling passages (Mark 1:24). BiTod 39 (2001) 371-372.

5252 *Krause, Deborah* Simon Peter's mother-in-law—disciple or domestic servant?: feminist biblical hermeneutics and the interpretation of Mark 1.29-31. A feminist companion to Mark. 2001 ⇒5147. 37-53.

5253 *Small, Joseph D.* Who's in, who's out?. ThTo 58 (2001) 58-71 [Mk 2, 13-3,6].

5254 *Ellingworth, Paul* 'To save life or to kill?' (Mark 3.4). BiTr 52 (2001) 245-246.

5255 *Skeat, Theodore C.* ἄρτον φαγεῖν: a note on Mark iii. 20-21. ᶠTHO-MAS, J. 2001 ⇒107. 29-30.

5256 **Rabuske, Irineu J.** Jesus exorcista: estudo exegético e hermenêutico de Mc 3,20-30. Bíblia e História: São Paulo 2001, Paulinas 415 pp. 85-356-0765-X. Bibl. 371-415.

5257 **Humphries, Michael L.** Christian origins and the language of the Kingdom of God. 1999 ⇒15,5233. ᴿJBL 120 (2001) 563-565 (*Elliott, Scott S.*).

5258 **Agbihounko, Hyacinthe Jérôme** Les caractéristiques de la vraie famille de Jésus selon l'évangile de Marc: Mc 3,31-35 et ses thèmes dominants. Diss. Gregoriana 2001, ᴰ*Stock, Klemens*: R 2001, 207 pp. Bibl. 187-198.

5259 *Derrett, J. Duncan M.* Preaching to the coast (Mark 4:1). EvQ 73 (2001) 195-205.

5260 *North, Robert* How loud was Jesus's voice: Mark 4:1. ET 112 (2001) 117-120 [Resp. ET 112,279].

5261 **Mell, Ulrich** Die Zeit der Gottesherrschaft: zur Allegorie und zum Gleichnis von Markus 4,1-9. BWANT 144: 1998 ⇒14,4745. ᴿZKTh 122 (2001) 224-225 (*Huber, Konrad*); RBLit 3 (2001) 391-393 (*Balla, Peter*).

5262 *Derrett, J. Duncan M.* 'He who has ears to hear, let him hear' (Mark 4:9 and parallels). DR 119 (2001) 255-268.

5263 *Hurley, Robert* Allusion et traces d'ironie dans un texte de Marc. SR 30 (2001) 293-305 [Mk 4,10-12].

5264 *Friedrichsen, Timothy A.* The parable of the mustard seed: Mark 4,30-32 and Q 13,18-19: a surrejoinder for independence. EThL 77 (2001) 297-317.

5265 *Rius-Camps, Josep* Les variants del text occidental de l'evangeli de Marc (VIII) (Mc 4,35-5,20). RCatT 26 (2001) 169-186.

5266 *Torchia, Natale J.* Eschatological elements in Jesus' healing of the Gerasene demoniac: an exegesis of Mk. 5:1-20. IBSt 23 (2001) 2-27.

5267 *Rius-Camps, Josep* Les variants del text occidental de l'evangeli de Marc (IX) (Mc 5,21-6,6a). RCatT 26 (2001) 365-383.

5268 *Cotter, Wendy J.* Mark's hero of the twelfth-year miracles: the healing of the woman with the hemorrhage and the raising of Jairus's daughter (Mark 5.21-43). A feminist companion to Mark. 2001 ⇒ 5147. 54-78.

5269 **Estévez López, Maria Elisa** La curación de la mujer con flujo de sangre a la luz de su contexto socio-cultural: Mc 5,24b-34. Diss. Deusto, 2001.

5270 *Dube, Musa W.* Fifty years of bleeding: a storytelling feminist reading of Mark 5:24-43. Other ways. 2001 ⇒260. 50-60.

5271 *Kotansky, Roy D.* Jesus and the lady of the Abyss (Mark 5:25-34): Hieros Gamos, cosmogony, and the elixir of life. ꟳBETZ, H. 2001 ⇒5. 77-120.

5272 *Moloney, Francis J.* Mark 6:6b-30: mission, the Baptist, and failure. CBQ 63 (2001) 647-663.

5273 *Focant, Camille* La tête du prophète sur un plat, ou, l'antirepas d'alliance (Mc 6.14-29). NTS 47 (2001) 334-353.

5274 *Bambi Kilunga, Godez* Quand l'exultation conduit à l'homicide: la danse de Salome, le meurtre du precurseur. Telema 105 (2001) 59-68 [Mk 6,17-29].

5275 *Henderson, Suzanne Watts* 'Concerning the loaves': comprehending incomprehension in Mark 6,45-52. JSNT 83 (2001) 3-26.

5276 **Enste, Stefan** Kein Markustext in Qumran: eine Untersuchung der These: Qumranfragment 7Q5 = Mk 6,52-53. NTOA 45: 2000 ⇒16, 5254. ꟳDSD 8 (2001) 312-315 (*Brooke, George J.*); OLZ 96 (2001) 572-574 (*Bull, K.-M.*); CBQ 63 (2001) 335-336 (*Harrington, Daniel J.*); WZKM 91 (2001) 378-384 (*Jaroš, Karl*).

5277 **Svartvik, Jesper** Mark and mission: Mk 7:1-23 in its narrative and historical contexts. CB.NT 32: 2000 ⇒16,5256. ꟳSvTK 77 (2001) 39-41 (*Fredriksen, Paula*); JThS 52 (2001) 794-800 (*Foster, Paul*); RBLit 3 (2001) 393-397 (*Fredriksen, Paula*).

5278 *Gnanadason, Aruna* Jesus and the Asian woman: a post-colonial look at the Syro-Phoenician woman/Canaanite woman from an Indian perspective. StWC 7 (2001) 162-177 [Mk 7,24-30].

5279 *Ranjini Wickramaratne, Rebera* The Syrophoenician women: a south Asian feminist perspective;

5280 *Ringe, Sharon* A gentile woman's story, revisted: rereading Mark 7, 24-31a. Feminist companion to Mark. 2001 ⇒5147. 101-10/79-100.

5281 *Keller, Marie Noël* Opening blind eyes: a revisioning of Mark 8:22-10:52. BTB 31 (2001) 151-157.

5282 *Stowasser, Martin* Das verheißene Heil: narratologische und textpragmatische Überlegungen zur markinischen Motivation der Leidensnachfolge in Mk 8,22-10,52. SNTU.A 26 (2001) 5-25.

5283 *Mele, Salvatore Antonio* Simbologia e teologia nella guarigione del cieco di Betsaida (Mc 8,22-26) e di Gerico (Mc 10,46-52): chiavi di lettura per la comprensione del vangelo di Marco. FolTh 12 (2001) 109-122.

5284 *Camacho Acosta, Fernando* Jesús pone a Pedro en su sitio (Mc 8, 33//Mt 16,23). Communio 34/1 (2001) 181-200.

5285 *Dewey, Joanna* 'Let them renounce themselves and take up their cross': a feminist reading of Mark 8.34 in Mark's social and narrative world. A feminist companion to Mark. 2001 ⇒5147. 23-36.

5286 *Becker, Uwe* Elia, Mose und Jesus: zur Bedeutung von Mk 9,2-10. BN 110 (2001) 5-11.

5287 *Viviano, Benedict T.* The titles Rabbi/Rabbouni and Mark 9:5. Trinity—kingdom—church. NTOA 48: 2001 <1990> ⇒223. 64-74.

5288 *Nicklas, Tobias* Formkritik und Leserrezeption: ein Beitrag zur Methodendiskussion am Beispiel Mk 9,14-29. Bib. 82 (2001) 496-514.

5289 *Heckel, Ulrich* Die Kindersegnung Jesu und das Segnen von Kindern: neutestamentliche und praktisch-theologische Überlegungen zu Mk 10,13-16 par. ThBeitr 32 (2001) 327-345.

5290 *Landgrave G., Daniel R.* Tensión permanente iglesia-reino: un aporte desde Mc 10,17-31. Qol 26 (2001) 19-37.

5291 *Stowasser, Martin* "... und im kommenden Aion ewiges Leben" (Mk 10,30): "ewiges Leben"—eine Vertröstung auf das Jenseits?. PzB 10 (2001) 57-72 [Mk 10,17-31].

5292 *Kollmann, Bernd* Die Heilung des blinden Bartimäus (Mk 10,46-52)—ein Wunder für Grundschulkinder. ZNT 7 (2001) 59-66.

5293 *Prostmeier, Ferdinand R.* Der 'Nachkomme Davids': Deutungen und Bedeutung für die Christologie. FSCHMUTTERMAYR, G. 2001 ⇒101. 209-236 [Mk 10,46-52].

5294 *Puykunnel, Shaji Joseph* Beggar by the roadside, disciple on the way: a study of Mark 10:46-52. FKAROTEMPREL, S. 2001 ⇒57. 49-63.

5295 *Derrett, J. Duncan M.* πάλιν: the ass again (Mk 11,3d). FgNT 14 (2001) 121-129.

5296 *Chávez, Emilio G.* Quiso Jesús purificar el templo según el evangelista Marcos?. AnáMnesis 11/2 (2001) 63-77 [Mk 11,15-17].

5297 *Collins, Adela Yarbro* Jesus' action in Herod's temple. FBETZ, H. 2001 ⇒5. 45-61 [Mk 11,15-18].

5298 *Masvie, Torkild* A response to Sevrin's paper;

5299 *Sevrin, Jean-Marie* Mark's use of Isaiah 56:7 and the announcement of the temple destruction. Jerusalem: house of prayer: SBFA 52: 2001 ⇒536. 57-65/45-56 [Mk 11,15-19].

5300 **Siluvaipichi, Maria John J.R.** The intervention of Jesus in the temple in Mark 11,15-19. Diss. Rome, Urbaniana 2001, ^D*Biguzzi, G.* [RTL 33,641].

5301 *Pool, Jeff B.* Toward a christian hermeneutic of love: problem and possibility. Ment. *Augustinus*: PRSt 28/3 (2001) 257-283 [Mk 12,28-34].

5302 *Malbon, Elizabeth Struthers* The poor widow in Mark and her poor
rich readers. A feminist companion to Mark. 2001 ⇒5147. 111-127
[Mk 12,41-44].

5303 *Schlaepfer, Carlos Frederico* Marcos 13: apocalipse, violência e vi-
gilância: uma pista para a violência e mercado hoje?. Estudos Bíblicos 69 (2001) 42-49.

5304 *Pitre, Brant James* Blessing the barren and warning the fecund:
Jesus' message for women concerning pregnancy and childbirth.
JSNT 81 (2001) 59-80 [Mk 13,17-19; Lk 23,28-31].

5305 *Martin, Troy W.* Watch during the watches (Mark 13:35). JBL 120
(2001) 685-701.

F6.8 Passio secundum Marcum, 14,1...[F5.3]

5306 **Bara, Shailendra J.G.** Mark's passion as story: the presence and the
absence of the twelve: narrative and reader-response criticisms of Mk
14: 1-16:8. Diss. Innsbruck 2001, ᴰ*Hasitschka, M.* [RTL 33,636].

5307 *Crossan, John Dominic* The power of the dog. Postmodern interpretations. 2001 ⇒229. 187-194.

5308 **Pérez Herrero, Francisco** Pasión y pascua de Jesús según san Marcos: del texto a la vida. Diss. Burgos 2001. Publicaciones de la Facultad de Teología del Norte de España 67: Burgos 2001, Facultad
de teología del Norte de España 445 pp. 84-95405-13-X. Bibl. 403-
432. ᴿRevista teología 41 (2001) 251-252 (*Fernández, Victor M.*).

5309 **Schwemer, Anna Maria** Antijudaismus in der Markuspassion?.
ThBeitr 32 (2001) 6-25;

5310 Die Passion des Messias nach Markus und der Vorwurf des Antijudaismus. Der messianische Anspruch Jesu. WUNT 138: 2001 ⇒276.
133-163.

5311 *MacDonald, Dennis R.* Renowned far and wide: the women who a-
nointed Odysseus and Jesus. A feminist companion to Mark. 2001 ⇒
5147. 128-135 [Mk 14,1-11; 13].

5312 **Ossom-Batsa, George** The institution of the eucharist in the gospel
of Mark: a study of the function of Mark 14,22-25 within the gospel
narrative. Diss. Gregoriana 2000, ᴰ*Vanhoye, Albert.* Bern 2001, Lang
312 pp. 3-906767-20-5. Bibl. 271-312.

5313 *Herzer, Jens* Freund und Feind: Beobachtungen zum alttestament-
lich-frühjüdischen Hintergrund und zum impliziten Handlungsmodell
der Gethsemane-Perikope Mk 14,32-42. Leqach 1 (2001) 107-136
[BuBB 36,61].

5314 **Schützeichel, Rudolf** Zu Mc 14,36 Bahuvrihi und Derivation im Althochdeutschen. NAWG Phil.-hist. Kl. 2001,7: Gö 2001, Vandenhoeck & R. 25 pp.

5315 *Hatton, Stephen B.* Mark's naked disciple: the semiotics and comedy
of following. Neotest. 35 (2001) 35-48 [Mk 14,51-52].

5316 **Perego, Giacomo** La nudità necessaria: il ruolo del giovane di Mc
14,51-52 nel racconto marciano della passione-morte-risurrezione di
Gesù. 2000 ⇒16,5305. [R]CivCatt 152/4 (2001) 410-11 (*Scaiola, D.*).

5317 *Thériault, Jean-Yves* Le "jeune homme" dans le récit de la passion
chez Marc. SémBib 104 (2001) 24-42 [Mk 14,51-52; 16,5-7].

5318 **Bock, Darrell L.** Blasphemy and exaltation in Judaism: the charge
against Jesus in Mark 14:53-65. 2000 <1998> ⇒16,5306. [R]CTJ 36
(2001) 379-382 (*Overduin, Nick*).

5319 **Borrell, Augustí** The good news of Peter's denial: a narrative and
rhetorical reading of Mark 14:54.66-72. 1998 ⇒14,4808; 16,5307.
[R]RCatT 26 (2001) 399-402 (*Puig i Tàrrech,Armand*).

5320 **Bock, Darrell L.** Blasphemy and exaltation in Judaism and the final
examination of Jesus: a... study of the key Jewish themes impacting
Mark 14:61-64. WUNT 2/106: 1998 ⇒14, 4809; 16,5309. [R]JSJ 32
(2001) 90-92 (*Frey, Jörg*); JThS 52 (2001) 245-247 (*Casey,
Maurice*); ThLZ 126 (2001) 162-164 (*Böttrich, Christfried*).

5321 *Kinukawa, Hisako* Women disciples of Jesus (15.40-41; 15.47; 16.1).
A feminist companion to Mark. 2001 ⇒5147. 171-190.

5322 *Combet-Galland, Corina* L'évangile de Marc et la pierre qu'il a déjà
roulée. Résurrection: l'après-mort. MoBi 45: 2001 ⇒296. 93-109
[Mk 16].

5323 *Böhm, Martina* Wo Markus aufhörte—und seine Leserinnen und Leser zu denken beginnen: zur erzählerischen Intention des kurzen Mar-
kusschlusses Mk 16,1-8. Leqach 1 (2001) 73-89 [BuBB 33,18].

5324 *Sieg, Franciszek* Ewangelia (Mk 16,1-8) o zmartwychwstaniu Jezusa
w szerszym kontekście biblijnym: studium egsegetyczno-teologizne
[The gospel of the resurrection of Jesus (Mk 16,1-8) in the broader
biblical context: an exegetical-theological study]. Studia Bobolanum
1/2 (2001) 111-137 Sum. 137. **P.**

5325 *Moloney, Francis J.* Mark 16:6-8 and the christian community. [F]KA-
ROTEMPREL, S. 2001 ⇒57. 108-121;

5326 'He is going before you into Galilee': Mark 16: 6-8 and the christian
community. Charism, leadership 2001 ⇒456. 64-75 Reaction by *A.
G. Ygrubay* 76-79; *B. Yocum* 80-82.

5327 *Holmes, Michael W.* To be continued ... the many endings of the gospel of Mark. BiRe 17/4 (2001) 13-23, 48-50 [Mk 16,9-20].

5328 Kelhoffer, James A. The witness of EUSEBIUS' *Ad Marinum* and other christian writings to text-critical debates concerning the original conclusion to Mark's gospel. ZNW 92 (2001) 78-112 [Mk 16,9-20].

5329 **Kelhoffer, James A.** Miracle and mission: the authentication of missionaries and their message in the longer ending of Mark. WUNT 2/112: 2000 ⇒16,5316. ᴿJThS 52 (2001) 248-250 (*Elliott, J.K.*); ThLZ 126 (2001) 639-642 (*Heckel, Theo K.*) [Mk 16,9-20].

X. Opus Lucanum

F7.1 *Opus Lucanum*—Luke-Acts

5330 **Barro, Jorge Henrique** Luke's theology of God's mission in the city. Diss. Fuller 2001, 354 pp. 9998898.

5331 *Bauckham, Richard* The restoration of Israel in Luke-Acts. Restoration. JSJ.S 72: 2001 ⇒319. 435-487.

5332 **Bonz, Marianne Palmer** The past as legacy: Luke-Acts and ancient epic. 2000 ⇒16,5321. ᴿJR 81 (2001) 110-112 (*Tannehill, Robert C.*); CBQ 63 (2001) 334-335 (*Sterling, Gregory E.*).

5333 **Böhm, Martina** Samarien und die Samaritai bei Lukas. WUNT 2/111: 1999 ⇒15,5319. ᴿThG 44 (2001) 303-304 (*Giesen, Heinz*); CBQ 63 (2001) 543-544 (*Bauer, David R.*); ThLZ 126 (2001) 922-923 (*Pokorný, Petr*) [Lk 9,1-56; 10,25-37; 17,11-19; Acts 8,4-25].

5334 **Constant, Pierre** Le psaume 118 et son emploi christologique dans Luc et Actes: une étude exégétique, littéraire et herméneutique. Diss. Trinity Evang. Divinity 2001, 522 pp. 3003779.

5335 **Decock, Paul B.** Isaiah in Luke-Acts. Exc. Diss. Gregoriana 1977, ᴰ*Rasco, Emilio*: Cedara, S. Africa 2001, ix; 111 pp. Bibl. updated.

5336 *Denaux, Adelbert; Delobel, Joël* De oorspronkelijke bestemmeling van Lukas-Handelingen: de 'gemeente van Lukas'?. Vroegchristelijke gemeenten. 2001 ⇒460. 115-133.

5337 **Fusco, Vittorio** Da Paolo a Luca: studi su Luca-Atti, 1. StBi 124: 2000 ⇒16,5333. ᴿRivBib 49 (2001) 495-497 (*Rossé, Gerard*); CivCatt 152/3 (2001) 553-554 (*Scaiola, D.*).

5338 **Ganser-Kerperin, Heiner** Das Zeugnis des Tempels: Studien zur Bedeutung des Tempelmotivs im Lukanischen Doppelwerk. NTA 36: 2000 ⇒16,5334. ᴿCBQ 63 (2001) 337-338 (*Phillips, Thomas E.*); ThLZ 126 (2001) 1042-1044 (*Böttrich, Christfried*).

5339 **Gregory, Andrew** The reception of Luke and Acts in the period before IRENAEUS. Diss. Oxford 2001, *DRowland, Christopher* [TynB 53,153-156].

5340 **Harms, Richard B.** Paradigms from Luke-Acts for multicultural communities. AmUSt.TR 216: NY 2001, Lang xiii; 214 pp. $52. 0-8-204-5209-2 [ThD 49,374—Heiser, W. Charles].

5341 **Hur, Ju** A dynamic reading of the Holy Spirit in Luke-Acts. JSNT.S 211: Shf 2001, Sheffield A. 372 pp. 1-84127-192-6. Bibl. 302-329.

5342 *Hurley, Michael* Reconciliation: a meditation on St Luke. DoLi 51 (2001) 356-361.

5343 **Jacobsen, David Schnasa; Wasserberg, Günter** Preaching Luke-Acts. Nv 2001, Abingdon 160 pp. 0-687-09972-2.
        Karlsen Seim, T. Abraham...Luke-Acts. 2001 ⇒3080.

5344 *Kealy, Seán P.* A fresh look at Luke. BiTod 39 (2001) 100-104.

5345 **Kim, Kyoung-Jin** Stewardship and almsgiving in Luke's theology. JSNT.S 155: 1998 ⇒14,4834; 15,5347. *RJThS* 52 (2001) 105-123 (*Capper, Brian J.*).

5346 *Knöppler, Thomas* Beobachtungen zur lukanischen theologia resurrectionis. *FHAHN, F.* 2001 ⇒41. 51-62.

5347 **Leonardi, Giovanni** Opera di Luca, 1: il vangelo; 2, Atti degli Apostoli. 2000 ⇒16,5352. *RBen.* 48/1 (2001) 277-278 (*Pierini, Piero Maria*).

5348 *Mainville, Odette* La question de la liberté en Luc-Actes: une question impertinente. Theoforum 32/1 (2001) 45-62.

5349 *Marguerat, Daniel* Luc-Actes: la résurrection à l'oeuvre dans l'histoire. Résurrection: l'après-mort. MoBi 45: 2001 ⇒296. 195-214.

5350 *Meiser, Martin* Das Alte Testament im lukanischen Doppelwerk. Im Brennpunkt. BWANT 8,13: 2001 ⇒1629. 167-195.

5351 **Mendez-Moratalla, Fernando** A paradigm of conversion in Luke. Diss. Durham 2001, *DBarton, S.C.*: 369 pp. [RTL 33,640].

5352 *EMoessner, David P.* Jesus and the heritage of Israel: Luke's narrative claim upon Israel's legacy. 1999 ⇒15,5312. *RCBQ* 63 (2001) 183-185 (*Smiga, George M.*).

5353 **Müller, Christoph Gregor** Mehr als ein Prophet: die Charakterzeichnung Johannes des Täufers im lukanischen Erzählwerk. Diss.-Habil. Würzburg 2000/01. Herders Biblische Studien 31: FrB 2001, Herder xii; 395 pp. €55. 3-451-27622-4. Bibl. 331-377.

5354 *Neirynck, Frans* Luke 4,16-30 and the unity of Luke-Acts. Evangelica III. BEThL 150: 2001 <1999> ⇒187. 167-206.

5355 *O'Toole, Robert F.* Ἡ ἐξουσία στήν Ἐκκλησία, σύμφωνα μέ τό κατά Λουκᾶν Εὐαγγέλιο καί τίς Πράξεις τῶν Ἀποστόλων [Authority in the church, according to Luke-Acts]. DBM 20/2 (2001) 5-46. **G.**

5356 *Paffenroth, Kim* Famines in Luke-Acts. ET 112 (2001) 405-407.

5357 **Phillips, Thomas E.** Reading issues of wealth and poverty in Luke-Acts. SBEC 48: Lewiston, NY 2001, Mellen xi; 393 pp. 0-7734-7473-0. Bibl. 289-361.

5358 **Pokorny, Petr** Theologie der lukanischen Schriften. FRLANT 174: 1998 ⇒14,4849... 16,5361. [R]SNTU.A 23 (1998) 259-260 (*Fuchs, Albert*); JBL 119 (2000) 364-366 (*Spencer, F. Scott*).

5359 **Rakocy, Waldemar** Obraz i funkcja faryzeuszy w dziele Łukaszowym (Łk-Dz): studium literacko-teologiczne [L'image et la fonction des pharisiens dans l'oeuvre de saint Luc (Lc-Ac): étude littéraire et théologique]. Diss.-Habil. Lublin 2001, 288 pp [RTL 33,640]. **P**.

5360 *Räisänen, Heikki* The redemption of Israel: a salvation-historical problem in Luke-Acts. Challenges to biblical interpretation. BiblInterp 59: 2001 <1991> ⇒200. 61-81.

5361 **Rusam, Dietrich** Alles muss(te) erfüllt werden: Intertextualität im lukanischen Doppelwerk. Diss.-Habil. Bonn 2001, [D]*Wolter, M.* [RTL 33,640].

5362 **Sánchez, Héctor** Das lukanische Geschichtswerk im Spiegel heilsgeschichtlicher Übergänge. PaThSt 29: Pd 2001, Schöningh 196 pp. €34.80. 3-506-76279-6.

5363 *Steffek, Emmanuelle* Luc-Actes et l'Ancien Testament. FV 100/4 (2001) 31-40.

5364 *Stenschke, Christoph W.* Some comments on a recent study of the characterisation of Judaism and the Jews in Luke-Acts. CV 43/3 (2001) 244-266.

5365 **Stenschke, Christoph W.** Luke's portrait of gentiles prior to their coming to faith. WUNT 2/108: 1999 ⇒15,5396; 16,5370. [R]ThLZ 126 (2001) 58-60 (*Bull, Klaus-Michael*); RBLit 3 (2001) 402-405 (*Karris, Robert J.*).

5366 **Stronstad, Roger** The prophethood of all believers: a study in Luke's charismatic theology. JPentec.S 16: 1999 ⇒15,5397. [R]JThS 52 (2001) 258-259 (*Beck, B.E.*).

5367 **Tyson, Joseph B.** Luke, Judaism, and the scholars: critical approaches to Luke-Acts. 1999 ⇒15,5406; 16,5375. [R]RBLit 3 (2001) 405-408 (*Weidemann, Frederick W.*).

5368 [E]**Verheyden, Joseph** The unity of Luke-Acts. BEThL 142: 1999 ⇒ 15,5410; 16,5378. [R]RivBib 49 (2001) 101-104 (*Rossé, Gerard*); JThS 52 (2001) 255-258 (*Franklin, E.*); LouvSt 26 (2001) 87-88 (*Harrington, Jay M.*); SNTU.A 25 (2000) 246-248 (*Fuchs, Albert*).

5369 **Woods, Edward J.** The 'Finger of God' and pneumatology in Luke-Acts. JSNT.S 205: Shf 2001, Sheffield A. 305 pp. £53.50. 1-84127-175-6. Bibl. 262-282.

5370 **Yanos, Susan** Woman, you are free: a spirituality for women in Luke. Cincinnati 2001, St. Anthony Messenger 138 pp. $9. 0-86716-413-1 [BiTod 40,66—Senior, Donald].

5371 *Zwiep, Arie W.* Assumptus est in caelum: rapture and heavenly exaltation in early Judaism and Luke-Acts. Auferstehung—Resurrection. WUNT 135: 2001 ⇒452. 323-349 [Lk 24; Acts 1,9-11].

F7.3 *Evangelium Lucae*—Textus, commentarii

5372 **Barclay, William** The New Daily Study Bible: the gospel of Luke. E 2001, Saint Andrew Pr. xxvi; 355 pp. 0-7152-0783-0.

5373 **Bock, Darrell L.** Luke 9:51-24:53. 1996 ⇒13,5259; 14,4862. [R]SNTU.A 22 (1997) 259-260 (*Fuchs, Albert*).

5374 **Bovon, François** Das Evangelium nach Lukas: Lk 9,51-14,35. 1996 ⇒12,5033; 16, 5383. [R]SNTU.A 22 (1997) 261-262 (*Fuchs, Albert*);

5375 L'Évangile selon Saint Luc, 3: Lk 15,1-19,27. Commentaire du N.T. 3c: Genève 2001, Labor et F. 266 pp. €33.54. 2-8309-1008-7;

5376 Das Evangelium nach Lukas (Lk 15,1-19,27). Evangelisch-Katholischer Kommentar zum NT 3/3: Z 2001, Benzinger 304 pp. €61.36. 3-545-23133-X;

5377 Lk 1,1-19,27. 1989-2001 ⇒5,5057...17,5376. [R]RBBras 18 (2001) 535-537.

5378 **Green, Joel B.** The gospel of Luke. NICNT: 1997 ⇒13,5269... 16, 5389. [R]ThLZ 126 (2001) 49-51 (*März, Claus-Peter*); SNTU.A 23 (1998) 260-262 (*Fuchs, Albert*);

5379 La teologia del vangelo di Luca. Teologia del NT, letture bibliche 16: Brescia 2001, Paideia 193 pp. 88-394-0626-3.

5380 **Hahn, Scott; Mitch, Curtis** The gospel of Luke, with introduction, commentary, and notes. SF 2001, Ignatius 82 pp. $10. 0-89870-819-2. Study questions by *Dennis Walters* [ThD 49,174—Heiser, W.C.].

5381 **Hendrickx, Herman** The third gospel for the third world, 4A: Jesus in the temple (Luke 19:45-21:38). ColMn 2001, Liturgical viii; 237 pp. $20. 0-8146-5119-4 [BiTod 40,265—Senior, Donald].

5382 [T]**Karris, Robert J.** Works of BONAVENTURE, 8/1: commentary on the gospel of Luke: chapters 1-8. Saint Bonaventure, NY 2001, Franciscan Institute 796 pp. $50. 1-57659-179-4 [BiTod 40,64—Senior, D.].

5383 **Kosch, Daniel; Schäfer, Brigitte; Zanetti, Claudia** Jesus im Alltag begegnen: Lebenssinn und Lebensstil nach Lukas. Werkstattbibel 1: Stu 2001, Kathol. Bibelwerk 80 pp. €11.80/10.70. 3-460-08501-0.

5384 **Lafon, Guy** L'esprit de la lettre: lectures de l'évangile selon saint Luc. P 2001, DDB 240 pp. €20,58.

5385 **Maggioni, Bruno** Il racconto di Luca. Assisi 2000, Citadella 402 pp. €15.49. [R]CivCatt 152/4 (2001) 525-526 (*Scaiola, D.*).

5386 **Nickle, Keith F.** Preaching the gospel of Luke: proclaiming God's royal rule. 2000 ⇒16,5395. [R]CTJ 36 (2001) 146-147 (*Deppe, Dean*).

5387 **Schweizer, Eduard** Il vangelo secondo Luca. NT 2. ser. 3. 2000 ⇒ 16,5398. [R]CivCatt 152/2 (2001) 88-89 (*Scaiola, D.*).

5388 **Walker, Thomas W.** Luke. Interpretation Bible Studies 15: LVL 2001, Geneva vi; 114 pp. 0-664-50075-7 [RB 108,480].

F7.4 *Lucae themata*—Luke's Gospel, topics

5389 **Abignente, D.** Conversione morale nella fede: una riflessione etico-teologica a partire da figure di conversione del vangelo di Luca. 2000 ⇒16,5403. [R]StPat 48 (2001) 289-290 (*Segalla, Giuseppe*).

5390 *Bailey, James L.* Reading and preaching Luke contextually. CThMi 28 (2001) 17-26.

5391 **Bieberstein, Sabine** Verschwiegene Jüngerinnen—vergessene Zeuginnen: gebrochene Konzepte im Lukasevangelium. NTOA 38: 1998 ⇒14,4885; 16,5404. [R]JThS 52 (2001) 250-255 (*Nolland, John L.*); RB 108 (2001) 464-467 (*Viviano, Benedict T.*); CBQ 63 (2001) 542-543 (*Karris, Robert J.*); JBL 119 (2000) 574-576 (*Thompson, Richard P.*).

5392 **Boismard, Marie-Émile** Comment Luc a remanié l'évangile de Jean. CRB 51: P 2001, Gabalda 111 pp. €20. 28502-1131X [BuBB 33,99].

5393 **Bormann, Lukas** Recht, Gerechtigkeit und Religion im Lukasevangelium. StUNT 24: Gö 2001, Vandenhoeck & R. 420 pp. €84. 3-525-53378-0. Bibl. 361-392.

5394 *Böhm, Martina* 'Schaffe mir Recht!'—Frauen im Lukasevangelium. Forschungsstelle Judentum, Mitteilungen und Beiträge 18 (2001) 4-36 [BuBB 33,110].

5395 **Brambilla, Franco Giulio** Alla ricerca di Gesù. CinB 2001, San Paolo 94 pp [Hum(B)58,204—Montagnini, Felice].

5396 **Byrne, Brendan** The hospitality of God: a reading of Luke's gospel. 2000 ⇒16,5409. [R]ABR 49 (2001) 59-60 (*Squires, John T.*); CBQ 63 (2001) 739-740 (*Hamm, Dennis*).

5397 **Chrupcała, Lesław Deniel** Il regno opera della Trinità nel vangelo di Luca. ASBF 45: 1998 ⇒14,4889; 15,5441. [R]EstB 59 (2001) 395-396 (*Ibarzábal, S.*).

5398 *Collins, Raymond F.* The primacy of Peter: a Lukan perspective. LouvSt 26 (2001) 268-281.

5399 *Danker, Frederick W.* St. Luke for a new millennium: the middle and the end are in the beginning. CThMi 28 (2001) 5-16.

5400 *Du Plessis, Isak J.* The Lukan audience: rediscovered?: some reactions to Bauckham's theory. Neotest. 34 (2000) 243-261.

5401 *Jensen, Richard A.* Preaching the Spirit in the year of Luke. CThMi 28 (2001) 27-33.

5402 *Kilgallen, John* Self-interest in the teaching of Jesus. ChiSt 40 (2001) 185-194.

5403 **Kimball, Charles A.** Jesus' exposition of the Old Testament in Luke's gospel. JSNT.S 94: 1994 ⇒10,4945... 13,5300. [R]WThJ 63 (2001) 459-461 (*Smuts, Peter*).

5404 **Klassen-Wiebe, Sheila Anne** Called to mission: a narrative-critical study of the character and mission of the disciples in the gospel of Luke. Diss. Richmond 2001, [D]*Kingsbury, J.D.*: 548 pp. 3019386 [RTL 33,639].

5405 *Larkin, William J. Jr.* Mission in Luke. Mission in the NT. ASMS 27: 2001 ⇒367. 152-169.

5406 **Lavatori, Renzo; Sole, Luciano** Ritratti dal vangelo di Luca: persone e relazioni. Lettura pastorale della Bibbia, Bibbia e spiritualità 14: Bo 2001, EDB 295 pp. €19.11. 88-10-21109-X. Bibl. 285-292.

5407 *Leonardi, Giovanni* L'evangelista Luca promotore del pluralismo cristiano—solo inter-culturale, o anche inter-religioso?. StPat 48 (2001) 99-104.

5408 *Lombardini, Pietro* 'Poiché molti hanno posto mano': Luca, il terzo evangelo. Qol(I) 91; 92-93 (2001) 5-15; 4-12.

5409 *Masotcha Moyo, Aynos* The gospel and common humanity: Jesus' tolerant attitude towards the Samaritans in the gospel of Luke: African Theological Journal 24/2 (2001) 91-97.

5410 *Moxnes, Halvor* Kingdom takes place: transformations of place and power in the kingdom of God in the gospel of Luke. [F]MALINA, B. BiblInterp 53: 2001 ⇒67. 176-209.

5411 *Parsons, Mikeal* Who wrote the gospel of Luke?. BiRe 17/2 (2001) 12-21, 54-55.

5412 **Pereira, Francis** Jesus: the human and humane face of God: a portrait of Jesus in Luke's gospel. 2000 ⇒16,5425. [R]VJTR 65 (2001) 854-856 (*Lesser, R.H.*).

5413 *Rakocy, Waldemar* Entos hymon (Łk 17,21): Królestwo Boze "w was" czy "pośród was"?. CoTh 71/1 (2001) 31-40. **P.**

5414 **Rodríguez Palafox, Alberto** Seguir a Jesús para anunciar el reino: el discipulado en Lc 9,57-62; 14,25-35; 18,18-30. Diss. extr. Studium Biblicum Franciscanum, [D]*Bottini, C.*: J 2001, Franciscan Printing Press 157 pp.

5415 **Wasserberg, Günter** Aus Israels Mitte—Heil für die Welt: eine narrativ-exegetische Studie zur Theologie des Lukas. BZNW 92: 1998

⇒14,4917. [R]CBQ 63 (2001) 165-167 (*O'Toole, Robert F.*); CV 43 (2001) 244-266 (*Stenschke, Christoph*); ThLZ 126 (2001) 645-647 (*Horn, Friedrich W.*).

5416 **Weissenrieder, Annette** Krank in Gesellschaft—Krankheitskonstrukte im Lukas-Evangelium auf dem Hintergrund antiker medizinischer texte. Diss. Heidelberg 2001, [D]*Theissen, G.* [RTL 33,642].

F7.5 *Infantia, cantica*—**Magnificat, Benedictus: Luc. 1-3**

5417 *Blanco Berga, José Ignacio* Zacarías: cuando el mudo toma la palabra (la recuperación de la esperanza). Personajes del NT. 2001 ⇒231. 121-132.

5418 **Boismard, Marie-Émile** L'évangile de l'enfance (Luc 1-2) selon le Proto-Luc. EtB 35: 1997 ⇒13,5334... 16,5438. [R]JBL 119 (2000) 362-364 (*Chartrand-Burke, Tony*).

5419 *Bonney, Gillian* The exegesis of the gospel of Luke in the Expositio evangelii secundum Lucam of AMBROSE and in the In Lucae evangelium expositio of BEDE as observed in the figure of Elizabeth. ZAC 5 (2001) 50-64.

5420 *Cárdenas Pallares, José* La inmensa alegría. Qol 26 (2001) 69-75.

5421 *Farris, Stephen* The canticles of Luke's infancy narrative: the appropriation of a biblical tradition. Into God's presence. 2001 ⇒ 294. 91-112.

5422 **Jung, C.W.** An examination of the Greek of the Lukan infancy narrative. Diss. V.U. Amsterdam 2001, [D]*De Boer, M.C.*: vi; 198 pp.

5423 **Mikołajczak, Mieczysław** Teologia świątyni w dwudziele św. Łukasza [La théologie du temple dans le diptyque de saint Luc]. Diss.-Habil. Lublin 2001, 227 pp. [RTL 33,640]. **P**.

5424 *Vanni, Ugo* La sagrada familia en el evangelio de la infancia de Lucas. La Sagrada Familia en la biblia. 2001 ⇒4792. 139-147.

5425 **Coleridge, Mark** Nueva lectura de la infancia de Cristo: la narrativa como cristología en Lucas 1-2. 2000 ⇒16,5439. [R]EstJos 55 (2001) 178-180 (*Llamas, Román*); RevAg 42 (2001) 893-894 (*Sabugal, Santos*); CDios 214 (2001) 861-862 (*Gutiérrez, J.*)

5426 *Kuhn, Karl A.* The point of the step-parallelism in Luke 1-2. NTS 47 (2001) 38-49.

5427 *Lohfink, Norbert* Das Alte Testament und der christliche Tageslauf. BiKi 56 (2001) 26-34.

5428 *Harmon, Steven R.* Zechariah's unbelief and early Jewish-Christian relations: the form and structure of Luke 1:5-25 as a clue to the narrative agenda of the gospel of Luke. BTB 31 (2001) 10-16.

5429 *Janssen, Claudia* Eine alte Frau wird schwanger. JK 62/6 (2001) 9-17 [Lk 1,5-80].

5430 *Brown, David* The annunciation as true fiction. Theol. 104 (2001) 123-130 [Lk 1,26-38].

5431 *La Potterie, Ignace de* 'Concepirai nel grembo' (*Lc* 1,31): l'angelo annuncia a Maria il suo concepimento verginale. [F]KASPER, W.: 2001 ⇒58. 23-34.

5432 **Mathieu, J.-M.** Le nom de Josué-Jésus en hébreu et en arabe. 1998 ⇒15,5487. [R]ATG 64 (2001) 399-400 (*Verd, G.M.*) [Lk 1,31].

5433 *Kilgallen, John J.* A comment on Luke 1:31-35. ET 112 (2001) 413-414.

5434 *Reeling Brouwer, Rinse* Und seines Königreiches wird kein Ende sein: ein klassischer Widerspruch: Lukas 1:33 oder Korinther 15:28?. [F]DEURLOO, K.: ACEBT.S 2: 2001 ⇒23. 293-301.

5435 *Bell, Theo* Das Magnificat—verdeutscht und ausgelegt durch D. Martin LUTHER: Vorrede und Eingang. Luther 72 (2001) 124-136 [Lk 1,46-55].

5436 *Karris, Robert J.* Mary's Magnificat. BiTod 39 (2001) 145-149 [Lk 1,46-55].

5437 **Nolan, Mary Catherine** Mary's song: living her timeless prayer. ND 2001, Ave Maria 128 pp. $10. 0-87793-701-X [ThD 48,382—Heiser, W. Charles] [Lk 1,46-55].

5438 *Sell, Nancy A.* The Magnificat as a model for ministry: proclaiming justice, shifting paradigms, transforming lives. Liturgical ministry 10/1 (2001) 31-40 [Lk 1,46-55].

5439 *Valentini, Alberto* Il Dio cantato da Maria serva del Signore nel Magnificat. Maria e il Dio. 2001 ⇒547. 155-186 [Lk 1,46-55].

5440 *McKenzie, Alyce M.* Luke 1:68-79. Interp. 55 (2001) 413-416.

5441 *Thurston, Bonnie B.* Who was Anna?: Luke 2:36-38. PRSt 28/1 (2001) 47-55,

5442 *Mazzinghi, Luca* 'Perché mi cercavate?: non sapevate che io devo occuparmi delle cose del padre mio?' (*Lc* 2,49). Maria e il Dio. 2001 ⇒547. 187-219 [Lk 2,41-52].

5443 *Neirynck, Frans* The first synoptic pericope: the appearance of John the Baptist in Q. Evangelica III. BEThL 150: 2001 <1996> ⇒187. 219-244 [Lk 3,7-9].

F7.6 Evangelium Lucae 4,1...

5444 *D'Sa, Thomas* 'Devils! Are you there?' (the interpretation of Lk 4,1-13 and 8,26-29 from the point of view of a pastor). BiBh 27 (2001) 106-119.

5445 *Venema, René* 'Today this scripture has been fulfiled in your ears': mimetic representation in Luke 4:14-21. ᶠDEURLOO, K. ACEBT.S 2: 2001 ⇒23. 303-307.

5446 *Abernathy, David* A study on Lk 4,16-30. BiBh 27 (2001) 223-236.

5447 *Irudhayasamy, Raymond Joseph* The prophetic character of Jesus: an analysis of Lk 4,16-30 in the background of Isaianic citation and Elijah-Elisha references. Diss. Innsbruck 2001, ᴰ*Hasitschka, M.*: 314 pp. [RTL 33,638].

5448 *Van Minnen, Peter* Luke 4:17-20 and the handling of ancient books. JThS 52 (2001) 689-690.

5449 *Prete, Benedetto* Dati cristologici nel racconto della pesca miracolosa (Lc 5,1-11). DT(P) 104 (2001) 138-182.

5450 *Cárdenas Pallares, José* Jesús hermanado con los indeseables (Lc. 5,27-32). Qol 26 (2001) 39-44.

5451 *Neirynck, Frans* Q 6,20b-21; 7,22 and Isaiah 61. Evangelica III. BEThL 150: 2001 <1997> ⇒187. 129-166.

5452 **Topel, L. John** Children of a compassionate God: a theological exegesis of Luke 6:20-49. ColMn 2001, Liturgical xvii; 340 pp. $30. 0-8146-5085-6. Bibl. 297-314 [BiTod 40,66—Senior, Donald].

5453 *Puig i Tàrrech, Armand* Une parabole à l'image antithétique Q 6,46-49. The sayings source Q. 2001 ⇒477. 681-693 [Mt 7,24-27].

5454 *Shantz, Colleen* Wisdom is as wisdom does: the use of folk proverbs in Q 7:31-35. TJT 17 (2001) 249-262.

5455 *Kilgallen, John J.* Faith and forgiveness: Luke 7,36-50. RB 108 (2001) 214-227.

5456 *Rauchwarter, Barbara* Vergebung als Ermöglichung der Liebe: Lukas 7,36-50. JK 62/4 (2001) 56-59.

5457 **Seluvappan, Lawrence J.W.** The sinful woman accepts Jesus at the house of Simon the pharisee: text, characters and theology of Luke 7,36-50. Diss. Rome, Angelicum 2001, ᴰ*De Santis, Luca* R 2001, vii; 93 pp.

5458 *Karris, Robert J.* BONAVENTURE and Talbert on Luke 8:26-39: christology, discipleship, and evangelization. PRSt 28 (2001) 57-66.

5459 *Neirynck, Frans* Lk 9,22 and 10,25-28: the case for independent redaction. Evangelica III. 2001 <1999> ⇒187. 295-306.

5460 *Smyth, Geraldine* Looking to be transfigured. DoLi 51 (2001) 170-177 [Lk 9,28-36].

5461 *Luther, Donald J.* The mystery of the transfiguration: Luke 9:28-36 (37-43). WaW 21/1 (2001) 92-102.

F7.7 *Iter hierosolymitanum—Lc 9,51...*—**Jerusalem journey**

5462 **Bendemann, Reinhard von** Zwischen ΔΟΧΑ und ΣΤΑΥΡΟΣ: eine exegetische Untersuchung der Texte des sogenannten Reiseberichts im Lukasevangelium. Diss.-Habil. 1999, Bonn. BZNW 101: B 2001, De Gruyter xvi; 512 pp. €126.8. 3-11-016732-8. ᴿBZ 45 (2001) 270-272 (*Klauck, Hans-Josef*).

5463 *Reid, Robert S.* On preaching "fictive argument": a reader-response look at a Lukan parable and three sayings on discipleship. RestQ 43/1 (2001) 13-31 [Lk 9,51-19,48].

5464 **Sobradillo Casado, Conceso** Relatos de vocación en Lc 9,57-62: la radicalidad de la llamada de Jesús. Diss. Pampelune 2001, ᴰ*Balaguer Beltrán, V.* 361 pp. [RTL 33,641].

5465 *McFarland, Ian A.* Who is my neighbour?: the Good Samaritan as a source for theological anthropology. MoTh 17 (2001) 57-66 [Lk 10].

5466 *Palumbo, Paul K.* Eating what is set before you (Luke 10:1-11, 16-20). WaW 21 (2001) 297-301.

5467 *Neirynck, Frans* Luke 10,25-28: a foreign body in Luke <1994>;

5468 The minor agreements and Lk 10,25-28 <1995>. Evangelica III. BEThL 150: 2001 ⟹187. 267-282/283-294.

5469 *Couto, António* Desafios bíblicos à prática da vida humana e cristã, uma leitura de Lc 10,25-37. Igreja e missão 54 (2001) 193-210.

5470 *Puthenpurackal, Anthony* Relevance of the parable of the Good Samaritan today. Inter Fratres 51 (2001) 149-157 [Lk 10,25-37].

5471 *Talmon, Shemaryahu* Der "barmherzige Samariter"—ein 'guter Israelit'? Kul 16 (2001) 149-160 [Lk 10,25-37].

5472 *Fee, Gordon D.* 'One thing is needful'? (Luke 10:42). To what end exegesis?. 2001 <1981> ⟹143. 3-16.

5473 *Waetjen, Herman C.* The subversion of "world" by the parable of the friend at midnight. JBL 120 (2001) 703-721 [Lk 11,5-8].

5474 *Labahn, Michael* Jesu Exorzismen (Q 11,19-20) und die Erkenntnis der ägyptischen Magier (Ex 8,15): Q 11,20 als bewährtes Beispiel für Schrift-Rezeption Jesu nach der Logienquelle. The sayings source Q. BEThL 158: 2001 ⟹477. 617-633.

5475 *Sauter, André* Luc 12,16-21: quel est mon destin?. Lire et Dire 48 (2001) 21-29.

5476 *Schröter, Jens* Verschrieben?: klärende Bemerkungen zu einem vermeintlichen Schreibfehler in Q und tatsächlichen Irrtümern. ZNW 92 (2001) 283-289 [Lk 12,22-31];

5477 Rezeptionsprozesse in der Jesusüberlieferung: Überlegungen zum historischen Charakter der neutestamentlichen Wissenschaft am Beispiel der Sorgensprüche. NTS 47 (2001) 442-468 [Lk 12,24; 12,27].

5478 *Robinson, James M.; Heil, Christoph* Noch einmal: der Schreibfehler in Q 12,27. ZNW 92 (2001) 113-122.

5479 *Friedrichsen, Timothy A.* A note on καὶ διχοτομήσει αὐτὸν (Luke 12:46 and the parallel in Matthew 24:51). CBQ 63 (2001) 258-264.

5480 *Cárdenas Pallares, José* Mientras llega lo inevitable (Lc. 12,49-59);

5481 No dejen escapar la oportunidad (Mc. [sic! leg. Lc.] 13,1-9). Qol 25 (2001) 39-44/61-65.

5482 *Sorg, Theo* Galgenfrist oder Gnadenzeit?: Bibelarbeit über Lukas 13, 6-9. ThBeitr 32 (2001) 291-298.

5483 *Kilgallen, John J.* The obligation to heal (Luke 13,10-17). Bib. 82 (2001) 402-409.

5484 *Phelps, Stephen H.* Luke 13:10-17. Interp. 55 (2001) 64-66.

5485 *Cárdenas Pallares, José* El comienzo engañoso (Lc 13,18-21). Qol 25 (2001) 79-83;

5486 La fiesta esperada (Lc 13,23-30). EfMex 19 (2001) 267-272.

5487 *Ferraro, Giuseppe* 'Oggi e domani e il terzo giorno': osservazioni su Luca 13,32-33. Gli autori divini. 2001 <1968> ⇒144. 25-34.

5488 *Baldermann, Ingo* Von Mitläufern und vom Hass gegen die Nächsten: Lukas 14,25-33. JK 62/3 (2001) 60-63.

5489 *Ceccherelli, Ignazio Marino* Se uno viene a me e non odia... (Lc 14,26). BeO 43 (2001) 131-132.

5490 *Baisas, Bienvenido Q.* Luke 15: an invitation to church leaders' conversion to Jesus' God image—a journey onto mindfulness (an interreligious reading). Charism, leadership. 2001 ⇒456. 83-98.

5491 **Bartolomé, J.J.** La alegría del Padre: estudio exegético de Lc 15. Assoc. Bíblica Española 37: 2000 ⇒16,5516. [R]Salm. 48 (2001) 171-173 (*Miquel, Esther*).

5492 **Denis, Henri** Jésus le prodigue du Père. P 2001, Paulines 120 pp. €13.42 [EeV 60,32—Rastoin, Cécile] [Lk 15].

5493 *Lombard, Denis* Une lecture de Luc 15. SémBib 101 (2001) 50-55.

5494 **Betto, Frei** Os dois irmãos: versão atualizada da parábola do Filho Pródigo, do evangelho de Lucas 15,11 a 32. São Paulo 2001, Salesiana 29 pp. 85-87997-56-4.

5495 **Holgate, David A.** Prodigality, liberality and meanness in the parable of the prodigal son: a Greco-Roman perspective on Luke 15.11-32. JSNT.S 187: 1999 ⇒15,5558. [R]JBL 120 (2001) 570-572 (*Sheeley, Steven M.*); RBLit 3 (2001) 400-402 (*Sheeley, Steven M.*).

5496 *Räisänen, Heikki* The prodigal gentile and his Jewish christian brother: Lk 15,11-32. Challenges to biblical interpretation. BiblInterp 59: 2001 <1992> ⇒200. 37-60.

5497 *Sugirtharajah, R.S.* Son(s) behaving badly: the prodigal in foreign hands. Postmodern interpretations. 2001 ⇒229. 195-206 [Lk 15,11-32].

5498   *Greene, M. Dwaine* The parable of the unjust steward as question and challenge. ET 112 (2001) 82-88 [Lk 16,1-8].

5499   *Morschauser, Scott N.* Revolutionary economics?: once again, the parable of the Steward. JHiC 8/1 (2001) 49-67 [Lk 16,1-8].

5500   **Cheong, C.-S. Abraham** A dialogic reading of the steward parable (Luke 16:1-9). Studies in Biblical Literature 28: NY 2001, Lang xxiv; 239 pp. $36. 0-8204-5002-2. Bibl. 217-233.

5501   *Bowen, Edward C.* The parable of the unjust steward: *oikos* as the interpretative key. ET 112 (2001) 314-315 [Lk 16,1-13].

5502   *Lys, Daniel* Les richesses injustes: Luc 16/1-13. ETR 76 (2001) 391-398.

5503   *Neirynck, Frans* The divorce saying in Q 16,18 <1995>;

5504   Saving/losing one's life: Luke 17,33 (Q?) and Mark 8,35 <1998>. Evangelica III. BEThL 150: 2001 ⇒187. 462-479/480-503.

5505   *Wetzlaugk, Sigrun* "Schaffe mir Recht ...!"—eine Witwe kämpft um ihr Recht: Lukas 18,1-8. JK 62/5 (2001) 55-58.

5506   *Dietz, François* Luc 19,1-10: Zachée ou le salut sans condition. Lire et Dire 48 (2001) 13-19.

5507   *Parsons, Mikeal C.* 'Short in stature': Luke's physical description of Zacchaeus. NTS 47 (2001) 50-57 [Lk 19,1-10].

5508   *Baarda, Tjitze* The 'foolish' or 'deaf' fig-tree: concerning Luke 19:4 in the Diatessaron. NT 43 (2001) 161-177.

5509   *Janzen, Anna* Wer hat, bekommt mehr—Lob oder Urteil?: das Gleichnis vom anvertrauten Geld in der Logienquelle. Zeitschrift für Theologie und Gemeinde 6 (2001) 40-59 [{Lk 19,11-27].

5510   *Denaux, Adelbert* The parable of the talents/pounds (Q 19,12-27): a reconstruction of the Q text. The sayings source Q. BEThL 158: 2001 ⇒477. 429-460 [Mt 25,14-30].

5511   **Grangaard, Blake R.** Conflict and authority in Luke 19:47 to 21:4. 1999 ⇒15,5578. ᴿCBQ 63 (2001) 145-146 (*Bridge, Steven L.*).

5512   *Birot, Antoine* Drame divin, côté Père: une exégèse théologique de la parabole des vignerons. Com(F) 26/4 (2001) 97-114 [Lk 20,9-15].

F7.8 **Passio**—Lc 22...

5513   **Matson, Mark A.** In dialogue with another gospel?: the influence of the fourth gospel on the passion narrative of the gospel of Luke. Diss. Duke. SBL.DS 178: Atlanta, GA 2001, SBL xiii; 479 pp. $54. 1-58983-010-5. Bibl. 449-479.

5514   **Scaer, Peter** The Lukan passion and the praiseworthy death. Diss. Notre Dame 2001, ᴰ*Neyrey, J.* 191 pp. [RTL 33,640].

5515 *Sterling, Greg* Mors philosophi: the death of Jesus in Luke. HThR 94 (2001) 383-402.

5516 **Ponessa, Joseph** Doubling elements in Luke 22:15-20 and 1 Corinthians 11:23-26 in the light of ancient languages and literatures. Diss. Pont. Biblical Institute 2001, ᴰ*Vanhoye, Albert*: Sum. AcBib 10,873.

5517 *McGowan, Andrew* The inordinate cup: issues of order in early eucharistic drinking. StPatr 35 (2001) 283-291 [Lk 22,17-20; 1 Cor 10, 16].

5518 *Gramaglia, Pier Angelo* Analisi linguistica di Lc xxii,28-30: eucaristia ed escatologia. ATT 7 (2001) 255-298.

5519 **Gonsalves, Max** The passion of Jesus according to Luke: a narrative critical study of Luke 22:39-23:49. Extr. Diss. Urbaniana 2001, ᴰ*Biguzzi, Giancarlo*: R 2001, 140 pp. [Lk 22,39-49].

5520 **Harrington, Jay M.** The Lukan passion narrative: the Markan material in Luke 22,54-23,25: a historical survey: 1891-1997. NTTS 30: 2000 ⇒16,5547. ᴿThLZ 126 (2001) 1149-1152 (*Lang, Manfred*); Bib. 82 (2001) 573-576 (*Kilgallen, John J.*).

5521 **Bielinski, Krzystof** Prophet im Widerspruch: eine narrativ-sozialgeschichtliche Untersuchung zu Lk 23,6-12. Diss. München 2001, ᴰ*Gnilka, Joachim*: 231 pp. [RTL 33,636].

5522 *Byrne, Brendan* Peter as resurrection witness in the Lucan narrative. ᶠO'COLLINS, G. 2001 ⇒111. 19-33.

5523 *Schwemer, Anna Maria* Der Auferstandene und die Emmausjünger. Auferstehung—Resurrection. WUNT 135: 2001 ⇒452. 95-117 [Lk 24].

5524 *Neirynck, Frans* Once more Luke 24,12. Evangelica III. BEThL 150: 2001 <1994> ⇒187. 549-578.

5525 *Correia, João Alberto Sousa* O caminho do reconhecimento em do anúncio: Lc 24,13-35 em perspectiva cristológica. Theologica 36 (2001) 359-402.

5526 *Johnson, Luke Timothy* The eucharist and the identity of Jesus. PrPe 15 (2001) 230-235 [Lk 24,35].

5527 *Mierzwa, Tadeusz* Gesù risorto l'adempimento delle scritture e la pienezza escatologica: analisi del brano Lc 24,44-49. CoTh 71A (2001) 53-66.

5528 **Mekkattukunnel, Andrews George** The priestly blessing of the risen Christ: an exegetico-theological analysis of Luke 24,50-53. Diss. Gregoriana. EHS.T 714: Fra 2001, Lang 261 pp. $42. 3-906765-91-1. Bibl. 231-255.

F8.1 *Actus Apostolorum*, **Acts**—*text, commentary, topics*

5529   *Adoniran, Marcos* O Espírito Santo no livro dos Atos: o agitador social de Deus. Estudos Bíblicos 70 (2001) 110-118.

5530   *Ballabio, Fabio* Tra ebrei e gentili: la chiesa negli Atti degli Apostoli. Studi Fatti Ricerche 94 (2001) 3-11.

5531   *Barbi, Augusto* Le cronologie degli Atti. RStB 13/2 (2001) 25-63.

5532   **Barrett, Charles Kingsley** A critical and exegetical commentary on the Acts of the Apostles, 1-2. ICC: 1994-1998 ⇒14,5082; 16,5563. ᴿJThS 52 (2001) 691-703 (*Alexander, Loveday*).

5533   **Beilner, Wolfgang** Der Geist treibt seine Kirche. Vermittlung 82: Salzburg 2000, n.p. 156 pp.

5534   **Chocheyras, Jacques** Les actes des apôtres Pierre et Paul: histoire, tradition et légende. Faits religieux et société: P 2001, L'Harmattan 312 pp. €24.65. 2-7475-1179-0.

5535   *Comblin, José* A ressurreição nos Atos dos Apóstolos. Estudos Bíblicos 70 (2001) 65-72.

5536   *Correia, João Luiz* Atos dos Apóstolos: texto e contexto. Estudos Bíblicos 70 (2001) 10-29.

5537   **Darù, Jean** Dio ha aperto anche ai pagani la porta della fede (At 14,27): una lettura degli Atti degli Apostoli. Bibbia e Preghiera 40: R 2001, ADP 175 pp. 88-7357-254-5. Bibl. 169-171.

5538   **Dumais, Marcel** Communauté et mission: une lecture des Actes des Apôtres. Montréal 2000, Bellarmin 206 pp. Préf. de *Jacques Dupont*.

5539   **Eckey, Wilfried** Die Apostelgeschichte: der Weg des Evangeliums von Jerusalem nach Rom, 1-2. 2000 ⇒16,5568. ᴿThLZ 126 (2001) 1147-1149 (*Schille, Gottfried*).

5540   **Fitzmyer, Joseph A.** The Acts of the Apostles. AncB 31: 1998 ⇒14, 5086... 16,5569. ᴿJBL 119 (2000) 144-146 (*Tannehill, Robert C.*).

5541   *Fontana, Raniero* L'"opera" di Luca: storia dello Spirito e alchimia dell'umano (At 1-15). BeO 43 (2001) 215-234.

5542   *Freire, Anízio* A imagem de Jesus em Atos. Estudos Bíblicos 70 (2001) 48-64.

5543   **Gabba, Emilio** Gli Atti degli apostoli e la storiografia greca e romana nel I sec. a.C. RStB 13/2 (2001) 9-13.

5544   **Gargano, Innocenzo** Lectio divina sugli Atti degli Apostoli: conversazioni bibliche: Bo ²2001, Dehoniane 220 pp. €12.91.

5545   Die Geschichte der Apostel. Fischer Taschenbuch 14503: Fra 2000, Fischer 96 pp. 3-596-14503-1. Mit einer Einleitung von *P.D. James*.

5546   **Gonzalez, Justo L.** Acts: the gospel of the Spirit. Mkn 2001, Orbis xviii; 291 pp. $30. 1-57075-398-9 [BiTod 40,63—Senior, Donald].

5547 *Gräßer, Erich* Studien zur Acta-Forschung: Rückblick und Ausblick;

5548 Die Lösung des Problems der Parusieverzögerung in der Apostelgeschichte <1957, 1960, 1977>;

5549 Die Apostelgeschichte in der Forschung der Gegenwart <1960>;

5550 Acta-Forschung seit 1960 <1976-1977>;

5551 Vorwort zur 7. Auflage des Acta-Kommentars von Ernst Haenchen <1977>;

5552 Die Parusieerwartung in der Apostelgeschichte <1979>;

5553 Ta peri tès Basileias (Apg 1,3; 19,8). Forschungen zur Apostelgeschichte <1985>. WUNT 137: 2001 ⇒152. 1-47/48-58/59-133/134-287/288-291/292-320/321-333.

5554 *Green, Joel B.* Persevering together in prayer: the significance of prayer in the Acts of the Apostles. Into God's presence. 2001 ⇒294. 183-202.

5555 *Guttenberger, Gudrun* Ist der Tod der Apostel der Rede nicht wert?: Vorstellungen von Tod und Sterben in den lukanischen Acta. Das Ende des Paulus. BZNW 106: 2001 ⇒281. 273-305.

5556 *Haacker, Klaus* Das Bild der Kirche in der Apostelgeschichte des Lukas. ThBeitr 32 (2001) 70-89.

5557 *Hengel, Martin* Der Jude Paulus und sein Volk: zu einem neuen Acta-Kommentar. ThR 66 (2001) 338-368.

5558 *Jankowski, Gerhard* Und sie werden hören: die Apostelgeschichte des Lukas, erster Teil (1,1-9,31)—eine Auslegung. TeKo 24/3 (2001) 1-169.

5559 **Jervell, Jacob Stephan** Die Apostelgeschichte. KEK 3: 1998 ⇒14, 5087... 16,5572. [R]NTT 102 (2001) 75-85 (*Larsson, Edvin*); ThR 66 (2001) 338-368 (*Hengel, Martin*); JBL 119 (2000) 141-144 (*Stenschke, Christoph*).

5560 *Jossa, Giorgio* Gli ellenisti e i timorati di Dio. RStB 13/2 (2001) 103-122;

5561 Gli ellenisti e i timorati di Dio negli Atti degli Apostoli. I gruppi giudaici. 2001 ⇒5195. 105-131.

5562 *Kea, Perry* Source theories for the Acts of the Apostles. FORUM 4/1 (2001) 7-26.

5563 **Kisau, Paul** 'As many as the Lord our God shall call to Himself': a study of the theme of inclusiveness in the Acts of the Apostles. Diss. Aberdeen 2001, [D]*Bond, H.* [RTL 33,639].

5564 **Kollmann, Bernd** Joseph Barnabas: Leben und Wirkungsgeschichte. 1998 ⇒14,11859. [R]SNTU.A 25 (2000) 261-263 (*Tiwald, M.*).

5565 *Larkin, William J. Jr.* Mission in Acts. Mission in the NT. ASMS 27: 2001 ⇒367. 170-186.

5566 **Latham, Tony Glenn** Affirming the witness: Luke's narrative techniques of affirmation in the book of Acts. Diss. Southwestern Baptist Sem. 2001, 258 pp. 3010750.

5567 **Malas, William Holder** The literary structure of Acts: a narratological investigation into its arrangement: plot, and primary themes. Diss. Richmond 2001, ᴰ*Kingsbury, J.D.* 269 pp. 3019383 [RTL 33,639].

5568 **Marguerat, Daniel L.** La première histoire du christianisme: les Actes des apôtres. LeDiv 180: 1999 ⇒15,5357; 16,5606. ᴿCEv 115 (2001) 66 (*Stricher, Joseph*); NT 43 (2001) 302-304 (*Read-Heimerdinger, Jenny*); AnnTh 15 (2001) 374-375 (*Tábet, M.*); RHPhR 81 (2001) 457-459 (*Grappe, Ch.*); RCatT 26 (2001) 208-211 (*Puig i Tàrrech, Armand*).

5569 **Matthews, Shelly** First converts: rich pagan women and the rhetoric of mission in early Judaism and christianity. Contraversions: Jews and their differences: Stanford, CA 2001, Stanford University Press xiv; (2) 164 pp. $49.50. 0-8047-3592-1. Bibl. 143-160.

5570 **Mosconi, Luis** Atos dos Apóstolos: como ser igreja no início do terceiro milênio?. São Paulo ²2001, Filhas de São Paulo 232 pp. [REB 61,516].

5571 **Neuberth, Ralph** Demokratie im Volk Gottes: Untersuchungen zur Apostelgeschichte. SBB 46: Stu 2001, Kath. Bibelwerk xvi; 420 pp. €45.90. 3-460-00461-4 [Acts 6,1-7; 13,1-3; 15,1-41; 20,17-38].

5572 No caminho das comunidades: Atos dos Apóstolos: roteiros e subsídios para encontros. Do povo para o povo: São Paulo 2001, Paulus 148 pp. Centro Bíblico Verbo [REB 61,755].

5573 **Nodet, Étienne; Taylor, J. Justin** Le origini del cristianesimo. 2000 ⇒16,5611. ᴿCivCatt 152/4 (2001) 314-316 (*Mazzolini, D.*).

5574 *Penna, Romano* Il tema del 'viaggio' negli *Atti* lucani e nella letteratura dell'ambiente. Vangelo e inculturazione. 2001 ⇒193. 110-144 & RStB 13/2 (2001) 143-170.

5575 *Pervo, Richard I.* Meet right—and our bounden duty: community meetings in Acts. FORUM 4/1 (2001) 45-62.

5576 *Pitta, Antonio* Gli Atti degli apostoli: storiografia e biografia: introduzione. RStB 13/2 (2001) 5-8.

5577 *Redalié, Yann* L'immagine di Paolo negli Atti degli apostoli. RStB 13/2 (2001) 123-141.

5578 **Richard, Pablo** O movimento de Jesus depois da ressurreição, uma interpretação libertadora dos Atos dos Apóstolos. 1999 ⇒16,5619. ᴿEstudos Bíblicos 71 (2001) 78-80 (*Farias, Jacir de Freitas*).

5579 **Rius-Camps, Josep** Comentari als Fets dels Apòstols. 2000, 4 vols. ⇒16,5580. ᴿRCatT 26 (2001) 403-408 (*Puig i Tàrrech, Armand*).

5580 *Rius-Camps, Josep* Las variantes del texto occidental de los Hechos de los Apóstoles ((XIII) (Hch 7,23-8,1a). FgNT 14 (2001) 131-148.

5581 *Salvador, J.* Atos dos Apóstolos: introdução. RCB 97/98 (2001) 5-18.

5582 *Santos, Ederivaldo Guerra, al.*, Meditação do livro dos Atos dos Apóstolos. RCB 97/98 (2001) 95-151.

5583 *Simonet, Jean-Louis* Les citations des Actes des Apôtres dans les chapitres édités du *Kᵉtábá dᵊrêš mellê* de Jean BAR PENKAYE. Muséon 114 (2001) 97-119.

5584 ᴱ**Terra, João Evangelista Martins** Atos dos Apóstolos. RCB 97/98 (2001) 167 pp.

5585 *Terra, João Evangelista Martins* Atos dos Apóstolos;

5586 Uma leitura espiritual dos Atos dos Apóstolos. RCB 97/98 (2001) 19-45/46-94.

5587 *Trebilco, Paul* I 'Timorati di Dio'. Gli ebrei nell'impero romano. 2001 <1991> ⇒415. 161-193.

5588 *Troiani, Lucio* Gli Atti degli apostoli e il mondo ebraico-ellenistico. RStB 13/2 (2001) 15-24.

5589 *Tyson, Joseph B.* The legacy of F.C. BAUR & recent studies of Acts. FORUM 4/1 (2001) 125-144.

5590 Vorarbeiten zum Johannesevangelium und zur Apostelgeschichte. BVLI 45 (2001) 27.

5591 *Wander, Bernd, al.*, Judenchristen. RGG², 4. 2001 ⇒664. 601-609.

5592 **Williams, Benjamin E.** Miracle stories in the biblical book Acts of the Apostles. Mellen 59: Lewiston, NY 2001, Mellen (10) vi; 223 pp. 0-7734-7585-0. Bibl. 209-218.

5593 *Winter, Sarah C.* Antioch in Acts & Maccoby's 'two-tiered' christianity. FORUM 4/1 (2001) 27-44.

5594 **Witherington, Ben, III** The Acts of the Apostles: a socio-rhetorical commentary. 1998 ⇒14,5097... 16,5587. ᴿSNTU.A 23 (1998) 268-271 (*Fuchs, Albert*); JThS 52 (2001) 691-703 (*Alexander, Loveday*); JDh 26 (2001) 552-554 (*Pathrapankal, Joseph*)

F8.3 *Ecclesia primaeva Actuum*—Die Urgemeinde

5595 *Bohlen, Reinhold* Judentum und Kirche im 1. Jahrhundert: Vortrag anlässlich eines Studientages... Oktober 2000 im St. Josefs-Stift, Trier. Katholische Bildung 102/1 (2001) 28-35.

5596 *Bovon, François* Names and numbers in early christianity. NTS 47 (2001) 267-288.

5597 *Braun, Willi* The past as simulacrum in the canonical narratives of christian origins. R & T 8 (2001) 213-228.

5598 *Dassmann, Ernst* Beten am Anfang der Kirche. Lebendige Katechese 23 (2001) 106-108.

5599 *Fabris, Rinaldo* La comunità di Gerusalemme. RStB 13/2 (2001) 65-82 [Acts 1,1-8,4].

5600 *Feuillet, A.* Crenças fundamentais e vida comunidade primitiva segundo os Atos dos Apóstolos. RCB 97/98 (2001) 152-167.

5601 *Freyne, Seán* The geography of restoration: Galilee-Jerusalem relations in early Jewish and christian experience. NTS 47 (2001) 289-311.

5602 *Georgi, Dieter* Was the early church Jewish?. BiRe 17/6 (2001) 33-37, 51-52.

5603 **Gnilka, Joachim** Die frühen Christen: Ursprünge und Anfang der Kirche. HThK.S 7: 1999 ⇒15,5656. [R]ThRv 97 (2001) 44-46 (*Dassmann, Ernst*); SaThZ 5 (2001) 58-59 (*Huber, Konrad*); Biblos 50 (2001) 369-370 (*Henner, Jutta*).

5604 *Leutzsch, Martin* Zeit und Geld im Neuen Testament. 'Leget Anmut'. Jabboq 1: 2001 ⇒350. 44-104 [Lk 16,1-8].

5605 **Manns, Frederic** L'Israele di Dio: sinagoga e chiesa alle origini cristiane. CSB 32: 1998 ⇒14,5151; 16,5659. [R]Asp. 48 (2001) 456-457 (*Di Palma, Gaetano*).

5606 **Nam, Jong Sung** Roots and tensions. worship patterns developed from the synagogue to the Jerusalem church. Diss. Fuller Sem. 2001, 344 pp. 3003173.

5607 *Otten, Willemien* Early christianity between divine promise and earthly politics. Religious identity. 2001 ⇒549. 60-83.

5608 *Rivas Rebaque, Fernando* Protagonismo y marginación de la mujer en el cristianismo primitivo: Asia Menor (siglos I-II). MCom 59 (2001) 709-737.

5609 *Schmeller, Thomas* Urchristliche Gemeindebildung in ihrem sozialen Kontext. BiKi 56 (2001) 212-218.

5610 *Schultze, Harald* "Zufällige Geschichtswahrheiten": LESSING und SEMLER im Streit. ZThK 98 (2001) 449-463.

5611 *Söding, Thomas* Der Gottesdienst der Urgemeinde: Perspektiven des lukanischen Bildes in Apg 2,42. [F]LEHMANN, K. 2001 ⇒63. 81-96.

5612 *Stegemann, Wolfgang* Christentum als universalisiertes Judentum?: Anfragen an G. Theißens "Theorie des Urchristentums". KuI 16 (2001) 130-148.

5613 *Taylor, Justin* The community of goods among the first Christians and among the Essenes. Historical perspectives. StTDJ 37: 2001 ⇒ 612. 147-161.

5614 *Theobald, Michael* 'Wir haben hier keine bleibende Stadt, sondern suchen die zukünftige' (Hebr 13,14): die Stadt als Ort der frühen christlichen Gemeinde. Studien zum Römerbrief. WUNT 136: 2001 <1988> ⇒219. 538-562.

5615 *Venetz, Hermann-Josef* Die Gemeinde des Messias Jesu und die Praxis der Königsherrschaft Gottes: Gedanken zu den "Anfängen der Kirche". BiKi 56 (2001) 194-202.

5616 *Wenning, Robert* Treffpunkte. BiKi 56 (2001) 224-227.

F8.5 Ascensio, Pentecostes; ministerium Petri—*Act 1*...

5617 *Bazlez, Marie-Françoise* L'Ascension dans la pensée grecque et le judaïsme hellénisé. MoBi 133 (2001) 46-47 [BuBB 32,56].

5618 *Casalá, Luis* Esperando un nuevo Pentecostés: 'Es verdad, resucitó el Señor' (Lucas 24,34). CuMon 36/1 (2001) 45-55.

5619 *Chenu, Bruno* L'Ascension facette du mystère de Pâques. MoBi 133 (2001) 48-49 [BuBB 32,56].

5620 **Donne, Christian** L'annonce de la bonne nouvelle de Dieu: une analyse de la figure narrative de Dieu dans les discours pétriniens d'évangélisation des Actes des Apôtres (Ac 2,14-40; 3,12-26; 4,8-12; 5,29-32; 10,34-43). Diss. Ottawa 2001, [D]*Dumais, M.* [RTL 33,637].

5621 *Ellis, Edward Earle* 'The end of the earth' (Acts 1:8). History and interpretation. BiblInterp 54: 2001 ⇒141. 53-63.

5622 *Dunn, James D.G.* The ascension of Jesus: a test case for hermeneutics. Auferstehung—Resurrection. WUNT 135: 2001 ⇒452. 301-322 [Acts 1,9-11].

5623 *Alvarez Valdes, Ariel* ¿Quiénes estuvieron presentes el día de Pentecostés?. CuesTP 28 (2001) 135-140 [Acts 2].

5624 *Jobling, David* Postmodern pentecost: a reading of Acts 2. Postmodern interpretations. 2001 ⇒229. 207-218.

5625 *Kilgallen, J.J.* The use of Psalm 16:8-11 in Peter's pentecost speech. ET 113 (2001) 47-50 [Acts 2].

5626 *Penna, Romano* Il racconto lucano della pentecoste: dalla teofania del Sinai al dono dello Spirito di Cristo. Vangelo e inculturazione. 2001 <2000> ⇒193. 705-728 [Acts 2].

5627 *Valério, Paulo F.* Babel e pentecostes (Gn 11,1-9 e At 2,1-13). Estudos Bíblicos 70 (2001) 73-82.

5628 *Granados, Juan Manuel* Conversión, arrepentimiento y don del Espíritu en Hechos 2,38. ThX 51 (2001) 355-380.

5629 *Lawson, Steven J.* The priority of biblical preaching: an expository study of Acts 2:42-47. BS 158 (2001) 198-217.

5630 *Strelan, Rick* Keys to the Gate Beautiful. JBS 1/3 (2001). http://journalofbiblicalstudies.org/issu [Acts 3,1-10].

5631 *Ferraro, Giuseppe* 'Kairoi anapsyxeos': annotazioni su Atti 3,20. Gli autori divini. 2001 <1975> ⇒144. 50-59.

5632 **Lloyd-Jones, David Martyn** Authentic christianity: sermons on the Acts of the Apostles, 2: Acts 4-5. E 2001, Banner of Truth Trust vii; 328 pp. 0-85151-807-9.

5633 *Cifrak, Mario* "Pattern": Juda galilejac-Kvirinijev popis, bez Kvirinija u DJ 5,37. BoSm 71 (2001) 147-152. **Croatian.**

5634 **Dobbeler, Axel von** Der Evangelist Philippus in der Geschichte des Urchristentums: eine prosopographische Skizze. TANZ 30: 2000 ⇒ 16,5672. ᴿBZ 45 (2001) 139-142 (*Erlemann, Kurt*); ThLZ 126 (2001) 278-281 (*Schenke, Hans-Martin*) [Acts 6,1-6; 8,4-40; 21,8-9].

5635 *Strus, Andrzej* Bet Gemal: pathway to the tradition of Saints Stephen and Gamaliel. R 2001, Pont. Univ. Salesiana 69 pp. Bibl. 65-67 [Acts 6-7].

5636 **Jeska, Joachim** Die Geschichte Israels in der Sicht des Lukas: Apg 7,2b-53 und 13,17-25 im Kontext antik-jüdischer Summarien der Geschichte Israels. FRLANT 195: Gö 2001, Vandenhoeck & R 336 pp. €64. 3-525-53879-0. Bibl. 302-329.

5637 *Stowasser, Martin* Am 5,25-27; 9,11 f. in der Qumranüberlieferung und in der Apostelgeschichte: text- und traditionsgeschichtliche Überlegungen zu 4Q174 (Florilegium) III 12/CD VII 16/Apg 7,42b-43; 15,16-18. ZNW 92 (2001) 47-63.

5638 **Heintz, Florent** Simon "le Magicien": Actes 8, 5-25 et l'accusation de magie contre les prophètes thaumaturges dans l'antiquité. 1997 ⇒ 13,5573... 16,5678. ᴿRBLit 3 (2001) 419-421 (*Gilbert, Gary*).

5639 *Noja Noseda, Sergio* Le Coran, le *Sāmirī* et Simon le Mage. ᴹCAGNI, L., 4. SMDSA 61: 2001 ⇒15. 1925-1935 [Acts 8,9].

5640 *Lof, Andreas* Actes 8,26-40: le baptême de l'eunuque éthiopien. Lire et Dire 48 (2001) 21-31 [BuBB 33,137].

5641 *Monaco, David G.* Filippo e l'eunuco (At 8,26-40): un analisi esegetica. LSDC 16 (2001) 273-288.

5642 *Dehn, Ulrich* Weggefährten: Unwägbarkeiten einer Reise (Apg 8,29-39). ZMiss 27 (2001) 107-108.

5643 *Strelan, Rick* The running prophet (Acts 8:30). NT 43 (2001) 31-38.

5644 **Peace, Richard V.** Conversion in the New Testament: Paul and the Twelve. 1999 ⇒15,5688; 16,5684. ᴿThLZ 126 (2001) 642-644 (*Roloff, Jürgen*) [Acts 9,1-22].

5645 *Barthes, Roland* The structural analysis of narrative: apropos of Acts 10-11. The postmodern bible reader. 2001 <1988> ⇒287. 58-77.

5646 **Zetterholm, Magnus** Synagogue and separation: a social-scientific approach to the formation of christianity in Antioch. Diss. Lund 2001 [Acts 11].

5647 *Morton, Russell* Acts 12:1-19. Interp. 55 (2001) 67-69.

5648 *Gramaglia, Pier Angelo* La clandestinità di Pietro (*At* 12,17). ᴹCAGNI, L., 3. SMDSA 61: 2001 ⇒15. 1589-1609.

F8.7 Act 13...*Itinera Pauli*; Paul's journeys

5649 *Bauer, Dieter; Hecht, Anneliese; Kaiser, Helga* Die Reisen des Paulus durch Kleinasien und Griechenland. WUB 20 (2001) 30-54.

5650 **Clark, Andrew C.** Parallel lives: the relation of Paul to the apostles in the Lucan perspective. Paternoster biblical and theological monographs: Carlisle 2001, Paternoster xviii; 385 pp, 1-84227-035-4. Bibl. 342-372.

5651 *Deutschmann, Anton* Die paulinischen Gemeinden aus Juden und Heiden in der Apostelgeschichte. [F]HAINZ, J. 2001 ⇒42. 200-222.

5652 **Elledge, Casey Deryl** Resurrection and the end of history: the resurrection motif in Paul's preaching and defense in the Acts of the Apostles. Diss. Princeton Sem. 2001, 379 pp. 3006827.

5653 **Mauck, J.W.** Paul on trial: the book of Acts as a defense of christianity. Nv 2001, Nelson xviii; 236 pp. $15. 0-7852-4598-7.

5654 *Peregrino, Artur* A igreja peregrina. Estudos Bíblicos 70 (2001) 40-47.

5655 **Porter, Stanley E.** The Paul of Acts: essays in literary criticism, rhetoric, and theology. WUNT 115: 1999 ⇒15,5694; 16,5702. [R]Salm. 48 (2001) 351-357 (*Trevijano, Ramón*); SNTU.A 25 (2000) 248-249 (*Fuchs, Albert*);

5656 Paul in Acts. Peabody 2001, Hendrickson ix; 233 pp. $25. 1-56563-613-9 [BiTod 40,403—Senior, Donald].

5657 **Reichardt, Michael** Psychologische Erklärung der paulinischen Damaskusvision?: ein Beitrag zum interdisziplinären Gespräch zwischen Exegese und Psychologie seit dem 18. Jahrhundert. SBB 42: 1999 ⇒15,5695. [R]ThRv 97 (2001) 37-39 (*Möde, Erwin*); ThLZ 126 (2001) 931-933 (*Merk, Otto*); SNTU.A 25 (2000) 260-261 (*Oberforcher, R.*).

5658 *Sanday, William* Paul's attitude towards Peter and James. Essays in biblical criticism. JSNT.S 225: 2001 <1896> ⇒205. 217-223.

5659 **Maryono, Petrus** Luke's use of biblical history and promise in Acts 13:16-41. Diss. Dallas Sem. 2001, 304 pp. 3002967.

5660 **Deutschmann, Anton** Synagoge und Gemeindebildung: christliche Gemeinde und Israel in der Apostelgeschichte des Lukas untersucht am Beispiel von Apg 13,42-52. Diss. München 2000, [D]*Laub, F.*: Rg 2001, Pustet 279 pp. €34.90. 3-7917-1765-0.

5661 *Hoppe, Rudolf* Schöpfungstheologie und Anthropologie: Überlegungen zu Apg 14,8-18 und 17,16-34. [F]SCHMUTTERMAYR, G. 2001 ⇒ 101. 173-186.

5662   *Bechard, Dean P.* Paul among the rustics: the Lystran episode (Acts 14:8-20) and Lucan apologetic. CBQ 63 (2001) 84-101.

5663   **Bechard, Dean Philip** Paul outside the walls: a study of Luke's socio-geographical universalism in Acts 14:8-20. AnBib 143: 2000 ⇒ 16,5711. [R]CBQ 63 (2001) 737-738 (*Gormley, Joan Frances*).

5664   **Okoronkwo, Michael Enyinwa** The Jerusalem compromise as a conflict-resolution model: a rhetoric-communicative analysis of Acts 15 in the light of modern linguistics. Diss. Bonn, [D]*Merklein, Helmut*: Arbeiten zur Interkulturalität 1: Bonn 2001, Borengässer xiii; 302 pp. €26.80. 3-923946-52-X. Bibl. 281-302. [R]VSVD 42 (2001) 510-512 (*Gaioni, Dominic*).

5665   *Rothgangel, Martin* Apg 15 als Darstellung des Jerusalemer Apostelkonvents?: eine "einleitungswissenschaftliche Reminiszenz". [F]SCHMUTTERMAYR, G. 2001 ⇒101. 237-246.

5666   *Segal, Alan F.* Acts 15 as Jewish & christian history;

5667   *Taussig, Hal* Jerusalem as occasion for conversation: the intersection of Acts 15 and Galatians 2;

5668   *Tyson, Joseph B.* Themes at the crossroads: Acts 15 in its Lukan setting. FORUM 4/1 (2001) 63-87/89-104/105-124.

5669   **Wehnert, Jürgen** Die Reinheit des "christlichen Gottesvolkes" aus Juden und Heiden: Studien zum historischen und theologischen Hintergrund des sogenannten Aposteldekrets. FRLANT 173: 1997 ⇒13, 5595 ... 16,5717. [R]Henoch 23 (2001) 387-389 (*Gianotto, Claudio*).

5670   *Taylor, Justin* The Jerusalem decrees (Acts 15.20,29 and 21.25) and the incident at Antioch (Gal 2.11-14). NTS 47 (2001) 372-380.

5671   *McMillan, David K.* Acts 15:22-31. Interp. 55 (2001) 420-422.

5672   *Sanday, William* The text of the apostolic decree (Acts 15:29). Essays in biblical criticism. JSNT.S 225: 2001 <1913> ⇒205. 224-237.

5673   **Cara, Robert J.** The ambiguous characterization of Barnabas in Acts 15:36-41. Diss. Westminster Theol. Sem. 2001, 192 pp. 3010598.

5674   *Rakotojoelinandrasana, Daniel* The gospel in adversity: reading Acts 16:16-34 in African context. WaW 21/2 (2001) 191-197.

5675   **Dahle, Lars** Acts 17:16-34: an apologetic model then and now?. Diss. Open 2001, [D]*Cook, E. David* [TynB 53,313-316].

5676   **Darlington, Obhafuorieso Victor** The Lukan Paul's encounter with the Athenians (Acts 17,16-34): a contextual theological study for the Nigerian Church. Extr. Diss. Angelicum, R 2001, 98 pp. Bibl. 85-95.

5677   *Penna, Romano* Paolo nell'agorà e all'areopago di Atene (At 17,16-34): un confronto tra vangelo e cultura. Vangelo e inculturazione. 2001 <1995> ⇒193. 365-390.

5678 *Quesnel, Michel* Paul prédicateur dans les Actes des Apôtres. NTS 47 (2001) 469-481 [Acts 20].

5679 *Horn, Friedrich Wilhelm* Die letzte Jerusalemreise des Paulus [Acts 20-21; Rom 15,22-33];

5680 *Ballhorn, Geeske* Die Miletrede—ein Literaturbericht [Acts 20,17-35]. Das Ende des Paulus. BZNW 106: 2001 ⇒281. 15-35/37-47.

5681 *Guillet, Jacques* Les Actes des apôtres (11), (12). Croire aujourd'hui 106, 107 (2001) 30-31 [Acts 21-28].

5682 *Brenk, Frederick E.; Canali de Rossi, Filippo* The 'notorious' Felix, procurator of Judaea, and his many wives (Acts 23-24). Bib. 82 (2001) 410-417.

5683 *Reiser, Marius* Von Caesarea nach Malta: literarischer Charakter und historische Glaubwürdigkeit von Act 27;

5684 *Labahn, Michael* Paulus—ein homo honestus et iustus: das lukanische Paulusportrait von Act 27-28 im Lichte ausgewählter antiker Parallelen. Das Ende des Paulus. 2001 ⇒281. 49-74/75-106.

5685 *Hummel, Adrian* Factum et fictum: literarische und theologische Erwägungen zur Romreise des Paulus in der Apostelgeschichte (Apg 27,1-28,16). BN 106 (2001) 99.

5686 *Tilly, Michael* Das Ende des Paulus und die syrische Texttradition Act 28,17-31 in der Überlieferung der Peschitto;

5687 *Omerzu, Heike* Das Schweigen des Lukas: Überlegungen zum offenen Ende der Apostelgeschichte [Acts 28,30-31]. Das Ende des Paulus. BZNW 106: 2001 ⇒281. 107-125/127-156.

X. Johannes

G1.1 *Corpus johanneum*: **John and his community**

5688 *Blanchard, Yves-Marie* Le sacrifice dans l'évangile et les épîtres de Jean. CEv 118 (2001) 39-47.

5689 **Culpepper, R. Alan** John, the son of Zebedee: the life of a legend. 2000 <1994> ⇒16,5744. ᴿStMon 43 (2001) 405-406 (*Pou, A.*); ThLZ 126 (2001) 1037-1039 (*Nagel, Titus*).

5690 **Engel, Werner** Die Gemeinde des Johannes: Untersuchungen zur Ekklesiologie und zum Selbstverständnis der johanneischen Gemeinde. Diss. Wien 2001, ᴰ*Pratscher, W.* 201 pp [RTL 33,637].

5691 *Erdmann, Martin* Mission in John's gospel and letters. Mission in the NT. ASMS 27: 2001 ⇒367. 207-226.

5692 **Ferraro, Giuseppe** La gioia di Cristo: nel quarto vangelo, nelle lettere giovannee e nell'Apocalisse. Letture bibliche (Vaticano) 13: 2000
⇒16,5750. [R]Ang. 78 (2001) 734-736 (*Marcato, Giorgio*); LSDC 16
(2001) 397-398 (*Iodice, Michele*); Ho Theologos 19 (2001) 470-473
(*Nicolaci, M.A.*); CivCatt 152/1 (2001) 316-317 *Simone, M.*).

5693 *Ferraro, Giuseppe* Lo Spirito Santo negli scritti giovannei. Gli autori
divini. 2001 ⇒144. 200-239.

5694 [E]**Fortna, Robert Tomson; Thatcher, Tom** Jesus in Johannine tradition. LVL 2001, Westminster xviii; 381 pp. $30. 0-664-22219-6.
Bibl. 359-368.

5695 **Frey, Jörg** Die johanneische Eschatologie, 3: die eschatologische
Verkündigung in den johanneischen Texten. WUNT 117: 2000 ⇒16,
5751. [R]TThZ 110 (2001) 82-83 (*Reiser, Marius*); OrdKor 43 (2001)
134-135 (*Giesen, Heinz*); BZ 45 (2001) 273-276 [mit Bd. 2] (*Labahn, Michael*); RSR 89 (2001) 578-580 (*Morgen, Michèle*).

5696 **Ihenacho, David Asonye** The community of eternal life: a study of
the meaning of life for the Johannine community. Lanham 2001, University Press of America xxi; 411 pp. 0-7618-1638-0. Bibl. 367-411.

5697 *Levieils, Xavier* Juifs et Grecs dans la communauté johannique. Bib.
82 (2001) 51-78.

5698 **Lingad, Celestino G.** The problems of Jewish christians in the Johannine community. TGr.T 73: R 2001, E.P.U.G 487 pp. $34. 88-76-
52-887-3. Bibl. 437-469.

5699 *Mara, Maria Grazia* 'Giovanni, figlio de Zebedeo' nella più antica
interpretazione cristiana. VIII Simposio di Efeso. Turchia 15: 2001
⇒488. 133-141 [Mt 20,20-23].

5700 *Menken, Maarten* Afgezanten van Gods afgezant: over de johanneï-
sche gemeenten. Vroegchristelijke gemeenten. 2001 ⇒460. 134-147.

5701 *Morgen, Michèle* Bulletin johannique. RSR 89 (2001) 561-591.

5702 [E]**Nissen, Johannes; Pedersen, Sigfred** New readings in John: literary and theological perspectives. JSNT.S 182: 1999 ⇒15,5724; 16,
5801. [R]ThLZ 126 (2001) 54-56 (*Lang, Manfred*).

5703 *Orselli, Alba Maria* Tradizioni di culto di San Giovanni apostolo tra
Efeso Costantinopoli e Ravenna. VIII Simposio di Efeso. Turchia 15:
2001 ⇒488. 187-200.

5704 *Papaconstantinou, Arietta* La manne de Saint Jean: à propos d'un ensemble de cuillers inscrites. REByz 59 (2001) 239-246 [Heb 9,4; Rev
2,17].

5705 *Pasquetto, Virgilio* Il lessico antropologico del vangelo e delle lettere
di Giovanni. Antropologia cristiana. 2001 ⇒371. 207-260.

5706 **Pasquetto, Virgilio** In comunione con Cristo e con i fratelli: lessico
antropologico del vangelo e delle lettere di Giovanni. R 2001, Teresianum 387 pp. Bibl. 375-376.

5707 *Ruiz Martorell, Julián* Juan: cuando la teología toma alas. Personajes del NT. 2001 ⇒231. 9-23.

5708 *Schoenborn, Margret* "... als wie ein Lamm": die Deutung eines neutestamentlichen Schlüsselwortes. Evangelische Aspekte 11/1 (2001) 50-52.

5709 *Scholtissek, Klaus* Johannine studies: a survey of recent research with special regard to German contributions II. CurResB 9 (2001) 277-305.

5710 **Scholtissek, Klaus** In ihm sein und bleiben: die Sprache der Immanenz in den Johanneischen Schriften. 2000 ⇒16,5757. ᴿBZ 45 (2001) 134-136 (*Frey, Jörg*); OrdKor 43 (2001) 136-137 (*Giesen, Heinz*); StPat 48 (2001) 206-209 (*Segalla, Giuseppe*); Anton. 76 (2001) 576-579 (*Gruber, Margareta*); ThPh 76 (2001) 572-575 (*Beutler, J.*); RSR 89 (2001) 580-582 (*Morgen, Michèle*); TS 62 (2001) 828-829 (*Smith, D. Moody*); SNTU.A 26 (2001) 234-238 (*Schreiber, S.*) [Jn 13,31-14,31; 6; 15-17; 10].

5711 *Schwankl, Otto* Die johanneische Gemeinde in der Welt von damals: zu einem problematischen und exemplarischen Verhältnis. ᶠHAINZ, J. 2001 ⇒42. 255-294.

5712 *Tang Nielsen, Jesper* Den johannaeiske eskatologi: anmeldelse af Jörg Freys trebindsvaerk. DTT 64 (2001) 63-73.

5713 *Tiwald, Markus* Der Jünger, der bleibt bis zum Kommen des Herrn: eine textpragmatische Verortung der "Johanneischen Schule". PzB 10 (2001) 1-32 [Jn 3,1-21].

5714 **Weidmann, Frederick W.** Polycarp and John: the Harris fragments and their challenge to the literary tradition. 1999 ⇒15,5739; 16, 5762. ᴿVigChr 55 (2001) 104-107 (*Dehandschutter, Boudewijn*); JBL 120 (2001) 185-187 (*Ehrman, Bart D.*).

5715 *Wilckens, Ulrich* Gott, der Drei-Eine: zur Trinitätstheologie der johanneischen Schriften. ᶠLEHMANN, K. 2001 ⇒63. 55-70.

G1.2 **Evangelium Johannis**: *textus, commentarii*

5716 *Attridge, Harold W.* Johannesevangelium RGG², 4: I-K. 2001 ⇒664. 552-562.

5717 **Barclay, William** The New Daily Study Bible: the gospel of John. E 2001, Saint Andrew Pr. 2 vols. 0-7152-.

5718 **Bazzi, Carlo** Vangelo di Giovanni: testo e commento. 2000 ⇒16, 5766. ᴿRdT 42 (2001) 938-939 (*Simoens, Yves*).

5719 **Brown, Raymond E.** El evangelio según San Juan, 1 (1-129, 2 (13-21). 1999-2000 ⇒15,5745. ᴿEsVe 31 (2001) 342-345 (*Sánchez Mielgo, Gerardo*).

5720 *Browne, Gerald M.* An old Nubian lectionary fragment. Or. 70 (2001) 113-116

5721 **Castro Sánchez, Secundino** Evangelio de Juan: comprensión exegético-existencial. Biblioteca de teología Comillas: Bilbao 2001, Desclée de B. 528 pp. ᴿREsp 60 (2001) 447-451 (*Llamas, Román*); EstJos 55 (2001) 361-363 (*Llamas, Román*).

5722 **Dietzfelbinger, Christian** Das Evangelium nach Johannes, 1: Johannes 1-12; 2: 13-21. Zürcher Bibelkommentare 4,1-2: Z 2001, Theol. Verl. 406 + 387 pp. €82. 3-290-14743-6.

5723 **Konings, Johan** Evangelho segundo João: amor e fidelidade. 2000 ⇒16,5770. ᴿPerTeol 33 (2001) 126-130 (*Gruen, Wolfgang*); Estudos Bíblicos 71 (2001) 80-85 (*Gruen, Wolfgang*).

ᶠLEROY, H. Johannes aenigmaticus 2000 ⇒64.

5724 ᴱᵀLivrea, E. Di Panopoli NONNO: parafrasi del vangelo di san Giovanni: canto B. Biblioteca patristica 36: 2000 ⇒16,5774. ᴿEfMex 19 (2001) 273-274 (*López Rosas, Ricardo*).

5725 **Malina, Bruce J.; Rohrbaugh, Richard L.** Social-science commentary on the gospel of John. 1998 ⇒14,5271; 16,5775. ᴿJBL 119 (2000) 368-370 (*Segovia, Fernando F.*).

5726 **Schneiders, Sandra M.** Written that you may believe: encountering Jesus in the fourth gospel. 1999 ⇒15,5756; 16,5782. ᴿHeyJ 42 (2001) 493-494 (*Reinhartz, Adele*); StMon 43 (2001) 404-405 (*Pou, A.*); CBQ 63 (2001) 560-561 (*Sloyan, Gerard S.*).

5727 **Simoens, Yves** Secondo Giovanni: una tradizione e un'interpretazione 1997 ⇒15,5759. ᴿGr. 82 (2001) 791-793 (*Ferraro, Giuseppe*) [²2001].

5728 **Smith, D. Moody** John. 1999 ⇒15,5761; 16,5785. ᴿJThS 52 (2001) 811-812 (*Stibbe, Mark*).

5729 **Thayse, André** Jean: l'évangile revisité. Bru 2001, Racine 288 pp. Vorarbeiten zum Johannesevangelium...2001 ⇒5590.

5730 **Wengst, Klaus** Das Johannesevangelium, 1. Teilband: Kapitel 1-10. TKNT 4/1: 2000 ⇒16,5787. ᴿFrRu 8 (2001) 225-227 (*Gollinger, Hildegard*); ThLZ 126 (2001) 1046-1050 (*Zimmermann, Ruben*);

5731 Das Johannesevangelium, 2. Teilband: Kapitel 11-21. TKNT 4/2: Stu 2001, Kohlhammer 350 pp. €30.60. 3-17-016981-5.

5732 **Wilckens, Ulrich** Das Evangelium nach Johannes. NTD 4: ¹⁷1998 ⇒ 14,5280; 16,5788. ᴿJBL 119 (2000) 366-368 (*Luomanen, Petri*).

G1.3 Introductio *in Evangelium Johannis*

5733 **Ashton, John** Comprendere il quarto vangelo. 2000 ⇒16,5790. ᴿOrpheus 22 (2001) 304-307 (*Rotondo, Arianna*).

5734 **Burge, Gary M.** Interpreting the gospel of John. Guides to New Testament Exegesis 3: GR 2001, Baker 187 pp. 0-8010-1021-7. Bibl. 185-187.

   Katz, P. Von Markus zu Johannes... 'und siehe'. 2001 ⇒5198.

5735 *Köstenberger, Andreas J.* Introduction to John's gospel <2000>;

5736 Early doubts of the apostolic authorship of the fourth gospel in the history of modern biblical criticism <1996>. Studies on John and gender. 2001 ⇒169. 7-16/17-47.

5737 **López Fernández, Enrique** El mundo joánico: introducción al cuarto evangelio. 1998 ⇒14,5286. [R]EstB 59 (2001) 397-398 (*Sánchez Mielgo, G.*).

5738 **Nagel, Titus** Die Rezeption des Johannesevangeliums im 2. Jahrhundert. ABiG 2: 2000 ⇒16,5799. [R]BZ 45 (2001) 280-281 (*Frey, Jörg*); ThPh 76 (2001) 570-572 (*Wucherpfennig, A.*); EstAg 36 (2001) 630-631 (*De Luis, P.*).

5739 *Neirynck, Frans* John and the synoptics: 1975-1990 <1992>;

5740 John and the synoptics in recent commentaries <1998>;

5741 The question of John and the synoptics: D. Moody Smith 1992-1999 <2000>. Evangelica III. 2001 ⇒187. 3-64/601-615/616-628.

5742 Neuer Wettstein: Texte zum Neuen Testament aus Griechentum und Hellenismus, 1/2: Texte zum Johannesevangelium. [E]**Schnelle, Udo**: B 2001, De Gruyter 988 pp. €128. 3-11-016807-3. Mitarb. *Michael Labahn, Manfred Lang.*

5743 *Scholtissek, Klaus* Neue Wege in der Johannesauslegung: ein Forschungsbericht II. ThGl 91 (2001) 109-133;

5744 Eine Renaissance des Evangeliums nach Johannes: aktuelle Perspektiven der exegetischen Forschung. ThRv 97 (2001) 267-287.

5745 *Smith, Dwight M.* Johannine studies since BULTMANN. WaW 21 (2001) 343-351.

5746 **Smith, Dwight Moody** John among the gospels. Columbia, South Carolina [2]2001 <1992>. University of South Carolina Press xix; 262 pp. $15. 1-57003-446-X. Bibl. 243-252.

G1.4 *Themata de evangelio Johannis*—**John's Gospel, topics**

5747 [E]**Bieringer, Reimund; Pollefeyt, D.; Vandecasteele-Vanneuville, F.** Anti-Judaism and the fourth gospel: papers of the Leuven Colloquium, 2000. Jewish and Christian Heritage Series 1: Assen 2001, Van Gorcum xvi; 612 pp. $97.50. 90-232-3712-9. Bibl. 549-570.

5748 *Aerathedathu, Thomas* Discipleship and mission in the fourth gospel: Philip as a model missionary. [F]KAROTEMPREL, S. 2001 ⇒57. 15-25.

5749   *Anderson, Paul N.* John and Mark: the bi-optic gospels;

5750   *Ashton, John* Riddles and mysteries: the way, the truth, and the life. Jesus in Johannine tradition. 2001 ⇒5694. 175-188/333-342.

5751   **Asiedu-Peprah, Martin** Johannine sabbath conflicts as juridical controversy. WUNT 2/132: Tü 2001, Mohr S. xiii; 280 pp. €50.11. 3-16-147530-5. Bibl. 247-261.

5752   *Barrett, C.K.* John and Judaism. Anti-Judaism and the fourth gospel. 2001 ⇒5747. 401-417.

5753   *Bauckham, Richard* The audience of the fourth gospel. Jesus in Johannine tradition. 2001 ⇒5694. 101-111.

5754   **Bennema, Cornelis** The power of saving wisdom: an investigation of spirit and wisdom in relation to the soteriology of the fourth gospel. Diss. London Bible College/Brunel Univ. 2001, ᴰ*Turner, Max* [TynB 52,295-298].

5755   *Beutler, Johannes* The identity of the 'Jews' for the readers of John;

5756   *Bieringer, Reimund; Pollefeyt, Didier; Vandecasteele-Vanneuville, Frederique* Wrestling with johannine anti-judaism: a hermeneutical framework for the analysis of the current debate. Anti-Judaism and the fourth gospel. 2001 ⇒5747. 229-238/3-44.

5757   *Blanco Berga, José Ignacio* Nicodemo: el complejo del creyente: ser creyente en tiempos difíciles. Personajes del NT. 2001 ⇒231. 91-101.

5758   *Blomberg, Craig L.* The historical reliability of John: rushing in where angels fear to tread?. Jesus in Johannine tradition. 2001 ⇒ 5694. 71-82.

5759   **Blomberg, Craig L.** The historical reliability of John's gospel. Nottingham 2001. IVP 346 pp. $26. 0-85111-484-9. Bibl. 295-327.

5760   *Boismard, Marie-Émile* L'évangile de Jean et les Samaritains. Le judéo-christianisme. 2001 ⇒484. 86-96 [BuBB 36,33].

5761   *Branco, Frei Carlos A.* Fotografia teológica de Maria em João. Grande Sinal 55 (2001) 205-212.

5762   *Broadhead, Edwin K.* The fourth gospel and the synoptic sayings source: the relationship reconsidered;

5763   *Broer, Ingo* Knowledge of Palestine in the fourth gospel?. Jesus in Johannine tradition. 2001 ⇒5694. 291-301/83-90..

5764   **Brunson, Andrew** The coming one: an intertextual study of Psalm 118 in the gospel of John. Diss. Aberdeen 2001, ᴰ*Marshall, I.H.* [RTL 33,636].

5765   *Burge, Gary M.* Situating John's gospel in history. Jesus in Johannine tradition. 2001 ⇒5694. 35-46.

5766   *Burggraeve, Roger* Biblical thinking as the wisdom of love. Anti-Judaism and the fourth gospel. 2001 ⇒5747. 202-225.

5767 *Büttner, Gerhard; Roose, Hanna* Mit Johannes (etwas) anfangen?!. KatBl 126 (2001) 352-356.

5768 *Caba, José* Jesús, Palabra encarnada, en el IV evangelio. StMiss 50 (2001) 23-72.

5769 *Calloud, Jean* Quatrième évangile: le témoignage de Jean (2ème partie). SémBib 103 (2001) 22-55.

5770 *Caragounis, Chrys C.* The kingdom of God: common and distinct elements between John and the synoptics. Jesus in Johannine tradition. 2001 ⇒5694. 125-134.

5771 **Caron, Gérald** Qui sont les 'juifs' de l'évangile de Jean?. RFTP 35: 1997 ⇒13,5685; 14,5308. ^RRB 108 (2001) 614-618 (*Devillers, Luc*).

5772 **Cebulj, Christian** Ich bin es: Studien zur Identitätsbildung im Johannesevangelium. SBB 44: 2000 ⇒16,5826. ^RBZ 45 (2001) 276-278 (*Frey, Jörg*); RSR 89 (2001) 571-572 (*Morgen, Michèle*); SNTU.A 26 (2001) 233-234 (*Fuchs, Albert*).

5773 *Charlesworth, James H.* The gospel of John: exclusivism caused by a social setting different from that of Jesus (John 11:54 and 14:6). Anti-Judaism and the fourth gospel. 2001 ⇒5747. 479-513 [Jn 11,54; 14,6].

5774 *Chatelion Counet, Patrick* Het messiasgeheim in Johannes: analyse van het impliciete gebod tot zwijgen. TTh 41 (2001) 253-279.

5775 **Chatelion Counet, Patrick** John, a postmodern gospel: introduction to deconstructive exegesis applied to the fourth gospel. 2000 ⇒16, 5828. ^RBZ 45 (2001) 132-134 (*Frey, Jörg*) [Jn 6; 17; 21,24-25].

5776 **Clark-Soles, Jaime Anne** Scripture cannot be broken: the social function of the use of scripture in the fourth gospel. Diss. Yale 2001, 450 pp. 9991137.

5777 *Collins, Raymond F.* Speaking of the Jews: 'Jews' in the discourse material of the fourth gospel. Anti-Judaism and the fourth gospel. 2001 ⇒5747. 281-300.

5778 **Coloe, Mary L.** God dwells with us: temple symbolism in the fourth gospel. ColMn 2001, Liturgical x; 252 pp. $25. 0-8146-5952-7. Bibl. 223-239. ^RABR 49 (2001) 65-66 (*Byrne, Brendan*).

5779 **Conway, Colleen M.** Men and women in the fourth gospel: gender and Johannine characterization. SBL.DS 167: 1999 ⇒15,5796; 16, 5832. ^REThL 77 (2001) 220-222 (*Van Belle, G.*); RBLit 3 (2001) 408-411 (*Swartley, Willard M.*).

5780 **Crosby, Michael H.** Do you love me?: Jesus questions the church. Mkn 2000, Orbis xxvii; 255 pp. 1-57075-236-2.

5781 *Culpepper, R. Alan* Anti-judaism in the fourth gospel as a theological problem for christian interpreters. Anti-Judaism and the fourth gospel. Jewish and Christian heritage series 1: 2001 ⇒5747. 68-9;

5782   The origin of the "Amen, Amen" sayings in the gospel of John. Jesus
       in Johannine tradition. 2001 ⇒5694. 253-262.

5783   **Daly-Denton, Margaret** David in the fourth gospel: the Johannine
       reception of the Psalms. AGJU 47 2000 ⇒16,5835. ᴿETR 76 (2001)
       124-126 (*Rüsen-Weinhold, Christina; Rüsen-Weinhold, Ulrich*); BZ
       45 (2001) 136-137 (*Frey, Jörg*); JThS 52 (2001) 262-265 (*North,
       Wendy Sproston*); ThLZ 126 (2001) 525-528 (*Metzner, Rainer*).

5784   *De Boer, M.C.* The depiction of 'the Jews' in John's gospel: matters of
       behavior and identity;

5785   *De Jonge, Henk Jan* The 'Jews' in the gospel of John. Anti-Judaism
       and the fourth gospel. 2001 ⇒5747. 260-280/239-259.

5786   *DeConick, April D.* John rivals Thomas: from community conflict to
       gospel narrative. Jesus in Johannine tradition. 2001 ⇒5694. 303-311.

5787   **DeConick, April D.** Voices of the mystics: early christian discourse
       in the gospels of John and Thomas and other ancient christian litera-
       ture. JSNT.S 157: Shf 2001, Academic 191 pp. £31.50/$52.50. 1-
       84127-190-X. ᴿVigChr 55 (2001) 436-440 (*Quispel, Gilles*);
       Neotest. 35 (2001) 178-179 (*Draper, Jonathan A.*).

5788   **Desjeux, Xavier** Voir l'invisible: l'évangile de Jean, un chemin de
       contemplation. P 2001, Béatitudes 295 pp.

5789   **Destro, Adriana; Pesce, Mauro** Come nasce una religione: antropo-
       logia ed esegesi del vangelo di Giovanni. Percorsi 8: 2000 ⇒16,
       5838. ᴿArOr 69 (2001) 39-40 (*Guijarro, Santiago*); StPat 48 (2001)
       201-206 (*Segalla, Giuseppe*); Salm. 48 (2001) 173-176 (*Guijarro,
       Santiago*); VetChr 38 (2001) 347-351 (*Infante, Renzo*); ATT 7
       (2001) 214-219 (*Ghiberti, Giuseppe*).

5790   *Destro, Adriana; Pesce, Mauro* Un confronto di sistemi: il *Vangelo
       di Giovanni* et la *Regola della comunità* di Qumran. VIII Simposio di
       Efeso. Turchia 15: 2001 ⇒488. 81-107.

5791   *Dewey, Arthur J.* The eyewitness of history: visionary consciousness
       in the fourth gospel;

5792   *Dewey, Joanna* The gospel of John in its oral-written media world.
       Jesus in Johannine tradition. 2001 ⇒5694. 59-70/239-252.

5793   *Dietzfelbinger, Christian* Pilatus im Johannesevangelium. ᶠHAHN, F.
       2001 ⇒41. 101-116.

5794   **Dumm, Demetrius R.** A mystical portrait of Jesus: new perspectives
       on John's gospel. ColMn 2001, Liturgical xxi; 177 pp. $17. 0-8146-
       2760-9. Bibl. 171-172 [BiTod 40,133—Senior, D.].

5795   *Dunn, James D.G.* The embarrassment of history: reflections on the
       problem of 'anti-judaism' in the fourth gospel. Anti-Judaism and the
       fourth gospel. 2001 ⇒5747. 47-67.

5796   **DuToit, David S.** Theios anthropos: zur Verwendung von theios an-
       thropos und sinnverwandten Ausdrücken in der Literatur der Kaiser-

zeit. WUNT 2/91: 1997 ⇒13,5694... 16,5843. ᴿSNTU.A 23 (1998) 242-244 (*Schreiber, S.*).

5797 **Elson, Thomas O.** Disciples and christology in the gospel of John: the contrasting function of disciples in Greco-Roman biography and the fourth gospel. Diss. Fuller Sem. 2001, 271 pp. 3003171.

5798 *English, Adam C.* Feeding imagery in the gospel of John: uniting the physical and the spiritual. PRSt 28/3 (2001) 203-214.

5799 **Fehribach, Adeline** The women in the life of the bridegroom: a feminist historical-literary analysis and interpretation of the female characters in the fourth gospel. 1998 ⇒14,5323; 16,5848. ᴿJBL 119 (2000) 773-775 (*D'Angelo, Mary Rose*).

5800 *Felton, Tom; Thatcher, Tom* Stylometry and the signs gospel. Jesus in Johannine tradition. 2001 ⇒5694. 209-218.

5801 **Fernando, Charles Anthony** The relationship between law and love in the gospel of John. Diss. Ottawa 2001, ᴰ*Michaud, J.-P.* [RTL 33, 637].

5802 *Ferraro, Giuseppe* Gli autori divini dell'insegnamento nel quarto vangelo: Dio Padre, Gesù Cristo, lo Spirito <1988>;

5803 Eucaristia—incarnazione—pneumatologia: osservazioni su Giovanni 6,51c, 1,14: 6,63. Gli autori divini. 2001 ⇒144. 156-175/176-199.

5804 **Ferreira, Johan** Johannine ecclesiology. JSNT.S 160: 1998 ⇒14, 5327. ᴿJThS 52 (2001) 258-262 (*Williams, Catrin H.*); EThL 77 (2001) 222-224 (*Van Belle, G.*) [Jn 17].

5805 *Fortna, Robert T.* Jesus tradition in the signs gospel. Jesus in Johannine tradition. 2001 ⇒5694. 199-208.

5806 **Frey, Jörg** Die johanneische Eschatologie, II: das johanneische Zeitverständnis. WUNT 110: 1998 ⇒14,5330... 16,5852. ᴿRSR 89 (2001) 577-578 (*Morgen, Michèle*); RBLit 3 (2001) 411-413 (*Ferreira, G.R. Johan*).

5807 *Frühwald-König, Johannes* Die "größere Schuld": Antijudaismus in der Auslegung des Johannesevangeliums?. ᶠSCHMUTTERMAYR, G. 2001 ⇒101. 153-172.

5808 *Gadecki, Stanisław* Mysterium Incarnationis według pism Janowych. CoTh 71/3 (2001) 31-49. **P.**

5809 **García Moreno, Antonio** Jesús el nazareno, el rey de los judíos: estudio de cristología joánica. Fac. Teologia Univ. Navarra, Teologica 103: Pamplona 2001, EUNSA 455 pp. 84-3131-8627. Bibl. 397-417;

5810 Temi teologici del vangelo di Giovanni, 3: i sacramenti. Lett. pastor. della bibbia, bibbia e spiritualità 13: Bo 2001, EDB 240 pp. €21.17.

5811 ᵀ**Garzón Bosque, Isabel** Juan CRISÓSTOMO: Homilías sobre el evangelio de San Juan, 2-3 [30-60, 61-88]. ᴱ*Marcelo, Merin*: M 2001, Ciudad N. 344+360 pp. €19.23+18.03. v.2: 849715-0082 v.3: -0015.

5812 **González-Gullón, José Luis** La fecundidad de la cruz: estudio exegético y teológico-patrístico de la exaltación y de la atracción de Cristo en los textos joánicos. Diss. Pont. Univ. Santa Croce. R 2001 Som. [AHIg 11 (2002) 444-448].

5813 *Hargreaves, Cecil* WESTCOTT, India, and 'John'. ET 112 (2001) 333-335.

5814 *Hartenstein, Judith; Petersen, Silke* Zur Übersetzung von Texten aus dem Johannesevangelium in 'gerechte Sprache': Anmerkungen zu einem schwierigen Projekt. YESW 9 (2001) 163-177.

   Heise, J. Auslegen...johanneischer Texte 2001 ⇒159.

5815 *Hoet, Hendrik* "Abraham is our father" (John 8:39): the gospel of John and Jewish-Christian dialogue. Anti-Judaism and the fourth gospel. 2001 ⇒5747. 187-201.

5816 **Howard-Brook, Wes** Becoming children of God: John's gospel and radical discipleship. The Bible & liberation: Mkn 2001, Orbis xviii; 510 pp. 0-88344-983-8.

5817 **Hutchinson, Anthony** Semitic interference in the syntax of the gospel of John. Diss. Cath. Univ. of America 2001, ^D*Gignac, F.T.* [RTL 33,638].

5818 *Igirukwayo, Antoine M.Z.* Exaltation de Jésus en croix dans l'évangile selon saint Jean et vie morale. AETSC 6 (2001) 287-320.

5819 *Kanagaraj, Jey* The profiles of women in John: house-bound or Christ-bound?. BTF 33/2 (2001) 60-79;

5820 The implied ethics of the fourth gospel: a reinterpretation of the decalogue. TynB 52 (2001) 33-60 [Ex 20,1-17].

5821 **Kanagaraj, Jey J.** 'Mysticism' in the gospel of John: an inquiry into its background. JSNT.S 158: 1998 ⇒14,5342; 16,5866. ^RJBL 120 (2001) 572-574 (*Neufeld, Dietmar*).

5822 **Kim, Stephen S.** The relationship of the seven sign-miracles of Jesus in the fourth gospel to the Old Testament. Diss. Dallas Sem. 2001, 249 pp. 3002963.

5823 *Kirk, Alan* The Johannine Jesus in the gospel of Peter: a social memory approach. Jesus in Johannine tradition. 2001 ⇒5694. 313-321.

5824 *Klappert, Bertold* The coming Son of Man became flesh: high christology and anti-judaism in the gospel of John?. Anti-Judaism and the fourth gospel. 2001 ⇒5747. 159-186.

5825 *Koester, Craig R.* Jesus the way, the cross, and the world according to the gospel of John. WaW 21 (2001) 360-369.

5826 *Kowalski, Beate* "Wollt auch ihr weggehen?" (Joh 6,67)—Aspekte des johanneischen Gemeindemodells. ^FHAINZ, J. 2001 ⇒42. 360-76.

5827 *Köstenberger, Andreas J.* Jesus as rabbi in the fourth gospel <1998>;

5828 The seventh Johannine sign: a study in John's christology <1995>;

5829 The two Johannine verbs for sending: a study of John's use of words with reference to general linguistic theory <1999>;

5830 The challenge of a systematized biblical theology of mission: missiological insights from the gospel of John <1995>. Studies on John and gender. 2001 ⇒169. 65-98/99-116/129-147/149-169.

5831 **Kriener, Tobias** "Glauben an Jesus"—ein Verstoß gegen das zweite Gebot?: die johanneische Christologie und der jüdische Vorwurf des Götzendienstes. Neuk. Theol. Dissertationen und Habilitationen 29: Neuk 2001, Neuk ix; 159 pp. €25. 3-7887-1816-1 [Jn 20,28; 9; 10].

5832 **Kušmirek, Anna** Oryginalność posłannictwa Jezusa według czwartej ewangelii [L'originalité de la mission de Jésus selon le quatrième évangile]. Diss. Warsaw 2001, ᴰ*Wojciechowski M.*: 337 pp. [RTL 33, 639]. P.

5833 *Kurz, William S.* The Johannine Word as revealing the Father: a christian credal actualization. PRSt 28 (2001) 67-84.

5834 **Kügler, Joachim** Der andere König: religionsgeschichtliche Perspektiven auf die Christologie des Johannesevangeliums. SBS 178: 1999 ⇒15,5847; 16,5870. ᴿZKTh 122 (2001) 212-213 (*Hasitschka, Martin*); EThL 77 (2001) 475-479 (*Van Belle, G.*); SNTU.A 25 (2000) 259-260 (*Labahn, M.*).

5835 *Kysar, Robert* "As you sent me": identity and mission in the fourth gospel. WaW 21 (2001) 370-376.

5836 **Labahn, Michael** Jesus als Lebensspender: Untersuchungen zu einer Geschichte der johanneischen Tradition anhand ihrer Wundergeschichten. 1999 ⇒15,5851; 16,5871. ᴿJBL 120 (2001) 381-383 (*Koester, Craig R.*); JThS 52 (2001) 805-809 (*Smith, D. Moody*); RSR 89 (2001) 565-566 (*Morgen, Michèle*); ThLZ 126 (2001) 1155-159 (*Metzner, Rainer*); RBLit 3 (2001) 413-415 (*Koester, Craig R.*).

5837 *Lang, Walter* Was Christsein nach dem Johannesevangelium bedeutet. Theologisches 31 (2001) 161-166.

5838 **Larsson, Tord** God in the fourth gospel: a hermeneutical study of the history of interpretations. Diss. Lund 2001. CB.NT 35: Sto 2001, Almqvist & W. xiv; 319 pp. 91-22-01909-X. Bibl. 278-298.

5839 **Leijgraaf, Monique** Brood en wijn binnen de spanning van Gods verkiezing: een bijbels-theologische interpretatie van het brood des levens (Johannes 6), de wijn van de bruiloft van Kana (Johannes 2:1-12) en de betrouwbare wijnstok (Johannes 15:1-8). Diss. Amsterdam, ᴰ*Bakker, N.T.*: Baarn 2001, Ten Have xi; 212 pp. €20.37. 90-259-5271-2.

5840 **Leung, Donald Chung-Yiu** Peter in the fourth gospel: character development and reader empathy. Diss. Dallas Sem. 2001, 373 pp. 3002965.

5841 *Lieu, Judith M.* Anti-judaism in the fourth gospel: explanation and hermeneutics. Anti-Judaism and the fourth gospel. 2001 ⇒5747. 126-143.

5842 **Lincoln, Andrew T.** Truth on trial: the lawsuit motif in the fourth gospel. 2000 ⇒16,5875. [R]TrinJ 22 (2001) 269-272 (*Köstenberger, Andreas J.*).

5843 *Lincoln, Andrew T.* God's name, Jesus' name, and prayer in the fourth gospel. Into God's presence. 2001 ⇒294. 155-180.

5844 *Loader, William* "Your law"—the Johannine perspective. [F]HAHN, F. 2001 ⇒41. 63-74.

5845 *Marshall, Ronald F.* Our serpent of salvation: the offense of Jesus in John's gospel. WaW 21 (2001) 385-393 [Num 21,8-9; Jn 3,14].

5846 **Martignani, Luigi** "Il mio giorno": indagine esegetico-teologica sull'uso del termine ἡμέρα nel quarto vangelo. AnGr 275: 1998 ⇒ 14,5355; 15,5860. [R]RivBib 49 (2001) 497-499 (*Segalla, Giuseppe*).

5847 **Mashahu, Emmanuel** Le dualisme johannique. Diss. Angelicum 2001, [D]*Marcato, Giorgio*: R 2001, 202 pp. Bibl. 171-177.

5848 **Mazzocchi, Luciano** Il vangelo secondo Giovanni e lo Zen: volume secondo. Bo 2001, Dehoniane 332 pp. 88-10-80808-8.

5849 **McGrath, James Frank** John's apologetic christology: legitimation and development in Johannine christology. MSSNTS 111: C 2001, CUP xii; 269 pp. $60. 0-521-80348-9. Bibl. 236-260. [R]IBSt 23 (2001) 185-187 (*McCullough, J.C.*).

5850 **Menken, Maarten J.J.** Old Testament quotations in the fourth gospel. Contributions to Biblical Exegesis and Theology 15: 1996 ⇒12, 5445; 13,5732. [R]ThLZ 126 (2001) 1044-1046 (*Hübner, Hans*).

5851 *Menken, Maarten J.J.* Scriptural dispute between Jews and christians in John: literary fiction or historical reality?: John 9:13-17,24-34 as a test case. Anti-Judaism and the fourth gospel. 2001 ⇒5747. 445-460.

5852 **Metzner, Rainer** Das Verständnis der Sünde im Johannesevangelium. WUNT 122: 2000 ⇒16,5878. [R]CBQ 63 (2001) 346-348 (*Neufeld, Dietmar*); FgNT 14 (2001) 149-152 (*Stenschke, Christoph*).

5853 *Moloney, Francis J.* When is John talking about sacraments? <1982>;

5854 The gospel of John: a story of two paracletes <1998>;

5855 'God so loved the world': the Jesus of John's gospel <1998>. 'A hard saying'. 2001 ⇒184. 109-130/149-166/167-180.

5856 *Motyer, Stephen* The fourth gospel and the salvation of Israel: an appeal for a new start. Anti-Judaism and the fourth gospel. 2001 ⇒ 5747. 92-110.

5857 *Müller, Jean J.* Les citations de l'écriture dans le quatrième évangile. FV 100/4 (2001) 41-57.

5858 **Namita** The third millenium [!] in the light of mission in the gospel according to St. John and the early Upanishads. 2000 ⇒16,5883. ^RITS 38 (2001) 107-111 (*Francis, B. Joseph*).

5859 **Newheart, Michael Willett** Word and soul: a psychological, literary, and cultural reading of the fourth gospel. Glazier: ColMn 2001, Liturgical xxviii; 165 pp. $20. 0-8146-5924-1. Bibl. 141-147 [BiTod 39,389—Senior, Donald].

5860 **Ng, Wai-yee** Water symbolism in John: an eschatological interpretation. Studies in Biblical Literature 15: NY 2001, Lang xiv; 241 pp. $57. 0-8204-4453-7. Bibl. 195-235.

5861 **Nicklas, Tobias** Ablösung und Verstrickung: "Juden" und Jüngergestalten als Charaktere der erzählten Welt des Johannesevangeliums und ihre Wirkung auf den impliziten Leser. RSTh 60: Fra 2001, Lang 484 pp. €65.40. 3-631-37615-4.

5862 *O'Day, Gail R.* John's voice and the church's preaching. WaW 21 (2001) 394-403;

5863 The gospel of John: reading the incarnate words. Jesus in Johannine tradition. 2001 ⇒5694. 25-32.

5864 *Okorie, A.M.* The self-revelation of Jesus in the 'I am' sayings of John's gospel. CThMi 28 (2001) 486-490.

5865 *Onuki, Takashi* Fleischwerdung des Logos und Fehltritt der Sophia— Erwägungen zur johanneischen und gnostischen Lichtsprache. ^FHAHN, F. 2001 ⇒41. 75-86.

5866 *Palatty, Paul* The beloved disciple and apostle Thomas. BiBh 27 (2001) 161-173.

5867 *Papathanassiou, Constantine* 'Light of world' (John 8:12) and the human perspective (contribution to the universality of the fourth gospel). DBM 20/2 (2001) 47-79. **G.**;

5868 Ο κοσμος ως "κοσμος" ετο Δ'Ευαγγελιο [The world as 'world' (impropriety of creation) in the fourth gospel]. DBM 20/1 (2001) 5-37. **G.**

5869 *Perry, John M.* The sacramental tradition in the fourth gospel and the synoptics. Jesus in Johannine tradition. 2001 ⇒5694. 155-164.

5870 *Pesce, Mauro* Il *Vangelo di Giovanni* e le fasi giudaiche del giovannismo: alcuni aspetti. Verus Israel. BCR 65: 2001 ⇒524. 47-67.

5871 **Philippe, Marie-Dominique** Wherever he goes: a retreat based on the gospel of John. 2000 ⇒16,5890. ^RNBl 82 (2001) 405-406 (*Saward, John*).

5872 *Ramos, José C.* El ministerio de Jesús según el evangelio de San Juan: un cuadro ampliado de la transfiguración. Theologika 16 (2001) 170-185.

5873 *Reinhartz, Adele* 'Jews' and Jews in the fourth gospel. Anti-Judaism and the fourth gospel. 2001 ⇒5747. 341-356.

5874   **Reinhartz, Adele** Befriending the beloved disciple: a Jewish reading
       of the gospel of John. NY 2001, Continuum 206 pp. $25. 0-8264-
       1319-6 [BiTod 39,322—Senior, Donald].

5875   **Reis, Francisco Helton dos** O acontecer da fé no evangelho de João:
       estudo a partir de uma obra de Xavier LEÓN-DUFOUR. Diss. de me-
       strado Belo Horizonte 2001, *DKonings, Johan* [REB 62,495].

5876   *Rensberger, David* The messiah who has come into the world: the
       message of the gospel of John. Jesus in Johannine tradition. 2001 ⇒
       5694. 15-23.

5877   **Resseguie, James L.** The strange gospel: narrative design and point
       of view in John. BiblInterp 56: Lei 2001, Brill xi; 222 pp. €71. 90-
       04-12206-0. Bibl. 203-211.

5878   **Riedl, Hermann** Zeichen und Herrlichkeit: die christologische Rele-
       vanz der Semeiaquelle in den Kanawundern Joh 2,1-11 und Joh 4,46-
       54. RSTh 51: 1996 ⇒12,5463; 15,5892. *R*SNTU.A 23 (1998) 263-
       265 (*Fuchs, Albert*).

5879   **Ringe, Sharon H.** Wisdom's friends: community and christology in
       the fourth gospel. 1999 ⇒15,5894. *R*CBQ 63 (2001) 558-560 (*Bowe,
       Barbara E.*); RBLit 3 (2001) 415-418 (*Just, Felix*).

5880   *Schmidl, Martin* Johannes und Paulus: Überlegungen zur Methode ei-
       nes Vergleichs. *F*HAINZ, J. 2001 ⇒42. 223-254.

5881   *Schnelle, Udo* Recent views of John's gospel. WaW 21 (2001) 352-
       359.

5882   *Scholtissek, Klaus* "Rabbi, wo wohnst du?": zur Theologie der Imma-
       nenz-Aussagen im Johannesevangelium. BiLi 74 (2001) 240-253;

5883   Mystik im Johannesevangelium?: Reflexionen zu einer umstrittenen
       Fragestellung. *F*HAINZ, J. 2001 ⇒42. 295-324.

5884   *Schoon, Simon* Escape routes as dead ends: on hatred toward Jews
       and the New Testament, especially in the gospel of John. Anti-
       Judaism and the fourth gospel. 2001 ⇒5747. 144-158.

5885   **Schröder, Jörn-Michael** Das eschatologische Israel im Johannese-
       vangelium: eine Untersuchung der johanneischen Israel-Konzeption
       in Joh 2-4 und Joh 6. Diss. Bethel 2001, *DVouga, F.*: 331 pp. [RTL
       33,640].

5886   **Schwankl, Otto** Licht und Finsternis: ein metaphorisches Paradigma
       in den johanneischen Schriften. 1995 ⇒11/1,4096... 14,5253. *R*RB
       108 (2001) 109-117 (*Devillers, Luc*).

5887   *Sevrin, Jean-Marie* The Nicodemus enigma: the characterization and
       function of an ambiguous actor of the fourth gospel. Anti-Judaism
       and the fourth gospel. 2001 ⇒5747. 357-369.

5888   *Söding, Thomas* Die Wahrheit des Evangeliums: Anmerkungen zur
       Johanneischen Hermeneutik. EThL 77 (2001) 318-355 [Jn 14,6].

5889 *Spriggs, Steven* Christian mission according to the gospel of John. Evangel 19 (2001) i-iv; i-viii. Global Connections Occasional Paper 8 & 9.

5890 *Staley, Jeffrey L.* What can a postmodern approach to the fourth gospel add to contemporary debates about its historical situation?. Jesus in Johannine tradition. 2001 ⇒5694. 47-57.

5891 *Thatcher, Tom* Introduction;

5892 The legend of the beloved disciple;

5893 The signs gospel in context;

5894 The riddles of Jesus in the Johannine dialogues;

5895 Conclusion: new directions. Jesus in Johannine tradition. 2001 ⇒ 5694. 1-9/91-99/191-197/263-277/353-358.

5896 **Thatcher, Tom** The riddles of Jesus in John. SBL.MS 53: 2000 ⇒ 16,5908. [R]Bib. 82 (2001) 576-580 (*Segalla, Giuseppe*).

5897 *Thompson, Marianne M.* What is the gospel of John?. WaW 21 (2001) 333-342.

5898 **Thompson, Marianne Meye** The God of the gospel of John. GR 2001, Eerdmans x; 269 pp. $22/£15. 0-8028-4734-X. Bibl. 241-252.

5899 *Tomson, Peter J.* 'Jews' in the gospel of John as compared with the Palestinian Talmud, the synoptics and some New Testament apocrypha. Anti-Judaism and the fourth gospel. 2001 ⇒5747. 301-340.

5900 **Tovey, Derek** Narrative art and act in the fourth gospel. 1997 ⇒13, 5762... 16,5910. [R]EvQ 73 (2001) 349-351 (*Johnson, Brian D.*)

5901 *Trudinger, Paul* St John: a subtle sacramentalist. DR 119 (2001) 1-10;

5902 'In my father's house': expository note on a Johannine theme. ET 112 (2001) 229-230.

5903 *Tuckett, Christopher M.* The fourth gospel and Q;

5904 *Twelftree, Graham H.* Exorcisms in the fourth gospel and the synoptics. Jesus in Johannine tradition. 2001 ⇒5694. 281-290/135-143.

5905 **Urban, Christina** Das Menschenbild nach dem Johannesevangelium: Grundlagen johanneischer Anthropologie. Diss. Kiel 2000. WUNT 137: Tü 2001, Mohr S. ix; 499 pp. €74. 3-16-147604-2. Bibl. 463-484

5906 *Van Belle, Gilbert* Prolepsis in the gospel of John. NT 43 (2001) 334-347.

5907 *Van der Merwe, D.G. Imitatio Christi* in the fourth gospel;

5908 *Van der Watt, Jan Gabriël* Die funksie van verwysings na fisiese families in die Johannesevangelie. VeE 22 (2001) 131-148/158-177.

5909 *Vandecasteele-Vanneuville, Frederique* Johannine theology of revelation, soteriology, and the problem of Anti-Judaism. SNTU.A 26 (2001) 165-188.

5910 **Vignolo, Roberto** Personaggi nel quarto vangelo: figure della fede in San Giovanni. 1994 ⇒10,5329... 12,5490. ^RATT 7 (2001) 211-213 (*Ghiberti, Giuseppe*).

5911 *Vignolo, Roberto* Segni di gloria e sensi spirituali: bellezza della rivelazione e accoglienza della fede nel quarto vangelo. La bellezza. PSV 44: 2001⇒240. 95-126.

5912 *Viviano, Benedict T.* The Spirit in John's gospel: a Hegelian perspective. Trinity—kingdom. NTOA 48: 2001 <1996> ⇒223. 114-134;

5913 The missionary program of John's gospel. Trinity—kingdom—church NTOA 48: 2001 <1984> ⇒223. 223-231.

5914 **Webster, Jane** Ingesting Jesus: eating and drinking in the gospel of John. Diss. McMaster 2001, ^D*Reinhartz, A.* 233 pp. [RTL 33,642].

5915 *Wehr, Lothar* "Er wird euch alles lehren und euch an alles erinnern, was ich euch gesagt habe" (Joh 14,26): die hermeneutische Funktion des Geist-Parakleten und die Kriterien der Traditionsbildung im Johannesevangelium. ^FHAINZ, J. 2001 ⇒42. 325-359.

5916 **Westermann, Claus** The gospel of John: in the light of the Old Testament. ^T*Schatzmann, Siegfried S.*: 1998 ⇒14,5411; 16,5916. ^RRSR 89 (2001) 566-569 (*Morgen, Michèle*); VeE 22 (2001) 198-199 (*Van der Watt, J.G.*); EvQ 73 (2001) 179-180 (*Bodner, Keith*).

5917 **Wierenga, L.** Verhalen als bewijzen: strategieën van de narratieve retoriek in Johannes: verslag van een cursorischelectuur van het Johannes-evangelie. Kampen 2001. Kok 400 pp. €37.75. 90435-03320.

5918 *Williams, Catrin H.* "I am" or "I am He"?: self-declaratory pronouncements in the fourth gospel and rabbinic tradition;

5919 *Wink, Walter* "The son of the man" in the gospel of John;

5920 *Winter, Sara C.* Little flags: the scope and reconstruction of the signs gospel. Jesus in Johannine tradition. 2001 ⇒5694. 343-352/117-123/ 219-235.

5921 *Zumstein, Jean* Foi et vie éternelle selon Jean. Résurrection: l'après-mort. MoBi 45: 2001 ⇒296. 215-235.

G1.5 Johannis Prologus 1,1...

5922 *Paqué, Ruprecht* Die Stimme Gottes als Ursprung aller Sprache: ein altindischer Spruch vom Anfang der Welt und seine biblische "logos"-Parallele in Joh 1,1. WuA(M) 42/1 (2001) 29-35.

5923 *Mondati, Franco* Struttura letteraria di Gv 1,1-2,12. RivBib 49 (2001) 43-81.

5924 *Baldwin, John T.* The *Logos*: Lord of the cosmos, and recent trends in science and religion. AUSS 39 (2001) 101-107 [Jn 1,1-3].

5925 *Amphoux, Christian-B.* Les variantes de la tradition grecque du Prologue de Jean et leurs enjeux. Graphè 10 (2001) 11-34 [Jn 1,1-18].

5926 *Blanchard, Yves M.* La notion de Logos dans le Judaïsme ancien du premier siècle et sa réinterprétation chrétienne dans le Prologue de Jean. Graphè 10 (2001) 47-60 [Jn 1,1-18].

5927 *Denzey, Nicola Frances* Genesis traditions in conflict?: the use of some exegetical traditions in the Trimorphic Protennoia and the Johannine prologue. VigChr 55 (2001) 20-44 [Jn 1,1-18].

5928 *Goddard, Jean-Christophe* L'interprétation métaphysique du Prologue de Jean par FICHTE dans l'*Initiation à la vie bienheureuse*;

5929 *Hubaut, Michael A.* Rédactions et réceptions du prologue;

5930 *Jasper, Alison* The Word but lately could not speak: anti-theological reflections on John's Prologue. Graphè 10 (2001) 143-157/35-45/ 219-229 [Jn 1,1-18].

5931 **Jasper, Alison** The shining garment of the text: gendered readings of John's Prologue. JSNT.S 165: 1998 ⇒14,5420... 16,5924. ᴿJBL 120 (2001) 383-385 (*Conway, Colleen M.*) [Jn 1,1-18].

5932 *Kopenhagen-Urian, Judith* Anatomie du 'Verbe-qui-s'est-fait-chair' dans l'oeuvre de Saint-John PERSE face à la tropologie d'ELIOT et de CLAUDEL. Graphè 10 (2001) 181-198 [Jn 1,1-18].

5933 *Patterson, Stephen J.* The prologue to the fourth gospel and the world of speculative Jewish theology. Jesus in Johannine tradition. 2001 ⇒5694. 323-332 [Jn 1,1-18].

5934 *Renaud-Chamska, Isabelle* Les fondements johanniques d'*Une somme de poésie* de Patrice de LA TOUR DU PIN;

5935 *Rosaye, Jean-Paul* De l'idée d'absolu au Verbe: l'herméneutique de T.S. ELIOT. Graphè 10 (2001) 199-217/159-180 [Jn 1,1-18].

5936 *Van Tilborg, Sjef* 'Een God was het Woord': theologen vóór Nicea over de proloog van Johannes. TTh 41 (2001) 356-375 [Jn 1,1-18].

5937 *Vannier, Marie-Anne* ECKHART et le prologue de Jean. Graphè 10 (2001) 125-142 [Jn 1,1-18].

5938 *Waetjen, Herman C.* Logos πρὸς τὸν θεόν and the objectification of truth in the prologue of the fourth gospel. CBQ 63 (2001) 265-286.

5939 *Trudinger, Paul* Nicodemus's encounter with Jesus and the structure of St John's Prologue. DR 119 (2001) 145-148 [Jn 3,13-14].

5940 *Bernard, Jacques* Lectures des v. 9-13 du prologue de Jean. Graphè 10 (2001) 61-101.

5941 *Prior, J. Bruce* Who is 'full of grace and truth' in the Wˢ text of John 1:14?. BBR 11 (2001) 233-238.

5942 *Blumenthal, Christian* χάρις ἀντὶ χάριτος (Joh 1,16). ZNW 92 (2001) 290-294.

5943 *Dulaey, Martine* Jean 1,16-17 dans l'interprétation patristique. Graphè 10 (2001) 103-123.

5944 *Baarda, Tjitze* John 1,17b: the origin of a Peshitta reading. EThL 77 (2001) 153-162.

5945 *Haemig, Mary J.* The other John in John: LUTHER and ECK on John the Baptist (John 1:19-28). WaW 21 (2001) 377-384.

5946 *Suski, Andrzej* Przekaz świadectwa Jana Chrzciciela w czwartej Ewangelii. CoTh 71/1 (2001) 91-102 [Jn 1,19-34]. **P**.

5947 *Devillers, Luc, al.*, Les noces de Cana. CEv.S 117 (2001) 5-102 [Jn 2,1-11].

5948 *Ferraro, Giuseppe* Gesù e la madre alle nozze di Cana: Giovanni 2,1-11. Gli autori divini. 2001 <1999> ⇒144. 77-105.

5949 *Ternynck, Marie J.* Le signe de Cana: de quelles noces s'agit-il?: portée christologique du récit. Aletheia 20 (2001) 103-110 [Jn 2,1-11].

5950 *García-Moreno, Antonio* La fe de María (Jn 2,4). VIII Simposio di Efeso. Turchia 15: 2001 ⇒488. 27-46.

5951 *O'Neill, John C.* Jesus' reply to his mother at Cana of Galilee (John 2:4). IBSt 23 (2001) 28-35.

5952 *Rhodes, James N.* 'What do you want from me?' (John 2.4). BiTr 52 (2001) 445-447.

5953 *Matson, Mark A.* The temple incident: an integral element in the fourth gospel's narrative. Jesus in Johannine tradition. 2001 ⇒5694. 145-153 [Jn 2,12-22].

5954 *Gärtner, Helga; Gärtner, Hans Armin* Die Reinigung des Tempels (Johannes 2,13-17) bei NONNOS. ᶠSCHÄFER, J. 2001 ⇒99. 265-269.

5955 **López Rosas, Ricardo** La señal del templo: Jn 2,13-22: redefinición cristológica de lo sacro. Diss. St. Georgen, Fra 1999, ᴰ*Beutler, Johannes*: Biblioteca Mexicana 12: México 2001, UPM 426 pp. 968-5-448-00-0. Bibl. 349-421. ᴿEfMex 19 (2001) 415-420 (*J unco Garza, Carlos*).

5956 *Agourides, Savas* Varieties of approach to faith in Jesus (Jn. 2,23-3,36). DBM 20/2 (2001) 99-137. **G**.

G1.6 Jn 3ss... Nicodemus, Samaritana

5957 *Beutler, Johannes* Jésus en conflit—histoire et théologie en Jean 5-12. SIDIC 34/3 (2001) 3-11 Eng. ed. 2-7 [AcBib 10,910].

5958 **Cimbumba Ndayango, Antoine Cilumba** Wunder, Glaube und Leben bei Johannes: eine exegetisch-hermeneutische Studie am Beispiel von Joh 3 im Hinblick auf die Inkulturationsaufgabe. Arbeiten zur Interkulturalität 3: Bonn 2001, Borengässer x; 331 pp. €27.61. 3-923946-55-4. Bibl. 295-323.

5959 *Jong, Dick de* Hoe gebeurt zoiets?: over de ontmoeting van Nicodemus met Jezus. ITBT 9/4 (2001) 16-17 [Jn 3].

5960 **Popp, Thomas** Grammatik des Geistes: literarische Kunst und theologische Konzeption in Johnannes 3 und 6. Arbeiten zur Bibel und ihrer Geschichte 3: Lp 2001, Evangelische Verlagsanstalt 558 pp. €45. 3-374-01851-3.

5961 *Roy Michel, Aude* Jean 3,1-8: ma vieille veste. Lire et Dire 47 (2001) 31-38 [BuBB 33,125].

5962 *Ferraro, Giuseppe* Vedere il regno e nascere da acqua e da Spirito: aspetti del dialogo di Gesù con Nicodemo: Giovanni 3,1-21. Gli autori divini. 2001 <1997> ⇒144. 106-123.

5963 *Moloney, Francis J.* Adventure with Nicodemus: an exercise in hermeneutics. 'A hard saying'. 2001 <1998> ⇒184. 259-279 [Jn 3,1-21].

5964 *Derrett, J.Duncan M.* Correcting Nicodemus (John 3:2, 21). ET 112 (2001) 126.

5965 *Neyrey, Jerome H.; Rohrbaugh, Richard L.* "He must increase, I must decrease" (John 3:30): a cultural and social interpretation. CBQ 63 (2001) 464-483 [Jn 3,22-30].

5966 *Chennattu, Rekha* Women in the mission of the church: an interpretation of John 4. VJTR 65 (2001) 760-773.

5967 *Unamuno, Miguel de* El texto inédito de UNAMUNO: Jesús y la Samaritana. CDios 214 (2001) 579-612 [Jn 4].

5968 *Ferraro, Giuseppe* Il dono dell'acqua viva: l'adorazione in Spirito e verità: aspetti del dialogo di Gesù con la donna samaritana: Giovanni 4,1-26. Gli autori divini. 2001 <1994> ⇒144. 124-138.

5969 *Betto, Frei* A mulher samaritana: versão atualizada do relato evangélico de João 4,1 a 42. São Paulo 2001, Salesiana 28 pp. 85-87997-53-X.

5970 *Görrig, Detlef* Biblische Besinnung: Begegnung am Brunnen (Joh 4, 1-42). ZMiss 27 (2001) 242-243.

5971 **John, Brother of Taizé** At the wellspring: Jesus and the Samaritan woman. NY 2001, Alba 93 pp. $10 [BiTod 39,319—Senior, Donald] [Jn 4,1-42].

5972 **Schapdick, Stefan** Auf dem Weg in den Konflikt: exegetische Studien zum theologischen Profil der Erzählung vom Aufenthalt Jesu in Samarien (Joh 4, 1-42) im Kontext des Johannesevangeliums. BBB 126: 2000 ⇒16,5951. [R]BZ 45 (2001) 137-139 (*Frey, Jörg*).

5973 *Galot, Jean* Tu conosci "il dono di Dio"?. CivCatt 152/3 (2001) 224-235 [Jn 4,10].

5974 *Van Belle, Gilbert* "Salvation is from the Jews": the parenthesis in John 4:22b. Anti-Judaism and the fourth gospel. 2001 ⇒5747. 370-400.

5975 *Ferraro, Giuseppe* La donna samaritana e la fede in Gesù dei suoi concittadini: Giovanni 4,27-30.39-45. Gli autori divini. 2001 <2000> ⇒144. 139-155.

5976 *Neirynck, Frans* Jean 4,46-54: une leçon de méthode. Evangelica III. BEThL 150: 2001 <1995> ⇒187. 590-600.

5977 **Lozada, Francisco** A literary reading of John 5: text as construction. 2000 ⇒16,5958. [R]CBQ 63 (2001) 554-556 (*Moloney, Francis J.*); VeE 22 (2001) 480-482 (*Van der Watt, J.G.*).

5978 *Fee, Gordon D.* On the inauthenticity of John 5:3b-4. To what end exegesis?. 2001 <1982> ⇒143. 17-28.

5979 *Ferraro, Giuseppe* Il significato di 'heos arti' in Giovanni 5,17. Gli autori divini. 2001 <1972> ⇒144. 60-73.

5980 **Kammler, Hans-Christian** Christologie und Eschatologie: Joh 5,17-30 als Schlüsseltext johanneischer Theologie. WUNT 126: 2000 ⇒ 16,5962. [R]CBQ 63 (2001) 344-345 (*Swetnam, James H.*); ATG 64 (2001) 393-394 (*Contreras Molina, Francisco*).

5981 *Bales, David O.* John 5:31-47. Interp. 55 (2001) 416-419.

G1.7 Panis Vitae—*Jn 6...*

5982 **Labahn, Michael** Offenbarung in Zeichen und Wort: Untersuchungen zur Vorgeschichte von Joh. 6,1-25 a und seiner Rezeption in der Brotrede. WUNT 2/117: 2000 ⇒16,5966. [R]ThPh 76 (2001) 271-272 (*Scholtissek, K.*); ThLZ 126 (2001) 1269-271 (*Haldimann, Konrad*).

5983 *Scholtissek, Klaus* Die Brotrede Jesu in Joh 6,1-71: exegetische Beobachtungen zu ihrem Johanneischen Profil. ZKTh 123 (2001) 35-55.

5984 *Stimpfle, Alois* Fremdheit und Wirklichkeit: Überlegungen zu Joh 6, 16-21 aus konstruktivistischer Perspektive. [F]SCHMUTTERMAYR, G. 2001 ⇒101. 265-281.

5985 *García-Moreno, Antonio* El pan de vida (Jn 6,35-50). ScrTh 33 (2001) 13-42.

5986 *Łach, Jan* Znamienny zapis z dyskusji na temat pochodzenia Mesjasza (J 7,25-27.40-43). [F]JANKOWSKI, A. 2001 ⇒53. 240-246. **P**.

5987 *Fee, Gordon D.* Once more—John 7:37-39. To what end exegesis?. 2001 <1978> ⇒143. 83-87.

5988 **Shidemantle, Curtis Scott** The use of the Old Testament in John 7: 37-39: an examination of the Freed-Carson proposal. Diss. Trinity Evang. Divinity 2001, 313 pp. 3003801.

5989 **Tescione, Cesare** "Fiumi di acqua viva sgorgheranno dal suo seno" (Gv 7,38). N 2001, RCE 96 pp. Bibl. 85-93 [Jn 7,37-39].

5990 *Sánchez, Eduardo* El comentario de AMBROSIO y AGUSTÍN sobre la perícopa de la adúltera (Jn 7,53-8,11): parte primera: los materiales ambrosiano y agustiniano. Augustinus 46 (2001) 291-344.

5991 *Hoog, Pierre-Marie* L'impossible première pierre. Christus 48 (2001) 413-417 [Jn 8,1-11].

5992 *Philippe, Marie D.* Commentaire de l'Evangile de saint Jean: "Je suis la lumière du monde"—"Je suis" (1). Aletheia 20 (2001) 157-168 [Jn 8,12].

5993 **Vanneuville, Frederique** Jesus and 'the Jews' in John 8,31-59: an interdisciplinary investigation into the problem of anti-Judaism in the gospel of John. Diss. Leuven 2001, *DBieringer, R.* xxviii; 223 pp. [RTL 33,642].

5994 *Derrett, J. Duncan M.* Oriental sources for John 8,32-36?. BeO 43 (2001) 29-32.

5995 *Von Wahlde, Urban C.* "You are of your father the devil" in its context: stereotyped apocalyptic polemic in John 8:38-47. Anti-Judaism and the fourth gospel. 2001 ⇒5747. 418-444.

5996 *Nicklas, Tobias* "Söhne Kains": Berührungspunkte zwischen Textkritik und Interpretationsgeschichte am Beispiel Joh 8,44 bei APHRAHAT. RB 108 (2001) 349-359.

5997 *Adinolfi, Marco* Il cieco nato del vangelo di Giovanni e i ciechi delle stele di Epidauro. VIII Simposio di Efeso. Turchia 15: 2001 ⇒488. 7-14 [Jn 9].

5998 *Ito, Hisayasu* Johannine irony demonstrated in John 9: part I: part II. Neotest. 34 (2000) 361-371, 373-387.

5999 **Rein, Matthias** Die Heilung des Blindgeborenen (Joh 9). WUNT 2/ 73: 1995 ⇒11/1,4204... 16,5987. RSNTU.A 23 (1998) 265-266 (*Fuchs, Albert*).

6000 *Ito, H.* The significance of Jesus' utterance in relation to the Johannine son of man: a speech act analysis of John 9:35. AcTh(B) 21/1 (2001) 57-82.

6001 *Visschers, Lodewijk* Der gute Hirte (Joh 10): ein Gespräch mit Ferdinand Hahns Johannesexegese. FHAHN, F. 2001 ⇒41. 87-100.

6002 **Kowalski, Beate** Die Hirtenrede (Joh 10,1-18) im Kontext des Johannesevangeliums. SBB 31: 1996 ⇒12,5572... 16,5992. RSNTU.A 22 (1997) 264-266 (*Fuchs, Albert*).

6003 *Dehandschutter, Boudewijn* 'I and the Father are one': Johannine exegesis and intersubjectivity. AF (2001) 535-540 [Jn 10,30].

6004 **Sproston North, Wendy E.** The Lazarus story within the Johannine tradition. Diss. Wales 1997. JSNT.S 212: Shf 2001, Sheffield A. 184

pp. £37. 1-84127-195-0. Bibl. 164-172. ᴿPIBA 24 (2001) 123-124 (*Mangan, Céline*) [Jn 11].

6005 *Agourides, Savas* Η ανάσταση του Λαζάρου στο κατά Ιωάννην ευαγγέλιο (κεφ. 11) [The resurrection of Lazarus in the fourth gospel (ch. 11)]. DBM 20/1 (2001) 97-115. **G.**

6006 *Kiessel, Marie-Élisabeth* La séquence narrative Jn 11,1-12,50: analyse d'une mise en récit. Diss. Lv(N) 2001, ᴰ*Sévrin, J.-M.* xxvi; 435 pp. sum. 318-320.

6007 *Köstenberger, Andreas J.* A comparison of the pericopae of Jesus' anointing. Studies on John. 2001 ⇒169. 49-63 [Mt 26,6-13; Mk 14, 3-9; Lk 7,36-50; Jn 12,1-8].

6008 *Poli, Gianfranco* Betania ... armonizzare condivisione e missione. VitaCon 37/1 (2001) 38-58 [Jn 12,1-11].

6009 *Draper, Jonathan A.* Holy seed and the return of the diaspora in John 12:24. Neotest. 34 (2000) 347-359.

6010 *Reim, Günter* Wie der Evangelist Johannes gemäß Joh 12,37 ff. Jesaja 6 gelesen hat ZNW 92 (2001) 33-46.

G1.8 Jn 13... Sermo sacerdotalis et Passio

6011 **Boer, Martinus C. de** Johannine perspectives on the death of Jesus. Contributions to Biblical Exegesis and Theology 17: 1996 ⇒12, 5583; 13,5864. ᴿSNTU.A 22 (1997) 266-268 (*Niemand, Chr.*).

6012 *Frey, Jörg* Zur johanneischen Deutung des Todes Jesu .ThBeitr 32 (2001) 346-362.

6013 *Zumstein, Jean* The farewell discourses (John 13:31-16:33) and the problem of anti-judaism. Anti-Judaism and the fourth gospel. 2001 ⇒5747. 461-478.

6014 *Beutler, Johannes* La despedida de Jesús: discursos de adiós en Jn 13-17 en perspectiva bíblica. Qol 26 (2001) 45-67.

6015 **Derickson, Gary; Radmacher, Earl** The disciplemaker. Salem, OR 2001, Charis 480 pp. $25/18 [BS 160,377s—Howe, Frederic R.] [Jn 13-17].

6016 *Vakayil, Prema* An Indian approach to John 13,1-11. BiBh 27 (2001) 19-33.

6017 **Hoegen-Rohls, Christina** Der nachösterliche Johannes: die Abschiedsreden als hermeneutischer Schlüssel zum vierten Evangelium. WUNT 2/84: 1996 ⇒12,5588... 15,6038. ᴿStPat 48 (2001) 742-743 (*Segalla, Giuseppe*) [Jn 13-17].

6018 *Bekker, Ype* The beloved disciple in John 13:23. ᶠDEURLOO, K. ACEBT.S 2: 2001 ⇒23. 309-314.

6019 *Beutler, Johannes* Synoptic Jesus tradition in the Johannine farewell discourse. Jesus in Johannine tradition. 2001 ⇒5694. 165-173 [Jn 13,31-16,33].

6020 *Mikołajczak, Mieczysław* Obietnice Pocieszyciela—Ducha Prawdy w mowie pożegnalnej Jezusa (J 14-16) **P**.;

6021 *Oczachowski, Andrzej* 'Przydę znów do was' (J 14,3.28). [F]JANKOWS-KI, A. 2001 ⇒53. 275-280/297-308. **P**.

6022 *Köstenberger, Andreas J.* The 'greater works' of the believer according to John 14:12. Studies on John. 2001 <1995> ⇒169. 117-128.

6023 **Haldimann, Konrad** Rekonstruktion und Entfaltung: exegetische Untersuchungen zu Joh 15 und 16. BZNW 104: 2000 ⇒16,6018. [R]BZ 45 (2001) 278-280 (*Frey, Jörg*).

6024 *Castaño Fonseca, Adolfo M.* Análisis retórico de Jn 15,1-5. EstB 59 (2001) 537-550 & Qol 25 (2001) 45-60.

6025 *Untergaßmair, Franz Georg* Die johanneische "Bildrede vom Fruchtbringen" (15,1-17) im Kontext der biblischen Rechtfertigungslehre. [F]HAINZ, J. 2001 ⇒42. 377-387.

6026 *Piper, Ronald A.* Glory, honor and patronage in the fourth gospel: understanding the Doxa given to disciples in John 17. [F]MALINA, B., BiblInterp 53: 2001 ⇒67. 281-309.

6027 *Browne, Gerald M.* The Old Nubian translation of John 17:1. Muséon 114 (2001) 255-257.

6028 *Barlow, Michel* 'Que tous soient un' (Jean 17,21). Unité chrétienne 144 (2001) 10-14.

6029 *Stancari, Pino* La passione di Gesù secondo Giovanni (Gv 18-19). Bailamme 27/5 (2001) 229-240.

6030 **Lang, Manfred** Johannes und die Synoptiker: eine redaktionsgeschichtliche Analyse von Joh 18-20. FRLANT 182: 1999 ⇒15,6069; 16,6031. [R]ThRv 97 (2001) 51-54 (*Dunderberg, Ismo*); ThLZ 126 (2001) 397-402 (*Thyen, Hartwig*).

6031 *Jenkins, Allan K.* The case of Malchus's ear: narrative criticism and John 18.1-12. ET 112 (2001) 8-11.

6032 *Manns, Frédéric* 'Jésus dit à Pierre: remets le glaive au fourreau: le calice que le Père m'a donné, est ce que je ne le boirai pas?' (Jn 18, 11). VIII Simposio di Efeso. Turchia 15: 2001 ⇒488. 15-25.

6033 *Moloney, Francis J.* John 18:15-27 : a Johannine view of the church. 'A hard saying'. 2001 <1994> ⇒184. 131-147.

6034 *Fernando, G. Charles A.* The law of God and law of the 'Jews' in John 19,7. BiBh 27 (2001) 34-43.

6035 *Neirynck, Frans* Short note on John 19,26-27. Evangelica III. BEThL 150: 2001 <1995> ⇒187. 585-589.

6036 *Carvalho, José Carlos da Silva* The symbology of αἷμα καὶ ὕδωρ in John 19,34: a reappraisal. Did(L) 31 (2001) 41-59.

6037 *Rigato, Maria Luisa* La sepoltura regale e provvisoria di Gesù secondo Gv 19,38-40. VIII Simposio di Efeso. Turchia 15: 2001 ⇒488. 47-79.

6038 *Zumstein, Jean* Lecture narratologique du cycle pascal du quatrième évangile. ETR 76 (2001) 1-15 [Jn 20].

6039 *Lange, Ulrich-Paul* Er sah und glaubte (zu Joh 20,1-9): eine Vorschau auf Ostern. Theologisches 31 (2001) 66-70.

6040 *Aerathedathu, Thomas* Commission and mission: a biblical reflection on Jn 20:21b. MissTod 3 (2001) 444-446.

6041 *Weidemann, Hans-Ulrich* Nochmals Joh 20,23: weitere philologische und exegetische Bemerkungen zu einer problematischen Bibelübersetzung. MThZ 52 (2001) 121-127.

6042 **Kaniarakath, George** Person and faith of apostle Thomas in the gospels. 2000 ⇒16,6044. ᴿETJ 5 (2001) 102-103 (*Edasseril, P.*); BiBh 27 (2001) 155-156 (*Kottackal, Joseph*) [Jn 20,24-29].

6043 *Fee, Gordon D.* On the text and meaning of John 20:30-31. To what end exegesis?. 2001 <1992> ⇒143. 29-42.

6044 *Savasta, Carmelo* Gv 20,30-31 e 21,24-25: una doppia finale?. BeO 43 (2001) 130.

6045 *Mędala, Stanisław* Funkcja i treść opowiadania o trzecim objawieniu się Jezusa uczniom po zmartwychwstaniu (J 21,1-14). ᶠJANKOWSKI, A. 2001 ⇒53. 247-274. **P.**

G2.1 Epistulae Johannis

6046 **Akin, Daniel L.** 1,2,3 John. NAC 38: Nv 2001, Broadman 296 pp. $30. 0-8054-0138-5. Bibl. 281-284.

6047 **Beutler, Johannes** Die Johannesbriefe. Regensburger Neues Testament: 2000 ⇒16,6049. ᴿRdT 42 (2001) 145-146 (*Simoens, Yves*); ThLZ 126 (2001) 919-921 (*Horn, Friedrich W.*).

6048 **Hodges, Zane** The epistles of John: walking in the light of God's love. 1999 ⇒15,6102. ᴿBS 158 (2001) 501-503 (*Zuck, Roy B.*).

6049 *Köstenberger, Andreas J.* Mission in the general epistles. Mission in the NT. ASMS 27: 2001 ⇒367. 189-206.

6050 **Kruse, Colin G.** The letters of John. 2000 ⇒16,6052. ᴿABR 49 (2001) 70-71 (*Coloe, Mary*); ThLZ 126 (2001) 919-921 (*Horn, Friedrich W.*); Neotest. 35 (2001) 177 (*Van der Watt, Jan G.*).

6051 **Rensberger, David** The epistles of John. Westminster Bible companion: LVL 2001, Westminster viii; 130 pp. 0-664-25801-8. Bibl. 129-130.

6052 **Strecker, Georg** The Johannine letters: a commentary on 1, 2, and 3 John. [T]*Maloney, Linda M.*: Hermeneia: 1996 ⇒12,5643... 16,6056. [R]JBL 119 (2000) 776-780 (*Smith, D. Moody*).

6053 **Uebele, Wolfram** "Viele Verführer sind in die Welt ausgegangen": die Gegner in den Briefen des IGNATIUS von Antiochien und in den Johannesbriefen. BWANT 151: Stu 2001, Kohlhammer 195 pp. €38.50. 3-17-016725-1. Bibl. 165-188.

6054 **Giurisato, Giorgio** Struttura e teologia della prima lettera di Giovanni: analisi letteraria e retorica, contenuto teologico. AnBib 138: 1998 ⇒14,5528...16,6059. [R]Neotest. 35 (2001) 185-86 (*Decock, Paul B.*).

6055 **Lietaert Peerbolte, Lambertus J.** The antecedents of antichrist. 1996 ⇒12,5661... 16,6062. [R]ThLZ 126 (2001) 417-419 (*Kinzig, Wolfram*).

6056 *Mills, Donald W.* The eschatology of 1 John. Looking into the future. 2001 ⇒505. 97-111.

6057 *Studer, Basil* L'esegesi patristica della *Prima Ioannis*. VIII Simposio di Efeso. Turchia 15: 2001 ⇒488. 143-151.

6058 *Wilckens, Ulrich* 'Simul iustus et peccator' in 1 Joh 1,5-2,2. Gerecht und Sünder zugleich?. 2001 ⇒378. 82-91.

G2.3 *Apocalypsis Johannis*—Revelation: text, commentaries

6059 [E]**Acinas, Blanca** En torno al Apocalipsis. BAC, Teologia 14: M 2001, Biblioteca de Autores Cristianos xiv; 331 pp. €13.29. 84-7914-562-5. Bibl. 326-331. [R]ATG 64 (2001) 387-389 (*Contreras Molina, Francisco*); VyV 59 (2001) 577-579 (*Álvarez Barredo, Miguel*).

6060 *Afnulf, Arwed* Johannes-Apokalypse/Johannesoffenbarung. RGG[2], 4: I-K. 2001 ⇒664. 540-549.

6061 **Aune, David** Revelation. WBC 52a-c: 1998 ⇒14,5549-5551... 16, 6067. [R]RSR 89 (2001) 582-584 (*Morgen, Michèle*); EThL 77 (2001) 479-482 (*Verheyden, J.*).

6062 [E]**Backhaus, Knut** Theologie als Vision: Studien zur Johannes-Offenbarung. SBS 191: Stu 2001, Kathol. Bibelwerk 207 pp. €24.90. 3-460-04911-1.

6063 **Beale, Gregory K.** The book of Revelation: a commentary on the Greek text. NIGTC: 1999 ⇒16,6072. [R]EThL 77 (2001) 479-482 (*Verheyden, J.*); JBL 119 (2000) 158-160 (*Morton, Russell*); EvQ 73 (2001) 363-366 (*Mathewson, Dave*).

6064 **Donelson, Lewis R.** From Hebrews to Revelation: a theological introduction. LVL 2001, Westminster v; 161 pp. 0-664-22236-6. Bibl. 159-161.

6065 **Garrow, Alan John Philip** Revelation. New Testament Readings: 1997 ⇒13,5933. [R]JBL 119 (2000) 157-158 (*Kerkeslager, Allen*).

6066 **Giesen, Heinz** Die Offenbarung des Johannes. RNT: 1997 ⇒13, 5935... 16,6084. [R]RBLit 3 (2001) 466-468 (*McDonough, Sean M.*).

6067 [E]**Groote, Marc de** OECUMENII commentarius in Apocalypsin. 1999 ⇒15,6135; 16,6086. [R]VigChr 55 (2001) 442-446 (*Uthemann, Karl-Heinz*).

6068 *Gryson, R.* Verschiedene Arbeiten rings um die Apokalypse. BVLI 45 (2001) 28-35.

6069 [E]**Gryson, Roger** BEDA Venerabilis: expositio Apocalypseos. CChr. SL 121 A; Bedae Opera 2/5: Turnhout 2001. Brepols 606 pp. 2-503-01213-2;

6070 Apocalypsis Johannis: 3. Lief., Apc 2,7-4,1. BVLI 26/2: FrB 2001, Herder 161-240 pp [RBen 112,171—Bogaert, P.-M.].

6071 *Hamanishi, Masako* Die Trierer Apokalypse. BVLI 45 (2001) 35-36.

6072 **Joy, C.I. David** Revelation: a post-colonial viewpoint. Delhi 2001, ISPCK xiii; 104 pp. Rs85/$8/£6. 81721-46264 [VJTR 66,702 Jothi].

6073 **Kistemaker, Simon J.** New Testament commentary: exposition of the book of Revelation. GR 2001, Baker x; 635 pp. $40. 0-9810-2252-5.

6074 **Klein, Peter K.** Die Trierer Apokalypse: Codex 31 der Stadtbibliothek Trier. Graz 2001, ADEVA 84 pp. €89. 3-201-01762-0. Komm. *P. Klein*; Beitr. von *Richard Laufner* u. *Gunther Franz*; 74 Faks.

6075 **Koester, Craig R.** Revelation and the end of all things. GR 2001, Eerdmans xiv; 209 pp. $16. 0-8028-4660-2. Bibl. xiii-xiv.

6076 **Lindsay, Stan A.** Revelation: the human drama. Bethlehem, PA 2001, Lehigh University Pr. 216 pp. 0-934223-71-8. Bibl. 185-201.

6077 **Malina, Bruce J.; Pilch, John J.** Social-science commentary on the book of Revelation. 2000 ⇒16,6091. [R]CBQ 63 (2001) 757-758 (*Skemp, Vincent*).

6078 **Marshall, John William** Parables of war: reading John's Jewish Apocalypse. Studies in Christianity and Judaism 10; Études sur le christianisme et le judaïsme 10: Waterloo, Ontario 2001, Wilfrid Laurier University Pr. vii; 258 pp. $30. 08892-03741. Bibl. 208-239.

6079 **Mounce, Robert H.** The book of Revelation. [2]1998 ⇒14,5560... 16, 6092. [R]SNTU.A 23 (1998) 280-281 (*Fuchs, Albert*).

6080 [E]**Moyise, Steve** Studies in the book of Revelation. E 2001, Clark xvii; 206 pp. £17. 0-567-08804-9.

6081 Die Offenbarung des Johannes. Fischer Taschenbuch 14512: Fra 2000, Fischer 59 pp. 3-596-14512-0. Einleitung von *Will Self.*

6082 **Pikaza Ibarrondo, Xabier** Apocalisse. Guide alla lettura del Nuovo Testamento 17: R 2001, Borla 348 pp. 88-263-1368-7. Bibl. 333-43.

6083 **Prigent, P.** Les secrets de l'Apocalypse: mystique, ésoterisme et apocalypse. P 2001, Cerf 102 pp. 2-204-06965-5 [ATG 65,321—Contreras Molina, F.];

6084 L'Apocalypse. LiBi 117: 1998 ⇒14,5563; 15,6149. [R]EstB 59 (2001) 408-409 (*Asenjo, J.*);

6085 L'Apocalypse de Saint Jean. CNT 14: [2]2000 ⇒16,6097. [R]EstTrin 35 (2001) 456-457 (*Vázquez Allegue, Jaime*); EeV 42 (2001) 25-27 (*Cothenet, Edouard*);

6086 Commentary on the Apocalypse of St. John. [T]*Pradels, Wendy*: Tü 2001, Mohr xiv; 717 pp. $126. 3-16-147399-X. Bibl. 654-676.

6087 **Richard, Pablo** L'Apocalypse: reconstruction de l'espérance. Montréal 2001, Paulines 246 pp. CAD35/€30. 2-920912-41-0 [RTL 33, 576—Gérard, J.-P.].

6088 **Rossing, Barbara R.** The choice between two cities: whore, bride, and empire in the Apocalypse. HThS 48: 1999 ⇒15,6244; 16,6099. [R]BZ 45 (2001) 150-151 (*Klauck, Hans-Josef*); RBLit 3 (2001) 475-478 (*Seesengood, Robert Paul*) [Rev 17-19; 21,1-22,5].

6089 **Rozman, France** Apokalipsa–razodetje: komentar. 2000 ⇒16,6100. [R]BoSm 71 (2001) 203-204 (*Rebić, Adalbert*). **Croatian.**

6090 **Saout, Yves** Je n'ai pas écrit l'Apocalypse pour vous faire peur!: par Jean de Patmos. 2000 ⇒16,6101. [R]SR 30 (2001) 448-450 (*Mbonimpa, Melchior*).

6091 **Scheele, Paul-Werner** Würzburger Apokalypse: Apokalyptisches im Wandel der Zeit. Wü 2001, Echter 123 pp. 3-429-02393-9.

6092 **Smith, Robert H.** Apocalypse: a commentary on Revelation in words and images. 2000 ⇒16,6102. [R]ScrB 31/1 (2001) 51-53 (*O'-Kane, Martin*); CThMi 28 (2001) 498-499 (*Tietjen, John H.*).

6093 **Tenney, Merrill Chapin** Interpreting Revelation: a reasonable guide to understanding the last book in the bible. Peabody, MASS 2001, Hendrickson xi; 13-220 pp. 1-56563-655-4. Bibl. 207-211.

6094 *Untergaßmair, Franz Georg* Das Buch der Offenbarung (1): Einführung. BiLi 74 (2001) 61-64.

6095 **Valdes, Jorge Luis** The first printed Apocalypse of St. John: the Complutensian Polyglot and its influence in ERASMUS' Greek New Testament text. Diss. Loyola, Chicago 2001, 168 pp. 3015534.

6096 **Villefranche, Henry de** Lire l'*Apocalypse* de saint Jean. Les Cahiers de l'Ecole Cathédrale 46: P 2001, Parole et Silence 135 pp. €12.04. 2-84573-056-X.

6097 [E]**Vögele, Wolfgang; Schenk, Richard** Aktuelle Apokalyptik!. Loccumer Protokolle 20/99: Loccum 2001, Evangelische Akademie 288 pp. €11. 3-8172-2099-5.

G2.4 *Apocalypsis, themata*—**Revelation, topics**

6098 **Adinolfi, Marco** Apocalisse: testo, simboli e visioni. Piemme, Religione: CasM 2001, Piemme 171 pp. 88-384-6418-9.

6099 *Akerboom, T.H.M.* 'Er zullen grote tekenen zijn': een verkenning van LUTHERs verstaan van de Apocalyps in de context van zijn tijd. Luther Digest 9 (2001) 188-193 <Luther-Bulletin 7,62-75.

6100 *Arcari, Luca* La titolatura dell'Apocalisse di Giovanni: "Apocalisse" o "profezia"?: appunti per una ri-definizione del "genere apocalittico" sulla scorta di quello "profetico". Henoch 23 (2001) 243-265.

6101 *Ausloos, Hans* Als de nood het hoogst is, is de redding nabij!: Jehovah's getuigen en het boek Openbaring. TTh 41 (2001) 13-36.

6102 *Backhaus, Knut* Die Vision vom ganz Anderen: geschichtlicher Ort und theologische Mitte der Johannes-Offenbarung. Theologie als Vision. SBS 191: 2001 ⇒6062. 10-53.

6103 *Bandera, Armando* La iglesia de Roma en el Apocalipsis: un proyecto que espera desarrollo. Ang. 78 (2001) 23-48 Res. 48.

6104 **Barker, Margaret** The revelation of Jesus Christ, which God gave to him to show to his servants what must soon take place (Revelation 1.1). 2000 ⇒16,6108. ᴿBZ 45 (2001) 291-293 (*Giesen, Heinz*); AUSS 39 (2001) 323-327 (*Winkle, Ross E.*); SNTU.A 26 (2001) 243-245 (*Giesen, H.*).

6105 *Barr, David L.* Waiting for the end that never comes: the narrative logic of John's story. Studies in...Revelation. 2001 ⇒6080. 101-112.

6106 *Bauckham, Richard* Prayer in the book of Revelation. Into God's presence. 2001 ⇒294. 252-271.

6107 *Baumert, Norbert* Ein Ruf zur Entscheidung: Aufbau und Botschaft der Offenbarung des Johannes. Studien zu den Paulusbriefen. SBAB 32: 2001 <1991> ⇒123. 296-309.

6108 *Beale, G.K.* A response to Jon Paulien on the use of the Old Testament in Revelation. AUSS 39 (2001) 23-33.

6109 **Beale, Gregory K.** John's use of the Old Testament in Revelation. JSNT.S 166: 1998 ⇒14,5575; 16,6109. ᴿJBL 120 (2001) 583-585 (*Newport, Kenneth*); RSR 89 (2001) 589-590 (*Morgen, Michèle*).

6110 **Briggs, Robert A.** Jewish temple imagery in the book of Revelation. 1999 ⇒15,6179; 16,6116. ᴿCBQ 63 (2001) 139-140 (*Spatafora, Andrea*); WThJ 63 (2001) 466-467 (*Mbuvi, Andrew M.*).

6111 *Broadhead, Edwin K.* Sacred imagination and social protest. RExp 98 (2001) 77-85.

6112 **Brokoff, Jürgen** Die Apokalypse in der Weimarer Republik. Mü 2001, Fink 188 pp. €30.60. 3-7705-3603-7.

6113 *Campbell, Gordon* How to say what: story and interpretation in the book of Revelation. IBSt 23 (2001) 111-134.

6114 *Carey, Greg* The Apocalypse and its ambiguous ethos. Studies in the book of Revelation. 2001 ⇒6080. 163-180;

6115 Teaching and preaching the book of Revelation in the church. RExp 98 (2001) 87-100.

6116 **Carey, Greg** Elusive Apocalypse: reading authority in the Revelation to John. 1999 ⇒15,6181. [R]CBQ 63 (2001) 546-547 (*Winkler, Jude*).

6117 **Choi, Byong Kie** The 'arnion', lamb, as a christological figure in the visions of the Apocalypse (4:1-22:5): a christological study of the 'Book of Revelation'. Diss. Drew 2001, 255 pp. 3005854.

6118 [E]**Couch, Mal** A bible handbook to Revelation. GR 2001, Kregel 328 pp. $22.

6119 **Court, John M.** The book of Revelation and the Johannine apocalyptic tradition. JSNT.S 190: 2000 ⇒16,6129. [R]NT 43 (2001) 188-189 (*Elliott, J.K.*); CBQ 63 (2001) 549-550 (*Thompson, Leonard L.*); ThLZ 126 (2001) 923-924 (*Böcher, Otto*).

6120 *Cuvillier, Élian* Christ ressuscité ou bête immortelle?: proclamation pascale et propagande impériale dans l'Apocalypse de Jean. Résurrection: l'après-mort. MoBi 45: 2001 ⇒296. 237-254;

6121 L'immolation du Christ, de la bête et des croyants dans l'Apocalypse: sacrifice ou séduction trompeuse. CEv 118 (2001) 48-56.

6122 *Doglio, Claudio* Lo splendore della novità: l'Apocalisse come rivelazione della bellezza. La bellezza. PSV 44: 2001 ⇒240. 143-158.

6123 **Duff, Paul Brooks** Who rides the beast?: prophetic rivalry and the rhetoric of crisis in the churches of the Apocalypse. NY 2001, OUP xiii; 189 pp. £32.50. 0-19-513835-X. Bibl. 169-175.

6124 **Emonet, Pierre-Marie** L'église dans les images de l'Apocalypse. 1999 ⇒15,6193; 16,6080. [R]RThom 109 (2001) 498-499 (*Antoniotti, Louise-Marie*).

6125 *Fiorenza, Elisabeth Schüssler* The words of prophecy: reading the Apocalypse theologically. Studies in...Revelation. 2001 ⇒6080. 1-19.

6126 *Frey, Jörg* Die Bildersprache der Johannesapokalypse. ZThK 98 (2001) 161-185.

6127 **Friesen, Steven J.** Imperial cults and the Apocalypse of John: reading Revelation in the ruins. Oxf 2001, OUP xiii; 285 pp. £40. 0-19-513153-3. Bibl. 259-272.

6128 *Gloer, Hulitt* Worship God!: liturgical elements in the Apocalypse. RExp 98 (2001) 35-57.

6129 *Gloor, Daniel A.* G.K. Beale: "John's use of the Old Testament in Revelation"—notes de lecture. FV 100/4 (2001) 93-100.

6130 **Hanna, Kamal Fahim Awad** La passione di Cristo nell'Apocalisse. Diss. Gregoriana, ^D*Vanni, Ugo*: TGr.T 77: R 2001, E.P.U.G. 473 pp. €25.82. 88-7652-897-0. Bibl. 441-464.

6131 *Hasitschka, Martin* Bedrängtes und verherrlichtes Gottesvolk: Kirchenverständnis der Apokalypse. Wort zum Leben. 2001 ⇒284. 143-155.

6132 **Heinze, André** Johannesapokalypse und johanneische Schriften.. BWANT 142: 1998 ⇒14,5607... 16,6158. ^RStPat 48 (2001) 227-228 (*Segalla, Giuseppe*); JBL 120 (2001) 181-183 (*Koester, Craig R.*).

6133 **Hirschberg, Peter Dieter** Das eschatologische Gottesvolk: Untersuchungen zum Gottesvolkverständnis der Johannesoffenbarung. WMANT 84: 1999 ⇒15,6210. ^RThLZ 126 (2001) 528-530 (*Holtz, Traugott*).

6134 **Howard-Brook, Wes; Gwyther, Anthony** Unveiling empire: reading Revelation then and now. 1999 ⇒15,6211; 16,6162. ^RCBQ 63 (2001) 149-151 (*Harrington, Wilfrid J.*).

6135 **Hultberg, Alan David** Messianic exegesis in the Apocalypse: the significance of the Old Testament for the christology of Revelation. Diss. Trinity Evang. Divinity 2001, 460 pp. 3003781.

6136 *Jack, Alison* Out of the wilderness: feminist perspectives on the book of Revelation. Studies in...Revelation. 2001 ⇒6080. 149-162.

6137 *Kampling, Rainer* Vision der Kirche oder Gemeinde eines Visionärs?: auf der Suche nach der Ekklesiologie der Johannes-Offenbarung. Theologie als Vision. SBS 191: 2001 ⇒6062. 121-150.

6138 *Keller, Catherine* Eyeing the Apocalypse. Postmodern interpretations. 2001 ⇒229. 253-277.

6139 **Kerner, Jürgen** Die Ethik der Johannesapokalypse im Vergleich mit der des 4. Esra: ein Beitrag zum Verhältnis von Apokalyptik und Ethik. BZNW 94: 1998 ⇒14,5613. ^RJBL 120 (2001) 390-391 (*Schnabel, Eckhard J.*); RBLit 3 (2001) 468-470 (*Schnabel, Eckhard J.*).

6140 *Klauck, Hans-Josef* Do they never come back?: NERO redivivus and the Apocalypse of John. CBQ 63 (2001) 683-698.

6141 *Kowalski, Beate* "... sie werden Priester Gottes und des Messias sein; und sie werden König sein mit ihm—tausend Jahre lang" (Offb 20,6): Martyrium und Auferstehung in der Offenbarung. SNTU.A 26 (2001) 139-163.

6142 *Lambrecht, Jan* Synagogues of Satan (cf. Rev 2,9 and 3,9): Anti-Judaism in the Apocalypse. Collected studies. AnBib 147: 2001 ⇒170. 341-356 & Anti-Judaism and fourth gospel. 2001 ⇒5747. 514-530;

6143 The people of God in the book of Revelation. Collected studies. AnBib 147: 2001 ⇒170. 379-394;

6144 Het volk van God in de Openbaring van Johannes. Vroegchristelijke gemeenten. 2001 ⇒460. 163-177.

6145 *Lassus, Alain M. de* L'adoration dans l'Apocalypse (2. partie). Aletheia 19 (2001) 129-174.

6146 *Lockmann, Paulo* A violência do império e a justiça do reino. Estudos Bíblicos 69 (2001) 61-71.

6147 **Malina, Bruce J.** The New Jerusalem in the Revelation of John: the city as symbol of life with God. 2000 ⇒16,6171. [R]ScrB 31/1 (2001) 50-51 (*Docherty, Susan*).

6148 *Maniparampil, Jose* A spiral-teleological literary structure (an overall structure to the book of Revelation). BiBh 27 (2001) 44-75.

6149 *Mathews, Susan F.* Salvific suffering in John's Apocalypse: the church as sacrament of salvation. The bible on suffering. 2001 ⇒ 326. 188-210.

6150 **McCormack, Philip** The nature of judgment in the book of Revelation. Diss. Belfast 2001, [D]*Hibbert, A.*: 271 pp [RTL 33,639].

6151 *Meyer-Abich, Klaus-Michael* Kosmisches Christentum in der Offenbarung des Johannes—eine Vision der Hoffnung auch in der Naturkrise unserer Zeit. Aktuelle Apokalyptik!. Loccumer Protokolle 20/99: 2001 ⇒6079. 43-58.

6152 *Miller, Johnny V.* Mission in Revelation. Mission in the NT. ASMS 27: 2001 ⇒367. 227-238.

6153 *Moyise, Steve* Does the lion lie down with the lamb?. Studies in the book of Revelation. 2001 ⇒6080. 181-194;

6154 Seeing the Old Testament through a lens. Ment. *Beale, G.* IBSt 23 (2001) 36-41;

6155 Authorial intention and the book of Revelation. AUSS 39 (2001) 35-40.

6156 *Nakhro, Mazie* The meaning of worship according to the book of Revelation. BS 158 (2001) 75-85;

6157 The manner of worship according to the book of Revelation. BS 158 (2001) 165-180.

6158 *Nanz, Christian* "Hinabgeworfen wurde des Ankläger unserer Brüder ..." (Offb 12,10): das Motiv vom Satanssturz in der Johannes-Offenbarung. Theologie als Vision. SBS 191: 2001 ⇒6062. 151-171.

6159 *Nápole, Gabriel M.* Desarrollo y evolución de los estudios sobre "la apocaliptica". EstB 59 (2001) 325-363.

6160 *Neubrand, Maria* "Halte, was du hast" (Offb 3,11): zur sozioreligiösen Standortbestimmung der Offenbarung des Johannes. [F]HAHN, F. 2001 ⇒41. 180-191.

6161 *Nikolakopoulos, Konstantin* Rhetorische Auslegungsaspekte der Theologie in der Johannesoffenbarung. [F]HAHN, F. 2001 ⇒41. 166-180.

6162 *Oegema, Gerbern S.* Auferstehung in der Johannesoffenbarung: eine rezeptionsgeschichtliche Untersuchung zu der Vorstellung zweier

Auferstehungen in der Offenbarung des Johannes. Auferstehung—Resurrection. WUNT 135: 2001 ⇒452. 205-227.

6163   *Palmer, Gesine* Die Idee der Einfürallemaligkeit in apokalyptischen Vorstellungen: ein Versuch über eschatologische Müdigkeit. ZRGG 53 (2001) 97-114.

6164   *Pasquetto, Virgilio* 'Vieni, Signore Gesù' (Ap. 22,20): la speranza secondo il libro dell'Apocalisse. RVS 55 (2001) 636-659.

6165   *Paul, Ian* The book of Revelation: image, symbol and metaphor;

6166   *Paulien, Jon* Criteria and the assessment of allusions to the Old Testament in the book of Revelation. Studies in the book of Revelation. 2001 ⇒6080. 131-147/113-129;

6167   Dreading the whirlwind: intertextuality and the use of the Old Testament in Revelation. AUSS 39 (2001) 5-22.

6168   *Pilch, John J.* Dragons in the bible. BiTod 39 (2001) 301-305.

6169   **Pisano, Ombretta** La radice e la stirpe di David: salmi davidici nel libro dell'Apocalisse. Exc. Diss. Gregoriana, ᴰ*Vanni, Ugo*: R 2001, 171 pp .

6170   *Popielewski, Wojciech* Zwiazek religii imperialnej z czasem ucisku: *Sitz im Leben* Apokalipsy. ᶠJANKOWSKI, A. 2001 ⇒53. 365-382. **P.**

6171   **Portone, Paolo** L'ultimo sigillo: l'Apocalisse nel XXI secolo. 1999 ⇒15,6238. ᴿNRS 85 (2001) 207-212 (*De Rosa, Riccardo*).

6172   **Resseguie, James L.** Revelation unsealed: a narrative critical approach to John's Apocalypse. BiblInterp 32: 1998 ⇒14,5642; 16, 6192. ᴿRSR 89 (2001) 586-588 (*Morgen, Michèle*); RBLit 3 (2001) 472-475 (*Just, Felix*).

6173   **Riemer, Ulrike** Das Tier auf dem Kaiserthron?: eine Untersuchung zur Offenbarung des Johannes als historischer Quelle. 1998 ⇒14, 5644. ᴿGn. 73 (2001) 716-718 (*Molthagen, Joachim*).

6174   **Roose, Hanna** Das Zeugnis Jesu: seine Bedeutung für die Christologie, Eschatologie...in der Offenbarung des Johannes. TANZ 32: 2000 ⇒16,6195. ᴿThLZ 126 (2001) 56-8 (*Holtz, Traugott*).

6175   *Scholtissek, Klaus* "Mitteilhaber an der Bedrängnis, der Königsherrschaft und der Ausdauer in Jesus" (Offb 1,9): partizipatorische Ethik in der Offenbarung des Johannes. Theologie als Vision. SBS 191: 2001 ⇒6062. 172-207.

6176   ᴱ**Simoens, Yves; Theobald, Ch.** Sous le signe de l'imminence: l'Apocalypse de Jean pour penser l'histoire. P 2001, Médiasèvres 190 pp. 2-900-388-57-11. Session du Centre Sèvres [ATG 65,323– Contreras Molina, F.].

6177   **Soeting, A.G.** Auditieve aspecten van het boek Openbaring van Johannes. Diss. Amsterdam, ᴰ*Van Henten, J.W.*: Zoetermeer 2001, Boekencentrum 263 pp. €23.90. 90-239-0882-1 .

6178 *Söding, Thomas* Gott und das Lamm: Theozentrik und Christologie in der Johannesapokalypse. Theologie als Vision. SBS 191: 2001 ⇒ 6062. 77-120

6179 *Spencer, Richard A.* Violence and vengeance in Revelation. RExp 98 (2001) 59-75.

6180 **Stevenson, Gregory** Power and place: temple and identity in the book of Revelation. BZNT 107: B 2001, De Gruyter xvii; 368 pp. $71.23. 3-11-017008-6. Bibl. 307-342. ᴿWThJ 63 (2001) 468-469 (*Mbuvi, Andrew M.*).

6181 *Svigel, Michael J.* The Apocalypse of John and the rapture of the church: a reevaluation. TrinJ 22 (2001) 23-74.

6182 **Timossi, Innocenzo** Apocalisse: Rivelazione di Gesù Cristo: una cristologia per simboli. Per approfondire la bibbia: Leumann (Torino) 2001, Elle Di Ci 222 pp. 88-01-02177-1.

6183 *Untergaßmair, Franz Georg* Das Buch der Offenbarung (3): das Buch mit den sieben Siegeln. BiLi 74 (2001) 194-199;

6184 (4): Gericht und Vollendung. BiLi 74 (2001) 268-272.

6185 *Van Henten, Jan Willem* Anti-judaism in Revelation?: a response to Peter Tomson. Anti-Judaism and the fourth gospel. 2001 ⇒5747. 111-125 [Rev 2,9; 3,9].

6186 **Vanni, Ugo** "Divenire nello Spirito": l'Apocalisse guida di spiritualità. 2000 ⇒16,6201. ᴿCivCatt 152/3 (2001) 103-104 (*Scaiola, D.*).

6187 *Vanni, Ugo* La giustizia tipica dell'Apocalisse. Giustizia-giustificazione nella bibbia. DSBP 28: 2001 ⇒307. 228-246.

6188 *Vinson, Richard B.* The social world of the book of Revelation. RExp 98 (2001) 11-33.

6189 *Zbroja, Bogdan* Terminy własne Apokalipsy i ich znaczenie [La signification théologique des termes propres de l'Apocalypse]. ACra 33 (2001) 587-599 Rés. 599. P.

G2.5 *Apocalypsis*, **Revelation 1,1...**

6190 *Vögele, Wolfgang* Andacht über Apk 1,3. Aktuelle Apokalyptik!. Loccumer Protokolle 20/99: 2001 ⇒6079. 280-281.

6191 **McDonough, Sean M.** YHWH at Patmos: Rev. 1:4 in its Hellenistic and early Jewish setting. WUNT 2/107: 1999 ⇒15,6270; 16,6206. ᴿJSJ 32 (2001) 328-331 (*Mussies, Gerard*).

6192 *Untergaßmair, Franz Georg* Das Buch der Offenbarung (2): Johannes an die sieben Gemeinden in der Provinz Asien (Offb 1,4). BiLi 74 (2001) 132-136 [Rev 1,4-3,22].

6193 *Räisänen, Heikki* The Nicolaitans: Apoc 2; Acta 6. Challenges to biblical interpretation. BiblInterp 59: 2001 <1995> ⇒200. 141-189.

6194 **Hemer, Colin J.** The letters to the seven churches of Asia in their local setting. GR 2001 <1986>, Eerdmans xxii; 338 pp. £20. 0-8028-4714-5. Foreword *David Aune*; Bibl. ᴿScrB 31 (2001) 116-118 (*Clarke, Fern*); VJTR 65 (2001) 784-86 (*Meagher, P.M.*) [Rev 2-3].

6195 *Kowalski, Beate* Das Verhältnis von Theologie und Zeitgeschichte in den Sendschreiben der Johannes-Offenbarung. Theologie als Vision. SBS 191: 2001 ⇒6062. 54-76 [Rev 2-3].

6196 *Frankfurter, David* Jews or not?: reconstructing the "other" in Rev 2:9 and 3:9. HThR 94 (2001) 403-425.

6197 *Lambrecht, Jan* Jewish slander: a note on Revelation 2,9-10. Collected studies. AnBib 147: 2001 <1999> ⇒170. 329-339.

6198 *Tarocchi, Stefano* Il soggetto interpretante nella lettera alla chiesa di Laodicea (AP 3,14-21). VivH 12/2 (2001) 299-327.

6199 *Sordet, Jean-Michel* Apocalypse 3,20: choix banal et choix spirituel. Lire et Dire 49 (2001) 39-48 [BuBB 34,49].

6200 *Morton, Russell* Glory to God and to the lamb: John's use of Jewish and Hellenistic/Roman themes in formatting his theology in Revelation 4-5. JSNT 83 (2001) 89-109.

6201 *Stevenson, Kenneth* Animal rites: the four living creatures in patristic exegesis and liturgy. StPatr 34 (2001) 470-492 [Ez 1; Rev 4,6-11].

6202 *Parker, Floyd O.* 'Our Lord and God' in Rev 4,11: evidence for the late date of Revelation?. Bib. 82 (2001) 207-231.

6203 *Giesen, Heinz* Zur Christologie der Thronsaalvision (Offb 5). ThG 44 (2001) 25-35.

6204 *Stefanovic, Ranko* The meaning and significance of the ἐπὶ τὴν δεξιάν for the location of the sealed scroll (Revelation 5:1) and understanding the scene of Revelation 5. BR 46 (2001) 42-54.

6205 *Knight, Jonathan* The enthroned Christ of Revelation 5:6 and the development of christian theology. Studies in the book of Revelation. 2001 ⇒6080. 43-50.

6206 **Lumsden, Douglas W.** And then the end will come: early Latin christian interpretation of the opening of the seven seals. Diss. Medieval History and Culture: NY 2001, Garland xii; 112 pp. $60 [Rev 6,1-8,1].

6207 *Lambrecht, Jan* The opening of the seals (Revelation 6,1-8,6). Collected studies: AnBib 147: 2001 <1998> ⇒170. 357-377.

6208 *Martin, François* "Quand le septième ange sonnera de la trompette ...": Apg 8,1-11,19. Le judaïsme à l'aube de l'ère chrétienne. LeDiv 186: 2001 ⇒450. 247-268.

6209 *Holmes, James L.* Clothed with the sun. HPR 101/4 (2001) 20-27 [Rev 12].

6210 **Kalms, Jürgen H.** Der Sturz des Gottesfeindes: traditionsgeschichtliche Studien zu Apokalypse 12. Diss. Münster 2000, ᴰ*Taeger, J.-W.*:

WMANT 93: Neuk 2001, Neuk xii; 300 pp. €59. 3-7887-1859-5. Bibl. 281-300.

6211 *Poniży, Bogdan* Niewiasta—wizja autora protoewangelii (Rdz 3,15) i autora Apokalipsy (Ap 12). ᶠJANKOWSKI, A. 2001 ⇒53. 346-364. **P**.

6212 *Sumney, Jerry L.* The dragon has been defeated—Revelation 12. RExp 98 (2001) 103-115.

6213 **Ulland, Harald** Die Vision als Radikalisierung der Wirklichkeit in der Apokalypse des Johannes: das Verhältnis der sieben Sendschreiben zu Apokalypse 12-13. TANZ 21: 1997 ⇒13,6035... 15,6286. ᴿSNTU.A 23 (1998) 278-279 (*Fuchs, Albert*).

6214 *Roure, Damià* Del text al lector: estudi exegètic d'Ap 12,1-18. El text. Scripta Biblica 3: 2001 ⇒310. 61-74.

6215 **Abir, Peter Antonysamy** The cosmic conflict of the church: an exegetico-theological study of Revelation 12,7-12. EHS.T 547: 1995 ⇒11/1,4457. ᴿSNTU.A 22 (1997) 278-279 (*Fuchs, Albert*).

6216 *Bowles, Ralph G.* Does Revelation 14:11 teach eternal torment?: examining a proof-text on hell. EvQ 73 (2001) 21-36.

6217 *Alvarez Valdés, Ariel* Le sens biblique de la bataille de Harmagedôn. NRTh 123 (2001) 19-26 [Rev 16,16].

6218 *Heller, Jan* Armagedon: der Name als Programm. ᶠDEURLOO, K. ACEBT.S 2: 2001 ⇒23. 341-345.

6219 *Biguzzi, Giancarlo* Gli enigmi di Ap 17 e le sue allusioni alla storia contemporanea. RivBib 49 (2001) 173-201.

6220 *Boxall, Ian* The many faces of Babylon the Great: *Wirkungsgeschichte* and the interpretation of Revelation 17. Studies in the book of Revelation. 2001 ⇒6080. 51-68.

6221 *Biguzzi, Giancarlo* Interpretazione antiromana e antigerosolimitana di Babilonia in Ap. RivBib 49 (2001) 439-471 [Rev 17-18].

6222 **Popielewski, Wojciech** Alleluja!: liturgia godów baranka eschatologicznyn zwyciestwem Boga (Ap 19,1-8). Studia Biblica (Kielce) 1: Kielce 2001, "Verbum" 321 pp. 83-915855-0-6. Bibl. 12-43. **P**.

6223 *Bullard, Roger A.* Pictures at an exhibition: Revelation 19:1-10. RExp 98 (2001) 117-126.

6224 *Ruiz, Jean-Pierre* Praise and politics in Revelation 19:1-10. Studies in the book of Revelation. 2001 ⇒6080. 69-84.

6225 **Bøe, Sverre** Gog and Magog: Ezekiel 38-39 as pre-text for Revelation 19,17-21 and 20,7-10. WUNT 2/135: Tü 2001, Mohr S. xvi; 449 pp. €65.45. 3-16-147520-8. Bibl. 392-421.

G2.7 Millenniarismus, *Apc 20*...

Allison, D. Jesus of Naz.: millenarian prophet 1998 ⇒4287.

6226 ᴱ**Bateman, Herbert W.** Three central issues in contemporary dispensationalism: a comparison of traditional and progressive views. 1999 ⇒15,6312. ᴿBS 158 (2001) 120-123 (*Berghuis, Kent*).

6227 *Bradstock, Andrew* Reading the signs of the times: millenarian and apocalyptic movements then and now. Faith in the millennium. 2001 ⇒540. 298-309.

6228 *Brunotte, Ulrike* God's own country: die puritanischen Gründungslegenden Amerikas als Exodus ins Millennium;

6229 *Dannowski, Hans Werner* Apokalyptik im gegenwärtigen Hollywood-Film: AG-Bericht. Aktuelle Apokalyptik!. Loccumer Protokolle 20/99: 2001 ⇒6079. 26-42/212-213.

6230 **Fanlo, Jean-Raymond; Tournon, André** Formes de millénarisme en Europe à l'aube des temps modernes. P 2001, Champion 480 pp €32.80. 2-74530-465-8.

6231 *Fauvarque, Bertrand* La représentation du millenium dans quelques manuscrits médiévaux de l'Apocalypse. MSR 58 (2001) 5-21.

6232 *Goebel, Bernd* Die Apokalyptik in der aktuellen Philosophie: Hans Blumenberg. Aktuelle Apokalyptik!. 2001 ⇒6079. 90-118.

6233 ᴱ**Goldish, Matt; Popkin, Richard H.** Millenarianism and messianism in early modern European culture, 1: Jewish messianism in the early modern world. Dordrecht 2001, Kluwer xix; 238 pp. £68.25. 0-792-368-509.

6234 **Hill, Charles Evan** Regnum caelorum: patterns of millennial thought in early christianity. GR ²2001, Eerdmans xx; 324 pp. $30. 0-8028-4-634-3. Bibl. 273-298.

6235 *Hryniewicz, Wacław* Ten, który przychodzi: Chrystus 'Apokalipsy' w myśli Sergiusza Bułgakowa [Celui qui vient: Christ de 'l'Apocalypse' dans l'oeuvre de Sergiusza Bułgakowa]. AtK 136 (2001) 235-249 Sum. 249. **P.**

6236 ᴱ**Hunt, Stephen** Christian millenarianism: from the early church to Waco. Bloomington 2001, Indiana Univ. Pr. xii; 285 pp. $50/22. 0-253-34013-6/21491-2 [ThD 49,63—Heiser, W. Charles].

6237 *Kirwan, Michael* 'Such beautiful dignity in self-abuse': millennial refusals and the appetites of somatocracy. Faith in the millennium. 2001 ⇒540. 348-358.

6238 *Körtner, Ulrich H.J.* Die Entdeckung der Endlichkeit: zur theologischen Herausforderung apokalyptischen Denkens an der Jahrtausendwende. Aktuelle Apokalyptik!. 2001 ⇒6079. 223-239.

6239 *Lapide, Ruth* Neues Vertrauen aus altem Grauen. Aktuelle Apokalyptik!. 2001 ⇒6079. 59-78.

6240 **McKelvey, R.J.** The millennium and the book of Revelation. 1999 ⇒15,6324; 16,6264. ᴿEvQ 73 (2001) 264-65 (*Marshall, I. Howard*).

6241	*McKelvey, R.J.* The millennium and the Second Coming. Studies in the book of Revelation. 2001 ⇒6080. 85-100.

6242	*Nebeker, Gary L.* The theme of hope in dispensationalism. BS 158 (2001) 3-20.

6243	*Peters, Tiemo Rainer* Biblische Apokalyptik und Politische Theologie. Aktuelle Apokalyptik!. 2001 ⇒6079. 14-25.

6244	*Porter, Stanley E.* Was early christianity a millenarian movement?. Faith in the millennium. 2001 ⇒540. 234-259.

   ᴱ**Ruiz Sánchez, J.** Milenarismos 2001 ⇒543.

6245	*Schenk, Richard* Aktuelle Apokalyptik: Kommentar;

6246	Einleitung;

6247	*Stoellger, Philipp* Arbeit an der Apokalyptik zur Dehnung der Zeit: überspannte Erwartung und phänomenologische Entspannungsübungen;

6248	*Stümke, Volker* Das Jüngste Gericht—apokalyptischer Mythos oder unverzichtbarer Bestandteil evangelischer Dogmatik?. Aktuelle Apokalyptik!. 2001 ⇒6079. 240-245/8-13/248-279/119-138.

6249	**Walvoord, John F.** Prophecy in the new millennium. GR 2001, Kregel 176 pp. $11 [BS 160,375s—Witmer, John A.].

6250	*Withrow, Brandon G.* A future of hope: Jonathan EDWARDS and millennial expectations. TrinJ 22 (2001) 75-98.

6251	*Fauvarque, Bertrand* La représentation du millenium dans quelques manuscrits médiévaux de l'Apocalypse. MSR 58/1 (2001) 5-21 [Rev 20,1-6].

6252	*Lambrecht, Jan* Final judgments and ultimate blessings: the climactic visions of Revelation 20,11-21,8. Collected studies. AnBib 147: 2001 <2000> ⇒170. 395-417.

6253	**Gage, Warren Austin** St. John's vision of the heavenly city. Diss. Dallas, Univ. 2001, 225 pp. 3021465 [Rev 21].

6254	*Sauer, Gustav W.* Apokalypse 21—oder die Zeit als apokalyptischer Parameter. Aktuelle Apokalyptik!. 2001 ⇒6079. 139-211.

6255	**Lee, Pilchan** The New Jerusalem in the book of Revelation: a study of Revelation 21-22 in the light of its background in Jewish tradition. WUNT 2/129: Tü 2001, Mohr S. xvi; 342 pp. $54. 3-16-147477-5. Bibl. 307-319. ᴿWThJ 63 (2001) 467-468 (*Mbuvi, Andrew M.*).

6256	*Longenecker, Bruce W.* 'Linked like a chain': Rev 22.6-9 in light of an ancient transition technique. NTS 47 (2001) 105-117.

XII. Paulus

G3.1 Pauli biographia

6257 **Reicke, Bo Ivar** Re-examining Paul's letters: the history of the Pauline correspondence. *EMoessner, David P.; Reicke, Ingalisa*: Harrisburg, Pennsylvania 2001, Trinity xii; 164 pp. $20. 1-56338-350-0.

6258 **Ashton, John** The religion of Paul the apostle. 2000 ⇒16,6284. RRSR 89 (2001) 137-38 (*Aletti, Jean-Noël*); CBQ 63 (2001) 332-334 (*Murphy-O'Connor, Jerome*); ET 112 (2001) 181-183 (*Rodd, C.S.*).

6259 *Álvarez Cineira, David* Pablo, el indocumentado. EstAg 36 (2001) 377-384.

6260 **Cassidy, Richard J.** Paul in chains: Roman imprisonment and the letters of St. Paul. NY 2001, Herder and H. xv; 317 pp. $25. 0-8245-1920-5. Bibl. 283-304.

    EDonati, A. Pietro e Paolo 2000 ⇒4987.

6261 **Dreyfus, Paul** Paolo di Tarso: un grande reporter sulle tracce dell' apostolo. CasM 2000, Piemme 446 pp. €19.63. RCivCatt 152/3 (2001) 314-315 (*Scaiola, D.*).

6262 *Elsdon, Ron* Was Paul "converted" or "called"?: questions of methodology. PIBA 24 (2001) 17-47 [Gal 1].

6263 **Gnilka, Joachim** Paolo di Tarso: apostolo e testimone. CTNT.S 6: 1998 ⇒14,5730. RSal. 63 (2001) 385-386 (*Heriban, J.*); ED 54/1 (2001) 225-226 (*Giglioni, Paolo*).

6264 **Haacker, Klaus** Paulus: der Werdegang eines Apostels. SBS 171: 1997 ⇒13,6079; 15,6372. RJBL 119 (2000) 146-147 (*Kim, Seyoon*).

6265 **Hengel, Martin; Schwemer, Anna Maria** Paulus zwischen Damaskus und Antiochien: die unbekannten Jahre des Apostels. WUNT 108: 1998 ⇒14,5732... 16,6291. RZKTh 122 (2001) 221-222 (*Oberforcher, Robert*); RB 108 (2001) 294-298 (*Murphy-O'Connor, J.*); OLZ 96 (2001) 728-733 (*Wilk, Florian*).

6266 *Horn, Friedrich W.* Was wissen wir heute eigentlich über Paulus?. WUB 20 (2001) 11-19;

6267 Einführung. Das Ende des Paulus. BZNW 106: 2001 ⇒281. 1-13.

6268 *Löhr, Hermut* Zur Paulus-Notiz in 1 Clem 5,5-7. Das Ende des Paulus. BZNW 106: 2001 ⇒281. 197-213.

6269 *Marucci, Corrado* La cittadinanza romana di Paolo. FMÜHLSTEIGER, J. KStT 46: 2001 ⇒77. 13-34 [Acts 16,37-38; 22,25-29; 23,27].

6270 *Meeks, W.A.* Judaism, Hellenism, and the birth of christianity. Paul beyond . 2001 ⇒262. 17-27.

6271 **Meggitt, Justin J.** Paul, poverty and survival. 1998 ⇒14,5734. [R]JSNT 84 (2001) 51-64 (*Martin, Dale B.*); JSNT 84 (2001) 65-84 (*Theißen, Gerd*).

6272 *Meggitt, Justin J.* Response to Martin and Theissen. JSNT 84 (2001) 85-94.

6273 *Mimouni, Simon Claude* Paul de Tarse: éléments pour une réévaluation historique et doctrinale. Le judéo-christianisme. 2001 ⇒484. 97-125 [BuBB 36,118].

6274 *Moessner, David P.* Introduction. Re-examining Paul's letters. 2001 ⇒6257. 1-6.

6275 *Penna, Romano* Le notizie di DIONE di Prusa su Tarso e il loro interesse per le lettere di S. Paolo <1996>;

6276 Tre tipologie di conversione raccontate nell'antichità: POLEMONE di Atene, IZATE dell'Adiabene, Paolo di Tarso <1996>;

6277 Un fariseo del secolo I: Paolo di Tarso <1999>;

6278 Aperture universalistiche in Paolo e nella cultura del suo tempo <1998>. Vangelo e inculturazione. 2001 ⇒193. 255-274/275-296/ 297-322/323-364.

6279 **Ramsay, William Mitchell** St Paul, the traveler and Roman citizen. [E]*Wilson, Mark*: GR 2001, Kregel 319 pp. $23. 0-8254-3639-7. Revised & updated. [ThD 49,283—W. Charles Heiser].

6280 **Riesner, Rainer** Paul's early period: chronology, mission strategy, and theology. [T]*Stott, Doug* 1998 ⇒14,5740; 16,6300. [R]JThS 52 (2001) 827-829 (*Hickling, C.J.A.*).

6281 **Roetzel, Calvin J.** Paul: the man and the myth. 1998 ⇒14,5742... 16,6301. [R]JBL 119 (2000) 775-776 (*Richardson, Peter*); JJS 52 (2001) 164-166 (*Bockmuehl, Markus*); JThS 52 (2001) 265-268 (*Richardson, Neil*); ABR 49 (2001) 69-70 (*Watson, Nigel M.*); TJT 17 (2001) 301-302 (*Fox, Kenneth A.*).

6282 *Ruiz Martorell, Julián* Pablo: la necesaria conversión del religioso. Personajes del NT. 2001 ⇒231. 103-120.

6283 **Sanchez Bosch, Jordi** Nacido a tiempo: una vida de Pablo, el apostol. Estudios Biblicos: 1994 ⇒10,5589... 13,6087. [R]Sal. 63 (2001) 387-388 (*Buzzetti, Carlo*).

6284 *Sanday, William* The early visits of St Paul to Jerusalem <1896>;

6285 St Paul the traveller <1896>. Essays in biblical criticism. JSNT.S 225: 2001 ⇒205. 209-216/198-208.

6286 **Sanders, Ed Parish** Paul: A very short introduction. Very short introductions 42: Oxf 2001, OUP viii; 165 pp. 0-19-285451-8. Bibl. 153-156.

6287 *Scriba, Albrecht* Von Korinth nach Rom: die Chronologie der letzten
      Jahre des Paulus, Das Ende des Paulus. BZNW 106: 2001 ⇒281.
      157-173.
6288 *Söding, Thomas* Paulus—Legende und Wirklichkeit. Wort zum Le-
      ben. 2001 ⇒284. 113-141.
6289 **Wallace, Richard; Williams, Wynne** The three worlds of Paul of
      Tarsus. 1998 ⇒14,5745; 16,6307. [R]LTP 57 (2001) 394-395 (*Gignac,
      Alain*); SCI 20 (2001) 312-313 (*Almagor, Eran*).

G3.2 Corpus paulinum; *generalia, technica epistularis*

6290 **Adams, Edward** Constructing the world: a study in Paul's cosmolo-
      gical language. 2000 ⇒16,6313. [R]RRT (2001/1) 34-37 (*Campbell,
      Jonathan*); CBQ 63 (2001) 330-331 (*Paffenroth, Kim*).
6291 **Akenson, Donald Harman** Saint Saul: a skeleton key to the histori-
      cal Jesus. 2000 ⇒16,6315. [R]TJT 17 (2001) 277-278 (*Crook, Zeba
      Antonin*); CBQ 63 (2001) 539-540 (*Murphy-O'Connor, Jerome*).
6292 *Aletti, Jean-Noël* Bulletin Paulinien. RSR 89 (2001) 115-145;
6293 Wie man zur Zeit von Paulus Briefe schrieb. WUB 20 (2001) 71.
6294 *Alexander, Loveday IPSE DIXIT*: citation of authority in Paul and in
      the Jewish and Hellenistic schools. Paul beyond. 2001 ⇒262. 103-
      127.
6295 **Anderson, Dean R.** Ancient rhetorical theory and Paul. [2]1999 ⇒15,
      6390. [R]RSR 89 (2001) 128-130 (*Aletti, Jean-Noël*).
6296 **Bortolini, José** Introdução a Paulo e suas cartas. Como ler a Biblia:
      São Paulo 2001, Paulus 108 pp. 85-349-1780-9.
6297 *Brodie, Thomas L.* Towards tracing the gospel's literary indebtedness
      to the epistles. Mimesis. 2001 ⇒568. 104-116 [BuBB 34,2].
6298 *Buchegger, Jürg* Mögliche paulinische Neologismen: ein Beitrag zur
      Erforschung des paulinischen griechischen Wortschatzes. JETh 15
      (2001) 11-35.
6299 *Burnet, Régis* Les adresses pauliniennes: simple adaption ou véritable
      "christianisation"?. SémBib 102 (2001) 29-42.
6300 **Downing, F. Gerald** Cynics, Paul and the Pauline churches: Cynics
      and christian origins II. 1998 ⇒14,5752; 16,6329. [R]JThS 52 (2001)
      830-833 (*Hickling, C.J.A.*).
6301 *Dunn, James D.G.* Diversity in Paul. Religious diversity. BiSe 79:
      2001 ⇒398. 107-123.
6302 *Dupont-Roc, Roselyne* Quand Paul lit les écritures à partir de Jésus-
      Christ ... FV 100/4 (2001) 59-73.
6303 *Ellis, Edward Earle* Paul and his co-workers revisited. History and
      interpretation. BiblInterp 54: 2001 ⇒141. 85-97.

6304 *Förster, Hans* Papyrusfragmente eines sahidischen Corpus Paulinum. ZAC 5 (2001) 3-22.

6305 *Giuliani, Massimo* Jacob TAUBES e la teologia politica di San Paolo. Hum(B) 56 (2001) 568-604.

6306 **Harvey, John D.** Listening to the text: oral patterning in Paul's Letters. ETS Studies 1: 1998 ⇒14,5756... 16,6335. ᴿJBL 119 (2000) 576-577 (*Winger, Michael*).

6307 ᴱ**Hawthorne, Gerald F.**, *al.*, Dizionario di Paolo e delle sue lettere. 1999 ⇒15,6403; 16,6336. ᴿED 54/1 (2001) 227-228 (*Giglioni, Paolo*); RAMi 69 (2001) 607-609 (*Pedrini, Arnaldo*).

6308 ᴱ**Janssen, Claudia; Schottroff, Luise; Wehn, Beate** Paulus: umstrittene Traditionen—lebendige Theologie: eine feministische Lektüre. Gü 2001 <2000>, Kaiser 208 pp. FS37.50. 3-579-05318-3 [=JSNT 79 (2000)].

6309 **Kreitzer, Larry Joseph** Pauline images in fiction and film: on reversing the hermeneutical flow. BiSe 61: 1999 ⇒15,6408; 16, 6344. ᴿRBLit 3 (2001) 425-428 (*Seesengood, Robert Paul*).

6310 *Krentz, Edgar* The sense of senseless oxymora. CThMi 28 (2001) 577-584.

6311 **Langkammer, Hugolin** Apostol Pawel i jego dzielo. Opolska Biblioteka Teologiczna 46: Opole 2001, Wydzial Teologiczny Uniwersytetu 368 pp. 83-88939-08-4. Bibl. 21-50. **P.**

6312 *Lémonon, Jean-Pierre* Paul a-t-il déjudaïsé Jésus?. Théophilyon 6 (2001) 89-124 [BuBB 34,3].

6313 ᴱ**Martín, Melquiades Andrés** La revelación de San Pablo. M 2001, Fundación Univ. Española 172 pp. Anónimo [Cart. 19,215s—Sanz Valdivieso, R.].

6314 *Mitchell, Margaret M.* A patristic perspective on Pauline περιαυτο-λογια. NTS 47 (2001) 354-371.

6315 *Mowery, Robert L.* Egocentricity in the Pauline corpus. EThL 77 (2001) 163-168.

6316 ᴱ**Olbricht, Thomas H.; Sumney, Jerry L.** Paul and pathos. SBL. Symposium 16: Atlanta 2001, SBL xiii; 245 pp. $40. 1-58983-011-3. Bibl. 203-223.

6317 *Penna, Romano* L'origine del *corpus* epistolare paolino: problemi, analogie, ipotesi <1994>;

6318 Anonimia e pseudepigrafia nel Nuovo Testamento: comparativismo e ragioni di una prassi letteraria <1985>. Vangelo e inculturazione. 2001 ⇒193. 612-641/795-816.

6319 **Poucouta, Paulin** Paul, notre ancêtre, introduction au corpus paulinien. Yaoundé 2001, UCAC 189 pp.

6320 *Puigdollers i Noblom, Rodolf* Classificació i datació de les glosses en les colleccions de cartes paulines (I). RCatT 26 (2001) 229-266.

6321 **Quesnel, Michel** Paul et les commencements du christianisme. P
2001, Desclée de Brouwer 149 pp. €14.50. 2-220-05014-9.

6322 *Reicke, Bo Ivar* History of the Pauline correspondence. Re-examining
Paul's letters. 2001 ⇒6257. 27-102.

6323 *Reiser, Marius* Paulus als Stilist. SEÅ 66 (2001) 151-165.

6324 **Rosenmeyer, P.A.** Ancient epistolary fictions: the letter in Greek literature. C 2001, CUP x; 370 pp. £45. 0-521-80004-8.

6325 *Sandnes, Karl O.* Kroppen som tegn hos Paulus: om magens sug.
Ung teologi 34/2 (2001) 19-29.

6326 **Sánchez Bosch, Jordi** Escritos paulinos. 1998 ⇒14,5782; 15,6421.
^REstB 59 (2001) 399-401 (*Pastor-Ramos, F.*);

6327 Scritti paolini. ^EZani, Antonio: Introduzione allo studio della Bibbia
7: Brescia 2001, Paideia 440 pp. 88-394-0625-5. Bibl. 427-430.

6328 *Silva, Moisés* The Greek Psalter in Paul's letters: a textual study.
^FPIETERSMA, A.: JSOT.S 332: 2001 ⇒87. 277-288.

6329 **Son, Sang-Won (Aaron)** Corporate elements in Pauline anthropology: a study of selected terms, idioms, and concepts in the light of
Paul's usage and background. AnBib 148: R 2001, E.P.I.B. xvii; 240
pp. €15.49. 88-7653-148-3. Bibl. 191-218.

6330 *Staats, Reinhart* Kaiser KONSTANTIN, Apostel Paulus und die
deutsche Verfassung: eine kirchengeschichtliche Rücksicht. DtPfrBl
101 (2001) 118-122.

6331 *Tassin, Claude* Brève chronique paulinienne. Spiritus 42 (2001) 451-
455.

6332 **Tellbe, Mikael** Paul between synagogue and state: christians, Jews,
and civic authorities in 1 Thessalonians, Romans, and Philippians.
Diss. Lund 2001, ^DOlsson, Birger: CB.NT 34: Sto 2001, Almqvist &
W. xii; 340 pp. SEK270. 91-22-01908-1. Bibl. 298-333.

6333 **Thompson, James** Preaching like Paul: homiletical wisdom for
today. LVL 2001, Knox xi; 177 pp. $20. 0-664-22294-3.

6334 *Tkacz, Magdalena* Z badań nad retoryka w Listach św. Pawła. CoTh
71/1 (2001) 103-112. **P.**

6335 *Topczewska, Urszula* Paulusbriefe als Diskurs: zur pragmalinguisti-
schen Analyse der paulinischen Texte. CoTh 71A (2001) 67-99.

6336 **Walker, William O.** Interpolations in the Pauline letters. JSNT.S
213: Shf 2001, Sheffield A. 271 pp. 1-84127-198-5. Bibl. 243-256.

6337 **Warren, David Harold** The text of the apostle in the second century: a contribution to the history of its reception. Diss. Harvard 2001,
350 pp. 3008238 [HThR 94,500].

6338 **Wilk, Florian** Die Bedeutung des Jesajabuches für Paulus. FRLANT
179: 1998 ⇒14,5785; 15,6426. ^RJThS 52 (2001) 269-272 (*Watts,
Rikki E.*).

G3.3 Pauli theologia

6339 **Adamczewski, Bartosz** Madrościowy wymiar pneumatologii św. Pawła [La dimension sapientiale de la pneumatologie de saint Paul]. Diss. Lublin 2001, ᴰ*Langkammer, H.* 279 pp [RTL 33,636]. **P.**

6340 **Adams, Edward** Constructing the world: a study in Paul's cosmological language. 1999 ⇒15,6428. ᴿJThS 52 (2001) 273-275 (*Moule, C.F.D.*).

6341 *Adeyemi, Moses E.* Οι θέσεις του Απ. Παύλου για τη σωτηρία από τις δυνάμεις του κακού [The Pauline conception of deliverance from the powers of evil]. DBM 20/1 (2001) 82-96. **G.**

6342 **Alkier, Stefan** Wunder und Wirklichkeit in den Briefen des Apostels Paulus: ein Beitrag zu einem Wunderverständnis jenseits von Entmythologisierung und Rehistorisierung. WUNT 134: Tü 2001, Mohr S. xvi; 354 pp. €89. 3-16-147415-5. Bibl. 309-336.

6343 *Alvarez Verdes, Lorenzo* Dinamismo creador de la libertad cristiana. StMor 39 (2001) 333-370.

6344 **Baldanza, Giuseppe** La metafora sponsale in S. Paolo e nella tradizione liturgica siriaca: studi. BEL.S 114: R 2001, Liturgiche 154 pp. €12.91. 88-86655-98-3. Bibl. 133-141. ᴿCivCatt 152/4 (2001) 617-619 (*Teani, M.*).

6345 **Barbaglio, Giuseppe** La teologia di Paolo: abbozzi in forma epistolare. 1999 ⇒15,6433; 16,6367. ᴿRSR 89 (2001) 130-131 (*Aletti, Jean-Noël*); RivBib 49 (2001) 105-109 (*Redalié, Yann*).

6346 **Benzi, Guido** Paolo e il suo vangelo. Interpretare la Bibbia oggi 25: Brescia 2001, Queriniana 172 pp. 88-399-2464-7. Bibl. 169-170.

6347 *Betz, Hans Dieter* Der Mensch in seinen Antagonismen aus der Sicht des Paulus. Der neue Mensch in Christus. 2001 ⇒239. 39-56.

6348 *Bormann, Lukas* Reflexionen über Sterben und Tod bei Paulus. Das Ende des Paulus. BZNW 106: 2001 ⇒281. 307-330.

6349 **Burgos Núñez, M. de** Pablo, predicador del evangelio. 1999 ⇒15, 6436; 16,6373. ᴿHumTeo 22 (2001) 127-28 (*Carvalho, José Carlos*).

6350 *Burke, Trevor* Pauline adoption: a sociological approach. EvQ 73 (2001) 119-134.

6351 **Buscemi, A.M.** Gli inni di Paolo: una sinfonia a Christo Signore. SBFA 48: 2000 ⇒16,6374. ᴿRSR 89 (2001) 133-135 (*Aletti, Jean-Noël*); CDios 214 (2001) 212-213 (*Gutiérrez, J.*); CBQ 63 (2001) 141-142 (*Branick, Vincent*); Ang. 78 (2001) 733-734 (*Jurič, Stipe*) [Phil 02,6-11; Eph 1,3-14; 2,14-18; Col 1,15-20].

6352 *Buscemi, Marcello* Dio Padre in S. Paolo. Anton. 76 (2001) 247-269.

6353 *Butting, Klara* Paulinische Variationen zu Gen 2,24: die Rede vom
      Leib Christi im Kontext der Diskussion um Lebensformen. Paulus.
      2001 ⇒6308. 103-114.

6354 **Casalini, Nello** Le lettere di Paolo: esposizione del loro sistema di
      teologia. SBFA 54: J 2001, Franciscan Printing Pr. 304 pp. 965-516-
      003-3.

6355 *Dautzenberg, Gerhard* Freiheit im hellenistischen Kontext. Der neue
      Mensch in Christus. QD 190: 2001 ⇒239. 57-81.

6356 **Dornisch, Loretta** Paul and third world women theologians. 1999 ⇒
      15,6442. ᴿPacifica 14 (2001) 92-94 (*Elvey, Anne*).

6357 **Dunn, James D.G.** The theology of Paul the apostle. 1998 ⇒14,
      5800... 16,6382. ᴿJDh 26 (2001) 549-552 (*Pathrapankal, Joseph*);

6358 La teologia dell'apostolo Paolo. 1999 ⇒15,6445; 16,6383. ᴿOrpheus
      22 (2001) 344-347 (*Osculati, Roberto*).

6359 *Dunn, James D.G.* Jesus the judge: further thoughts of Paul's christo-
      logy and soteriology. ᶠO'COLLINS, G.: 2001 ⇒81. 34-54.

6360 **Eastman, Brad** The significance of grace in the letters of Paul.
      Studies in Biblical Literature 11: 1999 ⇒15,6447. ᴿHBT 23 (2001)
      106-107 (*Williams, H.H. Drake*).

6361 *Eckert, Jost* "Die neue Schöpfung" und die Kirche in der Verkündi-
      gung des Apostels Paulus. ᶠHAINZ, J. 2001 ⇒42. 46-68.

6362 *Ellis, Edward Earle* Performed traditions and their implications for
      the origins of Pauline christology. History and interpretation. BiblIn-
      terp 54: 2001 ⇒141. 133-150.

6363 **Eskola, Timo** Theodicy and predestination in Pauline soteriology.
      WUNT 2/100 1998 ⇒14,5803; 15,6449. ᴿRSR 89 (2001) 125-127
      (*Aletti, Jean-Noël*); JBL 119 (2000) 147-149 (*Moo, Douglas J.*).

6364 *Fee, Gordon D.* Paul and the Trinity: the experience of Christ and the
      Spirit for Paul's understanding of God <1999>;

6365 Wisdom christology in Paul: a dissenting view <2000>. To what end
      exegesis?. 2001 ⇒143. 330-350/351-378.

6366 *Fitzgerald, John T.* Paul and paradigm shifts: reconciliation and its
      linkage group. Paul beyond. 2001 ⇒262. 241-262.

6367 *Forbes, Chris* Paul's principalities and powers: demythologizing a-
      pocalyptic?. JSNT 82 (2001) 61-88.

6368 **Gager, John G.** Reinventing Paul. 2000 ⇒16,6391. ᴿDialog 40
      (2001) 314-316 (*Aageson, James*); PerTeol 33 (2001) 415-417 (*Mar-
      ques, Valdir*).

6369 *Heil, John Paul* Paul and the law. BiTod 39 (2001) 277-282.

6370 **Hillert, Sven** Limited and universal salvation: a text-oriented and
      hermeneutical study of two perspectives in Paul. CB.NT 31: 1999 ⇒
      15,6455. ᴿBiblInterp 9 (2001) 95-97 (*Murr*); CBQ 63 (2001) 148-

149 (*Pascuzzi, Maria*); JThS 52 (2001) 833-835 (*Byrne, B.J.*); Bib. 82 (2001) 286-288 (*Lambrecht, Jan*).

6371 **Janse, S.** Paulus en Jeruzalem: een onderzoek naar de heilshistorische betekenis van Jeruzalem in de brieven van Paulus. 2000 ⇒16, 6406. [R]KeTh 52 (2001) 196-199 (*Witkamp, L.Th.*).

6372 **Keesmaat, Sylvia C.** Paul and his story: (re)interpreting the Exodus tradition. JSNT.S 181: 1999 ⇒15,6464. [R]TJT 17 (2001) 291-292 (*Bertone, John A.*); EvQ 73 (2001) 351-53 (*Longenecker, Bruce W.*).

6373 *Kertelge, Karl* Gottes Selbstoffenbarung im Gekreuzigten: zur Paulusinterpretation von Helmut MERKLEIN. TThZ 110 (2001) 145-150.

6374 **Kim, Hyoung Kook** Paul's eschatological use of paristemi and its contribution to his eschatology and concept of ministry. Diss. Trinity Evang. Divinity 2001, 335 pp, 3003782.

6375 *Kirchhoff, Renate* Was lernten die verschiedenen Anfängerinnen und Angänger im Glauben bei Paulus?. Zeitschrift für Pädagogik und Theologie 53 (2001) 153-161.

6376 *Koester, Helmut* Paul's letters as theology for the community. [F]BETZ, H. 2001 ⇒5. 215-225.

6377 *Kraftchick, Steven J.* πάθη in Paul: emotional logic of "original argument". Paul and pathos. SBL Symposium 16: 2001 ⇒6316. 39-68.

6378 *Lémonon, Jean-Pierre* Les images de l'église dans les lettres de Paul. Unité chrétienne 144 (2001) 5-9.

6379 **Limbeck, Meinrad** Zürnt Gott wirklich?: Fragen an Paulus. Stu 2001, Kath. Bibelwerk 128 pp. 3-460-33164-X.

6380 *Lindner, Helgo* Israels Geschick im Unterschied der Zeiten bei Paulus und JOSEPHUS. Internationales Josephus-Kolloquium 2000. 2001 ⇒474. 279-292.

6381 *Lips, Hermann von* Die "Leiden des Apostels" als Thema paulinischer Theologie. [F]HAHN, F.: 2001 ⇒41. 117-128.

6382 *Löning, Karl* Kultmetaphorik im Neuen Testament. Kult, Konflikt. AOAT 285: 2001 ⇒387. 229-267 [Rom 3,19-26; Eph 2,11-22].

6383 *Martin, Dale B.* Instances of 'Judaism'–'Hellenism' in the interpretation of Paul and early christianity. Paul beyond. 2001 ⇒262. 29-61.

6384 *Meyer, John R.* Sharing in Christ's death and the Holy Spirit. IThQ 66 (2001) .25-140

6385 *Natoli, Salvatore* Paolo e l'escatologia. Bailamme 27/5 (2001) 19-32.

6386 *Parsons, Michael* Time and location: aspects of eschatological motivation in Paul. RTR 60/3 (2001) 109-122.

6387 *Pasquetto, Virgilio* La speranza nelle lettere paoline (III): attesa della piena manifestazione della salvezza. RVS 55 (2001) 254-272.

6388 *Penna, Romano* Aspetti originali dell'escatologia paolina: tradizione e novità <1999>. Vangelo e inculturazione. 2001 ⇒193. 581-611.

6389 *Punt, Jeremy* Paul and the scriptures of Israel: how much hermeneuti-
      cal awareness did he display?. Neotest. 34 (2000) 311-327.

6390 *Quesnel, Michel* Le sacrifice chez Paul. CEv 118 (2001) 13-21;

6391 Vertraten Paulus und Jesus die gleiche Religion?. WUB 20 (2001)
      62-66.

6392 *Räisänen, Heikki* Interpreting Paul. Challenges to biblical interpreta-
      tion. BiblInterp 59: 2001 <1999> ⇒200. 85-99.

6393 *Sanday, William* Some leading ideas in the theology of St Paul
      <1878>;

6394 St Paul's equivalent for the 'Kingdom of Heaven' <1878>. Essays in
      biblical criticism. JSNT.S 225: 2001 ⇒205. 175-187/188-197.

      Schmidl, M. Johannes und Paulus 2001 ⇒5880.

6395 *Schnelle, Udo* Transformation und Partizipation als Grundgedanken
      paulinischer Theologie. NTS 47 (2001) 58-75.

6396 *Schottroff, Luise* Die Lieder und das Geschrei der Glaubenden:
      Rechtfertigung bei Paulus. Paulus. 2001 ⇒6308. 44-66.

6397 *Schrage, Wolfgang* Unterwegs zur Einzigkeit und Einheit Gottes:
      zum "Monotheismus" des Paulus und seiner alttestamentlich-jüdi-
      schen Tradition. EvTh 61/3 (2001) 190-203.

6398 **Schreiner, Thomas R.** Paul, apostle of God's glory in Christ: a Paul-
      ine theology. DG 2001, InterVarsity 504 pp. $25. 0-8308-2651-3.

6399 *Schwöbel, Christoph* Die "Botschaft der Versöhnung" (2 Kor 5,19)
      und die Versöhnungslehre: Bemerkungen zu den Wechselwirkungen
      exegetischer und systematisch-theologischer Interpretationsperspekti-
      ven. Biblischer Text. BThSt 44: 2001 ⇒252. 163-190.

6400 **Seifrid, Mark A.** Christ, our righteousness: Paul's theology and justi-
      fication. New Studies in Biblical Theology 9: 2000 ⇒16,6430.
      ᴿHBT 23 (2001) 108-109 (*Rowe, C. Kavin*).

6401 *Skrzyp, Benita* Duch Święty a królestwo Boże w ujęciu św. Pawła.
      ᶠJANKOWSKI, A. 2001 ⇒53. 394-404. **P.**

6402 **Smith, Robert S.** Justification and eschatology: a dialogue with 'The
      new perspective on Paul'. RTR.S 1: Doncaster, Victoria 2001, RTR
      xii; 151 pp. 0-646-41479-8.

6403 *Son, S. Aaron* Implications of Paul's 'one flesh' concept for his un-
      derstanding of the nature of man. BBR 11 (2001) 107-122.

6404 *Söding, Thomas* Verheißung und Erfüllung im Lichte paulinischer
      Theologie. NTS 47 (2001) 146-170;

6405 Die Rechtfertigung der Sünder und die Sünden der Gerechtfertigten:
      Anmerkungen zum Streit um '*simul iustus et peccator*' im Lichte
      paulinischer Theologie. Gerecht und Sünder zugleich? 2001 ⇒378.
      30-81 [Rom 7,25].

6406 *Standhartinger, Angela* Weisheit in Joseph und Aseneth und den
      paulinischen Briefen. NTS 47 (2001) 482-501.

6407 *Stowers, Stanley K.* Does Pauline christianity resemble a Hellenistic philosophy. Paul beyond. 2001 ⇒262. 81-102.

6408 **Strecker, Christian** Die liminale Theologie des Paulus: Zugänge zur paulinischen Theologie aus kulturanthropologischer Perspektive. FRLANT 185: 1999 ⇒15,6497. [R]BZ 45 (2001) 143-145 (*Hoegen-Rohls, Christina*); BTB 31 (2001) 79 (*DeMaris, Richard E.*); JBL 120 (2001) 777-780 (*Schröter, Jens*); ThLZ 126 (2001) 172-175 (*Karter, Martin*).

6409 **Stuhlmacher, Peter** Revisiting Paul's doctrine of justification: a challenge to the new perspective. DG 2001, InterVarsity 108 pp. $13. 0-8308-26610. Essay by *Donald A. Hagner* [ThD 49,87–Heiser, W.].

6410 *Theobald, Michael* 'Sohn Gottes' als christologische Grundmetapher bei Paulus. Studien zum Römerbrief. 2001 <1994> ⇒219. 119-141;

6411 Rechtfertigung und Ekklesiologie nach Paulus: Anmerkungen zur 'Gemeinsamen Erklärung zur Rechtfertigungslehre' <1998>;

6412 Das Gespräch geht weiter! Replik auf W. Löser, Rechtfertigung und sakramentale Kirche: ThPh 73 (1998) 321-333 <2000>. Studien zum Römerbrief. WUNT 136: 2001 ⇒219. 226-240/241-249.

6413 **Thurén, Lauri Toumas** Derhetorizing Paul: a dynamic perspective on Pauline theology and the law. WUNT 124: 2000 ⇒16,6434. [R]BiblInterp 9 (2001) 230-2 (*Donaldson, Terence L.*); JThS 52 (2001) 835-837 (*Kreitzer, Larry*); Sal. 63 (2001) 781-782 (*Vicent, R.*); CBQ 63 (2001) 564-566 (*Jaquette, James L.*).

6414 *Valentini, Alberto* Gesù Cristo secondo la teologia di Paolo. StMiss 50 (2001) 73-101.

6415 **Van Spanje, Teunis Erik** Inconsistency in Paul?: a critique of the work of Heikki RÄISÄNEN. WUNT 2/110: 1999 ⇒15,6499. [R]JThS 52 (2001) 275-278 (*Thielman, Frank*); JSNT 83 (2001) 125-126 (*Roo, J.C.R. de*); RBBras 18 (2001) 548-549.

6416 *Viviano, Benedict T.* The righteousness of God in Paul: a grammatical note. Trinity–kingdom–church. NTOA 48: 2001 ⇒223. 246-252.

6417 *Vouga, François* Paulus und der Entwurf einer neuen Welt. WUB 20 (2001) 57-61.

6418 **Walter, Matthias** Gemeinde als Leib Christi: Untersuchungen zum Corpus Paulinum und zu den "apostolischen Vätern". NTOA 49: FrS 2001, Univ.-Verl. 346 pp. €67.10. 3-7278-1367-9.

6419 *Wehr, Lothar* Funktion und Erfahrungshintergrund der Satansaussagen des Paulus: "...damit wir vom Satan nicht überlistet werden" (2 Kor 2,11). MThZ 52 (2001) 208-219.

6420 **Wilkinson, Steven Michael** Paul and his relationship to the apocalyptic tradition: an assessment of a neglected dimension: his revelatory experiences. Diss. Fuller Sem. 2001, 370 pp. 3003176.

6421 *Wright, N.T.* A fresh perspective on Paul?. BJRL 83/1 (2001) 21-39;
6422 Farewell to the rapture. BiRe 17/4 (2001) 8, 52.
6423 *Xavier, Aloysius* Faith vs law: a cultural identity crisis in Pauline theology. BiBh 27 (2001) 5-18.

G3.4 *Pauli stylus et modus operandi*—Paul's image

6424 **Glad, Clarence E.** Paul and PHILODEMUS: adaptability in Epicurean and early Christian psychagogy. NT.S 81: 1995 ⇒13,6196; 14,5855. ᴿBiblInterp 9 (2001) 99-101 (*Klutz, Todd E.*).
6425 **Légasse, Simon** L'antipaulinisme sectaire au temps des pères de l'église. CRB 47: 2000 ⇒16,6450. ᴿCBQ 63 (2001) 753-754 (*Luomanen, Petri*).
6426 *Loubser, J.A.* Media criticism and the myth of Paul, the creative genius, and his forgotten co-workers. Neotest. 34 (2000) 329-345.
6427 *Marguerat, Daniel* Das enfant terrible des Christentums. WUB 20 (2001) 5-10.
6428 *Polaski, Sandra Hack* Paul and the discourse of power. BiSe 62: 1999 ⇒15,6513; 16,6452. ᴿJBL 120 (2001) 171-3 (*Amador, J.D.H.*).
6429 **Walton, Steve** Leadership and lifestyle: the portrait of Paul in the Miletus speech and 1 Thessalonians. MSSNTS 108: 2000 ⇒16,6454. ᴿNT 43 (2001) 300-302 (*Weima, Jeffrey A.D.*); BiblInterp 9 (2001) 428-429 (*Witherington, Ben*) [Acts 20,17-38].

G3.5 **Apostolus Gentium** [⇒G4.6, Israel et Lex/Jews & Law]

6430 **Alvarez Cineira, David** Die Religionspolitik des Kaisers CLAUDIUS und die paulinische Mission. 1999 ⇒15,6515; 16,6457. ᴿBZ 45 (2001) 283-286 (*Hoppe, Rudolf*).
6431 **Barram, Michael D.** 'In order that they may be saved': mission and moral reflection in Paul. Diss. Union Theol. Sem. & Presbyterean School of Christian Edu. 2001, ᴰ*Carroll, J.T.* 283 pp. 3019380.
6432 **Beckheuer, Burkhard** Paulus und Jerusalem: Kollekte und Mission im theologischen Denken des Heidenapostels. EHS.T 611: 1998 ⇒ 16,6460. ᴿThLZ 126 (2001) 47-49 (*Böttrich, Christfried*).
6433 *Burnet, Régis* Paul: kérygme à transmettre, foi à faire vivre. Com(F) 26/4 (2001) 40-48.
6434 **Fabris, Rinaldo** Paolo: l'apostolo delle genti. 1997 ⇒13,6217; 15, 6522. ᴿSal. 63 (2001) 384-385 (*Heriban, J.*).

6435 **Fabris, Rinaldo** Paulo, apóstolo dos gentios. [T]**Balancin, Euclides Martins**: Luz do mundo: São Paulo 2001, Paulinas 807 pp [REB 61, 755].

6436 *Howell, Don N. Jr.* Mission in Paul's epistles: genesis, pattern, and dynamics. Mission in the NT. ASMS 27: 2001 ⇒367. 63-91;

6437 Mission in Paul's epistles: theological bearings. Mission in the NT. ASMS 27: 2001 ⇒367. 92-116.

6438 **Kraus, Wolfgang** Zwischen Jerusalem und Antiochia: die 'Hellenisten', Paulus und die Aufnahme der Heiden in das endzeitliche Gottesvolk. SBS 179: 1999 ⇒15,6526; 16,6471. [R]JBL 120 (2001) 774-777 (*Penner, Todd C.*); RBLit 3 (2001) 421-425 (*Penner, Todd C.*).

6439 **Krug, Johannes** Die Kraft des Schwachen: ein Beitrag zur paulinischen Apostolatstheologie. TANZ 37: Tü 2001, Francke 350 pp. €64. 3-7720-2829-2. Bibl. 321-350.

6440 **Legrand, Lucien** L'apôtre des nations?: Paul et la stratégie missionnaire des églises apostoliques. LD 184: P 2001, Cerf 153 pp. €20.58. 2-204-06532-3. [R]CEv 116 (2001) 64-65 (*Tassin, Claude*); Spiritus 42 (2001) 451-452 (*Tassin, Claude*); EeV 42 (2001) 24-25 (*Cothenet, Edouard*).

6441 **Plummer, Robert Lewis** The church's missionary nature: the apostle Paul and his churches. Diss. Southern Baptist Theol. Sem. 2001, 247 pp. 3015279.

6442 **Rodrigues, Antônio Márcio Alves** 'Paulo, servo de Jesus Cristo, chamado a ser apôstolo' (Rm 1,1): a autocompreensão da missão apostólica de Paulo na introdução das maiores epístolas. Diss. de mestrado Belo Horizonte 2001, [D]*Marques, Valdir* [REB 62,493].

6443 **Sywulka, Paul E.** A biblical-theological analysis of the terms euangelion/euangelizomai in the Pauline epistles. Diss. Dallas Sem.; 318 pp. 3002971.

6444 **White, John Lee** The apostle of God: Paul and the promise of Abraham. 1999 ⇒15,6530; 16,6482. [R]RSR 89 (2001) 131-133 (*Aletti, Jean-Noël*); TS 62 (2001) 610-611 (*Calef, Susan A.*).

G3.6 *Pauli fundamentum* philosophicum [⇒G4.3] *et* morale

6445 **Agamben, Giorgio** Le temps qui reste: un commentaire de l'Épître aux Romains. 2000 ⇒16,6484. [R]ETR 76 (2001) 429-430 (*Cuvillier, Élian*); EeV 46 (2001) 19-20 (*Rastoin, Cécile*).

6446 **Alvarez Verdes, Lorenzo** Caminar en el Espíritu: el pensamiento ético de S. Pablo. 2000 ⇒16,6485. [R]CTom 128 (2001) 199-200 (*García Cordoer, Maximiliano*).

6447 **Barcley, William B.** "Christ in you": a study in Paul's theology and ethics. 1999 ⇒15,6531. [R]CBQ 63 (2001) 736-737 (*Miller, Troy A.*).

6448 **Blumenfeld, Bruno** The political Paul: justice, democracy and kingship in a Hellenistic framework. JSNT.S 210: Shf 2001, Sheffield A. 507 pp. 1-84127-187-X. Bibl. 451-478.

6449 *Börschel, Regina* "Nicht wie die Heiden, die Gott nicht kennen ... " : Laster und Sünde bei Paulus. WuA(M) 42 (2001) 148-154.

6450 **Carrón Pérez, Julián** Acontecimiento y razón: principio hermenéutico paulino y la interpretación moderna de la escritura. Subsidia: M 2001, San Dámaso 35 pp. €2.

6451 *Dautzenberg, Gerhard* διακονία πνεύματος (2 Kor 3,8)—Paulus als Vermittler der eschatologischen Gabe des Geistes: Überlegungen zu einem besonderen Aspekt des paulinischen Selbstverständnisses. [F]HAINZ, J. 2001 ⇒42. 33-45.

6452 **Engberg-Pedersen, Troels** Paul and the Stoics. 2000 ⇒16,6491. [R]JThS 52 (2001) 278-280 (*Downing, F. Gerald*) BiblInterp 9 (2001) 233-236 (*Barclay, John M.G.*) LouvSt 26 (2001) 90-92 (*Koperski, Veronica*); Il Pensiero Politico 34 (2001) 503-505 (*Cucchi, D.*); CBQ 63 (2001) 743-744 (*Harrill, J. Albert*); RBLit 3 (2001) 12-15 *(Gaca, Kathy L.*): 16-20 (*Furnish, Victor Paul*): 20-24 (*Attridge, Harold W.*): 24-31 (*Stowers, Stanley K.*). Reply of author 31-41.

6453 **Given, Mark Douglas** Paul's true rhetoric: ambiguity, cunning, and deception in Greece and Rome. Emory Studies in Early Christianity 7: Harrisburg, PA 2001, Trinity xix; 219 pp. $25. 1-56338-341-1 [ThD 49,172—Heiser, W. Charles].

6454 **Heyer, Cornelis J. den** Paul: a man of two worlds. 2000 ⇒16,6493. [R]RBBras 18 (2001) 545-547.

6455 **Joubert, Stephan** Paul as benefactor: reciprocity, strategy and theological reflection in Paul's collection. WUNT 2/124: 2000 ⇒16, 6495. [R]BZ 45 (2001) 286-287 (*Backhaus, Knut*)

6456 *Murphy, William F.* The Pauline understanding of appropriated revelation as a principle of christian moral action. StMor 39 (2001) 371-409 [Rom 12,1-2].

6457 **Pearson, Brook W.R.** Corresponding sense: Paul, dialectic, and GADAMER. BiblInterp 58: Lei 2001, Brill xxiv; 370 pp. 90-04-12254-0. Bibl. 331-363.

6458 *Penna, Romano* Pentimento e conversione nelle lettere di San Paolo: la loro scarsa rilevanza soteriologica confrontata con lo sfondo religioso. Vangelo e inculturazione. 2001 <1993> ⇒193. 536-580.

6459 *Pitta, Antonio* Il vangelo paolino e la giustizia. Giustizia-giustificazione nella bibbia. DSBP 28: 2001 ⇒307. 170-208.

6460 **Reilly, Kevin** The interpretation of Paul and the social construction of sexuality. Diss. Princeton Sem. 2001, 292 pp. 3006828 [RTL 33, 640].

6461 *Theobald, Michael* 'Zur Freiheit berufen' (Gal 5,13)—die paulinische Ethik und das mosaische Gesetz <1991>;

6462 Das biblische Fundament der kirchlichen Morallehre <1994>. Studien zum Römerbrief. WUNT 136: 2001 ⇒219. 456-480/519-536.

6463 **Van Kooten, G.H.** The Pauline debate on the cosmos: Graeco-Roman cosmology and Jewish eschatology in Paul and in the Pseudo-Pauline letters to the Colossians and the Ephesians. Diss. R.U. Leiden 2001, *D_Jonge, H.J. de* xvii; 371 pp .

G3.7 *Pauli* communitates *et* spiritualitas

6464 *Bernabé Ubieta, Carmen* "Neither Xenoi nor paroikoi, sympolitai and oikeioi tou theou" (Eph 2.19): Pauline christian communities: defining a new territoriality. F_MALINA, B. 2001 ⇒67. 260-280.

6465 **Cipriani, S.** Il messaggio spirituale di San Paolo. Mi 2001. Ancora 170 pp. €12.39 [RdT 42,639].

6466 **De Vos, Craig Steven** Church and community conflicts: the relationships of the Thessalonian, Corinthian, and Philippian churches with their wider civic communities. SBL.DS 168: 1999 ⇒15,6550; 16,6508. R_ABR 49 (2001) 68-69 (*Dunnill, John*).

6467 *Du Toit, Andrie* 'In Christ', 'in the Spirit' and related prepositional phrases: their relevance for a discussion on Pauline mysticism. Neotest. 34 (2000) 287-298.

6468 **Fusco, Vittorio** Les premières communautés chrétiennes: traditions et tendances dans le christianisme des origines. T_Lucas, Noël: LeDiv 188: P 2001, Cerf 375 pp. €38.11. 2-204-06521-8. Préf. par *Jacques Schlosser*. R_NV 76/4 (2001) 94-95 (*Borel, Jean*); EeV 45 (2001) 20-21 (*Cothenet, Edouard*).

6469 **Gennaro, Giuseppe de; Salzer, Elisabetta C.** Literatura mística: San Pablo místico: Burgos 2001, Monte Carmelo 556 pp.

6470 **Gorman, Michael J.** Cruciformity: Paul's narrative spirituality of the cross. GR 2001, Eerdmans xi; 429 pp. $28. 0-8028-4795-1. Bibl. 402-412.

6471 **Kittredge, Cynthia Briggs** Community and authority: the rhetoric of obedience in the Pauline tradition. HThS 45: 1998 ⇒14,5897; 16, 6973. R_LTP 57 (2001) 194-195 (*Gignac, Alain*).

6472 *Köstenberger, Andreas J.* Women in the Pauline mission. Studies on John and gender. 2001 <2000> ⇒169. 323-352.

6473 *Longenecker, Richard N.* Prayer in the Pauline letters. Into God's presence. 2001 ⇒294. 203-227.

6474 *Murphy-O'Connor, Jerome* St Paul on love. PrPe 15 (2001) 129-33.

6475 *Obenhaus, Stacy R.* Sanctified entirely: the theological focus of Paul's instructions for church discipline. RestQ 43/1 (2001) 1-12.

6476 *O'Neill, John C.* Pedagogues in the Pauline corpus (1 Corinthians 4. 15; Galatians 3.24,25). IBSt 23 (2001) 50-65.

6477 **Orge, Manuel** ¿Es posible la virginidad?: criterios paulinos para su discernimiento. Monografías 9: M 2001, Claretianas 223 pp. 84-796-6-226-3. ᴿATG 64 (2001) 401-402 (*Contreras Molina, Francisco*); Salm. 48 (2001) 606-607 (*Trevijano, Ramón*).

6478 *Penna, Romano* Chiese domestiche e culti privati pagani alle origini del cristianesimo: un confronto. Vangelo e inculturazione. 2001 <1998> ⇒193. 746-770.

6479 **Pereira, Francis** Gripped by God in Christ: the mind and heart of St. Paul. Bandra 2001, St Pauls 157 pp. 81-7109-117-2. Bibl. 156-157.

6480 **Smith, Robert Wayne** Toward a Pauline theology of the christian ministry. Diss. Fuller Sem. 2001, 294 pp. 9999707.

6481 *Strieder, Inácio* O desafio de ser igreja no terceiro milênio: a proposta de Paulo. Estudos Bíblicos 70 (2001) 30-39.

6482 **Sumney, Jerry L.** 'Servants of Satan', 'false brothers' and other opponents of Paul. JSNT.S 188: 1999 ⇒15,6565. ᴿJBL 120 (2001) 578-81 (*Nanos, Mark D.*); RBLit 3 (2001) 428-32 (*Nanos, Mark D.*).

6483 **Szpyra, Szczepan** Pawłowa ocena fałszywych nauczycieli w pierwotnych gminach chrześcijańskich na podstawie jego wielkich listów [L'évaluation paulinienne des faux maîtres dans les communautés chrétiennes primitives selon les grandes épîtres]. Diss. Lublin 2001, ᴰ*Langkammer, H.*: 274 pp [RTL 33,641]. **P.**

6484 **Vanni, Ugo** L'ebbrezza nello Spirito (1Cor 12,13, Ef 5,18): una proposta di spiritualità paolina. Bibbia e Preghiera 38: 2000 ⇒16,6532. ᴿCivCatt 152/4 (2001) 312-313 (*Scaiola, D.*).

6485 *Viviano, Benedict T.* Saint Paul and the ministry of women. Trinity–kingdom–church. NTOA 48: 2001 <1978> ⇒223. 232-239.

G3.8 *Pauli receptio*, history of research

6486 *Giglioni, Paolo* La missione in San Paolo: teologia e prassi. ED 54/1 (2001) 225-229.

6487 *Sutter Rehmann, Luzia* Die aktuelle feministische Exegese der paulinischen Briefe: ein Überblick. Paulus. 2001 ⇒6308. 10-22.

G3.9 *Themata particularia de Paulo*, **details**

6488 *Schaller, Berndt* Zum Textcharakter der Hiobzitate im paulinischen Schrifttum. Fundamenta Judaica. StUNT 25: 2001 <1980> ⇒206. 156-161.

6489 **Winter, Bruce W.** PHILO and Paul among the sophists. 1997 ⇒13, 6273... 16,9069. [R]BiblInterp 9 (2001) 87-88 (*Klutz, Todd E.*).

G4.1 **Ad Romanos** *Textus, commentarii*

6490 **Abraha, Tedros** La lettera ai Romani: testo e commentari della versione etiopica. ÄthF 57: Wsb 2001, Harrassowitz 734 pp. €139. 3-4-47-04380-6.

6491 Der Brief des Apostels Paulus an die Römer. Fischer Taschenbuch 14510: Fra 2000, Fischer 58 pp. 3-596-14510-4. Mit einer Einleitung von *Ruth Rendell.*

6492 **Bryan, Christopher** A preface to Romans: notes on the epistle in its literary and cultural setting. 2000 ⇒16,6547. [R]JThS 52 (2001) 812-816 (*Bell, Richard H.*); RBLit 3 (2001) 435-437 (*Miller, James C.*); RBLit 3 (2001) 437-439 (*Nanos, Mark D.*).

6493 **Cranfield, Charles E.B.** Romans: a shorter commentary. E 2001, Clark xvii; 388 pp. 0-567-29118-9.

6494 **Fitzmyer, J.A.** Lettera ai Romani: commentario critico-teologico. 1999 ⇒15,6584. [R]EstTrin 35 (2001) 449-450 (*Vázquez Allegue, Jaime*).

6495 **Gargano, Innocenzo** Lectio divina sulla Lettera ai Romani, 1. Conversazioni bibliche: Bo 2001, Dehoniane 167 pp. 88-10-70978-1.

6496 **Grelot, Pierre** L'épître de Saint Paul aux Romains: une lecture pour aujourd'hui. Versailles 2001, Saint-Paul 227 pp. €18.30. 2-85049-86-3-7.

6497 **Haacker, Klaus** Der Brief des Paulus an die Römer. ThHK.NT 6: 1999 ⇒15,6585; 16,6551. [R]ThRv 97 (2001) 307-308 (*Theobald, Michael*).

6498 **Hume, C.R.** Reading through Romans. 1999 ⇒15,6586. [R]RBLit 3 (2001) 443-445 (*Daniels, John W.*).

6499 *Miller, James C.* The Romans debate: 1991-2001. CurResB 9 (2001) 306-349.

6500 [E]**Parker, T.H.L.; Parker, D.C.** Ioannis CALVINI: commentarius in epistolam Pauli ad Romanos. Opera Omnia 2/13: 1999 ⇒15,6592; 16,6553. [R]SCJ 32 (2001) 309-310 (*Blacketer, Raymond A.*).

6501 **Pitta, Antonio** Lettera ai Romani: nuova versione, introduzione e
       commento. I libri biblici, NT 6: Mi 2001, Paoline 632 pp. €31. 88-
       315-2117-9. ᴿLSDC 16 (2001) 200-201 (*Spera, Salvatore*); PaVi 46/
       5 (2001) 62-63 (*Ferrari, Pier Luigi*); FilTeo 15 (2001) 641-642
       (*Spera, Salvatore*).
6502 ᵀ**Scheck, Thomas P.** ORIGEN: commentary on the epistle to the Ro-
       mans: v.1, books 1-5. FaCh 103: Wsh 2001, Cath. Univ. of America
       Pr. xiii; (2) 411 pp. $40. 0-8132-0103-9. Bibl. ix-xiii;
6503 v.2, books 6-10. FaCh 104: Wsh 2001, The Catholic University of
       America Press xvi; 340 pp. $40. 0-8132-0104-7.
6504 **Schreiner, Thomas R.** Romans. 1998 ⇒14,5940; 16,6556. ᴿCTJ 36
       (2001) 149-151 (*Oostendorp, Derk*).
6505 **Segalla, Giuseppe** Lettera ai Romani: traduzione strutturata. 1999 ⇒
       15,6595. ᴿLat. 67 (2001) 371-372 (*Pulcinelli, Giuseppe*).
6506 ᵀ**Stroobant de Saint-Eloy, Jean-Eric** THOMAS d'Aquin: com-
       mentaire de l'épître aux Romains... lettre à Bernard Ayglier. 1999 ⇒
       15,6596; 16,6557. ᴿNBl 959 (2001) 49-50 (*Kerr, Fergus*).
6507 ᴱ**Swanson, Reuben J.** New Testament Greek manuscripts: variant
       readings arranged in horizontal lines against Codex Vaticanus Ro-
       mans. Wheaton, IL 2001, Tyndale xxxix; 391 pp. 0-86585-070-4.
6508 **Theobald, Michael** Der Römerbrief. EdF 294: 2000 ⇒16,6558.
       ᴿOrdKor 42 (2001) 424-425 (*Giesen, Heinz*).
6509 *Viviano, Benedict T.* Commentary on Romans by Ernest KÄSEMANN.
       Trinity—kingdom—church. NTOA 48: 2001 <1981> ⇒223. 253-58.

G4.2 *Ad Romans: themata*, **topics**

6510 **Burnett, Gary W.** Paul and the salvation of the individual. Bibl-
       Interp 57: Lei 2001, Brill ix; 246 pp. 90-04-12297-4. Bibl. 231-242
       [Rom 1-8].
6511 *Byrne, Brendan* Interpreting Romans theologically in a post-"new
       perspective" perspective. HThR 94 (2001) 227-241.
6512 **Cosgrove, Charles H.** Elusive Israel: the puzzle of election in Ro-
       mans. 1997 ⇒13,6296; 14,5946. ᴿJBL 119 (2000) 149-151 (*Nanos,
       Mark D.*).
6513 *Gieniusz, Andrzej* Identity markers csz solus Christus—o co toczy się
       bój w Pawłowej nauce o usprawiedliwieniu przez wiarę?. ᶠJANKOW-
       SKI, A. 2001 ⇒53. 118-137. P.
6514 ᴱ**Grenholm, Cristina; Patte, Daniel** Reading Israel in Romans: le-
       gitimacy and plausibility of divergent interpretations. 2000 ⇒16,471.
       ᴿCThMi 28 (2001) 512 (*Lull, David J.*); CBQ 63 (2001) 784-786
       (*Byrne, Brendan*).

6515 **Hartwig, Charlotte** Die Korintische Gemeinde als Nebenadressat des Römerbriefes: eine Untersuchung zur Wiederaufnahme von Themen aus dem 1. Korintherbrief im Römerbrief. Diss. Heidelberg 2001, [D]*Theissen, G.* 266 pp [RTL 33,638].

6516 *Keck, Leander E.* Pathos in Romans?: mostly preliminary remarks. Paul and pathos. SBL Symposium 16: 2001 ⇒6316. 71-96.

6517 *Lohse, Eduard* Das Evangelium für Juden und Griechen: Erwägungen zur Theologie des Römerbriefes. ZNW 92 (2001) 168-184;

6518 Doppelte Prädestination bei Paulus?. [F]LEHMANN, K. 2001 ⇒63. 71-80.

6519 **Mainville, Odette** Un plaidoyer en faveur de l'unité: la lettre aux Romains. 1999 ⇒15,6612; 16,6574. [R]RBLit 3 (2001) 446-448 (*Tobin, Thomas H.*).

6520 **Panattoni, Riccardo** Appartenenza ed eschaton: la lettera ai Romani di san Paolo e la questione 'teologico-politica'. N 2001, Liguori 147 pp.

6521 *Penna, Romano* Origine e dimensione del peccato secondo Paolo: echi della tradizione enochica. Vangelo e inculturazione. 2001 <1995> ⇒193. 391-418.

6522 *Pitta, Antonio* Un conflitto in atto: la legge nella lettera ai Romani. RivBib 49 (2001) 257-282 [Rom 7,7-25].

6523 **Reichert, Angelika** Der Römerbrief als Gratwanderung: eine Untersuchung zur Abfassungsproblematik. Diss.-Habil. Münster 2000, [D]*Taeger, J.-W.*: FRLANT 194: Gö 2001, Vandenhoeck & R. 366 pp. €64. 3-525-53878-2 .

6524 *Reiser, Marius* Sünde und Sündenbewusstsein in der Antike, bei Paulus und bei uns. EuA 77 (2001) 455-469.

6525 *Song, Changwon* Reading Romans through the macro-structure of the diatribe. SBL.SP 2001. SBL.SPS 40: 2001 ⇒494. 260-277.

6526 **Song, Changwon** Reading Romans as a diatribe. Diss. Drew 2001, 208 pp. 3005867.

6527 *Theobald, Michael* Zorn Gottes: ein nicht zu vernachlässigender Aspekt der Theologie des Römerbriefs;

6528 Concupiscentia im Römerbrief: exegetische Beobachtungen anlässlich der lutherischen Formel "simul iustus et peccator" [Rom 7,14-24; 1,24; 6,12; 8,13; 13,14; Gal 5,17];

6529 Warum schrieb Paulus den Römerbrief? <1983>;

6530 Verantwortung vor der Vergangenheit: die Bedeutung der Traditionen Israels für den Römerbrief <1982>;

6531 Glaube und Vernunft: zur Argumentation des Paulus im Römerbrief <1989>. Studien zum Römerbrief. WUNT 136: 2001 ⇒219. 68-100/ 250-276/2-14/15-28/417-431.

6532 *Verster, P.* Die implikasies van stellings as kategorie van nie-egte vrae in Romeine. AcTh(B) 21/1 (2001) 198-214.

6533 *Vos, Johan S.* Sophistische Argumentation im Römerbrief des Apostels Paulus. NT 43 (2001) 224-244.

6534 *Wong, Eric K.C.* The de-radicalization of Jesus' ethical sayings in Romans. NT 43 (2001) 245-263.

G4.3 *Naturalis cognitio Dei,* **Rom 1-4**

6535 *Gathercole, Simon J.* After the new perspective: works, justification and boasting in early Judaism and Romans 1-5. TynB 52 (2001) 303-306.

6536 **Gathercole, S.J.** After the new perspective: works, justification and boasting in early Judaism and Romans 1-5. Diss. Univ. of Durham 2001, ^D*Dunn, James D.G.* [TynB 52,303-306].

6537 *Lambrecht, Jan* God's own righteousness.: Dabourne's new reading of Romans 1-4. LouvSt 25 (2000) 260-274.

6538 *Meadors, Edward P.* Idolatry and the hardening of the heart in Romans 1-2. ProcGLM 21 (2001) 15-30.

6539 *Brown, Michael Joseph* Paul's use of δοῦλος χριστοῦ 'Ιησοῦ in Romans 1:1. JBL 120 (2001) 723-737.

6540 *Theobald, Michael* 'Dem Juden zuerst und auch dem Heiden': die paulinische Auslegung der Glaubensformel Röm 1,3f. Studien zum Römerbrief. WUNT 136: 2001 <1981> ⇒219. 102-118.

6541 **Dabourne, Wendy** Purpose and cause in Pauline exegesis: Romans 1.16-4.25 and a new approach to the letters. MSSNTS 104: 1999 ⇒ 15,6622; 16,6590. ^RBib. 82 (2001) 115-117 (*Campbell, William S.*); RBLit 3 (2001) 439-443 (*Given, Mark D.*).

6542 **Bell, Richard H.** No one seeks for God: an exegetical and theological study of Romans 1.18-3.20. WUNT 106: 1998 ⇒14,5978; 16, 6592. ^RJBL 119 (2000) 370-373 (*Stowers, Stanley K.*).

6543 *Hornsby, Teresa J.* Paul and the remedies of idolatry: reading Romans 1:18-24 with Romans 7. Postmodern interpretations. 2001 ⇒ 229. 219-232.

6544 *Theobald, Michael* Röm 1,26f.: eine paulinische Weisung zur Homosexualität?: Plädoyer für einen vernünftigen Umgang mit der Heiligen Schrift. Studien zum Römerbrief. WUNT 136: 2001 <1998> ⇒ 219. 511-518.

6545 **Berkley, Timothy W.** From a broken covenant to circumcision of the heart: Pauline intertextual exegesis in Romans 2:17-29. SBL.DS 175: 2000 ⇒16,6599. ^RCBQ 63 (2001) 540-41 (*Brodie, Thomas L.*).

6546 *Woyke, Johannes* 'Einst' und 'Jetzt' in Röm 1-3?: zur Bedeutung von Nυνὶ in Röm 3,21. ZNW 92 (2001) 185-206.

6547 *Theobald, Michael* Das Gottesbild des Paulus nach Röm 3,21-31. Studien zum Römerbrief. WUNT 136: 2001 <1981/2> ⇒219. 30-67.

6548 *Lambrecht, Jan* Paul's logic in Rom 3,29-30. Collected studies. AnBib 147: 2001 <2000> ⇒170. 3-5.

6549 *Theobald, Michael* "Abraham sah hin ...": Realitätssinn als Gütesiegel des Glaubens (Röm 4,18-22). Studien zum Römerbrief. WUNT 136: 2001 ⇒219. 398-416 = [F]SCHMUTTERMAYR, G. 2001 ⇒101. 283-301.

G4.4 *Redemptio cosmica*: Rom 5-8

6550 *Huber, Konrad* Being alive to God in Christ: some perspectives on human fulfillment from Paul's anthropology in Romans 5-8. Disputatio philosophica 3 (2001) 203-214.

6551 *Tobin, Thomas H.* The Jewish context of Rom 5:12-14. [F]HAY, D. 2001 ⇒45. 159-175.

6552 *Anderson, Gary A.* Biblical origins and the problem of the fall. ProEc 10 (2001) 17-30 [Rom 5,12-21].

6553 *Kolb, Robert* God kills to make alive: Romans 6 and LUTHER's understanding of justification (1535). Luther Digest 9 (2001) 207-210 <LuthQ 12/1,33-56.

6554 **Fox, Kenneth Allan** Paul's attitude toward the body in Romans 6-8: compared with PHILO of Alexandria. Diss. Toronto, St. Michael 2001, [D]*Lincoln, A.T.* vi; 300 pp. [RTL 33,638].

6555 **Agersnap, Søren** Baptism and the new life: a study of Romans 6.1-14. 1999 ⇒15,6645; 16,6608. [R]RBLit 3 (2001) 432-435 (*Hultgren, Arland J.*).

6556 *Boers, Hendrikus* The structure and meaning of Romans 6:1-14. CBQ 63 (2001) 664-682.

6557 *Gerber, Christine* Vom Waffendienst des Christenmenschen und vom Sold der Sünde: metaphorische Argumentation am Beispiel vom Röm 6,12-14.23. [F]HAHN, F. 2001 ⇒41. 129-142.

6558 **Bahr, Franck** Als aber das Gebot kam (Röm 7,9b): Funktion und Wirkung des Gesetzes in der Röm 7. Deutung vor ORIGENES' Römerbriefkommentar. Diss. Erlangen 2001, [D]*Brennecke, H.C.* [RTL 33, 636]

6559 *Stuhlmacher, Peter* Klage und Dank: exegetische und liturgische Überlegungen zu Römer 7. JBTh 16 (2001) 55-72.

6560 **Burton, Keith Augustus** Rhetoric, law, and the mystery of salvation in Romans 7:1-6. Studies in the Bible and early Christianity 44: Lewiston 2001, Mellen xiv; 162 pp. $80. 0-7734-7708-X. Bibl. 136-59.

6561 *Sutter Rehmann, Luzia* Vom Ende der Eifersucht: der Fall der "verdächtigten Ehefrau" in Röm 7,1-6. Paulus. 2001 ⇒6308. 67-82.

6562 *Bray, Gerald* Sin and the law (Romans 7:1-25). Evangel 19 (2001) 33-37.

6563 **Romanello, Stefano** Una legge buona ma impotente: analisi retorico-letteraria di Rm 7,7-25 nel suo contesto. SRivBib 35: 1999 ⇒16, 6648. ᴿEE 76 (2001) 294-296 (*Pastor-Ramos, Federico*); RivBib 49 (2001) 499-502 (*Penna, Romano*); CivCatt 152/3 (2001) 455-456 (*Scaiola, D.*).

6564 **Martin, Thomas Frank** Rhetoric and exegesis in AUGUSTINE's interpretation of Romans 7:24-25a. SBEC 47: Lewiston, NY 2001, Mellen xiv; 251 pp. $90. 0-7734-7535-4. Bibl. 227-242. ᴿLouvSt 26 (2001) 374-375 (*Verschoren, Marleen*).

6565 *Moreno García, Abdón* Los gemidos del Espíritu: la oración de la esperanza (Rom 8,26-27). EstTrin 35 (2001) 307-324.

6566 *Adewuya, J.A.* The Holy Spirit and sanctification in Romans 8.1-17. JPentec 18 (2001) 71-84.

6567 *Bray, Gerald* The work of the Spirit (Romans 8:1-17). Evangel 19 (2001) 65-69.

6568 *Lambrecht, Jan* The implied exhortation in Romans 8,5-8. Collected studies. AnBib 147: 2001 <2000> ⇒170. 7-17.

6569 *Fee, Gordon D.* Christology and pneumatology in Romans 8:9-11—and elsewhere: some reflections on Paul as a Trinitarian. To what end exegesis?. 2001 <1994> ⇒143. 218-239.

6570 *Giesen, Heinz* Söhne und Töchter Gottes kraft des Geistes: zur ekklesialen Dimension des Christseins (Röm 8,12-17). ᶠHAINZ, J. 2001 ⇒42. 69-101.

6571 *Theobald, Michael* Angstfreie Religiosität: Röm 8,15 und 1Joh 4,17f. im Licht der Schrift PLUTARCHs über den Aberglauben. Studien zum Römerbrief. WUNT 136: 2001 <1992> ⇒219. 432-454.

6572 *Watson, Nigel* "And if children, then heirs" (Rom 8:17)—why not sons?. ABR 49 (2001) 53-56.

6573 **Gieniusz, Andrzej** Romans 8:18-30: "suffering does not thwart the future glory". 1999 ⇒15,6659; 16,6624. ᴿBib. 82 (2001) 288-293 (*Byrne, Brendan*).

G4.6 *Israel et Lex*; **The Law and the Jews,** *Rom 9-11*

6574 **Aletti, Jean-Noël** Israël et la loi dans la lettre aux Romains. LeDiv 173: 1998 ⇒14,6006; 15,6661. [R]RHPhR 81 (2001) 460-461 (*Grappe, Ch.*).

6575 **Bell, Richard H.** Provoked to jealousy: the origin and purpose of the jealousy motif in Romans 9-11. WUNT 63: 1994 ⇒10,5801... 13, 6350. [R]BiblInterp 9 (2001) 85-86 (*Clarke, Andrew D.*)

6576 **Das, A. Andrew** Paul, the law, and the covenant. Peabody, MASS 2001, Hendrickson xix; 342 pp. $25. 1-56563-463-2. Bibl. 275-316. [E]**Dunn, J.** Paul and the Mosaic law 2001 ⇒462.

6577 **Gignac, Alain** Juifs et chrétiens à l'école de Paul de Tarse: enjeux i-dentitaires et éthiques d'une lecture de Romains 9-11. 1999 ⇒15, 6666; 16,6627. [R]CBQ 63 (2001) 338-339 (*Getty, Mary Ann*); Theoforum 32 (2001) 242-243 (*Bonneau, Normand*).

6578 **Kim, Johann D.** God, Israel, and the gentiles: rhetoric and situation in Romans 9-11. SBL.DS 176: 2000 ⇒16,6628. [R]CBQ 63 (2001) 152-154 (*Nanos, Mark D.*).

6579 *Mussner, Franz* The 'hardening' of Israel (Rom 9-11). ThD 48 (2001) 133-136.

6580 **Rapa, Robert Keith** The meaning of "works of the law" in Galatians and Romans. Studies in Biblical Literature 31: NY 2001, Lang xiv; 317 pp. $64. 0-8204-5119-3. Bibl. 267-269.

6581 *Talbert, Charles H.* Paul, Judaism, and the revisionists. CBQ 63 (2001) 1-22.

6582 *Theobald, Michael* Kirche und Israel nach Röm 9-11 <1987>;

6583 Der 'strittige Punkt' (Rh.a.Her.1,26) im Diskurs des Römerbriefs: die propositio 1,16f. und das Mysterium der Errettung ganz Israels. Studien zum Römerbrief. 2001 <1999> ⇒219. 324-349/278-323.

6584 **Yinger, Kent L.** Paul, Judaism and judgment according to deeds. MSSNTS 105: 1999 ⇒15,6675; 16,6640. [R]ETR 76 (2001) 127-128 (*Cuvillier, Elian*); JBL 120 (2001) 174-175 (*Seifrid, Mark A.*).

6585 *Zeller, Dieter* Paulus und das Gesetz des Mose. WUB 20 (2001) 67-71.

6586 *Räisänen, Heikki* Faith, works and election in Romans 9: a response to Stephen Westerholm. Challenges to biblical interpretation. BiblInterp 59: 2001 <1996> ⇒200. 101-110.

6587 *Seitz, Erich* Λόγον συντέμνων—eine Gerichtsankündigung? (zu Römer 9,27/28). BN 109 (2001) 56-82.

6588 *Heil, John Paul* Christ, the termination of the law (Romans 9:30-10: 8). CBQ 63 (2001) 484-498.

6589 *Lambrecht, Jan* The caesura between Romans 9,30-33 and 10,1-4. Collected studies. AnBib 147: 2001 <1999> ⇒170. 19-27.

6590 **Lowther, James Richard** Paul's use of Deuteronomy 30:11-14 in Romans 10:5-8 as a locus primus on Paul's understanding of the law in Romans. Diss. Fort Worth 2001, ᴰ*Corley, B.*: 205 pp [RTL 33,639].

6591 **Keller, Winfrid** Gottes Treue—Israels Heil: Röm 11,25-27—die These von 'Sonderweg' in der Diskussion. SBB 40: 1998 ⇒14,6026; 15,6684. ᴿFrRu 8 (2001) 135-137 (*Renker, Alwin*).

6592 *Scott, James M.* "And then all Israel will be saved" (Rom 11:26). Restoration. JSJ.S 72: 2001 ⇒319. 489-527.

6593 *Schaller, Berndt* "Ἥξει ἐκ Σιὼν ὁ ῥυόμενος: zur Textgestalt von Jes 59:20f. in Röm 11:26f. Fundamenta Judaica. StUNT 25: 2001 <1984> ⇒206. 162-166.

G4.8 Rom 12...

6594 *Jones, Peter Rhea* The new deadly sins: Romans 12:1-2. ExAu 17 (2001) 156-162.

6595 *Dal Covolo, Enrico* Romani 13,1-7 e i rapporti tra la chiesa e l'impero romano nel primo secolo. ᴹCᴀɢɴɪ, L., 3: 2001 ⇒15. 1481-1492.

6596 **MacKenzie, Edward E.M.** The state and the community of God: political motifs in Romans and the occasion for Romans 13:1-7. Diss. Edinburgh 2001, ᴰ*Hurtado, L.W.* 337 pp.

6597 *Waugh, Stuart G.* Heteron vs plesion: what's in a word?: an analysis of the canonical and Marcionite versions of Romans 13:8. JHiC 8/1 (2001) 73-90.

6598 **Reasoner, Mark** The strong and the weak: Romans 14,1-15,13 in context. MSSNTS 103: 1999 ⇒15,6694; 16,6663. ᴿJBL 120 (2001) 178-180 (*Nanos, Mark D.*).

6599 *Theobald, Michael* Der Einsamkeit des Selbst entnommen—dem Herrn gehörig: ein christologisches Lehrstück (Röm 14,7-9);

6600 Erkenntnis und Liebe: Kriterien glaubenskonformen Handelns nach Röm 14,13-23. Studien zum Römerbrief. WUNT 136: 2001 ⇒219. 142-161/481-510.

6601 *Gagnon, Robert A.J.* The meaning of ὑμων τὸ ἀγαθόν in Romans 14:16. JBL 117 (1998) 675-689.

6602 *Vreekamp, Hendrik* Dienaar van Israël: Romeinen 15:7-13. ThRef 44 (2001) 105-108.

6603 *Baumert, Norbert* Diener Gottes für Wahrheit und Barmherzigkeit: eine Rückmeldung zu J.R. Wagner's 'Fresh approach to Romans

15:8-9'. Studien zu den Paulusbriefen. SBAB 32: 2001 <2000> ⇒
123. 11-18.

6604 **Lambrecht, Jan** Syntactical and logical remarks on Romans 15,8-9a.
Collected studies. AnBib 147: 2001 <2000> ⇒170. 29-33.

6605 *Wander, Bernd* Warum wollte Paulus nach Spanien?: ein forschungs-
und motivgeschichtlicher Überblick. Das Ende des Paulus. BZNW
106: 2001 ⇒281. 175-195 [Rom 15,24].

6606 *Penna, Romano* Note sull'ipotesi efesina di Rom 16. VIII Simposio
di Efeso. Turchia 15: 2001 ⇒488. 109-114.

6607 *Burer, Michael H.; Wallace, Daniel B.* Was Junia really an apostle?:
a re-examination of Rom 16.7. NTS 47 (2001) 76-91.

6608 *Reid, Barbara E.* Puzzling passages (Romans 16:7). BiTod 39 (2001)
244-245.

G5.1 Epistulae ad Corinthios I (vel I-II), *textus, commentarii*

6609 [E]**Bray, Gerald** La biblia comentada por los Padres de la iglesia y o-
tros de la época patrística: Nuevo Testamento 7: 1-2 Corintios. [E]*Me-*
rino, Marcelo: M 2001, Ciudad Nueva 468 pp. €30. 84-9715-003-1.
Bibl. 17-24;

6610 1-2 Corinthians. ACCS.NT 7: 1999 ⇒15,6699; 16, 6673. [R]Biblos 50
(2001) 365-366 (*Henner, Jutta*).

6611 Die Briefe des Apostels Paulus an die Korinther. Fischer Taschenbuch 14511: Fra 2000, Fischer 76 pp. 3-596-14511-2. Mit einer Einleitung von *Fay Weldon*.

6612 *Mitchell, Margaret M.* Korintherbriefe. RGG², 4: I-K. 2001 ⇒664.
1688-1694.

6613 **Branick, Vincent P.** First Corinthians: building up the church.
Spiritual commentaries on the bible. Hyde Park, NY 2001, New City
151 pp. $12. 1-56548-162-3 [ThD 49,61—Heiser, W. Charles].

6614 **Collins, Raymond F.** First Corinthians. 1999 ⇒15,6705; 16,6677.
[R]ScrB 31/1 (2001) 47-50 (*Corley, Jeremy*); BZ 45 (2001) 146-147
(*Wehr, Lothar*); RB 108 (2001) 301-303 (*Murphy-O'Connor, J.*);
RivBib 49 (2001) 247-249 (*Barbaglio, Giuseppe*); CoTh (2001/4)
205-10 (*Załęski, Jan*); Bib. 82 (2001) 117-120 (*Talbert, Charles H.*).

6615 **Fabris, Rinaldo** Prima Lettera ai Corinzi. 1999 ⇒15,6706; 16,6678.
[R]Sal. 63 (2001) 196-197 (*Cimosa, Mario*).

6616 **Lindemann, Andreas** Der erste Korintherbrief. HNT 9/1: 2000 ⇒
16,6683. [R]RBBras 18 (2001) 551-552.

6617 **Merklein, Helmut** Der erste Brief an die Korinther, 2: Kapitel 5,1-11,1. ÖTBK 7/2: 2000 ⇒16,6685. [R]ThLZ 126 (2001) 760-761 (*Wolff, Christian*).

6618 **Schrage, Wolfgang** Der erste Brief an die Korinther, 3: 1 Kor 11,17-14,40. EKK 7/3: 1999 ⇒15,6714. [R]JBL 120 (2001) 574-576 (*Mitchell, Alan C.*); RBLit 3 (2001) 448-450 (*Mitchell, Alan C.*);

6619 4. Teilband 1Kor 15,1-16,24. EKK 7/4: Dü 2001, Benziger viii; 485 pp. €76.18. 3-545-23132-1. [R]RBBras 18 (2001) 552-553.

6620 **Speyr, Adrienne von** Première épître de saint Paul aux Corinthiens: méditations sur les chapitres 10 à 16. Bru 2000, Lessius 288 pp. €25.15 [EeV 51,35—Wallut, Matthieu].

6621 **Thiselton, Anthony C.** The first epistle to the Corinthians: a commentary on the Greek text. NIGTC: 2000 ⇒16,6689. [R]ScrB 31 (2001) 120-121 (*Stafford, Barbara*); RTR 60 (2001) 158-159 (*Ward, Rowland S.*); IBSt 23 (2001) 182-185 (*Ker, Donald P.*); LouvSt 26 (2001) 372-374 (*Koperski, Veronica*).

6622 **Trail, Ronald** An exegetical summary of 1 Corinthians 10-16. Dallas, TEX 2001, SIL I. 404 pp. 1-55671-116-6.

G5.2 *1 & 1-2 ad Corinthios*—themata, topics

6623 *Álvarez Cineira, D.* La misión de Pablo y sus enemigos en Corinto. EstAg 36 (2001) 461-494.

6624 **Bae, Hyunju** The symbolism of evil power in 1 and 2 Corinthians: power, wisdom, and community. Diss. Drew 2001, 303 pp. 3025582.

6625 *Barclay, John M.G.* Matching theory and practice: JOSEPHUS's constitutional ideal and Paul's strategy in Corinth. Paul beyond. 2001 ⇒ 262. 139-163.

6626 *Fee, Gordon D.* 'Another gospel which you did not embrace': 2 Corinthians 11:4 and the theology of 1 and 2 Corinthians. To what end exegesis?. 2001 <1994> ⇒143. 240-261.

6627 **Grant, Robert McQueen** Paul in the Roman world: the conflict at Corinth. LVL 2001, Westminster viii; 181 pp. $20. 0-664-22452-0. Bibl. 164-173.

6628 *Koch, Dietrich-Alex* Paulus in Korinth. WUB 20 (2001) 20-23.

6629 *Meeks, W.A.* Corinthian christians as artificial aliens. Paul beyond. 2001 ⇒262. 129-138.

6630 **Newton, Derek** Deity and diet: the dilemma of sacrificial food at Corinth. JSNT.S 169: 1998 ⇒14,6082; 16,6708. [R]RB 108 (2001) 304-305 (*Murphy-O'Connor, J.*).

6631 **Økland, Jorunn** Women in their space: Paul and the Corinthian discourse of gender and sanctuary space. Diss. Oslo 2001.

6632 *Polaski, Sandra Hack* Inside jokes: community and authority in the Corinthian correspondence. Postmodern interpretations. 2001 ⇒229. 233-242.

6633 **Robertson, Charles K.** Conflict in Corinth: redefining the system. Studies in Biblical Literature 42: NY 2001, Lang xv; 257 pp. 0-8204-5569-5. Bibl. 239-252.

6634 *Tronier, Henrik* The Corinthian correspondence between philosophical idealism and apocalypticism. Paul beyond. 2001 ⇒262. 165-196.

6635 **Winter, Bruce W.** After Paul left Corinth: the influence of secular ethics and social change. GR 2001, Eerdmans xxi; 344 pp. $28/£18. 0-8028-4898-2. Bibl. 302-321. [R]ScrB 31 (2001) 118-120 (*Corley, Jeremy*); ET 112 (2001) 325-327 (*Rodd, C.S.*).

6636 **Birge, Mary Katherine** The language of belonging: a rhetorical analysis of kinship language in First Corinthians. Diss. Cath. Univ. of America 2001, [D]*Moloney, F.J.*: 305 pp. 3004152.

6637 **Eriksson, Anders** Traditions as rhetorical proof: Pauline argumentation in I Corinthians. CB.NT 29: 1998 ⇒14,6068... 16,6702. [R]JBL 119 (2000) 152-153 (*Willis, Wendell Lee*).

6638 *Fee, Gordon D.* Toward a theology of 1 Corinthians. To what end exegesis?. 2001 <1989> ⇒143. 195-217.

6639 **Furnish, Victor Paul** The theology of the First Letter to the Corinthians. 1999 ⇒15,6724; 16,6703. [R]ProEc 10 (2001) 373-374 (*Keck, Leander E.*).

6640 *Hollander, Harm* Een verdeelde gemeente: de christelijke gemeente in Korinte volgens de eerste brief aan de Korintiërs. VroegchriHstelijke gemeenten. 2001 ⇒460. 40-53.

6641 *Neirynck, Frans* The sayings of Jesus in 1 Corinthians. Evangelica III. BEThL 150: 2001 <1996> ⇒187. 93-128.

6642 *Peng, Wang* On Paul's prohibitions on women in 1 Corinthians. CTR 15 (2001) 88-101.

G5.3 **1 Cor 1-7**: *sapientia crucis... abusus matrimonii*

6643 **Pate, C. Marvin** The reverse of the curse: Paul, wisdom, and the law. WUNT 2/114: 2000 ⇒16,6713. [R]TrinJ 22 (2001) 272-276 (*Moo, Douglas J.*); SNTU.A 26 (2001) 262-7 (*Wedderburn, A.J.M.*).

6644 *Tauwinkl, Wilhelm* Pregătirea in Vechiul Testament a paradoxului întelepciune/cryce din 1 Cor 1-4 [The wisdom-cross paradox in 1 Corinthians 1-4 and its foreshadowing in the Old Testament]. CICat 2/1 (2001) 30-40. **Roumanian**.

6645 *Fee, Gordon D.* Textual-exegetical observations on 1 Corinthians
      1:2, 2:1, and 2:10. To what end exegesis?. 2001 <1992> ⇒143. 43-
      56.

6646 *Lambrecht, Jan* The power of God: a note on the connection between
      1 Cor 1,17 and 18. Collected studies. AnBib 147: 2001 ⇒170. 35-
      42.

6647 *Penna, Romano* Logos paolino della croce e sapienza umana (1Cor
      1,18-2,16). Vangelo e inculturazione. 2001 <1993> ⇒193. 461-483.

6648 **Williams, H.H. Drake** The wisdom of the wise: the presence and
      function of scripture in 1 Cor 1:18-3:23. Diss. Aberdeen 2001, ᴰ*Ros-
      ner, Brian S.*: AGJU 49: Lei 2001, Brill xix; 409 pp. 90-04-11974-4.
      Bibl. 345-365 [TynB 52,315-317].

6649 *Le Gal, Frédéric* L'evangile de la folie sainte. RSR 89 (2001) 419-
      442 [1 Cor 1,18-31].

6650 *Winter, Franz* Erste Ergebnisse der Analyse des 1. Korintherbriefes
      auf dem Hintergrund der dokumentarischen Papyri. XXII Congresso
      di papirologia, 2. 2001 ⇒555. 1295-1306 [1 Cor 3,10; 1,4-6].

6651 *Azzali Bernardelli, Giovanna* 'Templum Dei estis' (1 Cor 3,16): os-
      servazioni sugli sviluppi dell'esegesi e del lessico dell'inabitazione
      divina negli scrittori africani da TERTULLIANO ad AGOSTINO. Cultura
      latina cristiana fra terzo e quinto secolo: atti del convegno, Mantova,
      5-7 novembre 1998. Accademia Naz. Virgiliana di Scienze Lettere e
      Arti, Misc. 9: F 2001, Olschki. 45-170 [REAug 48,346–Deléani, S.].

6652 *Tyler, Ronald L.* The history of the interpretation of *to me hyper ha
      gegraptai* in 1 Corinthians 4:6. RestQ 43/4 (2001) 243-252.

6653 *Lambrecht, Jan* Paul as example: a study of 1 Corinthians 4,6-21.
      Collected studies. AnBib 147: 2001 <1996> ⇒170. 43-62.

6654 *Renju, Peter M.* The passover lamb. BiTr 52 (2001) 229-234 [1 Cor
      5,7].

6655 *Hoskins, Paul M.* The use of biblical and extrabiblical parallels in the
      interpretation of First Corinthians 6:2-3. CBQ 63 (2001) 287-297.

6656 **Sánchez Rivera, César Orlando** Celibato-virginidad y matrimonio
      en 1Co 7 en el contexto de la corporeidad de 1Co. R 2001, 185 pp.
      Exc. Diss. Gregoriana.

6657 *Fee, Gordon D.* 1 Corinthians 7:1 in the NIV. To what end exegesis?.
      2001 <1980> ⇒143. 88-98.

6658 *Prete, Benedetto* Il significato della formula πρὸς καιρὸν (Vg.: ad
      tempus) in 1Cor 7,5. RivBib 49 (2001) 417-437.

6659 *Brewer, David I.* 1 Corinthians 7 in the light of the Graeco-Roman
      marriage and divorce papyri. TynB 52 (2001) 101-116 [1 Cor 7,10-
      15].

6660 *Kuck, David W.* The freedom of being in the world 'as if not' (1 Cor
      7:29-31). CThMi 28 (2001) 585-593.

G5.4 *Idolothyta... Eucharistia*: **1 Cor 8-11**

6661 **Cheung, Alex T.** Idol food in Corinth: Jewish background and Pauline legacy. JSNT.S 176: 1999 ⇒15,6755; 16,6731. [R]RB 108 (2001) 305-306 (*Murphy-O'Connor, J.*); JBL 120 (2001) 576-578 (*Brunt, John*); Bib. 82 (2001) 441-444 (*Willis, Wendell L.*).

6662 **Hawkins, Faith Kirkham** 1 Corinthians 8:1-11:1: the making and meaning of difference. Diss. Emory 2001, 305 pp. 3009437.

6663 **McGowan, Andrew** Ascetic eucharists: food and drink in early christian ritual meals. 1999 ⇒15,6775; 16,6733. [R]VigChr 55 (2001) 431-436 (*Rouwhorst, G.*).

6664 *Moreno García, Abdón; Saez Gonzalvez, Ramón* El problema de los idolotitos en 1 Co 8-11 como humus de los banquetes judeo-christianos. EstB 59 (2001) 47-77.

6665 *Troisfontaines, Claude* Les viandes sacrifiées: Saint Paul et les Corinthiens. [F]MOTTE, A. 2001, ⇒76. 257-268.

6666 *Fee, Gordon D.* Εἰδωλόθυτα once again: an interpretation of 1 Corinthians 8-10. To what end exegesis?. 2001 <1980> ⇒143. 105-128.

6667 **Lambrecht, Jan** Universalism in 1 Corinthians 8,1-11,1. Collected studies. AnBib 147: 2001 <1996> ⇒170. 63-70.

6668 **Galloway, Lincoln Emmanuel** Freedom in 1 Corinthians 9: Paul in conversation with EPICTETUS and PHILO. Diss. Emory 2001, 367 pp. 3009432.

6669 *Mitchell, Margaret M.* Pauline accommodation and 'condescension' (συγκατάβασις): 1 Cor 9:19-23 and the history of influence. Paul beyond. 2001 ⇒262. 197-214.

6670 *Joubert, Stephan* 1 Corinthians 9:24-27: an agonistic competition?. Neotest. 35 (2001) 57-68.

6671 **Ostmeyer, Karl-Heinrich** Taufe und Typos: Elemente und Theologie der Tauftypologien in 1. Korinther 10 und 1. Petrus 3. WUNT 2/118: 2000 ⇒16,6751. [R]BZ 45 (2001) 288-290 (*Zimmermann, Ruben*); JThS 52 (2001) 837-842 (*Wedderburn, A.J.M.*); RHPhR 81 (2001) 463-464 (*Grappe, Ch.*).

6672 *Gruenwald, Ithamar* Paul and ritual theory: the case of the "Lord's Supper" in 1 Corinthians 10 and 11. [F]BETZ, H. 2001 ⇒5. 159-187.

6673 **Inostroza Lanas, Juan Carlos** Moisés e Israel en el desierto: el midrás paulino de 1Cor 10,1-13. 2000 ⇒16,6752. [R]Salm. 48 (2001) 176-179 (*Sánchez Caro, José Manuel*); EstB 59 (2001) 558-560 (*Ribera-Florit, Joseph*); Revista teología 40 (2001) 98-102 (*Rivas, Luis Heriberto*).

6674   *Schaller, Berndt* 1 Kor 10,1-10(13) und die jüdischen Vorausset-
       zungen der Schriftauslegung des Paulus. Fundamenta Judaica..
       StUNT 25: 2001 ⇒206. 167-190.

6675   *Baumert, Norbert* 'Κοινωνία τοῦ αἵματος τοῦ Χριστοῦ'—1 Kor
       10,14-22. Studien zu den Paulusbriefen. SBAB 32: 2001 <1996>
       ⇒123. 43-48.

6676   *Ekem, John D.K.* Does 1 Cor 11:2-16 legislate for 'head covering'?.
       Neotest. 35 (2001) 169-176.

6677   *Graakjær Hjort, Brigitte* Gender hierarchy or religious androgyny?:
       male-female interaction in the Corinthian community—a reading of 1
       Cor. 11,2-16. StTh 55 (2001) 58-80.

6678   **Biguzzi, Giancarlo** Velo e silenzio: Paolo e la donna in 1Cor 11,2-
       16 e 14,33b-36. SRivBib 37: Bo 2001, Dehoniane 199 pp. 88-10-
       30225-7. Bibl. 159-171.

6679   *Powers, Janet E.* Recovering a woman's head with prophetic author-
       ity: a Pentecostal interpretation of 1 Corinthians 11.3-16. JPentec
       10/1 (2001) 11-37.

6680   *Betz, Hans Dieter* Gemeinschaft des Glaubens und Herrenmahl:
       Überlegungen zu 1 Kor 11,17-34. ZThK 98 (2001) 401-421.

6681   *Yde Iversen, Gertrud* Måltid og ritual, krop og konsum: eksegetiske
       belysninger af 1 Kor 11,17-34. Kritisk forum for praktisk teologi 83
       (2001) 41-51.

G5.5 1 Cor 12s... Glossolalia, charismata

6682   *Baumert, Norbert* Charisma und Amt bei Paulus <1986>;
6683   Charisma und Geisttaufe <1995>;
6684   Charisma und Recht <2000>. Studien zu den Paulusbriefen. SBAB
       32: 2001⇒123. 239-271/272-277/278-280.

6685   **Baumert, Norbert** Charisma—Taufe—Geisttaufe, 1: Entflechtung
       einer semantischen Verwirrung; 2: Normativität und persönliche Be-
       rufung. Wü 2001, Echter 320 + 399 pp. €39.90. 3-429-02317-3.

6686   *Claussen, Carsten* Die Frage nach der "Unterscheidung der Gei-
       ster"—Überlegungen auf dem Weg zu verantwortlichen Entscheidun-
       gen. ZNT 8 (2001) 25-33.

6687   *Green, Gene L.* 'As for prophecies, they will come to an end': 2 Peter,
       Paul and PLUTARCH on 'the obsolescence of oracles'. JSNT 82 (2001)
       107-122.

6688   **Hvidt, Niels Christian** The problem of christian prophecy: its pre-
       conditions, function, and status in the church. Exc. Diss. Gregoriana
       2001, ᴰ*Salmann, Elmar* 107 pp .

6689 **Levison, J.** Of two minds: ecstasy and inspired interpretation in the New Testament world. 1999 ⇒15,6787. ^RCBQ 63 (2001) 553-554 (*Clabeaux, John J.*).

6690 **Sionek, Andrzej** Posługa słowa we wspólnocie Korynckiej (1 Kor 12-14): studium egzegetyczno-teologizne [Le ministère du verbe dans la communauté de Corinthe (1 Co 12-14): étude exégétique et théologique]. Diss. Lublin 2001, ^D*Witczyk, H.* 347 pp [RTL 33,641]. **P.**

6691 *Theobald, Michael* 'Prophetenworte verachtet nicht!' (1 Thess 5,20): paulinische Perspektiven gegen eine institutionelle Versuchung. Studien zum Römerbrief. WUNT 136: 2001 <1991> ⇒219. 350-66.

6692 **Lee, Michelle Vidle** 'We are the parts of one great body': understanding the community as Christ's body in 1 Corinthians 12 in light of Hellenistic moral philosophy. Diss. Notre Dame 2001, ^D*D'Angelo, M.R.* 336 pp. 3000400.

6693 *Verspeeten, Frédéric* 1 Corinthiens 12,12-19: le 'déjà-là' de l'unité. Lire et Dire 48 (2001) 32-44.

6694 *Thurén, Lauri* "By means of hyperbole" (1 Cor 12:31b). Paul and pathos. SBL Symposium 16: 2001 ⇒6316. 97-113.

6695 **Sewodo Dovi, Michel** L'éloge de l'agapè en 1 Co 13. Diss. Rome, Urbaniana 2001, ^D*Biguzzi, G.* Diss. Rome, Urbaniana [RTL 33,641].

6696 *Sorg, Theo* Ein Geber—viele Gaben: 1. Korinther 14,1-3.23-25. ThBeitr 32 (2001) 1-5.

6697 **Masalles, Victor** La profecia en la asamblea cristiana: análisis retórico-literario de 1 Cor 14,1-25. TGr.T 74: R 2001, E.P.U.G. 410 pp. 88-7652-892-X. Bibl. 371-397.

6698 *Ramos, José C.* Dones, señales y ministerio: un estudio exegético de 1 Corintios 14:20-25. Theologika 16 (2001) 32-82.

6699 *Clarke, Graham* 'As in all the churches of the saints' (1 Corinthians 14.33). BiTr 52 (2001) 144-147.

6700 *Crüsemann, Marlene* Unrettbar frauenfeindlich: der Kampf um das Wort von Frauen in 1 Kor 14,34-35 im Spiegel antijudaistischer Elemente der Auslegung. Paulus. 2001 ⇒6308. 23-41.

G5.6 Resurrectio; *1 Cor 15*...[⇒F5.6]

6701 *Baumert, Norbert* Mit Christus sterben und auferstehen': Paulus zu Gegenwart und Zukunft der Auferstehung. Studien zu den Paulusbriefen. SBAB 32: 2001 <1998> ⇒123. 209-214.

6702 *Dunn, James D.G.* A response to Peter Stuhlmacher. Auferstehung—Resurrection. WUNT 135: 2001 ⇒452. 363-368.

6703 *Gourgues, Michel* La résurrection dans les credos et les hymnes des premières communautés chrétiennes;

6704 *Mainville, Odette* Les apparitions du ressuscité: fonctions et enjeux théologiques. Résurrection: l'après-mort. MoBi 45: 2001 ⇒296. 161-174/175-193.

6705 *Perera, James Dudley* The resurrection of the body: some biblical, theological and pastoral considerations. VJTR 65 (2001) 720-731.

6706 *Stuhlmacher, Peter* "Christus Jesus ist hier, der gestorben ist, ja vielmehr der auch auferweckt ist, der zur Rechten Gottes ist und uns vertritt". Auferstehung—Resurrection. 2001 ⇒452. 351-361.

6707 *Gignac, Alain* Comprendre notre résurrection dans une perspective paulinienne: les images de 1 Th 4,13-18, 1 Co 15 et 2 Co 5,1-10. Résurrection: l'après-mort. MoBi 45: 2001 ⇒296. 279-305.

6708 *Hengel, Martin* Das Begräbnis Jesu bei Paulus und die leibliche Auferstehung aus dem Grabe. Auferstehung—Resurrection. 2001 ⇒452. 119-183 [1 Cor 15].

6709 *Lambrecht, Jan* Three brief notes on 1 Corinthians 15. Collected studies. AnBib 147: 2001 ⇒170. 71-85.

6710 *Wischmeyer, Oda* 1. Korinther 15: der Traktat des Paulus über die Auferstehung der Toten. Was ist ein Text?. Neutestamentliche Entwürfe zur Theologie 1: 2001 ⇒335. 171-209.

6711 *Zeller, Dieter* Die angebliche enthusiastische oder spiritualistische Front in 1 Kor 15. ^FHAY, D. 2001 ⇒45. 176-189.

6712 *Eriksson, Anders* Fear of eternal damnation: pathos appeal in 1 Corinthians 15 and 16. Paul and pathos. SBL Symposium 16: 2001 ⇒6316. 115-126.

6713 *Alkier, Stefan* Die Vielfalt der Zeichen und die Aufgabe einer Theologie des Neuen Testaments. Religionskultur—zur Beziehung von Religion und Kultur in der Gesellschaft: Beiträge des Fachbereichs Evangelische Theologie an der Univ. Frankfurt/M. ^E**Witte, Markus**: Wü 2001, Religion & K. 177-198 [BuBB 34,19] [1 Cor 15,1-11].

6714 *De Saeger, Luc* "Für unsere Sünden": 1 Kor 15,3b und Gal 1,4a im exegetischen Vergleich. EThL 77 (2001) 169-191.

6715 **Babu, Chirayath** The nature of Paul's easter-experience: an exegetical-theological study of 1 Cor 15,8 in relation to Gal 1,15-17; 1 Cor 9,1-2; Phil 3,7-8; 2 Cor 4,6 and Acts 9,3-19; 22,6-21; 26,12-18. Extr. Diss. Rome, Urbaniana 2001, ^D*Biguzzi, G.* 70 pp. Bibl. 50-68.

6716 *Bachmann, Michael* 1 Kor 15,12f.: "Resurrection of the dead (= christians)"?. ZNW 92 (2001) 295-299.

6717 *Lambrecht, Jan* Just a possibility?: a reply to Johan S. Vos on 1 Corinthians 15,12-20. Collected studies. AnBib 147: 2001 <2000> ⇒170. 87-90.

6718 *Vincent, Jean Marcel* Avec quel corps les morts reviennent-ils?: l'usage des écritures dans 1 Corinthiens 15,36-45. FV 100/2 (2001) 63-70 [BuBB 37,9] [Gen 1-3].

6719 *Hodgens, David* Our resurrection body: an exegesis of 1 Corinthians 15:42-49. Melanesian Journal of Theology 17/2 (2001) 65-90.

6720 **Schneider, Sebastian** Vollendung des Auferstehens: eine exegetische Untersuchung von 1 Kor 15,51-52 und 1 Thess 4,13-18. FzB 97: 2000 ⇒16,6798. [R]CoTh (2001/3) 214-217 (*Załęski, Jan*); ThLZ 126 (2001) 1159-1161 (*Haufe, Günter*).

6721 *Baumert, Norbert* Maranatha: Gegenwart und Ankunft des Herrn—1 Kor 16,22: zur Adventsfrömmigkeit. Studien zu den Paulusbriefen. SBAB 32: 2001 <1985> ⇒123. 49-58.

G5.9 Secunda epistula ad Corinthios

6722 **Barnett, Paul William** The second epistle to the Corinthians. 1997 ⇒13,6519... 15,6821. [R]WThJ 63 (2001) 190-194 (*Hafemann, Scott*); SNTU.A 23 (1998) 276-277 (*Fuchs, Albert*).

6723 *Bieringer, Reimund* Een zelfbewuste gemeente: de christelijke gemeente in Korinte volgens de tweede brief aan de Korintiërs. Vroegchristelijke gemeenten. 2001 ⇒460. 54-67.

6724 **Chang, Steven** Fund-raising in Corinth: a socio-economic study of the Corinthian church, the collection and 2 Corinthians. Diss. Aberdeen 2001, [D]*Clarke, A.D.* [RTL 33,637].

6725 **Corsani, Bruno** La seconda lettera ai Corinzi: guida alla lettura. 2000 ⇒16,6801. [R]LSDC 16 (2001) 201-202 (*Spera, Salvatore*); RAMi 70 (2001) 610-611 (*Spera, Salvatore*); SapDom 54 (2001) 230-231 (*Spera, Salvatore*).

6726 *Doxtader, Erik* Reconciliation in a state of emergency: the middle voice of 2 Corinthians. JSR 14/1 (2001) 47-64.

6727 **Goodwin, Mark J.** Paul, apostle of the living God: kerygma and conversion in 2 Corinthians. Harrisburg, Pennsylvania 2001, Trinity ix; 261 pp. $28. 1-56338-318-7. Bibl. 231-242.

6728 **Goulder, Michael D.** Paul and the competing mission in Corinth. Library of Pauline Studies: Peabody, MASS 2001, Hendrickson xiv; 303 pp. £18. 1-56563-379-2. Bibl. 275-285.

6729 **Lambrecht, Jan** Second Corinthians. 1999 ⇒15,6826; 16,6822. [R]RBLit 3 (2001) 450-452 (*Furnish, Victor Paul*).

6730 **Plunkett-Dowling, Regina** Reading and restoration: Paul's use of scripture in 2 Corinthians 1-9. Diss. Yale 2001, [D]*Meeks, W.A.* [RTL 33,640].

6731 *Sumney, Jerry L.* Paul's use of πάθος in his argument against the op-
      ponents of 2 Corinthians;
6732 *Thompson, James W.* Paul's argument from pathos in 2 Corinthians.
      Paul and pathos. SBL Symposium 16: 2001 ⇒6316. 147-60/127-45.
6733 **Thrall, Margaret E.** A critical and exegetical commentary on the
      second epistle to the Corinthians, 2: commentary on II Corinthians
      VIII-XIII. ICC: 2000 ⇒16,6810. ᴿABR 49 (2001) 66-67 (*Watson,
      Nigel M.*);
6734 A commentary on the second epistle to the Corinthians, 1-2. ICC:
      1994-2000 ⇒16,6810. ᴿRBBras 18 (2001) 555-556.
6735 **Wan, Sze-kar** Power in weakness: conflict and rhetoric in Paul's
      second letter to the Corinthians. 2000 ⇒16,6812. ᴿRBLit 3 (2001)
      452-455 (*Hensell, Eugene*).

6736 *Fredrickson, David E.* "Through many tears" (2 Cor 2:4): Paul's
      grieving letter and the occasion of 2 Corinthians 1-7. Paul and
      pathos. SBL Symposium 16: 2001 ⇒6316. 161-179.
6737 *Welborn, L.L.* Paul's appeal to the emotions in 2 Corinthians 1.1-
      2.13; 7.5-16. JSNT 82 (2001) 31-60.
6738 *Fee, Gordon D.* ΧΑΡΙΣ in 2 Corinthians 1:15: apostolic parousia and
      Paul-Corinth chronology. To what end exegesis?. 2001 <1978> ⇒
      143. 99-104.
6739 **Gruber, M. Margareta** Herrlichkeit in Schwachheit: eine Ausle-
      gung der Apologie des zweiten Korintherbriefs 2 Kor 2,14-6,13. FzB
      89: 1998 ⇒14,6165... 16,6814. ᴿATG 64 (2001) 390-391 (*Carmona,
      A.R.*); ThLZ 126 (2001) 634-639 (*Wischmeyer, Oda*).
6740 *Clark Wire, Antoinette* Reconciled to glory in Corinth?: 2 Cor 2:14-
      7:4. ᶠBETZ, H. 2001 ⇒5. 263-275.
6741 **Ranzolin, Leo Santos** The rhetoric of 2 Corinthians 3:1-4:6: an en-
      comiastic proof in the service of deliberative oratory. Diss. Boston
      Univ. 2001, 210 pp. 3025227.
6742 *Grindheim, Sigurd* The law kills but the gospel gives life: the letter-
      spirit dualism in 2 Corinthians 3.5-18. JSNT 84 (2001) 97-115.
6743 *Frank, Karl Suso* Der verhüllte Glanz: 2 Kor 3,14-16 bei den Kir-
      chenvätern. ᶠLEHMANN, K. 2001 ⇒63. 147-156.
6744 *Dautzenberg, Gerhard* Überlegungen zur Exegese und Theologie
      von 2 Kor 4,1-6. Bib. 82 (2001) 325-344.
6745 *Avram, Wes* 2 Corinthians 4:1-18. Interp. 55 (2001) 70-73.
6746 *Marchesi, Giovanni* Sul volto di Cristo rifulge la gloria del Padre (2
      Cor 4,6). CivCatt 152/4 (2001) 240-253.
6747 *Aune, David E.* Anthropological duality in the eschatology of 2 Cor
      4:16-5:10. Paul beyond. 2001 ⇒262. 215-239.

6748 *Hoegen-Rohls, Christina* Wie klingt es, wenn Paulus von Neuer Schöpfung spricht?: stilanalytische Beobachtungen zu 2 Kor 5,17 und Gal 6,15. [F]HAHN, F. 2001 ⇒41. 143-153.

6749 **Adewuya, J. Ayodeji** Holiness and community in 2 Cor 6:14-7:1: Paul's view of communal holiness in the Corinthian correspondence. Diss. Manchester, [D]*Young, Frances*: Studies in Biblical Literature 40: NY 2001, Lang xvii; 230 pp. FS83. 0-8204-5557-1. Bibl. 201-23.

6750 *Fee, Gordon D.* 2 Corinthians 6:14-7:1 and food offered to idols. To what end exegesis?. 2001 <1976> ⇒143. 129-153.

6751 *Salvo, Mariarosaria* Un nuovo frammento della seconda lettera di Paolo ai Corinzi (7,6-11): P.Hamb.Inv. NS 1002. Analecta Papyrologica 13 (2001) 19-21.

6752 *Frettlöh, Magdalene* Der Charme der gerechten Gabe: Motive einer Theologie und Ethik am Beispiel der paulinischen Kollekte für Jerusalem. 'Leget Anmut'. 2001 ⇒350. 105-161 [Prov 22,8; 2 Cor 8-9].

6753 **Wodka, Andrzej** Una teologia biblica del dare nel contesto della colletta paolina (2Cor 8-9). TGr.T 68: 2000 ⇒16,6824. [R]Nuova Umanità 23 (2001) 567-569 (*Rossé, Gerard*); CivCatt 152/3 (2001) 207-208 (*Scaiola, D.*).

6754 *Lambrecht, Jan* Paul's boasting about the Corinthians: a study of 2 Cor. 8:24-9:5. Collected studies. AnBib 147: 2001 <1998> ⇒170. 91-106.

6755 *Bash, Anthony* A psychodynamic approach to the interpretation of 2 Corinthians 10-13. JSNT 83 (2001) 51-67.

6756 *Lambrecht, Jan* Dangerous boasting: Paul's self-commendation in 2 Cor 10-13. Collected studies. 2001 <1996> ⇒170. 107-129;

6757 The fool's speech in its context: Paul's particular way of arguing in 2 Cor 10-13. Bib. 82 (2001) 305-324.

6758 **Peterson, Brian K.** Eloquence and the proclamation of the gospel in Corinth. SBL.DS 163: 1998 ⇒14,6184; 16,6827. [R]JBL 120 (2001) 385-386 (*Gordon, J. Dorcas*) [2 Cor 10-13].

6759 *Lambrecht, Jan* Paul's appeal and the obedience to Christ: the line of thought in 2 Cor 10,1-6 <1996>;

6760 Strength in weakness: an answer to Scott B. Andrews on 2 Cor 11, 23b-33. Collected studies. AnBib 147: 2001 <1997> ⇒170. 131-148/149-156.

6761 *Wischmeyer, Oda* 2 Korinther 12,1-10: ein autobiographisch-theologischer Text des Paulus. Was ist ein Text?. Neutestamentliche Entwürfe zur Theologie 1: 2001 ⇒335. 29-41.

6762 *Abernathy, David* Paul's thorn in the flesh: a messenger of Satan?. Neotest. 35 (2001) 69-79 [2 Cor 12,7-8].

6763 *Lambrecht, Jan* Paulus vermag alles door de kracht van God: zwakheid en sterkte. NedThT 55/4 (2001) 273-285 [2 Cor 12,9-10].

6764   *Powers, Janet E.* A "thorn in the flesh": the appropriation of textual meaning. JPentec 18 (2001) 85-99 [2 Cor 12,10].

6765   *Motumi, Teboho Eliott; Zwilling, Anne-Laure* 2 Corinthiens 13,1-10: force et faiblesse. Lire et Dire 49 (2001) 43-52 [BuBB 34,23].

6766   *Herbst, Michael* Den Namen Gottes auf die Gemeinde legen: 2Kor 13,11-13. ThBeitr 32 (2001) 121-126.

G6.1 **Ad Galatas**

6767   **Borse, Udo** La lettera ai Galati 2000 ⇒16,6831. ^REstTrin 35 (2001) 455-456 (*Vázquez Allegue, Jaime*); CivCatt 152/1 (2001) 431-433 (*Scaiola, D.*).

6768   **Dognin, Paul-Dominique** 'La foi étant venue...': l'épître aux Galates. ConBib 25: Bru 2001, Lumen Vitae 64 pp. €6.25. 2-87324-168-3 [RB 110,154].

6769   **Esler, Philip F.** Galatians. 1998 ⇒14,6190; 15,6867. ^RBiblInterp 9 (2001) 101-105 (*Moxnes, Halvor*).

6770   **Jervis, L. Ann** Galatians. NIBC.NT: 1999 ⇒15,6868. $12. 1-56563-007-6. ^RRSR 89 (2001) 118-119 (*Aletti, Jean-Noël*).

6771   **Martyn, J. Louis** Galatians. AncB 33a: 1997 ⇒13,6561... 16,6836. ^RRBLit 3 (2001) 44-49 (*Barclay, John M.G.*): 49-59 (*Jervis, L. Ann*): 59-65 (*Hays, Richard B.*): 65-71 (*Stanton, Graham*): Resp. by author 71-85; JBL 119 (2000) 373-379 (*Hays, Richard B.*)

6772   **Saunders, Stanley P.** Philippians and Galatians. Interpretation Bible studies: LVL 2001, Geneva vi; 103 pp. 0-664-50102-8. Bibl. 91-93.

6773   ^E**Swanson, Reuben J.** New Testament Greek manuscripts: variant readings arranged in horizontal lines against Codex Vaticanus [Galatians]. 1999 ⇒15,6874. ^RNT 43 (2001) 178-180 (*Elliott, J.K.*).

6774   **Vanhoye, Albert** Lettera ai Galati. I libri biblici, NT 8: 2000 ⇒16, 6839. ^RCivCatt 152/2 (2001) 210-211 (*Scaiola, D.*).

6775   **Bachmann, Michael** Antijudaismus im Galaterbrief?: exegetische Studien zu einem polemischen Schreiben und zur Theologie des Apostels Paulus. NTOA 40: 1999 ⇒15,6862. ^RFrRu 8 (2001) 59-61 (*Maisich, Ingrid*); EstB 59 (2001) 551-552 (*González García, F.*).

6776   **Bryant, Robert A.** The risen crucified Christ in Galatians. SBL.DS 185: Atlanta 2001, SBL x; 272 pp. $48. 158-983-0210. Bibl. 247-72.

6777   *Burgos Núñez, Miguel de* La carta a los Gálatas, 'manifiesto' del cristianismo paulino. Communio 34/1 (2001) 201-228.

6778   *Dschulnigg, Peter* Überlegungen zur Bedeutung und Funktion der Geistaussagen im Galaterbrief. ^FHAINZ, J. 2001 ⇒42. 15-32.

6779 **Holmstrand, Jonas** Markers and meaning in Paul: an analysis of 1 Thessalonians, Philippians and Galatians. CB.NT 28: 1997 ⇒13, 6573... 16,6853. [R]RB 108 (2001) 151-152 (*Murphy-O'Connor, J.*).

6780 **Kern, Philip H.** Rhetoric and Galatians: assessing an approach to Paul's epistle. MSSNTS 101: 1998 ⇒14,6205; 16,6855. [R]AcTh(B) 21/1 (2001) 215-216 (*Tolmie, D.F.*); EvQ 73 (2001) 85-87 (*Van Neste, Ray*).

6781 **Kremendahl, Dieter** Die Botschaft der Form: zum Verhältnis von antiker Epistolographie und Rhetorik im Galaterbrief. NTOA 46: 2000 ⇒16,6856. [R]BZ 45 (2001) 148-150 (*Häfner, Gerd*).

6782 **Kuula, Kari** The law, the covenant and God's plan, 1: Paul's polemical treatment of the law in Galatians. SESJ 72: 1999 ⇒15, 6894. [R]JBL 120 (2001) 581-583 (*McGinn, Sheila E.*); Bib. 82 (2001) 121-126 (*Bachmann, M.*); RBLit 3 (2001) 455-458 (*McGinn, Sheila E.*).

6783 **Kwon, Yon** Eschatology in Galatians. Diss. London 2001, [D]*Campbell, D.* [RTL 33,639].

6784 *Lambrecht, Jan* Second thoughts: some reflections on the law in Galatians. Collected studies. AnBib 147: 2001 ⇒170. 257-265.

6785 **Lovett, Russell James** The metaphorical character of justification by faith in Galatians and Romans. Diss. Trinity Evang. Divinity 2001, 372 pp. 3003784.

6786 **Mapes, David L.** A covenantal basis for Paul's paradigm of law in Galatians and Romans. Diss. Mid-America Baptist Theol. Sem. 2001, 230 pp. 3004050.

6787 **Nanos, Mark D.** The irony of Galatians: Paul's Letter in first-century context. Mp 2001, Fortress xiii; 376 pp. Diss. St Andrews; Bibl. 333-359. $26. 0-8006-3214-1.

6788 *Nikolakopoulos, Konstantin* Aspekte der 'paulinischen Ironie' am Beispiel des Galaterbriefes. BZ 45 (2001) 193-208.

6789 **Oh, Boon** The social setting of Galatians. Diss. London 2001, [D]*Campbell, D.* [RTL 33,640].

6790 *Penna, Romano* Le opere della legge in Paolo e nel manoscritto qumraniano 4QMMT. Vangelo e inculturazione. 2001 <1997> ⇒193. 512-535.

6791 **Perkins, Pheme** Abraham's divided children: Galatians and the politics of faith. The New Testament in context: Valley Forge, PA 2001, Trinity v; 189 pp. $18. 1-56338-359-4. Bibl. 166-179.

6792 *Pindel, Roman* Epistolografia w interpretacji listu do Galatów. [F]JAN-KOWSKI, A. 2001 ⇒53. 336-345. **P**.

6793 *Rand, Thomas A.* Set free and set right: ritual, theology, and the inculturation of the gospel in Galatia. Worship 75 (2001) 453-468.

Rapa, R. The meaning of "works of the law" 2001 ⇒6580.

6794 **Scott, James M.** Paul and the nations: the Od Testament and Jewish background of Paul's mission to the nations with special reference to the destination of Galatians. WUNT 2/84: 1995 ⇒11/1,5026... 15, 6907. [R]EvQ 73 (2001) 180-182 (*Adams, Edward*).

6795 **Silva, Moisés** Interpreting Galatians: explorations in exegetical method. GR [2]2001, Baker 256 pp. 0-8010-2305-X.

6796 **Smiles, Vincent M.** The gospel and the law in Galatia. 1998 ⇒14, 6212. [R]JBL 119 (2000) 153-155 (*Dunn, James D.G.*).

6797 *Vos, Johan* Charismatisch en gevestigd gezag in de gemeente: een spanningsveld in de brief van Paulus aan de Galaten. Vroeg-christelijke gemeenten. 2001 ⇒460. 30-39.

6798 *Watson, Francis* Gospel and scripture: rethinking canonical unity. TynB 52 (2001) 161-182.

6799 **Witulski, Thomas** Die Adressaten des Galaterbriefes: Untersuchungen zur Gemeinde von Antiochia ad Pisidiam. FRLANT 193: 2000 ⇒16,6874. [R]SNTU.A 26 (2001) 246-247 (*Fuchs, Albert*).

6800 **Choi, Soon-Bong** Die Wahrheit des Evangeliums: eine traditionsgeschichtliche Untersuchung von Gal 1 und 2. Diss. Tübingen 2001, [D]*Betz, O.W.* [RTL 33,637].

6801 **Cummins, Stephen Anthony** Paul and the crucified Christ in Antioch: Maccabean martyrdom and Galatians 1 and 2. Diss. Oxford 1995, [D]*Wright, N.T.*: MSSNTS 114: C 2001, CUP xviii; 287 pp. $65. 0-521-66201-X. Bibl. 233-259.

6802 *Häfner, Gerd* Zur Auslegung von προειρήκαμεν in Gal 1,9. BZ 45 (2001) 101-104.

6803 **Na, Kang-Yup** The meaning of Christ in Paul: a reading of Galatians 1.11-2.21 in the light of Wilhelm DILTHEY's 'Lebensphilosophie'. Diss. Emory 2001, 225 pp. 3009459.

6804 *Reicke, Bo Ivar* The historical background of the apostolic council and the episode in Antioch (Gal. 2:1-14). Re-examining Paul's letters. 2001 <1953> ⇒6257. 16-25.

6805 *Clarke, Fern K.T.* 'Remembering the poor': does Galatians 2.10a allude to the collection?. ScrB 31/1 (2001) 20-28.

6806 *Lambrecht, Jan* Paul's reasoning in Galatians 2,11-21. Collected studies. AnBib 147: 2001 <1996> ⇒170. 157-181.

6807 *Mayer-Haas, Andrea J.* Identitätsbewahrung, kirchliche Einheit und die "Wahrheit des Evangeliums": der sogenannte "antiochenische Zwischenfall" im Spiegel von Gal 2,11-21. [F]HAINZ, J. 2001 ⇒42. 123-148.

6808 *Dumbrell, William J.* Galatians 2:14-21: a new covenant perspective. EurJT 10 (2001) 105-116.

6809 *Murphy-O'Connor, Jerome* Gal 2:15-16a: whose common ground?. RB 108 (2001) 376-385.

6810 *Theobald, Michael* Der Kanon von der Rechtfertigung (Gal 2,16; Röm 3,28): Eigentum des Paulus oder Gemeingut der Kirche?. Studien zum Römerbrief. WUNT 136: 2001 <1999> ⇒219. 164-225.

6811 *Schnelzer, Thomas* "Nicht mehr ich lebe, sondern Christus lebt in mir": das paulinische Damaskuserlebnis als Paradigma der Selbstfindung in tiefenpsychologischer und theologischer Sicht. ᶠSCHMUTTER-MAYR, G. 2001 ⇒101. 247-264 [Gal 2,20].

6812 *Eastman, Susan* The evil eye and the curse of the law: Galatians 3.1 revisited. JSNT 83 (2001) 69-87.

6813 **Wakefield, Andrew** Where to live: the hermeneutical significance of Paul's citations from scripture in Galatians 3:1-14.Diss. Duke 2000 [RTL 33,642].

6814 *Silva, Moisés* Abraham faith, and works: Paul's use of scripture in Galatians 3:6-14. WThJ 63 (2001) 251-267.

6815 **Wisdom, Jeffrey R.** Blessing for the nations and the curse of the law: Paul's citation of Genesis and Deuteronomy in Gal 3.8-10. WUNT 2/133: Tü 2001, Mohr S. xv; 272 pp. €50.11. 3-16-147533-X. Bibl. 225-249.

6816 **Carver, Andrew** Means or meaning: the logic of Paul's rhetoric in Galatians 3:10-14. Diss. Durham 2001, ᴰ*Dunn, J.D.G.* 325 pp [RTL 33,637].

6817 *Brondos, David* The cross and the curse: Galatians 3.13 and Paul's doctrine of redemption. JSNT 81 (2001) 3-32.

6818 *Damascelli, Andrea* Croce, maledizione e redenzione: un'eco di Purim in Galati 3,13. Henoch 23 (2001) 227-241.

6819 *Penna, Romano* Quando un testamento è irrevocabile: la promessa ad Abramo in Gal 3,15ss. Vangelo e inculturazione. 2001 <1994> ⇒ 193. 419-434.

6820 *Marcus, Joel* "Under the law": the background of a Pauline expression. CBQ 63 (2001) 72-83 [Gal 3,23].

6821 *Dupuy, Bernard* 'Ni juif ni grec': sur une formule controversée de saint Paul. Ist. 46 (2001) 229-233 [Gal 3,28].

6822 *De Campos Sampaio, Beatriz Augusta* O homem "filho e herdeiro" de Deus: um estudo sobre Gl 3-4. Annales theologici 15/1 (2001) 81-116 [Gal 3,29; 4,1-7].

6823 *Penna, Romano* 'Quando venne la pienezza del tempo...' (Gal 4,4): storia e redenzione nel cristianesimo delle origini. Vangelo e inculturazione. 2001 <1999> ⇒193. 435-460.

6824 *Lambrecht, Jan* Like a mother in the pain of childbirth again: a study of Galatians 4,12-20. Collected studies. AnBib 147: 2001 <1996> ⇒ 170. 183-199.

6825 *Martin, Troy W.* The voice of emotion: Paul's pathetic persuasion (Gal 4:12-20). Paul and pathos. SBL Symposium 16: 2001 ⇒6316. 181-202.

6826 *Fee, Gordon D.* Freedom and the life of obedience (Galatians 5:1-6: 18). To what end exegesis?. 2001 <1994> ⇒143. 154-172.

6827 *Lambrecht, Jan* Abraham and his offspring: a comparison of Galatians 5,1 with 3,13 <1999>;

6828 Is Galatians 5,11b a parenthesis?: a response to T. Baarda <1996>;

6829 The right things you want to do: a note on Galatians 5,17d <1998>. Collected studies. AnBib 147: 2001 ⇒170. 201-15/217-21/223-233.

6830 *Riches, John K.* Theological interpretation of the New Testament and the history of religions: some reflections in the light of Galatians 5:17. ^FBETZ, H. 2001 ⇒5. 245-262.

6831 **Wilder, William N.** Echoes of the Exodus narrative in the context and background of Galatians 5:18. Studies in Biblical Literature 23: NY 2001, Lang xv; 310 pp. $63. 0-8204-4579-7. Bibl. 279-294.

6832 *Baumert, Norbert* 'Mit Gewinn ernten': zur Paränese von Gal 5,25-6,10. Studien zu den Paulusbriefen. SBAB 32: 2001 <1994> ⇒123. 59-91.

6833 *Lambrecht, Jan* Paul's coherent admonition in Galatians 6,1-6: mutual help and individual attentiveness. Collected studies. AnBib 147: 2001 <1997> ⇒170. 235-255.

6834 *Ensminger, Charles* Paul the stigmatic. JHiC 8 (2001) 183-209 [Gal 6,17].

G6.2 Ad Ephesios

6835 **Aletti, Jean-Noël** Saint Paul: épitre aux Éphésiens: introduction, traduction et commentaire. EtB 42: P 2001, Gabalda 351 pp. €42.69. 2-85021-130-3. ^RETR 76 (2001) 431-432 (*Cuvillier, Élian*).

6836 **Best, Ernest** Essays on Ephesians. 1997 ⇒13,6619. ^REvQ 73 (2001) 356-357 (*Turner, Max*);

6837 A critical and exegetical commentary on Ephesians. ICC: 1998 ⇒14, 6245... 16,6921. ^REvQ 73 (2001) 357-359 (*Turner, Max*);

6838 Lettera agli Efesini. ^E*Zoroddu, Donatella*: Commentario NT 10: Brescia 2001, Paideia 782 pp. 88-394-0631-X. Bibl. 15-22.

6839 **Bortolini, José** Como ler a carta aos Efésios. Como ler a Biblia: São Paulo 2001, Paulus 66 pp [REB 62,247].

6840 **Dahl, Nils Alstrup** Studies in Ephesians. WUNT 131: 2000 ⇒16, 147. ^RNTT 102 (2001) 67-74 (*Hartman, Lars*).

6841 **MacDonald, Margaret Y.** Colossians and Ephesians. Sacra Pagina 17: 2000 ⇒16,6924. ^RPIBA 24 (2001) 119-120 (*Byrne, Patrick*).

6842 **Muddiman, John** The epistle to the Ephesians. Black's NT commentaries: NY 2001, Continuum xvi; 338 pp. £17. 0-8264-5202-7. Bibl. 306-318. [R]Studies in World Christianity 7 (2001) 256-260 (*Young, James*).

6843 **Nastepad, Th.J.M.** Schouwspelers van God: uitleg van Paulus' brief aan de Efeziers. Baarn 2001, Ten Have 344 pp. €18.10. 9025952666.

6844 **O'Brien, Peter Thomas** The letter to the Ephesians. 1999 ⇒15, 6943; 16,6925. [R]Pacifica 14 (2001) 90-92 (*Woods, Laurie*); BiTr 52 (2001) 350-351 (*Towner, Philip H.*); ThLZ 126 (2001) 284-286 (*Gese, Michael*); Bib. 82 (2001) 444-448 (*Lindemann, Andreas*).

6845 **Rossé, Gérard** Lettera ai Colossesi, lettera agli Efesini. Nuovo Testamento—commento esegetico e spirituale: R 2001, Città N. 209 pp. 88-311-3774-3. Bibl. 205.

6846 **Schnackenburg, Rudolf** The epistle to the Ephesians: a commentary. E 2001 <1991>, Clark 355 pp.

6847 **Boismard, Marie-Émile** L'énigme de la lettre aux Éphésiens. EtB 39: 1999 ⇒15,6945. [R]RSR 89 (2001) 121-124 (*Aletti, Jean-Noël*); CBQ 63 (2001) 137-139 (*Wild, Robert A.*); ScEs 53 (2001) 387-388 (*Doutre, Jean*).

6848 **Gese, Michael** Das Vermächtnis des Apostels: die Rezeption der paulinischen Theologie im Epheserbrief. WUNT 2/99: 1997 ⇒13, 6627; 15,6947. [R]JBL 119 (2000) 577-579 (*Standhartinger, Angela*).

6849 *Hartman, Lars* Nils Alstrup Dahl om Efeserbrevet. NTT 102 (2001) 67-74.

6850 **Kohlgraf, Peter** Die Ekklesiologie des Epheserbriefes in der Auslegung durch Johannes CHRYSOSTOMUS: eine Untersuchung zur Wirkungsgeschichte paulinischer Theologie. Diss. Bonn, [D]*Dassmann, E.*: Hereditas 19: Bonn 2001, Borengässer xii; 405 pp. €37.80. 3-92394-6-53-8.

6851 *Reicke, Bo Ivar* Caesarea, Rome, and the captivity epistles. Reexamining Paul's letters. 2001 <1970> ⇒6257. 131-140.

6852 *Viviano, Benedict T.* The letter to the Ephesians: a vision for the church. Trinity—kingdom. NTOA 48: 2001 <1979> ⇒223. 240-245.

6853 *Thomas, Rodney* The seal of the Spirit and the religious climate of Ephesus. RestQ 43/3 (2001) 155-166 [Eph 1,12].

6854 **Kil, Sungnam** The unity of Jews and gentiles in Christ: an exegetical study of Eph 2:11-22 with special reference to the relationship between Jews and gentiles. Diss. Trinity Evang. Divinity 2001, 321 pp. 3003802.

6855 **Rozario, Emmanuel** "For He is our peace": a study of Eph 2,13-18. Extr. Diss. Urbaniana 2001, [D]*Biguzzi, G.*: ix; 108 pp. Bibl. 13-31.

6856 *Fee, Gordon D.* Some exegetical and theological reflections on
      Ephesians 4:30 and Pauline pneumatology. To what end exegesis?.
      2001 <1994> ⇒143. 262-275.

6857 *Campbell-Reed, Eileen R.* Should wives "submit graciously"?: a fem-
      inist approach to interpreting Ephesians 5:21-33. RExp 98 (2001)
      263-276.

6858 **Dawes, Gregory W.** The body in question: metaphor and meaning in
      the interpretation of Ephesians 5:21-33. BiblInterp 30: 1998 ⇒14,
      6268; 15,6968. [R]RBLit 3 (2001) 460-463 (*Parker, David M.*).

6859 *Lambrecht, Jan* Christ and the church, husband and wife in Ephesi-
      ans 5,21-33. Collected studies. AnBib 147: 2001 <1997> ⇒170.
      295-308.

6860 *Köstenberger, Andreas J.* The mystery of Christ and the church: head
      and body, 'one flesh'. Studies on John and gender. 2001 <1991>
      ⇒169. 185-202 [Eph 5,22-33].

6861 *Baldanza, Giuseppe* L'originalità della metafora sponsale in Ef 5, 25-
      32: riflessi sull'ecclesiologia. Sal. 63/1 (2001) 3-21.

G6.3 Ad Philippenses

6862 **Galitis, G.,** *al.,* Per me il vivere è Cristo: (Filippesi 1,1 - 3,21).
      SMBen.BE 14: R 2001, Abbazia di S. Paolo 196 pp.

6863 **Abrahamsen, Valerie Ann** Women and worship at Philippi: Diana/
      Artemis and other cults in the early christian era. 1995 ⇒11/1,5092;
      13,6651. [R]Journal of Ancient History 237 (2001) 227-230 (*Paster-
      nak, A.V.*).

6864 **Bormann, Lukas** Philippi: Stadt und Christengemeinde zur Zeit des
      Paulus. NT.S 78: 1995 ⇒11/1,5097... 14,6279. [R]SNTU.A 22 (1997)
      272-275 (*Schreiber, S.*).

6865 **Davis, Casey Wayne** Oral biblical criticism: the influence of the
      principles of orality on the literary structure of Paul's epistle to the
      Philippians. JSNT.S 172: 1999 ⇒15,6980; 16,6971. [R]EvQ 73 (2001)
      359-360 (*Oakes, Peter*).

6866 **Ferguson, Sinclair B.** Let's study Philippians. 1997 ⇒13,6648.
      [R]SBET 19 (2001) 110-111 (*Smart, Dominic*).

6867 *Fowl, Stephen* Paul's riposte to Fr. Rodrigues: conceptions of martyr-
      dom in Philippians and ENDO's *Silence*. Postmodern interpretations.
      2001 ⇒229. 243-252.

6868 *Galitis, Georg* Die Einheit der Christen: ökumenische Erwägungen.
      Per me il vivere. 2001 ⇒6862. 181-187.

6869 *Günther, Hartmut* "Gemeinschaft am Evangelium" im Philipperbrief: eine pastoral-theologische Meditation. LuThK 25/1 (2001) 35-50.

6870 **Holloway, Paul A.** Consolation in Philippians: philosophical sources and rhetorical strategy. MSSNTS 112: C 2001, CUP xiii; 208 pp. $55. 0-521-80406-X. Bibl. 165-187.

     Holmstrand, J. Markers and meaning in Paul 1997 ⇒6779.

6871 **Oakes, Peter** Philippians: from people to letter. MSSNTS 110: C 2001, CUP xv; 231 pp. £37.50/$60. 0-521-79046-8. Bibl. 213-226. ^RRRT 8 (2001) 448-450 (*Wansbrough, Henry*).

     Saunders, S. Philippians and Galatians 2001 ⇒6772.

6872 *Hartman, Lars* Overseers and servants—for what?: Philippians 1:1-11 as read with regard to the implied readers of Philippians. Per me il vivere. 2001 ⇒6862. 13-43. Disc. 43-51.

6873 *Baumert, Norbert* Ja, ich muß mich wirklich freuen!—Phil 1,12-26. Studien zu den Paulusbriefen. 2001 <1985> ⇒123. 92-99.

6874 *Vos, J.S.* Phil. 1,12-26 und die Rhetorik des Erfolges. Disc. 78-87;

6875 *Mihoc, V.* L'hymne christologique de l'épître aux Philippiens dans son contexte (Phil. 1,27-2,18). Disc. 122-136. Per me il vivere. 2001 ⇒6862. 53-77/89-122.

6876 *MacLeod, David J.* Imitating the incarnation of Christ: an exposition of Philippians 2:5-8. BS 158 (2001) 308-330.

6877 *Fee, Gordon D.* Philippians 2:5-11: hymn or exalted Pauline prose?. To what end exegesis?. 2001 <1992> ⇒143. 173-191.

6878 *Clarey, Ricardo Eloy* Flp 2,6-11: la novedad del misterio de la encarnación. EstB 59 (2001) 487-500.

6879 *MacLeod, David J.* The exhalation of Christ: an exposition of Philippians 2:9-11. BS 158 (2001) 437-450.

6880 *Baumert, Norbert* 'Wirket euer Heil mit Furcht und Zittern'?—Phil 2,12f. Studien zu den Paulusbriefen. 2001 <1979> ⇒123. 100-108.

6881 *Standaert, Benoît* 'Prenez garde aux chiens': à la recherche des opposants visés par Paul en Philippiens 3. Per me il vivere. 2001 ⇒6862. 161-180.

6882 *Lange, Ulrich-Paul* Die Erkenntnis Jesu Christi (zu Phil 3,1-14). Theologisches 31 (2001) 157-162.

6883 *Gnilka, Joachim* Die Kehre des Paulus zu Christus (Phil. 3,2-21). Per me il vivere. 2001 ⇒ 6862. 137-152. Disc. 152-160.

6884 *O'Daly, Gerard* Time as *distentio* and St. AUGUSTINE's exegesis of *Philippians* 3,12-14. Platonism pagan and christian. 2001 <1977> ⇒ 188. 265-271.

6885 *Carls, Peter* Identifying Syzygos, Euodia, and Syntyche, Philippians 4:2f. JHiC 8 (2001) 161-182.

6886 *Baumert, Norbert* Ist Philipper 4,10 richtig übersetzt?. Studien zu den Paulusbriefen. SBAB 32: 2001 <1969> ⇒123. 109-116.
6887 *Fee, Gordon D.* To what end exegesis?: reflections on exegesis and spirituality in Philippians 4:10-20. To what end exegesis?. 2001 <1996> ⇒143. 276-289.

G6.4 Ad Colossenses

6888 *Aletti, Jean-Noël* Kolosser. RGG^4, 4: I-K. 2001 ⇒664. 1502-1504.
6889 *Barclay, John M.G.* Ordinary but different: Colossians and hidden moral identity. ABR 49 (2001) 34-52.
6890 *Bos, Abraham P.* Het metakosmische perspectief van de brief aan de Kolossenzen. GThT 101 (2001) 63-71.
6891 *Dettwiler, Andreas* La résurrection des croyants selon l'épître aux Colossiens. Résurrection: l'après-mort. 2001 ⇒296. 307-320.
6892 **Dunn, James D.G.** The epistles to the Colossians and to Philemon: a commentary on the Greek text. NIGTC: 1996 ⇒12,6450... 15,7001. ^{R}SNTU.A 22 (1997) 275-277 (*Fuchs, Albert*).
     MacDonald, M. Colossians and Ephesians 2000 ⇒6841.
6893 *Reicke, Bo Ivar* The historical setting of Colossians. Re-examining Paul's letters. 2001 <1973> ⇒6257. 121-130.
     Rossé, G. Lettera ai Colossesi... 2001 ⇒6845.
6894 *Standhartinger, Angela* Die Entstehung und Intention der Haustafel im Brief an die Gemeinde in Kolossä. Paulus. 2001 ⇒6308. 166-81.

6895 *Hofius, Otfried* "Erstgeborener vor aller Schöpfung"—"Erstgeborener aus den Toten": Erwägungen zu Struktur und Aussage des Christushymnus Kol 1,15-20. Auferstehung—Resurrection. WUNT 135: 2001 ⇒452. 185-203.
6896 **Otero Lázaro, Tomás** Col 1,15-20 en el contexto de la carta. TGr.T 48: 1999 ⇒15,7020; 16,6998. ^{R}Cart. 17 (2001) 447-448 (*Cuenca Molina, J.F.*); EstB 59 (2001) 403-404 (*Pastor-Ramos, F.*).
6897 *Kremer, Jacob* Was an den Bedrängnissen des Christus mangelt: Versuch einer bibeltheologischen Neuinterpretation von Kol 1,24. Bib. 82 (2001) 130-146.
6898 *Szarek, Jan* "Christus, in welchem verborgen liegen alle Schätze der Weisheit und der Erkenntnis" (Kol 2,3): zur Jahreslosung für 2001. LKW 48 (2001) 9-12.
6899 *Martin, Troy W.* Live unnoticed: an Epicurean maxim and the social dimension of Col 3:3-4. ^{F}BETZ, H. 2001 ⇒5. 227-244.

6900   **Thekkekara, Mathew** Christ is all and in all (Col 3:11b): its christo-
       logical, cosmic, and ecclesial significance. 1999 ⇒15,7025. ᴿCBQ
       63 (2001) 563-564 (*Mathews, Susan Fournier*).
6901   *Heymel, Michael* Wie einer dem anderen Christus zusingt: musikali-
       sche Seelsorge nach Kolosser 3,16. DtPfrBl 101 (2001) 181-182.

G6.6 Ad Thessalonicenses

6902   **Börschel, Regina** Die Konstruktion einer christlichen Identität: Pau-
       lus und die Gemeinde von Thessalonich in ihrer hellenistisch-römi-
       schen Umwelt. BBB 128: B 2001, Philo 501 pp. 3-8257-0236-7.
       Bibl. 462-489.
6903   **Brocke, Christoph vom** Thessaloniki—Stadt des Kassander und
       Gemeinde des Paulus: eine frühe christliche Gemeinde in ihrer heid-
       nischen Umwelt. WUNT 2/125: Tü 2001, Mohr S. xv; 310 pp.
       €60.33. 3-16-147345-0. Bibl. 273-296. ᴿFgNT 14 (2001) 157-162
       (*Stenschke, Christoph*).
6904   *Calabria, Nicola* Per una 'rilettura' dei testi sacri con sensibilità odi-
       erna: la comunità di Tessalonica, occasione e data degli scritti. PalCl
       1 (2001) 677-687.
6905   **Couch, Mal** The hope of Christ's return: premillennial commentary
       on 1 and 2 Thessalonians. Chattanooga, TN 2001, AMG 279 pp. $18
       [BS 159,500—Zuck, Roy B.].
6906   ᴱ**Donfried, Karl P.; Beutler, Johannes** The Thessalonians debate.
       2000 ⇒16, 255. ᴿCTJ 36 (2001) 143-145 (*Weima, Jeffrey A.D.*);
       JThS 52 (2001) 816-820 (*Griffith-Jones, R.*); CBQ 63 (2001) 375-77
       (*Ascough, Richard S.*); ThLZ 126 (2001) 1145-7 (*Pilhofer, Peter*).
6907   *Fee, Gordon D.* On text and commentary on 1 and 2 Thessalonians.
       To what end exegesis?. 2001 <1992> ⇒143. 57-79.
       Holmstrand, J. Markers and meaning in Paul 1997 ⇒6779.
6908   **Légasse, Simon** Les épîtres de Paul aux Thessaloniciens. 1999 ⇒15,
       7040. ᴿScEs 53 (2001) 400-402 (*Gignac, Alain*); CoTh (2001/3)
       218-221 (*Załęski, Jan*); Bib. 82 (2001) 580-584 (*Donfried, Karl P.*);
       RSR 89 (2001) 115-117 (*Aletti, Jean-Noël*).
6909   **Müller, Paul-Gerhard** Der erste und zweite Brief an die Thessaloni-
       cher. RNT: Rg 2001, Pustet 341 pp. €34.77. 3-7917-1764-2.
6910   *Peerbolte, Bert Jan Lietaert* Wachten op Jezus: de gemeente van
       Tessalonica. Vroegchristelijke gemeenten. 2001 ⇒460. 14-29.
6911   **Still, Todd D.** Conflict at Thessalonica: a Pauline church and its
       neighbours. JSNT.S 183: 1999 ⇒15,7050; 16,7008. ᴿTrinJ 22
       (2001) 115-118 (*Weima, Jeffrey A.D.*); ThLZ 126 (2001) 170-172
       (*Haufe, Günter*).

6912   **Verhoef, Eduard** De brieven aan de Tessalonicenzen. 1998 ⇒14,
       6344... 16,7011. ᴿJBL 119 (2000) 579-580 (*Boer, M.C. de*).
6913   **Young, Andrew W.** Let's study 1 & 2 Thessalonians. E 2001, Ban-
       ner of Truth Trust 194 pp.

6914   **Bickmann, Jutta** Kommunikation gegen den Tod: Studien zur pauli-
       nischen Briefpragmatik am Beispiel des ersten Thessalonicherbriefes.
       FzB 86: 1998 ⇒14,6347; 16,7012. ᴿRSR 89 (2001) 127-128 (*Aletti,
       Jean-Noël*).
6915   **Burke, Trevor J.** Family matters, an exegetical and socio-historical
       analysis of familial metaphors in 1 Thessalonians. Diss. Glasgow
       2001, ᴰ*Barclay, John M.G.* [TynB 52,299-302].
6916   **Haufe, Günter** Der erste Brief des Paulus an die Thessalonicher.
       ThHK 12/1: 1999 ⇒15,7055. ᴿThLZ 126 (2001) 1152-1153 (*Schra-
       ge, Wolfgang*).

6917   *Baumert, Norbert* Ὁμείρομαι in 1 Thess 2,8. Studien zu den Paulus-
       briefen. SBAB 32: 2001 <1987> ⇒123. 117-130.
6918   **Lambrecht, Jan** Connection or disjunction?: a note on 1 Thes-
       salonians 2,13 within 1,2-3,13. Collected studies: AnBib 147: 2001
       ⇒170. 267-277.
6919   *Schneider, Sebastian* Kirche und Andersgläubige: Versuch einer
       Auslegung von 1 Thess 2,13-16. ᶠHAINZ, J. 2001 ⇒42. 149-169.
6920   *Bockmuehl, Markus* 1 Thessalonians 2:14-16 and the church in Jeru-
       salem. TynB 52 (2001) 1-31.
6921   *Hoppe, Rudolf* Apostel ohne Gemeinde—Gemeinde ohne Apostel:
       Überlegungen zu Funktion und Pragmatik von 1 Thess 2,17-3,10.
       ᶠHAINZ, J. 2001 ⇒42. 102-122.
6922   *Lambrecht, Jan* A structural analysis of 1 Thessalonians 4-5. Col-
       lected studies. AnBib 147: 2001 <2000> ⇒170. 279-293.
6923   *Tosato, Angelo* I primi richiami di Paolo in tema matrimoniale (1Ts
       4,3-8). ᴹCAGNI, L., 4: SMDSA 61: 2001 ⇒15. 2193-2218.
6924   *Smith, Jay E.* Another look at 4Q416 2 ii.21, a critical parallel to
       First Thessalonians 4:4. CBQ 63 (2001) 499-504;
6925   1 Thessalonians 4:4: breaking the impasse. BBR 11 (2001) 65-105.
6926   *Konradt, Matthias* εἰδέναι ἕκαστον ὑμῶν τὸ ἑαυτοῦ σκεῦος κτᾶσθαι
       .... zu Paulus' sexualethischer Weisung in 1Thess 4,4 f. ZNW 92
       (2001) 128-135.
6927   *Zaleski, Jan* Paruzja a sytuacja zmarłych w Chrystusie według 1 Tes
       4,13-18. CoTh 71/1 (2001) 61-76. **P**.
6928   *Cotrozzi, Stefano* Where from and where to?—translating 1 Thessa-
       lonians 4.14b. BiTr 52 (2001) 424-430.

6929 *Jezierska, Ewa J.* Pawłowy warunek 'bycia z Panem' na końcu czasów (1 Tes 4,14): próba pogłębienia treści teologicznych. **P.**;

6930 *Załęski, Jan* Potrzeba czujności w obliczu niespodziewanej paruzji (1 Tes 5,1-11). [F]JANKOWSKI, A. 2001 ⇒53. 163-169/470-493. **P.**

6931 *Varickasseril, Jose* A programme of life in four present imperatives: a study of 1 Thessalonians 5:14. MissTod 3 (2001) 447-456.

6932 *Fee, Gordon D.* Pneuma and eschatology in 2 Thessalonians 2:1-2: a proposal about 'testing the prophets' and the purpose of 2 Thessalonians. To what end exegesis?. 2001 <1994> ⇒143. 290-308.

6933 *Lambrecht, Jan* Loving God and steadfastly awaiting Christ: a note on 2 Thessalonians 3,5. Collected studies. AnBib 147: 2001 <2000> ⇒170. 309-317.

G7.0 Epistulae pastorales

6934 **Cochand, Nicolas** Les ministères dans les épîtres pastorales. Diss. Neuchâtel 2001 [RTL 33,637].

6935 **Delbridge, Mary Lynette** 'Family' as a problem for the new religious movements: the Pastoral Epistles' collaboration with the Greco-Roman household. Diss. New York, Union 2001, [D]*Scroggs, R.* 353 pp. 3009990.

6936 *Ellis, Edward Earle* The origin and composition of the Pastoral Epistles. History and interpretation. BiblInterp 54: 2001 ⇒141. 65-83.

6937 *Frenschkowski, Marco* Pseudepigraphie und Paulusschule: Gedanken zur Verfasserschaft der Deuteropaulinen, insbesondere der Pastoralbriefe. Das Ende des Paulus. BZNW 106: 2001 ⇒281. 239-272.

6938 **Harding, Mark** What are they saying about the Pastoral Epistles?. NY 2001, Paulist ix; 146 pp. $13. 0-8091-3975-8. Bibl. 121-136.

6939 *Häfner, Gerd* Die Gegner in den Pastoralbriefen und die Paulusakten. ZNW 92 (2001) 64-77.

6940 **Looks, Carsten** Das Anvertraute bewahren: die Rezeption der Pastoralbriefe im 2. Jahrhundert. 1999 ⇒15,7079. [R]JECS 9 (2001) 410-411 (*Harmon, Steven R.*); JThS 52 (2001) 877-879 (*Elliott, J.K.*).

6941 **Marshall, I. Howard** The Pastoral Epistles. ICC: 1999 ⇒15,7080; 16,7059. [R]RB 108 (2001) 630-632 (*Murphy-O'Connor, J.*); JThS 52 (2001) 824-827 (*Barrett, C.K.*); SNTU.A 25 (2000) 250-251 (*Fuchs, Albert*); EvQ 73 (2001) 360-363 (*Ellingworth, Paul*).

6942 *Oberlinner, Lorenz* "Paulus" versus Paulus?: zum Problem des "Paulinismus" der Pastoralbriefe. [F]HAINZ, J. 2001 ⇒42. 170-199.

6943 *Prior, Michael* Revisiting the Pastoral Epistles. ScrB 31/1 (2001) 2-19.

6944 *Reicke, Bo Ivar* The chronology of the Pastoral Epistles. Re-examining Paul's letters. 2001 <1976> ⇒6257. 105-120.

6945 **Schlarb, E.** Die gesunde Lehre: Häresie und Wahrheit im Spiegel der Pastoralbriefe. MThSt 28: 1990 ⇒6,6663; 9,6378. ᴿSNTU.A 22 (1997) 277-278 (*Oberforcher, Robert*).

6946 *Schmidt, Peter* De kerksituatie achter de Pastorale Brieven. Vroeg-christelijke gemeenten. 2001 ⇒460. 148-162.

6947 **Stettler, Hanna** Die Christologie der Pastoralbriefe. WUNT 2/105: 1998 ⇒14,6374; 16,7069. ᴿRB 108 (2001) 632-633 (*Murphy-O'Connor, J.*); ThLZ 126 (2001) 934-936 (*Lips, Hermann von*); JBL 119 (2000) 777-778 (*Hultgren, Arland J.*).

G7.2 1-2 ad Timotheum, ad Titum

6948 **Johnson, Luke Timothy** The First and Second Letters to Timothy: a new translation with introduction and commentary. AncB 35A: NY 2001, Doubleday xiv; 494 pp. $40. 0-385-48422-4.

6949 **Quinn, Jerome D.; Wacker, William C.** The first and second letters to Timothy. 2000 ⇒16,7073. ᴿHeyJ 42 (2001) 75-78 (*Prior, Michael*); JThS 52 (2001) 282-284 (*Elliott, J.K.*); ETR 76 (2001) 273-274 (*Campbell, Gordon*); JBL 120 (2001) 180-181 (*Fiore, Benjamin*); AUSS 39 (2001) 149-151 (*Cosaert, Carl P.*); CBQ 63 (2001) 161-163 (*Béchard, Dean P.*).

6950 **Bortolini, José** Como ler a primeira carta a Timóteo. Como ler a Biblia: São Paulo 2001, Paulus 62 pp [REB 62,247].

6951 *Sumney, Jerry L.* God our Savior: the theology of 1 Timothy. LexTQ 36 (2001) 31-41 [BuBB 34,35].

6952 *Petit, Olivier* 1 Timothée 1: où Timothée est invité à servir l'évangile, appuyé sur l'exemplaire temoignage de Paul. SémBib 101 (2001) 8-20;

6953 1 Timothée 2: où l'exemplaire aventure de Paul devient transposable aux hommes et aux femmes. SémBib 102 (2001) 43-56.

6954 *Giles, Kevin* Women in the church: a rejoinder to Andreas Köstenberger. EvQ 73 (2001) 225-245 [1 Tim 2,9-15].

6955 *Köstenberger, Andreas* Women in the church: a response to Kevin Giles. EvQ 73 (2001) 205-224 [1 Tim 2,9-15];

6956 The crux of the matter: Paul's pastoral pronouncements regarding women's roles in 1 Timothy 2:9-15 <1997>;

6957 Syntactical background studies to 1 Timothy 2:12 in the New Testament and extra-biblical Greek literature <1995>. Studies on John and gender. 2001 ⇒169. 233-259/261-282.

6958 *Coupland, Simon* Salvation through childbearing?: the riddle of 1 Timothy 2:15. ET 112 (2001) 302-303.

6959 *Köstenberger, Andreas J.* Ascertaining women's God-ordained roles: an interpretation of 1 Timothy 2:15. Studies on John and gender. 2001 <1997> ⇒169. 283-322.

6960 *Petit, Olivier* 1 Timothée 3: où Paul pose la question du désir à propos de la piété. SémBib 104 (2001) 43-54.

6961 *Seidnader, Martin* Dienen, Apostolizität und Tugend: zur Aktualität von 1 Tim 3,8-9. MThZ 52 (2001) 103-112.

6962 *Tsuji, Manabu* Zwischen Ideal und Realität: zu den Witwen in 1 Tim 5.3-16. NTS 47 (2001) 92-104.

6963 *Byrne, Patrick J.* 1 Tim 6:6 "A window on the world of the pastorals". PIBA 24 (2001) 9-16.

6964 *Fee, Gordon D.* Toward a theology of 2 Timothy—from a Pauline perspective. To what end exegesis?. 2001 <1997> ⇒143. 309-329.

6965 **Martin, Seán Charles** Pauli testamentum: 2 Timothy and the last words of Moses. TGr.T 18: 1997 ⇒13,6734. ᴿEstB 59 (2001) 129-131 (*Urbán, A.*); RB 108 (2001) 633-635 (*Murphy-O'Connor, J.*).

6966 *Carvalho, José Carlos* O anúncio do evangelho na pós-modernidade: uma contextualização de 2 Tim 3,10-17. HumTeo 22 (2001) 261-86.

6967 *Fellows, Richard G.* Was Titus Timothy?. JSNT 81 (2001) 33-58.

6968 *Thompson, Dean K.* Titus 2:11-14. Interp. 55 (2001) 423-425.

G7.3 Ad Philemonem

6969 *Arzt-Grabner, Peter* The case of Onesimos: an interpretation of Paul's letter to Philemon based on documentary papyri and ostraca. ASEs 18 (2001) 589-614;

6970 Die Weberlehrverträge des 1. Jhs. und der Brief des Apostels Paulus an Philemon. XXII Congresso di papirologia, 1. 2001 ⇒555. 71-75.

6971 **Barth, Markus; Blanke, Helmut** The letter to Philemon. 2000 ⇒ 16,7088. ᴿJThS 52 (2001) 821-824 (*Moule, C.F.D.*); AUSS 39 (2001) 327-328 (*Cosaert, Carl*).

6972 *Baumert, Norbert* Ein Freundesbrief an einen Sklavenhalter?: der Brief des Paulus an Philemon. Studien zu den Paulusbriefen. SBAB 32: 2001 <2000> ⇒123. 131-160.

6973 *Bieberstein, Sabine* Brüche in der Alltäglichkeit der Sklaverei: eine feministische Lektüre des Philemonbriefs. Paulus. 2001 ⇒6308. 116-128.

6974 *Cassidy, Richard J.* Roman imprisonment and Paul's letter to Philemon. The bible on suffering. 2001 ⇒326. 144-164.

6975 **Combes, I.A.H.** The metaphor of slavery in the writings of the early church: from the New Testament to the beginning of the fifth century. JSNT.S 156: 1998 ⇒14,11369; 16,7091. ᴿJBL 120 (2001) 391-393 (*Glancy, Jennifer A.*).

6976 **Fitzmyer, Joseph A.** The letter to Philemon: a new translation with interpretation and commentary. AncB 34C: 2000 ⇒16,7093. ᴿJThS 52 (2001) 821-824 (*Moule, C.F.D.*); EstB 59 (2001) 554-556 (*Rodríguez Ruiz, M.*); CBQ 63 (2001) 744-745 (*Marrow, Stanley B.*).

6977 *Heil, John Paul* The chiastic structure and meaning of Paul's letter to Philemon. Bib. 82 (2001) 178-206.

6978 **Kieffer, René** Filemonbrevet, Judasbrevet, och Andra Petrusbrevet. KNT(U) 18: U 2001, EFS 168 pp. 91-7085-115-8.

6979 **Kumitz, Christopher** Der Brief als Medium der Agape: eine Untersuchung zur rhetorischen und epistolographischen Gestalt des Philemonbriefs. Diss. Marburg 2001, ᴰ*Harnisch, W.* [RTL 33,639].

6980 *Vos, Craig S. de* Once a slave, always a slave?: slavery, manumission and relational patterns in Paul's letter to Philemon. JSNT 82 (2001) 89-105.

6981 *Kraus, Thomas J.* Eine vertragsrechtliche Verpflichtung in Phlm 19: Duktus und juristischer Hintergrund. ᶠSchmuttermayr, G. 2001 ⇒ 101. 187-200.

G8 Epistula ad Hebraeos

6982 **Attridge, Harold W.** La lettera agli Ebrei: commento storico esegetico. 1999 ⇒15,7123; 16,7098. ᴿ Orpheus 22 (2001) 309-310 (*Osculati, Roberto*); Horeb 10 (2001) 88-89 (*Cervolo, Antonio*).

6983 **deSilva, David A.** Perseverance in gratitude: a socio-rhetorical commentary on the epistle to the Hebrews. 2000 ⇒16,7100. ᴿJThS 52 (2001) 285-287 (*Browne, Arnold S.*); Interp. 55 (2001) 191-192 (*Hay, David M.*); ThLZ 126 (2001) 1278-1279 (*März, Claus-Peter*); Bib. 82 (2001) 584-586 (*Attridge, Harold W.*); RBLit 3 (2001) 463-466 (*Goutzioudis, Moschos*).

Donelson, L. From Hebrews to Revelation 2001 ⇒6064.

6984 **Gordon, Robert P.** Hebrews. 2000 ⇒16,7101. ᴿJThS 52 (2001) 844-847 (*Browne, Arnold S.*).

6985 **Koester, Craig R.** Hebrews: a new translation with introduction and commentary. AncB 36: NY 2001, Doubleday xxiii; 604 pp. $47.50. 0-385-46893-8.

6986 **Manzi, Franco** Lettera agli Ebrei. NT—commento esegetico e spirituale: R 2001, Città N. 227 pp. 88-311-3773-5. Bibl. 219-223;

6987 Lettera agli Ebrei: un'omelia per cristiani adulti. Dabar... NT: Padova 2001, Messagero 204 pp.

6988 ^E**Mills, Watson Early** Hebrews. Bibliographies for biblical research, NT 20: Lewiston, NY, 2001 Mellen xv; 113 pp. 0-7734-2482-2.

6989 *Aitken, Ellen Bradshaw* Portraying the temple in stone and text: the arch of Titus and the epistle to the Hebrews. Religious texts. Studies in ancient Judaism: 2001 ⇒630. 73-88.

6990 **Anderson, David R.** The king-priest of Psalm 110 in Hebrews. Studies in Biblical Literature 21: NY 2001, Lang x; 342 pp 0-8204-4574-6. Bibl. 303-342.

6991 **Beatty, Mark Stanton** The mechanics and motivations of Greek word order applied to the exegesis of the epistle to the Hebrews. Diss. Texas at Arlington 2001, 316 pp. 3010029.

6992 *Berder, Michel* Le sacrifice dans l'épître aux Hébreux. CEv 118 (2001) 31-38.

6993 *Cortès, Enric* A l'encalç dels rebutjats i profans: a propòsit de l'obra de Jordi Cervera sobre la carta als Hebreus. RCatT 26 (2001) 187-193.

6994 **Di Giovambattista, Fulvio** Il giorno dell'espiazione nella lettera agli Ebrei. TGr.T 61: 2000 ⇒16,7110. ^REL 115 (2001) 379-382 (*Manzi, Franco*); CBQ 63 (2001) 740-741 (*Kealy, Seán P.*).

6995 **Emmrich, Martin** Pneumatological concepts in Hebrews. Diss. Westminster Sem. 2001, 224 pp. 3010603.

6996 *Gianotto, Claudio* Il sacrificio nell'epistola agli Ebrei. ASEs 18 (2001) 169-179.

6997 **Johnson, Richard W.** Going outside the camp: the sociological function of the Levitical critique in the epistle to the Hebrews. JSNT. S 209: Shf 2001, Sheffield A. 169 pp. 1-84127-186-1.

6998 *Kurianal, James* 'Multiplying I shall multiply you' (Gen 22,17): christians as the multiplicity of progeny promised to Abraham. ETJ 5 (2001) 23-33.

6999 *Manzi, Franco* Interrogativi, discussioni e conferme sul binomio Melchisedek e angelologia nell'epistola agli Ebrei e a Qumran. ScC 129 (2001) 683-729.

7000 **Manzi, Franco** Melchisedek e l'angelologia nell'epistola agli Ebrei e a Qumran. AnBib 136: 1997 ⇒13,6761... 16,7118. ^REstB 59 (2001) 405-408 (*Urbán, A.*).

7001 **Molinaro, Italo** "Ha parlato nel Figlio": progettualità di Dio e risposta del Cristo nella lettera agli Ebrei. SBFA 55: J 2001, Franciscan Printing Pr. 360 pp. 965-516-001-7. Bibl. 348-357. Diss. Lugano.

7002 **Rhee, Victor (Sung-Yul)** Faith in Hebrews: analysis within the context of christology, eschatology, and ethics. Studies in Biblical Literature 19: NY 2001, Lang xvi; 280 pp. 0-8204-4531-2. Bibl. 254-273. [R]IBSt 23 (2001) 187-190 (*McCullough, J.C.*).

7003 *Sterling, Gregory E.* Ontology versus eschatology: tensions between author and community in Hebrews. [F]HAY, D. 2001 ⇒45. 190-211.

7004 *Steyn, Gert J.* A quest for the Vorlage of the 'Song of Moses' (Deut 32) quotations in Hebrews. Neotest. 34 (2000) 263-272;

7005 "Jesus sayings" in Hebrews. EThL 77 (2001) 433-440.

7006 *Thomas, Mathew* The high priestly christology of Hebrews as a paradigm for an Indian christology. BiBh 27 (2001) 271-285.

7007 *Vanhoye, Albert* Il sacrificio di Cristo e la consacrazione sacerdotale. CivCatt 152/3 (2001) 114-126.

7008 **Wider, David** Theozentrik und Bekenntnis: Untersuchungen zur Theologie des Reden Gottes im Hebräerbrief. BZNW 87: 1997 ⇒13, 6772... 16,7125. [R]ThLZ 126 (2001) 413-414 (*März, Claus-Peter*).

7009 **Wray, Judith Hoch** Rest as a theological metaphor in the epistle to the Hebrews and the gospel of Truth: early christian homiletics of rest. SBL.DS 166: 1998 ⇒14,6415. [R]CBQ 63 (2001) 567-568 (*Sheridan, Mark*).

7010 *Schenck, Kenneth L.* A celebration of the enthroned son: the catena of Hebrews 1. JBL 120 (2001) 469-485.

7011 **Bateman, Herbert W.** Early Jewish hermeneutics and Hebrews 1:5-13: the impact of early Jewish exegesis on the interpretation of a significant New Testament passage. AmUSt TR 193: 1997 ⇒13,6776; 15,7154. [R]JBL 119 (2000) 379-380 (*Hay, David M.*).

7012 *Swetnam, James* The context of the crux at Hebrews 5,7-8. FgNT 14 (2001) 101-120.

7013 *Davidson, Richard M.* Christ's entry 'within the veil' in Hebrews 6:19-20: the Old Testament background. AUSS 39 (2001) 175-190.

7014 *Young, Norman H.* 'Where Jesus has gone as a forerunner on our behalf' (Hebrews 6:20). AUSS 39 (2001) 165-173.

7015 *Cockerill, Gareth Lee* Structure and interpretation in Hebrews 8:1-10:18: a symphony in three movements. BBR 11 (2001) 179-201.

7016 *Backhaus, Knut* Das Land der Verheißung: die Heimat der Glaubenden im Hebräerbrief. NTS 47 (2001) 171-188 [Heb 11,9-10].

7017 *Soggin, Jan Alberto* Jüdische Quellen zu Hebräer 11,17-19. [F]PURY, A. de. MoBi 44: 2001 ⇒89. 371-372.

7018 *Rhee, Victor (Sung-Yul)* Chiasm and the concept of faith in Hebrews 12:1-29. WThJ 63 (2001) 269-284.

7019 *Kasiłowsky, Piotr* Nie tak jak Ezaw (Hbr 12,14-17) [Not like Esau (Heb. 12,14-17)]. StBob 1/2 (2001) 83-110 Sum. 109. **P.**

7020 **Maddox, Roger Wayne** Paraenesis and exegesis: a paradigm for identification of constituent forms and interpretation of content applied to Hebrews 13:1-19. Diss. Fort Worth 2001, [D]*Corley, B.* 249 pp. 3010751 [RTL 33,639].

7021 *Seitz, Erich* Das doppelte ὤ (zu Hebr 13,3). BZ 45 (2001) 250-255.

G9.1 **1 Petri** (vel I-II)

7022 *Bosetti, Elena* La condotta 'bella' tra i pagani nella prima lettera di Pietro. La bellezza. PSV 44 (2001) 127-141.

7023 **Campbell, Barth L.** Honor, shame, and the rhetoric of 1 Peter. SBL.DS 160: 1998 ⇒14,6434; 16,7174. [R]JBL 119 (2000) 580-582 (*Davids, Peter H.*).

7024 [E]**Cervantes Gabarrón, José** Las cartas de Pedro. ResB 32 (2001) 2-51.

7025 *Cervantes Gabarrón, José* 1 Pe, un mensaje de esperanza. ResB 32 (2001) 33-41.

7026 **Corritore, Alfio** Pietro agli eletti della diaspora: identità storico-teologiche e dinamismi ecclesiali nella Prima Petri. Extr. Diss. Palermo 2000, Palermo 2001, 165 pp [RTL 33,637].

7027 *Dubis, Mark* First Peter and the 'sufferings of the Messiah'. Looking into the future. 2001 ⇒505. 85-96.

7028 **Elliott, John H.** 1 Peter. AncB 37B: 2000 ⇒16,7175. [R]CBQ 63 (2001) 741-742 (*Davids, Peter H.*).

7029 *Elliott, John H.* Elders as leaders in 1 Peter and the early church. CThMi 28 (2001) 549-559.

7030 **Herzer, Jens** Petrus oder Paulus?: Studien über das Verhältnis des ersten Petrusbriefes zur paulinischen Tradition. WUNT 103: 1998 ⇒ 14,6438... 16,7177. [R]JBL 119 (2000) 582-584 (*Herzer, Jens*).

7031 [E]**Lazzari, Loredana; Valente Bacci, Anna Maria** La figura di san Pietro nelle fonti del Medioevo: atti del convegno... 'Studiorum universitatum docentium congressus', Viterbo e Roma 5-8 settembre 2000. Textes et Études du Moyen Âge 17: Lv(N) 2001, Féderation Internationale des Instituts d'Études Médiévales viii; 708 pp. 18. ill.

7032 **Marconi, Gilberto** Prima lettera di Pietro. 2000 ⇒16,7180. [R]CivCatt 152/1 (2001) 539-540 (*Scaiola, D.*).

7033 *McDonald, Patricia M.* The view of suffering held by the author of 1 Peter. The bible on suffering. 2001 ⇒326. 165-187.

7034 **Pearson, Sharon Clark** The christological and rhetorical properties of 1 Peter. SBEC 45: Lewiston, NY 2001, Mellen xvii; 284 pp. 0-7734-7632-6. Bibl. 269-277.

7035 *Puig i Tàrrech, Armand* Los destinatarios de 1 Pe. ResB 32 (2001) 5-12.

7036 **Schweizer, Eduard** Der erste Petrusbrief. ZBK.NT 15: ⁴1998 ⇒14, 6430. ᴿThLZ 126 (2001) 538-540 (*Hoppe, Rudolf*).

7037 *Seland, Torrey* πάροικος καὶ παρεπίδημος; proselyte characterizations in 1 Peter?. BBR 11 (2001) 239-268.

7038 *Steenberg, P.F.* Christ: a solution to suffering in First Peter. VeE 22 (2001) 392-400.

7039 *Storm, Melvin R.* God's pilgrim people. RestQ 43/4 (2001) 267-279.

7040 *Tuñi Vancells, Josep Oriol* La figura de Jesucristo en 1 Pe. ResB 32 (2001) 13-22.

7041 *Vanhoye, Albert* Perspectivas eclesiales de 1 Pe. ResB 32 (2001) 23-32.

7042 **Yoo, Kenneth Keumsang** The classification of the Greek manuscripts of 1 Peter with special emphasis on methodology. Diss. Andrews 2001, ᴰ*Richards, W. Larry*: 395 pp. 3019344. AUSS 39,313.

7043 *Martini, Carlo M.* Dare testimonianza di gioia operosa e creativa. VitaCon 37/5 (2001) 451-460 [1 Pet 1,1-12].

7044 **Tite, Philip L.** Compositional transitions in 1 Peter: an analysis of the letter-opening. 1997 ⇒13,6811... 16,7186. ᴿSR 30 (2001) 120-121 (*Neufeld, Dietmar*) [1 Pet 1,1-14].

7045 *Rigato, Maria L.* Il carisma di interpretare la sacra scrittura in profeti cristiani (1Pt 1,10-12). Ricerche teologiche 12/2 (2001) 15-49.

7046 *Lambrecht, Jan* Christian freedom in 1 Pet 2,16: a grammatical and exegetical note. Collected studies. AnBib 147: 2001 ⇒170. 319-325.

7047 *Támez, Elsa* Giving an accounting of the hope that is in you. VFTW 24/2 (2001) 23-28 [1 Pet 3,13-16].

7048 *Klumbies, Paul-Gerhard* Die Verkündigung unter Geistern und Toten nach 1Petr 3,19f. und 4,6. ZNW 92 (2001) 207-228.

G9.2 2 Petri

7049 *Callan, Terrance* The christology of the second letter of Peter;

7050 The soteriology of the second letter of Peter. Bib. 82 (2001) 253-263/549-559.

7051 *Contreras Molina, Francisco* La segunda carta de Pedro. ResB 32 (2001) 43-51.

7052 **Gerdmar, Anders** Rethinking the Judaism-Hellenism dichotomy: a historiographical case study of Second Peter and Jude. CB.NT 36: Sto 2001, Almqvist & W. 174; (4) pp. $62.50. 91-22-01915-4. Bibl. 343-374. Diss. Uppsala.

7053 *Gilmour, Michael J.* Reflections on the authorship of 2 Peter. EvQ 73 (2001) 291-309.

      Kieffer, R. Filemonbrevet... Andra Petrusbrevet 2001 ⇒6978.

7054 *Kraus, Thomas J.* Grammatisches Problembewusstsein als regulativ für angemessene Sprachbeurteilung—das Beispiel der griechischen Negation und 2Petr. FgNT 14 (2001) 87-99.

7055 **Kraus, Thomas J.** Sprache, Stil und historischer Ort des zweiten Petrusbriefes. WUNT 2/136: Tü 2001, Mohr S. xvi; 486 pp. €69. 3-16-147550-X. Bibl. 415-452.

7056 *Müller, Peter* Der 2. Petrusbrief. ThR 66 (2001) 310-337.

7057 *Robertson, Terry* Relationships among the non-Byzantine manuscripts of 2 Peter. AUSS 39 (2001) 41-59.

7058 *Wall, Robert W.* The canonical function of 2 Peter. BiblInterp 9 (2001) 64-81.

7059 **Starr, James M.** Sharers in divine nature: 2 Peter 1:4 in its Hellenistic context. CB.NT 33: 2000 ⇒16,7198. ᴿCBQ 63 (2001) 764-765 (*Asher, Jeffrey R.*).

7060 *Charles, J. Daryl* On angels and asses: the moral paradigm in 2 Peter 2. ProcGLM 21 (2001) 1-12.

7061 *Bohren, Rudolf* Der Geschichte ins Rad greifen. ThFPr 27/2 (2001) 63-73 [2 Pet 3,11-12].

G9.4 Epistula Jacobi..data on both apostles James

7062 *Allison, Dale C.* The fiction of James and its Sitz im Leben. RB 108 (2001) 529-570.

7063 *Bauckham, Richard* James and Jesus. The brother of Jesus. 2001 ⇒256. 100-137.

7064 **Bottini, Giovanni Claudio** Giacomo e la sua lettera. SBFA 50: 2000 ⇒16,7200. ᴿCDios 214 (2001) 864-865 (*Gutiérrez, J.*).

7065 *Chilton, Bruce* James in relation to Peter, Paul, and the remembrance of Jesus. The brother of Jesus. 2001 ⇒256. 138-160.

7066 *Davids, Peter H.* James's message: the literary record. The brother of Jesus. 2001 ⇒256. 66-87.

7067 **Edgar, David Hutchinson** Has God not chosen the poor?: the social setting of the epistle of James. JSNT.S 206: Shf 2001, Sheffield A. 261 pp. £45. 1-84127-182-9. Bibl. 232-243.

7068 **Eisenman, Robert H.** James the brother of Jesus. 1997 ⇒13,6827; 14,6471. ᴿThe Brother of Jesus ⇒256. 186-197 (*Price, Robert M.*).

7069 *Evans, Craig A.* Comparing Judaisms: Qumranic, rabbinic, and Jacobean Judaisms compared. The brother of Jesus. 2001 ⇒256. 161-183.

7070 *Fabris, Rinaldo* Giustizia e giustificazione nelle lettere cattoliche. Giustizia-giustificazione nella bibbia. DSBP 28: 2001 ⇒307. 209-227.

7071 *Gianotto, Claudio* Giacomo e la comunità cristiana di Gerusalemme. RStB 13/2 (2001) 83-101;

7072 Giacomo e il giudeocristianesimo antico. Verus Israel. BCR 65: 2001 ⇒524. 108-119.

7073 **Hartin, Patrick J.** A spirituality of perfection: faith in action in the letter of James. 1999 ⇒15,7231. ᴿPacifica 14 (2001) 94-96 (*Forbes, Greg*).

7074 *Hoppe, Rudolf* Der Jakobusbrief als briefliches Zeugnis hellenistisch und hellenistisch-jüdisch geprägter Religiosität. Der neue Mensch in Christus. QD 190: 2001 ⇒239. 164-189.

7075 **Jackson-McCabe, Matt A.** Logos & law in the letter of James: the law of nature, the law of Moses, & the law of freedom. NT.S 100: Lei 2001, Brill 281 pp. €81/$100. 90-04-11994-9. ᴿETR 76 (2001) 432-433 (*Cuvillier, Élian*).

7076 ᴱ**Mills, Watson Early** James. Bibliographies for biblical research, NT 16: Lewiston 2001, Mellen xvi; 84 pp. 0-7734-2439-3.

7077 **Moo, Douglas J.** The letter of James. The Pillar New Testament Commentary: 2000 ⇒16,7204. ᴿCBQ 63 (2001) 349-350 (*Batten, Alicia*); AUSS 39 (2001) 335-338 (*Christian, Ed*).

7078 *Nodet, Etienne* James, the brother of Jesus, was never a christian. Le judéo-christianisme. 2001 ⇒484. 75-85 [BuBB 36,56];

7079 Procès de Jacques, procès de Jésus. Le judaïsme à l'aube de l'ère chrétienne. LeDiv 186: 2001 ⇒450. 51-62.

7080 **Painter, John** Just James. 1997 ⇒13,6833... 16,7205. ᴿTJT 17 (2001) 300-301 (*Batten, Alicia*).

7081 *Painter, John* Who was James?: footprints as a means of identification. The brother of Jesus. 2001 ⇒256. 10-65.

7082 **Piacentini, Giuseppe** La struttura e il messaggio della lettera di Giacomo. Sussidi biblici 72: Reggio Emilia 2001, San Lorenzo 123 pp. 88-8071-116-4.

7083 **Popkes, Wiard** Der Brief des Jakobus. ThHK 14: Lp 2001, Evangelische Verlagsanstalt xxxviii; 357 pp. 3-374-01813-0.

7084 *Popkes, Wiard* The mission of James in his time. The brother of Jesus. 2001 ⇒256. 88-99.

7085 **Taylor, Mark Edward** A textlinguistic investigation into the discourse structure of James. Diss. Fort Worth 2001, ^D*Corley, B.* 182 pp. 3010757 [RTL 33,641].

7086 *Verseput, Donald J.* PLUTARCH of Chaeronea and the epistle of James on communal behaviour. NTS 47 (2001) 502-518.

7087 **Kendall, R.T.** Justification by works: how works vindicate true faith: sermons on James 1-3. Carlisle 2001, Paternoster xii; 292 pp. 0-853-64-903-0.

7088 *Jackson-McCabe, Matt* The law of freedom (James 1:25): light from early exegesis. ProcGLM 21 (2001) 33-44.

7089 **Wachob, Wesley Hiram** The voice of Jesus in the social rhetoric of James. MSSNTS 106: 2000 ⇒16,7224. ^RAThR 83 (2001) 887-888 (*Sumney, Jerry L.*) [James 2,1-13].

7090 *Avemarie, Friedrich* Die Werke des Gesetzes im Spiegel des Jakobusbriefs: a very old perspective on Paul. ZThK 98 (2001) 282-309 [James 2,14-16].

7091 *Wall, Robert W.* The intertextuality of scripture: the example of Rahab (James 2:25). The bible at Qumran. 2001 ⇒267. 217-236 [James 2,21-26].

7092 *Carpenter, Craig* James 4.5 reconsidered. NTS 47 (2001) 189-205.

7093 *Wilson, Walter T.* Turning words: James 4:7-10 and the rhetoric of repentance. ^FBETZ, H. 2001 ⇒5. 357-382.

7094 *Böttrich, Christfried* Vom Gold, das rostet (Jak 5.3). NTS 47 (2001) 519-536.

G9.6 Epistula Judae

7095 **Bortolini, José** Como ler a carta de Judas. Como ler a Biblia: São Paulo 2001, Paulus 43 pp [REB 62,247].

7096 *Donelson, Lewis R.* Jude as text with excess of context. ^FBETZ, H. 2001 ⇒5. 279-295.

    Gerdmar, A. Rethinking the Judaism-Hellenism dichotomy 2001 ⇒7052.

7097 **Jones, Peter Russell** The epistle of Jude as expounded by the Fathers—CLEMENT of Alexandria, DIDYMUS of Alexandria, the Scholia of CRAMER's Catena, PSEUDO-OECUMENIUS, and BEDE. TSR 89: Lewiston, NY 2001, Mellen xvi; 128 pp. 077-347-4021. Bibl. 125-6.

    Kieffer, R. Filemonbrevet, Judasbrevet... 2001 ⇒6978.

7098 *Smith, Larry Douglas* The δοχας of Jude 8. BiTr 52 (2001) 147-148.

XIII. Theologia Biblica

H1.1 Biblical Theology [OT] God

7099   *Agus, Aharon R.E.* Literarische und visuelle Hermeneutik oder die Unmöglichkeit der Ikone Gottes. ᶠBARASCH, M. 2001 ⇒2. 181-196.

7100   *Becking, Bob* Only one God: on possible implications for biblical theology. Only one God?. BiSe 77: 2001 ⇒238. 189-201.

7101   *Biezeveld, Kune E.* Challenging the tradition of the bodiless God: a way to inclusive monotheism?. Religious identity. Studies in theology and religion 3: 2001 ⇒549. 84-96.

7102   **Boyd, Gregory A.** God of the possible: a biblical introduction to the open view of God. 2000 ⇒16,7241. ᴿTrinJ 22 (2001) 123-127 (*Nicholls, Jason A.*).

7103   *Cannuyer, Christian* Dieu est-il dans les cieux?. MoBi 133 (2001) 22-27 [BuBB 35,75].

7104   **Cazelles, Henri** La Bible et son Dieu. CJJC 40: ²1999 ⇒15,7268. ᴿEstB 59 (2001) 379-380 (*Asenjo, J.*).

7105   *Chopineau, Jacques* Face de Dieu, image de Dieu: les théophanies dans la bible hebraïque. AnBru 6 (2001) 74-90.

7106   **Coppedge, Allan** Portraits of God: a biblical theology of holiness. DG 2001, InterVarsity 432 pp. $23. 0-8308-1560-0 [ThD 49,64— Heiser, W. Charles].

7107   *Crenshaw, James L.* The reification of divine evil. PRSt 287/4 (2001) 327-332.

7108   *Dafni, Evangelia G.* Σάρξ μου ἐξ αὐτῶν (LXX-Hosea IX 12): zur Theologie der Sprache der Septuaginta. VT 51 (2001) 336-353.

7109   **Debray, Régis** Dieu, un itinéraire: matériaux pour l'histoire de l'É-ternel en Occident. P 2001, Jacob 399 pp. €27. 2-7381-1034-7 [RB 109,313].

7110   **Dietrich, Walter; Link, Christian** Die dunklen Seiten Gottes, 2: Allmacht und Ohnmacht. 2000 ⇒16,7248. ᴿThRv 97 (2001) 373-376 (*Neuhaus, Gerd*); ThLZ 126 (2001) 910-913 (*Reventlow, Henning Graf*).

7111   *Dietzel, Gabriele* Gott trauert: Zorn und Strafe. DtPfrBl 101 (2001) 633-634.

7112   *Duranti, Gian Carlo* Scienza e idea biblica del divino: cancellazione di un'antitesi. CiVi 156 (2001) 493-512.

7113   *Ebach, Jürgen* Fragmentale Reflexionen über biblisches Reden von Gott. JK 62/4 (2001) 20-24.

7114 *Feldmeier, Reinhard* Theodizee?: biblische Überlegungen zu einem unbiblischen Unterfangen. BThZ 18 (2001) 24-38.

7115 *Fleinert-Jensen, Flemming* Présence et absence de Dieu. PosLuth 49/1 (2001) 65-78.

7116 *García López, Félix* El Dios judeo-cristiano ante las utopías (Éxodo, reforma de Josías y exilio). EstTrin 35 (2001) 55-76.

7117 **Germinario, Mario** Chi ha paura del Dio biblico?. Brindisi 2001, Schena 236 pp [RRFC 98,95–Sartori, Silvana].

7118 *Grilli, Massimo* Il volto: rivelazione e mistero, alterità e responsabilità. CoSe 12 (2001) 11-15.

7119 *Gubler, Marie-Louise* Gott—kein Macher, sondern Schöpfer. Diak. 32 (2001) 381-385.

7120 *Häring, Hermann* From divine human to human God. [F]VAN DER VEN, J. 2001 ⇒109. 3-28.

7121 *Henrix, Hans Hermann* "Hinneni": Anmerkungen zur Gegenwart Gottes. BiLi 74 (2001) 211-215.

7122 **Hunziker-Rodewald, Regine** Hirt und Herde: ein Beitrag zum alttestamentlichen Gottesverständnis. BWANT 155: Stu 2001, Kohlhammer 256 pp. €35. 3-17-017090-2. Bibl. 231-250.

7123 *Jaffee, Martin S.* One God, one revelation, one people: on the symbolic structure of elective monotheism. JAAR 69 (2001) 753-775 [BuBB 36,37].

7124 *Janowski, Bernd* Königtum Gottes im Alten Testament. RGG², 4: I-K. 2001 ⇒664. 1591-1593.

7125 **Kaiser, Otto** Der Gott des Alten Testaments, 2: Wesen und Wirken: Jahwe, der Gott Israels, Schöpfer der Welt und des Menschen. 1998 ⇒14,6520. [R]CBQ 63 (2001) 114-115 (*Janzen, Waldemar*).

7126 **Klein, Joel T.** Through the name of God: a new road to the origin of Judaism and Christianity. CSRel 64: Westport, CT 2001, Greenwood xxv; 271 pp. 0-313-31656-2. Bibl. 253-257.

7127 *Kruger, H.A.J.* Myth, ideology, and wisdom: a brief survey. OTEs 14 (2001) 47-75 [Gen 3].

7128 **Lewandowski, Jerzy** Bóg i czlowiek. Wsz 2001, Wyd. Uniwersytetu Kardynala S. Wyszynkiego 245 pp. 83-7072-207-5. Bibl. 7-29. **P.**

7129 *Lindström, Fredrik* Guds långa näsa och blödande hjärta: gränser för Guds makt i Gamla Testamentet. SvTK 77 (2001) 2-12.

7130 *Loader, James Alfred* Zum Preis der Rechtfertigung Gottes im Alten Testament. BThZ 18 (2001) 3-23.

7131 *Lugo Rodríguez, Raúl H.* El defensor de los indefensos (pistas para la construcción de la imagen de Dios como ombudsman, a partir de la biblia). Qol 26 (2001) 77-96.

7132 **Magnani, Giovanni** Religione e religioni, 1: dalla monolatria al monoteismo profetico. R 2001, E.P.U.G. 671 pp. 88-7652-898-9;

7133   2: il monoteismo. R 2001, E.P.U.G. 573 pp. 88-7652-900-4.

7134   *Martens, Karen* "With a strong hand and an outstretched arm": the
       meaning of the expression נטויה וברוע חזקה ביד. SJOT 15 (2001) 123-
       141 [Ex 3,19; 7,3-12,37].

7135   **Messadié, Gerald** História geral de Deus—da antiguidade à época
       contemporânea. Mem Martins 2001, Europa-América 576 pp [Brot.
       156,96ss—F. Pires Lopes].

7136   **Nelson-Pallmeyer, Jack** Jesus against christianity: reclaiming the
       missing Jesus. Harrisburg 2001, Trinity 384 pp. $20. 1-56338-362-4
       [Interp. 56,334—Myers, Max A.].

7137   **Neufeld, Thomas R. Yoder** 'Put on the armour of God': the divine
       warrior from Isaiah to Ephesians. JSNT.S 140: 1997 ⇒13,6884; 15,
       7293. [R]JBL 119 (2000) 155-157 (*Huie-Jolly, Mary*) [Wis 5; Isa 59;
       Eph 6; 1 Thess 5].

7138   *Noll, K.L.* The kaleidoscopic nature of divine personality in the
       Hebrew Bible. BiblInterp 9 (2001) 1-24.

7139   *O'Brien, Mark* The nature of biblical monotheism: experience and
       ideology. Conc(US) 1 (2001) 66-73; Conc(P) 289,77-85; Conc(D)
       37/1,53-61; Conc(F) 69-77.

7140   **Penchansky, David** What rough beast?: images of God in the
       Hebrew Bible. 1999 ⇒15,7294. [R]BS 158 (2001) 492-494 (*Chisholm,
       Robert B.*).

7141   **Ravasi, Gianfranco** I monti di Dio: il mistero della montagna tra pa-
       rola e immagine. CinB 2001, San Paolo 123 pp. 88-215-4507-5.

7142   *Rusconi, Carlo* La verità nella bibbia. Hum(B) 56 (2001) 191-197.

7143   *Serra, Aristide M.* La "spada": simbolo della "Parola di Dio",
       nell'Antico Testamento biblico-giudaico e nel Nuovo Testamento.
       Ment. *Philo*; *Josephus*. Mar. 63 (2001) 17-89 [Wis 18,14-16; Isa
       49,1-2; 2 Macc 15,15-16; Eph 6,17; Heb 4,12-19].

7144   **Smith, Mark Stratton** Monotheistic re-readings of the biblical God.
       RStR 27/1 (2001) 25-31.

7145   *Sölle, Dorothee* Wo Liebe ist, da ist Gott. Schön bist du. 2001 ⇒274.
       167-181.

7146   *Spieckermann, Hermann* 'Barmherzig und gnädig ist der Herr...'.
       Gottes Liebe zu Israel. FAT 33: 2001 <1990> ⇒215. 3-19;

7147   'Die ganze Erde ist seiner Herrlichkeit voll': Pantheismus im Alten
       Testament?. Gottes Liebe zu Israel. 2001 <1990> ⇒215. 62-83.

7148   **Theissen, Gerd** Come cambia la fede: una prospettiva evoluzionisti-
       ca. Piccola biblioteca teologica 47: T 1999, Claudiana 252 pp. €18.
       59. [R]RSEc 19 (2001) 148-150 (*Morandini, S.*).

7149   *Virgili, Rosanna* La contesa di Dio con Israele. Servitium 35 (2001)
       611-623.

7150 *Werbick, Jürgen* Der Glaube an den allmächtigen Gott und die Krise des Bittgebets. BThZ 18 (2001) 40-59.

7151 *Wénin, André* "Le Seigneur est un homme de guerre". Christus 48 (2001) 403-411 [Gen 1-9].

7152 *Wright, J. Edward* Biblical versus Israelite images of the heavenly realm. JSOT 93 (2001) 59-75;

7153 Speaking of good and evil. BiRe 17/6 (2001) 10, 58.

H1.3 *Immutabilitas*—God's suffering; process theology

7154 **Gnuse, Robert K.** The Old Testament and process theology. 2000 ⇒16,7293. [R]BTB 31 (2001) 158 (*Eddinger, Terry W.*).

H1.4 *Femininum in Deo*—God as father and mother

7155 **Böckler, Annette** Gott als Vater im Alten Testament... Untersuchungen zur Entstehung und Entwicklung eines Gottesbildes, Jes 63,16. 2000 ⇒16,7298. [R]KuI 16 (2001) 90-91 (*Kirchberg, Julie*).

7156 *Cañellas, Gabriel* Dios como padre: la paternidad de Dios en el Antiguo Testamento. BiFe 27 (2001) 7-29.

7157 *Dabrowski, Wiesław* Dio Padre misericordioso alla luce dei commenti di san TOMMASO d'Aquino alle lettere di san Paolo apostolo. Ang. 78 (2001) 439-477.

7158 Dios, padre: la paternidad divina en la nueva conciencia del hombre. BiFe 27 (2001) 5-147.

7159 **Dumais, Marcel** A la rencontre d'un Dieu-Amour: Dieu le Père dans la bible. 1999 ⇒15,7321. [R]ScEs 53 (2001) 390-392 (*Côté, Julienne*).

7160 *Elders, Léo* La paternité de Dieu dans la théologie spirituelle de saint THOMAS d'Aquin. Sedes Sapientiae 77 (2001) 25-42.

7161 **Galot, Jean** Padre, ¿Quién eres?. 1998 ⇒15,7324. [R]ThX 51 (2001) 631-633 (*Cadena D., Orlando*).

7162 *Greene-McCreight, Kathryn* Back to Babel—that confounded language again: a response to David L. Jeffrey. [F]THISELTON, A. 2001 ⇒ 106. 280-283.

7163 **Grey, Mary** Introducing feminist images of God. Introductions in Feminist Theology 7: Shf 2001, Sheffield A. 133 pp. £13/$20. 1-84127-160-8. Bibl. 118-129.

7164 *Jeffrey, David L.* Naming the Father: the teaching authority of Jesus and contemporary debate. [F]THISELTON, A. 2001 ⇒ 106. 263-279.

7165 *Manrique, Andrés* Dios como padre: la paternidad de Dios en la época patrística. BiFe 27 (2001) 81-98.

7166 **Martini, Carlo Maria** Den Weg zum Vater finden: Gott-Vater in einer vaterlosen Gesellschaft. 1999 ⇒15,7339. ^RZKTh 123 (2001)
124-126 (*Hell, Silvia*).

7167 **Miller, John Wolf** Calling God "Father": essays on the bible, father-
hood and culture. ²1999 <1989> ⇒15,7340. 0-8091-3897-2. ^RGr. 82
(2001) 395-396 (*Pastor, Félix-Alejandro*).

7168 *Muñoz León, Domingo* Dios como padre: la paternidad de Dios en el
mensaje de Jesús. BiFe 27 (2001) 30-57.

7169 *Penna, Romano* I tre livelli della paternità di Dio nel NT: natura e
condizionamenti culturali. Vangelo e inculturazione. 2001 <1999>
⇒193. 645-679.

7170 *Salas, Antonio* Dios como padre: de la doctrina tradicional a la visión
holística. BiFe 27 (2001) 99-147.

7171 *Serrano, Vicente* Dios como padre: la paternidad de Dios en el cristianismo primitivo. BiFe 27 (2001) 58-80.

7172 **Thompson, Marianne Meye** The promise of the Father: Jesus and
God in the New Testament. 2000 ⇒16,7310. ^RJThS 52 (2001) 784-6
(*Richardson, Neil*); CBQ 63 (2001) 353-355 (*Boisclair, Regina A.*).

H1.7 Revelatio

7173 *Andresen, Dieter* Drucksache oder lebendiges Wort?: über das
Heilige an der "Heiligen Schrift". TeKo 24/1 (2001) 3-12.

7174 *Blanchard, Yves-Marie* L'oralité dans l'écriture. MD 226 (2001) 51-
72.

7175 **Brown, David** Tradition and imagination: revelation and change.
2000 ⇒16,1210. ^RTS 62 (2001) 386-388 (*Oakes, Edward T.*).

7176 **Goldsworthy, Graeme** According to plan: the unfolding revelation
of God in the bible. Nottingham 2001, Inter-Varsity Pr. 320 pp. 0-85-
110-955-1.

7177 *Gounelle, André* Révélation et foi selon TROELTSCH et TILLICH.
RHPhR 81 (2001) 13-28.

7178 **Gracia, Jorge J.E.** How can we know what God means?: the interpretation of revelation. NY 2001, Palgrave xiv; 229 pp. $19. 0-312-
24028-7. Bibl. 207-220.

7179 **Greco, Carlo** La rivelazione: fenomenologia, dottrina e credibilità.
2000 ⇒16,7325. ^RCivCatt 152/1 (2001) 530-531 (*Mazzolini, S.*).

7180 **Halivni, David Weiss** Restaurare la rivelazione: la scrittura divina e
le risposte della critica biblica. ^T*Ventura, Milka*: Schulim Vogelmann
85: F 2001, La giuntina 192 pp. €14.46. 88-8057-113-3. Pref. di
Peter Ochs e *Stanley M.Hauerwas*. ^RRasIsr 67/3 (2001) 119-123 (*Ascoli, Michael*);

7181 Revelation restored: divine writ and critical responses. L 2001, SCM xxiii; 114 pp. £14. 0-334-02860-4.

7182 *Helm, Paul* Speaking and revealing. RelSt 37 (2001) 249-258.

7183 *Quinn, Philip L.* Can God speak?: does God speak?. RelSt 37 (2001) 259-269.

7184 *Rodríguez, Angel Manuel* Ancient Near Eastern parallels to the bible and the question of revelation and inspiration. JATS 12/1 (2001) 43-64.

7185 *Sanday, William* Biblical criticism: the fullness of revelation in the New Testament. Essays in biblical criticism. JSNT.S 225: 2001 <1894> ⇒205. 14-21.

7186 **Stramare, Tarcisio** La teologia della divina revelazione. 2000 ⇒16, 7333. [R]MF 101 (2001) 398-400 (*Iammarrone, Luigi*).

7187 *Strange, John* Bibelsk arkaeologi og bibelsk teologi. DTT 64 (2001) 81-96.

7188 **Theobald, Christoph** La révélation... tout simplement. P 2001, Atelier 238 pp.

7189 *Westphal, Merold* On reading God the author;

7190 *Wolterstorff, Nicholas* Response to Helm, Quinn, and Westphal. RelSt 37 (2001) 271-291/293-306.

H1.8 Theologia fundamentalis

7191 *Broshi, Magen* Predestination in the bible and the Dead Sea scrolls. Bread, wine. JSPE.S 36: 2001 ⇒131. 238-251.

7192 **Canale, Fernando Luis** Back to revelation-inspiration: searching for the cognitive foundation of christian theology in a postmodern world. Lanham 2001, University Press of America xii; 177 pp. 0-7618-2082-5. Bibl. 163-173.

7193 **Feinberg, John S.** No one like him: the doctrine of God. Foundations of evangelical theology. Wheaton, IL 2001, Crossway 879 pp. $35. 1-58134-275-6 [ThD 49,68—Heiser, W. Charles].

7194 **Fisichella, R.** Jesús, profecía del Padre. M 2001, San Pablo 294 pp. €13.52.

7195 **Haight, Roger** Dynamics of theology. Mkn [2]2001 <1990>, Orbis xi; 207 pp. $24. 1-57075-387-3 [ThD 49,70—Heiser, W. Charles].

7196 **Hasenhüttl, Gotthold** Glaube ohne Mythos, 1: Offenbarung, Jesus Christus, Gott, 2: Mensch, Glaubensgemeinschaft, Symbolhandlungen, Zukunft. Mainz 2001, Grünewald 1612 pp. €39.80 + 39.80 (€69.50).

7197 *Johnson, William Stacy* Rethinking theology: a postmodern, post-holocaust, post-christendom endeavour. Interp. 55 (2001) 5-18.

7198 **Körtner, Ulrich H.J.** Theologie des Wortes Gottes: Positionen—Probleme—Perspektiven. Gö 2001, Vandenhoeck & R. 440 pp. €44.

7199 *Neufeld, Karl H.* Globalization: discovery of catholicity. ^FO'COLLINS, G. 2001 ⇒81. 126-135.

7200 **Patrick, Dale A.** The rhetoric of revelation in the Hebrew Bible. 1999 ⇒15,7382; 16,7339. ^RCBQ 63 (2001) 326-327 (*Craig, Kenneth M.*).

7201 *Sonderegger, Katherine* Theological realism. ^FDIETRICH, W., BJSt 329: 2001 ⇒24. 196-215.

7202 *Stirnimann, Heinrich* Biblische Grundbegriffe und Fundamentaltheologie: eine bibliographische Notiz. FZPhTh 48 (2001) 217-221.

H2.1 Anthropologia theologica—VT & NT

7203 **Aldeeb Abu-Sahlieh, Sami A.** Circoncision masculine, circoncision féminine: débat religieux, médical, social et juridique. P 2001, L'Harmattan 538 pp. €44.25. 27475-0445X. Préf. *Linda Weil-Curiel.*

7204 *Awi, Alexandre M.* ¿Qué dice la Biblia sobre la homosexualidad?. TyV 42 (2001) 377-398.

7205 *Barnouw, Jeffrey* Bible, science et souveraineté chez BACON et HOBBES. RThPh 133 (2001) 247-265.

7206 **Bar, Shaul** A letter that has not been read: dreams in the Hebrew Bible. ^T*Schramm, Lenn J.*: MHUC 25: Cincinnati 2001, Hebrew Union College Press xii; 257 pp. $40. 0-87820-424-5. Bibl. 233-252.

7207 *Baumert, Norbert* 'Alles ist durch Christus und auf Ihn hin geschaffen'. Studien zu den Paulusbriefen. SBAB 32: 2001 <1996> ⇒123. 192-200.

7208 *Beaude, Pierre-Marie* Introduction: le discours religieux, son sérieux, sa parodie. Le discours religieux. 2001 ⇒506. 7-12.

7209 La bible à plusieurs voix. Le discours religieux. 2001 ⇒506. 13-28.

7210 **Bénétreau, Samuel** Bonheur des hommes, bonheur de Dieu: spécificité et paradoxe de la joie chrétienne. Terre nouvelle: Vaux-sur-Seine 2001, Edifac 224 pp. €15. 2-914144-27-X.

7211 Das biblische Menschenbild und die Frage der Homosexualität. Lutherische Beiträge 6/1 (2001) 66-72.

7212 *Bird, Phyllis A.* Theological anthropology in the Hebrew Bible. The Blackwell companion to the Hebrew Bible. 2001 ⇒653. 258-275.

7213 *Blocher, Henri* Yesterday, today, forever: time, times, eternity in biblical perspective. TynB 52 (2001) 183-202.

7214 *Bricker, Daniel P.* Innocent suffering in Egypt. TynB 52 (2001) 83-100.

7215 **Brin, Gershon A.** The concept of time in the bible and the Dead Sea scrolls. StTDJ 39: Lei 2001, Brill xiii; 389 pp. £72.82. 90-04-12314-8. Bibl. 375-380.

7216 *Broyles, Craig C.* Interpreting the Old Testment: principles and steps. Interpreting the OT. 2001 ⇒248. 13-62.

7217 *Brueggemann, Walter* Epilogue. The bible on suffering. 2001 ⇒326. 211-216.

7218 *Burrows, Peter* Biblical models of leadership. PrPe 15 (2001) 402-406.

7219 *Ceccherelli, Ignazio Marino* Il 'nemico' nella bibbia. BeO 43 (2001) 214.

7220 *Chempakassery, Philip* Life and its value in the bible. Jeevadhara 31 (2001) 409-419.

7221 *Chilton, Bruce* Jesus' purity and the myth of liberal christianity. SBL.SP 2001. SBL.SPS 40: 2001 ⇒494. 108-130 [Mk 7].

7222 *Dafni, Evangelia G.* שׁ מאישׁ כי אשׁה—γυνή, ὅτι ἐκ τοῦ ἀνδρὸς αὐτῆς (Gen 2,23): zur Anthropologie von Genesis 1-11. Studies in the book of Genesis. BEThL 155: 2001 ⇒1936. 569-584.

7223 *Dahl, Nils Alstrup; Hellholm, David* Garment-metaphors: the old and the new human being. ᶠBETZ, H. 2001 ⇒5. 139-158.

7224 *David, Robert* L'indéterminisme biblique: une proposition du procès. Theoforum 32/1 (2001) 63-82.

7225 **Debergé, Pierre** L'amour et la sexualité dans la bible. P 2001, Nouveau Cité 208 pp. €15.40. 2-85313-397-4.

7226 *Deselaers, Paul* Liebesgeschichten: Liebe und Eros in der Anthropologie der Bibel. WUB 21 (2001) 65-67.

7227 *Dohmen, Christoph* Nicht ewig will ich leben: der Todeswunsch als Zumutung Gottes. AnzSS 110/11 (2001) 11-14 [Num 11; 1 Kgs 19].

7228 *Dondelinger, Patrick* Le discours démonologique. Le discours religieux. 2001 ⇒506. 99-110.

7229 **Estrada-Barbier, Bernardo** "Lieti nella speranza": la gioia nel Nuovo Testamento. Studi di teologia 8: R 2001, Ed. Univ. della Santa Croce 328 pp. €24.79. 88-8333-014-5. Bibl. 305-309.

7230 **Fernández Ramos, Felipe** Del mundo físico al tiempo bíblico. Teología en diálogo 20: S 2001, Universidad Pontificia de Salamanca 307 pp. 84-7299-495-3.

7231 *Ferraro, Giuseppe* Gioia dolore persecuzione in Matteo Marco e negli scritti giovannei. Gli autori divini. 2001 <2000> ⇒144. 243-265.

7232 *Fevel, Christian* Geweihte Frauen oder kultisch sanktionierte Unzucht?. WUB 21 (2001) 45-47.

7233 *Fontinoy, Charles* Existe-t-il un canon biblique de l'idéal féminin?. ᶠDESROCHES NOBLECOURT, C. 2001 ⇒22. 61-74.

7234 *García Bazán, Francisco* La complejidad antropológica del cristianismo primitivo. Epimelia 10 (2001) 7-37.

7235 **Gilders, William Keith** Representation and interpretation: blood
manipulation in ancient Israel and early Judaism. Diss. Brown 2001,
428 pp. 3006726.

7236 **Gilhus, Ingvild Saelid** Laughing gods, weeping virgins: laughter in
the history of religion. 1997 ⇒13,6949; 14,6612. ᴿHR 39 (2000)
372-376 (*Girardot, Norman J.*).

7237 **Girard, René** La vittima e la folla: violenza del mito e cristianesimo.
1998 ⇒14,6613. ᴿRdT 42 (2001) 311-312 (*Tanzarella, Sergio*);

7238 Celui par qui le scandale arrive. P 2001, Desclée de B. 195 pp. €19.
2-220-05011-4.

7239 *Gourgues, Michel* La "plénitudes des temps", ou le temps marqué de
façon décisive par la référence à Jésus Christ: polysémie d'une formule néotestamentaire (Mc 1,15; Ga 4,4; Ep 1,10). ScEs 53 (2001)
93-110.

7240 *Gruber, Margareta* "Verherrlicht Gott in eurem Leib" (1 Kor 6,20):
zu einer Theologie und Spiritualität des Leibes bei Paulus und im
Neuen Testament. ThG 44 (2001) 264-273.

7241 *Grund, Alexandra* Mitgeschöpflichkeit. rhs 44 (2001) 332-338.

7242 **Haag, Herbert,** *al.*, Kom, mijn geliefde, kom: liefde in de bijbel.
Kampen 2001, Kok 191 pp. [Coll. 32,110—Vanden Berghe, Eric].

7243 *Haag, Herbert; Elliger, Katharina* Einführung: Liebe, Eros, Sexualität. Schön bist du. 2001 ⇒274. 8-25.

7244 *Harrill, J. Albert* Invective against Paul (2 Cor 10:10), the physiog-
nomics of the ancient slave body, and the Greco-Roman rhetoric of
manhood. ᶠBᴇᴛᴢ, H. 2001 ⇒5. 189-213.

7245 **Harrington, Daniel J.** Why do we suffer?: a scriptural approach to
the human condition. 2000 ⇒16,7380. ᴿRRT (2001/1) 59-61 (*Wollaston, Isabel*); PIBA 24 (2001) 118-119 (*O'Leary, Anthony*); MillSt
48 (2001) 150-151 (*Mangan, Céline*).

7246 *Helewa, Giovanni* Il soffrire umano nell'Antico Testamento: pensiero
ed esperienza. Antropologia cristiana. 2001 ⇒371. 891-916.

7247 *Highfield, Ronald C.* Man and woman in Christ: theological ethics
after the egalitarian revolution. RestQ 43/3 (2001) 129-146.

7248 *Jankowski, Stanisław* Zbawczy charakter cierpienia w świetle tekstów biblijnych [Le sens salvifique de la souffrance à la lumière des
textes bibliques]. AtK 137 (2001) 206-226 Rias. 226. **P.**

7249 *Kartveit, Magnar* Kropp i eit gammaltestamentleg perspektiv. Ung
teologi 34/2 (2001) 7-18.

7250 **Karumathy, Gervasis** Out of my distress, O YHWH!: outcry in the
Hebrew Bible. Extr. Diss. PIB 2001, ᴰ*Pisano, Stephen*: R 2001,
E.P.I.B. viii; 156 pp. Bibl. 107-150.

7251 *Kegler, Jürgen* Beobachtungen zur Körpererfahrung in der hebräischen Bibel. Gesammelte Aufsätze. 2001 <1992> ⇒167. 247-260.

7252 **Klawans, Jonathan** Impurity and sin in ancient Judaism. 2000 ⇒16, 7384. ᴿJThS 52 (2001) 722-725 (*Houston, Walter J.*).

7253 *Koffi, Ettien* Rethinking the significance of the black presence in the pentateuch for translation and study bibles: part II. BiTr 52 (2001) 102-114.

7254 *Kristeva, Julia* Reading the bible. The postmodern bible reader. 2001 <1995> ⇒287. 92-101.

7255 *Kruger, Paul A.* A cognitive interpretation of the emotion of fear in the Hebrew Bible. JNSL 27/2 (2001) 77-89.

7256 **Lasine, Stuart** Knowing kings: knowledge, power, and narcissism in the Hebrew Bible. SBL Semeia Studies 40: Atlanta, GA 2001, SBL xv; 342 pp. $40. 1-58983-004-0. Bibl. 265-312.

7257 *Leyerle, Blake* Blood is seed. JR 81 (2001) 26-48.

7258 *Lloyd, J. William* Seelen-Verbindung. Irreale Glaubensinhalte. 2001 ⇒1066. 54-55.

7259 *Loader, James Alfred* 'Trembling, the best of being human': aspects of anxiety in Israel. OTEs 14 (2001) 260-280.

7260 *Mahlke, Hans P.* Die Frau im Verhältnis zu ihrem Ehemann: noch ein Beitrag zur hermeneutischen Frage in der Geschichte selbständiger evangelisch-lutherischer Kirchen in Deutschland. LuThK 25/2 (2001) 85-111.

7261 *Malamat, Abraham* Longevity: biblical concepts and some ancient Near Eastern parallels. History of biblical Israel. Culture and history of the ANE 7: 2001 <1951> ⇒182. 389-400.

7262 **Malina, Bruce J.** The New Testament world: insights from cultural anthropology. LVL ³2001, Westminster xv; 256 pp. $25. 0-664-22295-1. Bibl. [ThD 48,278—Heiser, W. Charles].

7263 *Martin, George* Suffering 'for the sake of' God. The bible on suffering. 2001 ⇒326. 18-33.

7264 *Martín-Moreno, Juan Manuel* 'El amigo fiel no tiene precio' (Si 6,15): carácter expansivo de la amistad en la biblia. SalTer 89 (2001) 781-794.

7265 *Mathews, Susan F.* Toward reclaiming an authentic bibical-christian view of the body. Linacre Quarterly 68 (2001) 277-295.

7266 **Miggelbrink, Ralf** Der Zorn Gottes: Geschichte und Aktualität einer ungeliebten biblischen Tradition. 2000 ⇒16,7407. ᴿThGl 91 (2001) 154-6 (*Bomhauer, Ralf*); ThRv 97 (2001) 214-218 (*Ruster, Thomas*).

7267 **Moltmann-Wendel, Elisabeth** Rediscovering friendship: awakening to the power and promise of women's friendships. ᵀ*Bowden, John* Mp 2001, Fortress viii; 127 pp. $15. 0-8006-3445-4 [ThD 49,78—Heiser, W. Charles].

7268 *Moriconi, Bruno* La filialità divina base dell'antropologia teologica cristiana. Antropologia cristiana. 2001 ⇒371. 335-371 [Jn 17,24-26; Gal 4,4-7].

7269 **Moschieri, Giovanna** Dal cuore di Dio: riflessioni su temi giubilari. Formazione 20: R 2001, ADP 143 pp. 88-7357-251-0.

7270 *Navone, John* Famine, hunger, and thirst in the bible. BiTod 39 (2001) 155-159.

7271 *Nkwoka, A.O.* The New Testament demonology and some pastoral concerns of the church in Africa. BiBh 27 (2001) 90-105.

7272 **Pham, Xuan Huong Thi** Mourning in the ancient Near East and the Hebrew Bible. JSOT.S 302: 1999 ⇒15,7433. [R]JThS 52 (2001) 719-20 (*Salters, Robert B.*); OLZ 96 (2001) 545-7 (*Berlejung, Angelika*).

7273 **Porter, Jeanne** Leading ladies: transformative biblical images for women's leadership. Ph 2000, Innisfree 158 pp. $14 [CThMi 31, 132—Connie Kleingartner].

7274 [E]**Pouthier, Jean-Luc** De la création aux rois mages: le ciel de la bible. MoBi 133 (2001) 3-53.

7275 *Prato, Ezio* Il ritorno dell'estetica: nichilismo postmoderno e verità del cristianesimo. La bellezza. PSV 44: 2001 ⇒240. 265-277.

7276 *Rattin, Piero* 'Non ha apparenza né bellezza': il rovescio della bellezza. La bellezza. PSV 44: 2001 ⇒240. 67-77.

7277 **Riches, John K.** Conflicting mythologies: identity formation in the gospels of Mark and Matthew. 2000 ⇒16,7433. [R]ABR 49 (2001) 63-65 (*Sim, David C.*).

7278 *Riezu, Jorge* Situación de frontera y situación de exilio. Communio 34 (2001) 473-482.

7279 *Rindone, Elio* La concezione biblica dell'amore. Il tetto 227 (2001) 41-52.

7280 *Schenker, Adrien* Quand les chrétiens se souviennent de Moïse!. Sources 27 (2001) 292-297.

7281 **Schroer, Silvia; Staubli, Thomas** Body symbolism in the bible. [T]*Maloney, Linda M.*: ColMn 2001, Liturgical xv; 249 pp. $40. 0-81-46-5954-3. Bibl. 227-235.

7282 *Sexson, Lynda* Bride's blood and God's laugh: reading the evidence of desire on "the blank page" of the Torah. RL 33/2 (2001) 37-57.

7283 *Smith, Carol* Biblical perspectives on power. JSOT 93 (2001) 93-110 [Gen 19; 38; 2 Sam 11; 1 Kgs 1; 2 Kgs 3].

7284 *Solà, Teresa* Sobre l'amor esponsal en la bíblia. RCatT 26 (2001) 385-389.

7285 *Soskice, Janet Martin* Blood and defilement: reflections on Jesus and the symbolics of sex. [F]O'COLLINS, G. 2001 ⇒81. 285-303.

7286 *Speyer, Wolfgang* Hellenistisch-römische Voraussetzungen der Verbreitung des Christentums. Der neue Mensch in Christus. QD 190: 2001 ⇒239. 11-38.

7287 *Stiebert, J.; Walsh, J.T.* Does the Hebrew Bible have anything to say about homosexuality?. OTEs 14 (2001) 119-152 [Gen 19; Lev 18,22; 20,13; Judg 19].

7288 *Stockham, Alice B.* Elternschaft. Irreale Glaubensinhalte. 2001 ⇒ 1066. 47-50.

7289 **Stol, Marten** Birth in Babylonia and the Bible. Cuneiform monographs 14: 2000 ⇒16,7443. [R]BiOr 58 (2001) 403-404 (*Jensen, Karen*); Phoe. 47 (2001) 163-164 (*Van Koppen, F.*).

7290 **Storkey, Elaine** Origins of difference: the gender debate revisited. GR 2001, Baker 156 pp. $14. 08010-22606 [ThD 49,87–Heiser, W.].

7291 *Sutter Rehmann, Luzia* Gebären als Arbeit gegen den Tod. JK 62/6 (2001) 18-23.

7292 *Tambasco, Anthony J.* Introduction: the bible and human suffering. The bible on suffering. 2001 ⇒326. 3-17.

7293 **Terrin, Aldo Natale** Antropologia e orizzonti del sacro: culture e religioni. Leitourgía: Assisi 2001, Citadella 400 pp. €27.37 [PaVi 47/5, 58—Giavini, Giovanni].

7294 **Thoennes, K. Erik** A biblical theology of godly human jealousy. Diss. Trinity Evang. Divinity 2001, 395 pp. 3003786.

7295 *Tillesse, Caetano Minette de* Ecclesiologia 6: o matrimônio em círculos o homem à imagem de Deus. RBBras 18 (2001) 379-406.

7296 **Tosato, Angelo** Il matrimonio israelitico: una teoria generale. AnBib 100: R [2]2001 <1982>, E.P.I.B. xxvi; 278 pp. €20. 88-7653-100-9. Nuova prefazione, presentazione, bibliografia.

7297 *Trublet, Jacques* Entre le temps et l'éternité: l'aujourd'hui dans la bible. Christus 48 (2001) 287-297 [Qoh 3,1-15].

7298 *Vanhoye, Albert* Milosierdzie w biblii [Mercy in the bible]. Pastores 13/4 (2001) 9-17 [AcBib 10,1032]. **P**.

7299 *Waschke, Ernst Joachim* 'Was ist der Mensch, daß du seiner gedenkst?' (Ps 8,5): theologische und anthropologische Koordinaten für die Frage nach dem Menschen im Kontext anthropologischer Aussagen. Der Gesalbte. 2001 <1991> ⇒227. 207-219.

7300 *Wendt, Matthias* Kirche und Sexualität;

7301 Die Verdrängung der Ursache des Leidens in den Religionen. Irreale Glaubensinhalte. 2001 ⇒1066. 51-52/23-38.

7302 *Wenzel, Knut* Erinnern—Versprechen—Vergeben: zur jesuanischen Dimension personalen Selbstvollzugs. [F]SCHMUTTERMAYR, G. 2001 ⇒ 101. 625-651.

7303 *Wetzel, Christoph* Biblische Paare. Schön bist du. 2001 ⇒274. 26-7.

7304 *Wilcken, John* Matthew 5.17-19 and aboriginal christians (part 2). ACR 78 (2001) 259-270.

7305 *Wirsching, Johannes* "So ihr nicht werdet wie die Kinder ...": der spielende Mensch und der Mensch des Evangeliums. LuThK 25/2 (2001) 73-84.

7306 **Zimmermann, Ruben** Geschlechtermetaphorik und Gottesverhältnis: Traditionsgeschichte und Theologie eines Bildfelds in Urchristentum und antiker Umwelt. WUNT 2/122: Tü 2001, Mohr xxv; 791 pp. €91. 3-16-147374-4. Bibl. 713-758.

7307 **Zuccotti, Ferdinando** Il giuramento nel mondo giuridico e religioso antico. 2000 ⇒16,7457. ᴿFilTeo 15 (2001) 643-645 (*Spera, Salvatore*); SapDom 54 (2001) 112-113 (*Spera, Salvatore*).

H2.8 Œcologia VT & NT—*saecularitas*

7308 **Bernal, Lisa Villanueva** Embodied relations and good human action: bases for a christian eco-justice ethic of creation. Diss. Princeton Theol. Sem. 2001, 239 pp. 3006841.

7309 **Boersema, Jan J.** The Torah and the Stoics on humankind and nature: a contribution to the debate on sustainability and quality. Lei 2001, Brill ix; 322 pp. $75. 90-04-11886-1. Bibl. 253-305.

7310 **Bouma-Prediger, Steven** For the beauty of the earth: a christian vision for creation care. GR 2001, Baker 234 pp. $22. 0-8010-2298-3 [Interp. 58,94—Towner, W. Sibley].

7311 *Draught, Gary F.* What if I don't want to compete against my neighbor down the road?. ᶠJANZEN, W. 2001 ⇒54. 198-207.

7312 *Field, David N.* The gospel, the church and the earth: reflections on an ecological ecclesiology. JTSA 111 (2001) 67-79.

7313 *Frymer-Kensky, Tikva* The end of the world and the limits of biblical ecology. ᶠBETZ, H. 2001 ⇒5. 15-26.

7314 *O'Mahony, Donal* An emerging christian perspective on ecology, as shaped by scripture, cosmology and contemporary science. JDh 26/1 (2001) 96-120.

7315 **Toolan, David** At home in the cosmos. Mkn 2001, Orbis xiii; 257 pp. $25. 1-57075-341-5 [ThD 48,290—Heiser, W. Charles].

7316 *Uehlinger, Christoph* Dem Segen Raum geben: biblische Impulse für eine umweltverträgliche Anthropologie. Diak. 32 (2001) 393-400.

7317 *Wahle, Hedwig* Human responsibility for God's creation in Jewish teaching and practice. JDh 26/1 (2001) 60-86.

H3.1 *Foedus*—The Covenant; *the Chosen People, Providence*

7318 **Bader-Saye, Scott** Church and Israel after christendom: the politics of election. 1999 ⇒15,9796; 16,7466. [R]ProEc 10/1 (2001) 108-110 (*Sonderegger, Katherine*).

7319 *Glorieux, Jean-Marie* Figures d'alliance: pédagogie de la liberté humaine et don de l'Esprit. VieCon 73 (2001) 364-378.

7320 **Gräbe, Petrus J.** Der neue Bund in der frühchristlichen Literatur: unter Berücksichtigung der alttestamentlich-jüdischen Vorausset-zungen. FzB 96: Wü 2001, Echter x; 246 pp. €19.90. 3-429-02247-9. Bibl. 211-233.

7321 **Groß, Walter** Zukunft für Israel: Alttestamentliche Bundeskonzepte und die aktuelle Debatte um den Neuen Bund. SBS 176: 1998 ⇒14, 6674; 16,7474. [R]ThRv 97 (2001) 114-116 (*Vogel, Manuel*).

7322 *Guenther, Titus F.* Missionary vision and practice in the Old Testa-ment. [F]JANZEN, W. 2001 ⇒54. 146-164.

7323 *Lemański, Janusz* Izrael jako krzew winny oraz winnica Jahwe w tek-stach Starego Testamentu. [F]JANKOWSKI, A. 2001 ⇒53. 220-239. **P.**

7324 *Lohfink, Norbert* La noción bíblica de alianza y el diálogo judeo-cri-stiano. CuesTP 28 (2001) 7-22;

7325 Ein Bund oder zwei Bünde in der Heiligen Schrift. L'interpretazione della bibbia nella chiesa. 2001 ⇒471. 273-297.

7326 **Novak, David** L'elezione d'Israele: l'idea di popolo eletto. [E]*Bassani, Franco*: BCR 64: Brescia 2001, Paideia 323 pp. €29.44. 88-394-0615-8. Bibl. 299-311.

7327 *Pieris, Aloysius* Multi-ethnic peoplehood and the God of the bible: a comment on the true nature of Yahweh's election of Israel. Dialogue 28 (2001) 66-78.

7328 **Römer, Thomas** Le peuple élu et les autres: l'Ancien Testament entre exclusion et ouverture. 1997 ⇒14,6683. [R]EstB 59 (2001) 108 (*Asenjo, J.*).

7329 *Salzmann, Jorg C.* Wer gehört zu Gottes Volk?: alttestamentliche Perspektiven zur Frage nach Volk, Gottesvolk und Mission. LuThK 25/3 (2001) 175-190.

7330 **Shepherd, Norman** The call of grace: how the covenant illuminates salvation and evangelism. 2000 ⇒16,7485. [R]TrinJ 22 (2001) 131-136 (*Karlberg, Mark W.*).

7331 *Troiani, Lucio* La circoncisione nel Nuovo Testamento e la testimo-nianza degli autori greci e latini. Verus Israel. 2001 ⇒524. 95-107.

7332 *Vanhoye, Albert* Réaction à l'exposé du Prof. Norbert Lohfink "Ein Bund oder zwei Bünde in der Heiligen Schrift". L'interpretazione del-la bibbia nella chiesa. 2001 ⇒471. 298-303.

7333   *Waschke, Ernst Joachim* Ein Volk aus vielen Völkern: die Frage
       nach Israel als die Frage nach dem Bekenntnis seiner Erwählung. Der
       Gesalbte. 2001 <1991> ⇒227. 235-252.
7334   **Wells, Jo Bailey** God's holy people: a theme in biblical theology.
       JSOT.S 305: 2000 ⇒16,7489. ᴿCBQ 63 (2001) 536-537 (*Dempsey,
       Carol J.*); Evangel 19 (2001) 88-89 (*Wilson, Alistair I.*).

H3.5 *Liturgia, spiritualitas VT*—OT prayer

7335   **Berger, Klaus** ¿Qué es la espiritualidad bíblica?: fuentes de la místi-
       ca cristiana. ᵀ*Tosaus Abadía, José Pedro*: El pozo de Siquem 127:
       Sdr 2001, Sal Terrae 232 pp. 84-293-1416-4.
7336   *Berghuis, Kent D.* A biblical perspective on fasting. BS 158 (2001)
       86-103.
7337   **Brunette, Pierre** Nos passos de Abraão. ᵀ*Vilela, Magno José*:
       Estudos bíblicos: São Paulo 2001, Paulinas 110 pp [REB 61,754].
7338   **Crainshaw, Jill Y.** Wise and discerning hearts: an introduction to
       wisdom liturgical theology. 2000 ⇒16,7494. ᴿThTo 58 (2001) 446,
       448 (*Huwiler, Elizabeth*).
7339   *Daval, Marcel* A palavra 'semente' no Antigo Testamento. Grande
       Sinal 55 (2001) 671-679.
7340   *Dohmen, Christoph* Am Ende muss gefeiert werden: Ex 24,11 und
       der Sijjum. ᶠSCHMUTTERMAYR, G. 2001 ⇒101. 27-36.
7341   ᴱ**Franz, Ansgar** Streit am Tisch des Wortes?: zur Deutung und Be-
       deutung des Alten Testaments und seiner Verwendung in der Litur-
       gie. PiLi 8: 1997 ⇒13,7034; 15,7493. ᴿALW 43-44 (2001-2002)
       128-132 (*Klöckener, Martin*).
7342   **Gafus, Georg** Das Alte Testament in der Perikopenordnung: bibel-
       theologische Perspektiven zur Auswahl der Lesungen an den Sonn-
       und Feiertagen. EHS.T 687: 2000 ⇒16,7496. ᴿThPQ 149 (2001)
       316-317 (*Haunerland, Winfried*).
7343   *Miller, Patrick D.* Prayer and worship. CTJ 36 (2001) 53-62.
7344   *Mosès, Stéphane* Tre preghiere per lo straniero. L'Eros e la legge.
       Schulim Vogelmann 80: 2001 <1997> ⇒185. 137-151.
7345   **Newman, Judith Hood** Praying by the book: the scripturalization of
       prayer in Second Temple Judaism. 1999 ⇒15,7505; 16,7501. ᴿCBQ
       63 (2001) 123-124 (*Hensell, Eugene*).
7346   *O'Kennedy, D.F.* Gebed en ou-testamentiese teologie. AcTh(B) 21/1
       (2001) 124-145.
7347   **Secondin, Bruno** La lettura orante della Parola: "Lectio divina" in
       comunità e in parrocchia. Padova 2001, Messaggero 288 pp. €17.50.
       88-250-0996-8.

7348 *Seitz, Christopher R.* Prayer in the Old Testament or Hebrew Bible. Into God's presence. 2001 ⇒294. 3-22.

7349 **Tita, Hubert** Gelübde als Bekenntnis: eine Studie zu den Gelübden im Alten Testament. OBO 181: Gö 2001, Vandenhoeck & R xvii; 251 pp. FS78. 3-525-53995-9. Bibl. 233-246.

7350 **Werline, Rodney Alan** Penitential prayer in second temple Judaism: the development of a religious institution. SBL Early Judaism and Its Literature 13: 1998 ⇒14,6742. [R]JBL 120 (2001) 550-552 (*Balentine, Samuel E.*).

H3.7 *Theologia moralis*—OT moral theology

7351 **Ball, Milner S.** Called by stories: biblical sagas and their challenge for law 2000 ⇒16,7511. [R]ThTo 58 (2001)94, 96-97 (*Brueggemann, Walter*).

7352 *Birch, Bruce C.* Old Testament ethics. The Blackwell companion to the Hebrew Bible. 2001 ⇒653. 293-307.

7353 **Blomberg, Craig L.** Neither poverty nor riches: a biblical theology of material possessions. New Studies in Biblical Theology 7: 1999 ⇒ 15,7511; 16,7514. [R]RBLit 3 (2001) 108-111 (*Reed, Stephen A.*).

7354 **Brown, William P.** The ethos of the cosmos: the genesis of moral imagination in the bible. 1999 ⇒15,7514; 16,7515. [R]ThTo 58 (2001) 442, 444, 446 (*Fager, Jeffrey A.*).

7355 *Holloway, Jeph* "From the beginning": the moral vision of Genesis 1-11. SWJT 44/1 (2001) 76-92.

7356 *Jeon, Jeong Koo* Covenant theology and Old Testament ethics: Meredith G. Kline's intrusion ethics. Kerux 16/1 (2001) 3-32.

7357 *Kegler, Jürgen* Das Zinsverbot in der hebräischen Bibel. Gesammelte Aufsätze. BEAT 48: 2001 <1992> ⇒167. 261-277 [Ex 22,24].

7358 *Kietliński, Krzysztof* Podstawy zobowiazań moralnych Izraela w nauczaniu proroków z VIII w. przed Chr. CoTh 71/4 (2001) 25-38. **P**.

7359 *Knierim, Rolf P.* Sünde II: Altes Testament. TRE 32 (2001) 365-372.

7360 *Koch, Timothy R.* A homoerotic approach to scripture. Theology and sexuality 14 (2001) 10-22 [2 Kgs 1,2-8].

7361 Cruising as methodology: homoeroticism and the scriptures [Judg 3,12-26; 2 Kgs 1,2-8; 2,23-25];

7362 *Liew, Tat-siong Benny* (Cor)Responding: a letter to the editor. Queer commentary. JSOT.S 334: 2001 ⇒325. 169-180/182-192.

7363 *Loader, James Alfred* Tertium datur: zum Wahrheitsbegriff der 'Ethischen Theologie'. Begegnung mit Gott. 2001 ⇒175. 291-301.

7364 **Mills, Mary E.** Biblical morality: moral perspectives in Old Testament narratives. Heythrop studies in contemporary philosophy, religion and theology: Aldershot 2001, Ashgate vii; 270 pp. £45/17. 0-7546-1579-0/80-4. Bibl. 263-270.

7365 **Neville, Richard W.** The relevance of creation and righteousness to intervention for the poor and needy in the Old Testament. Diss. Univ. of Cambridge 2001, ^D*Emerton, J.A.* [TynB 52,307-310].

7366 *Niccacci, Alviero* Giustizia e giustificazione nell'Antico Testamento. Giustizia-giustificazione nella bibbia. DSBP 28: 2001 ⇒307. 19-106.

7367 **Nissinen, Martti** Homoeroticism in the biblical world: a historical perspective. 1998 ⇒14,6771; 16,7524. ^RJBL 120 (2001) 143-145 (*Brawley, Robert L.*).

7368 *Provan, Iain* 'All these I have kept since I was a boy' (Luke 18:21): creation, covenant, and the commandments of God. ExAu 17 (2001) 31-46.

7369 *Reimer, Haroldo* Leis de mercado e direito dos pobres na Biblia Hebraica. Estudos Bíblicos 69 (2001) 9-18.

7370 **Rodd, Cyril S.** Glimpses of a strange land: studies in Old Testament ethics. Old Testament Studies: E 2001, Clark xiv; 402 pp. £30. 0-567-08753-0. Bibl. 335-364.

7371 *Rogerson, John W.* The Old Testament and christian ethics. Cambridge Companion to christian ethics. 2001 ⇒698. 29-41 [BuBB 35,78].

7372 **Ro, Un-Sok** Die sogenannte 'Armenfrömmigkeit' im nachexilischen Israel. Diss. Müns 2001, ^D*Pohlmann, K.F.* [RTL 33,634].

7373 *Sanders, Paul* Toen zei David: God verdoeme mij ... NedThT 55/4 (2001) 286-300.

7374 **Schroeder, Christoph O.** History, justice, and the agency of God: a hermeneutical and exegetical investigation on Isaiah and Psalms. BiblInterp 52: Lei 2001, Brill xiv; 236 pp. $79. 90-04-11991-4. Bibl. 225-229.

7375 **Segbers, Franz** Die Hausordnung der Tora: biblische Impulse für eine theologische Wirtschaftsethik. 1999 ⇒15,7538; 16,7529. ^RFrRu 8 (2001) 223-225 (*Zademach, Wieland*).

7376 *Spencer, Daniel T.* A gay male ethicist's response to queer readings on the bible. Queer commentary. JSOT.S 334: 2001 ⇒325. 193-209.

7377 *Stone, Ken* Queer commentary and biblical interpretation: an introduction. Queer commentary. JSOT.S 334: 2001 ⇒325. 11-34.

7378 **Verkindère, Gérard** La justicia en el Antiguo Testamento. Cuadernos bíblicos 105: Estella (Navarra) 2001, Verbo Divino 61 pp. 84-8169-421-5.

7379 **Wenham, Gordon J.** Story as torah: reading the Old Testament ethically. Old Testament Studies: 2000 ⇒16,7534. [R]ET 112 (2001) 327-328 (*Rodd, C.S.*).

7380 *Witte, Markus* Vom Wesen der alttestamentlichen Ethik. Religionskultur. 2001 ⇒6713. 139-161 [BuBB 35,72].

H3.8 *Bellum et pax VT-NT*—War and peace in the whole Bible

7381 *Bovati, Pietro* 'Per dirigere i nostri passi sulla via della pace' (Lc. 1,79): l'educazione alla pace nella sacra scrittura. Seminarium (2001) 717-741.

7382 **Boyd, Gregory A.** God at war: the bible and spiritual conflict. 1997 ⇒13,7104; 14,6792. [R]JBL 119 (2000) 114-116 (*Miller, Patrick D.*).

7383 *Brueggemann, Walter* Voice as counter to violence. CTJ 36 (2001) 22-33 [Ps 39].

7384 **Brueggemann, Walter** Peace. Understanding biblical themes: Saint Louis 2001, Chalice 205 pp. $25. 0-8272-3828-2 [BiTod 40,58—Bergant, Dianne].

7385 **Cazeaux, Jacques** La guerre sainte n'aura pas lieu. LeDiv 185: P 2001, Cerf 463 pp. €38.11. 2-204-06609-5.

7386 *Crisp, Beth R.* Reading scripture from a hermeneutic of rape. Theology and sexuality 14 (2001) 23-42.

7387 *Crüsemann, Frank* Damit "Kain nicht Kain wird": die Wurzeln der Gewalt und ihre Überwindung in biblischer Sicht. Evangelische Aspekte 11/3 (2001) 40-45.

7388 *Gonsalves, Francis* Gods of war and wars of God: religions and violence in contemporary society. Jahrbuch für kontextuelle Theologien 9 (2001) 33-59.

7389 *Herrmann, Wolfgang* Gott und Gewalt: vier Perspektiven. DtPfrBl 101 (2001) 627-633.

7390 *Lazar, Roy Anthonisamy* Peace on earth in spite of religions?. Jahrbuch für kontextuelle Theologien 9 (2001) 80-102.

7391 **Lefebure, Leo D.** Revelation, the religions, and violence. 2000 ⇒16, 7548. [R]AThR 83 (2001) 884-886 (*Webb, Stephen H.*).

7392 **McCarthy, Patricia** The word of God—the word of peace. ColMn 2001, Liturgical xii; 154 pp. $8. 0-8146-2789-7.

7393 *Moser, Barry* Blood and stone: violence in the bible and the eye of the illustrator. CrossCur 51/2 (2001) 219-228.

7394 *Müllner, Ilse* Die Gewalt benennen: Liebe und Eros ... und Gewalt in biblischen Texten. WUB 21 (2001) 59-63.

7395 *Ntambue Tshimbulu, Raphaël* Religions et violences: "une" lecture africaine. Jahrbuch für kontextuelle Theologien 9 (2001) 60-79.

7396 **Otto, Eckart** Krieg und Frieden in der Hebräischen Bibel und im Alten Orient. 1999 ⇒15,7557. ᴿCBQ 63 (2001) 323-325 (*Morschauser, Scott*); ThLZ 126 (2001) 1138-1139 (*Kessler, Rainer*).

7397 *Rayan, Samuel* Peace: biblical perspectives. JPJRS 4/2 (2001) 101-120.

7398 **Schwager, Raymund** Must there be scapegoats?: violence and redemption in the bible. 2000 <1987> ⇒16,7555. ᴿRfR 60 (2001) 551-552 (*Asen, Bernhard A.*); JThS 52 (2001) 706-709 (*Finlan, Stephen*).

7399 *Wénin, André* 'Le Seigneur est un homme de guerre'. Christus 48 (2001) 403-411.

H4.1 Messianismus

7400 *Alarcón, Juan José* La exposición 19 de Afrates *Contra los judíos*. Sef. 61 (2001) 227-242 Res., sum. 242.

7401 *Beall, Todd S.* History and eschatology at Qumran: Messiah. Judaism in late antiquity, 5: the Judaism of Qumran, 2. 2001 ⇒426. 125-146.

7402 **Bensussan, Gérard** Le temps messianique: temps historique et temps vécu. P 2001, Vrin 190 pp.

7403 **Cohn-Sherbok, Dan** Messianic Judaism. 2000 ⇒16,7565. ᴿThLZ 126 (2001) 1238-1239 (*Feldtkeller, Andreas*).

7404 *David, Pablo* The roots of collective messianism in Deutero-Isaiah and Daniel. Charism, leadership. 2001 ⇒456. 12-47. Reaction by *J.A.N. Aquino* 48-51; *C.G. Lingad* 52-55; *B. Dianzon* 56-61.

7405 *Gallego, Epifanio* Jesús, Mesías, en los evangelios. BiFe 27 (2001) 191-224.

7406 *Giesen, Heinz* Die Qumrangemeinde: ihre Texte und ihre Messiasvorstellungen. ThG 44 (2001) 142-149.

7407 *Hentschel, Georg* Tajemnica Wcielenia w perspektywie Starego Testamentu. CoTh 71/3 (2001) 17-29. **P**.

7408 **Horbury, William** Jewish messianism and the cult of Christ. 1998 ⇒14,6831... 16,7577. ᴿVT 51 (2001) 285-286 (*Baer, D.A.*); JBL 119 (2000) 351-353 (*Pomykala, Kenneth E.*).

7409 **Idel, Moshe** Messianic mystics. 1998 ⇒14,6833. ᴿJud. 57 (2001) 58-62 (*Necker, Gerold*).

7410 *Jongeneel, Jan A.B.* The messianic expectations and beliefs of Israel. ꟳKAROTEMPREL, S. 2001 ⇒57. 272-283.

7411 **Knohl, Israel** The messiah before Jesus: the suffering servant of the Dead Sea scrolls. ᵀ*Maisel, David* 2000 ⇒16,7581. ᴿDSD 8 (2001) 315-318 (*O'Neill, John C.*); Prudentia 33 (2001) 176-178 (*McKechnie, Paul*); HebStud 42 (2001) 367-371 (*Troxel, Ronald L.*);

7412 L'autre Messie. *TVeyret, Gabriel-Raphaël*: P 2001, Michel 190 pp. €14.94. [R]EeV 45 (2001) 19-20 (*Grelot, Pierre*).

7413 **Laato, Antti J.** A star is rising: the historical development of the OT royal ideology and the rise of the Jewish messianic expectations. 1998 ⇒14,6837; 15,7583. [R]JSSt 46 (2001) 147-151 (*Pomykala, Kenneth*).

7414 *Laperrousaz, E.-M.* Prophète, roi, prêtre, messie, principes ézéchiéliens et Judée postexilique entre modèles bibliques et réinterprétations intertestamentaires. TEuph 22 (2001) 79-96.

7415 *Marcus, Joel* The once and future messiah in early christianity and Chabad. NTS 47 (2001) 381-401.

7416 **Molka, Jacek** Mesjanizm biblijny w świetle tekstów z groty czwartiej w Qumran [Le messianisme biblique à la lumière des textes de la quatrième grotte de Qumran]. Diss. Lublin 2001, [D]*Tronina, A.* xxxvi; 204 pp [RTL 33,633]. P.

7417 *Müller, Denis* Le Christ, relève de la loi (Romains 10,4): la possibilité d'une éthique messianique à la suite de Giorgio Agamben. SR 30 (2001) 51-63 Rés., sum. 51.

7418 *Nerel, Gershon* Primitive Jewish christians in the modern thought of Messianic Jews. Le judéo-christianisme. 2001 ⇒484. 399-425 [BuBB 36,112].

7419 *Quelle, Constantino* La filiación divina y la expectación mesiánica en el Antiguo Testamento. BiFe 27 (2001) 163-190.

7420 **Rose, Wolter H.** Zemah and Zerubbabel: Messianic expectations in the early postexilic period. JSOT.S 304: 2000 ⇒16,7592. [R]JSJ 32 (2001) 341-344 (*Xeravits, Géza*); CBQ 63 (2001) 127-128 (*Redditt, Paul L.*); JJS 52 (2001) 361-363 (*Rooke, Deborah*).

7421 *Schaller, Berndt* Jüdische und christliche Messiaserwartungen. Fundamenta Judaica. StUNT 25: 2001 <1993> ⇒206. 201-210.

7422 [E]**Schäfer, Peter; Cohen, Mark R.** Toward the millennium: messianic expectations from the Bible to Waco. SHR 77: 1998 ⇒14,264; 16,324. [R]JR 81 (2001) 325-327 (*Collins, John J.*).

7423 *Schreiber, Stefan* König JHWH und königlicher Gesalbter: das Repräsentanzverhältnis in 4Q174. SNTU.A 26 (2001) 205-219.

7424 **Schreiber, Stefan** Gesalbter und König: Titel und Konzeptionen der königlichen Gesalbtenerwartung in frühjüdischen und urchristlichen Schriften. BZNT 105: 2000 ⇒16,7596. [R]RHPhR 81 (2001) 222-223 (*Grappe, Ch.*); BiLi 74 (2001) 203-204 (*Scholtissek, Klaus*); ThLZ 126 (2001) 1275-1278 (*Karrer, Martin*).

7425 *Schreiner, Stefan* "Der Messias kommt zuerst nach Polen": Jakob FRANKs Idee von Polen als gelobtem Land und ihre Vorgeschichte. Jud. 57 (2001) 242-268.

7426 *Shenk, Calvin E.* The Middle Eastern Jesus: Messianic Jewish and Palestinian christian understandings. Miss. 29 (2001) 403-416.

7427 **Stefani, Piero** Luce per le genti: prospettive messianiche ebraiche e fede cristiana. 1999 ⇒15,7598. [R]RSEc 19 (2001) 152-154 (*Morandini, Simone*).

7428 *Tromp, Johannes* The Davidic Messiah in Jewish eschatology of the first century BCE. Restoration. JSJ.S 72: 2001 ⇒319. 179-201.

7429 *Waschke, Ernst Joachim* Wurzeln und Ausprägung messianischer Vorstellungen im Alten Testament: eine traditionsgeschichtliche Untersuchung. Der Gesalbte. 2001 <1986> ⇒227. 3-104;

7430 Die Frage nach dem Messias im Alten Testament als Problem alttestamentlicher Theologie und biblischer Hermeneutik. Der Gesalbte. 2001 <1998> ⇒227. 157-169.

7431 *Weinfeld, Moshe* The roots of the messianic idea. Mythology and mythologies. 2001 ⇒589. 279-287.

7432 **Zimmermann, Johannes** Messianische Texte aus Qumran. WUNT 2/104: 1998 ⇒14,6864... 16,7603. [R]NT 43 (2001) 193-196 (*Schnabel, Eckhard J.*); BiOr 58 (2001) 239-242 (*Brooke, George J.*); RdQ 20 (2001) 321-322 (*Song, Chang-Hyun Michel*).

H4.3 *Eschatologia VT*—OT hope of future life

7433 *Albani, Matthias* 'Der HERR tötet und macht lebendig: er führt in die Unterwelt hinab und wieder herauf': zur Problematik der Auferstehungshoffnung im Alten Testament am Beispiel von 1 Sam 2,6. Leqach 1 (2001) 22-55 [BuBB 36,112].

7434 *Ausín, Santiago* La escatología en el Antiguo Testamento. ScrTh 33 (2001) 701-732.

7435 *Berlejung, Angelika* Tod und Leben nach den Vorstellungen der Israeliten: ein ausgewählter Aspekt zu einer Metapher im Spannungsfeld von Leben und Tod. Das biblische Weltbild. 2001 ⇒285. 465-502.

7436 *Bieberstein, Klaus* Die Pforte der Gehenna: die Entstehung der eschatologischen Erinnerungslandschaft Jerusalems. Das biblische Weltbild. FAT 32: 2001 ⇒285. 503-539.

7437 *Gilbert, Maurice* Immortalité? résurrection?: faut-il choisir?: témoignage du judaïsme ancien. Le judaïsme à l'aube de l'ère chrétienne. LeDiv 186: 2001 ⇒450. 271-297.

7438 **Gowan, Donald E.** Eschatology in the Old Testament. 2000 <1986> ⇒16,7608. [R]BiOr 58 (2001) 236-238 (*Becking, Bob*); OLZ 96 (2001) 257-261 (*Kaiser, Otto*).

7439 *Grappe, Christian* Naissance de l'idée de résurrection dans le judaïsme. Résurrection: l'après-mort. MoBi 45: 2001 ⇒296. 45-72.

7440 **Grey, Mary C.** The outrageous pursuit of hope: prophetic dreams for the twenty-first century. NY 2001, Crossroad vii; 118 pp. $15. 0-8245-1882-9. Sarum Lectures [ThD 48,271—Heiser, W. Charles].

7441 *Jedrzejewski, Sylwester* Jôm Jahwe jako kategoria eschatologiczna. CoTh 71/1 (2001) 51-59. **P.**

7442 *Jones, Ivor H.* Disputed questions in biblical studies, 4: exile and eschatology. ET 112 (2001) 401-405.

7443 *Lang, Bernhard* Vom *deus ludens* zum *deus victor*: Paradigmen biblischer Eschatologie. Abendländische Eschatologie. 2001 ⇒523. 61-74.

7444 *Pasquetto, Virgilio* La speranza del credente in Dio nella tradizione dell'Antico Testamento, 1-2. RVS 55 (2001) 6-30, 126-145.

7445 *Tamayo-Acosta, Juan-José* Prospettiva biblica: tra l'escatologia e l'apocalittica. Conc(I) 37 (2001) 284-295; Conc(E) 290, 247-255; Conc(GB) 2000/1, 65-73; Conc(D) 137, 190-198; Conc(F) 290,71-9.

7446 **Vos, Geerhardus** The eschatology of the Old Testament. [E]*Dennison, James T.*: Phillipsburg, NJ 2001, Presbyterian and Reformed ix; 176 pp. $12. 0-87552-181-9.

H4.5 *Theologia totius VT*—General Old Testament theology

7447 **Anderson, Bernhard Word** Contours of Old Testament Theology. 1999 ⇒15,7610; 16,7616. [R]TJT 17 (2001) 279-280 (*Peckham, Brian*); JBL 119 (2000) 749-750 (*Kselman, John S.*).

7448 *Bail, Ulrike* Von zerstörten Räumen und Barfußgehen: Anmerkungen zu Text-Räumen der Enge in der Hebräischen Bibel. EvTh 61/2 (2001) 92-101 [2 Sam 13; Mic 1,8].

7449 **Barr, James** The concept of biblical theology: an Old Testament perspective. 1999 ⇒15,7611; 16,7618. [R]JR 81 (2001) 298-299 (*Fretheim, Terence E.*); RStR 27 (2001) 233-238 (*Bellis, Alice Ogden*); JBL 120 (2001) 146-149 (*Anderson, Bernhard*); BTB 31 (2001) 44-52 (*Gnuse, Robert*); AUSS 39 (2001) 137-140 (*Pröbstle, Martin*); LouvSt 26 (2001) 180-181 (*Palmer, Sydney*).

7450 *Bellis, Alice Ogden* Walter BRUEGGEMANN and James BARR: Old Testament theology and inclusivity. RStR 27 (2001) 233-238.

7451 **Brueggemann, Walter** Theology of the Old Testament. 1997 ⇒13, 7170... 16,7623. [R]RStR 27 (2001) 233-238 (*Bellis, Alice Ogden*); AUSS 39 (2001) 140-142 (*Mattingly, Keith*); BN 110 (2001) 55-65 (*Čapek, Filip*); BTB 31 (2001) 90-95 (*Gnuse, Robert K.*).

7452 *Capek, Filip* The double rhetoric of BRUEGGEMANN's theology: hegemony as a rhetorical construct. CV 43/1 (2001) 60-76 = BN 110 (2001) 55-65.

7453 *Chopineau, Jacques* Toute théologie n'est-elle pas géocentrique?. AnBru 6 (2001) 26-36.

7454 *Dafni, Evangelia G.* Natürliche Theologie im Lichte des hebräischen und griechischen Alten Testaments. ThZ 57 (2001) 295-310.

7455 **Gerstenberger, Erhard S.** Theologien im Alten Testament: Pluralität und Synkretismus alttestamentlichen Gottesglaubens. Stu 2001, Kohlhammer 270 pp. €22.50. 3-17-015974-7. Bibl. 257-259.

7456 *Keel, Othmar* Religionsgeschichte Israels oder Theologie des Alten Testaments?. Wieviel Systematik?. QD 185: 2001 ⇒283. 88-109.

7457 *Loader, James Alfred* Logos spermatikos: die Sämlinge der Theologie. Begegnung mit Gott. 2001 ⇒175. 325-339.

7458 *Lohfink, Norbert* Alttestamentliche Wissenschaft als Theologie?: 44 Thesen. Wieviel Systematik?. QD 185: 2001 ⇒283. 13-47.

7459 *Martens, Elmer A.* The history of religion, biblical theology, and exegesis. Interpreting the OT. 2001 ⇒248. 177-199.

7460 **Melanchthon, Monica J.** Rejection by God: the history and significance of the rejection motif in the Hebrew Bible. Studies in Biblical Literature 22: NY 2001, Lang xix; 287 pp. $62. 0-8204-4577-0. Bibl. 259-277.

7461 *Murphy, Roland E.* Once again—the 'center' of the Old Testament. BTB 31 (2001) 85-89.

7462 **Nobile, Marco** Teologia dell'Antico Testamento. 1998 ⇒15,7620; 16,7642. [R]CBQ 63 (2001) 124-125 (*Boadt, Lawrence*).

7463 **Preuss, Horst Dietrich** Teología del Antiguo Testament, 1-2. 1999 ⇒15,7622; 16,7644. [R]EfMex 19 (2001) 284-285 (*López Rosas, Ricardo*).

7464 **Rad, Gerhard von** Old Testament theology. [T]*Stalker, D.M.G.*: OTL: LVL 2001 <1965>, Westminster 2 vols; xxxv; xiv; 470 pp. $30 + 30. 0-664-22407-5/8-3. Introd. *Walter Brueggemann* [ThD 48,384— Heiser, W. Charles].

7465 *Rendtorff, Rolf* Israels "Rest": unabgeschlossene Überlegungen zu einem schwierigen Thema der alttestamentlichen Theologie. Der Text in seiner Endgestalt. 2001 ⇒201. 265-271.

7466 **Rendtorff, Rolf** Theologie des Alten Testaments: ein kanonischer Entwurf, 1: kanonische Grundlegung. 1999 ⇒15,7625; 16,7647. [R]ThRv 97 (2001) 220-222 (*Groß, Walter*); ThPQ 149 (2001) 414-415 (*Hubmann, Franz*);

7467 2: thematische Entfaltung. Neuk 2001, Neuk ix; 353 pp. €24.90. 3-7887-1662-2;

7468 Teologia dell'Antico Testamento: v.1, sviluppo canonico. [T]*Di Pasquale, Marco*: Strumenti Biblica 5: T 2001, Claudiana 478 pp. 88-7016-365-2. Bibl. 449-467.

7469 *Reventlow, Henning Graf* Modern approaches to Old Testament theology. The Blackwell companion to the Hebrew Bible. Blackwell companions to religion 3: 2001 ⇒653. 221-240.

7470 *Rofé, Alexander* Il divenire del testo ebraico: correzioni di carattere teologico nella Bibbia Ebraica. RStB 13/1 (2001) 95-104.

7471 *Schenker, Adrian* Gott als Stifter der Religionen der Welt: unerwartete Früchte textgeschichtlicher Forschung. ᶠSCHENKER, A., OBO 179: 2001 ⇒100. 99-102 [Dt 32,8; Ps 82,6-7; Mic 4,5].

7472 *Schmitt, Hans-Christoph* Religionsgeschichte Israels oder Theologie des Alten Testaments?. Theologie in Prophetie. 2001 <1995> ⇒209. 346-366.

7473 *Schwienhorst-Schönberger, Ludger* Einheit und Vielheit: gibt es eine sinnvolle Suche nach der Mitte des Alten Testaments?. Wieviel Systematik?. QD 185: 2001 ⇒283. 48-87.

7474 *Seifrid, Mark A.* Righteousness language in the Hebrew scriptures and early Judaism. Justification, 1. 2001 ⇒251. 415-442.

7475 *Spieckermann, Hermann* Die Liebeserklärung Gottes: Entwurf einer Theologie des Alten Testaments. Gottes Liebe zu Israel. FAT 33: 2001 <2000> ⇒215. 197-223.

7476 *Waschke, Ernst Joachim* Zur Frage nach einer alttestamentlichen Theologie im Vergleich zur Religionsgeschichte Israels <1995>;

7477 Die Einheit der Theologie heute als Anfrage an das Alte Testament: ein Plädoyer für die Vielfalt <1992>. Der Gesalbte. 2001 ⇒227. 253-266/267-277.

7478 *Wessels, W.J.* Ou Testament teologie: quo vadis?: 'n bydrae tot die voortgaande debat. OTEs 14 (2001) 330-344.

7479 *Wilson, Jonathan R.* Theology and the Old Testament. Interpreting the OT. 2001 ⇒248. 245-264.

H5.1 *Deus*—NT—God [as Father ⇒H1.4]

7480 *Biezeveld, Kune E.* God opnieuw denken?: een andere weg naar de godsleer. NedThT 55/3 (2001) 196-212.

7481 *Dabek, Tomasz Maria* Granice doświadczenia religijnego w Nowym Testamencie. ᶠJANKOWSKI, A. 2001 ⇒53. 109-117. P.

7482 *Kasiłowski, Piotr* Kłopoty z miłosierdziem [Les problèmes avec la miséricorde]. PrzPow 118 (2001) 269-281. P.

H5.2 **Christologia ipsius NT**

7483 *Alfeev, Ilarion* La discesa di Cristo agli inferi nei primi testi cristiani. La Nuova Europa 2 (2001) 49-61.

7484 **Bauckham, Richard** God crucified: monotheism and christology in the New Testament. 1999 ⇒15,7643; 16,7663. ᴿThTo 58 (2001) 98, 100, 102 (*Floyd, Richard L.*).

7485 *Baumert, Norbert* Jesus Christus—die endgültige Offenbarung Gottes: biblische Sicht. Studien zu den Paulusbriefen. SBAB 32: 2001 <1991> ⇒123. 215-238.

7486 *Brandt, Pierre-Yves; Lukinovich, Alessandra* L'adresse à Jésus dans les évangiles synoptiques. Bib. 82 (2001) 17-50.

7487 **Brown, Raymond E.** Introducción a la cristología del Nuevo Testamento. Biblioteca de Estudios Bíblicos 97: S 2001, Sígueme 256 pp. 84-301-1325-8. ᴿSalTer 89 (2001) 922-924 (*Sanz Giménez-Rico, Enrique*); CTom 128 (2001) 627-629 (*González Blanco, Rafael*).

7488 **Cavalcoli, Giovanni** La gloria di Christo. SacDo.M 46/1: Bo 2001, Dehoniane 186 pp.

7489 *Corsi, Santi* Per un cristocentrismo teologico. DT 104 (2001) 83-106. Appendice: Per una lettura di *Matteo 23,11*, pp 108-118.

7490 **Davis, Carl J.** The name and way of the Lord: Old Testament themes, New Testament christology. JSNT.S 129: 1996 ⇒12,6915; 13,7212. ᴿEvQ 73 (2001) 176-177 (*Mathewson, Dave*).

7491 *Dreyer, Yolanda* Names of Jesus in Matthew and Luke: a synchronic perspective. APB 12 (2001) 86-104.

7492 **Eskola, Timo** Messiah and the throne: Jewish merkabah mysticism and early christian exaltation discourse. WUNT 2/142: Tü 2001, Mohr xiv; 439 pp. €64. 3-16-147641-7. Bibl. 391-413.

7493 **Furlani, Maria Aparecida** Jesus, o Messias na condição de servo. Diss. de mestrado Belo Horizonte 2001, ᴰ*Palácio, Carlos* [REB 62, 495].

7494 *Garcia de Presno, Jostein* Hvem skapte egentlig verden?. Ung teologi 34/3 (2001) 23-32.

7495 *Garuti, Paolo* Il primogenito, immaggine del Dio invisibile: qualche spunto di cristologia da *Col* 1,15-20 ed *Ef* 2,14-18. DT(P) 104 (2001) 119-137.

7496 *Gebauer, Roland* Die Einzigartigkeit Jesu im Kontext hellenistischer Religionen. ThFPr 27/2 (2001) 74-90.

7497 **Gelpi, Donald L.** The firstborn of many: a christology for converting christians, 1: to hope in Jesus Christ; 2: synoptic narrative christology; 3: doctrinal and practical christology. Milwaukee 2001, Marquette Univ. Pr. 552+613+582 pp. $40+50+45. 087-4626-447/55/63.

7498 **Hogan, Maurice Patrick** Seeking Jesus of Nazareth: an introduction to the christology of the four gospels. Dublin 2001, Columba 160 pp. €11.41. 1-85607-331-9. Bibl. 160.

7499 *Houtman, Cornelis* God in een nieuwe gestalte: exegetische kanttekeningen bij het "Ad dexteram Dei". NedThT 55/1 (2001) 1-12.

7500 *Huber, Konrad* Jesus Christus im Spiegel der Evangelien. GuL 74 (2001) 406-419;

7501 Faszination der Person Jesu: Jesus Christus im Spiegel der Evangelien. Wort zum Leben. 2001 ⇒284. 95-112.

7502 *Jankowski, Augustyn* Mysterium Incarnationis jako poprawna i operatywna kategoria biblijna—Jej geneza i etapy objawienia w Nowym Testamencie. CoTh 71/3 (2001) 5-15. **P.**

7503 **Johnson, Luke Timothy** Living Jesus: learning the heart of the gospel. 1999 ⇒15,7669. [R]ThTo 57 (2001) 537-539 (*Black, C. Clifton*).

7504 **Karrer, Martin** Jesus Christus im Neuen Testament. GNT 11: 1998 ⇒14,6917; 15,7671. [R]JBL 119 (2000) 567-568 (*Frey, Jörg*).

7505 *Kasper, Walter* Jesus Christus—Gottes endgültiges Wort. IKaZ 30 (2001) 18-26.

7506 **Kozyra, Józef** Jezus Chrystus jako 'αρχη' [Jésus Christ en tant que 'αρχη']. Diss.-Habil. Lublin 2001[RTL 33,639]. **P.**

7507 **Kreplin, Matthias** Das Selbstverständnis Jesu: hermeneutische und christologische Reflexion: historisch-kritische Analyse. Diss. Zürich. WUNT 2/141: Tü 2001, Mohr S. xii; 393 pp. €59. 3-16-147633-6. Bibl. 349-363.

7508 **Lang, Hartmut G.** Christologie und Ostern: Untersuchungen im Grenzgebiet von Exegese und Systematik. TANZ 29: 1999 ⇒15, 7675. [R]ThLZ 126 (2001) 51-53 (*Becker, Jürgen*).

7509 **Liderbach, Daniel** Christ in the early christian hymns. 1998 ⇒14, 6919; 15,7677. [R]Theol. 104 (2001) 284-285 (*Yarnold, Edward*).

7510 *López Rosas, Ricardo* Diversidad de cristologías y un solo Cristo: repensar la cristología. Qol 27 (2001) 35-45.

7511 **Matera, Frank J.** New Testament christology. 1999 ⇒15,7681; 16, 7686. [R]EThL 77 (2001) 209-211 (*Verheyden, J.*); TJT 17 (2001) 294-295 (*Knight, James W.*); JBL 119 (2000) 764-766 (*Pilgrim, Walter E.*).

7512 *Monshouwer, Dirk* Biblical christology: 'Son of God' (Mark 1:1). [F]DEURLOO, K.: ACEBT.S 2: 2001 ⇒23. 281-291.

7513 **Mußner, Franz** Was hat Jesus Neues in die Welt gebracht?. Stu 2001, Katholisches Bibelwerk 80 pp. €8.60. 3-460-33165-8.

7514 **Penna, Romano** I ritratti originali di Gesù il Cristo: inizi e sviluppi della cristologia neotestamentaria: gli sviluppi. 1999 ⇒15,7690; 16, 7689. [R]CrSt 22 (2001) 213-216 (*Prigent, Pierre*).

7515 *Penna, Romano* Cristologia senza morte redentrice: un filone di pensiero del giudeo-cristianesimo più antico. Vangelo e inculturazione. 2001 ⇒193. 680-704 = Verus Israel. 2001 ⇒524. 68-94.

7516 *Piekarz, Danuta* Jezus Chrystus—pierworodny. [F]JANKOWSKI, A. 2001 ⇒53. 327-335. **P.**

7517 **Pikaza Ibarrondo, Xabier** Questo è l'uomo: manuale di cristologia. 1999 ⇒15,7693. ᴿAsp. 48 (2001) 459 (*Scognamiglio, Edoardo*).

7518 **Powers, Daniel G.** Salvation through participation: an examination of the notion of the believers' corporate unity with Christ in early christian soteriology. Diss. Leiden, ᴰ*Jonge, H.J. de*: Contributions to Biblical Exegesis and Theology 29: Lv 2001, Peeters (6) 267 pp. €35. 90-429-1049-6. Bibl. 237-257.

      Riley, G. One Jesus, many Christs 1997 ⇒4253.

7519 *Schrettle, Anton* Der Jude Jesus—der universale Christus. CPB 114 (2001) 10-14.

7520 **Schröter, Jens** Jesus und die Anfänge der Christologie: methodologische und exegetische Studien zu den Ursprüngen des christlichen Glaubens. BThSt 47: Neuk 2001, Neuk xi; 252 pp. €24.90. 3-7887-1877-3. Bibl. 225-244.

7521 *Schwemer, Anna Maria* Jesus Christus als Prophet, König und Priester: das *munus triplex* und die frühe Christologie. Der messianische Anspruch Jesu. Ment. *Eusebius C.*: 2001 ⇒276. 165-230.

7522 *Serrano, Vicente* La filiación divina de Jesús en el cristianismo primitivo. BiFe 27 (2001) 225-244.

7523 *Siebenrock, Roman A.* Das Geheimnis des Rabbi: eine Christologie der Begegnung. KatBl 126 (2001) 333-338.

7524 **Susin, L.C.** Così umano così divino: Gesù nella cristologia narrativa. Mi 2001, Paoline 263 pp. €8.26 [Asprenas 49,455s—Cumerlato, G.].

7525 **Sys, Jacques** Les imaginaires christologiques. Villeneuve d'Ascq 2000, Universitaires du Septentrion 285 pp.

7526 *Thompson, Marianne Meye* Jesus and his God. The Cambridge companion to Jesus. 2001 ⇒4236. 41-55.

7527 *White, R.E.O.* 'No one comes to the father but by me'. ET 113 (2001) 116-117.

7528 *Wojciechowski, Michał* Chrystologia Nowego Testamentu: próba podsumowania. ᶠJANKOWSKI, A. 2001 ⇒53. 443-450. **P**.

H5.3 *Christologia praemoderna*—Patristic to Reformation

7529 **Behr, John** The way to Nicaea. Formation of Christian Theology 1: Crestwood, NY 2001, St. Vladimir Seminary Press xii; 261 pp. 0-88-141-224-4. Bibl. 243-255.

7530 *Bouteneff, Peter C.* Placing the christology of DIDYMUS the Blind. StPatr 37. 2001 ⇒553. 389-395.

7531 *De Bhaldraithe, Eoin* The christology of IGNATIUS of Antioch. StPatr 36. 2001 ⇒553. 200-206.

7532 *Dorfmann-Lazarev, Igor* Christologie de l'église d'Arménie. MoBi 136 (2001) 32 [BuBB 36,106].

7533 **Fernández Lois, Abel H.A.** La cristología en los comentarios a Isaías de CIRILO de Alejandria y TEODORETO de Ciro. 1998 ⇒14,6947; 15,7708. [R]REByz 59 (2001) 282-283 (*Wolinski, Joseph*).

7534 *Fédou, Michel* L'unicité du Christ selon le *Contre Celse* d'ORIGÈNE. StPatr 36. 2001 ⇒553. 415-420.

7535 **Gieschen, Charles A.** Angelomorphic christology: antecedents and early evidence. AGJU 42: 1998 ⇒14,1921... 16,7702. [R]RBLit 3 (2001) 323-325 (*Hurtado, Larry W.*).

7536 **Grillmeier, A.** Gesù il Cristo nella fede della chiesa 2/2: la chiesa di Costantinopoli nel VI secolo. 1999 ⇒15,7710. [R]Asp. 48 (2001) 444-447 (*Cacciapuoti, Pierluigi*);

7537 Fragmente zur Christologie: Studien zum altkirchlichen Christusbild. [E]*Hainthaler, Theresia*: 1997 ⇒13,7261; 14,6951. [R]ThGl 91 (2001) 327-329 (*Hattrup, Dieter*);

7538 Gesù il Cristo nella fede della chiesa, 2/4: la chiesa di Alessandria, la Nubia e l'Etiopia dopo il 451. [E]*Zani, Antonio*: Biblioteca teologica 26: Brescia 2001, Paideia 508 pp. 88-394-0619-0. Collab. *Theresia Hainthaler.*

7539 *Haes, René de* Jésus le Christ avant les conciles. Telema 106-107 (2001) 51-60.

7540 *Hainthaler, Theresia* 'Anders konnte der Mensch nicht gerettet werden': ANASTASIUS von Antiochien und seine Christologie nach *Or.* III. StPatr 37. 2001 ⇒553. 505-513.

7541 *Langa Augilar, Pedro* La filiación divina de Jesús en la época patrística. BiFe 27 (2001) 245-274.

7542 *Lang, U.M.* Christological themes in RUSTICUS Diaconus' *Contra Acephalos disputatio.* StPatr 38. 2001 ⇒553. 429-434.

7543 *Logan, Alastair* Truth in a heresy? 4: Gnosticism. ET 112 (2001) 187-191.

7544 **Margerie, Bertrand de** Le Christ des Pères. 2000 ⇒16,7705. [R]RThom 101 (2001) 689-691 (*Deloffre, M.-H.*).

7545 **Newman, John Henry** The Arians of the fourth century. [E]*Williams, Rowan*: ND 2001, Univ. of Notre Dame Pr. xlvii; 510 pp. 0-268-02012-4. Introd., notes *Rowan Williams;* Bibl. 506-510.

7546 *Pettersen, Alvyn* Truth in a heresy? 3: Arianism. ET 112 (2001) 150-154.

7547 *Plested, Marcus* The christology of MACARIUS-SYMEON. StPatr 37. 2001 ⇒553. 593-596.

7548 **Pokorny, Petr** Jesus in the eyes of his followers: newly discovered manuscripts and old christian confessions. 1998 ⇒14,6954. [R]JBL 120 (2001) 561-3 (*Percer, Leo*).

7549   **Williams, Rowan A.** Arius: heresy and tradition. GR ²2001 <1987>,
       Eerdmans xiii; 378 pp. $24.

H5.4 *(Commentationes de) Christologia* **moderna**

7550   **Allossé, Léopold** Le Sèmevi dans la culture Pédah—Popo et le "Sein
       du Père" (Jn 1,1.18): contribution à une christologie de filiation au
       Benin. Diss. Teresianum 2001, ᴰ*Moriconi, Bruno*: 324 pp. Bibl. 319-
       324.

7551   **Amato, Angelo** Gesù il Signore: saggio di cristologia. ²1999 ⇒15,
       7722; 16,7713. ᴿAsp. 48 (2001) 604-605 (*Scognamiglio, Edoardo*).

7552   **Bellows, Krista Rosenlund Larsen** Paul VAN BUREN's christology
       and theology of Israel. Diss. Copenhagen 2001.

7553   *Brunstad, Paul Otto* Jesus in Hollywood—the cinematic Jesus in a
       christological and contemporary perspective. StTh 55 (2001) 145-56.

7554   **Chan, Mark L.Y.** Christology from within and ahead: hermeneutics,
       contingency and the quest for transcontextual criteria. BiblInterp 49:
       Lei 2001, Brill xii; 353 pp. 90-04-11844-6. Bibl. 307-344.

7555   **Coll, Niall** Christ in eternity and time—modern Anglican perspec-
       tives. Dublin 2001, Four Courts 208 pp. €24.95. 1-85182-599-1.
       ᴿDoLi 51 (2001) 639-640 (*Clarke, Richard*).

7556   *Dulles, Avery* Jesus and faith. ᶠO'COLLINS, G. 2001 ⇒81. 273-284.

7557   *Dupuis, Jacques* Le verbe de Dieu, Jésus Christ et les religions du
       monde. NRTh 123 (2001) 529-546;

7558   Universality of the Word and particularity of Jesus Christ. ᶠO'COL-
       LINS, G. 2001 ⇒81. 320-342.

7559   *Farmer, Ronald* Jesus in process christology. Jesus then and now.
       2001 ⇒483. 201-215.

7560   *Fédou, Michel* Bulletin de christologie. RSR 89 (2001) 289-314.

7561   *Geering, Lloyd* The global future and Jesus. Jesus then and now.
       2001 ⇒483. 271-281.

7562   *Gerwing, Manfred* Jesus, der ewige Sohn Gottes?: zur gegenwärtigen
       theologischen Reflexion über die Präexistenz Christi. ThGl 91 (2001)
       224-244.

7563   **Gesché, Adolphe** Dieu pour penser, 6: le Christ. P 2001, Cerf 258
       pp. ᴿVS 741 (2001) 754-756 (*Maldamé, Jean-Michel*).

7564   **González de Cardedal, Olegario** Cristología. Sapientia Fidei 24: M
       2001, BAC 601 pp. 84-7914-563-3.

7565   **Haight, Roger** Jesus, symbol of God. 1999 ⇒15,4472; 16,7723. ᴿJR
       81 (2001) 303-306 (*Oakes, Edward T.*); Theol. 104 (2001) 374-376
       (*Sykes, Stephen*); MillSt 47 (2001) 147-153 (*Moloney, Raymond*).

7566 *Hanc, Wojciech* Chrystus centrum teologicznej refleksji ekumenicz-
nej [Le Christ au centre de la réflexion théologique oecuménique].
AtK 136 (2001) 250-269 Riass. 269. **P.**

7567 *Heyward, Carter* Subverting authoritarian relation: Jeus' power and
ours. Jesus then and now. 2001 ⇒483. 216-228.

7568 *Hick, John* Literal and metaphorical christologies;

7569 *Hughes, Charles T.* Pluralism, inclusivism, and christology. Jesus
then and now. 2001 ⇒483. 143-153/154-169.

7570 ᴱ**Kabasélé, F.; Doré, J.; Luneau, R.** Chemins de la christologie africaine. CJJC 25: P 2001 <1986>, Desclée 354 pp. €27. 2-7189-0961.

7571 **Kessler, Hans** Cristologia. ᵀ*Canobbio, Giacomo*: Introduzioni e trattati 16: Brescia 2001, Queriniana 265 pp. €16.53. 88-399-2166-4.

7572 **Knight, Henry F.** Confessing Christ in a post-Holocaust world: a
midrashic experiment. 2000 ⇒16,7725. ᴿRRT 8 (2001) 169-171
(*Pinnock, Sarah K.*).

7573 **König, Adrio** Die helfte is my nooit oor Jesus vertel nie: 'n nuwe
kyk op Een wat jou lewe verander. Kaapstad 2001, Lux V. 200 pp.

7574 **Kraushar, Alexander** Jacob FRANK: the end of the Sabbataian
heresy. ᴱ*Levy, Herbert*: Lanham 2001, University Press of America
vi; 555 pp. 0-7618-1863-4. Annotated with an introductory essay.

7575 **Küster, Volker** Die vielen Gesichter Jesu Christi: Christologie inter-
kulturell 1999 ⇒15,7735. ᴿExchange 30 (2001) 384-386 (*Steen-
brink, Karel*);

7576 The many faces of Jesus Christ: intercultural christology. ᵀ*Bowden,
John*: Mkn 2001, Orbis xii; 242 pp. $25. 1-57075-354-7.

7577 **La Due, William J.** Jesus among the theologians: contemporary interpretations of Christ. Harrisburg 2001, Trinity vii; 216 pp. $21. 1-
56338-351-9 [ThD 49,273—W. Charles Heiser].

7578 *Langa Augilar, Pedro* La filiación divina de Jesús en la doctrina de la
iglesia: aproximación hermenéutica. BiFe 27 (2001) 275-302.

7579 **Manzi, Franco; Pagazzi, Giovanni Cesare** Il pastore dell'essere: fenomenologia dello sguardo del Figlio. Studi Cristologici: Assisi
2001, Cittadella 166 pp. €14.46. 88-308-0729-X. Pref. *Franco Giuli-
o Brambilla;* Bibl. 143-164.

7580 **Mazzotta, Francesco** I titoli cristologici nella cristologia cattolica
contemporanea: uno studio delle aree italiana, francofona, ispano-la-
tino americana. 1998 ⇒14,6988... 16,7729. ᴿBoSm 71 (2001) 206-
210 (*Karlić. Ivan*).

7581 *Mesa, José de* Making salvation concrete and Jesus real: trends in
Asian christology. Exchange 30 (2001) 1-17.

7582 *Metz, Johann Baptist* Toward a christology after Auschwitz. ThD 48
(2001) 103-106.

7583   **Neville, Robert Cummings** Symbols of Jesus: a christology of symbolic engagement. C 2001, CUP xxvi; 291 pp. £16. 0-521-00353-9. With plates of a painting From Caves to Cosmos by *Beth Neville*; Bibl. 262-270.

7584   *Nitsche, Bernhard* Menschliche Identitätssuche und gläubiges Christusbekenntnis. KatBl 126 (2001) 322-332.

7585   *Nossol, Alfons* Jezus Chrystus w teologii protestanckiej [Jésus Christ dans la théologie protestante]. AtK 136 (2001) 216-234 Zsfg. 234. **P**.

7586   *Okure, Teresa* The global Jesus. The Cambridge companion to Jesus. Cambridge companions to religion: 2001 ⇒4236. 237-249.

7587   **Pfüller, Wolfgang** Die Bedeutung Jesu im interreligiösen Horizont: Überlegungen zu einer religiösen Theorie in christlicher Perspektive. Theologie 41: Müns 2001, LIT 224 pp. €20.90. 3-8258-5382-9.

7588   *Pollefeyt, Didier* Christology after Auschwitz: a catholic perspective. Jesus then and now. 2001 ⇒483. 229-248.

7589   *Prior, John Mansford* Portraying the face of the Nazarene in contemporary Indonesia: literature as frontier-expanding mission. Pacifica 14 (2001) 172-190.

7590   *Reikerstorfer, Johann* Über die "Klage" in der Christologie. JBTh 16 (2001) 269-287.

7591   *Salas, Antonio* La filiación divina de Jesús en la visión holística de hoy. BiFe 27 (2001) 303-313.

7592   **Slater, Thomas B.** Christ and community: a socio-historical study of the christology of revelation. JSNT.S 178: 1999 ⇒15,7750; 16,7737. ᴿJBL 120 (2001) 388-390 (*Resseguie, James L.*); RSR 89 (2001) 588-589 (*Morgen, Michèle*).

7593   *Smith, Leonard* Truth in a heresy? 5: Socinianism. ET 112 (2001) 221-224.

7594   *Söding, Thomas* War Jesus wirklich Gottes Sohn?: die neue Debatte um Jesus und die Christologie. ZNT 8 (2001) 2-13.

7595   *Swinburne, Richard* Evidence for the incarnation. Jesus then and now. 2001 ⇒483. 170-185.

7596   **Tillich, Paul** Teologia sistematica: volume secondo: l'esistenza e il Cristo. ᴱ*Bertalot, Renzo*: Sola Scriptura 18: T 2001, Claudiana 220 pp. 88-7016-396-2.

7597   *Torjesen, Karen* Wisdom, christology, and women prophets. Jesus then and now. 2001 ⇒483. 186-200.

7598   **Ugwaka, Patrick Ifeanyichukwu** Beatific vision as prefigured in the gospel of the Transfiguration: a dogmatic study of the teachings of the Popes from LEO the Great through JOHN XXII to BENEDICT XII. R 2001, Urbaniana xi; 147 pp. Diss.; Bibl. 135-147 [Mt 17,1-9].

7599   **Vasel, Stephan** Philosophisch verantwortete Christologie und christlich-jüdischer Dialog: Schritte zu einer doppelt apologetischen Christologie in Auseinandersetzung mit den Entwürfen von H.-J. Kraus, F.-W. Marquardt, P.M. van Buren, P. Tillich, W. Pannenberg und W. Härle. Gü 2001, Gü 768 pp. €45. 3-579-05315-9.

7600 *Viviano, Benedict T.* SCHILLEBEECKX's *Jesus* and *Christ*—contributions to christian life. Trinity—kingdom. 2001 <1982> ⇒223. 75-87.

7601 **Wilson, Jonathan R.** God so loved the world: a christology for disciples. GR 2001, Baker 213 pp. $17. 0-8010-2277-0.

H5.5 *Spiritus Sanctus: pneumatologia*—The Holy Spirit

7602 *Cardon-Bertalot, Philippe* Auguste SABATIER, théologien du Saint-Esprit. RHPhR 81 (2001) 301-319.

7603 *Del Colle, Ralph* The Holy Spirit: presence, power, person. TS 62 (2001) 322-340.

7604 **Dingemans, G.D.J.** De stem van de roepende: pneumatheologie. 2000 ⇒16,7744. ᴿITBT 9/2 (2001) 32-33 (*Nijkamp, Martin*).
    ᴱ**Di Nola, G.** Lo Spirito Santo 1999 ⇒349.

7605 **Dünzl, Franz** Pneuma: Funktionen des theologischen Begriffs in frühchristlicher Literatur. JAC.E 30: 2000 ⇒16,7745. ᴿSal. 63 (2001) 789-791.

7606 **Hahn, Udo** Heiliger Geist. GTB 685: Gü 2001, Gü 63 pp. 3-579-00685-1. ᴿPerTeol 33 (2001) 279-280 (*Libanio, João Batista*).

7607 *Hildén, Helge* Der Geist und das Wort. Lutherische Beiträge 6/1 (2001) 57-65.

7608 **Keener, Craig S.** Gift & giver: the Holy Spirit for today. GR 2001, Baker 224 pp. $17. 0-8010-22665 [ThD 49,74—Heiser, W. Charles].

7609 *Loza Vera, José* El Espiritu Santo en la revelación bíblica. AnáMnesis 11/2 (2001) 17-61.

7610 **López Fernández, Enrique** El don del Espíritu. Oviedo 2001, Lux 326 pp. 84-607-2384-4.

7611 *Ostański, Piotr* Dwa tchnienia, jeden Dawca. ᶠJANKOWSKI, A. 2001 ⇒53. 309-326. P.

7612 **Pettegrew, Larry D.** The new covenant ministry of the Holy Spirit. GR 2001, Kregel xi; 281 pp. $15 [BS 160,374s–Johnson, Elliott E.].

7613 **Pikaza, X.; Silanes, N.** Los carismas en la iglesia: presencia del Espíritu Santo en la historia. Agape 20: 1998 ⇒15,7771. ᴿThX 51 (2001) 503-505 (*Martínez, Jorge*).

7614 *Quelle, Constantino* El Espíritu Santo en el Antiguo Testamento. BiFe 27 (2001) 321-341.

7615 *Rakocy, Waldemar* Duch Święty w początkach Kościoła (od proroków do nauczycieli). ᶠJANKOWSKI, A. 2001 ⇒53. 383-393. P.

7616 **Skrzyp, Benita** Misja Ducha Świetego w królestwie bożym Nowego Testamentu [The mission of the Holy Spirit in the kingdom of God's new covenant]. Kraków 2001, Naukowe PAT 292 pp. **P.**

7617 *Tillesse, Caetano Minette de* Ecclesiologia 1: Espírito Santo. RBBras 18 (2001) 187-217.

7618 *Vázquez Allegue, Jaime* El Espíritu Santo en la literatura intertestamentaria. BiFe 27 (2001) 342-368.

H5.6 *Spiritus et Filius*; 'Spirit-Christology'

7619 *Bonnin Barceló, Eduardo* La ley del espiritu de vida en Cristo Jesus. EfMex 19 (2001) 155-186.

7620 **Preß, Michael** Jesus und der Geist: Grundlagen einer Geist-Christologie. Neuk 2001, Neuk'er ix; 326 pp. €39.90. 3-7887-1880-3. Diss. Heidelberg 2001.

7621 *Waldmann, Helmut* Machtpolitisch motivierte Umdeutung biblischer Texte am Beispiel des *filioque*. HBO 31 (2001) 301-315.

H5.7 *Ssma Trinitas*—The Holy Trinity

7622 **Bobrinskoy, Boris** The mystery of the Trinity: trinitarian experience and vision in the biblical and patristic tradition. 1999 ⇒15,7780. [R]MoTh 17 (2001) 399-401 (*Wainwright, Geoffrey*).

7623 *Derickson, Gary W.* Incarnational explanation for Jesus' subjection in the eschaton. Looking into the future. 2001 ⇒505. 217-232.

7624 *Rikhof, Herwi* Invention of tradition?: Trinity as test. Religious identity. Studies in theology and religion 3: 2001 ⇒549. 97-110.

7625 **Sanders, Frederick Russell** The image of the immanent Trinity: implications of RAHNER's rule for a theological interpretation of scripture. Diss. Graduate Theol. Union 2001, 300 pp. 3007741.

7626 **Tanner, Kathryn** Jesus, humanity and the Trinity: a brief systematic theology. Mp 2001, Fortress xix; 134 pp. $15. 0-8006-3293-1 [ThD 49,88—Heiser, W. Charles].

7627 *Terra, João Evangelista Martins* Trinidade divina no Novo Testamento. RCT 24 (2001) 93-102. Cf. K.H. Schelke, "Theologie des Neuen Testaments", vol. 3.

7628 *Vallin, Philippe* La sagesse en personne, ou comment la Trinité se fit désirer. Com(F) 26/1 (2001) 47-60.

7629 *Viviano, Benedict T.* The Trinity in the Old Testament: from Daniel 7:13-14 to Matt 28:19. Trinity—kingdom—church. NTOA 48: 2001 <1998> ⇒223. 3-20.

H5.8 *Regnum messianicum, Filius hominis*— Messianic kingdom Son of Man

7630 *Annus, Amar* Ninurta and the Son of Man. Mythology and mythologies. 2001 ⇒589. 7-17.

7631 *Ball, Michael* The anointed one. ET 112 (2001) 125-126.

7632 *Bauckham, Richard* The future of Jesus Christ. The Cambridge companion to Jesus. Cambridge companions to religion: 2001 ⇒4236. 265-280.

7633 *Bock, Darrell L.* The kingdom of God in New Testament theology. Looking into the future. 2001 ⇒505. 28-60.

7634 **Burkett, Delbert R.** The Son of Man debate: a history and evaluation. MSSNTS 107: 1999 ⇒15,7787. ᴿCBQ 63 (2001) 140-141 (*Sullivan, Kevin*); Bib. 82 (2001) 438-440 (*Tuckett, Ch.M.*); JBL 119 (2000) 766-768 (*Allison, Dale C.*).

7635 **Condra, Charles Edwin** Salvation for the righteous: Jesus amid expectations of salvation in second temple Judaism. Diss. Dallas Theol. Sem. 2001, 366 pp. 3002960.

7636 **Grappe, Ch.** Le royaume de Dieu: avant et après Jésus. MoBi 42: Genève 2001, Labor et F. 299 pp. €27.44. 2-8309-0994-1. ᴿEstAg 36 (2001) 624-626 (*Cineira, D.A.*); EstTrin 35 (2001) 667-668 (*Pikaza, Xabier*); RBBras 18 (2001) 524-525.

7637 *Hengel, Martin* Jesus der Messias Israels. Der messianische Anspruch Jesu. WUNT 138: 2001 ⇒276. 1-80.

7638 **Inch, Morris A.** Two gospel motifs: the original quest & the messianic theophany. Lanham 2001, University Press of America v; 164 pp. 0-7618-2010-8. Bibl. 161-162.

7639 *Kudasiewicz, Józef* Królestwo Boże w teologii ewangelistów. ᶠJANKOWSKI, A. 2001 ⇒53. 213-219. P.

7640 **Merklein, Helmut** La signoria di Dio nell'annuncio di Gesù. 1994 ⇒10,7610. ᴿDid(L) 31 (2001) 175-8 (*Neves, Joaquim Carreira das*).

7641 *Müller, Ulrich B.* Parusie und Menschensohn. ZNW 92 (2001) 1-19.

7642 *Owen, Paul; Shepherd, David* Speaking up for Qumran, DALMAN and the son of Man: was Bar Enasha a common term for 'man' in the time of Jesus?. JSNT 81 (2001) 81-122.

7643 *Pikaza, Xabier* Jesús, Espíritu Santo y reino de Dios. BiFe 27 (2001) 369-412.

7644 *Riesner, Rainer* Vom Messias Jesus zum christlichen Bekenntnis: jüdische Voraussetzungen und judenchristliche Überlieferungen. ThBeitr 32 (2001) 373-392.

7645 *Sanday, William* On the title, 'Son of Man' Essays in biblical criticism. JSNT.S 225: 2001 <1891> ⇒205. 155-166.

7646 *Viviano, Benedict T.* The kingdom of God in the New Testament. Trinity—kingdom—church. NTOA 48: 2001 ⇒223. 137-184.

7647 *Waltke, Bruce K.* The kingdom of God in biblical theology. Looking into the future. 2001 ⇒505. 15-27.

7648 **Wolff, Peter** Die frühe nachösterliche Verkündigung des Reiches Gottes. FRLANT 171: 1999 ⇒15,7800; 16,7782. [R]JBL 120 (2001) 161-163 (*Viviano, Benedict T.*).

7649 *Xeravits, Géza* Does the figure of the "Son of man" have a place in the eschatological thinking of the Qumran community?. LouvSt 26 (2001) 334-345.

H6.1 *Creatio, sabbatum NT*; **The Creation** [⇒E1.6]

7650 *Berger, Klaus* Creatio non ex nihilo und die Theodizeefrage. [F]SCHMUTTERMAYR, G. 2001 ⇒101. 19-25 [2 Macc 7,28].

7651 *Brueggemann, Walter* Options for creatureliness: consumer or citizen. HBT 23 (2001) 25-50.

7652 *Cole, H. Ross* The christian and time-keeping in Colossians 2:16 and Galatians 4:10. AUSS 39 (2001) 273-282.

7653 *Davis, Ellen F.* Slaves or sabbath-keepers?: a biblical perspective on human work. AThR 83 (2001) 25-40.

7654 **Doering, Lutz** Schabbat. TSAJ 78: 1999 ⇒15,7806; 16,7785. [R]TThZ 110 (2001) 81-82 (*Haag, Ernst*); ZRGG 53 (2001) 79-81 (*Horn, Friedrich W.*); Bijdr. 62 (2001) 220-221 (*Ottenheijm, Eric*); ThG 44 (2001) 304-306 (*Giesen, Heinz*); ThLZ 126 (2001) 622-625 (*Avemarie, Friedrich*).

7655 *Kegler, Jürgen* Sabbat—Sabbatruhe—Sonntagsruhe—ein theologischer Beitrag zu einer aktuellen Diskussion. Gesammelte Aufsätze. BEAT 48: 2001 <1989> ⇒167. 147-170.

7656 **Löning, Karl; Zenger, Erich** To begin with, God created... biblical theologies of creation. 2000 ⇒16,1889. [R]ScrB 31/1 (2001) 40-41 (*Docherty, Susan*).

7657 *Schaller, Berndt* Jesus und der Sabbat: Franz-DELITZSCH-Vorlesung 1992. Fundamenta Judaica. StUNT 25: 2001 <1994> ⇒206. 125-47.

H6.3 *Fides, veritas in NT*—**Faith and truth**

7658 **Alberti, Jean** La foi d'un judéo-chrétien. P 2001, Cerf 322 pp. €18. 29. [R]EeV 41 (2001) 26-27 (*Pivot, Maurice*).

7659 *Antista, Aurelio* "La tua fede ti ha salvato". Horeb 28/1 (2001) 33-37.

7660 *Appelros, Erica* Playing and believing. StTh 55 (2001) 23-40.

7661 *Battaglia, Gregorio* Testimoni nella storia del viaggio della parola. Horeb 28/1 (2001) 62-68.

7662 **Berger, Klaus** Kann man auch ohne Kirche glauben?. 2000 ⇒16, 7789. [R]Zeitzeichen 2/11 (2001) 66 (*Zeddies, Helmut*).

7663 *Beutler, Johannes* Wahrheit III: biblisch-theologisch;

7664 Zeuge, Zeugnis, Zeugenschaft I: biblisch. LThK 10. 2001 ⇒655. 933-935/1440-1442.

7665 **Bourgeois, Henri** Intelligence et passion de la foi. P 2001, L'Atelier 381 pp. 2-220-04839-X. Préf.de *Xavier Lacroix*; Bibl. 369-376.

7666 *DelSignore, Gabriella* "Memori davanti a Dio per la nostra fede" (1 Ts 1,3). Horeb 28/1 (2001) 26-32.

7667 **Fiedrowicz, Michael** Apologie im frühen Christentum: die Kontroverse um den christlichen Wahrheitsanspruch in den ersten Jahrhunderten. Pd [2]2001, Schönigh 363 pp. 3-506-72733-8.

7668 **Gil Arbiol, Carlos Javier** La autoestimación en el movimiento de Jesús: ensayo de exégesis socio-científica. 2001. Diss. Deusto.

7669 *Gushee, David P.* The good news after Auschwitz: a biblical reflection. "Good News" after Auschwitz?. 2001 ⇒377. 157-172.

7670 *Haynes, Stephen R.* Beware good news: faith and fallacy in post-holocaust christianity. "Good News" after Auschwitz?. 2001 ⇒377. 3-20.

7671 *Labèque, Marcelo Horacio* El evangelio de la verdad: de la verdad de las escrituras a la concepción de la verdad. Studium(BA) 4 (2001) 181-197.

7672 **Landmesser, Christof** Wahrheit als Grundbegriff neutestamentlicher Wissenschaft. 1999 ⇒15,7815; 16,7792. [R]ThRv 97 (2001) 385-386 (*Scholtissek, Klaus*); JBL 119 (2000) 347-349 (*Syreeni, Kari*).

7673 *Maggioni, Bruno* Fedeltà di Dio e fedeltà dell'uomo: percorso biblico, appunti. Servitium 136 (2001) 15-21.

7674 **Middleton, J. Richard; Walsh, Brian J.** Truth is stranger than it used to be: biblical faith in a postmodern age. 1995 ⇒11/2,3754; 12, 7092. [R]SBET 19 (2001) 119-121 (*Kearsley, Roy*).

7675 **Pak, Joseph Kyung-Bum** A study of selected passages on distinguishing marks of genuine and false believers. Diss. Dallas Theol. Sem. 2001, 331 pp. 3002968.

7676 *Porro, Carlo* Per una lettura biblical della fede, 1-2. RCI 82 (2001) 207-218, 299-311.

7677 **Rossi De Gasperis, Francesco** Cominciando da Gerusalemme (Lc 24, 47): la sorgente della fede e dell'esistenza cristiana. 1997 ⇒13, 7449; 16,7795. [R]BeO 43 (2001) 33-44 (*Matteo, Armando*).

7678 *Schurr, Adolf Anselm* Philosophische Anmerkungen zum chassidischen und christlichen Glaubensverständnis. ᶠSCHMUTTERMAYR, G. 2001 ⇒101. 551-570.

7679 **Wallis, Ian G.** Holy Saturday faith. 2000 ⇒16,7797. ᴿTheol. 104 (2001) 281-282 (*Griffith-Jones, Robin*); JThS 52 (2001) 790-792 (*Harvey, A.E.*); Theol. 104 (2001) 281-282 (*Griffith-Jones, Robin*).

H6.6 *Peccatum NT*—Sin, evil [⇒E1.9]

7680 **Dembele, Youssouf** Salvation as victory: a reconsideration of the concept of salvation in the light of Jesus Christ's life and work viewed as a triumph over the personal powers of evil. Diss. Trinity Evang. Divinity 2001, 383 pp. 3003780.

7681 **Girard, René** Je vois Satan tomber comme l'éclair. 1999 ⇒15,7825; 16,7801. ᴿFilTeo 15 (2001) 197-199 (*Tugnoli, Claudio*);

7682 I see Satan fall like lightning. ᵀ*Williams, James G.*: NY 2001, Orbis xxiv; 199 pp. 1-57075-319-9;

7683 Vedo Satana cadere come la folgore. Saggi 36: Mi 2001, Adelphi 250 pp. €20.66. 88-459-1616-2.

7684 *Gubler, Marie-Louise* Der versperrte Himmel: biblische und literarische Spurensuche nach dem Bösen. Diak. 32 (2001) 89-97.

7685 *Karrer, Martin* Sünde IV: Neues Testament. TRE 32: 2001 ⇒665. 375-389.

H7.0 Soteriologia NT

7686 *Baumert, Norbert* Erlösung durch Christus. Studien zu den Paulusbriefen. SBAB 32: 2001 <1996> ⇒123. 201-208.

7687 *Gómez, Enrique* Dios nos reconcilia en Cristo (2 Cor 5,18-19): hacia una soteriología existencial. RevAg 42 (2001) 715-776.

7688 **Heijer, C.J. den** Verzoening, bijbelse notities bij een omstreden thema. Baarn ¹⁰2001, ten Have 194 pp. €14.90. 90-259-5279-8.

7689 *Hofius, Otfried* Sühne IV: Neues Testament. TRE 32: 2001 ⇒665. 342-347.

7690 ᴱ**House, Paul R.; Thornbury, Gregory A.** Who will be saved?: defending the biblical understanding of God, salvation, and evangelism. 2000 ⇒16,7808. ᴿRExp 98 (2001) 615 (*Gosnell, Rick*).

7691 *Janßen, Hans-Gerd* "Denn durch dein heil'ges Kreuz hast du die Welt erlöst"?: Genugtuung und Sühnopfer auf dem Prüfstand. WiWei 64 (2001) 214-231.

7692 **Jüngel, Eberhard** Il vangelo della giustificazione come centro della fede cristiana. BTCon 112: 2000 ⇒16,7810. ᴿProtest. 56 (2001) 310-312 (*Ferrario, Fulvio*).

7693 **Klaiber, Walter** Gerecht vor Gott: Rechtfertigung in der Bibel und heute. BTSP 20: 2000 ⇒16,7813. ᴿThLZ 126 (2001) 929-931 (*Landmesser, Christof*).

7694 *Klauck, Hans-Josef* Debate sobre la justificación: Pablo, Santiago y Martín LUTERO. Cart. 17 (2001) 67-86 Res., sum.

7695 *Knöppler, Thomas* Sühne im Neuen Testament: Studien zum urchristlichen Verständnis der Heilsbedeutung des Todes Jesu. Diss.-Habil. München 1998/99, ᴰ*Hahn, Ferdinand*: WMANT 88: Neuk 2001, Neuk xi; 371 pp. €69. 3-7887-1815-3. Bibl. 323-351.

7696 *Lehtonen, Tommi* "Christus Victor"—the meaning of atonement. StTh 55 (2001) 118-128.

7697 *Niemand, Christoph* Zur Heilsbedeutung des Todes Jesu: historischrekonstruktive und bibeltheologische Thesen und ihr biographischer Ort. Leben-Erleben-Begreifen: zur Verbindung von Person und Theologie: Festgabe für Johannes SINGER zum 80. Geburtstag. ᴱ**Sauer, Hanjo; Gmainer-Pranzl, Franz**: Linzer philosophisch-theologische Beiträge 5: Fra 2001, Lang. 59-75.

7698 *Pangrazzi, Arnaldo* Fundamentos bíblico-teológicos de la pastoral de la salud. Medellín 27 (2001) 187-202.

7699 *Pasquetto,Virgilio* La storia della salvezza tra presente e futuro: prospettive bibliche. RVS 55 (2001) 413-431.

7700 **Ray, Darby Kathleen** Deceiving the devil: atonement, abuse, and ransom. 1998 ⇒14,7106. ᴿJR 81 (2001) 306-307 (*Carr, Amy*).

7701 *Sattler, Dorothea* Simul iustus et peccator?: zur Geschichte, zu den Ergebnissen und offenen Fragen des ökumenische Gesprächs. Gerecht und Sünder zugleich?. 2001 ⇒378. 9-29.

7702 *Schöndorf, Harald* ¿Por qué Jesús tuvo que sufrir?: una nueva concepción de la soteriología. Strom. 57 (2001) 153-176.

7703 *Weaver, J. Denny* The nonviolent atonement. GR 2001, Eerdmans xiii; 246 pp. $22. 0-8028-4908-3. Bibl. 229-238.

7704 *Wright, N.T.* The shape of justification. BiRe 17/2 (2001) 8, 50.

H7.2 *Crux, sacrificium*; The Cross, the nature of sacrifice [⇒E3.4]

7705 *Bremmer, Jan N.* The scapegoat between Hittites, Greeks, Israelites and christians. Kult, Konflikt. 2001 ⇒387. 175-186 [Lev 16].

7706 **Chazelle, Celia** The crucified God in the Carolingian era: theology and art of Christ's passion. C 2001, CUP xiv; 338 pp. $70. 33 fig.

7707 **Contreras Molina, Francisco** Sonetos de Jesús crucificado. Estella 2001, Verbo Divino 206 pp.

7708 *Dauzat, Pierre-Emmanuel* L'échelle de Jacob dans la lecture des premiers chrétiens. MoBi 133 (2001) 36-39 [Gn 28,10-22].

7709 *Destro, Adriana* Il dispositivo sacrificale: strumento della morte e della vita. ASEs 18 (2001) 9-46.

    ^E**Dreyer, E.** The cross in christian tradition 2000 ⇒522.

7710 *Federici, Tommaso* Il fuoco divino consuma il sacrificio. ^FKASPER, W. 2001 ⇒58. 35-52.

7711 **Fitch Fairaday, Brenda** ISAAC of Nineveh's biblical typology of the cross. StPatr 35. 2001 ⇒553. 385-390.

7712 **Green, Miranda Aldhouse** Dying for the gods: human sacrifice in Iron Age & Roman Europe. Oxf 2001, Tempus R. 224 pp. 0-7524-1940-4. Bibl. 204-216.

7713 *Heid, Stefan* Frühe Kritik am Gekreuzigten und das Ringen um eine christliche Antwort. TThZ 110 (2001) 85-114.

7714 **Heid, Stefan** Kreuz Jerusalem Kosmos: Aspekte frühchristlicher Staurologie. JAC.E 31: Müns 2001, Aschendorff viii; 293 pp 3-402-08116-4.

7715 *Lang, Walter* Wusste Jesus Christus, dass er sich beim Kreuzestod zum Opfer brachte zur Erlösung der Welt?. Theologisches 31 (2001) 467-470.

7716 **Lewis, Brenda Ralph** Ritual sacrifice: an illustrated history. Thrupp 2001, Sutton x; 182 pp. 0-7509-2707-0. Bibl. 177-178.

7717 *Lizarralde, Joxe* Crucificado por nosotros (1). Staurós 36 (2001) 57-68.

7718 **Mölk, Ulrich** Das älteste französische Kreuzlied und der Erfurter Codex Amplonianus 8° 32. NAWG Phil.-hist. Kl. 2001,10: Gö 2001, Vandenhoeck & R. 36 pp. Bibl. 30; 6 pl.

7719 *Niemand, Christoph* Jesu Tod am Kreuz als Heilsereignis: will Gott Blut sehen?. CPB 114 (2001) 6-9.

7720 *Pietri, Luce* CONSTANTIN et/ou HÉLÈNE, promoteurs des travaux entrepris sur le Golgota: les comptes rendus des historiens ecclésiastiques grecs du Ve siècle. L'historiographie de l'église. 2001 ⇒541. 371-380 [BuBB 36,104].

7721 *Prieur, Jean-Marc* "Si vous ne faites ce qui est à droite comme ce qui est à gauche": crucifixion et renversement des attitudes dans la littérature chrétienne ancienne. RHPhR 81 (2001) 413-424.

7722 *Puech, Émile* La crucifixion comme peine capitale dans le judaïsme ancien. Le judéo-christianisme. 2001 ⇒484. 41-66.

7723 *Rigato, Maria-Luisa* Il "Titulus Crucis": retroscena di una "storia" della documentazione. RivBib 49 (2001) 337-342.

7724 **Robinson, Martin** Why the cross?. Thinking clearly: GR 2001, Monarch 159 pp. $11. 0-8254-6021-2 [ThD 49,84–Heiser, W.C.].

7725 **Saurat, P.** Le crucifix dans l'art. P 2001, Téqui 142 pp.

7726 *Stegemann, Wolfgang* Sacrifice as metaphor. ᶠMALINA, B., BiblInterp 53: 2001 ⇒67. 310-327.

7727 *Stichel, Rainer* Ein Ausspruch des HERAKLIT gegen das Opferwesen in einer byzantinischen Illustration zum letzten Lied des Mose (Dtn 32,1-43). Kult, Konflikt. AOAT 285: 2001 ⇒387. 287-319.

7728 **Stott, John** La croce di Cristo. R 2001, GBU 521 pp.

7729 *Taeger, Jens-Wilhelm, al.,* Kreuz/Kreuz Christi. RGG², 4: I-K. 2001 ⇒664. 1744-1754.

7730 1**Thiede, Carsen Peter; D'Ancona, Matthew** The quest for the true cross. 2000 ⇒16,7858. ᴿAevum 75 (2001) 217-219 (*Ramelli, Ilaria*).

7731 **Tidball, Derek** The message of the cross: wisdom unsearchable, love indestructible. The Bible speaks today: Leicester 2001, IVP 341 pp. 0-85111-543-8. Bibl. 14-19.

7732 **Wanke, Daniel** Das Kreuz Christi bei IRENÄUS von Lyon. BZNW 99: 2000 ⇒16,7862. ᴿCBQ 63 (2001) 566-567 (*Bernas, Casimir*).

7733 *Witakowski, Witold* Ethiopic and Hebrew versions of the legend of The finding of the Holy Cross. StPatr 35. 2001 ⇒553. 527-535.

H7.4 *Sacramenta, gratia*

7734 **Alule, Cosmas** Baptism and faith: their relationship in our salvific encounter with God today in the light of the New Testament baptismal theology and Vatican II sacramental theology. EHS.T 100: 2000 ⇒16,7863. ᴿVJTR 65 (2001) 69-70 (*Gisbert-Sauch, G.*).

7735 **Boismard, Marie-Émile** Le baptême chrétien selon le Nouveau Testament. Théologies: P 2001, Cerf 143 pp. €13.72. 2-204-06639-7. ᴿBrot. 153 (2001) 1043-1044 (*Silva, I. Ribeiro da*).

7736 **D'Acquisto, Benedetto** Trattato dei sacramenti della legge evangelica. ᴱ*Armetta, Francesco*: Storia e cultura di Sicilia 6: Caltanisetta 2001, Sciascia 319 pp. 88-8241-105-2. Due saggi di *Francesco Armetta* e *Cosimo Scordato.*

7737 *Dockery, David S.* Baptism in the New Testament. SWJT 43/2 (2001) 4-16.

7738 *Figura, Michael* Zur Sakramentalität des Wortes Gottes. IKaZ 30 (2001) 27-43.

7739 *Grasham, Bill* Archaeology and christian baptism. RestQ 43/2 (2001) 113-116.

7740 **Gray, Tim** Sacraments in scripture: salvation history made present. Steubenville, OH 2001, Emmaus Road 96 pp. $10.

7741 *Hoss, Stefanie; Ristow, Sebastian* "Untertauchen in lebendigem Wasser ...": das jüdische Reinigungsbad und die christliche Taufe: Gemeinsamkeiten und Unterschiede. WUB 21 (2001) 70-75.

7742 **Johnson, Maxwell E.** The rites of christian initiation: their evolution and interpretation. A Pueblo book 76: ColMn 1999, Liturgical xxii; 414 pp. 0-8146-6011-8.

7743 **Kizhakearanjaniyil, Mathew** East Syrian baptismal theology: a Judeo-Christian synthesis. Kottayam 2001, Oriental Institute of Religious Studies 258 pp. $12 [BiBh 29,163ss—Parackal, Joseph].

7744 *Peterson, Jeffrey* "The circumcision of the Christ": the significance of baptism in Colossians and the churches of the restoration. RestQ 43/2 (2001) 65-77.

7745 **Ravasi, Gianfranco** La vite e l'olivo: lezionario biblico del matrimonio: commento. Piemme, Religione: CasM 2001, Piemme 180 pp. 88-384-5135-4.

7746 *Spieckermann, Hermann* Gnade: biblische Perspektiven. Gottes Liebe zu Israel. FAT 33: 2001 ⇒215. 20-33.

7747 *Williams, Robert L.* Baptism in two early church orders. SWJT 43/2 (2001) 17-31.

H7.6 *Ecclesiologia, Theologia missionis, laici*—The Church

7748 *Aagaard, Anna Marie* Ecclesiology and ethics. StTh 55 (2001) 157-174.

7749 *Adadevoh, Dela* He went on his way rejoicing: the salvation experience of an African executive: Acts 8:26-40. African Journal of Evangelical Theology 20 (2001) 209-214.

7750 *Arens, Eduardo* Para que el mundo crea: evangelización... desde el evangelio. Páginas 171 (2001) 76-90.

7751 *Calduch-Benages, Núria* La biblia: un reto para la Europa del tercer milenio. AnVal 27 (2001) 275-286.

7752 *Cazelles, Henri* Histoire des religions, états et église. RICP 80 (2001) 171-186.

7753 *Comeau, Geneviève* Vocation universelle d'Israël et de l'église. Spiritus 42 (2001) 419-427.

7754 *Composta, Dario* I fondamenti biblici del diritto canonico. Div. 44 (2001) 272-298.

7755 *Conser, Walter H.* Moral order on the American frontier: Lutheran mission in the 1840s. FDIETRICH, W. BJSt 329: 2001 ⇒24. 120-137.

7756 *Dormeyer, Detlev* Werden der Catholica—neutestamentliche Thesen. Was ist heute noch katholisch?. QD 192: 2001 ⇒353. 17-35.

7757 *Frankemölle, Hubert* Zehn Gebote für die Kirche im dritten Jahrtausend: biblische Impulse aus dem Neuen Testament. Diak. 32 (2001) 205-212.

7758 *Gangel, Kenneth O.* Marks of a healthy Church. BS 158 (2001) 467-477.

7759 **Gnilka, Joachim** I primi cristiani: origini e inizio della chiesa. 2000 ⇒16,7891. [R]CivCatt 152/2 (2001) 419-420 (*Scaiola, D.*).

7760 **Harrington, Daniel J.** The church according to the New Testament. Ch 2001, Sheed & W. xii; 188 pp. $20 [BiTod 40,265—Senior, D.].

7761 *Hasitschka, Martin* "Er machte uns zu einem Königreich, zu Priestern seinem Gott und Vater" (Offb 1,6): Bezeugung der Würde der Christen als Stärkung im Glauben. [F]MÜHLSTEIGER, J.: KStT 46: 2001 ⇒77. 5-12.

7762 **Hellerman, Joseph H.** The ancient church as family. Mp 2001, Fortress xv; 295 pp. $23. 0-8006-3248-6. Bibl. 271-283.

7763 **Howard-Brook, Wes** The church before christianity. Mkn 2001, Orbis viii; 168 pp. $15. 1-57075-403-9. Bibl. 161-163.

7764 **Illanes, José Luis** Laicado y sacerdocio. Fac. Teol. Univ. de Navarra, Teológica 102: Pamplona 2001, Eunsa 304 pp. 84-313-1858-9.

7765 *Javier Gonzalez, Francisco* La iglesia, cuerpo de Cristo y comunión de carismas en 1 Cor 12,1-14,40. Nuevo Mundo 196 (2001) 215-224.

7766 *Johnston, Anna* The book eaters: textuality, modernity, and the London Missionary Society. Semeia 88 (2001) 13-40.

7767 **Kaiser, Walter C.** Mission in the Old Testament: Israel as a light to the nations. 2000 ⇒16,7897. [R]RExp 98 (2001) 457-458 (*Jones, Barry A.*); HBT 23 (2001) 103-104 (*Paul, Glendora B.*).

7768 *Kanagaraj, Jey J.* Jerusalem and diaspora mission. Dharma Deepika 5/2 (2001) 11-20. Ment. *Eliade, M.*.

7769 *Kirchschläger, Walter* Hoffnung für die Kirche!: eine biblische Skizze in die Zukunft. Diak. 32 (2001) 55-61;

7770 Volk Gottes unterwegs: zur Weg-Dimension von Kirche. ThPQ 149 (2001) 17-25.

7771 **Köstenberger, Andreas J.; O'Brien, Peter Thomas** Salvation to the ends of the earth: a biblical theology of mission. New Studies in Biblical Theology 11: Leicester 2001, Apollos 351 pp. $25. 0-85111-519-5. Bibl. 275-310.

7772 *Kritzinger, J.J.* Missionêre perspektiewe op teologiese opleiding. VeE 22 (2001) 72-84.

7773 *Lampe, Peter* Urchristliche Missionswege nach Rom: Haushalte paganer Herrschaft als jüdisch-christliche Keimzellen. ZNW 92 (2001) 123-127.

7774 *Larkin, William J. Jr.* Introduction Mission in the NT. ASMS 27: 2001 ⇒367. 1-7.

7775 **Le Grys, Alan** Preaching to the nations: the origins of mission in the early church. L 1998, SPCK 240 pp. £16. 0-28-105-1488. [R]EvQ 73 (2001) 88-89 (*Marshall, I. Howard*).

7776 *Lemcio, Eugene E.* Images of the church in 1 Corinthians and 1 Timothy: an exercise in canonical hermeneutics. AsbTJ 56/1 (2001) 45-59.

7777 **Lohfink, Gerhard** Does God need the church?. 1999 ⇒15,7943; 16, 7904. [R]NewTR 14 (2001) 93-94 (*Burkhard, John J.*); MoTh 17 (2001) 250-252 (*Bauerschmidt, Frederick Christian*); ProEc 10 (2001) 491-493 (*Cavanaugh, William T.*);

7778 Heeft God de kerk nodig?: over de theologie van het volk van God. Gent 2001, Carmelitana 452 pp. [R]Coll. 31 (2001) 432-433 (*Vanden Berghe, Eric*).

7779 *Luz, Ulrich* Ekklesiologie und Gelder der Kirche: neutestamentliche Perspektiven für heute. EvTh 61/1 (2001) 6-18.

7780 *Marangon, Antonio* Quale paternità nella chiesa?. [F]MARIN, B. 2001 ⇒68. 61-72.

7781 **Martuccelli, Paolo** Origine e natura della chiesa: la prospettiva storico-dommatica di Joseph RATZINGER. RSTh: Fra 2001, Lang 518 pp.

7782 *McDaniel, Ferris L.* Mission in the Old Testament. Mission in the NT. ASMS 27: 2001 ⇒367. 11-20.

7783 **McKechnie, Paul** The first christian centuries: perspectives on the early church. Nottingham 2001, Apollos 270 pp. 0-85111-479-2. Bibl. 251-261.

7784 *Mimouni, Simon C.* Los orígenes del cristianismo en Palestina y en la diáspora en los siglos I y II: una panorámica. Qol 27 (2001) 7-34.

7785 **Nissen, Johannes** New Testament and mission: historical and hermeneutical perspectives. 1999 ⇒15,7952; 16,7909. [R]Exchange 30 (2001) 93-7 (*Uzukwu, E.E.*); CBQ 63 (2001) 556-7 (*Kealy, Seán P.*).

7786 *Oduyoye, Mercy* A biblical perspective on the church. ER 53 (2001) 44-47.

7787 *Oliva, José Raimundo* Atos e evangelhos: o anúncio de Jesus no terceiro milênio. Estudos Bíblicos 70 (2001) 97-109.

7788 *Painter-Morland, M.* Dealing with difference and dissensus within the church as organisation. VeE 22 (2001) 115-130.

7789 **Patzia, Arthur G.** The emergence of the church: context, growth, leadership & worship. Nottingham 2001, IVP 272 pp. $20. 0-85111-483-0. Bibl. 252-260.

7790 *Porter, Lawrence B.* Sheep and shepherd: an ancient image of the church and a contemporary challenge. Gr. 82 (2001) 51-85.

7791 *Reck, Reinhold* Christliche Gemeindestrukturen-systemisch betrachtet. BiKi 56 (2001) 228-233.

7792 **Reinbold, Wolfgang** Propaganda und Mission im ältesten Christentum: eine Untersuchung zu den Modalitäten der Ausbreitung der frühen Kirche. FRLANT 188: 2000 ⇒16,7917. [R]ThRv 97 (2001) 222-226 (*Fürst, Alfons*); JAC 44 (2001) 197-199 (*Dassmann, Ernst*); SNTU.A 25 (2000) 255-257 (*Schreiber, S.*)

7793 *Repschinski, Boris* Menschen verkünden Christen: die Ausbreitung des Christentums und der urkirchliche Glaube. Wort zum Leben. 2001 ⇒284. 157-177.

7794 *Roloff, Jürgen* Kirche im Spannungsfeld gestaltender Kräfte: die Vielfalt von Bildern der Kirche im Urchristentum. BiKi 56 (2001) 203-211.

7795 *Royon, Claude* Réactions d'un ecclésiologue. Le judaïsme à l'aube de l'ère chrétienne. LeDiv 186: 2001 ⇒450. 365-382.

7796 **Sachot, Maurice** L'invention du Christ: genèse d'une religion. 1998 ⇒15,7959; 16,7918. [R]RB 108 (2001) 308-309 (*Nodet, Étienne*).

7797 **Sachot, Maurice** Christianisme et philosophie. 1999 ⇒15,7960. [R]JAC 44 (2001) 200-203 (*Dihle, Albrecht*).

7798 *Schelbert, Georg* Zur frühen Missionsgeschichte. NZM 57 (2001) 3-14.

7799 *Scheuchenpflug, Peter* Katholische Kirche im Exil?: zur begrenzten Geltung eines biblischen Leitbildes im Kontext der gegenwärtigen Gestalt von Kirche. [F]SCHMUTTERMAYR, G. 2001 ⇒101. 519-536.

7800 *Seemuth, David P.* Mission in the early church. Mission in the NT. ASMS 27: 2001 ⇒367. 50-60.

7801 **Sider, Ronald J.** Good news and good works: a theology for the whole gospel. 1999 ⇒15,7962. [R]AUSS 39 (2001) 344-346 (*Maier, Rudolf*).

7802 *Söding, Thomas* Zukunft der Kirche—Kirche der Zukunft: Orientierungen am Neuen Testament. ThGl 91 (2001) 87-108.

7803 *Spicacci,Virginio* Ancora sulla pastorale di evangelizzazione: le coordinate biblico-teologiche di ogni progetto di evangelizzazione. LSDC 16 (2001) 119-123.

7804 *Tillesse, Caetano Minette de* Ecclesiologia 2: a igreja no Novo Testamento. RBBras 18 (2001) 218-291.

7805 *Wieh, Hermann* Gleiche Probleme, andere Wege: Eindrücke vom Gemeindeleben in den USA. BiKi 56 (2001) 239-243.

7806 *Williams, Joel F.* Conclusion. Mission in the NT. ASMS 27: 2001 ⇒ 367. 239-247.

H7.7 *Œcumenismus*—The ecumenical movement

7807 *Baisas, Bienvenido Q.* A gospel inspiration for interreligious dialogue: the Syrophoenician woman of Mk 7:24-30. Religious Life
Asia 3/4 (2001) 23-33.

7808 *Beinert, Wolfgang* Der Pontifikat JOHANNES PAUL II. im Kontext der
ökumenischen Entwicklung. [F]SCHMUTTERMAYR, G. 2001 ⇒101. 317-
335.

7809 **Bluck, John** The giveaway God: ecumenical bible studies on divine
generosity. Geneva 2001, WCC 116 pp.

7810 *Grünwaldt, Klaus* Ökumenische Annäherung als Heimkehr: zur
päpstlichen Deutung der Emmaus-Geschichte. DtPfrBl 101 (2001)
123-124 [Lk 24,13-35].

7811 *Kuschel, Karl-Josef* Abrahamische Ökumene?: zum Problem einer
Theologie des Anderen bei Juden, Christen und Muslimen. ZMR 85
(2001) 258-278.

7812 *Rodríguez Garrapucho, Fernando* Lectura eclesial de la biblia y unidad cristiana. DiEc 114 (2001) 81-121.

7813 **Sagovsky, Nicholas** Ecumenism: christian origins and the practice of
communion. 2000 ⇒16,7935. [R]JThS 52 (2001) 983-985 (*Clements,
Keith*).

7814 *Stubenrauch, Bertram* Warum Konfessionen und warum Ökumene?:
oder: Exegese und Dogmatik im Dienst der Glaubenseinheit.
[F]SCHMUTTERMAYR, G. 2001 ⇒101. 585-599.

H7.8 **Amt**—*Ministerium ecclesiasticum*

7815 *Almeida, Antonio José de* A origem dos presbíteros-epíscopos na i-
greja do Novo Testamento (II), (III). PerTeol 33 (2001) 67-86, 217-
234.

7816 *Benedict, Hans J.* Die größere Diakonie: Versuch einer Neubestim-
mung in Anschluss an J.W. COLLINS. WzM 53 (2001) 349-358.

7817 **Brent, Allen** The imperial cult and the development of church order:
concepts and images of authority in paganism and early christianity
before the age of CYPRIAN. SVigChr 45: 1999 ⇒15,7977; 16,7941.
[R]JECS 9 (2001) 403-405 (*Drake, H.A.*); REAug 47 (2001) 185-189
(*Dufraigne, P.*); ThLZ 126 (2001) 61-63 (*Klauck, Hans-Josef*).

7818 **Chilton, Bruce David; Neusner, Jacob** Types of authority in formative Christianity and Judaism. 1999 ⇒15,9813. [R]HeyJ 42 (2001)
368-370 (*Rousseau, Philip*).

7819 **Clarke, Andrew D.** Serve the community of the church: christians as leaders and ministers. 2000 ⇒16,7944. ᴿTheol. 104 (2001) 209-210 (*Way, David*); BiblInterp 9 (2001) 224-226 (*Kloppenborg Verbin, John S.*); JThS 52 (2001) 847-849 (*Campbell, R. Alastair*); CBQ 63 (2001) 547-549 (*Love, Smart L.*); ThLZ 126 (2001) 1265-1267 (*Roloff, Jürgen*).

7820 **Eisen, Ute E.** Women officeholders in early christianity. ᵀ*Maloney, Linda M.* 2000 ⇒16,7946. ᴿWorship 75 (2001) 281-283 (*Perkins, Pheme*);

7821 Amtsträgerinnen im frühen Christentum. FKDG 61: 1996 ⇒12,7240. .. 14,7199. ᴿRBLit 3 (2001) 316-318 (*Brooten, Bernadette J.*)..

7822 **Haag, Herbert** Da Gesù al sacerdozio. ᴱ*Tognina, Paolo*: T 2001, Claudiana 128 pp. €9.81. ᴿRdT 42 (2001) 460-2 (*Cattaneo, Enrico*).

7823 *Hoet, Hendrik* Bijbelse inspiratie van de christelijke diaconie. Coll. 31 (2001) 357-369.

7824 *Jezierska, S. Ewa J.* Instytucje diakonis i wdów w kościele pierwszych wieków [Les institutions des diaconesses et des veuves dans l'église des premiers siècles]. ACra 33 (2001) 385-395 Rés. 395. **P.**

7825 *Köstenberger, Andreas J.* On the alleged apostolic origins of priestly celibacy. Studies on John and gender. 2001 <1992> ⇒169. 173-183.

7826 *Küchler, Max* Das Verschwinden der Frauen: ein Essay. BiKi 56 (2001) 220-223.

7827 *Mayer, Wendy* Patronage, pastoral care and the role of the bishop of Antioch. VigChr 55 (2001) 58-70.

7828 *O'Neill, J.C.* 'The work of ministry' in Ephesians 4:12 and the New Testament. ET 112 (2001) 336-340.

7829 **Perrot, Charles** Après Jésus: le ministère chez les premiers chrétiens. 2000 ⇒16,7956. ᴿMD 225 (2001) 143-145 (*Blanchard, Yves-Marie*); Spiritus 42 (2001) 455-458 (*Faivre, Christophe*); CBQ 63 (2001) 557-558 (*Broadhurst, Laurence*).

7830 ᴱ**Rittner, Reinhard** In Christus berufen: Amt und allgemeines Priestertum in lutherischer Perspektive. SThKAB 36: Hannover 2001, LVH 164 pp.

7831 *Roloff, Jürgen* Herrenmahl und Amt im Neuen Testament. KuD 47/2 (2001) 68-89.

7832 **Sullivan, Francis A.** From apostles to bishops: the development of the episcopacy in the early church. Mahwah 2001, Newman ix; 253 pp. $29. 0-8091-0534-9 [ThD 49,192—Heiser, W. Charles].

H8.0 **Oratio**, *spiritualitas personalis NT*

7833 La 'lectio divina': essai de définition. VS 741 (2001) 605-624 [Anon.].

7834 ^E**Allen, Pauline; Canning, Raymond; Cross, Lawrence** Prayer and spirituality in the early church. 1998 ⇒14,408; 16,7963. Conference Melbourne, 1996. ^RJECS9 (2001) 133-134 (*Finn, Thomas M.*).

7835 **Asi, Emmanuel** The human face of God at Nazareth. Bangalore 2000, Claretian 132 pp [Jn 1,43-48].

7836 *Barban, Alessandro* Lectio divina as prayed word. Clar. 41 (2001) 181-205.

7837 *Bartnicki, Roman* Asceza w Biblii. ^FJANKOWSKI, A. 2001 ⇒53. 59-67. **P.**

7838 *Baumert, Norbert* Exegese und Spiritualität. Studien zu den Paulus-briefen. SBAB 32: 2001 <1977> ⇒123. 281-295.

7839 **Benedetti, G.** Il vangelo della festa: intellegenza spirituale della parola di Dio secondo i padri della chiesa: omelie Anno A. Bo 2001, EDB 264 pp. €15 [RdT 43,157].

7840 **Berger, Klaus** Was gibt uns die Kraft zum Leben?. GTBS 1203: Gü 2001, Quell 315 pp. 3-579-03310-7.

7841 *Berghuis, Kent D.* A biblical perspective on fasting. BS 158 (2001) 86-103.

7842 *Bianchi, Enzo* Les enjeux de la 'lectio divina' aujourd'hui;

7843 Les difficultés de la 'lectio divina'. VS 81 (2001) 403-411/595-604.

7844 **Bluck, John** The give away God: ecumenical bible studies on divine generosity. Risk Book 93: Geneva 2001, WCC vii; 113 pp. $8/£5.25. 2-8254-1347-X.

7845 *Bonowitz, Bernard* Gleichförmigkeit mit Christus. CistC 108 (2001) 255-261.

7846 *Braun, Hermann* Reden mit Gott?: ein Versuch über das Gebet. WuD 26 (2001) 307-321.

7847 *Brindle, Wayne A.* Biblical evidence for the imminence of the rapture. BS 158 (2001) 138-151 [Jn 14,1-3; 1 Thess 1,9-10; 5,4-9; Titus 2,13; 1 Jn 3,2-3; Rev 22,7; 22,12; 22,20].

7848 *Bronkhorst, Johannes* Asceticism, religion, and biological evolution. Method and theory in the study of religion 13/4 (2001) 374-418.

7849 **Butler, Virginia Marie** Go to Galilee: the spiritual geography of the gospels. NY 2001, Alba xiv; 110 pp. $10.

7850 *Camille, Soeur* Jean CASSIEN: la sainte écriture dans la vie du moine. VS 81 (2001) 413-427.

7851 **Collins, Pat** Prayer in practice: a biblical approach. Mkn 2001, Orbis 246 pp. $14. 0-57075-353-9 [ThD 48,263—Heiser, W. Charles].

7852 *Combet-Galland, Corina* Etre Protestant: la bible au chevet. PosLuth 49/4 (2001) 305-317.

7853 *Dahlgrün, Corinna* Das Gebet im Seelsorgegespräch: theologische Notwendigkeit, methodischer Fehler oder heilende Intervention?. WuD 26 (2001) 353-365.

7854 *D'Alessio, Davide* Il racconto e la vita: lectio biblica come avventura della mente e del cuore. ScC 129/1 (2001) 103-144.

7855 *Dohmen, Christoph* Von Gott zu Gott sprechen: wenn die Theologie ins Gebet genommen wird. GuL 74 (2001) 326-335 [Ps 103].

7856 *Dörr, Elfriede* Sich auf die Seite des Lebens schlagen. JK 62/1 (2001) 2-7 [Col 2,3].

7857 *Frohnhofen, Herbert* Bei Lebzeiten das Todlose erreichen?: Jesu Weg und unser Weg. Christlicher Glaube. 2001 ⇒511. 417-432.

7858 **Gallivan, H.** The temple within: the rosary, the bible and the inner journey. Dublin 2001, Columba 96 pp. 1-85607-3343.

7859 *García, P.* La pasión de Jesús y la nuestra. Pedal 231: Sígueme 2001, 253 pp [LSDC 18/1,97s—De Prado, Luis].

7860 *Gruenwald, Ithamar* Prayers, words, and temptation. NTS 47 (2001) 232-236.

7861 **Gunkel, Lioba** 'Ich bin der Weg' Joh 14,6: Meditationen zu den Evangelien der Sonn- und Festtage: Lesejahr A, Bd. 1: Weihnachts- und Osterfestkreis; Bd. 2: im Jahreskreis. Lp 2001, Benno 140 pp. €9.90 + 9.90. 3-7462-1471-8/2-6[OrdKor 44,126].

7862 *Hennig, Gerhard* Wie redet die Bibel von der Seelsorge?. ThBeitr 32 (2001) 181-198.

7863 *Holzem, Andreas* "Kriminalisierung" der Klage?: Bittgebet und Klageverweigerung in der Frömmigkeitsliteratur des 19. Jahrhunderts. JBTh 16 (2001) 153-181.

7864 *Human, D.J.* Gebed: 'n proses wat verandering bemiddel. VeE 22 (2001) 58-71.

7865 **Hurtado, Larry W.** At the origins of christian worship: the context and character of earliest christian devotion. 2000 ⇒16,7985. [R]BS 158 (2001) 505-506 (*Parsons, Stuart; Horrell, J. Scott*); CBQ 63 (2001) 751-752 (*Daly-Denton, Margaret*).

7866 *Johnson, Sherry E.* One step closer: the implicit use of scripture in counseling. JPsC 20/1 (2001) 91-94.

7867 *Kabasele Mukenge, André* De l'emerveillement à l'engagement: itinéraires bibliques pour une spiritualité des temps de crise. Telema 105 (2001) 41-54.

7868 *Kothgasser, Alois* Mein Umgang mit der Bibel: eine persönliche Reflexion. Wort zum Leben. 2001 ⇒284. 179-190.

7869 **Kunz, Claudia Edith** Schweigen und Geist: biblische und patristische Studien zu einer Spiritualität des Schweigens. 1996 ⇒12,135. [R]CCist 63 (2001) [27]-[28] (*Aust, Magdalena*).

7870 *Lange, Ulrich-Paul* Der auferstandene Herr ist uns nahe—Gott und die Seele. Theologisches 31 (2001) 153-158.

7871 **Larsen, David L.** Biblical spirituality: discovering the real connection between the bible and life. GR 2001, Kregel 304 pp. $14.

7872 *Leloir, Louis* La 'lectio divina' chez les Pères du désert. VS 81 (2001) 429-460.

7873 **Linn, Matthew; Linn, Sheila Fabnicant; Linn, Dennis** Understanding difficult scriptures in a healing way. Mahwah 2001, Paulist 112 pp. $13. Ill. *Francisco Miranda* [BiTod 40,128—Bergant, D.].

7874 *Louf, André* Une expérience de 'lectio divina'. VS 81 (2001) 461-481.

7875 **Maestri, William F.** Figures around the cross. NY 2001, Alba xv; 234 pp. $13 [BiTod 40,135—Senior, D.].

7876 *Martini, Carlo M.* La forza di ricominiciare ogni giorno. Ambrosius 77/1 (2001) 63-69.

7877 **Masini, Mario** Spiritualità biblica: temi e percorsi. 2000 ⇒16,7993. ^RRivBib 49 (2001) 373-375 (*De Virgilio, Giuseppe*).

7878 **Mesters, Carlos** Fazer arder o coração: reflexões sobre a leitura o-rante da bíblia. R 2001, Curia Generalizia O. Carm..

7879 *Médevielle, Geneviève* La bible dans l'accompagnement spirituel. La bible, parole adressée. 2001 ⇒323. 81-97.

7880 *Michaels, J. Ramsey* Finding yourself an intercessor: NT prayer from Hebrews to Jude. Into God's presence. 2001 ⇒294. 228-251.

7881 **Miller, Patrick D.** They cried to the Lord: the form and theology of biblical prayer. 1994 ⇒10,8179... 13,7646. ^RJBTh 16 (2001) 397-406 (*Etzelmüller, Gregor*).

7882 *Monari, Luciano* Testo, preghiera e vita: presentazione del libro "La pratica del testo biblico" del Card. Martini. Ambrosius 77/1 (2001) 44-62.

7883 *Navone, John* Il pellegrinaggio alla montagna di dio: il paradigma della conversione. RdT 42 (2001) 165-175.

7884 *Neyrey, Jerome H.* Prayer, in other words: New Testament prayers in social-science perspective. ^FMALINA, B., 2001 ⇒67. 349-380.

7885 *Nouzille, Philippe* La bible dans la 'lectio divina'. La bible, parole adressée. 2001 ⇒323. 99-116.

7886 *Pasquetto, Virgilio* Fonti della teologia spirituale: il criterio normativo della S. Scrittura. Ter. 52 (2001) 489-500.

7887 **Pieri, Fabrizio** Paolo di Tarso e IGNAZIO di Loyola: affinità di due maestri del discernimento spirituale: ispirazione per la vita spirituale e pastorale oggi. Extr. Diss. Gregoriana 2001, ^D*Alphonso, Herbert*: T 2001, 187 pp .

7888 **Poupard, Bernard** Prends et lis: les pères de l'Ancien Testament, Jésus et nous: libres lectures des écritures. Cahiers de Clerlande 9: Ottignies 2001, Saint-André 175 pp. 1027-3832.

7889 **Rupp, Joyce** Inviting God in: scriptural reflections and prayers throughout the year. ND 2001, Ave Maria 157 pp. $13. 0-87793-958-6 [ThD 48,385—Heiser, W. Charles].

7890 *Saraceno, Lorenzo Scriptura crescit cum legente*: porterà frutti a suo tempo. VM 218 (2001) 27-36.

7891 *Schlingensiepen, Ferdinand* "Ihr Pfarrer lebt ja mit Bibel und Gesangbuch": eine Plauderei. DtPfrBl 101 (2001) 230-233.

7892 *Schröer, Henning* Mit Propheten und Poeten beten. PTh 90 (2001) 118-132.

7893 *Steinkamp, Hermann* Ohnmacht und Klage: praktisch-theologische Annäherungen. JBTh 16 (2001) 325-345.

7894 **Stock, Klemens** Po dorozi z Isusom [In cammino con Gesù]. ᴱ*Frankivsk, Ivano*: Samyydav 2001, 34 pp [AcBib 10,914]. **Ukrainian**.

7895 *Vergottini, Marco* "Nutrimento e regola" della vita ecclesiale. Ment. *Martini, C.M.*: Ambrosius 77/1 (2001) 36-43.

7896 *Viviano, Benedict T.* Hillel and Jesus on prayer. Trinity—kingdom—church. NTOA 48: 2001 <1997>⇒223. 88-113.

7897 **Vogl, Wolfgang** Aktion und Kontemplation in der Spiritualität des antiken Judentums und frühen Christentums mit einem hinführenden Teil zur Theorie-Praxis-Problematik in der Antike: Exzerpt zur akademischen Diskussion. Exc. Diss. Gregoriana 2001, ᴰ*García Mateo, Rogelio*: 225; cxiii pp .

7898 *Weber, Franz* Klagen und Anklagen: unterdrückte und befreite Klage in der Volksfrömmigkeit. JBTh 16 (2001) 303-324.

7899 **Wellens, A.** Le vin des écritures. P 2001, Desclée de B. 109 pp. €14.50.

H8.1 *Spiritualitas publica*: Liturgia, Via communitatis, Sancti

7900 **Angenendt, Arnold** Liturgik und Historik: gab es eine organische Liturgie-Entwicklung?. QD 189: FrB 2001, Herder 251 pp. 3-451-02189-7. Bibl. 209-245.

7901 *Aucante, Vincent* Le rôle de l'intuition chez Edith STEIN. RHPhR 81 (2001) 321-332.

7902 **Baawobr, Richard** Bible study and sharing on the gospel of Matthew [... Mark,... Luke] for christian communities. Nairobi 2001, Paulines 3 vols 9966-21-362-7 [v. A]; 9966-21-056-3 [v. B]; 9966-21-564-6 [v. C]. V.1: gospel of Matthew: Sundays of the Year A; v.2: gospel of Mark: Sundays of the Year B; v.3: gospel of Luke: Sundays of the Year C.

7903 Die Bibel in der Liturgie—persönliche Erfahrungen. HlD 55 (2001) 5-12.

7904 *Bracchi, Remo* Di pasqua in pasqua: tra culto e cultura. RivLi 88 (2001) 205-225.

7905 *Brulin, Monique* Quand la parole se prend aux mots. La bible, parole adressée. 2001 ⇒323. 69-79.

7906 *Burger, C.W.* Reformed liturgy in the South African context. AcTh(B) 21/2 (2001) 5-22.

7907 *Bux, Nicola* Il lezionario delle chiese orientali. RivLi 88 (2001) 909-916.

7908 **Casel, Odo** Fede, gnosi e mistero: saggio di teologia del culto cristiano. Padova 2001, EMP xxxviii; 226 pp. €18.07.

7909 *Ceresoli, Luigi* Valenze bibliche nel memoriale propositi. ATOR 32 (2001) 209-377.

7910 *Chadwick, Henry* The calendar: sanctification of time. IThQ 66 (2001) 99-107.

7911 *Chauvet, L.-M.* La bible dans son site liturgique. La bible, parole adressée. 2001 ⇒323. 49-68.

7912 *Cina, Giuseppe* Testimoni dell'amore misericordioso di Cristo e promotori di salute: riflessioni biblico-teologiche. Camillianum 3 (2001) 411-441.

7913 *Crocetti, Giuseppe* Presenza della bibbia nella liturgia delle ore. RivLi 88 (2001) 881-901.

7914 *D'Sa, Francis X.* Discipleship: the hermeneutics of following. Third Millennium 4/4 (2001) 107-118.

7915 **Devijver, J.** Zondagsvieringen in het A-jaar. Averbode 2001, Altiora 539 pp.

7916 *Devillers, Luc* Frère et ami: la vocation du disciple de Jésus. VS 81 (2001) 215-229.

7917 *De Zan, Renato* Leggere la bibbia nella liturgia. RivLi 88 (2001) 869-880.

7918 **Domergue, Marcel** Commentaires bibliques des dimanches et fêtes, années A, B et C: année A. P 2001, Salvator 184 pp. €14.94.

7919 **Dunn, James D.G.** La llamada de Jesús al seguimiento. Alcance 53: Sdr 2001, Sal Terrae 206 pp. 84-293-1378-8.

7920 **Eberle, Andrea** Ethos im koptischen Mönchtum: christliches Gedankengut oder kulturelles Erbe Altägyptens?. ÄAT 52: Wsb 2001, Harrassowitz xi; 314 pp. 3-447-04479-9. Bibl. 290-298.

7921 **Eliseo Gil, Alfonso** Hijos de Adán: los antepasados de Jesús cuentan su historia. M 2001, San Pablo 216 pp. €9.50.

7922 **Federici, T.** Cristo Signore risorto amato e celebrato: commento al lezionario domenicale cicli A,B,C. Quaderni di 'Oriente cristiano' 11: Palermo 2001, Eparchia di Piana degli Albanesi 2189 pp.

7923 *Ferraro, Giuseppe* Commento biblico alla colletta della domenica X 'Per annum'. Notitiae 37 (2001) 549-553.

7924 *Fioriti, Luigi* Il lezionario della chiesa italo-greca e italo-albanese. RivLi 88 (2001) 917-926.

7925 *Foresi, Pasquale* La vocazione a seguire Gesù. Nuova umanità 23 (2001) 593-600.

7926 *Forman, Mary* BENEDICT's use of scripture in the rule: introductory understandings. ABenR 52 (2001) 324-345.

7927 *Franz, Ansgar* Schriftgemäßheit als Anspruch an das Kirchenlied. HID 55 (2001) 21-36.

7928 *Fuchs, Guido* Den Boden lockern: Hinführungen zu den Schriftlesungen. Gottesdienst 35/21 (2001) 161-163.

7929 *Gaucher, Guy* La bible avec THÉRÈSE de Lisieux. VS 741 (2001) 671-693.

7930 *Genre, Ermanno* I lezionari delle chiese della riforma: rapporto tra bibbia e liturgia. RivLi 88 (2001) 947-959.

7931 *Gerhards, Albert* Kraft aus der Wurzel: zum Verhältnis christlicher Liturgie gegenüber dem Jüdischen: Fortschreibung oder struktureller Neubeginn. KuI 16 (2001) 25-44.

7932 *Giraudo, Cesare* Pasqua annuale, pasqua settimanale, pasqua quotidiana: dal ciclo pasquale ebraico al ciclo della pasqua cristiana. RivLi 88 (2001) 67-88.

7933 *Graham, Helen* Liturgical mini-torah. Charism, leadership. 2001 ⇒ 456. 118-122.

7934 *Grant, Robert M.* The structure of eucharistic prayers. ᶠBETZ, H. 2001 ⇒5. 321-332.

7935 *Greule, Albrecht* Was bedeutet widersagen?: die Versprachlichung der abrenuntiatio in der deutschen Sprache. ᶠSCHMUTTERMAYR, G. 2001 ⇒101. 419-425.

7936 *Haunerland, Winfried* "Lebendig ist das Wort Gottes" (Hebr 4,12): die Liturgie als Sitz im Leben der Schrift. ThPQ 149 (2001) 114-124.

7937 *Häußling, Angelus A.* Biblische Grundlegung christlicher Liturgie. HID 55 (2001) 13-20.

7938 *Himmelbauer, Markus; Ritter-Werneck, Roland* Israel und das Erste Testament in den Gesangsbüchern der Kirchen. KuI 16 (2001) 64-74.

7939 ᴱHoulden, Leslie; Rogerson, John The common worship lectionary: a scripture commentary, year A. L 2001, SCPK 291 pp. £20.

7940 *Hubmann, Franz* Von Gott gerufen: biblische Anmerkungen zu einem existentiellen Thema. CPB 114 (2001) 194-198.

7941 *Jeanson, Nicole* Pâques dans le plus vieil état chrétien. MoBi 136 (2001) 13 [BuBB 36,117].

7942 *Jenner, Konrad D.* The relation between biblical text and lectionary systems in the Eastern Church. ᴹWEITZMAN, M., JSOT.S 333: 2001 113. 376-411.

7943 ᴱJohnson, Marshall D. New proclamation, year A, 2001-2002. Mp 2001, Fortress x; 242 pp. $25 [BiTod 39,319—Senior, Donald].

7944 *Kaschewsky, Rudolf* "Liturgische Bibelverdunstung"—zu einem Aufsatz von N. LOHFINK. Una Voce-Korrespondenz 31 (2001) 294-297.

7945 *Koltun-Fromm, Naomi* Yokes of the holy-ones: the embodiment of a christian vocation. HThR 94 (2001) 205-218.

7946 **Kranemann, Daniela** Israelitica dignitas?: Studien zur Israeltheologie Eucharistischer Hochgebete. MThA 66: Altenberge 2001, Oros €30. 3-89375-199-8. Bibl. 253-282.

7947 *L'année en fêtes: les Pères commentent la liturgie de la parole. 2000* ⇒16,8036. ^RFV 100/3 (2001) 75-76 (*Gagnebin, Laurent*).

7948 *Lawrence, Richard T.* The altar bible: *digni, decori, et pulchri.* Worship 75 (2001) 386-402.

7949 *Lehmann, Leonard* FRANCESCO e la bellezza. La bellezza. PSV 44: 2001 ⇒240. 205-220.

7950 *Leonhard, Clemens* Pessachhaggada und Osternacht: gegenseitige Beeinflussung von jüdischer und christlicher Liturgie. KuI 16 (2001) 45-47.

7951 **Lewis, Alan E.** Between cross and resurrection: a theology of Holy Saturday. GR 2001, Eerdmans xiii; 477 pp. $30. 0-8028-4702-1.

7952 *Llewelyn, S.R.* The use of Sunday for meetings of believers in the New Testament. NT 43 (2001) 205-223 [Acts 20,7; 1 Cor 16,2; Rev 1,10].

7953 *Lohfink, Norbert* Neuübersetzung des Osterlobs—warum und wie?. BiLi 74 (2001) 24-26;

7954 Zur Perikopenordnung für die Sonntage im Jahreskreis. HlD 55 (2001) 37-57.

7955 *Lyonnet, Stanislas* La nature du culte chrétien dans le Nouveau Testament. StMiss 50 (2001) 103-137.

7956 *MacCall, Richard D.* The shape of the eucharistic prayer: an essay on the unfolding of an action. Ment. *Hippolytus*: Worship 75 (2001) 321-333.

7957 *Magnoli, Claudio* Il lezionario della chiesa di Milano. RivLi 88 (2001) 927-936.

7958 *Manzi, Franco* Allusions mainly biblical in two modern Marian prefaces. EL 115 (2001) 181-192;

7959 Commento biblico alla colletta della Domenica IV `Per annum';

7960 Commento biblico alla colletta della Domenica IX 'Per annum';

7961 Commento esegetico alla colletta della Domenica V `Per annum'. Notitiae 37 (2001) 68-70/541-545/76-80;

7962 Traduzioni bibliche, tradizione, ed esegesi nell'istruzione 'Liturgiam authenticam'. EL 115 (2001) 313-337.

7963 *Maritano, Mario* La pasqua nei primi secoli cristiani. RivLi 88 (2001) 89-101.

7964 **Meissner, W.W.** The cultic origins of christianity: the dynamics of religious development. 2000 ⇒16,8044. ᴿNBl 82 (2001)298-300 (*Taylor, Justin*); TS 62 (2001) 411-413 & 612-613 (*Gillespie, C. Kevin*); CBQ 63 (2001) 157-158 (*Pilch, John J.*).

7965 **Mitman, F. Russell** Worship in the shape of scripture. Cleveland 2001, Pilgrim 165 pp. $16. 0-8298-1421-3.

7966 **Murphy, Roland E.** Experiencing our biblical heritage. Peabody 2001, Hendrickson 185 pp. $20. 1-56563-496-9.

7967 **Neotti, Clarêncio** Ministério da palavra: comentários aos evangelhos dominicais e festivos—ano A. Pétropolis 2001, Vozes 319 pp [REB 244, 995].

7968 *Ortkemper, Franz-Josef* Ist unsere Liturgiesprache noch zeitgemäß?!!. BiKi 56 (2001) 60.

7969 **Pardilla, A.** La forma di vita di Cristo al centro della formazione alla vita religiosa: il quadro biblico e teologico della formazione. R 2001, Rogate 380 pp.

7970 *Perkins, Judith B.* Space, place, voice in the *Acts* of the martyrs and the Greek romance. Mimesis. 2001 ⇒568. 117-137 [BuBB 36,91].

7971 **Power, David Noel** "The Word of the Lord": liturgy's use of Scripture. Mkn 2001, Orbis viii; 168 pp. £15.39. 1-57075-397-0.

7972 *Ramis, Gabriel* Il lezionario del rito ispanico-mozarabico. RivLi 88 (2001) 937-946.

7973 *Raschzok, Klaus* Die Gegenwart Israels im evangelischen Gottesdienst: zum "Israelkriterium" des Evangelischen Gottesdienstbuches. KuI 16 (2001) 48-61.

7974 *Rayan, Samuel* Theologian as disciple: disciple as theologian. Third Millennium 4/4 (2001) 100-106.

7975 *Ros García, Salvador* Biblia y mística: la revelación de Dios por el símbolo en el poema 'Noche oscura'. Ment. *John of the Cross*. REsp 60 (2001) 351-392.

7976 **Ruiz de Gallareta, J.E.** Palabra y eucaristía: comentarios a los textos de las eucaristías dominicales del ciclo A. Bilbao 2001, Mensajero 431 pp.

7977 *Sahi, Jyoti* Biblical symbols and liturgy in the Indian context. WoWo 34 (2001) 181-204.

7978 *Sancho Fermín, Francisco Javier* La biblia con ojos de mujer: Edith STEIN y sus claves para escuchar la palabra. Claves 2: Avila 2001, Teresiano 223 pp. ᴿPhilipSac 36 (2001) 587-8 (*Ofilada, Macario*).

7979 *Sardini, Fausto* Leggere la bibbia oggi. BeO 43 (2001) 182 [Heb 5].

7980 *Schütz, Christian* "Rectissima norma vitae humanae" (RB 73,3): die Benediktusregel und ihr Umgang mit der Hl. Schrift. ᶠSCHMUTTERMAYR, G. 2001 ⇒101. 537-550.

7981 *Schwier, Helmut* Liturgie und Bibel. WuD 26 (2001) 379-392 & CV 43/3 (2001) 202-219.

7982 **Sodi, Manlio** La parola di Dio nella celebrazione eucaristica: tavole sinottiche. Città del Vaticano 2000, Vaticana xxxiii; 928 pp. €59.39. ᴿCivCatt 152/2 (2001) 87-88 (*Vanzan, P.*).

7983 *Sorci, Pietro* Nella proclamazione delle scritture l'annuncio del mistero pasquale. RivLi 88 (2001) 845-868.

7984 **Staubli, Thomas** Weisheit wurzelt im Volk: Begleiter zu den Sonntagslesungen aus dem Ersten Testament: Lesejahr A. Luzern 2001, Exodus 231 pp. €24. 3-905577-52-6. 73 ill. [EuA 79,351].

7985 **Staudacher, Joseph M.** Lector's guide to biblical pronunciations. Huntington 2001, Our Sunday Visitor 158 pp. $7 [BiTod 40,65— Senior, Donald].

7986 *Steins, Georg* "Dies ist die Nacht": die alttestamentlichen Schriftlesungen in der Struktur der Osternacht. Gottesdienst 35/3 (2001) 17-19.

7987 *Strauss, M.U.* Hoe lyk die spiritualiteit van die erediens met die draai van die millenium. AcTh(B) 21/2 (2001) 126-135.

7988 **Szmurlo, Roman** Zycie monastyczne w pismach Szenutego z Atripe. SAChr 16: Wsz 2001, Wydawnictwo Uniwersytetu Kardynala Stefana Wyszynskiego 271 pp. 83-7072-214-8. Bibl. 16-20. **P.**

7989 *Tagliaferri, Roberto* Estetica e liturgia. La bellezza. PSV 44: 2001 ⇒ 240. 221-250.

7990 *Taylor, Justin* The 'plêthos' of Jesus' disciples. Le judéo-christianisme. 2001 ⇒484. 67-74 [BuBB 36,109].

7991 **Theissen, Gerd** De godsdienst van de eerste christenen—een theorie van het oerchristendom. Kampen 2001, Agora 432 pp. €39.90. 90-391-08277.

7992 *Theokritoff, Elizabeth* Prier les Ecritures dans la tradition liturgique orthodoxe. Contacts 53 (2001) 6-30.

7993 **Tinat, Jürgen** LektorenDienst: Einführungen in die Lesungen der Sonntage, Feste und Hochfeste A/B/C. Konkrete Liturgie: Rg 2001, Pustet 280 pp. €19.90.

7994 *Udris, John* Scented tracks: Thérèse's *reading* of scripture. ScrB 31/1 (2001) 29-35 [Gal 2,10].

7995 *Vorster, J.N.* 'n Politiek tegnologie van die vroeë Christen se gepynigde liggaam. VeE 22 (2001) 434-454.

7996 *Wet, F.W. de; Venter, C.J.H.* Aangegryp deur die woord: teologiesestetiese riglyne vir die omgang met en bediening van die woord. AcTh(B) 21/2 (2001) 23-35.

7997 *Work, Telford* Annunciation as election. SJTh 54 (2001) 285-307 [Lk 1,46-55].

7998 ^E**Zevini, G.; Cabra, P.G.** Lectio divina per ogni giorno dell'anno: ferie del tempo ordinario (Sett. 9-17, anno dispari). Brescia 2001, Queriniana 396 pp. €16.53 [RdT 42,640];

7999 ferie del tempo ordinario (Sett. 18-25, anno dispari). Brescia 2001, Queriniana 336 pp. €14.46 [RdT 42,640];

8000 ferie del tempo ordinario (Sett. 1-8, anno pari). Brescia 2001, Queriniana 326 pp. €14.46 [RdT 43,160];

8001 domeniche del tempo ordinario (Ciclo A). Brescia 2001, Queriniana 328 pp. €14.46 [RdT 43,160];

8002 proprio dei santi 1 (gennaio-giugno). Brescia 2001, Queriniana 328 pp. €14.46 [RdT 43,160].

H8.2 Theologia moralis NT

8003 *Adam, Andrew Keith Malcolm* Walk this way: repetition, difference, and the imitation of Christ Interp. 55 (2001) 19-33.

8004 ^E*Amadon, James; Eklund, Rebekah* Annotated bibliography on biblical ethics. ExAu 17 (2001) 163-176.

8005 ^E**Balch, David L.** Homosexuality, science, and the 'plain sense' of scripture. 2000 ⇒16,231. ^RBiblInterp 9 (2001) 105-109 (*Lincoln, Andrew T.*); JThS 52 (2001) 312-314 (*Grayston, K.*); RRT 8 (2001) 176-178 (*Cöster, Henry*); ThTo 58 (2001) 90-92, 94 (*Sonderegger, Katherine*); CBQ 63 (2001) 370-372 (*Turro, James C.*).

8006 **Blount, Brian K.** Then the whisper put on flesh: New Testament ethics in an African American context. Nv 2001, Abingdon 232 pp. $21. 0-687-08589-6. Bibl. 213-222.

8007 *Boarini, Serge* Deux procédures de résolution des situations morales difficiles: aux origines des conférences de consensus. RHPhR 81 (2001) 171-187.

8008 **Bockmuehl, Markus** Jewish law in Gentile churches: halakhah and the beginning of christian public ethics. 2000 ⇒16,8074. ^RRRT 8 (2001) 147-149 (*Neusner, Jacob*); Theol. 104 (2001) 282-283 (*Horrell, David G.*); Theol. 104 (2001) 282-283 (*Horrell, David G.*); SNTU.A 26 (2001) 261-262 (*Repschinski, B.*); ET 112 (2001) 219-220 (*Rodd, C.S.*).

8009 **Borghi, Ernesto; Buzzi, Franco** La coscienza di essere umani: percorsi biblici e filosofici per un agire etico. In cammino: Mi 2001, Àncora 186 pp. 88-7610-900-5. Bibl. 177-181.

8010 *Botero Giraldo, J. Silvio* El amor al prójimo: el cónyuge es el prójimo más próximo. Strom. 57 (2001) 97-118.

8011 *Brewer, Ken* The ethics of Jerusalem and the morals of Athens: assessing Hans KÜNG's theological ethics. AsbTJ 56/1 (2001) 101-18.

8012 *Britz, J.J.* Inligtingsarmoede: 'n christelik etiese refleksie. VeE 22 (2001) 252-272.

8013 **Brooten, Bernadette J.** Love between women: early christian responses to female homoeroticism. 1996 ⇒12,7324... 16,8075. ᴿJBL 119 (2000) 127-129 (*Castelli, Elizabeth A.*).

8014 *Coda, Piero* Giustizia e grazia: il paradosso del Crocifisso. FilTeo 15 (2001) 514-525.

8015 **Collins, Raymond F.** Sexual ethics and the New Testament. 2000 ⇒ 16,8081. ᴿJThS 52 (2001) 310-312 (*Grayston, K.*); CBQ 63 (2001) 142-4 (*Harrington, Daniel J.*); EThL 77 (2001) 482-484 (*Selling, J.*).

8016 ᴱ**Compagnoni, Francesco; Privitera, Salvatore** Vita morale e beatitudini: sacra scrittura, storia, teoretica, esperienza. 2000 ⇒16,502. Congr. ATISM 1998. ᴿCivCatt 152/2 (2001) 513-515 (*Cultrera, F.*).

8017 **Coninck, Frédéric de** La justice et la puissance: dire et vivre sa foi dans la société d'aujourd'hui (II). Québec 1998, La Clairière 109 pp.

8018 *Connock, Evan B.; Van Rensburg, Fika J.* The literary context of the husband-wife code in the New Testament. APB 12 (2001) 68-85.

8019 *Da Spinetoli, Ortensio* La giustizia nel Nuovo Testamento: vangeli e Atti. Giustizia-giustificazione nella bibbia. DSBP 28: 2001 ⇒307. 128-169.

8020 **Debergé, Pierre** La justice dans le Nouveau Testament. CEv 115: P 2001, Cerf 5-59 pp.

8021 **De Gruchy, John W.** Christianity, art and transformation: theological aesthetics in the struggle for justice. C 2001, CUP xii; 273 pp. 0-521-77205-2. Bibl. 255-258.

8022 *Dijon, Xavier; Montero, Ètienne* La bible, source d'inspiration pour le droit en bioéthique?. Bible et droit. 2001 ⇒300. 87-120.

8023 *Dolamo, R.T.H.* Reconciliation and economic justice in South Africa: the role of the church and theology. VeE 22 (2001) 292-299.

8024 **Domanyi, Thomas** Der Toleranzgedanke im Neuen Testament: ein Beitrag zur christlichen Ethik. Basel 2000, Reinhardt 166 pp. €16.90. 3-724-511-299 [BiKi 58,252—Hartmann, Michael].

8025 *Dupree, Claretta* Biblical ethics at the end of life. ExAu 17 (2001) 142-154.

8026 *Echeverria, Eduardo J.* The moral life in biblical perspective. HPR 102/3 (2001) 28-32, 47-49.

8027 *Fernandes, José Flávio de C.* Hipocrisia. Estudos Bíblicos 70 (2001) 83-96.

8028 **Fernández, Aurelio** El mensaje moral de Jesús de Nazaret. 1998 ⇒ 14,7309; 15,8106. ᴿCart. 17 (2001) 235-237 (*Parada Navas, J.L.*).

8029 *Fields, Bruce* Response to Wheeler. ExAu 17 (2001) 73-76.

8030 **Gagnon, Robert A.J.** The bible and homosexual practice: texts and hermeneutics. Nv 2001, Abingdon 520 pp. $49. 0-687-08413-X.

8031 **Gauthier, André-Pierre** Paul RICOEUR et l'agir ensemble: les figures bibliques du prophète et du témoin. Lyon 2001, PROFAC 145 pp. €10.67. 2-85319-086-1. Préf. *Bruno-Marie Duffé.*

8032 *Gibbs, Robert* The disappearing God of ethical monotheism. ᶠDIETRICH, W. BJSt 329: 2001 ⇒24. 229-239.

8033 **Graham, Gordon** Evil and christian ethics. New Studies in Christian Ethics 20: C 2001, CUP xviii; 241 pp. 0-521-79745-4. Bibl. 230-34.

8034 *Grassi, Joseph A.* Animal rights and justice in the biblical tradition. BiTod 39 (2001) 373-378.

8035 *Guest, Pauline D.* Battling for the bible: academy, church and the gay agenda. Theology and sexuality 15 (2001) 66-93.

8036 *Haas, Peter J.* Ethical monotheism in an age of probability: what if God does play dice?. ᶠDIETRICH, W., BJSt 329: 2001 ⇒24. 216-228.

8037 *Hadley, Mark A.* Ethical monotheism or ethical polytheism?: reflections on TROELTSCH, WEBER, and JAMES. ᶠDIETRICH, W., BJSt 329: 2001 ⇒24. 155-178.

8038 **Hari, Albert; Verdoodt, Albert** I diritti dell'uomo nella bibbia e oggi. Città del Vaticano 2001, Libreria Editrice Vaticana 168 pp. 88-2-09-7185-2.

8039 **Hays, R.B.** La visione morale del Nuovo Testamento. 2000 ⇒16, 8096. ᴿStPat 48 (2001) 229-230 (*Segalla, Giuseppe*); StMon 43 (2001) 415-416 (*Busquets, P.*).

8040 *Heimbach-Steins, Marianne; Steins, Georg* Ornament, Fundament, Argument oder was sonst?: zur Rolle der Bibel als Kanon in theologischer Ethik und in gemeinsamen katholisch-evangelischen Texten. ZEE 45 (2001) 95-108.

8041 *Hossfeld, Frank-Lothar* Homosexualität und Homoerotik im Vorderen Orient—und in der Bibel?. WUB 21 (2001) 48-51.

8042 *Huarte Osácar, Juan* Presencia de los cristianos en el diálogo social. Communio 34/1 (2001) 229-260.

8043 *Human, L.H.; Liebenberg, J.; Müller, J.C.* Morality, imagination and human decision making. VeE 22 (2001) 300-313.

8044 *Huneke, Douglas K.* A post-Shoah interventionist christianity: expanding the ranks of the faithful remnant in the third millennium. "Good News" after Auschwitz?. 2001 ⇒377. 141-156.

8045 *Jackson, Winston* Biblical reflections on liberation and reconciliation from the South African experience. Journal of African Christian Thought 4/2 (2001) 2-7.

8046 **Knust, Jennifer Wright** Abandoned to lust: the politics of sexual slander in early christian discourse. Diss. Columbia 2001, 341 pp. 9999255.

8047 *Lange, Frits de* Weerloze aanspraak—over bijbel en ethiek. GThT 101 (2001) 140-149.

8048 *Lindemann, Andreas* Schwangerschaftsabbruch als ethisches Problem im antiken Judentum und im frühen Christentum. WuD 26 (2001) 127-148.

8049 *Maccoby, Hyam* How unclean were tax-collectors?. BTB 31 (2001) 60-63.

8050 *Maggioni, Bruno* Gesù e il denaro. VitaCon 37 (2001) 473-479.

8051 **Marshall, Christopher D.** Beyond retribution: a New Testament vision for justice, crime, and punishment. Studies in Peace and Scripture: GR 2001, Eerdmans xx; 342 pp. $24. 0-8028-4797-8. Bibl. 285-316 [BiTod 39,389—Senior, Donald].

8052 *Martini, Carlo Maria* El extranjero en la escritura. SalTer 89 (2001) 417-426;

8053 L'uso evangelico dei beni di questo mondo. VitaCon 37 (2001) 355-368.

8054 **Matera, Frank J.** Ética do Novo Testamento: os legados de Jesus e de Paulo. [T]*Costa, João Rezende*: 1999 ⇒15,8121. [R]REB 61 (2001) 473-477 (*Marques, Valdir*); PerTeol 33 (2001) 272-276 (*Marques, Valdir*).

8055 **Mcdonald, J. Ian H.** The crucible of christian morality. 1998 ⇒14, 7324... 16,8103. [R]CoTh (2001/3) 225-227 (*Dziuba, Andrzej F.*).

8056 *Mouton, Elna* A rhetoric of theological vision?: on scripture's reorienting power in the liturgy of (social) life. Neotest. 35 (2001) 111-127.

8057 *Müller, Hadwig* Option für die Armen: "das Schwache der Welt hat Gott erwählt, um das Starke zuschanden zu machen" (1 Kor 1,27). Jahrbuch für kontextuelle Theologien 9 (2001) 173-192.

8058 *Panimolle, Salvatore A.* Le vie del Signore sono giustizia!. Giustizia-giustificazione nella bibbia. DSBP 28: 2001⇒307. 9-18.

8059 *Penna, Romano* Osservazioni sull'anti-edonismo nel Nuovo Testamento in rapporto al suo ambiente culturale. Vangelo e inculturazione. 2001 <1985> ⇒193. 771-794.

8060 *Petracca, Vincenzo* Gott oder Mammon—Überlegungen zur neutestamentlichen Besitzethik. ZNT 8 (2001) 18-24.

8061 **Pfeiffer, Matthias** Einweisung in das neue Sein: neutestamentliche Erwägungen zur Grundlegung der Ethik. BEvTh 119: Gü 2001, Kaiser 348 pp. €39.95. 3-579-05314-0.

8062 *Poucouta, Paulin* Mémoire et réconciliation dans l'Écriture. AETSC 8 (2001) 63-81.

8063 *Reimer, Ivoni Richter* A lógica do mercado e a transgressão de mulheres: uma visão teológico-cultural a partir dos evangelhos. Estudos Bíblicos 69 (2001) 50-60.

8064 *Reiser, Marius* Love of enemies in the context of antiquity. NTS 47 (2001) 411-427.

8065 *Rizzi, Armido* I diritti umani nella bibbia. FilTeo 15 (2001) 504-513.

8066 *Salzman, Todd A.* The basic goods theory and revisionism: a methodological comparison of the use of scripture as a source of moral knowledge. LouvSt 26 (2001) 117-146.

8067 *Schmeller, Thomas* Neutestamentliches Gruppenethos. Der neue Mensch in Christus. QD 190: 2001 ⇒239. 120-134.

8068 **Schreiner, Josef; Kampling, Rainer** Il prossimo, lo straniero, il nemico. I temi della Bibbia 3: Bo 2001, EDB 159 pp. 88-10-22105-2. Bibl. 153-155.

8069 *Schüssler Fiorenza, Francis* Pluralism: a western commodity of justice for the other?. ᶠDIETRICH, W. BJSt 329: 2001 ⇒24. 278-306.

8070 **Segalla, Giuseppe** Un'etica per tre comunità: l'etica di Gesù in Matteo, Marco e Luca. 2000 ⇒16,8114. ᴿStPat 48 (2001) 230-232 (*De Virgilio, Giuseppe*); CivCatt 152/3 (2001) 300-302 (*Cultrera, F.*).

8071 **Shaw, Teresa M.** The burden of the flesh: fasting and sexuality in early christianity. 1998 ⇒14,7343. ᴿHeyJ 42 (2001) 367-368 (*Laird, Martin*).

8072 **Skillen, James W.** A covenant to keep: meditations on the biblical theme of justice. 2000 ⇒16,8116. ᴿCTJ 36 (2001) 203-204 (*Cooper, John W.*).

8073 *Slocum, Robert B.* Zacchaean effects and ethics of the Spirit. AThR 83 (2001) 585-593 [Lk 19,1-10].

8074 *Soards, Marion L.* Scripture and stem cells: seeking biblical guidance when there is no obvious biblical word. ExAu 17 (2001) 97-120.

8075 **Spohn, William C.** Go and do likewise: Jesus and ethics. 1999 ⇒15, 8136. ᴿMoralia 24 (2001) 142-144 (*Mingo Kaminouchi, Alberto de*).

8076 *Stanton, Graham* What is the law of Christ?. ExAu 17 (2001) 47-59.

8077 *Starnitzke, Dierk* Bezeichnungen diakonisch betreuter Menschen und das Liebesgebot. WuD 26 (2001) 289-306.

8078 **Stemm, Sönke von** Der betende Sünder vor Gott: Studien zu Vergebungsvorstellungen in urchristlichen und frühjüdischen Texten. AGJU 45: 1999 ⇒15,8138. ᴿJSJ 32 (2001) 355-359 (*Mulder, M.C.*); CBQ 63 (2001) 355-356 (*Mowery, Robert L.*).

8079 *Stenström, Hanna* En bit till på väg mot en etisk bibelkritik. SEÅ 66 (2001) 177-196.

8080 *Stone, Ken* Homosexuality and the bible or queer reading?: a response to Martti Nissinen. Theology and sexuality 14 (2001) 107-18.

8081 *Timmer, David E.* The bible and the christian moral life: a debate within the Reformed Church in America. RefR(H) 54/3 (2001) 157-167.

8082 *Tiwald, Markus* Die Nichterfüllung wanderradikaler Erwartungen als Geburt frühkirchlicher Ethik. PzB 10 (2001) 105-119.

8083   *Troiani, Lucio* Spunti per un'origine del perdono cristiano. ᴹCAGNI,
       L., 4. SMDSA 61: 2001 ⇒15. 2219-2236.
8084   *Van Tilborg, Sjef* Wie is de homo die gered wordt?: de interpetatie
       van Genesis in documenten over homoseksualiteit vanuit de katholike
       kerk. TTh 41 (2001) 3-12.
8085   *Vial, Theodore M.* Introduction. ᶠDIETRICH, W. 2001 ⇒24. 1-12.
8086   *Wheeler, Sondra* Creation, community, discipleship: remembering
       why we care about sex. ExAu 17 (2001) 60-72;
8087   Response to Soards. ExAu 17 (2001) 121-124.
8088   **Wheeler, Sondra Ely** Wealth as peril and obligation: the New Testa-
       ment on possessions. 1995 ⇒11/2,4719... 13,7755. ᴿSNTU.A 22
       (1997) 233-235 (*Giesen, H.*).
8089   **Woyke, Johannes** Die neutestamentlichen Haustafeln: ein kritischer
       und konstruktiver Forschungsüberblick. SBS 184: 2000 ⇒16,8123.
       ᴿITS 38 (2001) 255-257 (*Legrand, L.*).
8090   *Zeller, Dieter* Konkrete Ethik im hellenistischen Kontext. Der neue
       Mensch in Christus. QD 190: 2001 ⇒239. 82-98.
8091   *Zerbe, Gordon* Forgiveness and the transformation of conflict: the
       continuity of a biblical paradigm. ᶠJANZEN, W. 2001 ⇒54. 235-258.

H8.4 *NT de reformatione sociali*—Political action in Scripture

8092   **Pilgrim, Walter** Uneasy neighbors: church and state in the New
       Testament. 1999 ⇒15,8145; 16,8129. ᴿCoTh (2001/3) 211-214
       (*Załęski, Jan*) .

H8.5 Theologia liberationis latino-americana...

8093   *Cardenal, Ernesto* The Song of Mary (Luke 1:46-55). The post-
       modern bible reader. 2001 <1990> ⇒287. 183-187.
8094   *Cavalcanti, Tereza M.P.* Quand les pauvres lisent la bible: un regard
       latino-américain. LV.F 56 (2001) 413-422.
8095   **Ceci, L.** La teologia della liberazione in America latina: l'opera di
       Gustavo GUTIÉRREZ. 1999 ⇒15,8150. ᴿCrSt 22 (2001) 283-286 (*Vi-
       lanova, Evangelista*).
8096   *Dussel, Enrique* From *Ethics and community*. The postmodern bible
       reader. 2001 <1988> ⇒287. 296-318 [Gen 3,1-7].
8097   *George, Sherron Kay* From liberation to evangelization: new Latin
       American hermeneutical keys. Interp. 55 (2001) 367-377.

8098 *Pieris, Aloysius* Cristo más allá del dogma: hacer cristología en el contexto de las religiones de los pobres (II). RLAT 18 (2001) 107-124.

8099 **Sobrino, Jon** Jesucristo liberador: lectura histórico-teológica de Jesús de Nazaret. Estructuras y Procesos, Religión: M ⁴2001, Trotta 350 pp.

8100 **Tavares, Sinivaldo S.** Il mistero de la croce nei teologi della liberazione latino-americani. 1999 ⇒15,8160; 16,8144. ᴿRSR 89 (2001) 306-307 (*Fédou, Michel*); PerTeol 33 (2001) 407-411 (*Libanio, João Batista*).

8101 *Vedoato, João Marinot* Cristologia e teologia della croce in prospettiva latino-americana: un approccio che parte dai crocifissi nella storia. LSDC 16 (2001) 125-136.

8102 **Weber, Burkhard** Ijob in Lateinamerika: Deutung und Bewältigung von Leid in der Theologie der Befreiung. 1999 ⇒15,8162. ᴿNZM 57 (2001) 67-68 (*Piepke, Joachim*).

H8.6 *Theologiae emergentes*—**Theologies of emergent groups**

8103 **Alangaram, A.** Christ of the Asian peoples: toward an Asian contextual christology. Bangalore 2001, Asian Trading Corporation xxiii; 232 pp 81-7086-238-8. Based on the documents of Federation of Asian Bishops' Conferences; revised edition; bibl. 209-223.

8104 *Asante, Emmanuel* The gospel in context: an African perspective. Interp. 55 (2001) 355-366.

8105 *Fansaka, Bernard* Mgr. L. Monsengwo Pasinya et la théorie d'une inculturation dynamique enracinée dans la révélation. NRTh 123 (2001) 46-61.

8106 *Hones, Donald F.* The word: religion and literacy in the life of a Hmong American. RelEd 96/4 (2001) 489-509.

8107 *Horsfjord, Vebjorn L.* Challenging contexts: a study of two contemporary Indian christian theologians and a reflection on the need for intercontextual dialogue. StTh 55 (2001) 41-57.

8108 *Maluleke, Tinyiko S.* African 'Ruths,' ruthless Africas: reflections of an African Mordecai. Other ways. 2001 ⇒260. 237-251.

8109 *Mulackal, Shalini* Feminist christology in Asia. ThD 48 (2001) 107-110.

8110 *Plaatjie, Gloria Kehilwe* Toward a post-apartheid black feminist reading of the bible: a case of Luke 2:36-38. Other ways. 2001 ⇒260. 114-142.

8111 **Sugirtharajah, Rasiah S.** The bible and the third world: precolonial, colonial and postcolonial encounters. C 2001, CUP x; 306 pp. £45/ 16. 0-521-00524-8. Bibl. 283-297.

H8.7 *Mariologia*—The mother of Jesus in the NT

8112 **Beattie, Tina** Redescobrindo Maria a partir dos evangelhos. [T]*Ferreira, Silvio Neves*: São Paulo 2001, Filhas de São Paulo 152 pp [REB 61,516].

8113 **Becker, Jürgen** Maria: Mutter Jesu und erwählte Jungfrau. Biblische Gestalten 4: Lp 2001, Evangelische Verlagsanstalt 319 pp. €14.50. 3-374-01932-3.

8114 **Ben-Chorin, Schalom** Marie: un regard juif sur la mère de Jésus. P 2001, Desclée de B. 255 pp. €22.87. [R]EeV 41 (2001) 27-28 (*Rastoin, Cécile*).

8115 [E]*Billon, Gérard* Marie, mère de Dieu. DosB 88 (2001) 3-29.

8116 *Bravo, Arturo* Presencia de la Virgen María en la biblia. Revista católica 101 (2001) 289-293.

8117 *Buby, Bertrand* Biblical images of Mary from Blessed William Joseph CHAMINADE. EphMar 51 (2001) 181-201.

8118 **Calì, Rosa** I testi antimariologici nell'esegesi dei Padri: da Nicea a Calcedonia: per una mariologia in prospettiva ecclesiale. 1999 ⇒15, 8172. [R]Miles Immaculatae 37 (2001) 619-622 (*Costa, Francesco*); MF 101 (2001) 845-847 (*Costa, Francesco*); Mar. 63 (2001) 530-531 (*Mateo-Seco, Lucas F.*).

8119 *Corsato, Celestino* La tipologia 'Eva—chiesa—Maria' nella tradizione patristica prenicena. Theotokos 9 (2001) 153-190 Sum. 190.

8120 *Díez Merino, L.* La Santissima Trinidad y la madre de Jesús en pasajes neotestamentarios según algunos exegetas españoles. EstMar 67 (2001) 119-161.

8121 *Dorelli, Cesare A.* Karezza-Liebe (Auszug). Irreale Glaubensinhalte. 2001 ⇒1066. 56.

8122 [E]**Fiores, S. de; Meo, S.; Tourón, E.** Nuevo diccionario de mariología. M [3]2001, San Pablo 2128 pp.

8123 [E]**Gambero, L.** Testi mariani del secondo millennio 3,: Autori medievali dell'Occidente, sec. XI-XII; 4,: Autori medievali dell'Occidente, sec. XIII-XV. R 1996, Città Nuova 88-311-9234-5/3.

8124 *Gambero, Luigi* Maria 'vergine' e 'madre' nell'esegesi patristica del Nuovo Testamento nei primi tre secoli. Theotokos 9 (2001) 129-151 Sum. 151.

8125 **Gaventa, Beverly Roberts** Mary: glimpses of the mother of Jesus. 1999 ⇒15,8178. [R]TJT 17 (2001) 288-289 (*Campbell, Joan*); RBLit 3 (2001) 321-323 (*Collins, Raymond F.*).

8126 [E]**Gharib, Georges** Maria di Nazaret secondo gli apocrifi. Minima di Città Nuova: R 2001, Città N. 85 pp. 88-311-1424-7.

8127 *Gila, Angelo* La Vergine Madre e l'Antico Testamento secondo i primi padri della chiesa. Theotokos 9 (2001) 83-128 Sum. 127.
      Un grande segno nel cielo 2000 ⇒383.

8128 **Hahn, Scott** Hail, Holy Queen: the mother of God in the word of God. NY 2001, Doubleday xii; 191 pp. £11. Foreword by *Kilian Healy*: [R]Immacolata Mediatrix 1/1 (2001) 134-135 (*Calkins, Arthur Burton*).

8129 [E]**Heil, Johannes; Kampling, Rainer** Maria—Tochter Sion?: Mariologie, Marienfrömmigkeit und Judenfeindschaft. Pd 2001, Schöningh 271 pp. €41. 3-506-74254-X. [R]Mar. 63 (2001) 536-538 (*Stern, Jean*).

8130 **Jordan, Michael** Mary: the unauthorised biography. L 2001, Weidenfeld and N. xiii; 338 pp. 0-297-84252-8. Bibl. 315-324.

8131 **Landucci, Pier Carlo** Maria santissima nel vangelo. 2000 ⇒16, 8181. [R]Immacolata Mediatrix 1/2 (2001) 143-144 (*Manelli, Stefano Maria*).

8132 **Masciarelli, Michele Giulio** La discepola: Maria di Nazaret beata perché ha creduto. Città del Vaticano 2001, Vaticana 103 pp. 88-209-7240-9.

8133 *Norelli, Enrico* Maria nella letteratura apocrifa dei primi tre secoli. Theotokos 9 (2001) 191-225 Sum. 225.

8134 *Perera, James Dudley* Mary's discipleship: some exegetical and theological considerations. VJTR 65 (2001) 270-278.

8135 **Peretto, Elio** Percorsi mariologici nell'antica letteratura cristiana. Città del Vaticano 2001, LEV 324 pp. 88-209-7079-1. [R]Miles Immaculatae 37 (2001) 609-612 (*Olszewski, Jan M.*); Aug. 41 (2001) 560-562 (*Grossi, V.*); Mar. 63 (2001) 531-533 (*Mateo-Seco, Lucas F.*).

8136 **Ponce Cuéllar, Miguel** María, madre del Redentor y madre de la iglesia. Barc [2]2001, Herder 559 pp. 84-254-2218-3.

8137 *Ruiz Martorell, Julián* María: la mujer clave de la historia. Personajes del NT. 2001 ⇒231. 75-89.

8138 *Serra, Aristide M.* Il Padre celeste e la madre terrena: convergenze nella storia della salvezza. Maria e il Dio. 2001 ⇒547. 221-316;

8139 L'Assunta, segno di 'speranza e consolazione' per il peregrinante popolo di Dio. L'Assunzione. 2001 ⇒513. 203-246 [Wisd 18,14-16; 2 Macc 15,15-16; Eph 6,17; Heb 4, 12-19].

8140 **Sinoir, Michel** La 'démonocratie' et le triomphe de Marie dans la Sainte Écriture. P 2001, Téqui 150 pp. €10.52. 2-7403-0843-4.

8141 ᴱSpidlik, T.; Guaita, G.; Campatelli, M. Testi mariani del secondo
      millennio 2,: Autori dell'area russa, sec. XI-XX. R 2000, Città Nuova
      88-311-9256-6.
8142 Sri, Edward P. Queen Mother: a biblical theology of Mary's queen-
      ship. Diss. Angelicum 2001, ᴰHenchey, Joseph: R 2001, 232 pp.
8143 Stramare, Tarcisio Il matrimonio della Madre de Dio: i santi sposi.
      Verona 2001, Stimmatine 76 pp.
8144 ᴱSuprenant, Leon J. Catholic for a reason II: scripture and the mys-
      tery of the mother of God. 2000 ⇒16,377. ᴿImmacolata Mediatrix 1/
      1 (2001) 138-140 (Calkins, Arthur Burton).
8145 ᴱValentini, Alberto Maria secondo le scritture. Theotokos 8/2: R
      2001, Monfortane 373-949 pp.
8146 Van Beeck, Frans Josef "Born of the virgin Mary": toward a Sprach-
      regelung on a delicate point of doctrine. Pacifica 14 (2001) 121-143.

H8.8 Feminae NT—Women in the NT and church history

8147 Barbero, Mario A first-century couple, Priscilla and Aquila: their
      house churches and missionary activity. Diss. Cath. Univ. of America
      2001, ᴰCollins, R.F. 349 pp. 3004148 [Acts 18].
8148 Blaquière, G. L'altra metà del vangelo: il dono di essere donna. Mi
      2001 <1982>, Ancora 136 pp.
8149 Carpinello, Mariella Données à Dieu: figures féminines dans les
      premiers siècles chrétiens. Spiritualité orientale 78: Bégrolles-en-
      Mauges 2001, Abbaye de Bellefontaine 411 pp. €22.90. 2-85589-
      378-X [RHPhR 82,339s—Larchet, J.-C.].
8150 Cerrato, J.A. Martha and Mary in the commentaries of HIPPOLYTUS.
      StPatr 34. 2001 ⇒553. 294-297.
8151 Coletti, Theresa Paupertas est donum Dei: hagiography, lay religion,
      and the economics of salvation in the Digby Mary Magdalene. Spec.
      76 (2001) 337-378.
8152 Dauzat, Pierre-Emmanuel L'invention de Marie-Madeleine. P
      2001, Bayard 180 pp [PastSc 21,414s—Gauthier, Jacques].
8153 Eisen, Ute E. "Jesus und die Frauen": ein kritischer Rückblick. BZ 45
      (2001) 79-93.
8154 Fischer, Eva Maria Salome—femme fatale des Neuen Testaments?:
      ein Streifzug durch Rezeptions- und Wirkungsgeschichte. ᶠSCHMUT-
      TERMAYR, G. 2001 ⇒101. 383-401.
8155 Getty-Sullivan, Mary Ann Women in the New Testament. ColMn
      2001, Liturgical ix; 269 pp. $8. 0-8146-2546-0. Bibl. 261-262
      [BiTod 39,386—Senior, Donald].

8156 **Haskins, Susan** María Magdalena: mito y metáfora. 1996 ⇒12, 7468; 15,8218. [R]CTom 127 (2001) 621-623 (*Fueyo, Bernardo*).

8157 *Hintersberger, Benedikta* Maria aus Magdala: Patronin des Dominikanerordens. WuA(M) 42 (2001) 136-138.

8158 **Jansen, Katherine Ludwig** The making of the Magdalen: preaching and popular devotion in the later Middle Ages. 2000 ⇒16,8221. [R]TS 62 (2001) 382-384 (*Mueller, Joan*); ChH 70 (2001) 353-354 (*Fleming, Martha H.*).

[E]**Kraemer, R.** Women & christian origins 1999 ⇒289.

8159 **Küng, Hans** Women in christianity. [T]*Bowden, John*: L 2001, Continuum x; 129 pp. 0-8264-5686-3.

8160 **Malone, Mary T.** Women & christianity, 1: the first thousand years. Mkn 2001, Orbis 276 pp. $20. 1570753660 [TD 48,279–Heiser, W.].

8161 **Marjanen, Atti** The woman Jesus loved: Mary Magdalene in the Nag Hammadi library and related dcouments. NHS 40: 1996 ⇒12, 7475... 15,8224. [R]BiblInterp 9 (2001) 93-95 (*Klutz, Todd*).

8162 *Matthews, Shelly* Thinking of Thecla: issues in feminist historiography. JFSR 17/2 (2001) 39-55.

8163 *Moloney, Francis J.* Jesus and women. 'A hard saying'. 2001 <1988> ⇒184. 3-34.

8164 *Montagnes, Bernard* Le pèlerinage provençal à Marie-Madeleine au XVe siècle. RSPhTh 85 (2001) 679-695.

8165 **Petersen, Silke** 'Zerstört die Werke der Weiblichkeit!': Maria Magdalena, Salome und andere Jüngerinnen Jesu in christlich-gnostischen Schriften. NHMS 48: 1999 ⇒15,8229. [R]JECS 9 (2001) 275-276 (*Meconi, David Vincent*); YESW 9 (2001) 276-277 (*Boer, Esther A. de*); CBQ 63 (2001) 158-160 (*Perkins, Pheme*).

8166 *Polanowski,Tadeusz P.* Maria Magdalena w literaturze [Marie Madeleine en littérature]. PrzPow 7-8 (2001) 101-112. **P.**

8167 *Ruiz Martorell, Julián* Las mujeres: compañeras de Pablo;

8168 Lidia: la entrada del cristianismo en Europa. Personajes del NT. 2001 ⇒231. 37-46/47-58.

8169 *Schumacher, Joseph* Ein neues Frauenbild. Katholische Bildung 102/3 (2001) 97-113.

8170 **Tunc, Suzanne** También las mujeres seguían a Jesús. [T]*Pablos, Gregorio de*: Presencia Teológica 98: 1999 ⇒15,8236; 16,8236. [R]PerTeol 33 (2001) 132-133 (*Taborda, Francisco*).

8171 **Whitley, Katerina Katsarka** Seeing for ourselves: biblical women who met Jesus. Harrisburg 2001, Morehouse ix; 107 pp. $13 [BiTod 40,267—Senior, Donald].

H8.9 *Theologia feminae*—Feminist theology

8172 *Barton, Mukti* The skin of Miriam became as white as snow: the bible, western feminism and colour politics. Feminist Theology 27 (2001) 68-80 [Num 12].

8173 **Beattie,Tina** The Last Supper according to Mary and Martha. NY 2001, Continuum 127 pp. £10. 0-86012-290-5.

8174 *Bird, Phyllis A.* A North American feminist response. Other ways. 2001 ⇒260. 199-206.

8175 **Claassens, L. Juliana M.** The God who feeds: a feminist-theological analysis of key pentateuchal and intertestamental texts. Diss. Princeton Sem. 2001, 235 pp. 3006838.

8176 **Clifford, Anne M.** Introducing feminist theology. Mkn 2001, Orbis xi; 273 pp. $21.

8177 *Conti, Cristina* Hermenêutica feminista. Grande Sinal 55 (2001) 497-512.

8178 *Douglas, Kelly B.* Marginalized people, liberating perspectives: a womanist approach to biblical interpretation. AThR 83 (2001) 41-47.

8179 **Dube, Musa W.** Postcolonial feminist interpretation of the bible. 2000 ⇒16,8251. [R]JKTh (2001) 227-234 (*Heidemanns, Katja*).

8180 **Fiorenza, Elisabeth Schüssler** Rhetoric and ethic: the politics of biblical studies. 1999 ⇒15,8249; 16,8259. [R]RSR 89 (2001) 140-141 (*Aletti, Jean-Noël*); JR 81 (2001) 278-280 (*Calef, Susan A.*); MoTh 17 (2001) 406-408 (*Fowl, Stephen*); JThS 52 (2001) 856-859 (*Rowland, Christopher*);

8181 Jesus and the politics of interpretation. 2000 ⇒16,8260. [R]AThR 83 (2001) 886-887 (*Chilton, Bruce*);

8182 Wisdom ways: introducing feminist biblical interpretation. Mkn 2001, Orbis x; 229 pp. $20. 1-57075-383-0. Bibl. 217-220.

8183 **Fuchs, Esther** Sexual politics in the biblical narrative: reading the Hebrew bible as a woman. JSOT.S 310: 2000 ⇒16,8261. [R]BiblInterp 9 (2001) 433-435 (*Rooke, Deborah W.*); HebStud 42 (2001) 328-331 (*Franke, Chris*).

8184 **Hailer, Martin** Figur und Thema der Weisheit in feministischen Theologien: ein kommentierender Forschungsbericht. Internationale Theologie 7: Fra 2001, Lang 103 pp. 3-631-37832-7.

8185 **Isherwood, Lisa; McEwan, Dorothea** Introducing feminist theology. Shf [2]2001, Sheffield A. 167 pp. 1-84127-233-7. Bibl. 159-165.

8186 *Jackson, Glenna S.* The complete gospel: Jesus and women via the Jesus Seminar. Feminist Theology 28 (2001) 27-39.

8187 *Jacobs, Maretha M.* Feminist scholarship, biblical scholarship and the bible. Neotest. 35 (2001) 81-94.

8188 *Janssen, Claudia* Leibliche Auferstehung?: zur Diskussion um Auferstehung bei Karl BARTH, Rudolf BULTMANN, Dorothee SÖLLE und in der aktuellen feministischen Theologie. Paulus. 2001 ⇒6308. 84-102.

8189 *Jasper, Alison* Raising the dead?: reflections on feminist biblical criticism in the light of Pamela Sue Anderson's book "A feminist philosophy of religion", 1988. Feminist Theology 26 (2001) 110-120 [Jn 11,1-44].

8190 **Johnson, Elisabeth A.** Dieu au-delà du masculin et du féminin: celui/celle qui est. CFi 214: 1999 ⇒15,8262; 16,8265. [R]RTL 32 (2001) 113-116 (*Dermience, Alice*).

8191 *Jones, Serene* Bounded openness: postmodernism, feminism, and the church today. Interp. 55 (2001) 49-59.

8192 *Kahl, Brigitte* Nicht mehr männlich?: Gal 3,28 und das Streitfeld Maskulinität. Paulus. 2001 ⇒6308. 129-145.

8193 *Kawale, Winston R.* The role of women in social transformation in the Nkhoma Synod (Malawi). Scriptura 77 (2001) 211-223, 225-238.

8194 **Kern, Kathi** Mrs. Stanton's bible. Ithaca 2001, Cornell Univ. Pr. 288 pp. $40. 0-8014-3191-3.

8195 [E]**Korte, Anne-Marie** Women and miracle stories: a multidisciplinary exploration. SHR Numen Bookseries 88: Lei 2001, Brill xi; 350 pp. 90-04-11681-8.

8196 *Kuanrong, Chen* Women's status and the creation stories in Genesis. CTR 15 (2001) 102-107.

8197 *Laffey, Alice L.* The influence of feminism on christianity. Daughters of Abraham. 2001 ⇒528. 50-64.

8198 *Manda, Joel* Biblical interpretation and the role of women in the church of Central Africa, presbyterian. Scriptura 77 (2001) 239-249.

8199 *Masenya, Mmadipoane* A *bosadi* (womanhood) reading of Proverbs 31:10-31. Other ways. 2001 ⇒260. 145-157.

8200 *Merz, Annette* Warum die reine Braut Christi (2 Kor 11,2) zur Ehefrau wurde (Eph 5,22-33): Thesen zur intertextuellen Transformation einer ekklesiologischen Metapher. Paulus. 2001 ⇒6308. 148-165.

8201 *Monreal, Sarah A.* Algunos perfiles femeninos en la biblia. Qol 27 (2001) 59-74.

8202 *Njoroge, Nyambura J.* The bible and African christianity: a curse or a blessing?. Other ways. 2001 ⇒260. 207-236.

Pathak, Z. Pedagogy for postcolonial feminists 2001 ⇒3405.

8203 *Plietzsch, Susanne* '...nähert euch keiner Frau'—zum feministisch-theologischen Entwurf von Judith Plaskow 'Und wieder stehen wir am Sinai'. Leqach 1 (2001) 37-50 [BuBB 33,21].

8204 *Reimer, Margaret Loewen* If the bible is so patriarchal how come I love it so much?. ᶠJ ANZEN, W. 2001 ⇒54. 115-127.

8205 *Ress, Mary Judith* "Holistic ecofeminism:" a Latin American response to the search for meaning in a postmodern world. Jahrbuch für kontextuelle Theologien 9 (2001) 150-172.

8206 *Rondet, Michel* Quand la mystique réconcilie le masculin et le féminin. Christus 48 (2001) 143-149.

8207 **Saranyana, Josep-Ignasi** Teología de la mujer, teología feminista, teología mujerista y ecofeminismo en América Latina (1975-2000). Teologia 1: San José de Costa Rica 2001, Promesa 147 pp. ᴿRTLi 35 (2001) 264-266 (*Sánchez, Gustavo*).

8208 *Sawyer, Deborah F.* Disputed questions in biblical studies, 3: a male bible?. ET 112 (2001) 366-369.

8209 *Schaab, Gloria L.* Feminist theological methodology: toward a kaleidoscopic model. TS 62 (2001) 341-365.

      ᴱ**Schottroff, L.** Kompendium feministische Bibelauslegung ²1999 ⇒317.

8210 *Schroer, Silvia* Die Grerechtigkeit der Sophia: biblische Weisheitstraditionen und feministische Diskurse. ThZ 57 (2001) 281-290.

8211 **Smith, Elizabeth J.** Bearing fruit in due season: feminist hermeneutics and the bible in worship. 1999 ⇒15,8285. ᴿTS 62 (2001) 410-411 (*Dempsey, Deirdre*); Pacifica 14 (2001) 331-333 (*McKinlay, Judith E.*).

8212 **Thurston, Anne** Knowing her place: gender and the gospels. 1998 ⇒14,7522; 15,8288. ᴿNewTR 14 (2001) 88-89 (*Osiek, Carolyn*).

8213 **Winter, Miriam Therese** Il vangelo secondo Maria: un nuovo testamento per le donne. ᵀ*Dal Lago, Luigi*: Vicenza 1997, Neri Pozza 137 pp. 88-730-5538-9.

H9.0 Eschatologia NT, *spes*, hope

8214 **Balabanski, Vicky** Eschatology in the making: Mark, Matthew and the Didache. MSSNTS 97: 1997 ⇒13,7919... 16,8290. ᴿJBL 119 (2000) 361-362 (*Sim, David C.*) [Mt 24; 25; Mk 13].

8215 ᴱ**Bauckham, Richard; Hart, Trevor** Hope against hope: christian eschatology in contemporary context. 1999 ⇒15,304; 16,8292. ᴿThTo 57 (2001) 582, 584, 586 (*Volf, Miroslav*); CTJ 36 (2001) 156-159 (*Thompson, Thomas R.*).

8216 **Berger, Klaus** Ist mit dem Tod alles aus?. GTBS 1451: Gü 1999 <1997>, Gü'er 228 pp. 3-579-01451-X.

8217 **Blank, Renold J.** Escatologia do mundo: o projeto cósmico de Deus (Escatologia II). São Paulo 2001, Paulus 391 pp. BRL21. [R]RBBras 18 (2001) 523-524.

8218 **Bremmer, Jan Nicolaas** The rise and fall of the afterlife: the 1995 Read-Tuckwell lectures at the University of Bristol. L 2001, Routledge xi; 238 pp. $80/26. 0-415-14148-6. Bibl. 187-223.

8219 *Christophersen, Alf* Die Begründung der Apokalyptikforschung durch Friedrich LÜCKE: zum Verhältnis von Eschatologie und Apokalyptik. KuD 47/3 (2001) 158-179.

8220 *Countryman, Louis W.* Healing leaves: the bible as source of hope. AThR 83 (2001) 49-63.

8221 *Dabek, Tomasz Maria* Teksty eschatologiczne w Listach do siedmiu Kościołów (Ap 2-3). CoTh 71/1 (2001) 19-30. **P.**

8222 *Ebner, Martin* Klage und Auferweckungshoffnung im Neuen Testament. JBTh 16 (2001) 73-87.

8223 **Ellis, E. Earle** Christ and the future in New Testament history. NT.S 97: 2000 ⇒16,8301. [R]ThLZ 126 (2001) 166-8 (*Schweizer, Eduard*).

8224 *Fuchs, Ottmar* Unerhörte Klage über den Tod hinaus!: Überlegungen zur Eschatologie der Klage. JBTh 16 (2001) 347-379.

8225 **Fudge, Edward William; Peterson, Robert A.** Two views of hell: a biblical and theological dialogue. 2000 ⇒16,8303. [R]CTJ 36 (2001) 169-171 (*Roels, Edwin D.*).

8226 *Gnilka, Joachim* Acerca de la escatología del Nuevo Testamento. ScrTh 33 (2001) 753-772.

8227 *Green, M.D.* Reflections on christian hope. RExp 98 (2001) 433-438.

8228 **Greer, Rowan A.** Christian hope and christian life: raids on the inarticulate. NY 2001, Crossroad 282 pp. $25. 0-8245-1916-7 [Interp. 58,97—M.S. Burrows].

8229 *Karrer, Martin* In der Welt außerhalb der Welt: Beobachtungen zur neutestamentlichen Eschatologie. Christlicher Glaube. 2001 ⇒511. 477-500.

8230 *Khiok-khng, Yeo* An eschatological view of history in the New Testament: messianic and millenarian hope. AJTh 15/1 (2001) 38-51.

8231 **Klaine, Roger** Le devenir du monde et la bible 1-2. 2000 ⇒16,8309. [R]Cahiers de l'Atelier 492 (2001) 123-125 (*Sindt, Gérard*).

8232 *Lee, Sang M.* Marginalization and its driving force: eschatological / apocalyptic vision. JAAT 4 (2001) 29-46.

8233 *Marmorstein, Art* Eschatological inconsistency in the Ante-Nicene Fathers. AUSS 39 (2001) 125-132.

8234 *Meagher, P.M.* A reason for hope. VJTR 65 (2001) 877-890.

8235 *Meier, John P.* Jesus, the Twelve, and the restoration of Israel. Restoration. JSJ.S 72: 2001 ⇒319. 365-404.

8236 *Pietrobelli, Mario* I superstiti della parusia. Asp. 48 (2001) 503-524.

8237 *Pinnock, Clark H.* Toward a more inclusive eschatology. Looking into the future. 2001 ⇒505. 249-262.

8238 **Pippin, Tina** Apocalyptic bodies: the biblical end of the world in text and image. 1999 ⇒15,8330. [R]RBLit 3 (2001) 470-472 (*Barr, David L.*).

8239 *Reiser, Marius* Das Jenseits im Neuen Testament. TThZ 110 (2001) 115-132.

8240 *Sanday, William* The eschatology of the New Testament. Essays in biblical criticism. JSNT.S 225: 2001 <1908> 205. 28-32.

8241 **Schreiner, Thomas R.; Caneday, Ardel B.** The race set before us: a biblical theology of perseverance and assurance. DG 2001, InterVarsity. 344 pp. $22. 0-8308-1555-4.

8242 *Schwarz, Hans* Eschatologie als Kriterium für die Glaubwürdigkeit der christlichen Botschaft. [F]SCHMUTTERMAYR, G. 2001 ⇒101. 571-583.

8243 **Szczepaniak, Maciej** Symbolika swiatla w apokalipsach Starego Testamentu i w Apokalipsie swietego Jana. Studia i materialy 45: Poznan 2001, Uniw. Mickiewicza 160 pp. 8386360739. Bibl. 135-48. **P.**

8244 *Thomas, Robert L.* The place of imminence in recent eschatological systems. Looking into the future. 2001 ⇒505. 199-216.

8245 *Turek, Valdemar* Classica, biblica et patristica'spei' notio: similitudines ac dissimilitudines. Latinitas 49 (2001) 66-75.

8246 *Van McClain, T.* The pretribulation rapture: a doubtful doctrine. Looking into the future. 2001 ⇒505. 233-245.

8247 **Vena, Osvaldo D.** The parousia and its rereadings: the development of the eschatological consciousness in the writings of the New Testament. Studies in biblical literature 27: NY 2001, Lang ix; 284 pp. $62. 0-8204-4995-4. Bibl. 273-282.

8248 *Yeo, Khiok K.* An eschatological view of history in the New Testament: messianic and millenarian hope. AJTh 15/1 (2001) 38-51.

H9.5 *Theologia totius [VT-]NT*—General [OT-]NT theology

8249 **Balla, Peter** Challenges to New Testament theology: an attempt to justify the enterprise. WUNT 2/95: 1997 ⇒13,7955... 16,8323. [R]Bib. 82 (2001) 282-286 (*Claudel, Gérard*).

8250 *Bossman, David M.* Presenting the issue: biblical theology for a secular society. BTB 31 (2001) 2-3.

8251 *Breytenbach, Cilliers* Zwischen Exegese und systematischer Theologie: Ferdinand Hahns Auffassung von der Einheit der "Theologie des Neuen Testaments". [F]HAHN, F. 2001 ⇒41. 204-214.

8252 **Cardona Ramírez, Hernán** Bordeando el Mar de Galilea: ensayos de teología bíblica. Cuadernos de Formación Avanzada 8: Medellín 2001, Universidad Pontificia Bolivariana 149 pp.

8253 *Carr, David M.* Passion for God: a center in biblical theology. HBT 23 (2001) 1-24.

8254 *Chopineau, Jacques* L'ébranlement des fondations: vers une théologie biblique pour notre temps. AnBru 6 (2001) 17-25;

8255 Toute théologie n'est-elle pas géocentrique?. AnBru 6 (2001) 26-36.

8256 *Fitzmyer, Joseph A.* Unity and diversity of concepts in the New Testament. L'interpretazione della bibbia nella chiesa. 2001 ⇒471. 320-334.

8257 *Green, Joel B.* Modernity, history and the theological interpretation of the bible. SJTh 54 (2001) 308-329.

8258 *Hille, Rolf* Das Theodizeeproblem im Kontext neuzeitlicher Religionskritik und biblisch-theologischer Antworten. JETh 15 (2001) 49-68.
   ᴱHossfeld, F. Wieviel Systematik erlaubt die Schrift? 2001 ⇒ 283.

8259 **Hübner, Hans** Teologia biblica del Nuovo Testamento, 3: Lettera agli Ebrei, vangeli e Apocalisse. ᴱ*Tomasoni, Francesco*: CTNT.S 8: 2000 ⇒16,8334. ᴿCivCatt 152/2 (2001) 629-630 (*Scaiola, D.*).

8260 ᴱ**Hübner, Hans; Jaspert, Bernd** Biblische Theologie: Entwürfe der Gegenwart. Biblisch-theologische Studien 38: 1999 ⇒15,243. ᴿThLZ 126 (2001) 262-264 (*Pratscher, Wilhelm*).

8261 *Leproux, Alexis* Réflexion sur une pratique de la théologie biblique. Com(F) 26/1 (2001) 61-74.

8262 **Lohfink, Norbert; Cardona Ramírez, Hernán** *La alianza; *los milagros: "una aproximación bíblico-teológica". Cuadernos de Formación Avanzada 9: Medellín 2001, Universidad Pontificia Bolivariana 116 pp. Bibl. 113-114.

8263 **López Fernández, Enrique** Tras las huellas de la Palabra. Publicaciones Studium Ovetense 10: Oviedo 2001, Centro Superior de Estudios Teologicos de Oviedo 482 pp. 84-607-4091-9. Bibl. 463-482.

8264 **Marconi, Nazzareno** La Bibbia fa audience?. Fede e comunicazione 10: Mi 2000, Paoline 136 pp. 88-315-2012-1. Bibl. 129-131.

8265 *Martens, Elmer A.* Reaching for a biblical theology of the whole bible. ᶠJANZEN, W. 2001 ⇒54. 83-101.

8266 *McConville, J.G.* Biblical theology: canon and plain sense. SBET 19 (2001) 134-157. Finlayson memorial lecture 2001.

8267 *Müller, Peter* Die Metapher vom "Kind Gottes" und die neutestamentliche Theologie. ᶠHAHN, F. 2001 ⇒41. 192-203.

8268 **Navone, John** Lead, radiant spirit. ColMn 2001, Liturgical vii; 128 pp. $12 [BiTod 39,321—Senior, Donald].

8269 ^E**Pedersen, Sigfred** Bibelsk teologi. 2000 ⇒16,8344. ^RSEÅ 66 (2001) 221-224 (*Syreeni, Kari*).

8270 *Punt, Jeremy* The New Testament, theology and imperialism: some postcolonial remarks on beyond New Testament theology. Neotest. 35 (2001) 129-145.

8271 **Sacchi, Alessandro** Fede di Israele e messaggio cristiano: alle radici del cristianesimo. Interpretare la Bibbia oggi 2/7: Brescia 2001, Queriniana 190 pp. €13. 88-399-2466-3. Bibl. 177-178.

8272 *Schwier, Helmut* Praktische Theologie und Bibel: die Rolle von Bibel und Exegese in der derzeitigen Standortbestimmung der Praktischen Theologie. EvTh 61/5 (2001) 340-353.

8273 *Segalla, Giuseppe* La testimonianza dei libri del Nuovo Testamento ad un unico kerygma/evangelo, buon annuncio dell'evento orginario. L'interpretazione della bibbia nella chiesa. 2001 ⇒471. 304-319.

8274 **Strecker, Georg** Theology of the New Testament. ^T*Boring, M. Eugene*; ^E*Horn, Friedrich Wilhelm* 2000 ⇒16,8356. ^RTheol. 104 (2001) 450 (*Downing, F. Gerald*).

8275 **Stuhlmacher, Peter** Biblische Theologie des NT, 2: von der Paulusschule bis zur Johannesoffenbarung, der Kanon und seine Auslegung. 1999 ⇒15,8373; 16,8357. ^RZKTh 122 (2001) 220-21 (*Oberforcher, Robert*); JThS 52 (2001) 208-9 (*Morgan, Robert*); ActBib 38 (2001) 43-44 (*Boada, J.*); SNTU.A 25 (2000) 264-269 (*Fuchs, Albert*).

8276 **Theißen, Gerd** Die Religion der ersten Christen: eine Theorie des Urchristentums. 2000 ⇒16,8359. ^RBiKi 56 (2001) 109-110; 249-250 (*Kosch, Daniel*); SaThZ 5 (2001) 60-62 (*Huber, Konrad*); EstAg 36 (2001) 626-627 (*Cineira, D.A.*); Orpheus 22 (2001) 406-407 (*Osculati, Roberto*); ThLZ 126 (2001) 409-413 (*Zager, Werner*).

8277 **Thüsing, Wilhelm** Die neutestamentlichen Theologien und Jesus Christus: Grundlegung einer Theologie des Neuen Testaments, 3: Einzigkeit Gottes und Jesus-Christus-Ereignis. ^E*Söding, Thomas* 1999 ⇒15,8374; 16,8361. ^RAnton. 76 (2001) 356-358 (*Stamm, Heinz-Meinolf*); EstTrin 35 (2001) 452-455 [with vol. 1-2] (*Vázquez Allegue, Jaime*); JThS 52 (2001) 780-781 (*Morgan, Robert*); ThLZ 126 (2001) 540-542 (*Stuhlmacher, Peter*).

8278 **Vouga, François** Une théologie du Nouveau Testament. MoBi 43: Genève 2001, Labor et F. 474 pp. €36.59. 2-8309-0999-2. Bibl. 455-459. ^REstTrin 35 (2001) 443-445 (*Vázquez Allegue, Jaime*); EstAg 36 (2001) 628-629 (*De Luis, P.*); RThPh 133 (2001) 538-539 (*Freudiger, Marc-André*).

XIV. Philologia biblica

J1.1 Hebraica *grammatica*

8279 *Aaron, David H.* The doctrine of Hebrew language usage. The Blackwell reader in Judaism. 2001 ⇒423. 202-214.

8280 **Auvray, Paul** Iniciação ao Hebraico Bíblico—gramática elementar, textos comentados e vocabulário. Petrópolis 1997, Vozes 297 pp. RHermenêutica 1 (2001) 85-86 (*Almeida F., Edno José*).

8281 ^E**Avishur, Y.** Dictionaries and lexicography. Haivrit Weaḥyoteha 1 (2001) 1-156. Univ. of Haifa. RLeš. 63 (2000-2001) 131-140 *Bar-Asher, Moshe*).

8282 **Bachra, Bernard Nehemia** The phonological structure of the verbal roots in Arabic and Hebrew. SStLL 34: Lei 2001, Brill xv; 326 pp. €73/$90. 90-04-12008-4. Bibl. 189-193.

8283 **Basal, Nasir** Kitab al-Nutaf by Judah HAYYUJ: a critical edition. Texts and Studies in the Hebrew Language and Related Subjects 11: TA 2001, Tel Aviv University (10) 343; xiv pp. Bibl. 281-291. **H.**

8284 **Bergman, Nava** Bibelhebreiska för nybörjare: lärobok. Lund 2000, 461 pp. Studentlitteratur. RSvTK 77 (2001) 185-186 (*Hidal, Sten*).

8285 *Bombeck, Stefan* Das althebräische *w*-Perf. für Gegenwart und Vergangenheit in den hinteren Propheten und den Psalmen. ^FDENZ, A. 2001 ⇒21. 21-34.

8286 *Borger, Rykle* Johannisbrot in der Bibel und im Midrasch: über Fortschritt, Rückschritt und Stillstand in der biblischen Philologie. ZAH 14 (2001) 1-19 [Isa 1,19-20].

8287 **Bouchoc, Raymond** An analysis of disjunctive waw verbal clauses in the Biblical Hebrew narrative of the pentateuch. Diss. Southeastern Baptist Theol. Sem. 2001, 333 pp. 3007278.

8288 **Brettler, Marc Zvi** Biblical Hebrew for students of modern Israeli Hebrew. Yale Language: NHv 2001, Yale Univ. Pr. xii; 355 pp. $40.

8289 *Caën, Vincent de* Hebrew linguistics and biblical criticism: a minimalist programme. Journal of Hebrew Scriptures 3 (2001) [electr.].

8290 **Chisholm, Robert B., Jr.** From exegesis to exposition: a practical guide to using Biblical Hebrew. 1998 ⇒14,7594. RRExp 97 (2001) 129-30 (*Ellis, Robert E.*); WThJ 63 (2001) 183-186 (*Kelly, Michael*).

8291 *Cook, John A.* The Hebrew verb: a grammaticalization approach. ZAH 14 (2001) 117-143.

8292 **Deiana, Giovanni; Spreafico, Ambrogio** Guida allo studio
      dell'ebraico biblico. [T]*Pak, James Yeong-Sik*: Seoul 2001, St Pauls 2
      vols. 89-8015- + audio cassetta. **K.**

8293 **Deiana, Giovanni; Spreafico, Ambrogio** Wprowadzenie do he-
      brajszczyzny biblijnej. [T]*Bazylinski, Stanislaw*: Wsz 2001, Towar-
      zystwo Biblijne w Polsce 2 vols. 83-85260-. **P.**

8294 **Diehl, Friedrich** Die Fortführung des Imperativs im biblischen He-
      bräisch. Diss. Mainz 2001, [D]*Zwickel, W.* [RTL 33,631].

8295 **Dolgopolsky, Aron** From Proto-Semitic to Hebrew: phonology: ety-
      mological approach in a Hamito-Semitic perspective. SCS 2: 1999 ⇒
      16,8374. [R]UF 33 (2001) 713-717 (*Tropper, J.*).

8296 **Donnet-Guez, Brigitte** Grammaire de l'hébreu: simple et pratique.
      La Varenne [5]1998 <1993>, Vera Pax 248 pp.

8297 [TE]**Dotan, Aron** The dawn of Hebrew linguistics: the book of Ele-
      gance of the language of the Hebrews by SAADIA Gaon. 1997 ⇒13,
      8012; 15,8456. [R]REJ 160 (2001) 282-4 (*Olszowy-Schlanger, Judith*).

8298 **Durand, Olivier** La lingua ebraica: profilo storico-strutturale. Studi
      sul Vicino Oriente Antico 3: Brescia 2001, Paideia 236 pp. 88-394-
      0610-7. Bibl. 225-236.

8299 *Fassberg, Steven E.* The movement from *qal* to *pi[cc]el* in Hebrew and
      the disappearance of the *qal* internal passive. HebStud 42 (2001)
      243-255.

8300 **García-Jalón de la Lama, Santiago** Inventario de las gramáticas
      hebreas del siglo XVI de la Biblioteca General de la Universidad de
      Salamanca. BSal.E 183: 1996 ⇒12,7634. [R]REJ 160 (2001) 531-533
      (*Kessler-Mesguich, Sophie*);

8301 La gramática hebrea en Europa en el siglo XVI: guía de lectura de las
      obras impresas. BSal.E 204: 1998 ⇒14,7605. [R]REJ 160 (2001) 533-
      534 (*Kessler-Mesguich, Sophie*).

8302 *Greenfield, Jonas C.; Naveh, Joseph* Hebrew and Aramaic in the
      Persian period. 'Al kanfei yonah, 1. 2001 <1984> ⇒153. 232-246.

8303 **Gross, Walter** Doppelt besetztes Vorfeld: syntaktische, pragmati-
      sche und übersetzungstechnische Studien zum althebräischen Verbal-
      satz. BZAW 305: B 2001, De Gruyter xiv; 348 pp. 3-11-017009-4.
      Bibl. 319-332.

8304 *Groß, Walter* Die Stellung der Zeitangabe in Sätzen mit zwei oder
      mehr nominalen / pronominalen Satzteilen vor dem Verbum finitum
      in alttestamentlicher Poesie. [F]DENZ, A. 2001 ⇒21. 35-50.

8305 *Harlap, Luba* The concept of the gender of nouns in Biblical Hebrew
      in the Middle Ages. [F]AHITUV, S. 2001 ⇒1. 205-215. **H.**

8306 *Heckl, Raik* Die starke Bildung des Imperfekts bei einigen Formen
      der Verba primae Nun—ein Problem des Verbalsystems?. ZAH 14
      (2001) 20-33.

8307 *Hoftijzer, Jacob* Zukunftsaussagen und Modalität. KUSATU 2 (2001) 5-45.

8308 *Holmstedt, Robert D.* Headlessness and extraposition: another look at the syntax of אשׁר. JNSL 27/1 (2001) 1-16.

8309 **Horsnell, Malcolm J.A.** A review and reference grammar for Biblical Hebrew. 1999 ⇒15,8406. ᴿRExp 98 (2001) 279-280 (*Ellis, Robert*); HebStud 42 (2001) 289-297 (*Gentry, Peter J.*).

8310 *Huwyler, Beat* "Wenn Gott mit mir ist ..." (Gen 28,20-22): zum sprachlichen und theologischen Problem des hebräischen Konditionalsatzes. ThZ 57 (2001) 10-25.

8311 **Jenni, Ernst** Die hebräischen Präpositionen, 3: die Präposition Lamed. 2000 ⇒16,8388. ᴿThQ 181 (2001) 76-77 (*Groß, Walter*).

8312 *Joosten, Jan* A forma alongada do imperfeito no que se refere ao tempo passado do Hebraico Bíblico. Hermenêutíca 1 (2001) 31-44.

8313 *Kroeze, Jan H.* Alternatives for the nominative in Biblical Hebrew. JSSt 46 (2001) 33-50.

8314 **Lambdin, Thomas Oden** Introducción al Hebreo bíblico. ᵀ*Melero Gracia, María Luisa; Reyes Bravo, Noé*: Instrumentos para el estudio de la Biblia: Estella 2001, Verbo Divino xxviii; 359 pp 8481694282.
　　　Ljungberg, B. Verbal meaning:...Ruth 2001 ⇒2736.

8315 *Meyer, Esias E.* The particle כי , a mere conjunction or something more?. JNSL 27/1 (2001) 39-62 [Ps 83].

8316 *Muraoka, Takamitsu* 'Three of them' and 'the three of them' in Hebrew. ANESt 38 (2001) 215-216.

8317 *Müller, Augustin R.* Die Freiheit, ein *Und* zu gebrauchen: zur hebräischen Konjunktion *w*. ᶠDENZ, A. 2001 ⇒21. 85-105.

8318 **Pratico, Gary D.; Van Pelt, Miles V.** Basics of Biblical Hebrew. GR 2001, Zondervan 476 pp. $40 [BiTod 40,60—Bergant, Dianne].

8319 *Qimron, Elisha* The letter *waw* as a marker for a glide. AHITUV, S. 2001 ⇒1. 362-375. **H.**

8320 **Regt, Lénart J. de** Participants in Old Testament texts and the translator: reference devices and their rhetorical impact. SSN 39: 1999 ⇒ 15,8433; 16,8402. ᴿCTJ 36 (2001) 142-143 (*Rubingh, Eugene*); JSSt 46 (2001) 329-331 (*Coetzee, Andries W.*).

8321 *Rendsburg, Gary A.* Hebrew philological notes (II). HebStud 42 (2001) 187-195 [Gen 38,25; Ex 32,18; Prov 30,4; 22,19];

8322 Once more the dual: with replies to J. Blau and J. Blenkinsopp. ANESt 38 (2001) 28-41.

8323 *Rosik, Mariusz* The meaning and the function of "he-locale". PJBR 1/2 (2001) 207-212.

8324 **Ross, Allen P.** Introducing Biblical Hebrew. GR 2001, Baker 565 pp. $40. 0-8010-2147-2.

8325 *Rössler, Otto* Eine bisher unerkannte Tempusform im Althebräischen. Gesammelte Schriften. 2001 <1961> ⇒202. 431-437;

8326 Die Präfixkonjugation qal der Verba I^ae nûn im Althebräischen und
das Problem der sogenannten Tempora <1962>;

8327 Zum althebräischen Tempussystem: eine morpho-syntaktische Untersuchung <1977>. Gesammelte Schriften. 2001 ⇒202. 453-469/613-
637.

8328 *Rubin, Aaron* A note on the conjugation of לייה verbs in the derived
patterns. ZAH 14 (2001) 34-42.

Rubinstein, E. Syntax and semantics 1998 ⇒203.

8329 **Sarfatti, Gad B.** Semantic aspects of Hebrew. J 2001, Academy of
the Hebrew Language 304 pp. ^RLeš. 63 (2000-2001) 341-344 [Sum.
IX] (*Nir, Raphael*).

8330 *Sasson, Victor* The waw consecutive/waw contrastive and the perfect:
verb tense, context, and texture in Old Aramaic and Biblical Hebrew,
with comments on the Deir 'Alla dialect and post-Biblical Hebrew.
ZAW 113 (2001) 602-617.

8331 **Schneider, Wolfgang** Grammatik des biblischen Hebräisch: ein
Lehrbuch. Mü 2001, Claudius xii; 281 pp. 3-532-71151-6.

8332 *Seidl, Theodor* Wunschsätze mit *mī yittin* im Biblischen Hebräisch.
^FDenz, A. 2001 ⇒21. 129-142.

8333 *Shulman, Ahouva* Imperative and second person indicative forms in
Biblical Hebrew prose. HebStud 42 (2001) 271-287.

8334 **Van der Merwe, Christo H.J.; Naudé, Jackie A.; Kroeze, Jan H.**
A Biblical Hebrew reference grammar. 1999 ⇒15,8448; 16,8422.
^RAUSS 39 (2001) 156-160 (*Pröbstle, Martin*); JSSt 46 (2001) 310-
313 (*Van Peursen, Wido*); JBL 119 (2000) 109-110 (*Greenspahn,
Frederick E.*).

8335 *Vanoni, Gottfried* Ist *wa=yiqtol* im Althebräischen Ausdruck für
Regreß und Korrektur?. ^FDenz, A. 2001 ⇒21. 143-150.

8336 *Verheij, Arian* A cloud of witnesses: towards a linguistic typology of
Biblical Hebrew texts. ^FDeurloo, K., 2001 ⇒23. 257-263.

8337 *Young, Ian* Observations on the third person masculine singular
pronominal suffix -*h* in Hebrew biblical texts. HebStud 42 (2001)
225-242

8338 *Zewi, Tamar* Biblical Hebrew word order and Saadya Gaon's translation of the pentateuch. ANESt 38 (2001) 42-57.

8339 *Zewi, Tamar; Van der Merwe, Christo H.J.* Biblical Hebrew nominal
clause: definitions of subject and predicate. JNSL 27/1 (2001) 81-99.

J1.2 Lexica et inscriptiones hebraicae; *later Hebrew*

8340 *Anbar, Moshé* Le lettre de Yavneh-Yam et les archives royales de Mari. UF 33 (2001) 49-52.

8341 **Bar-Ascher, Moshé** L'hébreu mishnique: études linguistiques. 1999 ⇒15,8463; 16,8433. ᴿJSJ 32 (2001) 289-292 (*Pérez Fernández, Miguel*); REJ 160 (2001) 261-263 (*Hadas-Lebel, Mireille*); Leš. 63 (2000-2001) 155-158 *(Sarfatti, Gad B.)*.

8342 ᴱ**Bar-Asher, Moshe; Fassberg, Steven E.** Studies in Mishnaic Hebrew. ScrHie 37: 1998 ⇒15,8464. ᴿJSSt 46 (2001) 317-320 *(Elwolde, J.F.)*.

8343 *Bar, Tali* Expression of temporality, modality and perfectivity in contemporary Hebrew conditionals as compared with non-conditionals. WZKM 91 (2001) 49-83.

8344 *Becking, Bob; Wagenaar, Jan A.* Personal name or royal epithet?: a remark on ostracon 1027 from Tell el-Farʿah (south). BN 107/108 (2001) 12-14.

8345 *Casanellas, Pere* Transliteració i transcripció de l'hebreu: una nova proposta. El text. Scripta Biblica 3: 2001 ⇒310. 233-371.

8346 *Charlap, Luba* Another view on Rabbi Abraham IBN-EZRA's contribution to medieval Hebrew grammar. HebStud 42 (2001) 67-80.

8347 ᴱ**Clines, David J.A.** The dictionary of Classical Hebrew, 5: כ-נ. Shf 2001, Sheffield Academic 957 pp. £110. 1-84127-217-5.

8348 *Cotton, Hannah M.* Documentary texts from the Judaean Desert: a matter of nomenclature. SCI 20 (2001) 113-119.

8349 *Cross, Frank Moore* A fragment of a monumental inscription from the City of David. IEJ 51 (2001) 44-47.

8350 **Eisenberg, Joyce; Scolnic, Ellen** The JPS dictionary of Jewish words. Ph 2001, Jewish Publ. Society xxi; 202 pp. 0-8276-0723-7.

8351 *Emerton, J.A.* Were the Lachish letters sent to or from Lachish?. Ment. *Yadin, Y.* PEQ 133 (2001) 2-15.

8352 **Gogel, Sandra Landis** A grammar of epigraphic Hebrew. SBL Resources for Biblical Study 23: 1998 ⇒14,8090... 16,8456. ᴿJSSt 46 (2001) 141-142 (*Gibson, J.C.L.*); JBL 120 (2001) 347-348 (*Zevit, Ziony*); HebStud 42 (2001) 323-326 (*Gentry, Peter J.*); Syr. 78 (2001) 737 (*Briquel Chatonnet, Françoise*).

8353 *Greenfield, Jonas C.* Lexicographical notes I <1958>;

8354 Lexicographical notes II <1959>;

8355 Etymological semantics <1993>. ʿAl kanfei yonah, 2. 2001 ⇒153. 653-678/679-689/821-832.

8356 *Haber, Heriberto* Theophoric names in the bible. JBQ 29/1 (2001) 56-59.

8357 **Halevy-Nemirovsky, Rivka** Between syntax and lexicon: restricted collocations in contemporary Hebrew. 1999 ⇒15,8484; 16,8459. ᴿLeš. 63 (2000-2001) 159-165 *(Kaddari, Menahem Zevi).* **H.**

8358 **Heller, Jan** Vocabularium biblicum septem linguarum. 2000 ⇒16, 8460. ᴿOLZ 96 (2001) 69-71 *(Thiel, W.).*

8359 *Heltzer, Michael* The South-Judean family *bny glg(w)l* between the VIII century B.C.E. and the II century A.D. AltOrF 28 (2001) 185-9.

8360 **Hempel, Charlotte** The laws of the Damascus document: sources, tradition and redaction. StTDJ 29: 1998 ⇒14,7664. ᴿJThS 52 (2001) 767-768 *(Lim, Timothy H.).*

8361 *Hess, Richard S.* Typology of a late Bronze Age administrative table from Hazor. UF 33 (2001) 237-243.

8362 *Israel, Felice* Studi di lessico ebraico epigrafico II. ᴹCᴀɢɴɪ, L., 3. SMDSA 61: 2001 ⇒15. 1617-1636.

8363 **Jaroš, Karl** Inschriften des Heiligen Landes aus vier Jahrtausenden. Mainz 2001, Von Zabern. CD-ROM.

8364 *Knauf, Ernst Axel; Niemann, H.M.* Weitere Überlegungen zum neuen Ostracon 1027 vom Tell el-Faraʿ Süd. BN 109 (2001) 19-20.

8365 ᴱ**Koehler, Ludwig; Baumgartner, Walter** The Hebrew and Aramaic lexicon of the Old Testament, 1-4. ᵀᴱ*Richardson, M.E.J.* 1999 ⇒ 15,8487; 16,8472. ᴿNT 43 (2001) 196-197 *(Elliott, J.K.);*

8366 1-5. ᵀᴱ*Richardson, M.E.J.* 1994-2000 ⇒16,8473. ᴿArOr 69 (2001) 636-638 *(Segert, Stanislav);*

8367 Hebrew and Aramaic dictionary of the Old Testament: study edition. Lei 2001, Brill 2 vols. 90-04-12445-4.

8368 **Landes, George M.** Building your Biblical Hebrew vocabulary: learning words by frequency and cognate. SBL.Resources for Biblical Study 41: Atlanta, GA 2001, SBL xiv; 218 pp. $20. 1-58983-003-2. Bibl. 40.

8369 **Mankowski, Paul V.** Akkadian loanwords in Biblical Hebrew. HSS 47: 2000 ⇒16,8477. ᴿOLZ 96 (2001) 697-700 *(Heltzer, Michael);* CBQ 63 (2001) 528-529 *(Fleming, Daniel E.);* Bib. 82 (2001) 586-588 *(Hess, Richard S.);* JNSL 27/1 (2001) 147-49 *(Muntingh, L.M.).*

8370 **Mittler, Doron** Grammatica ebraica. Bo 2000, Zanichelli x; 338 pp. €24.79. ᴿQol(I) 92-93 (2001) 22 *(Anderlini, Gianpaolo).*

8371 **Muraoka, Takamitsu** Modern Hebrew for biblical scholars. ²1998 <1982> ⇒14,7676; 16,8482. ᴿEstB 59 (2001) 384 *(Ródenas, A.).*

8372 *Naudé, Jackie A.* The distribution of independent personal pronouns in Qumran Hebrew. JNSL 27/2 (2001) 91-112.

8373 *Naveh, Joseph* Hebrew graffiti from the first temple period. IEJ 51 (2001) 194-207.

8374 **Pérez Fernàndez, Miguel** An introductory grammar of Rabbinic Hebrew. 1997 ⇒13,8118. [R]ANESt 38 (2001) 221-223 (*Van Peursen, W.Th.*).

8375 *Rapallo, Umberto* Il lessico ebraico di base: fra generalità e universalità. [M]CAGNI, L., 4. SMDSA 61: 2001 ⇒15. 2017-2041.

8376 *Renz, Johannes* Der Beitrag der althebräischen Epigraphik zur Exegese des Alten Testaments und zur Profan- und Religionsgeschichte Palästinas.: Leistung und Grenzen, aufgezeigt am Beispiel der Inschriften des (ausgehenden) 7. Jahrhunderts vor Christus;

8377 *Rüterswörden, Udo* Der Prophet in den Lachisch-Ostraka. Steine-Bilder-Texte. 2001 ⇒ 613. 123-158/179-192.

8378 *Shveka, Avi* 'And they disregarded my sabbaths': a re-examination of Arad Ostracon no. 7. Tarb. 70/3-4 (2001) 317-325 Sum. v. **H**.

8379 [E]**Soggin, J. Alberto; Bianchi, Francesco** Dizionario di ebraico e aramaico biblici. R [2]2001, Società Biblica Britannica e Forestiera 595 pp. 88-237-8041-1. 2ᵃ ed. aumentata da: Dizionario dei nomi biblici, dei nomi di luogo e dei lemmi di incerto significato (a cura di *Francesco Bianchi*).

8380 *Wambutda, Daniel N.* Hebrewisms in West Africa. BOTSA 11 (2001) 9-10.

8381 **Yardeni, Ada** Textbook of Aramaic, Hebrew and Nabataean texts. 2000 ⇒16,8507. [R]ThLZ 126 (2001) 630-631 (*Beyer, Klaus*).

J1.3 Voces *ordine alphabetico consonantium* hebraicarum

8382 *Grätz, Sebastian; Heckl, Raik* Lexikalisches Material. ZAH 14 (2001) 220-232.

8383 *Lipiński, Edward* Syro-Mesopotamian figures in biblical dress [Nimrod, Nisroch, Amraphel, Sheshak]. [M]CAGNI, L., 3. SMDSA 61: 2001 ⇒15. 1693-1707.

Akkadian

8384 *niggalu*: *Cohen, Haim; Klein, Jacob* חרמש and מגל in the bible and their parallels—Ugaritic ḥrmṯ and Akkadian *niggalu*. [F]AHITUV, S. 2001 ⇒1. 245-268. **H**.

8385 *šql*: *Greenfield, Jonas C.* The root *šql* in Akkadian, Ugaritic and Aramaic. 'Al kanfei yonah, 2. 2001 <1979> ⇒153. 731-733.

8386 *tubkinnu*: [Aram.] קלקלתא: *Greenfield, Jonas C.; Shaffer, Aaron* QLQLTᵓ, TUBKINNU, refuse tips and treasure trove. 'Al kanfei yonah, 1. 2001 <1983> ⇒153. 225-231.

Arabic

8387 *rhn*: Greenfield, Jonas C. *Kullu nafsin bimā kasabat rahīnā*: the use of *rhn* in Aramaic and Arabic. 'Al kanfei yonah, 1. 2001 <1991> ⇒ 153. 453-459.

Aramaic

8388 דחשפט: *Greenfield, Jonas C.* Nergol DḤŠPṬ' <1989>;

8389 הנצל: Aramaic HNṢL and some biblical passages <1983> [Gen 31,9; Hos 2,10-11];

8390 טכונה: The meaning of *ṬKWNH* <1985>. 'Al kanfei yonah, 1 2001 ⇒ 153. 418-426/214-216/258-262.

8391 מרועא: *Joosten, Jan* Targumic Aramaic מרועא, 'oppression' (Isa. lxvii 2 [! Read xlvii 2], Hos. xi 7, Mic. vi 3). VT 51 (2001) 552-555.

8392 פחז: *Greenfield, Jonas C.* The meaning of פחז. 'Al kanfei yonah, 2. 2001 <1978> ⇒153. 725-730.

קלקלתא ⇒8386.

רהן ⇒8387.

שקל ⇒8385.

Eblaite

8393 *mabtaḥū*: [Heb.] מבטחים: *Artzi, Pinhas* Eblaite *mabtaḥū* (pl.) = *mibṭaḥīm* (pl.). MCAGNI, L., 1. SMDSA 61: 2001 ⇒15. 13-24.

Emar

8394 *makrittu*: *Dietrich, Manfred; Loretz, Oswald* Bezeichnungen für 'bewässertes Feld' in Ugarit und Emar (*miyt-maʾitu* ~ *makrittu*). UF 33 (2001) 193-199.

Hebrew

8395 אולי: *Livnat, Zohar* אולי From Biblical to Modern Hebrew: a semantic-textual approach. HebStud 42 (2001) 81-104.

8396 אלמנה: *Leeb, Carolyn S.* The widow in the Hebrew Bible: homeless and post-menopausal. ProcGLM 21 (2001) 61-67 [Isa 52,13-53,12].

8397 אָמוֹן: *Schwartz, Baruch J.; Focht, Adam* אָמוֹן—constantly. ZAH 14 (2001) 43-49 [Prov 8,30].

8398 אֲמֶתַחת: *Greenfield, Jonas C.* The etymology of אֲמֶתַחת. 'Al kanfei yonah, 2. 2001 <1965> ⇒153. 701-703.

8399 בראשית: *Warning, Wilfried* Terminological patterns and the first word of the Bible: Br'syt "(in the) beginning". TynB 52 (2001) 267-274.

8400 ברית: *Lepore, Luciano* La berît nella duplice accezione di obbedienza e di comunione. RdT 42 (2001) 867-890.

8401 גבל: *Greenfield, Jonas C.* The root 'GBL' in Mishnaic Hebrew and in the hymnic literature from Qumran. 'Al kanfei yonah, 2. 2001 <1960> ⇒153. 690-697.

8402 גמר: *Scibona, Rocco* 'Gomer' (Os 1,3): nota critica (area filologica sumerica e semitica). BeO 43 (2001) 3-28.

8403 גר: *Bonola, Gianfranco* "Lo straniero nelle tue porte": un confronto tra Gerhard KITTEL e Martin BUBER (1933). ASEs 18 (2001) 559-87;

8404 *Ramírez Kidd, José E.* Alterity and identity in Israel: the "ger" in the Old Testament. BZAW 283: 1999 ⇒15,8530; 16, 8523. ᴿThZ 57 (2001) 88-89 (*Zehnder, Markus*).

8405 {Hebrew}דֶּרֶךְ: **Zehnder, Markus** Wegmetaphorik im Alten Testament. 1999 ⇒15,8531; 16,8525. ᴿOLZ 96 (2001) 556-560 (*Krispenz, Jutta*); RBLit 3 (2001) 128-130 (*Wiggins, Steve A.*).

8406 הוא *Tropper, Josef* Das genusindifferente hebräische Pronomen HWꞋ im Pentateuch aus sprachvergleichender Sicht. ZAH 14 (2001) 159-172.

8407 הנה: *Dorn, Louis O.* 'Lo' and 'behold'—translating the Hebrew word *hinneh*. BiTr 52 (2001) 222-229.

8408 הנה: *Sadka, Yitshak* Hinne in Biblical Hebrew. UF 33 (2001) 479-93.

8409 זנה: **Riegner, Irene Erna** The vanishing Hebrew harlot: a diachronic and synchronic study of the root znh. Diss. Temple 2001, 388 pp. 9997291.

8410 חלב: *Heckl, Raik* Ḥēleb oder ḥālāb?: ein möglicher Einfluss der frühjüdischen Halacha auf die Vokalisation des MT in Ex 23,19b; Ex 34,26b; Dtn 14,21b. ZAH 14 (2001) 144-158.

8411 {Hebrew}חמס: *Piedad Sánchez, Jorge* El uso del término [חמס] תָּמָס en la biblia hebrea. Qol 26 (2001) 11-18.

8412 חרם: **Wochna, Marek** Herem—l'atto culminante della guerra santa. Extr. Diss. Angelicum 2001, 80 pp.
חרמש: ⇒8384.

8413 כי: *Follingstad, Carl Martin* Deictic viewpoint in Biblical Hebrew text: a syntagmatic and paradigmatic analysis of the particle כי. Dallas 2001, SIL Intern. xxix; 683 pp. 1-55671-113-1. Bibl. 643-676.

8414 כמס: *Greenfield, Jonas C.* Three related roots: *kms, kns* and *knš.* 'Al kanfei yonah, 2. 2001 <1996> ⇒153. 840-846.
כנס: ⇒8414.

8415 כנען: *Tammuz, Oded* Canaan—a land without limits. UF 33 (2001) 501-543.

כנש: ⇒8414.

8416 כפר: *Albertz, Rainer* KPR: kultische Sühne und politische und gesellschaftliche Versöhnung. Kult, Konflikt. AOAT 285: 2001 ⇒387. 135-149.

8417 כפר: *Schenker, Adrian* Sühne II: Altes Testament TRE 32: 2001 ⇒ 665. 335-338.

8418 {Hebrew}כשר: *Leshem, Yosi* Likshor kesher—to form a conspiracy. BetM 168 (2001) 57-64 Sum. 94. **H**.

8419 {Hebrew}כתב: **Schaack, Thomas** Die Ungeduld des Papiers: Studien zum alttestamentlichen Verständnis des Schreibens anhand des Verbums *ktb* im Kontext administrativer Vorgänge. BZAW 262: 1998 ⇒ 14,7725; 16,8533. [R]JBL 119 (2000) 543-544 (*Handy, Lowell K.*).
מבטחים: ⇒8393.
מגל: ⇒8384.

8420 מלא: *Migsch, Herbert* Zur Bedeutung von מלא Niph'al in Num 14,21 und Ps 72,19. Bib. 82 (2001) 79-83.

8421 מרזח: *Greenfield, Jonas C.* The *marzeah* as a social institution. 'Al kanfei yonah, 2. 2001 <1974> ⇒153. 907-911.

8422 משיח: *Thompson, Thomas L.* The Messiah epithet in the Hebrew Bible. SJOT 15 (2001) 57-82.

8423 נבל: *Jacobson, Howard* Nebel. ZAH 14 (2001) 84-85.

8424 {Hebrew}נער; נערה: **Leeb, Carolyn S.** Away from the father's house: the social location of the na'ar and na'arah in Ancient Israel. 2000 ⇒ 16,8543. [R]CBQ 63 (2001) 524-525 (*Frick, Frank S.*); HebStud 42 (2001) 326-328 (*Matthews, Victor H.*).

8425 עדה: *Young, Ian 'Edah* and *Qahal* as collective nouns in Hebrew biblical texts. ZAH 14 (2001) 68-78.

8426 על־כן: *Jenni, Ernst* Eine hebräische Abtönungspartikel: *'al-ken.* [F]SEYBOLD, K.: AOAT 280: 2001 ⇒102. 201-215.

8427 עם: *Margalit, Baruch* The biblical עם־הארץ: a Ugaritic parallel. [M]CAGNI, L., 4. SMDSA 61: 2001 ⇒15. 1775-1788.

8428 עתק: *Loretz, Oswald* Ugaritisch *'tq* I-II, *'tq* und hebräisch *'tq* in Ps 6,8: zur Nominalform *qtly* (*şrry*) in KTU 1.16 I 2-9a. UF 33 (2001) 303-324.

8429 פחז: *Lange, Armin* Die Wurzel *phz* und ihre Konnotationen. VT 51 (2001) 497-510 [Gen 49,4; Zeph 3,4].

8430 פנים: *Simian-Yofre, Horacio* pānîm, face. TDOT 10: 2000 ⇒16,625. 589-615.
קהל ⇒8425.

8431 ראה: *Emerton, J.A.* Looking on one's enemies. VT 51 (2001) 186-96.

8432 רוח: *Gaß, Erasmus* Genus und Semantik am Beispiel von "theologischem" רוח. BN 109 (2001) 45-55.

8433 רעה: *Van Hecke, Pierre* Polysemy or homonymy in the root(s) *rʿh* in Biblical Hebrew: a cognitive-linguistic approach. ZAH 14 (2001) 50-67.

8434 שאול: *Rudman, Dominic* The use of water imagery in descriptions of Sheol. ZAW 113 (2001) 240-244.

8435 שלג: *Amar, Zohar* 'Like snow in summer': a luxury product in the land of Israel and Syria. Cathedra 102 (2001) 51-62 Sum. 209. **H.**

8436 שלום: **Savage, Joseph Michael** Shalom and its relationship to health/ healing in the Hebrew scriptures: a contextual and semantic study of the books of Psalms and Jeremiah. Diss. Florida State 2001, 227 pp. 3021535.

8437 שמים: *Bartelmus, Rüdiger* šamajim-Himmel: semantische und traditionsgeschichtliche Aspekte. Das biblische Weltbild. FAT 32: 2001 ⇒ 285. 87-124.

8438 תחש: *Görg, Manfred* Das Lexem תחש—Herkunft und Bedeutung. BN 109 (2001) 5-9.

8439 תקע ;כף: *Rogland, Max* 'Striking a hand' (*tqʿ kp*) in Biblical Hebrew. VT 51 (2001) 107-109.

8440 תרדמה: *Görg, Manfred* Tardema—"Tiefschlaf", "Ekstase" oder?. BN 110 (2001) 19-24 [Gen 2,21].

8441 תתן: *Tropper, Josef* Das unerkannte Verbalsubstantiv *ttn* "Geben" im Hebräischen und Ugaritischen. ZAH 14 (2001) 200-206 [1 Kgs 6,19; 17,14].

Philistine

8442 *ptgyh*: *Alonso, Carlos* El teónimo *PTGYH* de la inscripción filistea de Ecrón. Sef. 61 (2001) 259-264 Res., sum. 264.

Phoenician

8443 *hbrk*: *Müller, Hans-Peter* Ein wanderndes Kulturwort?: Isoglossen zu Phönizisch *hbrk* KAI 26 A I 1. RSFen 29 (2001) 13-26.

8444 *ḥzt*: *Mosca, Paul G.* For the birds: the term ṢṢP and ḤZT in the Marseilles Tariff (Line 11). UF 33 (2001) 403-418.

8445 *mš*: *Xella, Paolo* Fenicio *m(ʾ)š*, 'statua' (matériaux pour le lexique phénicien—III). ᶠHuß, W., OLA 104: 2001 ⇒51. 21-40. *ššp* ⇒8444.

8446 *trpy*: *Sznycer, Maurice* A propos du 'trophée' dans l'inscription phénicienne de Milkyatôn, roi de Kition et d'Idalion. ᶠHuß, W., OLA 104: 2001 ⇒51. 99-110.

Ugaritic

8447 *bmt*: Loretz, *Oswald* Literarische Quellen zur Stele des 'Baal au foudre' (RS 4.427): Ug. *bmt* I, *bmt* II, akkadische und hebräische Parallelen. UF 33 (2001) 325-376.

8448 *gdlt*: Tropper, *Josef* Brot als Opfermaterie in Ugarit: eine neue Deutung der Lexeme *dqt* und *gdlt*. UF 33 (2001) 545-565.
      dqt ⇒8448.

8449 *ḫšt*: Loretz, *Oswald* Der ugaritische architektonische Begriff *ḫšt* 'Totenheiligtum'. UF 33 (2001) 377-385.
      miyt-maʾitu ⇒8394.

8450 *mdl*: Greenfield, *Jonas C.* Ugaritic *mdl* and its cognates. 'Al kanfei yonah, 2. 2001 <1964> ⇒153. 847-854.
      ʿtq ⇒8428.

8451 *ġbr*: Mazzini, *Giovanni* The term *ġbr* in KTU 1.40: a possible Arabic-Ugaritic isogloss. StEeL 18 (2001) 51-53.
      ṣrry ⇒8428.
      qtly ⇒8428.

8452 *šakinu*: Van Soldt, *Wilfred* Studies on the *šakinu*-official (1): the spelling and the office-holders at Ugarit. UF 33 (2001) 579-599.

8453 *tqnn*: Ford, *J.N.* The verb *tqnn* in RS 1992.2014. UF 33 (2001) 201-212.

8454 *ṯrtnm*: Vita, *Juan-Pablo* À propos de la vocalisation du mot *ṯrtnm* dans le texte ougaritique RS 15.094. Sem. 50 (2001) 220-221.

       J1.5 *Phoenicia, ugaritica*—**Northwest Semitic** [⇒T5.4]

8455 *Allan, Robert* KTU 1.24 (= RS 5.194):15: a revised reading. StEeL 18 (2001) 45-50.

8456 *Amadasi Guzzo, Maria Giulia* Sur la prononciation spirante de *k* en phénicien. ᶠHuß, W.: OLA 104: 2001 ⇒51. 13-19.

8457 **Battaglini, Sergio** Le lamine di Pyrgi: la bilingue etrusco-fenicia e il problema delle origini etrusche. R 2001, Il Calamo 86 pp. 88-88039-14-7. Bibl. 79-80.

8458 **Beckman, Gary** Texts from the vicinity of Emar in the collection of Jonathan Rosen. 1996 ⇒12,7774... 15,8574. ᴿOr. 70 (2001) 133-136 (*Huehnergard, John*).

8459 *Bordreuil, Pierre* A propos de l'inscription de Meshaʿ: deux notes. ᶠDion, P.-E. 3: JSOT.S 326: 2001 ⇒25. 158-167.

8460 *Bordreuil, Pierre; Pardee, Dennis* Épigraphie moabitique—nouvel examen du 'papyrus du marzeaḥ'. Sem. 50 (2001) 224-226.

8461 *Chmiel, Jerzy* Ugarit a Stary Testament. CoTh 71/1 (2001) 41-49. **P.**

8462 *Clemens, David M.* KTU 1.45 and 1.6 I 8-18, 1.161, 1.101. UF 33 (2001) 65-116.

8463 *Duarte Castillo, Raúl* La inscripción filistea en favor de Padi. Qol 25 (2001) 85-88.

8464 *El-Khayari, Abdelaziz* Une stèle funéraire portant une inscription néopunique découverte dans le temple C à Volubilis. Sem. 50 (2001) 55-68.

8465 *Greenfield, Jonas C.* Notes on the Phoenician letter from Saqqara. 'Al kanfei yonah, 2. 2001 <1984> ⇒153. 756-758;

8466 A bronze *phialē* with a Phoenician dedicatory inscription <1982>;

8467 Scripture and inscription: the literary and rhetorical element in some early Phoenician inscriptions <1971>;

8468 Philological observations on the Deir 'Alla inscription <1991>;

8469 The epithets *rbt//ṯrrt* in the Krt epic <1987>;

8470 Ugaritic lexicographical notes <1967>;

8471 Amurrite, Ugaritic and Canaanite <1969>;

8472 Some glosses on the Keret epic <1969>;

8473 Some Phoenician words <1990>;

8474 *Greenfield, Jonas C.; Blau, Joshua* Ugaritic glosses <1970>. 'Al kanfei yonah, 2. 2001 ⇒153. 738-749/704-719/803-814/898-900/855-863/875-884/864-874/799-802/885-891.

8475 *Greenstein, Edward L.* The Ugaritic epic of Kirta in a wisdom perspective. Studies in Judaica. 2001 ⇒408. 1-13 Sum. xi-xii. **H.**

8476 *Kottsieper, Ingo* 'ŠTRM—eine südarabische Gottheit in der Scharonebene. ZAW 113 (2001) 245-250.

8477 **Krahmalkov, Charles R.** Phoenician-Punic dictionary. OLA 90: 2000 ⇒16,8568. [R]IEJ 51 (2001) 112-113 (*Naveh, Joseph*);

8478 A Phoenician-Punic grammar. HO 1/54: Lei 2001, Brill xix; 309 pp. €64. 90-04-11771-7. [R]RSO 75 (2001) 279-281 (*Garbini, Giovanni*).

8479 *Loretz, Oswald* Die Figur *Hysteron proteron* in KTU 1.14 I 28-30. UF 33 (2001) 299-302.

8480 *Lutz, R. Theodore* Phoenician inscriptions from Tell el-Maskhuta. [F]DION, P.-E. 3: JSOT.S 326: 2001 ⇒25. 190-212.

8481 *Müller, Hans-Peter* Ein phönizischer Totenpapyrus aus Malta. JSSt 46 (2001) 251-265.

8482 *Pardee, D.* Épigraphie et structure dans les textes administratifs en langue ougaritique: les exemples de RS 6.216 et RS 19.017. Or. 70 (2001) 235-282;

8483 Corrigenda au fac-similé. RS 15.116. Sem. 50 (2001) 222-223.

8484 *Peckham, Brian* Phoenicians and Aramaeans: the literary and epigraphic evidence. [F]DION, P.-E. 2: JSOT.S 325: 2001 ⇒25. 19-44.

8485 *Prosser, Miller* Reconsidering the reconstruction of KTU 1.4 VII 19. UF 33 (2001) 467-478.

8486 *Rainey, Anson F.* Mesha' and syntax. ᶠMILLER, J. JSOT.S 343: 2001 ⇒74. 287-307.

8487 *Rössler, Otto* Ghain im Ugaritischen. Gesammelte Schriften. 2001 <1961> ⇒202. 438-452.

8488 *Saporetti, Claudio* L'alfabeto di Ugarit. La decifrazione. Rivista della Fondazione Europea Dragan 13: 2001 ⇒436. 83-94.

8489 *Sivan, Daniel* The status of Ugaritic among the Northwest Semitic languages in the wake of recent research. ᶠAHITUV, S. 2001 ⇒1. 287-297. **H.**

8490 **Streck, Michael P.** Das amurritische Onomastikon der altbabylonischen Zeit, Bd. 1: die Amurriter. AOAT 271/1: 2000 ⇒16,8584. ᴿWZKM 91 (2001) 403-407 (*Pruzsinszky, Regine*).

8491 *Sznycer, Maurice* Les inscriptions néopuniques conservées au Musée national de Copenhague. Sem. 50 (2001) 41-54;

8492 Une ancienne inscription phénicienne découverte à Abul (Portugal). Sem. 50 (2001) 226-228.

8493 *Steiner, Richard C.* Albounout "frankincense" and alsounalph "oxtongue": Phoenician-Punic botanical terms with prothetic vowels from an Egyptian papyrus and a Byzantine codex. Or. 70 (2001) 97-103.

8494 *Tropper, Josef* 'Anats Kriegsgeschrei (KTU 1.3 II 23);

8495 Themen der ugaritischen Grammatik in der Diskussion;

8496 Umstrittene Verbalformen in ugaritischen Ritualtexten;

8497 *Tropper, Josef; Vita, Juan-Pablo* Pächter für den Hafen und die Landzugänge von Ugarit: neue Überlegungen zu KTU 4.172, 4.266, 4.336 und 4.388. UF 33 (2001) 567-571/621-639/679-696/573-578.

8498 **Westenholz, Joan Goodnick** Cuneiform inscriptions in the collection of the Bible Lands Museum Jerusalem: the Emar tablets. Cuneiform monographs 13: 2000 ⇒16,8593. ᴿSEL 18 (2001) 119-121 (*Seminara, Stefano*).

8499 *Wimmer, Stefan Jakob* Sichimitica Varia I: zur sog. Sichem-Plakette. BN 109 (2001) 21-26.

J1.6 Aramaica

8500 **As'ad, K.; Yon, J.-B.** Inscriptions de Palmyre: promenades épigraphiques dans la ville antique de Palmyre. Guides archéologiques 3: Beyrouth 2001, Direction générale des Antiquités... de la République arabe syrienne 128 pp. 2-912738-12-1.

8501 *Aufrecht, W.* A legacy of Syria: the Aramaic language. Canadian research on ancient Syria. 2001 ⇒581. 145-155.

8502 *Bengtsson, Per Å.* Semitic inscriptions in Rome. The synagogue of ancient Ostia. 2001 ⇒427. 151-165.

8503 **Beyer, Klaus** Die aramäischen Inschriften aus Assur, Hatra und dem übrigen Ostmesopotamien (datiert 44 v.Chr. bis 238 n. Chr.). 1998 ⇒14,7796; 16,8600. ᴿJBL 120 (2001) 366-368 (*Klingbeil, Gerald A.*); RBLit 3 (2001) 97-99 (*Klingbeil, Gerald A.*).

8504 **Brock, Sebastian P.,** *al.*, The hidden pearl: the Syrian Orthodox Church and its ancient Aramaic heritage, 1: the ancient Aramaic heritage, 2: the heirs of the ancient Aramaic heritage, 3: at the turn of the third millennium. R 2001, Trans World Film Italia 3 vols; 201+265+262 pp. $165. Plus 3 1-hour video tapes.

8505 *Cohen, Nahum* The Abiʾor Cave—Greek and Aramaic papyri. XXII Congresso di papirologia, 1. 2001 ⇒555. 251-254.

8506 ᴱ**Cotton-Paltiel, Hannah M.; Yardeni, Ada** Aramaic, Hebrew and Greek documentary texts. DJD 27: 1997 ⇒13,8228... 16,8602. ᴿEstB 59 (2001) 114-119 (*Chapa, J.*).

8507 *Couturier, Guy* Quelques observations sur le *bytdwd* de la stèle araméenne de Tel Dan. ᶠDION, P.-E. 2: JSOT.S 325: 2001 ⇒25. 72-98.

8508 *Cussini, Eleonora* Palaeography of the Aramaic epigraphs from Tell Neirab. ᴹCAGNI, L., 3: SMDSA 61: 2001 ⇒15. 1459-1479.

8509 *DeCaen, Vincent* The morphosyntactic argument for the waw consecutive in Old Aramaic. VT 51 (2001) 381-385.

8510 *Ehrlich, Carl Stephan* The *bytdwd*-inscription and Israelite historiography: taking stock after half a decade of research. ᶠDION, P.-E. 2: JSOT.S 325: 2001 ⇒25. 57-71.

8511 **Estelle, Bryan Daniel** Know before whom you stand: the language of deference in some ancient Aramaic and Hebrew documents. Diss. Cath. Univ. of America 2001, 259 pp. 3004162.

8512 *Fassberg, Steven* The 1st sg. suffix -ay in western neo-Aramaic: a historical perspective. Or. 70 (2001) 104-112.

8513 *Frame, Grant* A Neo-Babylonian tablet with an Aramaic docket and the surety phrase *put šep(i)...našû.* ᶠDION, P.-E. 3: JSOT.S 326: 2001 ⇒25. 100-133.

8514 *Galil, Gershon* A re-arrangement of the fragments of the Tel Dan inscription and the relations between Israel and Aram. PEQ 133 (2001) 16-21;

8515 The Aramaic royal inscription from Tel Dan. ᶠAHITUV, S. 2001 ⇒1. 67-74. **H.**

8516 *Greenfield, Jonas C.* The use of the targum in a Mandaic incantation text. ʿAl kanfei yonah, 1. 2001 <1992> ⇒153. 493-496;

8517 Some Arabic loanwords in the Aramaic and Nabatean texts from Naḥal Ḥever. ʿAl kanfei yonah, 1 2001. <1992> ⇒153. 497-508:

8518 The verbs for washing in Aramaic <1992> 465-471;

8519 The Babylonian forerunner of a Mandaic formula <1993> 509-512;

8520 The 'defension clause' in some documents from Naḥal Ḥever and Naḥal Ṣeʾelim <1992> 460-464;

8521 A Mandaic miscellany <1984> 397-404;

8522 Notes on some Aramaic and Mandaic magic bowls <1974> 353-360;

8523 Aramaic and its dialects <1978> 361-375;

8524 An Aramaic inscription from Tyre from the reign of DIOCLETIAN preserved in the Palestinian talmud <1991> 449-452;

8525 Some glosses on the Sefire inscriptions <1991> 327-333;

8526 Notes on the Early Aramaic lexicon. <1984-86> 251-257;

8527 Stylistic aspects of the Sefire Treaty inscriptions <1965> 22-39;

8528 Asylum at Aleppo: a note on Sfire III,4-7 <1990> 320-326;

8529 The 'periphrastic imperative' in Aramaic and Hebrew <1969> 56-67;

8530 Two proverbs of Aḥiqar <1990> 313-319;

8531 On Mandaic poetic technique <1989> 427-434;

8532 The Zakir inscription and the Danklied <1969> 75-92;

8533 The background and parallel to a proverb of Ahiqar <1972> 93-103;

8534 Un rite religieux araméen et ses parallèles <1973> 104-110;

8535 Standard literary Aramaic <1974> 111-120;

8536 The Aramaic legal texts of the Achaemenian period <1990> 305-12;

8537 Iranian or Semitic?. <1975> 138-143;

8538 On some Iranian terms in the Elephantine papyri: aspects of continuity <1977> 148-153;

8539 Some reflections on the vocabulary of Aramaic in relationship to the other Semitic languages <1978> 154-159;

8540 The dialects of early Aramaic <1978> 160-166;

8541 Early Aramaic poetry <1979> 167-173;

8542 Aramaic studies and the bible <1981> 174-194;

8543 Babylonian-Aramaic relationships <1982> 203-213;

8544 Aspects of archives in the Achaemenid period <1986> 276-282;

8545 ana urdūti kabāsu=לעבד כבש <1984> 247-250;

8546 *HAMARAKARA>ʾAMARKAL <1970> 68-74;

8547 Studies in Aramaic lexicography I <1962> 6-21;

8548 *Greenfield, Jonas C.; Cotton, Hannah* Babatha's property and the law of succession in the Babatha archive <1994> 540-553;

8549 *Greenfield, Jonas C.; Porten, Bezalel* The Aramaic papyri from Hermopolis <1968> 40-55;

8550 Hermopolis letter 6 <1974> 121-137;

8551 *Greenfield, Jonas C.; Shaffer, Aaron* Notes on the Akkadian-Aramaic bilingual statue from Tell Fekherye <1983> 217-224;

8552 Notes on the curse formulae of the Tell Fekherye inscription <1985> 263-275;

8553 *Greenfield, Jonas C.; Sokoloff, Michael* An astrological text from Qumran (4Q318) and reflections on some zodiacal names <1994> 554-572. Astronomical considerations by *David Pingree,* 517-519; Paleographic analysis by *Ada Yardeni,* 567-569;

8554 Astrological and related omen texts in Jewish Palestinian Aramaic <1989> 435-448;

8555 The contribution of Qumran Aramaic to the Aramaic vocabulary <1992> 472-492;

8556 *Greenfield, Jonas C.; Yadin, Yigael; Yardeni, Ada* Babatha's *Ketubba* <1994> 513-539;

8557 **Gropp, Douglas M.** , *al.,* Wadi Daliyeh II: the Samaria papyri from Wadi Daliyeh; Qumran Cave 4, XXVIII:2 Miscellanea, part 2. DJD 28; Qumrân Cave 4/28; Qumran 4Q368,371-373,377. Oxf 2001, Clarendon xv; 255 pp. $135. 0-19-92495-3. In consultation with *James Vanderkam* and *Monica Brady;* 63 pl.

8558 *Gropp, Douglas M.* The Samaria papyri from Wadi Daliyeh. Wadi Daliyeh II. DJD 28: 2001 ⇒8557. 1-116.

8559 *Hayajneh, Hani* Marcus Ulpius Suʿaidu in einem Bruchstück einer nabatäischen Inschrift aus Süd-Jordanien. ZDPV 117 (2001) 171-85.

8560 *Heltzer, Michael* An alabaster cup with an Aramaic inscription. ᴹCAGNI, L., 3: SMDSA 61: 2001 ⇒15. 1611-1615.

8561 **Herranz Marco, Mariano** Huellas de arameo en los evangelios y en la catequesis cristiana primitiva. Studia Semitica NT 5: 1997 ⇒13, 3983 ... 15,8608. ᴿRBLit 3 (2001) 351-352 (*Rodgers, Lloyd W.*).

8562 *Ilan, Tal* Witnesses in the Judaean Desert documents: prosopographical observations. SCI 20 (2001) 169-178.

8563 **Khan, Geoffrey** A grammar of Neo-Aramaic: the dialect of the Jews of Arbel. HO 1/47: 1999 ⇒15,8611. ᴿBiOr 58 (2001) 440-443 (*Murre-van den Berg, H.L.*).

8564 ᴱ**Kottsieper, Ingo** Aramäisches Wörterbuch. THWAT 9/1: Stu 2001, Kohlhammer 128 col. €34. 3-17-015616-0.

8565 *Laffitte, Roland* Du babylonien *zibānītu(m)* à l'arabe *al-zubānā* par le mandéen *zabānītā?*. Sem. 50 (2001) 193-197.

8566 **Lemaire, André** Nouvelles tablettes araméennes. E.P.H.E. Sciences historiques et philologiques II, Hautes Études Orientales 34, Moyen et Proche-Orient 1: Genève 2001, Droz 160 pp. FS68. 2-600-00614-1. 81 photo [RB 109,157].

8567 *Lewis, Naphtali* The demise of the Aramaic document in the Dead Sea region. SCI 20 (2001) 179-181.

8568 *Lindenberger, James M.* What ever happened to Vidranga?: a Jewish liturgy of cursing from Elephantine. ᶠDION, P.-E. 3: JSOT.S 326: 2001 ⇒25. 134-157.

8569 *Makujina, John* A critical note on two old Persian calques in official Aramaic. ANESt 38 (2001) 178-185.

8570 *Muraoka, T.* The prefix conjugation in circumstantial clauses in the Tel Dan inscription?. VT 51 (2001) 389-392.

8571 **Muraoka, Takamitsu; Porten, Besalel** A grammar of Egyptian Aramaic. HO 1/32: 1998 ⇒14,7822; 16,8625. ᴿOLZ 96 (2001) 574-577 (*Oelsner, Joachim*); Or. 69 (2000) 183-185 (*Gianto, Agustinus*).

8572 *Nehmé, Laïla* Cinq *graffiti* nabatéens du Sinaï. Sem. 50 (2001) 69-80.

8573 **Nosek, Bedřich** Aramejština babylónského talmudu: praktická gramatika [Das Aramäisch des babylonischen Talmuds: eine praktische Grammatik]. Praha 2001, Karolinum 279 pp. 80-246-0079-X. **Czech**.

8574 ᴱᵀ**Porten, Bezalel; Yardeni, Ada** אוסף תעודות ארמיות ממצרם העתיקה Textbook of Aramaic documents from ancient Egypt, 4: חרסים ושונות Ostraca and assorted inscriptions. 1999 ⇒15,8626; 16,8632. ᴿBiOr 58 (2001) 668-670 (*Lemaire, A.*); Syr. 78 (2001) 235-236 (*Lozachmeur, Hélène*).

8575 *Puech, Émile* Notes d'épigraphie christo-palestinienne cisjordanienne. RB 108 (2001) 61-72.

8576 **Puech, Émile** Qumrân Grotte 4 XXII: textes araméens première partie 4Q529-549. DJD 31: Oxf 2001, Clarendon xviii; 441 pp. £80. 0-19-827026-7. 22 pl. ᴿCRAI (2001/3) 1342-1343 (*Caquot, André*).

8577 *Röllig, Wolfgang* Aramaica Haburensia V: Limu-Datierungen in aramäischen Urkunden des 7. Jh. v. Chr. ᶠDION, P.-E. 2: JSOT.S 325: 2001 ⇒25. 45-56.

8578 *Schniedewind, William M.; Zuckerman, Bruce* A possible reconstruction of the name of Haza'el's father in the Tel Dan inscription. IEJ 51 (2001) 88-91.

8579 **Sokoloff, Michael; Yahalom, Joseph** Jewish Palestinian Aramaic poetry from late antiquity: critical edition with introduction and commentary. 1999 ⇒15,8632; 16,8640. ᴿREJ 160 (2001) 228-231 (*Danan, Jules*). **H**.

8580 *Steiner, Richard C.* The scorpion spell from Wadi Hammamat: another Aramaic text in demotic script. JNES 60 (2001) 259-268.

8581 **Tal, Abraham** A dictionary of Samaritan Aramaic. HO 1/50/1-2: 2000 ⇒16,8643. ᴿOr. 70 (2001) 142-143 (*Beyer, Klaus*).

8582 *Tavernier, Jan* An Achaemenid royal inscription: the text of paragraph 13 of the Aramaic version of the Bisitun inscription. JNES 60 (2001) 161-176.

8583 *Taylor, David G.K.* An annotated index of dated Palmyrene Aramaic texts. JSSt 46 (2001) 203-219.

8584 *Tropper, Josef* Dialektvielfalt und Sprachwandel im frühen Aramäischen: soziolinguistische Überlegungen. [F]DION, P.-E. 3: JSOT.S 326: 2001 ⇒25. 213-222.

8585 *Wesselius, Jan-Wim* The road to Jezreel: primary history and the Tel Dan inscription. SJOT 15 (2001) 83-103.

8586 *Yardeni, Ada* The decipherment and restoration of legal texts from the Judaean Desert: a reexamination of *Papyrus Starcky (P.Yadin* 36). SCI 20 (2001) 121-137.

8587 **Younansardaroud, Helen** Der neuostaramäische Dialekt von Särdä:rïd. Semitica Viva 26: Wsb 2001, Harrassowitz xxiv; 261 pp. €72. 3-447-04430-6. Bibl. 251-261.

J1.7 Syriaca

8588 *Abou Samra, Gaby* Petites inscriptions syriaques sur une tablette de pierre (Vallée de la Qadicha, Liban). Sem. 50 (2001) 91-98.

8589 *Briquel Chatonnet, Françoise* De l'écriture édessenienne à l'*Estrangelā* et au *Serṭō*. Sem. 50 (2001) 81-90.

8590 [ET]**Drijvers, Hendrik Jan Willem; Healey, John F.** The Old Syriac inscriptions of Edessa and Osrhoene: text, translations and commentary. HO 42: 1999 ⇒15,8639. [R]ZDMG 151 (2001) 207-208 (*Joosse, N. Peter*).

8591 *Edzard, Lutz* Problems with post-vocalic spirantization in Syriac: cyclic rule ordering vs. 'early phonemization with paradigmatic levelling'. JSSt 46 (2001) 77-95.

8592 **Falla, Terry C.** A key to the Peshitta gospels, 2: hē-yōdh. 2000 ⇒ 16,8649. [R]NT 43 (2001) 413-415 (*Lane, D.J.*); ABR 49 (2001) 71-72 (*Glover, Tim*); ANESt 38 (2001) 218-220 (*Van Peursen, W.Th.*).

8593 *Jullien, Christelle; Jullien, Florence* La Chronique d'Arbèles: proposition pour la fin d'une controverse. OrChr 85 (2001) 41-83.

8594 *Kaufhold, Hubert* Anhang: Julius Aßfalgs Rolle bei der Identifizierung des in Speyer gefundenen Blattes des Codex Argenteus. OrChr 85 (2001) 13-22.

8595 *Kuty, Renaud* The position of the particle dên in New Testament Syriac. ANESt 38 (2001) 186-199.

8596 *Leonhard, Clemens* Observations on the date of the Syriac Cave of Treasures. [F]DION, P.-E. 3: JSOT.S 326: 2001 ⇒25. 255-293.

8597 **Muraoka, Takamitsu** Classical Syriac: a basic grammar with a chrestomathy. PLO 19: 1997 ⇒13,8264; 15,8643. [R]Or. 70 (2001) 339-345 (*Morrison, Craig*); JSSt 46 (2001) 321-322 (*Healey, John F.*).

8598 *Qing, Duan* Bericht über ein neuentdecktes syrisches Dokument aus Dunhuang/China. OrChr 85 (2001) 84-93.

8599 *Rogland, Max* Performative utterances in classical Syriac. JSSt 46 (2001) 243-250.

8600 *Weninger, Stefan* Die Wochentagsbezeichnungen im Syrischen. ᶠDENZ, A. 2001 ⇒21. 151-166.

8601 *Wertheimer, Ada* The functions of the Syriac particle d-. Muséon 114 (2001) 259-289 [Jn 17,1];

8602 Special types of cleft sentences in Syriac. JSSt 46 (2001) 221-241.

J1.8 Akkadica (sumerica)

8603 **Black, Jeremy A.** Reading Sumerian poetry. 1998 ⇒4,7853... 16, 8659. ᴿJSSt 46 (2001) 132-137 (*Geller, M.J.*).

8604 **Bodi, Daniel** Petite grammaire de l'Akkadien à l'usage des débutants. P 2001, Geuthner 263 pp. 2-7053-3693-1 [RHPhR 82,200— Heintz, J.-G.].

8605 *Cohen, Eran* Focus marking in Old Babylonian. WZKM 91 (2001) 85-104.

8606 *Cooper, Jerrold* Literature and history: the historical and political referents of Sumerian literary texts. Proceedings of the XLVe Rencontre Assyriologique, 1. 2001 ⇒577. 131-147.

8607 ᴱ**D'Agostino, Franco** Testi umoristici babilonesi e assiri. 2000 ⇒16, 8663. ᴿRivBib 49 (2001) 343-345 (*Lucci, Laila*).

8608 *Donbaz, Veysel* Some late Babylonian texts: gleaned from the Assur collection. Proceedings of the XLVe Rencontre Assyriologique, 1. 2001 ⇒577. 163-179.

8609 **Eidem, Jesper; Læssøe, Jørgen** The Shemshara Archives 1: the letters. DVSS.HF 23: K 2001, Det kongelige Danske Videnskabernes Selskab 185 pp. 87-7876-245-6. Bibl. 172-180.

8610 ᴱ**Englund, Robert K.; Nissen, Hans Jörg** Archaische Verwaltungstexte aus Uruk: die Heidelberger Sammlung. Ausgrabungen der Deutschen Forschungsgemeinschaft in Uruk-Warka 17; Archaische Texte aus Uruk 7: B 2001, Mann 72 pp. 3-7861-2402-7. Mit einem Beitrag von *Rainer B. Boehmer*; 102 pl.

8611 *Giorgieri, Mauro* Der Löwe und der Fuchs in dem Brief KBo 1.14. Or. 70 (2001) 89-96.

8612 *Greenfield, Jonas C.* našû-nadānu and its congeners. ʿAl kanfei yonah, 2. 2001 <1977> ⇒153. 720-724.

8613 ᴱ**Hunger, Hermann** Astronomical diaries and related texts from Babylonia, 5: lunar and planetary texts. DÖAW 299: W 2001, ÖAW xii; 399 pp. 3-7001-3028-7. Collab. *Abraham J. Sachs; John M. Steele.*

8614 *Kogan, L.* *ǧ in Akkadian. UF 33 (2001) 263-298.

8615 *Krebernik, Manfred šumman lā qabīʾat ana balāṭim...* wärst du nicht zum Leben berufen...der Irrealis im Altbabylonischen. [F]DENZ, A. (2001) 51-78.

8616 *Larsen, M.T.* Affect and emotion. [F]VEENHOF, K. 2001 ⇒111. 275-86.

8617 *Lundström, Steven M.* 'Für die Dauer der Tage ... für die Tage, die verbleiben': zur Funktion der akkadischen Grabinschriften des 2. und 1. Jts. v. Chr. WZKM 91 (2001) 211-258.

8618 **Malbran-Labat, Florence** Manuel de langue akkadienne. PIOL 50: Lv(N) 2001, Institut Orientaliste x; 407 pp. 90-429-0982-X. Bibl. 393.

8619 *Marchesi, Gianni* Alleged SIG7 = agar4 and related matters. Or. 70 (2001) 313-317.

8620 **Martin, Harriet P.,** *al.,* The Fara tablets in the University of Pennsylvania Museum of Archaeology and Anthropology. Bethesda, MD 2001, CDL xxvii; 163 pp. 1-88305-366-8.

8621 [T]**Michel, Cécile** Correspondance des marchands de Kanish au début du IIe millénaire avant J.-C. LAPO 19: P 2001, Cerf 601 pp. €36.59. 2-204-06700-8.

8622 **Novotny, Jamie R.** The standard Babylonian Etana epic: cuneiform text, transliteration, score, glossary, indices and sign list. SAA.Cuneiform Texts II: Univ. of Helskini 2001, Neo-Assyrian Text Corous Project xxvii; 62 pp. $25. 951-45-9047-3.

8623 **Pentiuc, Eugen J.** West Semitic vocabulary in the Akkadian texts from Emar. Harvard Semitic Studies 49: WL 2001, Eisenbrauns xvii; 278 pp. $37. 1-57506-910-5. Bibl. 251-266.

8624 **Römer, Willem H.** Philibert Hymnen und Klagelieder in sumerischer Sprache. AOAT 276: Müns 2001, Ugarit-Verlag xi; 275 pp. 3-927120-94-4.

8625 [E]**Saggs, Henry William Frederick** The Nimrud Letters, 1952. Cuneiform Texts from Nimrud 5: L 2001, British School of Archaeology in Iraq xii; 327 pp. 0-903472-20-1. Bibl. vii-x.

8626 *Scafa, Paola Negri* La decifrazione del cuneiforme. La decifrazione. Rivista della Fondazione Europea Dragan 13: 2001 ⇒436. 10-26.

8627 **Schaudig, Hanspeter** Die Inschriften Nabonids von Babylon und Kyros' des Großen: samt den in ihrem Umfeld entstandenen Tendenzschriften. AOAT 256: Müns 2001, Ugarit-Verlag xlii; 766 pp. 3-927-120-75-8. Textausgabe und Grammatik; Bibl. xxxix-xlii.

8628 **Schramm, Wolfgang** Bann, Bann!: eine sumerisch-akkadische Beschwörungsserie. Göttinger Arbeitshefte zur altorientalischen Literatur 2: Gö 2001, Seminar für Keilschriftforschung vi; 121 pp. 3-00-008707-9. Bibl. 103-111.

8629 *Selz, Gebhard J.* Irano-Sumerica. WZKM 91 (2001) 259-267.

8630 *Seminara, Stefano* I sumeri e il 'pensiero agglutinante': considerazioni sull'agglutinazione in sumerico tra lingua, scrittura e forme letterarie. StEeL 18 (2001) 1-26.

8631 **Seminara, Stefano** La versione accadica del Lugal-E: la tecnica babilonese della traduzione dal sumerico e le sue regole.Materiali per il vocabolario sumerico 8: R 2001, Università degli Studi di Roma "La Sapienza" 595 pp. Bibl. 559-575.

8632 ᴱ**Sjöberg, Åke W.** The Sumerian dictionary of the University Museum of the University of Pennsylvania, 1: A.—Pt. 3. 1998 ⇒14, 7898. ᴿBiOr 58 (2001) 152-156 (*Schretter, Manfred*).

8633 **Spar, Ira; Dassow, Eva von** Private archive texts from the first millennium B.C. Cuneiform Texts in the Metropolitan Museum of Art 3: Turnhout 2000, Brepols civ; 304 pp. 2-503-50927-3. Contrib. *J.N. Postgate; Linda B. Bregstein*; 126 pl.

8634 **Stein, Peter** Die mittel- und neubabylonischen Königsinschriften bis zum Ende der Assyrerherrschaft: grammatische Untersuchungen. Jenaer Beiträge zum Vorderen Orient 3: 2000 ⇒16,8685. ᴿOLZ 96 (2001) 515-518 (*Streck, Michael P.*); WZKM 91 (2001) 411-418 (*Schaudig, Hanspeter*).

8635 *Taylor, J.* A new OB Proto-Lu-Proto-Izi combination tablet. Or. 70 (2001) 209-234.

J2.7 Arabica

8636 *Abdul-Raof, Hussein* On the subject in Arabic. JSSt 46 (2001) 97-120.

8637 **Bron, François** Ma'in. Inventaire des inscriptions sudarabiques 3: 1998 ⇒16,8698. ᴿSyr. 78 (2001) 259-261 (*Ryckmans, Jacques*).

8638 *Bron, François* Deux inscriptions sabéennes sur bronze provenant d'al-Bayḍā'. Sem. 50 (2001) 228-229;

8639 Antiquités qatabanites (II). Sem. 50 (2001) 230-233.

8640 **Gacek, Adam** The Arabic manuscript tradition: a glossary of technical terms and bibliography. HO 1/58: Lei 2001, Brill xvi; 269 pp. 90-04-12061-0. Bibl. 179-269.

8641 *Gajda, Iwona* Coupe en argent portant une inscription sudarabique. Sem. 50 (2001) 99-111.

8642 **Kinberg, Naphtali** Studies in the linguistic structure of classical Arabic. SStLL 31: Lei 2001, Brill ix; 275 pp. 90-04-11765-2.

8643 *Masliyah, Sadok* Curses and insults in Iraqi Arabic. JSSt 46 (2001) 267-308.

8644 *Nebes, Norbert* Das Inzidsenzschema im klassischen Arabischen: ein Vorbericht. ᶠDᴇɴᴢ, A. 2001 ⇒21. 113-128.

8645 *Sima, Alexander* Altsüdarabische Konditionalsätze. Or. 70 (2001) 283-312;

8646 Untersuchungen zur Phraseologie altsüdarabischer Inschriften: Paronomasie, Merismus und Klangfiguren. WZKM 91 (2001) 269-315.

8647 *Wagner, Ewald* Neues Material zum Studium des Neusüdarabischen: die Stroomer'sche Edition der Mehri-Texte von Jᴏʜɴsᴛᴏɴᴇ. WZKM 91 (2001) 331-346.

J3.0 Aegyptia

8648 **Allen, James P.** Middle Egyptian: an introduction to the language and culture of hieroglyphs. 2000 ⇒16,8708. ᴿCÉg 76 (2001) 89-99 (*Malaise, Michel*).

8649 *Assmann, Jan* Pictures versus letters: William Wᴀʀʙᴜʀᴛᴏɴ's theory of grammatological iconoclasm. ᶠBᴀʀᴀsᴄʜ, M. 2001 ⇒2. 297-311.

8650 *Baud, Michel; Farout, Dominique* Trois biographies d'Ancien Empire revisitées. BIFAO 101 (2001) 43-57.

8651 *Betrò, Marilina* La decifrazione della scrittura geroglifica. La decifrazione. Rivista della Fondazione Dragan 13: 2001 ⇒436. 27-41.

8652 **Cauville, Sylvie** Dendara IV: traduction. OLA 101: Lv 2001, Peeters viii; 929 pp. 90-429-0935-8. Phot. A. Lecler; 217 pl.

8653 **Collier, Mark; Manley, Bill** How to read Egyptian hieroglyphs: a step-by-step guide to teach yourself. 1998 ⇒14,7932. ᴿJSSt 46 (2001) 137-138 (*Richardson, M.E.J.*).

8654 *Czerny, Ernst* Ein früher Beleg für ḥwt-wʿrt auf einem Siegelabdruck aus Tell el-Dabʿa. Ä&L 11 (2001) 13-26.

8655 **Derchain-Urtel, Maria-Theresia** Epigraphische Untersuchungen zur griechisch-römischen Zeit in Ägypten. ÄAT 43: 1999 ⇒15,8710. ᴿBiOr 58 (2001) 354-357 (*Hallof, Jochen*).

8656 **Dodson, Aidan** The hieroglyphs of ancient Egypt. L 2001, New Holland 144 pp. £17. 1-85974-918-6.

8657 *Feder, Frank* Der Wert einer lexikologischen Untersuchung der koptischen Bibelübersetzung für die ägyptische Lexikographie. ZÄS 128 (2001) 7-23.

8658 **Galán, José M.** Cuatro viajes en la literatura del antiguo Egipto. 1998 ⇒14,7941. ᴿRBLit 3 (2001) 99-100 (*Dupertuis, Rubén R.*).

8659 *Goelet, Ogden* The anaphoric style in Egyptian hymnody. JSSEA 28 (2001) 75-89.

8660 *Görg, Manfred* Israel in Hieroglyphen. BN 106 (2001) 21-27;

8661 Afrika, Asien und Europa in einer Völkerliste des Tempels von Komir/Oberägypten. [F]Huß, W.: OLA 104: 2001 ⇒51. 371-383.

8662 **Graefe, Erhart** Mittelägyptische Grammatik für Anfänger. Wsb [6]2001, Harrassowitz xix; 262 pp. 3447044691. Mit *Jochem Kahl*.

8663 **Grallert, Silke** Bauen—Stiften—Weihen: ägyptische Bau- und Restaurierungsinschriften von den Anfängen bis zur 30. Dynastie. ADAI.Ä 18/1-2: B 2001, Achet 2 vols. 3-933684-10-2. 59 pl.

8664 **Gülden, Svenja A.** Die hieratischen Texte des P. Berlin 3049. KÄT 13: Wsb 2001, Harrassowitz xx; 89 pp. 3-447-04220-6. 17 pl.; Abgk. Lit. xi-xii.

8665 *Hofmann, Tobias* Majestät und Diener—zur Dialektik des Begriffes ḥm. ZÄS 128 (2001) 116-132.

        [F]Israelit-Groll, S. Structuring Egyptian syntax 2001 ⇒52.

8666 **Jansen-Winkeln, Karl** Biographische und religiöse Inschriften der Spätzeit aus dem Ägyptischen Museum Kairo: Teil 1: Übersetzungen und Kommentare; Teil 2: Texte und Tafeln. ÄAT 45,1-2: Wsb 2001, Harrassowitz v.1, xii; 1-330; v.2, vi; 331-441 pp. €78. 3447-04416-0.

8667 **Junge, Friedrich** Late Egyptian grammar: an introduction. [T]*Warburton, David*: Oxf 2001, Griffith Institute 391 pp. £20. 0-900-416-76-9.

8668 *Kaplony-Heckel, Ursula* Theben-Ost III: die r-rḫ=w-Tempel-Quittungen und ähnliche Texte: erster Teil: Allgemeiner Teil und Texte Nr. 18-25. ZÄS 128 (2001) 24-40.

8669 **Kitchen, Kenneth A.** Poetry of ancient Egypt. 1999 ⇒15,8721; 16, 8722. [R]BiOr 58 (2001) 350-354 (*Burkard, Günter*); CÉg 76 (2001) 100-115 (*Gillam, Robyn A.*).

8670 [E]**Leclant, Jean** Les textes de la Pyramide de Pépy Ier. Mémoires de l'Institut Français d'Archéologie Orientale du Caire 118,1-2: Le Caire 2001, Institut Français d'Archéologie Orientale 2 vols. 2-7247-0282-4. Bibl. v. 1 13-17.

8671 **Leitz, Christian** Magical and medical papyri in the British Museum. 1999 ⇒15,8723; 16,8726. [R]Or. 70 (2001) 193-195 (*Roccati, Alessandro*).

8672 *Migahid, Abd-El-Gawad* Eine spätdemotische Zahlungsquittung auf dem Palimpsest einiger Abrechnungslisten (P. Vindob. D 6819). ZÄS 128 (2001) 142-145.

8673 **Moers, Gerald** Fingierte Welten in der ägyptischen Literatur des 2. Jahrtausends v. Chr.: Grenzüberschreitung, Reisemotiv und Fiktionalität. PÄ 19: Lei 2001, Brill viii; 338 pp. €65/$76. 90-04-12125-0. Bibl. 285-317.

8674 **Peden, Alexander J.** The graffiti of Pharaonic Egypt: scope and roles of informal writings (c. 3100-332 B.C.). PÄ 17: Lei 2001, Brill xxii; 348 pp. €77. 90-04121-12-9.

8675 *Quack, Joachim Friedrich* Ein neuer Versuch zum Moskauer literarischen Brief. ZÄS 128 (2001) 167-181.

8676 *Rainey, Anson F.* Israel in Merenptah's inscription and reliefs. IEJ 51 (2001) 57-75.

8677 *Redford, Donald B.* New perspectives on ancient Egyptian texts. Archaeology and society. 2001 ⇒443. 104-110.

8678 *Rössler, Otto* Das Ägyptische als semitische Sprache. Gesammelte Schriften. 2001 <1971> ⇒202. 543-606.

8679 *Schoville, Keith* The Rosetta Stone in historical perspective. JATS 12/1 (2001) 1-21.

8680 **Sweeney, Deborah** Correspondence and dialogue: pragmatic factors in late Ramesside letter writing. ÄAT 49: Wsb 2001, Harrassowitz (8) v; 327 pp. 3-447-04419-5. Bibl. 255-276.

8681 **Takács, Gábor** Etymological dictionary of Egyptian, 1: a phonological introduction. HO 1/48: 1999 ⇒15,8737. ᴿJRAS 11 (2001) 54-55 (*Kitchen, K.A.*); BiOr 58 (2001) 565-581 (*Osing, Jürgen*);

8682 2: b-, p-, f-. HO 1/48/2: Lei 2001, Brill xxviii; 644 pp. €148. 90-04-12121-8.

8683 ᴱᵀ**Thissen, Heinz Josef** Des Niloten HORAPOLLON Hieroglyphenbuch. APF.B 6: Mü 2001, Saur xxiv; 109 pp. 3-598-77539-3.

8684 **Vandekerckhove, Hans; Müller-Wollermann, Renate** Die Felsinschriften des Wadi Hilâl. Elkab 6,1-2: Turnhout 2001, Brepols 2 vols. 2-503-51023-X. Beitrag und Karten von *Frans Depuydt* und Fotos von *Arpag Mekhitarian*; Bibl. v.I 401-413.

8685 **Verhoeven, Ursula** Untersuchungen zur späthieratischen Buchschrift. OLA 99: Lv 2001, Peeters xii; (2) 374 pp. €90. 90-429-0932-3. Bibl. 347-364.

8686 **Vittmann, Günter** Der demotische Papyrus Rylands 9, Teil II: Text und Übersetzung: Körperlichkeit im 1. Jahrtausend n. Chr. ᴱ*Görg, Manfred*: ÄAT 38: Wsb 1998, Harrassowitz 777 pp; 2 vols. 3-447-03969-8.

8687 **Vleeming, Sven P.** Some coins of Artaxerxes and other short texts in the Demotic script found on various objects gathered from many publications. Studia Demotica 5: Lv 2001, Peeters xxxviii; 341 pp. 90-429-1061-5.

J3.4 Coptica

8688 ᴱ**Azevedo, Joaquim** A simplified Coptic dictionary (Sahidic dialect). Tools for exegesis 1: Cachoeira, Brazil 2001, Centro de Pesquisa xl; 186 pp.

8689 **Biedenkopf-Ziehner, Anneliese** Koptische Schenkungsurkunden aus der Thebais: Formeln und Topoi der Urkunden, Aussagen der Urkunden, Indices. GOF.Ä 41: Wsb 2001, Harrassowitz xi; 152 pp. 3-447-04464-0. Bibl. 148-149.

8690 [E]**Gardner, Iain; Alcock, Anthony; Funk, Wolf-Peter Paul** Coptic documentary texts from Kellis, 1: P.Kell V (P.Kell.Copt.10-52; O.Kell.Copt.1-2). Dakhleh Oasis Project, Monograph 9,1: 1999 ⇒ 15,354. [R]Apocrypha 12 (2001) 287-289 (*Dubois, J.-D.*).

8691 *Krause, Martin* Referat der koptischen Urkunden von 1998 und 1999. APF 47 (2001) 229-244.

8692 **Layton, Bentley** A Coptic grammar, with chrestomathy and glossary: Sahidic dialect. 2000 ⇒16,8745. [R]Sef. 61 (2001) 210-211 (*Torallas Tovar, S.*); Enchoria 27 (2001) 231-242 (*Schenke, Hans-Martin*).

8693 *Lucchesi, Enzo* Deux pages inédites d'une instruction d'Horsièse sur les amitiés particulières. Or. 70 (2001) 183-192.

8694 **Plisch, Uwe-Karsten** Einführung in die koptische Sprache: Sahidischer Dialekt. Sprachen und Kulturen des Christlichen Orients 5: 1999 ⇒15,8746. [R]BiOr 58 (2001) 629-631 (*Hasitzka, Monika*).

8695 *Richter, Siegfried; Wurst, Gregor* Koptische literarische Texte (1998-2000). APF 47 (2001) 196-228.

8696 *Robinson, Gesine Schenke* A plea for gender equality in a partially restored Coptic codex (Papyrus Berolinensis 20 915). Muséon 114 (2001) 15-39 [Gen 2,23; 46,26].

8697 **Smith, Richard** A concise Coptic-English lexicon. SBL, Resources for Biblical Study 35: [2]1999 ⇒15,8749. [R]RBLit 3 (2001) 100-103 (*Williams, Michael A.*).

J3.8 Aethiopica

8698 *Drewes, A.J.* Noms propres dans les documents épigraphiques de l'Éthiopie, II. Sem. 50 (2001) 199-210.

8699 **Hayajneh, Hani** Die Personennamen in den qatabänischen Inschriften.. 1998 ⇒14,7995. [R]JRAS 11 (2001) 76-77 (*Gajda, J.*).

8700 **Weninger, Stefan** Das Verbalsystem des Altäthiopischen: eine Untersuchung seiner Verwendung und Funktion unter Berücksichtigung des Interferenzproblems. VOK 47: Wsb 2001, Harrassowitz (8) 387 pp. €49. 3-447-04484-5. Bibl. 345-360.

J4.0 Anatolica

8701 *De Martino, Stefano* L'interpretazione dell'ittita, la decifrazione del luvio geroglifico e l'interpretazione del hurrico. La decifrazione. Rivista della Fondazione Europea Dragan 13: 2001 ⇒436. 72-82.

8702 *Groddek, Detlev* 'Mausoleum' (É.NA₄) und 'Totentempel' (^É*ḫišta*) im Hethitischen. UF 33 (2001) 213-218.

8703 *Hutter, Manfred* Luwische Sprache und Kultur in der Eisenzeit: zum "Corpus of Hieroglyphic Luwian Inscriptions". WZKM 91 (2001) 161-181.

8704 *Kitchen, Kenneth A.* A preliminary look at Hurrian poetics. ^MCAGNI, L., 1. SMDSA 61: 2001 ⇒15. 555-561.

8705 ^E**Lebrun, R.** Syro anatolica scripta minora I. Muséon 114 (2001) 245-253.

8706 ^E**Neu, Erich; Otten, Heinrich; Rüster, Christel** Textfunde der neunziger Jahre. KBo 42: B 2001, Mann xviii pp. 28 Ill. 3-7861-2420-5 [Hittite].

8707 **Puhvel, Jaan** Hittite etymological dictionary, 5: words beginning with L; indices to volumes 1-5. Trends in linguistics, documentation 18: B 2001, De Gruyter x; 187 pp. €130.89. 3-11-016931-2.

8708 **Tischler, Johann; Neumann, Günter; Neu, Erich** Hethitisches etymologisches Glossar, Teil 2, Lfg. 11/12, P. Innsbrucker Beiträge zur Sprachwissenschaft 20: Innsbruck 2001, Inst. für Sprachwiss. d. Univ. Innsbruck 355-679 pp. 3-85124-682-9.

8709 **Tischler, Johann** Hethitisches Handwörterbuch. Innsbrucker Beiträge zur Sprachwissenschaft 102: Innsbruck ²2001 <1982>, Inst. für Sprachwiss. d. Univ. Innsbruck 208 pp. 3-85124-681-0.

J4.8 Armena, georgica

8710 **Olsen, Birgit Anette** The noun in Biblical Armenian: origin and word-formation with special emphasis on the Indo-European heritage 1999 ⇒15,8758. ^RSal. 63 (2001) 413-414 (*Bracchi, R.*).

8711 ^T**Mahé, Jean-Pierre** Le nouveau manuscrit Géorgien Sinaïtique N SIN 50: édition en fac-similé. CSCO 586; CSCO.Sub 108: Lv 2001, Peeters (6) 285 pp. 90-429-0981-1. Introd. *Z. Aleksidzé*; Bibl. 61-70.

J5.1 Graeca grammatica

8712 **Anderson, Dean R.** Glossary of Greek rhetorical terms connected to methods of argumentation, figures and tropes from ANAXIMENES to QUINTILIAN. 2000 ⇒16,8763. ^RTJT 17 (2001) 280-281 (*Kloppenborg Verbin, John S.*).

8713 **Bauer, Walter** A Greek-English lexicon of the New Testament and other early christian literature. ^E*Danker, Frederick William*: ³2000 ⇒

16,8764. ^RJBL 120 (2001) 780-784 (*Blomqvist, Jerker*); AThR 83 (2001) 883-884 (*Adam, A.K.M.*); RBBras 18 (2001) 445-446.

8714 *Baumert, Norbert* Konsekutives ὅτι im biblischen Griechisch?. BN 107/108 (2001) 5-11 = Studien zu den Paulusbriefen. SBAB 32: 2001 ⇒123. 183-191;

8715 Ἐις τό mit Infinitiv. Studien zu den Paulusbriefen. SBAB 32: 2001 <1998> ⇒123. 161-182.

8716 **Blass, Friedrich; Debrunner, Albert; Rehkopf, Friedrich** Grammatik des neutestamentlichen Griechisch: Joachim Jeremias zum 75. Geburtstag. GTL: Gö ¹⁸2001, Vandenhoeck & R. xxi; 511 pp. 3-525-52106-5.

8717 ^E**Boned Colera, Pilar; Rodríguez Somolinos, Juan** Repertorio bibliográfico de la lexicografía griega (RBLG). 1998 ⇒14,8012; 16, 8766. ^RJSJ 32 (2001) 296-298 (*Hilhorst, A.*).

8718 ^E**Christidis, Anastasios-Phoibos** Histoire de la langue grecque: des origines à l'antiquité tardive. Thessalonica 2001, Centre de la Langue Grecque 1213 pp. 960-231-094-4.

8719 **Colwell, Ernest Cadman** A beginner's reader grammar for New Testament Greek. Peabody, MASS 2001, Hendrickson 111 pp. $13. 1-56563-599-X. Collab. *Ernest W. Tune.*

8720 **DeMoss, Matthew S.** Pocket dictionary for the study of New Testament Greek. DG 2001, InterVarsity 138 pp. $8 [BiTod 40,133—Senior, D.].

8721 **Devine, A.M.; Stephens, Laurence D.** Discontinuous syntax: hyperbaton in Greek. Oxf 2000, OUP xi; 348 pp [IJCT 9,446s–Irigoin, J.].

8722 ^E**Easterling, Pat; Handley, Carol** Greek scripts: an illustrated introduction. L 2001, Society for the Promotion of Hellenic Studies vii; 72 pp. 0-902984-17-9.

8723 **Goodrich, Richard; Diewert, David** A summer Greek reader. GR 2001, Zondervan 112 pp. $15 [BiTod 39,387—Senior, Donald].

8724 **Haubeck, Wilfrid; Siebenthal, Heinrich von** Neuer sprachlicher Schlüssel zum griechischen Neuen Testament I: Matthäus-Apostelgeschichte; II: Römer-Offenbarung. 1997 ⇒13,8358; 16,8774. ^RSNTU.A 23 (1998) 229-230 (*Fuchs, Albert*).

8725 *Horsley, G.H.R.* Towards a lexicon of the New Testament with documentary parallels. XXII Congr. papirologia, 1. 2001 ⇒555. 655-667.

8726 ^E**Kramer, Johannes** Glossaria bilinguia altera: (C. Gloss. Biling. II). APF.B 8: Mü 2001, Saur ix; 128 pp. €78. 3598775423. Bibl. vii-viii.

　　　Kraus, T. Grammatisches Problembewusstsein... das Beispiel der griechischen Negation und 2Petr 2001 ⇒7054.

8727 **Kytzler, Bernhard; Redemund, Lutz; Eberl, Nikolaus** Unser tägliches Griechisch: Lexikon des griechischen Spracherbes. Kulturgeschichte der antiken Welt 88: Mainz 2001, Von Zabern xli; (2) 1209 pp. 3-8053-2816-8. Mitarbeit *Elke Steinmeyer*.

8728 **Murachco, Henrique** Língua grega: visão semântica, lógica, orgânica e funcional, 1: teoria, 2: prática. Petrópolis 2001, Discurso 735 + 675 pp [Estudos Bíblicos 69,94].

8729 [E]**Nesselrath, Heinz-Günther** Einleitung in die griechische Philologie. 1997 ⇒13,8368. [R]ClR 51 (2001) 83-7 (*Mastronarde, Donald*).

8730 New Testament Greek: a reader. C 2001, CUP xv; 212 pp. 0-521-65447-5. Joint Association of Classical Teachers' Greek Course.

8731 *Porter, Stanley E.; O'Donnell, Matthew Brook* The Greek verbal network viewed from a probabilistic standpoint: an exercise in Hallidayan linguistics. FgNT 14 (2001) 3-41.

8732 **Rodríguez Adrados, Francisco** Nueva Sintaxis del Griego Antiguo. Manuales: M 1992, Gredos 839 pp. [R]Gn. 73 (2001) 193-201 (*Calboli, Gualtiero*).

8733 **Romizi, Renato** Greco antico: vocabolario greco italiano etimologico e ragionato. [E]*Negri, Mario*: Bo 2001, Zanichelli 1488 pp. 88-08-08915-0.

8734 *Scafa, Enrico* La decifrazione della Lineare B Micenea. La decifrazione. Rivista Fondazione Europea Dragan 13: 2001 ⇒436. 42-71.

8735 **Schoch, Reto** Griechischer Lehrgang zum Neuen Testament. UTB 2140: 2000 ⇒16,8794. [R]NT 43 (2001) 393-395 (*Black, David Alan*).

8736 *Tiller, Patrick A.* Reflexive pronouns in the New Testament. FgNT 14 (2001) 43-63.

8737 **Van Voorst, Robert E.** Building your New Testament Greek vocabulary. [2]1999 ⇒15,8794. [R]BS 158 (2001) 243-244 (*Meeker, Kyle; Smith, Jay E.*);

8738 SBL, Resources for Biblical Study 43: Atlanta, GA [3]2001, SBL xii; 119 pp. $15. 1-58983-002-4.

8739 *VanderKam, James C.* Greek at Qumran. Hellenism in the land of Israel. CJAn 13: 2001 ⇒399. 175-181.

8740 **Walser, Georg** The Greek of the ancient synagogue: an investigation on the Greek of the Septuagint, Pseudepigrapha and the New Testament. Studia Graeca et Latina Lundensia 8: Lund 2001, Almqvist & Wiksell xxv; 197 pp. SK288. 91-22-01928-6. Bibl. xiii-xxiii.

8741 **Wenham, John W.; Pennington, Jonathan T.; Young, Norman H.** The elements of New Testament Greek: based on the earlier work by H.P.V. NUNN. C 2001, CUP 2 vols. 0-521-00257-5. 2 CD set.

8742 **Young, Norman H.** Syntax lists for students of New Testament Greek. C 2001, CUP iv; 132 pp. 0-521-00257-5.

J5.2 *Voces ordine alphabetico consonantium* **graecarum**

8743 ἀγαλλιάομαι: *Graczyk, Anna* Some remarks on ἀγαλλιάομαι, ἀγαλλίαμα, ἀγαλλίασις in the bible: a linguistic commentary to the most interesting passages. FolOr 37 (2001) 55-57.

8744 Αἴγυπτος: *Hasitschka, Martin* Ägypten im Neuen Testament: eine bibeltheologische Skizze. PzB 10 (2001) 75-83 [Judg 5; Mt 2,15; Acts 7,39; Heb 11, 26; Rev 11,8].

8745 αἰών: *Folliet, Georges* L'ambiguité du concept biblique αἰών (*saeculum* vel *aeternum*) dénoncée et interprétée par AUGUSTIN. WSt 114 (2001) 575-596 [RBen 112,158—Bogaert, P.-M.].

8746 ἀκούω: *Danove, Paul* A comparison of the usage of ἀκούω and ἀκούω-compounds in the Septuagint and New Testament. FgNT 14 (2001) 65-85.

8747 ἀμήν: *Stuiber, Alfred* Amen. RAC, Suppl. Bd. 1. 2001 ⇒661. 310-323.

8748 δόξα: **Raurell, Frederic** "Doxa" en la teologia i antropologia dels LXX. 1996 ⇒12,7932. ᴿRivBib 49 (2001) 227-233 (*Passoni dell'Acqua, Anna*).

8749 δόξα: *Vironda, Marco* La gloria di Dio sul volto di Cristo. La bellezza. PSV 44: 2001 ⇒240. 159-171.

8750 ἐγγαστρίμυθοι: *Torallas Tover, Sofía* Between necromancers and ventriloquists: the ἐγγαστρίμυθοι in the *Septuaginta*. Sef. 61 (2001) 419-438 Res., sum. 438.

8751 θεομάχος: *Passoni Dell'Acqua, Anna* La figura del θεομάχος nella letteratura giudaico-ellenistica: un ritratto per antitesi del monarca ellenistico ideale. ᴹCAGNI, L., 4. SMDSA 61: 2001 ⇒15. 1963-1981.

8752 ἱλάσκεσθαι: *Gosling, F.A.* Where is the God of justice?: an examination of C.H. DODD's understanding of ἱλάσκεσθαι and its derivatives. ZAW 113 (2001) 404-414.

8753 ἰουδαΐζω: *Déroche, Vincent* Iudaizantes. RAC 19: 2001 ⇒660. 130-142.

8754 καιρός: *Berciano, Modesto* Καιρός: superación del tiempo nel cristianismo. NatGrac 48 (2001) 167-200.

8755 κτίσις: *Meiattini, Giulio* Creatura umana o cosmo creato?: ancora su ktísis nel Nuovo Testamento. Rivista di scienze religiose 15 (2001) 19-64.

8756 λόγος: *Lawson, Jack N.* Mesopotamian precursors to the Stoic concept of Logos. Mythology and mythologies. 2001 ⇒589. 69-91.

8757 μαθητής *Kany, Roland* Jünger. RAC 19. 2001 ⇒660. 258-346.

8758 ὁδήγειν: *Mazurel, Jan* Welche Bedeutung hat das Verbum ὁδήγειν?: eine Untersuchung anlässlich Apostelgeschichte 8:31. [F]DEURLOO, K. ACEBT.S 2: 2001 ⇒23. 315-323.

8759 παρρησία: **Scarpat, Giuseppe** Parrhesia greca, parrhesia cristiana. StBi 130: Brescia 2001, Paideia 187 pp. €17.04. 88-394-0623-9. Rev. ed.; Bibl. 173-176.

8760 συνεργος: **Manjaly, Thomas** Collaborative ministry: an exegetical and theological study of synergos in Paul. Bangalore 2001, ATC xxii; 397 pp. 81-7086-265-5. Bibl. 360-397.

J5.4 *Papyri et inscriptiones graecae*—Greek epigraphy

8761 *Arfken, Ernst* Der Diskus von Phaistos und die Psalmen. ITE 10 (2001) 209-227.

8762 *As'ad, Khaled; Yon, Jean-Baptiste* Textes et fragments grecs de Palmyre. Syria 78 (2001) 153-162.

8763 *Atallah, Nabil* Des inscriptions du nord de la Jordanie. Epigraphica Anatolica 33 (2001) 199-207.

8764 **Bagnall, Roger S.; Frier, B.W.; Rutherford, I.C.** The census register P.Oxy. 984: the reverse of Pindar's Paeans. PapyBrux 29: 1997 ⇒15,8819. [R]BASPap 38 (2001) 147-151 (*Scheidel, Walter*).

8765 *Bar-Oz, Guy* An inscribed astragalus with a dedication to Hermes. NEA(BA) 64/4 (2001) 215-217.

8766 **Bernand, Étienne** Inscriptions grecques d'Alexandrie ptolémaïque. BEt 133: Cairo 2001, Inst. français d'archéologie orientale xi; 202 pp. €30. 2-7247-0298-0. 35 pl.

8767 [E]**Bodel, John** Epigraphic evidence: ancient history from inscriptions. Approaching the ancient world: NY 2001, Routledge xxvi; 246 pp. $75/25. 0-415-11624-4. 27 fig.

8768 *Bowman, Alan K.* Documentary papyrology and ancient history;

8769 *Carlini, Antonio* Il corpus dei papiri filosofici greci e latini. XXII Congresso di papirologia, 1. 2001 ⇒555. 137-145/187-195.

8770 **Clackson, S.J.** Coptic and Greek texts relating to the Hermopolite monastery of Apa Apollo. 2000 ⇒16,8814. [R]Muséon 114 (2001) 457-459 (*Schmidt, Th.*).

Cohen, N. The Abiʾor Cave—Greek... papyri 2001 ⇒8505.

8771 [E]**Coles, R.A.**, *al.*, The Oxyrhynchus papyri, 67. PEES.GR 87: L 2001, Egypt Expl. Society xiv; 294 pp.

8772 Corpus e papiri filosofici greci e latini: testi e lessico nei papiri di cultura greca e latina, I: autori noti, 1. (NICOLAUS Damascenus - ZENO Tarsensis) 1999. ⇒15,8826. [R]Analecta Papyrologica 13 (2001) 247-251 (*Fassino, Marco*).

8773 ^T**Costa, C.D.N.** Greek fictional letters: a selection with introduction, translation and commentary. Oxf 2001, OUP xxiii; 189 pp. 0-19-924001-9. Bibl. xxii-xxiii.

8774 **Cribiore, Raffaella** Gymnastics of the mind: Greek education in Hellenistic and Roman Egypt. Princeton 2001, Princeton Univ. Pr. xiii; 270 pp. €39.50. 0-691-00234-9.

8775 **Derderian, Katherine** Leaving words to remember: Greek mourning and the advent of literacy. Mn.S 209: Lei 2001, Brill vi; 206 pp [AfR 5,386f—Casey, Eric].

8776 *Devreker, John; Verreth, Herbert* New inscriptions from Pessinous and elsewhere (VI). Epigraphica Anatolica 33 (2001) 57-68.

8777 **Drew-Bear, Th.; Thomas Chr. M.; Yildizturan, M.** Phrygian votive steles. 1999 ⇒15,8831. ^REpigraphica Anatolica 33 (2001) 195-198 *(Ricl, Marijana).*

8778 *Faraone, Christopher A.* A collection of curses against Kilns (Homeric Epigram 13.7-23). ^FBETZ, H. 2001 ⇒5. 435-449.

8779 **Farioli, Marcella** Mundus alter: utopie e distopie nella commedia greca antica. Letteratura greca e latina: Mi 2001, Vita e P xii; 293 pp. 88-343-0720-8; Bibl. 241-277.

8780 *Fikhman, Itzhak F.* La description physique des Juifs égyptiens d'après les papyrus grecs. XXII Congresso di papirologia, 1. 2001 ⇒ 555. 461-468

8781 **Friggeri, Rosanna** La collezione epigrafica del Museo nazionale romano alle Terme di Diocleziano. Mi 2001, Electa 204 pp. 88-435-7875-8. Bibl. 199-204.

8782 **Ghinatti, F.** Profilo di epigrafia greca. 1998 ⇒15,8832. ^RAnCl 70 (2001) 414-415 *(Msarasco, Gabriele).*

8783 **Gigante, Marcello** Die deutsche Forschung über die herkulanensischen Papyri in den letzten drei Jahrzehnten. NAWG Phil.-hist. Kl. 2001,11: Gö 2001, Vandenhoeck & R. 16 pp.

8784 **Gonis, N.,** *al.,* The Oxyrhynchus papyri, 66 [nos 4494-4544]. PEES. GR 86: 1999 ⇒15,8834. ^RCÉg 76 (2001) 300-304 *(Lenaerts, Jean).*

8785 ^T**Guidorizzi, Giulio; Beta, Simone** La metafora: testi greci e latini tradotti e commentati 3. 2000 ⇒16,8821. ^RREG 114 (2001) 306-308 *(Chiron, P.);* Rhetorica 19 (2001) 419-420 *(Spina, Luigi).*

8786 *Haensch, Rudolf* Zum Verständnis von P.Jericho 16 gr. SCI 20 (2001) 155-167.

8787 ^E**Hallof, Klaus** Inscriptiones Graecae: volumen IX: pars I: fasc. IV. B 2001, De Gruyter 396 pp. 3-11-017411-1.

8788 *Ilan, Tal* An inscribed ossuary from a private collection. IEJ 51 (2001) 92-95.

8789 ^E**Jones, Alexander** Astronomical papyri from Oxyrhynchus (P. Oxy. 4133-4300a). 1999 ⇒15,8839. ^RIsis 35 (2001) 745-748 (*Rochberg, Francesca*).

8790 *Jones, Christopher P.* Imperial letters at Ephesos. Epigraphica Anatolica 33 (2001) 39-44.

8791 ^E**Kaltsas, D.** Dokumentarische Papyri des 2. Jh. v. Chr. aus dem Herakleopolites (P.Heid. VIII). Heid 2001, Winter xxx; 355 pp. €87. 3-8253-1100-7.

8792 *Kant, Laurence H.* Earliest christian inscription: Bishop Avercius's last words document emergence of the church. BiRe 17/1 (2001) 10-19, 47.

8793 *Kroll, John H.* The Greek inscriptions of the Sardis synagogue. HThR 94 (2001) 5-127.

8794 *Lightfoot, Jane L.* Μαμβογαῖος. Epigraphica Anatolica 33 (2001) 113-118.

8795 *Lührmann, Dieter* Petrus als Evangelist—ein bemerkenswertes Ostrakon. NT 43 (2001) 348-367.

8796 ^T**Maclean, Jennifer K. B.; Aitken, Ellen B.** Flavius PHILOSTRATUS: Heroicus. SBL.Writings from the Greco-Roman World 1: Atlanta 2001, SBL xcvii; 318 pp. 1-58983-008-3. Prologue *Gregory Nagy*, epilogue by *Helmut Koester*; Bibl. 245-255. Greek text with trans.

8797 *Merkelbach, Reinhold; Stauber, Josef* Epigramme aus Sinope und Amaseia. Epigraphica Anatolica 33 (2001) 69-78;

8798 Ein paegniarius. Epigraphica Anatolica 33 (2001) 79.

8799 ^E**Merkelbach, Reinhold** Steinepigramme aus dem griechischen Osten, 2: die Nordküste Kleinasiens (Marmarameer und Pontos). Mü 2001, Saur xii; 399 pp. 3-598-77447-8;

8800 3: der "Ferne Osten" und das Landesinnere bis zum Tauros. Mü 2001, Saur xii; 416 pp. 3-598-77448-6.

8801 *Naldini, Mario* Nuovi contributi nelle lettere cristiane su papiro dei primi quattro secoli;

8802 *Nevius, Richard C.* On using the nomina sacra as a criteria [!] for dating early christian papyri. XXII Congresso di papirologia, 2. 2001 ⇒555. 1017-1024/1045-1050.

8803 *Nielsen, Bruce; Worp, Klaas A.* New papyri from the New York University collection: II. ZPE 136 (2001) 125-144.

8804 *Niemeier, Wolf-Dietrich* Archaic Greeks in the Orient: textual and archaeological evidence. BASOR 322 (2001) 11-32.

8805 **Oates, John F.**, *al.*, Checklist of editions of Greek and Latin papyri, ostraca and tablets. BASPap.S 9: NHv ⁵2001, American Society of Papyrologists xiii; 121 pp. £21. 0-970059-4-0.

8806 The Oxyrhynchus papyri, 65. ^E**Haslam, M.W.**, *al.*: PEES.GR 85: 1998 ⇒14,8095; 16,8824. ^RGn. 73 (2001) 1-5 (*Luppe, Wolfgang*).

8807 ᴱᵀPatillon, Michel APSINÈS: art rhétorique: problèmes à faux-sem-
blant. Collection des Universités de France, Association Guillaume
Budé: P 2001, Les Belles Lettres cxii; 214 pp. 2-251-00492-0.

8808 Petsas, Ph.M., al., Inscriptions du sanctuaire de la mère des dieux
autochtone de Leukopétra (Macédoine). Meletemata 28: Athens
2000, 260 pp. 104 pl.

8809 Petzl, Georg Varia epigraphica. Epigraphica Anatolica 33 (2001) 51-
56.

8810 Pilhofer, Peter Philippi, Bd. II: Katalog der Inschriften von Philippi.
WUNT 119: 2000 ⇒16,8836. ᴿBiblInterp 9 (2001) 444-446 (Van
der Horst, Pieter W.);

8811 Philippi, Bd. I-II. WUNT 87, 119: 2000 ⇒16,8836. ᴿRBBras 18
(2001) 557-559.

8812 ᴱPoethke, Günter Griechische Papyrusurkunden spätrömischer und
byzantinischer Zeit aus Hermupolis Magna. ÄgU.G 17; APF.B 7: Mü
2001, Saur xxxix; 184 pp. 3-598-77541-5. 60 pl.

8813 ᴱᵀPreisendanz, Karl Papyri Graecae magicae: die griechischen Zau-
berpapyri. ᴱHenrichs, Albert: Sammlung Wissenschaftlicher Com-
mentare: Saur 2001 <= 1973>, Mü 2 vols 3-519-. Ergänzungen von
Karl Preisendanz.

8814 ᴱRupprecht, Hans-Albert Sammelbuch griechischer Urkunden aus
Ägypten, 19 (Index zu Band 18), 2/9: Wsb 2001, Harrassowitz iii;
196 pp. €34.77. Mitarbeit von Andrea Jördens;

8815 22 (Nr. 15205-15874). Wsb 2001, Harrassowitz xvi; 451 pp. €96.12.
3-4476-04436-5. Mitarbeit von Joachim Hengstl.

8816 Russo, Simona I gioielli nei papiri di età greco-romana. 1999 ⇒15,
8849. ᴿBASPap 38 (2001) 153-155 (Verhoogt, Arthur).

8817 Rutherford, Ian Canons of style in the Antonine age: idea—theory
and its literary context. 1998 ⇒14,8114; 16,8841. ᴿGn. 73 (2001)
498-501 (Hose, Martin).

8818 Schubert, Paul Vivre en Égypte gréco-romaine: une sélection de
papyrus. Le Chant du Monde: Vevey 2000, L'Aire 200 pp.;

8819 A Yale papyrus (P Yale III 137) in the Beinecke Rare Book and
Manuscript Library III. ASP 41: Oakville, Conn. 2001, American
Society of Papyrologists xii; 112 pp. 0-970-0591-16.

8820 ᴱStrubbe, J.H.M., al., Supplementum epigraphicum graecum: vols
46-47. Amst 2000, Gieben xxx; 868 pp. €145.21.

8821 Van der Horst, Pieter Willem Greek in Jewish Palestine in light of
Jewish epigraphy. Hellenism in the land of Israel. CJAn 13: 2001 ⇒
399. 154-174.

8822 Wachter, Rudolf Non-Attic Greek vase inscriptions. Oxf 2001,
OUP xx; 398 pp. £100. 0-19-814093-2. Ill.

8823 **Walde, Christine** Die Traumdarstellungen in der griechisch-römischen Dichtung. Mü 2001, Saur viii; 487 pp. Diss.-Hab. Basel 1998.

8824 *Wischmeyer, Wolfgang* Die Aberkios-Inschrift: Reflexionen über den Umgang mit Texten anhand einer Inschrift. Was ist ein Text?. Neutestamentliche Entwürfe zur Theologie 1: 2001 ⇒335. 65-79.

J6.0 Elamite

8825 *Rossi, Adriano Valerio* L'iscrizione originaria di Bisotun: DB Elam. A+L. ᴹCAGNI, L., 4: SMDSA 61: 2001 ⇒15. 2065-2107.

J6.5 Latina

8826 **Albrecht, Michael von** Roman epic: an interpretative introduction. Mn.S 189: 1999 ⇒15,8862. ᴿGn. 73 (2001) 720-722 (*Boyle, A.J.*).

8827 ᴱ**Annas, Julia** Cicero: On moral ends. ᵀ*Woolf, Raphael*: Texts in the History of Philosophy: C 2001, CUP xxxix; 158 pp. 0-521-66061-0. Bibl. xxxii-xxxiii.

8828 **Barton, Carlin A.** Roman honor: the fire in the bones. Berkeley, CA 2001, University of California xiii; 326 pp. 0-520-22525-2. Bibl. 297-316.

8829 **Courtney, Edward** A companion to PETRONIUS. Oxf 2001, OUP xii; 238 pp. 0-19-924552-5. Bibl. ix-xii.

8830 *Eck, Werner* Ein Spiegel der Macht: lateinische Inschriften römischer Zeit in Iudaea/Syria Palaestina. ZDPV 117 (2001) 47-63.

8831 **Ficca, Flaviana** Remedia doloris: la parola come terapia nelle "Consolazioni" di SENECA. Studi latini 43: N 2001, Loffredo 224 pp. 88-8096-878-5. Bibl. 197-209.

8832 *Gilula, Dwora* La satira degli ebrei nella letteratura latina. Gli ebrei nell'impero romano. 2001 <1986> ⇒415. 195-215.

8833 **Laird, Andrew** Powers of expression, expressions of power: speech presentation and Latin literature. 1999 ⇒15,8869. ᴿAnCl 70 (2001) 288-89 (*Rochette, Bruno*); AJP 122 (2001) 596-599 (*Oliensis, Ellen*).

8834 **Novak, Ralph Martin** Christianity and the Roman Empire: background texts. Harrisburg, Pennsylvania 2001, Trinity x; 340 pp. $28. 1-56338-347-0. Bibl. 310-327.

8835 *Olbricht, Thomas H.* Pathos as proof in Greco-Roman rhetoric. Paul and pathos. SBL Symposium 16: 2001 ⇒6316. 7-22.

8836 ᴱᵀ**Patillon, Michel; Brisson, Luc** LONGINUS; RUFUS Perinthius: Fragments, art rhétorique. CUFr Assoc. Guillaume Budé: P 2001, Belles Lettres (4) 390 pp. 2-251-00495-5.

8837 **Piso, Ioan** Inscriptions d'Apulum: (Inscriptions de la Dacie Romaine - III 5). Mémoires de l'Académie des inscriptions et Belles-Lettres, 24: P 2001, De Boccard 2 vols. 2-877754-121-5.

8838 **Ramelli, Ilaria** I romanzi antichi e il cristianesimo: contesto e contatti. Diss. Milano, ᴰ*Zanetto, G.*: Graeco-Romanae Religionis Electa Collectio 6: M 2001, Signifer L. 300 pp .

8839 **Smith, Lesley** Masters of the sacred page: manuscripts of theology in the Latin West to 1274. The Bible in the Latin West 1: ND 2001, Univ. of ND Pr. ix; 190 pp. $49. 0-268-04213-6. Bibl. 171-179 [TD 48,288—Heiser, W. Charles].

8840 *Starr, Raymond J.* The flexibility of literary meaning and the role of the reader in Roman antiquity. Latomus 60 (2001) 433-445.

J8 Language, writing and the Bible

8841 **Aichele, George** Sign, text, scripture: semiotics and the bible. 1997 ⇒13,8472; 15,8875. ᴿJBL 119 (2000) 747-749 (*Moore, Stephen D.*).

8842 *Asher, Nicholas; Hardt, Daniel; Busquets, Joan* Discourse parallelism, ellipsis, and ambiguity. Journal of Semantics 18 (2001) 1-25.

8843 *Azevedo, Joaquim* The origin of the proto-Canaanite alphabet. Hermenêutica 1 (2001) 3-29.

8844 **Bennett, Patrick R.** Comparative Semitic linguistics: a manual. 1998 ⇒14,8135... 16,8873. ᴿJSSt 46 (2001) 122-124 (*Lipiński, Edward*); WO 31 (2001) 180-189 (*Voigt, Rainer*).

8845 **Blake, Barry J.** Case Cambridge Textbooks in Linguistics. C ²2001, CUP xx; 227 pp. 0-521-01491-3. Bibl. 208-218.

8846 **Boyle, Leonard E.** Integral palaeography. Textes et Études du Moyen Age 16: Turnhout 2001, Brepols xviii; 174 pp. 2-503-51177-5. Introd. *F. Troncarelli.*

8847 **Casson, Lionel** Libraries in the ancient world. NHv 2001, Yale Univ. Pr. xii; 177 pp. 0-300-08809-4.

8848 **de Boer, Bart** The origins of vowel systems. Studies in the evolution of language 1: Oxf 2001, OUP xiii; 168 pp. 0-19-829965-6. Bibl. 145-153.

8849 **Edzard, Lutz** Polygenesis, convergence and entropy: an alternative model of linguistic evolution applied to Semitic linguistics. 1998 ⇒ 14,8142. ᴿJSSt 46 (2001) 124-128 (*Tropper, Josef*).

8850 *Gai, Amikam* Several points of Semitic and Akkadian grammar. Muséon 114 (2001) 1-13.

8851 *Gianto, Agustinus* Historical linguistics and the Hebrew Bible. ᴹCAGNI, L., 3: SMDSA 61: 2001 ⇒15. 1553-1571.

8852 **Gibson, Arthur** Biblical semantic logic: a preliminary analysis. BiSe 75: Shf 2001, Sheffield A. xxxvi; 244 pp. 1-84127-338-4. Bibl. xxv-xxxvi.

8853 **Givón, Talmy** Syntax: an introduction. Amst 2001, Benjamins 2 vols. 90-272-.

8854 *Greenfield, Jonas C.* Of scribes, scripts and languages. 'Al kanfei yonah, 2. 2001 <1991> ⇒153. 926-938.

8855 *Grottanelli, Cristiano* La scrittura nell'ambiente della bibbia: valori culturali e religiosi dello "scritto" nel contesto storico che ha generato l'Antico Testamento. RStB 13/1 (2001) 11-26.

8856 **Harris, Roy** SAUSSURE and his interpreters. E 2001, Univ. Pr. vii; 224 pp. 0-7486-1308-0. Bibl. 214-220.

8857 *Herr, L.G.* The influence of Syrian Iron Age scripts on the writing of Transjordan. Canadian research on ancient Syria. 2001 ⇒581. 163-8.

8858 **Kienast, Burkhart** Historische semitische Sprachwissenschaft. Wsb 2001, Harrassowitz xxxi; 641 pp. €99. 3-447-04359-8. Mit Beiträgen von *Erhart Graefe* (Altaegyptisch) und *Gene B. Gragg* (Kuschitisch). [R]UF 33 (2001) 721-731 (*Tropper, J.*).

8859 **Korenjak, M.** Publikum und Redner: ihre Interaktion in der sophistischen Rhetorik der Kaiserzeit. Zetemata 104: 2000 ⇒16,8893. [R]ClR 51 (2001) 34-36 (*Trapp, M.B.*).

8860 **Lipinski, Edouard** Semitic languages: outline of a comparative grammar. OLA 80: 1997 ⇒13,8492; 16,8898. [R]WO 31 (2001) 165-172 (*Voigt, Rainer*);

8861 [2]2001, Peeters 780 pp. 90-42908-15-7.

8862 **Millard, Alan R.** Reading and writing in the time of Jesus. BiSe 69: 2000 ⇒16,10851. [R]JThS 52 (2001) 222-224 (*Noy, David*); BiblInterp 9 (2001) 409-410 (*Chilton, Bruce*).

8863 *Naumann, Ralf* Aspects of changes: a dynamic event semantics. Journal of Semantics 18 (2001) 27-81.

8864 **Petrucci, Armando** Writing the dead: death and writing strategies in the western tradition. 1998 ⇒14,8160. [R]ClR 51 (2001) 136-137 (*Scourfield, J.H.D.*).

8865 **Sawyer, John F.A.** Sacred languages and sacred texts: religion in the first christian centuries. 1999 ⇒15,8912; 16,8907. [R]JThS 52 (2001) 124-129 (*Millard, Alan*); Studies in World Christianity 7 (2001) 260-266 (*Prior, H.A.F.*); RBLit 3 (2001) 126-128 (*Mathews, Edward G.*).

8866 [E]**Spencer, Andrew; Zwicky, Arnold M.** The handbook of morphology. Blackwell handbooks in linguistics: Oxf 2001, Blackwell xvi; 815 pp. 0-631-22694-X. Bibl. 737-790.

8867 **Stempel, Reinhard** Abriß einer historischen Grammatik der semitischen Sprachen. Nordostafrikanisch-westasiatische Studien 3: 1999 ⇒15,8916. [R]WO 31 (2001) 172-180 (*Voigt, Rainer*).

8868   **Tognini-Bonelli, Elena** Corpus linguistics at work. Studies in corpus
       linguistics 6: Amst 2001, Benjamins xi; 223 pp. 90-272-2276-2. Bibl.
       187-201.

8869   *Tropper, Josef* Die Herausbildung des bestimmten Artikels im Semi-
       tischen. JSSt 46 (2001) 1-31.

XV. Postbiblica

K1.1 Pseudepigrapha [=catholicis 'Apocrypha'] *VT generalis*

8870   *Alba Cecilia, Amparo* El *Libro de Zorobabel*. Sef. 61 (2001) 243-
       258. Res., sum. 258.

8871   **Aranda Pérez, Gonzalo; García Martínez, Florentino; Pérez Fer-
       nàndez, Miguel** Letteratura giudaica intertestamentaria. 1998 ⇒14,
       8180; 16,8919. ᴿAsp. 48 (2001) 573-575 (*Di Palma, Gaetano*).

8872   **Atkinson, Kenneth** An intertextual study of the Psalms of Solomon:
       Pseudepigrapha. Studies in the bible and early Christianity 49: Lew-
       iston, NY 2001, Mellen xxii; 471 pp. $110. 0-7734-7596-6.

8873   *Bar.Kochva, Bezalel On Abraham and the Egyptians*: a Hellenistic-
       Greek or a Hellenistic-Jewish composition?. Tarb. 70/3-4 (2001)
       327-352 Sum. v. **H**.

8874   *Berger, Klaus* Die Bedeutung der zwischentestamentlichen Literatur
       für die Bibelauslegung. ZNT 8 (2001) 14-17.

8875   **Charlesworth, James Hamilton** Critical reflections on the Odes of
       Solomon. JSPE.S 22: 1998 ⇒14,8190; 15,8928. ᴿSal. 63 (2001)
       381-382 (*Vicent, R.*).

8876   *Craven, Toni* Women as teachers of torah in the apocryphal/deutero-
       canonical books. Passion. 2001 ⇒295. 275-289.

8877   *Davies, Philip R.* Didactic stories. Justification, 1: second temple
       Judaism. WUNT 2/140: 2001 ⇒251. 99-133.

8878   *DiTommaso, Lorenzo* A report on pseudepigrapha research since
       CHARLESWORTH's Old Testament pseudepigrapha. JSPE 12 (2001)
       179-207.

8879   **Díez Macho, A.; Piñero Sáenz, A.** Apócrifos del Antiguo Testa-
       mento, 3. M 2000 <1982>, Cristiandad 612 pp.

8880   ᴱ**Ejmnaes, Bodil; Otzen., Benedikt** De gammeltestamentlige Pseu-
       depigrafer. K ²2001, Danske Bibelselskab xv; 958 pp. DKR800. 87-
       7523-440-8.

8881   *Enns, Peter* Expansions of scripture.;

8882 *Evans, Craig A.* Scripture-based stories in the pseudepigrapha. Justification, 1. WUNT 2/140: 2001 ⇒251. 73-98/57-72.

8883 **Harrington, Daniel J.** Invitation to the Apocrypha 1999 ⇒15,8936; 16,8928. ᴿHorizons 27 (2001) 392-393 (*Burton, William L.*).

8884 ᴱ**Kümmel, Werner Georg; Lichtenberger, Hermann** Unterweisung in lehrhafter Form, Lfg. 1(1974) - 7(2001). Jüdische Schriften aus hellenistisch-römischer Zeit 3: Gü 1974-2001, Mohn 880 pp. 3-579-03928-8.

8885 **Lattke, Michael** Oden Salomos: Text, Übersetzung, Kommentar, 1: Oden 1 und 3-14. NTOA 41: 1999 ⇒15,8939. ᴿJThS 52 (2001) 319-321 (*Gelston, A.*);

8886 Oden Salomos. NTOA 41/1-2: Gö 1999-2001, Vandenhoeck & R. 2 vols. €59.20 + 64. 3-525-53941-X/8-7. V.1: Oden 1 und 3-14; v.2: Oden 15-28; Bibl. v.2 299-329.

8887 *Noffke, Eric* Apocrifi dell'Antico Testamento. Protest. 56 (2001) 39-41.

8888 *Norelli, Enrico* "Apocryphes de l'Ancien Testament"?: le troisième volume d'apocryphes de l'Ancien Testament de Paolo Sacchi. Apocrypha 12 (2001) 263-271.

8889 **Porter, J.R.** The lost bible: forgotten scriptures revealed. L 2001, Baird 256 pp. £25. 0-226-67579-3. 180 pl.

8890 ᴱ**Sacchi, Paolo** Apocrifi dell'Antico Testamento 3. 1999 ⇒15,8952. ᴿProtest. 56 (2001) 39-41 (*Noffke, Eric*); Sal. 63 (2001) 768-769 (*Vicent, R.*); Apocrypha 12 (2001) 301-302 (*Norelli, E.*).

8891 *Schmelz, Georg* Zwei neue Fragmente des Apokryphons über die Zauberer Jannes und Jambres. XXII Congresso di papirologia, 2. 2001 ⇒555. 1199-1212.

8892 *Urbán, Angel* Algunas peculiaridades bíblico-literarias en el anónimo De ortu et obitu patriarcharum. EstB 59 (2001) 501-536.

8893 ᵀ**Van der Horst, Pieter W.** De profeten: joodse en christelijke legenden uit de oudheid. Amst 2001, Athenaeum-Polak 188 pp. €17. 75. 90-253-4179-9. Inleiding. [Bijdr. 63,494].

8894 *Waschke, Ernst Joachim* 'Richte ihnen auf ihren König, den Sohn Davids'—Psalmen Salomos 17 und die Frage nach den messianischen Traditionen. Der Gesalbte. 2001 <1994> ⇒227. 127-140.

8895 **Wojciechowski, Michal** Apokryfy z Biblii greckiej: 3 i 4 Ksiega Machabejska, 3 Ksiega Ezdrasza, oraz Psalm 151 i Modlitwa Manassesa. Rozprawy i Studia Biblijne 8: Wsz 2001, Oficyna Wydawnicza "Vocatio" 328 pp. 83-7146-163-1. **P.**

K1.2 **Henoch**

8896 *Bhayro, Siam* A Karshuni (Christian Arabic) account of the descent of the watchers. ᴹWEITZMAN, M.: JSOT.S 333: 2001 ⇒113. 365-74.

8897 *Greenfield, Jonas C.; Stone, Michael E.* The Enochic pentateuch and the date of the Similitudes <1977>;

8898 The books of Enoch and the traditions of Enoch <1981>. 'Al kanfei yonah, 2. 2001 ⇒153. 595-609/618-632.

8899 *Knibb, Michael A.* Christian adoption and transmission of Jewish pseudepigrapha: the case of 1 Enoch. JSJ 32 (2001) 396-415;

8900 The translation of 1 Enoch 70.1: some methodological issues. ᴹWEITZMAN, M. JSOT.S 333: 2001 ⇒113. 340-354.

8901 **Nickelsburg, George W.E.** 1 Enoch 1: a commentary on the book of 1 Enoch, chapters 1-36; 81-108. Hermeneia: Mp 2001, Fortress xxxviii; 618 pp. $58. 0-8006-6074-9. Bibl. 561-571.

8902 *Orlov, Andrei A.* Overshadowed by Enoch's greatness: "two tablets" traditions from the book of Giants to Palaea Historica. JSJ 32 (2001) 137-158.

8903 ᴱ**Pincherle, Mario** Enoch: il primo libro del mondo, 1. Diegaro (Forlì Cesena) 2000, Macro 182 pp. €12.40. 88-7507-284-1.

8904 *Reed, Annette Yoshiko* From Asael and Šemiḥazah to Uzzah, Azzah, and Azael: 3 Enoch 5 (§7-8) and Jewish reception-history of 1 Enoch. JSQ 8 (2001) 105-136.

8905 *Tite, Philip L.* Textual and redactional aspects of the Book of Dreams (1 Enoch 83-90). BTB 31 (2001) 106-120.

8906 *VanderKam, James C.* The interpretation of Genesis in *1 Enoch*. The bible at Qumran. 2001 ⇒267. 129-148.

K1.3 **Testamenta**

8907 Allison, Dale C. Job in the Testament of Abraham. JSPE 12 (2001) 131-147.

8908 *Kugler, Robert* Testaments. Justification, 1: second temple Judaism. WUNT 2/140: 2001 ⇒251. 189-213.

8909 **Kugler, Robert A.** The Testaments of the Twelve Patriarchs. Guides to the Apocrypha and Pseudepigrapha 10: Shf 2001, Sheffield A. 122 pp. £9/$15. 1-84127-193-4. Bibl. 101-111.

8910 **La Torre Castillo, Jordi** El Testament de Levi: estudi de la teología sacerdotal. Extr. Diss. Barcelona 2000, ᴰ*Cortès, E.*: Barc 2001, Fac. de Teol. de Catalunya 93 pp [RTL 33,632].

8911 **Munoa, Phillip B. III** Four powers in heaven: the interpretation of Daniel 7 in the Testament of Abraham. JSPE.S 28: 1998 ⇒14,8223; 16,8975. [R]JSSt 46 (2001) 172-173 (*Casey, Maurice*).

8912 [ET]**Roddy, Nicolae** The Romanian version of the Testament of Abraham: text, translation, and cultural context. Early Judaism and Its Literature 19: Atlanta, GA 2001, SBL x; 140 pp. $40. 0-58983-012-1. Bibl. 128-134.

8913 *Schaller, Berndt* Zur Komposition und Konzeption des Testaments Hiobs. Fundamenta Judaica. StUNT 25: 2001 <1989> ⇒206. 28-66.

K1.6 Adam, Asenet, Jubilaea

8914 [E]**Anderson, Gary A.; Stone, Michael Edward; Tromp, Johannes** Literature on Adam and Eve. SVTP 15: 2000 ⇒16,346. [R]JThS 52 (2001) 195-196 (*Jeffers, Ann*); Henoch 23 (2001) 395-396 (*Ubigli, Liliana Rosso*); OrChr 85 (2001) 241-242 (*Van Esbroeck, Michel*).

8915 **Anderson, Gary A.** The Genesis of perfection: Adam and Eve in Jewish and christian imagination. LVL 2001, Westminster 257 pp. $25. 0-664-22403-2. Bibl. 239-249 [BiTod 40,56—Bergant, D.].

8916 **Stone, Michael Edward** A concordance of the Armenian Apocryphal Adam books. Hebrew University Armenian Studies 1: Lv 2001, Peeters xv; 292 pp. 90-429-0941-2.

8917 *Artés Hernández, José Antonio* José y Asenet y el estilo καί. EstB 59 (2001) 281-306.

8918 *Burfeind, Carsten* Der Text von Joseph und Aseneth im Palimpsest Rehdiger 26 der Universitätsbibliothek Wroclaw (Breslau). JSJ 32 (2001) 42-53.

8919 **Hirt, Susan Christine** Erotic vision in the conversions of Aseneth and Thecla. Diss. Stanford 2001, 239 pp. 3000041.

8920 *Inowlowcki, Sabrina* Le *Roman d'Aséneth*: un roman féministe?. [F]DESROCHES NOBLECOURT, C. 2001 ⇒22. 111-118.

8921 **Kraemer, Ross Shepard** When Aseneth met Joseph: a late antique tale of the biblical patriarch and his Egyptian wife, reconsidered. 1998 ⇒14,8237... 16,9019. [R]JBL 119 (2000) 760-762 (*Chesnutt, Randall D.*).

Standhartinger, A. Weisheit in Joseph u. Aseneth 2001 ⇒6406.

8922 *Berger, Klaus* Jubiläenbuch. RAC 19. 2001 ⇒660. 31-38.

8923 **Halpern-Amaru, Betsy** The empowerment of women in the book of Jubilees. JSJ.S 60: 1999 ⇒15,8983. [R]JJS 52 (2001) 161-164 (*Ilan, Tal*); JSJ 32 (2001) 305-307 (*Lange, Armin*).

8924 **VanderKam, James C.** The book of Jubilees. Guides to the Apocry-
      pha and Pseudepigrapha: Shf 2001, Sheffield A. 167 pp. $15. 1-
      85075-767-4. Bibl. 150-154.

8925 *Wacholder, Ben Zion* Calendar wars between the 364 and the 365-
      day year. RdQ 20 (2001) 207-222.

8926 *Werman, Cana* The book of Jubilees in Hellenistic context. Zion 66
      (2001) 275-296 Sum. xxi. **H.**

K1.7 Apocalypses, ascensiones

8927 *Bauckham, Richard* Apocalypses. Justification, 1: second temple
      Judaism. WUNT 2/140: 2001 ⇒251. 135-187.

8928 **Henze, Matthias** The Syriac Apocalypse of Daniel: introduction,
      text, and commentary. STAC 11: Tü 2001, Mohr v; (2) 158 pp. €34.
      3-16-147594-1. Bibl. 119-129.

8929 *Lienkamp, Christoph* Aufhalten der Krisis oder Aufschub des Ge-
      richts: zwei Denkfiguren apokalyptischer Zeiterfahrung. ZRGG 53
      (2001) 319-329.

8930 *Schreiber, Stefan* Hoffnung und Handelsperspektive in der Assump-
      tio Mosis. JSJ 32 (2001) 252-271.

8931 [E]**Silverstein, Theodore; Hilhorst, Anthony** Apocalypse of Paul: a
      new critical edition of three long Latin versions. 1997 ⇒13,8582...
      16,9031. [R]Spec. 76 (2001) 229-230 (*Carey, John*).

8932 *Trumbower, Jeffrey A. Apocalypse of Peter* 14,1-4 in relation to con-
      fessors' intercessions for the non-christian dead. StPatr 36. 2001 ⇒
      553. 307-312.

K2.1 Philo judaeus alexandrinus

8933 **Alexandre, Manuel** Rhetorical argumentation in Philo of Alexandri-
      a. BJSt 322: 1999 ⇒15,9033; 16,9033. [R]JBL 120 (2001) 763-765
      (*Olbricht, Thomas H.*).

8934 *Birnbaum, Ellen* Philo on the Greeks: a Jewish perspective on culture
      and society in first-century Alexandria. [F]HAY, D. 2001 ⇒45. 37-58.

8935 *Borgen, Peder* Application and commitment to the laws of Moses:
      observations on Philo's treatise *On the embassy to Gaius.* [F]HAY, D.
      2001 ⇒45. 86-101.

8936 [E]**Borgen, Peder; Fuglseth, Kåre; Skarsten, Roald** The Philo index.
      2000 ⇒16,9036. [R]VigChr 55 (2001) 215-216 (*Geljon, A.C.*); JSJ 32
      (2001) 298-9 (*Hilhorst, A.*); JThS 52 (2001) 864-7 (*North, J. Lionel*).

8937 *Calabi, Francesca* I sacrifici e la loro funzione conoscitiva in Filone di Alessandria. ASEs 18 (2001) 101-127.

8938 *Collins, John J.* Spells pleasing to God: the Binding of Isaac in Philo the epic poet. [F]BETZ, H. 2001 ⇒5. 3-13.

8939 *Feldman, Louis H.* Philo's interpretation of Joshua. JSPE 12 (2001) 165-178.

8940 *Fernández E., Samuel* Filón de Alejandría: entre Moisés y Platón. Revista católica 101 (2001) 39-41.

8941 **Fisk, Bruce Norman** Do you not remember?: scripture, story and exegesis in the rewritten bible of Pseudo-Philo. JSPE.S 37: Shf 2001, Sheffield A. 375 pp. £50/$80. 1-84127-207-8. Bibl. 332-349.

8942 **Frick, Peter** Divine Providence in Philo of Alexandria. TSAJ 77: 1999 ⇒15,9042; 16,9046. [R]JSJ 32 (2001) 299-302 (*Runia, David*); Sal. 63 (2001) 583-584 (*Vicent, R.*); RBLit 3 (2001) 284-288 (*Casiday, Augustine*).

8943 *Gemünden, Petra von* La figure de Jacob à l'époque hellénistico-romaine: l'exemple de Philon d'Alexandrie. [F]PURY, A. de: MoBi 44: 2001 ⇒89. 358-370.

8944 *Hay, David M.* Philo of Alexandria. Justification, 1: second temple Judaism. WUNT 2/140: 2001 ⇒251. 357-379.

8945 **Leonhardt, Jutta** Jewish worship in Philo of Alexandria. TSAJ 84: Tü 2001, Mohr S. xiv; 347 pp. €79. 3-16-147597-6. Bibl. 297-320.

8946 [E]**Lévy, Carlos** Philon d'Alexandrie et le langage de la philosophie. 1998 ⇒14,433; 16,9051. [R]RHPhR 81 (2001) 107-109 (*Hummel, P.*).

8947 *Matusova, Ye.D.* Philo of Alexandria and Greek doxography. Journal of Ancient History 1 (2001) 40-52 Sum. 52. **R**.

8948 **McNutt, Walter Buswell** Philo of Alexandria: an exegete of scripture. Diss. Missouri, Kansas City 2001, 358 pp. 3010619.

8949 **Niehoff, Maren R.** Philo on Jewish identity and culture. TSAJ 86: Tü 2001, Mohr xvii; 319 pp. €91. 3-16-147611-5. Bibl. 267-294.

8950 **Noack, Christian** Gottesbewußtsein: exegetische Studien zur Soteriologie und Mystik bei Philo von Alexandria. WUNT 2/116: 2000 ⇒ 16,9054. [R]ThRv 97 (2001) 322-324 (*Früchtel, Edgar*); JSJ 32 (2001) 333-335 (*Geljon, Albert-Kees*); CBQ 63 (2001) 760-761 (*Adler, William*); ThLZ 126 (2001) 407-409 (*Sellin, Gerhard*).

8951 *Phillips, Thomas E.* Revisting Philo: discussions of wealth and poverty in Philo's ethical dicourse. JSNT 83 (2001) 111-121.

8952 *Regev, Eyal* The two sins of Nob: biblical interpretation, an anti-priestly polemic and a geographical error in the Liber antiquitatum biblicarum. JSPE 12 (2001) 85-104 [Judg 19,14-15; 1 Sam 22,6-23].

8953 *Royse, James R.* Philo's division of his works into books. [F]HAY, D. 2001 ⇒45. 59-85.

8954 **Runia, David T.** Filone di Alessandria nella prima letteratura cristiana. [T]*Radice, Roberto*: Platonismo, studi e testi 14: 1999 ⇒15,9056.
[R]Vivens Homo 12 (2001) 441-443 (*Pellegrini, Angelo*).

8955 *Runia, David T.* Philo's reading of the psalms. [F]HAY, D. 2001 ⇒45.
102-121.

8956 *Runia, David T., al.,* Philo of Alexandria: an annotated bibliography
1998. [F]HAY, D. 2001 ⇒45. 250-290.

8957 *Runia, David T.* Philon d'Alexandrie devant le pentateuque. Le pentateuque d'Alexandrie. 2001 ⇒1616. 99-105.

8958 [T]**Runia, David T.** Philo of Alexandria: on the creation of the cosmos
according to Moses. Philo of Alexandria Commentary Series 1: Lei
2001, Brill xviii; 443 pp. $120. 90-04-12169-2. Introd., commentary;
Bibl. 404-423.

8959 *Sandelin, Karl-Gustav* Philo's ambivalence towards statues. [F]HAY, D.
2001 ⇒45. 122-138.

8960 *Schaller, Berndt* Philo von Alexandreia und das 'Heilige Land.' Fundamenta Judaica. StUNT 25: 2001 <1983> ⇒206. 13-27.

8961 [T]**Siegert, Folker; Roulet, Jacques de** Pseudo-Philon: prédications
synagogales. SC 435: 1999 ⇒15,9060. [R]JJS 52 (2001) 160-161
(*Lieu, Judith*); ScEs 53 (2001) 406-407 (*Valevičius, Andrius*).

8962 *Taylor, Joan E.* Virgin mothers: Philo on the women therapeutae.
JSPE 12 (2001) 37-63.

8963 *Termini, Cristina* La creazione come ἀρχή della legge in Filone di
Alessandria (Opif. 1-3). RivBib 49 (2001) 283-318.

8964 *Tulbure, Sabina* Biblical rewriting Pseudo-Philo: *Liber Antiquitatum
Biblicarum* LIX-LX (MT: 1 Sam 16,1-23). CICat 2/2 (2001) 105-
112. Sum 112. **Romanian.**

8965 **Weber, Reinhard** Das 'Gesetz' bei Philon von Alexandrien und
Flavius Josephus: Studien zum Verständnis und zur Funktion der
Thora bei den beiden Hauptzeugen des hellenistischen Judentums.
ARGU 11: Fra 2001, Europ. Verl. der Wissenschaften 437 pp.
€60.30. 3-631-37270-1.

8966 *Winston, David* Philo of Alexandria and Ibn al-ʿArabī. [F]HAY, D. 2001
⇒45. 139-155;

8967 Philo's theory of eternal creation: *Prov.* 1.6-9. Ancestral philosophy.
2001 <1980> ⇒228. 117-127:

8968 Theodicy and creation <1986> 128-134;

8969 Freedom and determinism in Philo of Alexandria <1976> 135-150;

8970 Was Philo a mystic? <1978> 151-170;

8971 Sage and super-sage in Philo of Alexandria <1995> 171-180;

8972 Judaism and Hellenism: hidden tensions in Philo's thought <1990>
181-198;

8973 Philo and the rabbis on sex and the body <1998> 199-219.
Winter, B. Philo and Paul among the sophists 1997 ⇒6489.

K2.4 *Evangelia apocrypha*—**Apocryphal gospels**

8974 *Backus, Irena* PRAETORIUS' anthology of New Testament apocrypha (1595). Apocrypha 12 (2001) 211-236.

8975 **Baum, Armin Daniel** Pseudepigraphie und literarische Fälschung im frühen Christentum: mit ausgewählten Quellentexten samt deutscher Übersetzung. WUNT 2/138: Tü 2001, Mohr S. xvi; 313 pp. €49. 3-16-147591-7. Bibl. 263-292.

8976 *Blackhirst, Rob* The exile of Jesus to Damascus in the medieval gospel of Barnabas. JHiC 8/1 (2001) 1-17.

8977 *Browne, Gerald M.* An Old Nubian apocryphal text from Qaṣr Ibrīm. Journal of Coptic Studies 3 (2001) 129-132.

8978 *Calzolari, Valentina* La bible et les textes apocryphes dans l'Arménie ancienne. Connaissance des Pères de l'Église 81 (2001) 38-51.

8979 *Charron, Régine; Painchaud, Louis* 'God is a dyer': the background and significance of a puzzling motif in the *Coptic Gospel according to Philip* (CG II,3). Muséon 114 (2001) 41-50.

8980 **Da Spinetoli, Ortensio,** *al.,* Gli apocrifi cristiani. 1999 ⇒16,9079. ᴿApocrypha 12 (2001) 297-298 (*Roessli, J.-M.*).

8981 *DeConick, April D.* The true mysteries: sacramentalism in the gospel of Philip. VigChr 55 (2001) 225-261.

8982 *Droge, A.J.* Discerning the body: early christian sex and other apocryphal acts. ᶠBETZ, H. 2001 ⇒5. 297-320.

8983 *Kraus, Thomas J.* P.Vindob.G 2325: das sogenannte Fayûm-Evangelium-Neuedition und kritische Rückschlüsse. ZAC 5 (2001) 197-212.

8984 *Létourneau, Pierre* Les apparitions du Sauveur dans la littérature apocryphe chrétienne. Résurrection: l'après-mort. MoBi 45: 2001 ⇒ 296. 255-275.

8985 Il libro dell'infanzia di Cristo: vangelo apocrifo armeno. Genova 2001, Marietti 145 pp. 88-211-8941-4. Pref. *Bruno Maggioni*; 8 tavole di *Albrecht Dürer*.

8986 ᴱᵀ**Lührmann, Dieter H.; Schlarb, Egbert** Fragmente apokryph gewordener Evangelien in griechischer und lateinischer Sprache. MThSt 59: 2000 ⇒16,9088. ᴿThLZ 126 (2001) 906-907 (*Hofius, Otfried*).

8987 **Martín, S.** Il vangelo segreto di Maria. Dimensioni dello Spirito: CinB 2001, San Paolo 248 pp. €16.53.

8988 ᴱMcNamara, Martin J., al., Apocrypha Hiberniae, 1: evangelia infantiae. CChr.SA 13-14: Turnhout 2001, Brepols xvi; 487 + 1,203 pp. €290./240. 2-503-41131-2. Irish Biblical Assoc.; bibl. ix-xvi.

8989 Morard, Françoise L'Évangile de Marie: un message ascétique?. Apocrypha 12 (2001) 155-171.

8990 Nicklas, Tobias Die 'Juden' im Petrusevangelium (PCair 10759): ein Testfall. NTS 47 (2001) 206-221.

8991 Nicklas, Tobias Erzähler und Charakter zugleich: zur literarischen Funktion des "Petrus" in dem nach ihm benannten Evangelienfragment. VigChr 55 (2001) 318-326.

8992 Peretto, Elio Giustizia e giustificazione nella letteratura apocrifa neotestamentaria, in IRENEO di Lione e in alcuni apologisti. Giustizia-giustificazione nei Padri della Chiesa. DSBP 29: 2001 ⇒308. 27-109.

8993 Porter, Stanley E. POxy II 210 as an apocryphal gospel and the development of Egyptian christianity. XXII Congresso di papirologia, 2. 2001 ⇒555. 1095-1108.

8994 Puig i Tàrrech, Armand La sagrada familia en los evangelios apócrifos. La Sagrada Familia en la biblia. 2001 ⇒4792. 149-166.

8995 Pulcini, Theodore In the shadow of Mount Carmel: the collapse of the `Latin East' and the origins of the gospel of Barnabas. ICMR 12 (2001) 191-209.

8996 Santos Otero, A. de Los evangelios apócrifos. Estudios y ensayos BAC 22, Ser. Teol.: M 2001, BAC xxx; 412 pp. 84-7914-504-8.

8997 ᴱStarowieyski, Marek Apokryfy Nowego Testamentu: Listy i Apokalipsy chrzescijanskie. Kraków 2001, WAM 411 pp. 83-7097-789-8. P.

K2.7 Alia apocrypha NT—Apocryphal acts of apostles

8998 Amerise, Marilena La scrittura e l'immagine nella cultura tardoantica: il caso di Abgar Edessa. OCP 67 (2001) 437-445.

8999 Amsler, Frédéric Acta Philippi: commentarius. CChr.SA 12: 1999 ⇒15,9112. ᴿApocrypha 12 (2001) 308-310 (Reynard, J.).

9000 ᵀᴱAranda Pérez, Gonzalo; García Lázar, C. Hechos de Andrés y Mateo en la ciudad de los antropófagos: martirio del apóstol San Mateo. Apócrifos cristianos 4: M 2001, Ciudad Nueva 279 pp. €17.50. 84-9715-007-4. Pres. e introd 1a parte G. Aranda Pérez, 2a parte C. García Lázaro. ᴿSalm. 48 (2001) 572-574 (Trevijano, Ramón).

9001 Boismard, Marie-Émile La lettre de Saint Paul aux Laodicéens. CRB 42: 1999 ⇒15,9115; 16,9118. ᴿRSR 89 (2001) 120-121 (Aletti, Jean-Noël).

9002 *Bombeck, Stefan* Pseudo-Kyrillos 'In Mariam virginem': Text und Übersetzung von Pierpont Morgan M 597 fols. 46-74. Or. 70 (2001) 40-88.

9003 ^E**Bovon, François; Graham Brock, Ann; Matthews, Christopher R.** The apocryphal acts of the Apostles. 1999 ⇒15,200; 16,9097. ^RThLZ 126 (2001) 1012-1016 (*Schröter, Jens*).

9004 ^E**Bremmer, Jan M.** The apocryphal Acts of Paul and Thecla. 1996 ⇒12,8136; 14,8339. ^RSNTU.A 25 (2000) 285-287 (*Raml, R.*);

9005 The apocryphal Acts of Andrew. 2000 ⇒16,9101. ^RApocrypha 12 (2001) 303-305 (*Prieur, J.-M.*).

9006 *Büllesbach, Claudia* Das Verhältnis der Acta Pauli zur Apostelgeschichte des Lukas: Darstellung und Kritik der Forschungsgeschichte. Das Ende des Paulus. BZNW 106: 2001 ⇒281. 215-237.

9007 *Cairus, Aecio E.* Sabbath and covenant in the epistle of Barnabas. AUSS 39 (2001) 117-123.

9008 **Chalmet, Philippe** Signes, miracles et prodiges: les Actes apocryphes des apôtres: des récits chrétiens de miracles dans le monde gréco-romain des trois premiers siècles. Diss. Strasbourg; ^D*Faivre, A.* 2001, 400 pp [RTL 33,642].

9009 *Congourdeau, Marie-Hélène* Jérusalem et Constantinople dans la littérature apocalyptique. Le sacré et son inscription dans l'espace à Byzance et en Occident: études comparées. ^E**Kaplan, Michel**: P 2001, Sorbonne. 125-136 [BuBB 36,98].

9010 **Cooper, Kate** The virgin and the bride: idealized womanhood in late antiquity. London ²1999 <1996>, Harvard University Press xii; 180 pp. 0-674-93950-6. Bibl.

9011 *D'Anna, Alberto* Sacrificio e scrittura nell'epistola di Barnaba. ASEs 18 (2001) 181-195.

9012 *Faerber, Robert* La lettre du Christ tombée du ciel en anglais ancien: les sermons Napier 43-44. Apocrypha 12 (2001) 173-209.

9013 *Gray, Patrick* Abortion, infanticide, and the social rhetoric of the Apocalypse of Peter. JECS 9 (2001) 313-337.

9014 **Hovhanessian, Vahan** Third Corinthians: reclaiming Paul for christian orthodoxy. 2000 ⇒16,9126. ^RJThS 52 (2001) 854-856 (*Elliott, J.K.*).

9015 **Hvalvik, Reidar** The struggle for scripture and covenant: the purpose of the epistle of Barnabas and Jewish-Christian competition in the second century. WUNT 2/82: 1996 ⇒12,10844... 14,8344. ^RSNTU.A 23 (1998) 244-246 (*Fuchs, Albert*).

9016 *Jacobson, Howard* Antonius and Judah the prince. OCP 67 (2001) 179 [Acts of John].

9017 *Jones, F. Stanley* Eros and astrology in the Περιοδοι Πετρου: the sense of the Pseudo-Clementine novel. Apocrypha 12 (2001) 53-78.

9018 ^T**Jullien, Christelle; Jullien, Florence** Les Actes de Mar Mari: l'apôtre de la Mésopotamie. Apocryphes, (L'Aelac) 11: Turnhout 2001, Brepols 175 pp. 2-503-51296-8. Bibl. 151-152.

9019 *Junod, Éric* De l'introduction de l'historiographie dans la littérature apocryphe ancienne: les *Actes de Jean à Rome*. L'historiographie. 2001 ⇒541. 97-104 [BuBB 36,16].

9020 *Kaestli, Jean-Daniel* Le Protoévangile de Jacques latin dans l'homélie Inquirendum Est pour la fête de la nativité de Marie. Apocrypha 12 (2001) 99-153.

9021 **Klijn, A.F.J.** Apokriefe handelingen van de Apostelen: buitenbijbelse verhalen uit de vroege kerk. Ten Have 2001, Baarn 149 pp. €14.24. 90-259-5235-6;

9022 Apokriefe oepenbaringen, orakels en brieven: buitenbijbelse aanvullingen op het Nieuwe Testament. Ten Have 2001, Baarn 126 pp. €12. 95. 90-259-5241-0.

9023 *Lambert, David* The pseudonymity of SALVIAN's *Timotheus ad ecclesiam*. StPatr 38. 2001 ⇒553. 423-428.

9024 *Misset-van de Weg, Magda* Magic, miracle and miracle workers in the *Acts of Thecla*. Women and miracle stories. 2001 ⇒8195. 29-52.

9025 **Molinari, Andrea Lorenzo** I never knew the man: the Coptic Act of Peter (Papyrus Berolinensis 8502.4): its independence from the Apocryphal Acts of Peter: genre and legendary origins. Bibliothèque copte de Nag Hammadi, Etudes 5: Québec 2000, Presses de l'Univ. Laval xxxv; 182 pp. 2-7637-7760-0.

9026 *Norelli, Enrico* La lettre aux Laodicéens: essai d'interprétation. ArBob 23 (2001) 45-70 [REAug 48,347—Chapot, Frédéric].

9027 *Paschoud, François* Refléxions sur le problème de la fiction en historiographie. L'historiographie de l'église. 2001 ⇒541. 23-35 [BuBB 36,98].

9028 *Schneider, Horst* Thekla und die Robben. VigChr 55 (2001) 45-57.

9029 *Wehn, Beate* "Selig die Körper der Jungfräulichen"—Überlegungen zum Paulusbild der Thekla-Akten. Paulus. 2001 ⇒6308. 182-198.

9030 **Westerhoff, Matthias** Auferstehung und Jenseits im koptischen 'Buch der Auferstehung Jesu Christi, unseres Herrn'. 1999 ⇒15, 9137; 16,9142. ^RJAC 44 (2001) 237-243 (*Schenke, Hans-Martin*); OrChr 85 (2001) 272-274 (*Müller, C. Detlef G.*).

9031 *Zarzeczny, Rafał* Apokryficzny żywot świętego Jana Chrzciciela przypisywany świętemu Markowi Ewangeliście (BHG 834; ClAp 181) [The apocryphal life of Saint John the Baptist ascribed to Saint Mark the Evangelist (BHG 834; ClAp 181)]. Studia Bobolanum 1/2 (2001) 171-181 Sum. 181. P.

K3.1 **Qumran**—*generalia*

9032 *Ahrnke, Stephan, al.,* Qumran. ZAH 14 (2001) 207-219.
9033 *Ahrnke, Stephan; Hoffmann, Matthias; Stuckenbruck, Loren* Bibliographische Dokumentation: Qumran. ZAH 14 (2001) 99-115.
9034 *Bar-Gal, Gila Kahila, al.,* The genetic signature of the Dead Sea scrolls. Historical perspectives. StTDJ 37: 2001 ⇒612. 165-171.
9035 *Broshi, Magen* Qumran and its scrolls: stocktaking. Cathedra 100 (2001) 165-182 Sum. 402. **H.**;
9036 The archaeology of Qumran: a reconsideration <1992>;
9037 Anti-Qumranic polemics in the talmud <1993>;
9038 Was Qumran, indeed, a monastery?: the consensus and its challengers: an archaeologist's view <1998>;
9039 A day in the life of Hananiah Nothos: a story <1997>. Bread, wine. JSPE.S 36: 2001 ⇒131. 198-210/211-222/259-273/284-295.
9040 *Callaway, Phillip R.* The Qumran Scrolls and textual reconstruction. FMILLER, J. JSOT.S 343: 2001 ⇒74. 278-286.
9041 *Carson, Cindy Alberts* The application of American copyright law to the Dead Sea scrolls controversy. On scrolls. JSPE.S 38: 2001 ⇒ 416. 74-98.
9042 *Chilton, Bruce D.* Reading the scrolls systemically. Judaism in late antiquity, 5: the Judaism of Qumran 2. HO I,57: 2001 ⇒426. 233-46.
9043 The Dead Sea scrolls Calliope: world history for young people 12/4. Peterborough, N.H. 2001, Cobblestone 47 pp. $5. 1050-7086.
9044 *Dombrowski, Bruno W.W.* Qumranologica IX;
9045 Qumranologica X. FolOr 37 (2001) 205-220/221-234.
9046 *Emmanuel, David* Orion Center bibliography of the Dead Sea scrolls (November 2000- September 2001). RdQ 20 (2001) 323-355.
9047 *Frerichs, Ernest S.; Silberman, Neil Asher* Introduction: the Dead Sea scrolls and archaeology: looking back and looking ahead. Archaeology and society. 2001 ⇒443. 1-10.
9048 *Freund, Richard A.; Arav, Rami* Return to the cave of letters: what still lies buried?. BArR 27/1 (2001) 25-39.
9049 *Gorski, Azriel* Analysis of microscopic material and the stitching of the Dead Sea scrolls: a preliminary study. Historical perspectives. StTDJ 37: 2001 ⇒612. 173-178.
9050 *Gruber, Mayer I.* Women in the religious system of Qumran. Judaism in late antiquity, 5: the Judaism of Qumran, 1. HO I,56: 2001 ⇒425. 173-196.
9051 *Gunneweg, Jan* How neutron activation analysis can assist research into the provenance of the pottery at Qumran. Historical perspectives. StTDJ 37: 2001 ⇒612. 179-185.

9052 **Hodge, Stephen** The Dead Sea scrolls: an introductory guide. L
      2001, Piattkus v; 234 pp. £17. 0-7499-2165-X.

9053 *Kowalski, Wojciech* Legal aspects of the recent history of the Qumran
      scrolls: access, ownership title and copyright. On scrolls, artefacts
      and intellectual property. JSPE.S 38: 2001 ⇒416. 128-158.

9054 ^E**Lim, Timothy H.** The Dead Sea scrolls in their historical context.
      2000 ⇒16,419. ^RRRT 8 (2001) 142-145 (*Williams, Catrin H.*); JSJ
      32 (2001) 315-317 (*Tigchelaar, Eibert*).

9055 *MacQueen, Hector L.* Copyright law and the Dead Sea scrolls: a Brit-
      ish perspective. On scrolls. JSPE.S 38: 2001 ⇒416. 99-115.

9056 *Maier, Johann* Zum Stand der Qumranforschung. Qumran. NTOA
      47: 2001 ⇒608. 23-95.

9057 **Nimmer, David** Copyright in the Dead Sea Scrolls: authorship and
      originality. Houston Law Review 38/1 (2001) 217 pp.

9058 *Pinnick, Avital* Orion Center bibliography of the Dead Sea scrolls
      (May-October 2000). RdQ 20 (2001) 139-163.

9059 **Pinnick, Avital** The Orion Center Bibliography of the Dead Sea
      Scrolls (1995-2000). StTDJ 41: Lei 2001, Brill viii; 228 pp. €50/$59.
      90-04-12366-0.

9060 *Richardson, John* To publish or not to publish?: anecdotes from the
      secret history of epigraphy. On scrolls, artefacts and intellectual
      property. JSPE.S 38: 2001 ⇒416. 216-222.

9061 *Rohrhirsch, Ferdinand; Röhrer-Ertl, Olav* Die Individuen der Grä-
      berfelder von Ḫirbet Qumran aus der Collectio Kurth: eine Zusam-
      menfassung. ZDPV 117 (2001) 164-170.

9062 **Roitman, A.** Sectarios de Qumrán: vida cotidiana de los esenios.
      2000 ⇒16,9188. ^RSalm. 48 (2001) 605-606 (*Trevijano, Ramón*).

9063 *Roitman, Adolfo* Exhibiting the Dead Sea scrolls: some historical and
      theoretical considerations;

9064 *Schiffman, Lawrence H.* Reclaiming the Dead Sea scrolls: the sig-
      nificance of the scrolls for Judaism and christianity;

9065 The many 'battles of the scrolls'. Archaeology and society. 2001 ⇒
      443. 41-66/160-168/188-210.

9066 ^E**Schiffman, Lawrence H.; VanderKam, James C.** The Encyclope-
      dia of the Dead Sea Scrolls. 2000 2 vols ⇒16,9193. ^RJSJ 32 (2001)
      351-352 (*Tigchelaar, Eibert*); CThMi 28 (2001) 500-501 (*Klein,
      Ralph W.*); DSD 8 (2001) 200-203 (*Goranson, Stephen*); RdQ 20
      (2001) 133-136 (*Berthelot, Katell*).

9067 *Schremer, Adiel* "[T]he[y] did not read in the sealed book": Qumran
      halakhic revolution and the emergence of torah study in second
      temple Judaism. Historical perspectives. 2001 ⇒612. 105-126.

9068 *Shanks, Hershel* The new struggle for the scrolls: will they go to the
      Palestinians?. BArR 27/3 (2001) 49-50;

9069 Intellectual property law and the scholar: cases I have known. On scrolls. JSPE.S 38: 2001 ⇒416. 63-72.

9070 *Silberman, Neil Asher* The politics of the Dead Sea scrolls. Archaeology and society. 2001 ⇒443. 11-20.

9071 *Steudel, Annette* Probleme und Methoden der Rekonstruktion von Schriftrollen. Qumran. NTOA 47: 2001 ⇒608. 97-109.

9072 *Strange, James F.; Riley Strange, James* The archaeology of everyday life at Qumran. Judaism in late antiquity, 5: the Judaism of Qumran, 1. HO I,56: 2001 ⇒425. 45-73.

9073 *Strugnell, John* The original team of editors. On scrolls, artefacts and intellectual property. JSPE.S 38: 2001 ⇒416. 178-192.

9074 ᴱ**Talmon, Shemaryahu; Ben-Dov, Jonathan; Glessmer, Uwe** Qumran Cave 4, XVI: calendrical texts. DJD 21: Oxf 2001, Clarendon xii; 265 pp. £60. 0-19-827016-X. 13 pl.

9075 *Torremans, Paul* Choice of law regarding copyright and the Dead Sea scrolls: the basic principles;

9076 *Tov, Emanuel* The publication of the Dead Sea scrolls. On scrolls. JSPE.S 38: 2001 ⇒416. 116-127/199-213;

9077 Die Veröffentlichung der Schriftrollen vom Toten Meer. Qumran. NTOA 47: 2001 ⇒608. 1-21;

9078 The decipherment and publication of the Dead Sea scrolls. Archaeology and society. 2001 ⇒443. 96-103.

9079 ᴱ**Trebolle Barrera, Julio Cesar** Paganos, judíos y cristianos en los textos de Qumrán. 1999 ⇒15,9139. ᴿSef. 61 (2001) 207-210 (*González Salinero, R.*).

9080 *Vermes, Geza* Access to the Dead Sea scrolls: fifty years of personal experience. On scrolls. JSPE.S 38: 2001 ⇒416. 193-198.

K3.4 *Qumran,* libri biblici et parabiblici

9081 ᵀ**Abegg, Martin; Flint, Peter; Ulrich, Eugene** The Dead Sea scrolls bible. 1999 ⇒15,9227; 16,9219. ᴿNT 43 (2001) 197-198 (*Elliott, J.K.*); JThS 52 (2001) 759-761 (*Lim, Timothy H.*).

9082 *Bernstein, Moshe J.* Contours of Genesis interpretation at Qumran: contents, context, and nomenclature. Studies in ancient midrash. 2001 ⇒290. 57-85.

9083 **Berrin, Shani L.** 4QpNah (4Q169, Pesher Nahum): a critical edition with commentary, historical analysis, and in-depth study of exegetical method. Diss. New York 2001, 601 pp. 3009286.

9084 *Brooke, George J.* 4Q158: reworked pentateuch a or reworked pentateuch A?. DSD 8 (2001) 219-241.

9085 *Charlesworth, James* XJudges. Qumran Cave 4 xxviii. DJD 28: 2001 ⇒8557. 231-233 [Judg 4,5-6].

9086 *Dimant, Devorah* 4QPseudo-Ezekiel;

9087 Apocryphon of Jeremiah. Qumran Cave 4 xxi: parabiblical texts: part 4: pseudo-prophetic texts. DJD 30: 2001 ⇒9088. 5-88/89-260.

9088 **Dimant, Devorah** Qumran Cave 4 XXI: parabiblical texts, part 4: pseudo-prophetic texts [4Q383-391]. Ment. *Strugnell, John.* DJD 30: Oxf 2001, Clarendon xiv; 279 pp. £55. 0-19-924542-8. 12 pl.

9089 **Doudna, Gregory L.** 4Q Pesher Nahum: a critical edition. JSPE.S 35; Copenhagen International Seminar 8: Shf 2001, Sheffield A. 813 pp. $95. 1-84127-156-X [Bibl. 769-789].

9090 *Evans, Craig A.* Biblical interpretation at Qumran. Judaism in late antiquity, 5/2. HO I,57: 2001 ⇒426. 105-124.

9091 *Fabry, Heinz-Josef* Die Schriftfunde aus Qumran und ihre Bedeutung für den hebräischen Bibeltext. Qumran. NTOA 47: 2001 ⇒608. 111-128.

9092 **Fincke, Andrew** The Samuel Scroll from Qumran: 4QSam[a] restored and compared to the Septuagint and 4QSam[c]. StTDJ 43: Lei 2001, Brill viii; 329 pp. €114. 90-04-12370-9. Bibl. 328.

9093 *Flint, Peter W.* The shape of the "Bible" at Qumran. Judaism in late antiquity, 5/2. HO I,57: 2001 ⇒426. 45-103;

9094 4QWords of judgement (pl. XL). Wadi Daliyeh II. DJD 28: 2001 ⇒ 8557. 119-123 [BuBB 37,33] [Lev 8,26].

9095 *Gold, Sally L.* Targum or translation: new light on the character of Qumran Job (11Q10) from a synoptic approach. JAB 3 (2001) 101-120.

9096 *Greenfield, Jonas C.* The small caves of Qumran <1969>;

9097 The Genesis Apocryphon: observations on some words and phrases <1980>;

9098 Two notes on the apocryphal psalms <1992>;

9099 *Greenfield, Jonas C.; Qimron, Elisha* The Genesis Apocryphon col. XII. 'Al kanfei yonah, 2. 2001 <1992> ⇒153. 573-594/610-617/ 640-645/646-652.

9100 **Herbert, Edward D.** Reconstructing biblical Dead Sea scrolls: a new method applied to the reconstruction of 4QSam[a]. 1997 ⇒13, 8817... 16,9240. [R]JBL 119 (2000) 558-560 (*VanderKam, James C.*).

9101 *Kugel, James L.* Some instances of biblical interpretation in the hymns and wisdom writings of Qumran. Studies in ancient midrash. 2001 ⇒290. 155-169.

9102 *Kugler, R.A.; VanderKam, J.C.* A note on *4Q225* (*4QPseudo-Jubilees*). RdQ 20 (2001) 109-116.

9103 *Loader, James Alfred* Das Vorbild des Priesterlichen Segens in 1QS. Begegnung mit Gott. 2001 ⇒175. 237-243 [Num 6,24-26].

9104 **Martone, Corrado** The Judaean Desert Bible: an index. Quaderni di Henoch 11: T 2001, Zamorani 156 pp. €24.79. 88-7158-097-4. Bibl. 135-156.

9105 *Miller, Robert D.* The Greek biblical fragments from Qumran in text-critical perspective. BeO 43 (2001) 235-248.

9106 *Newsom, Carol A.* Apocalyptic subjects: social construction of the self in the Qumran Hodayot. JSPE 12 (2001) 3-35.

9107 *Puech, Emile* Identification de nouveaux manuscrits bibliques: *Deutéronome* et *Proverbes* dans les débris de la Grotte 4. RdQ 20 (2001) 121-127 [Dt 14,28-29; 12,31-13,3; Prov 9,16; 10,30-32];

9108 Un autre fragment du *Psaume* 122 en *4Q522* (*4Q522 26*). RdQ 20 (2001) 129-132;

9109 530-533, 203 1: 4QLivre des géants[b-e] ar. Qumrân Grotte 4 xxii. DJD 31: 2001 ⇒8576. 9-117:

9110 534-536: 4QNaissance de Noé[a-c] ar. 117-170;

9111 537: 4QTestament de Jacob? ar (4QTJa? ar). 171-190;

9112 538: 4QTestament de Juda ar. 191-199;

9113 539: 4QTestament de Joseph ar. 201-211;

9114 540-541: 4QApocryphe de Lévi[a-b]? ar. 213-256;

9115 542: 4QTestament de Qahat ar. 257-288;

9116 543: 4QVisions de 'Amram ar. 289-318;

9117 544: 4QVisions de 'Amram[b] ar. 319-329;

9118 545: 4QVisions de 'Amram[c] ar. 331-349;

9119 546: 4QVisions de 'Amram[d] ar. 351-374;

9120 547: 4QVisions de 'Amram[e] ar. 375-390;

9121 548: 4QVisions de 'Amram[f] ar. 391-398;

9122 549: 4QVisions de 'Amram[g] ar. 399-405.

9123 **Pulikottil, Paulson** Transmission of biblical texts in Qumran: the case of the large Isaiah scroll 1QIsa[a]. JSPE.S 34: Shf 2001, Sheffield A. 240 pp. £55. 1-84127-140-3. Bibl. 219-228.

9124 *Schmitt, Armin* Die hebräischen Textfunde zum Buch Tobit aus Qumran 4QTobe (4Q200). ZAW 113 (2001) 566-582.

9125 *Scibona, Rocco* 7Q5 e il 'calcolo delle probabilità' nella sua identificazione. BeO 43 (2001) 133-138.

9126 *Shemesh, Aharon* A note on *4Q339* 'list of false prophets'. RdQ 20 (2001) 319-320.

9127 *Steinmetz, Devora* Sefer HeHago: the community and the book. JJS 52 (2001) 40-58 [Prov 25,4-5].

9128 [TE]**Steudel, Annette** Die Texte aus Qumran II: Hebräisch/Aramäisch und Deutsch: mit masoretischer Punktation, Übersetzung, Einführung und Anmerkungen. Da:Wiss 2001, xx; 277 pp. €49.90. 3-534-11613-5. Var. collab.; Bibl. xvii-xx.

9129 *Tov, Emanuel* A categorized list of all the "biblical texts" found in the Judean desert. DSD 8 (2001) 67-84.

9130 *Ulrich, Eugene* The bible in the making: the scriptures found at Qumran. The bible at Qumran. 2001 ⇒267. 51-66.

9131 ^E**Ulrich, Eugene Charles** Qumran Cave 4, X: the Prophets. DJD 15: 1997 ⇒13,8835... 16,9278. ^RDSD 8 (2001) 100-104 (*Lange, Armin*).

9132 *VanderKam, James C.; Brady, Monica* QApocryphal pentateuch A (Pls. xliv-xlv). Wadi Daliyeh II. DJD 28: 2001 ⇒8557. 131-149 [BuBB 37,31] [Ex 33,11-33,13].

9133 **Venturini, Simone** Alcune caratteristiche editoriali di 4QSam^a. Extr. Diss. Pontificio Istituto Biblico, ^D*Pisano, Stephen*: R 2001, E.P.I.B. (4) v; 106 pp. Bibl. 100-105.

9134 *Vielhauer, Roman* Materielle Rekonstruktion und historische Einordnung der beiden Pescharim zum Hoseabuch (4QpHos^a und 4QpHos^b) (1). RdQ 20 (2001) 39-91.

9135 *Wechsler, Michael G.* 'Who can restore it...?': an alternative reading of *11QTgJob* XXV,5 (*AD* 34:29). RdQ 20 (2001) 117-119.

9136 **Wood, Marcus** History and prophecy in the Qumran pesharim. Diss. Durham 2001, ^D*Hayward, C.T.R.*: 304 pp [RTL 33,636].

9137 *Young, Ian* Notes on the language of 4QCant^b. JJS 52 (2001) 122-31.

K3.5 *Qumran*—varii rotuli et fragmenta

9138 *Amit, Yairah* The Shunammite, the Shulamite and the professor between midrash and midrash. JSOT 93 (2001) 77-91 [2 Kgs 4,27].

9139 *Baumgarten, Joseph M.* The seductress of Qumran. BiRe 17/5 (2001) 21-23, 42.

9140 ^E**Baumgarten, Joseph** Qumran Cave 4 XIII: the Damascus Document (4Q266-273). DJD 18: 1996 ⇒12,8283... 14,8490. ^RJNES 60 (2001) 151-153 (*Wise, Michael O.*);

9141 Qumrân Grotte 4 Halakhic texts. DJD 25: 1999 ⇒15,9270. ^RDSD 8 (2001) 85-89 (*Harrington, Hannah K.*); HebStud 42 (2001) 363-365 (*Lim, Timothy H.*).

9142 *Ben-Dov, Jonathan* 319: 4QOtot Qumran Cave 4 xvi: calendrical texts. DJD 21: 2001 ⇒9074. 195-244.

9143 *Bernard, Jacques* Pour lire 4QMMT: quelques-unes des mises en pratique de la Torah. Le judaïsme à l'aube de l'ère chrétienne. LeDiv 186: 2001 ⇒450. 63-94.

9144 *Bockmuehl, Markus* 1QS and salvation at Qumran. Justification, 1: second temple Judaism. WUNT 2/140: 2001 ⇒251. 381-414.

9145 *Broshi, Magen* Visionary architecture and town planning in the Dead Sea scrolls. Bread, wine. JSPE.S 36: 2001 <1995> ⇒131. 223-237.

9146 *Caquot, André* Poésie religieuse de Qoumrân. RHPhR 81 (2001) 131-157.

9147 [E]**Charlesworth, James H.**, *al.*, The Dead Sea scrolls: Hebrew, Aramaic, and Greek texts with English translations: Angelic liturgy: songs of the sabbath sacrifice. 1999 ⇒15,9278. [R]Protest. 56 (2001) 300-301 (*Noffke, Eric*); DSD 8 (2001) 306-308 (*Hughes, Julie A.*); JAC 44 (2001) 193-196 (*Maier, Johann*);

9148 Miscellaneous texts from the Judaean Desert. DJD 38: 2000 ⇒16, 9290. [R]HebStud 42 (2001) 366-367 (*Crawford, Sidnie White*).

9149 **Chyutin, Michael** The new Jerusalem scroll from Qumran: a comprehensive reconstruction. JSPE.S 25: 1997 ⇒13,8853... 16,9293. [R]JBL 119 (2000) 560-561 (*Patton, Corrine*).

9150 *Crawford, Sidnie White* The meaning of the phrase עיר המקדש in the Temple scroll. DSD 8 (2001) 242-254.

9151 **Davila, James R.** Liturgical works. Eerdmans Commentaries on the Dead Sea Scrolls 6: 2000 ⇒16,9298. [R]Cart. 17 (2001) 439-440 (*Sanz Valdivieso, R.*); RRT 8 (2001) 548-550 (*Norton, Gerard J.*);TrinJ 22 (2001) 262-264 (*Schnabel, Eckhard J.*).

9152 *Dorner, Dalia* The judgment. On scrolls, artefacts and intellectual property. JSPE.S 38: 2001 ⇒416. 26-62.

9153 [E]**Eshel, Esther**, *al.*, Qumran Cave 4, XX. Poetical and liturgical texts, 2. DJD 29: 1999 ⇒15,9264. [R]HebStud 42 (2001) 361-363 (*Davila, James R.*); JJS 52 (2001) 371-373 (*Lim, Timothy H.*).

9154 *Eshel, Hanan* 4Q348, 4Q343 and 4Q345: three economic documents from Qumran Cave 4?. JJS 52 (2001) 132-135;

9155 Three new fragments from Qumran cave 11. DSD 8 (2001) 1-8;

9156 The Kittim in the War Scroll and in the Pesharim. Historical perspectives. StTDJ 37: 2001 ⇒612. 29-44.

9157 *Flint, Peter, al.*, Qumran, miscellanea, part 2. Qumran Cave 4 xxviii. DJD 28: 2001 ⇒8557. 119-233.

9158 *Flint, Peter W.* Noncanonical writings in the Dead Sea scrolls: apocrypha, other previously known writings, pseudepigrapha and the canon of scripture in the time of Jesus. The bible at Qumran. 2001 ⇒ 267. 80-126.

9159 [E]**Garcia Martinez, Florentino** Qumran Cave 11, 2: 11Q2-18, 11Q20-31. DJD 23: 1998 ⇒14,8505... 16,9308. [R]DSD 8 (2001) 92-100 (*Hempel, Charlotte*); JThS 52 (2001) 197-199 (*Campbell, Jonathan*).

9160 *Garcia Martínez, Florentino* Discoveries in the Judaean desert: textes legaux (I). JSJ 32 (2001) 71-89.

9161 *Gillet-Didier, Véronique* Calendrier lunaire, calendrier solaire et gardes sacerdotales: recherches sur *4Q321*. RdQ 20 (2001) 171-205.

9162 *Glessmer, Uwe* 334: 4QOrdo. Qumran Cave 4 xvi: calendrical texts. DJD 21: 2001 ⇒9074. 167-194.

9163 *Grossman, Maxine L.* Reading *4QMMT*: genre and history. RdQ 20 (2001) 3-22.

9164 **Jefferies, Daryl Foy** Wisdom at Qumran: a form-critical analysis of the admonitions in 4QInstruction. Diss. Wisconsin 2001, 342 pp. 3012580.

9165 **Lefkovits, Judah K.** The copper scroll—3Q15: a reevaluation: a new reading, translation, and commentary. StTDJ 25: 2000 ⇒16, 9322. [R]JSJ 32 (2001) 311-313 (*Muchowski, Piotr*); DSD 8 (2001) 318-321 (*Brooke, George J.*).

9166 *Lim, Timothy H.* The alleged reference to the tripartite division of the Hebrew Bible. RdQ 20 (2001) 23-37 [4QMMT].

9167 *Nimmer, David* Assaying Qimron's originality. On scrolls, artefacts and intellectual property. JSPE.S 38: 2001 ⇒416. 159-176.

9168 *Philonenko-Sayar, Belkis; Philonenko, Marc* Sur l'expression 'temps de justice' en 4Q215a, dans l'*Apocalypse d'Abraham* et dans l'*Epître à Diognète*. Sem. 50 (2001) 234-235.

9169 **Pike, Dana M.; Skinner, Andrew C.** Qumran Cave 4 XXIII: unidentified fragments. DJD 33: Oxf 2001, Clarendon xiii; 380 pp. $135. 0-19-924955-5. Contrib. *Terrence L. Szink*, in consultation with *James VanderKam* and *Monica Brady*; 41 pl.

9170 *Puech, Emile* 529: 4QParoles de Michel ar. Qumrân Grotte 4 xxii. DJD 31: 2001 ⇒8576. 1-8.

9171 **Puech, Émile** Qumrân Grotte 4.XVIII: textes hébreux (4Q521-4Q528, 4Q576-4Q579). DJD 25: 1998 ⇒14,8530... 16,9333. [R]JSSt 46 (2001) 170-2 (*Crawford, Sidnie White*); JBL 120 (2001) 370-371 (*Kugler, Robert A.*); RBLit 3 (2001) 299-300 (*Kugler, Robert A.*).

9172 *Qimron, Elisha* An interpretation of an enigmatic scroll [4Q439, 4Q469]. Tarb. 70/3-4 (2001) 627-630 Sum. xiii. **H.** [Jer 8,23-9,2].

9173 **Riska, Magnus** The Temple Scroll and the biblical text traditions: a study of columns 2-13:9. Diss. Helsinki 2001, [D]*Veijola, T.*: 213 pp [RTL 33,633].

9174 *Schuller, Eileen* Some contributions of the cave four manuscripts (4Q427-432) to the study of the Hodayot. DSD 8 (2001) 278-287.

9175 *Scott, James M.* Korah and Qumran. The bible at Qumran. 2001 ⇒ 267. 182-202.

9176 [E]**Strugnell, John; Harrington, Daniel J.; Elgvin, Torleif** Qumrân Grotte 4 Sapiential texts, Pt. 2, 4Q Instruction (מוּסָר לְמֵבִין): 4Q415ff. DJD 24: 1999 ⇒15,9265. With a re-ed. of 1Q26 by *John Strugnell*; ed. of 4Q423 by *Torleif Elgvin.* [R]JR 81 (2001) 274-276 (*Goff, Matthew*); JJS 52 (2001) 369-371 (*Lim, Timothy H.*); JSSt 46 (2001) 333-335 (*Collins, John J.*).

9177 *Talmon, Shemaryahu; Ben-Dov, Jonathan* Calendrical documents and mishmarot: 320-330, 337, 394 1-2. Qumran Cave 4 xvi: calendrical texts. DJD 21: 2001 ⇒9074. 1-166.

9178 **Tigchelaar, Eibert J.C.** To increase learning for the understanding ones: reading and reconstructing the fragmentary early Jewish sapiential text 4QInstruction. StTDJ 44: Lei 2001, Brill xv; 267 pp. €110/ $130. 90-04-11678-8. Bibl. 249-252.

9179 *Vázquez Allegue, Jaime* "Jurar por Dios en Qumrán" (CD 15,1-2). Salm. 48 (2001) 123-148.

9180 **Vázquez Allegue, Jaime** Los hijos de la luz y los hijos de las tinieblas: el prólogo de la Regla de la Comunidad de Qumrán. Biblioteca midrásica 21: 2000 ⇒16,9354. [R]Salm. 48 (2001) 335-340 (*Trevijano, Ramón*); Henoch 23 (2001) 393-394 (*Martone, Corrado*).

9181 *Wacholder, Ben Zion* The omer polemics in 4Q513 fragments 3-4: is Ananni their author?. RdQ 20 (2001) 93-108.

9182 *Zahn, Molly M.* Schneiderei oder Weberei?: zum Verständnis der Diachronie der Tempelrolle. RdQ 20 (2001) 255-286.

9183 *Zissu, Boaz* The identification of the Copper Scroll's Kaḥelet at ʿEin Samiya in the Samarian desert. PEQ 133 (2001) 145-158.

K3.6 **Qumran et Novum Testamentum**

9184 *Abegg, Martin G., Jr.* 4QMMT, Paul, and 'works of the law'. The bible at Qumran. 2001 ⇒267. 203-216.

9185 *Bengtsson, Håkan* Jakten på det stora avslöjandet—om Dödahavsrullarna och deras uttolkare under ett halvt sekel. SEÅ 66 (2001) 119-138.

9186 **Cryer, Frederick H.; Thompson, Thomas L.** Qumran between the Old and New Testaments. JSOT.S 290: 1998 ⇒14,327; 16,9365. [R]JThS 52 (2001) 199-201 (*Campbell, Jonathan*).

9187 *Destro, Adriana; Pesce, Mauro* The gospel of John and the Community Rule of Qumran: a comparison of systems. Judaism in late antiquity, 5: the Judaism of Qumran, 2. HO I,57: 2001 ⇒426. 201-229.

Fitzmyer, J. Dead Sea scrolls and christian origins 2000 ⇒146.

9188 *Frey, Jörg* Die Bedeutung der Qumranfunde für das Verständnis des Neuen Testaments. Qumran. NTOA 47: 2001 ⇒608. 129-208.

9189 *Harrington, Daniel J.* Jesus and the Dead Sea scrolls. Jesus: a colloquium. 2001 ⇒461. 27-44.

9190 *Räisänen, Heikki* Paul's and Qumran's Judaism. Challenges to biblical interpretation. BiblInterp 59: 2001 ⇒200. 111-139 = Judaism in late antiquity, 5/2. HO I,57: 2001 ⇒426. 173-200;

9191 Exorcisms and the kingdom: is Q 11:20 a saying of the historical Jesus?. Challenges to biblical interpretation. BiblInterp 59: 2001 <1996> ⇒200. 15-36.

9192 *Sievers, Joseph* Judaísmo y cristianismo a través de los rollos del Mar Muerto. CuTe 20 (2001) 37-54 [AcBib 10,1031].

9193 **Thiede, Carsten Peter** The Dead Sea scrolls and the Jewish origins of christianity. 2000 ⇒16,9378. [R]DSD 8 (2001) 323-326 (*Crossley, James*);

9194 NY 2001, Palgrave 256 pp. 0-312-29361-5.

9195 **Tronina, Antoni** Biblia w Qumran: wprowadzenie w lekturę biblijnych rękopisów znad Morza Martwego. Biblioteka Zwojów, Tło NT 8: Kraków 2001, Enigma 148 pp. [R]CoTh (2001/4) 199-202 (*Chrostowski, Waldemar*). **P**.

9196 **Ulrich, Eugene Charles** The Dead Sea scrolls and the origins of the bible. 1999 ⇒15,9378; 16,9379. [R]JThS 52 (2001) 201-204 (*Campbell, Jonathan*); JBL 120 (2001) 549-550 (*Crawford, Sidnie White*); RBLit 3 (2001) 297-298 (*Crawford, Sidnie White*).

K3.8 Historia et doctrinae Qumran

9197 *Abegg, Martin G.* The calendar at Qumran. Judaism in late antiquity, 5: the Judaism of Qumran, 1. HO I,56: 2001 ⇒425. 145-171.

9198 *Broshi, Magen; Eshel, Hanan* Radiocarbon dating and *The Messiah before Jesus*. RdQ 20 (2001) 311-317.

9199 *Collins, John J.* The construction of Israel in the sectarian rule books. Judaism in late antiquity, 5/2. HO I,56: 2001 ⇒425. 25-42.

9200 [E]**Collins, John Joseph; Kugler, Robert A.** Religion in the Dead Sea scrolls. 2000 ⇒16,393. [R]JThS 52 (2001) 761-764 (*Bockmuehl, M.*); BASOR 322 (2001) 95-96 (*Crawford, Sidnie White*).

9201 *Cook, Edward M.* What did the Jews of Qumran know about God and how did they know it?: revelation and God in the Dead Sea scrolls. Judaism in late antiquity, 5/2. HO I,57: 2001 ⇒426. 3-22.

9202 *Davies, Philip R.* The torah at Qumran;

9203 *Elgvin, Torleif* Wisdom at Qumran. Judaism in late antiquity, 5: the Judaism of Qumran, 2. HO I,57: 2001 ⇒426. 23-44/147-169.

9204 *Fàbrega, Valentí* La escatología de Qumrán. ActBib 38 (2001) 5-17.

9205 **Fisdel, Steven A.** The Dead Sea Scrolls: understanding their spiritual message. 1997 ⇒13,8920. [R]DSD 8 (2001) 194-96 (*Brooke, George*).

9206 *Goodblatt, David* Judean nationalism in the light of the Dead Sea scrolls. Historical perspectives. StTDJ 37: 2001 ⇒612. 3-27.

9207 *Hacham, Noah* Communal fasts in the Judean Desert scrolls. Historical perspectives. StTDJ 37: 2001 ⇒612. 127-145.

9208 *Harrington, Hannah K.* Holiness and law in the Dead Sea scrolls;

9209 *Himmelfarb, Martha* Impurity and sin in 4QD, 1QS, and 4Q512. DSD 8 (2001) 124-135/9-37.

9210 *Ilan, Tal* Shelamzion in Qumran: new insights. Historical perspectives. StTDJ 37: 2001 ⇒612. 57-68 [4Q322; 4Q324].

9211 *Jokiranta, Jutta M.* 'Sectarianism' of the Qumran 'sect': sociological notes. RdQ 20 (2001) 223-239.

9212 *Kister, Menahem* 5Q13 and the 'Avodah: a historical survey and its significance. DSD 8 (2001) 136-148.

9213 *Lichtenberger, Hermann* Auferstehung in den Qumranfunden. Auferstehung—Resurrection. WUNT 135: 2001 ⇒452. 79-91.

9214 *Maier, Johann* Purity at Qumran: cultic and domestic. Judaism in late antiquity, 5: Judaism of Qumran, 1. HO I,56: 2001 ⇒425. 91-124.

9215 *Martone, Corrado* Osservazioni sul tema del dolore nella letteratura qumranica e negli apocrifi. ATT 7 (2001) 7-17 Som., sum. 17.

9216 *Neusner, Jacob* What is "a Judaism"?: seeing the Dead Sea library as the statement of a coherent Judaic religious system. Judaism in late antiquity, 5: the Judaism of Qumran, 1. HO I,56: 2001 ⇒425. 3-21.

9217 *Nitzan, Bilha* The concept of the covenant in Qumran literature. Historical perspectives. StTDJ 37: 2001 ⇒612. 85-104.

9218 *Olyan, Saul M.* The exegetical dimensions of restrictions on the blind and the lame in texts from Qumran. DSD 8 (2001) 38-50.

9219 *Puech, Emile* Dieu le Père dans les écrits péritestamentaires et les manuscrits de la mer Morte. RdQ 20 (2001) 287-310.

9220 *Schiffman, Lawrence H.* The Pharisees and their legal traditions according to the Dead Sea scrolls. DSD 8 (2001) 262-277;

9221 Jewish law at Qumran. Judaism in late antiquity, 5: the Judaism of Qumran, 1. HO I,56: 2001 ⇒425. 75-90;

9222 The concept of restoration in the Dead Sea scrolls. Restoration. JSJ.S 72: 2001 ⇒319. 203-221.

9223 *Schuller, Eileen* Worship, temple, and prayer in the Dead Sea scrolls. Judaism in late antiquity, 5/2. HO I,56: 2001 ⇒425. 125-143;

9224 Prayer in the Dead Sea scrolls. Into God's presence. 2001 ⇒294. 66-88.

9225 **Se, Heng Kei** They shall be neither early nor late: a study of the time reckoning system in the Qumran calendrical documents. Diss. Edinburgh 2001, ^D*Lim, T.*: 328 pp [RTL 33,635].

9226 *Van Peursen, Wido* Qumran origins: some remarks on the Enochic/ Essene hypothesis. RdQ 20 (2001) 241-253.

K4.1 Sectae iam extra Qumran notae: Esseni, Zelotae

9227 **Boccaccini, Gabriele** Beyond the Essene hypothesis: the parting of the ways between Qumran and Enochic Judaism. 1998 ⇒14,8607; 16,9437. [R]BZ 45 (2001) 118-121 (*Fabry, Heinz-Josef*); DSD 8 (2001) 89-92 (*Jastram, Natham*); JBL 120 (2001) 372-373 (*Schnabel, Eckhard J.*); Sal. 63 (2001) 568-569 (*Vicent, R.*).

9228 *Broshi, Magen* Matrimony and poverty: Jesus and the Essenes. Bread, wine. JSPE.S 36: 2001 <2000> ⇒131. 252-258;

9229 Hatred: an Essene religious principle and its christian consequences. Bread, wine. JSPE.S 36: 2001 <1999> ⇒131. 274-283.

9230 *Hempel, Charlotte* The Essenes. Religious diversity. BiSe 79: 2001 ⇒398. 65-80.

9231 *Jossa, Giorgio* Gli zeloti e i sicari. I gruppi giudaici. 2001 <1980> ⇒ 5195. 11-78.

9232 *Kraft, Robert A.* PLINY on Essenes, Pliny on Jews. DSD 8 (2001) 255-261.

9233 **Riesner, Rainer** Esseni e prima comunità cristiana a Gerusalemme: nuove scoperte e fonti. Città del Vaticano 2001, Libreria Editrice Vaticana 310 pp. 88-209-7165-8. Bibl. 203-271.

9234 **Theissen, Gerd** L'ombre du Galiléen. [T]*Bagot, J.-P.*: P 2000, Cerf 270 pp. €21.34 [EeV 45,18—Rastoin, Cécile].

9235 *Wenning, Robert* Kein Essener-Dorf bei En-Gedi. WUB 21 (2001) 79

K4.3 Samaritani

9236 **Crown, Alan David** Samaritan scribes and manuscripts. TSAJ 80: Tü 2001, Mohr xiii; 555 pp. €116.57. 3-16-147490-2. Bibl. 517-536.

9237 **Faü, Jean-François; Crown, Alain-David** Les samaritains: rescapés de 2700 ans d'histoire. P 2001, Maisonneuve et L. 120 pp. €15. 2-7068-1535-3. Bibl. 112-114.

9238 [ET]**Florentin, Moshe** The Tulida: a Samaritan chronicle, text—translation—commentary. 1999 ⇒15,9432. [R]FJB 28 (2001) 175-178 (*Dexinger, Ferdinand*).

9239 *Fossum, Jarl* The angel of the Lord in Samaritanism. JSSt 46 (2001) 51-75.

9240 **Hjelm, Ingrid** The Samaritans and early Judaism: a literary analysis. JSOT.S 303: 2000 ⇒16,9450. [R]RRT 8 (2001) 145-147 (*Kugler, Robert A.*); BiblInterp 9 (2001) 437-440 (*Grabbe, Lester L.*); JBL 120

(2001) 557-559 (*Roddy, Nicolae*); CBQ 63 (2001) 340-342 (*Murphy, Frederick J.*); ThLZ 126 (2001) 382-385 (*Böhm, Martina*); RBLit 3 (2001) 291-293 (*Roddy, Nicolae*).

9241 Schorch, Stefan Das Lernen der Tora bei den Samaritanern heute und drei samaritanische Erzählungen über das Lernen. WuD 26 (2001) 107-126.

9242 *Van der Horst, Pieter Willem* The Samaritan languages in the pre-Islamic period. JSJ 32 (2001) 178-192.

9243 **Zsengellér, József** Gerizim as Israel: northern tradition of the Old Testament and early history of the Samaritans. 1998 ⇒15,9437. [R]FJB 28 (2001) 171-173 (*Dexinger, Ferdinand*).

K4.5 *Sadoqitae, Qaraitae*—Cairo Genizah; Zadokites, Karaites

9244 **Baker, F.Colin; Polliack, Meira** Arabic and Judaeo-Arabic manuscripts in the Cambridge Genizah Collections: Arabic Old Series (T-S Ar. 1a-54). CULGS 12: C 2001, CUP xxii; 616 pp. $190. 0-521-79280-0. Advisor *Haggai Ben-Shamai*; 24 pl.; Bibl. 551-571.

9245 *Blumfield, Fiona* Yefet BEN ELI on the identity of the 'Redeemer' in his commentary on the book of Ruth. Exegesis and grammar. 2001 ⇒413. 65-75 [Ruth 3,13; 4,1; 4,4].

9246 *Erder, Yoram* The altar of the covenant at Mount Sinai (Exodus 24:4-5). Studies in Judaica. Te'uda 16-17: 2001 ⇒408. 315-357 Sum. xxv-xxvi. **H**.

9247 *Fenton, Paul B.* 'De la perfection de la torah et des voies de sa révélation': un commentaire piétiste sur le Psaume XIX provenant de la genizah du Caire. Torah et science: perspectives historiques et théoriques: études offertes à Charles TOUATI. Ment. *Philoponus*. [E]**Freudenthal, Gad; Rothschild, Jean-Pierre; Dahan, Gilbert:** Collection.REJ 22: Lv 2001, Peeters vi; 284 pp. €60. 90-429-1028-3. 97-117 [BuBB 37,114].

9248 [E]**Friedman, Mordechai A.** A century of Geniza research. Te'uda 15: 1999 ⇒15,9446. [R]OLZ 96 (2001) 276-279 (*Leicht, Reimund*); REJ 160 (2001) 518-520 (*Khan, Geoffrey*).

9249 *Gallego, María Ángeles* The transmission in medieval manuscripts of *al-Kitāb al-Kāfī* by Abū al-Faraj Hārūn ibn al-Faraj. Exegesis and grammar. 2001 ⇒413. 151-178.

9250 *Goldstein, Miriam* The beginnings of the transition from *derash* to *peshat* as exemplified in Yefet BEN ELI's comment on Psa. 44:24. Exegesis and grammar. 2001 ⇒413. 41-64.

9251 *Khan, Geoffrey* Biblical exegesis and grammatical theory in the Karaite tradition. Exegesis and grammar 2001 ⇒413. 127-149.

9252 *Niessen, Friedrich* An anonymous Karaite commentary on the book of Hosea. Exegesis and grammar 2001 ⇒413. 77-126 [Hos 2,1-15]:

9253 *Olszowy-Schlanger, Judith* The *Explanation of difficult words* by ʾAbū al-Faraj Hārūn ibn al-Faraj. 179-194;

9254 *Outhwaite, Benjamin* Karaite epistolary Hebrew: the letters of Ṭoviyyah BEN MOSHE. 195-234;

9255 *Polliak, Meira; Schlossberg, Eliezer* Historical-literary, rhetorical and redactional methods of interpretation in Yefet BEN ELI's Introduction to the Minor Prophets. 1-39.

9256 **Reif, Stefan C.** A Jewish archive from Old Cairo: the history of Cambridge University's Genizah collection. 2000 ⇒16,9479. [R]JJS 52 (2001) 179-180 (*Olszowy-Schlanger, Judith*).

9257 **Schäfer, Peter; Shaked, Shaul** Magische Texte aus der Kairoer Geniza, 3. TSAJ 72: 1999 ⇒15,9459. [R]JSJ 32 (2001) 111-113 (*Davila, James R.*); Sal. 63 (2001) 765-767 (*Vicent, R.*).

K5 Judaismus prior vel totus

9258 *Anderson, Gary A.* The garments of skin in apocryphal narrative and biblical commentary. Studies in ancient midrash. 2001 ⇒290. 101-143 [Gen 2,25; 3,7; 3,21].

9259 *Andreasen, Niels-Erik A.* Sabbath and synagogue. Passion. 2001 ⇒295. 189-211.

9260 *Aviam, Mordechai* The ancient synagogues at Barʿam. Judaism in late antiquity, 3/4. HO I,55: 2001 ⇒424. 155-177.

9261 *Bar-Kochva, Bezalel* Second temple-period research: training, means, methods, and aims. Cathedra 100 (2001) 121-164 Sum. 403. **H.**

9262 *Baumgarten, A.I.* Literacy and the polemics surrounding biblical interpretation in the second temple period. Studies in ancient midrash. 2001 ⇒290. 27-41.

9263 **Baumgarten, Albert I.** The flourishing of Jewish sects in the Maccabean era: an interpretation. JSJ.S 55: 1997 ⇒13,8972; 15,9463. [R]Zion 66 (2001) 379-381 (*Schiffman, Lawrence H.*).

9264 *Bedell, Clifford H.* Mission in intertestamental Judaism. Mission in the NT. ASMS 27: 2001 ⇒367. 21-29.

9265 *Berquist, Jon L.* The social context of postexilic Judaism. Passion. 2001 ⇒295. 20-54.

9266 *Bodenheimer, Alfred* Das Problem des Bösen in der jüdischen Bibelexegese. BSGJ 10 (2001) 9-21.

9267 *Carson, D.A.* Introduction;

9268 Summaries and conclusions Justification, 1: second temple Judaism. WUNT 2/140: 2001 ⇒251. 1-5/505-548.

9269 **Castaldini, Alberto** L'ipotesi mimetica: contributo a una antropologia dell'ebraismo. F 2001, Olschki 164 pp. €18.07.

9270 *Cohen, Shaye J.* Die Anfänge des Judeseins. KuI 16 (2001) 101-111.

9271 **Cohen, Shaye J.J.** The beginnings of Jewishness: boundaries, varieties, uncertainties. 1999 ⇒15,9473; 16,9498. [R]JBL 120 (2001) 159-161 (*Janowitz, Naomi*); REJ 160 (2001) 273-274 (*Hadas-Lebel, Mireille*).

9272 **Cohn-Sherbok, D.; Cohn-Sherbok, L.** Breve storia dell'ebraismo. Bo 2001, Il Mulino 185 pp. €9.30.

9273 *Davies, Philip R.* Judaism and the Hebrew scriptures. The Blackwell reader in Judaism. 2001 ⇒423. 31-41.

9274 *De Benedetti, Paolo* La lettura sinagogale della Torà. RivLi 88 (2001) 903-908.

9275 *Deines, Roland* The Pharisees between "Judaisms" and "Common Judaism". Justification, 1: second temple Judaism. WUNT 2/140: 2001 ⇒251. 443-504.

9276 *Diebner, Bernd Jørg* Annotations concerning the relation between "Judaism" since the Persian period and Juda's belonging to "Israel". TEuph 21 (2001) 119-131.

9277 *Dohmen, Christoph* "... als er uns die Schrift erschloss" (Lk 24,32): jüdische Kommentare als Weg zur Gegenwart Gottes in der Schrift. BiLi 74 (2001) 254-259.

9278 **Elliott, Mark Adam** The survivors of Israel: a reconsideration of the theology of pre-christian Judaism. 2000 ⇒16,9505. [R]EThL 77 (2001) 203-204 (*Lust, J.*); JThS 52 (2001) 772-775 (*Tromp, Johannes*).

9279 *Endres, John C.* Joyful worship in second temple Judaism. Passion. 2001 ⇒295. 155-188.

9280 *Finkel, Asher* Prayer in Jewish life of the first century as background to early christianity. Into God's presence. 2001 ⇒294. 43-65.

9281 *Georgi, Dieter* Synkretismus IV: Judentum. TRE 32: 2001 ⇒665. 534-538.

9282 **Giordano, Carlo; Kahn, Isidoro** Testimonianze ebraiche a Pompei, Ercolano, Stabia e nelle città della Campania. [E]*Felix García y García, Laurentino*: Coll. archeologica 2: R [3]2001, Bardi 119 pp. 88-8569-9-90-1;

9283 The Jews in Pompeii, Herculaneum, Stabiae and in the cities of Campania. [T]*Felix Jashemski, Wilhelmina F.*: Archaeological collection 2: R [3]2001, Bardi 120 pp. 88-85699-91-X.

9284 *Gnandt, Georg* Das Gebet im Judentum. Lebendige Katechese 23 (2001) 103-105.

9285 *Görtz-Wrisberg, Irene von* A sabbath service in Ostia: what do we know about the ancient synagogal service?. The synagogue of ancient Ostia. 2001 ⇒427. 167-202.

9286 *Gruen, Erich S.* Ebrei, Greci e Romani nel terzo oracolo sibillino. Gli ebrei nell'impero romano. 2001 <1998> ⇒415. 57-76.

9287 **Hachlili, Rachel** Ancient Jewish art and archaeology in the diaspora. HO 1/35: 1998 ⇒14,8675; 15,9497. [R]PEQ 133 (2001) 61-62 (*Rosenberg, Stephen G.*).

9288 **Hadas-Lebel, Mireille** Un sage juif au temps de Jésus. Ment. *Hillel.* 1999 ⇒15,9498. [R]REJ 160 (2001) 276-277 (*Nahon, Gérard*).

9289 *Harrelson, Walter* Critical themes in the study of the postexilic period. Passion. 2001 ⇒295. 290-301.

9290 **Harrington, Hannah K.** Holiness: rabbinic Judaism in the Graeco-Roman world. Religion in the first Christian centuries: L 2001, Routledge xiv; 242 pp. 0-415-14986-X. Bibl. 231-240.

9291 **Hezser, Catherine** Jewish literacy in Roman Palestine. TSAJ 81: Tü 2001, Mohr S. ix; 557 pp. €126.80. 3-16-147546-1. Bibl. 505-535.

9292 **Ilan, Tal** Mine and yours are hers: retrieving women's history from rabbinic literature. AGJU 41: 1997 ⇒13,8996; 15,9511. [R]SCI 20 (2001) 314-318 (*Stein, Dina*).

9293 **Jacobs, Martin** Die Institution des jüdischen Patriarchen: eine quellen- und traditionskritische Studie zur Geschichte der Juden in der Spätantike. TSAJ 52: Tü 1995, Mohr 401 pp. [R]CV 43 (2001) 81-84 (*Sláma, Petr*).

9294 **Jaffee, Martin S.** Torah in the mouth: writing and oral tradition in Palestinian Judaism, 200 BCE-400 CE. Oxf 2001, OUP xi (2) 239 pp. £40. 0-19-514067-2. Bibl. 211-228.

9295 **Kieweler, Hans Volker** Erziehung zum guten Verhalten und zur rechten Frömmigkeit: die hiskianische Sammlung, ein hebräischer und ein griechischer Schultext. BEAT 49: Fra 2001, Lang 476 pp. FS103. 3-631-37668-5. Bibl. 405-433.

9296 *Kugel, James L.* Ancient biblical interpretation and the biblical sage. Studies in ancient midrash. 2001 ⇒290. 1-26.

9297 **Lange, Nicholas de** El judaísmo. M 2000, CUP 313 pp;

9298 An introduction to Judaism. 2000 ⇒16,9525. [R]RRT (2001/1) 80-81 (*Harvey, Graham*).

9299 *Lenhardt, Pierre* À l'origine du mouvement pharisien, la tradition o-rale et la résurrection. Le judaïsme à l'aube de l'ère chrétienne. LeDiv 186: 2001 ⇒450. 123-176.

9300 *Lesses, Rebecca* Exe[o]rcising power: women as sorceresses, exorcists and demonesses in Babylonian Jewish society of late antiquity. JAAR 69 (2001) 343-375 [BuBB 36,29].

9301 **Levine, Lee I.** The ancient synagogue: the first thousand years. 2000 ⇒16,9529. [R]BZ 45 (2001) 265-268 (*Claußen, Carsten*); TJT 17 (2001) 292-294 (*Kloppenborg Verbin, John S.*).

9302 *Levine, Lee I.* Synagoge. TRE 32. 2001 ⇒665. 499-508.

9303 *Lémonon, Jean-Pierre* Le judaïsme avait-il une pensée et une pratique missionnaires au début du Ier siècle de notre ère?. Le judaïsme à l'aube de l'ère chrétienne. LeDiv 186: 2001 ⇒450. 299-329.

9304 *Liebeschuetz, Wolf* L'influenza del giudaismo sui non-ebrei nel periodo imperiale. Gli ebrei nell'impero romano. 2001 ⇒415. 143-159.

9305 *Lindemann, Andreas* Schwangerschaftsabbruch als ethisches Problem im antiken Judentum und im frühen Christentum. WuD 26 (2001) 127-148.

9306 **Loewenberg, Frank M.** From charity to social justice: the emergence of communal institutions for the support of the poor in ancient Judaism. New Brunswick, NJ 2001, Transaction 222 pp. 0-7658-0052-7. Bibl. 195-201.

9307 *Luker, Lamontte M.* Passion for torah and prophetic vitality. Passion. 2001 ⇒295. 1-19.

9308 *Massonnet, Jean* Les Pharisiens et le sens communautaire. Le judaïsme à l'aube de l'ère chrétienne. LeDiv 186: 2001 ⇒450. 177-205.

9309 *Middleburgh, Charles H.* Reliable account of Judaism. ET 112 (2001) 341.

9310 *Murphy, Frederick J.* Second temple Judaism. The Blackwell reader in Judaism. Blackwell readings in religion: 2001 ⇒423. 42-59.

9311 **Navé Levinson, Pnina** Volk Israel—eine Kulturgeschichte des Judentums. [E]*Zepf, I.*: Hannover 2001, Lutherisches Verlagshaus 340 pp. €24.90. 3-7859-0838-5. 14 ill.

9312 *Neusner, Jacob* Defining Judaism;

9313 The doctrine of torah;

9314 The doctrine of Israel. The Blackwell reader in Judaism. Blackwell readings in religion: 2001 ⇒423. 3-18/159-172/187-201;

9315 Introduction: what is a Judaism?. The brother of Jesus. 2001 ⇒256. 1-9.

9316 **Neusner, Jacob** Recovering Judaism: the universal dimension of Judaism. Mp 2001, Augsburg F. xiii; 201 pp. $20. 0-8006-3268-0 [RB 108,317];

9317 The unity of rabbinic discourse, v.2: halakhah in the aggadah; v.3: halakhah and aggadah in concert. Studies in ancient Judaism: Lanham 2001. University Press of America 0-7618-;

9318 The theology of the halakhah. Brill Reference Library of Ancient Judaism 6: Lei 2001, Brill liv; 396 pp. €97. 90-04-12291-5.

9319 [E]**Neusner, Jacob** Dictionary of Judaism in the biblical period, 450 B.C.E. to 600 C.E. [E]*Green, William S.*: [2]1999 <1996> ⇒15,9532; 16,9547. [R]Theoforum 32 (2001) 235-236 (*Laberge, Léo*).

9320 **Neusner, Jacob; Sonn, Tamara; Brockopp, Jonathan E.** Judaism and Islam in practice: a sourcebook. 2000 ⇒16,9548. [R]RRT 8 (2001) 508-510 (*Wilkes, George*).

9321 *Penna, Romano* Che cosa significava essere giudeo al tempo e nella terra di Gesù: problemi e proposte. Vangelo e inculturazione. 2001 ⇒193. 63-88.

9322 *Porten, Bezalel* The Jews of Elephantine who are named after ancestors. [F]AHITUV, S. 2001 ⇒1. 332-361. **H.**

9323 *Rabello, Alfredo M.* La situazione giuridica degli Ebrei nell'impero romano. Gli ebrei nell'impero romano. 2001 ⇒415. 125-142.

9324 *Rajak, Tessa* The Jewish community and its boundaries <1992>;

9325 Jews and christians as groups in a pagan world <1985>;

9326 Benefactors in the Greco-Jewish diaspora <1996>;

9327 The synagogue in the Greco-Roman city <1999>;

9328 *Rajak, Tessa; Noy, David Archisynagogoi*: office, title and social status in the Greco-Jewish synagogue <1993>. The Jewish dialogue. AGJU 48: 2001 ⇒199. 225-354/344-372/373-391/463-478/393-429.

9329 **Rodríguez Carmona, Antonio** La religión judía: historia y teología. M 2001, BAC xxix; 761 pp. €33.52. 84-7914-583-8. [R]EstTrin 35 (2001) 664-666 (*Pikaza, Xabier*).

9330 **Runesson, Anders** The origins of the synagogue: a socio-historical study. CB.NT 37: Sto 2001, Almqvist & W. 573 pp. SEK366. 91-22-01946-4. Diss. Lund 2001; bibl. 507-553.

9331 **Rutgers, Leonard Victor** The hidden heritage of diaspora Judaism. 1998 ⇒14,8719; 15,9544. [R]JBL 119 (2000) 124-25 (*Barclay, John*).

9332 *Sacchi, Paolo* Giustizia e giustificazione nel mondo giudaico ellenistico. Giustizia-giustificazione nella bibbia. DSBP 28: 2001 ⇒307. 107-127.

9333 **Sanders, Ed Parish** Il giudaismo: fede e prassi (63 a.C. - 66 d.C.). [E]*Capelli, Piero*: 1999 ⇒15,9546. [R]AnnTh 15 (2001) 352-354 (*Tábet, M.*); CivCatt 152/1 (2001) 633-635 (*Prato, G.L.*).

9334 **Satlow, Michael L.** Jewish marriage in antiquity. Princeton, NJ 2001, Princeton Univ. Pr. xxvi; 431 pp. $55. 0-691-00255-X. Bibl. 367-400.

9335 [E]**Schiffman, Lawrence H.** Texts and traditions: a source reader for the study of second temple and rabbinic Judaism. 1998 ⇒15,9547. [R]RBLit 3 (2001) 274-276 (*Garber, Zev*).

9336 **Schmidt, Francis** How the temple thinks: identity and social cohesion in ancient Judaism. [T]*Crowley, J. Edward*: BiSe 78: Shf 2001, Sheffield A. 307 pp. £20/$30. 1-84127-208-6. Bibl. 276-292.

9337 [E]**Schoeps, Julius H.; Wallenborn, Hiltrud** Juden in Europa: ihre Geschichte in Quellen, 1: von den Anfängen bis zum späten Mittelalter. Da:Wiss 2001, viii; 309 pp. €39.88. 3-89678-402-1.

9338 *Schreiner, Stefan* Sühne III: Judentum. TRE 32: 2001 ⇒665. 338-42;

9339 Sünde III: Judentum. TRE 32: 2001 ⇒665. 372-375.

9340 *Schwartz, Seth* Imperialism and Jewish society, 200 BCE to 640 CE. Princeton 2001, Princeton Univ. Pr. xi; 320 pp. $39.50. 0691088500.

9341 *Schwartz, Seth; Gotzmann, Andreas; Meyer, Michael A.* Judentum. RGG², 4: I-K. 2001 ⇒664. 610-627.

9342 *Sievers, Joseph* JOSEPHUS, first Maccabees, Sparta, the three Harei-seis—and CICERO. JSJ 32 (2001) 241-251.

9343 *Stemberger, Günter* Juden. RAC 19: 2001 ⇒660. 160-228.

9344 **Stern, Marc** Was ist Judentum?: die häufigsten Fragen und ihre Antworten. Fra 2001, Lembeck 168 pp. €8.30. 3-89710-167-X.

9345 **Stern, Sacha** Calendar and community: a history of the Jewish calendar second century BCE-tenth century CE. NY 2001, OUP xvi; 306 pp. £45. 0-19-827034-8. Bibl. 285-302.

9346 *Steussy, Marti J.* The vitality of story in second temple judaism. Passion. 2001 ⇒295. 212-241.

9347 *Strange, James F.* The synagogue as metaphor. Judaism in late antiquity, 3/4. HO I,55: 2001 ⇒424. 93-120.

9348 *Talmon, Shemaryahu* "Exile" and "restoration" in the conceptual world of ancient Judaism. Restoration. 2001 ⇒319. 107-146.

9349 ᵀ**Teugels, Lieve M.** Aggadat Bereshit. Jewish and Christian Perspectives 4: Lei 2001, Brill xxxvi; 305 pp. €111/$130. 90-04-12173-0. Introd., notes.

9350 *Thondiparambil, Joseph* Religious conversion in the Israelite community. Living Word 107/1 (2001) 16-26.

9351 *Vana, Liliane* La *birkat ha-minim* è una preghiera contro i giudeocristiani?. Verus Israel. BCR 65: 2001 ⇒524. 147-189.

9352 **VanderKam, James C.** An introduction to early Judaism. 2000 ⇒ 16,9567. ᴿJSJ 32 (2001) 359-360 (*Xeravits, Géza*).

9353 *Veltri, Giuseppe* The meal of the spirits, the three Parcae and Lilith: apotropaic strategies for coping with birth anxieties and child mortality. Henoch 23 (2001) 343-359;

9354 Der Magier im antiken Judentum: von empirischer Wissenschaft zur Theologie. Der Magus: seine Ursprünge und seine Geschichte in verschiedenen Kulturen. ᴱ**Grafton, Anthony; Idel, Moshe**: B 2001, Akademie 147-167 [BuBB 36,22].

9355 ᴱ**Visotzky, Burton; Fishma, David** From Mesopotamia to modernity: introduction to Jewish history and literature. 1999 ⇒15,398; 16, 9569. ᴿMillSt 47 (2001) 166-170 (*Rogers, Patrick*).

9356 **Walters, Kerry S.; Portmess, Lisa** Religious vegetarianism: from HESIOD to the DALAI LAMA. Albany 2001, SUNY 216 pp. $16. 0-79-14-4972-6.

9357　*Whitters, Mark F.* Some new observations about Jewish festal letters. JSJ 32 (2001) 272-288.

9358　*Wick, Peter* Vom Tempelgottesdienst (Avodah) zum Wortgottes- dienst. KuI 16 (2001) 9-24.

9359　**Yahalom, J.** Poetry and society in Jewish Galilee of late antiquity. 1999 ⇒15,9568. H. [R]JSJ 32 (2001) 113-115 (*Van Bekkum, Wout*).

K6.0 Mišna, *tosepta: Tannaim*

9360　*Alexander, Philip S.* Torah and salvation in tannaitic literature. Justi- fication, 1: second temple Judaism. 2001 ⇒251. 261-301.

9361　*Cohen, Jonathan* Charitable contributions, communal welfare organi- zations, and allegiance to the community according to RASHBA. HUCA 72 (2001) 85-100.

9362　[E]**Cohen, Shaye J.D.** The synoptic problem in rabbinic literature. 2000 ⇒16,9578. [R]JBL 120 (2001) 784-790 (*Bakhos, Carol*).

9363　*Ego, Beate* Israels Not und Gottes Klage: zu einem Theologumenon der rabbinischen Literatur. JBTh 16 (2001) 91-108.

9364　*Hepner, Gershon* Verbal resonance in the bible and intertextuality. JSOT 96 (2001) 3-27.

9365　*Hezser, Catherine* Tannaiten. TRE 32. 2001 ⇒665. 639-642.

9366　*Hirshman, Marc* Qohelet's reception and interpretation in early rab- binic literature. Studies in ancient midrash. 2001 ⇒290. 57-85.

9367　**Kalmin, Richard** The sage in Jewish society of late antiquity. 1999 ⇒15,9574. [R]JBL 120 (2001) 589-591 (*Hayes, Christine*); JSSt 46 (2001) 337-340 (*Levine, Lee*); RBLit 3 (2001) 301-304 (*Hayes, Christine*).

9368　[T]**Mayer, Günter; Lisowsky, Gerhard** Die Tosefta: Seder I: Zeraim, 4: Maaser scheni—Halla—Bikkurim. Rabbinische Texte, Reihe 1/4: Stu 2001, Kohlhammer 185 pp. 3-17-017592-0 [BuBB 36,79].

9369　*Milikowsky, Chaim* Trajectories of return, restoration and redemption in Rabbinic Judaism: Elijah, the Messiah, the war of Gog and the world to come. Restoration. JSJ.S 72: 2001 ⇒319. 265-280.

9370　*Neudecker, Reinhard* "Die Stimmen sehen können": Bibel und Zen. Edith-Stein-Jahrbuch 7 (2001) 56-70 [Exod 20,18; Acts 2,3];

9371　Dialog zwischen Bibel und Zen: 'Das ganze Volk sah die Stimmen' (Exodus 20,18). Kiyo 25 (2001) 1-20. Collab. *K. Suzawa* [AcBib 10,804].

9372　*Neusner, Jacob* Sacrifice in rabbinic Judaism: the presentation of the atonement-rite of sacrifice in tractate Zebahim in the Mishnah, Tosefta, Bavli and Yerushalmi. ASEs 18 (2001) 225-253;

9373 Intersecting realms of sanctification: the slaughter of animals for secular purposes in the context of sanctification in rabbinic Judaism: Tractate Hullin in the Mishnah, Tosefta, Yerushalmi, and Bavli;

9374 Sin, repentance, atonement and resurrection: the perspective of rabbinic theology on the views of James 1-2 and Paul in Romans 3-4. ASEs 18 (2001) 255-280/409-431;

9375 The canon of rabbinic Judaism: the mishnah and the midrash. The Blackwell reader in Judaism. 2001 ⇒423. 73-85.

9376 *Rabello, Alfredo Mordechai* Il diritto e le feste degli ebrei. Gli ebrei nell'impero romano. 2001 ⇒415. 295-334.

9377 *Reif, Stefan C.* Some notions of restoration in early rabbinic prayer. Restoration. JSJ.S 72: 2001 ⇒319. 281-304.

9378 *Sarason, Richard S.* The "intersections" of Qumran and rabbinic Judaism: the case of prayer texts and liturgies. DSD 8 (2001) 169-81.

9379 *Shemesh, Aharon* King Manasseh and the halakhah of the sadducees. JJS 52 (2001) 27-39.

9380 *Stemberger, Günter* The formation of rabbinic Judaism, 70-640 CE. The Blackwell reader in Judaism. 2001 ⇒423. 60-72.

κ6.5 Talmud; midraš

9381 **Agus, Aharon R.E.** Das Judentum in seiner Entstehung: Grundzüge rabbinisch-biblischer Religiosität. Judentum und Christentum 4: Stu 2001, Kohlhammer 260 pp. €20.40. 3-17-016422-8.

9382 **Akenson, Donald Harman** Surpassing wonder: the invention of the bible and the talmuds. Ch 2001, Univ. Press vii; 658 pp. $25. 0-226-01073-2 [ThD 48,351—Heiser, W. Charles].

9383 **Albeck, Shalom** Introduction to Jewish law in talmudic times. 1999 ⇒15,9587. H. ᴿREJ 160 (2001) 510-512 (*Rothschild, Jean-Pierre*).

9384 *Arndt, Timotheus* Abraham aus der Ur Kasdim: Midrasch-Motive. Forschungsstelle Judentum, Mitteilungen und Beiträge 18 (2001) 51-74 [BuBB 35,40] [Gen 11,31].

9385 **Banon, David** Il midrash: vie ebraiche alla lettura della bibbia. ᵀ*Genta, Elsa*: CinB 2001, San Paolo 160 pp.

9386 **Becker, Hans-Jürgen** Die grossen rabbinischen Sammelwerke Palästinas: zur literarischen Genese von Talmud Yerushalmi und Midrash Bereshit Rabba. TSAJ 70: 1999 ⇒15,9593; 16,9591. ᴿJJS 52 (2001) 176-177 (*Neusner, Jacob*); JAC 44 (2001) 196-197 (*Maier, Johann*).

9387 *Becker, Hans-Jürgen* Talmud. TRE 32. 2001 ⇒665. 626-636.

9388 *Bernstein, Marc S.* Midrash and marginality: the "Agunot" of S.Y. AGNON and Devorah BARON. HebStud 42 (2001) 7-58.

9389 ^E**Bodendorfer, Gerhard; Millard, Matthias** Bibel und Midrasch. FAT 22: 1998 ⇒14,8766... 16,9597. ^RDBM 20 (2001) 116-125 (*Belezos, Const. I.*); OrthFor 15 (2001) 231-238 (*Belezos, Konstantin*); RBLit 3 (2001) 307-311 (*Ulmer, Rivka*).

9390 *Brito, Jacil Rodrígues de* Midraxe e história. Estudos Bíblicos 71 (2001) 53-61.

9391 **Bruckstein, Almut Sh.** Die Maske des Moses: Studien zur jüdischen Hermeneutik. B 2001, Philo 200 pp. €19.50. 3-8257-0230-8.

9392 *Cohen, Avinoam* The contrastive term "אתון מתניתש ... אנן מתנינן ..." in the Babylonian Talmud and its historical significance. HUCA 72 (2001) 45-60.

9393 *Derrida, Jacques* Whom to give to (knowing not to know). The postmodern bible reader. 2001 <1995> ⇒287. 333-352.

9394 **Egger, Peter** Verdienste vor Gott?: der Begriff der *zekhut* im arabischen Genesiskommentar *Bereshit Rabba.* NTOA 43: 2000 ⇒16, 9606. ^RThRv 97 (2001) 296-298 (*Stemberger, Günter*); ThZ 57 (2001) 472-474 (*Schori, Kurt*); ThLZ 126 (2001) 1259-1261 (*Avemarie, Friedrich*).

9395 *Ehrlich, Ernst Ludwig* Die Bedeutung des Talmud für die Verbindlichkeit der Tora. Wieviel Systematik?. QD 185: 2001 ⇒283. 192-199.

9396 *Ehrlich, Uri* An additional source of the *Sitz im Leben* of midrash and aggada. Studies in Judaica. Teʻuda 16-17: 2001 ⇒408. 123-135 Sum. xvii-xviii. **H.**

9397 *Feldman, Seymour* 'In the beginning God created the heavens': PHILOPONUS' De Opificio mundi and rabbinic exegesis: a study in comparative midrash. ^FTOUATI, C. Collection.REJ 22: 2001 ⇒9247. 37-69 [BuBB 37,8] [Gen 1].

9398 **Ginzberg, Louis** Les légendes des juifs, 3. ^T*Sed-Rajna, Gabrielle*: Patrimoines judaïsme: P 2001, Cerf 391 pp. €38. 2-204-06827-6.

9399 **Goshen-Gottstein, Alon** The sinner and the amnesiac: the rabbinic invention of Elisha BEN ABUYA and Eleazar BEN ARACH. 2000 ⇒16, 9617. ^RRRT 8 (2001) 550-551 (*Neusner, Jacob*).

9400 **Grohmann, Marianne** Aneignung der Schrift: Wege einer christlichen Rezeption jüdischer Hermeneutik. 2000 ⇒16,9618. ^RJud. 57 (2001) 62-64 (*Morgenstern, Matthias*); KuI 16 (2001) 89-90 (*Kirchberg, Julie*).

9401 ^{ET}**Guggenheimer, Heinrich W.** The Jerusalem Talmud: first order: Zeraïm: tractates Kilaim and Seviit. SJ 147: B 2001, De Gruyter xiii; 677 pp. €148. 3-11-017122-8.

9402 *Haubig, Hans-Michael* Zur Diskussion um den Talmud im 19. Jahrhundert: die Kontroverse zwischen Abraham GEIGER und den Brüdern DEUTSCH. HBO 31 (2001) 197-206.

9403 *Hayman, Pinhas* Disputation terminology and edetorial activity in the academy of Rava Bar Yosef Bar Hama. HUCA 72 (2001) 61-83.

9404 *Hoffer, Victoria* And he prayed to him: Manasseh's repentance and its reception in the midrash. Hermenêutíca 1 (2001) 55-78 [2 Chr 33].

9405 *Holtz, Shalom E.* 'To go and marry any man that you please': a study of the formulaic antecedents of the rabbinic writ of divorce. JNES 60 (2001) 241-258.

9406 ᴱKellner, Menachem Commentary on Song of Songs by Rabbi Levi BEN GERSHOM. Ramat-Gan 2001, Bar-Ilan Univ. 178 pp.

9407 *Kister, Menahem* 'Leave the dead to bury their own dead'. Studies in ancient midrash. 2001 ⇒290. 43-56 [Gen 12,1].

9408 ᵀLehnardt, Andreas Rosh ha-Shana—Neujahr. Übersetzung des Talmud Yerushalmi 2/7: 2000 ⇒16,9632. ᴿJSJ 32 (2001) 313-315 (*Stemberger, Günter*);

9409 Talmud Yerushalmi: Besa: Ei. Übersetzung des Talmud Yerushalmi 2/8. Tü 2001, Mohr S. xxxv; 186 pp. 3-16-147589-5. Bibl. xvi-xxxii.

9410 *Lenhardt, Pierre* Talmud torà degli ebrei e studi ebraici dei cristiani. Qol(I) 95-96 (2001) 14-18.

9411 *Levinas, Emmanuel* On the Jewish reading of scriptures. The postmodern bible reader. 2001 <1994> ⇒287. 319-332.

9412 *Mandel, Paul* Midrashic exegesis and its precedents in the Dead Sea scrolls.DSD 8 (2001) 149-168.

9413 **Manns, Frédéric** Le midrash: approche et commentaire de l'Écriture. SBFA 56: J 2001, Franciscan Printing Press 200 pp. $15. 965-516-005-X. Bibl. 191-197.

9414 *Menn, Esther M.* Praying king and sanctuary of prayer, part 1: David and the Temple's origins in rabbinic Psalms commentary (Midrash Tehillim). JJS 52 (2001) 1-26.

9415 *Minkoff, Dinah* Kedusha, holiness, and ethics. JBQ 29 (2001) 106-112 [Gen 18,22].

9416 *Morfino, Mauro Maria* 'La torah non si acquista a meno di quarant-otto condizioni': tipologie maestro-discepolo nel trattato *Pirqé 'Abot* e nel midrash *'Abot [!] De-Rabbi Natan.* ᶠMARIN, B. 2001 ⇒68. 75-172.

9417 *Neudecker, Reinhard; Scanu, Maria Pina* 'Dove sei?' (Gen 3,9): motivi salienti di antropologia nel giudaismo. Antropologia cristiana. 2001 ⇒371. 605-651.

9418 **Neusner, Jacob** The reader's guide to the talmud. Brill Reference Library of Ancient Judaism 5: Lei 2001, Brill xxx; 374 pp. €97. 90-04-12187-0. Bibl. xxii-xxx;

9419   The social teaching of rabbinic Judaism. Lei 2001, Brill 3 vols. €159.
90-04-12261-3. V.1: Corporate Israel and the individual Israelite;
v.2: Between Israelites; v.3: God's presence in Israel;

9420   The halakhah and the aggadah: theological perspectives. Lanham
2001, University Press of America xi; 193 pp. $34. 0-7618-1929-0;

9421   The aggadic role in halakhic discourse. Lanham 2001, University
Press of America xxix; 162 + xi; 188 + xiii; 278 pp; 3 vols. $33 + 34
+ 41. 0-7618-1931-2/2-0/3-9;

9422   Dual discourse, single judaism: the category-formation of the halakhah and the aggadah defined, compared, and contrasted. Studies in
Ancient Judaism: Lanham 2001, University Press of America xxii;
179 pp. $34. 0-7618-1928-2.

9423   **Oberhänsli-Widmer, Gabrielle** Biblische Figuren in der rabbinischen Literatur: Gleichnisse und Bilder zu Adam, Noah und Abraham
im Midrasch Bereschit Rabba. JudChr 17: 1998 ⇒14,8803; 15,9653.
RFrRu 8 (2001) 140-141 (*Vonach, Andreas*).

9424   *Perani, Mauro; Stemberger, Günter* The Yerushalmi fragments discovered in the diocesan library of Savona. Henoch 23 (2001) 267-
303.

9425   **Petuchowski, Jakob J.** Das große Buch der rabbinischen Weisheit:
Geschichten der Meister. EPetuchowski, Elizabeth: FrB 2001, Herder
221 pp.

9426   *Petzel, Paul* Kommentar—signifikante Denkform im Judentum: eine
erkenntnistheologische Studie. Orien. 65 (2001) 33-36, 38-42, 50-53.

9427   *Rizzi, Giovanni* Il *Midrash haggadah* nella versione greca di Abaquq, Abdia, Nahum e Sofonia come esegesi trasformante nel giudaismo del periodo ellenistico. MCAGNI, L., 4: SMDSA 61: 2001
⇒15. 2043-2064.

9428   **Rubenstein, Jeffrey L.** Talmudic stories: narrative art, composition,
and culture. 1999 ⇒15,9657. RJJS 52 (2001) 379-381 (*Stern,
Sacha*); JBL 120 (2001) 790-792 (*Bakhos, Carol*); HebStud 42
(2001) 382-385 (*Schofer, Jonathan*); RBLit 3 (2001) 304-307
(*McEntire, Mark*).

9429   ESchäfer, Peter; Becker, Hans-Jürgen Synopse zum Talmud Yerushalmi. Ordnung Mo'ed: shabbat—yoma. TSAJ 82/2/1-4: Tü 2001
Mohr x; 218 pp. €188.16. 3161475550 [JSJ 33,342–Stemberger, G.];

9430   Ordnung Mo'ed: sheqalim-mo'ed qatan. TSAJ 83/2/5-12: Tü 2001,
Mohr v; 371 pp. €203.49. 3161475569 [JSJ 33,342–Stemberger, G.].

9431   **Scherman, Nosson** The Early Prophets with a commentary antholo-
gized from the rabbinic writings: Joshua - Judges. ArtScroll Brooklyn, NY 2001, Mesorah xxiv; 263 pp. 1-57819-331-1.

9432   *Scholem, Gershom G.* Révélation et tradition comme catégories religieuses dans le judaïsme. VS 81 (2001) 485-513.

9433 *Shea, William H.* Three notes on relations between early rabbinic and early christian sources. JATS 12/1 (2001) 78-82.

9434 *Shraga Lichtenstein, Yechezkel* The RAMBAM's approach regarding prayer, holy objects and visiting the cemetery. HUCA 72 (2001) 1*-34*. **H.**

9435 *Smelik, Willem F.* Language, locus, and translation between the talmudim. JAB 3 (2001) 199-224.

9436 ᴱ**Sussmann, Yaacov** Talmud Yerushalmi: according to Ms. Or. 4720 (Scal. 3) of the Leiden University Library with restorations and corrections. J 2001, The Academy of the Hebrew Language pag. varia. 965-481-018-2. Introd. *Yaacov Sussmann.* **H.**

9437 *Teugels, Lieve* Gap filling and linkage in the midrash on the Rebekah cycle. Studies in the book of Genesis. BEThL 155: 2001 ⇒1936. 585-598 [Gen 22,20-23; 24; 25,19-28; 27].

9438 ᵀ**Thoma, Clemens,** *al.,* Die Gleichnisse der Rabbinen. Judaica et Christiana 10, 13, 16: 1986-1996 ⇒12,8562. ᴿSIDIC 34/2 (2001) 27-28 *(Wahle, Hedwig).*

9439 *Ulmer, Rivka* The semiotics of the dream sequence in Talmud Yerushalmi Maʿaser Sheni. Henoch 23 (2001) 305-323;

9440 Further manuscript evidence of Pesiqta Rabbati: a description of MS JTS 8195 (and MS Moscow 214). JJS 52 (2001) 269-307.

9441 *Unchelen, N.A.* Rabbinic updating of the torah: Isaiah 49:14 and 15 in BavliBerkhot 32b. ᶠDEURLOO, K. ACEBT.S 2: 2001 ⇒23. 355-62.

9442 *Veltri, Giuseppe* Letteratura talmudica Palestinese: edizioni, traduzioni e studi recenti. Laur. 42 (2001) 543-556.

9443 **Verhelst, Stéphane** Trois remarques sur la *Pesiqta de-Rav Kahana* et le christianisme. Le judéo-christianisme. 2001 ⇒484. 366-380 [BuBB 36,81].

9444 **Zetterholm, Karin** Portrait of a villain: Laban the Aramean in rabbinic literature. Diss. Lund 2001, 243 pp.

κ7.1 Judaismus mediaevalis, *generalia*

9445 *Astren, Fred* The Dead Sea scrolls and medieval Jewish studies: methods and problems. DSD 8 (2001) 105-123.

9446 *Bauer, Uwe F.W.* "Die Stimme, die so wimmert": ein Pijut aus Meinz zu Jom Kippur. WuD 26 (2001) 89-106.

9447 **Baumgarten, Jean** Récits hagiographiques juifs. Patrimoines, Judaïsme: P 2001, Cerf 573 pp. €52. 2-204-06819-5. Bibl. 521-549.

9448 **Brody, Robert** The Geonim of Babylonia and the shaping of medieval Jewish culture. 1998 ⇒14,8822. ᴿDR 414 (2001) 72-74 *(Derrett, J. Duncan M.)*; JSSt 46 (2001) 175-177 *(Reif, Stefan C.)*.

9449   **Collini, Paolo** Famiglia. Indice concettuale del Medio Giudaismo 1:
       2000 ⇒16,9673. ᴿSEL 18 (2001) 121-23 (*Lancelotti, Maria Grazia*);
9450   Sessualità. Indice concettuale del Medio Giudaismo 2: 2000 ⇒16,
       9674. ᴿSEL 18 (2001) 121-123 (*Lancelotti, Maria Grazia*).
9451   ᴱ**De Lange, Nicholas Robert Michael** Hebrew scholarship and the
       medieval world. C 2001, CUP xiv; 247 pp. 0-521-78116-7. Bibliog-
       raphy of the writings of *Raphael Loewe* 240-245.
9452   *Katsumata, Naoya* Hebrew style in the liturgical poetry of Shemu'el
       HaShelishi. JJS 52 (2001) 308-322.
9453   *Marcus, Ivan G.* The dynamics of Jewish renaissance and renewal in
       the twelfth century. Jews and christians in twelfth-century Europe.
       2001 ⇒442. 27-45.
9454   **Marcus, Jacob Rader** The Jew in the medieval world: a source
       book, 315-1791. ᴱ*Saperstein, Marc* 1999 <1938> ⇒15,9690. ᴿJJS
       52 (2001) 177-178 (*Skinner, Patricia*).
9455   *Mondschein, Aaron* Concerning the inter-relationship of the com-
       mentaries of R. Abraham Iʙɴ Ezʀᴀ and R. Samuel B. Meɪʀ to the
       pentateuch: a new appraisal. Studies in Judaica. Teʿuda 16-17: 2001
       ⇒408. 15-46 Sum. xii-xiii. **H**.
9456   *Nahon, Gérard* From the Rue aux Juifs to the Chemin du Roy: the
       classical age of French Jewry, 1108-1223. Jews and christians in
       twelfth-century Europe. 2001 ⇒442. 311-339.
9457   *Reguer, Sara* Judaism in the Muslim world. The Blackwell reader in
       Judaism. Blackwell readings in religion: 2001 ⇒423. 101-113.
9458   **Reif, Stefan C.** Why Medieval Hebrew studies?: an inaugural lecture
       delivered before the University of Cambridge in the School of Pytha-
       goras, St. John's College, 11.11.1999. C 2001, CUP 53 pp. 0-521-
       01047-0.
9459   **Romero, Elena** Andanzas y prodigios de Ben-Sirá: edición del texto
       judeoespañol y traducción del texto hebreo. Publicaciones de Est.
       Sef. 7: M 2001, Consejo Sup. de Investigaciones Científicas 280 pp.
9460   *Tamani, Giuliano* La simbiosi medievale fra pensiero ebraico e pen-
       siero greco: linee di ricerca. Pensiero e istituzioni. 2001 ⇒580. 277-
       295.
9461   *Wolfson, Elliot R.* Martyrdom, eroticism, and asceticism in twelfth-
       century Ashkenazi piety. Jews and christians in twelfth-century
       Europe. 2001 ⇒442. 171-220.

κ7.2 **Maimonides**

9462   **Arbel, Ilil** Maimonides: a spiritual biography. Lives & Legacies: NY
       2001, Crossroad 192 pp. 0-8245-2359-8. Bibl. 184-186.

9463 ^T**Brague, Rémi** Maïmonide, traité d'éthique ('Huit chapitres'). P 2001, Desclée de B. 186 pp.

9464 ^E**Cohen, Robert S.; Levine, Hillel** Maimonides and the sciences. Boston Studies in the Philosophy of Science 211: Dordrecht 2000, Kluwer xv; 251 pp.

9465 *Dietrich, Jan* Negative Theologie bei Pseudo-Dionysios AREOPAGITA und Mose ben Maimon. ThPh 76 (2001) 161-184.

9466 *Dureau, Yona* La conduite de sa santé (de Moïse Maïmonide). Représentations des maladies. 2001 ⇒482. 45-55.

9467 ^{ET}**Hayoun, Maurice-Ruben** Solomon Maïmon—Commentaires de Maïmonide. 1999 ⇒15,9702. ^RREJ 160 (2001) 247-250 (*Freudenthal, Gad*).

9468 **Idel, Moshé** Maimonide e la mistica ebraica. Genova 2000, Melangolo 198 pp.

9469 *Kaplan, Lawrence* Philosophy and the divine law in Maimonides and al-Farabi in light of Maimonides' *Eight chapters* and al-Farabi's *Chapters of the statesman*. Jewish-Muslim encounters. 2001 ⇒379. 1-34.

9470 **Kreisel, Howard T.** Maimonides' political thought: studies in ethics, law and the human ideal. 1999 ⇒15,9703. ^RREJ 160 (2001) 525-526 (*Brague, Rémi*).

9471 *Zwiep, Irene E.* Did Maimonides write nonsense?: intellect, sense and sensibility in Ruach Chen. ^FDEURLOO, K. 2001 ⇒23. 363-367.

K7.3 Alteri magistri Judaismi mediaevalis

9472 *Blau, Joshua* The linguistic character of SAADIA Gaon's translation of the pentateuch. Oriens 36 (2001) 1-9.

9473 ^{ET}**Gatti, Roberto** Shelomoh IBN GABIROL: Meqor hayyîm. Opera 21: Genova 2001, Il melangolo 330 pp. 88-7018-383-1. Bibl. 183-198.

9474 *Gómez Aranda, Mariano* Exégesis filosófica en las interpretaciones de Abraham IBN EZRÁ al libro de *Job*. Sef. 61 (2001) 367-380 Res., sum. 380;

9475 Aspectos científicos en el comentario de Abraham IBN EZRA al libro de Job. Henoch 23 (2001) 81-96.

9476 ^T**Lockshin, Martin I.** RASHBAM's commentary on Leviticus and Numbers: an annotated translation. BJSt 330: Providence 2001, Brown Univ. x; 309 pp. $40. 1-930675-07-0. Bibl. 299-309.

9477 *Tamani, Giuliano* Le edizioni dei commenti biblici di Levi BEN GERSHOM. ^MCAGNI, L., 4: SMDSA 61: 2001 ⇒15. 2165-2176.

9478 *Todaro, Maria Novella* Il commento di RABANO Mauro a Geremia. StMed 42 (2001) 41-119.

9479   *Zewi, Tamar* Energicus in SAADYA Gaon's translation of the pentateuch. ᴹHETZRON, R. 2001 ⇒46. 223-230.

K7.4 *Qabbalâ, Zohar, Merkabā*—Jewish mysticism

9480   *Blumenthal, David R.* Three is not enough: Jewish reflections on trinitarian thinking. DIETRICH, W.: BJSt 329: 2001 ⇒24. 181-195.

9481   *Boyarin, Daniel* The gospel of the Memra: Jewish binitarianism and the prologue to John. HThR 94 (2001) 243-284.

9482   **Davila, James R.** Descenders to the chariot: the people behind the hekhalot literature. JSJ.S 70: Lei 2001, Brill xi; 343 pp. 90-04-11541-2. Bibl. 313-323.

9483   *DeConick, April D.* 'Early Jewish and christian mysticism': a collage of working definitions. SBL.SP 2001. SBL.SPS 40: 2001 ⇒494. 278-304.

9484   *Deghaye, Pierre Gedulla et Gebura*: le *Dictionnaire biblique et emblématique* de Friedrich Christoph OETINGER (1976). ᶠFAIVRE, A. 2001 ⇒29. 233-247.

9485   **Deutsch, Nathaniel** L'immaginazione gnostica: gnosticismo, mandeismo e misticismo della merkavah. ᵀ*Bovolenta, Daniela*: Hermetica: R 2001, Arkeios 175 pp. 88-86495-52-8. Bibl. 167-174.

9486   ᵀ**Faierstein, Morris M.** Jewish mystical autobiographies: book of visions and book of secrets. ClWS 94: 1999 ⇒15,9726. ᴿTheoforum 32 (2001) 244-245 (*Laberge, Léo*).

9487   **Giller, Pinchas** Reading the Zohar: the sacred text of the kabbalah. Oxf 2001, OUP xviii; 246 pp. $60. 0-19-511849-9. Bibl. 225-240.

9488   *Goetschel, Roland* Kabbale théosophique et piétisme juif rhénan au XIVe siècle. RevSR 75 (2001) 544-562.

9489   *Idel, Moshe* Kabbalah and hermeticims in Dame Frances A. YATES's Renaissance. ᶠFAIVRE, A. 2001 ⇒29. 71-90;

9490   Torah: between presence and representation of the divine in Jewish mysticism. ᶠBARASCH, M. 2001 ⇒2. 197-235.

9491   ᴱ**Idel, Moshe** Natan BEN SAⱠDYAH Har'ar: le porte della giustizia (Ša're ṣedeq). ᴱ*Mottolese, Maurizio*: Mi 2001, Adelphi 544 pp. €51. 65. Saggio di *Moshe Idel.* ᴿRasIsr 67/3 (2001) 125-132 (*Lelli, Fabrizio*).

9492   *Jelonek, Tomasz* Ksiego Jecira [Il libro di Jecirah]. ACra 33 (2001) 369-384 Riass. 384. P.

9493   *Kilcher, Andreas; Dan, Joseph* Kabbala. RGG², 4: I-K. 2001 ⇒664. 724-727.

9494   **Laenen, J.H.** Jewish mysticism: an introduction. ᵀ*Orton, D.E.*: LVL 2001, Westminster xiv; 292 pp. $20. 0-664-22457-1.

9495 **Mecklenburg, Tzevi** Haketav vehakabbalah: torah commentary. ^T*Munk, Eliyahu*: J 2001, Lambda xxv; 3060 pp. 7 vols. 96571-08292.

9496 *Meroz, Ronit* The chariot of Ezekiel: an unknown Zoharic commentary. Studies in Judaica. Te'uda 16-17: 2001 ⇒408. 567-616 Sum. xxxvii-xxxviii. **H**. [Ezek 1].

9497 **Schneider, Sarah** Kabbalistic writings on the nature of masculine & feminine. Northvale, NJ 2001, Aronson xvi; 349 pp. 0-7657-6148-3. Bibl. 323-327.

9498 *Swartz, Michael D.* The Dead Sea scrolls and later Jewish magic and mysticism. DSD 8 (2001) 182-193.

9499 *Williams-Hogan, Jane* Emanuel SWEDENBORG and the kabbalistic tradition. ^FFAIVRE, A. 2001 ⇒29. 343-360.

K7.5 Judaismus saec. 14-18

9500 *Chiesa, Bruno* DANTE e la cultura ebraica del Trecento. Henoch 23 (2001) 325-342.

9501 ^E**Feiner, Shmuel; Sorkin, David** New perspectives on the Haskalah. Littman Library of Jewish Civilization: L 2001, The Littman Library of Jewish Civilization ix; 260 pp. 1-874774-61-7. Bibl. 225-250.

9502 *Gailus, Manfred* Die Erfindung des "Korn-Juden": zur Geschichte eines antijüdischen Feindbildes des 18. und frühen 19. Jahrhunderts. HZ 272 (2001) 597-622.

9503 *Goetschel, Roland* La tour de Babel dans le commentaire de Bahya BEN ASHER (XIIIe siècle). RHPhR 81 (2001) 3-12 [Gen 11].

9504 *Netzer, Zvi H.* Further clarifications on the work of NORZI. HebStud 42 (2001) 257-269.

9505 *Sáenz-Badillos, Angel* Hebräische Dichtung im christlichen Spanien: Dichter und ihre Absichten. Jud. 57 (2001) 2-19; 82-93.

9506 ^T**Weinberg, Joanna** Azariah de' ROSSI: The light of the eyes. YJS 31: NHv 2001, Yale Univ. Pr. xlix; 802 pp. $120. 0-300-07906-0. Introd. & annotations [TD 48,286—Heiser, W. Charles].

K7.7 Hasidismus et Judaismus saeculi XIX

9507 *Danieli, Natascia* La "restaurazione universale" (tiqqun ha-kelali) nell'insegnamento di NAHMAN di Bratslav. Henoch 23 (2001) 97-112.

9508 **Jacobs, Louis** La preghiera chassidica. ^T*Romagnoli, Gloria*: Mi 2001, Gribaudi 220 pp.

9509　*Kampmann, Christoph* Protest gegen die Obrigkeit?: zur Deutung der judenfeindlichen Unruhen während des Vormärz. HJ 121 (2001) 471-500.

9510　**Lifschitz, Daniel** L'Haggadah di Pasqua con commento chassidico. Mi 2001, Gribaudi 144 pp. Illustr. di *Paolo Foresti*.

9511　**Necker, Gerold** Das Buch des Lebens: Edition, Übersetzung und Studien. Diss. Freie Univ. Berlin 1999, ᴰ*Schäfer, Peter*: TSMJ 16: Tü 2001, Mohr S. xi; 222; 78* pp .

9512　*Sias, Giovanni* Nel nome del padre. Ment. *Freud, S.*: BeO 43 (2001) 249-255.

9513　*Vargon, Shmuel* S.D. LUZZATTO on מקרא של פשוטו. HebStud 42 (2001) 167-186.

9514　**Wineman, Aryeh** The Hasidic parable: an anthology with commentary. Ph 2001, Jewish Publication Society of America xxv; (2) 191 pp. $20. 0-8276-0707-5. Bibl. 185-191.

K7.8 Judaismus contemporaneus

9515　*Avery-Peck, Alan J.* The doctrine of God;

9516　*Baskin, Judith R.* Women in contemporary Judaism. The Blackwell reader in Judaism. 2001 ⇒423. 173-186/316-332.

9517　ᴱ**Bekhor, Shlomo** Lekhàyim: guida di tutte le feste e ricorrenze felici: riti, canti e commenti in ebraico traslitterato e tradotto. ᵀ*Khana Dell'Acqua, Annalisa*: Mi 2001, DLI 289 pp. 88-86674-25-2. Trasliterazione e testi ebraici: *Eliyàhu Hadad*.

9518　*Berner, Leila Gal* Hearing Hannah's voice: the Jewish feminist challenge and ritual innovation. Daughters of Abraham. 2001 ⇒528. 35-49 [1 Sam 1,9-16].

9519　*Beyrich, Tilman* "Kann ein Jude Trost finden in KIERKEGAARDs Abraham?": jüdische Kierkegaard-Lektüren: BUBER, FACKENHEIM, LEVINAS. Jud. 57 (2001) 20-40.

9520　*Bodenheimer, Aron Ronald* Ein Zwischenruf aus Not und voll Empörung. KuI 16 (2001) 161-170.

9521　*Boschki, Reinhold* Schweigen und schreien zugleich: Anklage Gottes im Werk von Elie WIESEL. JBTh 16 (2001) 109-132.

9522　*Breslauer, S. Daniel* Philosophy in Judaism: two stances. The Blackwell reader in Judaism. 2001 ⇒423. 128-144.

9523　*Brocke, Edna* Birkat Kohanim—Priestersegen für Israel. KuI 16 (2001) 62-63.

9524　*Brown, Benjamin* Orthodox Judaism. The Blackwell reader in Judaism. 2001 ⇒423. 232-255.

9525 *Cappellini, M. Roberta* La corporeità nella bibbia secondo visuali rabbiniche contemporanee. FilTeo 15 (2001) 101-107.

9526 **Cohn-Sherbok, Dan** Ebraismo. 2000 ⇒16,9767. [R]Studi Fatti Ricerche 93 (2001) 13-14 (*De Benedetti, Paolo*); PaVi 46/3 (2001) 59-61 (*Ferrari, Pier Luigi*); Vivens Homo 12 (2001) 440-441 (*Tarocchi, Stefano*); CivCatt 152/4 (2001) 413-415 (*Prato, G.L.*).

9527 *Danzger, M. Herbert* The "return" to traditional Judaism at the end of the twentieth century: cross-cultural comparisons. The Blackwell reader in Judaism. 2001 ⇒423. 411-431.

9528 *Davidowicz, Klaus* Jüdischer Gottesdienst und seine Liturgie. KuI 16 (2001) 3-8.

9529 *De Benedetti, Paolo* La lettura sinagogale della torà. RivLi 88 (2001) 903-908.

9530 *Domhardt, Yvonne* Auswahlbibliographie von Werken mit jüdisch-judaistischer Thematik, die seit Sommer 2000 bis Redaktionsschluss 2001 in Schweizer Verlagen erschienen sind bzw. durch den Inhalt oder Verfasser/in die Schweiz betreffen. BSGJ 10 (2001) 22-37.

9531 **Donin, Hayim Halevy** To pray as a Jew: a guide to the prayer book and the synagogue service. NY 2001 <1991>, Basic B. 416 pp. $13.30. 0-4650-8633-0.

9532 *Dorff, Elliot N.* Ethics of Judaism;

9533 *Elazar, Daniel J.* Judaism as a theopolitical phenomenon. The Blackwell reader in Judaism. 2001 ⇒423. 287-315/333-362.

9534 **Firestone, Reuven** Children of Abraham: an introduction to Judaism for Muslims. Hoboken, NJ 2001, KTAV xxiv; 322 pp. 0-88125-721-4. Bibl. 303-306.

9535 *Frank, Évelyne* Lecture d'un poème de Claude VIGÉE: "Sommeil: extase noire ...". FV 100/5 (2001) 31-40.

9536 **Gal-Ed, Efrat** Das Buch der jüdischen Jahresfeste. Insel-Taschenbuch 2597: Fra 2001, Insel 411 pp. 3-458-34297-4.

9537 *Gellner, Christoph* 'Die Antwort der Literatur ist: keine Antwort': Theologie im Gespräch mit Günter KUNERT. Orien. 65 (2001) 79-84.

9538 *Gillman, Neil* Theology in contemporary Judaism;

9539 *Gordis, Daniel* Conservative Judaism: the struggle between ideology and popularity;

9540 *Gorny, Yosef* Judaism and Zionism. The Blackwell reader in Judaism. Blackwell readings in religion: 2001 ⇒423. 363-377/256-267/397-410.

9541 **Halivni, David Weiss** Revelation restored: divine writ and critical responses. 1997 ⇒14,8884. [R]JJS 52 (2001) 147-150 (*Solomon, Norman*).

9542 **Hartman, David** Love and terror in the God encounter: the theological legacy of Rabbi Joseph B. SOLOVEITCHIK. Woodstock, VT 2001, Jewish Lights xi; 219 pp. 1-58023-112-8. Bibl. 213-214.

9543 *Havers, Grant* Leo STRAUSS and the politics of biblical religion. SR 30 (2001) 353-363 [Mk 4,10-12].

9544 *Holländer, Katarina* Die Frage nach der jüdischen Kunst: sechzig Jahre "Omanut, Verein zur Förderung jüdischer Kunst in der Schweiz". Jud. 57 (2001) 204-221.

9545 *Homolka, Walter; Geiger, Abraham* Judentum im 21. Jahrhundert: zwischen Fundamentalismus und Synkretismus. GuL 74 (2001) 256-260.

9546 **Jacobs, Louis** Beyond reasonable doubt. 1999 ⇒15,9769. [R]JJS 52 (2001) 150-151 (*Solomon, Norman*).

9547 *Jutrin, Monique* Benjamin FONDANE: un "Ulysse juif". FV 100/5 (2001) 19-30.

9548 *Kam, Abraham Y.; Kwun-cheung, Lo* The myth of river Sambatyon: a review of modern studies of Chinese Judaism. Jian Dao 15 (2001) 165-222 Sum. 221. **C.**

9549 *Kaplan, Dana Evan* Reform Judaism. The Blackwell reader in Judaism. Blackwell readings in religion: 2001 ⇒423. 217-231.

9550 **Kellner, Menachem** Must a Jew believe anything?. 1999 ⇒15,9771. [R]JJS 52 (2001) 152-154 (*Solomon, Norman*); JJS 52 (2001) 202-206 (*Statman, Daniel*).

9551 *Kopciowski, Elia* Cura del corpo, norme igieniche, alimentari, digiuni ... quali insegnamenti per l'oggi?. Studi Fatti Ricerche 93 (2001) 4-7.

9552 **Krupp, Michael** Die Geschichte des Zionismus. GTBS 1212: Gü 2001, Gü'er 128 pp. 3-579-01212-6.

9553 **Kuzar, Ron** Hebrew and Zionism: a discourse analytic cultural study. Language, Power and Social Process 5: B 2001, Mouton de Gruyter xii; 324 pp. 3-11-016992-4. Bibl. 297-315.

9554 *Meghnagi, David* L'ebraismo. ED 54/2 (2001) 123-127.

9555 *Mendes-Flohr, Paul* Secular forms of Jewishness. The Blackwell reader in Judaism. 2001 ⇒423. 378-396.

9556 *Morgenstern, Matthias* Drama als Geschichtsbewältigung: Moshe Shamirs Stück über Alexander JANNAI und SHIMON ben Shetach Krieg der Söhne des Lichts. Jud. 57 (2001) 120-136.

9557 *Neusner, Jacob* How Judaism reads the bible. JHiC 8 (2001) 210-50.

9558 **Neusner, Jacob** Contemporary views of ancient Judaism: disputes and debates. Academic Studies in the History of Judaism: Binghamton 2001, Global xix; 349 pp. 1-586841-14-9.

9559 *Newman, Louis E.* The law of nature and the nature of the law: David NOWAK and the role of natural law in Judaism;

9560 *Novak, David* Emmanuel LEVINAS and ethical monotheism. [F]DIET-RICH, W., BJSt 329: 2001 ⇒24. 259-277/240-258;

9561 Karl BARTH on divine command: a Jewish response. SJTh 54 (2001) 463-483.

9562 **Olin, Margaret Rose** The nation without art: examining modern discourses on Jewish art. Texts and Contexts: Lincoln, NE 2001, University of Nebraska Press xxvii; 275 pp. 0-8032-3564-X.

9563 *Petry, Erik* Akkulturation versus Zionismus?: der galut-Begriff bei Heinrich LOEWE. Jud. 57 (2001) 41-57;

9564 Die "Erste Alija": Geschichte und Wirkung der ersten jüdischen Einwanderung 1882-1904. [F]CARMEL, A., 2001 ⇒17. 91-100.

9565 *Roth, John K.* Good news after Auschwitz: does christianity have any?. "Good News" after Auschwitz?. 2001 ⇒377. 173-85 [Jn 1,14].

9566 *Salkin, Jeffrey K.* New Age Judaism. The Blackwell reader in Judaism. Blackwell readings in religion: 2001 ⇒423. 268-283.

9567 **Schulweis, Harold M.** Finding each other in Judaism?: meditation on the rites of passage from birth to immortality. NY 2001, UAHC 118 pp. $13. 0-8074-0764-X. Artwork by *Jeanette Kuvin Oren* [ThD 48,386—Heiser, W. Charles].

9568 **Seidler, Meir** Schma Jisrael: Einheit—die jüdische Sicht. 1998 ⇒ 14,8904. [R]FrRu 8 (2001) 306 (*Thoma, Clemens*).

9569 *Shavit, Ari* Der Tag, an dem der Frieden starb: Ari Shavit interviewt Shlomo BEN AMI. KuI 16 (2001) 171-190.

9570 [E]**Shire, Michael** The Jewish prophet: visionary words from Moses and Miriam to Henrietta SZOLD and A.J. HESCHEL. Woodstock, VT 2001, Jewish Lights 125 pp. 1-58023-168-3.

9571 **Sicker, Martin** Between man and God: issues in Judaic thought. CSRel 66: Westport, CONN 2001, Greenwood xii; (2) 260 pp. 0-313-31904-9. Bibl. 239-254.

9572 **Stingl, Wolfgang** Jüdisches Leben in Nidda im 19. und 20. Jahrhundert: Untersuchungen zur Lokalgeschichte des oberhessischen Landjudentums unter Berücksichtigung biblisch-theologischer Aspekte. Diss. Frankfurt, Univ. 2001, [D]*Wittstadt*, K [RTL 33,650].

9573 *Suied, Alain* Rêver la lettre. FV 100/5 (2001) 53-55.

9574 *Thoma, Clemens* Das Fach "Judaistik"/"Jüdische Studien" in der Schweiz. BSGJ 10 (2001) 6-8.

9575 *Vincent, Jean M.* "Ça m'oblige": regard sur quelques aspects de la poésie juive contemporaine. FV 100/5 (2001) 57-85.

9576 *Voigts, Manfred J.G.* FICHTE und das Judentum: eine Kritik des Buches Fichtes Idee der Nation und das Judentum von Hans Joachim BECKER. Jud. 57 (2001) 284-292.

9577 **Wiese, Christian** Wissenschaft des Judentums und protestantische Theologie im wilhelminischen Deutschland: ein Schrei ins Leere?. SWALBI 61: 1999 ⇒15,9790. [R]Jud. 57 (2001) 137-149 (*Deines, Roland*).

9578 **Wyschogrod, Michael** Gott und Volk Israel: Dimensionen jüdischen Glaubens. [T]*Karkowski, Annerose; Stegemann, Wolfgang*: Stu 2001, Kohlhammer 247 pp. €21.45. 3-17-015344-7.

9579 *Zahavy, Tzvee* Jewish piety. The Blackwell reader in Judaism. Blackwell readings in religion: 2001 ⇒423. 145-156.

9580 **Zemer, Moshe** Jüdisches Religionsgesetz heute: progressive Halacha. [T]*Birkenhauer, Anne* 1999 ⇒15,9791. [R]ThLZ 126 (2001) 43-45 (*Agus, Aharon*).

9581 *Zola, Gary P.* The common places of American Reform Judaism's conflicting platforms. HUCA 72 (2001) 155-191.

K8 *Philosemitismus*—Jewish Christian relations

9582 **Altermatt, Urs** Katholizismus und Antisemitismus: Mentalitäten, Kontinuitäten, Ambivalenzen: zur Kulturgeschichte der Schweiz 1918-1945. 1999 ⇒15,9794. [R]KuI 16 (2001) 194-195 (*Kirchberg, Julie*).

9583 *Andrei, Osvalda* Il provvedimento anticristiano di Settimio SEVERO (SHA, Sev. 17,1): una tappa della 'divisione delle vie' fra giudaismo e cristianesimo. Henoch 23 (2001) 43-79.

9584 *Arndt, Timotheus* Eine jüdische Sicht auf die Trennung der Kirche von Israel. Leqach 1 (2001) 56-72 [BuBB 36,112].

9585 *Asbury, Bev. Allen* Can I still be a christian after Auschwitz?. "Good News" after Auschwitz?. 2001 ⇒377. 29-35.

9586 *Barkenings, Hans Joachim* Der Jom HaSchoa-gottesdienstliche Herausforderung für uns Christen?. KuI 16 (2001) 75-82.

9587 *Barnett, Victoria J.* The message and the means: some historical reflections on the "good news". "Good News" after Auschwitz?. 2001 ⇒377. 131-139.

9588 [E]**Bellis, Alice Ogden; Kaminsky, Joel S.** Jews, christians, and the theology of Hebrew scriptures. SBL Symposium 8: 2000 ⇒16,237. [R]ABR 49 (2001) 58-59 (*Tonson, Paul*).

9589 **Ben-Chorin, Schalom** Werke, 1: Jugend an der Isar. [E]*Lenzen, Verena*: Gü 2001, Kaiser xxii; 154 pp. 3-579-05340-X.

9590 *Ben-Chorin, Tovia* Universalismus im Judentum. Christen und Juden gemeinsam. 2001 ⇒352. 235-247.

9591 *Blanchetière, François* La contribution du Doyen Marcel SIMON à l'étude du judéo-christianisme. Le judéo-christianisme. 2001 ⇒484. 19-30.

9592 **Blanchetière, François** Enquête sur les racines juives du mouvement chrétien (30-135). Initiations: P 2001, Cerf 587 pp. €44.21. 2-204-06215-4 [RB 108,637].

9593 *Bodendorfer, Gerhard* Gott und Völker im Kontext von Exil und Leidbewältigung. Jud. 57 (2001) 162-181.

9594 *Bolgiani, Franco* Erik PETERSON e il giudeocristianesimo. Verus Israel. BCR 65: 2001 ⇒524. 339-374.

9595 *Boulton, Maureen* Anti-Jewish attitudes in twelfth-century French literature. Jews and christians in twelfth-century Europe. 2001 ⇒442. 234-254.

9596 *Boyarin, Daniel* Als Christen noch Juden waren: Überlegungen zu den jüdisch-christlichen Ursprüngen. KuI 16 (2001) 112-129.

9597 **Boyarin, Daniel** Dying for God: martyrdom and the making of christianity and Judaism. 1999 ⇒15,9806; 16,9831. [R]HeyJ 42 (2001) 81-83 (*Reinhartz, Adele*); MoTh 17 (2001) 393-395 (*Young, Robin Darling*); HebStud 42 (2001) 385-389 (*Eliav, Yaron Z.*); ASEs 18 (2001) 679-681 (*Neusner, Jacob*).

9598 **Boys, Mary C.** Has God only one blessing?: Judaism as a source for christian self-understanding. 2000 ⇒16,9832. [R]TS 62 (2001) 393-395 (*Gaudin, Gary A.*); RRT 8 (2001) 505-508 (*Wollaston, Isabel*); Theoforum 32 (2001) 246-248 (*Baum, Gregory*); AThR 83 (2001) 891-892 (*Sharp, Carolyn*).

9599 [E]**Brändle, Rudolf** Johannes CHRYSOSTOMUS: acht Reden gegen Juden. BGrL 41: 1995 ⇒11/2,7587; 12,8643. [R]JAC 44 (2001) 210-214 (*Schatkin, Margaret A.*).

9600 *Breuning, Wilhelm* Elemente einer nicht-antijudaistischen Christologie. Christen und Juden gemeinsam. 2001 ⇒352. 183-215.

9601 *Brunschwig-Ségal, Annette* "der jude habe si gemint": verbotene Beziehungen zwischen Juden und Christen im Spätmittelalter. Jud. 57 (2001) 182-203.

9602 *Bullock, Robert W.* After Auschwitz: Jews, Judaism, and christian worship. "Good News" after Auschwitz?. 2001 ⇒377. 69-83.

9603 *Cahn, Walter* The expulsion of the Jews as history and allegory in painting and sculpture of the twelfth and thirteenth centuries. Jews and christians in twelfth-century Europe. 2001 ⇒442. 94-109.

9604 *Carr, David R.* Judaism in christendom. The Blackwell reader in Judaism. Blackwell readings in religion. 2001 ⇒423. 114-127.

9605 **Carroll, James** CONSTANTINE's sword: the church and the Jews: a history. Boston 2001, Houghton M. xii; 756 pp. 0-395-77927-8. Bibl. 696-719.

9606 **Chalier, Catherine; Faessler, Marc** Judaïsme et christianisme: l'écoute en partage. Patrimoines: P 2001, Cerf 506 pp. 2-204-06740-7 [FV 101/2,89—Keller, Bernard].

9607 *Chazan, Robert* From the first crusade to the second: evolving perceptions of the Christian-Jewish conflict. Jews and christians in twelfth-century Europe. 2001 ⇒442. 46-62.

9608 *Chiappini, Azzolino* La sinagoga e la chiesa. RTLu 6 (2001) 319-34.

9609 *Chilton, Bruce* Judaism and christianity in the formative age. The Blackwell reader in Judaism. 2001 ⇒423. 86-100.

9610 *Chu, Jolene; Pellechia, James N.* Good news after Auschwitz: binding the brokenhearted. "Good News" after Auschwitz?. 2001 ⇒377. 85-98 [Isa 61,1-2].

9611 *Cohen, Jeremy* A 1096 complex?: constructing the first crusade in Jewish historical memory, medieval and modern. Jews and christians in twelfth-century Europe. 2001 ⇒442. 9-26.

9612 *Cohen, Shaye J.D.* Between Judaism and christianity: the semicircumcision of christians according to Bernard GUI, his sources and R. ELIEZER of Metz. HThR 94 (2001) 285-321.

9613 **Comeau, Geneviève** Juifs et chrétiens: le nouveau dialogue. Questions ouvertes: P 2001, Atelier 160 pp. RSpiritus 42 (2001) 462-463 (*Berder, Michel*).

Crossan, J. Wer tötete Jesus? 1999 ⇒5058.

9614 *Crouter, Richard* SCHLEIERMACHER's *Letters on the occasion* and the crisis of Berlin Jewry. FDIETRICH, W.: BJSt 329: 2001 ⇒24. 74-91.

9615 ECrüsemann, Frank; Theissmann, Udo Ich glaube an den Gott Israels: Fragen und Antworten zu einem Thema, das im christlichen Glaubensbekenntnis fehlt. Gü ²2001, Kaiser 159 pp. €11.90.

9616 **Cunningham, Philip A.** A story of shalom: the calling of Christians and Jews by a covenanting God. Studies in Judaism and Christianity: NY 2001, Paulist xiii; 106 pp. $12. 0-8091-4014-4. Bibl. 100-104.

9617 **Dabru emet:** parlons franchement: un dialogue religieux véritable entre juifs et chrétiens est-il maintenant possible?. Ist. 46 (2001) 416-423.

9618 **Dacy, Marianne** The separation of early christianity from Judaism. Diss. Sidney 2000, 300 pp [SIDIC 36,59ss—Pawlikowski, John T.].

9619 **Davies, W.D.** Christian engagements with Judaism. 1999 ⇒15,4676. RChH 70 (2001)148-149 (*Setzer, Claudia*).

9620 *Degenhardt, Johannes Joachim; Brandt, Henry; Sorg, Manfred* Möglichkeiten und Grenzen im christlich-jüdischen Verhältnis: Podiumsgespräch am 5. Juni 2000. Christen und Juden gemeinsam. 2001 ⇒352. 249-271.

9621 **Detmers, Achim** Reformation und Judentum: Israel-Lehren und Einstellungen zum Judentum von LUTHER bis zum frühen CALVIN. Judentum und Christentum 7: Stu 2001, Kohlhammer viii; 392 pp. €35. 3-17-016968-8. Diss. Gießen 2000 [RHPhR 82,370s—Arnold, M.].

9622 *Dirscherl, Erwin* Die je andere einzigartige Erwählung in der Zeit: die Besonderheit des christlich-jüdischen Verhältnisses und seine Konsequenzen für uns. BiLi 74 (2001) 218-230.

9623 *Dobbeler, Axel von* Wo liegen die Wurzeln des christlichen Antijudaismus?. ZNT 8 (2001) 42-47.

   EDonfried, K.arl P.; **Richardson, Peter** Judaism and christianity in first-century Rome 1998 ⇒259.

9624 *Dramm, Sabine* Wo die Kirche hätte schreien müssen: Dietrich BONHOEFFER und die Juden. Orien. 65 (2001) 148-153.

9625 *Einbinder, Susan* Signs of romance: Hebrew prose and the twelfth-century renaissance;

9626 *Elukin, Jonathan M.* The discovery of the self: Jews and conversion in the twelfth century. Jews and christians in twelfth-century Europe. 2001 ⇒442. 221-233/63-76.

9627 *Erlemann, Kurt* Einleitung zur Kontroverse. ZNT 8 (2001) 35-36.

   EFarmer, W. Anti-Judaism & the gospels 1999 ⇒464.

9628 *Favreau, Robert* Controverses judéo-chrétiennes et iconographie: l'apport des inscriptions. CRAI 3 (2001) 1267-1303.

9629 *Fiedler, Peter* Die Bibel—ein Buch für Juden und Christen. LS 52 (2001) 290-295.

9630 **Fields, Lee Morrison** 'An anonymous dialog with a Jew': an introduction and annotated translation. Diss. Hebrew Union 2001, 259 pp. 3003303.

9631 *Fontana, Raniero* Alla scuola d'Israele: variazioni sul tema dell'ascolto cristiano di Israele. Qol(I) 91 (2001) 2-5.

9632 *Frankemölle, Hubert* Christen und Juden gemeinsam ins dritte Jahrtausend?: Thesen und Impulse. Christen und Juden gemeinsam. 2001 ⇒352. 273-297.

9633 *Freyer, Thomas* Die Bedeutung der jüdisch-christlichen Tradition für die christliche Theologie: erkenntnistheoretische Anmerkungen im Kontext der Spätmoderne. ThG 44 (2001) 36-49.

9634 **Gardenal, Gianna** L'antigiudaismo nella letteratura cristianan antica e medievale. Shalom: Brescia 2001, Morcelliana 340 pp. €15.50. 88-372-1821-4. RStudi, Fatti, Ricerche 95 (2001) 13-14 (*Menestrina,, Giovanni*).

9635 *Greschat, Martin* Die Rolle des Vatikans in der NS-Zeit. Christen und Juden gemeinsam. 2001 ⇒352. 79-98.

9636 *Groppe, Lothar* Rom und die Juden. Theologisches 31 (2001) 245-260.

9637 *Guggenheim, Antoine* Entre lettre et esprit: Juifs et chrétiens autour de la bible aux IXe-XIIIe siècles. Com(F) 26/1 (2001) 75-88.

9638 **Halevi, Yossi Klein** At the entrance to the Garden of Eden: a Jew's search for God with Christians and Muslims in the Holy Land. NY 2001, Morrow xv; 315 pp. 0-688-16908-2.

9639 *Haverkamp, Alfred* Baptised Jews in German lands during the twelfth century. Jews and christians in twelfth-century Europe. 2001 ⇒442. 255-310.

9640 *Hennings, Ralph* EUSEBIUS von Emesa: zwei Osterpredigten gegen die Juden. StPatr 37. 2001 ⇒553. 535-542.

9641 *Henrix, Hans Hermann* Canon—revelation—reception: problems of a biblically oriented theology in the face of Israel. Anti-Judaism and the fourth gospel. 2001 ⇒5747. 533-548;

9642 Mit einem Tumor im Gedächtnis: Erfahrungen und Herausforderungen des christlich-jüdischen Dialogs. Christen und Juden gemeinsam. 2001 ⇒352. 13-46.

9643 ^E**Henrix, Hans Hermann; Kraus, Wolfgang** Die Kirchen und das Judentum, 2: Dokumente von 1986 bis 2000. Pd 2001, Bonifatius 1036 pp. €49.95. 3-89710-122-X. Buch u. CD-ROM. ^RLuThK 25 (2001) 217-219 (*Stolle, Volker*).

9644 *Heschel, Susannah* How the Jews invented Jesus and Muhammed: christianity and Islam in the work of Abraham GEIGER. ^FDIETRICH, W. BJSt 329: 2001 ⇒24. 49-73.

9645 **Hilton, Michael** 'Wie es sich christelt, so jüdelt es sich': 2000 Jahre christlicher Einfluß auf das jüdische Leben. 2000 ⇒16,9876. ^RFrRu 8 (2001) 63-65 (*Thoma, Clemens*).

9646 **Horbury, William** Jews and christians: in contact and controversy. 1998 ⇒14,8978. ^RRBLit 3 (2001) 327-330 (*Visotzky, Burton L.*); JBL 119 (2000) 780-782 (*Visotsky, Burton L.*).

9647 **Horoszewicz, Michal** Przez dwa millenia do rzymskiej Synagogi: Szkice o ewolucji postawy Kosciola katolickiego wobec Zydów i judaizmu. Kosciól a Zydzi i Judaizm 7: Wsz 2001, Wydawnictwa Uniw. Wyszynkiego 452 pp. 83-7072-172-9. Bibl. 415-437. **P**.

9648 **Huguet, Marie-Thérèse** Un peuple unique pour le Dieu unique: 'Israël'. P 2001, Parole et S. 120 pp. €12. 2-84573-046-2. ^REeV 41 (2001) 28 (*Rastoin, Cécile*).

9649 *Jansen, Reiner* Die Antwort blieb aus: Leo BAECKs "Wesen des Judentums" als Reaktion auf Adolf VON HARNACKs "Wesen des Christentums". Jud. 57 (2001) 94-119.

9650 *Jefford, Clayton N.* Reflections on the role of Jewish christianity in second-century Antioch [BuBB 36,113];

9651 *Jones, F. Stanley* HEGESIPPUS as a source for the history of Jewish christianity [BuBB 36,112]. Le judéo-christianisme. 2001 ⇒484. 147-167/201-212;

9652 Jewish-Christian chiliastic restoration in Pseudo-Clementine Recognitions 1.27-71. Restoration. JSJ.S 72: 2001 ⇒319. 529-547.

9653 *Jordan, William Chester* Adolescence and conversion in the Middle Ages: a research agenda. Jews and christians in twelfth-century Europe. 2001 ⇒442. 77-93.

9654 **Joubert, Jean-Marc** Foi juive et croyance chrétienne. Midrash: P 2001, Desclée de B. 339 pp.

9655 **Jucquois, Guy; Sauvage, Pierre** L'invention de l'antisémitisme racial: l'implication des catholiques français et belges (1850-2000). Science et enjeux 2: Lv(N) 2001, Academia Bruylant 513 pp. 2-87209-610-8.

9656 *Kampling, Rainer* Bilder des Missverstehens: Dokumente der Judenfeindschaft in der europäischen Kunst. Christen und Juden gemeinsam. 2001 ⇒352. 99-129.

9657 ᴱ**Kampling, Rainer** Nun steht aber diese Sache im Evangelium...": zur Frage nach den Anfängen des christlichen Antijudaismus. 1999 ⇒15,319. ᴿFrRu 8 (2001) 217-218 (*Oberforcher, Robert*); ThLZ 126 (2001) 523-525 (*Sänger, Dieter*).

9658 *Kessler, Edward* Un avenir différent: juifs et chrétiens peuvent-ils tirer des leçons de l'histoire?. SIDIC 34/2 (2001) 5-12;

9659 The exegetical encounter between the Greek Church Fathers and the Palestinian rabbis. StPatr 34. 2001 ⇒553. 395-412.

9660 Kirche und Israel: ein Beitrag der reformatorischen Kirchen Europas zum Verhältnis von Christen und Juden. ᴱ**Schwier, H.**: Fra 2001, Lembeck 161 pp. €5. 3-87476-392-7. Im Auftrag des Exekutivausschusses für die Leuenberger Kirchengemeinschaft.

9661 **Klappert, Bertold** Miterben der Verheißung: Beiträge zum jüdisch-christlichen Dialog. NBST 25: 2000 ⇒16,9890. ᴿFrRu 8 (2001) 298-299 (*Hoffmann, Klaus*).

9662 *Knight, Henry F.* The holy ground of hospitality: good news for a Shoah-tempered world. "Good News" after Auschwitz?. 2001 ⇒377. 99-116.

9663 *Kraft, Robert A.* Setting the stage and framing some central questions. JSJ 32 (2001) 371-395.

9664 *Lauer, Simon* Christologie ohne Antijudaismus?: ist aus jüdischer Sicht ein Neuansatz denkbar?. Christen und Juden gemeinsam. 2001 ⇒352. 217-233.

9665 **Lemke, Hella** Judenchristentum—zwischen Ausgrenzung und Integration: zur Geschichte eines exegetischen Begriffes. Hamburger Theologische Studien 25: Müns 2001, Lit x; 329 pp. 3-8258-5759-X.

9666 *Lenzen, Verena* Wesen der Erinnerung und jüdische Gedächtniskultur. LebZeug 56 (2001) 254-264.

9667 *Leonardi, Giovanni; Girolami, Maurizio* Il giudeo-cristianesimo nel I e II sec. d.C.: IX Convegno di Studi neotestamentari 13-15 settembre 2001, Napoli. StPat 48 (2001) 631-640.

9668 *Lémonon, Jean-Pierre* Un exégète catholique enseigné par la tradition juive. LV.F 56 (2001) 365-373.

9669 **Lipton, Sara** Images of intolerance: the representation of Jews and Judaism in the bible moralisée. 1999 ⇒15,9869; 16,9914. [R]HeyJ 42 (2001) 85-86 (*Swanson, R.N.*).

9670 *Locke, Hubert G.* Christian integrity after Auschwitz. "Good News" after Auschwitz?. 2001 ⇒377. 37-42.

9671 **Magonet, Jonathan** Abraham—Jesus—Mohammed: interreligiöser Dialog aus jüdischer Perspektive. GTB 735: 2000 ⇒16,9920. [R]ÖR 50 (2001) 414-415 (*Graebe, Uwe*).

9672 **Manns, Frédéric** Le Judéo-christianisme: mémoire ou prophétie?. ThH 112: 2000 ⇒16,9924. [R]Brotéria 152 (2001) 105-106 (*Silva, I. Ribeiro da*).

9673 *Menestrina, Giovanni* Antigiudaismo nella letteratura cristiana. Studi Fatti Ricerche 95 (2001) 13-14.

9674 **Mimouni, Simon Claude** Le judéo-christianisme ancien: essais historiques. 1998 ⇒14,9002; 15,9877. [R]OCP 67 (2001) 486-489 (*Poggi, V.*); EstB 59 (2001) 409-412 (*Urbán, A.*); Henoch 23 (2001) 389-391 (*Gianotto, Claudio*).

9675 *Mußner, Franz* Das jüdische Nein zu Jesus und zum Evangelium: Gründe und Konsequenzen für die Juden. TThZ 110 (2001) 47-66.

9676 *Neuhaus, Richard John* 'Salvation is from the Jews'. First things 117 (2001) 17-22.

9677 **Neusner, Jacob; Chilton, Bruce** Jewish and christian doctrines: the classics compared. 2000 ⇒16,9934. [R]CBQ 63 (2001) 583-584 (*Jacobson, Arland D.*).

9678 *Ochs, Peter* Ethical monotheism when the word is wounded: Wendell Dietrich reread. [F]DIETRICH, W., BJSt 329: 2001 ⇒24. 15-45.

9679 *Parente, Fausto Verus Israel* di Marcel SIMON a cinquant'anni dalla pubblicazione. Verus Israel. BCR 65: 2001 ⇒524. 19-46.

9680 *Petersen, William L.* Constructing the matrix of Judaic christianity from texts [BuBB 36,112];

9681 *Pixner, Bargil* Nazoreans on Mount Zion (Jerusalem) [BuBB 36, 112]. Le judéo-christianisme. 2001 ⇒484. 126-144/289-316.

9682 Il popolo ebraico e le sue sacre scritture nella bibbia cristiana. Documenti Vaticani: Città del Vaticano 2001, Libreria Editrice Vaticana 213 pp. 88-209-7218-2. Pontificia Commissio Biblica.

9683 [E]**Porter, Stanley E.; Pearson, Brook W.R.** Christian-Jewish relations through the centuries. JSNT.S 192: 2000 ⇒16,433. [R]RRT 8 (2001) 502-505 (*Wollaston, Isabel*).

9684 *Rajak, Tessa* Jews, pagans and christians in late antique Sardis: models of interaction. The Jewish dialogue. 2001 ⇒199. 447-462.

9685 *Ramelli, Ilaria* Elementi comuni della polemica antgiudaica e di quella anticristiana fra I e II sec. d.C. StRo 49 (2001) 245-274.

9686 *Rau, Johannes* Ansprache von Bundespräsident Johannes RAU am 16. Februar 2000 vor der Knesset in Jerusalem. Christen und Juden gemeinsam. 2001 ⇒352. 301-310.

9687 *Räisänen, Heikki* MARCION and the origins of christian anti-Judaism: a reappraisal. Challenges to biblical interpretation. BiblInterp 59: 2001 <1997> ⇒200. 191-205.

9688 *Reicke, Bo Ivar* Judeo-christianity and the Jewish establishment, A.D. 33-66. Re-examining Paul's letters. 2001 <1984> ⇒6257. 9-15.

9689 *Reimer, Ingo* Das Dogma von der leiblichen Aufnahme Mariens in den Himmel durch Pius XII. im Jahre 1950: auch der Versuch einer Antwort auf die Gräuel des Nationalsozialismus?. KuI 16 (2001) 83-85.

9690 **Remaud, Michel** Chrétiens et juifs entre le passé et l'avenir. 2000 ⇒ 16,9945. ᴿSIDIC 34/2 (2001) 28-30 (*Cuche, Jacqueline*);

9691 Cristiani ed ebrei tra passato e avvenire. Bo 2001, EDB 158 pp.

9692 *Rendtorff, Rolf* Theologische Vorarbeiten zu einem christlich-jüdischen Dialog;

9693 Christliche Identität in Israels Gegenwart;

9694 Die Bibel Israels als Buch der Christen;

9695 Israel, die Völker und die Kirche. Der Text in seiner Endgestalt. 2001 ⇒201. 1-19/20-29/30-46/47-58.

9696 *Rittner, Carol* What can a christian say about forgiveness after Auschwitz?. "Good News" after Auschwitz?. 2001 ⇒377. 117-128.

9697 *Rittner, Carol; Roth, John K.* The courage to try. "Good News" after Auschwitz?. 2001 ⇒377. 187-191.

9698 *Roentgen, Markus* Abgeschlossene oder unabgeschlossene Vergangenheit?: die Novemberpogrome und die Vernichtung der europäischen Juden als Krise der Rede von Gott—Eingedenken und Verantwortung. LebZeug 56 (2001) 287-304.

9699 *Rosenblatt, Eloise* Canonizing Edith STEIN and recognizing catholic antisemitism. "Good News" after Auschwitz?. 2001 ⇒377. 45-68.

9700 **Sandmel, David Fox; Catalano, Rosann M.; Leighton, Christopher M.** Irreconcilable differences?: a learning resource for Jews and Christians. Boulder, CO 2001, Westview xii; 228 pp. $22. 0-8133-6568-6. Bibl. 211-214.

9701 *Schaller, Berndt, al.,* Judentum und Christentum. RGG², 4: I-K. 2001 ⇒664. 628-637.

9702 **Sicker, Martin** Between Rome and Jerusalem: 300 years of Roman-Judaean relations. Westport, CONN 2001, Praeger xii; 201 pp. 0-27-5-97140-6. Bibl. 191-194.

9703 *Signer, Michael A.* Conclusion. Jews and christians in twelfth-century Europe. 2001 ⇒442. 355-359.

9704 *Smith, Stephen D.* The failure of goodness: in search of the christian christian. "Good News" after Auschwitz?. 2001 ⇒377. 21-28.

9705 *Solomon, Norman* Auf dem Wege zu einer jüdischen Theologie des jüdisch-christlich-muslimischen Gespräches. Jud. 57 (2001) 269-283.

9706 **Spence, Stephen** The separation of the church and the synagogue in first-century Rome. Diss. Fuller Sem. 2001, 461 pp. 3006184.

9707 *Stacy, Robert C.* Jews and christians in twelfth-century England: some dynamics of a changing relationship. Jews and christians in twelfth-century Europe. 2001 ⇒442. 340-354.

9708 *Stemberger, Günter* Judenchristen. RAC 19. 2001 ⇒660. 228-245.

9709 *Stöhr, Martin* Schritte zur Erneuerung der Beziehungen von Juden und Christen in evangelischer Sicht. Christen und Juden gemeinsam. 2001 ⇒352. 47-77.

9710 *Theobald, Michael* Mit verbundenen Augen?: Kirche und Synagoge nach dem Neuen Testament. Studien zum Römerbrief. WUNT 136: 2001 ⇒219. 367-395.

9711 *Van Engen, John* Introduction: Jews and christians together in the twelfth century. Jews and christians in twelfth-century Europe. 2001 ⇒442. 1-8.

9712 *Van Henten, Jan Willem; Schaller, Berndt* Christianization of ancient Jewish writings. JSJ 32 (2001) 369-370.

9713 *Vanlaningham, Michael G.* Should the church evangelize Israel?: a response to Franz MUSSNER and other *Sonderweg* proponents. TrinJ 22 (2001) 197-217.

9714 *Van Luyn, A.H.* Gedeelde hoop in een verdeelde wereld: gemeenschappelijk spreken vanuit christendom en jodendom over maatschappelijke kwesties. TTh 41 (2001) 117-127.

9715 *Visotzky, Burton L.* Jewish-christianity in rabbinic documents: an examination of *Leviticus-Rabbah*. Le judéo-christianisme. 2001 ⇒ 484. 335-349 [BuBB 36,46].

9716 *Walter, Meinrad* Antijudaismus in der geistlichen Musik?: am Beispiel der Passionskompositionen von Johann Sebastian BACH. Christen und Juden gemeinsam. 2001 ⇒352. 131-150.

9717 **Whale, Hedwig** Ebrei e cristiani in dialogo: un patrimonio comune da vivere. Cammini nello Spirito, Teologia 62: Mi 2001, Paoline 203 pp. €14.46 [R]CredOg 125-126 (2001) 173-174 (*Cappelletto, Gianni*).

9718 *Ziolkowski, Jan M.* Put in no-man's land: GIUBERT of Nogent's accusations against a judaizing and Jew-supporting christian. Jews and christians in twelfth-century Europe. 2001 ⇒442. 110-122.

XVI. Religiones parabiblicae

M1.1 Gnosticismus classicus

9719 *Edwards, M.J.* Hebraism, Hellenism and the Gnostic fall. StPatr 35. 2001 ⇒553. 222-226.

9720 *Filoramo, Giovanni* Il sacrificio nei testi gnostici. ASEs 18 (2001) 211-223.

9721 *Holzhausen, Jens* Gnostizismus, Gnosis, Gnostiker: ein Beitrag zur antiken Terminologie. JAC 44 (2001) 58-74.

9722 *Hyldahl, Jesper* "Gnosticisme" eller "gnosis"?: overvejelser over en vanskelig forskningsterminologi. DTT 64 (2001) 111-129.

9723 *Inglebert, Hervé* L'histoire des hérésies chez les hérésiologues. L'historiographie de l'église. 2001 ⇒541. 105-125 [BuBB 36,83].

9724 **Jonas, Hans** Gnosis: die Botschaft des fremden Gottes. ᴱ*Wiese, Christian* 1999 ⇒16,9998. ᴿThLZ 126 (2001) 148-151 (*Kartel, Rainer*).

9725 **Koslowski, Peter** Philosophien der Offenbarung: antiker Gnostizismus, Franz von BAADER, SCHELLING. Pd 2001, Schöningh xxxiii; 918 pp. 3-506-74795-9.

9726 **Lancellotti, Maria Grazia** The Naassenes: a Gnostic identity among Judaism, christianity, classical and ancient Near Eastern traditions. FARG 35: 2000 ⇒16,10003. ᴿRHR 218 (2001) 412-413 (*Turcan, Robert*).

9727 **Lancri, Solomon** Introduzione allo studio della dottrina segreta. ᵀ*Orafi, Neda*: Teosofia: T 2001, Valerio 87 pp. 88-88132-31-7.

9728 **Magris, Aldo** La logica del pensiero gnostico. Scienze delle religioni: 1997 ⇒13,9314. ᴿApocrypha 12 (2001) 284-85 (*Bechtle, G.*).

9729 **Markschies, Christoph** Die Gnosis. Beck'sche Reihe 2173: Mü 2001, Beck 127 pp. 3-406-44773-2.

9730 *Pearson, Birger A.* Early christianity and gnosticism in the history of religions. StTh 55 (2001) 81-106.

9731 **Rudolph, Kurt** Gnosis und spätantike Religionsgeschichte: gesammelte Aufsätze. 1996 ⇒12,147; 14,9075. ᴿZRGG 53 (2001) 282-283 (*Klein, Wassilios*);

9732 La gnosi: natura e storia di una religione tardoantica. 2000 ⇒16, 10011. ᴿAnton. 76 (2001) 574-575 (*Nobile, Marco*); CivCatt 152/4 (2001) 99-101 (*Prato, G.L.*).

9733 *Scholer, David M.* Bibliographia gnostica: Supplementum II/4. NT 43 (2001) 39-88.

9734 *Shoemaker, Stephen J.* Rethinking the "Gnostic Mary": Mary of Nazareth and Mary of Magdala in early christian tradition. JECS 9 (2001) 555-595.

9735 *Tite, Philip L.* Categorical designations and methodological reductionism: Gnosticism as case study. Method and Theory in the Study of Religion 13 (2001) 269-292 [BuBB 36,82].

9736 **Tröger, Karl-Wolfgang** Die Gnosis—Heilslehre und Ketzerglaube. FrB 2001, Herder 221 pp. €3.50. 3-4510-4953-8.

9737 **Turner, John D.** Sethian Gnosticism and the Platonic tradition. Bibliothèque copte de Nag Hammadi, Etudes 6: Québec 2001, Presses de l'Univ. Laval xix; 842 pp. €80. 2-7637-7834-8 [RB 110,159].

9738 **Williams, Michael Allen** Rethinking 'Gnosticism': an argument for dismantling a dubious category. 1996 ⇒12,8754; 14,9084. ᴿRBLit 3 (2001) 492-495 (*Zyla, Roy T.*).

9739 *Wilson, Robert McL.* Gnosticism. Religious diversity. BiSe 79: 2001 ⇒398. 164-181.

M1.3 Valentinus; Corpus hermeticum; Orphismus

9740 *Douglass, J. Robert* The epistle to Rheginos: christian-gnostic teaching on the resurrection. Looking into the future. 2001 ⇒505. 115-23.

9741 *Edwards, M.J.* Pauline platonism: the myth of Valentinus;

9742 *Förster, N.* Mark the magician and Valentinian syncretism. StPatr 35. 2001 ⇒553. 205-221/227-233.

9743 **Förster, Niclas** Marcus Magus: Kult, Lehre und Gemeindeleben einer valentianischen Gnostikergruppe: Sammlung der Quellen und Kommentar. WUNT 114: 1999 ⇒15,9937; 16,10028. ᴿThPh 76 (2001) 576-9 (*Wucherpfennig, A.*); ThLZ 126 (2001) 64-7 (*Frenschkowski, Marco*); Apocrypha 12 (2001) 286-287 (*Dubois, J.-D.*).

9744 *Neugebauer-Wölk, Monika* 'Denn dis ist müglich, lieber Sohn!': zur esoterischen Übersetzungstradition des Corpus Hermeticum in der frühen Neuzeit. ᶠFAIVRE, A. 2001 ⇒29. 131-144.

9745 **O'Regan, Cyril** Gnostic return in modernity. Albany 2001, SUNY 288 pp. $21.32. 0-7914-5022-8 [BuBB 36,86].

9746 *Sabbah, Guy* Sozomène et la politique religieuse des Valentiniens. L'historiographie de l'église. 2001 ⇒541. 293-394 [BuBB 36,87].

M1.5 **Mani,** *dualismus*; **Mandaei**

9747 *Alcock, Anthony* The sale of Mani. VigChr 55 (2001) 99-100.

9748 *BeDuhn, Jason* The metabolism of salvation: Manichaean concepts of human physiology. Light and darkness. 2001 ⇒421. 5-37.

9749 **BeDuhn, Jason David** The Manichaean body: in discipline and ritual. 2000 ⇒16,10030. ᴿOLZ 96 (2001) 289-290 (*Schmidt-Glintzer, Helwig*).

9750 *Bennett, Byard* DIDYMUS the Blind's knowledge of Manichaeism;

9751 *Iuxta unum latus erat terra tenebrarum*: the division of primordial space in anti-Manichaean writers' descriptions of the Manichaean cosmogony;

9752 *Coyle, J. Kevin* Prolegomena to a study of women in Manichaeism. Light and darkness. 2001 ⇒421. 38-67/68-78/79-92.

9753 *Dubois, Jean-Daniel* La redécouverte actuelle du manichéisme. ConnPE 83 (2001) 3-15.

9754 ᴱ**Funk, Wolf-Peter** Kephalaia, I/2: Lfg. 13/14. Manichäische Handschriften der Staatlichen Museen zu Berlin I/2. 1999 ⇒16,10034. ᴿApocrypha 12 (2001) 289-291 (*Dubois, J.-D.*);

9755 Lfg. 15/16. 2000 ⇒16,10035. ᴿWZKM 91 (2001) 367-369 (*Hutter, Manfred*).

9756 *Gardner, Iain* The reconstruction of Mani's Epistles from three Coptic codices (Ismant el-Kharab and Medinet Madi). Light and darkness. 2001 ⇒421. 93-104.

9757 *Griffith, Sidney H.* The thorn among the tares: MANI and Manichaeism in the works of St. EPHRAEM the Syrian. StPatr 35. 2001 ⇒553. 395-427.

9758 *Gulácsi, Zsuzsanna* Reconstructing Manichaean book paintings through the technique of their makers: the case of The work of the religion scene on MIK III 4974 recto;

9759 *Harrison, Geoffrey; BeDuhn, Jason* The authenticity and doctrine of (Ps.?)Mani's *Letter to Menoch*. Light and darkness. 2001 ⇒421. 105-127/128-172.

9760 **Heuser, Manfred; Klimkeit, Hans-Joachim** Studies in Manichaean literature and art. NHMS 46: 1998 ⇒14,339. ᴿVigChr 55 (2001) 218-220 (*Lieu, Samuel N.C.*).

9761 *Koch, Carsten* Die Nerigpolemiken und der Kanonisierungsprozeß des Johannesbuches der Mandäer als Beispiele für unterschiedliche Formen der Textbearbeitung im Dienste religiöser Existenzsicherung. HBO 31 (2001) 223-248.

9762 *Levitt, Stephan Hillyer* Where does "Barlaam and Josaphat" take place?. OCP 67 (2001) 263-273.

9763 *Lieu, Samuel N.C.* Lexicographica Manichaica: Dictionary of Manichaean texts, vol. 1: texts from the Roman empire (texts in Syriac, Greek, Coptic and Latin)—an interim report and discussion on methodology. Augustine and Manichaeism. 2001 ⇒550. 137-147.

9764 *Mirecki, Paul* Manichaean allusions to ritual and magic: spells for invisibility in the Coptic *Kephalaia*;

9765 *Mirecki, Paul; BeDuhn, Jason* Introduction: the light and the darkness: studies in Manichaeism and its world. Light and darkness. 2001 ⇒173-180/1-4.

9766 *Poirier, Paul-Hubert* Une nouvelle hypothèse sur le titre des psaumes manichéens dits de Thomas. Apocrypha 12 (2001) 9-27.

9767 *Richter, S.G.* Bemerkungen zu verschiedenen "Jesusfiguren" im Manichäismus. Augustine and Manichaeism. 2001 ⇒550. 174-184.

9768 **Richter, Siegfried G.** The Manichaean Coptic papyri in the Chester Beatty Library: Psalm Book II, Fasc. 2: die Herakleides-Psalmen. Corpus Fontium Manichaeorum, Series Coptica, I/2/2: 1998 ⇒16, 10041. [R]Enchoria 27 (2001) 243-254 (*Schenke, Hans-Martin*).

9769 *Scibona, Concetta Giuffré* How monotheistic is Mani's dualism?: once more on monotheism and dualism in Manichaean gnosis. Numen 48 (2001) 444-467.

9770 *Scopello, Madeleine* Femmes et propagande dans le manichéisme. ConnPE 83 (2001) 35-44.

9771 *Sundermann, Werner* Das Manichäerkapitel des Skand Gumanig WIZAR in der Darstellung und Deutung Jean de MENASCES. Augustine and Manichaeism. 2001 ⇒550. 325-337.

9772 On human races, semi-human beings and monsters;

9773 A Manichaean liturgical instruction on the act of almsgiving. Light and darkness. 2001 ⇒421. 181-199/200-208.

9774 *Tardieu, Michel* Les Symmachiens de Marius VICTORINUS et ceux du manichéen FAUSTUS. Le judéo-christianisme. 2001 ⇒484. 322-334 [BuBB 36,89].

9775 *Tremblay, Xavier* Pour une histoire de la Sérinde: le manichéisme parmi les peuples et religions d'Asie Centrale d'après les sources primaires. SÖAW.PH 690; Veröffentlichungen der Kommission für Iranistik 28: W 2001, Verlag der Österreichischen Akademie der Wissenschaften vi; 337 pp. 3-7001-3034-1. Bibl. 247-275.

9776 *Tubach, Jürgen; Zakeri, Mohsen* MANI's name. Augustine and Manichaeism. NHMS 49: 2001 ⇒550. 272-286.

9777 *Van Oort, Johannes* Le Codex manichéen de Cologne et son importance. ConnPE 83 (2001) 17-24.

9778 [T]**Vermes, Mark** HEGEMONIUS: Acta Archelai: (the acts of Archelaus). Manichaean Studies 4: Turnhout 2001, Brepols xii; 177 pp.

€45. 2-503-51156-2. Bibl. 160-171; introd., comm. *Samuel N.C. Lieu; K. Kaatz.*

9779 *Wurst, Gregor* Le psautier manichéen copte de Medinet Mâdi. ConnPE 83 (2001) 25-34.

9780 *Zieme, Peter* A Manichaean-Turkic dispute in runic script. The light and the darkness. NHMS 50: 2001 ⇒421. 209-219.

M2.1 Nag Hammadi, *generalia*

9781 **Funk, Wolf-Peter** Concordance des textes de Nag Hammadi, les codices VIII et IX. 1997 ⇒14,9116. [R]BiOr 58 (2001) 141-142 (*Beltz, Walter*).

9782 *Goehring, James E.* The provenance of the Nag Hammadi codices once more. StPatr 35. 2001 ⇒553. 234-253.

9783 [E]**Schenke, Hans-Martin; Bethge, Hans-Gebhard; Kaiser, Ursula Ulrike** Nag Hammadi deutsch, 1: NHC I,1-V,1. Die griechischen christlichen Schriftsteller der ersten Jahrhunderte 8: B 2001, De Gruyter xxi; 397 pp. €98. 3-11-017234-8. Eingeleitet, übersetzt von Mitgliedern d. Berliner Arbeitskreises f. koptisch-gnostische Studien.

9784 *Valantasis, Richard* Nag Hammadi and asceticism: theory and practice. StPatr 35. 2001 ⇒553. 172-190.

M2.2 *Evangelium etc. Thomae*—The Gospel of Thomas

9785 [E]**Bremmer, Jan Nicolaas** The Apocryphal Acts of Thomas. Studies in Early Christian Apocrypha 6: Lv 2001, Peeters xii; 189 pp. 90-429-1070-4. Bibl. 171-175:

9786 *Adamik, Tamás* The serpent in the Acts of Thomas 115-124;

9787 *Bolyki, János* Human nature and character as moving factors of plot in the Acts of Thomas 91-100;

9788 *Bremmer, Jan N.* The Acts of Thomas: place, date and women 74-90;

9789 The apocryphal Acts: authors, place, time and readership 149-170;

9790 Bibliography of Acts of Thomas 171-175.

9791 **Chartrand-Burke, Tony** The infancy gospel of Thomas: the text, its origins, and its transmission. Diss. Toronto, Univ. 2001, [D]*Vaage, L.E.* 448 pp [RTL 33,637].

9792 *Connors-Nelson, Catherine* The way of perfection in the *Acts of Thomas.* Studies in Spirituality 11 (2001) 144-165.

9793 *Czachesz, István* The bride of the demon: narrative strategies of self-definition in the Acts of Thomas. The apocryphal Acts of Thomas. Studies on early christian apocrypha 6: 2001 ⇒9785. 36-52.

9794 **DeConick, April D.** Seek to see Him: ascent & vision mysticism in the gospel of Thomas. SVigChr 33: 1996 ⇒12,8792; 13,9376. ᴿHenoch 23 (2001) 391-393 (*Gianotto, Claudio*).

9795 *Hilhorst, A.* The heavenly palace in the Acts of Thomas;

9796 *Klijn, A.F.J.* The Acts of Thomas revisited. The apocryphal Acts of Thomas. 2001 ⇒9785. 53-64/1-10.

9797 *Laurence, Patrick* Eglise, femmes et pouvoir dans les *Actes de Thomas*. RevAg 42 (2001) 193-220.

9798 *Luttikhuizen, Gerard P.* The hymn of Jude Thomas, the apostle, in the country of the Indians (ATh 108-113). The apocryphal Acts of Thomas. 2001 ⇒9785. 101-114.

9799 *Meyer, Marvin* Albert SCHWEITZER and the image of Jesus in the *Gospel of Thomas*. Jesus then and now. 2001 ⇒483. 72-90.

9800 *Nagel, Peter* Das Gleichnis vom zerbrochenen Krug: EvThom Logion 97. ZNW 92 (2001) 229-256.

9801 **Patterson, Stephen J.; Robinson, James McConkey** The fifth gospel: the gospel of Thomas comes of age. ᵀ*Bethge, Hans-Gebhard*: 1998 ⇒14,9128. ᴿJBL 119 (2000) 385-386 (*Valantasis, Richard*).

9802 *Pesthy, Monika* Thomas, the slave of the Lord. The apocryphal Acts of Thomas. 2001 ⇒9785. 65-73.

9803 *Robinson, James M.; Heil, Christoph* The lilies of the field: Saying 36 of the gospel of Thomas and secondary accretions in Q 12.22b-31. NTS 47 (2001) 1-25 [Mt 6,25-34; Lk 12,22-31].

9804 *Schenke, Hans-Martin* Bemerkungen zu #71 des Thomas-Evangeliums. Enchoria 27 (2001) 120-126.

9805 *Sellew, Philip* Thomas christianity: scholars in quest of a community;

9806 *Van den Bosch, Lourens P.* India and the apostolate of St. Thomas. The apocryphal Acts of Thomas. 2001 ⇒9785. 11-35/125-148.

9807 **Zöckler, Thomas** Jesu Lehren im Thomasevangelium. NHMS 47: 1999 ⇒15,9988; 16,10062. ᴿJThS 52 (2001) 315-318 (*Wilson, R.McL.*); CBQ 63 (2001) 569-570 (*Timbie, Janet*).

M2.3 *Singula scripta*—**Various titles** [⇒K3.4]

9808 ᴱ**Barry, Catherine** Zostrien (NH VIII,1). BCNH.T 24: 2000 ⇒16, 10064. ᴿMSR 58/2 (2001) 70-71 (*Cannuyer, Christian*); JThS 52 (2001) 875-877 (*Wilson, R. McL.*).

9809 ᴱ**Funk, Wolf-Peter Paul; Gianotto, Claudio** Melchisédek (NH IX, 1): oblation, baptême et vision dans la gnose séthienne. ᵀ*Mahé, Jean-Pierre*: BCNH.T 28: Lv 2001, Peeters xix; 188 pp. €60. 90-429-1021-6. Bibl. ix-xvi.

9810 ^{TE}**Plisch, Uwe-Karsten** Die Auslegung der Erkenntnis. TU 142: 1996 ⇒12,8798; 13,9407. ^RJAC 44 (2001) 234-237 (*Wurst, Gregor*).

9811 ^E**Roberge, Michel** La Paraphrase de Sem (NH VII,1). BCNH.T 25: 2000 ⇒16,10071. ^RJThS 52 (2001) 872-875 (*Wilson, R. McL.*); BiOr 58 (2001) 670-672 (*Beltz, Walter*).

9812 ^{ET}**Schenke, Hans-Martin** Das Philippus-Evangelium (Nag-Hammadi-Codex II,3). TU 143: 1997 ⇒13,9408. ^RJAC 44 (2001) 230-234 (*Krause, Martin*).

9813 *Valantasis, Richard* Demons, adversaries, devils, fishermen: the asceticism of *Authoritative teaching* (NHL, VI, 3) in the context of Roman asceticism. JR 81 (2001) 549-565 [BuBB 36,85].

9814 **Williams, Francis E.** Mental perception: a commentary on NHC VI,4: the concept of our great power. NHMS 51: Lei 2001, Brill lix; 284 pp. $103. 90-04-11692-3. Bibl. 264-271.

M3.2 Religio comparativa

9815 *Aschim, Anders* Den "nye religionshistoriske skole" i nytestamentlig forskning. TTK 72 (2001) 37-50.

9816 *Assmann, Jan* Das Geheimnis der Wahrheit: das Konzept der 'doppelten Religion' und die Erfindung der Religionsgeschichte. AfR 3 (2001) 108-134.

9817 **Bernal, Martin** Black Athena writes back: Martin Bernal responds to his critics. ^E*Moore, David Chioni*: Durham, NC 2001, Duke University Press xxvi; 550 pp. 0-8223-2706-6. Bibl. 473-534.

9818 **Kolakowski, Leszek** Religion: if there is no God...: on God, the devil, sin and other worries of the so-called philosophy of religion. South Bend, Indiana 2001, St. Augustine's vii; 9-221 pp. 1-890318-87-6.

9819 *Lüpkes, Gerhard* Kritische Gedanken zur christlichen Religion. Irreale Glaubensinhalte. 2001 ⇒1066. 8-22.

9820 **Slaczka, Zbigniew** Offenbarung und Heil in den nichtchristlichen Religionen?: eine Untersuchung zu W. PANNENBERG, H.R. SCHLETTE und G. GÄDE: EHS.T 718: Fra 2001, Lang 218 pp. 3-631-38013-5. Bibl. 207-218.

9821 *Wendt, Matthias* Das All, der ewige Keim;

9822 Wiedergeburt?;

9823 Es gibt noch ein anderes Glauben. Irreale Glaubensinhalte. 2001 ⇒ 1066. 39-46/61-64/65-66.

M3.5 Religiones mundi cum christianismo comparatae

9824 **Dhavamony, Mariasusai** Christian theology of religions: a systematic reflection on the christian understanding of world religions. Studies in Intercultural History of Christianity 108; Bern [2]2001, Lang 252 pp. 3-906765-81-4.

9825 **Favaro, Gaetano** Letture della Bibbia nel contesto religioso e socioculturale dell'India contemporanea. Interpretare la Bibbia oggi 53: Brescia 2001, Queriniana 188 pp. €12.91. 88-399-2485-X. Bibl. 184-185.

9826 **Ratzinger, J.** La chiesa, Israele e le religioni del mondo. Saggi teologici: CinB 1998, San Paolo 82 pp. €6.20. [R]Sacrum Ministerium 6/1 (2001) 175-176 (*Moraglia, Francesco*).

9827 **Seelig, Gerald** Religionsgeschichtliche Methode in Vergangenheit und Gegenwart: Studien zur Geschichte und Methode des religionsgeschichtlichen Vergleichs in der neutestamentlichen Wissenschaft. Arbeiten zur Bibel und ihrer Geschichte 7: Lp 2001, Evang. Verl.-Anst. 354 pp. €38.50. 3-374-01909-9.

M3.6 *Sectae*—Cults

9828 **Adamo, David Tuesday** Reading and interpreting the bible in African indigenous churches. Eugene 2001, Wipf and S. iii; 120 pp. $15. 1-57910-700-1 [BOTSA 11,23].

9829 *Barnard, M.* Prinses Diana als postmoderne heilige en een kerkdienst in een museum: tendensen in de dynamiek van cultus en cultuur vanuit een West-Europees perspectief. VeE 22 (2001) 209-230.

9830 *Bastian, Jean-Pierre* De l'autorité prophétique chez les dirigeants pentecôtistes. RHPhR 81 (2001) 189-202.

9831 *Boutter, Bernard* Le pentecôtisme à l'Île de la Réunion: "Protestantisme émotionnel" ou nouvelle "religion populaire"?. RHPhR 81 (2001) 45-61.

9832 *Ens, Adolf* The Old Testament in Mennonite preaching. [F]JANZEN, W. 2001 ⇒54. 22-32.

9833 **Friesen, Abraham** ERASMUS, the Anabaptists, and the Great Commission. 1998 ⇒14,4655... 16,10089. [R]CrSt 22 (2001) 245-247 (*Weiler, A.G.*) [Mt 28,19].

9834 **Hammer, Olav** Claiming knowledge: strategies of epistemology from theosophy to the new age. SHR 90: Lei 2001, Brill xviii; 547 pp. 90-04-12016-5. Bibl. 519-533.

9835 *Harder, Helmut* The use of the Old Testament in the *Confession of faith in a Mennonite perspective.* [F]JANZEN, W. 2001 ⇒54. 34-47.

9836 *Hunt, Stephen* 'At the cutting edge of what God is doing': millenarian aspects of British Neo-Pentecostalism. Faith in the millennium. 2001 ⇒540. 324-346.

9837 *Janzen, Waldemar* A canonical rethinking of the Anabaptist-Mennonite New Testament orientation. [F]JANZEN, W. 2001 ⇒54. 3-21.

9838 [E]**Jospe, Raphael; Madsen, Truman G.; Ward, Seth** Covenant and chosenness in Judaism and Mormonism. Madison, NJ 2001, Associated University Presses 225 pp. 0-8386-3927-5.

9839 **McKim, Donald K.** Introducing the Reformed faith: biblical revelation, christian tradition, contemporary significance. LVL 2001, Westminster xvii; 261 pp. $28. 0-664-25644-9. Bibl. 196 [ThD 48,387— Heiser, W. Charles].

9840 *Meiring, P.G.J.* Die hoop beskaam nie: die N G Kerk se rol ten opsigte van versoening, armoede en morele herstel. VeE 22 (2001) 102-114.

9841 *Stiewe, Martin* Aus der wechselhaften Geschichte des Buß- und Bettags. WuD 26 (2001) 235-247.

9842 *Stoffels, Hijme C.* The roaring lion strikes again: modernity vs. Dutch orthodox Protestantism. Religious identity. 2001 ⇒549. 292-301.

9843 *Surridge, Robert* Seventh-Day Adventism: self-appointed Laodicea. Studies in the book of Revelation. 2001 ⇒6080. 21-42 [Rev 2-3].

9844 *Van der Water, D.* The United Congregational Church of Southern Africa (UCCSA)—a case study of a united and ecumenical church. VeE 22 (2001) 149-157.

9845 *Van Niekerk, A.S.* "But where's the bloody horse?": die NG teologie in Afrika. VeE 22 (2001) 418-433.

9846 *Villiers, D.E. de* Teologiekroniek—die kerk en ekonomiese globalisering. VeE 22 (2001) 465-477.

M3.8 Mythologia

9847 **Allen, Douglas** Myth and religion in Mircea ELIADE. 1998 ⇒14, 9192. [R]AmA 103/1 (2001) 264-265 (*Caldwell, Sarah*).

9848 **Burkert, Walter** Savage energies: lessons of myth and ritual in ancient Greece. [T]*Bing, Peter*: Ch 2001, University of Chicago Press xiv; 110 pp. $28/£18. 0-226-08085-4.

9849 **Dumas-Reungoat, Christine** La fin du monde: enquête sur l'origine d'un mythe. Vérité des mythes: P 2001, Belles Lettres 401 pp. 2-251-32433-X. Bibl. 387-400.

9850 **Ellwood, Robert** The politics of myth: a study of C.G. JUNG, Mircea ELIADE, and Joseph CAMPBELL. 1999 ⇒15,10032. ᴿJR 81 (2001) 173-175 (*McCutcheon, Russell T.*).

9851 **Grimal, Pierre** Enciclopedia della mitologia. Le garzantine: Mi 2000, Garzanti xxxii (2) 853 pp. 88-11-50482-1. Prefazione *Charles Picard*.

9852 **Inconnu-Bocquillon, Danielle** Le mythe de la déesse Lointaine à Philae. Bibliothèque d'étude 132: Le Caire 2001, Institut Français d'Archéologie Orientale viii; 360 pp. 2-7247-00236-0. Bibl. 10-14.

9853 **Izre'el, Shlomo** Adapa and the south wind: language has the power of life and death. Mesopotamian Civilizations 10: WL 2001, Eisenbrauns xii; 183 pp. $36.50. 1-57506-048-5. Bibl. 151-172.

9854 *Kaiser, Otto* Der Mythos als Grenzaussage. Gerechtigkeit und Leben. BZAW 296: 2001 ⇒56. 87-116.

9855 **Marderness, William Anthony** How to read a myth, and the case of mythic homeland narratives. Diss. State Univ. of NY, Stony Brook 2001, 89 pp. 3024874.

9856 **Payne, Craig** Where myth and history meet: a christian response to myth. Lanham 2001, University Press of America viii; 59 pp. 0-7618-2148-1. Bibl. 51-55.

9857 **Segal, Robert Alan** Theorizing about myth 1999 ⇒15,170; 16, 10114. ᴿZygon 36/1 (2001) 179-182 (*Hendy, Andrew von*); ASSR 114 (2001) 114-115 (*Tarot, Camille*).

9858 **Walls, Neal H.** Desire, discord and death: approaches to ancient Near Eastern myth. ASOR Books 8: Boston, MA 2001, ASOR viii; 211 pp. 0-89757-055-3. Bibl. 183-204.

M4.0 Religio romana

9859 *Aune, David E.* Prayer in the Greco-Roman world. Into God's presence. 2001 ⇒294. 23-42.

9860 *Baslez, Marie-Françoise* Le corps, l'âme et la survie: anthropologie et croyances dans les religions du monde gréco-romain. Résurrection: l'après-mort. MoBi 45: 2001 ⇒296. 73-89.

9861 **Beard, Mary; North, John; Price, Simon R.F.** Religions of Rome v.1: a history; v.2: a sourcebook. 1998 2 vols ⇒14,9207... 16,10116. ᴿSCI 20 (2001) 191-208 (*Bendlin, Andreas*).

9862 **Brown, John Pairman** Israel and Hellas, 2: sacred institutions with Roman counterparts. BZAW 276: 2000 ⇒16,10119. ᴿThRv 97 (2001) 294-296 (*Woschitz, Karl M.*); CBQ 63 (2001) 512-513 (*Hawk, L. Daniel*); OTEs 14 (2001) 169-173 (*Muntingh, L.M.*).

9863 *Cancik, Hubert; Cancik-Lindemaier, Hildegard* The truth of images: CICERO and VARRO on image worship. ᶠBARASCH, M. 2001 ⇒2. 43-61.

9864 ᵀᴱ**Chapot, Frédéric; Laurot, Bernard** Corpus de prières grecques et romaines. Recherches sur les Rhétoriques Religieuses 2: Turnhout 2001, Brepols 446 pp. €67. 2-503-50953-3.

9865 **Clauss, Manfred** Kaiser und Gott: Herrscherkult im römischen Reich. 1999 ⇒15,10046; 16,10122. ᴿPrudentia 33 (2001) 152-154 (*Stevenson, Tom*).

9866 **De Carolis, Ernesto** Gods and heroes in Pompeii. Pompeii - Thematic Guides: R 2001, "L'Erma" 80 pp. 88-8265-128-2. Bibl. 80.

9867 **Di Dario, Beniamino M.** La via romana al divino: Julius EVOLA e la religione romana. Paganitas 7: Padova 2001, Ar 160 pp. Bibl. Evola cit. 155-156.

9868 ᴱ**Edwards, Mark; Goodman, Martin; Price, Simon R.F.** Apologetics in the Roman Empire: pagans, Jews, and christians. 1999 ⇒15, 10047; 16,10124. ᴿJECS 9 (2001) 140-141 (*Trumbower, Jeffrey A.*); JJS 52 (2001) 377-379 (*Lange, Nicholas de*).

9869 *Estienne, Sylvia* Les 'dévots' du Capitole: le 'culte des images' dans la Rome impériale, entre rites et superstition. MEFRA 113/1 (2001) 189-210.

9870 **Feeney, Denis** Literature and religion at Rome: cultures, contexts, and beliefs. 1998 ⇒14,9213... 16,10127. ᴿRHR 218 (2001) 284-286 (*Reydellet, Maud*).

9871 **Hopkins, Keith** A world full of gods: pagans, Jews and christians in the Roman Empire. 1999 ⇒15,10050; 16,10129. ᴿNumen 48 (2001) 122-24 (*Martin, Luther H.*); SvTK 77 (2001) 38-39 (*Rydbeck, Lars*).

9872 *Hübner, Wolfgang* Ἀποπομπή und ἐπιπομπή in der römischen Kriegsführung. Kult, Konflikt. AOAT 285: 2001 ⇒387. 187-210.

9873 **Janowitz, Naomi** Magic in the Roman world: pagans, Jews and christians. Religion in the first Christian centuries: L 2001, Routledge xiii; 145 pp. $75/25. 0-415-20207-8. Bibl. 117-128.

9874 *Kragelund, Patrick* Dreams, religion and politics in Republican Rome. Hist. 50 (2001) 53-95.

9875 **Magini, Leonardo** Astronomy and calendar in ancient Rome: the eclipse festivals. R 2001, "L'Erma" di Bretschneider 133 pp. 88-8265-118-5.

9876 **North, J.A.** Roman religion. 2000 ⇒16,10134. ᴿSCI 20 (2001) 191-208 (*Bendlin, Andreas*).

9877 **Ogden, Daniel** Greek and Roman necromancy. Princeton 2001, Princeton Univ. Pr. xxii; 313 pp. $47.50.

9878 *Ramelli, Ilaria L.E.* L'omen per Acilio GLABBIONE e per TRAIANO: una corona?. RSCI 55 (2001) 389-394.

9879   **Requena, Miguel** El emperador predestinado: los presagios de poder en época imperial romana. M 2001, Pastor de E. 225 pp. 84-920-465-1-1.

9880   **Rüpke, Jörg** Die Religion der Römer: eine Einführung. Mü 2001, Beck 264 pp. €19.90. 3-406-47175-7.

9881   **Scheid, John** Religion et piété à Rome. Sciences des religions: P ²2001 <1985>, Michel 202 pp. €14.94. 2-226-12134-X.

9882   **Vigourt, Annie** Les présages impériaux d'AUGUSTE à DOMITIEN. Etudes d'archéologie et d'histoire ancienne: P 2001, Boccard 532 pp.

9883   **Wallraff, Martin** Christus Verus Sol: Sonnenverehrung und Christentum in der Spätantike. JAC.E 32: Müns 2001, Aschendorff 248 pp. 3-402-08115-6. 8 pl.; bibl. 207-231.

M4.5 **Mithraismus**

9884   *Albanese, Luciano* Saturno nei misteri di Mithra. SMSR 67 (2001) 53-74.

9885   **Betz, Hans Dieter** Gottesbegegnung und Menschwerdung: zur religionsgeschichtlichen und theologischen Bedeutung der 'Mithrasliturgie' (PGM IV.475-820). Hans-Lietzmann-Vorlesungen 6: B 2001, De Gruyter x; (2) 56 pp. 3-11-017088-4.

9886   **Clauss, Manfred** The Roman cult of Mithras: the god and his mysteries. ᵀ*Gordon, Richard*: E 2000, Edinburgh Univ. Pr. xxiv; 198 pp. £15. 0-7486-1396-X.

9887   *Court, John M.* Mithraism among the mysteries. Religious diversity. BiSe 79: 2001 ⇒398. 182-195.

9888   *Schütte-Maischatz, A.; Winter, E.* Mithrasheiligtum in Doliche gefunden. WUB 19 (2001) 71.

9889   **Ulansey, David** Die Ursprünge des Mithraskults: Kosmologie und Erlösung in der Antike. 1998 ⇒14,9230. ᴿAfR 3 (2001) 320-322 (*Weiß, Maria*).

M5.1 *Divinitates Graeciae*—**Greek gods and goddesses**

9890   **Baumgarten, R.** Heiliges Wort und heilige Schrift bei den Griechen: Hieroi Logoi und verwandte Erscheinungen. 1998 ⇒14,9233. ᴿClR 51 (2001) 281-283 (*Graf, Fritz*).

9891   **Bettinetti, Simona** La statua di culto nella pratica rituale greca. Le rane, Studi 30: Bari 2001, Levante 264 pp. €24.79. 88-7949-256-X. Bibl. 239-259.

9892 **Burkert, W.** La tradition orientale dans la culture grecque. [T]*Leclercq-Neveu, B.*: P 2001, Macula 49 pp. 2-86589-036-8 [REA 105/ 1,323s–Pierre Lévêque].

9893 **Calame, C.** Thésée et l'imaginaire athénien: légende et culte en Grèce. [2]1996 ⇒12,8862; 14,9243. [R]HR 41 (2001) 81-84 (*Borgeaud, Philippe*).

9894 [E]**Deacy, S.; Villing, A.** Athena in the classical world. Lei 2001, Brill xii; 435 pp. 90-0412-142-0. Bibl.

9895 [E]**De Caro, Stefano** Ercole: l'eroe, il mito. Mi 2001, Biblioteca di via Senato 143 pp. 88-87945-06-3.

9896 **Dickie, M.W.** Magic and magicians in the Greco-Roman world. L 2001, Routledge viii; 380 pp. £55. 0-415-24982-1.

9897 **Di Donato, Ricardo** Hierà: prolegomena ad uno studio storico antropologico della religione greca. Didattica e ricerca, manuali: Pisa 2001, Plus 368 pp. 88-8492-091-4.

9898 **Faraone, Christopher A.** Ancient Greek love magic. CM 2001: Harvard Univ. Pr. xii; 223 pp. $20. 0-674-00696-8.

9899 **Fowler, R.L.** Early Greek mythography, 1: text and introduction. Oxf 2001, OUP xlvii; 459 pp. £55. 0-19-814740-6.

9900 **Furley, William D.; Bremer, Jan Maarten** Greek hymns: selected cult songs from the archaic to the Hellenistic period. Studien und Texte zu Antike und Christentum 9-10: Tü 2001, Mohr 2 vols. €39 + 64. 3-16-147527-5/542. Bibl. v.I 383-392; v.II 437-443; v.1, the texts in translation; v.2, Greek texts and commentary.

9901 **Garland, Robert** The Greek way of death. NY 2001, Cornell Univ. Pr. 198 pp [REG 116,726s—Queyrel, Anne].

9902 *Gebhard, Elizabeth R.* The gods in transit: narratives of cult transfer. [F]BETZ, H. 2001 ⇒5. 451-476.

9903 *Hallo, William W.* Polymnia and Clio. Proceedings of the XLVe Rencontre Assyriologique, 1. 2001 ⇒577. 195-209.

9904 **Johnston, Sarah Iles** Restless dead: encounters between the living and the dead in ancient Greece. 1999 ⇒15,10072; 16,10159. [R]AJP 122 (2001) 433-436 (*Felton, D.*); At. 89 (2001) 652-655 (*Bardi, F.*).

9905 **Karageorghis, Vassos** Greek gods and heroes in ancient Cyprus. 1998 ⇒15,10073. [R]RAr (2001) 372-374 (*Hermary, Antoine*).

9906 **Le Bris, Anne** La mort et les conceptions de l'au-delà en Grèce ancienne à travers les épigrammes funéraires. P 2001, Harmattan 189 pp.

9907 *Lupu, Eran* The sacred law from the cave of Pan at Marathon (*SEG* XXXVI 267). ZPE 137 (2001) 119-124.

9908 **Mikalson, Jon D.** Religion in Hellenistic Athens. 1998 ⇒14,9250; 16,10163. [R]Gn. 73 (2001) 315-319 (*Albinus, Lars*).

9909 *Penna, Romano* Componenti essenziali della religiosità del mondo ellenistico. Vangelo e inculturazione. 2001 <1988> ⇒193. 89-109.

9910 *Piettre, Renée* Images et perception de la présence divine en Grèce ancienne. MEFRA 113/1 (2001) 211-224.

9911 **Price, Simon** Religions of the ancient Greeks. 1999 ⇒15,10078. ᴿRH 67 (2001) 158-161 (*Sineux, Pierre*); AnCl 70 (2001) 370-371 (*Van Liefferinge, Carine*).

9912 **Rosenberger, Veit** Griechische Orakel: eine Kulturgeschichte. Da:Wiss 2001, 213 pp.

9913 **Rudhardt, Jean** Thémis et les Hôrai: recherche sur les divinités grecques de la justice et de la paix. 1999 ⇒15,10081; 16,10170. ᴿAnCl 70 (2001) 373-375 (*Pirenne-Delforge, Vinciane*).

9914 *Schmidt, Jens-Uwe* Das Schicksal des reichen Krösus und die Religiosität des Historikers Hᴇʀᴏᴅᴏᴛ. WuD 26 (2001) 23-41.

9915 **Sissa, Giulia; Detienne, Marcel** The daily life of the Greek gods. ᵀ*Lloyd, Janet*: Stanford, CA 2001, Stanford University Press xiii (2) 287 pp. 0-8047-3613-8.

9916 *Stein, Markus* Die Verehrung des theos hypsistos: ein allumfassender pagan-jüdischer Synkretismus?. Epigraphica Anatolica 33 (2001) 119-126.

9917 *Thom, Johan C.* Cleanthes' hymn to Zeus and early christian literature. ᶠBᴇᴛᴢ, H. 2001 ⇒5. 477-499.

9918 *Wildberg, Christian* Die Gerechtigkeit des Zeus in den Dramen des Eᴜʀɪᴘɪᴅᴇꜱ. Gerechtigkeit und Leben. BZAW 296: 2001 ⇒56. 1-20.

9919 **Zolla, Elémire** Catàbasi e anàstasi: discesa nell'ade e resurrezione: katábasis kai anástasis. Alpignano (T) 2001, Tallone 200 pp. €9.

M5.2 *Philosophorum critica religionis*—**Greek philosopher religion**

9920 ᴱ**Berner, U.**, *al.*, Pʟᴜᴛᴀʀᴄʜ: Ist 'Lebe im Verborgenen' eine gute Lebensregel?. Da:Wiss 2000, 176 pp. €25.05. ᴿSNTU.A 26 (2001) 284-286 (*Schreiber, S.*).

9921 **Boys-Stones, G.R.** Post-Hellenistic philosophy: a study of its development from the Stoics to Oʀɪɢᴇɴ. Oxf 2001, OUP viii; 241 pp. $45.

9922 *Brenk, Frederick* In the image, reflection and reason of Osiris: Pʟᴜᴛᴀʀᴄʜ and the Egyptian cults. Estudios sobre Plutarco. 2001 ⇒572. 83-98.

9923 **Carfora, Anna** Morte e presente nelle meditazioni di Mᴀʀᴄᴏ Aᴜʀᴇʟɪᴏ e negli Atti dei martiri contemporanei. Il pensiero e la storia 86: N 2001, La Città del sole 126 pp.

9924 ᵀ**Ebner, Martin,** *al.*, Lᴜᴋɪᴀɴ, Die Lügenfreunde, oder: Der Ungläubige. Sapere 3: Da:Wiss 2001, 214 pp. €26.70.

9925 ^TKlauck, Hans-Josef DION von Prusa: Olympische Rede oder Über die erste Erkenntnis Gottes. Sapere 2: Da:Wiss 2000, 256 pp. €26.40. Archäologischen Beitrag von *Balbina Bäbler*.

M5.3 *Mysteria eleusinia; Hellenistica*—Mysteries; Hellenistic cults

9926 **Adinolfi, Marco** Scintille del verbo: ellenismo e bibbia a confronto. Odorifera verba Domini 2: Montella 2001, Dragonetti 237 pp. €15. 49. Bibl. 209.

9927 *Anderson, Graham* Greek religion in the Roman Empire: diversities, convergences, uncertainties. Religious diversity. BiSe 79: 2001 ⇒ 398. 143-163.

9928 **Casadio, Giovanni** Il vino dell'anima: storia del culto di Dioniso a Corinto, Sicione, Trezene. 1999 ⇒15,10088; 16,10185. ^RAnCl 70 (2001) 375-376 (*Van Liefferinge, Carine*).

9929 ^E**Frangoulis, H.** NONNOS de Panopolis: les dionysiaques, 13: chant xxxvii. 1999 ⇒15,10089. ^RREG 114 (2001) 336-337 (*Fournet, Jean-Luc*).

9930 *Henrichs, Albert* Demythologizing the past, mythicizing the present: myth, history, and the supernatural at the dawn of the Hellenistic period. From myth to reason?. 2001 ⇒395. 223-248.

9931 **Klauck, Hans-Josef** The religious context of early christianity: a guide to Graeco-Roman religions. ^T*McNeil, Brian*: 2000 ⇒16,10191. ^RCBQ 63 (2001) 154-155 (*Talbert, Charles H.*).

9932 **Le Guen, Brigitte** Les associations de technites dionysiaques à l'époque hellénistique. Etudes d'archéologie classique: Nancy 2001, De Boccard 2 vols; 355 +224 pp. ^RCRAI (2001/3) 1303-1304 (*Chamoux, François*).

9933 *Lichtenberger, Achim* Die Einweihung MARK AURELS in die Mysterien von Eleusis und der Beginn der Ära von Philadelphia. ZDPV 117 (2001) 140-148.

9934 *Minore, Paolo* I misteri eleusini nelle fonti cristiane. PalCl 1 (2001) 791-798.

9935 **Morand, Anne-France** Études sur les *Hymnes orphiques*. RGRW 143: Lei 2001, Brill xvi; 374 pp. 90-04-12030-0. Bibl. 350-361.

9936 ^{TE}**Simon, B.** NONNOS de Panopolis: les dionysiaques, xiv, chants xxxviii-xl. 1999 ⇒15,10096. ^RClR 51 (2001) 236-237 (*Whitby, Mary*); REA 103 (2001) 556-557 (*Cusset, Christophe*).

9937 **Stroumsa, Guy G.** Hidden wisdom: esoteric traditions and the roots of christian mysticism. 1996 ⇒13,9500... 15,10097. ^RCrSt 22 (2001) 216-218 (*Gianotto, Claudio*).

9938 **Tripolitis, Antonia** Religions of the Hellenistic-Roman age. GR 2001, Eerdmans 165 pp. $16. 0-8028-4913-X.

M5.5 Religiones anatolicae

9939 *Haas, Volkert* Die Frauen mit den verstümmelten Nasen: eine Notiz zum hethitischen Ištar-Kult. ᴹCAGNI, L., 1. SMDSA 61: 2001 ⇒15. 421-431;

9940 Verfluchungen am hethitischen Hof und deren rituelle Beseitigung. Kult, Konflikt. AOAT 285: 2001 ⇒387. 53-71.

9941 *Hutter, Manfred* Luwische Religion in den Traditionen aus Arzawa. IV. Internationaler Kongress. 2001 ⇒650. 224-234.

9942 *Melchert, H. Craig* Hittite *damnaššara-* 'domestic'/ᵈ*damnaššareš* 'household deities'. JANER 1 (2001) 150-157;

9943 A Hittite fertility rite?. IV. Internationaler Kongress. 2001 ⇒650. 404-409.

9944 *Orlamünde, Julia* Überlegungen zum hethitischen KIN-Orakel. ᶠHAAS, V. 2001 ⇒39. 295-311.

9945 *Richter, Thomas* Theophore Elemente ḫurritischer Personennamen altbabylonischen Datums aus Syrien und dem Osttigrisgebiet. IV. Internationaler Kongress. 2001 ⇒650. 563-575.

9946 **Roller, Lynn E.** In search of god the mother: the cult of Anatolian Cybele. 1999 ⇒15,10103; 16,10202. ᴿHR 41 (2001) 86-88 (*Johnston, Sarah Iles*).

9947 *Taracha, Piotr* Aspekte der Hurritisierung Kleinasiens: ein Beschwörungsritual aus mittelhethitischer Zeit. IV. Internationaler Kongress. 2001 ⇒650. 685-695.

9948 *Tassignon, Isabelle* Les éléments anatoliens du mythe et de la personnalité de Dionysos. RHR 218 (2001) 307-337.

9949 **Torri, Giulia** Lelwani: il culto di una dea ittita. Vicino Oriente, 2: 1999 ⇒15,10104. ᴿBiOr 58 (2001) 430-432 (*Hutter, Manfred*).

9950 *Van den Hout, Theo P.J.* Bemerkungen zu älteren hethitischen Orakeltexten. ᶠHAAS, V. 2001 ⇒39. 423-440.

9951 **Van Gessel, Ben H.L.** Onomasticon of the Hittite pantheon, 3. HO I/33,3: Lei 2001, Brill xviii; 401 pp. 90-04-12116-1.

9952 *Vassileva, Maya* Further considerations on the cult of Kybele. AnSt 51 (2001) 51-63.

M6.0 Religio canaanaea, syra

9953 *Anbar, Moshe* Les sentiments religieux dans la correspondance de Zimri-lim, roi de Mari, et de ses fonctionnaires. ^MCAGNI, L., 1: SMDSA 61: 2001 ⇒15. 1-11.

9954 *Avner, Uzi* Sacred stones in the desert. BArR 27/3 (2001) 30-41.

9955 **Baldacci, Massimo** Prima della bibbia: sulle tracce della religione arcaica del proto-Israele. 2000 ⇒16,10208. ^RRasIsr 67/3 (2001) 113-119 (*Di Segni, Riccardo*).

9956 *Becking, Bob* The gods, in whom they trusted... Assyrian evidence for iconic polytheism in ancient Israel. Only one God?. BiSe 77: 2001 ⇒238. 151-163.

9957 **Belayche, Nicole** Iudaea-Palaestina: the pagan cults in Roman Palestine (second to fourth century). Religion der Römischen Provinzen 1: Tü 2001, Mohr xxiv; 386 pp. €89. 3-16-147153-9. Bibl. 311-358.

9958 **Blazquez Martinez, José Maria** Dioses, mitos y rituales de los semitas occidentales en la antigüedad. M 2001, Cristiandad 319 pp. 84-7057-439-6.

9959 *Bonnet, Corinnne* Encore sur Astarté. ^MCAGNI, L., 3: SMDSA 61: 2001 ⇒15. 1289-1301.

9960 *Boshoff, Willem* Archaeological publications and the history of ancient Israelite religions: primary and secondary publications on the archaeology, history and religion of ancient Israel. OTEs 14 (2001) 371-391.

9961 *Crowell, Bradley L.* The development of Dagan: a sketch. JANER 1 (2001) 32-83.

9962 *Daviau, P.M. Michèle* Family religion: evidence for the paraphernalia of the domestic cult. ^FDION, P.-E. 2. 2001 ⇒25. 199-229.

9963 **Day, John** Yahweh and the gods and goddesses of Canaan. JSOT.S 265: 2000 ⇒16,10217. ^RBib. 82 (2001) 589-591 (*Gnuse, Robert*); ET 112 (2001) 291-292 (*Rodd, C.S.*).

9964 *Dietrich, Manfried* '(Nur) einer, der von Sünde nichts weiß, eilt zu seinen Göttern': der altorientalische Mensch vor seiner Gottheit. Kult, Konflikt. AOAT 285: 2001 ⇒387. 73-97.

9965 *Dijkstra, Meindert* I have blessed you by YHWH of Samaria and his Asherah: texts with religious elements from the soil archive of ancient Israel. Only one God?. BiSe 77: 2001 ⇒238. 17-44;

9966 Women and religion in the Old Testament. Only one God?. BiSe 77: 2001 ⇒238. 164-188.

9967 *Ernst-Pradal, Françoise* Ougarit—Qodeš-Amrour et la pêche au feu. Sem. 50 (2001) 217-220.

9968 *Fantar, Mhamed* Propos sur les divinités féminines dans l'univers li-byco-punique. [F]Huß, W.: OLA 104: 2001 ⇒51. 221-233.

9969 **Frantsouzoff, Serguei** Raybun: Hadran, Temple de la déesse 'Athta-rum/'Astarum. Inventaire des inscriptions sudarabiques 5: P 2001, De Boccard 2 vols. 2-87754-110-X. Bibl. Fasc. A 303-314; collab. *Se-dov, Aleksandr*.

9970 **Grabbe, Lester L.** Judaic religion in the second temple period: belief and practice from the exile to Yavneh. 2000 ⇒16,10227. [R]JThS 52 (2001) 757-759 (*Bray, Jason*).

9971 *Greenfield, Jonas C.* The Aramean God Rammān/Rimmōn.<1976>;

9972 Aspects of Aramean religion <1987>;

9973 To praise the might of Hadad <1987>. 'Al kanfei yonah, 1. 2001 ⇒153. 144-147/283-294/295-304.

9974 *Gruenwald, Ithamar* Ritual, economy, and the religion of ancient Is-rael. Mythology and mythologies. 2001 ⇒589. 29-46.

9975 *Gulde, Stefanie* Unterweltsvorstellungen in Ugarit. Das biblische Weltbild. FAT 32: 2001 ⇒285. 393-429.

9976 **Hadley, Judith M.** The cult of Asherah in ancient Israel and Judah. UCOP 57: 2000 ⇒16,10228. [R]BTB 31 (2001) 39 (*Burns, John Bar-clay*); RRT 8 (2001) 134-136 (*Taylor, David*); CBQ 63 (2001) 520-521 (*Fulco, William J.*); BASOR 323 (2001) 102-103 (*Wiggins, Steve A.*); NEA 64 (2001) 218-219 (*Nakhai, Beth Alpert*).

9977 *Hämeen-Anttila, Jaakko; Rollinger, Robert* HERODOT und die arabi-sche Göttin 'Alilat'. JANER 1 (2001) 84-99.

9978 **Healey, John F.** The religion of the Nabataeans: a conspectus. RGRW 136: Lei 2001, Brill xvi; 242 pp. €75/$87. 90-04-10754-1. Bibl. 211-234.

9979 *Hentrich, T.* The fertility pair Ba'al and 'Anat in the Ugaritic texts. Canadian research on ancient Syria. 2001 ⇒581. 115-122.

9980 *Keel, Othmar* "Das Land der Kanaanäer mit der Seele suchend". ThZ 57 (2001) 245-261 [2 Kgs 18,4].

9981 *Korpel, Marjo C.A.* Asherah outside Israel. Only one God?. BiSe 77: 2001 ⇒238. 127-150.

9982 *Lancellotti, Maria Grazia* Le thème du 'dieu qui meurt' à l'époque perse: les aspects méthodologiques. TEuph 22 (2001) 51-62.

9983 *Lemaire, A.* Épigraphie et religion en Palestine à l'époque achémé-nide. TEuph 22 (2001) 97-113;

9984 Les religions du sud de la Palestine au IVe siècle av. J.-C. d'après les ostraca araméens d'Idumée. CRAI 2 (2001) 1141-1158.

9985 *Loretz, Oswald* Sparagmos und Omophagie in Māri und Ugarit. [M]CAGNI, L., 3. SMDSA 61: 2001 ⇒15. 1719-1730.

9986 **Merlo, Paolo** La dea Asratum—Atiratu—Asera: un contributo alla storia della religione semitica del nord. 1998 ⇒14,9309... 16,10237. [R]JSSt 46 (2001) 138-139 (*Watson, Wilfred G.E.*).

9987 **Mettinger, Tryggve N.D.** The riddle of resurrection: "Dying and rising Gods" in the ancient Near East. CB.OT 50: Sto 2001, Almqvist & W. 275 pp. SEK238. 91-22-01945-6.

9988 **Miller, Patrick D.** The religion of ancient Israel. 2000 ⇒16,10238. [R]ThTo 58 (2001) 254, 256-257 (*Dearman, Andrew*); RRT 8 (2001) 510-512 (*Norton, Gerard J.*); CV 43 (2001) 269-274 (*Ber, Viktor*); CBQ 63 (2001) 529-530 (*Jacobs, Paul F.*).

9989 **Nakhai, Beth Alpert** Archaeology and the religions of Canaan and Israel. ASOR 7: Boston 2001, ASOR xi; 262 pp. 0-89757-057-X. Bibl. 205-251.

9990 **Niehr, H.** Religionen in Israels Umwelt: Einführung in die nordwest-semitischen Religionen Syrien-Palästinas. 1998 ⇒14,9315; 16, 10251. [R]ZKTh 123 (2001) 101-102 (*Oberforcher, Robert*); ETR 76 (2001) 606-607 (*Bauks, Michaela*); Or. 69 (2000) 336-338 (*Bonnet, Corinne*).

9991 *Niehr, Herbert* Die Wohnsitze des Gottes El nach den Mythen aus Ugarit: ein Beitrag zu ihrer Lokalisierung. Das biblische Weltbild. FAT 32: 2001 ⇒285. 325-360.

9992 *Novák, Mirko* Zur Verbindung von Mondgott und Wettergott bei den Aramäern im 1. Jahrtausend v. Chr. UF 33 (2001) 437-465.

9993 [TE]**Olmo Lete, Gregorio del** Mitos, leyendas y rituales de los semitas occidentales. 1998 ⇒14,9318. [R]Sef. 61 (2001) 448-450 (*Such Gutiérrez, M.*).

9994 *Patrón de Smith, Ana Fund* Canaan: cultural crossroads for gods and heroes. [M]CAGNI, L., 3. SMDSA 61: 2001 ⇒15. 1529-1541.

9995 *Penchansky, David* Is Hokmah an Israelite goddess, and what should we do about it?. Postmodern interpretations. 2001 ⇒229. 81-92.

9996 **Robertson, Dale N.** The biblical ciphers unsealed: a revival of the Hebrew goddess. St. Paul, MN 2001, Paragon xviii; 652 pp. 1-55778-797-2. Bibl. 637-646.

9997 *Röllig, Wolfgang* Phönizisches aus Nordsyrien und der Gott Kurra. [F]HUß, W.: OLA 104: 2001 ⇒51. 41-52.

9998 *Sallaberger, Walther* Zu einer Urkunde aus Ekalte über die Rückgabe der Hausgötter.UF 33 (2001) 495-499 [Gen 31,30].

9999 *Sasson, Jack M.* Ancestors divine?. [F]VEENHOF, K. 2001 ⇒111. 413-428.

10000 *Smith, Mark S.* The divine familiy at Ugarit and Israelite monotheism. [M]MORSE, J.: JSOT.S 336: 2001 ⇒75. 40-68.

10001 **Smith, Mark S.** The origins of biblical monotheism: Israel's polytheistic background and the Ugaritic texts. NY 2001, OUP xviii; 325 pp. $60. 0-19-513480-X.

10002 **Stark, Rodney** One true God: historical consequences of monotheism. Princeton 2001, Princeton Univ. Pr. 319 pp. $18. 0691-08923X.

10003 *Stern, Ephraim* Pagan Yahwism: the folk religion of ancient Israel. BArR 27/3 (2001) 20-29.

10004 *Stolz, Fritz* Synkretismus II: Altes Testament. TRE 32. 2001 ⇒665. 530-533.

10005 *Sweeney, Marvin A.* The religious world of ancient Israel to 586. The Blackwell reader in Judaism. 2001 ⇒423. 19-30.

10006 **Theuer, Gabriele** Der Mondgott in den Religionen Syrien-Palästinas: unter besonderer Berücksichtigung von KTU 1.24. OBO 173: 2000 ⇒16,10267. ᴿETR 76 (2001) 414-415 (*Smyth, Françoise*); BiOr 58 (2001) 423-425 (*Spronk, Klaas*); CBQ 63 (2001) 734-735 (*Rollston, Chris A.*).

10007 *Vriezen, Karel J.H.* Archaeological traces of cult in ancient Israel. Only one God?. BiSe 77: 2001 ⇒238. 45-80.

10008 **Weippert, Manfred** Jahwe und die anderen Götter: Studien zur Religionsgeschichte des antiken Israel in ihrem syrisch-palästinischen Kontext. FAT 18: 1997 ⇒13,9567... 16,10268. ᴿOTEs 14 (2001) 356-358 (*Nel, Philip J.*).

10009 *Wenning, Robert* Die Religion der Nabatäer. WUB 19 (2001) 19-26.

10010 *Wiggins, Steve A.* Of Asherahs and trees: some methodological questions. JANER 1 (2001) 158-187.

10011 *Xella, Paolo* Le soi-disant 'dieu qui meurt' en domaine phénico-punique. TEuph 22 (2001) 63-77;

10012 Les plus anciens témoignages sur le dieu Eshmoun: une mise au point. ᶠDION, P.-E. 2. JSOT.S 325: 2001 ⇒25. 230-242;

10013 Yhwh e la sua *'šrh*: la dea o il suo simbolo?: (una risposta a J.A. Emerton). StEeL 18 (2001) 71-81;

10014 Da Baal di Ugarit agli dei fenici: una questione di vita o di morte. Quando un dio muore. 2001 ⇒449. 73-96.

10015 **Zevit, Ziony** The religions of ancient Israel: a synthesis of parallactic approaches. NY 2001, Continuum xx; 821 pp. $150. 0-8264-4728-7.

M6.5 **Religio aegyptia**

10016 **Armour, Robert A.** Gods and myths of ancient Egypt. Cairo [2]2001, The American University in Cairo Press x; 207 pp. 977-424-669-1. Bibl. 197-201.

10017 **Assman, Jan** The search for God in ancient Egypt. [T]*Lorton, David* Ithaca 2001, Cornell Univ. Pr. xii; 275 pp. £13. 0-8014-8729-3. Bibl. 259-267;

10018 Tod und Jenseits im Alten Ägypten. Mü 2001, Beck xiv; 624 pp. €40. 3-406-46570-6.

10019 *Assmann, Jan* Echnaton und das Trauma des Monotheismus. WUB 22 (2001) 19-25.

10020 [E]**Aufrère, Sydney H.** Encyclopédie religieuse de l'univers végétal. 1999 ⇒15,10179. [R]BiOr 58 (2001) 115-120 (*Koemoth, Pierre P.*).

10021 *Baines, John* Egyptian letters of the New Kingdom as evidence for religious practice. JANER 1 (2001) 1-31.

10022 **Bakhoum, Soheir** Dieux égyptiens à Alexandrie sous les Antonins, recherches numismatiques et historiques. 1999 ⇒15,10181; 16, 10277. [R]CÉg 76 (2001) 312-314 (*Bingen, Jean*).

10023 **Bakos, Margaret** Marchiori Fatos e mitos do Antigo Egito. Porto Alegre [2]2001, EDIPUCRS 187 pp. [REB 61,515].

10024 **Barguet, Paul** Aspects de la pensée religieuse de l'Égypte ancienne. Fuveau 2001, La Maison de Vie 236 pp. 2-909-816-38-9. Préf. *Christian Jacq*.

10025 **Beinlich, Horst** Das Buch vom Ba. 2000 ⇒16,10280. [R]DiscEg 49 (2001) 99-102 (*DuQuesne, Terence*); Enchoria 27 (2001) 209-211 (*Quack, Joachim Friedrich*).

10026 *Borghouts, J.F.* De religie van Achnaton. Phoe. 47 (2001) 5-35.

10027 [E]**Bos, Gerrit; Burnett, Charles** Hermetis Trismegisti: astrologica et divinatoria. CChr.CM 144 C: Turnhout 2001, Brepols 454 pp. 2-503-04447-6.

10028 *Breyer, Francis A.K.* Ptahhotep—von Ptahs Gnaden der Weise mit dem dreifachen Palindrom. WO 31 (2001) 19-22.

10029 **Bricault, Laurent** Atlas de la diffusion des cultes isiaques: (IVe S. AV. J.-C. - IVe S. Apr. J.-C.). Mémoires de l'Académie des inscriptions et Belles-Lettres 23: P 2001, De Boccard xxiv; 192 pp. 2-87754-123-1. Préf. *Jean Leclant*; Bibl. xvii-xxi.

10030 [TE]**Cauville, Sylvie** Dendara: les chapelles osiriennes, 1: transcription et traduction, 2: commentaire, 3: index. 1997 3 vols ⇒13, 9585... 16,10284. [R]WO 31 (2000-2001) 201-206 (*Derchain-Urtel, Maria-Theresia*).

10031　*Coulon, Laurent* Quand Amon parle à Platon (la statue Caire JE 38033). RdE 52 (2001) 85-125.

10032　*Curto, Silvio* Some notes concerning the religion and statues of divinities of ancient Egypt <1984>;

10033　Serapide, dio egiziano ed europeo <1986>. Attraverso l'egittologia. 2001 ⇒136. 351-370/383-400.

10034　**Dunand, Fr.** Isis: mère des dieux. 2000 ⇒16,10288. [R]BiOr 58 (2001) 101-105 (*Bricault, Laurent*).

10035　*DuQuesne, Terence* Dictionaries and databases of Egyptian religious texts. DiscEg 50 (2001) 15-24;

10036　Concealing and revealing: the problem of ritual masking in ancient Egypt. DiscEg 51 (2001) 5-31.

10037　**El-Sabban, Sherif** Temple festival calendars of ancient Egypt. LMAOS: 2000 ⇒16,10289. [R]BiOr 58 (2001) 584-587 (*Bomhard, A.S. von*).

10038　**Fischer-Elfert, Hans-W.** Die Vision von der Statue im Stein: Studien zum altägyptischen Mundöffnugsritual. Schriften der Phil.-hist. Kl. der Heidelberger Akad. der Wissenschaften 5 (1998): Heid 1998, Winter x; 105 pp. €19.43. 3-8253-0678-X. Zoologischer Beitrag von *Friedhelm Hoffmann.*

10039　**Frankfurter, David T.M.** Religion in Roman Egypt: assimilation and resistance. 1998 ⇒14,9358... 16,10294. [R]CIR 51 (2001) 74-76 (*Lee, A.D.*); BiOr 58 (2001) 126-132 (*Kaper, Olaf E.*); JBL 120 (2001) 368-370 (*Johnston, Sarah Iles*); RBLit 3 (2001) 499-501 (*Johnston, Sarah Iles*).

10040　**Gasse, Annie** Le Livre des Morts de Pacherientaihet au Museo Gregoriano Egizio. Museo Gregoriano Egizio Aegyptiaca Gregoriana 4: Città del Vaticano 2001, Monumenti, Musei e Gallerie Pontificie 379 pp. 35 pl.; Bibl. 305-307.

10041　**Goyon, Jean-Claude** Rê, Maât et Pharaon ou le destin de l'Egypte antique. 1998 ⇒14,9361. [R]BiOr 58 (2001) 97-100 (*Tobin, Vincent/Vladimir*).

10042　**Görg, Manfred** Die Barke der Sonne. Kleine Bibliothek der Religionen 7: FrB 2001, Herder 212 pp. 3-451-23847-0.

10043　**Haring, B.J.J.** Divine households: administrative and economic aspects of the New Kingdom memorial temples in western Thebes. Egyptologische Uitgaven 11: 1997 ⇒13,9601; 15,10197. [R]OLZ 96 (2001) 185-193 (*Römer, Malte*); BiOr 58 (2001) 364-365 (*Dodson, Aidan*).

10044　*Hornung, Erik* Die neue Religion des Echnaton. WUB 22 (2001) 11-16.

10045 **Hornung, Erik** Das esoterische Ägypten: das geheime Wissen der Ägypter und sein Einfluß auf das Abendland. 1999 ⇒15,10203. RThLZ 126 (2001) 157-160 (*Blumenthal, Elke*);

10046 The secret lore of Egypt: its impact on the West. ^T*Lorton, David*: Ithaca 2001, Cornell University Press viii (2) 229 pp. $20 0-8014-3847-0. Bibl. 209-219.

10047 *Janák, Jiří* How to drive a *Ka*: cars and computers in ancient Egyptian religion. ArOr 69 (2001) 586-588.

10048 *Jansen-Winkeln, Karl* Eine Familie im Totenkult. ZÄS 128 (2001) 133-141.

10049 *Kahl, Jochem* Die ältesten schriftlichen Belege für den Gott Seth. GöMisz 181 (2001) 51-57.

10050 **Kahl, Jochem** Siut—Theben: zur Wertschätzung von Traditionen im alten Ägypten. PÄ 13: 1999 ⇒15,10204; 16,10300. ^RDiscEg 50 (2001) 109-113 (*Morenz, Ludwig D.*); BiOr 58 (2001) 590-592 (*Meulenaere, H. de*).

10051 *Karkajian, Lourik* La mort et l'après-mort dans le Proche-Orient ancien. Résurrection: l'après-mort. MoBi 45: 2001 ⇒296. 23-44.

10052 *Magness, Jodi* The cults of Isis and Kore at Samaria-Sebaste in the Hellenistic and Roman periods. HThR 94 (2001) 157-177.

10053 *Meyer, Béatrice* Magie et bains publics. XXII Congresso di papirologia, 2. 2001 ⇒555. 937-942.

10054 **Munro, Irmtraut** Das Totenbuch des Pa-en-nesti-taui aus der Regierungszeit des Amenemope (pLondon BM 10064). Handschriften des altägyptischen Totenbuches 7: Wsb 2001, Harrassowitz pag. var. €108. 3-447-03950-7. CD; Bibl. 69;

10055 Spruchvorkommen auf Totenbuch-Textzeugen der Dritten Zwischenzeit. Studien zum altägyptischen Totenbuch 5: Wsb 2001, Harrassowitz x; 139 pp. €35. 3-447-04477-2.

10056 *Nel, Christiaan* The changing face of Nubian religion: the lion temples at Musawwarat es Sufra and Naqa and the three-headed and four-armed Apedemak. JNSL 27/1 (2001) 101-120.

10057 *Preys, René* La fête de la prise de pouvoir d'Ihy "le grand dieu" à Dendera. ZÄS 128 (2001) 146-166.

10058 *Quack, Joachim Friedrich* Die rituelle Erneuerung der Osirisfigurinen. WO 31 (2001) 5-18.

10059 **Quirke, Stephen G.J.** The cult of Ra: sun-worship in ancient Egypt. L 2001, Thames & H. 184 pp. 0-500-05107-0. Bibl. 174-77.

10060 *Refai, Hosam* Nebet-Hetepet, Iusas und Temet: die weiblichen Komplemente des Atum. GöMisz 181 (2001) 89-94.

10061 *Rondot, Vincent* Le dieu à la bipenne, c'est Lycurgue. RdE 52 (2001) 219-49.

10062   **Rößler-Köhler, Ursula** Zur Tradierungsgeschichte des Totenbuches zwischen der 17. und 22. Dynastie (Tb 17). 1999 ⇒15,10225. [R]OLZ 96 (2001) 488-491 (*Kahl, Jochem*).

10063   *Spieser, Cathie* Serket, protectrice des enfants à naître et des défunts à renaître. RdE 52 (2001) 251-264.

10064   **Spieser, Cathie** Les noms du Pharaon: comme êtres autonomes au Nouvel Empire. OBO 174: 2000 ⇒16,10327. [R]DiscEg 50 (2001) 103-107 (*Koemoth, Pierre P.*); BiOr 58 (2001) 360-363 (*Brand, Peter J.*).

10065   **Sternberg-El Hotabi, Heike** Untersuchungen zur Überlieferungsgeschichte der Horusstelen. ÄA 62: 1999 2 vols ⇒15,10227. [R]BiOr 58 (2001) 598-601 (*Kákosy, László*).

10066   **Taylor, John Hammond** Death and the afterlife in Ancient Egypt. L 2001, British Museum Pr. 272 pp. £15. 0-7141-1917-2. Bibl. 264-265; 198 fig.

10067   **Traunecker, Claude** The gods of Egypt. [T]*Lorton, David*: Ithaca, NY 2001, Cornell University Press x; 134 pp. $28. 0-8014-3834-9. Bibl. 127-128.

10068   *Wettengel, Wolfgang* Zwischen Sonnnenkult und Vielgötterei: eine Betrachtung von Religion und Götterkult des Pharaonenreiches. WUB 22 (2001) 44-47.

10069   *Zecchi, Marco* The god Hedjhotep. CÉg 76 (2001) 5-19.

10070   **Zeidler, Jürgen** Pfortenbuchstudien. GOF.Ä 36: 1999 2 vols ⇒15, 10231; 16,10332. [R]OLZ 96 (2001) 193-195 (*Hornung, Erik*); WO 31 (2001) 190-194 (*Leitz, Christian*).

M7.0 Religio mesopotamica

10071   **Annus, Amar** The standard Babylonian epic of Anzu. State Archives of Assyria Cuneiform texts 3: Helsinki 2001, The Neo-Assyrian Text Corpus Project xli; 61 pp. $25. 951-45-9051-1. Introd., cuneiform text, translit., score, glossary, sign list by *Amar Annus*.

10072   *Beaulieu, Paul-Alain* The abduction of Ištar from the Eanna Temple: the changing memories of an event. Proceedings of the XLVe Rencontre Assyriologique, 1. 2001 ⇒577. 29-40.

10073   **Bottéro, Jean** Religion in ancient Mesopotamia. [T]*Fagan, Teresa Lavender*: Ch 2001, University of Chicago Press xiii; 246 pp. $36. 0-226-06717-3. Bibl. 233-235.

10074   **Brown, D.** Mesopotamian planetary astronomy-astrology. Cuneiform Mon. 18: 2000 ⇒16,10338. [R]BiOr 58 (2001) 156-163 (*Koch, Johannes*); SEL 18 (2001) 115-119 (*Casaburi, Maria C.*).

10075 *Charvát, Petr* Guides to the netherworld, protectors or demons?: cone-headed females in Mesopotamian pre- and protohistory. ^MCAGNI, L., 1: SMDSA 61: 2001 ⇒15. 101-106.

10076 **Chiodi, Silvia Maria** Offerte "funebri" nella Lagas presargonica. Materiali per il vocabolario sumerico 5,1-2: 1997 ⇒13,2026; 14,9415. ^RAfO 48-49 (2001-2002) 175-180 (*Foxvog, Daniel A.*).

10077 *Chiodi, Silvia Maria* Rapporto cielo, terra ed inferi nel mondo mesopotamico. ^MCAGNI, L., 1: SMDSA 61: 2001 ⇒15. 107-124.

10078 *Conti, Giovanni* A proposito di Gibil, dio del fuoco;

10079 *Dietrich, Manfried* Der unheilbringende Wurm: Beschwörung gegen den 'Zahnwurm' (CT 17,50). ^MCAGNI, L., 1. SMDSA 61: 2001 ⇒15. 125-134/209-220.

10080 *Groddek, Detlev* '[Diese Angelegenheit] höre Ištar von Ninive nicht!': eine neue Episode einer Erzählung des Kumarbi-Kreises. WO 31 (2001) 23-30.

10081 *Groneberg, Brigitte* Die Liebesbeschwörung *MAD* V 8 und ihr literarischer Kontext. RA 95 (2001) 97-113.

10082 *Hirsch, Hans* Zur Vorstellung von einem barmherzigen Gott im alten Mesopotamien: eine Annäherung. ^MCAGNI, L., 1. SMDSA 61: 2001 ⇒15. 451-462.

10083 **Hunger, Hermann; Pingree, David** Astral sciences in Mesopotamia. HO 1/44: 1999 ⇒15,10244. ^RBiOr 58 (2001) 41-59 (*Brown, David*); OLZ 96 (2001) 503-510 (*Oelsner, Joachim*); WO 31 (2000-2001) 229-235 (*Koch, Johannes*).

10084 *Klein, Jacob* The so-called 'Spell of Nudimmud' (ELA 134-155): a re-examination. ^MCAGNI, L., 2: SMDSA 61: 2001 ⇒15. 563-584.

10085 *Koch, Heidemarie* Früheste Götterdarstellungen in Elam und Mesopotamien. ^MCAGNI, L., 2: SMDSA 61: 2001 ⇒15. 585-605.

10086 *Koch, Johannes* Neues von den babylonischen Planeten-Hypsomata. WO 31 (2001) 46-71.

10087 *Lundström, Steven* 'Wenn du in die Unterwelt hinabsteigen willst...': mesopotamische Vorstellungen von der Ordnung der Unterwelt. ^FHAAS, V. 2001 ⇒39. 245-253.

10088 *Mander, Pietro* Antecedents in the cuneiform literature of the Attis tradition in late antiquity. JANER 1 (2001) 100-149;

10089 General considerations on main concerns in the religion of ancient Mesopotamia. ^MCAGNI, L., 2: SMDSA 61: 2001 ⇒15. 635-664.

10090 *Mayer, Walter* Waffenreinigung im assyrischen Kriegsritual. Kult, Konflikt. AOAT 285: 2001 ⇒387. 123-133.

10091 *Müller-Kessler, Christa* Lilit(s) in der aramäisch-magischen Literatur der Spätantike, Teil 1: Wüstenbeherrscherin, Baum-Lilit und Kindesräuberin. AltOrF 28 (2001) 338-352.

10092 *Nissinen, Martti* Akkadian rituals and poetry of divine love. Mythology and mythologies. 2001 ⇒589. 93-136.

10093 *Pettinato, Giovanni* Discesa di Enki agli inferi?. ^MCAGNI, L., 2: SMDSA 61: 2001 ⇒15. 863-879.

10094 **Pettinato, Giovanni** Mitologia sumerica. Classici delle religioni, sezione prima: le religioni orientali: T 2001, UTET 575 pp. 88-02-05807-5. Bibl. 79-87.

10095 *Pomponio, Francesco* Bunene, un dio che non fece carriera. ^MCAGNI, L., 2: SMDSA 61: 2001 ⇒15. 887-904.

10096 *Pongratz-Leisten, Beate* Mental map und Weltbild in Mesopotamien. Das biblische Weltbild. FAT 32: 2001 ⇒285. 261-279.

10097 **Pongratz-Leisten, Beate** Herrschaftswissen in Mesopotamien: Formen der Kommunikation zwischen Gott und König im 2. und 1. Jahrtausend v.Chr. State Archives of Assyria Studies 10: 1999 ⇒ 15,10254. ^RArOr 69 (2001) 526-527 (*Pečirková, Jana*).

10098 *Pongratz-Leisten, Beate* The other and the enemy in the Mesopotamian conception of the world. Mythology and mythologies. 2001 ⇒589. 195-231.

10099 **Reiner, Erica** Babylonian planetary omens, 3. 1998 ⇒15,10255. ^ROLZ 96 (2001) 510-515 (*Oelsner, Joachim*).

10100 *Renger, Johannes* Aus-der-Geschichte-lernen: das en-Priesteramt von Ur unter den Dynastien von Akkade und Ur III. ^FHAAS, V. 2001 ⇒39. 373-376.

10101 *Richardson, Seth* An Assyrian garden of ancestors: room 1, northwest palace, Kalḫu. SSA Bulletin 13 (1999-2001) 145-216.

10102 **Richter, Thomas** Untersuchungen zu den lokalen Panthea Süd- und Mittelbabyloniens in altbabylonischer Zeit. AOAT 257: 1999 ⇒15,10258. ^RBiOr 58 (2001) 173-176 (*Stol, M.*).

10103 **Rochberg, Francesca R.** Babylonian horoscopes. TAPhS 88,1: 1998 ⇒14,9446; 15,10262. ^RJNES 60 (2001) 62-65 (*Koch, Johannes*); Or. 69 (2000) 122-125 (*Brown, David*).

10104 *Röllig, Wolfgang* Myths about the netherworld in the ancient Near East and their counterparts in the Greek religion. La questione delle influenze. 2001 ⇒574. 307-114.

10105 *Sanders, Seth L.* A historiography of demons: preterit-thema, para-myth, and historiola in the morphology of genres. Proceedings of the XLVe Rencontre Assyriologique, 1: 2001 ⇒577. 429-440.

10106 **Schwemer, Daniel** Die Wettergottgestalten Mesopotamiens und Nordsyriens im Zeitalter der Keilschriftkulturen: Materialien und Studien nach den schriftlichen Quellen. Wsb 2001, Harrassowitz xiv; 1024 pp. €101.24. 3-447-04456-X. Bibl. 735-811. ^RUF 33 (2001) 657-677 (*Dietrich, Manfred*).

10107 **Sherwin, Simon J.** Mesopotamian religious syncretism: the interaction of religion and politics in the 3rd and 2nd millennia BC. Diss. Cambridge 2001, ^D*Postgate, J.N.* [TynB 52,311-313].

10108 **Vanstiphout, Herman** Helden en goden van Sumer. 1998 ⇒14, 9452. ^RBiOr 58 (2001) 404-411 (*Römer, W.H.Ph.*).

10109 ^T**Walker, Christopher; Dick, Michael B.** The induction of the cult image in ancient Mesopotamia: the Mesopotamian *mis pî* ritual. SAA.Literary Texts 1: Helsinki 2001, The Neo-Assyrian Text Corpus Project vii; 267 pp. $75. 951-45-9048-1. Transliteration... commentary; bibl. 248-259; incl. CD-Rom.

10110 *Westenholz, Joan Goodnick* Intimations of mortality. ^MCAGNI, L., 2: SMDSA 61: 2001 ⇒15. 1179-1201.

10111 *Zgoll, Annette* Sumerische Religion. TRE 32. 2001 ⇒665. 457-62.

M7.5 Religio persiana

10112 **Boyce, Mary** Zoroastrians: their religious beliefs and practices. Library of religious beliefs and practices: L 2001, Routledge xxv; 252 pp. $25. 0-415-23902-8. Bibl. 229-236.

10113 **Gignoux, Philippe** Man and cosmos in ancient Iran. Serie orientale Roma 91: R 2001, Istituto Italiano per l'Africa e l'Oriente 147 pp. Bibl. 127-136.

10114 *Grillot-Susini, Françoise* Le monde d'en bas en Susiane. RA 95 (2001) 141-148.

10115 *Reeves, John C.* Adam meets the evil Archon: the biblical roots of a Persian religion. BiRe 17/4 (2001) 34-41, 51-52.

10116 *Steve, Marie-Joseph* L'au-delà zoroastrien: le 'Paradis des lumières infinies'. Akkadica 122 (2001) iii-xii.

M8.2 *Muḥammad et asseclae*—Qur'an and early diffusion of Islam

10117 *Abugideiri, Hibba* Hagar: a historical model for 'gender jihad'. Daughters of Abraham. 2001 ⇒528. 81-107.

10118 **Anzuini, Carlo Aberto** I manoscritti coranici della Biblioteca Apostolica Vaticana e delle biblioteche romane. StT 401: Città del Vaticano 2001, Biblioteca Apostolica Vaticana xiii; 489 pp. 88-210-0724-3. Bibl. 447-455; 459-462.

10119 *Bauschke, Martin* Der koranische Jesus und die christliche Theologie. MThZ 52 (2001) 26-33.

10120 **Borrmans, Maurice** Gesù Cristo e i musulmani del XX secolo. 2000 ⇒16,10374. ^RRdT 42 (2001) 146-149 (*Poggi, Vincenzo*).

10121 *Broşteanu, Monica* A comparison of incomparables: God's personal name and a few names regarding various attributes of the divine essence in the scriptures of the great monotheist religions. CICat 2/2 (2001) 18-32 Rés. 32. **Romanian.**

10122 *Busse, Heribert* Aaron (Harun) im Islam. WUB 19 (2001) 64-65.

10123 *Khan, Irfan Ahmad* The Qur'anic view of Moses as a messenger of God from the children of Israel to Pharaoh. Jewish-Muslim encounters. 2001 ⇒379. 35-50.

10124 *Lupaşcu, Silviu* Rewritten bible, rewritten gospel and rewritten Qur'an in *Mathnawi* by Jalal-ud-din RUMI: 'The tale of Moses'. CICat 2/2 (2001) 113-121. Sum 121. **Romanian.**

10125 **Masood, Steven** The Bible and the Qur'an: a question of integrity. L 2001, Om xix; 228 pp. 1-85078-369-1. Bibl. 220-228.

10126 *Mohagheghi, Hamideh* Apokalyptik im Q'uran. Aktuelle Apokalyptik!. Loccumer Protokolle 20/99: 2001 ⇒6097. 79-87.

Neusner, J. Judaism and Islam in practice 2000 ⇒9320.

10127 ᴱ**Paret, Rudi** Der Koran. Digitale Bibliothek 46: B 2001, Directmedia 1: CD-ROM. 3-89853-146-5.

10128 *Peters, F.E.* Jesus in Islam. Jesus then and now. 2001 ⇒483. 260-270.

10129 *Reynolds, Gabriel* Said Jesus, the Qā'im and the end of the world. RSO 75 (2001) 55-86.

10130 **Rippin, Andrew** The Qur'an and its interpretative tradition. CStS 715: Aldershot, Hampshire 2001, Ashgate xx; 336 pp. 0-86078-848-2.

10131 *Robin, Christian* Les 'Filles de Dieu' de Saba' à la Mecque: reflexions sur l'agencement des pantheons dans l'Arabie ancienne. Sem. 50 (2001) 113-192.

10132 **Rubin, Uri** Between bible and Qur'an: the children of Israel and the Islamic self-image. Princeton, NJ 1999, Darwin 293 pp $30.

10133 **Sfar, Mondher** Le Coran, la Bible et l'Orient ancien. ²1998 ⇒14, 9473; 16,10394. ᴿThLZ 126 (2001) 24-26 (*Heine, Peter*).

10134 **Tottoli, Roberto** I profeti biblici nella tradizione islamica. StBi 121: 1999 ⇒15,10291; 16,10396. ᴿSal. 63 (2001) 389-390 (*Vicent, R.*); Protest. 56 (2001) 303-304 (*La Torre, Giuseppe*); RTL 32 (2001) 564-5 (*Platti, E.*); OM 20 (2001) 482-483 (*Branca, Paolo*).

10135 *Veinstein, Gilles* Les usages du livre saint dans l'islam et le christianisme: présentation. RHR 218 (2001) 5-12.

M8.3 Islam, *evolutio recentior*—later theory and practice

10136   Jacov, Marko L'Europa tra conquiste ottomane e leghe sante. StT
         403: Città del Vaticano 2001, Biblioteca Apostolica Vaticana 283
         pp. 88-210-0730-8.
10137   ᴱKhoury, Adel Theodor; Hagemann, Ludwig; Heine, Peter
         Lexikon des Islam: elektronische Ressource: Geschichte—Ideen—
         Gestalten. Digitale Bibliothek 47: B 2001, Directmedia. 1 CD-
         ROM. 3-89853-147-3.
10138   Miehl, Melanie 99 Fragen zum Islam. GTBS 1203: Gü ²2001,
         Gü'er 144 pp. 3-579-01203-7.
10139   Scarcia, Gianroberto Ripensare la creazione: riflessioni autobio-
         grafiche sulla teoria del diritto musulmano. Saggi 15: R 2001, Jou-
         vence 233 pp. 88-7801-303-X.
10140   Il terrorismo sconfigge le grandi trasversali teologiche del monote-
         ismo biblico e coranico. Servitium 35 (2001) 680-684.
10141   Watt, W. Montgomery Breve storia dell'Islam. Bo 2001, Mulino
         144 pp. €9.30.

M8.4 Islamic-Christian relations

10142   *Borrmans, Maurice* Qui est Jésus pour les musulmans d'aujourd'-
         hui?. StMiss 50 (2001) 251-270,
10143   Koscielniak, Krysztof Tradycja Muzulmanska na tle akulturacji
         chrzescijansko-islamskiej od VII do X wieku: Geneza, historia i
         znaczenie zapozyczen nowotestamentowych w hadisach. Kraków
         2001, UNUM 384 pp. 83-87022-60-8. Bibl. 315-341. P.
10144   Leirvik, Oddbjørn Images of Jesus Christ in Islam. SMU: 1999 ⇒
         15,10301. ᴿTS 62 (2001) 197-198 (*McAuliffe, Jane Dammen*);
         RSR 89 (2001) 310-311 (*Fédou, Michel*).
10145   Meynet, Roland, *al.*, Rhétorique sémitique: textes de la bible et de
         la tradition musulmane. 1998 ⇒14,4109...16,10404. ᴿRhetorica 19
         (2001) 173-174 & RHPhR 81 (2001) 204-5 (*Heintz, Jean-George*).
10146   *Ortkemper, Franz-Josef* Feindbild Islam?. BiKi 56 (2001) 252-253.
10147   *Punt, Jeremy* The Bible and multiscripturality in South Africa:
         moving beyond the boon-or-bane debate. R & T 8/1 (2001) 61-95.
10148   *Sakowicz, Eugeniusz* Jezus i muzulmanie [Jésus et les musulmans].
         AtK 136/1 (2001) 40-52 Sum. 52. P.

M8.5 **Religiones Indiae**, *Extremi Orientis, Africae, Amerindiae*

10149   *Adamo, David Tuesday* African influence on ancient Israel. BOTSA 11 (2001) 11-14.

10150   *Ahirika, Edwin A.* Priesthood in Israelite and Igbo religions: a comparison. BiBh 27 (2001) 120-133.

10151   ᴱ**Emilsen, William W.** GHANDI's bible. Delhi 2001, ISPCK xlii; 185 pp. Rs95/$9/£7.

10152   **Fic, Leonard** Buddyzm a chrześcijaństwo: problem 'Boga' i Jezusa Chrystusa w buddyzmie [Bouddhisme et christianisme: le problème de 'Dieu' et de Jésus Christ dans le bouddhisme]. AtK 136/1 (2001) 22-39 Zsfg. 39. **P.**

10153   *Harris, Elizabeth* Avatāra, bodhisattva or prophet: meeting Jesus through the eyes of other faiths. Dialogue 28 (2001) 106-129.

10154   *Khiok-khng, Yeo* Messianic predestination in Romans 8 and classical Confucianism. SBL.SP 2001. SBL.SPS 40: 2001 ⇒494. 58-80.

10155   *Kłodkowski, Piotr* Chrystus a hinduizm [Jésus Christ et hindouisme]. AtK 136/1 (2001) 53-72 Sum. 72. **P.**

10156   *Lavik, Marta Høyland* Some critical remarks to Le Roux, Wambutda and Adamo. BOTSA 11 (2001) 15-16.

10157   **Leong, Kenneth S.** The Zen teachings of Jesus. NY 2001, Crossroad 239 pp. 0-8245-1883-7. Rev. edition.

10158   ᴱ**Notz, Klaus-Josef** Lexikon des Buddhismus: Grundbegriffe–Traditionen–Praxis. Digitale Bibliothek 48: B 2001, Directmedia 1 CD-ROM. 3-89853-148-1.

10159   *Park, Andrew Sung* A theology of the way (Tao). Interp. 55 (2001) 389-399.

10160   ᴱ**Sharf, Robert H. & Elizabeth Horton** Living images: Japanese Buddhist icons in context. Asian Religions & Cultures: Stanford, CA 2001, Stanford University Pr. xiii (2); 266 pp. 0-8047-3989-7.

10161   *Susaimanickam, J.* Protest: the language of prophecy. JDh 26 (2001) 311-335.

10162   **Young, R.F.; Jebanesan, S.** The bible trembled: the Hindu-Christian controversies of nineteenth-century Ceylon. 1995 ⇒13, 9707; 15,10317. ᴿABORI 82 (2001 267-269 (*Anand, Subhash*).

XVII. Historia Medii Orientis Biblici

Q1   *Syria prae-Islamica, Canaan* Israel Veteris Testamenti

10163   **Albertz, Rainer** Die Exilzeit: 6. Jahrhundert v. Chr. Biblische Enzyklopädie 7: Stu 2001, Kohlhammer 344 pp. €22.80. 3-17-012336-X.

10164   **Ash, Paul S.** David, Solomon and Egypt: a reassessment. JSOT.S 297: 1999 ⇒15,10320. [R]JBL 120 (2001) 152-153 (*Chavalas, Mark W.*); OLZ 96 (2001) 719-727 (*Schipper, Bernd U.*).

10165   *Bieniada, Michal* Factors which effected changes in settlement pattern and the character of "Israelite settlement" during the transitional Late Bronze and Early Iron Age in Palestine. PJBR 1/2 (2001) 157-199.

10166   *Bondi, Sandro Filippo* Interferenza fra culture nel Mediterraneo antico: Fenici, Punici, Greci. I Greci oltre la Grecia. 2001 ⇒440. 369-400.

10167   **Bright, John** A history of Israel. [4]2000 ⇒16,10443. [R]Estudos Bíblicos 69 (2001) 90-93 (*Garmus, Ludovico*).

10168   **Brown, John Pairman** Israel and Hellas. BZAW 231: 1995 ⇒11/2,9197...15,10620. [R]Cart. 17 (2001) 211-12 (*Álvarez Barredo, M.*).

10169   *Cardellini, Innocenzo* L'esilio: un normale evento storico riletto con innovativa forza ideale. [M]CAGNI, L., 3. SMDSA 61: 2001 ⇒15. 1331-1353.

10170   **Carter, E. Charles** The emergence of Yehud in the Persian period: a social and demographic study. JSOT.S 294: 1999 ⇒15,10325. [R]VT 51 (2001) 559-560 (*Gillingham, Susan*); BiOr 59 (2002) 373-377 (*Labahn, Antje*).

10171   *Cazelles, Henri* La bible et la culture cunéiforme. [M]CAGNI, L., 3: SMDSA 61: 2001 ⇒15. 1385-1399.

10172   *Coggins, Richard J.* Disputed questions in biblical studies, 1: history and story in the Old Testament. ET 112 (2001) 257-260.

10173   *Cooper, E.N.* Archaeological perspectives on the political history of the Euphrates Valley, during the early second millenium [!] B.C. Canadian research on ancient Syria. 2001 ⇒581. 79-86.

10174   *Davies, Graham I.* Genesis and the early history of Israel: a survey of research. Studies in the book of Genesis. BEThL 155: 2001 ⇒ 1936. 105-134.

10175   *Dever, William G.* Excavating the Hebrew Bible, or burying it again?. BASOR 322 (2001) 67-77;

10176   Archaeology and the history of Israel. The Blackwell companion to the Hebrew Bible. 2001 ⇒653. 119-126.

10177   **Dever, William G.** What did the biblical writers know and when did they know it?: what archaeology can tell us about the reality of Ancient Israel. GR 2001, Eerdmans xiii; 313 pp. $25. 0-8028-4794-3. [R]America 185/1 (2001) 33-35 (*Coogan, Michael*); Igreja e missão 54 (2001) 235-236 (*Couto, A.*); ArOr 69 (2001) 638-640 (*Segert, Stanislav*).

10178   **Dion, Paul Eugène** Les araméens à l'Âge du fer: histoire politique et structures sociales. ÉtB 34: 1997 ⇒13,9736... 15,10329. [R]ThLZ 126 (2001) 501-505 (*Kreuzer, Siegfried*).

10179   **Fox, Nili Sacher** In the service of the king: officialdom in ancient Israel and Judah. MHUC 23: 2000 ⇒16,10455. [R]BASOR 323 (2001) 103-104 (*McKenzie, Steven L.*).

10180   *Freu, Jacques* Ugarit et les puissances à l'époque amarnienne (c. 1350-1310 av. J.-C.). Sem. 50 (2001) 9-39.

10181   **Gallagher, William R.** Sennacherib's campaign to Judah: new studies. 1999 ⇒15,10337. [R]JRAS 11 (2001) 55-57 (*Millard, Alan*); BiOr 58 (2001) 227-229 (*Rudman, Dominic*); JBL 120 (2001) 539-541 (*Roberts, J.J.M.*); RBLit 3 (2001) 144-146 (*Roberts, J.J.M.*).

10182   *Gane, Roy E.* El fin de la monarquia israelita. Theologika 16 (2001) 84-127.

10183   **Garbini, Giovanni** Il ritorno dall'esilio babilonese. StBi 129: Brescia 2001, Paideia 230 pp. €20.66. 88-394-0614-X. [R]Protest. 56 (2001) 299-300 (*Noffke, Eric*).

10184   *Gruber, Mayer I.* The ancient Israel debate: a Jewish postcolonial perspective. ANESt 38 (2001) 3-27.

10185   *Gunn, David M.* The myth of Israel: between present and past. Did Moses speak Attic?. JSOT.S 317: 2001 ⇒270. 182-199.

10186   *Harrison, Timothy P.* Tell Taʻyinat and the kingdom of Unqi. [F]DION, P.-E. 2. JSOT.S 325: 2001 ⇒25. 115-132.

10187   *Heltzer, M.* The political institutions of ancient Emar as compared with contemporary Ugarit (13.-beginning of the 12. century B.C. E.). UF 33 (2001) 219-236.

10188   *Hoppe, Leslie J.* The history of Israel in the monarchic period. The Blackwell companion to the Hebrew Bible. Blackwell companions to religion 3: 2001 ⇒653. 87-101.

10189   **Isserlin, Benedikt Sigmund Johannes** Das Volk der Bibel: von den Anfängen bis zum Babylonischen Exil. [T]*Jaros-Deckert, Brigitte*: Kulturgeschichte der antiken Welt 84: Mainz 2001, Von Zabern vii; 327 pp. €45. 3-8053-2713-7. Bibl. 304-317;

10190   The Israelites. Mp 2001, Fortress 304 pp. $23. 0-8006-3426-8 [BiTod 39,382—Bergant, Dianne].

10191 **Keel, Othmar; Uehlinger, Christoph** Göttinnen, Götter und Gottessymbole: neue Erkenntnisse zur Religionsgeschichte Kanaans und Israels aufgrund bislang unerschlossener ikonographischer Quellen. QD 134: [4]1998 ⇒14,9544. [R]ArOr 69 (2001) 530-532 (*Břeňová, Klára*).

10192 **Kinet, Dirk** Geschichte Israels. NEB.E 2 z. AT: Wü 2001, Echter 239 pp. €25.44. 3-429-02315-7. [R]RevAg 42 (2001) 894-895 (*Sabugal, Santos*); EstTrin 35 (2001) 457-459 (*Vázquez Allegue, Jaime*); ActBib 38 (2001) 201-202 (*Boada, J.*).

10193 *Krebernik, Manfred* Neues zu den Eponymen unter Jasmaḫ-Addu. AltOrF 28 (2001) 1-7.

10194 *Kuan, Jeffrey K.* Šamši-ilu and the realpolitik of Israel and Aram-Damascus in the eighth century BCE. [F]MILLER, J.: JSOT.S 343: 2001 ⇒74. 135-151 [2 Kgs 10,32-33; 12,17-18].

10195 **Langston, Scott M.** Cultic sites in the tribe of Benjamin: Benjamite prominence in the religion of Israel. AmUSt.TR 200: 1998 ⇒14,9549. [R]CBQ 63 (2001) 116-117 (*Fulco, William J.*).

10196 *Lemaire, André* Les premiers rois araméens dans la tradition biblique. [F]DION, P.-E. 1: JSOT.S 324: 2001 ⇒25. 113-143 [Gen 36, 31-39; 1 Kgs 11,14-25].

10197 **Lemche, Niels Peter** The Israelites in history and tradition. 1998 ⇒14,9550; 15,10356. [R]JSSt 46 (2001) 327-329 (*Provan, Iain*); JBL 119 (2000) 544-547 (*Zorn, Jeffrey R.*).

10198 **Lopasso, Vincenzo** Breve storia di Israele: da Abramo a Bar Kokhbà. Quaderni di Vivarium 3: Catanzaro 2001, Ursini 130 pp. Bibl. 129-130.

10199 [E]**MacDonald, Burton; Younker, Randall W.** Ancient Ammon. 1999 ⇒15,8566. [R]ThLZ 126 (2001) 505-507 (*Knauf, Ernst Axel*).

10200 *Malamat, Abraham* 'Distant land' as a specific category in international relations in the bible and the ancient Near East. [F]AHITUV, S. 2001 ⇒1. 283-286. H.;

10201 The proto-history of Israel: a study in method <1983>;

10202 Mari and early Israel <1985>;

10203 Pre-monarchical social institutions in Israel in the light of Mari. History of biblical Israel. 2001 <1988> ⇒182. 3-16/17-27/28-40.

10204 *Mazzoni, Stefania* La Siria e il mondo greco arcaico. I Greci oltre la Grecia. 2001 ⇒440. 283-328.

10205 *Meyers, Carol* Early Israel and the rise of the Israelite monarchy. The Blackwell companion to the Hebrew Bible. Blackwell companions to religion 3: 2001 ⇒653. 61-86.

10206 **Nissen, Hans J.** Geschichte Altvorderasiens. Oldenbourg Grundriß der Geschichte 25: 1999 ⇒15,10368; 16,10480. [R]BiOr 58 (2001)

147-148 (*Snell, Daniel C.*); OLZ 96 (2001) 208-211 (*Van De Mie-roop, Marc*).

10207 **Noll, K.L.** Canaan and Israel in antiquity: an introduction. BiSe 83: Shf 2001, Sheffield A. 331 pp. 1-84127-258-2.

10208 **Noort, E.** Die Seevölker in Palästina. 1994 ⇒10,12196... 12, 10015. [R]ZDPV 117 (2001) 76-79 (*Ehrlich, Carl S.*).

10209 **Olmo Lete, Gregorio del** El *continuum* cultural cananeo: pervivencias cananeas en el mundo fenicio-púnico. AuOr.S 14: 1996 ⇒ 12,9148. [R]OLZ 96 (2001) 538-539 (*Blázqez Martínez, José M.*).

10210 *Pardee, Dennis* Canaan. The Blackwell companion to the Hebrew Bible. Blackwell companions to religion 3: 2001 ⇒653. 151-168.

10211 **Pixley, Jorge** Heilsgeschichte von unten: eine Geschichte des Volkes Israel aus der Sicht der Armen (1220 v.Chr.-135 n.Chr.). 1997 ⇒14,9564. [R]BiLi 74 (2001) 205-206 (*Silber, Stefan*).

10212 *Rainey, Anson F.* Stones for bread: archaeology versus history. NEA(BA) 64/3 (2001) 140-149.

10213 *Rossi, Marco* La Siria e il mondo greco dopo l'età arcaica. I Greci oltre la Grecia. 2001 ⇒440. 329-368.

10214 *Ruby, J.* Assyrian provincial governors in Syria. Canadian research on ancient Syria. 2001 ⇒581. 169-174.

10215 **Sacchi, Paolo** The history of the second temple period. JSOT.S 285: 2000 ⇒16,10485. [R]RHPhR 81 (2001) 223-224 (*Grappe, Ch.*).

10216 **Schams, Christine** Jewish scribes in the Second-Temple period. JSOT.S 291: 1998 ⇒14,9570. [R]DSD 8 (2001) 196-200 (*Brooke, George J.*); JBL 120 (2001) 553-554 (*Wright, John W.*); RBLit 3 (2001) 282-284 (*Newman, Judith H.*).

10217 *Schäfer-Lichtenberger, Christa* Hazor—a city state between the major powers. SJOT 15 (2001) 104-122.

10218 *Scheffler, Eben* Beyond the judges and the amphictyony: the politics of tribal Israel (1200-1020 BCE). OTEs 14 (2001) 494-509.

10219 **Schipper, Bernd Ulrich** Israel und Ägypten in der Königszeit: die kulturellen Kontakte von Salomo bis zum Fall Jerusalems. OBO 170: 1999 ⇒15,10372. [R]BiOr 58 (2001) 376-385 (*Kitchen, K.A.*); CÉg 76 (2001) 159-162 (*Lipiński, Edward*).

10220 *Silva, Airton José da* A história de Israel na pesquisa atual. Estudos Bíblicos 71 (2001) 62-74.

10221 *Stern, E.* The Phoenicians—major role players of the ancient Mediterranean world. OTEs 14 (2001) 102-118.

10222 *Tadmor, Haim* Chronological remarks on the conquest of Samaria. [F]AHITUV, S. 2001 ⇒1. 433-436. **H.**

10223 *Thompson, Thomas L.* Methods and results: a review of two recent publications. SJOT 15 (2001) 306-325.

10224 **Thompson, Thomas L.** Early history of the Israelite people from the written and archaeological sources. 1994 ⇒8,b848...15,10377. [R]RBBras 18 (2001) 441-443.

10225 **Veenhof, Klaas R.** Geschichte des Alten Orients bis zur Zeit ALE-XANDERs des Großen. [T]*Weippert, Helga*: GAT 11: Gö 2001, Vandenhoeck & R 360 pp. €39. 3-525-51685-1. [R]RBBras 18 (2001) 439-440.

10226 **Wellhausen, Julius** Prolegomena zur Geschichte Israels. De-Gruyter-Studienbuch: B 2001 <1882>, De Gruyter viii; 444 pp. 3-11-017155-4.

10227 **Wilson, Kevin Arnold** The campaign of Pharaoh Shoshenq I into Palestine. Diss. Johns Hopkins 2001, 226 pp. 3006368.

10228 *Zwickel, Wolfgang* Biblische Archäologie. ThR 66 (2001) 288-309;

10229 Syrien I: Zeit des Alten Testaments. TRE 32. 2001 ⇒665. 585-87.

Q2 Historiographia—*theologia historiae*

10230 **Amit, Yairah** History and ideology: introduction to historiography in the Hebrew Bible. BiSe 60: 1999 ⇒15,10387. [R]HebStud 42 (2001) 322-323 (*Dyson, Anne R.*).

10231 **Barr, James** History and ideology in the Old Testament: biblical studies at the end of a millennium. 2000 ⇒16,10504. [R]RRT 8 (2001) 138-140 (*Pietsch, Michael*); BiblInterp 9 (2001) 221.224 (*Provan, Iain*); JThS 52 (2001) 717-718 (*Johnston, William*); OTEs 14 (2001) 544-545 (*Spangenberg, I.J.J.*); ET 112 (2001) 253-254 (*Rodd, C.S.*).

10232 *Bauks, M.* Quelques réflexions pour ou contre l'apparition d'historiographies bibliques à l'époque perse. TEuph 21 (2001) 43-59.

10233 *Bermejo Barrera, José Carlos* Making history, talking about history. HTh 40 (2001) 190-205.

10234 **Bordreuil, Pierre; Briquel-Chatonnet, Françoise** Le temps de la bible. 2000 ⇒16,10507. [R]SEL 18 (2001) 125-126 (*Bonnet, Corinne*).

10235 **Bottéro, Jean** The birth of God: the bible and the historian. [T]*Bolle, Kees W.*: 2000 ⇒16,10509. [R]Augustinus 46 (2001) 379 (*De Silva, Alvaro*).

10236 **Boyer, Alain; Hayoun, Maurice-Ruben** L'historiographie juive. QSJ 3616: P 2001, P.U.F. 128 pp. 2-13-052064-2.

10237 *Brettler, Marc* Memory in ancient Israel. Memory and history. 2001 ⇒441. 1-17.

10238 *Breukelman, Frans H.* "Geschichte" als theologischer Begriff. TeKo 24/2 (2001) 42-51.

10239   *Capomacchia, Anna Maria G.* Heroic dimension and historical per-
        spective in the ancient Near East. Proceedings of the XLVe Ren-
        contre Assyriologique, 1. 2001 ⇒577. 91-97.
10240   *Chopineau, Jacques* Bible et histoire: la transformation des études
        bibliques dans la deuxième moitié du XIX. siècle. AnBru 6 (2001)
        37-47.
10241   **Cortese, Enzo** Le tradizioni storiche di Israele: da Mosé a Esdra.
        La Bibbia nella storia 2: Bo 2001, EDB 432 pp. €33.57. 88-10-40-
        269-3. Bibl. 393-425.
10242   *Davies, Philip R.* The intellectual, the archaeologist and the bible.
        ᶠMILLER, J.: JSOT.S 343: 2001 ⇒74. 239-254.
10243   *Fales, Frederick Mario* Assyrian royal inscriptions: newer
        horizons. SSA Bulletin 13 (1999-2001) 115-144.
10244   *Finkelstein, Israel; Silberman, Neil A.* Archaeology and biblical
        history in the beginning of the third millennium: a view from the
        center. Cathedra 100 (2001) 47-64 Sum. 404. **H.**
10245   *Gibert, Pierre* Les premiers repères historiques. MoBi 137 (2001)
        14-17 [BuBB 35,39].
10246   *Grabbe, Lester L.* Introduction to *Did Moses speak Attic?*;
10247   Jewish historiography and scripture in the Hellenistic period;
10248   Reflections on the discussion;
10249   Who were the first real historians?: on the origins of critical histori-
        ography. Did Moses speak Attic?. JSOT.S 317: 2001 ⇒270. 16-27/
        129-155/320-340/156-181.
10250   *Herr, Bertram* Hat das Alte Testament als Quelle der Geschichte
        Israels ausgedient?: die Probe auf das Exempel 2 Reg. XII 5-17.
        VT 51 (2001) 42-54.
10251   *Hertog, Gerard C. den* Uit de hemel of uit de mensen?: de verhou-
        ding tussen geschiedenis en theologie in Tomson's Benadering van
        het Nieuwe Testament. ThRef 44 (2001) 158-173.
10252   *Japhet, Sara* Was the history of Israel 'invented' during the Persian
        period?. Cathedra 100 (2001) 109-120 Sum. 403. **H.**
10253   *Kallai, Zecharia* EA 288 and biblical historiography. RB 108
        (2001) 5-20;
10254   Punishment and sin in historiography. ᶠAHITUV, S. 2001 ⇒1. 376-
        381. **H.**
10255   *Konings, Johan* A historiografia de Israel nos 'livros históricos'.
        Estudos Bíblicos 71 (2001) 8-31.
10256   **Maier, H.** Cronologia: contare gli anni da cristiano. 2000 ⇒16,
        10538. ᴿASEs 18 (2001) 703-704 (*Ruggiero, Fabio*).
10257   *Malamat, Abraham* Doctrines of causality in Hittite and biblical
        historiography: a parallel <1955>;

10258 Distant lands and cities as a specific category in international relations in the bible and in the ancient Near East. History of biblical Israel. 2001 ⇒182. 341-352/406-410.

10259 *Marone, Corrado* Cronologie bibliche e tradizioni testuali. AnScR 6 (2001) 167-190.

10260 *Mazar, Amihai* On the relation between archaeological research and the study of the history of Israel in the biblical period. Cathedra 100 (2001) 65-88 Sum. 404. **H.**

10261 **Mehl, Andreas** Römische Geschichtsschreibung: Grundlagen und Entwicklungen: eine Einführung. Stu 2001, Kohlhammer 232 pp. €22.80.

10262 *Müller, Hans-Peter* "Jhwh gebe seinem Volk Kraft": zum Hintergrund der alttestamentlichen Geschichtsreligion. ZThK 98 (2001) 265-281 [Ps 29,11; 68,36].

10263 *Niemann, Hermann Michael* Von Oberflächen, Schichten und Strukturen: was leistet die Archäologie für die Erforschung der Geschichte Israels und Judas?. Steine–Bilder–Texte. Arbeiten zur Bibel und ihrer Geschichte 5: 2001 ⇒613. 79-121.

10264 *Nobile, Marco* Possibili incidenze o influssi della storiografia greca sulla storiografia veterotestamentaria (Genesi - 2Re). ᴹCAGNI, L., 4: SMDSA 61: 2001 ⇒15. 1893-1923.

10265 **Pani, Mario** Le ragioni della storiografia in Grecia e a Roma: una introduzione. Documenti e Studi 28: Bari 2001, Edipuglia 155 pp. €18.08. 88-7228-289-6.

10266 *Penna, Romano* Pienezza del tempo e teologia della storia. Vangelo e inculturazione. 2001 <1998> ⇒193. 729-745.

10267 **Porciani, Leone** Prime forme della storiografia greca: prospettiva locale e generale nella narrazione storica. Historia, Einzelschriften 152: Stu 2001, Steiner 156 pp. 3-515-07869-X.

10268 *Sebastiani, Silvia* Conjectural history vs. the bible: eighteenth-century Scottish historians and the idea of history in the *Encyclopaedia Britannica*. Storia della storiografia 39 (2001) 51-61.

10269 **Ska, Jean-Louis** Les énigmes du passé: histoire d'Israël et récit biblique. ᵀ*Di Pede, Elena*: Le livre et le rouleau 14: Bru 2001, Lessius 144 pp. €14.50. 2-87299-113-1. Bibl. 135-136.

10270 **Snell, Daniel C.** Flight and freedom in the Ancient Near East. Culture and history of the Ancient Near East 8: Lei 2001, Brill xi; 200 pp. €48. 90-04-12010-6. Bibl. 179-191.

10271 **Thompson, T.L.** The bible in history: how writers create a past. 1999 ⇒15,10449; 16,10556. ᴿBib. 82 (2001) 293-298 (*Zwickel, Wolfgang*); SJOT 14 (2000) 117-139 (*Grabbe, Lester L.*).

10272 *Tronina, Antoni* Biblijna wizja ludzkich dziejów [Biblical vision of human history]. Ethos 14/4 (2001) 75-83. **P.**

10273   *Tucker, Aviezer* The future of the philosophy of historiography.
        HTh 40 (2001) 37-56.

10274   *Uehlinger, Christoph* Bildquellen und 'Geschichte Israels': grund-
        sätzliche Überlegungen und Fallbeispiele. Steine–Bilder–Texte.
        Arbeiten zur Bibel und ihrer Geschichte 5: 2001 ⇒613. 25-77.

10275   **Vaahtera, Jyri** Roman augural lore in Greek historiography: a
        study of the theory and terminology. Hist.Einzelschriften 156: Stu
        2001, Steiner 194 pp. 3-515-07946-7. Bibl. 169-179.

Q3 *Historia Ægypti*—Egypt

10276   **Alston, R.** Soldier and society in Roman Egypt: a social history.
        1998 <1995> ⇒11/2,c564;15,10456. ᴿAt. 89 (2001) 263-264 (*Fo-
        raboschi, Daniele*).

10277   **Assmann, Jan** Herrschaft und Heil: politische Theologie in Altä-
        gypten, Israel und Europa. 2000 ⇒16,10562. ᴿZRGG 53 (2001)
        375-377 (*Mehring, Reinhard*).

10278   *Ayud, Mariam* Some thoughts on the disappearance of the office of
        the god's wife of Amun. JSSEA 28 (2001) 1-14.

10279   **Baud, Michel** Famille royale et pouvoir sous l'Ancien Empire é-
        gyptien. 1999 2 vols ⇒15,10460; 16,10565. ᴿOLZ 96 (2001) 178-
        183 (*Altenmüller, Hartwig*).

10280   *Beckerath, Jürgen von* Überlegungen zum Zeitabstand zwischen
        Ramses II. und dem Ende der XXI. Dynastie. GöMisz 181 (2001)
        15-18.

10281   **Beckerath, Jürgen von** Chronologie des pharaonischen Ägypten:
        die Zeitbestimmung der ägyptischen Geschichte von der Vorzeit bis
        332 v. Chr. MÄST 46: 1997 ⇒13,9858... 16,10567. ᴿCÉg 76
        (2001) 116-118 (*Spalinger, Anthony*);

10282   Handbuch der ägyptischen Königsnamen. MÄSt 49: ²1999 <1984>
        ⇒15,10461. ᴿCÉg 76 (2001) 119-120 (*Meulenaere, Herman de*).

10283   *Bierbrier, Morris L.* What's in a name?. ArOr 69 (2001) 583-585.

10284   **Brewer, Douglas J.; Teeter, Emily** Egypt and the Egyptians. 1999
        ⇒15,10465. ᴿJournal of African History 42 (2001) 117-118
        (*Morris, Ellen*).

10285   **Casson, Lionel** Everyday life in ancient Egypt. Baltimore ²2001
        <1975>, Johns Hopkins Univ. Pr. xi; 163 pp. 0-8018-6600-6/1-4.

10286   **Ciałowicz, K.M.** La naissance d'un royaume: l'Égypte dès la péri-
        ode prédynastique à la fin de la Iᵉʳᵉ dynastie. Kraków 2001, Uniw.
        Jagielloński 259 pp. 83-7188-483-4.

10287   *Clancy, Frank* Errors and assumptions: a reply to Kenneth Kitchen.
        JSOT 93 (2001) 13-15.

10288 *Depuydt, Leo* Glosses to JEROME's Eusebios as a source for Pharaonic history. CÉg 76 (2001) 30-47.

10289 [E]**Eide, Tormod,** *al.*, Fontes historiae nubiorum: textual sources for the history of the Middle Nile region between the eighth century BC and the sixth century AD, 4: Corrigenda and indices. 2000 ⇒16,10578. [R]Or. 70 (2001) 328-330 (*Hofmann, Inge*).

10290 **Fisher, Marjorie M.** The sons of Ramesses II. ÄAT 53: Wsb 2001, Harrassowitz 2 vols. 3-447-04486-1. Bibl. v.2 215-232.

10291 *Fox, Michael V.* Deine Liebe ist ein berauschendes Getränk: die Liebeslyrik im Alten Ägypten. WUB 21 (2001) 21-25.

10292 **Gabolde, Marc** D'Akhenaton à Toutânkhamon. 1998 ⇒14,9643. [R]BiOr 58 (2001) 91-97 (*Eaton-Krauss, M, Krauss, Rolf*).

10293 **Grajetzki, Wolfram** Die höchsten Beamten der ägyptischen Zentralverwaltung zur Zeit des Mittleren Reiches: Prosopographie, Titel und Titelreihen. 2000 ⇒16,10583. [R]JEA 87 (2001) 197-200 (*Franke, Detlef*).

10294 *Green, L.* In search of ancient Egyptian virgins: a study in comparative values. JSSEA 28 (2001) 90-98.

10295 **Gurrid, John** Ancient Egypt and the Old Testament. 1997 ⇒14, 9650. [R]PEQ 133 (2001) 59-60 (*Uphill, Eric*).

10296 *Haring, Ben* Hoe bestuurt een ketter zijn land? [Achnaton]. Phoe. 47 (2001) 36-52.

10297 **Hartung, Ulrich,** *al.*, Umn El-Qaab II: Importkeramik aus dem Friedhof U in Abydos (Umm el-Qaab) und die Beziehungen Ägyptens zu Vorderasien im 4. Jahrtausend v. Chr. Archäologische Veröffentlichungen 92: Mainz 2001, Von Zabern xvi; 481 pp. 3-8053-2784-6. 101 pl.

10298 *Hengstl, Joachim* Rechtsanthropologie, Rechtssoziologie und die Rechtsordnung im ptolemäischen Ägypten. XXII Congresso di papirologia, 1. 2001 ⇒555. 619-639.

10299 **Higginbotham, Carolyn R.** Egyptianization and elite emulation in Ramesside Palestine: governance and accommodation on the imperial periphery. 2000 ⇒16,10587 [R]JRAS 11 (2001) 253-254 (*Kitchen, K.A.*)

10300 **Hölbl, Günther** A history of the Ptolemaic Empire. [T]*Saavedra, Tina*: L 2001, Routledge xxxvi; 373 pp. £20. 0-415-20145-4. Bibl.

10301 **Huss, Werner** Ägypten in hellenistischer Zeit, 332-30 v. Chr. Mü 2001, Beck 885 pp. FS148. 3-406-47154-4. Bibl. 761-853.

10302 *Istasse, Nathaël* Trois notes sur les affranchis dans les papyrus de l'Égypte romaine. CÉg 76 (2001) 202-208.

10303 *Kitchen, Kenneth Anderson* The Shoshenqs of Egypt and Palestine. JSOT 93 (2001) 3-12.

10304   *Knauf, Ernst Axel* Shoshenq at Megiddo. BN 107/108 (2001) 31.

10305   *Koyano, Akira* The concept of borders or frontiers, and their geographical locations in ancient Egypt. Nippon Oriento Garkai 44/1 (2001) 1-24 Sum. 1-2. **J.**

10306   *Krol, A.A.* Sed-festival and the origins of the Ancient Egyptian state. Journal of Ancient History 4 (2001) 3-11 Sum. 10. **R.**

10307   **Lesko, Barbara S.** The remarkable women of ancient Egypt. Providence 1996, Scribe 68 pp. Ill. [R]JEA 87 (2001) 190-193 (*Fletcher, Joann*).

10308   *Lieven, Alexandra von* Kleine Beiträge zur Vergöttlichung Amenophis' I.. II: der Amenophis-Kult nach dem Ende des Neuen Reiches. ZÄS 128 (2001) 41-64.

10309   **Lohwasser, Angelika** Die königlichen Frauen im antiken Reich von Kusch: 25. Dynastie bis zur Zeit des Nastasen. Meroitica 19: Wsb 2001, Harrassowitz xxiv; 407 pp. €75.67. 3-447-04407-1. Bibl. 350-381.

10310   *Lurson, Benoît* La légitimation du pouvoir royal par l'observance des rites osiriens: analyse d'une séquence de scènes de la grande salle hypostyle de Karnak. [F]DESROCHES NOBLECOURT, C. 2001 ⇒ 22. 303-332.

10311   *Manning, Joseph G.* Twilight of the gods: economic power and the land tenure regime in Ptolemaic Egypt. XXII Congresso di papirologia, 2. 2001 ⇒555. 861-878.

10312   **McDowell, A.G.** Village life in ancient Egypt: laundry lists and love songs. 1999 ⇒15,10496. [R]CamArchJ 11 (2001) 123-130 (*Kemp, Barry*); BSOAS 64 (2001) 268-269 (*Kuhrt, Amélie*).

10313   **Montserrat, Dominic** Akhenaten: history, fantasy and Ancient Egypt. 2000 ⇒16,10600. [R]DiscEg 50 (2001) 137-140 (*Wilkinson, Toby A.H.*); BiOr 58 (2001) 587-590 (*Tobin, Vladimir A.*).

10314   *Morales, Antonio J.* The suppression of the high priest Amenhotep: a suggestion to the role of Panhesi. GöMisz 181 (2001) 59-75.

10315   **Moreno Garcia, Juan Carlos** Études sur l'administration, le pouvoir et l'idéologie en Égypte, de l'Ancien au Moyen Empire. 1997 ⇒13,9902; 15,10499. [R]Or. 70 (2001) 328-330 (*Hofmann, Inge*).

10316   *Morkot, Robert* Egypt and Nubia. Empires. 2001 ⇒388. 227-251.

10317   [E]*Pouthier, Jean-Luc* Le Nil: fleuve sacré d'Égypte. MoBi 138 (2001) 3-59.

10318   *Redford, Donald B.* The so-called "codification" of Egyptian law under Darius I. Persia and torah. 2001 ⇒1919. 135-159.

10319   **Reeves, Nicholas** Akhenaten: Egypt's false prophet. L 2001, Thames & H 208 pp. £19. 0-500-05106-2. Num. ill. [R]EgArch 19 (2001) 42 (*Montserrat, Dominic*).

10320 *Reiter, Fabian* Die arsinoitischen Nomarchen im römischen Ägypten. XXII Congresso di papirologia, 2. 2001 ⇒555. 1119-1133.

10321 **Rose, Lynn E.** Sun, moon, and Sothis: a study of calendars and calendar reforms in ancient Egypt. Osiris 2: 1999 ⇒15,10510. ᴿAnCl 70 (2001) 392-394 (*Deman, Albert*).

10322 **Roth, Silke** Die Königsmütter des Alten Ägypten: von der Frühzeit bis zum Ende der 12. Dynastie. ÄAT 46: Wsb 2001, Harrassowitz xlvi; 584 pp. €85.90. 3-447-04368-7. Bibl. xviii-xxxvi.

ᴱ**Rowlandson, J.** Women and society in... Egypt 1998 ⇒435.

10323 ᴱ**Shaw, Ian** The Oxford history of ancient Egypt. 2000 ⇒16, 10617. ᴿPrudentia 33 (2001) 201-204 (*Spalinger, Anthony*).

10324 **Storm, Elfriede** Massinissa: Numidien im Aufbruch. SWGF.G 10: Stu 2001, Steiner 222 pp. FS41.60. 3-515-07829-0. 19 ill.

10325 *Thijs, Ad* Reconsidering the end of the twentieth dynasty, 6: some minor adjustments and observations concerning the chronology of the last Ramessides and the *wḥm mswt*. GöMisz 181 (2001) 95-103.

10326 *Thomas, J. David* The administration of Roman Egypt: a survey of recent research and some outstanding problems;

10327 *Thompson, Dorothy J.* Ethnê, taxes and administrative geography in early Ptolemaic Egypt. XXII Congresso di papirologia, 2. 2001 ⇒555. 1245-1254/1255-1263.

10328 *Uphill, Eric* The question of Pharaonic co-regency. DiscEg 49 (2001) 81-97.

10329 *Van Dijk, Jacobus* Toetanchamon: de contrarevolutie van een kind. Phoe. 47 (2001) 90-110.

10330 *Van Soldt, Wilfred* De internationale betrekkingen in de Amarnaperiode. Phoe. 47 (2001) 53-68.

10331 *Van Walsem, René* Sporen van een revolutie in Saqqara: het nieuw ontdekte graf van Meryneith alias Meryre en zijn plaats in de Amarnaperiode. Phoe. 47 (2001) 69-89.

10332 *Verner, Miroslav* Archaeological remarks on the 4ᵗʰ and 5ᵗʰ dynasty chronology. ArOr 69 (2001) 363-418.

10333 ᴱ**Walker, Susan; Higgs, Peter** Cleopatra of Egypt: from history to myth. L 2001, British Museum Pr. 384 pp. £25. 0-7141-1943-1. Bibl. 372-373.

10334 **Warburton, David** Egypt and the Near East: politics in the Bronze Age. Civilisations du Proche-Orient, 4. Histoire—Essais 1: Neuchâtel 2001, Recherches et Publications xv; 363 pp. 2-940032-12-2. Bibl. 228-342.

10335 **Wilkinson, T.A.H.** Early dynastic Egypt. L ²2001 <1999>, Routledge xxxiv; 413 pp. £15. 0-415-26011-6;

10336   Royal Annals of ancient Egypt. 2000 ⇒16,10631. ᴿDiscEg 49
        (2001) 95-97 (*Dodson, Aidan*).

Q4.0 Historia Mesopotamiae

10337   *Altman, Amnon* EA 59:27-29 and the efforts of Mukiš, Nuḫašše and
        Niya to establish a common front against Šuppiluliuma I;
10338   The submission of Šarrupši of Nuḫašše to Šuppiluliuma I (*CTH* 53:
        A, obv. i, 2-11). UF 33 (2001) 1-25/27-47.
10339   **André-Salvini, Béatrice** Babylone. QSJ 292: P 2001, PUF 127 pp.
        €6.50. Ill. ᴿAkkadica 122 (2001) 73-74 (*Gasche, Hermann*).
10340   ᴱ**Baker, Heather D.; Parpola, Simo** The prosopography of the
        Neo-Assyrian empire, 2: Part 2, L - N: using the electronic data
        base of the Neo-Assyrian Text Corpus Project and with the col-
        laboration of numerous colleagues. Helsinki 2001, The Neo-
        Assyrian Text Corpus Project ix; 647-975 pp. 951-45-9055-4.
10341   *Beaulieu, Paul-Alain* A land grant on a cylinder seal and Assur-
        banipal's Babylonian policy. ᴹCAGNI, L., 1: 2001 ⇒15. 25-45.
10342   *Blackham, M.* Factions, foreigners, and fads: changes of state in the
        Levant Early Bronze Age. Canadian research on ancient Syria.
        2001 ⇒581. 47-59.
10343   *Blocher, Felix* Assyrische Würdenträger und Gouverneure des 9.
        und 8. Jh.: eine Neubewertung ihrer Rolle. AltOrF 28 (2001) 298-
        324.
10344   **Bottéro, Jean**, *al.*, Everyday life in ancient Mesopotamia. ᵀ*Nevill,
        Antonia*: E 2001, University Press xii; 276 pp. $19. 0-7486-1388-9.
        Bibl. 270-272.
10345   *Cohen, Andrew C.* Dehistoricizing strategies in third-millennium B.
        C.E. royal inscriptions and rituals. Proceedings of the XLVe Ren-
        contre Assyriologique, 1. 2001 ⇒577. 99-111.
10346   *D'Agostino, Franco* 'Il re è un pazzo furioso!': appunti su uno stra-
        no caso di propaganda mesopotamica. StEeL 18 (2001) 55-61.
10347   *Dalley, Stephanie* Assyrian court narratives in Aramaic and Egyp-
        tian: historical fiction. Proceedings of the XLVe Rencontre Assyri-
        ologique, 1. 2001 ⇒577. 149-161.
10348   *Da-Riva, Rocío* Sippar in the reign of Sîn-šum-līšir (626 BC).
        AltOrF 28 (2001) 40-64.
10349   *Fincke, Jeanette C.* Der Assur-Katalog der Serie enuma anu enlil
        (EAE). Or. 70 (2001) 19-39.
10350   **Flückiger-Hawker, Esther** Urnamma of Ur in Sumerian literary
        tradition. OBO 166: 1999 ⇒15,10528; 16,10645. ᴿMes. 36 (2001)
        132-133 (*D'Agostino, F.*).

10351 *Foster, Benjamin* The forty-nine sons of Agade. ᴹCᴀɢɴɪ, L., 1: SMDSA 61: 2001 ⇒15. 309-318.

10352 **Fuchs, Andreas; Parpola, Simo** The correspondence of Sargon II Part III: letters from Babylonia and the eastern provinces. State Archives of Assyria 15: Helsinki 2001, University Press lviii; 281 pp. 951-570-497-9. Illustrations edited by *Julian Reade.*

10353 **Galil, Gershon** Israel and Assyria. Haifa 2001, Univ. of Haifa 184 pp. ᴿUF 32 (2000) 749-751 (*Heltzer, M.*). **H.**

10354 *Garelli, Paul* Réflexions sur 'le péché de Sargon'. ᴹCᴀɢɴɪ, L., 1: SMDSA 61: 2001 ⇒15. 341-343;

10355 Notes sur les éponymes de l'empire assyrien. ꜰVᴇᴇɴʜᴏꜰ, K. 2001 ⇒111. 145-149.

10356 **Gasche, Hermann** Dating the fall of Babylon: a reappraisal of second-millennium chronology. 1998 ⇒14,9724... 16,10649. ᴿBiOr 58 (2001) 163-173 (*Seal, Th.*).

10357 *Gentili, Paolo* Il re sognatore. ᴹCᴀɢɴɪ, L., 1: 2001 ⇒15. 355-373.

10358 Nabonedo: un percorso. Nabonedo e Sela'. 2001 ⇒438. 89-109.

10359 *Glassner, Jean-Jacques* Le devin historien en Mésopotamie. Proc. XLVe Rencontre Assyriologique, 1. 2001 ⇒577. 181-193;

10360 L'historien mésopotamien et la fin des empires. ᴹCᴀɢɴɪ, L., 1: SMDSA 61: 2001 ⇒15. 383-393.

10361 *Grayson, A.K.* Assyria and the Orontes valley. Canadian research on ancient Syria. 2001 ⇒581. 185-187.

10362 **Grayson, Albert Kirk** Assyrian rulers of the early first millennium BC II (858-745 BC). 1996 ⇒12,9226... 15,10535. ᴿAfO 44-45 (1997-98) 393-396.

10363 *Gruntfest, Yaakov; Heltzer, Michael* Nabonid, king of Babylon (556-539 B.C.E.) in Arabia in light of new evidence. BN 110 (2001) 25-30.

10364 *Harrak, Amir* Tales about Sennacherib: the contribution of the Syriac sources. ꜰDɪᴏɴ, P.-E. 3: JSOT.S 326: 2001 ⇒25. 168-189 [Gen 8,3; 2 Kgs 19,37].

10365 *Holloway, Steven W.* The giš Kakki Aššur and Neo-Assyrian loyalty oaths. Proc. XLVe Rencontre Assyriologique, 1. 2001 ⇒577. 239-266.

10366 **Horsnell, Malcolm J.A..** The year-names of the first dynasty of Babylon. 1999 ⇒15,10538. ᴿRA 95 (2001) 89-92 (*Charpin, D.*).

10367 **Hrouda, Barthel** Mesopotamia. M 2001, Acento 140 pp.

10368 **Ivantchik, Askold I.** Kimmerier und Skythen: kulturhistorische und chronologische Probleme der Archäologie der osteuropäischen Steppen und Kaukasiens in vor- und frühskythischer Zeit. Steppenvölker Eurasiens 2: Mainz 2001, Von Zabern 325 pp. €75.80. 5-89526-009-8.

10369 **Joannes, F.** La Mésopotamie au 1er millénaire avant J.-C. 2000 ⇒ 16,10654. ᴿREA 103 (2001) 581-582 (*Breniquet, Catherine*).

10370 *Kahn, Dan'el* The inscription of Sargon II at Tang-i Var and the chronology of Dynasty 25. Or. 70 (2001) 1-18.

10371 *Klein, Jacob* The genealogy of Nanna-Suen and its historical background. Proc. XLVe Rencontre Assyriologique, 1. 2001 ⇒577. 279-301.

10372 *Kupper, Jean-Robert* Les débuts du règne d'Ibâl-Addu. RA 95 (2001) 33-38.

10373 **Lamprichs, Roland** Die Westexpansion des neuassyrischen Reiches: eine Strukturanalyse. AOAT 239: 1995 ⇒11/2,9460... 16, 10657. ᴿWO 31 (2000-2001) 236-240 (*Faist, Betina*).

10374 *Liverani, Mario* Mesopotamian historiography and the Amarna letters. Proc. XLVe Rencontre Assyriologique, 1. 2001 ⇒577. 303-311;

10375 The fall of the Assyrian empire: ancient and modern interpretations. Empires. 2001 ⇒388. 374-391.

10376 **Liverani, Mario** International relations in the ancient Near East, 1600-1100 BC. Studies in Diplomacy: Houndmills 2001, Palgrave xvii; 241 pp. 0-333-76153-7.

10377 *Magid, Glenn* Micromanagement in the é-mi/dBa-ú: notes on the organization of labor at early dynastic Lagash. Proceedings of the XLVe Rencontre Assyriologique, 1. 2001 ⇒577. 313-328.

10378 **Masetti-Rouault, Maria Grazia** Cultures locales du Moyen-Euphrate: modèles et événements IIe-Ier mill. av. J.-C. Subartu 8: Turnhout 2001, Brepols (6) 200 pp. 2-503-99116-5. Bibl. 143-185.

10379 **Mattila, Raija** The King's magnates: a study of the highest officials of the Neo-Assyrian Empire. SAAS 11: 2000 ⇒16,10662. ᴿBiOr 58 (2001) 197-206 (*Dalley, Stephanie*).

10380 *Michaux-Colombot, Danièle* Magan and Meluḫḫa: a reappraisal through the historiography of Thalassocratic powers. Proceedings of the XLVe Rencontre Assyriologique, 1: 2001 ⇒577. 329-355.

10381 *Mora, Clelia* Per una migliore utilizzazione della corrispondenza reale assiro-ittita come fonte storica. ᴹCAGNI, L., 2: SMDSA 61: 2001 ⇒15. 765-782.

10382 *Müller, Walter W.; Al-Said, Said F.* Der babylonische König Nabonid in taymanischen Inschriften. BN 107/108 (2001) 109-119.

10383 *Na'aman, Nadav* An Assyrian residence at Ramat Raḥel?. TelAv 28 (2001) 260-280;

10384 The conquest of Yadnana according to the inscriptions of Sargon II. Proc. XLVe Rencontre Assyriologique, 1. 2001 ⇒577. 357-363.

10385 *Nevling Porter, Barbara* The importance of place: Esarhaddon's stelae at Til Barsip and Sam'al. Proceedings of the XLVe Rencontre Assyriologique, 1. 2001 ⇒577. 373-390.

10386 *Novotny, J.R.* Daughters and sisters of Neo-Hitttite and Aramaean rulers in the Assyrian harem. Canadian research on ancient Syria. 2001 ⇒581. 175-184.

10387 *Oded, Bustanai* Fundamental lines in the policies of exile of the Assyrian and Babylonian empires and their relevance to the study of the exiles of Israel and Judah in Mesopotamia. [F]AHITUV, S. 2001 ⇒ 1. 298-318. **H.**

10388 *Pecha, Lukáš* Die *igisûm*-Abgabe in den altbabylonischen Quellen. ArOr 69 (2001) 1-20.

10389 **Pečirková, Jana** Asýrie: od městského státu řiši [Assyrien: vom Stadtstaat zum Reich]. 2000 ⇒16,10667. [R]ArOr 69 (2001) 93-94 (*Hruška, Blahoslav*). CZECH.

10390 **Pollock, Susan** Ancient Mesopotamia: the Eden that never was. 1999 ⇒15,10552; 16,10669. [R]AmA 103/1 (2001) 226-8 (*Lamberg-Karlovsky, C.C.*); BiOr 58 (2001) 677-681 (*Helwing, Barbara*).

10391 *Potts, Timothy* Reading the Sargonic "historical-literary" tradition: is there a middle course? (thoughts on the great revolt against Naram-Sin). Proceedings of the XLVe Rencontre Assyriologique, 1. 2001 ⇒577. 391-408.

10392 *Prosecký, Jiří* A hymn glorifying Ashurnasirpal II. ArOr 69 (2001) 427-436.

10393 *Qatamin, Hamed* The role of Babylonia in the south of Syria: historical background. Nabonedo e Sela'. 2001 ⇒438. 83-88.

10394 [E]**Radner, Karen** The prosopography of the Neo-Assyrian Empire. 1998 ⇒15,10550. [R]VT 51 (2001) 417-419 (*Millard, A.R.*).

10395 *Reade, Julian* Assyrian king-lists, the royal tombs of Ur, and Indus origins. JNES 60 (2001) 1-30.

10396 *Rehm, Ellen* Kleine Gaben für große Götter. AltOrF 28 (2001) 102-107.

10397 **Robson, Eleanor** Mesopotamian mathematics 2100-1600 BC. 1999 ⇒15,10553. [R]Mes. 36 (2001) 133-134 (*D'Agostino, F.*); BiOr 58 (2001) 639-642 (*Freydank, H.*).

10398 *Rollinger, Robert* The ancient Greeks and the impact of the ancient Near East: textual evidence and historical perspective (ca. 750-650 BC). Mythology and mythologies. 2001 ⇒589. 233-264.

10399 **Sallaberger, Walther; Westenholz, Aage** Mesopotamien: Akkade-Zeit und Ur-III-Zeit. OBO 160/3: 1999 ⇒15,10556; 16,10674. [R]BiOr 58 (2001) 149-151 (*Snell, Daniel C.*); WZKM 91 (2001) 387-403 (*Koslova, Natalia*).

10400   *Saporetti, Claudio* Due punti sulla cronologia di Ešnunna. ᴹCᴀɢɴɪ,
        L., 2: SMDSA 61: 2001 ⇒1. 913-920.

10401   *Sassmannshausen, Leonhard* Administrative texts as a source for
        historiography. Proceedings of the XLVe Rencontre Assyriolo-
        gique, 1. 2001 ⇒577. 441-453.

10402   **Sassmannshausen, Leonhard** Beiträge zur Verwaltung und Ge-
        sellschaft Babyloniens in der Kassitenzeit. Baghdader Forschungen
        21; Deutsches Archäologisches Institut, Orient-Abteilung: Mainz
        2001, Von Zabern xv; 525 pp. €74. 3-8053-2471-5. Bibl. vii-xiii.

10403   **Schuol, Monika** Die Charakene: ein mesopotamisches Königreich
        in hellenistisch-parthischer Zeit. Oriens et Occidens 1: 2000 ⇒16,
        10676. ᴿBiOr 58 (2001) 421-423 (*Boiy, T.*).

10404   *Selz, Gebhard J.* 'Guter Hirte, weiser Fürst'—zur Vorstellung von
        Macht und zur Macht der Vorstellung im altmesopotamischen
        Herrschaftsparadigma. AltOrF 28 (2001) 8-39.

10405   *Sharlach, T. M.* Beyond chronology: the Šakkanakkus of Mari and
        the kings of Ur. Proceedings of the XLVe Rencontre Assyriolo-
        gique, 2. 2001 ⇒582. 59-70.

10406   *Sigrist, Marcel* "... du bist wahrhaftig mein Geliebter": die Liebes-
        lyrik in Mesopotamien. WUB 21 (2001) 15-20.

10407   **Swerdlow, Noel M.** The Babylonian theory of the planets. 1998 ⇒
        14,9762; 15,10561. ᴿJNES 60 (2001) 65-69 (*Koch, Johannes*).

10408   *Tanret, M.* As years went by in Sippar-Amnanum... Proceedings of
        the XLVe Rencontre Assyriologique, 1. 2001 ⇒577. 455-466.

10409   *Visicato, Giuseppe* The journey of the Sargonic King to Assur and
        Gasur;

10410   *Waters, Matthew W.* Mesopotamian sources and Neo-Elamite his-
        tory. Proc. XLVe Rencontre Assyriologique, 1. 2001 ⇒577. 467-
        472/473-482.

10411   **Yamada, Shigeo** The construction of the Assyrian Empire: a his-
        torical study of the inscriptions of Shalmanesar III (859-824 B.C.)
        relating to his campaigns to the west. 2000 ⇒16,10683. ᴿIHR 23
        (2001) 876-877 (*Postgate, Nicholas*).

Q4.5 *Historia Persiae*—Iran

10412   *Bodi, D.* La clémence des Perses envers Néhémie et ses compatri-
        otes: faveur ou opportunisme politique?. TEuph 21 (2001) 69-86.

10413   **Briant, Pierre** Bulletin d'histoire achéménide II (=BHAch II,
        1997-2000). Persika 1: P 2001, Thotm 334 pp. €42.70. 2-9145-
        3100-1. 30 fig.

10414 **Brown, John Pairman** Israel and Hellas, 3: the legacy of Iranian imperialism and the individual, with cumulative indexes to vols. I-III. BZAW 299: B 2001, De Gruyter xxxii; 548 pp. €126.80. 3-11-016882-0. [R]EtCl 69 (2001) 468-469 (*Rochette, Br.*); RBBras 18 (2001) 437-439.

10415 *Carroll, Robert P.* Exile, restoration, and colony: Judah in the Persian empire. The Blackwell companion to the Hebrew Bible. Blackwell companions to religion 3: 2001 ⇒653. 102-116.

10416 **Derakhshani, Jahanshah** Die Arier in den nahöstlichen Quellen des 3. und 2. Jahrtausends v. Chr. 1998 ⇒14,9774. [R]Mes. 36 (2001) 134-136 (*Jasink, A.M.*).

10417 *Frei, Peter* Persian imperial authorization: a summary;

10418 *Grabbe, Lester L.* The law of Moses in the Ezra tradition: more virtual than real?;

10419 *Knoppers, Gary N.* An Achaemenid imperial authorization of torah in Yehud?. Persia and torah. 2001 ⇒1919. 5-40/91-113/115-134.

10420 *Kuhrt, Amélie* The Achaemenid Persian empire (c. 550-c. 330 BCE): continuities, adaptations, transformations. Empires. 2001 ⇒ 388. 93-123.

10421 **Meinhold, Arndt** Serubbabel, der Tempel und die Provinz Jehud. Steine–Bilder–Texte. 2001 ⇒613. 193-217.

10422 **Potts, Daniel T.** The archaeology of Elam: formation and transformation of an ancient Iranian state. 1999 ⇒16,10693. [R]Or. 70 (2001) 204-205 (*Koch, Heidemarie*).

10423 *Shea, William H.* Who succeeded Xerxes on the throne of Persia?;

10424 The search for Darius the Mede (concluded), or, the time of the answer to Daniel's prayer and the date of the death of Darius the Mede. JATS 12/1 (2001) 83-88/97-105.

10425 *Ska, Jean Louis* "Persian imperial authorization": some question marks. Persia and torah. 2001 ⇒1919. 161-182.

10426 **Wiesehöfer, J.** Ancient Persia from 550 BC to 650 AD. [T]*Azodi, A.*: L 2001, Tauris xiv; 332 pp. 1-86064-675-1. 32 pl. [Ancient West & East 1/1,200—Boardman, John].

Q5 *Historia Anatoliae*—Asia Minor, Hittites [⇒T8.2]

10427 *Cohen, Yoram* The image of the "other" and Hittite historiography. Proc. XLVe Rencontre Assyriologique, 1. 2001 ⇒577. 113-12 9.

10428 **Debord, Pierre** L'Asie Mineure au IVe siècle (412-323 a.C.): pouvoirs et jeux politiques. 1999 ⇒15,10589. [R]AnCl 70 (2001) 458-460 (*Bertrand, Jean-Marie*).

10429   *Hutter-Braunsar, Sylvia* The formula "to become a God" in Hittite historigraphical texts. Proceedings of the XLVe Rencontre Assyriologique, 1. 2001 ⇒577. 267-277.

10430   *Jasink, Anna Margherita* Šuppiluliuma and Hartapu: two 'Great Kings' in conflict?;

10431   *Klengel, Horst* Einige Bemerkungen zur hethitischen Herrschaftsordnung in Syrien. IV. Internationaler Kongress. 2001 ⇒650. 235-240/255-271;

10432   Nochmals zur Rolle der Herrscher von Ḫalab und Karkamiš in der hethitischen Großreichszeit. ᶠHAAS, V. 2001 ⇒39. 191-196.

10433   *Klinger, Jörg* Historiographie als Paradigma: die Quellen zur hethitischen Geschichte und ihre Deutung;

10434   *Miller, Jared L.* Ḫattušili I's expansion into northern Syria in light of the Tikunani Letter;

10435   *Orlamünde, Julia* Zur Datierung und historischen Interpretation des hethitischen Orakelprotokolls KUB 5.1+;

10436   *Ökse, A. Tuba* Hethitisches Territorium am oberen Maraššantia: ein Rekonstruktionsversuch. IV. Internationaler Kongress. 2001 ⇒650. 272-291/410-429/511-523/499-510.

10437   ᴱ*Pouthier, Jean-Luc* L'Arménie: mémoire de la bible. MoBi 136 (2001) 12-53.

10438   **Schuler, Chr.** Ländliche Siedlungen und Gemeinden im hellenistischen und römischen Kleinasien. 1998 ⇒14,9796. ᴿAt. 89 (2001) 265-270 (*Boffo, Laura*); Gn. 73 (2001) 416-421 (*Herz, Peter*).

10439   *Sommer, Michael* Der Untergang des hethitischen Reiches: Anatolien und der östliche Mittelmeerraum um 1200 v.Chr. Saec. 52 (2001) 157-176.

10440   *Taracha, Piotr* Mycenaeans, Ahhiyawa and Hittite imperial policy in the west: a note on KUB 26.91. ᶠHAAS, V. 2001 ⇒39. 417-422.

10441   *Van den Hout, Theo* Zur Geschichte des jüngeren hethitischen Reiches;

10442   *Wazana, Nili* Border descriptions and cultural barriers;

10443   *Yakar, Jak, al.,* The territory of the appanage kingdom of Tarḫuntassa: an archaeological appraisal. IV. Internationaler Kongress. 2001 ⇒650. 213-223/696-710/711-720.

Q6.1 Historia Graeciae classicae

10444   **Baurain, Claude** Les grecs et la méditerranée orientale: des 'siècles obscurs' à la fin de l'époque archaïque. 1997 ⇒14,9808. ᴿGn. 73 (2001) 66-68 (*Haider, Peter W.*).

10445 **Gehrke, Hans-Joachim** Kleine Geschichte der Antike. 1999 ⇒15, 10600. ^RGn. 73 (2001) 728-729 (*Kienast, Dietmar*).

10446 **Hornblower, Simon** The Greek world 479-323 B.C. Routledge history of the ancient world. L 2001, Routledge xii; 354 pp. 0-415-06557-7. Bibl. 323-328.

10447 **Miller, Margaret Christina** Athens and Persia in the fifth century BC: a study in cultural receptivity. 1997 ⇒13,9995; 14,9829. ^RCRAI (2001/2) 1044-1058 (*Bernard, Paul*).

10448 **Nevett, Lisa C.** House and society in the ancient Greek world. 1999 ⇒15,10607. ^RAJA 105 (2001) 553-54 (*Becker, Marshall J.*).

10449 **Osborne, Robin** Greece in the making 1200-479 BC. Routledge history of the ancient world: L 2001, Routledge xx; 396 pp. 0-415-0353-X.

10450 **Pritchett, William Kendrick** Athenian calendars and ekklesias. Archaia Hellas 8: Amst 2001, Gieben xiii; 250 pp. 90-5063-258-0.

Q6.5 Alexander, Seleucidae; historia Hellenismi

10451 *Albertz, Rainer* An end to the confusion?: why the Old Testament cannot be a Hellenistic book!. Did Moses speak Attic?. JSOT.S 317: 2001 ⇒270. 30-46.

10452 *Alexander, Philip S.* Hellenism and hellenization as problematic historiographical categories. Paul beyond. 2001 ⇒262. 63-80.

10453 *Asmis, Elizabeth* Choice in EPICTETUS' philosophy. ^FBETZ, H. 2001 ⇒5. 385-412.

10454 ^T**Auberger, Janick** Historiens d'Alexandre. Fragments: P 2001, Les Belles Lettres 518 pp. 2-251-74200-X. Textes traduits et annotés par *Janick Auberger*; bibl. 501-505.

10455 *Austin, Michel* War and culture in the Seleucid empire. War. 2001 ⇒596. 90-109.

10456 *Baslez, Marie-Françoise* Des auteurs en prise sur leur temps à l'époque hellénistique. MoBi 137 (2001) 28-31 [BuBB 35,34].

10457 *Becking, Bob* The Hellenistic period and ancient Israel: three preliminary statements. Did Moses speak Attic?. 2001 ⇒270. 78-90.

10458 **Boardman, John; Griffin, Jasper; Murray, Oswyn** The Oxford illustrated history of Greece and the Hellenistic world. Oxf 2001, <1986>, OUP viii; 445 pp. £15. 0-192-85438-0. 151 ill.

10459 The Cambridge history of Hellenistic philosophy. ^E**Algra, Keimpe**, *al.*, 1999 ⇒15,10612. ^RAnCl 70 (2001) 362-63 (*Stevens, Annick*).

10460 *Carroll, Robert P.* Jewgreek Greekjew: the Hebrew Bible is all Greek to me: reflections on the problematics of dating the origins

of the bible in relation to contemporary discussions of biblical historiography. Did Moses speak Attic?. 2001 ⇒270. 91-107.

10461 **Clarke, Katherine** Between geography and history: Hellenistic
constructions of the Roman world. 1999 ⇒15,10621. [R]At. 89
(2001) 291-294 (*Gabba, Emilio*); ClR 51 (2001) 325-327 (*Swain,
Simon*).

10462 *Cohen, Shaye J.D.* Hellenism in unexpected places;

10463 *Collins, John J.* Cult and culture: the limits of hellenization in
Judea. Hellenism in the land of Israel. 2001 ⇒399. 216-243/38-61.

10464 **Collins, John J.** Between Athens and Jerusalem: Jewish identity in
the Hellenistic Diaspora. [2]2000 ⇒16,10729. [R]JJS 52 (2001) 363-
367 (*Barclay, John M.G.*); Sal. 63 (2001) 772-773 (*Vicent, R.*).

10465 *Davies, Philip R.* Judaeans in Egypt: Hebrew and Greek stories.
Did Moses speak Attic?. JSOT.S 317: 2001 ⇒270. 108-128.

10466 **Del Monte, Giuseppe F.** Testi dalla Babilonia ellenistica. Studi el-
lenistici 9: 1997 ⇒13,10011. [R]Or. 69 (2000) 433-438 (*Van der
Spek, R.J.*).

10467 *Doran, Robert* The high cost of a good education. Hellenism in the
land of Israel. CJAn 13: 2001 ⇒399. 94-115.

10468 **Droysen, Johann Gustav** Geschichte des Hellenismus, 1. Geschichte ALEXANDERS des Großen; 2, Geschichte der Diadochen; 3,
Geschichte der Epigonen. [E]*Bayer, Erich* 1998 <1952-1953> ⇒14,
9850. [R]SNTU.A 25 (2000) 283-284 (*Schwendtner, F.*).

10469 *Ehling, Kay* Zwei 'seleukidische' Miszellen[: 1, Wer war der älteste Sohn des Demetrios I?; 2, Selbstmorde von Seleukidenkönigen].
Hist. 50 (2001) 374-378.

10470 *Freyne, Seán* Galileans, Phoenicians, and Itureans: a study of
regional contrasts in the hellenistic age. Hellenism in the land of Israel. CJAn 13: 2001 ⇒399. 182-215.

10471 **Gera, Dov** Judaea and Mediterranean politics, 219 to 161 B.C.E.
1998 ⇒14,9857; 15,10627. [R]JSJ 32 (2001) 302-304 (*Grabbe,
Lester L.*).

10472 *Greenfield, Jonas C.* The languages of Palestine 200 B.C.E.-200
C.E. 'Al kanfei yonah, 1. 2001 <1978> ⇒153. 376-387.

10473 **Gruen, Erich S.** Heritage and Hellenism: the reinvention of Jewish
tradition. 1998 ⇒14,9861... 16,10740. [R]Gn. 73 (2001) 224-229
(*Siegert, Folker*); SCI 20 (2001) 209-224 (*Honigman, Sylvie*).

10474 *Gruen, Erich S.* Jewish perspectives on Greek culture and ethnicity.
Hellenism in the land of Israel. CJAn 13: 2001 ⇒399. 62-93.

10475 *Hengel, Martin* Judaism and hellenism revisited. Hellenism in the
land of Israel. CJAn 13: 2001 ⇒399. 6-37.

10476 **Hengel, Martin** Giudaismo ed ellenismo: studi sul loro incontro,
con particolare riguardo per la Palestina fino alla metà del II secolo

a.C. ^E*Monaco, Sergio*: BSSTB 14: Brescia 2001, Paideia 763 pp. 88-394-0621-2. Bibl. 651-704.

10477 *Lemche, Niels Peter* How does one date an expression of mental history?: the Old Testament and Hellenism;

10478 The Old Testament—a Hellenistic book?. Did Moses speak Attic?. JSOT.S 317: 2001 ⇒270. 200-224/287-318.

10479 **Lewis, Naphtali** Greeks in Ptolemaic Egypt: case studies in the social history of the Hellenistic world. Oakville 2001 <1986>, American Society of Papyrologists xii; 184 pp.

10480 **Long, A.A.; Sedley, D.N.** Les philosophes hellénistiques. ^T*Brunschwig, Jacques; Pellegrin, Pierre*: P 2001, Flammarion 3 vols; 312 + 570 + 254 pp;

10481 Die hellenistischen Philosophen: Texte und Kommentare. ^T*Hülser, Karlheinz*: Stu 2000, Metzler 640 pp. €39.90. 3-467-01574-2.

10482 **Magris, Aldo** La filosofia ellenistica: scuole, dottrine e interazioni col mondo giudaico. Filosofia Brescia 2001, Morcelliana 124 pp. 88-372-1853-2.

10483 **Ma, John** Antiochos III and the cities of western Asia Minor. 1999 ⇒15,10637. ^RSCI 20 (2001) 303-305 (*Shipley, Graham*); ClR 51 (2001) 320-322 (*Erskine, Andrew*); RH 306 (2001) 970-975 (*Bertrand, Jean-Marie*).

10484 **Morgan, Teresa** Literate education in the Hellenistic and Roman worlds. 1998 ⇒14,9873... 16,10752. ^RLatomus 60 (2001) 1030-1032 (*Rochette, Bruno*).

10485 **Ogden, Daniel** Polygamy, prostitutes and death: the Hellenistic dynasties. 1999 ⇒15,10641; 16,10754. ^RClR 51 (2001) 112-113 (*Weber, Gregor*).

10486 *Poster, Carol* The affections of the soul: pathos, protreptic, and preaching in hellenistic thought. Paul and pathos. SBL Symposium 16: 2001 ⇒6316. 23-37.

10487 *Rajak, Tessa* Judaism and Hellenism revisited;

10488 Roman intervention in a Seleucid siege of Jerusalem? <1981>;

10489 JUSTUS of Tiberias as a Jewish historian <1973> . The Jewish dialogue. AGJU 48: 2001 ⇒199. 3-10/81-98/161-176.

10490 *Sacchi, Paolo* From righteousness to justification in the period of Hellenistic Judaism. Henoch 23 (2001) 11-26.

10491 *Sanday, William* Greek influence on christianity. Essays in biblical criticism. JSNT.S 225: 2001 <1891> ⇒205. 108-122.

10492 **Sartre, Maurice** D'ALEXANDRE à ZÉNOBIE: histoire du Levant antique, IVe siècle avant J.-C.-IIIe siècle après J.-C. P 2001, Fayard 1194 pp. 2-213-60921-7.

10493 *Schwartz, Daniel R.* Antiochus IV Epiphanes in Jerusalem. Historical perspectives. StTDJ 37: 2001 ⇒612. 45-56.

10494   **Shipley, Graham** The Greek world after ALEXANDER, 323-30 B.C.
        2000 ⇒16,10759. ᴿClR 51 (2001) 109-112 (*Gruen, E.S.*); IHR 23
        (2001) 381-382 (*Archibald, Zofia H.*); AnCl 70 (2001) 454-455
        (*Straus, Jean A.*).

10495   *Sterling, Gregory E.* Judaism between Jerusalem and Alexandria.
        Hellenism in the land of Israel. CJAn 13: 2001 ⇒399. 263-301.

10496   *Thompson, Thomas L.* The bible and hellenism: a response. Did
        Moses speak Attic?. JSOT.S 317: 2001 ⇒270. 274-286.

10497   *Troiani, Lucio* Greci ed ebrei, ebraismo ed 'ellenismo'. I Greci ol-
        tre la Grecia. 2001 ⇒440. 203-230;

10498   Aspetti dell'ellenismo nel pensiero ebraico antico (III sec. a.C.-I
        d.C.). Gli ebrei nell'impero romano. 2001 ⇒415. 47-56.

10499   *Tunny, Jennifer Ann* The health of Ptolemy II Philadelphus. BAS-
        Pap 38 (2001) 119-134.

10500   **Vasunia, Phiroze** The gift of the Nile: hellenizing Egypt from AES-
        CHYLUS to ALEXANDER. Classics and contemporary thought 8:
        Berkeley 2001, California Univ. Pr. xiv; 346 pp. 0-520-22820-0.
        Bibl. 309-334.

10501   **Virgilio, Biagio** Lancia, diadema e porpora: il re e la regalità elle-
        nistica. Studi ellenistici 11: 1999 ⇒15,10653. ᴿREG 114 (2001)
        296-297 (*Martinez-Sève, Laurianne*); AnCl 70 (2001) 457-458
        (*Bertrand, Jean-Marie*).

10502   *Zonta, Mauro* 'Sapienza straniera': la cultura greca nella tradizione
        ebraica. I Greci oltre la Grecia. 2001 ⇒440. 673-704.

Q7 Josephus Flavius

10503   *Bardet, Serge* Une approche épistémologique et christologique des
        problèmes posés par le *Testimonium Flavianum* (Flavius Josèphe,
        Antiquités juives XVIII, §63-64). Le judéo-christianisme. 2001 ⇒
        484. 168-200 [BuBB 36,49].

10504   *Bar-Kochva, Bezalel* A distorted account of the Jewish origo (C 1:
        305-311). Josephus-Kolloquium 2000. 2001 ⇒474. 11-28.

10505   *Bazlez, Marie-Françoise* Une nouvelle méthode historique. MoBi
        135 (2001) 34-39 [BuBB 36,49].

10506   *Begg, Christopher* The Ai-Achan story (Joshua 7-8) according to
        Josephus. Jian Dao 16 (2001) 1-20 [Josh 7-8];

10507   Josephus' retelling of Genesis 34. Studies in the book of Genesis.
        BEThL 155: 2001 ⇒1936. 599-605.

10508   **Begg, Christopher T.** Josephus' story of the later monarchy (AJ
        9,1-10, 185). BEThL 145: 2000 ⇒16,10767. ᴿJSJ 32 (2001) 294-

295 (*Spilsbury, Paul*); ThRv 97 (2001) 382-384 (*Gerber, Christine*); BiOr 58 (2001) 438-440 (*Höffken, Peter*); LouvSt 26 (2001) 183-185 (*Leemans, Johan*).

10509 Begg, C.T. The dynastic promise according to Josephus. SE 39 (2000) 5-19.

10510 **Ben Zeev, Miriam Pucci** Jewish rights in the Roman world: the Greek and Roman documents quoted by Josephus Flavius. TSAJ 74: 1998 ⇒16,9488. ᴿJSJ 32 (2001) 337-340 (*Sievers, Joseph*); REJ 160 (2001) 277-279 (*Hadas-Lebel, Mireille*); Gn. 73 (2001) 684-688 (*Ceccarelli, Paola*).

10511 Bilde, Per La foi juive présentée aux gréco-romains. MoBi 135 (2001) 24-27 [BuBB 36,49].

10512 Broshi, Magen The credibility of Josephus. Bread, wine. JSPE.S 36: 2001 <1982> ⇒131. 71-77.

10513 Caillet, Jean-Pierre Les *Antiquités judaïques* vues par FOUQUET. MoBi 135 (2001) 28-33 [BuBB 36,49].

10514 Carleton Paget, James Some observations on Josephus and christianity. JThS 52 (2001) 539-624.

10515 Castelli, Silvia Riferimenti a Flavio Giuseppe nella letteratura siriaca. Henoch 23 (2001) 199-226;

10516 Antiquities 3-4 and Against Apion 2:145ff: different approaches to the law. Josephus-Kolloquium 2000. 2001 ⇒474. 151-169.

10517 **Colautti, Federico Moisés** La pascua en la obra de Flavio Josefo. Extr. Diss. Gregoriana, ᴰSievers, Joseph, R 2001, 128 pp .

10518 Dochhorn, Jan Die auf MEANDER von Ephesus zurückgehende Liste der Könige von Tyrus in C 1:116-126: ein Beitrag zur Textkritik des Josephus und des Meander sowie zur absoluten Chronologie von Tyrus. Josephus-Kolloquium 2000. 2001 ⇒474. 77-102.

10519 Dormeyer, Detlev Des Josephus zwei suasoriae (Übungsreden) über das Volk der Juden: die beiden Vorworte (Proömien) *Contra Apionem* 1:1-5; 2:1-7 und die beiden Vorworte Lukas 1,1-4; Acta 1,1-14. Josephus-Kolloquium 2000. 2001 ⇒474. 241-261.

10520 Feldman, Louis H. Josephus' liberties in interpreting the bible in the *Jewish War* and in the *Antiquities*. JSQ 8 (2001) 309-325;

10521 On Professor Mark RONCACE's portraits of Deborah and Gideon in Josephus. JSJ 32 (2001) 193-220.

10522 **Feldman, Louis H.** Josephus's interpretation of the bible. 1998 ⇒ 14,9909...16,10803. ᴿBiOr 58 (2001) 242-244 (*Tromp, Johannes*); Gr. 82 (2001) 787-791 (*Prato, Gian Luigi*); ThLZ 126 (2001) 38-40 (*Vogel, Manuel*); JBL 119 (2000) 126-127 (*Spilsbury, Paul*);

10523 Studies in Josephus' rewritten Bible. JSJ.S 58: 1998 ⇒14,9908; 16,10802. ᴿGn. 73 (2001) 488-492 (*Bilde, Per*); ThLZ 126 (2001) 38-40 (*Vogel, Manuel*).

10524   *Feldman, Louis H.* Restoration in Josephus. Restoration. JSJ.S 72:
        2001 ⇒319. 223-261.
10525   *Förster, Niclas* Der Exorzist El'azar: Salomo, Josephus und das alte
        Ägypten. Josephus-Kolloquium 2000. 2001 ⇒474. 205-221.
10526   *Fuks, Gideon* Josephus' Tobiads again: a cautionary note. JJS 52
        (2001) 354-356.
10527   *Gerber, Christine* Die Bezeichnungen des Josephus für das jüdi-
        sche Volk, insbesondere in *Contra Apionem*: von der Wortwahl
        und ihrer Wirkung. Internationales Josephus-Kolloquium 2000.
        2001 ⇒474. 135-149.
10528   **Gruenenfelder, Regula** Frauen an den Krisenherden: eine rheto-
        risch-politische Deutung des Bellum Judaicum. Diss. Fribourg
        2001, ᴰ*Küchler, M.* [RTL 33,635].
10529   *Hadas-Lebel, Mireille* Flavius-Josèphe, de l'action à l'histoire.
        MoBi 135 (2001) 12-17 [BuBB 36,49].
10530   *Halpern-Amaru, Betsy* Flavius Josephus and the book of Jubilees: a
        question of source. HUCA 72 (2001) 15-44.
10531   *Hansen, Günther Christian* Das letzte Werk des Josephus und seine
        Textgestalt. Josephus-Kolloquium 2000. 2001 ⇒474. 65-75.
10532   *Höffken, Peter* Zum Kanonbewusstsein des Josephus Flavius in
        Contra Apionem und in den Antiquitates. JSJ 32 (2001) 159-177;
10533   Bekehrung von Nichtjuden als (Nicht-)Thema bei Josephus Flavius.
        ThZ 57 (2001) 391-401.
10534   *Jacobson, Howard* Apion, the Jews, and human sacrifice. CQ 51
        (2001) 318-319.
10535   *Jonquière, Tessel M.* Prayer in *Contra Apionem* 2:195-197. Inter-
        nationales Josephus-Kolloquium 2000. 2001 ⇒474. 171-188.
10536   *Jossa, Giorgio* 'Novatori' e 'briganti' negli scritti di Flavio Giusep-
        pe <1992>;
10537   La missione di Giuseppe in Galilea agli inizi della guerra giudaica
        <1992>;
10538   Chi sono i galilei nella *Vita* di Flavio Giuseppe? <1992>. I gruppi
        giudaici. 2001 ⇒5195. 132-146/147-161/162-175.
10539   *Lambers-Petry, Doris* Proselytenwerbung bei Josephus?: Überle-
        gungen zur Absicht der Schrift *Contra Apionem*;
10540   *Leonhardt, Jutta* εὐχαι και θυσιαι (A 14:260)—Opfer in der jüdi-
        schen Synagoge von Sardes?. Internationales Josephus-Kolloquium
        2000. 2001 ⇒474. 223-238/189-203.
10541   *Lindner, Helgo* Porträt eines Historikers: Otto Michel über Flavius
        Josephus. ThBeitr 32 (2001) 363-372.
10542   **Madden, Shawn Clarke** Josephus's use of the book of Daniel: a
        study of Hellenistic-Jewish historiography. Diss. Texas, Arlington
        2001, 209 pp. 3010040.

10543　**Mader, Gottfried** Josephus and the politics of historiography: apologetic and impression management in the Bellum Judaicum. Mn.S 205: 2000 ⇒16,10812. [R]JSJ 32 (2001) 325-328 (*Spilsbury, Paul*); ClR 51 (2001) 242-244 (*Landau, Tamar*); CBQ 63 (2001) 756-757 (*Feldman, Louis H.*).

10544　*Marguerat, Daniel* Le cinquième évangéliste?. MoBi 135 (2001) 44-47 [BuBB 36,49].

10545　**Mason, Steve** Flavius Josephus und das Neue Testament. UTB.W; UTB 2130: 2000 ⇒16,10815. [R]ThLZ 126 (2001) 1271-1272 (*Gerber, Christine*);

10546　Flavius Josephus on the pharisees: a composition-critical study. Lei 2001 <1991>, Brill 424 pp. €25.50. 0-391-04154-1;

10547　Giuseppe Flavio e il Nuovo Testamento. [T]*Comba, A.*: PBT: T 2001, Claudiana 272 pp. €19.62. 88-7016-3792.

10548　[T]**Mason, Steve** Life of Josephus: translation and commentary. Flavius Josephus, translation and commentary 9: Lei 2001, Brill liv; 287 pp. $134. 90-04-11793-8 [RB 109,316].

10549　*Martinez-Seve, Laurianne* Un historien de l'Orient hellénistique. MoBi 135 (2001) 40-43 [BuBB 36,49].

10550　*McLaren, James S.* Ananus, James, and earliest christianity: Josephus' account of the death of James. JThS 52 (2001) 1-25.

10551　**McLaren, James S.** Turbulent times?: Josephus and scholarship on Judaea in the first century CE. 1998 ⇒14,9930... 16,10817. [R]RBLit 3 (2001) 288-291 (*Feldman, Louis H.*); JBL 119 (2000) 586-588 (*Sievers, Joseph*).

10552　*Mendels, Doron* The sources of the *Ecclesiastical history* of EUSEBIUS: the case of Josephus. L'historiographie de l'église. 2001 ⇒ 541. 195-205 [BuBB 36,49].

10553　*Miller, Stuart S.* Josephus on the cities of Galilee: factions, rivalries and alliances in the first Jewish revolt. Hist. 50 (2001) 453-467.

10554　*Nodet, Etienne* Les bibles et Josèphe. MoBi 135 (2001) 18-23 [BuBB 36,49];

10555　Un nouveau commentaire des oeuvres de Josèphe. RB 108 (2001) 386-421;

10556　Jewish features in the "Slavonic" War of Josephus. Internationales Josephus-Kolloquium 2000. 2001 ⇒474. 105-131.

10557　[T]**Nodet, Étienne** Flavius Josèphe: les antiquités juives, 3: livres VI et VII. P 2001, Cerf liv; 487 pp. €36.59. 2-204-06595-1.

10558　[E]*Pouthier, Jean-Luc* Flavius Josèphe: historien du temps de Jésus. MoBi 135 (2001) 3-53.

10559　*Prestel, Peter* Kain und Abel (Gen 4,1-16) bei Flavius Josephus. WD 26 (2001) 73-88 [Gen 4,1-16].

10560 *Rajak, Tessa* Greeks and barbarians in Josephus. Hellenism in the land of Israel. CJAn 13: 2001 ⇒399. 244-262;

10561 Moses in Ethiopia: legend and literature. The Jewish dialogue. AGJU 48: 2001 <1978> ⇒199. 257-272:

10562 Josephus and the 'archaeology' of the Jews <1983> 241-255;

10563 Was there a Roman charter for the Jews? <1984> 301-333;

10564 The sense of history <1986> 11-37;

10565 Josephus and JUSTUS of Tiberias <1987> 177-193;

10566 Friends, Romans, subjects: Agrippa II's speech in Josephus' *Jewish war* <1991> 147-159;

10567 Ciò che Flavio Giuseppe vide: Josephus and the Essenes <1994> 219-240;

10568 The *Against Apion* and the continuities in Josephus' political thought <1998> 195-217;

10569 The Parthians in Josephus <1998> 273-297;

10570 Ethnic identities in Josephus 137-146.

10571 *Sementchenko, Lada* On the two conceptions of just war in the 'Jewish Antiquities' of Flavius Josephus.REA 103 (2001) 485-495.

10572 *Siegert, Folker* Eine "neue" Josephus-Handschrift: kritischer Bericht über den Bologneser Codex Graecus 3568. Internationales Josephus-Kolloquium 2000. 2001 ⇒474. 31-63.

10573 **Siegert, Folker; Schreckenberg, Heinz; Vogel, Manuel** Flavius Josephus: aus meinem Leben (Vita): kritische Ausgabe, Übersetzung und Kommentar. Tü 2001, Mohr S. 218 pp. €64. 3-1614-7407-4.

10574 **Spilsbury, Paul** The image of the Jew in Flavius Josephus' Paraphrase of the Bible. TSAJ 69: 1998 ⇒14,9941; 16,10827. [R]JThS 52 (2001) 205-206 (*Downing, F. Gerald*); JBL 120 (2001) 183-184 (*McLaren, James S.*); ThLZ 126 (2001) 390-393 (*Herzer, Jens*).

10575 *Spilsbury, Paul* Josephus. Justification, 1: second temple Judaism. WUNT 2/140: 2001 ⇒251. 241-260.

10576 **Thackeray, Henry St. John** Flavius Josèphe: l'homme et l'historien. 2000 ⇒16,10828. [R]RB 108 (2001) 274-284 (*Schwartz, Daniel R.*).

10577 *Villeneuve, François* Les archéologues et Flavius Josèphe. MoBi 135 (2001) 48-53 [BuBB 35,10].

       Weber, R. Das 'Gesetz' bei Philon... Josephus 2001 ⇒8965.

Q8.1 *Roma Pompeii et Caesaris*—Hyrcanus to Herod

10578 *Baltrusch, Ernst* Königin Salome-Alexandra (76-67 v.Chr.) und die Verfassung des hasmonäischen Staates. Hist. 50 (2001) 163-179.

10579 *Brenner, Sandy Charles* Herod the Great remains true to form.
NEA(BA) 64/4 (2001) 212-214.

10580 *Goodblatt, David* The union of priesthood and kingship in second
temple Judea. Cathedra 102 (2001) 7-28 Sum. 209. **H.**

10581 *Jacobson, David M.* Herod the Great shows his true colors.
NEA(BA) 64/3 (2001) 100-104;

10582 Three Roman client kings: Herod of Judaea, Archelaus of Cappa-
docia and Juba of Mauretania. PEQ 133 (2001) 22-38.

10583 **Kokkinos, Nikos** The Herodian dynasty: origins, role in society
and eclipse. JSP.S 30: 1998 ⇒14,9949... 16,10831. [R]JSJ 32 (2001)
101-105 (*Sievers, Joseph*).

10584 **Lichtenberger, Achim** Die Baupolitik Herodes des Großen.
ADPV 26: 1999 ⇒15,10711; 16,10832. [R]IJCT 8 (2001) 286-288
(*Roller, Duane W.*).

10585 *Rajak, Tessa* Hasmonean kingship and the invention of tradition.
The Jewish dialogue. AGJU 48: 2001 <1996> ⇒199. 39-60;

10586 The Hasmoneans and the uses of Hellenism. The Jewish dialogue.
AGJU 48: 2001 <1990> ⇒199. 61-80.

10587 **Richardson, Peter** Herod: king of the Jews and friend of the Romans. 1996 (1999) ⇒12,9411... 16,10834. [R]JSJ 32 (2001) 109-111
(*Grabbe, Lester L.*); [R]EvQ 73 (2001) 366-367 (*Brewer, David I.*).

10588 **Schalit, Abraham Chaim** König Herodes: der Mann und sein
Werk. B [2]2001, De Gruyter xxxii; 890 pp. €40. 3-11-017036-1.
Vorwort von *Daniel R. Schwartz*; Bibl. 870-889.

10589 *Schatzman, Israel* L'integrazione della Giudea nell'impero romano.
Gli ebrei nell'impero romano. 2001 ⇒415. 17-46.

10590 *Winterling, Aloys* Die römische Republik im Werk Max WEBERs:
Rekonstruktion—Kritik—Aktualität. HZ 273 (2001) 595-635.

10591 *Zur, Yiphtah* Shimon BEN SHETAH as the preacher of deceit. RB 108
(2001) 360-375.

Q8.4 **Zeitalter Jesu Christi**: *particular/general*

10592 **Absil, M.** Les préfets du prétoire d'AUGUSTE à COMMODE: 2 avant
Jésus-Christ 192 après Jésus-Christ. De l'archéologie à l'histoire: P
1998, De Boccard 293 pp. 2-7018-0111-7. Bibl.

10593 **Álvarez Gómez, Jesús** Historia de la iglesia, 1: edad antigua. BAC
Manuales 25: M 2001, BAC xxiv; 355 pp. [R]EfMex 19 (2001) 422-
424 (*Jaramillo Escuria, Roberto*); Augustinus 46 (2001) 374-375
(*Eguiarte, Enrique*).

10594 *Baarlink, Heinrich* Jezus en de wetsopvattingen in zijn tijd. ThRef
44 (2001) 114-134.

10595 *Barclay, John M.G.* Diaspora Judaism. Religious diversity. BiSe 79: 2001 ⇒398. 47-64.

10596 **Bartman, Elizabeth** Portraits of Livia: imaging the imperial woman in Augustan Rome. 1999 ⇒15,10716; 16,10836. [R]CIR 51 (2001) 143-144 (*Smith, R.R.R.*); AnCl 70 (2001) 537-539 (*Balty, Jean Ch.*).

10597 *Berlejung, Angelika* Die Liebenden sind den Göttern gleich: Liebe und Eros im Kulturraum des Vorderen Orients. WUB 21 (2001) 3-7.

10598 **Camps, Abel** Camins de Jerusalem: camins d'amor i odis. Barc 2001, Claret 284 pp. [R]RCatT 26 (2001) 414-415 (*Ricart, Ignasi*).

10599 *Chilton, Bruce* From economic culture to theological interpretation: Nazareth, Capernaum, and Jerusalem as environments of Jesus' teaching. Religious texts. Studies in ancient Judaism: 2001 ⇒630. 63-71.

10600 *Court, John M.* Introduction. Religious diversity. BiSe 79: 2001 ⇒ 398. 11-20.

10601 **Crossan, John Dominic** The birth of christianity: discovering what happened in the years immediately after the execution of Jesus. 1998 ⇒14,8302... 16,9078. [R]HThR 94 (2001) 369-374 (*Bovon, François*); EvQ 73 (2001) 178-179 (*Marshall, I. Howard*); JBL 119 (2000) 129-131 (*Reed, Jonathan L.*); HeyJ 42 (2001) 503-505 (*Turner, Geoffrey*).

10602 **Declercq, Georges** Anno Domini: les origines de l'ère chrétienne. 2000 ⇒16,10841. [R]MÂ 107 (2001) 335-6 (*Guyotjeannin, Olivier*); REByz 59 (2001) 264-5 (*Failler, Albert*); RHE 96 (2001) 447-449 (*Verbist, Peter*); VetChr 38 (2001) 362-364 (*Aulisa, Immacolata*).

10603 *Esler, Philip F.* Palestinian Judaism in the first century. Religious diversity. BiSe 79: 2001 ⇒398. 21-46.

10604 *Feldtkeller, Andreas* Syrien II: Zeit des Neuen Testaments. TRE 32. 2001 ⇒665. 587-589.

10605 *Freyne, Seán* The geography of restoration: Galilee-Jerusalem relations in early Jewish and christian experience. Restoration. JSJ.S 72: 2001 ⇒319. 405-433.

10606 *Hertog, Gerard C. den* Inleiding op het themanummer: "Jezus Christus in de context van het Israël van de eerste eeuw". ThRef 44 (2001) 110-113.

10607 **Hurlet, F.** Les collègues du prince sous AUGUSTE et TIBÈRE. Ecole française de Rome 227: 1997 ⇒14,9963. [R]CIR 51 (2001) 119-120 (*Hall, Lindsay G.H.*).

10608 **Jossa, Giorgio** I cristiani e l'impero romano: da TIBERIO a MARCO AURELIO. 2000 ⇒16,10847. [R]RivBib 49 (2001) 362-370 (*Troiani, Lucio*).

10609 *Kany, Roland* Grecità e cristianesimo. I Greci oltre la Grecia. 2001 ⇒440. 563-591.

10610 **Loreto, Luigi** Il comando militare nelle province procuratorie 30 a.C.-280 d.C.: dimensione militare e dimensione costituzionale. Pubbl. della Fac. di Giurisprudenza della Seconda Univ. di Napoli 12: N 2000, Jovene 92 pp.

10611 **Miano, Peter J.** The word of God and the world of the bible: an introduction to the cultural backgrounds of the New Testament. L 2001, Melisende 196 pp.

10612 *Muñoz León, Domingo* La memoria de los 'padres' y de las 'madres' en el judaísmo de los siglos II a.C.-II d.C. Maria e il Dio. 2001 ⇒547. 99-153.

10613 *Paul, André* Les "écritures" dans la société juive au temps de Jésus. RSR 89 (2001) 13-42.

10614 [E]**Pietri, Luce** Histoire du christianisme, 1: le nouveau peuple: des origines à 250. P 2001, Desclée 938 pp. €64.03. 2-7189-0631-6. Introd. *Daniel Marguerat* [BCLF 634,26].

10615 **Richard, François** Situation politique en Orient et en Judée-Palestine à la veille de l'ère chrétienne. Le judaïsme à l'aube de l'ère chrétienne. LeDiv 186: 2001 ⇒450. 15-28.

10616 **Rizzo, Francesco Paolo** La chiesa dei primi secoli: lineamenti storici. 1999 ⇒15,10734; 16,10856. [R]RSLR 37 (2001) 606-607 (*Bossina, Luciano*).

10617 **Saldarini, Anthony J.** Pharisees, Scribes and Sadducees in Palestinian society: a sociological approach. GR [2]2001 <1988>, Eerdmans xxv; 326 pp. $28. 0-8028-4358-1 [RB 109,159].

10618 *Sanday, William* The language spoken in Palestine at the time of our Lord. Essays in biblical criticism. 2001 <1878> ⇒205. 80-93.

10619 **Schürer, Emil** Storia del popolo giudaico al tempo di Gesù Cristo (175 a.C.-135 d.C.). [E]*Vermes, Geza, al.,* : BSSTB 12-13/3/1-2: 1998 ⇒ 15,10738; 16,10859. [R]Asp. 48 (2001) 437-440 (*Di Palma, Gaetano*).

10620 *Shemesh, Aharon* King Manasseh and the halakhah of the Sadducees. JJS 52 (2001) 27-39.

10621 *Skeat, T.C.* The Egyptian calendar under AUGUSTUS. ZPE 135 (2001) 153-156.

10622 *Taylor, N.H.* Popular opposition to CALIGULA in Jewish Palestine. JSJ 32 (2001) 54-70.

10623 **Wellhausen, Julius** The Pharisees and the sadducees: an examination of internal Jewish history. [T]*Biddle, Mark E.*: Mercer Library of Biblical Studies: Macon, GA 2001, Mercer University Press viii; 115 pp. $30. 0-86554-729-7.

10624　**Witherington, Ben** New Testament history: a narrative account. GR 2001, Baker 430 pp. $27. 0-8010-2293-2.

Q8.7 *Roma et Oriens*, prima decennia post Christum

10625　**Aberbach, Moshe; Aberbach, David** The Roman-Jewish wars and Hebrew cultural nationalism. 2000 ⇒16,10862. [R]IHR 23 (2001) 629-630 (*Feldman, Louis H.*).

10626　*Benoist, Stéphane* Le prince, la cité et les événements: l'année 68-69 à Rome. Hist. 50 (2001) 279-311.

10627　*Ben Zeev, Miriam Pucci* La sovranità sopra i paramenti del sommo sacerdote: un capitolo nei rapporti ebraico-romani. Gli ebrei nell'impero romano. 2001 ⇒415. 99-112.

10628　**Birley, Anthony R.** HADRIAN: the restless emperor. 1998 ⇒14, 9975. [R]AnCl 70 (2001) 476-478 (*Dondin-Payre, Monique*).

10629　*Blanchetière, François* De l'importance de l'an 135 dans l'évolution respective de la synagogue et du christianisme. L'historiographie de l'église. 2001 ⇒541. 91-96 [BuBB 36,102].

10630　**Cassidy, Richard J.** Christians and Roman rule in the New Testament: new perspectives. Companions to the NT: NY 2001, Herder and H. xiv; 145 pp. $26. 0-8245-1903-5. Bibl. 136-139.

10631　*Cotton, Hannah M.* L'impatto dei papiri documentari del deserto di Giudea sullo studio della storia ebraica dal 70 al 135/6 e.v. Gli ebrei nell'impero romano. 2001 <1999> ⇒415. 217-231.

10632　**Eshel, Hanan; Amit, Dor** מערות המפלט מתקופת מרד בר־כוכבא [Refuge caves of the Bar Kokhba revolt]. 1999 ⇒15,10750. [R]Zion 66 (2001) 107-108 [Hebr.] (*Dar, Shimon*). **H**.

10633　[E]**Jones, Brian W.** SUETONIUS: VESPASIAN. 2000 ⇒16,10869. [R]Prudentia 33/1 (2001) 82-85 (*Wardle, David*).

10634　*Jossa, Giorgio* Sul problema dell'identità giudaica nell'impero romano. I gruppi giudaici. 2001 ⇒5195. 176-191.

10635　**Levick, Barbara** VESPASIAN. 1999 ⇒15,10755; 16,10871. [R]REA 103 (2001) 602-603 (*Roddaz, Jean-Michel*).

10636　**Malitz, Jürgen** NERO. 1999 ⇒15,10757; 16,10873. [R]AnCl 70 (2001) 471-472 (*Birley, Anthony R.*).

10637　*Mercier, Raymond* Intercalation in the era of the province of Arabia. RB 108 (2001) 101-108.

10638　**Perea Yébenes, Sabino** Berenice: reina y concubina. 2000 ⇒16, 10877. [R]Sef. 61 (2001) 450-451 (*González Salinero, R.*).

10639　*Price, Jonathan J.* La 'Grande rivolta'. Gli ebrei nell'impero romano. 2001 ⇒415. 113-124.

10640   *Price, Jonathan J.* Jüdischer Krieg. RGG², 4: I-K 2001 ⇒664. 644-647.

10641   *Rosen, Klaus* Die römische Welt des Paulus. WUB 20 (2001) 25-29.

10642   **Timpe, Dieter** Römische Geschichte und Heilsgeschichte. Hans-Lietzmann-Vorlesungen 5: B 2001, De Gruyter ix; 135 pp. 3-11-0116942-8.

Q9.1 *Historia Romae generalis et* post-christiana

10643   **Aldrete, Gregory** Gestures and acclamations in ancient Rome. 1999 ⇒15,10761. ᴿEM 69 (2001) 187-189 (*Arce, Javier*).

10644   **Bauman, Richard A.** Human rights in ancient Rome. 1999 ⇒15, 10763. ᴿClR 51 (2001) 79-81 (*Rees, Roger*); AnCl 70 (2001) 571-573 (*Deman, Albert*).

10645   *Bérenger-Badel, Agnès* Les recensements dans la partie orientale de l'empire: le cas de l'Arabie. MEFRA 113 (2001) 605-619.

10646   **Cantarella, Eva** Les peines de mort en Grèce et à Rome: origines et fonctions des supplices capitaux dans l'antiquité classique. 2000 ⇒16,10888. ᴿAnnales 56/1 (2001) 245-247 (*Lovisi, Claire*).

10647   **Chadwick, Henry** The Church in ancient society: from Galilee to GREGORY the Great. Oxford history of the Christian church. Oxf 2001, OUP ix; 730 pp. £80. 0-19-924695-5. Bibl. 694-713.

10648   *Decret, François* Premiers chrétiens en terre d'Afrique. MoBi 132 (2001) 17-23 [BuBB 36,102].

10649   ᴱ**Dixon, Susanne** Childhood, class and kin in the Roman world. L 2001, Routledge xvi; 282 pp. £50. 0-415-23578-2.

10650   **Dixon, Suzanne** Reading Roman women: sources, genres and real life. L 2001, Duckworth xiv; 242 pp. £17. 0-715-62981-6. 16 pl.

10651   *Dorival, Gilles* Un gruppo giudeocristiano misconosciuto: gli ebrei. Verus Israel. BCR 65: 2001 ⇒524. 190-219.

10652   *Dubuisson, Michel* Barbares et barbarie dans le monde gréco-romain: du concept au slogan. AnCl 70 (2001) 1-16.

10653   **Gardner, Jane F.** Family and familia in Roman law and life. 1998 ⇒14,9996. ᴿGn. 73 (2001) 229-232 (*Linke, Bernhard*).

10654   *Geraci, Giovanni* Le dichiarazioni di nascità e di morte a Roma e nelle province. MEFRA 113 (2001) 675-711.

10655   ᴱ**Goldhill, Simon** Being Greek under Rome: cultural identity, the second Sophistic and the development of Empire. C 2001, CUP viii; 395 pp. $45. 0-521-66317-2 [Bibl. 362-389].

10656   **Gourevitch, Danielle; Raepsaet-Charlier, Marie-Thérèse** La femme dans la Rome antique. La Vie Quotidienne; P 2001, Hachette 301 pp. €22. 2-01-2353-310-X. 20 fig. [AnCl 72,555s—Mekacher, Nina].

10657   *Guijarro Oporto, Santiago* Cristianos en el mundo: las comunidades cristianas de la segunda generación en la sociedad helenístico-romana. Salm. 48 (2001) 5-39.

10658   **Hausamann, Susanne** Alte Kirche: zur Geschichte und Theologie in der ersten vier Jahrhunderten, 2: Verfolgungs- und Wendezeit der Kirche: Gemeindeleben in der Zeit der Christenverfolgungen und Konstantinische Wende. Neuk 2001, Neuk vi; 209 pp. €24.90. 3-7887-1807-2.

10659   *Hidal, Sten* The Jews as the Roman authors saw them. The synagogue of ancient Ostia. 2001 ⇒427. 141-144.

10660   *Hugoniot, Christophe* Église et cité: le conflit des spectacles. MoBi 132 (2001) 24-27 [BuBB 36,102].

10661   *Isaac, Benjamin* עמדות הרומאים כלפי היהודים והיהדות [Roman attitudes towards Jews and Judaism]. Zion 66 (2001) 41-72 Sum. v. **H.**

10662   *Jossa, Giorgio* Giudei e greci nel primo secolo dell'era cristiana: osservazioni in margine al volume di L. TROIANI, Il perdono cristiano, Paideia, Brescia 1999. RivBib 49 (2001) 83-89.

10663   *Jullien, Christelle; Jullien, Florence* "Aux temps des disciples des apôtres": les sabbatiens d'Édesse. RHR 218 (2001) 155-170.

10664   *Lancel, Serge* Un schisme africain, le donatisme. MoBi 132 (2001) 29-33 [BuBB 36,102].

10665   **Lapin, Hayim** Economy, geography, and provincial history in later Roman Palestine. TSAJ 10: Tü 2001, Mohr S. x; 227 pp. €70.56. 3-16-147588-7. Bibl. 195-212.

10666   *Lo Cascio, Elio* Il census a Roma e la sua evoluzione dall'età 'serviana' alla prima età imperiale. MEFRA 113 (2001) 565-603.

10667   **MacMullen, Ramsay** Romanization in the time of AUGUSTUS. 2000 ⇒16,10902. [R]JIntH 32 (2001) 452-3 (*Champion, Craige B.*).

10668   **Mattern, Susan P.** Rome and the enemy: imperial strategy in the principate. 1999 ⇒15,10782. [R]AJP 122 (2001) 451-454 (*Talbert, Richard J.A.*).

10669   *Mesters, Carlos; Orofino, Francisco* A violência do império romano e a sua influência na vida das comunidades cristãs do fim do primero século. Estudos Bíblicos 69 (2001) 72-82.

10670   **Peachin, Michael** *Iudex vice Caesaris*: deputy emperors and the administration of justice during the principate. 1996 ⇒14,10011. [R]Gn. 73 (2001) 328-332 (*Spengler, Hans-Dieter*).

10671 **Phang, Sara Elise** The marriage of Roman soldiers (13 B.C. - A.D. 235): law and family in the imperial army. CSCT 24: Lei 2001, Brill ix; 471 pp. 90-04-12155-2. Bibl. 425-449.

10672 **Philip, T.V.** East of Euphrates: early christianity in Asia. 1998 ⇒ 14,10012. [R]Pacifica 14 (2001) 100-101 (*Spykerboer, Hans*).

10673 *Rajak, Tessa* Jews, Semites and their cultures in Fergus Millar's *Roman Near East.* Jewish dialogue. 2001 <2000> ⇒199. 503-9.

10674 **Riley, Gregory John** The river of God: a new history of christian origins. SF 2001, Harper Collins iii; 252 pp. 0-06-066979-9.

10675 **Rizakis, A.D.; Zoumbakel, S.** Roman Peloponnese, 1: Roman personal names in their social context (Achaia, Arcadia, Argolis, Corinthia and Eleia). Meletêmata 31: Athens 2001, Research Center for Greek and Roman Antiquity 643 pp. 960-7905-13-X. Collab. *M. Kantirea* [RB 110,158].

10676 **Roller, Matthew B.** Constructing autocracy: aristocrats and emperors in Julio-Claudian Rome. Princeton, NJ 2001, Princeton Univ. Pr. xii; 319 pp. $20. 0-691-05021-X.

10677 **Ross, Steven K.** Roman Edessa: politics and culture on the eastern fringes of the Roman Empire, 114-242 CE. L 2001, Routledge xiii; 204 pp. 0-415-18787-7. Bibl. 185-195.

10678 [E]**Rowe, Christopher; Schofield, Malcolm** The Cambridge History of Greek and Roman political thought. 2000 ⇒16,10911. [R]HeyJ 42 (2001) 403-406 (*Waterfield, Robin*).

10679 **Salmon, Pierre** La limitation des naissances dans la société romaine. 1999 ⇒15,10786. [R]RH 306 (2001) 982-984 (*Benoist, Stéphane*).

10680 **Schumacher, Leonhard** Sklaverei in der Antike: Alltag und Schicksal der Unfreien. Mü 2001, Beck 368 pp. €34.90. 146 ill.

10681 **Thome, Gabriele** Zentrale Wertvorstellungen der Römer, 1-2: Text—Bilder—Interpretationen. Auxilia: Bamberg 2000, Buchners 151 + 152 pp. 15 pl. [Gn. 75,447—Hellegouarc'h, Joseph].

10682 **Weber, Gregor** Kaiser, Träume und Visionen in Prinzipat und Spätantike. Historia, Einzelschriften 143: Stu 2000, Steiner xiii; 585 pp. €84 3-515-07681-6.

10683 *Wehnert, Jürgen* 'Falsi fratelli, attori, superapostoli': per una storia dalla missione giudeocristiana ai pagani nel I e II secolo d.C. Verus Israel. BCR 65: 2001 ⇒524. 265-279.

10684 **Wood, Susan Elliott** Imperial women: a study in public images, 40 B.C.-A.D. 68. Mn.S 194: 1999 ⇒15,10801. [R]AJA 105 (2001) 745-746 (*Rose, C. Brian*).

10685 *Woolf, Greg* Inventing empire in ancient Rome. Empires. 2001 ⇒ 388. 311-322.

10686   *Zadok, Ran* The ethno-linguistic character of the Semitic-speaking
        population of Mesopotamia and adjacent regions between the 1st
        and 7th centuries A.D.: a preliminary survey of the onomastic evi-
        dence. [M]CAGNI, L., 4: SMDSA 61: 2001 ⇒15. 2237-2270.

Q9.5 Constantine, Julian, Byzantine Empire

10687   *Hahn, Johannes* Tempelzerstörung und Tempelreinigung in der
        Spätantike. Kult, Konflikt. AOAT 285: 2001 ⇒387. 269-286.
10688   *Hansen, Günther Christian* Le monachisme dans l'historiographie
        de l'église ancienne [BuBB 36,103];
10689   *Lançon, Bertrand* La contribution à l'histoire de l'église de la
        Chronique de MARCELLIN d'Illyricum [BuBB 36,104]. L'historio-
        graphie de l'église. 2001 ⇒541. 139-147/469-480 .
10690   *Landes, Christian* Tunisie: du christianisme à l'Islam, IVe-XIVe
        siècle. MoBi 132 (2001) 52-53 [BuBB 36,102].
10691   *Laurence, Patrick* La *Vie de sainte Mélanie*: la part de l'histoire
        [BuBB 36,104];
10692   *Le Boulluec, Alain* L'historiographie dans les écrits théologiques de
        l'Empereur JUSTINIEN [BuBB 36,104];
10693   *Lusini, Gianfrancesco* L'église axoumite et ses traditions historio-
        graphiqes (IVe-VIIe siècle) [BuBB 36,102]. L'historiographie de
        l'église. 2001 ⇒541. 159-179/511-529/41-557.
10694   *Mahé, Jean-Pierre* Aux sources d'une histoire nationale. MoBi 136
        (2001) 48-53 [BuBB 36,103].
10695   [E]**Necipoglu, Nevra** Byzantine Constantinople: monuments, topog-
        raphy and everyday life. The Medieval Mediterranean 33: Lei
        2001, Brill xv; 363 pp. 90-04-11625-7.
10696   **Noethlichs, Karl Leo** Die Juden im christlichen Imperium Roma-
        num (4.-6. Jahrhundert). Studienbücher: B 2001, Akademie 271 pp.
10697   *Pérès, Jacques-Noël* Les origines du christianisme en Éthiopie: hi-
        stoire, tradition et liturgie. L'historiographie de l'église. 2001
        ⇒541. 531-540 [BuBB 36,103].
10698   *Phidas, Vlassios* The Johannine apostolicity of the throne of Con-
        stantinople. GOTR 45 (2000) 23-55.
10699   *Renoux, Charles* Les Arméniens et la liturgie de Jérusalem. MoBi
        136 (2001) 26-31 [BuBB 36,103].
10700   **Rosser, John H.** Historical dictionary of Byzantium. Historical
        Dictionaries of Ancient Civilizations and Historical Eras 4: Lanham
        2001, Scarecrow xli; 479 pp. 0-8108-3979-2. Bibl. 426-478.

10701   *Silberman, Neil Asher* Thundering hordes: the image of the Persian and Muslim conquests in Palestinian archaeology. ᴹEssᴇ, D.: SAOC 59: 2001 ⇒28. 611-623.

XVIII. Archaeologia terrae biblicae

T1.1 General biblical-area archaeologies

10702   *Boardman, John* Aspects of "colonization". BASOR 322 (2001) 33-42.

10703   **Braudel, Fernand** The Mediterranean in the ancient world. ᴱ*De Ayala, R.; Braudel, P.*; ᵀ*Reynolds, S.*: L 2001, PBR 408 pp. £20. 0-71-399331-6. Introd. *O. Murray*; Pref., notes *G. Guilaine; P. Rouillard*.

10704   *Broshi, Magen* Religion, ideology and politics and their impact on Palestinian archaeology. Bread, wine. 2001 <1987> ⇒131. 14-38.

10705   **Currid, John D.** Doing archaeology in the land of the bible: a basic guide. 1999 ⇒15,10818. ᴿCTJ 36 (2001) 221 (*Van Elderen, Bastiaan*).

10706   **Deist, Ferdinand E.** The material culture of the bible: an introduction. ᴱ*Carroll, Robert P.* BiSe 70: 2000 ⇒16,10933. ᴿBiblInterp 9 (2001) 435-436 (*Edelman, Diana*); OLZ 96 (2001) 711-715 (*Zwickel, Wolfgang*); CBQ 63 (2001) 715-716 (*Penchansky, David*); OTEs 14 (2001) 347-350 (*Nel, P.J.*); ET 112 (2001) 75-77 (*Rodd, C.S.*).

10707   *Dever, William G.* Biblical and Syro-Palestinian archaeology. The Blackwell companion to the Hebrew Bible. Blackwell companions to religion 3: 2001 ⇒653. 127-147.

10708   *Gafni, Isaiah M.* A generation of scholarship on Eretz Israel in the talmudic era: achievement and reconsideration. Cathedra 100 (2001) 199-226 Sum. 402. **H**.

10709   *Hess, Richard S.* Ancient Near Eastern studies. Interpreting the OT. 2001 ⇒248. 201-220.

10710   **Horden, P.; Purcell, N.** The corrupting sea: a study of Mediterranean history. 2000 ⇒16,10941. ᴿCIR 51 (2001) 99-102 (*Laurence, Ray*); AJA 105 (2001) 334-335 (*Knapp, A. Bernard*): IHR 23 (2001) 377-379 (*Hodges, Richard*).

10711   **King, Philip J.; Stager, Lawrence E.** Life in biblical Israel. Library of Ancient Israel: LVL 2001, Westminster xxii; 440 pp. $40. 0-664-22148-3 [ThD 49,74—Heiser, W..Charles].

10712   **Laughlin, John Charles Hugh** Archaeology and the bible. 2000
        ⇒16,10942. ^RVeE 22 (2001) 201-202 (*Le Roux, J.H.*).

10713   **Lavigne, Jean-Claude; Berten, Ignace** Nations et patries: échos
        bibliques. Connaître la bible 21/22: Bru 2001, Lumen Vitae 105
        (111) pp. €9.45. 2-87324-141-1 [RB 109,157].

10714   *Reich, Ronny* Recent achievements of archaeology from the Hel-
        lenistic to the Byzantine periods. Cathedra 100 (2001) 183-198
        Sum. 402. **H**.

10715   **Ridolfi, F.F.** I luoghi dello spirito. R 2001, Bardi 220 pp. €24. 88-
        8599-93-6.

10716   *Shanks, Hershel* How to stop looting. Archaeology and society.
        2001 ⇒443. 132-137.

10717   **Stern, Ephraim** Archaeology of the land of the bible, 2: the
        Assyrian, Babylonian & Persian periods (732-332 B.C.E.). Anchor
        Bible reference library: NY 2001, Doubleday li; 665 pp. $45. 0-
        385-42450-7.

10718   **Wyatt, Nicolas** Space and time in the religious life of the Near
        East. BiSe 85: Shf 2001, Sheffield A. 368 pp. 1-84127-288-4. Bibl.
        333-354.

10719   *Zwickel, Wolfgang* Scherben bringen Glück: die neueren Erkennt-
        nisse der biblischen Archäologie und die Exegese. HerKorr 55
        (2001) 531-536.

T1.2   **Musea, organismi,** *displays*

10720   **Antica Persia: I tesori del Museo Nazionale di Teheran e la ricerca
        italiana in Iran** [29 maggio - 22 luglio 2001]. R 2001, De Luca lv;
        182 pp. 88-8016-437-6. Bibl. 173-182.

10721   **Ayalon, Etan; Sorek, Chagit** Bare bones: ancient artifacts from
        animal bones. 1999 ⇒15,10836. ^RBASOR 322 (2001) 94-95 (*Lie-
        bowitz, Harold*).

10722   **Bénazeth, Dominique** Catalogue général du Musée copte du Caire:
        1, objets en métal. Mémoires 119: Le Caire 2001. Institut Français
        d'Archéologie Orientale viii; 453 pp. 2-7247-0302-2. Bibl. 439-51.

10723   ^E**Borriello, Maria Rosaria; Giove, Teresa** The Egyptian collec-
        tion of the National Archaeological Museum of Naples. Guide to
        the collections: N 2000, Electa 61 pp. 88-435-8524-X. Bibl. 61.

10724   **Brehme, Sylvia** Ancient Cypriot art in Berlin: Antikensammlung
        Museum für Vor- und Frühgeschichte, Münzkabinett. Nicosia
        2001, Leventis xii; 232 pp. Cyp£20. 9963-560-46-6. Num. ill. [RB
        109,312].

10725 *Broshi, Magen* Archaeological museums in Israel: reflections on problems of national identity. Bread, wine. JSPE.S 36: 2001 <1994> ⇒131. 52-59.

10726 ᴱ**De Caro, Stefano** La natura morta nelle pitture e nei mosaici delle città vesuviane. Guide tematiche: N 2001, Electa 117 pp. 88-435-8772-2. Museo Archeologico di Napoli - Guide.

10727 ᴱ**Guidotti, Maria Cristina** Le mummie del Museo egizio di Firenze. MAAT 1: F 2001, Giunti 64 pp. 88-09-02058-8. Bibl. 63.

10728 The Holy Land: David Roberts, Dead Sea scrolls, house of David inscription. Santa Ana, CA 2001, Bowers Museum of Cultural Art Oct. 6, 2001-Jan. 13, 2002.

10729 ᴱ**Karageorghis, Vassos; Vanchugov, Vladimir P.** Greek and Cypriot antiquities in the archaeological museum of Odessa. Nicosia 2001, Leventis 96 pp. Cyp£15. 9963-560-45-8. Num. ill. [RB 109,315].

10730 **Manera, Fausta; Mazza, Claudia** Le collezioni egizie nel Museo nazionale romano. Mi 2001, Electa 135 pp. 88-435-7870-7. Bibl. 133-135.

10731 **Mathews, Thomas F.; Taylor, Alice** The Armenian gospels of Gladzor: the life of Christ illuminated. LA 2001, Getty Museum 119 pp. £30/19. 0-89236-626-5/7-3. Catalogue Exhib. for 17th centenary of Armenian church.

10732 *Nevejan, Geneviève* Le sacré dans l'Egypte ancienne. Choisir Déc. (2001) 31-34. Reflets du divin, antiquités pharaoniques et classiques d'une collection privée, au Musée d'art et d'histoire de Genève, 30.8.2001-3.2.2002.

10733 ᴱ**Nigro, Lorenzo; Amato, Pietro** Animals in western art from the Vatican Museums. Tokyo 2001, Toyota Municipal Museum of Art 363 pp. **J.**, **Italian.**

10734 **O'Neill, John P.** Egyptian art in the age of the pyramids. 1999 ⇒15,11033. ᴿCÉg 76 (2001) 124-126 (*Baud, Michel*).

10735 *Sorgue, Pierre* Die Rettung des Nationalmuseums in Beirut. WUB 21 (2001) 80-83.

10736 ᴱ**Suckale-Redlefsen, Gude; Schemmel, Bernhard** Das Buch mit 7 Siegeln: die Bamberger Apokalypse: Katalog. 2000 ⇒16,10973. Ausstellung der Staatsbibliothek Bamberg. ᴿScr. 55 (2001) 175*-176* (*Cames, G.*).

10737 *Welte, Michael* Wie entstand unser Bibeltext?: das "Bibelmuseum Münster" präsentiert die spannende Geschichte der Handschriften und Drucke bis zum heutigen Text. WUB 19 (2001) 76-78.

10738 ᴱ**Willems, Harco; Clarysse, Willy** Les empereurs du Nil. ᵀ*Preys, René*: 2000 ⇒16,10977. ᴿBiOr 58 (2001) 393-397 (*Kiss, Zsolt*).

T1.3 *Methodi*—Science in archaeology

10739 *Anderson, Richard C.* Kite aerial photography for archaeology: an assessment and short guide. ᶠMEGAW, A. 2001 ⇒70. 167-180.

10740 *Bunimovitz, Shlomo* Cultural interpretation and the bible: biblical archaeology in the postmodern era. Cathedra 100 (2001) 27-46 Sum. 405. **H.**

10741 *Gous, Ignatius G.P.* The 'Tell'-tale of the mind: about cognitive archaeology. OTEs 14 (2001) 404-418.

10742 **Johnson, Matthew** Archaeological theory: an introduction. 1999 ⇒15,10870. ᴿAJA 105 (2001) 330 (*Hitchcock, Louise A.*).

10743 **Klejn, Leo S.** Meta archaeology. ᴱ*Sindbræk, Soren M.; Simpson, Ian R.; Randsborg, Klaus*: AcAr 72/1; AcAr.S 3: K 2001, Munksgaard (6) 149 pp. Bibl. 134-149.

10744 *Knauf, Ernst Axel* History, archaeology, and the bible. ThZ 57 (2001) 262-268.

10745 *Shanks, Hershel* The age of BAR: scholars talk about how the field has changed. BArR 27/2 (2001) 21-25, 29-31, 35.

10746 *Sievertsen, Uwe* Archäologie und Internet. BaghM 32 (2001) 313-325.

10747 **Thomas, Julian** Time, culture and identity: an interpretive archaeology. 1998 ⇒14,10082. ᴿAJA 105 (2001) 330-331 (*Hitchcock, Louise A.*).

T1.4 *Exploratores*—Excavators, pioneers

10748 *Bodine, Walter R.; Bohrer, Frederick N.* LAYARD and BOTTA: archaeology, imperialism, and aesthetics. Proceedings of the XLVe Rencontre Assyriologique, 1. 2001 ⇒577. 55-63.

10749 *Fauveaud, Catherine; Lozachmeur, Hélène* Une lettre inédite d'Ernest RENAN: conseils à un voyageur au Proche-Orient. Sem. 50 (2001) 235-240.

10750 **Fox, Edward** Palestine twilight: the murder of Dr. Albert GLOCK and the archaeology of the Holy Land. SF 2001, Harper Collins ix; 277 pp. 0-00-255607-3.

10751 **Hankey, Julie** A passion for Egypt: Arthur WEIGALL, Tutankhamun and the "Curse of the Pharaohs". L 2001, Tauris xi; 380 pp. 1-86064-566-6. Bibl. 349-352.

10752 **MacGillivray, Joseph Alexander** Minotaur: Sir Arthur EVANS and the archaeology of the Minoan myth. 2000 ⇒16,10996. ᴿIsis 35 (2001) 756-758 (*Marchand, Suzanne*).

10753 **McCall, Henrietta** The life of Max MALLOWAN: archaeology and Agatha CHRISTIE. L 2001, British Museum Pr. 208 pp. 0-7141-1149-X.

T1.5 *Materiae primae*—metals, glass

10754 **Dussart, Odile** Le verre en Jordanie et en Syrie du Nord. BAH 152: 1998 ⇒14,10088. ᴿSyr. 78 (2001) 264-266 (*Foy, Danièle*).

10755 *Levene, Dan; Rothenberg, Beno* Tin and tin-lead alloys in Hebrew and Jewish Aramaic. ᴹWEITZMAN, M.: JSOT.S 333: 2001 ⇒113. 100-112.

10756 *Levy, Thomas E., al.,* Early metallurgy, interaction, and social change: the Jabal Ḥamrat Fidan (Jordan) research design and 1998 archaeological survey: preliminary report. ADAJ 45 (2001) 159-187.

10757 **Lilyquist, C.; Brill, R.H.** Studies in Early Egyptian glass. ²1995 ⇒ 15,10884. ᴿCÉg 76 (2001) 154-155 (*Guidotti, M. Cristina*).

10758 *Lomoro, Romolo* La metallurgia svelata dalla bibbia. BeO 43 (2001) 183-196.

10759 **Müller, H.W.; Thiem, E.** The royal gold of ancient Egypt. 1999 ⇒15,10885. ᴿBiOr 58 (2001) 601-603 (*Ertman, Earl L.*).

10760 *Nenna, Marie-Dominique* Verres de l'antiquité gréco-romaine: cinq ans de publication (1995-1999). RAr 2 (2001) 303-342.

10761 *Ross, Jennifer C.* Text and subtext: precious metals and politics in Old Akkadian Mesopotamia. Proceedings of the XLVe Rencontre Assyriologique, 1. 2001 ⇒577. 417-428.

10762 **Stern, E.M.** Roman, Byzantine, and early medieval glass: 10 BCE-700 CE. Ernesto Wolf Collection: Ostfildern-Ruit 2001, Cantz 427 pp. 3-7757-9042-X. Bibl.; ill.

10763 *Yamahana, Kyoko* Ancient Egyptian glass vessels from the New Kingdom: a comparative analysis with Roman glass. Nippon Oriento Garkai 44/1 (2001) 25-41 Sum. 24-25. J.

10764 **Yener, K. Aslihan** The domestication of metals: the rise of complex metal industries in Anatolia. 2000 ⇒16,11009. ᴿAJA 105 (2001) 729-730 (*Muhly, James D.*); ZDMG 151 (2001) 209-211 (*Bonatz, Dominik*); BASOR 324 (2001) 114-117 (*Yakar, Jak*).

T1.7 **Technologia antiqua; architectura**

10765 *Chabot, J.* Persistance des outils en pierre taillée à l'Age du Bronze
Ancien en Syrie du nord. Canadian research on ancient Syria. 2001
⇒581. 61-68.

10766 **Pedde, Fr.** Vorderasiatische Fibeln. 2000 ⇒16,11011. [R]BiOr 58
(2001) 458-462 (*White Muscarella, Oscar*).

10767 **Sauvage, Martin** La brique et sa mise en oeuvre en Mésopotamie:
des origines à l'époque achéménide. 1998 ⇒14,10127; 16,11051.
[R]Mes. 36 (2001) 122-123 (*Fiorina, P.*); RAr (2001) 365-367
(*Treuil, René*); Syr. 78 (2001) 227-230 (*Castel, Corinne*); Or. 69
(2000) 180-182 (*Rova, Elena*).

10768 *Banning E.* On these foundations: the first 5,000 years of domestic
architecture in Syria. Canadian research on ancient Syria. 2001 ⇒
581. 33-39.

10769 **Barletta, Barbara A.** The origins of the Greek architectural
orders. NY 2001, CUP xi; 220 pp. $70. 0-521-79245-2. 87 fig.

10770 **Battini-Villard, Laura** L'espace domestique en Mésopotamie de
la IIIe dynastie d'Ur à l'époque paléo-babylonienne. 1999 ⇒15,
10901. [R]Mes. 36 (2001) 125-126 (*Fiorina, P.*).

10771 *Chadwick, R.* Iron Age gate architecture in Jordan and Syria. Canadian research on ancient Syria. 2001 ⇒581. 125-134.

10772 **DeVries, LaMoine F.** Cities of the biblical world. 1997 ⇒13,
10204; 14,10102. [R]RBLit 3 (2001) 86-88 (*Krieger, William H.*).

10773 **Dezzi Bardeschi, Chiara** Architettura domestica nella Mesopotamia settentrionale nel II millennio a.C. Eothen 8: F 1998, LoGisma
xxvi; 405 pp. Bibliografia 371-405.

10774 **Ellis, Simon P.** Roman housing. 2000 ⇒16,11021. [R]Prudentia 33/1
(2001) 67-70 (*Bligh, Lisa*).

10775 *Fiandra, Enrica; Monticone, Mara; Simonetti, Cristina* Elementi
per la chiusura delle porte nel Vicino Oriente antico e in Egitto.
[M]CAGNI, L., 1: SMDSA 61: 2001 ⇒15. 283-307.

10776 *Flesher, Paul V.M.* Prolegomenon to a theory of early synagogue
development. Judaism in late antiquity, 3/4: the special problem of
the synagogue. HO I,55: 2001 ⇒424. 121-153.

10777 Imperial art as christian art, christian art as imperial art: expression
and meaning in art and architecture from CONSTANTINE to JUSTINI-
AN. AAAHP n.s. 1: R 2001, Bardi 336 pp. 88-85699-94-4.

10778 **Jones, Mark Wilson** Principles of Roman architecture. 2000 ⇒16,
11029. [R]BiOr 58 (2001) 685-687 (*Wright, G.R.H.*).

10779 *Kanellopoulos, Chrysanthos* The architecture of the shops and colonnaded street in Petra. BASOR 324 (2001) 9-22.

10780 **Kubba, S.A.A.** Architecture and linear measurement during the Ubaid period in Mesopotamia. BAR internat. ser. 707: 1998 ⇒14, 10113; 16,11032. ᴿOLZ 96 (2001) 389-395 (*Sievertsen, Uwe*).

10781 *Magness, Jodi* The question of the synagogue: the problem of typology;

10782 A response to Eric M. Meyers and James F. Strange. Judaism in late antiquity, 3/4: the special problem of the synagogue. HO I,55: 2001 ⇒424. 1-48/79-91.

10783 ᴹMARTIN, Roland: Architettura, urbanistica, società nel mondo antico. ᴱGreco, E.: Tekmeria 2: Paestum 2001, Pandemos 110 pp. 88-87744-07-6. Ill.; Giornata di studi in ricordo di Roland Martin, Paestum, 21 febb. 1998.

10784 **Miglus, Peter A.** Städtische Wohnarchitektur in Babylonien und Assyrien. 1999 ⇒15,10919; 16,11035. ᴿMes. 36 (2001) 123-124 (*Fiorina, P.*).

10785 *Miroschedji, Pierre de* Notes on Early Bronze Age metrology and the birth of architecture in ancient Palestine. ᴹESSE, D.: SAOC 59: 2001 ⇒28. 465-491.

10786 **Negev, Avraham** The architecture of Oboda: final report. Qedem 36: 1997 ⇒13,10217... 16,11037. ᴿRB 108 (2001) 152-154 (*Murphy-O'Connor, J.*).

10787 **Oredsson, Dag** Moats in ancient Palestine. CB.OT 48: 2000 ⇒16, 11043. ᴿSEÅ 66 (2001) 201-210 (*Strange, John*); CBQ 63 (2001) 530-532 (*Hauer, Christian E.*).

10788 **Pfälzner, Peter** Haus und Haushalt: Wohnformen des dritten Jahrtausends vor Christus in Nordmesopotamien. Damaszener Forschungen 9: Mainz 2001, Von Zabern xxii; 419 pp. €101.24. 3-8053-2416-2. Num. ill. [RB 109,158].

10789 **Roller, Duane W.** The building program of Herod the Great. 1998 ⇒14,9952; 15,10930. ᴿGn. 73 (2001) 180-183 (*Fittschen, Klaus*); JNES 60 (2001) 155-156 (*Magness, Jodi*).

10790 **Russell, John Malcolm** The writing on the wall: studies in the architectural context of late Assyrian palace inscriptions. 1999 ⇒ 15,10554. ᴿAJA 105 (2001) 548 (*Sack, Ronald H.*); Or. 70 (2001) 330-335 (*Braun-Holzinger, Eva A.*).

10791 *Strange, James F.* Synagogue typology and Khirbet Shema': a response to Jodi Magness. Judaism in late antiquity, 3/4: the special problem of the synagogue. HO I,55: 2001 ⇒424. 71-78.

10792 **White, Michael L.** Social origins of christian architecture. 1997 ⇒ 13,10224; 14,10135. ᴿRStR 27 (2001) 223-225 (*Friesen, Steven*

J.); RStR 27 (2001) 225-227 (*Krentz, Edgar*); RStR 27 (2001) 227-228 (*Outschar, Ulrike*); RStR 27 (2001) 228-231 (*Oșiek, Carolyn*).

10793   Zertal, Adam The 'corridor-builders' of central Israel: evidence for the settlement of the 'northern sea peoples'?. Defensive settlements. 2001 ⇒619. 215-232.

T2.1 *Res militaris*—military matters

[E]**Bekker-Nielsen, T.** War as a cultural force 2001 ⇒596.

10794   *Briend, Jacques* Der Krieger und seine Ausrüstung: in der Zeit des Alten Testaments. WUB 19 (2001) 74-75.

10795   **Chevereau, Pierre-Marie** Prosopographie des cadres militaires égyptiens du Nouvel Empire. Études et Mémoires d'Égyptologie 3: P 2001 <1994>, Cybèle 254 pp. €36. 2-9512-0928-2.

10796   *Hobbs, T.R.* Soldiers in the gospels: a neglected agent. [F]MALINA, B.: BiblInterp 53: 2001 ⇒67. 328-348.

10797   **Kern, Paul Bentley** Ancient siege warfare. Bloomington 1999, Indiana Univ. Pr. xiii; 419 pp. $35. 0-25333-5469. [R]JRS 91 (2001) 202-203 (*Gilliver, Kate*).

10798   *Malamat, Abraham* Millitary rationing in papyrus Anastasi I and the bible. History of biblical Israel. 2001 <1957> ⇒182. 353-361.

10799   *Quesnel, Michel* Der Krieger und seine Ausrüstung: in der Zeit des Neuen Testaments. WUB 19 (2001) 75.

10800   *Seeber, Rudolfine* Restauratorische Bemerkungen zur Bergung und Konservierung des Sichelschwertes aus A/II-p/14, Grab 18 [L 468]. Ä&L 11 (2001) 221.

10801   **Sekunda, N.** Hellenistic infantry reform in the 160's B.C. Studies on the history of ancient and medieval art of warfare 5: Lodz 2001, Oficyna Naukowa MS 189 pp. 83-85874-04-6.

10802   *Zawadzki, S.; Jursa, M.* Šamaš-tirri-kuṣur, a smith manufacturing weapons in the Ebabbar temple at Sippar. WZKM 91 (2001) 347-363.

T2.2 *Vehicula, nautica*—transport, navigation

10803   **Bollweg, Jutta** Vorderasiatische Wagentypen: im Spiegel der Terracottaplastk bis zur Altbabylonischen Zeit. OBO 167: 1999 ⇒15, 10945. [R]BiOr 58 (2001) 456-458 (*Miglus, Peter A.*).

10804   *Özgüç, Nimet* Notes on the bronze vehicle from the Sarikaya palace at Acemhöyük. [F]VEENHOF, K. 2001 ⇒111. 361-366.

10805 *Van Soldt, Wilfred* Te land, ter zee en op de vlucht: reizen en trekken in de Levant in de late bronstijd. Phoe. 47 (2001) 148-162.

10806 *Meyer, Jan-Waalke* Zur Bedeutung der Bootsmodelle aus dem Alten Orient. [F]Haas, V. 2001 ⇒39. 267-283.

10807 **Morton, Jamie** The role of the physical environment in ancient Greek seafaring. Mn.S 213: Lei 2001, Brill ix; 363 pp. 90-04-11717-2. Bibl. 333-346.

10808 **Ward, Cheryl A.** Sacred and secular: Ancient Egyptian ships and boats. 2000 ⇒16,12193. [R]DiscEg 50 (2001) 115-122 (*Nibbi, Alessandra*)

T2.4 *Athletica*—sport, games

10809 **Beacham, Richard C.** Spectacle entertainments of early imperial Rome. 1999 ⇒15,10951. [R]CIR 51 (2001) 117-9 (*Van Nijf, Onno*).

10810 **Herb, Michael** Der Wettkampf in den Marschen: quellenkritische, naturkundliche und sporthistorische Untersuchungen zu einem altägyptischen Szenentyp. Nikephoros.B 5: Hildesheim 2001, Weidmann (10) 504 pp. €65.45. 3-615-00226-1 [Bibl. 473-482].

10811 [E]**Köhne, Eckart; Ewigleben, Cornelia** Caesaren und Gladiatoren: die Macht der Unterhaltung im antiken Rom. 2000 ⇒16,11085. [R]AJA 105 (2001)378 (*Cerutti, Steven M.*).

10812 **Kyle, Donald G.** Spectacles of death in ancient Rome. 1998 ⇒14, 10156; 16,11086. [R]Latomus 60 (2001) 489-491 (*Robert, Jean-Noël*); CIR 51 (2001) 347-349 (*Bodel, John*); HR 41 (2001) 170-172 (*Belayche, Nicole*).

10813 **Lee, Hugh M.** The program and schedule of the ancient Olympic Games. Nikephoros.B 6: Hildesheim 2001, Weidmann (8) 122 pp. 3-615-00235-0. Bibl. 110-116.

10814 *Malamat, Abraham* Foot-runners in Israel and Egypt in the third intermediate period. History of biblical Israel. Culture and history of the ANE 7: 2001 <1994> ⇒182. 362-365 [Jer 12,5].

10815 *Sebbane, Michael* Board games from Canaan in the early and intermediate Bronze Ages and the origin of the Egyptian Senet game. TelAv 28 (2001) 213-230 [Arad].

T2.5 *Musica, drama, saltario*—music, drama, dance

10816 *Arledler, Giovanni* Johann Sebastian BACH, musicista e teologo. CivCatt 152/2 (2001) 30-39.

10817 *Batnitzky, Leora* SCHOENBERG's "Moses und Aron" and the Judaic ban on images. JSOT 92 (2001) 73-90.

10818 **Bermond, Cristina** La danza negli scritti di FILONE, CLEMENTE Alessandrino e ORIGENE: storia e simbologia. Fra 2001, Domus Editoria Europaea 163 pp. 3-927884-56-1. Bibl. 141-145.

10819 *Borland, James A.* The meaning and identification of God's eschatological trumpets. Looking into the future. 2001 ⇒505. 63-73.

10820 **Braun, Joachim** Die Musikkultur Altisraels/Palästinas. OBO 164: 1999 ⇒15,339. ᴿFrRu 8 (2001) 129-130 (*Salmen, Walter*); BiOr 58 (2001) 656-658 (*Geus, C.H.J. de*); NEA(BA) 64/1-2 (2001) 93 (*Burgh, Theodore W.*).

10821 *Buetubela, Balembo* Danser à la louange de son nom (Ps 149,2). Telema 105 (2001) 55-58.

10822 **Chuaqui, Carmen** Musicología griega. Cuadernos del Centro de Estudios clásicos 45: Mexico 2000, Univ. Autónoma 268 pp. 968-36-8822-5.

10823 *Detwiler, David F.* Church music and Colossians 3:16. BS 158 (2001) 347-369.

10824 *Doerksen, Victor* The poetry of praise: some comments on the Old Testament and the new music. ᶠJANZEN, W. 2001 ⇒54. 105-114.

10825 *Elder, Linda Bennett* Virgins, viragos and virtuo(u)si among Judiths in opera and oratorio. JSOT 92 (2001) 91-119.

10826 **Flynn, William T.** Medieval music as medieval exegesis. 1999 ⇒ 15,10966; 16,11092. ᴿChH 70 (2001)153-4 (*Westerfield, Karen*).

10827 *Frederichs, Henning; Meyer-Blanck, Michael* Evangelische Apokalyptik: zur Konzeption einer Millenniums-Messe nach der Offenbarung des Johannes. JLH 40 (2001) 9-26.

10828 **Geck, Martin** BACH: Leben und Werk. 2000 ⇒16,11093. ᴿBiLi 74 (2001) 71-72 (*Fischer, Michael*).

10829 **Landels, John G.** Music in ancient Greece and Rome. 1999 ⇒15, 10967; 16,11095. ᴿAJP 122 (2001) 148-150 (*Solomon, Jon*).

10830 *Legrais, Michelle* Le chant grégorien ou la bible commentée. Sedes Sapientiae 76 (2001) 20-30.

10831 *Loader, James Alfred* Johannes BRAHMS, Agnostizismus und andere Weisheiten. Begegnung mit Gott. 2001 ⇒175. 257-268.

10832 **Marissen, Michael** Lutheranism, anti-Judaism, and BACH's 'St. John Passion' with an annotated translation of the libretto. 1998 ⇒ 14,10171. ᴿJR 81 (2001) 120-121 (*Westermeyer, Paul*).

10833 *Matoušová-Rajmová, Marie* Dance in Mesopotamia. ArOr 69 (2001) 21-32;

10834 Der verheimlichte Tanz. ᴹCAGNI, L., 2: SMDSA 61: 2001 ⇒15. 693-708.

10835 *Porter, Wendy J.* Sacred music at the turn of the millennia. Faith in the millennium. 2001 ⇒540. 423-444.

10836 *Seidel, Hans* Kritische Anmerkungen zur sogenannten Instrumentalmusik der Samaritaner. Leqach 1 (2001) 151-158 [BuBB 35,17].

10837 *Steinmetz, Agnes* Johann Sebastian BACH—ein Exeget der Bibel: eine Untersuchung der Kantate BWV 131 mit Hinweisen zum Unterricht. rhs 44 (2001) 215-234.

10838 *Vendrix, Philippe* La musique et la bible aux XVII. et XVIII. siècles: le cas de la "Passion selon Saint Jean" de Jean-Sébastien BACH. RThPh 133 (2001) 421-432.

10839 **West, M.L.** Ancient Greek music. 1992 ⇒8,d859... 10,11763*. ᴿAJP 122 (2001) 436-440 (*Feaver, Douglas*).

10840 **Winter, David** Ich weiß, dass mein Erlöser lebt: 40 Tage mit HÄNDELS 'Messias'. Wu 2001, Brockhaus 158 pp. €15.24. 3-417-1168-0-5. CD.

10841 **Wolff, Christoph** Johann Sebastian BACH. 2000 xv; 623 pp. ⇒16, 11109. ᴿBiLi 74 (2001) 70-71 (*Fischer, Michael*).

10842 **Younger, John G.** Music in the Aegean Bronze Age. 1998 ⇒14, 10176; 15,10978. ᴿRAr (2001/1) 109-112 (*Bélis, Annie*).

10843 **Zimmermann, Heidy** Tora und Shira: Untersuchungen zur Musikauffassung des rabbinischen Judentums. 2000 ⇒16,11111. ᴿFrRu 8 (2001) 228-229 (*Salmen, Walter*).

T2.6 *Vestis*, clothing; *ornamenta*, jewellry

10844 *Eder, Manfred* Die Aachener Heiligtumsfahrt des Jahres 1902: ein Beitrag zur Verehrungsgeschichte und Echtheitsfrage "biblischer" Reliquien. ᶠSCHMUTTERMAYR, G. 2001 ⇒101. 349-382.

10845 **Montembault, V.** Catalogue des chaussures de l'antiquité égyptienne. 2000 ⇒16,11114. ᴿBiOr 58 (2001) 375-376 (*Vogelsang-Eastwood, G.M.*).

10846 *Caubet, Annie* Die Waffen der Verführung: von der Bedeutung des Schmucks und des Sich-Schmückens. WUB 21 (2001) 9-12.

10847 **Derriks, Claire** Les miroirs cariatides Egyptiens en bronze: typologie, chronologie et symbolique. MÄSt 51; MüPF. Mainz 2001, Von Zabern xii; 232 pp. 3-8053-2819-2.

10848 *Michel, Cécile* Le lapis-lazuli des Assyriens au début du IIᵉ millénaire av. J.-C. ᶠVEENHOF, K. 2001 ⇒111. 341-359.

10849 **Pavesi, Giuseppina; Gagetti, Elisabetta** Arte e materia: studi su oggetti di ornamento di età romana. ᴱ*Chiesa, Gemma Sena*: Quaderni di ACME 49: Mi 2001, Cisalpino xii; 512 pp. 88-323-4598-6.

10850 **Plantzos, Dimitris** Hellenistic engraved gems. 1999 ⇒15,10983.
        RAJA 105 (2001) 367-368 (*Gerring, Britta*).
10851 *Schenke, Gesa* Der Schmuck der Frauen: Mumienporträts im Kon-
        text papyrologischer Zeugnisse. XXII Congresso di papirologia, 2.
        2001 ⇒555. 1187-1198.
10852 **Ubaldelli, Marco-Leopoldo** Corpus gemmarum: dactylotheca cap-
        poniana: collezionismo romano di intagli e cammei nella prima me-
        tà del XVIII secolo. Bollettino di numismatica, mon. 8/1: R 2001,
        Ministero per i Beni e le Attività Culturali 539 pp. Bibl. 497-513.

T2.8 Utensilia

10853 **Lilyquist, Christine** Egyptian stone vessels: Khian through Thut-
        mosis IV. 1995 ⇒13,10258; 14,10183. RCÉg 76 (2001) 155-157
        (*Guidotti, M. Cristina*).
10854 *Schoske, Sylvia* Die "Bonbonnieren-Kanope". WUB 22 (2001) 74.
10855 **Siebert, Anne-Viola** Instrumenta sacra: Untersuchungen zu römi-
        schen Opfer-, Kult- und Priestergeräten. RVV 44: 1999 ⇒15,
        10991; 16,11132. RAJA 105 (2001) 376-378 (*Stewart, Roberta*).

T2.9 *Pondera et mensurae*—weights and measures

10856 *Deutsch, Robert* A lead weight of Shimon Bar Kokhba. IEJ 51
        (2001) 96-98.
10857 *Gelander, S.* On the biblical concept of time. Beit Mikra 165
        (2001) 121-127. **H**.
10858 *Heltzer, Michael* A new weight from Hamath and trade relations
        with the south in the ninth-eighth centuries BCE. FDion, P.-E. 2:
        JSOT.S 325: 2001 ⇒25. 133-135.
10859 *Kletter, Raz; Beit-Arieh, Itzhaq* A heavy scale weight from Tel
        Malhata and the maneh (mina) of Judah. UF 33 (2001) 245-261.
10860 *Kupper, Jean-Robert* De l'usage frauduleux des poids et mesures.
        Akkadica 121 (2001) 1-4.
10861 EMichailidou, **Anna** Manufacture and measurement: counting,
        measuring and recording craft items in early Aegean societies.
        Athens 2001, Research Center for Greek and Roman Antiquity xv;
        349 pp. 960-7905-12-1. Num. ill. [RB 110,157].
10862 *Zaccagnini, Carlo* A note on Old Assyrian weight stones and
        weight system. MCAGNI, L., 2: SMDSA 61: 2001 ⇒15. 1203-1213.

T3.0 **Ars antiqua**, *motiva, picturae* [icones T3.1 infra]

10863 **Bahrani, Zainab** Women of Babylon: gender and representation in Mesopotamia. L 2001, Routledge xii; 212 pp. 0-415-21830-6. Bibl. 189-209.

10864 *Barkay, Gabriel; Im, MiYoung* Egyptian influence on the painted human figures from Kuntillet ʿAjrud. TelAv 28 (2001) 288-300.

10865 *Basirov, Oric* Evolution of the Zoroastrian iconography and temple cults. ANESt 38 (2001) 160-177.

10866 **Beard, Mary; Henderson, John** Classical art: from Greece to Rome. Oxf 2001, OUP vi; 298 pp. £11. 0192-84237-4. 223 ill.

10867 *Berlejung, Angelika* Die Kraft der Erotik: Sexualitä in der Bildwelt des Vorderen Orients. WUB 21 (2001) 52-58.

10868 *Bonatz, Dominik* Mnemohistory in Syro-Hittite iconography. Proceedings of the XLVe Rencontre Assyriologique, 1. 2001 ⇒577. 65-77.

10869 *Brandl, Baruch* Two engraved tridacna shells from Tel Miqne-Ekron. BASOR 323 (2001) 49-62.

10870 [E]**Chappaz, Jean-Luc; Vuilleumier, Sandrine** "Sortir au jour": art égyptien de la Fondation Martin Bodmer. Cahiers de la Société d'Égyptologie 7: Genève 2001, Société d'Égyptologie 180 pp. FS48. 2-940011-09-5.

10871 **Clarke, John R.** Looking at lovemaking: constructions of sexuality in Roman art. 100 B.C.-A.D. 250. 1998 ⇒14,10205. [R]Gn. 73 (2001) 440-444 (*Jacobelli, Luciana*).

10872 [E]**Davies, W.V.** Colour and painting in Ancient Egypt. L 2001, British Museum Press xvi; 192 pp. £30. 0-7141-1928-8.

10873 **Ewald, Björn Christian** Der Philosoph als Leitbild: ikonographische Untersuchungen an römischen Sarkophagreliefs. RM-EH 34: 1999 ⇒15,11016. [R]AJA 105 (2001) 365-366 (*D'Ambra, Eve*).

10874 *Finkelberg, Margalit* Two kinds of representation in Greek religious art. [F]BARASCH, M. 2001 ⇒2. 27-41.

10875 **Fullerton, Mark D.** Greek art. 2000 ⇒16,11169. [R]Prudentia 33/1 (2001) 71-74 (*Rankin, Elizabeth*).

10876 **Germond, Philippe** Bestiaire égyptien. [E]*Livet, J.*: P 2001, Citadelles & M. 223 pp. 2850881740. Iconographie réunie par *Jacques Livet*; Bibl. 220-221.

10877 **Gros De Beler, Aude** Vivre en Égypte au temps de Pharaon: le message de la peinture égyptienne. P 2001, Errance 221 pp. 2-87772-214-7. Bibl. 217-219.

10878 *Gurney, Oliver R.* The iconography of the Hasanlu bowl. [M]CAGNI, L., 1: SMDSA 61: 2001 ⇒15. 417-420.

10879   **Heinz, Susanna Constanze** Die Feldzugsdarstellungen des Neuen
        Reiches: eine Bildanalyse. DÖAW 18; Untersuchungen der Zweig-
        stelle Kairo des Österr. Archäologischen Institutes 17: W 2001,
        Verlag der ÖAW 327 pp. €152.36. 3-7001-2922-X. Bibl. 12-16.

10880   **Isler-Kerényi, Cornelia** Dionysos nella Grecia arcaica, il contribu-
        to delle immagini. R 2001, Istituti editoriali e poligrafici internazio-
        nali 272 pp. €40. 88-8147-230-9. 133 fig.

10881   **Kaplan, Irene** Grabmalerei und Grabreliefs der Römerzeit: Wech-
        selwirkungen zwischen der ägyptischen und griechisch-alexandrini-
        schen Kunst. VIAÄ 86; Beiträge zur Ägyptologie 16: W 1999,
        Institut für Ägyptologie iv; 217 pp. €69.77. 111 pl.

10882   **Karageorghis, Vassos; Vassilika, Eleni; Wilson, Penelope** The
        art of ancient Cyprus in the Fitzwilliam Museum, Cambridge. 1999
        ⇒15,11023. [R]BASOR 323 (2001) 98-100 (*Knoblauch, Ann-
        Marie*).

10883   **Karageorghis, Vassos** Excavating at Salamis in Cyprus, 1952-
        1974. 1999 ⇒15,11024. [R]BASOR 321 (2001) 88-90 (*Reyes, A.T.*);

10884   Ancient Cypriote art in the Severis Collection. 1999 ⇒15,11025.
        [R]BASOR 321 (2001) 95-96 (*Barlow, Jane A.*).

10885   **Keel, Othmar** Goddesses and trees, new moon and Yahweh: an-
        cient Near Eastern art and the Hebrew bible. JSOT.S 261: 1998 ⇒
        14,10217. [R]JBL 119 (2000) 338-339 (*Burns, John Barclay*).

10886   **Keel, Othmar; Uehlinger, Christoph** Dieux, déesses et figures di-
        vines: les sources iconographiques de l'histoire de la religion d'Isra-
        ël [T]*Prignaud, Jean*: P [2]2001 <1992>, Cerf 489 pp. €53.36. 2-204-
        06565-X. Bibl. 435-467. [R]RSR 89 (2001) 555-556 (*Gibert, Pierre*).

10887   *Knauf, Ernst Axel* Hirte, Jäger, Bauer, Gott?: zu einem ikonogra-
        phischen Problem aus der FB-III-Zeit. BN 107/108 (2001) 26-30.

10888   **Langner, Martin** Antike Graffitizeichnungen: Motive, Gestaltung
        und Bedeutung. Palilia 11: Wsb 2001. Reichert 173 pp. €49.90. 3-
        89500-188-0. CD-Rom [AnCl 72,667s—Raepsaet, Georges].

10889   **Leitz, Christian** Die Aussenwand des Sanktuars in Dendara: Un-
        tersuchungen zur Dekorationssystematik. MÄSt 50: Mainz 2001,
        Von Zabern xiii; 364 pp. €65.45. 3-8053-2722-6. Bibl. 343-351.

10890   **Marinatos, Nanno** The goddess and the warrior: the naked god-
        dess and mistress of animals in early Greek religion. 1999 ⇒15,
        11029. [R]AnCl 70 (2001) 376-378 (*Pirenne-Delforge, Vinciane*).

10891   **Málek, Jaromir** Egyptian art. 1999 ⇒15,11031. [R]AJA 105 (2001)
        101-102 (*Foster, Karen P.*).

10892   **Nunn, Astrid** Der figürliche Motivschatz Phöniziens, Syriens und
        Transjordaniens vom 6. bis zum 4. Jahrhundert v. Chr. OBO.A 18:
        2000 ⇒16,11186. [R]BiOr 58 (2001) 464-466 (*Amiet, Pierre*).

10893 **Onians, John** Classical art and the cultures of Greece and Rome. 1999 ⇒15,11034; 16,11188. [R]IHR 23 (2001) 379-380 (*Stewart, Peter*); IJCT 8 (2001) 265-268 (*Pollitt, J.J.*).

10894 *Ornan, Tallay* The bull and its two masters: moon and storm deities in relation to the bull in ancient Near Eastern art. IEJ 51 (2001) 1-26.

10895 *Passoni Dell'Acqua, Anna* Appunti sulla terminologia dei colori nella bibbia e nei papiri. XXII Congresso di papirologia, 2. 2001 ⇒ 555. 1067-1075.

10896 *Roussin, Lucille A.* Helios in the synagogue: did some ancient Jews worship the sun god?. BArR 27/2 (2001) 53-56.

10897 *Schmid, Stephan G.* König, nicht Königin: ein nabatäisches Herrscherporträt in Paris. AA 1 (2001) 91-105.

10898 **Schmitt, Rüdiger** Bildhafte Herrschaftsrepräsentation im eisenzeitlichen Israel. AOAT 283: Müns 2001, Ugarit-Verlag viii; 231 pp. 3-934628-05-2. Bibl. 199-219.

10899 *Schörner, Günther* Helios und ALEXANDER: zum Einfluss der Herrscherikonographie auf das Götterbild. AA 1 (2001) 59-68.

10900 **Stansbury-O'Donnell, Mark** Pictorial narrative in ancient Greek art. 1999 ⇒15,11036; 16,11193. [R]AJA 105 (2001) 354-355 (*Castriota, David*).

10901 **Teissier, Beatrice** Egyptian iconography on Syro-Palestinian cylinder seals of the Middle Bronze Age. OBO.A 11: 1996 ⇒12, 9701; 13,10302. [R]OLZ 96 (2001) 668-678 (*Eder, Christian*).

10902 *Thomason, Allison Karmel* Representations of the north Syrian landscape in neo-Assyrian art. BASOR 323 (2001) 63-96.

10903 *Thomsen, Marie-Louise* The identity of the lion-man. [M]CAGNI, L., 2: SMDSA 61: 2001 ⇒15. 1049-1063.

10904 **Volokhine, Youri** La frontalité dans l'iconographie de l'Égypte ancienne. 2000 ⇒16,11200. [R]DiscEg 49 (2001) 119-126 (*Warburton, David*).

T3.1 *Icones*—ars postbiblica

10905 *Amodei, Tito* Le crocifissioni di PIRANDELLO. LSDC 16 (2001) 185-192.

10906 *Barasch, Moshe* The idol in the icon: some ambiguities. [F]BARASCH, M. 2001 ⇒2. 1-26.

10907 *Baudienville, Marie-Paule* Iconographie de l'Apocalypse et histoire de l'art. MSR 58 (2001) 23-38 Rés., sum. 23.

10908 **Belting, Hans** Il culto delle immagini: storia dell'icona dall'età imperiale al tardo Medioevo. R 2001, Carocci 695 pp. €61.90. Ill.

10909 **Ben-Arieh, Yehoshua** Painting the Holy Land in the nineteenth century. 1997 ⇒14,10253. ᴿPEQ 133 (2001) 56-58 (*Searight, Sarah*).

10910 **Bisconti, Fabrizio** Temi di iconografia paleocristiana. 2000 ⇒16, 11206. ᴿSMSR 67 (2001) 206-209 (*Mazzoleni, Danilo*).

10911 *Bohn, Babette* Rape and the gendered gaze: Susanna and the elders in early modern Bologna. BiblInterp 9 (2001) 259-286 [Dan 13].

10912 *Bolard, Laurent* Le mur surmonté de frondaisons: un motif du quattrocento. RHPhR 81 (2001) 159-170.

10913 **Bord, Lucien-Jean; Skubiszewski, Piotr** L'image de Babylone aux Serpents dans les *Beatus*—contribution à l'étude des influences du Proche-Orient antique dans l'art du haut Moyen Âge. 2000 ⇒16,11210. ᴿRHPhR 81 (2001) 207-208 (*Heintz, J.-G.*).

10914 *Böhmisch, Franz* Exegetische Wurzeln des Antijudaismus im Ecclesia-Synagoge-Motiv. FrRu 8 (2001) 258-268.

10915 *Busi, Gianluca* La bellezza del Cristo nella tradizione iconografica. La bellezza. PSV 44: 2001 ⇒240. 251-263.

10916 *Cannuyer, Christian* Le poisson ιχθυς, symbole du Christ, serait-it d'origine égyptienne?. ᶠDESROCHES NOBLECOURT, C. 2001 ⇒22. 255-292.

10917 **Cartlidge, David R.; Elliott, J. Keith** Art and the christian apocrypha. L 2001, Routledge xvi; 277 pp. $30. 0-415-23391-7. Bibl. 257-265.

10918 **Cavarnos, Constantine** Guide to Byzantine iconography, 2. Boston 2001, Holy Transfiguration Monastery 160 pp. $23. 0-943405-11-4 [ThD 49,263—W. Charles Heiser].

10919 *Charalampidis, Costantino P.* L'evangelista Giovanni e il discepolo Procoro nell'iconografia bizantina. VIII Simposio di Efeso. Turchia 15: 2001 ⇒488. 239-253.

10920 **Christe, Yves** Jugements derniers. Les Formes de la Nuit 12: 2000 ⇒16,11216. ᴿScr. 55/1 (2001) 29*-30* (*Westerman, J.*);

10921 Das Jüngste Gericht. ᵀ*Lauble, Michael*: Rg 2001, Schnell & S. 215 pp. 195 ill.

10922 *Cifani, Arabella; Monetti, Franco* Un inedito capolavoro di Pierre-Charles LE METTAY: 'La natività': già della distrutta chiesa dell'Eremo di Torino. ACr 89 (2001) 439-444.

10923 **Cocke, Richard Paolo** VERONESE: piety and display in an age of religious reform. Aldershot 2001, Ashgate 270 pp. £50.

10924 **Cohn-Wiener, Ernst** Jewish art: its history from the beginning to the present day. ᵀ*Bell, Anthea*: Yelvertoft Manor, Northampton 2001, Pilkington 276 pp. 1-899044-27-2. Afterword *Hannelore Künzl*.

10925 *Collomb, Michel* Le possédé de Gérasia: sur un tableau de Sébastien BOURDON. Représentations des maladies. 2001 ⇒482. 261-270 [Mk 5,1-20].

10926 **Corona, Raimondo** L'infanzia di Gesù in alcune opere dell'arte in Abruzzo: sec. XII-XIX: lettura storico-teologica e note iconografiche. L'Aquila 2001, n.p. 127 pp. Bibl. 119-123.

10927 *Cutler, Anthony* The propriety of Peter: on the nature and authenticity of the Bryn Athyn apostle plaque. [F]MEGAW, A. 2001 ⇒70. 27-32.

10928 **De Borchgrave, Helen** A journey into christian art. 2000 ⇒16, 11221. [R]Dialog 40 (2001) 316-317 (*Meadows-Rogers, Robert D.*).

10929 **Di Blasio, Tiziana Maria** Veronica: il mistero del volto: itinerari iconografici, memoria e rappresentazione. R 2000, Città Nuova 236 pp. €41.32. Ill. [R]CivCatt 152/4 (2001) 620-621 (*Fantuzzi, V.*).

10930 **Dulaey, Martine** 'Des forêts de symboles': l'initiation chrétienne et la bible (Ier-VIe siècle). P 2001, Librairie générale française 287 pp. €8.30. 2-253-90574-7. Bibl. 261-272; ill.

10931 *Elliott, J.K.* Art and the christian apocrypha. ET 113 (2001) 84-87.

10932 [E]**Felmy, Karl Christian; Haustein-Bartsch, Eva** Die Weiheit baut ihr Haus': Untersuchungen zu hymnischen und didaktischen Ikonen. 1999 ⇒15,11067. [R]Iren. 73 (2001) 593-594.

10933 **Fournier, Dominique** Psaumes. P 2001, Soceval 128 pp. €35 [EeV 57,33—Pousseur, Robert].

10934 **Gerhard, Romana** Die Opferung Isaaks in der jüdischen und christlichen Literatur und in der Kunst des 11. und 13. Jahrhunderts in Italien. Diss. Bochum 2001, [D]*Berg, W.*: 350 pp. [RTL 33,631] [Gn 22].

10935 **Gulácsi, Zsuzsanna** Manichaean art in Berlin collections: a comprehensive catalogue of Manichaean artifacts belonging to the Berlin state museums of the Prussian Cultural Foundation... Corpus Fontium Manichaeorum, Series Archaeologica et Iconographica 1: Turnhout 2001, Brepols vii; 283 pp. 2-503-50649-6. Bibl. 271-278.

10936 **Hall, Rachel; Roberts, Helene E.** Iconographic index to New Testament subjects represented in photographs and slides of paintings in the visual collections, Fine Arts Library, Harvard University, 2. Christian Devotional Painting of the Italian School: NY 2001, Routledge xi; 618 pp. £175. 0-8153-3422-2 [NT 44,308—Cartlidge, David R.].

10937 [E]**Hari, Albert** Cantique des cantiques et Qohélet. Strasbourg 2001, Signe 80 pp.

10938 [E]*Heck, Christian; Boespflug, François; Da Costa, Valérie* Cristo nell'arte. Il Mondo della Bibbia 57 (2001) 2-72.

10939 **Heiser, Lothar** Äthiopien erhebe seine Hände zu Gott!: die äthiopische Kirche in ihren Bildern und Gebeten. Schriftenreihe des Patristischen Zentrums Koinonia-Oriens 49: St. Ottilien, 2000 EOS 396 pp. €24.60. 3-8306-8048-6.

10940 *Hornik, Heidi J.; Parsons, Mikeal C.* Ambrogio LORENZETTI's "Presentation in the temple": a "visual exegesis" of Luke 2:22-38. PRSt 28/1 (2001) 31-46 [Lk 2,22-38].

10941 **Imesch, Kornelia** Franziskanische Ordenspolitik und Bildprogrammatik: die Leben-Jesu-Fresken von Santa Maria delle Grazie in Bellinzona. Oberhausen 1998, Athena 268 pp. 3-9327-40246. [R]FF 67 (2001) 206-209 (*Lehmann, Leonhard*).
   Imperial art as christian art 2001 ⇒10777.

10942 *Janocha, Michał* Ofiarowanie Chrystusa w ukraińskim i białoruskim malarstwie ikonowym [The Presentation of Christ in the Ukrainian and Bylorussian icon painting]. Saeculum Christianum 7/2 (2001) 147-160 Sum. 160 [Lk 2,22-38].

10943 **Jensen, Robin Margaret** Understanding early christian art. 2000 ⇒16,11233. [R]RRT 8 (2001) 152-154 (*Young, Frances*); NT 43 (2001) 410-413 (*Elliott, J.K.*); JThS 52 (2001) 882-883 (*Charles-Murray, Mary*); Studies in World Christianity 7 (2001) 267-269 (*Russell, Ada*).

10944 *Künzl, Hannelore* Jewish artists and the representation of God. [F]BARASCH, M. 2001 ⇒2. 149-159.

10945 **Landesmann, Peter** Die Himmelfahrt des Elijas (2 Kön 2,1-18), ihre Wirkungsgeschichte und ihre Ikonologie bis in das 5. Jahrhundert. Diss. Wien 2001, [D]*Wischmeyer, W.* [RTL 33,652].

10946 **Landsberg, Jacques de** L'Art en croix: le thème de la crucifixion dans l'histoire de l'art. Tournai 2001, La Renaissance du Livre 166 pp. €60.22. 2-8946-0498-5. 163 pl. [ETR 78,592s—Cottin, J.].

10947 **Lia, Pierluigi** Il cantico di CHAGALL: tra arte e teologia. Mi 2001, Àncora 80 pp. €14.45. Ill.

10948 *Lipton, Sara* The un-moralized Bible. BiRe 17/2 (2001) 30-37, 48, 50.

10949 *Lo Paro, Vittorio* Marc CHAGALL (Moise Zaharovic Segal): la sua cultura russo-ebraica, i termini del dialogo con le Avanguardie, la bibbia sorgente zampillante della sua opera. Itinerarium 9 (2001) 131-142.
   Lowden, J. The making of the bibles moralisées 2000 ⇒2737.

10950 **MacGregor, Neil; Langmuir, Erika** Seeing salvation: images of Christ in art. 2000 ⇒16,11240. [R]NT 43 (2001) 410-413 (*Elliott, J.K.*).

10951 *Martens-Czarnecka, Malgorzata* Wall paintings discovered in Old Dongola. Dongola-Studien. 2001 ⇒411. 253-284.

10952 **Martin, Pierre** La résurrection en images: le cheminement des symboles de la résurrection. Préf. *Yves Christé*: Saint-Maurice 2001, Saint Augustin 162 pp. €22.50.

10953 **Marzolph, Ulrich** Narrative illustration in Persian lithographed books. HO 1/60: Lei 2001, Brill xii; 302 pp. 90-04-12100-5. Bibl. 295-302.

10954 **Mathews, Thomas F.** The clash of gods: a reinterpretation of early christian art. ²1999 ⇒15,11079. ᴿCrSt 22 (2001) 473-476 (*Prigent, Pierre*); ByZ 94 (2001) 736-741 (*Deckers, Johannes G.*).

10955 **Meyer zu Capellen, Jürg** RAPHAEL, a critical catalogue of his paintings, 1. ᴱᵀ*Polter, Stefan B.*: Landshut 2001, Arcos 328 pp. 3-93533-900-3.

10956 **Neipp, Bernadette** REMBRANDT et la mort de Jésus. Bible et images 1: Saint-Maurice 2001, Saint-Augustin 175 pp. €21.19. 2-88011-234-6. 20 pl. [ETR 78,594—Cottin, Jérôme].

10957 *Nikolaou, Theodor* 'Du sollst dir kein Gottesbild machen': die Undarstellbarkeit Gottes bzw. der HeiligenTrinität. OrthFor 15 (2001) 5-15.

10958 ᴱ**O'Grady, Ron** Christ for all people. Mkn 2001, Orbis 159 pp. $30. 1-57075-378-4.

10959 ᴱ**O'Grady, Ron** Christ for all people: celebrating a world of christian art. Auckland, New Zealand 2001, Pace 159 pp. $30. 2-8254-1339-9 [ThD 48,358—Heiser, W. Charles].

10960 **Plazaola Artola, J.** Historia del arte cristiano. 1999 ⇒15,11088. ᴿVyV 59 (2001) 175-176 (*Sanz Montes, Jesús*).

10961 **Plazaola, Juan** Arte e iglesia: veinte siglos de arquitectura y pintura cristiana. Hondarribia 2001, Nerea 236 pp. €59.80. 84-89569-57-6. Ill.

10962 ᴱ*Pouthier, Jean-Luc* Les trésors cachés des églises: fresques, retables et statues. MoBi 139 (2001) 3-67.

10963 **Prinz, Wolfram** Die Storia oder die Kunst des Erzählens in der italienischen Malerei und Plastik des späten Mittelalters und der Frührenaissance 1260-1460. 2000 ⇒16,11261. ᴿZRGG 53 (2001) 368-370 (*Sprenger, Hans*).

10964 **Rauchenberger, Johannes** Biblische Bildlichkeit: Kunst—Raum theologischer Erkenntnis. 1999 ⇒15,11093. ᴿThPQ 149 (2001) 90-91 (*Rombold, Günter*); ThPh 76 (2001) 306-307 (*Splett, J.*); ThGl 91 (2001) 178-180 (*Mennekes, Friedhelm*).

10965 **Ridez, Louis** Jésus en images: l'attente du Sauveur dans l'évangéliaire d'Egbert. P 2001, Cerf 60 pp. €18. 2-204-06811-X [CEv 118,65].

10966   **Schade, Herbert** Lamm Gottes und Zeichen des Widders: zur kosmologisch-psychologischen Hermeneutik der Ikonographie des 'Lammes Gottes'. 1998 ⇒14,10318. [R]RivBib 49 (2001) 249-252 (*Prato, Gian Luigi*).

10967   **Schmidt, Peter** In de handen van mensen: 2000 jaar Christus in kunst en cultuur. 2000 ⇒16,11269. [R]Str. 68 (2001) 376-377 (*Koenot, Jan*).

10968   *Schneider, Jan Heiner* Emil NOLDE: Christus und die Kinder. KatBl 126 (2001) 362-366 [Mk 10,13-16].

10969   *Scholz, Piotr O.* Das nubische Christentum und seine Wandmalereien. Dongola-Studien. 2001 ⇒411. 177-251.

10970   **Schreckenberg, Heinz** Christliche Adversus-Judaeos-Bilder: das AT und NT im Spiegel der christlichen Kunst. EHS.T 650: 1999 ⇒ 15,11098; 16,11272. [R]Sal. 63 (2001) 566-567 (*Vicent, R.*).

10971   *Seasoltz, R. Kevin* Transcendence and immanence in sacred art and architecture. Worship 75 (2001) 403-431.

10972   *Sed-Rajna, Gabrielle* Le songe de Jacob à Béthel: interprétations visuelles. [F]PURY, A. de: 2001 ⇒89. 394-396 [Gn 28,10-17].

10973   **Sekules, Veronica** Medieval art. Oxford History of Art: Oxf 2001, OUP 228 pp. £11 [ScrB 31,110].

10974   *Sills, David L.* What's in a name?: the strange case of VERONESE's Last Supper. BiRe 17/5 (2001) 34-39.

10975   *Snoek, Godefridus J.C.* De passiespelen te Oberammergau in 2000: traditionele en transitionele aspecten. TTh 41 (2001) 167-185.

10976   *Spijkerboer, Anne Marijke* REMBRANDT und Hagar. [F]DEURLOO, K.: ACEBT.S 2: 2001 ⇒23. 21-31.

10977   **Steinberg, Leo** LEONARDO's incessant Last Supper. NY 2001, Zone xiii; 413 pp. $43.

10978   *Sturtevant, Henry H.* MANTEGNA's *Agonies*. Parabola 26/1 (2001) 58-64.

10979   *Tomić, Radoslav* Il dipinto 'Cristo e la Samaritana' di PIER PAOLO da Santa Croce in Dalmazia. ACr 89 (2001) 315-316.

10980   **Tracz, Catherine Brown** The key to the Brescia Casket: typology and the early christian imagination. EAug, Ant. 165: P 2001, Inst. des Etudes Augustiniennes 282 pp. €60.50. 2-85121-178-1. Num. ill. [RBen 113,199—Bogaert, P.-M.].

10981   *Treiber, Karl Heinz* Über die Apokalypse in der Bildenden Kunst: der Versuch einer Annäherung. Aktuelle Apokalyptik!. Loccumer Protokolle 20/99: 2001 ⇒6097. 214-222.

10982   *Troyas, Alain* Le deuil de l'unité art—science—religion. Représentations des maladies. 2001 ⇒482. 231-242.

10983 *Utro, Umberto* L'immagine di Maria nell'arte delle origini: dalle prime raffigurazioni al Concilio di Nicea (325). Theotokos 9 (2001) 455-480.

10984 *Van den Hoek, Annewies; Herrmann, John J.* Thecla the beast fighter: a female emblem of deliverance in early christian popular art. [F]HAY, D. 2001 ⇒45. 212-249.

10985 **Van Laarhoven, Jan** Storia dell'arte cristiana. Sintesi: Mi 1999, Mondadori 368 pp. 88-4249-3694. [R]Rivista di teologia dell'evangelizzazione 5/9 (2001) 206-207 (*Ziviani, Giampietro*).

10986 *Vardanyan, Edda* Un psautier arménien illustré du XVe siècle. HandAm 115 (2001) 256-279.

10987 **Verdon, Timothy** L'arte sacra in Italia: dai mosaici paleocristani alle espressioni contemporanee. Mi 2001, Mondadori 398 pp. €21.69. Num. ill.

10988 *Volti, Panayota* L'art, miroir de la dévotion: fin du Moyen Âge. MoBi 139 (2001) 40-45 [BuBB 36,99].

10989 *Wataghin, Gisella Cantino* Biblia pauperum: a proposito dell'arte dei primi cristiani. Antiquité Tardive 9 (2001) 259-274 Sum. 259.

10990 **Weitzmann, Kurt; Bernabò, Massimo** The Byzantine octateuchs. The illustrations in the manuscripts of the Septuagint 2: 1999 2 vols ⇒15,11118. [R]JAC 44 (2001) 252-258 (*Zimmermann, Barbara*).

10991 *Young, Robin Darling* EVAGRIUS the iconographer: monastic pedagogy in the Gnostikos. JECS 9 (2001) 53-71.

T3.2 **Sculptura**

10992 **Ashton, Sally-Ann** Ptolemaic royal sculpture from Egypt: the interaction between Greek and Egyptian traditions. Oxf 2001, Archaeopress 121 pp. 1-84171-221-3.

10993 **Baumer, Lorenz E.** Vorbilder und Vorlagen: Studien zu klassischen Frauenstatuen und ihrer Verwendung für Reliefs und Statuetten des 5. und 4. Jahrhunderts vor Chr. Acta Bernensia 12: 1997 ⇒ 13,10384; 14,10346. [R]RAr (2001) 393-394 (*Muller, Arthur*).

10994 **Brand, Peter James** The monuments of Seti I: epigraphic, historical and art historical analysis. PÄ 16: 2000 ⇒16,11284. [R]BiOr 58 (2001) 358-360 (*Hornung, Erik*); JRAS 11 (2001) 382-384 (*Kitchen, K.A.*).

10995 *Curto, Silvio* The history of the Great Sphinx. Attraverso l'egittologia. 2001 <1992> ⇒136. 413-426.

10996 *Daltrop, Georg* Das Ethos des Verlierers: Gedanken zur Laokoongruppe. Der neue Mensch in Christus. 2001 ⇒239. 190-202.

10997 **Damaskos, Dimitris** Untersuchungen zu hellenistischen Kultbildern. 1999 ⇒15,11125. [R]Gn. 73 (2001) 437-440 (*Flashar, Martin*); AnCl 70 (2001) 519-520 (*Hermary, Antoine*).

10998 *Elayi, Josette* Nouvelle recherche sur les cavaliers perses. [M]CAGNI, L., 1: SMDSA 61: 2001 ⇒15. 243-259.

10999 *Friedland, Elise A.* The Roman marble sculptures from the east baths at Jarash. ADAJ 45 (2001) 461-477.

11000 **Hannestadt, Niels** Tradition in late antique sculpture: conservation, modernization, production. AJut 69/2: Aarhus 1994, Aarhus UP 166 pp. DKR198. 105 ill. [R]Gn. 73 (2001) 56-66 (*Bergmann, Marianne*).

11001 **Harvey, Julia** Wooden statues of the Old Kingdom: a typological study. Egyptological Memoirs 2: Lei 2001, Brill ix; 666 pp. €156/$182. 90-04-12357-1. Bibl. 643-652.

11002 *Hölzl, Regina* Die Statuengruppe des Minmose im Ashmolean Museum Oxford (Inv. Nr. 1888.298). ZÄS 128 (2001) 108-115.

11003 *Jones, Christopher P.* A statuette of Nemesis. Epigraphica Anatolica 33 (2001) 45-48.

11004 *Kaim, Barbara* Killing and dishonouring the royal statue in the Mesopotamian world. [M]CAGNI, L., 1: SMDSA 61: 2001 ⇒15. 515-20.

11005 **Kissas, Konstantin** Die attischen Statuen- und Stelenbasen archäischer Zeit 2000 ⇒16,11296. [R]AJA 105 (2001) 126-127 (*Keesling, Catherine M.*).

11006 *Kletter, Raz* Between archaeology and theology: the pillar figurines from Judah and the asherah. Archaeology of the Iron Age. JSOT.S 331: 2001 ⇒625. 179-216.

11007 *Klinger, Sonia* A terracotta statuette of Artemis with a deer at the Israel Museum. IEJ 51 (2001) 208-224.

11008 *Kruchten, Jean-Marie* Le pharaon sculpteur des images divines. [F]DESROCHES NOBLECOURT, C. 2001 ⇒22. 299-302.

11009 **Lapatin, Kenneth D.S.** Chryselephantine statuary in the ancient Mediterranean world. Oxford monographs on classical archaeology: Oxf 2001, OUP xvi; 242 pp. £75. 0-19-8153-11-2. 14 pl.; 249 fig.

11010 *Lurson, Benoît* La typologie des statuettes tenant un vase è onguent offertes par le roi dans les scènes rituelles des temples du Nouvel Empire: à propos de deux bas-reliefs du temple de Ramsès II à Ouadi es-Seboua. ZÄS 128 (2001) 65-70.

11011 Topographical bibliography of Ancient Egyptian hieroglyphic texts, statues, reliefs and paintings, 8: objects of provenance not known. 1999 ⇒15,11139 [R]BiOr 58 (2001) 76-78 (*Meulenaere, H.J.A. de*).

11012 **Neils, Jenifer** The Parthenon frieze. C 2001, CUP xxii; 294 pp. £45. 0-521-64161-6.

11013 **Page Gasser, Madeleine** Götter bewohnten Ägypten: Bronzefiguren der Sammlungen "Bibel+Orient" der Universität Freiburg Schweiz. OBO 183: Gö 2001, Vandenhoeck & R. xvii; 178 pp. FS48. 3-7278-1359-8. 38 pl.; bibl. 155-176.

^EPalagia, O. Regional schools in Hellenistic sculpture 1998 ⇒633.

11014 *Prag, Kay* Figurines, figures and contexts in Jerusalem and regions to the east in the seventh and sixth centuries BCE. Archaeology of the Iron Age. JSOT.S 331: 2001 ⇒625. 217-234.

11015 **Reade, Julian** Assyrian sculpture. CM 1999, Harvard Univ. Pr. 96 pp. $19. 109 phot. ^RRBLit 3 (2001) 92-94 (*Power, Bruce A.*).

11016 **Ridgway, Brunilde Sismondo** Hellenistic sculpture, 2: the styles of ca. 200-100 B.C. 2000 ⇒16,11302. ^RAJA 105 (2001) 740-742 (*Stansbury-O'Donnell, Mark D.*).

11017 *Ritter, Stefan* Fremde Götter und Heroen in attischen Urkundenreliefs. JdI 116 (2001) 129-162.

11018 **Robins, Gay** Egyptian statues. Shire Egyptology 26: Princes Risborough, Buckinghamshire 2001, Shire 64 pp. £5. 0-7478-0520-2. Bibl. 59-60.

11019 *Rolley, Claude* Les bronzes grecs et romains: recherches récentes. RAr 2 (2001) 343-358.

11020 **Skupinska-Lovset, Ilona** Portraiture in Roman Syria: a study in social and regional differentiation within the art of portraiture. 1999 ⇒15,11146. ^RIEJ 51 (2001) 115-117 (*Segal, Arthur*).

11021 **Steiner, Deborah Tarn** Images in mind: statues in archaic and classical Greek literature and thought. Princeton 2001, Princeton Univ. Pr. xviii; 360 pp. $39.50. 0-691-04431-7. 28 fig. [AJA 106,331—Pollitt, J.J.].

11022 *Watanabe, Chikako Esther* Mythological associations implied in the Assyrian royal bull hunt. ^MCAGNI, L., 2: 2001 ⇒ 15. 1149-61.

11023 *Weber, Thomas* Syrien: König Herodes Agrippa und seine Leibgarde: ein Statuendenkmal in der syrischen Basaltwüste (Trachonitis). WUB 21 (2001) 78-79.

T3.3 *Glyptica*; **stamp and cylinder seals**; *scarabs, amulets*

11024 *Amadasi Guzzo, Maria Giulia* Une empreinte de sceau de Tell Afis. Or. 70 (2001) 318-324.

11025 **Avigad, N.; Heltzer, M.; Lemaire, A.** West Semitic seals: eighth-sixth centuries B.C.E. Hecht Museum Collection B. Haifa 2000, Univ. of Haifa 180 pp. 965-7045-02-7.

11026 *Baker, Heather D.; Wunsch, Cornelia* Neo-Babylonian notaries and their use of seals. XLVe Rencontre Assyriologique, 2. 2001 ⇒582. 197-213.

11027 **Beyer, Dominique** Emar IV: les sceaux: mission archéologique de Meskéné-Emar: recherches au pays d'Astata. OBO.A 20: Gö 2001, Vandenhoeck & R. xvii; (4) 491 pp. FS185. 3-525-53001-3. 50 pl.; Bibl. 460-471. ᴿRA 95 (2001) 184-186 (*Amiet, Pierre*).

11028 *Bikai, Pierre M.; Eggler, Jürg* A stamp seal of the Persian period from Khirbet Salameh ('Amman). JNSL 27/1 (2001) 63-70.

11029 *Blocher, Felix* Sealing tablets in early second-millennium Babylonia: wealth and significance of the Yale Babylonian collection. XLVe Rencontre Assyriologique, 2. 2001 ⇒582. 133-148.

11030 *Bosshard-Nepustil, Erich; Morenz, Stäfa; Morenz, Ludwig D.* Layout als Schriftspiel—zu einem edomitischen Siegel aus Horvat Qidmit. WO 31 (2001) 72-74.

11031 *Carruba, Onofrio* Tauanana II: De magnae filiae regis cognominis significatione atque usu. ᴹCAGNI, L., 1: 2001 ⇒15. 71-83.

11032 *Charvát, Petr; Gil Fuensanta, Jesús* Seals and seal impressions from Tilbes Höyük, south-eastern Turkey (1996-1999). ArOr 69 (2001) 559-570.

11033 **Collon, Dominique** Catalogue of the western Asiatic seals in the British Museum: cylinder seals 5: neo-Assyrian and neo-Babylonian periods. L 2001, British Museum Pr. 204 pp. £90. 0-7141-1147-3. Collab. *Margaret Sax; C.B.F. Walker*; 48 ill.

11034 *Collon, Dominique* How seals were worn and carried: the archaeological and iconographic evidence. Proceedings of the XLVe Rencontre Assyriologique, 2. 2001 ⇒582. 15-30.

11035 **Dickers, Aurelia** Die spätmykenischen Siegel aus weichem Stein: Untersuchungen zur spätbronzezeitlichen Glyptik auf dem griechischen Festland und in der Ägäis. Internationale Archäologie 33: Rahden 2001, Marie Leidorf 258 pp. €66.37. 3-89646-305-5. 26 ill.; 51 pl.; 10 maps.

11036 *Dinçol, Ali M.* Ein interessanter Siegelabdruck aus Boğazköy und die damit verknüpften historischen Fragen;

11037 *Dinçol, Belkis* Bemerkungen über die hethitischen Siegelinhaber mit mehreren Titeln. IV. Internationaler Kongress 2001 ⇒650. 89-97/98-105.

11038 *Ehrenberg, Erica* Sixth-century Urukaen seal impressions at Yale. XLVe Rencontre Assyriologique, 2. 2001 ⇒582. 185-195.

11039 **Feghali-Gorton, Andrée** Egyptian and Egyptianizing scarabs: a typology of steatite, faience and paste scarabs from Punic and other Mediterranean sites. 1996 ⇒14,10377. ᴿBiOr 58 (2001) 109-115 (*Schlick-Nolte, Birgit*).

11040 **Garrison, Mark B.; Root, Margaret** Cool Seals on the Persepolis fortification tablets: images of heroic encounter, 1: text; 2: plates. The University of Chicago, Oriental Institute Publications 117: Ch 2001, Oriental Instit. of Univ. of Chicago 2 vols. $140. 1-885923-12-0. Bibl. v.1, xxi-xxxiii.

11041 *Göhde, Hildegard* The rhomb, a god's symbol. ᴹCᴀɢɴɪ, L., 1: SMDSA 61: 2001 ⇒15. 395-415.

11042 *Görg, Manfred* Zur sogenannten "anra"-Gruppe auf palästinischen Skarabäen. BN 107/108 (2001) 22-25.

11043 *Greenberg, Raphael* Early Bronze Age II-III Palestinian cylinder seal impressions and the North Canaanite metallic ware jar. ᴹEssᴇ, D.: SAOC 59: 2001 ⇒28. 189-197.

11044 *Greenfield, Jonas C.* A group of Phoenician city seals. ʿAl kanfei yonah, 2. 2001 <1985> ⇒153. 759-765.

11045 *Győry, Hedvig* The history of early amulets. JSSEA 28 (2001) 99-110.

11046 **Gyselen, Rika** Catalogue des sceaux, camées et bulles sassanides de la Bibliothèque Nat. et du... Louvre, 1: collection générale. 1993 ⇒11/2,a699. ᴿJNES 60 (2001) 138-140 (*Azarpay, Guitty*).

11047 *Hallo, William W.* Seals and seal impressions;

11048 *Hattori, Atsuko* Sealing practices in Ur III Nippur. XLVe Rencontre Assyriologique, 2. 2001 ⇒582. 239-254/71-99.

11049 *Helzer, Michael* Two early West Semitic seals. ᶠAʜɪᴛᴜᴠ, S. 2001 ⇒1. 161-162. **H.**

11050 *Joffe, Alexander H.* Early Bronze Age seal impressions from the Jezreel valley and the problem of sealing in the southern Levant. ᴹEssᴇ, D.: SAOC 59: 2001 ⇒28. 355-375.

11051 *Kawami, Trudy S.* The cattle of Uruk: stamps seals and animal husbandry in the Late Uruk/Jemdet Nasr period. Proceedings of the XLVe Rencontre Assyriologique, 2. 2001 ⇒582. 31-47.

11052 **Keel, Othmar** Corpus der Stempelsiegel-Amulette aus Palästina/Israel: von den Anfängen bis zur Perserzeit: Einleitung. 1995 ⇒11/2, a706...15,11169. ᴿOr. 69 (2000) 125-128 (*De Salvia, Fulvio*).

11053 *Klock-Fontanille, Isabelle* Écritures et langages visuels sur les sceaux royaux digraphes de l'empire hittite: quelques propositions pour une rhétorique de l'écriture. IV. Internationaler Kongress. 2001 ⇒650. 292-307.

11054 *Lubetski, Meir* King Hezekiah's seal revisited: small object reflects big geopolitics. BArR 27/4 (2001) 44-51, 59.

11055 *Mayr, R.* Intermittent recarving of seals in the Neo-Sumerian period. XLVe Rencontre Assyriologique, 2. 2001 ⇒582. 49-58.

11056 **Merrillees, Parvine H.** Ancient Near Eastern glyptic in the
National Gallery of Victoria, Melbourne, Australia. Studies in
Mediterranean archaeology 129: Jonsered 2001, Åström viii; 95, vii
pp. 91-7081-181-4. Bibl. 62-72.

11057 *Millard, Alan* The corpus of West Semitic stamp seals: review arti-
cle. IEJ 51 (2001) 76-87.

11058 *Mlinar, Christa* Die Skärabäen aus dem Grabungsareal A/II-o/14-
A/II-p/15 von Tell el-Dab'a. Ä&L 11 (2001) 223-264.

11059 ᴱ**Müller, Walter; Pini, Ingo** Die Siegelabdrücke von Aj. Triada
und anderen zentral- und ostkretischen Fundorten: unter Ein-
beziehung von Funden aus anderen Museen. 1999 ⇒15,11180.
ᴿAJA 105 (2001) 118-120 (*Krzyszkowska, Olga*).

11060 *Nachtergael, Georges* Sceaux et timbres de bois d'Égypte, 2: les
sceaux de grand format. CÉg 76 (2001) 231-257.

11061 *Naveh, Joseph* A sixth-century BCE Edomite seal from 'En Ḥaẓeva.
'Atiqot 42 (2001) 197-198;

11062 Appendix: an Aramaic amulet from Bar'am. Judaism in late antiquity, 3/4: the special problem of...synagogue. 2001 ⇒424. 179-185.

11063 **Nijhowne, Jeanne** Politics, religion, and cylinder seals: a study of
Mesopotamian symbolism in the second millennium B.C. BAR international 772: 1999 ⇒15,11181. ᴿMes. 36 (2001) 127-128 (*Cel-
lerino, A.*).

11064 *Ornan, Tallay* Ištar as depicted on finds from Israel. Archaeology
of the Iron Age. JSOT.S 331: 2001 ⇒625. 235-256.

11065 **Otto, Adelheid** Die Entstehung und Entwicklung der klassisch-sy-
rischen Glyptik. UAVA 8: 2000 ⇒16,11330. ᴿOLZ 96 (2001) 703-
706 (*Klengel-Brandt, E.*); RA 95 (2001) 84-86 (*Amiet, Pierre*).

11066 *Peilstöcker, Martin; Sass, Benjamin* A Hebrew seal from Jaffa and
the Hebrew script in the post-first temple period. 'Atiqot 42 (2001)
199-210.

11067 *Reichel, Clemens D.* Seals and sealings at Tell Asmar: a new look
at an Ur III to early Old Babylonian place. Proceedings of the
XLVe Rencontre Assyriologique, 2. 2001 ⇒582. 101-131.

11068 **Reyes, A.T.** The stamp-seals of ancient Cyprus. Oxf 2001, Oxbow
xvii; 286 pp. £45. 0-947816-52-6.

11069 **Salje, B.** Der 'Common Style' der Mitanni-Glyptik und die Glyptik
der Levante und Zyperns in der späten Bronzezeit. 1990 ⇒7,d108
... 11/2,a725. ᴿJNES 60 (2001) 133-138 (*Garrison, Mark B.*).

11070 *Selz, Gebhard* Der sogenannte 'geflügelte Tempel' und die 'Himmelfahrt' der Herrscher: Spekulationen über ein ungelöstes Prob-

lem der altakkadischen Glyptik und dessen möglichen rituellen
Hintegrund [!]. ^MCAGNI, L., 2: SMDSA 61: 2001 ⇒15. 961-983.

11071 *Shanks, Hershel* Solomon's blessings: would museums purchase
these good-luck tokens today?. BArR 27/5 (2001) 46-47.

11072 *Stadler, Martin Andreas* Der Skarabäus als osirianisches Symbol
vornehmlich nach spätzeitlichen Quellen. ZÄS 128 (2001) 71-83.

11073 *Staubli, Thomas* Stabile Politik—florierende Wirtschaft und umgekehrt: eine rechteckige, beidseitig gravierte Platte der Hyksoszeit.
ZDPV 117 (2001) 97-115.

11074 *Stein, Diana L.* Nuzi glyptic: the eastern connection. Proceedings
of the XLVe Rencontre Assyriologique, 2. 2001 ⇒582. 149-183.

11075 *Vanlathem, Marie-Paule* Scarabées de coeur *in situ*. CÉg 76 (2001)
48-56.

11076 *Wallenfels, Ronald* Fourth-century Babylonian sealed archival
texts;

11077 *Winter, Irene J.* Introduction: glyptic, history, and historiography.
XLVe Rencontre Assyriologique, 2. 2001 ⇒582. 215-238/1-13.

T3.4 Mosaica

11078 *Abramowski, Luise* Die Mosaiken von S. Vitale und S. Apollinare
in Classe und die Kirchenpolitik Kaiser JUSTINIANS. ZAC 5 (2001)
289-341.

11079 *Besonen, Joanne* The Yattir mosaic: a visual journey to Christ.
BArR 27/4 (2001) 37-43.

11080 **Bucci, Giovanna** L'albero della vita nei mosaici pavimentali del
Vicino Oriente. Studi e scavi 15: Bo 2001, University Press 135 pp.
88-86946-54-6. Bibl. 105-124.

11081 **Dunbabin, Katherine M.D.** Mosaics of the Greek & Roman
world. 1999 ⇒15,11202. ^RAntiquity 75 (2001) 448-450 (*Michaelides, Demetrios*); AnCl 70 (2001) 507-509 (*Balty, Janine*).

11082 ^E**Ennaïfer, M.; Rebourg, A.** La mosaïque gréco-romaine VII/1-2.
1999 ⇒15,11203. ^RCRAI (2001/1) 624-625 (*Lavagne, Henri*).

11083 *Jacoby, Ruth* The four seasons in zodiac mosaics: the Tallaras
baths in Astypalaea, Greece. IEJ 51 (2001) 225-230.

11084 *Kühnel, Bianca* Jewish art and 'iconoclasm': the case of Sepphoris.
^FBARASCH, M. 2001 ⇒2. 161-180.

11085 *Ling, Roger* Roman mosaics: a success story of classical archaeology. AJA 105 2001 325-329.

11086 **Ling, Roger** Ancient mosaics. 1998 ⇒14,10403. ^RAJA 105 (2001)
569 (*Ramage, Nancy H.*).

11087   *Metzger, Martin* Hananja, Mischael und Asarja auf der Mosaikin-
        schrift der Synagoge von En Gedi. [F]SEYBOLD, K.: AOAT 280: 2001
        ⇒102. 261-279.
11088   *Perrin, Michel-Yves* La paternité du Christ: à propos d'une mosa-
        ïque de la catacombe de Domitille. RivAC 77 (2001) 481-518.
11089   Victory on the harbor: Greek remains found at Dor. BArR 27/4
        (2001) 17.

T3.5 *Ceramica; lampas*, pottery; lamps

11090   *Aston, David* The pottery from H/VI Süd strata a and b: preliminary
        report. Ä&L 11 (2001) 167-196.
11091   *Attoura, Hala* Zur Funktion der Tonstreifen. Anatolien. 2001 ⇒
        414. 13-24.
11092   [E]**Ballet, Pascale** Cahiers de la céramique égyptienne 4-5. 1996-97
        ⇒15,11215. [R]CÉg 76 (2001) 148-154 (*López Grande, María J.*).
11093   **Boardman, John** The history of Greek vases: potters, painters and
        pictures. L 2001, Thames & H. 320 pp. £30. 0-500-23780-8. 321
        fig. [R]Antiquity 75 (2001) 900-901 (*Spivey, Nigel*).
11094   *Boileau, M.-C.* Etude multidisciplinaire de la céramique de Tell
        'Atij, Syrie. Canadian research on ancient Syria. 2001 ⇒581. 69-
        78.
11095   *Botto, M.* Indagini archeometriche sulla ceramica fenicia e punica
        del Mediterraneo centro-occidentale. RSFen 29 (2001) 159-181.
11096   *Cohen-Weinberger, Anat; Wolff, Samuel R.* Production centers of
        collared-rim pithoi from sites in the Carmel coast and Ramat Mena-
        she regions. [M]ESSE, D.: SAOC 59: 2001 ⇒28. 639-657.
11097   **Coldstream, J.N.; Eiring, L.J.; Forster, G.** Knossos pottery
        handbook, Greek and Roman. ABSA Studies 7: L 2001, British
        School at Athens 224 pp. £47. 0-9048-8738-3.
11098   *Dessel, J.P.* The relationship between ceramic production and so-
        ciopolitical reconfiguration in fourth millennium Canaan;
11099   *Dever, William G.* Iron Age kernoi and the Israelite cult. [M]ESSE, D.:
        SAOC 59: 2001 ⇒28. 99-118/119-133.
11100   *Di Paolo, Silvana* Una collezione di ceramiche palestinesi nel
        Santuario di S. Maria dell'Oriente (L'Aquila). SMEA 43 (2001)
        203-239.
11101   *Fuscaldo, Perla* Preliminary report on the 18th Dynasty pottery
        from 'Ezbet Helmi, area H/III-t-u/17 (the bathroom). Ä&L 11
        (2001) 149-166.
11102   *Gal, Zvi* Regional aspects of the Iron Age pottery in the Akko plain
        and its vicinity. [M]ESSE, D.: SAOC 59: 2001 ⇒28. 135-142.

11103 *Gilboa, Ayelet* The significance of Iron Age 'wavy-band' pithoi along the Syro-Palestinian littoral, with reference to the Tel Dor pithoi. [M]ESSE, D.: SAOC 59: 2001 ⇒28. 163-173.

11104 **Güntner, Wolfgang** Figürlich bemalte mykenische Keramik aus Tiryns. Deutsches Archaeologisches Institut Athen, Tiryns, Forschungen und Berichte 12: Mainz 2000, Von Zabern 391 pp. €85.90. 3-8053-1887-1. 88 pl..

[E]**Hausleiter, A.** Iron Age pottery 1999 ⇒614.

11105 *Hein, Irmgard* Untersuchungen und vorläufige Bilanz zur Keramik aus 'Ezbet Helmi, speziell Areal H/V. Ä&L 11 (2001) 121-147.

11106 **Hope, C.A.** Egyptian pottery. Princes Risborough, Bucks. [2]2001, Shire 64 pp. £5. 0-7478-0494-X.

11107 *Killebrew, Ann E.* The collared pithos in context: a typological, technological, and functional reassessment. [M]ESSE, D.: SAOC 59: 2001 ⇒28. 377-398.

11108 **Lissarrague, François** Greek vases: the Athenians and their images. [T]*Allen, Kim*: NY 2001, Riverside 241 pp. $75. 1-878351-57-5. 33 fig; [AJA 106,334—Spivey, Nigel].

11109 *Lawall, Mark L.* Amphoras in the 1990s: in need of archaeology. AJA 105 (2001) 533-537.

11110 **Loffreda, Stanislao** Ceramica del tempo di Gesù: vasi della Terra Santa nel periodo romano antico 63 a.C. - 70 d.C. Studium Biblicum Franciscanum.Museum 14: 2000 ⇒16,11370. [R]RivAC 77 (2001) 615-616 (*De Rossi, Gianfranco*).

11111 *Magrill, Pamela; Middleton, Andrew* Did the potter's wheel go out of use in Late Bronze Age Palestine?. Antiquity 75 (2001) 137-144.

11112 *Milano, Lucio; Rova, Elena* Ceramic provinces and political borders in Upper Mesopotamia in the late early dynastic period. [M]CAGNI, L., 2. SMDSA 61: 2001 ⇒15. 709-749.

11113 **Nielsen, Anne Marie; Sørensen, Lone Wriedt** The vase collection in the Odense University. [E]*Nys, Karin; Åström, Paul*: Studies in Mediterranean Archaeology 20,22; Corpus of Cypriote antiquities 22: Jonsered 2001, Aström 45 pp. 91-7081-185-7. 73 pl.; Bibl. 42-45.

11114 **Postgate, Carolyn; Oates, David; Oates, Joan** The excavations at Tell al Rimah: the pottery. 1997 ⇒13,10466... 16,11377. [R]Syr. 78 (2001) 244-249 (*Lyonnet, Bertille*).

11115 *Raban, Avner* Standardized collared-rim pithoi and short-lived settlements. [M]ESSE, D.: SAOC 59: 2001 ⇒28. 493-518.

11116 *Reid Hocking, Nancy* Lessons from the kiln: reduction firing in Cypriot Iron Age pottery. NEA(BA) 64/3 (2001) 132-139.

11117 **Sabetal, V.** Corpus vasorum antiquorum, Greece, Fasc. 6: Thebes, Archaeological Museum I. Athens 2001, Research Centre for Antiquity 367 pp. 960-7099-93-1. 43 ill, 89 pl.

11118 **Sallaberger, Walther** Der babylonische Töpfer und seine Gefässe nach Urkunden altsumerischer bis altbabylonischer Zeit sowie lexikalischen und literarischen Zeugnissen. 1996 ⇒14,10451. [R]JNES 60 (2001) 140-141 (*Hempel, Wolfgang*).

11119 [E]**Scheffer, Charlotte** Ceramics in context: proceedings of the Internordic Colloquium on ancient pottery, Stockholm, 13-15 June 1997. 65 ill. Stockholm Studies in Classical Archaeology 12: Sto 2001, Stockholm Univ. 170 pp. Kr223. 91-22-01913-8.

11120 *Schreiber, Nicola* A word of caution: black-on-red pottery at Tel Mevorakh in the 'tenth century' B.C. PEQ 133 (2001) 132-135.

11121 **Shanks, Michael** Art and the Greek city state: an interpretive archaeology. 1999 ⇒15,11241; 16,11379. [R]AJA 105 (2001) 120-122 (*Papalexandrou, Nassos*); Antiquity 75 (2001) 890-891 (*Johnston, Alan*).

11122 *Sharon, Ilan* Philistine bichrome painted pottery: scholarly ideology and ceramic typology. [M]ESSE, D.: 2001 ⇒28. 555-609.

11123 *Tietz, Werner* Wild goats: Wechselwirkungen über die Ägäis hinweg bei Vasendarstellungen wildlebender Paarhufer in der archaischen Epoche. Anatolien. 2001 ⇒414. 181-247.

11124 *Van der Steen, Eveline J.* Putting Khirbet Balamah on the archaeological map. PEQ 133 (2001) 111-131.

11125 *Yellin, Joseph; Broshi, Magan; Eshel, Hanan* Pottery of Qumran and Ein Ghuweir: the first chemical exploration of provenience. BASOR 321 (2001) 65-78.

11126 [E]**Yon, Marguerite; Karageorghis, Vassos; Hirschfeld, Nicolle** Céramiques mycéniennes d'Ougarit. 2000 ⇒16,11385. [R]AJA 105 (2001) 547-548 (*Koehl, Robert B.*).

11127 *Zorn, Jeffrey R.* Wedge- and circle-impressed pottery: an Arabian connection. [M]ESSE, D.: SAOC 59: 2001 ⇒28. 689-698.

11128 **Loffreda, Stanislao** Light and life: ancient christian oil lamps of the Holy Land. SBF.Museum 13: J 2001, Franciscan Printing Press 56 pp. 965-516-004-1.

T3.7 *Cultica*—cultic remains

11129 **Arnold, Dieter** Temples of the last pharaohs. 1999 ⇒15,11247. [R]CamArchJ 11 (2001) 284-288 (*Spence, Kate*); ArOr 69 (2001) 633-635 (*Smoláriková, Květa*).

11130 **Binder, Donald D.** Into the temple courts: the place of the synagogues in the Second Temple period. SBL.DS 169: 1999 ⇒15, 11250; 16,11393. ^RJR 81 (2001) 171-172 (*Levine, Lee I.*); BZ 45 (2001) 265-268 (*Claußen, Carsten*); JBL 120 (2001) 555-556 (*Fine, Steven*); HebStud 42 (2001) 375-378 (*Meyers, Eric M.*).

11131 *Biran, Avraham* The high places of biblical Dan. Archaeology of the Iron Age. JSOT.S 331: 2001 ⇒625. 148-155.

11132 **Bongenaar, A.C.V.M.** The Neo-Babylonian Ebabbar temple at Sippar: its administration and its prosopography. 1997 ⇒13,9643; 15,10235. ^ROLZ 96 (2001) 518-523 (*Oelsner, Joachim*).

11133 *Brizzi, Massimo; Mastrogiacomo, Mariella; Sepio, Daniele* Jarash: excavations of the trapezoidal square in the sanctuary of Artemis: preliminary report of the 1999-2000 seasons. ADAJ 45 (2001) 447-459.

11134 **Forest, Jean-Daniel** Les premiers temples de Mésopotamie (4e et 3e millénaires). 1999 ⇒15,11259; 16,11403. ^RMes. 36 (2001) 120-122 (*Fiorina, P.*).

11135 *Groenewoud, Elvira M.C.* Use of water in Phoenician sanctuaries. ANESt 38 (2001) 139-159.

11136 **Gruben, Gottfried** Griechische Tempel und Heiligtümer. ⁵2001, Da:Wiss 535 pp. Aufnahmen von *Max* und *Albert Hirmer*.

11137 *Gruber, Mayer I.* Neusner's tannaitic synagogue in the light of philology & archaeology: reponse to Jacob Neusner, 'The synagogue in law'. Religious texts. 2001 ⇒630. 175-181.

11138 **Hachlili, Rachel** The menorah, the ancient seven-armed candelabrum: origin, form and significance. JSJ.S 68: Lei 2001, Brill xxviii; 541 pp. €150. 90-04-12017-3. Bibl. 481-499.

11139 *Herzog, Ze'ev* The date of the temple at Arad: reassessment of the stratigraphy and the implications for the history of religion in Judah. Archaeology of the Iron Age. 2001 ⇒625. 156-178.

11140 *Joukowsky, Martha Sharp* Brown University 2000 excavations at the Petra great temple. ADAJ 45 (2001) 325-342.

11141 *Joukowsky, Martha Sharp; Basile, Joseph J.* More pieces in the Petra Great Temple puzzle. BASOR 324 (2001) 43-58.

11142 *Klein, Holger A.* Niketas und das wahre Kreuz: kritische Anmerkungen zur Überlieferung des Chronicon Paschale ad annum 614. ByZ 94 (2001) 580-587.

11143 **Kohlmeyer, Kay** Der Tempel des Wettergottes von Aleppo. 2000 ⇒16,11413. ^ROLZ 96 (2001) 539-541 (*Wartke, R.-B.*).

11144 **Levine, Lee I.** The ancient synagogue: the first thousand years. 1999 ⇒15,11270. ^RBSOAS 64 (2001) 106-107 (*Rosenberg, Stephen Gabriel*); Zion 66 (2001) 238-241 (*Safrai, Ze'ev*).

11145	*Lindner, Manfred* An important archaeological site opposite the ad-Dayr monument of Petra (Jordan), deplorably neglected by science. ADAJ 45 (2001) 393-394.

11146	*Magness, Jodi* When were the Galilean-type synagogues built?. Cathedra 101 (2001) 39-70 Sum. 205. **H**.

11147	*Meyers, Eric M.* The dating of the Gush Halav synagogue: a response to Jodi Magness. Judaism in late antiquity, 3/4: the special problem of the synagogue. HO I,55: 2001 ⇒424. 49-70.

11148	^E**Muss, Ulrike** Der Altar des Artemisions von Ephesos: Tafelbd.; Textbd. Forschungen in Ephesos 12,2: W 2001, Verl. d. Österr. Akad. d. Wiss. 306 + 163 pp. 3-7001-2979-3. 526 ill..

11149	*Mussell, M.-L.* The oldest known christian churches: Dura Europos and Aqaba. Canadian research on ancient Syria. 2001 ⇒581. 189-199.

11150	*Neusner, Jacob* The synagogue in law: what the texts lead us to expect to find. Religious texts. 2001 ⇒630. 151-173.

11151	*Puech, Émile* Un nouvel autel à encens de Palmyre. ^FDION, P.-E. 2: JSOT.S 325: 2001 ⇒25. 243-256.

11152	*Rapuano, Yehudah* The Hasmonean period 'synagogue' at Jericho and the 'council chamber' building at Qumran. IEJ 51 (2001) 48-56.

11153	*Shanks, Hershel* Is it or isn't it–a synagogue?: archaeologists disagree over buildings at Jericho and Migdal. BArR 27/6 (2001) 51-7.

11154	*Stern, E.* ראש הגורגונה ובנייתם של ראשוני המקדשים היוונים בדור ובחופי פניקיה וארץ־ישראל [A Gorgon's head and the building of the first Greek temples at Dor and along the coast]. Qad. 34 (2001) 44-8. **H**.

11155	*Strange, James F.* The archaeology of religion at Capernaum, synagogue and church. Religious texts. 2001 ⇒630. 43-62.

11156	**Uphill, Eric P.** Pharaoh's gateway to eternity: the Hawara Labyrinth of King Amenemhat III. 2000 ⇒16,11425. ^RDiscEg 51 (2001) 143-146 (*Dodson, Aidan*); WZKM 91 (2001) 369-373 (*Jánosi, Peter*).

11157	**Van Ess, Margarete** Uruk: Architektur II: von der akkad- bis zur mittelbabylonischen Zeit, Teil 1: das Eanna-Heiligtum zur Ur III- und altbabylonischen Zeit. Ausgrabungen in Uruk-Warka Endberichte 15/1: Mainz 2001, Von Zabern 2 vols. €144. 3-8053-2812-5. Deutsches Archäologisches Inst. Orient-Abteilung; Bibl. v.1 371-6.

11158	**Wilkinson, Richard H.** The complete temples of Ancient Egypt. 2000 ⇒16,11431. ^RAJA 105 (2001) 730-731 (*Shaw, Ian*); BiOr 58 (2001) 581-584 (*Degardin, Jean-Claude*).

11159	**Winlock, Herbert Eustis** In search of the woman Pharaoh, Hatshepsut: excavations at Deir el-Bahri 1911-1931. The Kegan Paul

Library of Ancient Egypt: L 2001, Kegan Paul x; 237 pp. 0-7103-0708-X.

T3.8 Funeraria; *Sindon*, the Shroud

11160 *Alexanddre, Yardenna; Stern, Edna J.* Phoenician cremation burials at Tel Bira. 'Atiqot 42 (2001) 183-195.

11161 *Belli', Oktay; Konyar, Erkan* Excavations at Van-Yoncatepe fortress and necropolis. TelAv 28 (2001) 169-212.

11162 *Bikai, Patricia Maynor; Perry, Megan A.* Petra north ridge tombs 1 and 2: preliminary report. BASOR 324 (2001) 59-78.

11163 **Bonatz, Dominik** Das syro-hethitische Grabdenkmal: Untersuchungen zur Entstehung einer neuen Bildgattung in der Eisenzeit im nordsyrisch-südostanatolischen Raum. Mainz 2000, Von Zabern 232 pp. €60..33 3-8053-2603-3. 23 ill.

11164 *Bonatz, Dominik* Il banchetto funerario: tradizione e innovazione di un soggetto sociale nella Siria-Anatolia dal Bronzo Antico all'età del Ferro. EVO 24 (2001) 159-174.

11165 *Braun, Eliot* Iron Age II burials and archaeological investigations at Ḥorbat Menorim (El-Manara), Lower Galilee. 'Atiqot 42 (2001) 171-182.

11166 **Castel, Georges; Pantalacci, Laure; Cherpion, Nadine** Le mastaba de Khentika: tombeau d'un gouverneur de l'Oasis à la fin de l'Ancien Empire: Balat V. FIFAO 40,1-2: Cairo 2001, Institut Français d'Archéologie Orientale du Caire 2 vols. 2-7247-0291-1. Bibl. v.1 311-315.

11167 **Davies, Penelope J.E.** Death and the Emperor: Roman imperial funerary monuments, from AUGUSTUS to MARCUS AURELIUS. 2000 ⇒16,11449. [R]AJA 105 (2001) 570-571 (*Broucke, Pieter B.F.J.*).

11168 **Davis, Theodore M.; Daressy, Georges; Maspero, Gaston C.C.** The tombs of Harmhabi and Touatankhamanou; the discovery of the tombs; King Harmhabi and Touatânkhamanou: catalogue of the objects discovered. Duckworth Egyptology: L 2001, Duckworth 135 pp. 0-7156-3072-5. 92 pl.

11169 **Eisa, Khider Adam** Le mobilier et les coutumes funéraires koushites à l'époque méroitique. Meroitica 16: Wsb 1999, Harrassowitz xx; 151 pp. €75.67. 3-447-04094-7.

11170 [E]**Empereur, Jean-Yves; Nenna, Marie-Dominique** Nécropolis 1. Études alexandrines 5: Le Caire 2001, Institut français d'archéologie orientale vii; 527 pp. 2-7247-0297-2.

11171 *Fine, Steven* Why bone boxes?: splendor of Herodian Jerusalem reflected in burial practices. BArR 27/5 (2001) 38-44, 57.

11172   *Fitzenreiter, Martin* Statue und Kult: Aspekte der funerären Praxis an nichtköniglichen Grabanlagen der Residenz im Alten Reich. GöMisz 185 (2001) 67-90.

11173   *Frangipane, M., al.*, New symbols of a new power in a 'royal' tomb from 3000 BC Arslantepe, Malatya (Turkey). Paléorient 27 (2001) 105-139.

11174   *Garfinkel, Yosef* Warrior burial customs in the Levant during the early second millennium B.C. ᴹEsse, D.: 2001 ⇒28. 143-161.

11175   *Getzov, Nimrod; Stern, Edna J.; Parks, Danielle* A burial cave at Lower Ḥorbat Manot: additional evidence for the intermediate Bronze Age (EB IV-MB I) settlement pattern in the ʿAkko plain and western Galilee. ʿAtiqot 42 (2001) 133-138.

11176   **Gomaà, Farouk; Hegazy, El Sayed Aly** Die neuentdeckte Nekropole von Athribis. ÄAT 48: Wsb 2001, Harrassowitz (8) 94 pp. €60.33. 3-447-04418-7. Ill.

11177   ᴱ**Grimm, Alfred; Schoske, Sylvia** Das Geheimnis des goldenen Sarges: Echnaton und das Ende der Amarnazeit. Schriften aus der Ägyptischen Sammlung 10: Mü 2001, Staatliches Museum Ägyptischer Kunst 162 pp. 3-874-90-722-8. Ausstellung 2001-02; 135 ill.

11178   *Hallote, Rachel S.* Tombs, cult, and chronology: a reexamination of the Middle Bronze Age strata of Megiddo. ᴹEsse, D.: SAOC 59: 2001 ⇒28. 199-214.

11179   **Hallote, Rachel S.** Death, burial, and afterlife in the biblical world: how the Israelites and their neighbors treated the dead. Ch 2001, Dee 237 pp. $26.50. 1-56663-401-6. Bibl. 223-227.

11180   *Harrison, Timothy P.* Early Bronze social organization as reflected in burial patterns from the southern Levant. ᴹEsse, D. SAOC 59: 2001 ⇒28. 215-236.

11181   **Hawass, Zahi** Das Tal der goldenen Mumien: die neueste und großartigste archäologische Entdeckung unserer Tage. 2000 ⇒16, 11455. ᴿOLZ 96 (2001) 688-692 (*Bisping, Dana*).

11182   **Helck, Hans Wolfgang** Das Grab Nr 55 im Königsgräbertal: sein Inhalt und seine historische Bedeutung. ᴱ*Schoske, Sylvia; Grimm, Alfred*: Deutsches Archäologisches Institut, Abt. Kairo, Sonderschrift 29: Mainz 2001, Von Zabern viii; 67 pp. 3-8053-2860-5.

11183   **Hoskin, Michael** Tombs, temples and their orientations: a new perspective on Mediterranean prehistory. Bognor Regis 2001, Ocarina viii; 264 pp. 0-9540867-1-6.

11184   *Hussein, Mahmoud I.* Anatomy of the Egyptian tomb: 'the Egyptian tomb as a womb'. DiscEg 49 (2001) 26-33.

11185   **Jean-Marie, Marylou** Tombes et nécropoles de Mari. BAH 153: 1999 ⇒15,11326. ᴿBiOr 58 (2001) 682-684 (*Meyer, J.-W.*).

11186 **Jørgensen, Morgens** Catalogue Egypt 3: coffins, mummy adorn-ments and mummies form the third Intermediate, Late, Ptolemaic and the Roman periods (1080 BC-AD 400). K 2001, Ny Carlsberg 376 pp. 87-7452-253-1. Phot. *Ole Haupt.*

11187 **Kanawati, Naguib** The tomb and beyond: burial customs of Egyp-tian officials. Wmr 2001, Aris & P. viii; 134 pp. £28. 0-85668-734-0. Bibl. 130-131.

11188 **Lembke, K.** Phönizische anthropoide Sarkophage. Damaszener Forschungen 10: Mainz 2001, Von Zabern xiv; 169 pp. €75.67. 3-8053-2662-9. 61 pl.

11189 *Lev-Tov, Justin S.E.; Maher, Edward F.* Food in late Bronze Age funerary offerings: faunal evidence from tomb I at Tell Dothan. PEQ 133 (2001) 91-110.

11190 *Magen, Y.* בית הקברות בבית ענון שבהר חברון [The cemetery at Beit ʿAnun in the Hebron hills]. Qad. 34 (2001) 53-59. **H.**

11191 *Magness, Jodi* Where is Herod's tomb at Herodium?. BASOR 322 (2001) 43-46;

11192 A Near Eastern ethnic element among the Etruscan elite. Religious texts. Studies in ancient Judaism: 2001 ⇒630. 3-39.

11193 *Malantrucco, Alessandro* La teologia di fronte alla Sindone. Ricer-che teologiche 12/2 (2001) 123-146.

11194 **Martin, Geoffrey Thorndike** The tomb of Tia and Tia: a royal monument of the Ramesside period in the Memphite necropolis. L 1997, Egypt Exploration Society xxv; 113 pp. 58th Excavation Memoir; 175 pl. [R]Or. 69 (2000) 108-110 (*Valloggia, Michel*);

11195 The tombs of three Memphite officials: Ramose, Khay and Pabes. Excavation Memoir 66: L 2001, Egypt Exploration Society xv; 70 pp. £52. 0-85698-148-6. Collab. *Hans D. Schneider; René van Walsem*; 81 ill.; bibl. xiv.

11196 **Meyer-Dietrich, Erika** Nechet und Nil: ein ägyptischer Frauensarg des Mittleren Reiches aus religionsökologischer Sicht. AUU.HR 18: U 2001, Uppsala University 327 pp. 91-554-5172-1. Bibl. 310-320; Diss. Uppsala 2001.

11197 **Nasrabadi, Behzad Mofidi** Untersuchungen zu den Bestattungssit-ten in Mesopotamien in der ersten Hälfte des ersten Jahrtausends v. Chr. [T]Attoura, Hala: Baghdader Forschungen 23: 1999 ⇒15, 11338. [R]OLZ 96 (2001) 523-530 (*Hausleiter, Arnulf; Lundström, Steven*).

11198 *Niehr, Herbert* Ein weiterer Aspekt zum Totenkult der Könige von Samʾal. StEeL 18 (2001) 83-97.

11199 *Niveau de Villedary y Mariñas, Ana María* Pozos púnicos en la ne-crópolis de Cádiz: evidencias de práticas rituales funerarias. RSFen 29 (2001) 183-239.

11200 **O'Farrell, Gerald** The Tutankhamun deception: the true story of the mummy's curse. L 2001, Sidgwick & Jackson xvii; 234 pp. 0-283-072-938. Bibl. 218-225.

11201 **Pearson, M. Parker** The archaeology of death and burial. 2000 ⇒ 16,11478. [R]AJA 105 (2001) 110-112 (*Rife, Joseph L.*);

11202 Gloucester 2001, Sutton vi; 250 pp. 0-7509-1777-6. Bibl. 217-243.

11203 *Polz, Daniel* Nub-Cheper-Re Intef: ein wiederentdecktes Pharaonengrab der 17. Dynastie. WUB 22 (2001) 70-72.

11204 *Porten, Bezalel; Gee, John* Aramaic funerary practices in Egypt. [F]DION, P.-E. 2: JSOT.S 325: 2001 ⇒25. 270-307.

11205 *Rajak, Tessa* The rabbinic dead and the diaspora dead at Beth She-'arim. Jewish dialogue. AGJU 48: 2001 <1998> ⇒199. 479-499.

11206 *Randl-Gadora, Ulrike G.; Großschmidt, Karl* Erste Untersuchungen von Zahnschmelzhypoplasien bei hyksoszeitlichen Kinderskeletten aus Tell el-Dab'a/Unterägypten. Ä&L 11 (2001) 273-281;

11207 Metrische Analyse der Bezahnung von hyksoszeitlichen (1640-1530 v. Chr.) Kinderskeletten aus Tell el-Dab'a (Unterägypten);

11208 Nicht-metrische Zahnmerkmale bei hyksoszeitlichen (1640-1530 v. Chr.) Kinderskeletten aus Tell el-Dab'a: erste Ergebnisse;

11209 *Randl-Gadora, Ulrike G.* Rasterelektronenmikroskopische (REM) Bestimmung des Sterbealters bei hyksoszeitlichen (1640-1530 v. Chr) Kinderskeletten aus Tell el-Dab'a (Unterägypten) anhand der Perikymatien der Dauerzähne. Ä&L 11 (2001) 283-287/289-299/265-271.

11210 **Raven, Maarten J.**, *al.*, The tomb of Maya and Meryt II: objects and skeletal remains. Excavation Memoir 65: Lei 2001, National Museum of Antiquities xxiv; 111 pp. 0-85698-139-7. Bibl. xvii-xx.

11211 *Regev, Eyal* The individualistic meaning of Jewish ossuaries: a socio-anthropological perspective on burial practice. PEQ 133 (2001) 39-49.

11212 *Riggs, Christina* Forms of the *Wesekh* collar in funerary art of the Graeco-Roman period. CÉg 76 (2001) 57-68.

11213 **Roth, Ann Macy** A cemetery of palace attendants including G 2084-2099, G 2230+2231, and G 2240. 1995 ⇒14,10544; 16, 11484. [R]CÉg 76 (2001) 133-135 (*Bolshakov, Andrey O.*).

11214 *Rowan, Yorke M.* Prismatic blades and periodization: the case of the fourth millennium B.C.E. "cave of the warrior". ZDPV 117 (2001) 1-4.

11215 **Sartre-Fauriat, Annie** Des tombeaux et des morts, monuments funéraires et culture en Syrie du Sud du Ier s. av. J.-C. au VIIe s. apr. J.-C. BAHI 158: Beyrouth 2001, Institut français d'Archéologie vi; 291 + vi; 299 pp. 2 vols. 2-9127-3808-3.

11216 **Seeher, Jürgen** Die bronzezeitliche Nekropole von Demircihüyük-Sarıket: Ausgrabungen des Deutschen Archäologischen Instituts in Zusammenarbeit mit dem Museum Bursa, 1990-1991. IF 44: Tü 2000, Wasmuth xi; 300 pp. €101.24. 3-8030-1765-3. 28 pl.

11217 *Segal, A.* מבני הקליבה—מקדשים לפולחן הקיסרים בחורן ובטרכון ניתוח היסטורי/ארכיטקטוני [The Kalibe buildings—temples for the worship of emperors in Hauran and in Trachonitis—a historical-archaeological analysis]. Qad. 34 (2001) 60-66. **H.**

11218 *Spieser, Cathie* Amarna et la négation du cycle solaire. CÉg 76 (2001) 20-29.

11219 **Teitelbaum, Dina** The relationship between ossuary burial and the belief in resurrection during late second temple period Judaism. M.A. Diss. Carleton University, Canada 1997. ⇒14,10556. [R]JJS 52 (2001) 166-167 (*Triebel, Lothar*).

11220 **Thomas, Thelma K.** Late antique Egyptian funerary sculpture. 2000 ⇒16,11494. [R]AJA 105 (2001) 379-380 (*Bolman, Elizabeth S.*); CÉg 76 (2001) 340-341 (*Rassart-Debergh, Marguerite*).

11221 *Vitto, Fanny* An Iron Age burial cave in Nazareth. 'Atiqot 42 (2001) 159-169.

11222 *Walker, Bethany J.* The late Ottoman cemetery in field L, Tall Hisban. BASOR 322 (2001) 47-65.

11223 **Washbourne, Rose Mary** Out of the mouth of pots: towards an interpretation of the symbolic meaning of Cypriot Bronze Age funerary artifacts including examples in the University of Canterbury's Logie Collection. Pocketbook 158: Jonsered 2000, Åström v; 393 pp. £35.50. 91-7081-105-9.

11224 **Weeks, Kent R.** The lost tomb: the greatest discovery at the Valley of the Kings since Tutankhamun. L 2001, Phoenix xvii; (2) 330 pp. 0-75380-681-9.

11225 *Wenning, Robert* Neues zum Grab des Herodes. WUB 22 (2001) 74.

11226 **Wrede, Henning** Senatorische Sarkophage Roms. Monumenta Artis Romanae 29: Mainz 2001, Von Zabern 146 pp. €55.22. 3-8053-2696-3. 24 pl.

11227 [E]**Zaccone, Gian Maria** Le due facce della Sindone: pellegrini e scienziati alla ricerca di un volto. T 2001, ODPF 151 pp. 88-88441-00-X. Bibl. 148.

T3.9 *Numismatica*, **coins**

11228 **Alföldi, Maria R.** Bild und Bildersprache der römischen Kaiser: Beispiele und Analysen. 1999 ⇒15,11366. [R]AJA 105 (2001) 746-747 (*Tanner, Jeremy*).

11229 ᴱAngeli Bufalini, Gabriella La moneta romana: Museo nazionale
       romano: Palazzo Massimo alle Terme - Medagliere. Mi 2001,
       Electa 146 pp. 88-435-7291-1.
11230 *Auge, Christian* Note sur le trésor de monaies Ptolémaïques de 'Iraq
       al-Amir. ADAJ 45 (2001) 483-486.
11231 ᴱBalmuth, Miriam S. Hacksilber to coinage: new insights into the
       monetary history of the Near East and Greece: a collection of eight
       papers presented at the 99th annual meeting of the Archaeological
       Institute of America. Numismatic Studies 24: NY 2001, American
       Numismatic Society 134 pp. $50. 0-89722-281-4. 22 fig.; 21 pl.
11232 *Burgers, P.* Coinage and state expenditure: the reign of CLAUDIUS
       AD 41-54. Hist. 50 (2001) 96-114.
11233 Carradice, Ian Greek coins. Austin 1995, Univ. of Texas Press
       112 pp. 327 ill. ᴿAJA 105 (2001) 357-358 (*Bauslaugh, Robert*).
11234 *Elayi, J.; Elayi, A.G.* La divinité marine des monnaies préalexan-
       drines d'Arwad. TEuph 21 (2001) 133-148.
11235 Elayi, Josette; Lemaire, André Graffiti et contremarques ouest-
       sémitiques sur les monnaies grecques et proche-orientales. 1998 ⇒
       14,10569; 15,11372. ᴿANESt 38 (2001) 217-8 (*Röllig, Wolfgang*).
11236 *Gerson, Stephen N.* Fractional coins of Judea and Samaria in the
       fourth century BCE. NEA(BA) 64/3 (2001) 106-121.
11237 Harl, Kenneth W. Coinage in the Roman economy: 300 B.C. to
       A.D. 700. 1996 ⇒12,10001... 16,11511. ᴿAt. 89 (2001) 261-263
       (*Foraboschi, Daniele*).
11238 Howgego, Christopher Ancient history from coins. 1995 ⇒11/2,
       a887. ᴿAJA 105 (2001) 358-359 (*Bauslaugh, Robert*).
11239 Ireland, Stanley Greek, Roman and Byzantine coins in the Muse-
       um at Amasya (Ancient Amaseia), Turkey. 2000 ⇒16,11513.
       ᴿBiOr 58 (2001) 688-689 (*Meadows, Andrew*).
11240 ᴱMeadows, Andrew; Shipton, Kirsty Money and its uses in the
       ancient Greek world. Oxf 2001, OUP xx; 167 pp. £55.
11241 Meshorer, Ya'akov A treasury of Jewish coins: from the Persian
       period to Bar Kokhba. J 2001, Yad Ben-Zvi x; 356 pp. 965-217-
       189-1.
11242 Noeske, H.-Chr. Die Münzen der Ptolemäer. 2000 ⇒16,11520.
       ᴿBiOr 58 (2001) 627-629 (*Meadows, A.R.*).
11243 ᴱSheedy, K., *al.*, Pella in Jordan 1979-1990: the coins. Adapa 1:
       Sydney 2001, Near Eastern Archaeology Foundation xi; 183 pp.
       AUD$75.
11244 *Waner, Mira; Safrat, Zeev* Hoards and revolts: the chronological
       distribution of coin hoards in Eretz Israel during the Roman and
       Byzantine periods. Cathedra 101 (2001) 71-90 Sum. 206. H.

11245 **Wolters, R.** Nummi signati: Untersuchungen zur römischen Münz-
prägung und Geldwirtschaft. 1999 ⇒15,11381. ᴿCIR 51 (2001) 96-
97 (*Williams, J.H.C.*).

T4.3 **Jerusalem,** *archaeologia* **et historia**

11246 *Abbad, Abdul Rahman* Ethnic and religious pluralism in Jerusalem
according to Quran and the Islamic traditions. Jerusalem: house of
prayer. SBFA 52: 2001 ⇒536. 81-96.

11247 *Amit, D.; Zeligman, J.; Zilberbod, I.* A quarry and workshop for the
production of stone vessels on the eastern slope of Mount Scopus.
Qad. 34 (2001) 102-110. **H.**

11248 ᴱ**Ariel, Donald T.** Excavations at the City of David V 1978-1985:
extramural areas. Qedem 40: 2000 ⇒16,11535. ᴿBASOR 321
(2001) 85-86 (*Herr, Larry G.*).

11249 **Auld, A. Graeme; Steiner, Margreet** Jerusalem: from the Bronze
Age to the Maccabees. Cities of the Biblical World 1: 1996 ⇒12,
10020; 14,10598. ᴿOTEs 14 (2001) 166-168 (*Boshoff, W.S.*).

11250 *Bahat, D.* Re-examining the history of 'Solomon's stables'. Qad. 34
(2001) 125-130.

11251 *Baruch, Y.; Avni, J.* Excavations east of Herod's Gate;

11252 *Baruch, Y.; Reich, R.* Second temple period finds from new excavations at the Ophel, south of the Temple Mount. Qad. 34 (2001) 96-
101/93-95. **H.**

11253 ᴱ**Bauer, Dieter; Herbers, Klaus; Jaspert, Nikolas** Jerusalem im
Hoch- und Spätmittelalter: Konflikte und Konfliktbewältigung
—Vorstellungen und Vergegenwärtigungen. Fra 2001, Campus 492
pp. €56. Conferences Erlangen &Weingarten 1999 [EHR 118,171s
—Morris, Colin].

11254 *Bermejo Cabrera, Enrique* La settimana santa al santo sepolcro di
Gerusalemme: una riforma liturgica problematica. RivLi 88 (2001)
227-238.

11255 *Broshi, Magen* Estimating the population of ancient Jerusalem.
Bread, wine. JSPE.S 36: 2001 <1975> ⇒131. 110-120;

11256 The expansion of Jerusalem in the reigns of Hezekiah and Manasseh. Bread, wine. JSPE.S 36 2001 <1974> ⇒131. 174-180;

11257 Jerusalem, the City of David and the other capitals of the land of Israel. Bread, wine. JSPE.S 36: 2001 <1982> ⇒131. 181-187.

11258 *Burrell, David B.* Jerusalem after Jesus. The Cambridge companion
to Jesus. Cambridge companions to religion: 2001 ⇒4236. 250-64.

11259 *Chopineau, Jacques* Jérusalem, ville forte ou symbole: la signification de la destruction de ses murailles. AnBru 6 (2001) 97-104.

11260   **Cohen, Amnon** The guilds of Ottoman Jerusalem. The Ottoman Empire and its heritage 21: Lei 2001, Brill vi; 305 pp.

11261   *Cortese, Enzo* Dialogue in Jerusalem on Jerusalem. Jerusalem: house of prayer. SBFA 52: 2001 ⇒536. 25-30.

11262   *Ego, Beate* Die Wasser der Gottesstadt: zu einem Motiv der Zionstradition und seinen kosmologischen Implikationen. Das biblische Weltbild. FAT 32: 2001 ⇒285. 361-389.

11263   **Ellis, Marc H.** O, Jerusalem!: the contested future of the Jewish covenant. 1999 ⇒15,11404. [R]Month 34 (2001) 178-179 (*Prior, Michael*).

11264   *Furlong, Jude* Jerusalén en la historia. Eccl(R) 15 (2001) 453-459.

11265   *Gat, Shimon* The Seljuks in Jerusalem. Cathedra 101 (2001) 91-124 Sum. 206. **H.**

11266   *Geva, H.* Innovations in archaeological research in Jerusalem during the 1990s. Qad. 34 (2001) 70-77. **H.**

11267   *Goldfuss, H.; Arubas, B.* The kilnworks of the tenth legion at the Jerusalem Convention Center. Qad. 34 (2001) 111-118.

11268   *Guillaume, Ph.* Jerusalem 586 B C: katastrophal?. BN 110 (2001) 31-32.

11269   *Heid, Stefan* Kreuz Christi, Titulus Crucis und das Heilige Grab in neuesten Publikationen. FKTh 17 (2001) 161-178.

11270   **Hoppe, Leslie J.** The Holy city: Jerusalem in the theology of the Old Testament. 2000 ⇒16,11574. [R]CBQ 63 (2001) 521-522 (*Wiggins, Steve A.*).

11271   **Israël, Gérard** Jérusalem la sainte. P 2001, Jacob 204 pp. €19.82. 2-7381-1005-3. Bibl. 199-201[BCLF 641,20].

11272   **Jeremias, Joachim** Jerusalén en tiempos de Jesús: estudio económico y social del mundo del Nuevo Testamento. [4]2000 ⇒16, 11577. [R]EstJos 55 (2001) 177-178 (*Llamas, Román*).

11273   **Jondot, Michel** Aujourd'hui à Jérusalem. Le temps de la bible: P 2001, Cerf 218 pp [IslChr 27,286—Borrmans, Maurice].

11274   *Kartveit, Magnar* Sions dotter. TTK 72 (2001) 97-112.

11275   *Kegler, Jürgen* Die Verarbeitung der Zerstörung Jerusalems 587/6 in den prophetischen Überlieferungen Jeremias und Ezechiels. Gesammelte Aufsätze. BEAT 48: 2001 <1988> ⇒167. 138-146.

11276   *Knauf, Ernst Axel* Hezekiah or Manasseh?: a reconsideration of the Siloam tunnel and inscription. TelAv 28 (2001) 281-287.

11277   *Lenhardt, Pierre* Dal particolare all'universale: la terra, Gerusalemme e il tempio. Qol(I) 94 (2001) 8-9.

11278   *Lipschits, O.* Judah, Jerusalem and the temple 586-539 B.C. TEuph 22 (2001) 129-142.

11279   *Lucchesi, Enzo* La légende d'Eudoxie et du saint sépulcre dans un papyrus copte de Berlin. VigChr 55 (2001) 427-429.

11280 *Marcuzzo, Giacinto B.* Comment on Wadi's paper literature;

11281 *Niccacci, Alviero* Jerusalem for the three monotheistic religions: a theological synthesis;

11282 *Noujaim, Halim* A response to Dr. Abbad's paper. Jerusalem: house of prayer. SBFA 52: 2001 ⇒536.113-114/163-182/97-101.

11283 *Otto, Eckart, al.,* Jerusalem. RGG², 4: I-K. 2001 ⇒664. 428-448.

11284 *Paczkowski, Mieczysław Celestyn* The centrality of Jerusalem in the reflections of the fathers of the church. Jerusalem: house of prayer. SBFA 52: 2001 ⇒536. 115-134.

11285 *Patrich, Joseph* The lost circus of Aelia Capitolina. Cathedra 102 (2001) 29-50 Sum. 209. **H.**

11286 **Peri, Oded** Christianity under Islam in Jerusalem: the question of the holy sites in early Ottoman times. The Ottoman Empire and its Heritage 23: Lei 2001, Brill xi; 219 pp. €64. 90-04-12042-4. Bibl. 207-213.

11287 *Prag, Kay* Kenyon's Jerusalem excavation reports. On scrolls. JSPE.S 38: 2001 ⇒416. 223-229.

11288 *Re'em, Amit* Two second-temple-period burial caves in Abu Ṭor, Jerusalem. 'Atiqot 42 (2001) 3*-8* Sum. 319. **H.**

11289 *Reich, R.; Billig, Y.* A group of theatre seats from Jerusalem. Qad. 34 (2001) 88-92. **H.**

11290 *Reich, R.; Shukrun, E.* New excavations on the eastern slope of the City of David. Qad. 34 (2001) 78-87. **H.**

11291 **Sandri, Luigi** Città santa e lacerata: Gerusalemme per ebrei, cristiani e musulmani. Saronno 2001, Monti 416 pp. [Studi Fatti Ricerche 99,14—Livia Lesma].

11292 *Sevrin, Jean-Marie* Comment on Niccacci's paper. Jerusalem: house of prayer. SBFA 52: 2001 ⇒536. 183-184.

11293 *Steiner, Margreet* Jerusalem in the tenth and seventh centuries BCE: from administrative town to commercial city. Archaeology of the Iron Age. JSOT.S 331: 2001 ⇒625. 280-288.

11294 *Tass, Andrey* Rishon Le-Zion (B-145). TelAv 28 (2001) 312.

11295 *Tilly, Michael* Jerusalem–Nabel der Welt: Stadt und Tempel im Schnittpunkt dreier Weltreligionen. Materialdienst 5 (2001) 2-9.

11296 *Tzaferis, Vassilios* The Monastery of the Cross: where heaven and earth meet. BArR 27/6 (2001) 32-41.

11297 *Wadi, Abullif* The centrality of Jerusalem in the Arabic-Christian literature. Jerusalem: house of prayer. 2001 ⇒536. 103-112

11298 **Walker, Peter W.L.** Jesus and the Holy City: 1996 ⇒12,10091... 15,11460. ᴿEvQ 73 (2001) 182-185 (*Stenschke, Christoph W.*); SNTU.A 23 (1998) 235-236 (*Oberforcher, R.*).

11299   *Zeligman, J.; Avni, G.* Recent excavations and studies at the
        Church of the Holy Sepulcher compound. Qad. 34 (2001) 119-124.
        H.

T4.4 Judaea, Negeb; *situs alphabetice*

11300   *Bienkowski, Piotr; Van der Steen, Eveline* Tribes, trade, and towns:
        a new framework for the late Iron Age in southern Jordan and the
        Negev. BASOR 323 (2001) 21-47.
11301   *Broshi, Magen* Fire, soil and water: the settlement of the hilly
        regions of Palestine in the early Iron Age. Bread, wine. JSPE.S 36:
        2001 <1996> ⇒131. 60-70.
11302   *Chancey, Mark A.; Porter, Adam* The archaeology of Roman
        Palestine. NEA(BA) 64/4 (2001) 164-204.
11303   Digs. BArR 27/1 (2001) 46-61.
11304   *Gibson, Shimon* Agricultural terraces and settlement expansion in
        the highlands of early Iron Age Palestine: is there any correlation
        between the two?;
11305   *Ofer, Avi* The monarchic period in the Judaean highland: a spatial
        overview. Archaeology of the Iron Age. JSOT.S 331: 2001 ⇒625.
        113-146/14-37.
11306   *Wagner-Lux, Ute* Judaea. RAC 19. 2001 ⇒660. 63-130.
11307   *Yekutieli, Yuval* The Early Bronze Age IA of southwestern Canaan.
        ᴹESSE, D.: SAOC 59: 2001 ⇒28. 659-688.

11308   **an-Nabi**: *Amit, David; Yezerski, Irit* An Iron Age II cemetery and
        wine presses at an-Nabi Danyal. IEJ 51 (2001) 171-193.
11309   **Arad; Ai**: *Ilan, Ornit* Household archaeology at Arad and Ai in the
        Early Bronze Age II. ᴹESSE, D.: SAOC 59: 2001 ⇒28. 317-354.
11310   **Ashdod**: *Finkelstein, Israel; Singer-Avitz, Lily* Ashdod revisited.
        TelAv 28 (2001) 231-259.
11311   **Beersheba**: *Wenning, Robert* Beer Sheva: Tell Abu Matar—nicht
        gefährdet?. WUB 22 (2001) 75-76.
11312   **Beth Shemesh**: *Bunimovitz, Shlomo; Lederman, Zvi* The Iron Age
        fortifications of Tel Beth Shemesh: a 1990-2000 perspective. IEJ
        51 (2001) 121-147.
11313   **Bethlehem**: **Teyssier D'Orfeuil, Yves** Betlemme 2000 anni di
        storia. Città del Vaticano 2001, Libreria Editrice Vaticana 231 pp.
        88-209-7179-8. Bibl. 221-225.
11314   **Ein Gedi**: *Cotton, Hannah M.* Ein Gedi between the two revolts.
        SCI 20 (2001) 139-154.

11315 *es-Sultan*: *Broshi, Magen* Troy and Jericho. Bread, wine. JSPE.S 36: 2001 <1988> ⇒131. 39-45;

11316 ^E**Marchetti, Nicola; Nigro, Lorenzo** Scavi a Gerico, 1997: relazione preliminare sulla prima campagna di scavi e prospezioni archeologiche a Tell es-Sultan, Palestina. 1998 ⇒14, 10701. ^RPEQ 133 (2001) 66-67 (*Cartwright, Caroline*);

11317 **Netzer, Ehud** Hasmonean and Herodian palaces at Jericho: final reports of the 1973-1987 excavations, v.1: stratigraphy and architecture. J 2001, Israel Exploration Society xxvii; 354 pp. 965-221-044-7. 16 pl.; bibl. 343-345.

11318 *Gath*: *Maeir, Aren M.; Ehrlich, Carl Stephan* Excavating Philistine Gath: have we found Goliath's hometown?. BArR 27/6 (2001) 22-31.

11319 *Gaza*: *Miroschedji, P. de, al.*, Les fouilles de Tell es-Sakan (Gaza): nouvelles données sur les contacts égypto-cananéens aux IVe-IIIe millénaires. Paléorient 27 (2001) 75-104.

11320 *'Illin Taḥtit*: *Segal, Dror; Carmi, Israel* A series of radiocarbon dates from the late Early Bronze Age I site at Ḥorvat 'Illin Taḥtit. ^MESSE, D.: SAOC 59: 2001 ⇒28. 551-554.

11321 *Masada*: *Gill, Dan* It's a natural: Masada ramp was not a Roman engineering miracle. BArR 27/5 (2001) 22-31, 56-57;

11322 *Reich, Ronny* Women and men at Masada: some anthropological observations based on the small finds (coins, spindles). ZDPV 117 (2001) 149-163;
^E**Talmon, S.** Masada VI 1999 ⇒3648.

11323 *Masada; Herodium; Qumran*: **Laperrousaz, Ernest-Marie** Trois hauts lieux de Judée: les palais-forteresses hérodiens de Massada et de l'Herodium: le couvent essénien de Qoumrân et ses 'Manuscrits de la mer Morte'. P 2001, Paris-Méditerranée 127 pp. €21.19. 2-84272-106-3. Num. ill.

11324 *Megiddo*: ^E**Finkelstein, Israel; Ussishkin, David; Halpern, Baruch** Megiddo III—the 1992-1996 seasons. 2000 ⇒16,11690. ^RBiOr 58 (2001) 449-453 (*Van der Steen, Eveline J.*).

11325 *Naḥal Tillah*: *Levy, Thomas E., al.*, The protodynastic/dynasty 1 Egyptian presence in southern Canaan: a preliminary report on the 1994 excavations at Naḥal Tillah, Israel. ^MESSE, D.: 2001 ⇒28. 411-445.

11326 *Soreq*: *Braun, Eliot, al.*, New evidence for Egyptian connections during a late phase of Early Bronze I from the Soreq basin in south-central Israel. ^MESSE, D.: SAOC 59: 2001 ⇒28. 59-97.

11327 *Timnah*: **Mazar, Amihai; Panitz-Cohen, Nava** Timnah (Tel Batash) II: the finds from the first millennium BCE. J 2001,

Institute of Archaeology, Hebrew Univ. 2 vols; xi; 305 pp. $64. 18 fig.; 55 tables; 15 graphs; plates vol.: 106 pl.

11328   *Yattir*: *Eshel, Hanan; Magness, Jodi; Shenhav, Eli* Surprises at Yattir: unexpected evidence of early christianity. BArR 27/4 (2001) 32-36, 59.

11329   *Yavne-Yam*: *Fantalkin, Alexander* Meẓad Ḥashavyahu: its material culture and historical background. TelAv 28 (2001) 3-165.

T4.5 Samaria, Sharon

11330   *Rainey, Anson F.* HERODOTUS' description of the east Mediterranean coast. BASOR 321 (2001) 57-63.

11331   *Zertal, Adam* The heart of the monarchy: pattern of settlement and historical considerations of the Israelite kingdom of Samaria. Archaeology of the Iron Age. JSOT.S 331: 2001 ⇒625. 38-64.

11332   **Zwingenberger, Uta** Dorfkultur der frühen Eisenzeit in Mittelpalästina. OBO 180: Gö 2001, Vandenhoeck & R. xx; 593 pp. FS175/ €115. 3-525-53994-0. Bibl. 553-592.

11333   *Akko*: *West, David R.* Akko, Alphito and Akkû. UF 33 (2001) 601-603.

11334   *Aphek*: *Kochavi, Moshe; Gadot, Yuval* The Roman forum at Aphek-Antipatris. TelAv 28 (2001) 310.

11335   *Apollonia-Arsuf*: [E]Roll, Israel; Tal, Oren Apollonia-Arsuf: final report of the excavations, v.1: Persian and Hellenistic periods. 1999 ⇒15,11529. [R]BASOR 322 (2001) 89-91 (*Berlin, Andrea M.*).

11336   *Caesarea M*: [E]Donaldson, Terence L. Religious rivalries and the struggle for success in Caesarea Maritima. 2000 ⇒16,11708. [R]TJT 17 (2001) 283-285 (*Beck, Roger*); SR 30 (2001) 429-430 (*Arnal, William*);

11337   *Elliger, Winfried* Kaisareia II (in Palästina). RAC 19. 2001 ⇒660. 1026-1057;

11338   *Geiger, Joseph* קלון קריין -שמע- אלוניסתין יהודים, נכרים וחכמת יוונית בקיסריה ['Voices reciting the Sh'maʿ in Greek': Jews, gentiles, and Greek wisdom in Caesarea]. Cathedra 99 (2001) 27-36 Sum. 209.

11339   *Patrich, Joseph* Israel: neue erkenntnisse bei Ausgrabungen in Cäsarea am Meer: ein zweites Prätorium in Cäsarea. WUB 21 (2001) 76-77;

11340   **Castra Samaritanorum**: *Finkielsztejn, Gerald* Die Schätze einer byzantinischen Stadt: Gespräch mit Gerald Finkielsztejn (israelischer Archäologe) über Kfar Samir/Porphyrion. WUB 19 (2001) 72-73;

11341 *Tass, Andrey* Shoham (B-206). TelAv 28 (2001) 310-311.

11342 *Maqatir*: **Wood, Bryant G.** Khirbet el-Maqatir, 2000. IEJ 51 (2001) 246-252.

11343 *Michal*: **Grossmann, Eva Martime,** *al.*, Tel Michal and Apollonia: results of the underwater survey 1989-1996. Oxf 2001, Archaeopress xii; 131 pp £27. 95 fig. Diss. MacQuarie.

11344 *Ramat Hanadiv*: **Hirschfeld, Yizhar** Ramat Hanadiv excavations: final report of the 1984-1998 seasons. 2000 ⇒16,11735. [R]IEJ 51 (2001) 107-110 (*Merker, Gloria S.*).

11345 *Samaria*: **Tappy, Ron E.** The archaeology of Israelite Samaria, 2: the eighth century BCE. WL 2001, Eisenbrauns xxxi; 668 pp. $90. 1-57506-916-4. 85 fig.; 67 tables.

11346 *Sumaqa*: [E]**Dar, Shimon** Sumaqa: a Jewish village on the Carmel. 1998 ⇒14,10733. [R]BASOR 324 (2001) 117-8 (*Porter, Adam L.*).

T4.6 **Galilaea**; *Golan*

11347 **Bagatti, Bellarmino** Ancient christian villages of Galilee. [T]*Rotondi, Paul*: SBF.CMi 37: J 2001, Franciscan Printing Pr. 288 pp. €30. 965-516-034-3. 153 fig.; Bibl. 11-18.

11348 *Lehmann, Gunnar* Phoenicians in western Galilee: first results of an archaeological survey in the hinterland of Akko. Archaeology of the Iron Age. JSOT.S 331: 2001 ⇒625. 65-112.

11349 [E]**Meyers, Eric M.** Galilee through the centuries: confluence of cultures. 1999 ⇒15,548; 16,11754. [R]AJA 105 (2001) 548-549 (*Kraabel, A.T.*).

11350 **Nun, Mendel** Der See Genezareth und die Evangelien: archäologische Forschungen eines jüdischen Fischers. Biblische Archäologie und Zeitgeschichte 10: Giessen 2001, Brunnen 255 pp. 3-7655-9810-0. [R]FgNT 14 (2001) 152-157 (*Stenschke, Christoph*).

11351 *Perkams, Matthias* Der Comes Josef und der frühe Kirchenbau in Galiläa. JAC 44 (2001) 23-32.

11352 **Sawicki, Marianne** Crossing Galilee: architecture of contact in the occupied land of Jesus. 2000 ⇒16,11756. [R]CBQ 63 (2001) 763-764 (*Hoppe, Leslie J.*).

11353 *Tiedemann, Holger* Töpfe, Texte, Theorien—Archäologie und Neues Testament. ZNT 8 (2001) 48-58.

11354 *'Ain Assawir*: *Yannai, Eli; Braun, Eliot* Anatolian and Egyptian imports from late EB at Ain Assawir, Israel. BASOR 321 (2001) 41-56.

11355   *Beit Yeraḥ*: *Mazar, Amihai* On the significance of the Early Bronze
         III granary building at Beit Yeraḥ. [M]ESSE, D. 2001 ⇒28. 447-464.

11356   *Beth Shean*: *Mazar, Amihai* Beth Shean during the Iron Age II:
         stratigraphy, chronology and Hebrew ostraca. Archaeology of the
         Iron Age. JSOT.S 331: 2001 ⇒625. 289-309.

11357   *Bethsaida*: *Arav, Rami* Bethsaida, 2000. IEJ 51 (2001) 239-246;

11358   **Bernett, Monika; Keel, Othmar** Mond, Stier und Kult am Stadt-
         tor: die Stele von Betsaida (et-Tell). OBO 161: 1998 ⇒14, 10749...
         16,11763. [R]Syr. 78 (2001) 243-244 (*Dion, Paul-Eugène*).

11359   *Caesarea P.*: [E]**Wilson, John F.** Rediscovering Caesarea Philippi:
         the ancient city of Pan. Malibu 2001, Pepperdine University Press
         72 pp. 0-932612-26-1;

11360   *Wenning, Robert* Ziegen im Heiligtum. WUB 22 (2001) 77-79.

11361   *Cana*: *Edwards, Douglas R.* Auf der Hochzeit in Kana ... WUB 22
         (2001) 73;

11362   **Herrojo, Julián** Cana de Galilea y su localización: un examen crí-
         tico de las fuentes. CRB 45: 1999 ⇒15,11564. [R]JThS 52 (2001)
         809-810 (*Mayordomo, Moisés*); EstB 59 (2001) 561-2 (*Urbán, A.*).

11363   *Capernaum*: *Fischer, Moshe* Kapharnaum: eine Retrospektive.
         JAC 44 (2001) 142-167.

11364   *ʿEn Ṣippori*: *Dessel, J.P.; Meyers, Carol L.; Meyers, Eric M.* Tel
         ʿEn Ṣippori. IEJ 51 (2001) 99-105.

11365   *Hazor*: *Ben-Ami, Doron* The Iron Age I at Tel Hazor in light of the
         renewed excavations. IEJ 51 (2001) 148-170;

11366   *Ben-Tor, Amnon* Tel Hazor, 2001. IEJ 51 (2001) 235-238;

11367   Responding to Finkelstein's addendum (on the dating of Hazor X-
         VII). TelAv 28/2 (2001) 301-304.

11368   *Kinneret*: *Fritz, Volkmar* Kinneret, eine Stadt als Spiegel der Ge-
         schichte Israels. WUB 20 (2001) 77-79.

11369   *Magdala*: **Zangenberg, Jürgen** Magdala am See Gennesaret:
         Überlegungen zur sogenannten "mini-sinagoga" und einige andere
         Beobachtungen zum kulturellen Profil des Ortes in neutestamentli-
         cher Zeit. Kleine Arbeiten zum Alten und Neuen Testament 2:
         Waltrop 2001, Spenner 81 pp. 3-933688-49-3.

11370   *Megiddo*: *Ilan, David* The riddle of structure 5239 at Megiddo,
         stratum IX. [M]ESSE, D.: SAOC 59: 2001 ⇒28. 307-316;

11371   *Kedar, Benjamin Z.* Eine Luftaufnahme von Schumachers Aus-
         grabungen in Megiddo. [F]CARMEL, A.: 2001 ⇒17. 13-19.

11372   *Nain*: *Bagatti, Bellarmino* Nain of the gospel. Holy Land Summer
         (2001) 33-40.

11373   *Sepphoris*: *Chancey, Mark* The cultural milieu of ancient Sep-
         phoris. NTS 47 (2001) 127-145;

11374 *Weiss, Zeev* בצירפורי דיוניסוס בית תושבי של לזיהוים ליהדות פגניזם בין
הרומית [Between paganism and Judaism: toward an identification of
the 'Dionysiac building' residents at Roman Sepphoris]. Cathedra
99 (2001) 7-26 Sum. 209. **H**.

11375 *Yodefat*: *Aviam, Mordechai* Yodefat—eine Stadt des ersten jüdischen Aufstands in Galiläa wird entdeckt. WUB 20 (2001) 76-77;

11376 *Green, William Scott* It takes a village: preliminary reflections on
Yodefat in the history of Judaism. Religious texts. Studies in ancient Judaism: 2001 ⇒630. 141-149.

T4.8 *Transjordania*: (East-)Jordan

11377 *'Amr, Khairieh; al-Momani, Ahmed* Preliminary report on the
archaeological component of the Wadi Musa water supply and
wastewater project. ADAJ 45 (2001) 253-285.

11378 *Bartl, Karin, al.*, Palaeoenvironmental and archaeological studies in
the Khanaṣiri region/Northern Jordan: preliminary results of the
archaeological survey 1999. ADAJ 45 (2001) 119-134.

11379 *Batayneh, Amjad* Dar Saraya Irbid. ADAJ 45 (2001) 67*-79*. **A**.

11380 *Ben David, Chaim* Mountain strongholds of Edom. Cathedra 101
(2001) 7-18 Sum. 205. **H**.

11381 *Bienkowski, Piotr* New evidence on Edom in the Neo-Babylonian
and Persian periods. ᶠMILLER, J.: JSOT.S 343: 2001 ⇒74. 198-
213;

11382 Iron Age settlement in Edom: a revised framework. ᶠDION, P.-E. 2:
JSOT.S 325: 2001 ⇒25. 257-269.

11383 *Bisheh, Ghazi* The protection and preservation of the archaeological heritage of Jordan: the challenge for constructing a responsible
stewardship. Archaeology and society. 2001 ⇒443. 67-74.

11384 *Caneva, Isabella, al.*, The Wadi az-Zargaʾ/Wadi aḍ Ḍulayl
archaeological project: report on the 1997 and 1999 fieldwork seasons. ADAJ 45 (2001) 83-117.

11385 *Edwards, Phillip C., al.*, Archaeology and environment of the Dead
Sea plain: preliminary results of the first season of investigations by
the Joint la Trobe University / Arizona State University project.
ADAJ 45 (2001) 135-157.

11386 *Farès-Drapeau, Saba; Zayadine, Fawzi; Abbes, Frédéric* Preliminary report on the fourth season of the Wadi Iram epigraphical,
geographical and archaeological survey. ADAJ 45 (2001) 205-216.

11387 *Khalil, Lufti; Eichmann, Ricardo* Archaeological survey and
excavations at the Wadi al-Yutim and Magaṣṣ area-al-ʿAqaba

(Aseym): a preliminary report on the second season in 2000. ADAJ 45 (2001) 195-204.

11388 *Kokkinos, Nikos* A reconnaissance trip to Peraea (2-12 October 2000). ADAJ 45 (2001) 479-482.

11389 *MacDonald, Burton, al.*, The Ṭafila-Busayra archaelogical survey: phase 2 (2000). ADAJ 45 (2001) 395-411.

11390 ᴱ**MacDonald, Burton; Adams, Russell; Bienkowski, Piotr A.** The archaeology of Jordan. Levantine Archaeology 1: Shf 2001, Sheffield A. xv; 704 pp. 1-84127-136-5.

11391 *Maher, Lisa; Banning, Edward B.* Geoarchaeological survey in Wadi Ziqlab, Jordan. ADAJ 45 (2001) 61-70.

11392 *McKenzie, Judith S.* Keys from Egypt and the East: observations on Nabataean culture in the light of recent discoveries. BASOR 324 (2001) 97-112.

11393 *Melhem, Ismaeel* Preliminary results of the archaeological excavations at Zmal, al-Ashrafiyyah, Kufr al-Ma', 'Ayn al-Makhasha, Ṣir Saḥam 1992-2000. ADAJ 45 (2001) 25*-32*.

11394 *Olszewski, Deborah I.* The Eastern Al-Ḥasa late Pleistocene project: preliminary report on the 2000 season. ADAJ 45 (2001) 39-60.

11395 *Rast, Walter E.* Early Bronze Age state formation in the southeast Dead Sea plain, Jordan. ᴹEssE, D.: SAOC 59: 2001 ⇒28. 519-534.

11396 *Raz, Eli; Raz, Tal; Uchitel, Alexander* Selaᶜ—the rock of Edom. Cathedra 101 (2001) 19-38 Sum. 205. **H.**

11397 *Rollefson, Gary O.; Quintero, Leslie; Wilke, Philip J.* Azraq Wetlands survey 2000, preliminary report. ADAJ 45 (2001) 71-81.

11398 *Saidel, Benjamin Adam* Abandoned tent camps in southern Jordan. NEA(BA) 64/3 (2001) 150-157.

11399 *Saporetti, Claudio* Edom prima di Nabonedo. Nabonedo e Sela'. 2001 ⇒438. 59-82.

11400 *Savage, Stephen H.; Zamora, Kurt A.; Keller, Donald R.* Archaeology in Jordan. AJA 105 (2001) 427-461.

11401 *Savage, Stephen H.; Rollefson, Gary O.* The Moab archaeological resource survey: some results from the 2000 field seaon. ADAJ 45 (2001) 217-236.

11402 *Shmais, Adeib Abu* Survey and excavations at the Sadd ad-Wala basin. ADAJ 45 (2001) 15*-24*. **A.**

11403 ᴱ**Walmsley, Alan** Australians uncovering ancient Jordan: fifty years of Middle Eastern archaeology: a volume of studies and retrospectives prepared for the eighth international conference on the history and archaeology of Jordan, Sydney Univ. 9-13.7.2001. Sydney 2001, Univ. 287 pp. AUS$66. 0-9585-9973-2. Num. ill.

11404 *Whalen, Norman M.; Kolly, Christopher M.* Survey of Acheulean sites in the Wadi as-Sirḥan basin, Jordan, 1999. ADAJ 45 (2001) 11-18.

11405 *Abila*: **Wineland, John D.** Ancient Abila: an archaeological history. BAR-IS 989: Oxf 2001, Archeopress vi; 216 pp. £32. 1-8417-1-274-4. 83 fig.; 9 tables; 4 maps.

11406 *adh-Dhba*: *Falahat, Samia; Al-Nawafleh, Sami; Nuʿeimat, Fawzi* Khirbat adh-Dhba: the 2000 season. ADAJ 45 (2001) 51*-57*. **A.**

11407 *al-ʿAqaba*: *Fakhry, Sawson* The history of the al-ʿAqaba castle in the light of recent excavations. ADAJ 45 (2001) 59*-62*. **A.**

11408 *al-Karak*: *Hijazeen, Husan* The Orthodox Church excavation/ al-Karak: the 2001 season. ADAJ 45 (2001) 63*-65*. **A.**

11409 *al-Kharrar*: *Waheeb, M.* Recent discoveries east of the Jordan river. Wadi al-Kharrar archaeological: project preliminary report. ADAJ 45 (2001) 419-425.

11410 *al-Mafraq*: *al-Husan, Abdel-Qader* Preliminary results of the archaeological excavations at al-Mafraq, 1991-2001. ADAJ 45 £5*-13*. **A.**

11411 *al-ʿUmayri*: *Herr, Larry G.; Clark, Douglas R.; Trenchard, Warren C.* Madaba plains project: excavations at Tall al-ʿUmayri, 2000. ADAJ 45 (2001) 237-252.

11412 *an-Naqʾ; Tulayat Qaṣr Musa*: *Papadopoulos, Thanasis J.; Kontorli-Papadopoulou, Litsa; Politis, Konstantinos* Rescue excavations at an-Naqʾ and Tulayat Qaṣr Musa al-Ḥamid 2000. ADAJ 45 (2001) 189-193.

11413 *Arabah*: *Henry, Donald O., al.,* Survey of prehistoric sites, Wadi Araba, southern Jordan. BASOR 323 (2001) 1-19.

11414 *Bethany*: *Khouri, R.G.* Betanien—neue Ergebnisse der Ausgrabungen der Taufstelle. WUB 22 (2001) 76.

11415 *Busayra*: *Bienkowski, Piotr* Busayra and Judah: stylistic parallels in the material culture. Archaeology of the Iron Age. JSOT.S 331: 2001 ⟹625. 310-325.

11416 *Der ʿEn ʿAbaṭa*: *Politis, Konstantinos D.* Wo Lot Verehrung fand—Deir 'Ain 'Abata. WUB 19 (2001) 70.

11417 *el-ʿUmeiri*: *Herr, Larry G.; Clark, Douglas R.* Excavating the tribe of Reuben. BArR 27/2 (2001) 36-47, 64, 66.

11418 *Gadara*: *Meynersen, S. Felicia* The Tiberias gate of Gadara (Umm Qays): reflections concerning the date and its reconstruction. ADAJ 45 (2001) 427-432;

11419 —; *Madeba Arndt, Marian B.* Gadara i Madaba—raport z wykopalisk. CoTh 71/1 (2001) 77-81. **P.**

11420 *Gamla*: *Syon, D.; Yavor, Z.* גמלא—ישן וחדש [Gamla—old and new].
Qad. 34 (2001) 2-33.

11421 *Ğawa*: *Daviau, P.M. Michèle* Assyrian influence and changing
technologies at Tall Jawa, Jordan. ᶠMILLER, J. 2001 ⇒74. 214-238.

11422 *Gerasa*: *Braun, Jean-Pierre, al.*, The town plan of Gerasa in AD
2000: a revised edition. ADAJ 45 (2001) 433-436;

11423 *Kehrberg, Ina; Manley, John* New archaelogical finds for the
dating of the Gerasa Roman city wall. ADAJ 45 (2001) 437-446.

11424 *Harun*: *Frösén, Jaakko, al.*, The 1998-2000 Finnish Harun Project:
specialized reports. ADAJ 45 (2001) 377-392.

11425 *Hesban*: **Ray, Paul J.** Tell Hesban and vicinity in the Iron Age.
Diss. Andrews, ᴰ*Younker, Randall W.*: Hesban 6: Berrien Springs
2000, Andrews Univ. Pr. xv; 270 pp. 68 fig.; 37 pl.

11426 *Isin; Eshnunna*: *Kozyreva, N.V.* Amorites in the cities of Isin and
Eshnunna. Journal of Ancient History 3 (2001) 119-123 Sum. 123.
R.

11427 *Iskander*: *Richard, Suzanne* 2000 season of excavations at Khirbet
Iskander, Jordan. ProcGLM 21 (2001) 105-114.

11428 *Jarash*: *Brizzi, Massino; Mastrogiacomo, Mariella; Sepio, Daniele*
Jarash: excavations of the trapezoidal square in the sanctuary of Artemis: preliminary report of the 1999-2000 seasons. ADAJ 45
(2001) 447-459.

11429 *Khallit 'Isa-Şir*: *Melhem, Ismaeel; al-Husan, Abdel-Qader* First
season of excavation at Khallit 'Isa-Şir / Bayt Idis, 2000. ADAJ 45
(2001) 33*-50*. **A.**

11430 *Lehun*: *Homès-Fredericq, Denyse* Ontdek Lehun en de konings-
weg... : de belgische opgravingen in het antieke Jordanië. Phoe. 47
(2001) 117-147;

11431 A case study: Lehun between 'desert and sown' in Moab (central
Jordan): observations on the results of recent Belgian excavations
at Lehun. ᶠVEENHOF, K. 2001 ⇒111. 197-210.

11432 *Marajim*: *Nicolle, Christophe; Steimer, Tara; Humbert, Jean-Baptiste* Marajim, implantation rurale du IIIème millénaire en Jordanie
du nord. Akkadica 121 (2001) 77-86.

11433 *Petra*: *Al-Muheisen, Zeidun* Die Arbeit des "Petra Regional Council": der Umgang mit einer außergewöhnlichen Region. WUB 19
(2001) 66-67;

11434 *Bowersock, Glen W.* Petra—eine griechisch-römische Stadt?. WUB
19 (2001) 37-40;

11435 *Dentzer, Jean-Marie* Die nabatäische Herrschaft: ihre Epochen und
ihr Territorium. WUB 19 (2001) 6-9;

11436 ᴱFiema, T. Zbigniew The Petra church. ACOR 3: Amman 2001, American Center of Oriental Research xvi; 447 pp. $150. 9957-8543-0-5. Ill. [RB 109,314].

11437 *Fiema, Zbigniew T.* Petra in christlicher Zeit. WUB 19 (2001) 55-58.

11438 *Frösén, Jaakko* Die Papyri aus der Basilika. WUB 19 (2001) 60-1;

11439 *Joukowsky, Martha Sharp* Nabataean Petra. BASOR 324 (2001) 1-4;

11440 *Kanellopoulos, Chrysanthos; Akasheh, Talal S.* The Petra map. BASOR 324 (2001) 5-7;

11441 *Knauf, Ernst Axel* Juden und Nabatäer—eine schwierige Nachbarschaft. WUB 19 (2001) 34-35;

11442 Das Mirjams-Grab "bei Petra". WUB 19 (2001) 62-63;

11443 *Kolb, Bernhard* Die Patrizierhäuser von ez-Zantur. WUB 19 (2001) 52-53;

11444 *Kolb, Bernhard; Keller, Daniel* Swiss-Liechtenstein excavation at az-Zanṭur / Petra: the eleventh season. ADAJ 45 (2001) 311-324.

11445 *Lindner, Manfred* An important archaeological site opposite the ad-Dayr monument of Petra (Jordan), deplorably neglected by science. ADAJ 45 (2001) 393-394;

11446 *Nehmé, Laila* Die Ausgrabungsstätte und ihre natürliche Umgebung. WUB 19 (2001) 16-17;

11447 *Schmid, Stephan G.* The international Wadi Farasa project (IWFP) 2000 season. ADAJ 45 (2001) 343-357;

11448 The International Wadi Farasa Project (IWFP): between microcosm and macroplanning—a first synthesis. PEQ 133 (2001) 159-197;

11449 **Taylor, Jane** Petra and the lost kingdom of the Nabataeans. L 2001, Tauris 224 pp. 1-86064-508-9 [SCI 21,322s—Price, J.];

11450 *Villeneuve, Estelle* Einblicke in die Arbeit der Archäologen;

11451 Petra—neu entdeckt. WUB 19 (2001) 47-51/4-5;

11452 *Wenning, Robert* The betyls of Petra. BASOR 324 (2001) 79-95;

11453 Die nabatäische Stadt. WUB 19 (2001) 11-15;

11454 Petra als römische Stadt. WUB 19 (2001) 29-33;

11455 —; *Jerash; Amman* **Borgia, E.** Jordan: past & present: Petra, Jerash, Amman. R 2001, Vision 74 pp. 88-8162-124-X. ill.

11456 *Qaᶜ Abu Ṭulayḥa: Fujii, Sumio* Qaᶜ Abu Ṭulayḥa west, 2000: an interim report of the fourth season. ADAJ 45 (2001) 19-37.

11457 *Ramoth-Gilead: Knauf, Ernst Axel* The mists of Ramthalon, or: how Ramoth-Gilead disappeared from the archaeological record. BN 110 (2001) 33-36.

11458 *Şal*: *Kafafi, Zeidan; Vieweger, Dieter* Das chalkolithische und früh-
       bronzezeitliche Sal: eine auf geoelektrischer Erkundung basierende
       Rettungsgrabung im Norden Jordaniens. ZDPV 117 (2001) 5-46.

11459 *Sela'*: *Gentili, Paolo; Saporetti, Claudio* Nabonedo a Sela';

11460 *Qatamin, Hamed* The stele of Sela';

11461 Sela': history and archaeology. Nabonedo e Sela'. 2001 ⇒438. 39-
       58/25-37/11-24.

11462 *Umm Saysaban*: *Lindner, Manfred; Hübner, Ulrich; Genz, Her-
       mann* The early Bronze Age settlement on Umm Saysaban north of
       Petra (Jordan) and its topographical context: report on the 1998 /
       1999 survey. ADAJ 45 (2001) 287-310.

11463 *Wadi Šuʻeb*: *Simmons, Alan H., al.*, Wadi Shu'eib, a large neolithic
       community in central Jordan: final report of test investigations.
       BASOR 321 (2001) 1-39.

11464 *Yaʻmun*: *El-Najjar, Mahmoud* First season of excavation at Yaʻmun
       (1999). ADAJ 45 (2001) 413-417.

                T5.1 Phoenicia—*Libanus*, Lebanon; *situs mediterranei*

11465 **Aubet, Maria Eugenia** The Phoenicians and the West: politics,
       colonies and trade. [T]*Turton, Mary*: C [2]2001, CUP xv; 432 pp. 0-
       521-79161-8.

11466 **Blázquez, J.M.; Alvar, J.; Wagner, C.G.** Fenicios y Cartagineses
       en el Mediterráneo. 1999 ⇒15,11630. [R]OLZ 96 (2001) 245-247
       (*Vita, Juan-Pablo*).

11467 *Baalbek*: [E]**Sader, Hélène S.; Scheffler, Thomas; Neuwirth, An-
       gelika** Baalbek: image and monument 1898-1998. Beiruter Texte
       und Studien 69: 1998 ⇒14,10846. [R]Islam 78 (2001) 348-350 (*Zia-
       deh, Nicola A.*).

11468 *Garbini, Giovanni* Gli scavi del mondo fenicio occidentale come
       misura del mondo mediterraneo. Tre scavi. 2001 ⇒406. 15-33.

11469 *Byblos*: *Nibbi, Alessandra* The name of *Byblos*—again. DiscEg 49
       (2001) 35-41.

11470 *Kamid el-Loz*: [E]**Hachmann, Rolf; Penner, Silvia** Kamid el-Loz 3:
       der eisenzeitliche Friedhof und seine kulturelle Umwelt. 1999 ⇒
       15,11637. [R]OLZ 96 (2001) 212-216 (*Pedde, Friedhelm*); Or. 70
       (2001) 335-338 (*Lehmann, Gunnar*).

T5.4 Ugarit—*Ras Šamra*

11471 **Chanut, Claude** Bois, pierres et métaux à Ugarit-Ras Shamra (Syrie), à l'âge du Bronze récent, d'après les données des sciences naturelles, de l'archéologie et des textes. Diss. Institut Cath. de Paris 2001, [D]*Bordreuil, Pierre*: 324 pp [RLCP 79,204-209].

11472 **Clemens, David M.** Sources for Ugaritic ritual and sacrifice, 1: Ugaritic and Ugarit Akkadian texts. AOAT 284/1: Müns 2001, Ugarit-Verlag xxxix; 1407 pp. 3-934628-07-9. Bibl. 1281-1358. [R]UF 33 (2001) 712-713 (*Tropper, J.*).

11473 *Dietrich, Manfred* Der Brief des Kommandeurs Šumiyānu an den ugaritischen König Niqmepaʿ (RS 20.33): ein Bericht über Aktivitäten nach der Schlacht bei Qadeš 1275 v. Chr. UF 33 (2001) 117-91.

11474 *Mazzini, Giovanni* Dinamiche testuali nella tavoletta ugaritica KTU 1.4. EVO 24 (2001) 151-157.

11475 *Pardee, Dennis* Ugaritic science. [F]DION, P.-E. 3: JSOT.S 326: 2001 ⇒25. 223-254.

11476 **Pardee, Dennis** Les textes rituels. Ras Shamra - Ougarit 12: 2000 ⇒16,8578. [R]UF 33 (2001) 697-706 (*Wyatt, N.*).

11477 **Schloen, J. David** The house of the father as fact and symbol: patrimonialism in Ugarit and the ancient Near East. Studies in the archaeology and history of the Levant 2: WL 2001, Eisenbrauns xv; 414 pp. $57.50. 1-57506-907-5. Harvard Semitic Museum Publications. [R]UF 32 (2000) 769-775 (*Loretz, O.*).

11478 [E]*Schmidt, Brian* The mysteries of Ugarit: history, daily life, cult. NEA(BA) 63 (2001) 182-240.

11479 **Tropper, Josef** Ugaritische Gramatik. AOAT 273: 2000 ⇒16, 8587. [R]OLZ 96 (2001) 223-227 (*Schorch, Stefan*).

11480 [E]**Watson, W.G.E.; Wyatt, N.** Handbook of Ugaritic studies. HO 1/39: 1999 ⇒15,11640. [R]OLZ 96 (2001) 386-388 (*Streck, Michael P.*); JSSt 46 (2001) 309-310 (*Niehr, Herbert*); RBLit 3 (2001) 103-108 (*Hoop, Raymond de*).

11481 **Wyatt, Nick** Religious texts from Ugarit: the words of Ilimilku and his colleagues. BiSe 53: 1998 ⇒14,10905... 16,8595. [R]RB 108 (2001) 422-427 (*Tarragon, J.-M.*).

11482 [E]**Yon, Marguerite; Arnaud, Daniel** Études ougaritiques I: travaux 1985-1995. Ras Shamra-Ougarit 14: P 2001, Éditions Recherche sur les Civilisations 422 pp. €63. 2-86538-284-2. Bibl. 417-422. [R]UF 33 (2001) 745-747 (*Loretz, O.*).

T5.5 **Ebla**

11483   *Archi, Alfonso* The king-lists from Ebla. Proceedings of the XLVe
        Rencontre Assyriologique, 1. 2001 ⇒577. 1-13.
11484   *Bonechi, Marco* The dynastic past of the rulers of Ebla. UF 33
        (2001) 53-64.
11485   **Marchetti, Nicolò** La coroplastica eblaita e siriana nel bronzo me-
        dio: campagne 1964-1980. Materiali e studi archeologici di Ebla
        (MSAE V) 5: R 2001, Università degli Studi di Roma "La Sapien-
        za" 2 vols. 88-88233-01-6. Bibl. v.1 440-6; v.1: Testo; v.2: Tavole.
11486   *Waetzoldt, Hartmut* Bildnisse von Göttern und Menschen in Ebla.
        ᴹCAGNI, L., 2: SMDSA 61: 2001 ⇒15. 1135-1148.
11487   **Waetzoldt, Hartmut** Wirtschafts- und Verwaltungstexte aus Ebla:
        Archiv L. 2769. Materiali per il vocabolario sumerico 12: R 2001,
        694 pp.

T5.8 **Situs efossi Syriae in ordine alphabetico**

11488   *Archi, Alfonso* Text forms and levels of comparison: the rituals of
        Emar and the Syrian tradition. ᶠHAAS, V. 2001 ⇒39. 19-28.
11489   *Chazan, M.* Civilization and the lower paleolithic of Syria;
11490   *Dion, P.-E.* Les langues utilisées en Syrie vers 800 av. J.-C. Cana-
        dian research on ancient Syria 2001 ⇒581. 3-8/157-162.
11491   **Dirven, Lucinda** The Palmyrenes of Dura-Europos: a study of reli-
        gious interaction in Roman Syria. RGRW 138: 1999 ⇒15,11708.
        ᴿJRS 91 (2001) 204-205 (*Millar, Fergus*).
11492   ᴱ**Geyer, Bernard** Conquête de la steppe et appropriation des terres
        sur les marges arides du Croissant fertile. Lyon 2001, Maison de
        l'Orient méditerranéen 218 pp. Ill.
11493   *Hole, Frank* A radiocarbon chronology for the middle Khabur,
        Syria. Iraq 63 (2001) 67-98.
11494   ᴱ**Lyonnet, B.** Prospection archéologique du Haut-Khabur occiden-
        tal (Syrie du N.E.), 1. 2000 ⇒16,11887. ᴿMes. 36 (2001) 128-129
        (*Cellerino, A.*).
11495   *Miller, J. Maxwell* Arti-facts: Syria, land of civilizations. NEA(BA)
        64/3 (2001) 122-131.

11496   *Afis*: *Mazzoni, Stefania* Tell Afis and the Luʿash in the Aramaean
        period. ᶠDION, P.-E. 2: JSOT.S 325: 2001 ⇒25. 99-114.
11497   *Antioch*: ᴱ**Kondoleon, Christine** Antioch: the lost ancient city.
        2000 ⇒16,11900. ᴿAJA 105 (2001) 560-561 (*Ramage, Andrew*);

11498 *Van Henten, Jan Willem* De gemeente in Antiochië. Vroegchristelijke gemeenten. 2001 ⇒460. 193-206.

11499 *Brak*: Emberling, Geoff; McDonald, Helen Excavations at Tell
Brak 2000: preliminary report. Iraq 63 (2001) 21-54;

11500 **Oates, David; Oates, Joan; McDonald, Helen,** *al.*, Excavations at
Tell Brak, vol. 2: Nagar in the third millennium BC. McDonald
Institute Monographs: L 2001, British School of Archaeology in
Iraq. 0-9519420-9-3. Bibl. 626-643.

11501 *Emar*: **Adamthwaite, Murray R.** Late Hittite Emar: the chronology, synchronisms, and socio-political aspects of a late Bronze Age
fortress town. ANESt.S 8: Lv 2001, Peeters xxiii; 293 pp. 90-429-
0909-9. Bibl. 283-293;

11502 **Fleming, Daniel E.** Time at Emar: the cultic calendar and the
rituals from the diviner's archive. Mesopotamian Civilizations 11:
2000 ⇒16,11906. ᴿRA 95 (2001) 182-184 (*Lion, Brigitte*).

11503 *Hama; ʿAcharneh*: Fortin, M. Hama et Tell ʿAcharneh: deux sites
comparables de la vallée de l'Oronte. Canadian research on ancient
Syria. 2001 ⇒581. 87-105.

11504 *Jébel Wastani*: **Peña, Ignacio; Castellana, Pascal; Fernández,
Romuald** Inventaire du Jébel Wastani: recherches archéologiques
dans la région des villes mortes de la Syrie du Nord. SBF.CMi 36:
1999 ⇒15,11713. ᴿRivBib 49 (2001) 110-111 (*Prato, Gian Luigi*);
PEQ 133 (2001) 206-208 (*Dauphin, Claudine M.*).

11505 *Mari*: ᵀ**Durand, Jean-Marie** Les documents épistolaire du palais
de Mari, 3. LAPO 18: 2000 ⇒16,11914. ᴿETR 76 (2001) 605-606
(*Bauks, Michaela*).

11506 *Munbāqa*: **Mayer, Walter** Ausgrabungen in Tall Munbāqa—El-
kalte II: die Texte. Saarbrücken 2001, SDV 300 pp. $91. 3-9308-
4367-6. 86 pl.

11507 *Palmyra*: ᴱ**Charles-Gaffiot, Jacques; Lavagne, Henri; Hofmann, Jean-Marc** Moi, Zénobie reine de Palmyre. Mi 2001, Skira
375 pp. 88-8491-116-8. Bibl. 370;

11508 **De Micheli, Gianfranco** La visione di Palmyra. Le Sfere: Bo
2001, Pendragon 127 pp. 88-8342-068-3. Pref. *Paolo Portoghesi*;
64 fig.; bibl. 125-127;

11509 **Degeorge, Gérard** Palmyre: métropole caravanière. P 2001, Impri-
merie Nationale 311 pp. €68.60. 2-7433-0408-1. Préf. *Paul Veyne*;
bibl. 302-307;

11510 **Hartmann, Udo** Das palmyrenische Teilreich. Oriens et Occidens
2: Stu 2001, Steiner 533 pp. €96. 3-515-07800-2. Bibl. 480-519.

11511 *Qara Qūzāg*: ᴱ**Olmo Lete, Gregorio del,** *al.*, Qara Qūzāg II: cam-
pañas IV-VI (1992-1994). AuOr.S 17: Sabadell 2001, Ausa 505 pp.
84-88810-53-9.

11512   *Ras Ibn Hani*: **Bounni, Adnan**, *al.*, Ras Ibn Hani, 1: le palais nord du Bronze Récent: fouilles 1979-1995, synthèse préliminaire. BAH 151: 1998 ⇒14,10941... 16,11917. ᴿBASOR 322 (2001) 85-87 (*McClellan, Thomas L.*); Syr. 78 (2001) 232-233 (*Margueron, Jean-Claude*).

11513   *Selenkahiye*: ᴱVan Loon, M.N. Selenkahiye: final report on the University of Chicago and University of Amsterdam excavations in the Tabqa reservoir, northern Syria. Lei 2001, Ned. Inst. v. h. Nabije Oosten viii; 672 pp. €120. 90-6258-092-0.

11514   *Wardiyat*: *Hasan, H.* Tell Wardiyat: récentes recherches archéologiques (1997-1999). Canadian research on ancient Syria. 2001 ⇒ 581. 107-114.

T6.1 Mesopotamia, *generalia*

11515   *Bahrani, Zainab* History in reverse: archaeological illustration and the invention of Assyria. Proceedings of the XLVe Rencontre Assyriologique, 1. 2001 ⇒577. 15-28.

11516   **Balossi Restelli, Francesca** Formation processes of the first developed neolithic societies in the Zagros and the northern Mesopotamian plain. Studi di Preistoria Orientale 1: R 2001, Visceglia viii; 83 pp. 88-87320-12-8. Bibl. 75-83.

11517   *Brown, David* Misinformation on Mesopotamian exact science. XLVe Rencontre Assyriologique, 1. 2001 ⇒577. 79-89.

11518   *Casaburi, Maria C.* Il testo LBAT 1526 e la continuità della tradizione astromantica in Mesopotamia. ᴹCAGNI, L., 1: SMDSA 61: 2001 ⇒15. 85-99.

11519   *Chevalier, Nicole* Un voyage dans le sud de la Mésopotamie, il y a cent ans. ᶠHUOT, J. 2001 ⇒50. 79-90.

11520   *Cleuziou, Serge* Autrefois la Mésopotamie allait jusqu'à la mer...;

11521   *Glassner, Jean-Jacques* Quelques questions sur les femmes en Mésopotamie. ᶠHUOT, J. 2001 ⇒50. 91-104/211-214.

11522   **Haas, Volkert** Babylonischer Liebesgarten: Erotik und Sexualität im Alten Orient. 1999 ⇒15,12085; 16,11929. ᴿINTAMS review 7 (2001) 241-242 (*Lellek, Oliver*); WZKM 91 (2001) 408-411 (*Rubio, Gonzalo*).

11523   *Hauser, Stefan R.* Not out of Babylon?: the development of ancient Near Eastern studies in Germany and its current significance. XLVe Rencontre Assyriologique, 1. 2001 ⇒577. 211-237.

11524   *Holloway, Steven W.* Mad to see the monuments: how ancient Assyria saved Victorian bible scholarship. BiRe 17/6 (2001) 38-47, 55-57.

11525 **Kolinski, Rafal** Mesopotamian dimatu of the second millennium BC. BAR international series 1004: Oxf 2001, Archaeopress ix; 228 pp. 1-84171-283-3. Bibl. 135-147.

11526 **Lion, Brigitte; Stein, Diana L.** The Pula-Hali family archives. Studies on the civilization and culture of Nuzi and the Hurrians 11: Bethesda, MD 2001, CDL 377 pp. 1-883053-56-0.

11527 *Malul, Meir* Foot symbolism in the ancient Near East: imprinting foundlings' feet in clay in ancient Mesopotamia. ZAR 7 (2001) 353-367.

11528 *Müller, Hans-Peter* Der Mond und die Plejaden: griechisch-orientalische Parallelen. VT 51 (2001) 206-218 [Job 31,26; 9,8-10; Cant 6,10].

11529 **Nemet-Nejat, Karen Rhea** Daily life in ancient Mesopotamia. Peabody 2001, Hendrickson xxi; 346 pp. $25. 1-56563-712-7 [ThD 49,278—W. Charles Heiser].

11530 *Oates, Joan* Writing archaeology. Proceedings of the XLVe Rencontre Assyriologique, 1. 2001 ⇒577. 365-371.

11531 *Robson, Eleanor* The tablet house: a scribal school in Old Babylonian Nippur. RA 95 (2001) 39-66.

11532 ᴱ**Rothman, Mitchell S.** Uruk Mesopotamia & its neighbours: cross-cultural interactions in the era of state formation. School of American Research advanced seminar series: Santa Fe 2001, School of American Research Press xxi; 556 pp. 0-85255-461-3. Bibl. 477-535.

11533 *Waerzeggers, Caroline* A note on the marriage gift *biblu* in the Neo-Babylonian period. Akkadica 122 (2001) 65-70.

T6.5 Situs effossi Iraq *in ordine alphabetico*; **Arabia; Iran**

al Rimah: **Postgate, C.** The excavations 1997 ⇒11114.

11534 *Babylon*: *Saporetti, Claudio* Babilonia. Le sette meraviglie. Rivista della Fondazione Europea Dragan 14: 2001 ⇒437. 9-18.

11535 *Khorsabad*: *Franklin, Norma* A room with a view: images from room V at Khorsabad, Samaria, Nubians, the Brook of Egypt and Ashdod. Archaeology of the Iron Age. 2001 ⇒625. 257-277.

11536 *Nimrod*: **Hartal, Moshe** The Al-Subayba (Nimrod) Fortress: Towers 11 and 9. IAA Reports 11: J 2001, Israel Antiquities Authority 130 pp. 965-406-036-1. Contributions by *Reuven Amitai* and *Adrian Boas*;

11537 *Oates, Joan; Oates, David* Nimrud: an Assyrian imperial city revealed. L 2001, British School of Archaeology in Iraq ix; 309 pp. £20. 0-9034-7225-2. 172 fig.; 12 col. pl.

11538   *Nineveh*: **Barnett, Richard David; Bleibtreu, Erika S.; Turner, Geoffrey** Sculptures from the southwest palace of Sennacherib at Nineveh, 1: text; 2: plates. L 1998, British Museum Pr. 2 vols; xvi; 159 pp. £125. 0-7141-1126-0. 521 pl. [R]Syr. 78 (2001) 241-243 (*Muller, Béatrice*);

11539   **Gut, Renate Vera** Das prähistorisiche Ninive. 1995 ⇒11/2,b424... 16,11946. [R]Or. 70 (2001) 128-133 (*Peyronel, Luca*);

11540   *Turner, Geoffrey* Sennacherib's palace at Nineveh: the drawings of H.A. Churchill and the discoveries of H.J. Ross. Iraq 63 (2001) 107-138;

11541   **Matthiae, Paolo** Ninive: glanzvolle Hauptstadt Assyriens. 1999 ⇒ 15,11730. [R]OLZ 96 (2001) 534-538 (*Schmidt, Claudia*).

11542   *Nuzi*: [E]**Owen, David I.; Wilhelm, Gernot** Nuzi at seventy-five. 1999 ⇒15,11732. [R]OLZ 96 (2001) 376-386 (*Richter, Thomas*);

11543   [E]**Owen, David I.; Wilhelm, Gernot** General studies and excavations at Nuzi 10/2. 1998 ⇒14,10975. [R]BiOr 58 (2001) 185-190 (*Meinhold, Wiebke*).

11544   *Terqa*: *Rouault, Olivier* Terqa et sa région (6e-1er millénaires av. J.-C.): recherches récentes. Akkadica 122 (2001) 1-26.

11545   *Ur-Nammu*: **Canby, Jeanny Vorys** The "Ur-Nammu" stela. University museum monograph 110: Ph 2001, University of Pennsylvania xv; 58 pp. 0-924171-87-1. 64 pl.

11546   *Uruk*: **Kose, Arno** Uruk Teil 4, Architektur: von der Seleukidenbis zur Sasaniderzeit. 1998 ⇒16,11955. [R]BiOr 58 (2001) 473-482 (*Oettel, A.*).

11547   **Hoyland, Robert G.** Arabia and the Arabs: from the Bronze Age to the coming of Islam. L 2001, Routledge xii; 324 pp. £16. 0-415-19535-7. Bibl. 256-315.

11548   **Müller, Walter W.** Südarabien im Altertum: kommentierte Bibliographie der Jahre 1973 bis 1996. [E]**Nebes, Norbert**: Epigraphische Forschungen auf der arabischen Halbinsel 2: Rahden/Westf. 2001, Leidorf vii; 156 pp. 3-89646-682-8. Mitarbeit *E.-M. Wagner*.

11549   *Persepolis*: **Koch, Heidemarie** Persepolis: glänzende Hauptstadt des Perserreiches. Bildbände zur Archäologie. Mainz 2001, Von Zabern 112 pp. €34.80. 3-8053-2813-3. Num. ill. [BiKi 58,139— Niemann, H. Michael].

T7.1 Ægyptus, *generalia*

11550 **Aufrère, Sydney H.; Golvin, Jean-Claude; Goyon, Jean-Claude**
L'Égypte restituée, 3: sites, temples et pyramides de Moyenne et
Basse Égypte de la naissance de la civilisation pharaonique à l'é-
poque gréco-romaine. P 1997, Errance 363 pp. [R]CÉg 76 (2001)
122-124 (*Degardin, Jean-Claude*).

11551 *Bagnall, Roger S.* Archaeological work on Hellenistic and Roman
Egypt, 1995-2000. AJA 105 (2001) 227-243.

11552 [E]**Casini, Maria** One hundred years in Egypt: paths of Italian archaeology. Mi 2001, Electa 248 pp. 88-435-9628-4. Bibl. 243-248.
[E]**Cervelló Autuori, J.** África antigua 2001 ⇒602.

11553 **Clauss, Manfred** Das Alte Ägypten. Da:Wiss 2001, 511 pp. €30.
50.

11554 *Curto, Silvio* Lingua, scrittura e cultura nell'antico Egitto <1988>;

11555 La riscoperta dell'Egitto cristiano <1998>. Attraverso l'egittologia.
2001 ⇒136. 401-411/483-492.

11556 **Curto, Silvio** L'Antico Egitto: realtà e fantasia. T 2001, I libri di
La stampa 270 pp. 88-7783-135-9. Bibl. 251-256.

11557 **Dasen, Veronique** Dwarfs in ancient Egypt and Greece. 1993 ⇒9,
15153; 11/2,c428. [R]JEA 87 (2001) 187-190 (*Filer, Joyce M.*).

11558 **David, Rosalie** The experience of Ancient Egypt. 2000 ⇒16,
11962. [R]BiOr 58 (2001) 78-79 (*Green, L.*).

11559 **Dziobek, Eberhard** Denkmäler des Veziers User-Amun. Studien
zur Archäologie und Geschichte Altägyptens 18: Heid 2001,
Orientverlag x; 168 pp. 3-927552-34-8. 14 pl.

11560 *Grimal, Nicolas* La danse des peuples aux marches du royaume.
CRAI 2 (2001) 1159-1182.

11561 *Guiter, Jacques* Contraception en Égypte ancienne. BIFAO 101
(2001) 221-236.

11562 **Houlihan, Patrick F.** Wit and humour in ancient Egypt. L 2001,
Rubicon xxii; 170 pp. £22. 0-948695-69-2. Bibl. 155-163. [R]EgArch
19 (2001) 40 (*Hart, George*).

11563 *Kondo, Jiro; Uchida, Sugihiko* Egyptology: the land of Pharaohs
from a Japanese viewpoint. Orient 36 (2001) 57-77.

11564 *Leclant, Jean; Minault-Gout, Anne* Fouilles et travaux en Égypte et
au Soudan, 1999-2000. Or. 70 (2001) 349-476.

11565 **Manley, Deborah; Rée, Peta** Henry SALT: artist, traveller, diplo-
mat, egyptologist. L 2001, Libri xiv; 314 pp. 1-901965-04-X. Bibl.
301-307.

11566 **Mariette-Pacha, Auguste** Voyage dans la Haute Egypte. 1999
<1878> ⇒15,11748. [R]BiOr 58 (2001) 72-76 (*Raven, Maarten J.*).

11567   ᴱNicholson, Paul T.; Shaw, Ian Ancient Egyptian materials and
        technology. 2000 ⇒16,11970. ᴿAJA 105 (2001) 338-340 (*Malek,*
        Jaromir); DiscEg 50 (2001) 33-53 (*Nibbi, Alessandra*); BASPap
        38 (2001) 157-159 (*Wilfong, Terry G.*).

11568   **Piacentini, Patrizia; Orsenigo, Christian** Gli egizi: la civiltà della
        memoria. ᴱ*Gallina, Mariavittoria*: Civiltà mediterranee: CinB
        2001, Silvana 143 pp. 88-8215-357-6. Bibl. 141-143.

11569   **Romer, John** The Valley of the Kings. L 2001, Phoenix x; 373 pp.
        1-84212-045-X. Bibl. 353-363.

11570   **Scheidel, Walter** Death on the Nile: disease and the demography
        of Roman Egypt. Mn.S 228: Lei 2001, Brill xxx; 286 pp. €78.

11571   **Smith, W. Stevenson** The art and architecture of ancient Egypt.
        ³1999 ⇒15,11756; 16,11974. ᴿCÉg 76 (2001) 120-122 (*Tefnin,*
        Roland).

11572   **Stafford-Deitsch, Jeremy** The monuments of ancient Egypt. L
        2001, British Museum 167 pp. $40. 0-253-34038-1. Foreword *T.G.*
        H. James.

11573   **Toivari-Viitala, Jaana** Women at Deir El-Medina: a study of the
        status and roles of the female inhabitants in the workmen's com-
        munity during the Ramesside period. Egyptologische uitgaven 15:
        Lei 2001, Nederlands Instituut voor het Nabije Oosten viii; 293 pp.
        €55. 90-6258-215-X. Bibl. 239-279.

11574   **Vlora, Nedim R.** Le porte del cielo: l'eredità dei faraoni. Collana
        di astronomia culturale (Archeoastronomia): Bari 2001, Adda 255
        pp. 88-8082-434-1. Bibl. 251-254.

                T7.2 *Luxor*, **Karnak** [East Bank]—**Thebae** [West Bank]

11575   **Roehrig, Catharine H.** Explorers and artists in the Valley of the
        Kings. Cairo 2001, American University in Cairo Press 96 pp. 977-
        424-705-1. Bibl. 94.

11576   *Karnak*: *Ernst, Herbert* Ein Weihgeschenk Thutmosis' III. an
        Amun-Re: der Sonnenaltar im Re-Heiligtum im Achmenu zu Kar-
        nak. ZÄS 128 (2001) 1-6;

11577   **Jacquet, Jean** Karnak-Nord IX. FIFAO 44: Cairo 2001, Institut
        Français d'Archéologie Orientale vi; 75 pp. 2-7247-0300-6. Bibl.
        69-70.

11578   *Luxor*: ᴱ**Weeks, Kent R.** The treasures of the Valley of the Kings:
        tombs and temples of the Theban west bank in Luxor. Cairo 2001,
        The American University in Cairo Press 434 pp. 977-424-666-7.
        Phot. *Araldo De Luca.*

11579   *Thebes*: **Cabrol, A.** Les voies processionnelles de Thèbes. OLA
          97: Lv 2001, Peeters xxxviii; 853 pp. €137.80. 90-429-0866-1;
11580   *Jansen-Winkeln, Karl* Der thebanische 'Gottesstaat'. Or. 70 (2001)
          153-182.

T7.3 Amarna

11581   ᴱ**Cohen, Raymond; Westbrook, Raymond** Amarna diplomacy:
          the beginnings of international relations. 2000 ⇒16,11981. ᴿAJA
          105 (2001) 340-341 (*Cline, Eric H.*); BiOr 58 (2001) 416-419
          (*Fleming, Daniel E.*); RA 95 (2001) 95-96 (*Charpin, D.*).
11582   **Giles, F.J.** The Amarna Age: Egypt. Wmr 2001, Aris & P. xii; 285
          pp. 0-85668-820-7;
11583   The Amarna age: western Asia. 1997 ⇒13,10968; 15,11769.
          ᴿJNES 60 (2001) 141-142 (*Chavalas, Mark W.*); CÉg 76 (2001)
          157-159 (*Murnane, William J.*).
11584   **Kemp, Barry J.; Vogelsang-Eastwood, Gillian,** *al.,* The ancient
          textile industry at Amarna. Excavation Memoir 68: L 2001, Egypt
          Exploration Society 498 pp. 0-85698-153-2. Bibl. 483-498.
11585   ᴱ**Liverani, Mario** Le lettere di el-Amarna. 1998-1999 ⇒14,11018
          ... 16,11987. ᴿAsp. 48 (2001) 239-241 (*Di Palma, Gaetano*).
11586   *Rainey, Anson* The El-Amarna documents: a cultural phenomenon
          in the Late Bronze period. ᶠAHITUV, S. 2001 ⇒1. 391-408.
11587   *Reeves, Nicholas* An Amarna-period ostracon from the Valley of
          the Kings. Antiquity 75 (2001) 501-502.
11588   *Roellig, Wolfgang* Die Briefe aus Amarna—neues Licht in alte Ge-
          schichte. WUB 22 (2001) 48-50.
11589   *Schoske, Sylvia* Die Rolle der Frauen in Amarna. WUB 22 (2001)
          57-62.
11590   *Van der Westhuizen, Jasper P.* Substrate interferences and word
          order variation in non-verbal sentences in the Jerusalem-Amarna
          letters. ᴹCAGNI, L., 2: SMDSA 61: 2001 ⇒15. 1075-1094.
11591   *Vita, Juan-Pablo* La provenance de la lettre d'El-Amarna EA 308.
          Sem. 50 (2001) 1-7.
11592   *Waterhouse, S. Douglas* Who are the Ḫabiru of the Amarna Let-
          ters?. JATS 12/1 (2001) 31-42.
11593   *Zivie, Alain* Echnaton: ein Pharao hinter dem Schleier der Jahrtau-
          sende. WUB 22 (2001) 4-9.

T7.4 **Memphis,** *Saqqara*—**Pyramides,** *Giza* (Cairo)

11594   *Bauval, Robert G.* Carbon-14 dating the Giza pyramids?: the small relics found inside the pyramids. DiscEg 49 (2001) 5-21. Collab. *Javier Serra.*

11595   ^E**Bárta, Miroslav; Krejcí, Jaromír** Abusir and Saqqara in the year 2000. ArOr.S 9: Praha 2000, Academy of Sciences xxi; 612 pp. 80-85425-39-4.

11596   **Brovarsky, Edward** The Senedjemib Complex part I: the Mastabas of Senedjemib Inti (G 2370), Khnumenti (G 2374), and Senedjemib Mehi (G 2378). Giza Mastabas 7: Boston 2001, Museum of Fine Arts 2 vols 0-87846-479-4. Bibl. xxvii-xliv.

11597   **Giddy, Lisa** Kom Rabi'a: the New Kingdom and post-New Kingdom objects. 1999 ⇒15,11781. ^RAJA 105 (2001) 546 (*Smith, Stuart Tyson*).

11598   **Isler, Martin** Sticks, stones, and shadows: building the Egyptian pyramids. Norman, OK 2001, University of Oklahoma Press xiv; 352 pp. $30. 0-8061-3342-2. Bibl. 327-336.

11599   **Janosi, Peter** Österreich vor den Pyramiden. ÖAW.PHK 648, Bd. VÄK 3: 1997 ⇒14,11030. ^RBiOr 58 (2001) 105-106 (*Roth, Ann Macy*);

11600   Die Pyramidenanlagen der Königinnen: Untersuchungen zu einem Grabtyp des Alten und Mittleren Reiches. 1996 ⇒13,10984; 15, 11782. ^ROLZ 96 (2001) 356-359 (*Altenmüller, Hartwig*).

11601   **Kanawati, Naguib; Abdel-Raziq, Mahmud,** *al.,* The Teti Cemetery at Saqqara, Vol VII: the tombs of Shepsipuptah, Mereri (Merinebti), Hefi and others. The Australian Centre for Egyptology, Reports 17: Wmr 2001, Aris & P. 76 pp. £45. 0-85668-806-1. 57 pl.

11602   **Kanawati, Naguib,** *al.,* Tombs at Giza, Vol I: Kaiemankh (G4561) and Seshemnefer I(G4940). The Australian Centre for Egyptology, Reports 16: Wmr 2001, Aris & P. 68 pp. £45. 0-85668-805-3. Pref. *Zahi Hawass.* 51 pl.

11603   **Labrousse, Audran** Mission archéologique de Saqqara III: l'architecture des pyramides à textes: I-Saqqara Nord. 1996 ⇒12,10442. ^RZDMG 150 (2001) 602-605 (*Engel, Eva-Maria*); CÉg 76 (2001) 126-132 (*Legon, John A.R.*);

11604   L'architecture des pyramides à textes II: Saqqara Sud. 2000 ⇒16, 11997. ^RBiOr 58 (2001) 610-612 (*Jánosi, P.*).

11605   **Pincherle, Mario** La grande piramide e lo Zed: nuove scoperte nella piramide: come fu costruita e cosa nasconde. Diegaro (Forlì Cesena) 2001, Macro 267 pp. 88-7507-174-8. Bibl. 263-265.

11606 *Potter, Jeremy* The Great Pyramid: the tangents on the south shaft, queen's chamber, and the north and south shafts, king's chamber. DiscEg 51 (2001) 89-108.

11607 *Priskin, Gyula* The philosopher's stones: the Great Pyramid. DicEg 51 (2001) 109-120.

11608 **Rousseau, Jean** Construire la grande pyramide. P 2001, L'Harmattan 220 pp.

11609 *Tonner, Tobias* Auf der Suche nach den Erbauern der Pyramiden von Giza .WUB 22 (2001) 64-69.

11610 **Verner, Miroslav** The pyramids: the mystery, culture, and science of Egypt's great monuments. [T]*Rendall, Steven*: NY 2001, Grove xv; 495 pp. $35. 0-8021-1703-1. Bibl. 481-484.

T7.5 Delta Nili; *Alexandria*

11611 *Bietak, Manfred, al.*, Ausgrabungen in dem Palastbezirk von Avaris: Vorbericht Tell el-Dabʿa/ʿEzbet Helmi 1993-2000. Ä&L 11 (2001) 27-119.

11612 *Forstner-Müller, Irene* Vorbericht der Grabung im Areal A/II1 in Tell el-Dabʿa. Ä&L 11 (2001) 197-220.

11613 **Ballet, Pascale** La vie quotidienne à Alexandrie 331-30 avant J.-C. 1999 ⇒15,11787. [R]BiOr 58 (2001) 123-26 (*Młynarczyk, Jolanta*).

11614 *Empereur, Jean-Yves* Alexandrie (Égypte). BCH 125 (2001) 679-700.

11615 **Empereur, Jean-Yves** Alexandria rediscovered. 1998 ⇒14,11044; 15,11794. [R]ArOr 69 (2001) 95-97 (*Smoláriková, Květa*).

11616 **Jakab, Attila** Ecclesia Alexandrina: évolution sociale et institutionnelle du christianisme alexandrin (IIe-IIIe siècles.) Christianismes anciens 1: Bern 2001, Lang xv; 373 pp. $58. 3-906767-79-5. Bibl. 317-330.

11617 *Luttikhuizen, Gerard* Veronderstellingen over het vroegste christendom in Alexandrië. Vroegchristelijke gemeenten. 2001 ⇒460. 207-222.

11618 **Pfrommer, Michael** Alexandria. 1999 ⇒15,11791; 16,12006. [R]OLZ 96 (2001) 359-363 (*Effland, Andreas*).

11619 [E]**Sartorius, Joachim** Alexandria: Fata Morgana. 2001, Da:Wiss 316 pp.

11620 *Schimanowski, Gottfried* Hochburg griechischer Kultur der jüdischen Diaspora: Alexandrien in hellenistischer Zeit. BiKi 56 (2001) 76-80.

11621   *Varisco, Sergio* Il Faro di Alessandria. Le sette meraviglie. Rivista della Fondazione Europea Dragan 14: 2001 ⇒437. 86-93.

T7.6 *Alii situs Ægypti* alphabetice; *Nubia*

11622   ***Berenice Pancrisia***: **Castiglioni, Alfredo** Das Goldland der Pharaonen: die Entdeckung von Berenike Pancrisia. [T]*Lippert, Barbara*: 1998 ⇒15,11818. [R]CÉg 76 (2001) 162-168 (*Pierce, Richard H.*).

11623   ***Beydar***: **Van Lerberghe, Karel; Voet, Gabriella** Tell Beydar: environmental and technical studies. Subartu 6: Turnhout 2001, Brepols (6) ii; 224 pp. 2-503-99121-1.

11624   ***Dakhleh***: [E]**Marlow, C.A.; Mills, A.J.** The Oasis Papers 1: the proceedings of the first conference of the Dakhleh Oasis Project. Dakhleh Oasis Project, Monograph 6: Oxf 2001, Oxbow viii; 110 (2) pp. 1-900188-54-6. Durham 1994.

11625   ***Edfou***: **Kurth, Dieter** Edfou VIII. Die Inschriften des Tempels von Edfu Abteilung I. Übersetzungen 1: 1998 ⇒14,11054; 16,12010. [R]WO 31 (2000-2001) 196-201 (*Quack, Joachim Friedrich*).

11626   ***el-Balamun***: **Spencer, A.J.** Excavations at Tell el-Balamun 1995-1998. 1999 ⇒15,11807; 16,12012. [R]ArOr 69 (2001) 524-526 (*Smoláriková, Květa*).

11627   ***el-Dab'a***: **Bader, Bettina** Tell El-Daba c A XIII: Typologie und Chronologie der Mergel C-Ton Keramik: Materialien zum Binnenhandel des Mittleren Reiches und der Zweiten Zwischenzeit. DÖAW 22; Untersuchungen der Zweigstelle Kairo des Österr. Archäologischen Institutes 19: W 2001, Österreichische Akademie der Wissenschaften 250 pp. 3-7001-2972-6. Bibl. 235-239.

11628   **Habachi, Labib** Tell el-Dab'a I: Tell el-Dab'a and Qantir, the site and its connection with Avaris and Piramesse. DÖAW 23; Untersuchungen der Zweigstelle Kairo des Österr. Archäologischen Institutes 2: W 2001, Österr. Akademie der Wissenschaften 263 pp. 3-7001-2986-6. Aus dem Nachlass herausgegeben von *Eva-Maria Engel*; Mitarbeit von *Peter Jánosi* und *Christa Mlinar*.

11629   ***es-Sakan***: *Miroschedji, Pierre; Sadek, Moain* Gaza et l'Égypte de l'époque prédynastique à l'Ancien Empire: premiers résultats des fouilles de Tell es-Sakan. BSFE 152 (2001) 28-52.

11630   ***Fayyum***: **Hewison, R. Neil** The Fayoum history and guide. Cairo [3]2001, The American University in Cairo Press xi; 107 pp. 977-424-671-3. Phot.;

11631   *Rathbone, Dominic* Mapping the south-west Fayyum: sites and texts. XXII Congresso di papirologia, 2. 2001 ⇒555. 1109-1117;

11632 **Zecchi, Marco** Geografia religiosa del Fayyum: dalle origini al IV. secolo a.C. Archeologia e storia della civiltà egiziana e del vicino Oriente antico, materiali e studi 7: Imola 2001, La mandragora 307 pp. 88-88108-26-2. Bibl. 249-277.

11633 *Mahgar Dendera*: **Hendrickx, Stan; Midant-Reynes, Béatrix; Van Neer, Wim** Mahgar Dendera 2 (Haute Égypte), un site d'occupation Badarien. Egyptian Prehistory Monographs 3: Lv 2001, University Press 112 pp. 90-5867-163-1. 56 pl.

11634 *Nabta Playa*: **Wendorf, Fred**, *al.*, Holocene settlement of the Egyptian Sahara, 1: the archaeology of Nabta Playa, 2: the pottery of Nabta Playa. NY 2001, Kluwer 2 vols. Bibl. v.1, 676-694.

11635 *Naukratis*: **Leonard, Albert** Ancient Naukratis: excavations at a Greek emporium in Egypt. AASOR 54: 1997 ⇒13,11012; 16, 12016. ᴿSyr. 78 (2001) 252-254 (*Carrez-Maratray, Jean-Yves*);

11636 **Leonard, Albert**, *al.*, Ancient Naukratis, excavations at a Greek emporium, 2: the excavations at Kom Hadid. AASOR 55: Boston 2001, ASOR xix; 245 pp. $100. 76 fig.; 25 pl.; 8 tables;

11637 **Piekarski, Dirk** Die Keramik aus Naukratis im Akademischen Kunstmuseum Bonn. Bonner Sammlung von Aegyptiaca 4: Wsb 2001, Harrassowitz 63 pp. 3-447-04443-8. Bibl. 9-10.

11638 *Piye: Gozzoli, Roberto B.* The triumphal stele of Piye as sanctification of a king. GöMisz 182 (2001) 59-67.

11639 *Tanis: Brissaud, Philippe* Tanis: résultats récents 1997-2000. BSFE 150 (2001) 26-41.

11640 *Taposiris Magna*: **Vörös, Gy.** Taposiris Magna, port of Isis: Hungarian excavations at Alexandria (1998-2001). Budapest 2001, Egyptian Excavation Soc. of Hungary 204 pp. 963-00-7109-7/0-X.

T7.9 Sinai

11641 **Anati, Emmanuel** The riddle of Mount Sinai: archaeological discoveries at Har Karkom. Studi Camuni 21: Capo di Ponte 2001, Centro Camuno 192 pp. 88-86621-15-9. 205 ill.

11642 **Hobbs, Joseph J.** Mount Sinai. 1995 ⇒11/2,b734. ᴿIJMES 33 (2001) 613-615 (*Miller, James A.*).

11643 *Soumeka, Anna* The significance of Kuntillet 'Ajrud for the study of early Judahite history and religion. DBM 20/2 (2001) 80-98.

T8.1 **Anatolia** *generalia*

11644   *Blum, Hartmut* Die "homererische Gesellschaft": Adelsherrschaft oder "big-man society"?. Anatolien. 2001 ⇒414. 25-39;

11645   Homers Troia und die Luwier: Prof. Dr. Helmut Castritius zum 60. Geburtstag. Anatolien. 2001 ⇒414. 41-51.

11646   *Hoff, Corinna* Europa und Lykien: ein Beitrag zur Entstehungsgeschichte Lykiens im ausgehenden 18. und frühen 19. Jh.;

11647   *Hülden, Oliver* Überlegungen zur Bedeutung der Amazonomachie am Maussolleion von Halikarnassos. Anatolien. 2001 ⇒414. 67-81/83-105.

11648   *Laflı, Ergün* Geschichte und Perspektiven der archäologischen Erforschung des eisenzeitlichen Kilikien. IV. Internationaler Kongress. 2001 ⇒650. 308-325.

11649   *Lebrun, René* Des cités apostoliques de Lycaonie, de Lycie et de Pamphylie au second millénaire avant Jésus-Christ. ᴹCᴀɢɴɪ, L., 3: SMDSA 61: 2001 ⇒15. 1681-1691.

        ᴱ**Mikasa, T.** Essays on ancient Anatolia 1999 ⇒420.

11650   *Ruggieri, Vincenzo; Miranda, Luigi; Reyes, Fernando A. Harris* Affreschi in Caria, a Gündogan, e a Monastir Dag: rilivievi tecnici. OCP 67 (2001) 5-19.

11651   **Yakar, Jak** Ethnoarchaeology of Anatolia: rural socio-economy in the Bronze and Iron Ages. 2000 ⇒16,12035. ᴿBASOR 322 (2001) 83-85 (*Wilkinson, T.J.*).

T8.2 **Boğazköy**—*Hethaei*, **the Hittites**

11652   **Neve, Peter** Die Oberstadt von Hattusa: die Bauwerke: I, die Bastion des Sphinxtores und die Tempelviertel am Königs - und Löwentor. Bogazköy-Hattusa 17: Mainz 2001, von Zabern xi; 125 pp. 3-7861-2262-8. 120 pl.

11653   **Seeher, Jürgen** Die Ausgrabungen in Boğazköy-Ḫattuša 2000. AA 3 (2001) 333-362. Beitrag von *Reinder Neef.*

T8.3 **Ephesus; Pergamon**

11654   **Halfmann, Helmut** Städtebau und Bauherren im römischen Kleinasien: ein Vergleich zwischen Pergamon und Ephesos. IM.B 43: Tü 2001, Wasmuth x; 116 pp. 19 ill.

11655 *Londer, Lucilla* Il tempio di Artemide a Efeso. Le sette meraviglie. Rivista della Fondazione Europea Dragan 14: 2001 ⇒437. 37-51.

11656 *Pillinger, Renate* Paolo e Tecla ad Efeso: nuove scoperte nella grotta (chiesa rupestre) sul Bülbüldağ. <2000>;

11657 Piccola guida al cimitero dei Sette Dormienti ad Efeso. VIII Simposio di Efeso. Turchia 15: 2001 ⇒488. 213-237/275-286.

11658 *Pülz, Andreas* La cosidetta tomba di Luca ad Efeso con speciale riguardo al periodo paleobizantino;

11659 *Yalçin, Asnu Bilban; Büyükkolanci, Mustafa* I capitelli corinzi dell'atrio della basilica di S. Giovanni a Efeso: nuove considerazioni. VIII Simposio di Efeso. 2001 ⇒488. 255-274/287-297.

11660 **Börker, Christoph; Burow, Johannes** Die hellenistischen Amphorenstempel aus Pergamon: der Pergamon-Komplex [Börker]; die übrigen Stempel aus Pergamon [Burow]. 1998 ⇒14,11110. RBSOAS 64 (2001) 342-346 (*Jefremow, Nikolai*).

11661 **De Luca, G.; Radt, W.** Sondagen im Fundament des grossen Altars. 1999 ⇒15,11845. RAJA 105 (2001) 129-130 (*Rotroff, Susan*).

11662 **Garbrecht, Günther, al.,** Die Wasserversorgung von Pergamon. Altertümer von Pergamon 1/4; Stadt und Landschaft 4: B 2001, De Gruyter 2 vols 3-11-016947-9.

11663 EKoester, Helmut Pergamon, citadel of the gods: archaeological record, literary description, and religious development. HThS 46: 1998 ⇒14,11111; 16,12043. RRAr (2001) 409-411 (*Le Roy, Christian*).

T8.6 *Situs Anatoliae*—Turkey sites; Urartu

11664 EÇilingiroglu, Altan; Salvini, Mirjo Ayanis I: ten years' excavations at Rusahinili Eiduru-kai 1989-1998. Documenta Asiana 6: R 2001, Istituto per gli Studi Micenei ed Egeo-Anatolici 396 pp. 88-87345-04-X.

11665 *Greaves, Alan M.; Helwing, Barbara* Archaeology in Turkey: the Stone, Bronze, and Iron Ages, 1997-1999. AJA 105 (2001) 463-511.

11666 *Harrison, T.P.* The evidence for Aramaean cultural expansion in the Amuq plain. Canadian research on ancient Syria .2001 ⇒581. 135-144.

11667 *Masson, Emilia* Le complexe cultuel du 'Südburg' (Hattusa): quelques réflexions. IV. Internationaler Kongress. 2001 ⇒650. 364-91.

11668 *Patitucci, Stella* Kyme cristiana e il *Kastron* bizantino: l'evidenza archeologica. VIII Simposio di Efeso. 2001 ⇒488. 323-342.

11669 *Redford, Scott, al.*, Excavations at medieval Kinet, Turkey: a preliminary report. ANESt 38 (2001) 58-138.

11670 *Seeher, Jürgen* Die Zerstörung der Stadt Ḫattuša. IV. Internationaler Kongress. 2001 ⇒650. 623-634.

11671 *Uggeri, Giovanni* Kyme, antica metropoli dell'Eolide: profilo storico-topografico. VIII Simposio di Efeso. 2001 ⇒488. 299-322.

T9.1 Cyprus

11672 *Destrooper-Georgiades, A.* Témoignages des monnaies dans les cultes funéraires à Chypre à l'époque achéménide. TEuph 21 (2001) 101-118.

11673 **Frankel, David** Windows onto the Bronze Age: the view from Nicosia. Leventis Municipal Museum of Nicosia 10: Nicosia 2001, Leventis 24 pp. Cyp£3. 9963-560-13-X. Annual lecture [RB 108,638].

11674 *Hadjisavvas, Sophoklis* Chronique des fouilles et découvertes archéologiques à Chypre en 2000. BCH 125 (2001) 743-777.

11675 *Heltzer, Michael* Asylium on Alashia (Cyprus). ZAR 7 (2001) 368-373.

11676 *Hermary, A.* Lieux et formes du culte à Chypre sous la domination achéménide. TEuph 22 (2001) 9-20.

11677 **Karageorghis, Vassos; Demas, M.** Excavations at Kition, 5: the pre-Phoenician levels. 1985 ⇒5,e651. ᴿRAr (2001) 374-376 (*Aupert, Pierre*).

11678 **Karageorghis, Vassos** Ancient art from Cyprus: the Cesnola Collection of the Metropolitan Museum of Art. 2000 ⇒16,12069. ᴿBASOR 322 (2001) 87-89 (*Childs, William A.P.*).

11679 *Karageorghis, Vassos* Patterns of fortified settlements in the Aegean and Cyprus c. 1200 B.C. Defensive settlements. 2001 ⇒619. 1-12.

11680 **Karageorghis, Vassos** Ancient art from Cyprus in the cultural foundation of the Bank of Cyprus. Collection of George and Nefeli Giabra Pierides. Nicosia 2001, Leventis 220 pp. c.400 ill.

11681 **Karageorghis, Vassos, al.**, Ancient Cypriote art in Copenhagen: the collection of the National Museum of Denmark and the Ny Carlsberg Glyptotek. Nicosia 2001, Leventis Foundation xii; 145 pp. Cyp£12. 177 phot.

11682 *Knapp, Bernard; Kassianidou, Vasiliki; Donelly, Michael* Copper smelting in late Bronze Age Cyprus: the excavations at Politiko Phorades. NEA(BA) 64/4 (2001) 204-210.

11683 **Papasavvas, Giorgos** Bronze stands from Cyprus and Crete. Nicosia 2001, Leventis ix; 400 pp. Cyp£20. Diss. Athens 1997; 202 pl.; Eng. sum.

11684 **Raptou, Eustathios** Athènes et Chypre à l'époque perse (VIe-IVe s. av. J.-C.). CMOM 28, A 14: 1999 ⇒15,11865. [R]BASOR 321 (2001) 86-88 (*Nys, Karin*).

11685 *Stewart, J.R.* Corpus of Cypriot artefacts of the Early Bronze Age, 3/1. 1999 ⇒15,11870. [R]BiOr 58 (2001) 446-449 (*Merrillees, R.S.*).

11686 [E]**Swiny, Stuart** The earliest prehistory of Cyprus from colonization to exploitation. ASOR, Archaeological Reports 5; Cyprus American Archaeological Research Institute, MS 2: Boston, MA 2001, ASOR xiv; 171 pp. $85. 0-89757-051-0.

11687 **Webb, Jennifer M.** Corpus of Cypriote antiquities, 20: Cypriote antiquities in the Nicholson Museum at the University of Sydney. Studies in Mediterranean archaeology 20,20: Göteborg 2001, Åström 132, [66] pp. 91-7081-175-X.

11688 **Webb, Jennifer M.; Frankel, David** Corpus of Cypriote antiquities, 21: eight Middle Bronze Age tomb groups from Dhenia in the University of New England Museum of Antiquities. Studies in Mediterranean archaeology 20,21: Göteborg 2001, Åström iv, 51, [23] pp. 91-7081-183-0.

T9.3 *Graecia*, Greece

11689 **Blegen, Carl W.; Rawson, Marion** A guide to the palace of Nestor: Mycenaean sites in its environs and the Chora Museum. Princeton, NJ 2001, American School of Classical Studies at Athens 68 pp. 0-87661-640-6. Bibl. 66.

11690 *Boyd, Michael; Provost, Samuel* Application de la prospection géophysique à la topographie urbaine, 1: Philippes, les quartiers sud-ouest. BCH 125 (2001) 453-521;

11691 Philippes: prospection géophysique autour de l'édifice avec bain. BCH 125 (2001) 586-589.

11692 **Broodbank, Cyprian** An island archaeology of the early Cyclades. C 2000, CUP xviii; 414 pp. £50. 0-521-78272-4. 124 fig. [R]Antiquity 75 (2001) 438-440 (*Berg, Ina*).

11693 **Camp, John M.** The archaeology of Athens. NHv 2001, Yale University Press xii; 340 pp. $40. 0-300-08197-9.

11694 [E]**Cullen, Tracey** Aegean prehistory: a review. AJA.S 1: Boston 2001, Archaeological Institute of America xvii; 506 pp. 0-9609042-4-7.

11695 **Cultraro, Massimo** L'anello di Minosse: archeologia della regalità nell'Egeo Minoico. Biblioteca di archeologia 31: Mi 2001, Longanesi 446 pp. 88-304-1650-9. Bibl. 385-429.

11696 *Gaffney, Vince, al.*, Enclosure and defence: the context of Mycenaean contact within central Dalmatia;

11697 *Kanta, Athanasia; Stampolidis, Nicolas C.* Orné (AIPY) in the context of the defensive settlements of the end of the Bronze Age. Defensive settlements. 2001 ⇒619. 137-156/95-113.

11698 *Lambrinoudakis, Vassilios; Philaniotou-Hadjianastasiou, Olga* The town of Naxos at the end of the late Bronze Age: the Mycenaean fortification wall. Defensive settlements. 2001 ⇒619. 157-169.

11699 *Lolos, Yannos G.* Dark age citadels in southern Salamis. Defensive settlements. 2001 ⇒619. 115-136.

11700 **Merker, Gloria S.** Corinth, 18/4: the sanctuary of Demeter and Kore: terracotta figurines of the classical, Hellenistic and Roman periods. 2000 ⇒16,12081 ᴿAJA 105 (2001) 355-356 (*Biers, Jane*).

11701 ᴱ**Parlama, Liana; Stampolidis, Nikolaos Chr.** Athens: the city beneath the city: antiquities from the Metropolitan Railway excavations. Athens 2001, Goulandris Foundation, Museum of Cycladic Art 413 pp. 0-8109-6725-1. Bibl. 401-413.

11702 *Touchais, Gilles; Huber, Sandrine; Philippa-Touchais, Anna* Chronique des fouilles et découvertes archéologiques en Grèce en 2000. BCH 125 (2001) 779-1063.

11703 **Whitley, James** The archaeology of ancient Greece. Cambridge World Archaeology: C 2001, CUP xxvi; 484 pp. £60/$90; £22/$32. 0-521-62205-0/62733-8. Bibl. 429-476. 170 fig.

11704 **Wilson, David B.** Ayia Irini: periods I-III: the neoltihic and early Bronze Age settlements, 1: the pottery and small finds. 1999 ⇒15, 11882. ᴿAJA 105 (2001) 343-344 (*Wiencke, Martha Heath*).

T9.4 Creta

11705 *Aartun, Kjell* A brief comparative documentation of Semitic religious groups in antiquity. ᴹCAGNI, L., 3: SMDSA 61: 2001 ⇒15. 1219-1230.

11706 *Böhm, Stephanie* Abschied nehmen von einer schönen Idee: Kreta und die eingewanderten Orientalen. ᶠSCHÄFER, J. 2001 ⇒99. 125-130.

11707 ᴱ**Chaniotis, A.** From Minoan farmers to Roman traders: sidelights on the economy of ancient Crete. 1999 ⇒15,11878. ᴿCIR 51 (2001) 132-133 (*Sweetman, Rebecca*).

11708 **Driessen, Jan; MacDonald, Colin** The troubled island: Minoan Crete before and after the Santorini eruption. 1997 ⇒14,11168; 16, 12088. ᴿAJA 105 (2001) 115-118 (*Warren, Peter*).

11709 *Haggis, Donald C.* A dark age settlement system in east Crete, and a reassessment of the definition of refuge settlements;

11710 *Hayden, Barbara J.* Elias to Nisi: a fortified coastal settlement of possible Late Minoan IIIC date in the Vrokastro area, eastern Crete. Defensive settlements. 2001 ⇒619. 41-59/61-83.

11711 **Jones, Donald W.** External relations of Early Iron Age Crete, 1100-600 B.C. Archaeological Institute of America, Monographs 4: Ph 2000, Univ. Museum Publications x; 396 pp.

11712 *Kanta, Athanasia* Cretan refuge settlements: problems and historical implications within the wider context of the eastern Mediterranean towards the end of the Bronze Age;

11713 *Nowicki, Krzysztof* Sea-raiders and refugees: problems of defensible sites in Crete c. 1200 B.C. Defensive settlements. 2001 ⇒619. 13-21/23-40.

11714 *Perna, Massimo* L'amministrazione a Creta in epoca minoica e sue dipendenze dai modelli vicino-orientali. ᴹCAGNI, L., 2: SMDSA 61: 2001 ⇒15. 847-862.

11715 *Watrous, L. Vance* The Isthmus of Ierapetra in east Crete and the dark age refuge settlement of Profitis Elias: diaspora or local population change?. Defensive settlements. 2001 ⇒619. 85-94.

11716 *Woudhuizen, Fred C.* Defining Atlantis in space and time. UF 33 (2001) 605-620.

T9.6 Urbs Roma

11717 **Corbier, P.** Rome, ville et capitale, de la fin de la République à la fin des Antonins. Regards sur l'histoire, histoire ancienne 149: P 2001, SEDES 224 pp. 2-7181-9364-6 [EtCl 70,316s–Rochette, B.].

11718 **De Kleijn, Gerda** The water supply of ancient Rome: city area, water and population. Dutch Monographs on Ancient History and Archaeology 22: Amst 2001, Gieben (6) v; 353 pp. 90-5063-268-8. Bibl. 308-332.

11719 ᴱ**Ermini, Letizia Pani; Siniscalco, Paolo** La comunità cristiana di Roma: la sua vita e la sua cultura dalle origini all'alto Medio Evo. Atti e documenti 9: Città del Vaticano 2001, Vaticana 480 pp. €54.23.

11720 *Feldman, Louis H.* Financing the Colosseum. BArR 27/4 (2001) 20-31, 60-61.

11721   *Hedner-Zetterholm, Karin* The Jewish communities of ancient
        Rome. The synagogue of ancient Ostia. 2001 ⇒427. 131-140.
11722   **Kyle, Donald G.** Spectacles of death in ancient Rome. L 2001,
        Routledge xii; 288 pp. 0-415-24842-6. Bibl. 272-281.
11723   ᴱ**La Regina, Adriano** Sangue e arena. Mi 2001, Electa 410 pp. 88-
        435-7981-9. Bibl. 400-410.
11724   Opuscula Romana. Annual of the Swedish Institute in Rome
        27/2002: Sto 2001, Aströms 138 pp. 91-7042-166-8.
11725   **Packer, James E.** Il Foro di Traiano a Roma: breve studio dei mo-
        numenti. R 2001, Quasar xviii; 235 pp. 88-7140-198-0. Ricostruzi-
        oni architettoniche di *John Burge, James E. Packer*, e *Kevin Sar-
        ring*; bibl. 218-225.
11726   **Polia, Mario** Imperium: origine e funzione del potere regale nella
        Roma arcaica. Gli Archi: Rimini 2001, Il Cerchio 296 pp. 88-8474-
        007-X. Bibl. 281-283.
11727   *Rochette, Bruno* Juifs et romains: y a-t'il eu un antijudaïsme ro-
        main. REJ 160 (2001) 1-31.
11728   *Vismara, Cinzia* I monumenti ebraici di Roma. Gli ebrei nell'impe-
        ro romano. 2001 ⇒415. 247-257.
11729   *Walser, Georg* The Greek of the Jews in ancient Rome. The syna-
        gogue of ancient Ostia. 2001 ⇒427. 145-150.

T9.7 Catacumbae

11730   **Bisconti, Fabrizio** Mestieri nelle catacombe romane: appunti sul
        declino dell'iconografia del reale nei cimiteri cristiani di Roma.
        Studi e ricerche, Pont. Comm. di Archeologia Sacra 2: 2000 ⇒16,
        12118. ᴿSMSR 67 (2001) 387-388 (*Perraymond, Myla*).
11731   **Dorsch, Klaus-Dieter; Seeliger, Hans Reinhard** Römische Kata-
        kombenmalereien: im Spiegel des Photoarchivs Parker... 1864-
        1994. 2000 ⇒16,12120. ᴿActBib 38 (2001) 31-32 (*Borràs, Anto-
        ni*); ByZ 94 (2001) 711-716 (*Zimmermann, Norbert*).
11732   **Fiocchi Nicolai, Vincenzo; Bisconti, Fabrizio; Mazzoleni, Dani-
        lo** Le catacombe cristiane di Roma: origini, sviluppo, apparati de-
        corativi, documentazione epigrafica. 1998 ⇒14,11202; 15,11896.
        ᴿSal. 63 (2001) 378-380 (*Baruffa, Antonio*);
11733   Les catacombes chrétiennes de Rome: origine, développement, dé-
        cor, inscriptions. 2000 ⇒16,12123. ᴿMoBi 133 (2001) 62 (*Caillet,
        Jean-Pierre*).
11734   **Fiocchi Nicolai, Vincenzo** Strutture funerarie ed edifici di culto
        paleocristiani di Roma dal IV al VI secolo. Studi e ricerche / Ponti-

ficia commissione di archeologia sacra 3: Città del Vaticano 2001, IGER 206 pp. 88-88420-08-8. Num. ill.; bibl.141-161.

11735 *Foro, Philippe* La mémoire des catacombes de Rome. BLE 102 (2001) 25-38.

11736 *Rajak, Tessa* Inscription and context: reading the Jewish catacombs of Rome. The Jewish dialogue. AGJU 48: 2001 <1994> ⇒199. 431-446.

11737 *Seeliger, Hans Reinhard* A collection of historical photographs in the Bodleian Library at Oxford and its significance for investigations in Roman catacomb paintings. StPatr 34. 2001 ⇒553. 224-26.

T9.8 *Archaeologia paleochristiana*—early Christian archaeology

11738 ᴱ**Cecchelli, Margherita** Materiali e tecniche dell'edilizia paleocristiana a Roma. R 2001, De Luca 455 pp. Ministero per i beni culturali.

11739 **Íñiguez Herrero, J.A.** Arqueología cristiana. 2000 ⇒16,12128. ᴿCDios 214 (2001) 211-212 (*Gutiérrez, J.*); Mayéutica 27 (2001) 238-240 (*Eguiarte, Enrique*).

11740 **Laskaris, Nikolaos G.** Monuments funéraires paléochrétiens (et byzantins) de Grèce. 2000 ⇒16,12129. ᴿTheol(A) 72/1 (2001) 409-413 (*Theodoros, Euangelos D.*).

11741 *O'Loughlin, Thomas* The early church. Religious diversity. BiSe 79: 2001 ⇒398. 124-142.

11742 **Pergola, Philippe** Christian Rome: early christian Rome: catacombs and basilicas: past & present. R 2000, Vision 98 pp. 88-8162-101-0.

11743 *Sapelli, Marina* Sarcofagi tardoantichi e paleocristiani del Museo Nazionale Romano in Palazzo Massimo alle Terme;

11744 *Spinola, Giandomenico* I sarcofagi paleocristiani del Museo Pio Cristiano ex Lateranense nei Musei Vaticani. RivAC 77 (2001) 519-544/545-569.

11745 **Thümmel, Hans-Georg** Die Memorien für Petrus und Paulus in Rom. 1999 ⇒15,11903. ᴿJAC 44 (2001) 244-246 (*Seeliger, Hans Reinhard*).

11746 *Tremblay, Xavier* Das Christentum an der Seidenstraße: vergessene Spuren in Zentralasien. WUB Sonderheft (2001) 42-45.

11747 **Webb, Matilda** The churches and catacombs of early christian Rome: a comprehensive guide. Brighton 2001, Sussex Academic xxvi; 324 pp. $45 [ChH 71,870s—Meyers, Eric M.].

XIX. Geographia biblica

u1.0 Geographica

11748 **Alphin, George** A New Testament geography: description, perspectives, and implications for the field of geography. Diss. Louisiana State, 2001 317 pp. 30416524.

11749 **Aujac, Germaine** ERATOSTHÈNE de Cyrène, le pionnier de la géographie: sa mesure de la circonférence terrestre. P 2001, Comité des travaux historiques et scientifiques 224 pp. €14.

11750 **Belmonte Marín, Juan Antonio** Répertoire géographique des textes cunéiformes, 12,2: die Orts- und Gewässernamen der Texte aus Syrien im 2. Jt. v. Chr. ^ERöllig, Wolfgang; Kupper, Jean-Robert: BTAVO.B 24: Wsb 2001, Reichert vi; 430 pp. €59. 3-89500-266-6. ^RRA 95 (2001) 190-191 (Charpin, D.).

11751 ^TBerggren, J. Lennart; Jones, Alexander PTOLEMY's geography: an annotated translation of the theoretical chapters. 2000 ⇒16, 12131. ^RPrudentia 33 (2001) 149-151 (Spalinger, Anthony).

11752 ^EHübner, W. Geographie und verwandte Wissenschaften. Geschichte der Mathematik und der Naturwissenschaften in der Antike 2: Stu 2000, Steiner 258 pp.

11753 *Liverani, Mario* The Sargon geography and the Late Assyrian mensuration of the earth. SSA Bulletin 13 (1999-2001) 57-85.

11754 *Müller-Wollermann, Renate* Griechisch-römische Topographie zwischen pharaonischen und modernen Daten. XXII Congresso di papirologia, 2. 2001 ⇒555. 1009-1015.

u1.2 Historia geographiae

11755 *Carrez-Maratray, J.-Y.* De l'Oronte au Nil: Typhon et Saphon. Ment. *Herodotus*. TEuph 21 (2001) 87-100.

11756 *Frayne, Douglas* In Abraham's footsteps. ^FDION, P.-E. 1: JSOT.S 324: 2001 ⇒25. 216-236 [Gen 11].

11757 *Luciani, Marta* On Assyrian frontiers and the middle Euphrates. SSA Bulletin 13 (1999-2001) 87-114.

11758 *Rubin, Rehav* Historical geography in Israel—ideas, themes, and perspectives. Cathedra 100 (2001) 339-360 Sum. 401. **H**.

11759 **Wäfler, Markus** Tall al-Hamidiya 3: zur historischen Geographie von Idamaras zur Zeit der Archive von Mari(2) und Subat-enlil/

Sehna. OBO.A 21: Gö 2001, Vandenhoeck & R 304 pp. 3-525-53-002-1. Beiträge v. *Jimmy Brignoni; Henning Paul.*

U1.4 Atlas— maps; photographiae

11760 *Bagnall, Roger S.* Mapping Hellenistic and Roman Egypt: comment. XXII Congresso di papirologia, 1. 2001 ⇒555. 85-88.

11761 *Krieger, Klaus-Stefan* Maps of Palestine in Matthew 4,23-25 and Bellum 3:35-58. Internationales Josephus-Kolloquium 2000. 2001 ⇒474. 263-277.

11762 **Littell, Franklin H.** Historical atlas of christianity. NY [2]2001, Continuum xv; 440 pp. $35. 0-8264-1303-X. [R]Studies in World Christianity 7 (2001) 266-267 (*Dawson, Jane E.A.*).

11763 [E]**Mittmann, Siegfried; Schmitt, Götz** Tübinger Bibelatlas: auf der Grundlage des Tübinger Atlas des Vorderen Orients (TAVO). Stu 2001, Deutsche Bibelges. ca. 124 pp. €66. 3-438-06022-1. [R]UF 33 (2001) 709-711 (*Zwickel, W.*).

11764 [E]**Parpola, Simo; Porter, Michael** The Helsinki Atlas of the Near East in the Neo-Assyrian Period. Helsinki 2001, The Neo-Assyrian Text Corpus Project xiv; 46 pp. $30. 951-45-9050-3. Bibl. 36-45.

11765 *Sidebotham, Steven E.* The contribution of the Global Positioning System (GPS) to mapping the Eastern Desert. XXII Congresso di papirologia, 2. 2001 ⇒555. 1213.

11766 **Westrem, Scott D.** The Hereford map: a transcription and translation of the legends with commentary. Terrarum orbis 1: Turnhout 2001, Brepols lxii; 476 pp. 2-503-51056-6. Bibl. xlix-lvii.

11767 **Zwickel, Wolfgang** Calwer Bibelatlas. 2000 ⇒16,12168. [R]FgNT 14 (2001) 162-164 (*Stenschke, Christoph*).

11768 *Neumann, Thomas* Photographien als historische Dokumente: über die Quellen von Holyland-Photographs, einer Datenbank historischer Photographien aus Palästina. Steine-Bilder-Texte. Arbeiten zur Bibel und ihrer Geschichte 5: 2001 ⇒613. 159-178.

U1.6 Guide-books, *Führer*

11769 **Bourbon, Fabio; Lavagno, Enrico** The Holy Land: guide to the archaeological sites and historical monuments. Vercelli 2001, White Star 227 pp. 0-7607-2215-3. Bibl. 224-225.

11770 **Diwersy, A.; Wand, G.** Irak, Land zwischen Euphrat und Tigris. Blieskastel 2001, Gollenstein 444 pp. 3-933389-46-1. 490 phot.

11771 **Hoppe, Leslie J.** A guide to the lands of the bible. 1999 ⇒15, 11939. [R]NewTR 14 (2001) 89-90 (*Cook, Joan E.*) [Lk 18,35-24,53].

11772 **Kaswalder, Pietro Alberto; Bosetti, Elena** Sulle orme di Mosè: Egitto, Sinai, Giordania: nuova guida biblica e archeologica. 2000 ⇒16,12177. [R]CDios 214 (2001) 207-208 (*Gutiérrez, J.*): Vivens Homo 12 (2001) 439-440 (*Tarocchi, Stefano*).

11773 **Kilgallen, John J.** Prsewodnik po Ziemi Świętej: według Nowego Testamentu. [T]*Baraniak, Marek*: Wsz 2000, Rhetos 298 pp. 83-917849-0-8.

11774 **Mee, Christopher; Spawforth, Antony** Greece: an Oxford archaeological guide. Oxford Archaeological Guides: Oxf 2001, OUP xv; 464 pp. 0-19-288058-6. Bibl. 451-453.

11775 **Peña, Ignacio** Lieux de pèlerinage en Syrie. SBF.CMi 38: 2000 ⇒ 16,12180. [R]CDios 214 (2001) 517-518 (*Gutiérrez, J.*); POC 51 (2001) 225-226 (*Attinger, D.*).

U2.2 Geologia; *Hydrographia*; rivers, seas, salt

11776 *Frumkin, Amos; Elitzur, Yoel* The rise and fall of the Dead Sea. BArR 27/6 (2001) 42-50.

11777 **Manning, Sturt** A test of time: the volcano of Thera and the chronology and history of the Aegean and east Mediterranean in the mid-second millennium B.C. 1999 ⇒15,11943. [R]AJA 105 (2001) 527-532 (*Macdonald, Colin F.*).

11778 *Bedal, Leigh-Ann* A pool complex in Petra's city center. BASOR 324 (2001) 23-41.

11779 **Dierx, Wiel; Garbrecht, Günther,** *al.*, Wasser im Heiligen Land: Zeugnisse und archäologische Forschungen Schriftenreihe der Frontinus-Gesellschaft.S III: Mainz 2001, Von Zabern 238 pp. €40. 90. 3-8053-2721-8. 194 fig. [RB 109,155].

11780 **Hirschfeld, Yizhar** The Roman baths of Hammat Gader: final report. 1997 ⇒13,11128... 16,12189. [R]Or. 69 (2000) 451-459 (*Vismara, Cinzia*).

U2.3 *Clima*, climate

11781 *Futato, Mark D.* Sense relations in the "rain" domain of the Old Testament. [F]FITZGERALD, A.: CBQ.MS 32: 2001 ⇒31. 81-94.

11782 *Rosen, Arlene M.; Rosen, Steven A.* Determinist or not determinist?: climate, environment, and archaeological explanation in the Levant. ^MESSE, D.: SAOC 59: 2001 ⇒28. 535-549.

U2.5 *Fauna*, animalia

11783 **Brewer, Douglas J.; Clark, Terence; Phillips, Adrian** Dogs in antiquity: Anubis to Cerberus: the origins of the domestic dog. Wmr 2001, Aris & P. vi; 113 pp. £16.50/$35. 0-855668-704-9. Bibl. 107-111.

11784 ^E**Cannuyer, Christian; Fredericq-Homes, D.** L'animal dans les civilisations orientales; animals in the oriental civilizations. Acta Orientalia Belgica 14: Bru 2001, Société Belge d'Études Orientales xxvii; 256 pp. Bibl. xix-xxvii.

11785 **Chaix, Louis, Méniel, Patrice** Archéozoologie: les animaux et l'archéologie. Hespérides: P 2001, Errance 239 pp. €25.92. 2-877-72-218-X [AnCl 72,600—Raepsaet, Georges].

11786 **De Benedetti, P.** E l'asina disse... l'uomo e gli animali secondo la sapienza di Israele. 1999 ⇒15,11953. ^RAsp. 48 (2001) 613-615 (*Castello, Gaetano*).

11787 *Driesch, Angela von den* Frühe Pferde- und Maultierskelette aus Auaris (Tell el-Dabʿa), östliches Nildelta. Ä&L 11 (2001) 301-311.

11788 *Ehlers, Kathrin* Tiermetaphorik. rhs 44 (2001) 345-351.

11789 **Engels, Donald** Classical cats: the rise and fall of the sacred cat. 1999 ⇒15,11954; 16,12203. ^RAnCl 70 (2001) 398-401 (*Bodson, Liliane*).

11790 **Germond, Philippe** Das Tier im alten Ägypten. Mü 2001, Hirmer 223 pp. €79.80. 3-7774-9130-6.

11791 *Glatz, Ingrid* Tiernamen als Personennamen. Im Schatten deiner Flügel. 2001 ⇒412. 27-31.

11792 *Hesse, Brian; Wapnish, Paula* Commodities and cuisine: animals in the early Bronze Age of northern Palestine. ^MESSE, D.: SAOC 59: 2001 ⇒28. 251-282.

11793 **Hoffmann, Friedhelm; Steinhart, Matthias** Tiere vom Nil. Ägyptische Terrakotten in Würzburg (Schenkung Gütte) Heft 1: Wsb 2001, Reichert 104 pp. €36. 3-89500-225-9. Bibl. 101-103.

11794 *Keel, Othmar* Tiere als Gefährten und Feinde;

11795 Warum man sich Gott als Schlange oder Aal vorstellen konnte: Tiere als Gottessymbole. Im Schatten deiner Flügel. 2001 ⇒412. 25-26/75-77.

11796 *Kolska-Horwitz, Liora; Milevski, Ianir* The faunal evidence for socioeconomic change between the Middle and Late Bronze Age in the southern Levant. ^MEsse, D.: SAOC 59: 2001 ⇒28. 283-305.

11797 *Marzel, Shoshana-Rose* Maladies 'inhumaines', les maladies des objets et des animaux dans la bible. Représentations des maladies. 2001 ⇒482. 15-25 [Lev 13,47-59; 14,33-57].

11798 *McNamara, Martin* Symbolic animals. Way 41 (2001) 211-223.

11799 *Panagiotakopulu, E.* Fleas from pharaonic Amarna. Antiquity 75 (2001) 499-500.

11800 *Pilch, John* Snakes in the Hebrew Bible. BiTod 39 (2001) 239-243.

11801 *Riede, Peter* Tierfrieden. rhs 44 (2001) 352-358.

11802 *Schreiber, Stefan* Cavete canes!: zur wachsenden Ausgrenzungsrelevanz einer neutestamentlichen Metapher. BZ 45 (2001) 170-192.

11803 *Schroer, Silvia* 'Im Schatten deiner Flügel'. Im Schatten deiner Flügel. 2001 ⇒412. 8-12.

11804 *Sima, Alexander* Die Jagd im antiken Südarabien. WO 31 (2001) 84-109.

11805 *Staubli, Thomas* Warum im alten Israel Bären und Hirsche neben Nilpferd und Krokodilen lebten: historische Tiergeographie;

11806 Warum die Hebräerinnen ihren Tieren Namen wie 'Hund', 'Schaf', 'Esel' und 'Kuh' gaben: Haustierwerdung und Wertung der Tiere. Im Schatten deiner Flügel. 2001 ⇒412. 13-19/20-24.

11807 **Strawn, Brent Allen** 'What is stronger than a lion?': leonine image and metaphor in the Hebrew Bible and the ancient Near East. Diss. Princeton Sem. 2001, 594 pp. 3006835 [RTL 33,634].

11808 *Whitekettle, Richard* Rats are like snakes, and hares are like goats: a study in Israelite land animal taxonomy. Bib. 82 (2001) 345-362;

11809 Where the wild things are: primary level taxa in Israelite zoological thought. JSOT 93 (2001) 17-37.

U2.6 *Flora*; plantae biblicae et antiquae

11810 **Becker, Lothar** Rebe, Rausch und Religion: eine kulturgeschichtliche Studie zum Wein in der Bibel. Theologie 23: Müns 1999, LIT 288 pp.

11811 *Bosse-Griffiths, Kate* The fruit of the mandrake in Egypt and Israel. Amarna studies. 2001 <1983> ⇒128. 82-96 [Gen 30,14-15].

11812 **Boureux, Christophe** Les plantes de la bible et leur symbolique. P 2001, Cerf 127 pp. €32. 2-204-06727-X. Préf. Père *Thierry de l'Épine*; Ill. [RB 110,310].

11813 **Bouvier, Michel** Les saveurs du vin antique: vins d'hier, vignerons d'aujourd'hui. Hespérides: P 2001, Errance 200 pp. €24.39. 2-87772-209-X [AnCl 72,492s—Desy, Philippe].

11814 *Broshi, Magen* Wine in ancient Palestine: introductory notes. Bread, wine. JSPE.S 36: 2001 <1984> ⇒131. 144-172.

11815 *Clarysse, Willy* Use and abuse of beer and wine in Graeco-Roman Egypt. ᶠHuß, W.: OLA 104: 2001 ⇒51. 159-166.

11816 **Feliks, Yehuda** Trees: aromatic, ornamental, and of the forest in the bible and rabbinic literature. 1997 ⇒15,11972; 16,12228. ᴿLeš. 63 (2000-2001) 151-153 (*Amar, Zohar*). **H.**

11817 **Lefebvre, Philippe** 'Comme des arbres qui marchent': l'homme et l'arbre dans la bible. Connaître la bible 24: Bru 2001, Lumen Vitae 64 pp. €6.25. 2-87324-159-4 [RB 109,478].

11818 *Liphschitz, Nili; Bonani, Georges* Wild and cultivated date palm (Phoenix dactylifera) from Qumran Cave 24. TelAv 28 (2001) 305-309.

11819 *Penna, Romano* Il vino e le sue metafore nella grecità classica, nell'Israele antico, e nel Nuovo Testamento. Vangelo e inculturazione. 2001 <1997> ⇒193. 145-179.

11820 *Watson-Treumann, Brigitte* Beyond the cedars of Lebanon: Phoenician timber merchants and trees from the 'Black Mountain'. WO 31 (2001) 75-83.

U2.8 Agricultura, alimentatio

11821 *Brenner, Athalya; Van Henten, Willem* Food and drink in the bible: an existing new theme. ᶠDEURLOO, K.: 2001 ⇒23. 347-354.

11822 *Broshi, Magen* The diet of Palestine in the Roman period: introductory notes. Bread, wine. 2001 <1986> ⇒131. 121-143.

11823 **Cauvin, Jacques** The birth of the gods and the origins of agriculture. ᵀWatkins, Trevor 2000 ⇒16,12242. ᴿAntiquity 75 (2001) 620-621 (*Wright, Katherine I.*).

11824 **García Soler, María José** El arte de comer en la antigua Grecia. Cultura Clásica: M 2001, Biblioteca Nueva 462 pp. 84-7030-922-6.

11825 *Geyer, Patrick Scott* Evidence of flax cultivation from the temple-granary complex at et-Tell (Bethsaida/Julias). IEJ 51 (2001) 231-4.

11826 ᴱKlengel, H.; Renger, J. Landwirtschaft im Alten Orient. 1999 ⇒ 15,509; 16,12246. ᴿOLZ 96 (2001) 372-376; 693-697 (*Galter, Hannes*).

11827 *Moreno García, Juan Carlos* L'Organisation sociale de l'agriculture dans l'Égypte pharaonique pendant l'Ancien Empire (2650-2150 avant J.-C.). JESHO 44 (2001) 411-450 Sum., rés. 411.

11828   **Nathan, Joan** The foods of Israel today. NY 2001, Knopf x; 433 pp. $40. Ill.

11829   *Schmandt-Besserat, Denise* Le feste nel Vicino Oriente antico. ^MCAGNI, L., 2: SMDSA 61: 2001 ⇒15. 921-932.

11830   *Van Driel, G.* On villages. ^FVEENHOF, K.: 2001 ⇒111. 103-118.

11831   *Van Koppens, Frans* The organisation of institutional agriculture in Mari. JESHO 44 (2001) 451-504 Sum., rés. 451.

11832   **Webb, Stephen H.** Good eating. The christian practice of everyday life: GR 2001, Brazos 272 pp. $22. 1-58743-015-0 [ThD 49,292— W. Charles Heiser].

11833   *Winterling, Aloys* "Mit dem Antrag Kanitz also säßen die Cäsaren noch heute auf ihrem Throne": Max WEBERs Analysen der römischen Agrargeschichte. AKuG 83 (2001) 413-449.

U2.9 **Medicina** *biblica et antiqua*

11834   *Allen, E.A.* What is the church's healing ministry?: biblical and global perspectives. IRM 90 (2001) 46-54.

11835   ^E**Andorlini, Isabella** Greek Medical Papyri I. F 2001, "G. Vitelli" ix; 183 pp. 88-87829-23-3.

11836   *Aufrère, Sydney H.* Maladie et guérison dans les religions de l'Égypte ancienne: au sujet du passage de Diodore Livre I, §LXXXII. Représentations des maladies. 2001 ⇒482. 87-106.

11837   **Avalos, Hector I.** Health care and the rise of christianity. 1999 ⇒ 15,12016; 16,12253. ^RChH 70 (2001) 144-145 (*Martin, Dale*); JECS 9 (2001) 286-287 (*Shelton, W. Brian*); Salm. 48 (2001) 179-181 (*Guijarro, Santiago*); CBQ 63 (2001) 136-137 (*Just, Felix*); OCP 67 (2001) 481-482 (*Ruggieri, V.*).

11838   *Bengeloune, Ahlam* Maladie et guérison dans la tradition musulmane au Maghreb: le médicament magique;

11839   *Fainzang, Sylvie* Douleur, religion et médicaments;

11840   *Garrigue, Pierre* Le veau d'or. Représentations des maladies. 2001 ⇒482. 147-159/107-120/205-208.

11841   *Haussperger, Martha* Einige medizinische Anmerkungen zum Text BAM 3. ^MCAGNI, L., 1: SMDSA 61: 2001 ⇒15. 439-450.

11842   **Howard, James Keir** Disease and healing in the New Testament: an analysis and interpretation. Lanham 2001, University Press of America ix; 344 pp. $44. 0-7618-1979-7. Bibl. 303-333.

11843   ^FKOLLESCH, Jutta: Text and tradition: studies in ancient medicine and its transmission. ^E**Fischer, K.-D.; Nickel, D.; Potter, P.** 1998 ⇒14,56. ^RLatomus 60 (2001) 764-767 (*Garofalo, Ivan*).

ᴱ**Kottek, S.** From Athens to Jerusalem: medicine in Hellenistic Jewish lore and in early christian literature 2000 ⇒585.

11844 **Marganne, Marie-Hélène** La chirurgie dans l'Égypte gréco-romaine d'après les papyrus littéraires grecs. 1998 ⇒14,11326. ᴿRHS 54 (2001) 559-560 (*Samama, Évelyne*).

11845 **Mavroudis, Aimilios Dem.** Ἀρχιγένης Φιλίππου Ἀπαμεύς: vie et oeuvre d'un médecin grec dans la Rome impériale. Athènes 2000, Académie d'Athènes lxi; 469 pp.

11846 **Schulze, Christian** Celsus. Studienbücher Antike 6: Hildesheim 2001, Olms 158 pp. €15.80. 3-487-11293-5 [AnCl 72,494—Gourevitch, Danielle].

11847 **Wilson, Leslie S.** The serpent symbol in the ancient Near East: Nahash and Asherah: death, life and healing. Studies in Judaism: Lanham 2001, University Press of America ix; 243 pp. 0-7618-2124-4. Bibl. 221-238.

U3 *Duodecim tribus*; **Israel tribes;** *land ideology; adjacent lands*

11848 *Altman, Amnon* Claim of possession over occupied or conquered territory in the bible and in the ancient Near East. ZAR 7 (2001) 332-352 [Judg 11,12-27].

11849 **Bartusch, Mark Walter** Understanding Dan: an exegetical approach to Dan in the biblical traditions. Diss. Lutheran School of Theology 2001, 401 pp. 3001224.

11850 *Chapman, Colin* Whose promised land?: the use and misuse of scripture in the current debate. ThRev 22 (2001) 179-198.

11851 **Hartman, David** Israelis and the Jewish tradition: an ancient people debating its future. 2000 ⇒16,12280. ᴿArOr 69 (2001) 640-641 (*Břeňová, Klára*).

11852 *Jacobson, David* When Palestine meant Israel. BArR 27/3 (2001) 42-47.

11853 *Japhet, Sara* La tierra de Israel en el pensamiento bíblico. Voces 18 (2001) 143-153.

11854 *Jones, Dorothy* Surveying the promised land: Elizabeth Jolley's Milk and Honey. Semeia 88 (2001) 97-111.

11855 *Le Roux, Magdel* Are the Balemba in southern Africa a lost tribe of Israel?. BOTSA 11 (2001) 2-8.

11856 **Holes, Clive** Dialect, culture, and society in eastern Arabia, 1: Glossary. HO 1/51.1: Lei 2001, Brill lxiv; 576 pp. €155. 90-04-107-63-0.

U4.5 *Viae*, **roads, routes**

11857   *Ben-David, Chaim* The 'ascent of Luhith' and the 'road to Horona-im': new evidence for their identification. PEQ 133 (2001) 136-44.

11858   *Cavillier, Giacomo* The ancient military road between Egypt and Palestine reconsidered: a reassessment. GöMisz 185 (2001) 23-33.

11859   *Comfort, Anthony; Ergeç, Rifat* Following the Euphrates in antiquity: north-south routes around Zeugma. AnSt 51 (2001) 19-49.

11860   **Hübner, Ulrich; Kamlah, Jens; Reinfandt, Lucian** Die Seidenstraße: Handel und Kulturaustrausch in einem eurasiatischen Wegenetz. Asien und Afrika 3: Ha 2001, EB-Verlag vi; 259 pp. 3-930826-63-1.

11861   **Kolb, Anne** Transport und Nachrichtentransfer im Römischen Reich. B 2000, Akademie 380 pp. €63.40.

U5.0 *Ethnographia*, **sociologia**; *servitus*

11862   *Basson, Alec* Israel en die nasies: 'n kritiese nadenke oor die dokument Ras, Volk en Nasie. Scriptura 77 (2001) 185-192 [Dt 32,8].

11863   *Bimson, John* Old Testament history and sociology. Interpreting the OT. 2001 ⇒248. 125-155.

11864   *Blenkinsopp, Joseph* The household in ancient Israel and early Judaism. The Blackwell companion to the Hebrew Bible. Blackwell companions to religion 3: 2001 ⇒653. 169-185.

11865   **Bony, Paul** L'église et les pauvres. Tout Simplement 30: P 2001, L'Atelier 192 pp.

11866   *Buell, Denise Kimber* Rethinking the relevance of race for early christian self-definition. HThR 94 (2001) 449-476.

11867   *Bunimovitz, Shlomo; Faust, Avraham* Chronical separation, geographical segregation, or ethnic demarcation?: ethnography and the Iron Age low chronology. BASOR 322 (2001) 1-10.

11868   *Cannon, Katie Geneva* Slave ideology and biblical interpretation. The postmodern bible reader. 2001 <1995> ⇒287. 195-204.

11869   *Carter, Charles E.* Social scientific approaches. The Blackwell companion to the Hebrew Bible. 2001 ⇒653. 36-57.

11870   *Cavedo, Romeo* Ricchi e poveri al tempo di Gesù. Presbyteri 35 (2001) 263-270.

11871   *Clements, R.E.* The community of God in the Hebrew Bible. The Blackwell companion to the Hebrew Bible. Blackwell companions to religion 3: 2001 ⇒653. 276-292.

11872 *Craffert, Pieter F.* An exercise in the critical use of models: the "goodness of fit" of Wilson's sect model. [F]MALINA, B.: BiblInterp 53: 2001 ⇒67. 21-46.

11873 *Drinkard, Joel F.* An understanding of family in the Old Testament: maybe not as different from us as we usually think. RExp 98 (2001) 485-501.

11874 Duling, Dennis C. Recruitment to the Jesus movement in social-scientific perspective. [F]MALINA, B.: 2001 ⇒67. 132-175.

11875 *Elliott, John H.* On wooing crocodiles for fun and profit: confessions of an intact admirer. [F]MALINA, B.: 2001 ⇒67. 5-20

11876 *Emilsen, William W.* GANDHI, scripture and the bible. Pacifica 14 (2001) 71-86.

11877 **Fechter, Friedrich** Die Familie in der Nachexilszeit. BZAW 264: 1998 ⇒14,11383... 16,12310. [R]JSSt 46 (2001) 151-152 (*Janowski, Bernd*); JBL 120 (2001) 364-366 (*Pietsch, Michael*).

11878 **Fitzgerald, William** Slavery and the Roman literary imagination. Roman literature and its contexts: 2000 ⇒16,12311. [R]JRS 91 (2001) 210-211 (*Henderson, John*); AJP 122 (2001) 599-604 (*Shelton, Jo-Ann*).

11879 **Friedt, Corinna** Polygynie im Alten Mesopotamien und im Alten Israel: eine vergleichende sozial-geschichtliche Studie anhand rechtlicher Quellen. Diss. Berlin 1999, [D]*Liwak, R.* [RTL 33,631].

11880 **Gehring, Roger W.** Hausgemeinde und Mission: die Bedeutung antiker Häuser und Hausgemeinschaften—von Jesus bis Paulus. BWM 9: 2000 ⇒16,12313. [R]BZ 45 (2001) 281-283 (*Klauck, Hans-Josef*).

11881 **Gibson, E. Leigh** The Jewish manumission inscriptions of the Bosporus Kingdom. TSAJ 75: 1999 ⇒15,12080; 16,12315. [R]JBL 120 (2001) 559-560 & RBLit 3 (2001) 276-279 (*Noy, David*).

11882 **Gottwald, Norman Karol** The politics of ancient Israel. Library of Ancient Israel: LVL 2001, Westminster xvii; 366 pp. £25. 0-664-21977-2. [R]RRT 8 (2001) 512-513 (*Norton, Gerard J.*).

11883 *Grabbe, Lester L.* Sup-urbs or only hyp-urbs?: prophets and populations in ancient Israel and socio-historical method. Urbanism and prophecy. JSOT.S 330: 2001 ⇒271. 95-123.

11884 *Greenfield, Jonas C.* Adi balṭu: care for the elderly and its rewards. ʿAl kanfei yonah, 2. 2001 <1982> ⇒153. 912-919.

11885 **Hanson, Kenneth C.; Oakman, Douglas E.** Palestine in the time of Jesus: social structures and social conflicts. 1998 ⇒14,11393... 16,12319. [R]JBL 120 (2001) 765-767 (*DeMaris, Richard E.*).

11886 **Hanson, Paul D.** The people called: the growth of community in the bible. LVL 2001, Westminster xix; 564 pp. 0-664-22445-8. Bibl. 547-552.

11887 *Hobbs, T.R.* Hospitality in the First Testament and the 'teleological fallacy'. JSOT 95 (2001) 3-30 [1 Sam 25; 2 Kgs 3,8-34].

11888 **Inglebert, Hervé** Interpretatio christiana: les mutations des savoirs (cosmographie, géographie, ethnographie, histoire) dans l'antiquité chrétienne (30-630 après J.-C.). EAug, Antiquité 166: Turnhout 2001, Brepols 632 pp. €49.42. 2-85121-186-2.

11889 ^E**Jaramillo Rivas, Pedro; Pérez Tendero, Manuel** Los pobres en la biblia. ResB 29 (2001) 2-68.

11890 *Joubert, Stephan* Coming to terms with a neglected aspect of ancient Mediterranean reciprocity: SENECA's views on benefit-exchange in De beneficiis as the framework for a model of social exchange. ^FMALINA, B.: BiblInterp 53: 2001 ⇒67. 47-63;

11891 One form of social exchange or two?: 'euergetism,' patronage, and Testament studies. BTB 31 (2001) 17-25.

11892 *Kegler, Jürgen* Arbeitsorganisation und Arbeitskampfformen im Alten Testament. Gesammelte Aufsätze. BEAT 48: 2001 <1983> ⇒167. 90-106.

11893 *Klauck, Hans-Josef* Gemeinde und Gesellschaft im frühen Christentum: ein Leitbild für die Zukunft?. Anton. 76 (2001) 225-246.

11894 *Krobath, Evi* Jesus, ein "Freund der Zöllner und Sünder"—ein Gegner der Pharisäer?: eine sozialgeschichtliche Bibelauslegung. CPB 114 (2001) 2-5 [Mk 2,13-17].

11895 ^E**Laurence, Ray; Berry, Joanne** Cultural identity in the Roman Empire. 1998 ⇒14,11407. ^RCIR 51 (2001) 145-46 (*Bradley, Guy*).

11896 **Legrand, Lucien** The bible on culture: belonging or dissenting. 2000 ⇒16,12329. ^RVJTR 65 (2001) 537-539 (*Aleaz, K.P.*); AJTh 15 (2001) 474-481 (*Chung, Paul*); ITS 38 (2001) 265-268 (*Susaimanickarn, J.*).

11897 *Levin, Christoph* The poor in the Old Testament: some observations. R & T 8 (2001) 253-273.

11898 *Mack, Burton L.* Explaining religion: a theory of social interests;
11899 Explaining christian mythmaking: a theory of social logic;
11900 The christian myth and the christian nation;
11901 Annex: the christian origins project. The christian myth. 2001 ⇒ 181. 83-99/ 101-125/177-193/201-216.

11902 *Mahlangu, E.* The ancient Mediterranean values of honour and shame as a hermeneutical procedure: a social-scientific criticism in an African perspective. VeE 22 (2001) 85-101.

11903 **Malina, Bruce J.** The social gospel of Jesus: the kingdom of God in Mediterranean perspective. Mp 2001, Augsburg F. xiii; 178 pp. $19. 080-06-32478. ^RSalm. 48 (2001) 167-70 (*Guijarro, Santiago*).

11904 *Manjaly, Thomas* Gospel-culture interface: a biblical approach. BiBh 27 (2001) 195-222.

11905   **Markschies, Christoph** Between two worlds: structures of earliest christianity. 1999 ⇒15,12104; 16,12335. ᴿRBLit 3 (2001) 478-481 (*Ekaterini, Tsalampouni*).

11906   ᴱ**Männchen, Julia** Gustaf DALMAN: Arbeit und Sitte in Palästina, 8: Das häusliche Leben, Geburt, Heirat, Tod. B 2001, De Gruyter vii; 504 pp. €151.34. 3-11-016607-0. Fragment mit 66 Abbildungen sowie Gesamtregister für die Bände 1-8; im Auftrag des Gustaf-Dalman-Instituts Greifswald [ZRGG 54,283s–F.W. Horn].

11907   **McNutt, Paula M.** Reconstructing the society of Ancient Israel. 1999 ⇒15,12106; 16,12336. ᴿProcGLM 21 (2001) 139-143 (*Thimmes, Pamela*); ProcGLM 21 (2001) 145-149 (*Spencer, John R.*); ProcGLM 21 (2001) 151-154 (*Duling, Dennis C.*)

11908   *Mikołajczak, Mieczysław* I classi socialmente deboli alla luce del 2 Sam 11-12 e 1 Re 21. CoTh 71A (2001) 15-22.

11909   **Navia Velasco, Carmina** La ciudad interpela a la biblia. Quito 2001, Verbo Divino 158 pp.

11910   *Penna, Romano* Cultura e inculturazione nella bibbia: una panoramica. Vangelo e inculturazione. 2001 <1988> ⇒193. 41-59;

11911   Confrontare per capire: l'importanza del comparativismo culturale nello studio delle origini cristiane. Vangelo e inculturazione. 2001 ⇒193. 11-40.

11912   *Pilch, John* A window into the biblical world: individuals? or stereotypes?. BiTod 39 (2001) 171-176.

11913   **Pleins, J. David** The social visions of the Hebrew Bible: a theological introduction. Westminster 2001, Knox xii: 592 pp. £30. 0-664-22175-0. ᴿNBl 82 (2001) 248-249 (*O'Brien, Mark A.*); ET 112 (2001) 254-256 (*Rodd, C.S.*).

11914   *Rohrbaugh, Richard L.* Gossip in the New Testament. ᶠMALINA, B.: BiblInterp 53: 2001 ⇒67. 239-259.

11915   **Sadler, Rodney** Can a Cushite change his skin?: an examination of race, ethnicity, and othering in the Hebrew Bible. Diss. Duke 2001 [Lev 18] [RTL 33,634].

11916   *Sardini, Fausto* Leggere la bibbia oggi. BeO 43 (2001) 257-258.

11917   **Schmeller, Thomas K.** Schulen im Neuen Testament?: zur Stellung des Urchristentums in der Bildungswelt seiner Zeit. Herders Biblische Studien 30: FrB 2001, Herder xi; 396 pp. €55. 3-451-27-621-6. Beitrag von *Christian Cebuli* zur johanneischen Schule; Bibl. 352-379.

11918   **Snyder, Graydon F.** Inculturation of the Jesus tradition: the impact of Jesus on Jewish and Roman cultures. 1999 ⇒15,12133; 16, 12355. ᴿTS 62 (2001) 157-158 (*Prendergast, Terrence*); Miss. 29 (2001) 360-361 (*Bergquist, James A.*).

11919   *Spieckermann, Hermann* Die Stimme des Fremden im Alten Testament. Gottes Liebe zu Israel. FAT 33: 2001 <1994> ⇒215. 84-99.

11920   **Stegemann, Ekkehard W.; Stegemann, Wolfgang** The Jesus movement: a social history of its first century. 1999 ⇒15,12141; 16,12361. [R]JThS 52 (2001) 306-308 (*Harvey, A.E.*); CBQ 63 (2001) 561-563 (*Osiek, Carolyn*); RBBras 18 (2001) 516-517;

11921   Historia social del cristianismo primitivo: los inicios en el judaísmi y las comunidades cristianas en el mundo mediterráneo. [T]*Montes, Miguel*: Agora 8: Estella 2001, Verbo Divino 615 pp.

11922   **Testart, A.** L'esclave, la dette et le pouvoir: études de sociologie comparative. P 2001, Errance 238 pp. 2-87772-213-9. Bibl. [REA 104,612s—Annequin, Jacques].

11923   **Theissen, Gerd** The religion of the earliest churches. 1999 ⇒15, 12143; 16,12365. [R]Pacifica 14 (2001) 96-99 (*Martin, John Hilary*); Interp. 55 (2001) 78, 80 (*Meeks, Wayne A.*); RExp 97 (2001) 130-131 (*May, David M.*); JECS 9 (2001) 413-414 (*Paffenroth, Kim*); RBLit 3 (2001) 483-485 (*Kerkeslager, Allen*);

11924   Die Religion der ersten Christen: eine Theorie des Urchristentums. Gü [2]2001, Kaiser 455 pp. 3-579-02623-2.

11925   **Thomsen, Marie-Louise; Cryer, Frederick H.** Biblical & pagan societies. Witchcraft & Magic in Europe 1: L 2001, Athlone xvii; 168 pp. £50/18. 0-485-89001-1/89101-8.

11926   **T'sinai'n, Luciano** Ascolta o Israele!...: sulla schiavitù e sull'amore romantico. Bo 2001, Pendragon 182 pp. 88-8342-081-0.

11927   **Walzer, Michael** Exilpolitik in der Hebräischen Bibel / Politics of exile in the Hebrew Bible. [E]*Drehsen, Volker*; [T]*Riebe, Alexandra*: Tü 2001, Mohr S. 129 pp. €29.65. 3-16-147543-7.

11928   *Warrior, Robert Allen* Canaanites, cowboys, and Indians: deliverance, conquest, and liberation theology today. The postmodern bible reader. 2001 <1999> ⇒287. 188-194.

11929   **Weber, Cornelia** Altes Testament und völkische Frage: der biblische Volksbegriff in der alttestamentlichen Wissenschaft der nationalsozialistischen Zeit, dargestellt am Beispiel von Johannes HEMPEL. FAT 28: 2000 ⇒16,12371. [R]OLZ 96 (2001) 547-552 (*Weippert, Manfred*); ThLZ 126 (2001) 917-919 (*Christophersen, Alf*).

11930   *Zerfaß, Rolf* Exodus—Exil—Diaspora: Glaubensgemeinschaften in der Fremde. WuA(M) 42 (2001) 65-69.

U5.3 Commercium, oeconomica

11931   *Briend, Jacques* Seehandel und Fischfang: zur Zeit des Alten Testaments. WUB 20 (2001) 74.

11932 *Brown, S.C.* Ancient Syria and the lapis lazuli trade. Canadian research on ancient Syria. 2001 ⇒581. 43-46.

11933 *Dandamayev, Muhammad A.* State taxes in Neo-Babylonian and Achaemenid Mesopotamia. ^MCAGNI, L., 1: SMDSA 61: 2001 ⇒15. 147-162.

11934 *Dercksen, J.G.* 'When we met in Ḫattuš': trade according to Old Assyrian texts from Alishar and Boğazköy. ^FVEENHOF, K. 2001 ⇒ 111. 39-66.

11935 *Faist, Betina* Die Handelsbeziehungen zwischen Assyrien und Anatolien in der zweiten Hälfte des 2. Jt.s. v. Chr. unter besonderer Berücksichtigung des Metallhandels. Anatolien. 2001⇒414. 53-66.

11936 **Faist, Betina I.** Der Fernhandel des assyrischen Reiches zwischen dem 14. und 11. Jh. v. Chr. AOAT 265: Müns 2001, Ugarit-Verlag xxii; 323 pp. 3-927120-79-0. Bibl. 255-293.

11937 *Gabrielsen, Vincent* Economic activity, maritime trade and piracy in the Hellenistic Aegean. RET 103 (2001) 219-240.

11938 ^E**Grimal, Nicolas-Christophe; Menu, Bernadette** Le commerce en Égypte ancienne. 1998 ⇒14,11446... 16,12379. ^RWO 31 (2000-2001) 194-196 (*Haring, Ben*).

11939 **Hikade, Thomas** Das Expeditionswesen im ägyptischen Neuen Reich: ein Beitrag zu Rohstoffversorgung und Außenhandel. Studien zur Archäologie und Geschichte Altägyptens 21: Heid 2001, Orientverlag xxxix; 275 pp. €50. 3-927552-36-4. Bibl. xiii-xxxviii.

11940 *Hoffner, Harry A.* Some thoughts on merchants and trade in the Hittite kingdom. ^FHAAS, V. 2001 ⇒39. 179-189.

11941 *Holladay, John S.* Toward a new paradigmatic understanding of long-distance trade in the ancient Near East: from the Middle Bronze II to Early Iron II—a sketch. ^FDION, P.-E. 2: JSOT.S 325: 2001 ⇒25. 136-198.

11942 **Jursa, Michael** Der Tempelzehnt in Babylonien vom siebenten bis zum dritten Jahrhundert v.Chr. AOAT 254: 1998 ⇒14,11447; 15, 12162. ^RBZ 45 (2001) 121-123 (*Leonhard, Clemens*); Or. 69 (2000) 332-336 (*MacGinnis, John*).

11943 *Meijer, Diederik J.W.* Long-distance trade: some remarks on the ancient Syrian economy. ^FVEENHOF, K. 2001 ⇒111. 325-340.

11944 *Precedo Lafuente, Manuel Jesús* El comercio y su regulación en el Antiguo Testamento. Comp. 46 (2001) 103-116.

11945 *Quesnel, Michel* Seehandel und Fischfang: zur Zeit des Alten Testaments. WUB 20 (2001) 74-75.

11946 *Renger, Johannes* When tablets talk business: reflections on Mesopotamian economic history and its contribution to a general historyof [sic!] Mesopotamia. Proceedings of the XLVe Rencontre Assyriologique, 1: 2001 ⇒577. 409-415.

11947 **Skaist, Aaron** The Old Babylonian loan contract: its history and
       geography. 1994 ⇒11/2,c847... 13,11291. ᴿRA 95 (2001) 87-89
       (*Lafont, Sophie*).
11948 *Stager, Lawrence E.* Port power in the Early and the Middle
       Bronze Age: the organization of maritime trade and hinterland pro-
       duction. ᴹEssE, D.: SAOC 59: 2001 ⇒28. 625-638.
11949 *Vargyas, Péter* Babylonian interest rates: weren't they annual?.
       ᴹCᴀɢɴɪ, L., 2: SMDSA 61: 2001 ⇒15. 1095-1105.
11950 **Young, Gary Keith** Rome's eastern trade: international commerce
       and imperial policy, 31 BC-AD 305. L 2001, Routledge xv; 303 pp.
       £50. 0-415-24219-3. Bibl. 281-298.
11951 **Zeeb, Frank** Die Palastwirtschaft in Altsyrien nach den spätaltba-
       bylonischen Getreidelieferlisten aus Alalah (Schicht VII). AOAT
       282: Müns 2001, Ugarit-Verlag xiv; 757 pp. 3-934628-06-0. Bibl.
       719-757.

U5.7 Nomadismus, *ecology*; Urbanismus

11952 **Berman, Morris** Wandering god: a study in nomadic spirituality.
       2000 ⇒16,12392. ᴿAmA 103/1 (2001) 265-66 (*Daly, Richard H.*).
11953 **Redman, Charles L.** Human impact on ancient environments.
       1999 ⇒15,12172. ᴿAJA 105 (2001) 109-110 (*Blitzer, Harriet*).

11954 **Boatwright, Mary T.** HADRIAN and the cities of the Roman Em-
       pire. 2000 ⇒16,12395. ᴿAJA 105 (2001) 374-375 (*Keay, Simon*).
11955 **Goddeeris, A.** Townsmen, farmers and nomads: the development
       of urban institutions in northern Babylonia during the early Old
       Babylonian period (ca. 2000-1800 BC). Diss. Kath. Univ. Leuven
       2001, ᴰ*Van Lerberghe, K.*
11956 **Herzog, Ze'ev** Archaeology of the city: urban planning in ancient
       Israel and its social implications. 1997 ⇒13,11313... 16,12402.
       ᴿBASOR 321 (2001) 80-85 (*Daviau, P.M. Michèle*).
11957 **Liebeschuetz, John H.W.G.** The decline and fall of the Roman
       city. Oxf 2001, OUP xvii; 479 pp. 0-19-815247-7. Bibl. 417-462.
11958 *Nefzger, Ben D.* The sociology of preindustrial cities;
11959 *Nissinen, Martti* City as lofty as heaven: Arbela and other cities in
       neo-Assyrian prophecy. Urbanism and prophecy. JSOT.S 330:
       2001 ⇒271. 159-171/172-209.
11960 **Novak, M.** Herrschaftsform und Stadtbaukunst. 1999 ⇒15,12180.
       ᴿBiOr 58 (2001) 453-456 (*Van de Mieroop, Marc*); BiOr 58 (2001)
       547-550 (*Van de Mieroop, Marc*).

11961 **Van de Mieroop, Marc** The ancient Mesopotamian city. 1997 ⇒ 13,11335... 16,12410. [R]RA 95 (2001) 186-190 (*Charpin, D.*).

11962 **Wheatley, Paul** The places where men pray together: cities in Islamic lands seventh through the tenth centuries. Ch 2001, Univ. of Chicago Pr. xvii; 572 pp. 0-226-89428-2. Bibl. 517-552.

U5.9 Demographia

11963 *Broshi, Magen* The population of Iron Age Palestine <1993>;

11964 Methodology of population estimates: the Roman-Byzantine period as a case study <1993>;

11965 The population of western Palestine in the Roman-Byzantine period <1979>. Bread, wine. 2001 ⇒131. 80-85/86-92/93-109.

11966 *Cels Saint-Hilaire, Janine* Citoyens romains, esclaves et affranchis: problèmes de démographie. REA 103 (2001) 443-479.

U6 Narrationes peregrinorum et exploratorum; *loca sancta*

11967 **Adinolfi, Marco; Bruzzone, Giovanni Battista S.** Viaggio del cuore in Terra Santa. 2000 ⇒16,12415. [R]RivBib 49 (2001) 345-348 (*Rolla, Armando*).

11968 **Bedini, Alessandro** Testimone a Gerusalemme: il pellegrinaggio di un fiorentino del Trecento. Ment. *Sigoli, Simone*: 1999 ⇒15, 12188. [R]Rivista di teologia dell'evangelizzazione 5/9 (2001) 189-190 (*Mirri, Luciana Maria*).

11969 *Carile, Antonio* Luoghi santi e pellegrinaggi nelle chiese di oriente. VIII Simposio di Efeso. Turchia 15: 2001 ⇒488. 201-212.

11970 **Chareion, S.** Les pèlerins de Jérusalem au Moyen Age. 2000 ⇒16, 12422. [R]Oecumenica Civitas 1 (2001) 127-128 (*Ceccoli, Guido Bellatti*).

11971 [E]**David, Abraham** In Zion and Jerusalem: the itinerary of Rabbi Moses BASOLA (1521-1523). 1999 ⇒15,12193. [R]JJS 52 (2001) 181-183 (*Wagstaff, Malcolm*); Henoch 23 (2001) 127-128 (*Borbone, Pier Giorgio*); RasIsr 67/3 (2001) 132-136 (*Di Segni, Noemi*). **Eng. & H.**

11972 **Gabashvili, Timothy** Pilgrimage to Mount Athos, Constantinople and Jerusalem, 1755-1759. [T]*Ebanoidze, Mzia; Wilkinson, John*: Richmond, Surrey, UK 2001, Curzon 224 pp. £45. 0-7007-1264-X. Ill. [RB 108,473].

11973 **Gomez-Géraud, Marie-Christine** Le crépuscule du grand voyage: les récits des pèlerins à Jérusalem (1485-1612). 1999 ⇒15,12196. ᴿRHE 96 (2001) 163-165 (*Sigal, Pierre André*).

11974 *Gomez-Géraud, Marie-Christine* Salubrité, fécondité: le sens du prodige naturel dans les récits des pèlerins à Jérusalem entre Moyen Âge et Renaissance. Représentations des maladies. 2001 ⇒ 482. 135-145.

11975 *Homs i Guzmán, Antoni* Un altra relació sobre Terra Santa: el llibre de la mia peregrinació: del pare Antoni FLUXÀ, OFM (1732-1736). Annales Sacra Tarraconensia 74 (2001) 131-155.

11976 *Hunt, E.D.* The date of the *Itinerarium Egeriae*. StPatr 38. 2001 ⇒ 553. 410-416.

11977 ᴱ**Invernizzi, Antonio** PIETRO della Valle: in viaggio per l'Oriente: le mummie, Babilonia, Persepoli. Mnème Documenti 1: T 2001, Orso 270 pp. €25.82. 35 fig.; 29 pl.

11978 **Lane, Edward William** Description of Egypt: notes and views in Egypt and Nubia, made during the years 1825, -26, -27, and -28: chiefly consisting of a series of descriptions and delineations of the monuments, scenery... ᴱ*Thompson, Jason*: 2000 ⇒16,12430. ᴿNEA 64 (2001) 219-220 (*Wilfong, T.G.*).

11979 ᴱ**Lisac, Josip; Šokota, Mirjana** Jakov PLETIKOSA: putovanje k Jerozolimu god. 1752 [Jakov Pletikosa: journey to Jerusalem in 1752]. 2000 ⇒16,12434. ᴿCCP 47 (2001) 276-278 (*Čoralić, Lovorka*).

11980 *Mariniello, Giuliana* Memoria biblica e letteratura di viaggio: The pylgrymage of Sir Richard GUYLFORDE to the Holy Land, A.D. 1506. ᴹCAGNI, L., 4: SMDSA 61: 2001 ⇒15. 1789-1810.

11981 ᴱ**Merle, Alexandra** Voyage au Levant: les observations de Pierre BELON du Mans de plusieiurs singularités et choses mémorables, trouvées en Grèce, Turquie, Judée, Égypte, Arabie et autres pays étrangers (1553). P 2001, Chandeigne 607 pp. €37.50.

11982 *Rossi de Gasperis, Francesco* De Jérusalem, quel enseignement tirer de la visite de Jean-Paul II aux pays de la bible?. VieCon 73 (2001) 379-395.

11983 **Stemberger, Günter** Jews and christians in the Holy Land: Palestine in the fourth century. ᵀ*Tuschling, Ruth*: 2000 ⇒16,12440. ᴿJThS 52 (2001) 903-905 (*Lieu, Judith*).

11984 ᵀ**Yule, Henry** The travels of Friar ODORIC. Italian Texts & Studies on Religion & Society: GR 2001, Eerdmans xi; 174 pp. 0-8028-4963-6.

U7 *Crucigeri*—The Crusades

11985 ^E**Balard, Michel; Kedar, Benjamin Z.; Riley-Smith, Jonathan** Dei gesta per Francos: crusade studies im honour of Jean RICHARD. Aldershot 2001, Ashgate xxiv; 434 pp. £55. ^RCRAI (2001/4) 1552-1554 (*Contamine, Philippe*) [EHR 118,174—Luscombe, David].

11986 *Croizy-Naquet, Catherine* Deux représentations de la troisième croisade: l'*Estoire de la guerre sainte* et la *Chronique d'Ernoul et de Bernard le Trésorier.* CCMéd 44 (2001) 313-327.

11987 *Friedman, Yvonne* Crusades and the Latin Kingdom: crossroads in historical research. Cathedra 100 (2001) 259-286 Sum. 401. **H.**

11988 **Hillenbrand, Carole** The crusades: Islamic perspectives. L 1999, Routledge 648 pp. $55. 0-41592-9148. ^RDA 57/1 (2001) 306-307 (*Möhring, Hannes*); PEQ 133 (2001) 200-203 (*Pringle, Denys*).

11989 **Madden, Thomas F.** A concise history of the Crusades. 1999 ⇒ 15,12218; 16,12449. ^RByZ 94 (2001) 730-32 (*Bliznyuk, Svetlana*).

11990 *Mayer, Hans Eberhard* Die Register der Secrète des Königreichs Jerusalem. DA 57/1 (2001) 165-170.

11991 **Pahlitzsch, Johannes** Graeci und Suriani im Palästina der Kreuzfahrerzeit: Beiträge und Quellen zur Geschichte des griechisch-orthodoxen Patriarchats von Jerusalem. BHSt 33; Ordensstudien 15: B 2001, Duncker & H. 452 pp. €68. 3-428-09884-6. ^RMuséon 114 (2001) 461-465 (*Schmidt, A.B.*).

11992 ^E**Phillips, Jonathan; Hoch, Martin** The second crusade: scope and consequences. Manchester 2001, Manchester U.P. xxi; 234 pp. £16. 0-7190-5711-6.

11993 **Pringle, Denys** The churches of the Crusader Kingdom of Jerusalem: a corpus: II, L-Z 1998 ⇒14,11505; 15,12221. Churches outside Tyre. ^RCHR 87 (2001) 91-92 (*Riley-Smith, Jonathan*); Antiquity 75 (2001) 636-638 (*Biddle, Martin*).

U8 **Communitates Terrae Sanctae**

11994 **Heyer, Friedrich** 2000 Jahre Kirchengeschichte des Heiligen Landes: Märtyrer, Mönche, Mirchenväter, Kreuzfahrer, Patriarchen, Ausgräber und Pilger. Studien zur Orientalischen Kirchengeschichte 11: 2000 ⇒16,12447. ^RCFr 71 (2001) 651-652 (*Vadakkekara, Benedict*).

11995 *Kushner, David* Osmanische Reaktionen auf die fremde Infiltration in Eretz Israel. ^FCARMEL, A.: 2001 ⇒17. 21-30.

11996   *Laird, Lance D.* Meeting Jesus again in the first place: Palestinian christians and the bible. Interp. 55 (2001) 400-412.

11997   *Levy, Ze'ev* Palästina im Denken von Moses HESS und Hermann COHEN: zwei antagonistische Anschauungen. ᶠCARMEL, A. 2001 ⇒17. 101-109.

11998   **Marcus, Amy Dockser** Tempelberg und Klagemauer: die Rolle der biblische Stätten im Nahost-Konflikt. W 2001, Deuticke 335 pp. €26.90. 3-216-30440-X.

11999   *Perry, Yaron* Die englisch-preußische Zusammenarbeit im Heiligen Land. ᶠCARMEL, A. 2001 ⇒17. 31-45.

12000   *Prior, Michael* Israel-Palestine: a challenge to theology. Faith in the millennium. 2001 ⇒540. 59-84.

12001   *Thalmann, Rita* Der Einfluß Frankreichs als Schutzmacht in Palästina im 19. Jahrhundert. ᶠCARMEL, A. 2001 ⇒17. 53-60.

12002   **Wagner, Donald E.** Dying in the land of promise: Palestinian christianity from Pentecost to 2000. L 2001, Melisende 299 pp. ᴿIslChr 27 (2001) 300-301 (*Fitzgerald, Michael L.*).

XX. Historia scientiae biblicae

Y1.0 History of exegesis: General

12003   *Bañeza Román, Celso* El "exemplum" de los personajes bíblicos en las listas de pecados capitales en la patrística y poetas medievales españoles. EE 76 (2001) 259-292.

12004   **Breck, John** Scripture in tradition: the bible and its interpretation in the Orthodox Church. Crestwood, NY 2001, St Vladimir's Sem. Pr. xi; 238 pp. $16. 0-88141-226-0 [ThD 50,64—Heiser, W.C.].

12005   **Clark, Elizabeth Ann** Reading renunciation: asceticism and scripture in early christianity. 1999 ⇒15,12231; 16,12467. ᴿCIR 51 (2001) 76-78 (*Edwards, M.J.*); AugSt 32 (2001) 133-135 (*Finn, Thomas M.*); JR 81 (2001) 280-282 (*Valantasis, Richard*); JEH 52 (2001) 342-344 (*Rousseau, Philip*); CCist 63/3 (2001) [37-40] (*Sheridan, Mark*); AnCl 70 (2001) 335-338 (*Savon, Hervé*).

12006   *Dassmann, Ernst* Die verstummte Klage bei den Kirchenvätern. JBTh 16 (2001) 135-151.

12007   **Dognini, Cristiano; Ramelli, Ilaria** Gli apostoli in India nella patristica e nella letteratura sanscrita. Mi 2001, Medusa 190 pp. ᴿOCP 67 (2001) 491-497 (*Poggi, V.*).

12008 **Fiedrowicz, Michael** Prinzipien der Schriftauslegung in der Alten Kirche. 1998 ⇒14,11522. [R]ThRv 97 (2001) 195-199 (*Hübner, Hans*).

12009 **Fiedrowicz, Michael** Apologie im frühen Christentum: die Kontroverse um den christlichen Wahrheitsanspruch in den ersten Jahrhunderten. 2000 ⇒16,12472. [R]ActBib 38 (2001) 50-1 (*Boada, J.*).

12010 **Gounelle, Rémi** La descente du Christ aux enfers: institutionnalisation d'une croyance. EAug, Antiquité 162: 2000 ⇒16,12473. [R]Apocrypha 12 (2001) 291-292 (*Iourovskaia, Z.*) [1 Pet 3,19-22].

12011 **Hamman, A.G.** Leer la biblia en la escuela de los Padres: de JUSTINO Mártir a San BUENAVENTURA. 1999 ⇒15,12240. [R]San Juan de la Cruz 27 (2001) 136-137 (*Parejo, Juan Hidalgo*).

12012 **Hargis, Jeffrey W.** Against the christians: the rise of early antichristian polemic. 1999 ⇒15,12241. [R]HeyJ 42 (2001) 505-507 (*Rousseau, Philip*).

12013 *Harrison, Nonna Verna* Women, human identity, and the image of god: Antiochene interpretations. JECS 9 (2001) 205-249.

12014 **Lubac, Henri de** Typologie, Allegorie, geistiger Sinn: Studien zur Geschichte der christlichen Schriftauslegung. 1999 ⇒15,12244; 16, 12478. [R]OrthFor 15 (2001) 63-66 (*Fenske, Wolfgang*).

12015 *Mayeski, Marie Anne* Quaestio disputata: catholic theology and the history of exegesis. TS 62 (2001) 140-153.

12016 **Merkt, Andreas** Das patristische Prinzip: eine Studie zur theologischen Bedeutung der Kirchenväter. SVigChr 58: Lei 2001, Brill xiii; 288 pp. 90-04-12221-4. Bibl. 259-277.

12017 *Miller, Peter N.* The "antiquarianization" of biblical scholarship and the London Polyglot Bible (1653-57). JHI 62 (2001) 463-482.

12018 **Moreschini, Claudio; Norelli, Enrico** Antologia della letteratura cristiana antica greca e latina. V.1, Da Paolo all'età constantiniana; v.2, Dal concilio di Nicea agli inizi del Medioevo. Letteratura cristiana antica, Strumenti: 1999 ⇒15,12246. [R]CivCatt 152/4 (2001) 629-631 (*Cremascoli, G.*).

12019 *Paciorek, Piotr* Les diverses interprétations patristiques des quatre vivants d'Ezéchiel 1,10 et de l'Apocalypse 4,6-7 jusqu'au XIIe siècle. Aug(L) 51 (2001) 151-218.

12020 *Panimolle, Salvatore* Il Dio giusto che giustifica Giustizia-giustificazione nei Padri della Chiesa. DSBP 29: 2001 ⇒308. 7-18.

12021 **Poffet, Jean-Michel** Los cristianos y la biblia. [T]*Martínez de Lapera, Abelardo*: Iglesia y sociedad 3: M 2001, BAC 125 pp. €8. 84-7914-522-6 [ActBib 39, 193—Boada, J.].

12022 **Reventlow, Henning Graf** Storia dell'interpretazione biblica, 1: dall'Antico Testamento a ORIGENE; 2: dalla tarda antichità alla fine

del medioevo; 3: rinascimento, riforma, umanesimo. 1999 ⇒15,
12257; 16,12488. [R]CivCatt 152/1 (2001) 433-435 (*Prato, G.L.*);

12023   Epochen der Bibelauslegung, 4: von der Aufklärung bis zum 20.
Jahrhundert. Mü 2001, Beck 448 pp. €44.90. 3-406-34988-9.
[R]LuThK 25 (2001) 210-211 (*Stolle, Volker*).

12024   *Ruzer, Serge* The cave of treasures on swearing by Abel's blood
and expulsion from paradise: two exegetical motifs in context.
JECS 9 (2001) 251-271.

12025   [E]**Sæbø, Magne** Hebrew Bible/Old Testament: the history of its
interpretation, 1: From the beginnings to the Middle Ages, 1:
Antiquity. 1996 ⇒16,12491. [R]SNTU.A 22 (1997) 221-226
(*Böhmisch, F.*).

12026   *Souletie, Jean-Louis; Gagey, Henri-Jérôme* La bible en ses sites.
La bible, parole adressée. 2001 ⇒323. 7-21.

12027   **Trevijano Etcheverria, Ramón** La Biblia en el cristianismo antiguo: Prenicenos, Gnósticos, Apócrifos. Introducción al estudio de
la Biblia 10: Estella (Navarra), 2001 Verbo Divino 488 pp. 84-715-
1-911-9.

12028   **Vallée, Gérard** The shaping of christianity: the history and literature of its formative centuries (100-800). 1999 ⇒15,12261; 16,
12496. [R]JECS 9 (2001) 411-413 (*Paffenroth, Kim*); SR 30 (2001)
121-123 (*Hegedus, Tim*).

Y1.4 *Patres apostolici et saeculi II*—First two centuries

12029   [T]**Ayán, Juan José** Padres apostólicos. 2000 ⇒16,12499.[R]San Juan
de la Cruz 27 (2001)142-143 (*Sánchez, Manuel Diego*).

12030   *Bergian, Silke-Petra* How to speak about early christian apologetic
literature?: comments on the recent debate. StPatr 36. 2001 ⇒553.
177-183.

12031   *Bradshaw, Paul* A paschal root to the anaphora of the *Apostolic
Tradition*?: a response to Enrico Mazza. StPatr 35. 2001 ⇒553.
257-265.

12032   *Campbell, Ted A.* Charismatic prophecy as loyal opposition in the
second-century church. AsbTJ 56/1 (2001) 77-86.

12033   *Caspar, Philippe* Aux origines d'une tradition: culture de vie, culture de mort chez les Pères apostoliques. NV 76/3 (2001) 55-65.

12034   *De Spirito, Giuseppe* Le décor d'une religion nouvelle: période
paléochrétienne. MoBi 139 (2001) 16-21 [BuBB 36,98].

12035   **Ehrman, Bart D.** After the New Testament: a reader in early christianity. 1999 ⇒15,12267. [R]AThR 83 (2001) 132-133 (*Smith,
James V.*).

12036 *Finkelpearl, Ellen* Pagan traditions of intertextuality in the Roman world. Mimesis. 2001 ⇒568. 78-90 [BuBB 36,92].

12037 *Garstad, Benjamin* THEOPHILUS of Antioch, PSEUDO-JUSTIN, and THALLUS' treatment of Moses. StPatr 36. 2001 ⇒533. 207-209.

12038 **Hausamann, Susanne** Alte Kirche: zur Geschichte und Theologie in der ersten vier Jahrhunderten, 1: Frühchristliche Schriftsteller: 'Apostolische Väter'—Häresien—Apologeten. Neuk 2001, Neuk ix; 339 pp. €24.90. 3-7887-1806-4.

12039 ^E**Lenzuni, Anna** Il cristianesimo delle origini: i padri apostolici. Letture patristiche 9: Bo 2001, EDB 150 pp. 88-10-42046-2.

12040 *Mimouni, Simon Claude* Les représentations historiographiques du christianisme au Ier siècle. L'historiographie de l'église. 2001 ⇒541. 67-90 [BuBB 36,101].

12041 *Riley, Gregory J.* Mimesis of classic ideals in the second century. Mimesis. 2001 ⇒568. 91-103 [BuBB 36,91].

12042 *Rizzi, Marco* Il sacrificio nella polemica dell'apologetica cristiana del II secolo. ASEs 18 (2001) 197-209.

12043 *Torti, Giovanni* Giustizia e giustificazione nei Padri apostolici. Giustizia-giustificazione nei Padri della Chiesa. DSBP 29: 2001 ⇒ 308. 19-26.

12044 **Trumbower, Jeffrey A.** Rescue for the dead: the posthumous salvation of non-christians in early christianity. Oxford Studies in Historical Theology: NY 2001, OUP xv; 206 pp. $45.

12045 **Wartelle, André** Bibliographie historique et critique de saint Justin philosophe et martyr et des Apologistes du IIe siècle: 1494-1994 (avec un supplément 1995-1998). P 2001, Lanore 1032 pp.

12046 *Winston, David* Creatio ex nihilo revisited: a reply to Jonathan Goldstein. Ancestral philosophy. 2001 <1986> ⇒228. 78-82.

12047 *Zocca, Elena* Sacrificio e martirio nella letteratura agiografica del II e III secolo. ASEs 18 (2001) 281-306.

12048 *Young, Frances* The *Apostolic Constitutions*: a methodological case-study. StPatr 36. 2001 ⇒533. 105-115.

12049 CLEMENS A.: *Kovacs, Judith L.* Divine pedagogy and gnostic teacher according to Clement of Alexandria. JECS 9 (2001) 3-25.

12050 **Schneider, Ulrich** Theologie als christliche Philosophie: zur Bedeutung der biblischen Botschaft im Denken des Clemens von Alexandria. AKG 73: 1999 ⇒15,12407. ^RZKG 112 (2001) 101-104 (*Wyrwa, Dietmar*).

12051 ^E**Van den Hoek, Annewies** Clément d'Alexandrie: les Stromates: Stromate IV. ^T*Mondésert, Claude*: SC 463: P 2001, Cerf 368 pp. €26. 2-204-06733-4. Bibl. 44-50.

12052 CLEMENS R.: *Bakke, Odd Magne* The rhetorical composition of the first letter of Clement. StPatr 36. 2001 ⇒533. 155-162.

12053 **Bakke, Odd Magne** "Concord and peace": a rhetorical analysis of the first letter of Clement with an emphasis on the language of unity and sedition. WUNT 2/143: Tü 2001, Mohr xv; 390 pp. €59. 3-16-147637-9. Bibl. 343-367.

12054 *Cirillo, Luigi* L'antipaolinismo nelle Pseudoclementine: un riesame della questione. Verus Israel. BCR 65: 2001 ⇒524. 280-303.

12055 **Côté, Dominique** Le thème de l'opposition entre Pierre et Simon dans les Pseudo-Clémentines. EAug.Antiquité 167: P 2001, Institut d'Études Augustiniennes viii, 300 pp. €49. 2-85121-188-9. Bibl. 277-295. ᴿPOC 51 (2001) 446-447 (*Attinger, D.*).

12056 *Faivre, Alexandre* "Préceptes laïcs (λαικα προσταγματα) et commandements humains (ἐνταλματα ἀνθρωπων)": les fondements scripturaires de 1 Clement 40,5. RevSR 75 (2001) 288-308.

12057 *Geoltrain, Pierre* Le roman pseudo-clémentin depuis les recherches d'Oscar CULLMANN. Le judéo-christianisme. 2001 ⇒484. 31-38. [BuBB 36,20].

12058 *Gerber, Albrecht* Some remarkable aspects of Clement of Rome's letter to the Corinthians. Prudentia 33 (2001) 130-148.

12059 *Gianotto, Claudio* Alcune riflessioni a proposito di *Recognitiones* I,27-71: la storia della salvezza. Le judéo-christianisme. 2001 ⇒ 484. 213-230 [BuBB 36,21].

12060 *Hauge, Eirin H.* Det kristne liv som "bekjennelse": en retorisk undersøkelse av 2. Klemensbrev. TTK 72 (2001) 273-293.

12061 *Jakab, Attila* Quand les chrétiens de Rome conseillaient ceux de Corinthe. Choisir Dec. (2001) 19-21,

12062 **Löhr, Hermut** Das zweite christliche Gebet: Untersuchungen zu 1 Clem 39 bis 61 in seinem literarischen, historischen und theologischen Kontext. Diss.-Habil. Bonn, ᴰ*Grässer, E.* [RTL 33,639].

12063 **Lona, Horacio E.** Der erste Clemensbrief. 1998 ⇒14,11563; 16, 12523. ᴿBZ 45 (2001) 153-155 (*Löhr, Hermut*); JThS 52 (2001) 339-342 (*Maier, H.O.*); CrSt 22 (2001) 218-220 (*Penna, Romano*).

12064 *Pani, Giancarlo* Convergenze tra Giovanni e la *Prima Clementis*. VIII Simposio di Efeso. 2001 ⇒488. 115-132 [Rom 16];

12065 Il concetto di ἐπιείκεια nella struttura della *Prima Clementis*. StPatr 36. 2001 ⇒553. 282-292.

12066 ᵀ**Peretto, Elio** Clemente Romano: lettera ai Corinzi. SOCr 23: 1999 ⇒15,12288. ᴿRdT 42 (2001) 300-303 (*Cattaneo, Enrico*).

12067 *Pouderon, Bernard* Aux origines du roman clémentin: prototype païen, refonte judéo-hellénistique, remaniement chrétien. Le judéo-christianisme. 2001 ⇒484. 231-256 [BuBB 36,21].

12068 **Schmitt, Tassilo** Paroikie und Oikoumene: sozial- und mentalitäts-geschichtliche Untersuchungen zum 1. Clemensbrief. BZNT 110: B 2001, De Gruyter 161 pp. 3-11-017257-7.

12069 [T]**Schneider, André** Les Reconnaissances du pseudo-Clément: ro-man chrétien des premiers siècles. [E]*Cirillo, Luigi* Apocryphes, (L'Aelac) 10: 1999 ⇒15,12289; 16,12526. [R]Apocrypha 12 (2001) 306-307 (*Roessli, J.-M.*).

12070 [T]**Spada, Domenico; Salachias, Dimitrios** Costituzioni dei Santi Apostoli per mano di Clemente. Grandi Opere: R 2001. Urbaniana Univ. Pr. 320 pp. €28.41.

12071 *Verheyden, Jos* De christelijke gemeente in Korinte volgens de eer-ste brief van Clemens. Vroegchristelijke gemeenten. 2001 ⇒460. 68-83.

12072 DIDACHE: *Del Verme, Marcello* Did. 16 e la cosiddetta 'Apocalitti-ca giudaica'. Orpheus 22 (2001) 39-76;

12073 Didaché e origini cristiane: una bibliografia per lo studio della Didaché nel contesto del giudaismo cristiano. VetChr 38 (2001) 5-39, 223-245.

12074 **Niederwimmer, Kurt** The Didache: a commentary. Hermeneia: 1998 ⇒14,11570... 16,12529. [R]RTL 32 (2001) 109-111 (*Auwers, Jean-Marie*); JBL 119 (2000) 584-586 (*Hagner, Donald A.*).

12075 *Novo, Alfonso* La Didakhé y los evangelios canónicos: algunas con-sideraciones a partir del uso de κύριος. Comp. 46 (2001) 297-301.

12076 *Rordorf, Willy* La *Didachè* en 1999. StPatr 36. 2001 ⇒553. 293-299.

12077 **Schaff, Philip** The oldest church manual. L 2001 <1885>, Pendle-burys 301 pp. £20. 1-9007-9694-5. Fascimile ed.

12078 *Van de Sandt, Huub* Een gemeenschap op zoek naar haar identiteit: de gemeente van de Didachè. Vroegchristelijke gemeenten. 2001 ⇒460. 178-192.

12079 [T]**Visonà, Giuseppe** Didaché: insegnamento degli apostoli. 2000 ⇒ 16,12531. [R]RdT 42 (2001) 621-625 (*Cattaneo, Enrico*); VetChr 38 (2001) 195-196 (*Micunco, Giuseppe*); Lat. 67 (2001) 353-355 (*La-iti, Giuseppe*); ASEs 18 (2001) 682-686 (*Menestrina, Giovanni*).

12080 *Fonrobert, Charlotte Elisheva* The Didascalia Apostolorum: a mishnah for the disciples of Jesus. JECS 9 (2001) 483-509.

12081 [T]**Lona, Horacio E.** An Diognet. Kommentar zu frühchristlichen Apologeten 8: FrB 2001, Herder 378 pp. €104.81. 3-451-27679-8.

12082 HERMAS: *Durante Mangoni, Maria Beatrice* Comunione escatologica e comunità terrena nel Pastore di Erma. RdT 42 (2001) 39-54.

12083 *Fredrikson, Nadia Ibrahim* L'esprit saint et les esprits mauvais dans le Pasteur d'Hermas: sources et prolongements. VigChr 55 (2001) 262-280.

12084 *Lusini, Gianfrancesco* Nouvelles recherches sur le texte du Pasteur d'Hermans. Apocrypha 12 (2001) 79-97.

12085 **Osiek, Carolyn A.** The Shepherd of Hermas: a commentary. ᴱ*Köster, Helmut* 1999 ⇒15,12303; 16,12535. ᴿBiblInterp 9 (2001) 90-93 (*Alexander, James S.*); JThS 52 (2001) 342-345 (*Maier, H.O.*); RBLit 3 (2001) 488-490 (*Snyder, Graydon F.*).

12086 **Schneider, Athanasius** "Propter sanctam ecclesiam suam": die Kirche als Geschöpf, Frau und Bau im Bussunterricht des Pastor Hermae. SEAug 67: 1999 ⇒15,12304. ᴿJThS 52 (2001) 346-348 (*Hall, Stuart G.*).

12087 HIPPOLYTUS: *Bradshaw, Paul* The problems of a new edition of the *Apostolic Tradition*. Comparative liturgy. 2001 ⇒545. 613-622.

12088 *Markschies, Christoph* Neue Forschungen zur sogenannten 'Traditio Apostolica'. Comparative liturgy 12 (2001) 583-598.

12089 ᵀ**Stewart-Sykes, Alistair** Hippolytus: On the apostolic tradition. St Vladimir's Seminary Press Popular Patristics Series: Crestwood, NY 2001, St. Vladimir's Seminary Pr. 222 pp. $15/£10. 0-88141-233-3. Bibl. 207-214.

12090 IGNATIUS A.: *Bergamelli, Ferdinando* Dal Padre al Padre: il Padre come principio e termine del Cristo e del cristiano in Ignazio di Antiochia. StPatr 36. 2001 ⇒553. 168-176.

12091 *Hill, C.E.* Ignatius and the apostolate: the witness of Ignatius to the emergence of christian scripture. StPatr 36. 2001 ⇒553. 226-248.

12092 *Jefford, Clayton, N.* Conflict at Antioch: Ignatius and the *Didache* at odds. StPatr 36. 2001 ⇒553. 262-269.

12093 **Lechner, Thomas** Ignatius adversus VALENTINIANOS?: chronologische und theologiegeschichtliche Studien zu den Briefen des Ignatius von Antiochien. SVigChr 47: 1999 ⇒15,12308. ᴿSEÅ 66 (2001) 229-230 (*Isacson, Mikael*).

12094 *Norelli, Enrico* Ignazio di Antiochia combatte veramente dei cristiani giudaizzanti?. Verus Israel. BCR 65: 2001 ⇒524. 220-264.

12095 ᵀ**Rius-Camps, J.** Ignasi d'Antioquia: cartes. Barc 2001, Metge 2 vols; 266 + 312 pp.

12096 ᴱ**Urbán Fernandez, Angel C.** Ignatii epistularum concordantia. Concordantia in Patres Apostolicos 6: Hildesheim 2001, Olms 595 pp. 3-487-11322-8.

12097 *Vogt, Hermann J.* Sind die Ignatius-Briefe antimarkionitisch beeinflußt?. ThQ 181 (2001) 1-19.

12098 Iʀᴇɴᴀᴇᴜs: *Behr, John* Irenaeus on the word of God. StPatr 36. 2001 ⇒533. 163-167.

12099 *Bingham, D. Jeffrey* Irenaeus's reading of Romans 8. SBL.SP 2001. SBL.SPS 40: 2001 ⇒494. 131-150;

12100 Knowledge and love in Irenaeus of Lyons. StPatr 36. 2001 ⇒553. 184-199.

12101 ᴱ**Brox, Norbert** Adversus haereses: Gegen die Häresien, V. Fontes christiani 8/5: FrB 2001, Herder 310 pp. €34. 3-451-22129-2/-9.

12102 *Ferguson, Thomas C.K.* The rule of the truth and Irenaean rhetoric in book 1 of Against Heresies. VigChr 55 (2001) 356-375.

12103 *Gagliardi, Mauro* Un'ipotesi su Adversus haereses III 22,4. VetChr 38 (2001) 287-292.

12104 *Guevin, Benedict M.* The natural law in Irenaeus of Lyons' *Adversus Haereses*: a metaphysical or a soteriological reality?. StPatr 36. 2001 ⇒553. 222-225.

12105 *Holzhausen, Jens* Irenäus und die valentianische Schule: zur Praefatio von Adv. Haer. 1. VigChr 55 (2001) 341-355.

12106 (*a*) *Jacobsen, Anders-Chr. Lund* The philosophical argument in the teaching of Irenaeus on the resurrection of the flesh. StPatr 36. 2001 ⇒553. 256-261;
(*b*) *Kriegel, Nicolas* La figure d'Abraham chez Irénée de Lyon. Connaissance des Pères de l'Église 82 (2001) 57-60.

12107 **Meijering, Eginhard** Irenaeus: grondlegger van het christelijk denken. Amst 2001, Balans 232 pp. €17.92. 90-5018-453-7.

12108 **Osborn, Eric Francis** Irenaeus of Lyons. NY 2001, CUP xv; 307 pp. $65. 0-521-80006-4.

12109 (*a*) **Polanco Fermandois, Rodrigo** El concepto de profecía en la teología de San Ireneo. 1999 ⇒15,12551. ᴿLat. 67 (2001) 375-376 (*Pasquato, Ottorino*); Burg. 42 (2001) 634-635 (*Guerra Gómez, Manuel*);
(*b*) ᵀ**Romero-Pose, Eugenio** Ireneo de Lión: Demostración de la predicación apostólica. Fuentes Patrísticas—Textos 2: M ²2001, Ciudad N. 262 pp. 84-89651-96-5. Introd... notas (extractadas de la obra de *Antonio Orbe*). Bibl. 39-48.

12110 *Schüngel, Paul* Das Valentinreferat des Irenäus von Lyon (Haer I 11,1). VigChr 55 (2001) 376-405.

12111 JUSTIN: *Boyarin, Daniel* Justin Martyr invents Judaism. ChH 70 (2001) 427-461.

12112 ᴱ**D'Anna, Alberto** PSEUDO-GIUSTINO: sulla resurrezione: discorso cristiano del II secolo. Letteratura cristiana antica, testi: Brescia 2001, Morcelliana 328 pp. €18.08. 88-372-1832-X. Pres. *Enrico Norelli.*

12113 *Heid, Stefan* Iustinus Martyr I. RAC 19. 2001 ⇒660. 801-847.

12114 **Heimgartner, Martin** Pseudojustin—über die Auferstehung: Text und Studie. PTS 54: B 2001, De Gruyter xi; 362 pp. €98. 3-11-016-903-7. Bibl. 316-337.

12115 *Horner, Timothy J.* Listening to Trypho: uncovering the subtext of Justin's *Dialogue*. StPatr 36. 2001 ⇒553. 249-255.

12116 **Horner, Timothy J.** "Listening to Trypho": Justin Martyr's Dialogue reconsidered. Contributions to Biblical Exegesis and Theology 28: Lv 2001, Peeters (4) 222 pp. 90-429-1040-2. Bibl. 213-22.

12117 *Langella, Alfonso* Il vangelo di Maria in Giustino Martire. Theotokos 9 (2001) 329-352.

12118 *Meunier, Bernard* Le clivage entre juifs et chrétiens vu par Justin (vers 150). Le judaïsme à l'aube de l'ère chrétienne. LeDiv 186: 2001 ⇒450. 333-344.

12119 **Misiarczyk, Leszek** Il Midrash nel dialogo con Trifone di Giustino martire. 1999 ⇒15,12318; 16,12551. ᴿEE 76 (2001) 480-481 (*Uribarri, Gabino*).

12120 *Parvis, Paul* The textual tradition of Justin's *Apologies*: a modest proposal. StPatr 36. 2001 ⇒553. 54-60.

12121 *Rajak, Tessa* Talking at Trypho: christian apologetic as anti-Judaism in Justin's *Dialogue with Trypho the Jew*. The Jewish dialogue. AGJU 48: 2001 <1999> ⇒199. 511-533.

12122 *Riedweg, Christoph* Iustinus Martyr II (Pseudo-justinische Schriften). RAC 19. 2001 ⇒660. 848-873.

12123 **Rudolph, Anette** 'Denn wir sind jenes Volk...': die neue Gottesverehrung in Justins Dialog mit dem Juden Tryphon in historisch-theologischer Sicht. 1999 ⇒15,12320; 16,12553. ᴿCrSt 22 (2001) 476-478 (*Visonà, Giuseppe*); Salm. 48 (2001) 553-557 (*Trevijano, Ramón*).

12124 *Rudolph, Anette* Die Judenchristen in Justins Dialog mit Tryphon. StPatr 36. 2001 ⇒553. 300-306.

12125 **Sanchez, Sylvain J.G.** Justin apologiste chrétien: travaux sur le *Dialogue avec Tryphon* de Justin Martyr. CRB 50: 2000 ⇒16, 12554. ᴿREAug 47 (2001) 171-174 (*Pouderon, Bernard*).

12126 *Sánchez, Sylvain J.G.* Analyse littéraire du *Dialogue avec Tryphon* de Justin Martyr. RevAg 42 (2001) 1077-1114;

12127 Du bénéfice du De Resurrectione. RB 108 (2001) 73-100;

12128 Problèmes historiques du *Dialogue avec Tryphon* de Justin Martyr. RevAg 42 (2001) 653-714;

12129 La tradition du texte du *Dialogue avec Tryphon* de Justin Martyr, 1. RevAg 42 (2001) 221-262.

12130 *Widdicombe, Peter* Justin Martyr's apophaticism. StPatr 36. 2001 ⇒553. 313-319.

12131 MARCION: *McGowan, Andrew* Marcion's love of creation. JECS 9 (2001) 295-311.

12132 POLYCARP: ^T**Buschmann, Gerd** Das Martyrium des Polykarp. KAV 6: 1998 ⇒14,11592... 16,12559. ^RVigChr 55 (2001) 101-104 (*Dehandschutter, Boudewijn*); JBL 120 (2001) 585-87 (*Weidmann, Frederick W.*); RBLit 3 (2001) 485-488 (*Weidmann, Frederick W.*).

12133 TATIAN: *Petersen, William L.* Tatian (ca. 125-ca. 185). TRE 32. 2001 ⇒665. 655-659.

Y1.6 Origenes

12134 ^E**Balthasar, Hans Urs von** Origen: spirit and fire: a thematic anthology of his writings. ^T*Daly, Robert J.*: E 2001 <1984>, Clark xviii; 416 pp. £17.60. 0-567-08771-9. repr. [IThQ 68,88s—Madden, Nicholas].

12135 *Bendinelli, Guido* Origene e il descensus ad inferos. DT(P) 104 (2001) 183-210 [1 Pet 3,18-19].

12136 **Bendinelli, Guido** Il commentario a Matteo di Origene: l'ambito della metodologia scolastica dell'antichità. SEAug 60: 1997 ⇒14, 11594. ^RJThS 52 (2001) 890-892 (*Edwards, M.J.*).

12137 ^E**Bienert, Wolfgang A.; Kühneweg, Uwe** Origeniana Septima: Origenes in den Auseinandersetzungen des 4. Jahrhunderts. BEThL 137: 1999 ⇒15,450. ^REThL 77 (2001) 227-228 (*Verheyden, J.*); CDios 214 (2001) 518-519 (*Gutiérrez, J.*); CrSt 22 (2001) 478-488 (*Pazzini, Domenico*).

12138 *Buchinger, Harald* Ex. 12,11.27.48 LXX bei Origenes: Textkritik und Antijudaismus. StPatr 34. 2001 ⇒533. 285-293 [Ex 12,11; 12,27; 12,48].

12139 *Clements, Ruth* (Re)Constructing Paul: Origen's reading of Romans in *Peri Archōn*. SBL.SP 2001. SBL.SPS 40: 2001 ⇒494. 151-174.

12140 *Cocchini, Francesca* Giustizia-giustificazione in Origene. Giustizia-giustificazione nei Padri della Chiesa. DSBP 29: 2001 ⇒308. 176-195;

12141 L'"oggi" biblico: l'interpretazione origeniana di una scansione del tempo. SMSR 67 (2001) 221-227.

12142 *Dively Lauro, Elizabeth A.* Reconsidering Origen's two higher senses of scriptural meaning: identifying the psychic and pneumatic senses. StPatr 34. 2001 ⇒553. 306-317.

12143 *Dorival, Gilles* Le regard d'Origène sur les judéo-chrétiens. Le judéo-christianisme. 2001 ⇒484. 257-288 [BuBB 36,137].

12144 [ET]**Doutreleau, Louis** Origène: homélies sur les Nombres, 2. SC 442: 1999 ⇒15,12345; 16,12575. [R]JThS 52 (2001) 357-9 (*Meredith, Anthony*); REAug 47 (2001) 174-175 (*Pouderon, Bernard*);

12145 Origène: homélies sur les Nombres, 3: Homélies XX-XXVIII. SC 461: P 2001, Cerf 396 pp. €39.03. 2-204-06708-3. Texte latin de *W.A. Baehrens.* [R]EstTrin 35 (2001) 647-648 (*Silanes, N.*).

12146 [E]**Égron, Agnès, Soeur** Origène: exégèse spirituelle, 2: Exode et Lévitique. 2000 ⇒16,12576. [R]Brot. 153 (2001) 743-744 (*Silva, I. Ribeiro da*);

12147 3: les Nombres. FoiViv 418: P 2001, Cerf 184 pp. 2-204-06519-6. Préf. *J.-M. Poffet*; textes choisis et présentés par Soeur A. Egron.

12148 *Fédou, Michel* L'historien SOCRATE et la controverse origéniste du IVe siècle. L'historiographie de l'église. 2001 ⇒541. 271-280 [BuBB 36,102].

12149 *Heine, Ronald E.* The Prologues of Origen's Pauline commentaries and the *Schemata Isagogica* of ancient commentary literature. StPatr 36. 2001 ⇒553. 421-439.

12150 **Hombergen, Daniel** The second Origenist controversy: a new perspective on CYRIL of Scythopolis' monastic biographies as historical sources for sixth-century Origenism. StAns 132: R 2001, Ateneo S. Anselmo 448 pp.

12151 *Johnson, Allan E.* Allegorical narrative and evangelism: 'three days' journey' in Origen's homilies on Exodus. StPatr 36. 2001 ⇒ 553. 440-444.

12152 *Kingsmill, Edmée* Origen's *Commentary on the Song of Songs*: is there a Hebrew word behind his exposition at 1:2?;

12153 *Kuyama, Michihiko* Origen and Esther—a reflection on the 'Anti-Jewish' argument in early christian literature. StPatr 34. 2001 ⇒ 553. 420-423/424-435.

12154 **Lekkas, Georgios** Liberté et progrès chez Origène. Monothéismes et philosophie: Turnhout 2001, Brepols 277 pp. 2-503-50655-0. Bibl. 257-265.

12155 *Letellier, Joël* Le contact avec la parole de Dieu: force de guérison et de salut, dans l'oeuvre d'Origène. VS 741 (2001) 625-648.

12156 *Lust, J.* Colloquium Origenianum Octavum. EThL 78 (2001) 298-299. Pisa, 27-31 Aug. 2001.

12157 ^E**Marcovich, Miroslav** Origenes: Contra Celsum libri VIII. SVigChr 54: Lei 2001, Brill xxv; 637 pp. 90-04-11976-0. Bibl. xvii-xxiii.

12158 Perrone, Lorenzo Les commentaires d'Origène sur *Jean* et *Matthieu*: tradition, innovation et système. POC 51 (2001) 35-69.

12159 *Pouderon, Bernard* Origène, le Pseudo-Clément et la structure des Periodoi Petrou. Apocrypha 12 (2001) 29-51.

12160 *Rickenmann, Agnell* La dottrina di Origene sui sensi spirituali e la sua ricezione in Hans Urs VON BALTHASAR. RTLu 6 (2001) 155-68.

12161 ^E**Salvesen, Alison** Origen's Hexapla and fragments: papers presented at the Rich Seminar on the Hexapla, Oxford Centre for Hebrew and Jewish Studies, August 1994. TSAJ 58: 1998 ⇒14, 399... 16,12592. ^RNT 43 (2001) 400-402 (*Baarda, Tjitze*).

12162 *Simonetti, Manlio* Origene e le moltiplicazioni dei pani. VetChr 38 (2001) 85-101 [Mt 14,15-21].

12163 *Stewart, Columba* Origen on the journey to the promised land. BiTod 39 (2001) 27-32 [Num 33].

12164 **Vogt, Hermann Josef** Origenes als Exeget. ^E*Geerlings, Wilhelm*: 1999 ⇒15,12371; 16,12595. ^RThPh 76 (2001) 276-278 (*Voderholzer, R.*); ThRv 97 (2001) 405-406 (*Markschies, Christoph*).

12165 *Weinandy, Thomas* Origen and the suffering of God. StPatr 36. 2001 ⇒553. 456-460.

Y1.8 Tertullianus

12166 **Alexandre, J.** Une chair pour la gloire: l'anthropologie réaliste et mystique de Tertullien. ThH 115: P 2001, Beauchesne 554 pp. 2-7010-1422-0.

12167 ^T**Braun, René** Tertullien: contre Marcion tome IV. ^E*Moreschini, Claudio*: SC 456: 2001 545 pp. €47.26. 2-204-06585-4. Texte critique par *C. Moreschini*, introd. trad. et comm. par *René Braun*.

12168 *Dunn, Geoffrey D.* The ancestry of Jesus according to Tertullian: *Ex David per Mariam*. StPatr 36. 2001 ⇒553. 349-355.

12169 *Fernández E., Samuel* La salvación sin mediaciones según MARCIÓN y la respuesta de Tertuliano. TyV 42 (2001) 50-73.

12170 **Leal, Jerónimo** La antropología de Tertuliano: estudios de los tratados polémicos de los años 207-212 d.C. SEAug 76: R 2001, Institutum Patristicum Augustinianum 220 pp. 88-7961-017-1 [RTL 34, 382—Alexandre, J.].

12171 *Livermore, Paul* Reasoning with unbelievers and the place of the scriptures in Tertullian's Apology. AsbTJ 56/1 (2001) 61-75.

12172   *Lombino, Vincenzo* La giustizia nei primi apologeti latini. Giustizia-giustificazione nei Padri della Chiesa. DŞBP 29: 2001 ⇒308. 110-175.

12173   *Ruggiero, Fabio* La testimonianza di Tertulliano, "Apologeticum" 9,2-4 sul sacrificio dei bambini nell'ambito del culto di Saturno. ASEs 18 (2001) 307-333.

12174   *Schwarzkopf, Matthias* Tertullian als Beispiel für die Rezeption neutestamentlicher "Pädagogik" bei den Kirchenvätern. Zeitschrift für Pädagogik und Theologie 53 (2001) 162-169.

12175   ^{ET}**Vicastillo, Salvador** Tertulliano: 'Prescripciones' contra todas las herejías. Fuentes Patrísticas 14: M 2001, Ciudad Nueva 329 pp.

Y2.0 *Patres graeci*—**The Greek Fathers**—*in ordine alphabetico*

12176   *Cremaschi, Lisa* Lo spirito filocalico nella tradizione orientale. La bellezza. PSV 44: 2001 ⇒240. 193-203.

12177   *Girardi, Mario* L'uomo immagine somigliante di Dio (Gen 1,26-27) nell'esegesi dei Cappadoci. VetChr 38 (2001) 293-314.

12178   **Harnack, Karl Gustav Adolf von** Protokollbuch der Kirchenväter-Kommission der Preußischen Akademie der Wissenschaften 1897-1928. ^E*Rebenich, Stefan; Markschies, Christoph*: Berlin-Brandenburgische Akademie der Wissenschaften, Akademieunternehmen griechische christliche Schriftsteller: B 2000, De Gruyter (6) 173 pp. 3-11-016764-6. Diplomatische Umschrift: *Stefan Rebenich*, Einleitung, kommentierende Anmerkungen: *C. Markschies*.

12179   **Laporte, Jean** Les pères de l'église, 1: les pères latins, 2: les pères grecs. Initiations aux pères de l'église: P 2001, Cerf 311 + 279 pp.

12180   **Meredith, Anthony** The Cappadocians. 1995 ⇒11/2,g300. ^RArchaeus 5 (2001) 147-150 (*Neamţu, Mihail*).

12181   *Orlov, Andrei; Golitzin, Alexander* "Many lamps are lightened from the one": paradigms of the transformational vision in Macarian homilies. VigChr 55 (2001) 281-298.

12182   APOLLINARIUS: *McCarthy Spoerl, Kelley* Apollinarius on the Holy Spirit. StPatr 37. 2001 ⇒553. 571-592.

12183   ATHANASIUS: **Bouter, P.F.** Athanasius van Alexandrië en zijn uitleg van de Psalmen: een onderzoek naar de hermeneutiek en theologie van een psalmverklaring uit de vroege kerk. Diss. Utrecht, ^D*Van den Broek, R.*: Zoetermeer 2001, Boekencentrum 381 pp. €29.50. 90-239-1151-2.

12184   *Brakke, David* Jewish flesh and christian spirit in Athanasius of Alexandria. JECS 9 (2001) 453-481.

12185 *Ernest, James D.* Athanasian scripture citations;

12186 *Gonnet, Dominique* The salutary action of the Holy Spirit as proof of his divinity in Athanasius' *Letters to Serapion.* StPatr 36. 2001 ⇒553. 502-508./509-513.

12187 *Kannengiesser, Charles* L'*Histoires des Ariens* d'Athanase d'Alexandrie: une historiographie de combat au IVe siècle. L'historiographie de l'église. 2001 ⇒541. 127-138 [BuBB 36,102].

12188 *Leemans, J.* Thirteeen years of Athanasius research (1985-1998): a survey and bibliography. SE 39 (2000) 105-217.

12189 **Ng, Nathan Kwok-kit** The spirituality of Athanasius: a key for proper understanding of this important Church Father. EHS.T 733: Bern 2001, Lang 392 pp. 3-906767-99-X. Bibl. 357-383.

12190 BASILIUS: (*a*) **Girardi, Mario** Basilio di Cesarea interprete della Scrittura. QVetChr 26: 1998 ⇒14,11642... 16,12618. [R]JThS 52 (2001) 368-369 (*Vaggione, Richard Paul*); Aevum 75 (2001) 216-217 (*Bernardini, Anna Penati*); Orpheus 22 (2001) 362-366 (*Giardina, Alessandra*).
(*b*) *Filoramo, Giovanni* Giustizia-giustificazione in Basilio di Cesarea. Giustizia-giustificazione nei Padri della Chiesa. DSBP 29: 2001 ⇒308. 205-216.

12191 [E]**Schmidt, Thomas S.** Basilii Minimi in Gregorii Nazianzeni orationem XXXVIII commentarii. CChr.SG 46; Corpus Nazianzenum 13: Turnhout 2001, Brepols lxxxiii; 196 pp. 2-503-40461-8.

12192 CHRYSOSTOM: *Amirav, Hagit* Exegetical models and Chrysostomian homiletics: the example of Gen. 6.2;

12193 *Bady, Guillaume* La méthode exégétique du commentaire inédit sur les Proverbes attribué à Jean Chrysostome;

12194 *Broc, Catherine* La femme de Job dans la prédication de Jean Chrysostome. StPatr 37. 2001 ⇒553. 311-318/319-327/396-403.

12195 *Castagno, Adele* Monaci I giudaizzanti di Antiochia: bilancio e nuove prospettive di ricerca. Verus Israel. 2001 ⇒524. 304-338.

12196 [T]**Ciarlo, Domenico** Giovanni Crisostomo: commento a Isaia, omelie su Ozia. CTePa 162: R 2001, Città Nuova 338 pp. 88-311-3162-1. Bibl. 41-44.

12197 *Hill, Robert C.* Chrysostom on the obscurity of the Old Testament. OCP 67 (2001) 371-383;

12198 St John Chrysostom's homilies on Hannah. SVTQ 45 (2001) 319-338 [1 Sam 2,1-2];

12199 Two Antiochenes on the Psalms. StPatr 34. 2001 ⇒553. 353-369 [Theodoret].

12200   *Loader, James Alfred* Chrysostomos, Jesaja und die Antiochenische Sicht der Heiligen Schrift. Begegnung mit Gott. Wiener alttestamentliche Studien 3: 2001 ⇒175. 245-256.

12201   *Miranda, Americo* La resurrezione dei corpi nel Crisostomo (in 1 Cor 15): una nuova percezione della realtà "corporea" tra IV e V secolo. Ang. 78 (2001) 387-404.

12202   *Mitchell, Margaret M.* Reading rhetoric with patristic exegetes: John Chrysostom on Galatians. [F]BETZ, H.: 2001 ⇒5. 333-355.

12203   *Pradels, Wendy; Brändle, Rudolf; Heimgartner, Martin* Das bisher vermisste Textstück in Johannes Chrysostomus, Adversus Judaeos, Oratio 2. ZAC 5 (2001) 23-49.

12204   *Soler, Emmanuel* L'utilisation de l'histoire de l'église d'Antioche au IVe siècle par Jean Chrysostome dans les débuts de sa prédication. L'historiographie de l'église. 2001 ⇒541. 499-509 [BuBB 36, 103].

12205   *Thurén, Lauri* John Chrysostom as a rhetorical critic: the hermeneutics of an early father. BiblInterp 9 (2001) 180-218.

12206   *Torrance, Iain* 'God as physician': ecclesiology, sin and forgiveness in the preaching of St John Chrysostom. Le péché. [E]Doré, Joseph: P 2001, Cerf. 229-246 [BuBB 36,131].

12207   *Wallraff, Martin* Le conflit de Jean Chrysostome avec la cour chez les historiens ecclésiastiques grecs. L'historiographie de l'église. 2001 ⇒541. 361-370 [BuBB 36,131].

12208   *Tse, Mary W.* συγκατάβασις and ἀκρίβεια—the warp and woof of Chrysostom's hermeneutics a study based on Chrysostom's Genesis homilies. Jian Dao 15 (2001) 1-17 Sum. 17.

12209   *Zincone, Sergio* Giustizia-giustificazione nei Padri antiocheni. Giustizia-giustificazione nei Padri della Chiesa. DSBP 29. 2001 ⇒ 308. 217-224.

12210   CYRIL: [E]**Toniolo, C.** Ferrari Cyrilliana in psalmos: i frammenti del commento ai salmi di Cirillo di Alessandria nel codice Laudiano greco 42. 2000 ⇒16,12633. [R]VetChr 38 (2001) 206-207 (*Di Stasio, Rocco*).

12211   *Cassel, J. David* Key principles in Cyril of Alexandria's exegesis. StPatr 37. 2001 ⇒553. 413-420.

12212   DIONYSIUS: *Andia, Ysabel de* Symbole et mystère selon Denys l'Aréopagite. StPatr 37. 2001 ⇒553. 421-451.

12213   EPIPHANIUS: *Mimouni, Simon C.* Qui sont les jesséens dans la notice 29 du Panarion d'Épiphane de Salamine?. NT 43 (2001) 264-299;

12214   I nazorei a partire dalla notizia 29 del *Panarion* di Epifanio di Salamina. Verus Israel. BCR 65: 2001 ⇒524. 120-146.

12215 EUSEBIUS C: *Brennecke, Hanns Christof* Die Kirche als διαδοχαι των άποστολων: das Programm der έκκλησιαστικη ίστορια des Euseb von Caesarea (Eus., H.E. I 1). Was ist ein Text?. Neutestamentliche Entwürfe zur Theologie 1: 2001 ⇒335. 81-93.

12216 ᵀ**Carrara, Paolo** Eusebio di Cesarea: dimostrazione evangelica. LCPM 29: 2000 16,12635. ᴿAsp. 48 (2001) 602-3 (*Iaia, Gaetano*).

12217 *Gonnet, Dominique* L'acte de citer dans l'*Histoire ecclésiastique* d'Eusèbe. L'historiographie de l'église. 2001 ⇒541. 181-193 [BuBB 36,132].

12218 *Heid, Stefan* Die gute Absicht im Schweigen Eusebs über die Kreuzauffindung. RQ 96 (2001) 37-56.

12219 (*a*) *Mendels, Doron* The use of JOSEPHUS by Eusebius in his *Ecclesiastical History*. Internationales Josephus-Kolloquium 2000. 2001 ⇒ 474. 295-303.

(*b*) ᵀ**Migliore, Franzo; Borzi, Salvatore; Lo Castro, Giovanni** Eusebio di Cesarea: storia ecclesiastica. CTePa 158-159: R 2001, Città N. 2 vols. 88-311-.

12220 *Norelli, Enrico* La mémoire des origines chrétiennes: PAPIAS et HÉGÉSIPPE chez Eusèbe [BuBB 36,133];

12221 *Thelamon, Françoise* Écrire l'histoire de l'église: d'Eusèbe de Césarée à RUFIN d'Aquilée [BuBB 36,104]. L'historiographie de l'église. 2001 ⇒541. 1-22/207-235.

12222 EUSEBIUS E: *Hennings, Ralph* Eusebius von Emesa und die Juden. ZAC 5 (2001) 240-260.

12223 EVAGRIUS: *Dysinger, Luke* The *logoi* of providence and judgement in the exegetical writings of Evagrius Ponticus. StPatr 37. 2001 ⇒ 553. 462-471.

12224 GREGORIUS Naz: **Brubaker, Leslie** Vision and meaning in ninth-century Byzantium: image as exegesis in the homilies of Gregory of Nazianzus. 1999 ⇒15,12423; 16,12638. ᴿJThS 52 (2001) 404-407 (*Louth, Andrew*).

12225 *Calvet-Sebasti, Marie-Ange* L'évocation de l'affaire Sasimes par Grégoire de Nazianze. L'historiographie de l'église. 2001 ⇒541. 481-497 [BuBB 36,130].

12226 ᴱ**Haelewyck, Jean-Claude** Sancti Gregorii Nazianzeni opera: versio syriaca I: Oratio XL. CChr.SG 49; Corpus Nazianzenum 14: Turnhout 2001, Brepols xl; 221 pp. 2-503-40491-X.

12227 ᴱᵀ**Lequeux, Xavier** GREGORIUS Presbyter: vita Sancti Gregorii Theologi. CChr.SG 44; Corpus Nazianzenum 11: Turnhout 2001, Brepols xxii; 285 pp. 2-503-40441-3. Bibl. vii-xxii.

12228 ^T**Smith, Jennifer Nimo** Gregory of Nazianzus: a christian's guide to Greek culture: the PSEUDO-NONNUS commentaries on sermons 4, 5, 39 and 43. Translated texts for historians 37: Liverpool 2001, University Press xlviii; 156 pp. 0-85323-917-7. Bibl. 131-139.

12229 GREGORIUS Nys: *Bernardini, Anna Penati* Giustizia e giustificazione nei Padri Cappadoci: l'argomentazione di Gregorio di Nissa. Giustizia-giustificazione nei Padri della Chiesa. DSBP 29: 2001 ⇒ 308. 196-204.

12230 **Cortesi, A.** Le omilie sul Cantico dei cantici di Gregorio di Nisa. R 2000, Institutum Patristicum Agustinianum 296 pp.

12231 *Laird, Martin* Apophasis and logophasis in Gregory of Nyssa's *Commentarius in Canticum canticorum*. StPatr 37. 2001 ⇒553. 126-132.

12232 ^T**Martín, T.H.** Gregorio de Nisa: Semillas de contemplación: homilías sobre el Cantar de los Cantares, Vida de Moisés: historia y contemplación. Clásicas de Espiritualidad: M 2001, BAC 289 pp.

12233 *Meis Wörmer, Anneliese* Die Verborgenheit Gottes im Hohenliedkommentar Gregors von Nyssa und ihre Rezeption durch PSEUDO-DIONYSIUS Areopagita. EThL 77 (2001) 73-107;

12234 El ocultamiento de Dios en los *Comentarios al Cantar de los Cantares* de Gregorio de Nisa y PSEUDO-DIONISIO Areopagita. StPatr 37. 2001 ⇒553. 194-206.

12235 *Ritter, Adolf Martin* The Fathers as interpreters of Holy Scripture: Gregory of Nyssa's, *De beatitudinibus*. StPatr 34. 2001 ⇒553. 453-458 [Mt 5,3-12].

12236 LEONTIUS: ^T**Dell'Osso, Carlo** Leonzio di Bisanzio: le opere. CTePa 161: R 2001, Città Nuova 206 pp. 88-311-3161-3. Introduzione, traduzione e note a cura di *Carlo Dell'Osso*; Bibl. 47-49.

12237 MELITO: ^T**Di Domenico, Pier Giorgio** Melitone di Sardi: Clavis Scripturae. Visibile parlare 4: Città del Vaticano 2001, Libreria Editrice Vaticana 179 pp. 88-209-7207-7. Introd.

12238 ^T**Stewart-Sykes, Alistair** On Pascha: with the fragments of Melito and other material related to the Quartodecimans. St. Vladimir's Seminary Press "Popular Patristics": Crestwood, NY 2001, St. Vladimir's Seminary Press x; 103 pp. 0-88141-217-1. Bibl. 97-101.

12239 OECUMENIUS: ^E**De Groote, Marc** Index Oecumenianus: Wortindex zum Apokalypsekommentar des Oecumenius. Alpha-Omega, A 223: Hildesheim 2001, Olms (8), 170 pp. 3-487-11389-9.

12240 POLYCHRONIUS: *Bruns, Peter* Polychronius von Apamea—der Exeget und Theologe. StPatr 37. 2001 ⇒553. 404-412.

12241 PROCOPIOS: *Guérard, Marie-Gabrielle* Le contenu de l'*Épitomé* de Procope sur le *Cantique*. StPatr 36. 2001 ⇒553. 9-22.

12242 SERAPION: *West, Maxine* The law, a holy school, Serapion of Thmuis and scripture. StPatr 35. 2001 ⇒553. 198-201.

12243 SIMEON: ^T**Neyrand, L.** Syméon le Studite: discours ascétique. ^E*Alfeyev, Hilarion*: SC 460: P 2001, Cerf 154 pp. 2-204-06676-1. Introduction, texte critique et notes par *Hilarion Alfeyev*; Bibl. 7-9.

12244 THEODORET: *Bouffartigue, Jean* Le texte de Théodoret et le texte de ses documents [BuBB 36,139];

12245 *Guinot, Jean-Noël* La place et le rôle de l'histoire événementielle dans l'exégèse de Théodoret de Cyr [BuBB 36,139]. L'historiographie de l'église. 2001 ⇒541. 315-327/329-348.

12246 *Hill, Robert C.* Theodoret wrestling with Romans. StPatr 34. 2001 ⇒553. 347-352.

12247 ^T**Hill, Robert Charles** Theodoret of Cyrus: commentary on the letters of St. Paul. Brookline, MT 2001, Holy Cross 319 pp. $19. 1-885652-53-4 [IThQ 68,92s—Price, R.M.].

12248 *Martin, Annick* L'origine de l'arianisme vue par Théodoret. L'historiographie de l'église. 2001 ⇒541. 349-59 [BuBB 36,104].

12249 THEODORUS: *Hill, R.C.* Theodore of Mopsuestia, interpreter of the prophets. SE 40 (2001) 107-129.

12250 *Jakobi, R.* Studien zur lateinischen Fassung des Psalmenkommentars des Theodorus von Mopsuestia. SE 39 (2000) 81-97.

Y2.4 Augustinus

12251 Acta do congresso internacional: as Confessões de Santo Agostinho: 1600 anos depois: presença e actualidade. Lisboa 2001, Universidade Católica 788 pp.

12252 *Asiedu, Felix Baffour Asare* Paul and Augustine's retrospective self: the relevance of Epistula XXII. REAug 47 (2001) 145-164 [Rom 13,13-14].

12253 ^E**Atkins, E. Margaret; Dodaro, Robert** Augustine: political writings. Cambridge Texts in the History of Political Thought: C 2001, CUP li; 299 pp. 0-521-44697-X. Bibl. xli-l.

12254 *Bastiaensen, A.* Augustine's Pauline exegesis and AMBROSIASTER. Augustine: biblical exegete. 2001 ⇒331. 33-54.

12255 *Beatrice, Pier Franco* De RUFIN à CASSIODORE: la réception des *Histoires ecclésiastiques* grecques dans l'Occident latin. L'historiographie de l'église. 2001 ⇒541. 237-257 [BuBB 36,128].

12256 *Beltz, Walter* Augustins "Manichäischer Erbteil" dargestellt an *De mendacio* und *Contra mendacium* (*Ad consentium contra mendacium*). Augustine and Manichaeism. 2001 ⇒550. 16-23.

12257 *Bochet, Isabelle* L'unité du *De utilitate credendi* d'Augustin. Augustine and Manichaeism. NHMS 49: 2001 ⇒550. 24-42.

12258 [T]**Boulding, Maria** Augustine: expositions of the Psalms: 1-32. Works of St Augustine, 3/15: 2000 ⇒16,12690. [R]AugSt 32 (2001) 154-156 (*Cunningham, Lawrence S.*); JECS 9 (2001) 605-606 (*Van Slyke, Daniel*);

12259 33-50. Works of St Augustine, 3/16: 2000 ⇒16,12691. [R]AugSt 32 (2001) 281-282 (*Cunningham, Lawrence S.*).

12260 *Bourke, Vernon J.* Augustine on the Psalms. Augustine: biblical exegete. 2001 ⇒331. 55-70.

12261 [ET]**Bright, Pamela** Augustine and the bible. The Bible through the ages 2: 1999 ⇒15,12450; 16,12692. [R]AugSt 32 (2001) 129-132 (*Harmless, William*).

12262 **Brown, Peter** Agustín de Hipona: nueva edición con un epílogo del autor. [T]*Tovar, Santiago; Tovar, M. Rosa; Oldfield, John*: Las Luces: M 2001 <1970>, Acento 654 pp.

12263 *Burns, J. Patout* Augustine's use of the Song of Songs against the Donatists. Augustine: biblical exegete. 2001 ⇒331. 99-127.

12264 [T]**Carrozzi, L.; Tarulli, V.** Sant'Agostino: opere esegetiche X/3: otto questioni dell'Antico Testamento, annotazioni sul libro di Giobbe, specchio di precetti morali dalla sacra scrittura. 1999 ⇒15, 12454. [R]CivCatt 152/4 (2001) 407-409 (*Cremascoli, G.*).

12265 *Casiday, Augustine* St Augustine on deification: his homily on Psalm 81. Sob. 23/2 (2001) 23-44.

12266 **Chadwick, Henry** Agustín. M 2001, Cristiandad 202 pp.

12267 *Chmiel, Jerzy* Św. Augustyna pierwsze spotkanie z Biblia. [F]JAN-KOWSKI, A. 2001 ⇒53. 87-90. **P**.

12268 *Cocchini, Francesca* Il Giovanni di Agostino. VIII Simposio di Efeso. Turchia 15: 2001 ⇒488. 153-161.

12269 *Coyle, J. Kevin* What did Augustine know about Manichaeism when he wrote his two treatises *De moribus*?. Augustine and Manichaeism. NHMS 49: 2001 ⇒550. 43-56;

12270 Augustin et le manichéisme. ConnPE 83 (2001) 45-55.

12271 *Decret, François* Objectif premier visé par Augustin dans ses controverses orales avec les responsables manichéens d'Hippone. Augustine and Manichaeism. NHMS 49: 2001 ⇒550. 57-66.

12272 **Dixon, Sandra Lee** Augustine: the scattered and gathered self. 1999 ⇒15,12457. [R]MoTh 17 (2001) 404-06 (*Collinge, William J.*).

12273 *Djuth, Marianne* The royal way: Augustine's freedom of the will and the monastic tradition [Num 21,21-22; Jn 14,5-6];

12274 *Evans, G.R.* Augustine on exegesis against the heretics. Augustine: biblical exegete. 2001 ⇒331. 129-143/145-156.

12275 *Filoramo, Giovanni* Giustizia-giustificazione in Agostino. Giustizia-giustificazione nei Padri della Chiesa. DSBP 29: 2001 ⇒308. 274-287.

12276 ᴱ**Fitzgerald, Allan D.** Augustine through the ages: an encyclopedia. 1999 ⇒15,12462; 16,12702. ᴿAugSt 32 (2001) 142-146 (*Drobner, Hubertus*); Ancient Philosophy 21 (2001) 531-533 (*Maclean, Iain S.*); Annales Theologici 15 (2001) 606-612 (*Reale, V.*);

12277 Diccionario de San Agustín. Burgos 2001, Monte Carmelo 1354 pp. ᴿBurg. 42 (2001) 617-619 (*García, Jaime*); RelCult 47 (2001) 867-874 (*Langa, Pedro*).

12278 *Folliet, Georges Tolerabilior damnatio*: la thèse augustinienne de la mitigation des peines de l'enfer et ses sources scripturaires. Aug. 41 (2001) 149-167 [Ps 76,10; Mt 10,15].

12279 *Fortin, Anne; Pénicaud, Anne* Augustin, lecteur des écritures. SémBib 104 (2001) 3-23.

12280 *Fredriksen, Paula* Augustine and Israel: *Interpretatio ad litteram*, Jews, and Judaism in Augustine's theology of history. StPatr 38. 2001 ⇒553. 119-135.

12281 *Fuhrer, Therese* Zu Form und Funktion von Augustins exegetischen Schriften. StPatr 38. 2001 ⇒553. 136-152.

12282 *Genovese, Armando* Note sull'uso del Cantico dei Cantici in Sant'Agostino. Aug. 41 (2001) 201-212;

12283 La ricerca di Dio: il Cantico dei Cantici e le Confessioni. RVS 55 (2001) 685-696.

12284 *Gori, Franco* L'edizione critica delle Enarrationes in Psalmos graduum: questioni specifiche. Aug. 41 (2001) 99-112.

12285 **Gorman, Michael M.** The manuscript traditions of the works of St Augustine. Millennio medievale 2: F 2001, Sismel 374 pp.

12286 **Grossi, Vittorino** Leggere la bibbia con S. Agostino. 1999 ⇒15, 12470. ᴿRdT 42 (2001) 462-463 (*Marafioti, Domenico*).

12287 *Harrison, Carol* 'Not words but things:' harmonious diversity in the four gospels. Augustine: biblical exegete. 2001 ⇒331. 157-173.

12288 *Herrera, Robert* A shattered mirror: the presence of Africa in Augustine's exegesis. Augustine: biblical exegete. 2001 ⇒331. 175-188.

12289 *Hoffmann, Andreas* Erst einsehen, dann glauben: die nordafrikanischen Manichäer zwischen Erkenntnisanspruch, Glaubensforderung und Glaubenskritik. Augustine and Manichaeism. NHMS 49: 2001 ⇒550. 67-112.

12290 *Jackson, Michael* Miracles and 'spiritual correctness' in the theology of St. Augustine. StPatr 38. 2001 ⇒553. 184-189.

12291   **Janner, Sara; Jurot, Romain** Die handschriftliche Überlieferung der Werke des Heiligen Augustinus. DÖAW.PH 688; VKCLK 19: W 2001, Verlag der Österreichischen Akademie der Wissenschaften 2 vols. 3-7001-3020-1. Bibl. v.1 19-20; v.2 9-11.

12292   **Kaye, Sharon M.; Thomson, Paul** On Augustine. Wadsworth philosophers series: Belmont, CA 2001, Wadsworth (8) 83 pp. 0-534-58362-8. Bibl. 81-83.

12293   *Kelly, Joseph F.* BEDE's use of Augustine for his *Commentarium in principium Genesis*. Augustine: biblical exegete. 2001 ⇒331. 189-196.

12294   *Lamberigts, Mathijs* Was Augustine a Manichaean?: the assessment of JULIAN of Aeclanum. Augustine and Manichaeism. NHMS 49: 2001 ⇒550. 113-136.

12295   **Lancel, Serge** Saint Augustin. 1999 ⇒16,12715. ᴿZKG 112 (2001) 390-392 (*Drecoll, Volker Henning*).

12296   *Lienhard, Joseph T.* John the Baptist in Augustine's exegesis. Augustine: biblical exegete. 2001 ⇒331. 197-213.

12297   ᵀ**Longobardo, Luigi** Agostino d'Ippona: il discorso del Signore sulla montagna. Mi 2001, Paoline 354 pp. €23.24. ᴿASEs 18 (2001) 686-687 (*Ruggiero, Fabio*) [Mt 5-7].

12298   *Lössl, Josef* A shift in patristic exegesis: Hebrew clarity and historical verity in Augustine, JEROME, JULIAN of Aeclanum and THEODORE of Mopsuestia. AugSt 32 (2001) 157-175.

12299   *Madec, Goulven* Les *Confessions* comme prière biblique;

12300   Les deux en une seule chair: la lecture augustinienne de *Genèse*, 2, 24 <2000>. Lectures augustiniennes. 2001 ⇒12303. 111-120/271-280;

12301   Augustin et la bible. MoBi 132 (2001) 43-45.

12302   **Madec, Goulven** Le Christ de saint Augustin: la patrie et la voie. CJJC 36: P 2001 <1989>, Desclée 288 pp. 2-7189-0966-8;

12303   Lectures augustiniennes. EAug, Antiquité 168: P 2001, Institut d'Etudes Augustiniennes 388 pp.

12304   *Magris, Aldo* Augustins Prädestinationslehre und die manichäischen Quellen. Augustine and Manichaeism. 2001 ⇒550. 148-160.

12305   *Martin, Thomas F.* Paul the patient: *Christus medicus* and the '*stimulus carnis*' (2 Cor. 12:7): a consideration of Augustine's medicinal christology. AugSt 32 (2001) 219-256;

12306   Psalmus Gratiae Dei: Augustine's "Pauline" reading of Psalm 31. VigChr 55 (2001) 137-155.

12307   **Mathewes, Charles T.** Evil and the Augustinian tradition. C 2001, CUP xii; 271 pp. 0-521-80715-8. Bibl. 247-266.

12308   ᴱ**Mayer, C.** Augustinus-Lexikon: Deus-Donatistas (Contra-). 1999 ⇒15,12478 2/3-4. ᴿThPh 76 (2001) 280-282 (*Sieben, H.J.*).

12309 **Morrison, Angus** Augustine's use of scripture in the anti-Donatist writings, with special reference to the marks of the church. Diss. Edinburgh 2001, ^D*Wright, D.F.*: 378 pp [RTL 33,643].

12310 *Norris, John* Augustine and sign in *Tractatus in Johannis Euangelium*. Augustine: biblical exegete. 2001 ⇒331. 215-231;

12311 The 'palate of the heart' in St. Augustine and medieval spirituality;

12312 *O'Connell, Robert J.* Augustine's exegetical use of Ecclesiasticus 10:9-14;

12313 *Renna, Thomas* Zion and Jerusalem in the Psalms. Augustine: biblical exegete. 2001 ⇒331. 253-278/233-252/279-298.

12314 *Ries, Julien* Jésus Sauveur dans la controverse anti-manichéenne de saint Augustin. Augustine and Manichaeism. 2001 ⇒550. 185-194;

12315 Le jugement porté sur le Manichéisme par saint Augustin à la lumière de son expérience relatée dans les Confessions. StPatr 38. 2001 ⇒553. 264-274.

12316 *Rudolph, Kurt* Augustinus und Manichaicus—das Problem von Konstanz und Wandel. Augustine and Manichaeism NHMS 49: 2001 ⇒550. 1-15.

12317 *Sánchez, Eduardo* Algunos principios olvidados de hermenéutica agustiniana. Augustinus 46 (2001) 345-359.

12318 *Schipper, H.G.* Melothesia: a chapter of manichaean astrology in the west. Augustine and Manichaeism. 2001 ⇒550. 195-204.

12319 ^T**Schrama, Martijn; Saleddens, Wim; De Lil, Hugo** Aurelius Augustinus: zoals het hart verlangt: preken over de Psalmen. Sleutelteksten in godsdienst en theologie 24: Zoetermeer 2001, Meinema 189 pp. €20.21. 90-211-3793-3.

12320 *Scopello, Madeleine* L'*Epistula fundamenti* à la lumière des sources manichéennes du Fayoum;

12321 *Sfameni Gasparro, Giulia* Au coeur du dualisme manichéen: la polémique augustinienne contre la notion de "mutabilité" de Dieu dans le *Contra Secundinum*;

12322 *Smagina, Eugenia* Das manichäische Kreuz des Lichts und der Jesus patibilis. Augustine and Manichaeism. NHMS 49: 2001 ⇒550. 205-229/230-242/243-249.

12323 *Steinhauser, Kenneth B.* Job exegesis: the Pelagian controversy. Augustine: biblical exegete. 2001 ⇒331. 299-311.

12324 *Stein, Markus* Bemerkungen zum Kodex von Tebessa. Augustine and Manichaeism. NHMS 49: 2001 ⇒550. 250-271.

12325 ^E**Stump, E.; Kretzmann, N.** The Cambridge Companion to Augustine. C 2001, CUP 307 pp. $60/22. 0-521-65018-6/985-X.

12326 **Tack, Theodore E.** As one struggling christian to another: Augustine's christian ideal for today. ColMn 2001, Liturgical xii; 119 pp. 0-8146-2415-4.

12327   *TeSelle, Eugene* Exploring the inner conflict: Augustine's sermons on Romans 7 and 8;

12328   *Teske, Roland* The Good Samaritan (Lk 10:29-37) in Augustine's exegesis. Augustine: biblical exegete. 2001 ⇒331. 313-345/347-367.

12329   *Torchia, Joseph* The significance of the *communicatio idiomatum* in St. Augustine's christology, with special reference to his rebuttal of later Arianism. StPatr 38. 2001 ⇒553. 306-323.

12330   *Van Amersfoort, J.* Some remarks on the gospel tradition in the anti-Manichaean writings of Augustine of Hippo. StPatr 38. 2001 ⇒553. 324-330.

12331   *Van Fleteren, Frederick* Augustine's evolving exegesis of Romans 7:22-23 in its Pauline context. AugSt 32 (2001) 89-114;

12332   Principles of Augustine's hermeneutic: an overview. Augustine: biblical exegete. 2001 ⇒331. 1-32.

12333   *Vannier, Marie-Anne* L'interpretation augustinienne de la creation et l'emantisme manichéen;

12334   *Van Oort, Johannes* *Secundini manichaei epistula*: Roman Manichaean 'biblical' argument in the age of Augustine. Augustine and Manichaeism. NHMS 49: 2001 ⇒550. 287-297/161-173.

12335   *Vaz, Armindo* Dos Santos Narrativas bíblicas da criação e Confissões de Santo Agostinho. As Confessões. 2001 ⇒12261. 121-184.

12336   ᴱVessey, Mark, *al.*, History, Apocalypse, and the secular imagination: new essays on Augustine's *City of God*. 1999 ⇒15,12500. ᴿJThS 52 (2001) 392-393 (*Markus, R.A.*).

12337   ᴱᵀWalsh, Patrick Gerard Augustinus: De bono coniugali; De sancta virginitate. Oxford Early Christian Texts: Oxf 2001, Clarendon xxxv; 164 pp. 0-19-826995-1. Bibl. xxxiii-xxxiv.

12338   *Weber, Dorothea Augustinus, De Genesi contra Manichaeos*: zu Augustins Darstellung und Widerlegung der manichäischen Kritik am biblischen Schöpfungsbericht. Augustine and Manichaeism. NHMS 49: 2001 ⇒550. 298-306.

12339   *Williams, Thomas* Biblical interpretation. Cambridge Companion to Augustine. 2001 ⇒12325. 59-70.

12340   Wills, Garry Saint Augustine. 1999 ⇒15,12504; 16,12742. ᴿABenR 52 (2001) 214-215 (*Timko, Philip*); CTJ 36 (2001) 426-428 (*Vos, Arvin*).

12341   *Wurst, Gregor* Bemerkungen zu Struktur und genus litterarium der *Capitula* des FAUSTUS von Mileve. Augustine and Manichaeism. NHMS 49: 2001 ⇒550. 307-324.

Y2.5 **Hieronymus**

12342 *Adkin, N.* Apollonius of Tyana in Jerome. SE 39 (2000) 67-79.

12343 **Bartelink, G.J.M.** Hiëronymus als exegeet: een keuze van teksten in Nederlandse vertaling met inleiding en commentaar. Kerkvaderteksten met commentaar 12: Bonheiden 2001, Abdij Bethlehem 240 pp [Coll. 31,332s—Hoet, Hendrik].

12344 ᴱ**Canellis, Alina S.** Hieronymi presbyteri opera, 3: opera polemica, 4: altercatio Luciferiani et Orthodoxi. CChr.SL 79: 2000 ⇒16, 12744. ᴿScr. 55 (2001) 231*-232* (*Hamblenne, P.*).

12345 **Conring, Barbara** Hieronymus als Briefschreiber: ein Beitrag zur spätantiken Epistolographie. Studien und Texte zu Antike und Christentum 8: Tü 2001, Mohr 273 pp. €49. 3-16-147502-X. Bibl. 253-265. ᴿRHPhR 81 (2001) 347-348 (*Prieur, J.-M.*).

12346 **Cromwell, Bruce Nelson Grieser** Saint Jerome's defense of his Vulgate translation from the Hebrew. Diss. Saint Louis 2001, 212 pp. 3014197 [REAug 48,459].

ᵀ**Domínguez García, A.** Comentarios a los Profetas Menores. 2000 ⇒4111.

12347 *Duval, Yves-Marie* Jérôme et l'histoire de l'église du IVᵉ siècle. L'historiographie de l'église. 2001 ⇒541. 381-408 [BuBB 36, 102].

12348 ᴱ**Feiertag, J.-L.** S. Hieronymi presbyteri opera, opera III: opera polemica, 2: contra Johannem. CChr.SL 79A: 1999 ⇒15,12511. ᴿScr. 55/1 (2001) 73*-74* (*Hamblenne, P.*).

12349 *Jacobs, Andrew S.* The place of the biblical Jew in the early christian Holy Land. StPatr 38. 2001 ⇒553. 417-422.

12350 *Jeanjean, Benoît* L'utilisation antihérétique de Ps. 72,9 par saint Jérôme. StPatr 34. 2001 ⇒553. 376-387;

12351 De la *Chronique* à la *Consolation à Héliodore (Epist. 60)*: les mutations de la matière historique chez Jérôme. L'historiographie de l'église. 2001 ⇒541. 409-423 [BuBB 36,136].

Lössl, J. A shift in patristic exegesis: Hebrew clarity and historical verity in Augustine, Jerome... 2001 ⇒12298.

12352 ᴱᵀ**McManamon, John M.** Pierpaolo Vᴇʀɢᴇʀɪᴏ the Elder and Saint Jerome. MRTS 177: 1999 ⇒15,12519; 16,12754. ᴿJR 81 (2001) 123-125 (*Botterill, Steven*).

12353 *Newman, Hillel I.* Jerome's Judaizers. JECS 9 (2001) 421-452.

12354 **Prandini, Silvia** Girolamo santo antinoia. 2000 ⇒16,12757. ᴿRivista di scienze religiose 15 (2001) 214-215 (*Dell'Ossa, Carlo*).

12355 *Ratti, Stéphane* Les sources de la *Chronique* de Jérôme pour les années 357-364: nouveaux éléments. L'historiographie de l'église. 2001 ⇒541. 425-450 [BuBB 36,136].

12356 *Starowieyski, Marek* Les commentaires bibliques patristiques dans le *De viris illustribus* de S. Jérôme. StPatr 34. 2001 ⇒553. 459-69.

Y2.6 Patres Latini *in ordine alphabetico*

12357 **Bardy, Gustave** Storia della letteratura cristiana antica latina. [E]*Di Nola, Gerardo*: 1999 ⇒15,12526. [R]CivCatt 152/4 (2001) 316-317 (*Cremascoli, G.*).

12358 **Campenhausen, Hans von** Los padres de la iglesia, 2: padres latinos. [T]*Martínez de Lapera, V.A.*: Iglesia antigua y medieval: M 2001, Cristiandad 405 pp. 84-7057-442-6.
   Laporte, J. Les pères de l'église, 1: pères latins 2001 ⇒12179.

12359 AMBROSIASTER: *Stuiber, Alfred* Ambrosiaster. RAC, Suppl. Bd. 1. 2001 ⇒661. 301-310.

12360 AMBROSIUS: *Bonato, Antonio* Il tema della giustizia nel pensiero di Ambrogio. Giustizia-giustificazione nei Padri della Chiesa. DSBP 29: 2001 ⇒308. 225-273.

12361 *Burns, J. Patout* Creation and fall according to Ambrose of Milan. Augustine: biblical exegete. 2001 ⇒331. 71-97.

12362 *Kamesar, Adam* Ambrose, PHILO, and the presence of art in the bible. JECS 9 (2001) 73-103.

12363 **Moretti, Francesca Paola** Non harundo sed calamus: aspetti letterari della 'Explanatio Psalmorum XII' di Ambrogio. 2000 ⇒16,12780 [R]Aevum. 75 (2001) 219-221 (*Ramelli, Ilaria*).

12364 [T]**Riain, Ide M. Ni** Commentary of Saint Ambrose on the gospel according to Saint Luke. Dublin 2001, Halcyon xviii; 368 pp. $37. 1-902-232-26-7. Bibl. xvi-xvii [ThD 48,351—Heiser, W. Charles].

12365 *Trisoglio, Francesco* S. Ambrogio e l'esegesi di S. MASSIMO di Torino. ASEs 18 (2001) 615-635.

12366 *Turek, Waldemar* Il peccato contro lo Spirito Santo nell'esegesi ambrosiana. ED 54/1 (2001) 71-85 [Mt 12,31-32; Mk 3,20; Lk 12,10].

12367 APPONIUS: *Hamblenne, P.* Deux métaphores apponniennes (*In Cant.* III,1.92s. et IX,1.110-112). SE 39 (2000) 21-35 [Cant 1,11; 7,1].

12368 CAESARIUS: [TE]**Courreau, Joël** Césaire d'Arles: sermons sur l'Écriture: v.1, Sermons 81-105. [E]*Morin, G.*: SC 447: 2000 ⇒16,12788.

[R]JThS 52 (2001) 928-929 (*Winterbottom, Michael*); ThPh 76 (2001) 585-586 (*Sieben, H.-J.*).

12369 CASSIANUS: *Vannier, Marie-Anne* Jean Cassien, historiographe du monachisme égyptien?. L'historiographie de l'église. 2001 ⇒541. 149-158 [BuBB 36,104];

12370 Jean Cassien. EeV 42 (2001) 9-15.

12371 CYPRIANUS: *Torjesen, Karen Jo* The episcopacy—sacerdotal or monarchical?: the appeal to Old Testament institutions by Cyprian and the *Didascalia*. StPatr 36. 2001 ⇒553. 387-406.

12372 *Vallery-Radot, Maurice* Un Père de l'église à la pensée moderne: Cyprien, évêque de Carthage (248-258). L'historiographie de l'église. 2001 ⇒541. 559-586 [BuBB 36,131].

12373 EPHRAEM: [T]**Cassingena-Trévedy, François** Éphrem de Nisibe: hymnes sur la nativité. SC 459: P 2001, Cerf 344 pp. €37.19. 2-204-06675-3. Introduction par *François Graffin*; Bibl. 22-25.

12374 *Cerbelaud, Dominique* Je t'aime, je te hais: Éphrem le Syrien et le judaïsme. Le judaïsme à l'aube de l'ère chrétienne. LeDiv 186: 2001 ⇒450. 345-361.

12375 GREGORIO E: [E]**Pascual Torró, Joaquín** Gregorio de Elvira: comentario al Cantar de los cantares y otros tratados exegéticos. 2000 ⇒16,12800. [R]San Juan de la Cruz 27 (2001) 134-135 (*Sánchez, Manuel Diego*).

12376 GREGORIUS M: [T]**Bhattacharji, Santha** Reading the gospels with Gregory the Great: homilies on the gospels: 21-26. Petersham, MA 2001, St Bede's 122 pp. $12.

12377 *Clark, Francis* The unmasking of the pseudo-Gregorian *Commentary on Kings* and its relevance to the study of Benedictine origins. StPatr 36. 2001 ⇒553. 3-8.

12378 **Cremascoli, Giuseppe** L'esegesi biblica di Gregorio Magno. Interpretare la Bibbia oggi 36: Brescia 2001, Queriniana 166 pp. €11. 88. 88-399-2472-8. Bibl. 152-159. [R]Salm. 48 (2001) 609-610 (*Trevijano, Ramón*); VetChr 38 (2001) 341-346 (*Donnini, Mauro*).

12379 [E]**Étaix, Raymond** Gregorius Magnus: homiliae in Evangelia. CChr.SL 141: 1999 ⇒15,12544; 16,12803. [R]Scr. 55 (2001) 325-328 (*Hamblenne, Pierre*).

12380 *Ramos-Lisson, Domingo* En torno al exégesis de San Gregorio Magno sobre el "Cantar de los Cantares". TyV 42 (2001) 241-265.

12381 *Van Banning, J.H.A.* Gregory the Great and the surviving Arianism of his time: did he know the *Opus imperfectum in Matthaeum*?. StPatr 38. 2001 ⇒553. 481-495.

12382 GREGORIUS T: **Heinzelmann, Martin** Gregory of Tours: history and society in the sixth century. ^T**Carroll, Christopher**: C 2001, CUP xii; 235 pp. 0-521-63174-2. Bibl. 214-222.

12383 HILARIUS: *Manns, Frédéric* Une tradition judéo-chrétienne dans le *Traité des Mystères* de Hilaire de Poitiers. Le judéo-christianisme. 2001 ⇒484. 317-321 [BuBB 36,135].

12384 *Williams, D.H.* Defining orthodoxy in Hilary of Poitiers' Commentarium in Matthaeum. JECS 9 (2001) 151-171.

12385 JOHANNES PHILOPONOS: **Fladerer, L.** Johannes Philoponos: *De opificio mundi*: spätantikes Sprachdenken und christliche Exegese. 1999 ⇒15,12561. ^RCIR 51 (2001) 300-302 (*Haas, F.A.J. de*).

12386 JULIANUS A: **Lössl, Josef** Julian von Aeclanum: Studien zu seinem Leben, seinem Werk, seiner Lehre und ihrer Überlieferung. SVigChr 60: Lei 2001, Brill xvi; 406 pp. €96. 90-04-12180-3. Diss.-Habil. Münster.

12387 *Lößl, Josef* Julian of Aeclanum's Tractatus in Osee, Iohel, Amos: some notes on the current state of research. Aug(L) 51 (2001) 11-37.

12388 LEO M: *Cavalcanti, Elena* The sermon of Leo the First on the Transfiguration (*Serm.* LI Chavasse). StPatr 38. 2001 ⇒553. 371-376.

12389 ^E**Montanari, Elio** Leone Magno: i sermoni sul mistero pasquale. ^T*Cavalcanti, Elena*: BPat 38; Leone Magno–Sermoni 4: Bo 2001, EDB 488 pp. 88-10-42047-0. Introd. critica e costituzione del testo di *Elio Montanari*; Introd., trad. e commento di *Elena Cavalcanti*.

12390 MARIUS: *Voelker, John* Marius Victorinus' exegetical arguments for Nicene definition in *Adversus Arium*. StPatr 38. 2001 ⇒553. 496-502.

12391 PAULINUS: *Luongo, Gennaro* La recezione di Giovanni in Paolino di Nola. VIII Simposio di Efeso. Turchia 15: 2001 ⇒488. 163-185.

12392 PRUDENTIUS: *Sullivan, Lisa M.* Bursting the bonds of night: images of the Apocalypse in Prudentius' *Cathemerinon*. StPatr 38. 2001 ⇒ 553. 475-480.

12393 SULPICIUS: *Bertrand, Dominique* Chronologie et exégèse chez Sulpice Sévère. L'historiographie de l'église. 2001 ⇒541. 451-467 [BuBB 36,102].

12394 TICONIUS: *Marone, Paola* La continuità esegetica che caratterizza le opere di Ticonio ovvero l'applicazione delle *Regole* nel *Commento all'Apocalisse*. SMSR 67 (2001) 253-270.

12395 *Vercruysse, Jean-Marc* L'illustration scripturaire dans la Règle VII du *Liber Regularum* de Tyconius. StPatr 34. 2001 ⇒553. 511-517 [Isa 14,12-21; Ezek 28,2-19].

12396 VICTOR: JOANNES BICLARENSIS: [E]**Cardelle de Hartmann, Carmen; Collins, Roger** Victoris Tunnunensis et Iohannis Biclarensis: chronicon cum reliquiis ex Consularibus Caesaraugustanis. CChr.SL 173 A: Turnhout 2001, Brepols 160*; 160 pp. 2-503-01733-9. Commentaria historica ad Consularia Caesaraugustana et ad Iohannis Biclarensis Chronicon edidit *Roger Collins*.

Y2.8 Documenta orientalia

12397 *Albert, M.* À propos des citations scripturaires de la correspondance de JACQUES de Saroug. StPatr 35. 2001 ⇒553. 345-352.

12398 *Bettiolo, Paolo* Adamo in Eden e la liturgia celeste: temi della meditazione cristiana nella Siria del IV secolo, tra AFRAATE e il Liber Graduum. RSLR 37/1 (2001) 3-27.

12399 *Brock, Sebastian* La prière et la vie spirituelle selon les pères syriaques : (présentation générale): texte suivi d'extraits traduits en français: ÉPHREM, hymne sur la foi XX; "Livre des Degrés", sermon XII; ÉVAGRE Syriaque, "Admonition sur la prière"; ISAAC de N*. ParOr 26 (2001) 201-266.

12400 *Khalifé, Elias* Le monachisme syriaque: à propos d'un nouvel ouvrage. ParOr 26 (2001) 303-309.

12401 *Mathews, Edward G.* Water in the first creation account of Genesis 1 in the Commentary on Genesis of EPHREM the Syrian. [F]FITZGERALD, A.: CBQ.MS 32: 2001 ⇒31. 129-144.

12402 [ET]**Matthews, Edward G.** The Armenian commentaries on Exodus-Deuteronomy attributed to EPHREM the Syrian. CSCO.Ar 25-26; CSCO 587-588: Lv 2001, Peeters 2 vols. V.1: 90-429-1009-7, v.2: 90-429-1018-6.

12403 **Shaji, Thomas M.** The nativity of our Lord: a study based on the writings of St. EPHREM the Syrian. Diss. Rome, Pont. Inst. Orientale 2001, [D]*Yousif, P.*: xlviii; 277 pp [RTL 33,643].

12404 *Taylor, David G.K.* The christology of the Syriac Psalm commentary (AD 541/2) of DANIEL of Ṣalaḥ and the 'Phantasiast' controversy. StPatr 35. 2001 ⇒553. 508-515.

12405 *Teixidor, Javier* L'"oeil de l'intelligence" chez les Syriaques. Sem. 50 (2001) 211-216.

Y3.0 Medium aevum, *generalia*

12406 [E]**Bayless, Martha; Lapidge, Michael** Collectanea PSEUDO-BEDAE. Scriptores Latini Hiberniae 14: 1998 ⇒14,11752; 15,12569. [R]Apocrypha 12 (2001) 310-311 (*Gounelle, R.*).

12407   *Benad, Matthias* Auf die Methode kommt es an!: zum quellenkriti-
schen Umgang mit dem Inqisitionsregister Jacques FOURNIERs, Bischof von Pamiers 1318-1325. WuD 26 (2001) 207-215.

12408   *Borgehammar, Stephan* Perikoper och predikan under medeltiden.
SEÅ 66 (2001) 39-54.

12409   **Carmassi, Patrizia** Libri liturgici e istituzioni ecclesiastiche a
Milano in età medioevale. Corpus Ambrosiano-Liturgicum 4;
LWQF 85: Müns 2001, Aschendorff 439 pp. 3-402-04064-6. Bibl.
388-415.

12410   **Cartwright, Steven Richard** The Romans commentaries of WIL-
LIAM of St. Thierry and Peter ABELARD: a theological and methodological comparison. Diss. Western Michigan 2001, 305 pp. 3017-
308.

12411   *Dahan, Gilbert, al.,* L'Occident médiévale lecteur de l'écriture.
CEv.S 116 (2001) 5-99.

12412   **Dahan, Gilbert** L'exégèse chrétienne de la bible en occident médi-
éval, XIIe-XIVe siècle. 1999 ⇒15,12572; 16,12836. RRHEF 87
(2001) 207-208 (*Longère, Jean*); Iren. 73 (2001) 574-575; CrSt 22
(2001) 492-497 (*Berarducci, Silvia Cantelli*); RHE 96 (2001) 465-
468 (*Auwers, Jean-Marie*).

12413   **Daniel-Rops, Henri** The church in the dark ages. TButler, Audrey:
L 2001, Phoenix xi; 624 pp. 1-84212-465-X. Bibl. 609-611.

12414   **Fried, Johannes** Aufstieg aus dem Untergang: apokalyptisches
Denken und die Entstehung der modernen Naturwissenschaft im
Mittelalter. Mü 2001, Beck 262 pp. 3-406-48209-0.

12415   ETJonge, Lido; Voorwinden, Norbert Van den levene ons Heren:
kritische editie met inleiding, vertaling en commentaar. Middelne-
derlandse tekstedities 8: Hilversum 2001, Verloren 286 pp. €19.
ROGE 75 (2001) 296-299 (*Kuiper, Willem*).

12416   *Lluch Baixauli, Miguel* La interpretación del decálogo en los siglos
VII al IX: San ISIDORO de Sevilla, BEDA el Venerable y los escrito-
res Carolingios. ScrTh 33 (2001) 71-102 [Ex 20,1-17].

12417   *Mackay, Thomas W.* Apocalypse comments by PRIMASIUS, BEDE,
and ALCUIN: interrelationship, dependency and individuality. StPatr
36. 2001 ⇒553. 28-34.

12418   **Miller, Eric Patrick** The politics of imitating Christ: Christ the
King and christomimetic rulership in early medieval biblical commentaries. Diss. Virginia 2001, 349 pp. 3020379.

12419   *Ó Crónín, D.* A new seventh-century Irish commentary on Genesis.
SE 40 (2001) 231-265.

12420   **Santiago-Otero, Horacio; Reinhardt, Klaus** La biblia en la Pe-
nínsula ibérica durante la Edad Media (siglos XII-XV): el texto y

su interpretación. Coimbra 2001, Arquivo da Univ. Coimbra 155 pp.

12421 **Schlosser, Marianne** Lucerna in caliginoso loco: Aspekte des Prophetie-Begriffes in der scholastischen Theologie. VGI 43: 2000 ⇒16,12854. [R]Recherches de théologie et philosophie médiévales 68 (2001) 398-400 (*Decorte, J.*).

12422 *Signer, Michael A.* God's love for Israel: apologetic and hermeneutical strategies in twelfth-century biblical exegesis. Jews and christians in twelfth-century Europe. 2001 ⇒442. 123-149.

12423 *Tábet, Michelangelo* I preludi dei moderni trattati sulla natura e interpretazione della Sacra Scrittura nel periodo medievale. Annales theologici 15/1 (2001) 3-79.

12424 *Verkest, P.* The *praefatio* of the Irish 'Eglogae tractatorum in psalterium', edited with a critical introduction. SE 40 (2001) 267-292.

12425 *Young, D.J.* Biblical criticism in the late Middle Ages. ET 112 (2001) 155-160.

12426 *Ypenga, Anko* Allegorese, typologie en allegorie in de middeleeuwen; allegoresis, typology and allegory in the Middle Ages. Bijdr. 62 (2001) 3-27.

Y3.4 Exegetae mediaevales [Hebraei ⇒K7]

12427 ABAELARDUS: [E]**Ilgner, Rainer M.** Petrus Abaelardus: opera theologica IV: scito te ipsum. CChr.CM 190: Turnhout 2001, Brepols lxix; 109 pp. 2-503-04901-X. Bibl. lx-lxvii.

12428 AELRED: [T]**Pezzini, Domenico** Alfredo di Rievaulx: Gesù dodicenne: preghiera pastorale. Letture cristiane del secondo millennio. Mi 2001, Paoline 176 pp.

12429 **Schlubach, Jane** Friendship: Aelred of Rievaulx and scripture. Diss. Notre Dame 2001, [D]*Burrell, D.*: 217 pp [RTL 33, 644].

12430 ALCUIN: **Kieling, Michal** 'Terrena non amare sed coelestia': Theologie der Welt in Alkuins 'Commentaria super Ecclesiasten'. Diss. Frankfurt, St. Georgen 2001, [D]*Berndt, R.*: 275 pp [RTL 33,644].

12431 ALEXANDER: *Pasquale, Gianluigi An in Vetere Testamento gratia opus operans sit*: la teologia della storia della salvezza nella riflessione di Alessandro di Hales. StFr 98 (2001) 301-317.

12432 AQUINAS: *Bonnewijn, Olivier* Béatitudes et théologie morale chez Saint Thomas d'Aquin. Anthropotes 17 (2001) 295-309.

12433 **Ryan, Thomas F.** Thomas Aquinas as reader of the Psalms. Studies in spirituality and theology 6: ND 2001, Univ. of Notre Dame Pr. ix; 233 pp. $40. 0-2680-2003-5 [ThD 48,286–Heiser, W.C.].

12434   **Torrell, Jean-Pierre** Le Christ en ses mystères: la vie et l'oeuvre
de Jésus selon saint Thomas d'Aquin. 1999 ⇒15,12603; 16,12872.
^RNV 76/1 (2001) 97-98 (*Emery, Gilles*); RSR 89 (2001) 297-300
(*Fédou, Michel*).

12435   **Valkenberg, Wilhelmus G.B.M.** Words of the living God: place
and function of Holy Scripture in the theology of St. Thomas Aquinas. 2000 ⇒16,12873. ^RTS 62 (2001) 378-379 (*Levering, Matthew*); Thom. 65 (2001) 484-489 (*Donohoo, Lawrence J.*).

12436   AUGUSTINUS BELGICUS: *Parmentier, Martien* Was war die Sünde
Sodoms?: eine mittelalterliche Umfrage. IKZ 91 (2001) 274-288
[Gn 18-19].

12437   BACON: *Anheim, Étienne* Exégèse judéo-chrétienne, magie et linguistique: un recueil de *notes* inédites attribuées à Roger Bacon.
AHDL 68 (2001) 95-154.

12438   BAR SALIBI: **Ryan, Stephen Desmond** Studies in bar Salibi's *Commentary on the Psalms*. Diss. Harvard 2001 [HThR 97,112-113].

12439   BEDA: *Tugene, Georges* L'histoire ecclésiastique de Bède le Véné-
rable. L'historiographie de l'église. 2001 ⇒541. 259-270 [BuBB
36,104].

12440   *Ferraro, Giuseppe* Lo Spirito Santo nelle "omelie sui vangeli" di
Beda il Venerabile: i testi pneumatologici del quarto vangelo (parte
prima). Lat. 67 (2001) 31-69;

12441   Lo Spirito Santo nelle "omelie sui vangeli" di Beda il Venerabile: i
testi pneumatologici dei sinottici e di Paolo: il pensiero di Beda sullo Spirito (parte seconda). Lat. 67 (2001) 291-328.

12442   *Holder, Arthur G.* The patristic sources of Bede's commentary on
the Song of Songs. StPatr 34. 2001 ⇒553. 370-375.

12443   *Kelly, Joseph F.* Bede's use of the Fathers to interpret the Infancy
Narratives. StPatr 34. 2001 ⇒553. 388-394.

12444   *Petersen, William L.* Ephrem Syrus and the Venerable Bede: do
east and west meet?. StPatr 34. 2001 ⇒553. 443-452.

12445   BERNARD: ^T**Fassetta, Raffaele** Bernard de Clairvaux: sermons sur
le Cantique, 3: sermons 33-50. SC 452: 2000 ⇒16,12878. ^REThL
77 (2001) 488-490 (*Rebelo, S.*).

12446   *Marie-Bernard, Sr.* Saint Bernard et la 'lectio divina'. VS 741
(2001) 649-669.

12447   BONAVENTURA: *Karris, Robert J.* Bonaventure's commentary on
Luke: four case studies of his creative borrowing from Hugh of St.
Cher. FrS 59 (2001) 133-236.

12448 CUSANUS: *Egger, Wilhelm* Die Kirche von Brixen zur Heiligen Schrift hinführen: die Brixner Predigten des Nikolaus Cusanus. TThZ 110 (2001) 294-307.

12449 FIORE: *Blank, Andreas* Chiliasmus und Geschichte in Joachim von Fiore *Opera minora*. Florensia 15 (2001) 47-57.

12450 *Cross, Anthony R.* The bible, the Trinity and history: apocalypticism and millennialism in the theology of Joachim of Fiore. Faith in the millennium. 2001 ⇒540. 260-297.

12451 **Grundmann, Herbert** Gioacchino da Fiore: vita e opere. 1997 ⇒ 14,11757. [R]RSCI 54 (2001) 543-546 (*Accrocca, Felice*).

12452 **Reeves, Marjorie; Gould, Warwick** Gioacchino da Fiore e il mito dell'evangelo eterno nella cultura europea. 2000 ⇒16,12886. [R]CFr 71 (2001) 578-580 (*Maranesi, Pietro*).

12453 *Traver, Andrew G.* The *Liber de Antichristo* and the failure of Joachite expectations. Florensia 15 (2001) 87-98.

12454 *Wannenmacher, Julia Eva* Matthaeus GUERRA, Autor eines Kommentars zum *Psalterium decem chordarum*?. Florensia 15 (2001) 99-107.

12455 GERHOH: [ET]**Licciardello, Pierluigi** Gerhoh di Reichersberg: Tractatus in Psalmum LXIV: esegesi ed ecclesiologia nel secolo XII. Per verba 14: F 2001, SISMEL xcvi; 363 pp.

12456 GIORDANO: [E]**Grattarola, Serena** Giordano da Pisa: prediche sul secondo capitolo del Genesi. 1999 ⇒15,12614. [R]Burg. 42 (2001) 283-284 (*Berzosa Martínez, Raúl*); RSCI 55 (2001) 540-542 (*Pellegrini, Letizia*).

12457 GRADENIGO: *Gambino, Francesca* Un *Diatessaron* in terzine dantesche di fine trecento. La scrittura infinita. 2001 ⇒498. 537-580.

12458 GROSSETESTE: *MacEvoy, James* The edition of a sermon on the decalogue attributed to Robert Grosseteste. Recherches de théologie et philosophie médiévales 68 (2001) 228-244 [Ex 20,1-17; Dt 5,6-21].

12459 GUNDISALVO: *Fidora, Alexander* Domingo Gundisalvo y la sagrada escritura. EE 76 (2001) 243-258.

12460 HERBERT: **Goodwin, Deborah** A study of Herbert of Bosham's Psalms commentary (c.1190). Diss. Notre Dame 2001, [D]*Signer, M.* 326 pp. 3010291.

12461 HILDEGARDIS: [E]**Van Acker, L.; Klaes-Hachmöller, M.** Hildegardis Bingensis: epistolarium. CChr.CM 91 B: Turnhout 2001, Brepols xxxi; 352 pp. 2-503-03915-4. Bibl. xxx-xxxi.

12462 HROTSVIT: [E]**Berschin, Walter** Hrotsvita Gandeshemensis: opera omnia. BSGRT: Monachii 2001, Saur xxxiv; 334 pp. 35987-19124.

12463 HUGO: ᴱSicard, Patrick Hugo de Sancto Victore: de archa Noe: libellus de formatione arche. CChr.CN 176-176A: Turnhout 2001, Brepols 2 vols. 2-503-04761-0. Bibl. v.1 19*-24*.

12464 ISHODAD: *Leonhard, Clemens* Īšō'dād's commentary on Psalm 141,2: a quotation from THEODORE of Mopsuestia's lost commentary. StPatr 35. 2001 ⇒553. 449-457.

12465 JACOB: *Salvesen, Alison* Did Jacob of Edessa know Hebrew?. ᴹWEITZMAN, M.: JSOT.S 333: 2001 ⇒113. 457-467.

12466 JOANNES C: *Van Parys, Michel* L'interprétation des écritures saintes dans l'Échelle de saint Jean Climaque. Irén. 74 (2001) 515-537 [Ps 54,7; 103,19-22; Mt 11,28-30; Jn 11].

12467 JOHN F: ᵀᴱEmery, Pierre-Yves Jean de Ford: sermons sur le Cantique des cantiques, 2: sermons 44 à 87. 2000 ⇒16,12890. ᴿCCMéd 44 (2001) 180-181 (*Callerot, Françoise*) [Cant 6,1-7,9];

12468 3: sermons 88 à 120. Pain de Cîteaux 17: Oka 2001, Abbaye cistercienne Notre-Dame-du-Lac 525 pp. €21.34. 2-921592-21-5.

12469 MAXIMUS C: *Blowers, Paul M.* The passion of Jesus Christ in Maximus the Confessor: a reconsideration. StPatr 37. 2001 ⇒553. 361-377.

12470 Ihm, Sibylle Ps.-Maximus Confessor: erste kritische Edition einer Redaktion des sacro-profanen Florilegiums *Loci Communes* nebst einer Kollation einer zweiten Redaktion und weiterem Material. Palingenesia 73: Stu 2001, Steiner cviii; 1153 pp. €98. 3515-07758-8.

12471 Kattan, Assaad Elias Verleiblichung und Synergie: Grundzüge der Bibelhermeneutik bei Maximus Confessor. Diss. Marburg 2001, ᴰ*Bienert, W.* 400 pp [RTL 33,643].

12472 NICETAS H: *Van Deun, Peter* Nicétas d'Heraclée, commentaire sur l'évangile de S. Matthieu: édition critique du chapitre 4. Byz. 71 (2001) 517-551.

12473 NICHOLAS L.: ᴱKrey, Philip D.W.; Smith, Lesley Janette Nicholas of Lyra: the senses of scripture. SHCT 90: 2000 ⇒16,1466. ᴿMÂ 107 (2001) 359-361 (*Beyer de Ryke, Benoît*); RBLit 3 (2001) 506-510 (*Casiday, Augustine*).

12474 OCKHAM: *Leppin, Volker* Ockham und die Prophetie: Beobachtungen zur Selbstwahrnehmung eines philosophischen Theologen. FZPhTh 48 (2001) 470-475.

12475 OSWALDUS A: ᴱEgan, Belinda A. Oswaldi de Corda: opus pacis. CChr.CM 179: Turnhout 2001, Brepols 154*; 99 pp 2503-0479-12.

12476 PETER O: ᴱFlood, David Peter of John Olivi on the Acts of the Apostles. Franciscan Institute Publications, text series 25: NY 2001, St. Bonaventure Univ. xxv; 516 pp. $50. 1-57659-174-3. ᴿCFr 71 (2001) 587-588 (*Maranesi, Pietro*); WiWei 64 (2001) 327-330 (*Schlageter, Johannnes*).

12477 PICCOLOMINI A: ^E**Van Heck, Adrianus** Enee Silvii Piccolominei postea Pii PP. II De Europa. StT 398: Città del Vaticano 2001, Biblioteca Apostolica Vaticana 313 pp. 88-210-0707-3.

12478 SAVONAROLA: ^T**Carbone, Giorgio** Savonarola: il trionfo della croce: la ragionevolezza della fede. Sacra Dottrina, monografie 1: Bo 2001, Studio Domenicano 268 pp. 88-7094-416-6.

12479 SIMONE F: ^E**Eckermann, Willigis,** *al.*, Simonis Fidati de Cassia, OESA: De gestis Domini Salvatoris. CSA 7: R 1998, Augustinianum 2 vols.

12480 THEODORE; HADRIAN: *Löfstedt, Bengt* Zu den Bibelkommentaren von Theodor und Hadrian. Er. 99 (2001) 34-37.

12481 UBERTINO C: **Martinez Ruiz, Carlos Mateo** De la dramatización de los acontecimientos de la pascua a la cristología: el cuarto libro del Arbor Vitae Crucifixae Iesu, de Ubertino de Casale. 2000 ⇒16, 12911. ^RRTLi 35 (2001) 258-260 (*Jiménez, Donato*); Augustinus 46 (2001) 391-392 (*Eguiarte, Enrique*); CBQ 63 (2001) 759-760 (*Cahill, Michael*).

12482 VAN RUUSBROEC: ^E**Baere, G. de** Jan van Ruusbroec: een spieghel der eeuwigher salicheit. CChr.CM 108: Turnhout 2001, Brepols 489 pp. 2-503-04081-0. Bibl. 478-483.

12483 WILLIAM L: **Sulavik, Athanasius Andrew Thomas** Magistri Guillelmi de Luxi, OP: Postilla super Baruch et postilla super Ionam: editio critica. Diss. Rome, Angelicum 2001, ^D*Bataillon, Louis J.*: R 2001, xlix; 91 pp. Bibl. 85-87.

12484 WYCLIF: ^T**Levy, Ian Christopher** John Wyclif: on the truth of holy scripture. Commentary: Kalamazoo 2001, Medieval Institute x; 368 pp.

Y4.1 Luther

12485 *Arnold, Matthieu* Formation et dissolution du lien conjugal chez BUCER et Luther. RHPhR 81 (2001) 259-276.

12486 *Beutel, Albrecht* Biblischer Text und theologische Theoriebildung in Luthers Schrift "Von weltlicher Oberkeit, wie weit man ihr Gehorsam schuldig sei" (1523). Biblischer Text. BThSt 44: 2001 ⇒ 252. 77-104.

12487 **Bocquet, Catherine** L'art de la traduction selon Martin Luther, ou lorsque le traducteur se fait missionnaire. 2000 ⇒16,12917. ^RRHPhR 81 (2001) 373-374 (*Arnold, M.*).

12488 *Boendermaker, Joop* Abraham bei Luther. ^FDEURLOO, K.: ACEBT.S 2: 2001 ⇒23. 369-374 [Heb 11].

12489 *Brosseder, Johannes* Luthers Hermeneutik und ihre gegenwärtige ökumenische Bedeutung. CV 43/3 (2001) 220-243.

12490 **Burandt, Christian Bogislav** Der eine Glaube zu allen Zeiten— Luthers Sicht der Geschichte auf Grund der Operationes in psalmos 1519-1521. 1997 ⇒14,11777. [R]ZKG 112 (2001) 113-115 (*Basse, Michael*).

12491 *Bülow, Vicco von* Der Mann mit dem "Bombenschuss": Hans Joachim IWAND (1899-1960): Lutherforscher und Theologe im Widerstand der Bekennenden Kirche. WuD 26 (2001) 249-269.

12492 **Corsani, Bruno** Lutero e la bibbia. Interpretare la Bibbia oggi 310: Brescia 2001, Queriniana 118 pp. €8.78. 88-399-2476-0. Bibl. 113-116.

12493 **Holm, Bo Kristian** Leben und Gesetz: Luthers Verständnis des Christen im Lichte der Herausforderungen durch die neuere Paulusexegese untersucht. Diss. Aarhus 2001.

12494 **Kolb, Robert** Martin Luther as prophet, teacher, and hero: images of the reformer, 1520-1620. 1999 ⇒15,12637. [R]ChH 70 (2001) 355-357 (*Lehmann, Hartmut*).

12495 **Kunze, Johannes** ERASMUS und Luther: der Einfluss des Erasmus auf die Kommentierung des Galaterbriefs und der Psalmen durch Luther 1519-1521. 2000 ⇒16,12931. [R]LuThK 25 (2001) 214-215 (*Stolle, Volker*).

12496 **Lazareth, William H.** Christians in society: Luther, the bible, and social ethics. Mp 2001, Fortress xii; 274 pp. $22.

12497 **Lienhard, Marc** Martim Lutero, tempo, vida e mensagem. 1998 ⇒ 14,11781. [R]REB 241 (2001) 242-243 (*Lepargneur, Hubert*).

12498 Lutherbibliographie 2001. [E]*Junghans, Helmar, al.*, Lutherjahrbuch 68 (2001) 153-208.

12499 **Luther, Martin** Études sur les Psaumes. Martin Luther Oeuvres 18: Genève 2001, Labor et Fides 555 pp. €39.64. 2-8309-1027-3. Bibl. 551-554.

12500 *Mattox, Mickey L.* Sancta Sara, mater ecclesiae: Martin Luther's catholic exegesis of Genesis 18:1-15. ProEc 10 (2001) 295-320.

12501 *Mottu, Henri* Le choral de Luther et le Psaume 46. BCPE 53 (2001) 23-31.

12502 **Pelikan, Jaroslav; Lehman, Helmut T.** Luther's works on CD-ROM. St Louis 2001, Concordia. $169. 0-8006-0359-1.

12503 *Pesch, Otto Hermann* Simul iustus et peccator: Sinn und Stellenwert einer Formel Martin Luthers: Thesen und Kurzkommentare. Gerecht und Sünder zugleich?. 2001 ⇒378. 146-167.

12504 *Rasmussen, Larry* Luther und ein Evangelium der Erde. ÖR 50 (2001) 312-343 [Gen 1-2].

12505 **Trigg, Jonathan D.** Baptism in the theology of Martin Luther. Boston 2001, Brill vii; 234 pp. 0-391-04107-X. Bibl. 228-231.

12506 *Wicks, Jared* God and his grace according to Luther 1509-1517. Luther-Bulletin 10 (2001) 83-107.

Y4.3 Exegesis et controversia saeculi XVI

12507 *Bost, Hubert* La mise en scène genevoise d'*Abraham sacrifiant*. Ment. *Bèze, T. de*: ETR 76 (2001) 543-561 [Gen 22].

12508 *Kingdon, Robert M.* La discipline ecclésiastique vue de Zurich et Genève au temps de la Réformation: l'usage de Matthieu 18,15-17 par les réformateurs. RThPh 133 (2001) 343-355.

12509 ᴱ**Steinmetz, David C.** Die Patristik in der Bibelexegese des 16. Jahrhunderts. 1999 ⇒15,438; 16,12942. ᴿZRGG 53 (2001) 92-93 (*Brecht, Martin*); JThS 52 (2001) 422-425 (*Lane, Anthony N.S.*); ZKG 112 (2001) 418-419 (*Lexutt, Athina*).

Y4.4 Periti aetatis reformatoriae

12510 ÁLVAREZ: *Léon Azcárate, Juan Luis de* La biblia en la evangelización de América: el memorial a FELIPE II (1588) de Bartolomé Álvarez. RelCult 47 (2001) 543-586.

12511 ARIAS MONTANO: *Lazcano, R.* Benito Arias Montano: ensayo bibliográfico. M 2001, Revista Agustiniana 96 pp.

12512 CALVIN: ᴱ**Engammare, Max** Jean Calvin: sermons sur la Genèse, 1: chapitres 1,1-11,4; 2, chapitres 11,5-20,7. 2000 ⇒16,12947. ᴿRHE 96 (2001) 168-170 (*Gilmont, Jean-François*); SCJ 32 (2001) 1197-9 (*Lane, Tony*); ThLZ 126 (2001) 1291-4 (*Basse, Michael*).

12513 ᴱ**Feld, Helmut** Ioannis Calvini: commentariorum in Acta Apostolorum Ioannis Calvini. Opera exegetica Veteris et Novi Testamenti 12,1-2: Genève 2001, Droz 2 vols v.1, 2-600-00484-X; v.2, 2-600-00656-7.

12514 **Moehn, Wilhelmus H.Th.** 'God calls us to his service': the relation between God and his audience in Calvin's sermons on Acts. THR 345: Genève 2001, Droz 279 pp. €60. 2-600-00483-1. Diss. Utrecht 1996. ᴿRSLR .37 (2001) 610-611 (*Conconi, Bruna*).

12515 **Van't Spijker, Willem** Calvin: Biographie und Theologie. Die Kirche in ihrer Geschichte 3/J2: Gö 2001, Vandenhoeck & R. J101-J236 pp. €28. 3-525-52338-6.

12516   CARTWRIGHT T: *Reventlow, Henning Graf* Die Kirche nach bibli-
        schem Vorbild ordnen: Thomas Cartwright. Epochen der Bibelaus-
        legung 4. 2001 ⇒12023. 31-39.

12517   ERASMUS: ^E**Bateman, John J.** Collected works of Erasmus, 44.
        New Testament scholarship: paraphrasis D. Erasmi Roterodami in
        omnes epistulas apostolicas, 3: 1993 ⇒9,6363. ^RGn. 73 (2001)
        516-518 (*Jakobi, Rainer*).
        ILLYRICUS: ^T**Neri, U.** Comprendere le scritture 1998 ⇒1016.

12518   *Reventlow, Henning Graf* Das reformatorische Bibelverständnis
        methodisch begründen: Matthias Flacius Illyricus. Epochen der Bi-
        belauslegung 4. 2001 ⇒12023. 11-21.

12519   LUIS DE LÉON: *Perea Sillar, Francisco José* Genealogía y escritura
        en Fray Luis de León: valoración del campo léxico de *Linaje* en *De
        los nombres de Cristo.* RevAg 42 (2001) 1115-1137.

12520   MELANCHTHON: *Scheible, Heinz* L'importanza di Melantone nella
        storia e nel presente. Protest. 56 (2001) 110-123.

12521   ^E**Wengert, Timothy J.; Graham, M. Patrick** Philip Melanchthon
        (1497-1560) and the commentary. 1997 ⇒13,11633; 15,12668.
        ^RTrinJ 22 (2001) 118-122 (*Mattox, Mickey L.*).

12522   *Zschoch, Hellmut* "Colamus has nostras scholasticas amicitias":
        Philipp Melanchthons Briefe an Matthäus Collinus als Spiegel einer
        humanistisch-reformatorischen Lehrer-Schüler-Beziehung. WuD 26
        (2001) 217-233.

12523   NACHTGALL O: *Risse, Siegfried* Der deutsche Psalmenkommentar
        des Otmar Nachtgall von 1524: eine von der Rechtfertigungslehre
        geprägte Psalmenauslegung. MThZ 52 (2001) 128-143.

12524   SWYNNERTON T: ^E**Rex, Richard** A Reformation rhetoric: Thomas
        Swynnerton's tropes and figures of scripture. 1999 ⇒15,12670.
        ^RSCJ 32 (2001) 801-802 (*Aieta, Joseph*).

12525   TYNDALE: ^E**O'Donnell, Anne M.; Wicks, Jared** The independent
        work of William Tyndale, 3: *an Answere unto Sir Thomas Mores
        Dialoge.* 2000 ⇒16,12961. ^RERSY 21 (2001) 71-75 (*McCutcheon,
        Elisabeth*); JThS 52 (2001) 950-952 (*Brooks, Peter Newman*).

Y4.5 *Exegesis post-reformatoria*—Historical criticism to 1800

12526   BUXTORF J: *Reventlow, Henning Graf* Um Vokalzeichen und
        Akzente streiten: Elias LEVITA, Louis CAPPEL und die Buxtorfs.
        Epochen der Bibelauslegung 4. 2001 ⇒12023. 79-86:

12527   EDELMANN J: Gegen den 'Bibel-Götzen' kämpfen: Johann Christian
        Edelmann. 146-156:

12528 FRANCKE A: Philologisch-historische und erbauliche Bibelauslegung verbinden: August Hermann Francke. 135-146:

12529 GERHARD J: Die Bibel als Gottes Wort verteidigen: Johann Gerhard. Epochen der Bibelauslegung 4. 2001 ⇒12023. 21-30.

12530 *Steiger, Johann Anselm* Rabbinsk skriftutläggning och luthersk ortodoxi: den judiska skriftlärdomens reception hos Johann Gerhard med flera. KHÅ (2001) 47-60 Zsfg. 55s.

12531 GRIESBACH J: *Reventlow, Henning Graf* Den neutestamentlichen Text verbessern und die synoptische Frage voranbringen: Johann Jakob Griesbach. Epochen der Bibelauslegung 4. 2001 ⇒12023. 200-202.

12532 GUYON: *Heuberger, Jean M.* Les commentaires bibliques de Madame Guyon dans la "Bible de Berleburg". RThPh 133 (2001) 303-323.

12533 HERDER J: *Reventlow, Henning Graf* Die Bibel menschlich verstehen: Johann Gottfried Herder;

12534 HOBBES T: Den 'sterblichen Gott' zum Schutzherrn einsetzen: Thomas Hobbes;

12535 HUETIUS: Die christliche Wahrheit mit biblischer Prophetie verteidigen: Pierre-Daniel Huet (Huetius). Epochen der Bibelauslegung 4. 2001 ⇒12023. 189-200/39-57/114-125.

12536 LEIBNIZ: *Duchesneau, François* Leibniz: la bible et l'ordre des vérités. RThPh 133 (2001) 267-286.

12537 LESSING: *Reventlow, Henning Graf* Den Geist gegen den Buchstaben hochhalten: Gotthold Ephraim Lessing. Epochen der Bibelauslegung 4. 2001 ⇒12023. 166-175.

12538 *Strohschneider-Kohrs, Ingrid* Lessing und MENDELSSOHN: eine Freundschaft von historischem Rang. BN 109 (2001) 83-98.

12539 LOCKE J: EHiggins-Biddle, John C. The reasonableness of christianity as delivered in the scriptures. 1999 <1695> ⇒15,12684. RJThS 52 (2001) 433-438 (*Pailin, David A.*); IPQ 41 (2001) 501-502 (*Dixon, Philip*).

12540 *Reventlow, Henning Graf* Ethische Gebote aus dem Neuen Testament schöpfen: John Locke;

12541 REIMARUS: Die Vernunft-Religion zum Richter einsetzen: Hermann Samuel Reimarus. Epochen der Bibelauslegung 4. 2001 ⇒12023. 57-71/157-166.

12542 RENAN: **Goldziher, Ignaz** Renan als Orientalist: Gedenkrede am 27. November 1893. TZalán, Peter; ENiewöhner, Friedrich: 2000 ⇒16,12982. RJud. 57 (2001) 299-300 (*Schmelzer, Hermann Imre*).

12543 SEMLER J: *Reventlow, Henning Graf* Die biblischen Schriften aus ihrer Zeit heraus begreifen: Johann Salomo Semler;

12544 SIMON R: Historisch-philologische Kritik an der Bibel üben: Richard Simon. Epochen der Bibelauslegung 4. 2001 ⇒12023. 175-189/87-92.

12545 *Stroumsa, Guy G.* Richard Simon: from philology to comparatism. AfR 3 (2001) 89-107;

12546 SPENCER J: John Spencer and the roots of idolatry. HR 41 (2001) 1-23.

12547 SPENER P: *Reventlow, Henning Graf* Das Wort Gottes reichlicher unter uns bringen: Philipp Jakob Spener. Epochen der Bibelauslegung 4. 2001 ⇒12023. 126-135.

12548 SPINOZA: **Preus, James Samuel** Spinoza and the irrelevance of biblical authority. C 2001, CUP xvi; 228 pp. $55. 0-521-80013-7. Bibl. 212-224.

12549 *Ravven, Heidi M.* Some thoughts on what Spinoza learned from MAIMONIDES on the prophetic imagination, 1: MAIMONIDES on prophecy and the imagination. JHP 39 (2001) 193-214;

12550 2: Spinoza's Maimonideanism. JHP 39 (2001) 385-406.

12551 *Reventlow, Henning Graf* Vernunft und Offenbarung trennen: Baruch de Spinoza. Epochen der Bibelauslegung 4. 2001 ⇒12023. 92-113

12552 THALHOFER V: **Malcherek, Reinhold** Liturgiewissenschaft im 19. Jahrhundert: Valentin Thalhofer (1825-1891) und sein "Handbuch der katholischen Liturgik". LWQF 86: Müns 2001, Aschendorff xliv; 227 pp. 3-402-4065-4. Bibl. Thalhofer 194-212; Bibl. ix-xliv.

12553 TOLAND J: *Reventlow, Henning Graf* Nur Vernünftiges in der Bibel finden: John Toland. Epochen der Bibelauslegung 4. 2001 ⇒ 12021. 71-78.

12554 WOOLSTON T: **Woolston, Thomas** Six discours sur les miracles de notre Sauveur: deux traductions manuscrites du XVIII⁰ siècle, dont une de Mme Du Châtelet. Libre pensée et littérature clandestine 8: P 2001, Champion 394 pp. 2-7453-0504-2.

Y5.0 *Saeculum XIX*—Exegesis—19th century

12555 *Chopineau, Jacques* Bible et histoire—la transformation des études bibliques dans la deuxième moitié du XIXe siècle. Analecta Bruxellensia 6 (2001) 37-47.

12556 **Howard, Thomas Albert** Religion and the rise of historicism: W.M.L. DE WETTE, Jacob BURCKHARDT, and the theological origins of nineteenth-century historical consciousness. 2000 ⇒16,12983. ᴿJThS 52 (2001) 441-443 (*Chapman, Mark D.*); WThJ 63 (2001)

205-208 (*Snavely, Iren L.*); RRT 8 (2001) 523-525 (*Chandler, Andrew*).

12557 *Rajak, Tessa* Jews and Greeks: the invention and exploitation of polarities in the nineteenth century. The Jewish dialogue. AGJU 48: 2001 <1999> ⇒199. 535-557.

12558 **Waubke, Hans-Günther** Die Pharisäer in der protestantischen Bibelwissenschaft des 19. Jahrhunderts. BHTh 107: 1998 ⇒14, 11846; 16,12986. [R]ThLZ 126 (2001) 1019-1021 (*Merk, Otto*).

12559 BAUR F: *Christophersen, Alf* Zum Verhältnis von Gottesgerechtigkeit und Versöhnung bei Ferdinand Christian Baur. [F]HAHN, F: 2001 ⇒41. 154-165.

12560 *Reventlow, Henning Graf* In idealistischer Schau das Neue Testament historisch-kritisch untersuchen und geschichtlich verstehen: Ferdinand Christian Baur. Epochen der Bibelauslegung 4. 2001 ⇒ 12021. 269-278.

12561 DE WETTE W: *Bultmann, Christoph* Philosophie und Exegese bei W.M.L. de Wette: der Pentateuch als Nationalepos Israels. De Wette. 2001 ⇒12562. 44-61.

12562 [E]**Mathys, Hans-Peter; Seybold, Klaus** Wilhelm Martin Leberecht de Wette: ein Universaltheologe des 19. Jahrhunderts. Studien zur Geschichte der Wissenschaften in Basel N.F. 1: Ba 2001, Schwabe 153 pp. €29. 37965-1743-9. Kolloquium 1999 [ThLZ 129,37— Henning Graf Reventlow].

12563 *Reventlow, Henning Graf* Vernunft, Ästhetik, Glaube und historische Kritik verbinden: Wilhelm Martin Leberecht de Wette. Epochen der Bibelauslegung 4. 2001 ⇒12023. 227-240.

12564 *Rogerson, John W.* Neuentdeckte Briefe de Wettes und ihre Bedeutung für die heutige de Wette-Forschung. De Wette. 2001 ⇒12562. 30-43.

12565 *Seybold, Klaus* W.M.L. de Wettes Arbeit an den Psalmen. De Wette. 2001 ⇒12562. 62-78.

12566 *Smend, Rudolf* Ein Theologe zwischen den Fronten: Wilhelm Martin Leberecht de Wette 1780-1849. De Wette. 2001 ⇒12562. 11-29.

12567 *Stegemann, Ekkehard* "Die Halbierung der 'hebräischen' Religion": de Wettes Konstruktion von "Hebraismus" und "Judentum" zum Zwecke christlicher Aneignung des Alten Testaments;

12568 *Weder, Hans* Attraktive Auslegung: zur Hermeneutik der neutestamentlichen Exegese von W.M.L. de Wette. De Wette. 2001 ⇒ 12550. 79-95/96-107.

12569 DUHM B: *Reventlow, Henning Graf* Der originalen Prophetie nachspüren: Bernhard Duhm;

12570 EICHHORN J: Den biblischen Mythos als 'kindhafte' Sprechweise deuten: Johann Gottfried Eichhorn und Johann Philipp GABLER;

12571 EWALD H: Historische Bibelkritik zu positiven Ergebnissen führen: Heinrich Ewald. Epochen der Bibelauslegung 4. 2001 ⇒12023. 316-324/209-226/290-295.

12572 HEGEL: **Crites, Stephen** Dialectic and gospel in the development of Hegel's thinking. 1998 ⇒14,11837; 15,12691. [R]JThS 52 (2001) 444-445 (*Law, David R.*).

12573 HENGSTENBERG E: *Reventlow, Henning Graf* Das Alte Testament vom Rationalismus befreien: Ernst Wilhelm Hengstenberg;

12574 HOLTZMANN H: Die Quellen der Evangelien historisch-kritisch ermitteln: Heinrich Julius Holtzmann. Epochen der Bibelauslegung 4. 2001 ⇒12023. 278-290/295-302.

12575 KUENEN A: *Loader, James Alfred* Die Exilsperiode in Abraham Kuenens Darstellung der israelitischen Religion. Begegnung mit Gott. Wiener alttestamentliche Studien 3: 2001 ⇒175. 269-290.

12576 LIGHTFOOT J: **Treloar, Geoffrey R.** Lightfoot the historian. WUNT 2/103: 1998 ⇒15,12698. [R]RB 108 (2001) 467-69 (*Taylor, Justin*).

12577 LÜCKE, F: **Christophersen, Alf** Friedrich Lücke (1791-1855). TBT 94/1-2: 1999 ⇒16,12980. [R]ThLZ 126 (2001) 1016-9 (*Merk, Otto*).

12578 NEVIN J: **DiPuccio, William** The interior sense of scripture: the sacred hermeneutics of John W. Nevin. 1998 ⇒14,11838. [R]TJT 17 (2001) 306-307 (*Racine, Jean-François*).

12579 NEWMAN J: **Maceri, Francesco** La formazione della coscienza del credente: una proposta educativa alla luce dei *Parochial and Plain Sermons* di John Henry Newman. Aloisiana 31: R 2001, E.P.U.G. 327 pp. €23.24. 88-7652-899-7.

12580 NIETZSCHE F: *Cancik, Hubert; Cancik-Lindemaier, Hildegard* The "pre-existent form" (Präexistenz-Form) of christianity: philological observations concerning Nietzsche's early construction of the history of ancient religions. [F]BETZ, H. 2001 ⇒5. 413-434.

12581 PAULUS H: *Reventlow, Henning Graf* Wunder natürlich erklären: Heinrich Eberhard Gottlob Paulus. Epochen der Bibelauslegung 4. 2001 ⇒12023. 202-209.

12582 SCHLEIERMACHER F: *Herms, Eilert* Welt—Kirche—Bibel: zum hermeneutischen Zentrum und Fundament von Schleiermachers Verständnis der Christentums- und Sozialgeschichte. Biblischer Text. BThSt 44: 2001 ⇒252. 105-134.

12583 **Phillips, Buran** Didactic and rhetorical coherence in the thought of Friedrich Schleiermacher: the interrelationship of theology and preaching with special attention to Schleiermacher's sermons on the epistle to the Colossians. Diss. Vanderbilt 2001, [D]*Forstman* [RTL 33,648].

12584 **Schleiermacher, Friedrich D.E.** Kritische Ausgabe, 8: exegetische Schriften. [E]*Patsch, Hermann; Schmid, Dirk*: B 2001, De Gruyter lvii; 282 pp. €98. 3-1101-6893-6 [Col 1,15-20].

12585 **Schnur, Harald** Schleiermachers Hermeneutik und ihre Vorgeschichte im 18. Jahrhundert: Studien zur Bibelauslegung, zu HAMANN, HERDER und F. SCHLEGEL 1994 ⇒10, 14705*. [R]ThRv 97 (2001) 102-104 (*Reventlow, Henning Graf*).

12586 *Wyman, Walter E.* Testing liberalism's conceptuality: the relation of sin and evil in Schleiermacher's theology. [F]DIETRICH, W: BJSt 329: 2001 ⇒24. 138-154.

12587 STRAUß D: *Kuhn, Thomas K.* Strauß, David Friedrich (1808-1874). TRE 32. 2001 ⇒665. 241-246.

12588 *Reventlow, Henning Graf* Die Erzählungen der Evangelien als Mythen charakterisieren: David Friedrich Strauß. Epochen der Bibelauslegung 4. 2001 ⇒12023. 240-256.

12589 TISCHENDORF C: [E]**Böttrich, Christfried** Tischendorf-Lesebuch: Bibelforschung in Reiseabenteuern. 1999 ⇒15,12689. [R]NT 43 (2001) 199-200 (*Elliott, J.K.*).

12590 VAN Eß L: **Altenberend, Johannes** Leander van Eß (1772-1847): Bibelübersetzer und Bibelverbreiter zwischen katholischer Aufklärung und evangelikaler Erweckungsbewegung. SQWFG 41: Pd 2001, Bonifatius 448 pp. €29.90. 3-89710-177-7 [ThRv 99,132s— Wagner, Harald].

12591 VATKE W: *Reventlow, Henning Graf* Auf HEGEL und DE WETTE eine biblische Theologie begründen: Wilhelm Vatke;

12592 WELLHAUSEN J: Den Gang der Geschichte Israels neu bestimmen: Julius Wellhausen. Epochen der Bibelauslegung 4. 2001 ⇒12023. 256-269/302-316.

Y5.5 *Crisi modernistica*—The Modernist Era

12593 *Arnold, Claus* Die römische Indexkongregation und Alfred LOISY am Anfang der Modernismuskrise (1893-1903): mit besonderer Berücksichtigung von P. Thomas ESSER O.P. und einem Gutachten von P. Louis BILLOT S.J. RQ 96 (2001) 290-332.

12594 **Ciappa, Rosanna** Rivelazione e storia: il problema ermeneutico nel carteggio tra Alfred LOISY e Maurice BLONDEL (febbraio-marzo 1903). Univ. degli studi di Napoli, Pubb. del Dipart. di Discipline Storiche 14: N 2001, Liguori 198 pp. €10.33. 88-207-3145-2.

12595 **Guasco, Maurilio** El modernismo: los hechos, las ideas, los personajes. 2000 ⇒16,12988. [R]Isidorianum 10 (2001) 524-526 (*Riego, Manuel Martín*).

12596 *Hausberger, Karl* Dem Licht den Rücken gekehrt: zu den antimo-
dernistischen Rahmenbedingungen der katholischen Exegese zwischen 1870 und 1943. [F]SCHMUTTERMAYR, G. 2001 ⇒101. 427-440.

12597 **Loisy, Alfred** L'évangile et l'église; Autour d'un petit livre; Jésus
et la tradtion évangélique. P 2001, Noesis 482 pp.

12598 **Raurell, Frederic** L'antimodernismei el Cardenal VIVES I TUTÓ.
2000 ⇒16,12991. [R]RCatT 26 (2001) 214-218 (*Raguer, Hilari*).

Y6.0 *Saeculum XX-XXI*—20th-21st Century Exegesis

12599 *Bacq, Philippe* Les lectures de la bible dans l'église catholique.
CEv 116 (2001) 52-64.

12600 **Chapman, Mark D.** The coming crisis: the impact of eschatology
on theology in Edwardian England. JSNT.S 208: Shf 2001, Sheffield A. 189 pp. 1-84127-185-3. Bibl. 176-186.

12601 *Fernández Marcos, Natalio* Un siglo de investigación bíblica en
España, en los cien años de *Razón y fe*. RF 244 (2001) 129-142.

12602 **Mason, Nancy K.** Biblical scholars at the Catholic University of
America, 1889-1989: diverse, faithful, and sometimes irksome.
Diss. Washington, Cath. Univ. of America 2001, [D]FORD, J.T. 618
pp. 3004175 [RTL 33,648].

12603 **Smith, Mark S.** Untold stories: the bible and Ugaritic studies in the
twentieth century. Peabody, MASS 2001, Hendrickson xix; 252 pp.
$30. 1-56563-575-2.

12604 ALONSO SCHÖKEL L: *Beutler, Johannes* Alonso Schökel, Luis, SJ.
LThK 11. 2001 ⇒655. 4.

12605 BARCLAY W: **Rawlins, Clive** William Barclay—the authorized biography. 1998 ⇒14,11858. [R]SBET 19 (2001) 233-234 (*Macgregor,
Alan*).

12606 BARTH K: **Aguti, A.** La questione dell'ermeneutica in Karl Barth.
Bo 2001, EDB 306 pp. €18.08.

12607 Karl Barth-Gesamtausgabe. VF 46/1 (2001) 2-92.

12608 **Burnett, Richard E.** Karl Barth's theological exegesis: the hermeneutical principles of the Römerbrief period. WUNT 2/145: Tü
2001, Mohr xv; 312 pp. €49. 3-16-147677-8. Diss. Princeton
Theol. Sem. [Bibl. 293-305].

12609 *Chung, Sung Wook* Seeds of ambivalence sown: Barth's use of
CALVIN in *Der Römerbrief II* (1922). EvQ 73 (2001) 37-58 [Rev
14,11].

12610   *Jorgenson, Allen G.* Karl Barth's christological treatment of sin. SJTh 54 (2001) 437-462.

12611   *Reventlow, Henning Graf* Gott Gott sein lassen zu seiner Offenbarung in Kreuz und Auferstehung Jesu, des Christus: Karl Barth. Epochen der Bibelauslegung 4. 2001 ⇒12023. 366-380.

12612   *Smend, Rudolf* Vielfältige Virtuosität: Karl Barth, Gespräche 1959-1962 (IV/25), hg. von **Eberhard Busch**, xviii + 569 S. 1995. VF 46/1 (2001) 73-75.

12613   BEA A: *Schmidt, S.* Bea, Augustin. Diccionario histórico S.J., 1. 2001 ⇒717. 376-377.

12614   BONHOEFFER D: *Bitter, Stephan* Weichenstellungen 1932/1933. VF 46/2 (2001) 26-32.

12615   *Credaro, Giovanna* 'Poi giunse qualcosa di diverso': la bibbia nell'opera di Dietrich Bonhoeffer. NRS 85 (2001) 363-386.

12616   *Kelly, Geffrey B.; Nelson, F. Burton* Dietrich Bonhoeffer's theological interpretation of scripture for the church. ExAu 17 (2001) 1-30.

12617   BOUSSET W: *Reventlow, Henning Graf* Das Urchristentum in die antike Religionsgeschichte hineinstellen: Wilhelm Bousset. Epochen der Bibelauslegung 4. 2001 ⇒12023. 346-359.

12618   BREUKELMAN F: *Verbaas, Frans Willem* De partizaan en de professor: Frans Breukelman vergeleken met Walter BRUEGGEMANN. ITBT 9/2 (2001) 9-14.

12619   BUBER M: Werkausgabe, 1: frühe kulturkritische und philosophische Schriften 1898-1924. ᴱ**Mendes-Flohr, Paul; Schäfer, Peter; Urban, Martina**: Gü 2001, Kaiser 396 pp. 3-579-02675-5. Bearbeitet, eingeleitet und kommentiert von *Martin Treml.*

12620   **Bombaci, Nunzio** Ebraismo e cristianesimo a confronto nel pensiero di Martin Buber. N 2001, Dante & D. 214 pp.

12621   BULTMANN R: *Reventlow, Henning Graf* Die Botschaft des Neuen Testaments existential auslegen: Rudolf Bultmann. Epochen der Bibelauslegung 4. 2001 ⇒12023. 380-391.

12622   Nachlaßverzeichnis. ᴱ**Waßmann, Harry; Osthof, Jakob Matthias; Bruckhaus, Anna-Elisabeth**: Wsb 2001, Harrassowitz 410 pp. €45. 3-447-04414-4 [RB 109,313].

12623   CROSSAN J: *Sventsitskaya, I.S.* A new approach to the origin of christianity: works by J.D. Crossan. Journal of Ancient History 1 (2001) 88-97 Sum. 97. **R.**

12624   DAHOOD M: *Swetnam, James* Dahood, Mitchell. Diccionario histórico S.J., 2. 2001 ⇒717. 1038.

12625   DERRIDA J: *Collins, Guy* Defending Derrida: a response to Milbank and Pickstock. SJTh 54 (2001) 344-365.

12626   DEURLOO K: *Hoogewoud, F.J.; Deurloo-Sluijter, Jettie* Bibliography Karel Adriaan Deurloo. ᶠDEURLOO, K.: 2001 ⇒23. 393-416.

12627   *Zuurmond, Rochus* A man of letters: Karel Deurloo as a theologian. ᶠDEURLOO, K.: ACEBT.S 2: 2001 ⇒23. 1-8.

12628   DZUBBA H: *Marquardt, Friedrich W.* Horst Dzubba (19.7.1913-9.12.1978): ein Berliner Nachbar von Frans BREUKELMAN. TeKo 24/2 (2001) 4-31.

12629   ELIADE M: *Muthuraj, J. Gnanaseelan* The significance of Mircea Eliade for the study of the New Testament. BTF 33/2 (2001) 38-59.

12630   FITZGERALD A: *Blanchard, Monica J.* A list of the writings of Aloysius Fitzgerald, F.S.C. ᶠFITZGERALD, A.: CBQ.MS 32: 2001 ⇒31. 191-199.

12631   FLUSSER D: *Thoma, Clemens* David Flusser: Aussagen in :Briefen und Vorträgen. FrRu 8 (2001) 86-93.

12632   GAECHTER P: *Stock, Klemens* Gaechter, Paul. Diccionario histórico S.J. 2. 2001 ⇒717. 1546 [AcBib 10,1032].

12633   GANDHI: *Emilsen,William W.* Gandhi, scripture and the bible. Pacifica 14 (2001) 71-86.

12634   GIRARD R: **Tugnoli, Claudio** Girard: dal mito ai vangeli. Padova 2001, Messaggero 270 pp. €18.07.

12635   GOULDER M: **Goodacre, Mark S.** Goulder and the gospels. JSOT.S 133: 1996 ⇒12,11058; 14,11881. ᴿSNTU.A 25 (2000) 272-275 *(Fenske, Wolfgang)*.

12636   GUNKEL H: *Reventlow, Henning Graf* Die Religionsgeschichte Israels erforschen und eine alttestamentliche Literaturgeschichte entwerfen: Hermann Gunkel. Epochen der Bibelauslegung 4. 2001 ⇒ 12021. 327-346.

12637   HAHN F: *Hoegen-Rohls, Christina* Bibliographie der Veröffentlichungen von Ferdinand Hahn aus den Jahren 1990-2000. ᶠHAHN, F. 2001 ⇒41. 215-220.

12638   HAINZ J: *Bauer, Alexander* Veröffentlichungen von Josef Hainz. ᶠHAINZ, J. 2001 ⇒42. 388-395.

12639   HARNACK A von: ᴱ**Nowak, Kurt; Oexle, Otto Gerhard** Adolf von Harnack: Theologe, Historiker, Wissenschaftspolitiker. VMPIG 161: Gö 2001, Vandenhoeck & R. 448 pp. €47.30. Symposion, Ringberg 1998.

12640   KEGLER J: *Kegler, Jürgen* Rundfunkansprachen. Gesammelte Aufsätze. BEAT 48: 2001 ⇒167. 369-414.

12641   LAGRANGE M: *Gilbert, Maurice* M.-J. Lagrange et F. CUMONT: l'histoire des religions et la bible. EtCl 69 (2001) 3-22 [AcBib 10,802].

12642 LEVINAS E: **Ajzenstat, Oona** Driven back to the text: the premodern sources of Levinas's postmodernism. Pittsburgh 2001, Duquesne Uni. Pr. 388 pp. $54. 0820703257 [ThD 49,57–Heiser, W.].

12643 **Cohen, Richard A.** Ethics, exegesis and philosophy: interpretation after Levinas. C 2001, CUP vii; 361 pp. $65. 0-521-80158-3.

12644 *Meir, Ephraim* La philosophie de Lévinas, sacrificielle et naïve?: s'agit-il d'un drame?: à propos d'un ouvrage récent de Daniel Sibony. RHPhR 81 (2001) 63-79.

12645 **Plüss, David** Das Messianische: Judentum und Philosophie im Werk Emmanuel Lévinas'. Judentum und Christentum 8: Stu 2001, Kohlhammer 399 pp. €34. 3-17-016975-0.

12646 *Waaijman, Kees* The hermeneutics of Emmanuel Levinas. Studies in Spirituality 11 (2001) 71-125.

12647 LUBAC H de: **Kuther, Ulrich** Kirchliche Tradition als geistliche Schriftauslegung: zum theologischen Schriftgebrauch in Henri de Lubacs "Die Kirche: eine Betrachtung". Studien zur Traditionstheorie 5: Müns 2001, Lit 274 pp. 3-8258-5563-5.

12648 *Moulins-Beaufort, Eric de* Henri de Lubac: reader of *Dei Verbum*. Com(US) 28 (2001) 669-694.

12649 **Voderholzer, Rudolf** Die Einheit der Schrift und ihr geistiger Sinn: der Beitrag Henri de Lubacs zur Erforschung von Geschichte und Systematik christlicher Bibelhermeneutik. SlgHor 31: 1998 ⇒ 14,11895... 16,13044. ᴿSvTK 77 (2001) 43-45 (*Bexell, Peter*).

12650 **Wagner, Jean-Pierre** Henri de Lubac. Initiations aux théologiens: P 2001, Cerf 253 pp.

12651 **Wood, Susan K.** Spiritual exegesis and the church in the theology of Henri de Lubac. 1998 ⇒14,11896; 16,13045. ᴿProEc 10/1 (2001) 110-112 (*d'Ambrosio, Marcellino*).

12652 LYONNET S: *Places, E. des* Lyonnet, Stanislas. Diccionario histórico S.J., 3. 2001 ⇒717. 2448-2449.

12653 MACRAE G: *Harrington, D.J.* MacRae, George W. Diccionario histórico S.J., 3. 2001 ⇒717. 2458-2459.

12654 MALLON A: *Swetnam, James* Mallon, Alexis. Diccionario histórico S.J., 3. 2001 ⇒717. 2485-2486.

12655 METZGER B: **Metzger, Bruce Manning** Reminiscences of an octogenarian. 1997 ⇒13,11716... 16,13049. ᴿSBET 19 (2001) 114-115 (*Beckwith, Roger T.*).

12656 MVENG E: *Poucouta, Paulin E.* Mveng's African reading of the bible. ThD 48 (2001) 21-25 <NRT 120 (1998) 32-45.

12657 NOBER P: *Swetnam, James* Nober, Peter. Diccionario histórico S.J., 3. 2001 ⇒717. 2825.

12658   PEDERSEN J: *Loader, James Alfred* Eine Alternative zu Johannes
Pedersens Machtbegriff. Begegnung mit Gott. Wiener alttestamentliche Studien 3: 2001 ⇒175. 151-166.

12659   PIETERSMA A: *Pietersma, Margaret* Who is Albert Pietersma?.
ᶠPIETERSMA, A.: JSOT.S 332: 2001 ⇒87. 19-20.

12660   RAD G von: *Mathys, Hans-Peter* "Hier ist mehr als ...":
Anmerkungen zu Gerhard von Rad. ThZ 57 (2001) 230-242.

12661   RICOEUR P: *Orth, Stefan* Rätselhaftes Gedächtnis: Paul Ricoeurs
Thesen zu Erinnern und Vergessen. HerKorr 55 (2001) 80-85.

12662   ROSENZWEIG F: *Baccarini, Emilio* Eternità nella storia, ebraismo e
cristianesimo nella *Stella della redenzione* di F. Rosenzweig. Fil-
Teo 15 (2001) 297-312.

12663   *Bertoldi, Roberto* Il nuovo pensiero della verità in Franz Rosenzweig. Hum(B) 56 (2001) 605-626.

12664   *Bonagiuso, Giacomo* La dimensione dell'oltre': tentazione mistica
e utopia della storia in F. Rosenzweig. FilTeo 15 (2001) 313-327.

12665   **Ciglia, Francesco Paolo** Cinque studi su Rosenzweig. 1999 ⇒15,
12768. ᴿFilTeo 15 (2001) 651-653 (*Mancinelli, Paola*).

12666   **Rosenzweig, Franz** L'écriture, le verbe et autres essais. ᵀ*Evard,
Jean-Luc*: 1998 ⇒14,11911. ᴿRPL 99 (2001) 316-319 (*Jeanmart,
Gaëlle*); ETR 76 (2001) 625-626 (*Askani, Hans-Christoph*).

12667   *Janse, S.* Ervaring, schrift en traditie in Paulus' brieven: kritische
noten bij een stelling van E.P. Sanders. NedThT 55/3 (2001) 177-
195.

12668   SCHENKER A: Bibliographie d'Adrian Schenker (études bibliques).
ᶠSCHENKER, A.: OBO 179: 2001 ⇒100. 105-114.

12669   SCHWEITZER A: *Gräßer, Erich* Der Paulinismus als apostolisches
Urchristentum: Albert Schweitzers Paulusverständnis in seinen
Straßburger Vorlesungen. Forschungen zur Apostelgeschichte.
WUNT 137: 2001 <2000> ⇒152. 334-351.

12670   SEMKOWSKI L: *Swetnam, James* Semkowski, Ludwik;

12671   SIMON J: Simon, Jean. Diccionario histórico S.J., 4. 2001 ⇒717.
3553/3578.

12672   STREETER B: *Tuckett, Christopher M.* Streeter, Burnett Hillman
(1874-1937). TRE 32. 2001 ⇒665. 249-252.

12673   SUTCLIFFE E: *Meredith, A.* Sutcliffe, Edmund Felix. Diccionario
histórico S.J., 4. 2001 ⇒717. 3674.

12674   TALBERT C: *Dowd, Sharyn* Charles H. Talbert's contributions to
New Testament scholarship. PRSt 28/1 (2001) 5-13.

12675   TEITZ M: **Blau, Rivkah Teitz** Learn Torah, love Torah, live Torah:
haRav Mordechai Pinchas Teitz, the quintessential rabbi. Hoboken,
NJ 2001, KTAV xi; 371 pp. 0-88125-718-4.

12676 THOMPSON W: *Tobin, Thomas H.* The legacy of William G. Thompson, S.J. ^MTHOMPSON, W. 2001 ⇒108. 1-4.

12677 VISCHER W: **Felber, Stefan** Wilhelm Vischer als Ausleger der Heiligen Schrift: eine Untersuchung zum Christuszeugnis des Alten Testaments. FSÖTh 89: 1998 ⇒14,11924; 15,12783. ^RTrinJ 22 (2001) 276-280 (*Yarbrough, Robert W.*).

12678 VOGLER W: *Haufe, Günter* Werner Vogler: ein Blick in seine exegetisch-theologische Lebensarbeit. Leqach 1 (2001) 13-c.21.

12679 *Kähler, Christoph* Werner Vogler 1934-2000. Leqach 1 (2001) 6-c.12.

12680 VOGT E: *Wicki, J.; Gilbert, M.* Vogt, Ernest. Diccionario histórico S.J., 4. 2001 ⇒717. 3995.

12681 WEIß J: *Reventlow, Henning Graf* Jesu Verkündigung vom Reiche Gottes als Endzeitankündigung deuten: Johannes Weiß. Epochen der Bibelauslegung 4. 2001 ⇒12023. 359-365.

12682 WELBY V: *Petrilli, Susan* Light between sacred and profane: Victoria Welby from biblical exegesis to significs .Semiotica 136 (2001) 173-200.

12683 ZERWICK M: *Beutler, Johannes* Zerwick, Max, SJ. LThK 10. 2001 ⇒655. 1939-1940.

12684 *Swetnam, James* Zerwick, Maximilian. Diccionario histórico S.J., 4. 2001 ⇒717. 4075.

Y6.3 *Influxus Scripturae saeculis XX-XXI*—Survey of current outlooks

12685 *Bartal, Israel* Land and people, 2001. Cathedra 100 (2001) 21-26 Sum. 405. **H**.

12686 *Blomberg, Craig C.* Where should twenty-first-century evangelical biblical scholarship be heading?. BBR 11 (2001) 161-172.

12687 **Burns, Robert A.** Roman Catholicism after Vatican II. Wsh 2001, Georgetown University Press viii; 200 pp. 0-87840-822-3. Bibl. 183-194.

12688 *Court, John M.* Recent continental NewTestament literature. ET 112 (2001) 127-131.

12689 **Grenz, Stanley J.; Franke, John R.** Beyond foundationalism: shaping theology in a postmodern context. LVL 2001, Westminster xi; 298 pp. $25. 0-664-25769-0 [ThD 48,271–Heiser, W. Charles].

12690 **Gutting, Gary** French philosophy in the twentieth century. C 2001, CUP xiv; 419 pp. 0-521-66559-0. Bibl. 394-411.

12691 *Joubert, S.J.* Teologiekroniek: die relevansie van teologie in millenium drie. VeE 22 (2001) 191-197.

12692 **Pasquale, Gianluigi** La teologia della storia della salvezza nel secolo XX. Nuovi saggi teologici, series maior: Bo 2001, EDB 609 pp. 88-10-40563-3. Bibl. 547-591.

12693 *Rogerson, John W.* Recent continental Old Testament literature. ET 112 (2001) 88-91.

12694 *Verseput, Donald J.* Considering the needs of the church: a response to Craig Blomberg. BBR 11 (2001) 173-177.

Y7.2 *Congressus biblici*: nuntii, *rapports, Berichte*

Auwers, J. The biblical canons 2001 ⇒1224.

12695 *Capelli, Piero Septuaginta*: libri sacra della diaspora giudaica e dei cristiani: IV giornata di studio *Gerusalemme ed Alessandria: uno stesso pentateuco?*. Henoch 23 (2001) 113-114. Milano, Univ. Sacro Cuore, 10 maggio 2001.

12696 *Haquin, A.* Congrès de l'A.C.F.E.B. EThL 78 (2001) 293-294. Toulouse, 3-7 Sept. 2001.

12697 *Hoppe, Rudolf* 55. Meeting der Studiorum Novi Testamenti Societas vom 30. Juli-4. August 2000 in Tel Aviv. BZ 45 (2001) 156-58.

Izquierdo, A. Encuentro sobre la inspiración 2001 ⇒1195.

12698 *Leonardi, Giovanni* La tradizionale tomba di san Luca evangelista a Padova; II congresso internazionale su san Luca. PaVi 46/1 (2001) 56-60.

12699 *Leonardi, Giovanni; Girolami, Maurizio* Il giudeo-cristianesimo nel I e II sec. d.C.: IX convegno di studi neotestamentari 13-15 settembre 2001, Napoli. StPat 48 (2001) 631-640.

12700 *Libanori, Daniele* Il congresso sulle reliquie di San Luca evangelista. CivCatt 152/1 (2001) 497-501. 16-21 ott. 2000, Padova.

12701 *Marenco, Maria Rita* Associazione Biblica Italiana (ABI): XXXVI Settimana Biblica Nazionale, Roma, 11-15 settembre 2000. ATT 7 (2001) 519-533.

12702 [E]**Neirynck, Frans** Colloquium Biblicum Lovaniense: journées bibliques de Louvain 1-50, 1949-2001. SNTA 19: Lv 2001, Lv Univ. Pr. 116 pp. €10. 90-5867-150-X [RB 109,476].

12703 *Orth, Stefan* Aufhebung der Grenzen?: die Neutestamentler und der Gott des Juden Jesus. HerKorr 55 (2001) 298-301. Tagung der Arbeitsgemeinschaft der katholischen Neutestamentler im deutschen Sprachraum, Löwen, 2.-6. April 2001.

12704 *Pisarek, Stanisław* Sympozjum biblistów polskich: ostatnie w tym wieku oraz tysiacleciu [Symposium des biblistes polonais]. AtK 136 (2001) 366-368 Riass. 269. **P**.

12705 Proceedings of the 2nd General Assembly of the Catholic Biblical Association of the Philippines, July 20-22, 2001. Charism, leadership. 2001 ⇒456. 123-127.

12706 *Van Belle, G.* Annual convention of the 'Arbeitsgemeinschaft der [katholischen] deutschsprachigen Neutestamentler': Der Gott Israels im Zeugnis des Neuen Testaments. EThL 77 (2001) 252-53. Leuven, April 2-6;

12707 Studiorum Novi Testamenti Societas: 56th General Meeting, Montréal 31.7-4.8.2001. EThL 77 (2001) 550-552;

12708 Studiosorum Novi Testamenti Conventus: 51ste conferentie, Woudschouten te Heist, 11.6.2001. EThL 77 (2001) 559-560.

12709 *Verheyden, J.* Institutum Iudaicum: The images of the Judeo-Christians in ancient Jewish and Christian literature. EThL 78 (2001) 283.

12710 *Walsh, Jerome T.* Report of the 64th International Meeting of the Catholic Biblical Association of America. CBQ 63 (2001) 700-708.

12711 *Wehr, Lothar* Tagung der Arbeitsgemeinschaft der deutschsprachigen katholischen Neutestamentler in Leuven vom 2. bis 6. April 2001. BZ 45 (2001) 312-314.

12712 *Wénin, André* Symposium d'analyse narrative des textes bibliques (Réseau de recherche en analyse narrative des textes bibliques). RTL 32 (2001) 307-309. Paris, 9-10.2.2001.

12713 *Wischmeyer, Oda* Einführung: das erste Erlanger Textkolloquium: Ziele, Ablauf, Ergebnisse und Perspektiven;

12714 Was ist ein Text?: Zusammenfassung des Kolloquiums und Perspektiven für die Interpretation neutestamentlicher Texte. Was ist ein Text?. 2001 ⇒335. 1-14/211-225.

Y7.4 *Congressus theologici*: **nuntii**

12715 *Barea Amorena, Ernesto* XIII Simposio Internacional Mariológico, Roma, 2-5.10.2001. EphMar 51 (2001) 537-539.

12716 *Golasmici, Marilena* XIII simposio mariologico internazionale, Roma, 2-5 ottobre 2001. Theotokos 9 (2001) 491-495.

12717 *Ilunga Muya, Juvénal* "Who do you say I am?" (Mt 16,15): missiological and missionary responses in the context of religions and cultures: International Missiological Congress (Rome 17-20 October 2000). ZMR 85 (2001) 199-206.

12718 *Márquez Beunza, Carmen* 'Continuad soñando hermanas': IX conferencia internacional de la Asociación europea de mujeres en la investigación teológica (Salzburgo, 19-23 agosto 2001). TE 45 (2001) 367-372.

12719   *Prema* Indian Theological Association: 24th Annual General Body
Meeting and Seminar, April 24-28, 2001, St. Pius College, Mumbai. ITS 38 (2001) 247-250.

12720   *Russo, Marco* GIOACCHINO da Fiore tra BERNARDO di Clairvaux e
INNOCENZO III. Florensia 15 (2001) 149-154. San Giovanni in Fiore
(CS), sett. 1999.

12721   *Trudu, Fabio* La parola di Dio tra scrittura e rito. RivLi 88 (2001)
288-290. XXVIII settimana di studio: associazione professori e
cultri di liturgia, Pisa, 27.8-1.9.2000.

Y7.6 Reports of philological and archaeological meetings

12722   The 102nd annual meeting of the Archaeological Institute of America. AJA 105 (2001) 245-311.

12723   27th Archaeological Congress in Israel. IEJ 51 (2001) 105-106.
Jerusalem, 2-3.4.2001.

12724   *Geva, H.* The 27th archaeological congress in Israel; the 56th
annual convention of the Israel Exploration Society. Qad. 34
(2001) 135, 136. **H**.

12725   "Judaistische Forschung in der Schweiz: Bestandesaufnahme und
Ausblick": Zusammenfassung der Tagung der SGJF vom Sonntag,
19. November 2000 im Gemeindehaus der Jüdischen Gemeinde
Bern. BSGJ 10 (2001) 3-5.

Y8.0 *Periti*: Scholars, personalia, organizations

12726   **Aschheim, Steven E.** SCHOLEM, ARENDT, KLEMPERER: intimate
chronicles in turbulent times. Bloomington, IND 2001, Indiana
University Press ix; (2) 134 pp. 0-253-33891-3.

12727   *Baumann, Paul* Anthropology with a difference: Mary DOUGLAS at
80. Commonweal 128/14 (2001) 11-15, 18-19.

12728   *Bernard, Mathieu* Travaux de l'Institut français d'archéologie
orientale en 2000-2001. BIFAO 101 (2001) 449-610.

12729   [E]**Bosworth, Clifford Edmund** A century of British orientalists
1902-2001. Oxf 2001, OUP (4) 264 pp. 0-19-726243-0.

12730   *Dearman, J. Andrew* J. Maxwell MILLER, scholar and teacher: a
sketch. [F]MILLER, J.: JSOT.S 343: 2001 ⇒74. 16-35.

12731   *Eisler, Ejal Jakob* "Kirchler" im Heiligen Land—die evangelischen
Gemeinden in den württembergischen Siedlungen Palästinas (1886-
1914). [F]CARMEL, A.: 2001 ⇒17. 77-90.

12732 *Endress, Gerhard; Overwien, Oliver* Verzeichnis der Schriften von Franz ROSENTHAL. Oriens 36 (2001) xiii-xxxiv.

12733 *Fischer, Robert* Habsburg und das Heilige Land: Grundzüge der österreichischen Palästinapolitik 1840-1918. ᶠCARMEL, A.: Judentum und Christentum 9: 2001 ⇒17. 61-69.

12734 *Gilbert, Maurice* Bíblico, Pontificio Instituto. Diccionario histórico S.J., 1. 2001 ⇒717. 443-445;

12735 Šira, Josef. Diccionario histórico S.J., 4. 2001 ⇒717. 3582;

12736 Tierra santa. Diccionario histórico S.J., 4. 2001 ⇒717. 3796-3802.

12737 Il Pontificio Istituto Biblico di Gerusalemme. Vinea electa (Bollettino informativo dell'Associazione ex-alunni/e del PIB) 1 (2001) 2-3;

12738 Gli studi biblici in Sicilia. Notiziario (del Centro per lo studio della storia e della cultura in Sicilia della facoltà teologica di Sicilia) 2 (2001) 49-52 [AcBib 10,912].

12739 **Gordon, Cyrus Herzl** A scholar's odyssey. 2000 ⇒16,13141. ᴿET 112 (2001) 72 (*Rodd, C.S.*).

12740 **Green, Barbara** Mikhail BAKHTIN and biblical scholarship: an introduction. 2000 ⇒16,13142. ᴿRBLit 3 (2001) 111-114 (*Miller, Charles H.*).

12741 **Grondin, Jean** Einführung zu GADAMER. UTB.W 2139: 2000 ⇒ 16,13143. ᴿThRv 97 (2001) 507-508 (*Hammermeister, Kai*).

12742 *Haacker, Klaus* Martin Hengel zum 75. Geburtstag. ThBeitr 32 (2001) 289-290.

12743 *Habsburg-Lothringen, Michael-Salvator* Auf den Spuren familiärer Identität. ᶠCARMEL, A.: 2001 ⇒17. 71-76.

12744 *Hopwood, Derek* Die russische Präsenz in Palästina—religiöse Motive, politische Ambitionen. ᶠCARMEL, A: 2001 ⇒17. 47-52.

12745 **Idestrom, Rebecca G.S.** From biblical theology to biblical criticism: Old Testament scholarship at Uppsala Univ., 1866-1922. CB. OT 47: 2000 ⇒16,13155. ᴿJThS 52 (2001) 713-715 (*Davidson, R.*); SvTK 77 (2001) 186-187 (*Hidal, Sten*); CBQ 63 (2001) 725-726 (*Bundy, David*).

12746 **Jossua, Jean-Pierre** Une Vie. P 2001, Desclée de B 112 pp. 2-220-04993-0.

12747 **Lang, Bernhard** Eugen DREWERMANN: kleines Porträt eines Romantikers. Paderborner Universitätsreden, 78: ᴱ*Freese, Peter*: Pd 2001, Universität 42 pp.

12748 ᴱ**Noll, Mark A.** The Princeton theology, 1812-1921: scripture, science, and theological method from Archibald ALEXANDER to Benjamin Breckinridge WARFIELD. GR ²2001 <1983>, Baker 322 pp. $27. 0-8010-6737-5. [ThD 49,81—Heiser, W. Charles].

12749   **North, Robert** Bibliography 1936-2002. SubBi 21: R 2001,
        E.P.I.B. 126 pp. €12. 88-7653-616-7.

12750   ^E**Nothnagle, Almut; Abromeit, Hans-Jürgen; Foerster, Frank**
        Seht, wir gehen hinauf nach Jerusalem!: Festschrift zum 150
        jährigen Jubiläum von Talitha Kumi und des Jerusalemsvereins. Lp
        2000, Evangelische 348 pp. €15.30.

12751   *Ntyreh, Benjamin Abotchie* Ghana Association of Biblical Exe-
        getes. BOTSA 11 (2001) 21-22.

12752   *Pisano, Stephen* [Prof. J. Alberto Soggin]. AcBib 10/6 (1999-2000)
        636-638. Professore invitato al Pont. Ist. Biblico 1970/71-1998/99.

12753   *Rose, Martin* L'Ancien Testament à Neuchatel 1984-2001: un bilan.
        ThZ 57 (2001) 210-220.

12754   *Roueché, Charlotte* The prehistory of the Cyprus Department of
        Antiquities. ^FMEGAW, A.: 2001 ⇒70. 155-166.

12755   *Santos, Carlos de* La Pontificia Comisión Bíblica. Qol 27 (2001)
        83-86.

12756   **Scaglia, Franco** I custodi di Gesù: i francescani in Terra Santa
        dalle crociate ai nostri giorni. 2000 ⇒16,13177. ^RCredOg 123
        (2001) 140-141 (*Cappelletto, Gianni*).

12757   *Schöpsdau, Walter* Sola scriptura und kirchliche Tradition: zu einer
        Notifikation der vatikanischen Glaubenskongregation. MdKI 52/1
        (2001) 13-15.

12758   ^E**Seger, Joe D.** An ASOR mosaic: a centennial history of the Amer-
        ican Schools of Oriental Research. Boston 2001, ASOR xxii; 376
        pp. $75. Num. photos.

12759   *Smend, Rudolf* "Wo ist Professor ALT?": Stationen alttestament-
        licher Forschung in Basel. ThZ 57 (2001) 463-468.

12760   *Steck, Odil Hannes* Lehrstuhl für Alttestamentliche Wissenschaft
        und Spätisraelitische Religionsgeschichte an der Theologischen Fa-
        kultät der Universität Zürich. ThZ 57 (2001) 199-209.

12761   *VanderKam, James C.* Emanuel TOV at sixty. DSD 8 (2001) 213-
        216.

12762   *Watson, Nigel* The first fifty years of the fellowship for biblical
        studies and the Australian Biblical Review. ABR 49 (2001) 1-4.

12763   *Weingarten, Ralph* Schweizerische Gesellschaft für Judaistische
        Forschung (SGJF): Société Suisse des Etudes Juives (SSEJ): Jah-
        resbericht. BSGJ 10 (2001) 1-2.

12764   *Wevers, John William* Paul-Eugène DION: an appreciation. ^FDION,
        P.-E. 3: JSOT.S 326: 2001 ⇒25. 19-21.

Y8.5 *Periti*: in memoriam

12765 Abou-Ghazi, Dia Mahmoud 24.1.1924-10.4.2001 [DiscEg 54, 105-107—*Nibbi, Alessandra*].

12766 Beauchamp, Paul 28.7.1924-23.4.2001. REtudes (juin 2001) 793-794 (*Madelin, Henri*); CEv 117 (2001) 63-64 (*Farin, Michel*); RTeol(Br) 26 (2001) 115-119 (*Angelini, Giuseppe*).

12767 Bergman, Jan 1933-27.8.1999 ⇒15,12881; 16,13202. RSEÅ 66 (2001) 5-6 (*Kieffer, René*).

12768 Besques, Simone 2.7.1908-10.1.2001. RRAr (2001) 359-360 (bibl. 361-3) (*Fourmont, Martine*).

12769 Bosse-Griffiths, K. 1910-1998. *Griffiths, J. Gwyn* Introduction: Kate Bosse-Griffiths†. Amarna studies. 2001 ⇒128. 7-14.

12770 Cagni, Luigi Giovanni 4.3.1929-27.1.1998 ⇒14,12008.. RMCAGNI 2001 ⇒15. xxv-xxxiii (*Agrimi, Mario; Maisano, Riccardo; Marazzi, Ugo; Verardi, Giovanni*).

12771 Camps Reverter, Guiu ob. 15.5.2001. RResB 37 (2003) 69-71 (*Tragán, Pius-Ramón*).

12772 Carlson, Agge 1928-2001. RSEÅ 66 (2001) 11-12 (*Ottosson, Magnus*).

12773 Ceccherelli, Ignazio Marino 12.8.1915-27.2.2001. RBeO 43 (2001) 45-54 (*Sardini, Davide*).

12774 Ciasca, Antonia ob. 2000. RRSFen 29 (2001) 3-4 (*Bartoloni, P.*); RSFen 29 (2001) 5-6 (*Bondì, S.F.*).

12775 Coulson, William Donald Edward 17.9.1942-24.6.2001 [AJA 106, 103-105—*Wilkie, Nancy C.*].

12776 Daube, David 8.2.1908-24.2.1999 ⇒15,12887; 16,13209. RZSRG.R 118 (2001) xiv-lii (*Rodger, Alan*).

12777 Ebeling, Gerhard 1912-30.9.2001. RLuther-Bulletin 10 (nov. 2001) 5-7 (*Zwanepol, Klaas*).

12778 Epstein, Claire 1911-2000. RQad. 34 (2001) 136 (*Hartal, Moshe*); IEJ 50 (2000) 263-264; BAIAS 18 (2000) 111-114 (*Braun, Eliot*).

12779 Flossmann, Karel ob. 22.12.2000. RBiLi 74 (2001) 69 (*Höslinger, Norbert*).

12780 Flusser, David 15.9.1917-15.9.2000 ⇒16,13215. RFrRu 8 (2001) 76 (*Thoma, Clemens*).

12781 Freeman, Geoffrey Evelyn 26.9.1921-3.12.2001 [Society for the Study of Egyptian Antiquities Newsletter, Jan. 2002, 1—*Miosi, Terry*].

12782 Gelio, Roberto 1940-15.12.2000. RLat. 67 (2001) 197-200 (incl. bibl.).

12783   Gigante, Marcello 1923-2001.
12784   Gomà i Civit, Isidro 14.5.1917-4.11.2000 ⇒16,13217. ᴿResB 29 (2001) 68-69 (*Calduch-Benages, Nuria*).
12785   Gordon, Cyrus H. 29.6.1908-30.3.2001. ᴿEThL 77 (2001) 555 (*Collins, R.F.*); UF 32 (2000) xi-xxxvi (*Marblestone, Howard*); BArR 27/4 (2001) 18 (*Rendsburg, Gary A.*).
12786   Guillet, Jacques 3.4.1910-28.9.2001. ᴿRSR 89 (2001) 483-484 (*Gibert, Pierre*).
12787   Gurney, Oliver Robert 28.1.1911-11.1.2001. ᴿAnSt 50 (2001) iii-iv (*Hawkins, J.D.*); Iraq 63 (2001) v-vii (*Black, J.A.*).
12788   Haag, Herbert 11.2.1915-23.8.2001. ᴿBiKi 56 (2001) 256 (*Ortkemper, Franz-Josef*).
12789   Hammond, Nicholas Geoffrey Lempriére 14.11.1907-24.3.2001. ᴿAJA 105 (2001) 517-518 (*Graham, A.J.*).
12790   Hunger, Herbert 9.12.1914-9.7.2000 ⇒16,13223. ᴿGn. 73 (2001) 572-574 (*Trapp, Erich*).
12791   Karg, Norbert Viktor 27.11.1954-19.10.2001 [AfO 48-49,294-295 —*Edzard, D.O.*].
12792   Klein, Michael L. 1940-2000 ⇒16,13225. ᴿBArR 27/2 (2001) 18; JAB 3 (2001) 3 (*Ochs, Effie Wise*).
12793   Kraus, Hans-Joachim 17.12.1918-14.11.2000. ᴿFrRu 8 (2001) 234 (*Ehrlich, Ernst Ludwig*).
12794   Kronholm, Tryggve 1939-1999. ᴿSEÅ 66 (2001) 7-9 (*Mettinger, Tryggve N.D.*).
12795   Lauer, Jean-Philippe 7.5.1902-15.5.2001. ᴿBSFE 151 (2001) 5-10 (*Leclant, J.*).
12796   McHardy, William Duff ob. 9.4.2000, aet.88. ᴿZAW 113 (2001) 1 (*McKane, William*).
12797   Meurer, Siegfried 1931-8.9.2001. ᴿBiKi 56 (2001) 256 (*Ortkemper, Franz-Josef*); BiLi 74 (2001) 280.
12798   Michel, Diethelm 22.2.1931-2.7.1999 ⇒15,12904. ᴿKUSATU 1 (2000) 5-25 (*Smend, Rudolf*).
12799   Moraldi, Luigi 15.9.1915-11.2001 [AcBib 10,1092].
12800   O'Callaghan Martínez, José 7.10.1922-15.12.2001. ᴿAcBib 10 (2001-2002) 974-975.
12801   O'Mara, Patrick F. 1914-2001. ᴿGöMisz 185 (2001) 4.
12802   Peral Torres, Antonio 14.4.1922-5.2000. ᴿSef. 61 (2001) 439-440 (*Díaz Esteban, Fernando*).
12803   Polotsky, Hans Jakob 1905-1991 ⇒7,k347...9,17420. ᴿNEA(BA) 64/3 (2001) 146.
12804   Porsch, Felix 6.9.1928-24.2.2001. ᴿBiKi 56 (2001) 116 (*Ortkemper, Franz-Josef*).

12805 Riedl, Johannes ob. 11.11.2000 [R]BiLi 74 (2001) 69 (*Höslinger, Norbert*).

12806 Rozman, France 24.3.1931-6.8.2001. [R]BiLi 74 (2001) 279 (*Koncilja, Rudi*).

12807 Runciman, Steven 7.7.1903-1.11.2000. [R]AnSt 50 (2001) v-vi (*Bryer, Anthony*); ByZ 94 (2001) 911-912 (*Mango, Cyril*).

12808 Sabourin, Léopold 7.9.1919-14.1.2001 [AcBib 10, 977-978].

12809 Saldarini, Anthony J. 18.9.1941-16.9.2001. [R]BiRe 17/6 (2001) 12-13 (*Harrington, Daniel J.*).

12810 Schulman, Alan ob. 20.7.2000. [R]JSSEA 28 (2001) vii-x (*Delia, Robert D.*).

12811 Steck, Odil Hannes 26.12.1935-30.3.2001.

12812 Steve, Marie-Joseph 26.10.1911-27.10.2001. [R]Akkadica 122 (2001) 1-2 (*Gasche, Hermann*); RA 95 (2001) 1-4 (*Spycket, Agnès*).

12813 Stolz, Fritz 16.7.1942-10.12.2001 [ThLZ 127,362-363—Dalferth, Ingolf U.].

12814 Susini, Giancarlo 10.10.1927-23.10.2000. [R]REA 103 (2001) 325-327 (*Étienne, Robert*).

12815 Tångberg, Arvid 22.4.1946-16.10.2000 ⇒16,13250. [R]TTK 72 (2001) 3 (*Stordalen, Terje; Skarsaune, Oskar*); TTK 72 (2001) 5-14 (*Saebø, Magne*); TTK 72 (2001) 15-19 (*Knudsen, Ebbe E.*); TTK 72 (2001) 20-30 (with bibl.) (*Stordalen, Terje*).

12816 Trinquet, Joseph 1919-2001. [R]RICP 80 (2001) 224-225 (*Cazelles, Henri*).

12817 Van der Woude, Adam S. 1927-19.11.2000 ⇒16,13251. [R]KeTh 52 (2001) 1 (*Jongeneel, Jan A.B.*); EThL 77 (2001) 266-267 & JSJ 32 (2001) 1-4 (*García Martínez, F.*); Phoenix 46 (2001) 109.

12818 Vercoutter, Jean 20.1.1911-16.7.2000 ⇒16,13255. [R]Le Sceau (2001) 17-19 (*Geus, Francis*).

12819 Vermeule, Emily Dickinson Townsend 1928-6.2.2001. [R]AJA 105 (2001) 513-515 (*Morris, Sarah; Shelmerdine, Cynthia*).

12820 White, Leland J. 25.7.1940-27.9.2001. [R]BTB 31 (2001) 126.

12821 Zhenfang, Luo 4.1920-22.9.2000. [R]CTR 15 (2001) 108-111 (*Dingxin, Xu; Ruxi, Mo*).

Index Alphabeticus

Auctorum

Arav R 9048 11357
Arbel I 9462
Arcari L 6100
Arce J ᴿ10643
Archer K 927
Archi A 11483 11488
Archibald Z ᴱ592
  ᴿ10494
Arduini S 3082
Arendt H ᴹ12726
Arens E 1095 7750
Ares Fondevila S
  ᵀ4401
Arfken E 8761
Arias J 4517 **Montano**
  B 3164 ᴹ12511
Ariel D ᴱ389 11248
Arledler G 10816
Armetta F 7736
Armogathe J 928
  ᴱ1734
Armour P ᴿ1441 **R**
  10016
Armstrong D ᴱ451
Arnal W 4606 ᴿ4639
  11336
Arnaud D ᴱ11482
Arndt M 11420 **T** 9384
  9584 ᴿ2322
Arneth M 2957 3319
Arnold B 794 ᴱ234 **C**
  12593 **D** 2914 11129
  M 12485 ᴿ12487
Arnould J 1980
Arragel M ᴹ1731
Artés Hernández J
  8917
Arthur D 3679
Artus O 1502 ᴿ1913
Artzi P 8393
Arubas B 11267
Arzt S ᴿ158 **-Grabner**
  P 6969s
As'ad K 8500 8762
Asante E 8104
Asbury B 9585
Aschheim S 12726
Aschim A 9815
Ascoli M ᴿ7180
Ascough R 4729 ᴿ6906
Asen B ᴿ7398
Asenjo J ᴿ150 3379
  6084 7104 7328

Asgeirsson J ᴱ96
Ash P 10164
Ashby G ᴿ3356
Asher J ᴿ7059 **N**
  8842
Ashland B 3083
Ashton J 5733 5750
  6258 **S** 10992
Asi E 7835
Asiedu F 3448 12252
  -Peprah M 5751
Asirvatham S ᴱ390
Askani H ᴿ663
  12666
Asmis E 10453
Assmann J 118
  2332s 8649 9816
  10017ss 10277 ᴱ2
  ᴹ2378
Asten F ᴱ12
Aston D 11090
Astren F 9445
Asurmendi J 4094
  Ruiz J 3387
Aßfalg J ᴹ8594
Atallah N 8763
Atawolo A 3884
Athanasius ᴹ12183-9
Atkins E ᴱ12253 **P**
  4703
Atkinson J ᴿ1063 **K**
  8872
Atmatzides C 4978
Attinger D ᴿ11775
  12055
Attoura H 11091
  ᵀ11197
Attridge H 5716
  6982 ᴿ4409 6452
  6983
Auberger J ᵀ10454
Aubert P ᴿ323
Aubet M 11465
Aubin F ᴿ1820 **M**
  4908
Aucante V 7901
Aucker W 2939
Audinet J 854
Auffarth C ᴱ689 690
Auffret P 3272 3275
  3307 3326 3356
Aufrecht W 8501
Aufrère S 11550
  11836 ᴱ10020

Auge C 11230
Augustinus 3146 3151
  4891 ᴹ8 331 550
  2014 2033 3308
  3448 3453 4855
  4947 5301 5990
  6564 8745 12251-
  12341
Augustinus Ps Belgicus
  ᴹ12436
Aujac G 11749
Auld A 2658 2768
  11249 ᴰ2939 ᴿ2801
Aulisa I ᴿ10602
Aune D 4017 6061
  6747 9859 ᴱ108
  ᴿ1287
Aupert P ᴿ11677
Aurelius E 4607
Aurenche O ᴱ610
Ausín S 4043 7434
Ausloos H 2269 2562
  6101
Aust M ᴿ7869
Austermann F 3170
  3273 3353
Austin J ᴹ4179 **M**
  10455 **P** 3101
Auvray P 8280
Auwers J 1224 1723
  1873 3018 3171s ᴱ7
  ᴿ1724 1727 3096
  3132 3152 3156
  3179 3200 3207
  3220 3290 3352
  5044 12074
Avalos H 1503 11837
Avemarie F 7090 ᴱ452
  ᴿ7654 9394
Avent G 3301
Avery-Peck A 9515
  ᴱ423-6 337 716
Aviam M 9260 11375
Aviezer N 2029
Avigad N 11025
Avioz M 3897
Avis P 1323
Avishur Y ᴱ8281
Avner U 9954
Avni G 11299 **J** 11251
Avram W 6745
Awi A 7204
Awwad J 4288

Bardski K 1585 2185
Bardy G 12357
Barea Amorena E 12715
Bar-Gal G 9034
Barguet P 10024
Barkay G 10864
Barkenings H 9586
Barker K 1739 **M** 2871 2951 6104 2066
Bar-Kochva B 8873 9261 10504
Barletta B 10769
Barlow J ^{R}10884 **M** 6028
Barnard M 9829
Barnes M ^{E}339 **R** ^{R}3012
Barnet J 4730
Barnett P 6722 **R** 11539 **V** 9587
Barnouw J 7206
Baron D ^{M}9388
Bar-Oz G 8765
Barr D 6105 ^{R}8238 **J** 7449s 10231
Barram M 6431
Barrett C 5532 5752 ^{R}133 6941 **D** ^{E}1606
Barré M 1324
Barrick W 1821 2784 2859 2931 ^{R}2639
Barro J 5330
Barruffo A ^{F}3
Barry C ^{E}9808
Barsotti D 3388
Barstad H 2629 3680 ^{R}33
Bartal I 12685
Bartelink G 12343
Bartelmus R 2896 8437 ^{E}21
Barth K 1065 2033 8188 9560 12610 12612 ^{M}12606 12608s 12611 **M** 6971
Barthe C 1504 ^{E}236 1505
Barthes R 5645
Barthélemy D 120
Bartholomew C 930 3510 3585 ^{E}106

Bartina S 4790
Bartl K 11378
Bartlett J 3065 ^{R}3074
Bartman E 10596
Bartnicki R 7837
Bartolini E 1290 **P** 788
Bartolomé J 4290ss 4909 5491 ^{R}4953
Bartoloni P ^{R}12774
Barton C 8828 **J** 4044 4102 ^{E}314 931 1860 **M** 8172 S 121 4293 4996 ^{D}5351 ^{E}340
Bartusch M 11849
Baruch Y 11251s
Baruffa A ^{R}11732
Basal N 8283
Bash A 6755
Basile J 11141
Basilius C ^{M}12190 **M** ^{M}12191
Basirov O 10865
Baskin J 9516
Baslez M 2872 3019 5617 9860 10456 10505
Basola M 11971
Bass G ^{R}635
Bassani F ^{E}7326
Basse M ^{R}12490 12512
Basser H ^{E}2550 ^{R}2191
Basson A 11862
Bast R 2404
Bastiaensen A 12254
Bastian J 9830
Bastianini G ^{E}555
Baßler M ^{E}391
Bataillon L ^{D}12483
Batayneh A 11379
Bate S 4910
Bateman H 3314 7011 ^{E}6226 **J** ^{E}12517
Batey R 4294
Bathgate A ^{R}1221
Batnitzky L 10817
Batsch C ^{E}595
Battaglia G 7661 **V** ^{E}507

Battaglini S 8457
Batten A ^{R}7077 7080
Battini-Villard L 10770
Batto B 2659
Bauckham R 122 5331 5753 6106 7063 7484 7632 ^{E}237 8215
Baud M 8650 10279 ^{R}10734
Baude J 1268 1373
Bauder K ^{E}1740
Baudienville M 10907
Baudler G ^{M}899
Baudoz J 4835
Baudy G 4825
Bauer A 3899 12638 **D** 856 5649 ^{E}11253 ^{R}4950 5333 **U** 1856 2721s 2726s 3350 9446 ^{E}4594 ^{R}455 **W** 8713
Bauerschmidt F ^{R}7777
Baugh L 4532
Bauks M 1982s 2186 2239 3291 10232 ^{R}9990 11505
Baum A 4693 8975 ^{R}4945 **G** ^{R}9598
Bauman R 10644
Baumann G 3681 ^{R}4207 **P** 12727
Baumer L 10993
Baumert N 123 6107 6603 6675 6682 6683ss 6701 6721 6832 6873 6880 6886 6917 6972 7207 7485 7686 7838 8714s ^{R}1528 5186
Baumgarten A 9262s ^{E}2 **J** 9139 9447 ^{E}9140s **R** 9890
Baumgartner K 3228 **W** 8365ss
Baumstark A ^{M}545
Baur F ^{M}5589 12559s
Baurain C 10444
Bauschke M 4533 10119
Bauslaugh R ^{R}11233 11238

Benzi G 2918 6346
Ber V ᴿ3041 9988
Berarducci S ᴿ12412
Berciano M 8754
Berder M 3352 6993
  ᴿ9613
Beretta P ᴱ2296
Berg I ᴿ11692 W
  ᴰ10934
Bergamelli F 12090
Bergant D 837 1134
  3435
Berge K 4125 ᴿ166
Bergen W 1506 2932
Berger B 3588 K 934s
  2240 3010 7335
  7650 7662 7840
  8216 8874 8922
  ᵀ1765
Berges U 3230 3682
  3750 ᴿ3831 3834s
Bergey R 1894
Berggren J ᵀ11751
Berghuis K 7336 7841
  ᴿ6226
Bergian S 12030
Bergman J †12767 N
  8284
Bergmann M ᴿ11000 S
  936
Bergmeier R 125
Bergquist J ᴿ11918
Bergren T ᴱ828
Berkley T 6545
Berlejung A 7435
  10597 10867 ᴿ7272
Berlin A 3041s ᴿ604
  11335
Berlis A 762
Berman J 3043 M
  11952
Bermejo Barrera J
  10233 Cabrera E
  11254
Bermon P ᴿ538
Bermond C 10818
Bernabei E 1374
Bernabé Ubieta C
  6464
Bernabò M 10990
Bernal L 7308 M 9817
Bernand E 8766

Bernard J 4470 5940
  9143 ᴱ689s M
  12728 P ᴿ10447
Bernardelli M 1377
Bernardi L ᵀ2333 S
  1375
Bernardini A 12229
  ᴿ12190
Bernardus C
  ᴹ12445s
Bernas C ᴿ318 840
  4753 7732
Berndt R ᴰ12430
Berner L 9518 U
  ᴱ9920
Bernett M 11358
Bernstein M 1587
  9082 9388
Berquist J 2511 9265
Berrigan D 3389
  3633
Berrin S 9083
Berry D ᴿ176 2275 J
  ᴱ11895
Berschin W ᴱ12462
Bertalot R ᴱ7596
Berten I 10713
Berthelot K ᴿ9066
Berthoud P 1894
Bertoldi R 12663
Bertone J ᴿ6372
Bertrand D 12393
Bertrand J ᴿ10428
  10482 10501
Berzosa Martínez R
  ᴿ12456
Besch W 1766
Besonen J 11079
Besques S †12768
Besserman L ᴿ1746
Bessière G 4983
Bessire F 1483
Best E 6836ss
Beta S ᵀ8785
Bethge H ᴱ9783
  ᵀ9801
Betrò M 8651
Bettinetti S 9891
Bettiolo P 12398
Betto F 2571 5494
  5969
Betz H 126 6347
  6680 9885 ᴱ662ss
  ᶠ5 O 859 ᴰ6800

Beuken W 3751 ᴰ3883
  ᶠ6
Beutel A 1768 12486
Beutler J 1097 5755
  5957 6014 6019
  6047 7663s 12604
  12683 ᴰ5955 6906
  ᴱ239 ᴿ5710
Beuttler U 2052
Bexell O 1135 P
  ᴿ12649
Beyer B 794 de Ryke
  B ᴿ12473 D 11027 K
  8503 ᴿ1695 8381
  8581
Beyerle S 4045
Beyrich T 9519
Bélis A ᴿ10842
Bénazeth D 10722
Bénétreau S 7210
Bérard F 774
Bérenger-Badel A
  10645
Bèze T de ᴹ12507
Bhattacharji S ᵀ12376
Bhayro S 8896
Bianchi E 240 7842s
  ᵀ3100 F 3625 ᴱ8379
  ᴿ2986
Bibb B 2533
Bickmann J 6914
Biddle M ᴿ1648 3538
  3752 4106 4191s
  11993 ᵀ10623
Bieberstedt A 1769
Bieberstein K 3854
  7436 S 5391 6973
Biedenkopf-Ziehner A
  8689
Bielefeld P 3375
Bielinski K 5521
Bienert W ᴰ12471
  ᴱ12137
Bieniada M 10165
Bienkowski P 11300
Bienkowski P 11381s
  11416 ᴱ723 ᴱ11390
Bierbrier M 10283
Bieringer R 5756 6723
  ᴰ5993 ᴱ5747
Biers J ᴿ11700
Bietak M 11611 ᴱ597
Bietenhard S 2785

Bogaert P 3029s 3929
4276 E3028 F7 R4040
Bohlen R 5595 R2740
Bohlmann R 1226
Bohn B 10911
Bohren R 7061
Bohrer F 10748
Boice J 4694
Boileau M 11094
Boisclair R R7172
Boismard M 5088
5392 5418 5760
6847 7735 9001
M5152 R4405 4426
Boiy T R10403
Bolard L 10912
Bolgiani F 9594 R4252
Bolle K T10235
Bollweg J 10803
Bolman E R11220
Bolshakov A R11213
Bolt P 5168 E80
Bolyki J 4296 9787
Bombaci N 12620
Bombeck S 8285 9002
Bomhard A von
R10037
Bomhauer R R7266
Bonagiuso G 12664
Bonani G 11818
Bonati S 1377
Bonatz D 10868
11163s R10764
Bonaventura 5382
M5458 12447
Bond H 5053 D5563
R338
Bondí S 10166 R12774
Bonechi M 11484
Boned Colera P E8717
Boneva K 2671
Bonfante L E598
Bongenaar A 11132
Bonhoeffer D 1065
3231 9624 12614
12615s
Bonilla M 5169
Bonneau G 5138 5170
N 5171 R6577
Bonner G F8
Bonnet C 9959 E508
R453 9990 10234
Bonnewijn O 12432

Bonney G 5419
Bonnin Barceló E
7619
Bonola G 8403
Bonowitz B 7845
Bons E 4152
Bony P 11865
Bonz M 5332
Booij T 3357 3364
Boorer S 1896
Borbone P 1687
R11971
Borchers D E556
Bord L 2454 10913
Bordeyne P 1098
Bordoni M F9
Bordreuil P 1227
8459s 10234
D11471
Borel J R450 6468
Borgeaud P R9893
Borgehammar S
12408
Borgen P 8935 E8936
Borger J R3354
Borger R 8286 F10
Borghi E 4695 8009
E244
Borghouts J 10026
Borgia E 11455
Borgonovo G 1187
2480
Bori P 939
Boring M T8274
Borland J 10819
Bormann L 5393
6348 6864
Borokovsky E E203
Borragán V 796
Borras A 1099
R11731
Borrell A 5319
Borrelli C 1473
Borriello M E10723
Borrmans M 10120
10142 R3770
Borse U 4553 6767
Bortolini J 6296
6839 6950 7095
Bortone G E864
Borzi S T12219
Bos A 6890 G 10027
R 1137

Bosch Veciana A
R4138
Boschi B R322 2645
Boschki R 9521
Boscolo G 4696ss
E4238
Bosetti E 3436 7022
11772
Boshoff W 797 9960
R164 11249
Bosma C 1554
Bosman H 940 950
Bosse-Griffiths K 128
11811 †12769
Bosshard-Nepustil E
11030
Bossina L R10616
Bossman D 8250
Bost H 12507
Bostock D 5089
Bosworth C E708
12729
Botero Giraldo J 8010
Botha J E224 P 3358
4233
Botta E M10748
Bottai M 1450
Botterill S R12352
Botterweck G E670s
Bottéro J 10073
Bottéro J 10235 10344
Botti A E509
Bottiglieri C 1462
Bottini C D5414 G
7064
Botto M 11095
Bouchoc R 8287
Boud'Hors A ET1138
R1693
Boudreau P 1139
Bouffartigue J 12244
Boulding M T3146
12258s
Boulton M 9595
Bouma-Prediger S
7310
Bounni A 11512
Bourbon F 11769
Boureux C 11812
Bourgeois H 7665
Bourke V 12260
Bourquin Y 1080
Bousset W M12617

Brin G 7215
Brindle W 7847
Brinkman J 3147
Brinner W F12
Briquel Chatonnet F
  1227 8589 10234
  E557 578 R8352
Brissaud P 11639
Brisson E 3619 L
  ET8836
Brito E R1047 1480 J
  de 9390 M de R602
Britz J 8012
Brizzi M 11133 11429
Broadhead E K 4609
  5139 5762 6111
Broadhurst L R7829
Broc C 12194
Brock S 3753 8504
  12399
Brocke C vom 6903
Brocke E 9523
Brockmöller K 3563
Brockopp J 9320
Brodersen K 1623
  E558
Brodie N E394 T 1938
  1960 4610 6297
  R6545
Brody A R431 R 9448
Broer I 4237 5763
Brokoff J 6112
Bromiley G E696
Bron F 8637ss
Brondos D 6817
Bronkhorst J 7848
Bronstein H 4471
Bronte C M1435
Bronznick N 3552
Broodbank C 11692
Brooke G 3754 9084
  E758 R73 4129 5276
  7432 9165 9205
  10216
Brooks P R12525
Brooten B 8013 R7821
Broshi M 131 2875
  7191 9035-9 9145
  9198 9228s 10704
  10725 11125
  11255ss 11301
  11315 11814 11822
  11963ss

Brosseder J 12489
Broşteanu M 10121
Brottier L 1986
Broucke P R11167
Brovarsky E 11596
Brown B 9524 C
  5172 D 1210 5430
  7175 10074 11517
  R446 10083 10103
  J 9862 10168
  10414 M 6539 P
  12262 R 4238
  5054 5719 7487
  M4823 S 11932
  R615 4846 W 3568
  3589 7354 R162
  3542
Browne A R6983s G
  5720 6027 8977
  E3102
Brox N E12101
Broyles C 1229 3148
  7216 E248
Brubaker L 12224
Brucker R 4912
Bruckhaus A E12622
Bruckner J 2157
Bruckstein A 9391
Brueggemann W 132
  798 1140 2354
  2587 2944 3685
  3887 3900 4554s
  7217 7383s 7451
  7464 7651 E510
  F13 M4745 7450
  7452 12618 R3148
  3158 3694 4495
  7351
Bruehler B 4227
Brulé P E559
Brulin M 7905
Bruners W 4297
Brunette P 7337
Brunotte U 6228
Bruns P 12240
Brunschwig J E709
  T10480 -Ségal A
  9601
Brunson A 5764
  R3152
Brunstad P 7553
Brunt J R6661
Bruteau B E4467

Bruzzone G 11967
Brüning C 3375
Bryan C 6492 D R3012
  4345
Bryant R 6776
Bryer A R12807
Brzegowy T 1897
  2017 E3686
Bsteh A E511
Buber M 12619 M1788
  8403 9519 12620
Bubloz Y R2392
Buby B 8117
Bucci G 11080
Bucer M M2367 12485
Buchanan G 4027
Buchegger J 6298
Buchinger H 12138
Buchwalder C E570
Buckley T 4731
Budelmann F E27
Buell D 11866
Buetubela B 10821
Buis P 2512
Bułgakowa S M6235
Bułhakowa M M1436
Bulkeley T R1959
Bull K R5276 5365
Bullard R 6223
Bullock C 3135 R
  9602
Bultmann C 3901
  12561 R3903 R 4298
  12622 M4284 4428
  5745 8188 12621
Bundy D R678 1756
  2649 12745
Bunimovitz S 10740
  11312 11867
Burandt C 12490
Burchard C 133
Burckhardt J M12556
Burer M 6607
Burfeind C 8918
Burge G 5734 5765
Burger C 7906
Burgers P 11232
Burggraeve R 5766
Burgh T R10820
Burghardt W 1141
Burghart G 1771
Burgos Núñez M de
  6349 6777

Cappelletto G 801 1939 2955 ^{R}1237 2507 3159 5020 9717 12756
Cappellini M 9525
Capper B ^{R}5345
Capps D 1271
Caquot A 9146 ^{R}8576
Cara R 5673
Caragounis C 5770
Carasik M 3592
Carbajosa I 3344 ^{R}3262
Carbonaro D ^{E}537
Carbone G ^{T}12478 S 4104s
Cardelle de Hartmann C ^{E}12396
Cardellini I 2379 10169
Cardellino L 4875
Carden M 2158
Cardenal E 8093
Cardona Ramírez H 4914 8252 8262
Cardon-Bertalot P 7602
Carey G 6114ss ^{R}1501 8931
Carfora A 9923
Carile A 11969
Carleton Paget J 4300 10513
Carley K 3979
Carlini A 8769
Carls P 6885
Carlson A †12772 S 4611
Carmassi P 12409
Carmel A ^{F}17
Carmi I 11320
Carmichael C 1921 ^{E}416
Carmona A ^{R}6739
Carnevale L ^{R}217
Caron G 249 5771 R ^{E}29
Carpenter C 7092
Carpentier J ^{E}396
Carpinello M 8149
Carr A ^{R}7700 D 1961 2481 8253 9604 ^{R}3467

Carradice I 11233
Carrara P ^{T}12216
Carrera J 838
Carrez M ^{R}1724 - Maratray J 11755 ^{R}11635
Carrier R 5127
Carrière J 2588
Carroll C ^{T}12382
Carroll D ^{R}184 J 1272 9605 ^{D}6431 R M 4155 ^{E}250 R 3688 10415 10460 ^{E}10706
Carrozzi L ^{T}12264
Carrón Pérez J 4278 6450
Carruba O 11031
Carson C 9041 D 4587 9267s ^{E}251 ^{M}5988
Carstens P 3233
Carter C 11869 E 10170 W 1143 4732 4950 ^{R}4277
Cartledge T 2758
Cartlidge D 10917
Cartwright C ^{R}11316 S 12410 T ^{M}12516
Carvalho J 6036 6966 ^{R}6349
Carver A 6816
Casaburi M 11518 ^{R}10074
Casadesús Bordoy F ^{E}572
Casadeum T ^{E}2297
Casadio G 9928
Casalá L 5618
Casale U ^{R}4435
Casalini N 4239 6354
Casanellas P 8345
Casaretto F 1379
Casel O 7908
Casevitz M 1876
Casey M 5173 ^{R}4974 5006 5318 8911
Casiday A 12265 ^{R}518 1692 8942 12473
Casini M ^{E}11552
Caspar P 12033

Caspers C 5025
Cassel J 12211
Cassianus J ^{M}7850 12369s
Cassidy R 6260 6974 10630
Cassingena-Trévedy F ^{T}12373
Casson L 8847 10285
Castagno A 12195
Castaldini A 9269
Castaño A 733 6024
Castel C ^{R}10767 G 11166
Castelbajac I de 2708
Castellana P 11504
Castelli E ^{R}8013
Castelli F 4534 ^{R}5111 S 10514s
Castello G 2876 ^{R}2395 11786
Castiglioni A 11622
Castriota D ^{R}10900
Castro Sánchez S 5721
Catalano R 9700
Catastini A 1624 2819
Cattaneo E ^{E}3 ^{R}7822 12066 12079
Caubet A 10846
Causse J 2188 ^{R}1032 2080
Cauville S 8652 ^{TE}10030
Cauvin J 11823
Cavadini J ^{E}4915
Cavagnoli G 5026
Cavalcanti E 12388 ^{T}12389 T 8094
Cavalcoli G 7488
Cavanaugh W ^{R}7777
Cavarnos C 10918
Cavedo R 2846 11870
Cavigneaux A 2095
Cavillier G 11858
Cazeaux J 7385
Cazelles H 7104 7752 10171 ^{R}12816
Cárdenas Pallares J 5420 5450 5480s 5485s
Cebulj C 5772
Ceccarelli P ^{R}10510
Cecchelli M ^{E}397

Cuenca Molina J R6896
Cullen T E11694
Culley R E66 R3158 3188
Cullmann O 4240
Culpepper R 5689 5781s
Cultraro M 11695
Cultrera F R8016 8070
Cummins S 6801
Cumont F M508 12641
Cunneen J 2406
Cunningham L R12258s P 4310 9616 S R3172
Curkpatrick S 956 3597
Currid J 2302 10705
Currò S E868
Curtis J E606
Curto S 136 10032s 10995 11554ss
Cusanus N M12448
Cusset C R9936
Cussini E 8508
Custer J 4049
Cutler A 10927
Cuvillier É 4699 4918 6120s R4666 4704 4707s 4711 4715 4734 4744 4747s 4758 4767 4806 4846 5010 6445 6584 6835 7075
Cyprianus M12371s
Cyril S M12150
Cyrillus A 2349 7533 M12210s
Czachesz I 9793
Czerny E 8654
Çığ M 2124
Çilingiroglu A E11664

D'Acquisto B 7736
D'Agostino F 3480 10346 E8607 R10350 10397
D'Alario V 3624 R3596
D'Alatri A 1383
D'Alessio D 1326 7854
D'Altroy T E388

D'Ambra E R10873
d'Ambrosio M R12651 R 2920
D'Ancona M 7730
D'Angelo E 1385 M D6692 E289 R5799
D'Anna A 9011 E12112
d'Aurevilly B M1444
D'Lima E E348
D'Ottavi S 1384
D'Sa F 7914 T 5444
D'Souza F 1106 J 4556
Da Campo L 4798
Da Costa V E10938
Da Spinetoli O 8019 8980
Da Vinci L M10977
Dabek T 7481 8221
Dabney D 5093 E529
Dabourne W 6541
Dabrowski W 7157
Dacy M 9618
Dafni E 7108 7222 7454
Dahan G 12411s E9247
Dahl N 6840 7223 M6849
Dahle L 5675
Dahler E 839
Dahlgrün C 7853
Dahmen U 4157 R2600
Dahood M M12624
Dal Covolo E 6595 E517 1963 T3902
Dal Lago L T8213
Dale J R3381
Dalley S 10347 2097 E401 R3187 10379
Dalman G 11906
Daltrop G 10996
Daly R R11952 T12134 -Denton M 5783 R7865
Damascelli A 6818
Damaskos D 10997
Damerow P E409
Damm A R93 5236
Dan J 9493
Danaher J 957

Danan J R8579
Dancy J 1327
Dandamayev M 11933
Dangl O 4215 4219
Daniel S M12404
Daniele M E4700
Danieli N 9507
Daniel-Rops H 12413
Daniels A 1105 D T1583 J R6498
Danker F 5399 E8713
Dannowski H 6229
Danove P 1627 5175s 8746
Dante M1380 1441s 9500
Danzger M 9527
Dar S E11346 R10632
Daressy G 11168
Da-Riva R 10348
Darlington O 5676
Darr K 3972
Dartigues A 1328
Darù J 5537
Das A 6576
Dasen V 11557
Dassmann E 4158 5598 12006 D6850 E235 R5603 7792
Dassow E von 8633
Daube D †12776
Daumal R M1443
Dauphin C R11504
Dautzenberg G 137 6355 6451 6744
Dauzat P 7708 8152
Daval M 7339
Daviau M E25 P9962 11422 R11956
David A E11971 P 7404 R 7224 11558 R1974
Davidowicz K 9528
Davids P 7066 R4994 7023 7028
Davidson R 7013 R18 2353 12745
Davidzon I R415
Davies A 3769 E R2298 2553 G 10174 P 4050 8877 9202 9273 10242 10465 11167 W9619 E712 10872

Dupree C 8025
Dupuis J 7557s [R]5125
Dupuy B 1688 6821
DuQuesne T 10035s [R]10025
Durand J [T]11505
Durand O 8298
Durante Mangoni M 12082
Duranti G 7112
Dureau Y 9466
Durrwell F 5094
Dussart O 10754
Dussel E 8096
Dust S 1471
DuToit D 5183ss 5796
Dutton P 1710
Duval Y 12347 [E]541
Duvall J 872
Dünzl F 2247 7605
Dürer A [M]8985
Dyck J 2965
Dyk J 2125 [E]2677
Dysinger L 12223
Dyson A [R]10230
Dziobek E 11559
Dziuba A [R]8055
Dzubba H 1985 [M]12628

Eagleton T 4179
Easterling P [E]8722 [F]27
Eastman B 6360 S 6812
Eaton J [R]3148 3354 - Krauss M [R]10292
Ebach J 2100 2248 2358 7113 [D]3687 [E]350
Ebanoidze M [T]11972
Ebeling G †12777
Eberl N 8727
Eberle A 7920
Ebersohn M 4677
Ebertz M [E]4021
Ebner M 3655 4678 8222 [E]261 [T]9924
Echeverria E 8026
Eck J [M]5945 W 8830
Eckermann W [E]12479
Eckert J 6361 [E]42
Eckey W 5140 5539
Eckhart M [M]5937

Eckstein H 4738 5095
Eco U 2060
Edasseril P [R]6042
Edden V [R]722
Eddinger T [R]7154
Eddy P 4317
Edelman D 2789 [R]10706
Edelmann J [M]12527
Eder C [R]10901 M 10844
Edgar D 7067
Edney M [R]1448
Edwards B [ET]1884 C 1446 D 11361 J [M]6250 L 4477 M 9719 9741 [E]4588 9868 [R]1829 12005 12136 P 11385 R 4616 [R]148 4639
Edzard D [R]12791 L 8591 8849
Effland A [R]11618
Efron J 4022
Egan B [E]12475
Egelhaaf-Gaiser U [E]595
Egger P 9394 W 12448 -Wenzel R 3392 [E]3656 [R]840
Eggler J 11028
Ego B 1592 1990 3020 9363 11262 [E]285 2879 [R]1230
Eguiarte E [R]10593 11739 12481
Ehlers K 3185 11788 [R]324 W [E]403
Ehling K 10469
Ehrenberg E 11038
Ehrlich C 2337 8510 11318 [R]10208 E 140 9395 [R]12793 U 9396
Ehrman B 4318 4478 12035 [R]5714
Eichhorn J [M]12570
Eichler E 3482
Eichmann R 11387
Eichner J 3472
Eichrodt W 3973
Eichrodt-Kessel H 2743

Eickestedt K [E]99
Eide T [E]10289
Eidem J 8609
Einbinder S 9625
Eiring L 11097
Eisa K 11169
Eisele M [E]766
Eisen R 3046
Eisen U 7820s 8153
Eisenberg J 8350
Eisenman R 7068
Eisler E 12731
Eissfeldt O 808
Eissler F 3149
Ejmnaes B [E]8880
Ejrnæs B 1800 3186
Ekaterini T [R]11905
Ekem J 6676
Eklund R [E]8004
Elad-Bouskila A [E]86
Elayi A 11234 J 10998 11234s
Elazar D 9533
Eldarov G [R]3
Elder L 10825
Elders L 7160
Eleazar ben Arakh [M]9399
Elgavish D 2153
Elgvin T 9203 [E]9176
Eliade M [M]5819 7768 9847 9850 12629
Eliav Y [R]9597
Elior R 2880
Eliot G [M]1447s T [M]1449 1465 5932 5935
Eliseo Gil A 7921
Elisha ben Avuyah [M]9399
Elías Pérez M [R]709
El-Khayari A 8464
Elkis W [R]314
Elledge C 5652
Elliger K 2906 3452 3417 7243 W 11337
Ellington J [R]1847
Ellingworth P 5254 [R]1946 6941
Elliott J 740 7028s 11875 10917 10931 [R]772 1561 1711 4594 4666 5329

Falk D 3240 **Z** 2434
Falla T 8592 ^R1660
Falmagne T 2062
Fanlo J 6230
Fansaka B 8105
Fant C 809
Fantalkin A 11329
Fantar M 9968
Fantato S 4559
Fantino J 1991s ^E506
Fantuzzi V ^R10929
Fanuli A ^R1911 1914
  2379 4113
Fanwar W 3771
Faraone C 8778 9898
Farassino A 1387
Farès-Drapeau S
  11386
Farias J 3241 4513
  5578
Farin M ^R12766
Farioli M 8779
Farley M ^E97
Farmer K ^R1295 **R**
  7559 **W** ^E464 1863
  3857
Farout D 8650
Farris S 5421
Farrugia E ^E697 ^R4249
Fasano V 2435
Fassberg S 8299 8512
  ^E8343
Fassetta R ^T3466
  12445
Fassino M ^R8772
Faßbeck G 2881 ^R265
Fatica M 1801
Faur J ^R716
Faust A 11867
Fauvarque B 6231
  6251
Fauveaud C 10749
Faü J 9237
Fava C 1388
Favaro G 9825
Favreau R 9628
Fàbrega V 9204
Feaver D ^R10839
Fechter F 11877 ^R3824
Fedalto G 4323 5060
Feder F 3888 8657
Federici T 7710 7922

Fee G 143 1516
  5472 5978 5987
  6043 6364s 6569
  6626 6638 6645
  6657 6666 6738
  6750 6826 6856
  6877 6887 6907
  6932 6964
Feeney D 9870
Feghali-Gorton A
  11039
Fehribach A 5799
Feiertag J ^E12348
Feiler B 1899
Feinberg J 7193
Feiner S ^E9501
Feininger B 875
  ^R3162
Felber S 12677
Feld G 876 **H**
  ^E12513
Feldman L 2163
  8939 10519-23
  11720 ^R464 10542
  10550 10625 **S**
  9397
Feldmeier R 7114
Feldtkeller A 10604
  ^R7403
Feliks Y 11816
Fellous S 1731
Fellows R 6967
Felmy K ^E10932
Felton D ^R9904 **T**
  5800
Feneberg R 5186
Fenske W 1517 5061
  ^R5210 12014
  12635
Fenton J 5187s
Fenton P 9247 **T**
  3696
Ferguson S 6866 **T**
  12102
Fernandes J 8027
Fernando C 5801 **G**
  6034
Fernández A 8028 **E**
  S 8940 12169 **Lois**
  A 7533 **Marcos N**
  1632-7 2128 3376
  ^R2897 3164 **Ramos**
  F 7230 ^E675 **R**

11504 **Tejero E**
  1566 **V** ^R5308
Ferrante J^{.R}1441
Ferrari P ^R6501 9526
Ferrario F 2408 ^R7692
Ferraro G 144 4679
  5487 5631 5692s
  5802s 5948 5962
  5968 5975 5979
  7231 7923 12440s
  ^R5727
Ferreira G ^R5806 **J**
  5804 **S** ^T8112
Ferrie J 3850
Ferroni G 1466
Ferry J 2409 3904
Festorazzi F ^F30
Feuerverger A 3101
Feuillet A 5600
Fevel C 7232
Fewell D 2101 ^D2134
Fédou M 7534 7560
  12148 ^R9 5090 5103
  5125 8100 10144
  12434
Fénelon ^M1152
Fiandra E 10775
Fic L 10152
Ficca F 8831
Fichte J ^M5928 9576
Fidora A 12459
Fiedler P 9629 ^E265
Fiedrowicz M 7667
  12008s
Fieger M ^E608
Field D 7312
Fields B 8029 **L** 9630
Fiema Z 11438 ^E11437
Figueroa Jácome L
  ^R3438
Figura M 7738
Fikentscher W ^E609
Fikhman I 8780 ^R435
Filer J ^R11557
Fillion L 4324
Filoramo G 9720
  12190 12275 ^E524
Finan T ^E525
Finazzi R ^E564 580
Finch A 1389
Fincke A 9092 **J**
  10349
Fine S 11171 ^R11130

Frangipane M 11173
Frangoulis H E9929
Frank É 1482 9535 J
7574 K 6743
Franke C 3842 R8183
D R10293 H R782 J
12689
Frankel D 11673
11688
Frankemölle H 147
962 4704 4739 7757
9632 E268 352
Frankfurter D 6196
10039
Frankivsk I E7894
Franklin C R1709 E
R5368 N 11536
Frantsouzoff S 9969
Frantzen A 1391
Franz A 7927 E353
7341
Fraschetti A E405
Frayne D 11756 T2102
Frede D E527
Frederichs H 10827
Fredericq-Homes D
E22 11784
Fredouille J E611 R374
Fredricks C 1957
Fredrickson D 6736
Fredriksen P 4328
12280 R5277
Fredrikson N 12083
Freed E 4799 M5988
Freedman D 2410
3354 4191 E354 676
Freeman G †12781 M
R1744
Freese P E12747
Frei H M1009 P 10417
Freire A 5542
Frei-Stolba R E26
Freitag K 2461
Frenschkowski M
4617s 6937 R830
4550 9743
Frerichs E 9047 E443
F33
Fretheim T R2318
7449
Frettlöh M 6752 E355
Freu J 10180
Freud S M1493 1498
3956 9512

Freudenthal G E9247
R9467
Freudiger M R8278
Freund R 9048
Frevel C 1900 2623
Frey J 5695 5806
6012 6126 9188
M5712 R41 122 254
5318 5710 5738
5772 5775 5783
5972 6023 7504
Freydank H R10397
Freyer T 9633
Freyne S 148 4329
5601 10470 10605
R8424
Frick O 1772s P
8942
Fricke K 1774ss
E1763
Friebel K 3890
R3893
Fried J 12414 L
2991 R3894
Friedland E 10999
Friedlander A E119
Friedman M E9248 R
1880 1901 Y
11987
Friedrichsen T 5264
5479 R4956s
Friedt C 11879
Frier B 8764
Friesen A 9833 S
6127 R10792
Frigato S E3178
Friggeri R 8781
Fripp R 2031
Fritz V 11368
Froehlich K 3189
Frohnhofen H 7857
Frommann K M1790
Frosini G 5097
Frösén J 11425
11439
Früchtel E R8950
Frühwald W 1964
Köönig J 5807
E101
Fry G T3569
Frydrych T 3518
Frye N M1318
Frymer-Kensky T
2437 7313

Fuchs A 4619-22
10352 48 60 105 160
304 329 1517 1647
2888 4626 4645
4677 4686 4778
4845 4932 5059
5230 5236 5243
5358 5368 5373s
5378 5594 5655
5772 5878 5999
6002 6079 6213
6215 6722 6799
6892 6941 8275
8724 9015 E 8183
1295 3899 G 7928 O
1828 3242 8224
Fudge E 8225
Fueyo B R8156
Fuglseth K E8936
Fuhrer T 12281
Fuhs H 3519s
Fujii S 11456
Fuks G 10525
Fulco W R9976 10195
Fullerton M 10875
Fumagalli A 5020
Funk R 4330 W 9781
E8690 9754s 9809
Furlani M 7493
Furley W 9900
Furlong J 11264
Furnish V 6639 R1063
R6452 6729
Fuscaldo P 11101
Fusco V 5337 6468
Fuß B 4129
Futato M 11781
Fürst A R7792

Gabashvili T 11972
Gabba E 5543 R10461
Gabel H 1193 J 1334
Gabler J M12570
Gabolde M 10292
Gabrielsen V 11937
Gaca K R6452
Gacek A 8640
Gadamer H 149 M6457
12741
Gadecki S 5808
Gadot Y 11334
Gaechter P M12632
Gaffney V 11696

Gera D 10471
Geraci G 10654
Gerber A 12058 **C**
6557 10526 ^{R}10508
10544
Gerdmar A 7052
Gerhard J ^{M}12529s **R**
10934
Gerhards A 7931 ^{E}358
Gerhardsson B 4266
Gerhoh R ^{M}12455
Germain S ^{M}1451
Germinario M 7117
Germond P 10876
11790
Gerosa L ^{E}1508 1556
Gerring B ^{R}10850
Gerrish B ^{R}2035
Gershom 9406 ^{M}9477
Gerson J ^{M}1452 **S**
11236
Gerstenberger E 1148
3150 3137 3190
7455
Gertz J 2303 2483
Gerwing M 7562
Gesche B 2734 **P** 3484
Gesché A 7563
Gese M 6848 ^{R}6844
Getty M ^{R}6577 -
Sullivan M 8155
Getui M ^{E}466
Getzov N 11175
Geus C de ^{R}10820 **F**
^{R}12818 **K** ^{E}51
Geva H 11266 12724
Gex K ^{E}26
Geyer B ^{E}11492 **D**
5190 **P** 11825
Ghandi [vid Gandhi]
Gharib G ^{E}8126
Ghia F ^{R}330
Ghiberti G ^{R}4346 4388
5789 5910
Ghidelli C ^{R}1832
Ghinatti F 8782
Ghini E 2745
Giannarelli E 1393
Gianotto C 6997 7071s
12059 E524 9809
^{R}298 5669 9674
9794 9937
Gianto A 4055 8851
^{R}8571

Giardina A ^{R}12190
Giavini G 879
Gibbs R 8032
Gibert P 741 963
1149 2249 4988
10245 ^{R}323 1073
1936 2588 10886
12786
Gibson A 8852 **E**
11881 **J** 4890
^{R}8352 **S** 11304 ^{E}95
730
Giddy L 11597
Gieniusz A 6513
6573
Gieschen C 7535
Giesen H 4740 6066
6203 6570 7406
^{R}126 133 161 179
206 214 239 4237
5333 5695 5710
6104 6508 7654
8088
Giesler M 4823
Gigante M 12783
Gigante M 406 8783
Giglioni P 6486
^{R}6263 6307
Gigliotti M 3601
Gignac A 6577 6707
^{R}6289 6471 6908 **F**
^{D}5817
Gignoux P 10113
Gil Arbiol C 7668
Fuenōsanta J
11032
Gila A 8127
Gilbert G ^{R}5638 **M**
150 812 3393
3485ss 3521 3570
7437 12641 12680
12734-8 ^{F}34s **P**
2304
Gilboa A 11103 **R**
1966
Gilders W 7235
Gilead D 2650
Giles F 11582s **K**
6954
Gilhus I 7236
Gill D 11321 **R** ^{E}359
698
Gillam R ^{R}8669

Giller P 9487
Gillespie C ^{R}7964
Gillet-Didier V 2083
9161
Gillingham S ^{R}3086
3140 3176 10170
Gilliver K ^{R}10797
Gillman N 9538
Gillmayr-Bucher S
2189
Gilmont J ^{R}12512
Gilmore A 1479
Gilmour M 7053
Gilula D 8832
Gimeno Granero J
3488
Ginzberg L 9398
Giono J ^{M}1453
Giordano C 9282s
Giordano da P 12456
Giorello G 2032
Giorgieri M 8611
Giorgio G 3698
Giove T ^{E}10723
Girard M 3699 **R**
7237s 7681ss
^{M}12634
Girardi M 12177
12190
Girardot N ^{R}7236
Giraudo C 7932
Girolami M 9667
12699
Gisana R 2633
Gispert-Sauch G ^{R}84
696 7734
Gisel P ^{E}351 **Y** 3522
3700 3772
Gittins A ^{R}332
Giuliani M 6305
Giurisato G 6054
Given M 6453 ^{R}6541
Givens J ^{R}4243
Givón T 8853
Gjorgjevski G 3549
Glad C 6424
Gladigow B ^{E}693
Glancy J ^{R}6975
Glassé C ^{E}659
Glassner J 10359s
11521
Glatt-Gilad D 2966
^{R}2850

Hainthaler T 7540 [E]7537

Hainz J [F]42 [M]12638

Halbfas H 1864

Haldimann K 6023 [R]5982

Hale F 2305

Halevi Y 9638

Halevy-Nemirovsky R 8357

Halfmann H 11654

Halivni D 7180s 9541

Hall C 5154 **K** 1967 **L** [R]10607 **R** 10936 **S** [R]12086

Hallam P 1395

Hallo W 9903 11047 [E]407 582

Hallof J [R]8655 **K** [E]8787

Hallote R 11178s

Halmer M [E]59

Halpern B 2634 2791 [E]11324 [R]729 - **Amaru B** 8923 10529

Hamanishi M 6071

Hamann J [M]12585

Hamblenne P 12367 [R]12344 12348 12379

Hamel C de 842s

Hameline J 1152

Hamesse J [E]11

Hamilton A 3012 **J** [F]43 **M** [R]1360 **V** 2635

Hamm D 1153s [R]4328 5396 **M** [E]476

Hamman A 12011

Hammer J 1301 **O** 9834

Hammermeister K [R]149 12741

Hammond N 12789

Hamonville D 1641 [T]3524

Hanc W 7566

Handel G [M]1312

Handley C [E]8722

Handy L 2956 [R]8419

Haneke B [R]14

Hanhart R 1642

Hankey J 10751

Hanks D 4862

Hanna K 6130

Hannah D 2250

Hannestad L 596

Hannestadt N 11000

Hannick J [R]279

Hansen G 10530 10688 [E]20

Hanson K 11885 [E]155 **P** 11886

Hanspach A 3492

Haquin A 12696

Haraguchi T 2617

Haran M 3821

Haraway D 4538

Harder H 9835 **L** 3373

Harding M 6938

Hardmeier C 1521 3706 [E]613 [R]2600

Hardt D 8842

Hargis J 12012

Hargreaves C 5813

Hari A 8038 [E]10937

Haring B 10296 10043 [R]11938

Harl K 11237 **M** 1643ss [E]1616 [T]4114

Harlap L 8305

Harlow D 3963

Harman A 2591 [F]44

Harmless W [R]8 12261

Harmon S 5428 [R]6940

Harms R 5340

Harnack A von 12639 [M]1545 9649 12178

Harnisch W 4954 [D]6979 [R]4962

Harrak A 10364

Harrelson W 9289

Harrill J 7244 [R]6452

Harrington D 742 4742 7245 7760 8883 9189 12653 [E]750 9176 [R]1499 5276 8015 12809 **H** 9208 9290 [R]9141 **J** 5520 [R]5368 **W** [R]6134

Harris E 10153 **J** 1995 **R** 8856 [R]1286

Harrison C 12287 **G** 9759 **N** 12013 **P** 2035 **R** 814 **T** 10186 11666 11180

Hart G [R]11562 **T** [E]8215

Hartal M 11537 [R]12778

Hartenstein F 1996 2485 3196 **J** 5814

Hartin P 7073

Hartman D 6849 6872 9542 11851 **L** [R]6840

Hartmann M 4977 **U** 11510

Hartung U 10297

Hartwig C 6515

Harvey A [R]4512 7679 11920 **G** [R]9298 **J** 2770 4340 4743 6306 11001 **P** [R]680 **S** 1302

Hary B [E]12

Hasan H 11514

Hasenhütl G 7196

Hasitschka M 6131 7761 8744 [D]5248 5306 5447 [R]5834

Hasitzka M [R]8694

Haskins S 8156

Haslam M [E]8806

Hatch E [M]1660

Hatim B 1829

Hatton S 5315

Hattori A 11048

Hattrup D [R]7537

Haubeck W 8724

Haubig H 9402

Hauer C [R]1863 10787

Hauerwas S 157

Haufe G 6916 12678 [R]6720

Haug H 1568 1780

Hauge E 12060 **M** 2382 3197

Haunerland W 7936 [R]7342

Hausamann S 12038 10658

Hausberger K 12596

Hauser A [R]2298 **S** 11523

Hausleiter A [E]614 [R]11197

Herbst M 6766
Herder J M12533
  12585
Heriban J R6263 6434
Herion G E822
Hermans M E277
Hermant D 4627
Hermary A 11676
  R633 9905 10997
Hermisson H 162
Herms E 12582
Herodotus M2639 4068
  9914 11330 11755
Herr B 8857 10250
  11412 11418 R1580
  1648 11248
Herranz Marco M
  5191 8561
Herren M R1709
Herrera R 12288
Herrin J E70
Herrmann J 1781 1789
  10984 W 3815 4217
  7389
Herrojo J 11362
Hertig P 4744 5135
Hertog G den 10251
  10606
Hertzberg H 2652
Herz D T3598 P R117
  10438
Herzer J 5313 7030
  R10574
Herzog W 4345 Z
  11139 11956
Heschel S 4484 9644
Hesemann M 5064
Hesk J R1548
Heskett R 3557 3776
  R3443 3751
Hess M M11997
Hess R 8361 10709
  E278 R2678 8369
Hesse B 11792 H 3475
  M 973
Hetzron R M46
Heuberger J 12532
Heuser M 9760
Hewison R 11630
Heyer C den 1338
  4346 6454 F47 F
  11994 R 1443
Heymel M 6901

Heyse-Schäfer B E59
Heyward C 7567
Hezser C 9291 9365
  R5065
Hébert G 974
Hibbert A D2451
  6150
Hick J 7568 M4317
Hickling C R6280
  6300
Hidal S 10659 R8284
  12745
Hiebert R 1943 3109
  E87 R670 2140 T
  E16
Hieke T 1856 3906
  E4628 4594s
Hiers R 844
Higginbotham C
  10299
Higgins-Biddle J
  E12539
Higgs P E10333
Highfield R 7247
Hijazeen H 11409
Hikade T 11939
Hilaire Y E279
Hilarius P M12383s
Hildegardis B 12461
Hildén H 7607
Hilhorst A 9795
  E8931 R8717 8936
Hill C 4181 6234
  12091 E R3131 J
  3907 R 12197ss
  12246 12249 T3439
  3153ss 12247 T
  1396
Hille R 8258
Hillel M9288
Hillenbrand C 11988
Hillert S 6370
Hilton M 9645
Himbaza I 1569
  1804 1881 2704
Himmelbauer M
  7938
Himmelfarb M 9209
Hinson D 815
Hintersberger B 8157
Hinze B E529
Hippolytus M7956
  8150 12089

Hirsch H 10082
Hirschberg P 6133
Hirschfeld N E11126 Y
  11344 11780
Hirshman M 9366
Hirt S 8919
Hitchcock L R445
  10742 10747
Hjelde S 5021
Hjelm I 9240
Hlaváčková H E470
Hlungwani S 885
Hobbes T M7206
  12534
Hobbins J 4059
Hobbs J 11642 T
  10796 11887
Hoch M E11992
Hochschild R 1522
Hock R R126
Hodder I E725
Hodge S 9052
Hodgens D 6719
Hodges R R10710 Z
  6048
Hodgson P 1447s
Hoegen-Rohls C 6017
  6748 12637 R6408
Hoet H 5815 7823
  R2809
Hoff C 11646
Hoffer V 3395 9404
Hoffman L E344 Y
  3892 3938 3943
  E408
Hoffmann A 12289 F
  11793 H 2439 K
  R9661 M 9033 P
  1856 4629 P E4594s
  4666s F48
Hoffner H 11940
Hofius O 163 6895
  7689 R8986
Hofmann I R10289
  10315 J E11507 T
  8665 Y 4228
Hofrichter C 886
Hoftijzer J 2384 8307
Hogan M 4893 7498
  R3012
Hogeterp A R2879
Hohlfelder R E643
Holc M R2738

Hultgren A 4956 ^{R}4990 6555 6947
Human D 2386 7864 8043
Humbert J 11433
Hume C 6498 **D** ^{M}4923
Hummel A 5685 **P** ^{R}8946
Humphreys W 1968
Humphries M 5257 - **Brooks S** 4746
Huneke D 8044
Hung E 3908
Hunger H 10083 ^{E}8613 †12790
Hunt E 11976 **H** ^{D}2688 **J** 2636 S 9836 ^{E}6236
Hunter A 4187
Hunziker-Rodewald R 7122
Hunzinger C ^{E}573
Huot J ^{F}50
Hur J 5341
Hurault B & L 4590
Hurlet F 10607
Hurley M 5342 **R** 1524 3807 5017 5263 ^{R}2206
Hurowitz V 2253 3556 3559 3562 4232
Hurst L ^{R}95 104
Hurtado L 7865 ^{D}6596 ^{R}4527 7535
Hurter S ^{E}62
Hurth E ^{R}4542
Huskinson J ^{E}410
Huss W 10301 ^{F}51
Hussein M 11184
Husser J 2217 4080
Hutchinson A 5817
Hutchison J 4819
Hutter M 8703 9941 ^{R}375 9755 9949 - **Braunsar S** 10429
Huwiler E 3443 ^{R}7338
Huwyler B 4218 8310 ^{E}102
Hübner H 3634 4591 8259 ^{E}8260 ^{R}2441 4260 5850 12008 **U** 11462 ^{E}65 11752 11860 **W** 9872

Hülden O 11647
Hüllstrung W ^{R}3356
Hülser K ^{T}10481
Hüneburg M 4633ss
Hünermann P ^{E}531
Hvalvik R 9015
Hvidt N 6688
Hyldahl J 9722
Hyllier N ^{E}673
Hyman R 1745
Hyun C 3525

I aia G ^{R}257 349 1963 12216
Iammarrone L ^{R}7186
Ibarzábal S ^{R}7 4687 5397
Ibáñez M ^{R}808
Ibn Ezra A 2322 ^{M}8346 9474s
Ibn Gabirol S 9473
Ibn Kaspi J ^{M}3046
Idel M 7409 9468 9489 9490 ^{E}9354 9491
Idestrom R 12745
Igirukwayo A 5818 ^{R}5094
Ignatius A ^{M}6053 7531 12090-7 **L** ^{M}2227 7887
Ihenacho D 5696
Ihm S 12470
Ikeda J 777 **Y** 744
Ilan D 11370 **N** 2387 **O** 11309 **T** 1303s 8562 8788 9210 9292 ^{R}289 8923
Ilgner R ^{E}12427
Illanes J 7764
Illyricus M ^{M}12518
Ilunga Muya J 12717
Im M 10864
Imesch K 10941
Immink F 5032
Imparati F 2162
Inch M 7638
Inconnu-Bocquillon D 9852
Infante R ^{R}5789
Inglebert H 9723 11888
Ingolfsland D ^{R}4318

Ingraffia B 978
Inostroza Lanas J 6673
Inowlowcki S 8920
Instone-Brewer D 5033
Invernizzi A ^{E}11977
Iodice M ^{R}5692
Iourovskaia Z ^{R}12010
Iovino P 3602
Ireland S 11239
Irenaeus ^{M}1991 7732 8992 12098-110
Irsigler H 4212
Irudaya R 4351
Irudhayasamy R 5447
Irvine S 2947
Irwin W ^{R}3781
Isaac B 10661 **J** 4486 **N** ^{M}7711
Isacson M ^{R}12093
Isbell C 2486
Isherwood L 8185
Ishodad M ^{M}3355 12464
Isidore S ^{M}12416
Işik C ^{E}82
Isler M 11598 - **Kerényi C** 10880
Israel F 2616 8362
Israël G 11271
Israeli E 3013
Israelit-Groll S ^{F}52
Isserlin B 10189s
Istasse N 10302
Ito H 5998 6000
Ivantchik A 10368
Iwand H 12491
Izquierdo A 1195 ^{R}4332 4429 4754 5154
Izre'el S 9853
Izydorczyk Z ^{R}1404
Íñiguez Herrero J 11739

J ack A 1525 6136
Jackson B 2440 **G** 8186 **L** 2513 **M** 12290 **W** 8045 - **McCabe M** 7075 7088
Jacob E ^{M}12465 ^{T}2762
Jacobelli L ^{R}10871

Jong D de 5959 **H de** 1224 5034 5194 [D]7518 6463 **L** [ET]12415 **M de** 4356
Jongeneel J 7410 [R]12817
Jonker L 949ss 1512 1526 2105 982-5
Jonquière T 10534
Joosse N [R]8590
Joosten J 1649 1690 1882 3808 8312 8391
Jordan M 8130 **W** 9653
Jørgensen M 11186
Jorgenson A 12610
Josephus F [M]2163 2890 6380 6625 7143 8965 9342 10503-77 11761 12219
Joslin M 1945
Jospe R [E]9838
Jossa G 5195s 5560s 9231 10535ss 10608 10634 10662
Jossua J 12746
Joubert J 9654 **S** 1831 6455 6670 11891 11890 12691 [R]2054
Joukowsky M 11140s 11440
Joy C 6072
Jörns K [E]114
Jódar-Estrella C 2673
Jucquois G 9655
Julianus A [M]12298 12386s
Julien J 1458
Jullien C & F 8593 10663 [T]9018
Junco Garza C 816 3707 [R]5955
Jung C 5422 [M]1500 9850 **P** 363 **S** 2390
Junge F 8667
Junghans H [E]12498
Junod É 9019
Jurič S [D]3668 [R]2523 5249
Jurissevich E 2209
Jurot R 12291

Jursa M 10802 11942
Just F [R]5879 6172 11837
Justinianus [M]10692 11078
Justinus M [M]2146 12111-30
Justus T [M]10489 10564
Jutrin M 9547
Jülicher A [M]4962
Jüngel E 7692
Jüngling H [D]3318 [E]2515 [R]3096
Jürgens B 2518s

Kaatz K 9778
Kabasele Mukenge A 7867
Kabasélé F [E]7570
Kabuta N [R]3526
Kaddari M [R]8357
Kaestli J 9020 [E]737
Kafafi Z 11458
Kahl B 8192 **J** 10049s [R]10062
Kahn D 10370 **I** 9282s
Kaim B 11004
Kaiser G 2339 **H** 5649 **O** 165s 817 2018 3657 7125 9854 [F]56 [R]7438 **U** [E]9783 **W** 845 7767
Kalimi I 2276 2813 2970
Kallai Z 10253s
Kalmin R 9367
Kalms J 6210 [E]474
Kaltsas D [E]8791
Ka-lun L 3455
Kam A 9548
Kamesar A 12362 [R]3759
Kaminsky J 3844 [E]9588 [R]245 293
Kamionkowski S 4007
Kamlah J 2901 [E]11860
Kammerzell F [E]556
Kammler H 5980

Kampling R 4487 6137 8068 9656 [E]8129 9657
Kampmann C 9509
Kanagaraj J 5819ss 7768
Kanawati N 11187 11601s
Kanellopoulos C 10779 11441
Kaniarakath G 6042
Kannaday W [R]1613
Kannengiesser C 12187
Kant L 8792
Kanta A 11697 11712
Kany R 8757 10609
Kaper O [R]10039
Kapera Z [E]288
Kaplan D 9549 **I** 10881 **L** 9469 **M** [E]9009
Kaplony-Heckel U 8668
Karacolis C [R]163
Karageorghis V 9905 10882ss 11677-81 [E]598 619s 10729 11126
Karg N 12791
Kariapuram M [E]57
Karkajian L 10051
Karkowski A [T]9578
Karlberg M [R]7330
Karle I 890
Karlić I [R]7580
Karlsen Seim T 3080
Karman Y [R]820
Karotemprel S [F]57
Karrer C 2994 **M** 1650 7504 7685 8229 [R]7424
Karris R J 5436 5458 12447 [R]5053 5365 5391 [T]5382
Kartel R [R]9724
Karter M [R]6408
Karttunen K [E]83
Kartveit M 7249 11274
Karumathy G 7250
Kasack W 1397
Kaschewsky R 3308 7944

Kistemaker S 6073
Kister M 4361 9212
  9407
Kitchen K 2860 8669
  8704 10303 R8682
  10219 10299 10994
Kittel G 1789 M8403
Kittredge C 6471
Kitzberger I E988
Kiuchi N 2537
Kizhakearanjaniyil M
  7743
Kizhakkeyil S 3710
Klaes-Hachmöller M
  E12461
Klaiber W 7693 R125
Klaine R 8231
Klappert B 5824 9661
  E119
Klassen-Wiebe S 5404
Klauck H 6140 7694
  9931 11893 R5462
  6088 7817 11880
  T9925
Klaus N 2637 3302
Klausnitzer W 4362
Klawans J 2391 5035
  7252
Kleer M 3200
Klein G 2020 H 4747
  11142 J 7126 8384
  10084 10371 TE4469
  M 12792 P 5021
  6074 R 2219 2972
  R2658 9066 W R579
  9731
Kleiner D E621
Klejn L 10743
Klemperer V M12726
Klengel H 1043 1s
  E11826 -Brandt E
  R11065
Kletter R 10859 11006
Klijn A 9021s 9796
Klimkeit H 9760
Kline M M7356
Klingbeil G R1231
  2499 8503
Klinger J 10433 E39 S
  11007
Klinkott H E414
Klock-Fontanille I
  11053

Kłodkowski P 10155
Kloocke K 989
Klopfenstein M 4146
Kloppenborg J 4638s
  D4612 4673 E4666s
  R7819 8712 9301
Klose A 713
Klöckener M R7341
Klumbies P 5200
  7048
Klutz T R6424 6489
  8161
Knapp A R10710 B
  11682
Knauf E 2254 2674
  2775 2861 3711
  8364 10304 10744
  10887 11276
  11442s 11457 E65
  R2895 10199
Knellwolf C E714
Knesebeck H von
  dem 3111
Knibb M 1692 4060
  8899s
Knierim R 7359
Knight A E1398 H
  7572 9662 J 6205
  R7511 L 3332
Knoblauch A R10882
Knohl I 7411s
Knoppers G 2594
  2794 10419 R407
Knottenbelt E R1240
Knowles M 2884
Knöppler T 5346
  7695
Knudsen E R12815
Knust J 8046
Koch C 9761 D 5036
  6628 H 10085
  11549 R10422 J
  10086 R10074
  10083 10103
  10407 K 3713
  4035s 4061s R3839
  T 7360s
Kochavi M 11334
Koehl R R11126
Koehler L E8365ss
Koemoth P R10020
  10064
Koenen K 4023
  R3875 4112

Koenig J 5037
Koenot J R10967
Koester C 5825 6075
  6985 R5836 6132 H
  6376 E11663
Koffi E 7253
Kofsky A E364
Kogan L 8614
Kohl K E693 M T3832
Kohler G E280
Kohlgraf P 6850
Kohlmeyer K 11143
Kok J 990
Kokkinos N 10583
  11388
Kolakowski L 9818
Kolb A 11861 B
  11444s R 6553
  12494
Kolinski R 11525
Kollesch J F11843
Kollmann B 4868 5292
  5564
Kolly C 11405
Kolska-Horwitz L
  11796
Koltermann R 2037
Koltun-Fromm N 7945
Koncilja R R12806
Kondo J 11563
Kondoleon C E11497
Kongolo C 2488
Konings J 5723 10255
  D5875 R1728
Konkel M 4014
Konrad W 1156
Konradt M 6926
Kontorli-
  Papadopoulou L
  11413
Konyar E 11161
Koole J 3834 3872
Koopmans W R1867
Koopman-Thurlings M
  1444
Kooyman A R1819
Kopciowski E 9551
Kopenhagen-Urian J
  1465 5932
Koperski V R6452
  6621
Korenjak M 8859
Korpel M 2747 3835
  9981

Lenzuni A ᴱ12039
Leo M ᴹ12388s
Leonard A 11635s
Leonardi A 1442 **G**
  5146 5347 5407
  9667 12698s ᴿ1560
Leonas A 1655
Leong K 10157
Leonhard C 3355 7950
  8596 12464 ᴿ11942
Leonhardt J 8945
  10539
Leoni A di 3113
Leontius C ᴹ12236
Leopardi G ᴹ1459
Lepargneur H ᴿ12497
Lepore L 1001 8400
Leppin V 12474
Leproux A 8261
Lequeux X ᴱᵀ12227
Lerner B 3050 **M** 4491
  ᴱ2038
Leroy F ᴿ3833 **H** 4368
  ᶠ64
Lesch K 846
Lescow T 3279 3339
  3797
Leshem Y 2729 8418
Lesko B 10307
Leslie D 782
Lesser R ᴿ5412
Lesses R 9300
Lessing G ᴹ5610
  12537s
Letellier J 12155
Letis T 1561
Letsie S 1158
Leung D 5840
Leutzsch M 5604
Levene D 10755
Levenson J ᴿ1928
Levering M ᴿ12435
Levi della Torre S
  1401
Levi Y 2039
Levick B 10635 ᴿ5053
Levieils X 5697
Levin C 819 1970
  11897 ᴿ2638 **Y** 2973
Levinas E 174 9411
  ᴹ1059 2203 2880
  9519 9561 9792
  12643ss 12646

Levine A 1305 4749s
  4941 5202 ᴱ4709
  5147 **B** 2553 ᴱ618
  H ᴱ9464 **L** 9301s
  11144 ᴱ534 ᴿ9367
  11130
Levinsohn S 1074
Levinson B 2595
Levison J 6689 ᴱ309
  ᴿ2075
Levitt S 9762
Lev-Tov J 11189
Levy B 1572 **H**
  ᴱ7574 **I** ᵀ12484 **T**
  10756 11325 **Z**
  11997
Lewandowski J 7128
Lewin A ᴱ415
Lewis A 7951 **B**
  7716 **J** ᴿ1756 **N**
  8567 10479
Lexutt A ᴿ4250
  12509
Leyerle B 7257
Légasse S 5148 6425
  6908 ᴿ1724
Lémonon J-Pierre
  6312 6378 9303
  9668 ᴱ450
Léna M 894
Léon Azcárate J de
  12510 **-Dufour X**
  ᴱ679 ᴹ5875
Létourneau P 8984
Lévy C ᴱ8946 **E**
  ᴱ2471
Li T ᴿ2318
Lia P 10947
Libanio J ᴿ7606
  8100
Libanori D 12700
Licciardello P
  ᴱᵀ12455
Licharz W ᴱ119
Lichtenberger A
  9933 10584 **H**
  9213 ᴱ78 452 2985
  8884
Liderbach D 7509
Liebenberg J 4681
  8043
Lieber D ᴱ1885
Lieberg G 2001

Liebert E 3238
Liebeschuetz J 11957
  W 9304
Liebich F 4369
Liebowitz H ᴿ10721
Liem J 1002
Lienhard J 4803 12296
  ᴱ1886 **M** 1159 12497
Lienkamp C 8929
Liesen J 3671
Lietaert Peerbolte L
  6055
Lieu J 5841 ᴿ4512
  8961 11983 **S** 9763
  9778 ᴿ9760
Lieven A von 10308
Liew T 1003 7362
  ᴿ5159
Lifschitz D 9510
Ligato G 2885
Light G 3760 **L** 1712
Lightfoot J 8794
  ᴹ12576 ᴿ418
Likins-Fowler D 3860
Lilyquist C 10757
  10853
Lim J 1004s 2565 **T**
  9166 ᴰ9225 ᴱ416
  9054 8360 9081
  9141 9153 9176
Limbeck M 2441 6379
Limburg J 3158
Limet H 3398
Linafelt T 2735 3952
  3962 ᴱ13 293 ᴿ3848
Lincoln A 5842s
  ᴰ6554 ᴿ8005
Lind M 2492
Lindberg C 1746
  ᴱ1747
Lindemann A 4640s
  6616 8048 9305
  ᴱ477 ᴿ316 4243 6844
Lindenberger J M 8568
Linder A 3668
Lindner H 6380 10540
  M 11145 11446
  11462 ᶠ65
Lindsay S 6076
Lindström F 7129
Ling R 11085s
Lingad C 5698
Link C 7110

Marissen M 10832
Maritano M 7963
T3902
Marius V M12390
Marín i Torner J 4805
Marjanen A 8161
Mark M 3351
Markschies C 1241
9729 11905 12088
E12178 R12164
Markus R R12336
Marlett J R1756
Marlow C E11624
Marmorstein A 8233
Marocco G 2546 R120
Marone C 10259 P
12394
Marquardt F 3855
12628 M355
Marques F T2681 V
D6442 R934 4401
6368 8054
Marrou H M279
Marrow S R6976
Marshall C 8051 E
E616 I 4378 6941
D5007 5764 R1151
4356 6240 7775
10601 J 6078 R
5845
Martens E 7459 8265
K 7134 -Czarnecka
M 10951
Marti A 3115
Martignani L 5846
Martin A 12248 D
6383 F69 R6272
11837 de Vivies P
R1724 E 2887 F
1160 4879 6208
R189 G 7263 11194s
H 8620 Jiménez A
3082 J 3250 R11923
L R9871 Moreno J
7264 M E6313 Pet-
tegree A R3012 P
10952 R 1197 4379
E562 M10783 S 6965
8987 T 5305 6564
6825 6899 12305s
T12232
Martínez J R7613
Aldana H 5208 Bor-

rego P 847 de
Lapera A T120210
de Lapera V
T12358 Ferrer L
R692 Fresneda F
R5249 Puche J
E4380 Ruiz C
12481 -Sève L
10548 R62 10501
Martini C 5001 7043
7876 7166 8052s
4896 M7882 7895
Martone C 9104
9215 R9180
Martuccelli P 7781
Marty J 4827
Martyn J 6771
Marucci C 4643s
6269 R365 4959 F
R1467
Marx A 1906 2195
2222 S 1476
Maryono P 5659
Marz B E3980
Marzaroli D 4999
Marzel S 11797
Marzolph U 10953
Masalles V 6697
Maschke T E40
Masciarelli M 8132
Masenya M 1749
3051 3360 3402
8199
Masetti-Rouault M
10378
Mashahu E 5847
Masini M 1533 3862
7877
Masliyah S 8643
Mason M R359 N
12602 R R4192 S
10544ss T10547
Masood S 10125
Masotcha Moyo A
5409
Maspero G 11168
Massa D 4960
Masson E 11667 M
2925
Massonnet J 2394
9308
Master D 2777
Mastin B R4038

Mastrogiacomo M
11133 11429
Mastronarde D R8729
Masvie T 5298
Mateos J 1732 5150
Mateo-Seco L R8118
8135
Matera F 1161 4755
7511 8054
Matheson S E621
Mathewes C 12307
Mathews E 12401
ET1887 1949 R475
3129 8865 S 3403
4065 4154 6149
7265 R6900 T 10731
10954
Mathewson D R6063
7490
Mathieu J 5432
Mathison K 1198
Mathonnet-
VanderWell S 896
Mathys H-Peter 183
2223 2974 12660
D3786 4121 E102
12562
Matjaž M 5209s
Matlock M 2614
Matoušová-Rajmová
M 10833s
Matson M 5513 5953
R4685
Matsumoto K 791
Matt D 4493
Matteo A R7677
Mattern S 10668
Mattheeuws A 3251
Matthews C E750 9003
E ET12402 S 5569
8162 V 820 1871
3722 R8424
Matthiae P 11542
Matties G R678
Mattila R 10379
Mattingly D E419 K
2578 R7451
Mattox M 2169s
12500 R12521
Matusova Y 8947
Mauck J 5653
Maul S E10
Maupassant G de
M2819

Meijering E 12107
Meili J ᴿ1820
Mein A 3989s ᴿ3843 3992
Meineke B ᴱᵀ3447
Meinhold A 1835 10421 W ᴿ11534
Meir E 12644
Meiring P 9840
Meis A 12234 Wörmer A 12233
Meiser M 2765 4250 4685 5350
Meissner W 7964
Meistad T 4854
Mekkattukunnel A 5528
Melanchthon M 7460 P ᴹ12520ss
Melcher S ᴿ2470
Melchert H 9942s
Mele S 5283
Melero Gracia M ᵀ8314
Melhem I 11393 11430
Melito S ᴹ2380 12237s
Mell U 5261 ᴱ4 4962
Mello A 4715 ᵀ2395
Melnyk J 4081
Melo A de ᴿ5090
Melugin R ᴱ3761
Menaul M 2767
Menchén Carrasco J 3206
Mendels D 10551 12219
Mendelssohn M ᴹ12538 ᵀ1874
Mendenhall G 822
Mendes-Flohr P 9555 ᴱ12619
Mendez-Moratalla F 5351
Menestrina G 9673 ᴿ9634 1100 12079
Menichelli E 3254
Menken M 4824 4833 5700 5850s
Menn E 9414
Mennekes F ᴿ10964
Menu B ᴱ11938

Meo S ᴱ8122
Mercier R 10637
Meredith A 12180 12673 ᴿ12144
Merino M ᴱ6609 Rodríguez M ᵀ4588
Merk O ᴿ5657 12558 12577
Merkelbach R 8797s ᴱ8799s
Merker G 11700 ᴿ11344
Merklein H 4686 6617 7640 ᴰ5664 ᴹ71 4336 6373
Merkt A 12016
Merkur D 1496
Merle A ᴱ11981
Merling D 2665-8
Merlo P 9986
Merlos Arroyo F ᴿ3194
Meroz R 9496
Merrillees P 11056 R ᴿ11685
Merz A 4446 8200
Mesa J de 7581
Meshonnic H 3081
Meshorer Y 11241
Messadié G 2067 7135
Messori V 5110s
Mesters C 4756 7878 10669
Meßner R 4173 ᴹ12757
Mettinger T 9987 ᴿ12794
Metz J 7582
Metzger B 1242 1836 12655 ᴱ681 M 11087
Metzner R 5852 ᴿ5783 5836
Meulenaere H de ᴿ10050 10282 11011
Meunier B 12118
Meurer S 1786 ᴱ1763 †12797 T 897 2224 2717
Mewe T 1822

Meyer B 10053 E 8315 I 4564 J 6384 10806 ᴿ11185 M 9341 9799 ᴱ96 483 P ᴿ4358 zu Capellen J 10955 -Abich K 6151 -Blanck M 10827 -Dietrich E 11196
Meyers C 10205 11364 ᴱ1308 E 11147 11364 ᴱ729 11349 ᴿ11130
Meynell M 5067
Meynersen S 11419
Meynet R 1534 4597 4687s 4963 10145
Médevielle G 7879
Méniel P 11785
Mésoniat C 1347
Miano P 10611
Michael S ᴿ520
Michaeli H 3953
Michaelides D ᴿ11081
Michaels J 7880
Michailidou A ᴱ10861
Michaud J 4389 4646 5112 ᴰ5801 ᴿ4426
Michaux-Colombot D 10380
Micheel R 898
Michel A 2196 ᴱ38 C 10848 ᵀ8621 D 12798 O ᴹ10540 R 1451
Michelakis P ᴱ27
Micunco G ᴿ12079
Midant-Reynes B 11633
Middleburgh C 9309
Middleton A 11111 J 7674
Miehl M 10138
Miele M ᴿ277 2038
Mielgo C ᴿ2237 2626 2999 3609
Mierzwa T 5527
Mies F 3547 ᴱ35 300
Migahid A 8672
Miggelbrink R 7266
Migliore F ᵀ12219
Miglus P 10784 ᴿ10803

Prechel D ^{E}39
Preez J du 4169
Pregla A 1085
Preisendanz K ^{ET}8813
Prema 12719
Premstaller V ^{R}3988
Prendergast T ^{R}11918
Prestel P 10558
Preß M 7620
Prete B 5449 6658
Preus J 12548
Preuss H 7463
Prevost R 1025
Preys R 10057 ^{T}10738
Prévost J ^{T}1724
Price J 10639s **R** 4412
 ^{R}7068 **S** 9861 9911
 ^{E}9868
Prickett S ^{E}286 ^{M}5250
Prienne-Delforge V
 ^{R}615
Prieur J 4392 7721
 ^{R}1348 9005 12345
Prigent P 6083-6
 ^{R}7514 10954
Prignaud J ^{T}10886
Primasius ^{M}12417
Prime D 3055
Pringle D 11993
 ^{R}11988
Prinsloo G 4221
Prinz W 10963
Prior D 4116 **H** ^{R}8865
 J 5941 7589 **M** 6943
 12000 ^{R}3138 6949
 11263
Priotto M 2936
Priskin G 11607
Pritchett W 10450
Privat J 1414
Privitera S ^{E}8016
Probst M ^{R}358
Procopios C ^{M}12241
Prokurat M ^{R}1042
 1218
Pronzato A 4717
Propp W 2318
Prosecký J 10392
Prosser M 8485
Prostmeier F 5293
 ^{E}101
Protus K 4965
Proust M ^{M}1467

Provan I 3444 7368
 ^{R}3952 10197
 10231
Provost S 11690s
Pröbstle M ^{R}7449
 8334
Prudentius ^{M}12392
Prudky M 1168
Prusak B ^{R}525
Pruzsinszky R ^{R}8491
Prüller-Jagenteufel G
 ^{E}530
Pschibille J 3915
Ptolemy 11751
Puech E 3573 7722
 8575s 9107-22
 9170s 9219 11151
Puhvel J 8707
Puig i Tàrrech A 310
 1735 5453 7035
 8994 ^{E}490 ^{R}298
 4680 5319 5568
 5579
Puigdollers i Noblom
 R 6320
Pulatt S 4843
Pulcinelli G ^{R}5146
 6505
Pulcini T 8995
Pulikottil P 9123
 ^{R}3155
Pulsiano P ^{E}3119
Pulzer P ^{F}88
Punt J 1026 6389
 8270 10147
Punton A 4413
Purcell B ^{R}328 **N**
 10710
Pury A de 2144 2231
 ^{F}89
Puthenpurackal A
 5470 **C** 4942
Puthenveettil J ^{R}164
Puykunnel S 5294
Pülz A 11658
Pyeon Y 3408
Pyper H 3295 3956
 4414

Qatamin H 10393
 11460s
Qimron E 8319 9099
 9172 ^{M}9167

Qing D 8598
Quack J 8675 10058
 ^{R}10025 11625
Quast U ^{E}3098
Quelle C 7419 7614
Quesnel M 311 M 393
 1270 5678 6321
 6390s 10799 11945
 ^{E}85
Queyrel F ^{E}623
Quezada del Río J
 3409
Quincoces Loren A
 2283
Quinn J 6949 **P** 7183
 R 4992 -**Miscall P**
 3762
Quintero J 5072 **L**
 11398
Quinto R 4024
Quirke S 10059
Quispel G ^{F}90 ^{R}5787

Raabe P 4204
Raban A 11115
Rabano Mauro ^{M}9478
Rabello A 197 9323
 9376
Rabuske I 5256
Racine J ^{R}12578
Rad G von 7464
 ^{M}12660
Radcliffe T 198
Raddatz A ^{D}1787
Raddish M 809
Radermakers J ^{R}1245
 4245 4537
Radice R ^{T}8954
Radl W 4817
Radmacher E 6015
Radner K ^{E}10394
Radt W 11661
Raepsaet-Charlier M
 10656 ^{R}774
Raffelt A ^{E}63
Raguer H ^{R}12598
Raguse H 3410
Rahner J 1248 **K**
 ^{M}7625
Rahveh-Klemke S
 ^{T}3598
Rainey A 8486 8676
 10212 11330 11586
 ^{F}91

Rein M 5999
Reinbold W 7792
Reiner E 10099
Reinfandt L 11860
Reinhardt K 3461
  12420
Reinhart M ᵀᴱ4469
Reinhartz A 1088
  5873s ᴰ5914 ᴿ502
  5726 9597
Reinmuth E ᴿ1075
  3437
Reinsdorf W 5117
Reis F dos 5875
Reiser M 1031 1543
  5223 5683 6323
  6524 8064 8239
  ᴿ5695 **W** 5224
Reiter F 10320
Reiterer F ᴿ817
Remaud M 9690s
Rembrandt ᴹ1470
  10956 10976
Renan E ᴹ279 10749
  12542
Renaud-Chamska I
  1457 5934
Rendall S ᵀ11610
Rendsburg G 1973
  2321 8321s ᴿ685
  12785
Rendtorff R 201 1249s
  1909 1924 2175ss
  2371 2397 2421
  2425 2532 2615
  2766 3007 3784
  4119s 7465-8 9692-5
Renfrew C ᴱ394
Renger J 10100 11946
  ᴱ11826
Renju P 6654
Renkema J 3957
Renker A ᴿ5186 6591
Renna T 12313
Renoux C 10699
Rensberger D 5876
  6051
Renz J 779 8376 **T**
  3992 ᴿ4005 4015
Repschinski B 4418
  4767 7793 ᴱ284
  ᴿ5058 5140 8008
Requena M 9879

Ress M 8205
Resseguie J 5877
  6172 ᴿ7592
Revell E 2284 ᴿ1584
Reventlow H 7469
  12022s 12516
  12518 12526-9
  12531 12533ss
  12537 12540s
  12543s 12547
  12551 12553
  12560 12563
  12569ss 12573s
  12581 12588
  12591s 12611
  12617 12621
  12636 12681 ᴱ492
  ᴿ2515 7110 12585
Rex R ᴱ12524
Reydellet M ᴿ9870
Reyes A 11068
  ᴿ10883 **Bravo N**
  ᵀ8314 **F** 11650
Reymond E 3672
  3675
Reynard J ᴿ8999
Reynier C 1203
Reynolds G 10129 **S**
  ᵀ10703
Rée P 11565
Rhee V 7003 7018
Rhoads D ᴱ312 **J**
  2706 5952
Riain I ᵀ12364
Ribera-Florit J ᴿ6673
Ribichini S 788 ᴱ574
Ricart I ᴿ10598
Ricciotti G 4419
Richard F 10615 **J**
  1415 ᶠ92 **P** 5578
  6087 **S** 11428
Richards W ᴰ7042
Richardson J 9060 **M**
  2472 ᵀᴱ8365s
  ᴿ8653 **N** 10587
  ᴿ6281 7172 **P** ᴱ259
  ᶠ93 **S** 10101
Riches J 4600 5225
  6830 7277 ᴿ491
Richler B ᴱ1578
Richter H 3560 **S**
  2642 8695 9767s **T**
  9945 10102 ᴱ39
  ᴿ1693 11543

Rickenmann A 12160
Ricl M ᴿ8777
Rico C 1544 4575
Ricoeur P 291 1032
  ᴹ925 995 1037 1041
  1078 4282 8031
  12661
Ridez L 10965
Ridgway B 11016
Ridolfi F 10715
Riebe A ᵀ11927
Riede P 3428 11801
  ᴱ362
Riedl H 5878 **J** 12805
Riedweg C 12122
Riegner I 8409
Riego M ᴿ12595
Riemer U 6173
Ries J 12314s
Riesebrodt M ᴱ3714
Riesner R 4928 6280
  7644 9233
Riezu J 7278
Rife J ᴿ11201
Rigato M 6037 7045
  7723
Rigby C 3212
Riggs C 11212
Rikhof H 7624
Riley G 4253 10674
  12041 **Strange J**
  9072 -**Smith J** ᴱ92
  11985 ᴿ11993
Rinaldi G 4254
Rindone E 7279
Ring T 4947
Ringe S 5280 5879
  ᴱ1868
Ringgren H ᴱ670s
Riniker C 5006
Rippin A 10130
Riska M 9173
Risse S 12523
Rist J 3263
Ristow S 7741
Ritter A 12235 **S**
  11017 -**Werneck R**
  7938
Rittner C 9696s ᴱ377
  R ᴱ7830
Rius-Camps J 5265
  5267 5579s ᵀ12095
Rivas L ᴿ6673 **Reba-
  que F** 5608

Savage J 8436 S
11401s
Savasta C 6044
Savoca G ᴿ4105
Savon H ᴿ12005
Savonarola 12478
Saward J ᴿ5871
Sawicki M 5228 11352
Sawyer D F 3037s
8208 ᴿ320 J 3785
8865 ᴱ701
Sänger D 2418 ᴱ133
137 ᴿ5058 9657
Särkiö P 2866
Sáenz-Badillos A 9505
Scaer P 5514
Scafa E 8734 P 8626
Scaglia F 12756
Scaiola D 2900 2841
2943 ᴿ479 1089
2645 3159 3704
4753 5148 5316
5337 5385ss 6261
6484 6563 6753
6767 6774 7032
7759 8259
Scalabrini P 2602
Scalise P 3916
Scanlin H ᴿ1621
Scanu M 9417
Scarcia Amoretti B
ᴱ637 G 10139
Scardigli P 1419
Scarpat G 4902 8759
ᴱᵀ3639
Scarry E 1356
Scatolini S 4004
Schaab G 8209
Schaack T 8419
Schachner A ᴿ614
Schade H 10966
Schaefer K 3165
Schaff P 12077
Schalit A 10588
Schaller B 206 1170
3971 4501s 4883
6488 6593 6674
7421 7657 8913
8960 9701 9712
Schams C 10216
Schapdick S 5972
Schaper J 2999 3216
Scharbert J 2323

Scharer M ᴿ1359
Scharf G ᴿ1150
Schart A ᴿ1528 4136
Schatkin M ᴿ9599
Schatzman I 10589
Schatzmann S ᵀ5916
Schaudig H 8627
ᴿ8634
Schäfer B 5383 J ᶠ99
P 9257 ᴰ9511
ᴱ7422 9429s 12619
R 3 5 4 2 -
Lichtenberger C
2200 10217 ᴷ2658
Schäffer W 911
Scheck T ᵀ6502s
Scheele P 6091
Scheffczyk L 1124
Scheffer C ᴱ11119
Scheffler E 797
10218 T ᴱ11467
Schegget G ter 4857
Scheible H 12520
Scheid J 9881
Scheidel W 11570
ᴱ439 ᴿ8764
Schelbert G 7798
ᴿ233
Schelkens K ᴿ1113
Schellenberger B
ᵀ4992
Schellihg P 1338
Schelling W ᴹ9725
Schemmel B ᴱ10736
Schenck K 7010
Schenk R 6245s
ᴱ6097
Schenke G 10851 H
9804 ᴱ9783 ᴱᵀ4718
9812 ᴿ5634 8692
9030 9768
Schenker A 207 1033
1254 1579 1668
1881 2263 2426
2447 2897s 3217
3864 7280 7471
8417 ᴰ925 995
3451 ᶠ100 ᴹ12668
ᴿ1888
Scherer A 3472 3551
Scherman N 9431
Schertz M 1547
Scheuchenpflug P
7799

Scheuer M ᴿ211
Schiappa E 1548
Schiffman L 2890
9065 9220ss 9064
ᴱ639 1597 9066
9335 ᴿ9263
Schille G ᴿ5539
Schima S 4993
Schimanowski G
11620
Schipper B 10219
ᴿ10164 H 12318
ᴿ504
Schippmann K ᴿ386
Schlaepfer C 5303
Schlageter J ᴱᵀ3445
ᴿ12476
Schlarb E 6945 ᴱᵀ8986
Schlegel F ᴹ12585
Schleiermacher F
ᴹ9614 12582-6
Schleifer R ᴱ287
Schlick-Nolte B
ᴿ11039
Schlingensiepen F
7891
Schloen J 11477
Schlossberg E 9255
Schlosser J 4426 4670
5120 M 12421
Schlubach J 12429
Schmandt-Besserat D
11829
Schmeller T 5609
8067 11917 ᴿ316
1522 4311
Schmelz G 8891
Schmelzer H ᴿ12542
Schmid D ᴱ12584 H
3967 J 5121 K 2264
2501 2627 3404
3735 3763 ᴰ2575
ᴱ608 M 1472 S
10897 11447s V
ᴱ1734
Schmidinger H ᴱ315
Schmidl M 5880 ᴱ42
Schmidt A 4427 ᴱ4283
ᴿ11991 B ᴱ11478 C
ᴿ11542 F 4858 9336
J 2023 9914 L 1791
2448 4203 P 1420
6946 10967 S 12613

Schwarzkopf M 12174
Schweitzer A 4434ss
 4548 ^{M}9799 12669
Schweizer E 4720
 5387 7036 ^{R}5158
 8223 **H** 2290
Schwemer A 276
 5309s 5523 6265
 7521 ^{E}1647 **D** 10106
Schwendemann W
 ^{R}3226
Schwendtner F ^{R}10468
Schwienhorst-
 Schönberger L 7473
Schwier H 7981 8272
 ^{E}9660
Schwöbel C 6399
Scibona C 9769 **R**
 3946 8402 9125
Scognamiglio E ^{R}232
 7517 7551 **R** ^{T}4700
Scolnic E 8350
Scopello M 9770
 12320
Scoralick R 2503 ^{E}318
Scordato C 7736
Scott B 4969 **J** 4632
 6592 6794 9175
 ^{E}319
Scourfield J ^{R}8864
Scriba A 6287
Scroggs R ^{D}6935
 ^{R}1063
Scullion J 4437
Se H 9225
Seal T ^{R}10356
Searight S ^{R}10909
Seasoltz R 10971
Sebastiani S 10268
Sebbane M 10815
Sebesta J ^{R}621
Secher A 4503
Seckler M 1255
Secondin B 7347
Sedley D 10480s
Sedlmeier F 3820
Sed-Rajna G 10972
 ^{T}9398
Seebass H 1927 2557
 ^{R}2553 2626
Seeber R 10800
Seeher J 11216 11653
 11670

Seeley D 1549
Seelig G 9827
Seeliger H 11731
 11737 ^{R}11745
Seely P 2115
Seeman C ^{R}250 467
Seemuth D 7800
Seesengood R ^{R}6088
 6309
Segal A 5666 11217
 ^{R}11020 **D** 11320 **R**
 9857
Segalla G 4438 6505
 8070 8273 ^{R}4258
 4341 4346 4388
 5020 5389 5710
 5789 5846 5896
 6017 6132 8039
Segbers F 7375
Seger J ^{E}12758
Segert S ^{R}8366
 10177
Segovia F ^{E}320
 ^{R}5725
Seguin M 2116
Seidel H 10836
Seidl T 3739 8332
Seidler M 9568
Seidnader M 6961
Seifrid M 6400 7474
 ^{E}251 ^{R}6584
Seiler S 2804 3218
Seitz C 3836 4577
 7348 **E** 6587 7021
Sekine S 1036
Sekules V 10973
Sekunda N 10801
Seland T 7037
Selander I 3267
Selden R ^{E}720
Selengut C ^{E}379
Sell N 5438
Sellew P 9805
Sellin G ^{R}8950
Selling J ^{R}8015
Seluvappan L 5457
Selz G 8629 10404
 11070 ^{R}2095 2102
Sembrano L 2805
Sementchenko L
 10571
Seminara S 8630s
 ^{R}8498

Semkowski L ^{M}12670
Semler J ^{M}5610 12543
Seneca ^{M}8831 11890
Senior D 4772 5074
Seow C 3577
Sepio D 11429
Sequeri P 1256
Serapion T ^{M}12242
Şerban T 1037
Seripando G 4887
Serra A 7143 8138s
Serrano V 7171 7522
Serres M 1474
Seth S 912
Settis S ^{E}440
Setz C ^{R}4521
Setzer C ^{R}9619
Severus A 2315
Sevin M ^{T}1724
Sevrin J 4671 5299
 5887 11292 ^{D}6006
Sewell P 4672
Sewodo Dovi M 6695
Sexson L 7282
Seybold K 3092 12565
 ^{E}12562 ^{F}102
Seyferth S 1793
Sérandour A 4225
Sère B 913
Sfameni Gasparro G
 12321
Sfar M 10133
Sgargi G ^{E}4113
Shaffer A 8551s 8386
Shaji T 12403
Shaked S 1595 9257
Shakespeare W 1475ss
Shanks H 9068s 10716
 10745 11071 11121
 11153 ^{E}321
Shantz C 5454
Shapira D 1421
Shapiro R 4504
Sharf E ^{E}10160 **R**
 ^{E}10160
Sharlach T 10405
Sharma A 4439
Sharon I 11122
Sharp C 2713 ^{R}3899
 9598
Shavit A 9569
Shaw I ^{E}10323 11567
 ^{R}11158 **T** 8071

Stevenson G 6180 **K**
3993 4001 6202 **T**
^{R}9865
Stewart C 12163 **E**
4017 **J** 11685 **P**
^{R}10893 **R** ^{R}10855 -
Sykes A 1176 5044
T12089 12238
Steyn G 7004s
Stibbe M ^{R}5728
Stichel R 3123 7727
Stiebert J 1285 2730
7287 ^{R}2791
Stiewe M 4859 9841
Still T 6911
Stimpfle A 5984 ^{E}64
Stingl W 9572
Stipe J ^{D}3298
Stipp H 2011 3896 ^{E}38
Stirnimann H 7202
Stiver D 1041 4282
^{R}4530
Stock A 4778 **H** 899 **K**
4722 7894 12632
^{D}5207 5258
Stockham A 7288
Stoebe H 3927
Stoellger P 6247
Stoffels H 9842
Stol M 7289 ^{E}1286
^{R}10102
Stolle J 2203 **V** 5076
251 9643 12023
12495
Stolt B 1795
Stolz F 2347s 10004
12813
Stone K 4139 7377
8080 ^{E}325 **M** 1259
8897s 8916 ^{E}153 560
576 828 8914
Stordalen T 1260 2075
^{R}12815
Storkey E 7290
Storm E 10324 **M**
7039
Stos J 780
Stott D ^{T}6280 **J** 7728
Stout J 1484
Stowasser M 5282
5291 5637
Stowers S 6407 ^{R}6452
6542

Stöhr M 9709
Stökl D 2536
Straight J 1206
Stramare T 1716s
7186 8143 ^{R}2553
Strange J 7187 9072
9347 10791 11155
^{E}630 ^{R}10787
Strangio G ^{E}519
Straus J ^{R}10494
Strauss D ^{M}12587s **H**
3418 **L** 1953 **M**
7987
Stravinskas P ^{E}381
Strawn B 11807
Streck M 8491 ^{R}8634
11480
Strecker C 6408
^{R}1288 4927
Strecker G 4256
6052 8274
Streeter B ^{M}12672
Strelan R 5630 5643
Stricher J ^{R}5568
Strieder I 6481
Strohschneider-
Kohrs I 12538
Strola G 3310 5083
Strong J ^{R}3890
Stronstad R 5366
Stroobant de Saint-
Eloy J ^{T}6506
Stroumsa G 216
9937 12545s ^{E}364
642 ^{R}154
Strubbe J ^{E}8820
Strugnell J 9073
^{E}9176 ^{M}9088
Strus A 2076 5635
Stuart D 1553
Stubenrauch B 7814
Stuckenbruck L 4072
9033
Stuckrad K von ^{R}345
382
Studer B 217 6057
Stuhlmacher P 6409
6559 6706 8275
^{E}4593 ^{F}105 ^{R}8277
Stuiber A 8747
12359
Stulman L ^{E}3903
Stump E ^{E}12325

Sturbaut F 1427
Sturdy J ^{E}712
Sturm W 1177
Sturtevant H 10978
Stümke V 6248
Stylianopoulos T 1042
1218
Such Gutiérrez M
^{R}9993
Suckale-Redlefsen G
^{E}10736
Sudilovsky J 2891
Suermann H ^{R}4533
Suetonius 10633
Sugirtharajah R 1043
5497 8111 ^{E}695
1044
Suied A 9573
Sulavik A 3968 12483
Sullivan F 7832 **K**
^{R}7634 **L** 12392
Sulpicius S ^{M}12393
Sumney J 6212 6482
6731 6951 ^{E}6316
^{R}4591 7089
Sundermann W 218
9771ss ^{E}579
Sunquist S ^{E}706
Suprenant L ^{E}8144
Surridge R 9843
Susaimanickam J 3412
10161 ^{R}11896
Susin L 7524
Susini G 12814
Suski A 5946
Sussmann Y ^{E}9436
Sutcliffe E ^{M}12673
Suter D ^{R}337
Sutherland M 3413
Sutter Rehmann L
6487 6561 7291
Svartvik J 5277
Sventsitskaya I 12623
Svigel M 6181
Swain S ^{R}10461
Swanson R 1613 ^{E}6507
6773 ^{R}1751 9669
Swartley W ^{R}5779
Swartz M 9498
Swedenborg E ^{M}9499
Sweeney D 8680 ^{E}52
M 2938 3764 4123
4073 4201 10005

Terrinoni U 4185
Terstriep D 3503
Tescione C 5989
TeSelle E 12327
Teske R 12328
Testart A 11922
Teugels L 9437 ᵀ9349
Teuwsen B 4820
Tewes H ᴱ88
Teyssier D'Orfeuil Y
  11313
Thackeray H 10576
Thalhofer V ᴹ12552
Thalmann R 12001
Thatcher T 5800 5891-
  6 ᴱ5694
Thayse A 5729
Theissen G 4258
  4446ss 7148 7991
  8276 9234 11923s
  ᴰ4765 5416 6515
  ᴹ5612 ᴿ6272
Theissmann U ᴱ9615
Thekkekara M 6900
Thelamon F 12221
Thellung A 4259
Then R 920
Theobald C 7188
  ᴱ6176 M 219 1461
  5614 6461s 6410ss
  6529ss 6540 6571
  6582s 6544 6508
  6527s 6547 6549
  6599s 6691 6810
  9710 ᴰ4977 ᴱ186
  ᴿ5186 6497
Theodore A ᴹ12480
Mopsuestia ᴹ12298
Theodoretus C 3153s
  3439 ᴹ3804 4181
  12199 12244-8
Theodoros E ᴿ11740
Theodorus C ᴹ7533 M
  ᴹ3355 12249s 12464
Theokritoff E 7992
Theuer G 10006
Thérèse Lisieux ᴹ7929
  7994
Thériault J 5317
Thévenot S 4925
Thiede C 7730 9193s
Thiel J 1219 W ᴿ4194
  8358

Thiele W 3649s
Thielman F ᴿ6415
Thiem E 10759
Thierfelder J ᴱ866
Thijs A 10325
Thimmes P ᴿ11907
Thinès G 1455
Thiong'o N ᴹ1481
Thiselton A 1008
  1046 6621 ᶠ106
Thissen H ᴱᵀ8683
Thoennes K 7294
Thom J 9917
Thoma C 9574
  12631 ᴰ2261 ᴿ2879
  9568 9645 12780
  ᵀ9438
Thomas C 8777 J
  10326 10747 ᶠ107
  K 1849 M 7006 R
  6853 8244 T 11220
Thomason A 10902
Thome G 10681
Thompson A ᴿ676 D
  6968 10327 J 1313
  3126 6333 6732
  ᴱ11978 L ᴿ6119 M
  3837 4235 5897s
  7172 7526 ᴱ80 R
  1362 ᴿ5391 T 1917
  2628 8422 9186
  10224 10496
  10223 10271
  ᴿ8215 W ᴱ328
  ᴹ108 12676
Thomsen M 10903
  11925
Thomson P 12292 R
  1718
Thondiparambil J
  9350
Thornbury G ᴱ7690
Thottakara A ᴱ84
Thrall M 6733s
Throntveit M ᴿ2984
Thuesen P 1756
Thurén L 6413 6694
  12205
Thurston A 8212 B
  5156 5441
Thümmel H 11745
Thüsing W 8277
Thyen H ᴿ6030

Ticonius ᴹ12394
Tidball D 7731
Tiedemann H 11353
Tietjen J ᴿ6092
Tietz W 11123
Tigchelaar E 9178
  ᴿ9054 9066
Tiller P 8736
Tillesse C 2077 5045s
  7295 7617 7804
Tilley M ᴿ289
Tillich P 7596 ᴹ7177
Tilliette X 1047 4449
Tilly M 5686 11295
Timbie J ᴿ9807
Timko P ᴿ12340
Timm H 1048 S ᴰ2833
Timmer D 8081 J
  ᴿ4949
Timossi I 6182
Timotheus A 1138
Timpe D 10642
Tinat J 7993
Tischendorf C von
  12589 ᴹ12589
Tischler J 8708s
Tita H 7349
Titchener F ᴱ447
Tite P 7044 8905 9735
Titin S ᴱ33
Tiwald M 4450 4690
  5713 8082 ᴿ5564
Tkacz M 6334
Tobin T 6551 12676
  ᴿ6519 V ᴿ10041
  10313
Todaro M 9478
Toffanello G 4782
Tognina P ᴱ7822
Tognini-Bonelli E
  8868
Toivari-Viitala J 11573
Toland J ᴹ12553
Tollington J ᴿ4112
  4191
Tolmie D ᴱ771 ᴿ6780
  F 1090
Toloni G 2983
Tomasi G 5047
Tomasoni F ᴱ8259
Tombs D ᴱ540 5116
Tomes R 1869 ᴿ1231
  4195

Tyson J 5367 5589
5668
Tzaferis V 11296

Ubaldelli M 10852
Ubbiali S ᴱ330
Ubertino de Casale
  ᴹ12481
Ubigli L ᴿ1635 8914
Uchida S 11563
Uchitel A 11397
Udris J 7994
Uebele W 6053
Uehlinger C 2292 3143
  3465 3997 7316
  10191 10274 10886
  ᴱ100 644
Uemura S 3810
Uggeri G 11671
Uglione R ᴱ517
Ugwaka P 7598
Ukpong J 1049
Ulansey D 9889
Ulfgard H 2509
Ulland H 6213
Ullendorff E 1454
  ᴿ151
Ullmann M 786
Ulmer R 9439s ᴿ9389
Ulrich E 3766 4039
  9130 9196 ᴱ9131
  ᵀ9081
Unamuno M de 5967
Unchelen N 9441
Untergaßmair F 1556
  4260 6025 6094
  6183s 6192
Uphill E 10328 11156
  ᴿ10295
Urbainczyk T ᴿ3153s
Urbàn A 8892 ᴱ12096
  12619 ᴿ6965 7001
  9674 11362 C 5905
Urbrock W 3331
Uricchio F ᴿ1114
Uríbarri G ᴿ12119
Usque A ᴹ3113
Ussishkin D ᴱ11324
Uthemann K ᴿ6067
Utro U 10983
Utzschneider H 1677
  4197 ᴿ4192 4194
Uzukwu E ᴿ7785

Vaage L 4580
  ᴰ9791
Vaahtera J 10275
Vadakkekara B
  ᴿ11994
Vaggione R ᴿ12190
Vahrenhorst M 4581
Vakayil P 6016
Valantasis R 9784
  9813 ᴿ9801 12005
Valdés A 4934 J
  6095
Valente Bacci A
  ᴱ7031
Valentini A 2930
  4452 5439 6414
  ᴱ8145
Valevičius A ᴿ8961
Valério P 5627
Valkenberg W 12435
Vall G 4141
Vallery-Radot M
  12372
Vallet R 852
Vallée G 12028
Vallin P 7628
Valloggia M ᴿ11194
Valvo A ᴱ580
Van Aarde A 4453s
Van Acker L ᴱ12461
Van Amersfoort J
  12330
Van Andel J 4981
Van Baak E ᴿ695
Van Banning J 12381
Van Beeck F 8146
Van Bekkum W
  ᴿ9359
Van Belle G 772
  5906 5974 12706ss
  ᴿ988 5779 5804
  5834
Van Bemmelen P
  2012
Van Buren P 831
  ᴹ7552
Van Buuren L 2728
Van Cangh J 2529
Van Daalen L 2779
Van de Mieroop M
  11961 ᴿ10206
  11960

Van de Sandt H 12078
Van de Water R 1261
Van den Berg E 2948
  G 1486
Van den Bosch L 9806
Van den Broek R
  ᴰ12183 ᴱ90
Van den Eynde S 2118
  2980 3058 3918
  4012 ᴿ3437
Van den Hoek A
  10984 ᴱ12051
Van den Hout T 9950
  10441
Van der Horst P 8821
  9242 ᴱ685 ᴿ716 8810
  ᵀ8893
Van der Kooij A 1126
  1678 3071 3787
  3822 ᴰ2657 ᴱ501
  ᴿ2989
Van der Lans J 981
Van der Linde H 4455
Van der Meer M 2657
  2670
Van der Merwe C
  8334 8339 D 5907
Van der Plancke C
  3222
Van der Spek R
  ᴿ10466
Van der Steen E J
  11124 11300 ᴿ11324
Van der Toorn K 2325
  3580 4074 ᴱ501 685
  2427
Van der Ven J ᶠ109
Van der Water D 9844
Van der Watt J 5908
  ᴿ1090 5116 5122
  5916 5977 6050
Van der Westhuizen J
  11590
Van der Woude A 833
  †12817
Van Deun P 4821
  12472
Van Dijk J 10329
Van Driel G 11830
Van Duin K 3793
Van Elderen B ᴿ10705
Van Engen J 2530
  9711 ᴱ442

Vendrix P 10838
Venema R 5445
Venetz H 5615
Venter C 7996 **P** 4076
  R3568
Ventura M T7180
Venturini S 9133
Verardi G R12770
Verbaas F 12618
Verbist P R10602
Vercoutter J 12818
Vercruysse J 3816
  12395
Verd G R2887 5432
Verdeyen P T3466
Verdon T 10987
Verdoodt A 8038
Vergerio P 12352
Vergilius Maro P M130
Vergottini M 7895
Verheij A 8336
Verhelst S 9443
Verheyden J 749 755
  4674 12071 12709
  E767 5368 R96 187
  224 255 831 4707
  6061 6063 7511
  12137
Verhoef E 1262 6912
Verhoeven U 8685
Verhoogt A R8816
Verkest P 12424
Verkindère G 7378
Vermes G 4512 9080
  E10619 **M** T9778
Vermeule E 12819
Vermeulen U E645
Vermeylen J 832 2238
  2809 5238 E2788
V e r n e r M 1 0 3 3 2
  11610
Vernet J 4816
Vernus P T3504
Veronese P M10923
Verreth H 8776
Verschoren M R6564
V e r s e p u t D 7 0 8 6
  12694 R4751
Verspeeten F 6693
Verster P 6532
Vervenne M 2015 E6
Vespasian M10633
Vessey M E12336

Vetrali T 3667
Veyret G T7412
Vez C 4870
Vial T 8085 E24
Vian G 1263 R402
Vianney Infante R
  R2315
Vicari J 2119s
Vicastillo S ET12175
V i c e n t C e r n u d a A
  5081 **R** R216 2373
  4020 4277 6413
  8875 8890 8942
  9227 9257 10134
  10464 10970
Vichos Y E635
Viciano A E4876
Victor Tunnunensis
  M12396
Vidal M 2016 4513
Vidau E E519
Vidovic M 921 1127
Vielhauer R 9134
Vieweger D 11458
Viganò D 4549
Vigée C M1482 9535
Vignal M 2349
V i g n o l o R 1 0 5 5 s
  1930 3330 3545
  3617 5910s
Vigourt A 9882
Vilanova E R8095
Vilela M T7337
Villanueva Puig M
  E646
Villefranche H de
  6096
Villeneuve E 11450
  F 10577 11451
Villiers D de 9846
Villing A E9895
Vincent G D2743 **J**
  1615 6718 9575
  E493 2318 3904
  4023 4194 **Jurič S**
  R6351
Vines M 5239
Vinson R 6188 4358
  4409 4446 4463
  4466 4846
Virgili R 2783 2836
  7149 R4130
Virgilio B 10501

Vironda M 8749
Vischer W M12677
Visicato G 10409
V i s m a r a C 1 1 7 2 8
  R11780
V i s o n à G R12123
  T12079
Visotsky B R9646
V i s o t z k y B 9 7 1 5
  E9355
Visschers L 6001
V i t a J 8 4 5 4 8 4 9 7
  11591 R11466
Viterbi B 2403
Vitório J 4163
Vittmann G 8686
Vitto F 11221
Vives i Tutó J M12598
Viviano B 223 4460
  4583 4784 5016
  5287 5912s 6416
  6485 6509 6852
  7600 7629 7646
  7896 R2879 5391
  7648
Viviers H 3432
Vílchez J R3045
Vlaardingerbroek J
  4213
Vledder E 4939
V l e e m i n g S 8 6 8 7
  E1286
Vlora N 11574
Voderholzer R 12649
  R12164
Voegelin E M328
Voelker J 12390
Voet G 11623
Vogel Ettin A 4514 **M**
  10573 R7321 10521s
Vogelmann V T185
  2786
Vogels C R4098 **W**
  1264 1364 1974
  2327 3385 R296 893
  3087
Vogelsang-Eastwood
  G 11584 R10845
Vogl W 7897
V o g l e r W F1 1 2
  M12678s
Vogt E M12680 **H**
  12097 12164

Watrous J ^{E}390 **L**
11715
Watson C 1945 **D**
^{R}1501 **F** 1063 4462
6798 **N** 6572 12762
^{R}80 6281 6733 **W**
^{E}11480 ^{R}578 9986 -
Treumann B 11820
Watt W 10141
Wattiaux H ^{R}1472
Watts J 1933s 3414
3794 ^{E}75 1919 ^{R}1907
R 5240 ^{R}6338
Waubke H 12558
Waugh S 6597
Way D ^{R}7819
Wazana N 10442
Wächter L ^{R}302 422
Wäfler M 11759
Wälchli S 2868
Weaver D 2350 **J** 7703
W 4463 ^{E}457
Webb G ^{R}5206 **J**
11687s **M** 11747 **S**
11832 ^{R}451 7391 **W**
1064
Weber B 3167 3223
3315 3363 8102
^{E}102 ^{R}147 3197 3957
C 11929 **D** 12338 **F**
7898 **G** 10682
^{R}10485 **M** ^{M}2444
3714 3731 10590
11833 **R** 8965 **T**
11023
Webster J 1065 1266
5914
Wechsler M 3062s
9135
Wedderburn A 5124
^{R}6643 6671
Weder H 12568 ^{E}4593
4602
Weeks K 11224
^{E}11578
Wegenast K 4691
Wehn B 9029 ^{E}6308
Wehnert J 5669 10683
^{R}2250
Wehr L 5915 6419
12711 ^{R}137 6614
Wehrle J 2078 ^{R}2762
Weibling J 4884

Weidemann F ^{R}5367
H 6041
Weidmann F 5714
^{R}4256 12132
Weigall A ^{M}10751
Weigl M 3537 4208
^{E}25
Weil G ^{E}1582
Weiland F 3064
Weiler A ^{R}9833
Weill M 1314
Weima J ^{R}6429 6906
Weimar P 2328
Weinandy T 12165
Weinberg J 1366
^{T}9506
Weinfeld M 2183
7431
Weingarten R 12763
Weippert H 3361
^{T}10225 **M** 3849
10008 ^{R}11929
Weisberg D 2476
Weisman Z 1367
Weiss H 4786 **J**
^{M}12681 ^{R}2855 **M**
^{R}9889 **Z** 11374
Weissenrieder A
5416
Weitzman M 1704
^{M}113 **S** 1092
Weitzmann K 10990
Welborn L 6737
Welby V ^{M}12682
Welikadaarachchi
Daya A 2619
Wellens A 7899
Wellhausen J 10226
10623 ^{M}1907
12592
Wellings M ^{R}4854
Wells G 1557 **J** 7334
L 1287 **R** ^{R}3914
Welte M 10737
Welten P 922 ^{F}114
Wendland E 1851
1818 4011 4222
Wendorf F 11634
Wendt M 1066
7300s 9821ss
^{E}1066
Wengert T ^{E}12521
Wengst K 5730s

Wenham D 4263 **G**
7379 ^{E}278 **J** 8741
Wenig S ^{E}648
Weninger S 8600 8700
^{E}556
Wenning R 5616 9235
10009 11225 11311
11360 11452ss ^{E}65
Wente E ^{F}115
Wenz G ^{E}378
Wenzel K 7302
Werbick J 7150
Werding J 860
Weren W 1558 4464
4787 5015
Werline R 7350
Werlitz J 2911
Werman C 8926
Wermelinger O 550
Wertheimer A 8601s
Wesley J ^{M}4854
Wesselius J 1093 1605
4077 8585
Wessels W 7478
West D 11333 **G**
1067s 2839 ^{E}333 **J**
^{M}1206 **M** 3960
10839 12242 **T** 4531
Westbrook R 2477
^{E}649 11581 **V** 1760
Westcott B ^{M}5813
Westenholz A 10399 **J**
8498 10110
Westerfield K ^{R}10826
Westerhoff M 9030
Westerman J ^{R}10920
Westermann C 5916
Westermeyer P ^{R}10832
Westphal M 7189
Westrem S 11766
Wet F 7996
Weth R ^{E}552
Wettengel W 10068
Wetzel C 2810s 2818
2837 7303
Wetzlaugk S 5505
Wevers J 1683s 12764
^{E}25
Weyde K 3325 4234
Weyermann A 1181
Wénin A 1975 2184
2206s 3144 7151
7399 12712 ^{E}7 1936
^{R}323 1335 1913

Situs

Baal-Gad 2663
Barʿam 11062
Beit Yeraḥ 11355
Beth Sheʾarim 11205
Bethany 11415
Bethlehem 11313
Bethsaida 11358
Bet-Kerem 10383
Byblos 11469
Caesarea M 11337 **P**
  11360
Cana 11361s
Capernaum 11363
Castra Samaritanorum
  11341
Dan 8514 8570
Deir ʿAlla 8468
Deir el-Bahari 11159
Dendara 10889
Der ʿEn ʿAbaṭa 11417
Dor 11154
Dura-Europos 10972
el-Balamun 11626
el-Dabʿa 10800 11058
  1 1 1 0 1   1 1 2 0 7 s
  1 1 6 1 1 s   1 1 6 2 7 s
  11787
Elephantine 8568
el-ʿUmeiri 11418
Emar 11027 11501
ʿEn Ḥazeva 11061
ʿEn Ṣippori 11364
et-Tell 11825
Fayyum 11630
Gadara 11420
Gath 11318
Ǧawa 11422
Gaza 11319
Gerasa 11423

Hama 11503
Har Karkom 11641
Harun 11425
Ḥattuša 11667
Hauran 11217
Hazor 11365ss
Hesbon 2570
Hierapolis 8794
Ḥorbat 11165
Idamaras 11759
ʿIraq al-Amir 11230
Jaffa 11066
Jarash 11133 11429
Jericho 11317
Jébel Wastani 11504
K a d e s c h - B a r n e a
  1908
Kalḫu 10101
Kamid el-Loz 11470
Karnak 11576
Kinet 11669
Kinneret 11368
Kition 11677
Knossos 11097
K u n t i l l e t   ʿA j r u d
  11643
Lagash 10377
Lehun 11431s
Madeba 11420
Mari 9999 10202
Masada 1630 11321s
Megiddo 6218 10304
  11178
Menorim 11165
Michal 11343
Munbāqa 11506
Mycene 11689
Naxos 11698
Nazareth 4461 11221

Nimrod 11537
Nineveh 2097 11541
Nuzi 11543
Oboda 10786
Palmyra 8762 11509
  11151 11510
Petra 11140s 11145
  11162 11434 11438s
  11441s 11444 11446
  11454
Philippi 8810
Q a ʿ   A b u   Ṭ u l a y ḥ a
  11456
Qara Qūzāg 11511
Ramat Menashe 11096
Ramoth-Gilead 11457
Ṣal 11458
Saqqara 11604
Sardis 8793
Sela' 11459ss
Sepphoris 4294 11084
Sippar 10802
Tanis 11639
T a p o s i r i s   M a g n a
  11640
Telelat Ġassul 11818
Thebes 11579
Tiryns 11104
Trachonitis 11217
Umm Saysaban 11462
Ur 2109
Uruk 11532 11546
Van-Yoncatepe 11161
Wadi Šuʿeb 11463
Yaʿmun 11464
Yattir 11328
Zeugma 11859

Voces

Akkadicae	Aramaicae	Eblaitae
niggalu 8384	דחשפט 8388	*mabtaḫū* 8393
tubkinnu 8386	הנצל 8389	
šql 8385	קלקלתא 8386	
	שקל 8385	

Sacra Scriptura

1 Samuel

1-2 2767
1-3 2768s
1,1-2,21 2207
1,9-16 9518
2 1605
2-10 2770
2,1-2 12198
2,6 7433
4-6 2771
6,17-18 2772
8-12 2781
8-22 2782
9,1-10,16 3737
12 2638
13-15 2783
16-17 1093 2813
16,1-13 2812
16,1-23 8964
18-19 2814
18 2811
19 2811 2815
22-26 2816
22,6-23 8952
25 2817s 11887
25,31 2819
25,37 2820
27-31 2821
28 2822s

2 Samuel

3 2811
5-24 2790
5,6-8 2824
5,8 2825s
6 2771 2811
  2827
7 2828-31
7,1-17 2832ss
8 2835
9-12 2836
9-20 2798
11 7283
1 1 - 1 2 2 8 3 7
  11908
12 2828
13 2838 7448
13-21 2841
13,1-18,18 2840
13,1-22 2839
1 3 , 3 7 - 1 4 , 2 3
  2842

18 2843
22 1605 3191
  3288
23,1-7 1605
24 2844

1 Regum

1 2828 2896
  7283
1,2-17 2927
2-14 2897
2,28-34 2898
3,4-15 2899
3,16-27 2030
3,16-28 2900
4,7-19 2901s
6,19 8441
8 2638 2903
  3955
8,1-9,9 2904
9,15-19 2861
10 2906s
10,1-13 2905
10,26 2908
11 2334
11-14 2909
1 1 , 1 4 - 2 5
  10196
12,24 2909
12,32-33 2910
13 2911
13,11-32 2912
14-2K 17 2854
14,13 2913
17-19 2922
17-2K 2 2914
17,8-17 2929
17,14 8441
18,17-46 2927
19 2918 2926
  7227
19,9-13 2919
2 1 2 9 2 0 s
  11908

2 Regum

1,2-8 7360
1,2-8 7361
2-8 2939
2,1-18 10945
2,9-12 2940

2,23-25 7361
3 2941 7283
3,8-34 11887
4,1-8 2929
4,8-37 2942
4,27 9138
5 2943
5,2-3 2944
5,5-6 2945
6,24-7,2 2946
9 2921
9-10 2947
10,18-28 2927
1 0 , 3 2 - 3 3
  10194
12,5-17 10250
1 2 , 1 7 - 1 8
  10194
14,25 2634
1 8 - 2 0 2 9 4 8
  3706
18-21 2949
1 8 , 4 2 5 6 6
  9980
1 8 , 1 3 - 1 9 , 3 7
  2950
19-20 2951
19,37 10364
20,1-11 2952
21,1-18 2953
21,23 2954
22-23 2956
2 2 , 1 - 2 3 , 3 0
  2955
23,4-15 2957
23,29 2958
23,29-35 2959
2 3 , 3 1 - 2 5 , 3 0
  2960

1 Chronica

2,25-41 2982
16 3218
26,16 2983

2 Chronica

15,2-6 2963
19,1-11 2390
25,1-7 2963
29-32 2984
32 2951

33 9404

Esdras, **Ezra**

1 2992
1-6 2892
6,3-12 2872
7-10 3003s
7,12-26 2872
7,14 3001
9-10 2874
9 3928

Nehemias

1 3928
7,72-10,40 3005
8 3004
9 3006s
9-10 3008
9,9-11 4187
10,31-40 3009

Tobias

7-8 3024

Judith

8-16 3039
9,10 3032

Esther

3,1 3063
7,14-41 3045
8,1-17 3045
8,5 3063
9,10 3063
9,24 3063

1 Machab.

1,1-6,40 3066
  3113
14,25-49 3068
  3072

2 Machab.

2,13 2872
7,28 7650
8 3075

4,1-11 4848
4,13 4659
4,23-25 11761
5-7 1818 4973
  12297
5,3-12 12235
5,9 4874
5,13 4862s
5,14 4864
5,17-19 7304
5,17-20 4865
5,21-26 4866
5,27-30 4867
5,32 4882 4884
5,34 4868
5,38-42 4869
5,38-48 4870
5,39 4871
6,22-23 4872
6,24-34 4873
6,25-34 9803
6,28 4662
7,24-27 5453
8-9 4785 4939
9,9-13 4940
9,13 4766
9,18-26 4941
9,35-38 4942
10 4943
10,5-6 4944
10,15 12278
11 4945
11,26 4946
11,28-30 4344
  12466
12,4 4788
12,7 4766
12,31-32 4947
  12366
13,1-52 4975
13,3-23 4976
13,14-15 3810
13,31-32 888
13,53-58 940
  953 983 996
  1052 1062
14,3-12 4977
14,13-21 4978
14,15-21 12162
15,1-20 4979
15,21-28 4980ss
16,11-12 4788
16,23 5284

17,1-8 4995
17,1-9 4996s
  7598
17,27 4998
18 4999
18,12-14 3296
18,15 5000
18,15-17
  12508
18,21-25 5001
18,23-35 5002
19,3-12 5003
19,6-13 5004
19,9 4882
  4884
19,28 4626
20,1-16 5008s
20,20-23 5699
21,1-17 5010
21,12-13 5011
21,12-17 5012
21,23-27 4619
21,28-32 5013
21,32 4733
21,33-41 5014
22,1-14 5015
22,15-22 4620
22,23-33 4621
22,41-46 4622
23,1-12 5016
23,11 7489
23,34 5016
23,35 1246
24 5011 8214
25 5017 8214
25,1-13 5018
25,14-30 5019
  5510
25,31-46
  5020ss
25,32-33 5023
26,6-13 5050
  6007
26,26-29 5051
26,38 5083
27,3-10 5084
27,45-46 5085
27,57 5086
27,63-64 5127
28 5128
28,1 5129ss
28,9-10 5132
28,16-20
  5133ss

28,19 7629
  9833

Marcus

1,1 5245 7512
1,1-12 5171
1,1-15 5246
1,2 5244
1,12-13 4848
  5247
1,15 7239
1,16-2,17 5248
1,17 5249
1,21-28 5250
1,22 5207
1,24 5251
1,29-31 5252
2,13-3,6 5253
2,13-17 11894
2,27 4858
3,4 5254
3,6 5232
3,20 12366
3,20-21 5255
3,20-30 5256
3,22 5257
3,22-30 5189
3,31-35 5258
4,1 5259s
4,1-9 5261
4,9 5262
4,10-12 5263
  9543
4,10-13 3809
4,11-12 3810
4,30-32 5264
4,35-5,20 5265
5,1-20 5266
  10925
5,21-6,6 5267
5,21-43 5171
  5268
5,24-34 5269
5,24-43 5270
5,25-34 5271
6,6-30 5272
6,14-29 5273
6,17-29 5274
6,30-44 5236
6,34-44 4978
6,45-52 5275
6,52-53 5276

7 7221
7,1-23 5277
7,24-30 5278
  7807
7,24-31 5279s
8 4462
8,1-9 5236
8,15 5232
8,22-10,52
  5281s
8,22-26 5283
8,33 5284
8,34 5285
8,35 5504
9,2-8 4995
9,2-10 4996
  5286
9,5 5287
9,14-29 5288
9,50 4862
10 4884
10,9 4858
10,13-16 5289
  10968
10,17-31 5290s
10,46-52 5283
  5292ss
11,3 5295
11,15-17 5296
11,15-18 5297
11,15-19 5298ss
11,27-33 4619
12,13-17 4620
12,13-17 4515
  5232
12,18-27 4621
12,28-34 5301
12,35-37 4622
12,41-44 5302
13 5303 5311
  8214
13,17-19 5304
13,35 5305
14,1-11 5311
14,3-9 6007
14,22-25 5051
  5312
14,32-42 5313
14,34 5083
14,36 5314
14,51-52 5315ss
14,53-65 5320
14,54 5319

4,10 6886

Colossenses

1,15-20 6351
  6895s 7495
  12584
1,24 6897
2,3 6898 7856
2,16 7652
3,3-4 6899
3,11 6900
3,16 6901 10823

1 Thess.

1,3 7666
1,9-10 7847
2,8 6917
2,13 6918
2,13-16 6919
2,14-16 6920
2,17-3,10 6921
4-5 6922
4,3-8 6923
4,4 6924s
4,4-5 6926
4,13-18 6707
  6720 6927
4,14 6928s
5 7137
5,1-11 6930
5,4-9 7847
5,14 6931
5,20 6691

2 Thess.

2,1-2 6932
3,5 6933

1 ad Timoth.

1 6952
2 6953
2,9-15 6954ss

2,12 6957
2,15 6958s
3 6960
3,8-9 6961
5,3-16 6962
6,6 6963

2 ad Timoth.

3,10-17 6966

Ad Titum

2,11-14 6968
2,13 7847

Ad Philem.

19 6981

Ad Hebraeos

1 7010
1,5-13 7011
3-4 4945
4,12-19 7143
  8139
5 7979
5,7-8 7012
6,19-20 7013
6,20 7014
8,1-10,18 7015
9,4 5704
11 12488
11,9-10 7016
11,17-19 7017
11,26 8744
12,1-29 7018
12,14-17 7019
13,1-19 7020
13,5 7021

Jacobi, **James**

2,1-13 7089
2,14-16 7090

2,21-26 7091
4,5 7092
4,7-10 7093
5,3 7094

1 Petri

1,1-12 7043
1,1-14 7044
1,10-12 7045
2,16 7046
3 6671
3,13-16 7047
3,18-19 12135
3,19-20 7048
3,19-22 12010
4,6 7048

2 Petri

1,4 7059
2 7060
3,11-12 7061

1 Joannis

1,5-2,2 6058
3,2-3 7847
4,17-18 6571

Jude

8 7098

Apocalypsis
Revelation

1,3 6190
1,4 6191
1,4-3,22 6192
1,6 7761
1,10 7952
2 6193
2-3 6194s
  8221 9843

2,9 6142 6185
  6196
2,9-10 6197
2,17 5704
3,9 6142 6185
  6196
3,14-21 6198
3,20 6199
4-5 6201
4,6-7 12019
4,6-11 6202
4,11 6200
5 6203s
5,6 6205
6 4154
6,1-8,1 6206
6,1-8,6 6207
8,1-11,19 6208
11,8 8744
12 6158 6209-12
12-13 6213
12,1-18 6214
12,7-12 6215
14,11 6216
  12609
16,16 6217s
17 6219s
17-18 6221
17-19 6088
19,1-8 6222
19,1-10 6223s
19,17-21 6225
20,1-6 6251
20,6 6141
20,7-10 6225
20,11-21,8 6252
21 6253s
21-22 6255
21,1-22,5 6088
22,6-9 6256
22,7 7847
22,12 7847
22,20 7847

END

Finito di stampare
nel mese di Novembre 2004

presso la tipografia
"Giovanni Olivieri" di E. Montefoschi
00187 Roma • Via dell'Archetto, 10, 11, 12
Tel. 06 6792327 • E-mail: tip.olivieri@libero.it

49.43